THIRD EDITION

Shannon Pratt's

The Lawyer's Business Valuation Handbook

Understanding Financial Statements, Appraisal Reports, and Expert Testimony

Shannon P. Pratt and **ASA Educational Foundation**

ABA
AMERICAN BAR ASSOCIATION
Family Law Section
Real Property Trust and Estate Law Section

ASA
Providing Value Worldwide
Educational Foundation

Cover design by Jill Tedhams/ABA Design

Printed in the United States of America.

28 27 26 25 5 4 3 2

A catalog record for this book is available from the Library of Congress.

To all the attorneys
who work on business valuation matters and
to all judges
who hear cases involving business valuation:
We hope this book
will make your lives a little easier and more productive
in dealing with business valuation issues.

Contents

Table of Exhibits xxxv
Foreword—Perspective from the Bench xxxix
Foreword—Tax Law Perspective xli
Foreword—Family Law Perspective xliii
Foreword—Corporate Law Perspective xlv
About Shannon Pratt xlvii
About the Editors xlix
About the Editorial Advisory Board li
About the Authors liii
Preface lix
Acknowledgments lxiii

Chapter 1
Defining Value in the Relevant Context: Standards of Value 1

Roger J. Grabowski, FASA

Introduction 1
Commonly Used Definitions of Value 2
- Fair Market Value 3
- Fair Value under State Statutes 5
- Fair Value for Financial Reporting 6
- Investment Value 8
- Intrinsic or Fundamental Value 9

Other Terms Referring to Value 10
- Acquisition Value 10
- Book Value 10
- Going-Concern Value 11
- Enterprise Value 11
- Liquidation Value 12
- Strategic Value (Synergistic Value) 12
- Transaction Value 12

Sources of Authority for Definition of Value 13
Statutory Law 13
Federal Statutes 13
State Statutes 14
Legally Binding Rules and Regulations 14
Contractual Definitions of Value 14
Non–Legally Binding Administrative Rulings 15
Prior Court Decisions (i.e., Precedence) 15
Direction from the Court 16
Direction from the Attorney 16
Use of IRS Authority in Non-Tax Situations 16
Opinions of Other Attorneys and Appraisers 16
Summary 16
References for Defining Value in the Relevant Context 17

Chapter 2
Value to Whom? Levels and Premises of Value 19
Roger J. Grabowski, FASA

Introduction 19
Levels of Value 19
Premises of Value 21
Matching the Valuation Methodology with the Standard and Premises of Value 22
Sum of Parts Not Necessarily Equal to Whole 22
Summary 23
References for Levels and Premises of Value 23

Chapter 3
Overview of Business Valuation Approaches, Methods, and Procedures 25
Roger J. Grabowski, FASA

Introduction 25
Hierarchy of Approaches, Methods, and Procedures 25
Basic Appraisal Approaches 26
Methods Used within Appraisal Approaches 26
Income Approach Methods 26
Market Approach Methods 26
Asset-Based Approach Methods 27
Summary of Business Appraisal Approaches and Methods 27

Business Appraisal Procedures 28
 Invested Capital versus Equity 28
Approaches and Methods Not Totally Discrete 29
Ambiguities of Business Valuation Terminology 30
Summary 31
References for Overview of Business Valuation Approaches, Methods, and Procedures 31

Chapter 4
Financial Statement Terminology Used in Business Appraisal **33**
Alina Niculita, ASA, ARM, CFA
Introduction 33
The Basic Financial Statements 33
Balance Sheet Concepts 36
 Common Equity 36
 Invested Capital 36
 Capital Structure 36
 Book Value 36
 Book Value per Share 37
 Tangible Book Value versus Total Book Value 37
 Net Working Capital 37
Miscellaneous Expense Concepts 37
 Noncash Charges 37
 Owners' Compensation (Including Disclosed or Hidden Perks) 38
Levels of Economic Income 38
 Sales (Net Revenues) 38
 EBIT (Also Called *Operating Income*) 39
 EBITDA 39
 Discretionary Earnings 39
 Gross Cash Flow 39
 Debt-Free Net Income (DFNI), Also Called *NOPAT* (Net Operating Profit After Income Taxes) 40
 Debt-Free Gross Cash Flow (DFCF) 40
 Pretax Income 40
 Net Income 41
 Primary versus Diluted Net Income per Share 41
 Net Cash Flow to Invested Capital 41
 Net Cash Flow to Equity 42

Variables Affecting Net Cash Flow 43
Capital Expenditures 43
Changes in Net Working Capital 43
Changes in Debt 43
Cash versus Accrual Basis Accounting 43
Accrual Basis Accounting 44
Cash Basis Accounting 44
Conversion from Cash to Accrual Basis 44
Summary 44

Chapter 5
Company Information, Site Visits, and Interviews 45

Alina Niculita, ASA, ARM, CFA

Introduction 45
Gathering Company Information 45
Company-Specific Information 45
External Information—Impact on the Subject Company 46
Financial Statements 47
Income Tax Returns 49
Other Financial Information 49
Operating Information 51
Company Documents Relating to Owners' Rights 51
Site Visits and Interviews 52
Interviews 53
Court's View on Company Information 56
Summary 57
References for Company Information, Site Visits, and Interviews 58

Chapter 6
The Income Approach 59

Roger J. Grabowski, FASA

Introduction 59
The Concept of Discounting 62
The Concept of Capitalizing 62
The Basic Capitalized Economic Income Model 63
The Constant Income Capitalization Model 63
The Constant Growth Income Capitalization Model 64

The Basic Discounted Economic Income Model 66
The Discounted Economic Income Model for a Limited Life Investment 66
The Discounted Economic Income Method Using a "Terminal Value" 67
Capitalization Model versus Market Multiples for Estimating Terminal Value 71
Preference for Net Cash Flow in Income Approach 72
Net Cash Flow Is What You Get 73
Net Cash Flow Matches Empirical Data 73
Use of Net Cash Flow Strengthens the Corroborative Power of the Income Approach 73
Adjusting Formulas to Account for When Economic Income Is Received 73
Common Errors 74
Summary 75
References for Income Approach 79
Basic Income Approach References 79
Articles and Research Papers 79

Chapter 7
Developing a Discount Rate 81

Roger J. Grabowski, FASA

Introduction 81
Concept of the Discount Rate 81
Elements of the Discount Rate: Risk-Free Rate and a Premium for Risk 82
Estimating Discount Rates for Fixed-Income Securities 82
Estimating Discount Rates for Equity 83
Build-up Method 83
Risk-Free Rate 83
Equity Risk Premium 84
Industry Risk Premium in Build-up Method 85
Size Premium in Build-up Method 85
Summary Illustration of the Equity Discount Rate Using the Build-up Method 86
Capital Asset Pricing Model and Modified Capital Asset Pricing Model 87
Definition of Beta 87
Estimating Beta 87
Betas for Closely Held Companies 89
Incorporating Beta into the Equity Risk Premium 90
Size Premium in MCAPM 90
Company-Specific Risk Adjustment in MCAPM 91
Summary Illustration of the Equity Discount Rate Using MCAPM 91

Concept and Estimation of Capitalization Rates 92
Concept of a Capitalization Rate 92
Elements of the Capitalization Rate 92
Estimating Equity Capitalization Rates 93
Discount Rates for Smaller Closely Held Businesses 93
Measuring Equity Discount Rates for SMEs 94
Valuing Invested Capital versus Valuing Equity 96
Concept of Weighted Average Cost of Capital 96
Basic WACC Computation Model 96
Derivation of Weights for WACC 97
Matching the Discount Rate with the Definition of Economic Income 99
Common Errors 100
Summary 101
References for Developing Discount Rates 101
Basic Discount Rate References 101
Articles and Research Papers 102
Cost of Capital Data References 102

Chapter 8
The Market Approach **103**

Alina Niculita, ASA, ARM, CFA

Introduction 103
Market Approach Concept and Overview 103
Valuing Controlling versus Noncontrolling Interests 104
Valuing Total Invested Capital versus Direct Valuation of Equity 105
Using Sales of Entire Companies or Guideline Public Companies 105
Sources of Market Approach Data 106
Sales of Public Companies 106
Sales of Closely Held Companies 107
Guideline Public Company Data 107
Developing Market Multiples for Valuation 108
Invested Capital Multiples 108
Equity Multiples 109
Time Periods for Company Financial Statement Data 110
Criteria for Selecting Guideline Companies 110
How Many Guideline Companies? 111
Illustration of Developing Guideline Company Multiples 112

Deciding Where Subject Company Multiples Should Fall Relative to Observed Guideline Public Company Multiples 114
Relationship between Market Multiples and Capitalization Rates 115
Multiples Selected Based on Comparative Analysis 115
Different Multiples May Be Higher or Lower Relative to Guideline Companies 116
Relative Weights to Accord Various Multiples 117
Illustration of Valuation by Market Approach 117
Variations for Smaller Companies and Professional Practice Valuations 119
Involvement of the Owner 120
Availability of Comparative Accounting Data 120
Prior Transactions, Offers, and Buy-Sell Agreements 122
Arm's-Length Negotiations 122
Prior Transactions 122
Offers to Buy 124
Buy-Sell Agreements 124
Definition of Market Value in Some Fair Value Cases 124
Summary 124
References for the Market Approach 125
Basic Market Approach References 125
Private and Public Company Sale Databases 126
Public Company Data 127

Chapter 9
The Asset-Based Approach **129**

Roger J. Grabowski, FASA

Introduction 129
Discrete versus Collective Revaluation 129
Steps in the Asset Accumulation Method 130
Valuation Premises for Adjusting Balance Sheet Values 131
Illustrative Asset Accumulation Method 131
Breakup Value 132
Reliance on Experts 132
When Are Asset-Based Methods Used? 133
Summary 135
References for Asset-Based Approach 135

Chapter 10
The Excess Earnings Method **137**

Roger J. Grabowski, FASA

Introduction 137
Background of the Excess Earnings Method 137
Basic Steps in the Excess Earnings Method 138
Applying the Excess Earnings Method 138
A "Sanity Check" for Validity of an Excess Earnings Method Value 141
Critique of Excess Earnings Method in Revenue Ruling 68-609 142
Use of Historical Averages Impractical 144
"Required Return on Tangible Assets" Is Ambiguous 144
No Definition of "Earnings" 144
No Guidance for Intangibles Capitalization Rate 144
Common Errors in Applying the Excess Earnings Method 144
Undefined Earnings Stream 145
Unsupported Normalized Earnings Stream 145
Failure to Allow for Owner's Compensation 145
Unsupported Net Tangible Asset Value 145
Unsupported or Unrealistic Required Rate of Return on Tangible Assets 145
Unsupported or Unrealistic Capitalization Rate for Excess Earnings 145
Using Rates in the Revenue Ruling 68-609 Illustration Instead of Currently Supportable Rates 146
Claiming That the IRS Recommends Use of the Excess Earnings Method 146
Summary 146
References for Excess Earnings Method 147

Chapter 11
Rules of Thumb **149**

Alina Niculita, ASA, ARM, CFA

Introduction 149
Rules of Thumb Disclaimers 149
General Nature of Rules of Thumb 150
Rules of Thumb Are Not Cash-Equivalent Prices 151
Rule of Thumb Examples 151
Checking Alleged Rules of Thumb against Actual Transactions 151

Court Reaction to Rules of Thumb 153
Summary 154
References for Rules of Thumb 154
Transaction Databases with Price/Revenue and Price/Discretionary Earnings Ratios 155

Chapter 12
Personal versus Enterprise Goodwill **157**

Jay E. Fishman, FASA, FRICS, and Kenneth J. Pia, Jr., ASA, CPA/ABV, MCBA

Introduction 157
Distinction between Enterprise and Personal Goodwill 162
Enterprise Goodwill Characteristics 162
Personal Goodwill Characteristics 163
Case Examples 163
Divorce Cases 163
Income Tax Cases 164
Summary 164
References for Personal versus Enterprise Goodwill 164

Chapter 13
Reasonable Compensation **167**

Erin Hollis, ASA

Introduction 167
What Is Reasonable Compensation? 167
Tax Court and Reasonable Compensation 169
U.S. Tax Court's Five-Factor Test 169
IRS Job Aid 170
Adjusting Compensation 175
Reasonable Compensation in Corporations 176
Case Example: *Clary Hood, Inc. v. Commissioner* 177
Equity Incentives in LLCs 178
Common Errors 179
Compensation Resources 179
Summary 181
References for Reasonable Compensation 181

Chapter 14
Employment and Noncompetition Agreements **183**

Robert B. Morrison, FASA, BVIIA

Introduction 183
Noncompetition and Nonsolicitation Agreements 183
Noncompete Agreements, Tangible and Intangible Assets 184
Noncompete Agreements and Enforceability 184
Noncompetition Agreements and Public Policy 185
Noncompetition Agreements and Taxes 185
Noncompetition Agreements and Value 187
  IRS Weighs In 188
  Valuation of a Noncompetition Agreement 188
  With Model 189
  Without Model 191
  Noncompetition Agreements and Personal Goodwill 197
  Federal Income Tax Implications 198
  Marital Dissolution Implications 198
Employment Agreements 199
  Employment Agreements and Value 199
  Employment Agreements and Litigation 199
Summary 201
References for Employment and Noncompetition Agreements 201

Chapter 15
Financial Statement Adjustments **203**

Serena Morones, ASA, CPA/ABV, CFE, Paul Heidt, ASA, CPA/ABV, and Terry G. Whitehead, ASA, CPA/ABV

Introduction 203
Reasons for Financial Statement Adjustments 203
Normalizing Adjustments 205
  Nonrecurring Items 205
Personal Expenses 205
  Discontinued Operations 206
  Inventory Accounting Methods 206
  Depreciation and Depletion Methods and Schedules 207
  Net Operating Losses Carried Forward 207

Reserve and Allowance Accounts 208
Other Normalizing Adjustments 208
Control Adjustments 209
Reasonable Compensation 209
Related-Party Transactions 209
Separating Operating Assets from Nonoperating and Excess Assets 209
Comparisons with Other Entities 210
Treatment of Nonoperating and Excess Assets 210
Cash versus Accrual Accounting 210
Illustrative Financial Statement Adjustments 211
Income Statement Adjustments 212
Balance Sheet Adjustments 213
Summary 213
References for Financial Statement Adjustments 214
Books 214
Article 214

Chapter 16
Comparative Financial Statement Analysis 215

Serena Morones, ASA, CPA/ABV, CFE, Paul Heidt, ASA, CPA/ABV, and Terry G. Whitehead, ASA, CPA/ABV

Introduction 215
Tools of Comparative Financial Statement Analysis 216
Horizontal Analysis 217
Trend Analysis 219
Vertical Analysis 222
Analysis of Profitability 227
Analysis of Liquidity 233
Analysis of Risk 235
Industry Data Resources 236
Summary 237
References for Comparative Financial Statements 237

Chapter 17
Economic and Industry Analysis **239**

Kimberly Linebarger, ASA, CPA/ABV, CFA, CVA

Introduction 239
National Economy—Recent Status 240
National Economy—Outlook 242
Regional Information 244
International Information 245
Industry—General Data 245
Industry—Composite Company Data 247
Summary 249
References for Economic and Industry Analysis 250

Chapter 18
Discounts and Premiums **251**

William H. Frazier, ASA and Bruce A. Johnson, ASA

Introduction 251
Levels of Value 252
Measuring the Value Differential between Levels of Value 253
Distinguishing the Control Factor from the Marketability Factor 254
Lack of Control versus Control 255
 The Noncontrolling Owner's Situation 255
 Degrees of Control versus Lack of Control 255
 Other Forms of Noncontrolling Interests 256
 Quantifying Lack of Control (Minority) Discounts 257
Estimating Control Premiums 258
Discounts for Lack of Control 259
 Indirect Methodology 259
 Discount for Lack of Control Estimated from Acquisition Premiums for Publicly Traded Stocks 259
 Discount for Lack of Control Estimated from Secondary Market Prices 260
 Discounts for Lack of Control Estimated from Closed-End Funds 260
 Direct Procedure 261
Discounts for Lack of Marketability 262
 The Concept of Marketability 262
 Degrees of Marketability or Lack Thereof 263

Other Factors Affecting Discounts for Lack of Marketability 263
Benchmark for Marketability 264
Quantifying Lack of Marketability Discounts 265
Qualitative-Based Methods 265
Using Restricted Stock Studies 265
Using Pre-IPO Studies 269
Analytical Techniques 270
Option Pricing Models 270
Johnson/Park Empirical Method 271
Nonmarketable Investment Company Evaluation Method (NICE) 272
Quantitative Marketability Discount Model (QMDM) 273
Discounts for Lack of Liquidity and Lack of Marketability for Controlling Interests 273
How the Applicable Definition of Value Affects the Discounts for Lack of Control and Lack of Marketability 274
Fair Market Value 274
Fair Value under State Statute 274
Other Discounts 275
Key Person Discount 275
Tax on Built-In Capital Gains Adjustment 275
Voting versus Nonvoting Shares 276
Blockage 277
Summary 277
References for Discounts and Premiums 278
Basic Discount and Premiums References 278
References for Premium and Discount Court Cases 279
Premium and Discount Data References 279

Chapter 19
Reconciliation of Value Indications **281**

Roger J. Grabowski, FASA and Alina Niculita, ASA, ARM, CFA

Introduction 281
Overview of the Reconciliation Process 281
Did the Appraiser Appraise the Correct Property? 282
Did the Appraiser Appraise the Correct Property the Right Way? 284
Major Considerations in the Reconciliation Process 284
Reconciling Divergent Results among Business Valuation Methods 285

Weighting of Valuation Methods Results 285
Explicit Weighting 287
Implicit Weighting 288
Final Value Estimate 289
Summary 289
References for Reconciliation of Value Indications 289

Chapter 20
Valuations for Gift, Estate, and Charitable Contribution Matters 291

Ryan Montgomery, JD, LLM and Travis Harms, CFA, CPA/ABV

Introduction 291
Fair Market Value 292
Fair Market Value Assumes Adequate Knowledge 294
Must Consider Both Buyer and Seller—and Both Must Be Hypothetical 294
Qualifications of Appraisers 295
Burden of Proof 297
Adequate Disclosure of Gifts 298
Access to a Business's Sites, Management, and Records 298
Arm's-Length Transactions 298
Approaches to Value 299
Market Approach 300
Income Approach 301
Asset-Based Approach 302
Discounts 303
Discounts for Lack of Marketability (Noncontrolling Blocks) 303
Put Options 305
Put-Call Collars 305
Regression Analysis 306
Combined Noncontrol (Minority) and Lack of Marketability Discounts 306
Discounts for 50% Interests 306
Discounts for Lack of Liquidity/Marketability (Controlling Interests) 307
Discounts for Lack of Control 308
Blockage 309
Key Person Discount 309
Nonvoting versus Voting Stock 310
Premiums 310

Taxes on Trapped-In Capital Gains 311
Charitable Contributions 314
Contingent Liabilities 315
Subsequent Events and Information 315
  Proximity of Financial Information to Valuation Date 316
  Subsequent Sales 317
Buy-Sell Agreements 319
Weighting of Valuation Method Results 322
Pressure to Settle 323
Defined Value Formula Clauses 324
Summary 325
References for Valuations for Gift, Estate, and Charitable Contribution Matters 326
  Articles and Books 326
  Website 327

Chapter 21
Valuations for Federal Income Tax Matters 329

Roger J. Grabowski, FASA

Introduction 329
Federal Income Tax Reasons to Conduct an Appraisal 330
Standard of Value 331
U.S. Income Tax Considerations 332
Valuation of Property Received/Transferred in a Transaction 332
Determining Basis in a Property 333
  Property Received by Employees 334
Use of Financial Reporting Valuations for Income Tax Purposes 335
Valuation of Worthless and Abandoned Property 335
  Worthless Securities 335
  Abandoned Property 336
  Valuation Aspects of I.R.C. § 165 336
  Abandonment Loss for Nondepreciable Business Assets 337
  Worthless Stock Deduction 337
  Worthless Securities in Affiliated Corporations 338
Corporate Distribution of Appreciated Property to Shareholders 339
Valuation Aspects of Intercompany Transfer Pricing 340
  The Arm's-Length Principle 341

Transfer Pricing Guidance 341
Intangible Transfers and Valuation Approaches 342
Differences in Intangible Pricing for Transfer Pricing and Financial Reporting 344
Interaction of Transfer Pricing and Legal Entity Valuation 345
Pricing of Intercompany Debt 345
Summary 345
References for Valuations for Federal Income Tax Matters 346
Articles and Books 346
Website 346

Chapter 22
Marital Dissolution Valuations 347

Jay E. Fishman, FASA, FRICS and Kenneth J. Pia, Jr., ASA, CPA/ABV, MCBA

Introduction 347
Standard of Value for Marital Dissolutions 348
Premise of Value 350
Appreciation—Active versus Passive 350
Valuation Date 351
Goodwill 352
Buy-Sell Agreements 358
Covenants Not to Compete 362
Noncontrolling Interest and Lack of Marketability Discounts 363
Tax on Trapped-In Capital Gains 364
Adequacy of Evidence 366
Access to Records 367
The Persistent Problem of "Double-Dipping" 368
Summary 370
References for Marital Dissolution Valuations 371

Chapter 23
Shareholder and Partner Disputes 373

David G. Clarke, ASA, William P. McInerney, ASA, and Elise Scoles

Introduction 373
"Fair Value" Standard in Most Dissent and Dissolution Suits 374
Market Exception 376

Interpretation of the Fair Value Standard in Dissent Cases 377
 That Which Has Been Taken 377
 The Delaware Block Method 377
 Should Consider All Relevant Factors 377
 Consideration of Deal Price 378
Requirement for Entire Fairness 378
 Fair Consideration 378
 Procedural Fairness 379
Consequences of Lack of Entire Fairness 382
Noncontrolling Interest Dissolution Actions 382
Interpretation of the Fair Value Standard in Dissolution Cases 383
Readers Must Interpret Cases Carefully 384
High Risk Associated with Applying Novel Theories 384
Fair Value under State Statutes Is Not Fair Market Value 385
Premise of Value/Exclusion of Synergies 386
Breach of Fiduciary Duty Expands Plaintiffs' Potential Damages 388
Some States Use Acquisition Value Instead of Going-Concern Value 388
Other States Consider Market Value, Asset Value, and Investment Value 389
The Impact of Appraisal Arbitrage in Recent Delaware Decisions 390
 Dell Compliance/Approach to Valuation 391
Oppression Remedies Sometimes Differ from Appraisal 395
Corporate Dissolution in Shareholder Deadlock 396
Partnership and Limited Liability Company Dispute Cases 397
Discounts for Lack of Control and Lack of Marketability 398
Timely Actions Essential 401
Summary 401
References for Shareholder and Partner Disputes 402
 Website 403

Chapter 24
Valuations for Employee Stock Ownership Plans 405

Jeffrey S. Tarbell, ASA, CFA and Arlene L. Ashcraft, ASA, CFA

Introduction 405
ESOP Legal and Regulatory Framework 406
ESOP Structural Framework 407
 Leveraged ESOP Transaction 407

Unleveraged ESOP Transaction 408
Unique Advantages of ESOP Transactions 408
The ESOP Trustee 409
Fiduciary Process Agreements 410
Selection and Oversight of the Financial Advisor 410
Fiduciary Review Process 410
Valuation Issues with ESOP Stock 411
Independence of the Appraiser 411
When Appraisals Are Required 412
General Valuation Considerations 412
Level of Value Issues 412
ESOP Financial Statement Adjustments 413
Discount for Lack of Marketability 414
Repurchase Liability: Redemption or Recirculation 415
Relevant Case Law 415
Sommers v. Corrigan 415
U.S. News & World Report 416
Eyler v. Commissioner 417
Dole v. Farnum 417
Henry v. Champlain Enterprises 417
Reich v. Valley National Bank of Arizona 418
Chao v. Hall Holding Co., Inc. 418
Keach v. U.S. Trust Co. 419
Eckelkamp v. Beste 419
Armstrong v. LaSalle Bank National Association 420
Kennedy v. Trustmark 420
Perez v. Bruister 421
Fish v. GreatBanc 421
Brundle v. Wilmington Trust 422
Pizzella v. Vinoskey 422
Remy v. Lubbock National Bank 423
Lee v. Argent Trust 423
Walsh v. Bowers & Kubota 424
Summary 424
References for Valuation for Employee Stock Ownership Plans 425

Chapter 25
Valuing Professional Practices and Small Service Businesses 427

Alina Niculita, ASA, ARM, CFA

Introduction 427
Trade-off between Cash and Terms 427
Easy Terms 428
Earnouts 430
Valuation Approaches and Methods 430
Income Approach 430
Market Approach 431
Excess Earnings Method 431
Asset-Based Methods 431
Rules of Thumb 431
Summary 432
References for Valuing Professional Practices and Small Service Businesses 432

Chapter 26
Valuing Stock of S Corporations and Interests in Other Pass-through Entities 433

Roger J. Grabowski, FASA

Introduction 433
Value and Taxes 433
Understanding the Tax Avoided by the S Corp 434
Valuing S Corps by the Income Approach Requires Usage of Market Return Rates Derived from Publicly Traded C Corps 437
Public C Corporation versus S Corp Pricing under the Income Approach—an Example 438
Value of the Avoided Dividend Tax 441
Specific S Corporation Issues under Other Valuation Approaches and Methods 442
Summary 442
References for Valuing Stock in S-Corp and Interests in Pass-through Entities 442

Chapter 27
Valuing Interests in Real Property Holding Entities 445

Bruce A. Johnson, ASA and Roger J. Grabowski, FASA

Introduction 445
What Do Real Property Appraisers Do? 446
How Do Real Property Appraisers Analyze Going-Concern Properties? 447
Example 448
How Do Business Appraisers Value Interests in Real Estate Investment Trusts? 449
Using REIT Information for the Income Approach 449
Using REIT and Closed-End Fund Information for the Market Approach 450
How Do Business Appraisers Value Interests in Limited Partnerships and Limited Liability Companies? 451
Indirect Procedure for Valuing the Subject Interests 451
Direct Procedure for Valuing the Subject Interests 452
Liquidity Considerations 453
Using Limited Partnership Information for the Income Approach 453
Using Limited Partnership Information for the Market Approach 454
Discount for Lack of Marketability 454
Common Issues in Valuing Interests in Businesses Whose Principal Assets Are Real Property Interests 455
Example of a Shareholder Dispute 455
Valuation Issues 455
Valuing Business Interests When Real Property Used in the Business Is Owned by a Related Entity 456
Example 1: Ownership Is Identical 457
Example 2: Ownership Is Intermingled 457
Summary 457
References for Valuing Interests in Real Property Holding Entities 458
Articles and Books 458
Databases 458

Chapter 28
Valuing Intellectual Property and Intangible Assets 459

Christopher Bakewell, ASA, CLP, Julia Rowe, CPA, and Jill Kosonen

Introduction 459
Valuation of Legally Protected Intellectual Property in Litigation 459

Patent Infringement 460
Damages Period Considerations 461
Reasonable Royalty Damages 461
Additional Considerations for Standards-Essential Patents 465
Lost Profits Damages 467
Considerations Unique to Design Patents 468
Trade Secret Misappropriation 468
Trademark and Trade Dress Infringement 469
Copyright Infringement 470
Rights of Publicity 471
Valuation Considerations 473
Injunctive Relief 474
Income Tax and Transfer Pricing Considerations for Intangible Assets 475
Arm's-Length Standard 475
Intangible Property Transactions 475
Methods for Determining the Arm's-Length Price 476
Difference in Valuing Intangible Assets for Financial Reporting 477
Strategy and Licensing Valuations 478
Summary 479
Reference for Valuing Intellectual Property and Intangible Assets 479

Chapter 29
Valuation Provisions in Buy-Sell Agreements 481

Z. Christopher Mercer, FASA, CFA, ABAR and Jeffrey S. Tarbell, ASA, CFA

Introduction 481
Types of Buy-Sell Agreements 481
Entity Purchase Agreements 481
Cross-Purchase Agreements 481
Hybrid Agreements 482
Tag-Along Rights 482
Types of Valuation Provisions 482
Fixed Price 482
Formula Pricing 482
"Shotgun" Agreements 482
Valuation Process Pricing Agreements 483
Drafting a Good Buy-Sell Agreement 483
Definition of Value 483

The Valuation Date 485
Appraiser Qualifications and Business Appraisal Standards 485
Appraiser Selection and Procedures 485
Single Appraiser 485
Multiple Appraisers 486
Funding and Payment Mechanisms 487
Payment of Appraisers 490
Dealing with the Agreement When the Triggering Event Occurs 490
The Effect of the Agreement on Valuations for Purposes Other Than the Agreement Itself 490
Summary 491
References to Valuation Provisions in Buy-Sell Agreements 491

Chapter 30
Valuation in Fairness Matters 493

Jeffrey S. Tarbell, ASA, CFA

Introduction 493
Corporate Law Relevant to Fairness Opinions 494
The Role of the Board of Directors 495
Directors' Fiduciary Duties 495
Board Decisions in a Transactional Context 498
The Business Judgment Rule 498
Conflict Transactions and Going Private 500
Entire Fairness 500
Overview of Fairness Opinions 502
Why Do Boards Seek Fairness Opinions? 502
When Do Boards Seek Fairness Opinions? 503
What Do Fairness Opinions Say? 503
Standards and Regulation 505
SEC Disclosure Requirements 505
Underlying Financial Analyses 506
Scope of Work Issues 509
Summary 510
References to Valuation in Fairness Matters 511

Chapter 31
Valuation in Solvency Matters 513

Bob Bartell, CFA

Introduction 513
Claims of Fraudulent Conveyance/Transfers 513
Claims Regarding Breaches of Fiduciary Duties in the Context of Insolvency 515
Valuation Aspects of Cancellation of Indebtedness Income 516
Summary 518
Reference to Valuation in Solvency Matters 518

Chapter 32
Valuation in Lost Profits Damages Matters 519

William W. Thomsen, ASA, CFA

Introduction 519
Situations Requiring Calculation of Lost Profits or Lost Business Value 519
Prerequisites to Damage Recovery 519
Proximate Cause 519
Reasonable Certainty 520
Foreseeability 520
Key Concepts in Damage Calculations 520
Mitigation 521
Period of Damages 521
Time Value of Money 521
Ex Ante versus Ex Post Calculations 521
Damage Calculation Methods: Lost Profits and Lost Business Value 523
Measuring Lost Profit Damages 523
Measuring Lost Business Value Damages 525
When to Use Lost Profits, Lost Business Value, or Both 525
When Is a Loss of Profits Calculation Preferred? 525
When Is a Loss of Business Value Calculation Preferred? 525
When Should Both Lost Profits and Lost Business Value Calculations Be Used? 527
Key Differences between Lost Profits and Lost Business Value Calculations 527
Benefit Stream: Profit versus Cash Flow 528
Income Tax Treatment: Pretax versus After Tax 528

Discount Rate Calculation: Incremental versus Entire Business 529
Use of Hindsight: Ex Ante versus Ex Post 529
Standard of Value/Investor Perspective: Actual versus Hypothetical Investor 529
Present Value Calculations: Carrying Forward versus Discounting Back 530
When Lost Profits Might Be Greater Than Lost Business Value Damages 530
Using the Damages Expert 531
Summary 532
References for Lost Profits Damages 532

Chapter 33
Appraisal Reports **533**

Jay E. Fishman, FASA, FRICS and Jeffrey S. Tarbell, ASA, CFA

Introduction 533
Comprehensive Appraisal Reports 533
Introduction 534
Sources of Information 535
Qualitative Analysis of the Company 536
Subject Ownership Interest 537
Quantitative Analysis 537
Normalization and Control Adjustments 537
Valuation Approaches and Methods Considered 538
Valuation Approaches and Methods Used 538
Valuation Adjustments 540
Excess or Deficient Operating Assets 540
Nonoperating Items 540
Certification of the Appraiser Responsible for the Opinion 540
Conclusion of Value 541
Qualifications of the Appraiser 541
Summary Level Reports 541
Calculation Report 541
Oral Report 541
Summary 542
References for Appraisal Reports 542

Chapter 34
Checklist for Reviewing a Business Valuation Report 543

Timothy R. Lee, ASA and Lucas M. Parris, ASA, CFA

Introduction 543
Credentials of Report Preparer (Chapter 37) 543
Report Introduction (Chapters 1 and 2) 544
Economic Analysis (Chapter 17) 545
Industry Analysis (Chapter 17) 545
Interviews and Site Visits (Chapter 5) 545
Financial Statement Adjustments (Chapter 15) 546
Financial Statement Analysis (Chapter 16) 546
Reasonable Compensation (Chapter 13) 546
Discounts and Premiums (Chapter 18) 547
Valuation Methods Used (Chapter 3) 547
 Income Approach (Chapters 6 and 7) 547
 Market Approach (Chapter 8) 548
 Asset-Based Approach (Chapters 9 and 10) 548
Income Approach (Chapters 6 and 7) 548
 Discounted Cash Flow Method 548
 Discount/Capitalization Rates 549
Guideline Public Company Method (Chapter 8) 549
 Criteria for Selection 549
 Financial Metrics 550
 Statistics and Weightings 550
Guideline Transaction Method (Chapter 8) 550
 Criteria for Selection 550
 Financial Metrics 551
Past Transaction Method (Chapter 8) 551
 Criteria for Selection 551
 Financial Metrics 551
Excess Earnings Method (Chapter 10) 552
Rules of Thumb (Chapter 11) 552
Goodwill (Chapter 12) 553
Reconciliation of Indicated Values (Chapter 19) 553
Overall Assessment 553

Chapter 35
Admissibility and Impact of Expert Business Valuation Evidence 555

Anita M. Ventrelli, JD

Introduction 555
Supreme Court Affirms Courts' "Gatekeeper" Role 556
Daubert v. Merrell Dow Pharmaceuticals 556
General Electric Co. v. Joiner 558
Kumho Tire Co. v. Carmichael 558
Selecting and Evaluating the Appraiser 560
Professional Certifications and the Case for Peer Review 562
The CPA as Business Appraiser 563
Advantages 563
Disadvantages 563
The Financial Analyst as Business Appraiser 565
Advantages 565
Disadvantages 565
The Broker as Business Appraiser 566
Advantages 566
Disadvantages 566
The Academic as Business Appraiser 567
Advantages 567
Disadvantages 567
Engaging the Business Appraisal Expert 568
Court Cases Involving Appraiser Challenges 568
The Appraisal Opinion Must Stay within Expertise 571
Source Documents Must Be Those "Typically Relied Upon" by Appraisal Experts 572
Subjective Statements Must Be Documented 574
Superficial Treatment of Issues: The "Down and Dirty" Appraisal 575
Inaccurate or Inadequate Use of Accepted Methodologies—
the Expert Must Be Reliable 577
Original and Personally Developed Appraisal Methods Create Risk 579
Admissible Expert Evidence versus the Weight Accorded to It 580
Common Errors 582
Summary 583
References for Expert Witness Testimony 583

Chapter 36
Discovery and the Business Valuation Expert 585

Anita M. Ventrelli, JD

Introduction 585
- Expert Witnesses: Disclosure Requirements and Written Appraisal Report 594
- Federal Rule of Civil Procedure 26(a)(2) 594
- Jurisdictions That Follow or Deviate from FRCP 26(a)(2) 595

Requests for Production of Documents and Entry for Inspection and Interviews 596
- Documents 596
- Site Visit and Interviews 596
- Attorney's Role 597
- Preparation 597
- Mission 597
- Information to Be Gathered 597
- Individuals to Be Interviewed 598
- Confidentiality 598
- Adversarial Proceedings 598
- Federal Rule of Civil Procedure 34 599
- Limitations on the Scope of Discovery 599
- Sanctions for Failure to Comply with a Discovery Order 600

Subpoena for Production of Documents, Electronically Stored Information, or Tangible Things, or to Permit the Inspection of Premises 601
- Subpoena of Expert's Work Papers 602

Interrogatories: Timing of Service and Limitations 603
- Interrogatories Depend upon Written Report Requirement 603
- Timing of Service 603
- Limits on Number of Interrogatories That Can Be Served 604
- Form of Response 604

Requests for Admission 605

Depositions: Timing of Request and Special Rules 605
- Federal Rules of Civil Procedure 26(b)(4), 30, and 31 605

Depositions on Written Questions 607
- States That Do Not Allow Depositions of Expert Witnesses as a Matter of Course 607
- Ensuring an Expert Is Deposition Ready 607
- Timely Disclosure and Duty to Supplement 608
- Scope of Discovery—Some Specific Examples 611

Involving the Business Valuation Expert in Discovery 614
Preparing Discovery Requests 614
Preparing Deposition and Interrogatory Questions 614
Presence at Opposing Expert's Deposition 615
Involving Your Expert in Depositions of Opposing Experts 615
Rebutting the Opposition 616
Common Errors 617
Summary 617
Reference for Discovery and the Business Valuation Expert 618

Chapter 37
Business Valuation Standards and Credentials 619

Jay E. Fishman, FASA, FRICS and Kenneth J. Pia, Jr., ASA, CPA/ABV, MCBA

Introduction 619
Organizations Offering Professional Accreditation 619
Other Organizations Offering Business Valuation Guidance 620
Business Valuation Professional Standards 621
Uniform Standards of Professional Appraisal Practice 621
Other Professional Organization Standards 623
Internal Revenue Service Authority 623
Summary 623
References for Business Valuation Standards and Credentials 624

Chapter 38
Valuation and Appraiser Penalties 625

Michael A. Gregory, ASA, CVA

Introduction 625
Standards 625
History of the § 6695A Penalty on Appraisers and Definitions 626
Qualified Appraiser and Qualified Appraisal Defined 626
Qualified Appraiser 626
Qualified Appraisal 627
Additional Requirements Relating to Non-cash Charitable Contributions 627
2010 Developments 628
January 2020 Developments 628
Reaction by Professional Organizations 628

Follow Up to Letter 4477 629
Summary of the History 629
Key Elements of the IRS Penalty Handbook 629
I.R.C. § 6695A and Two Examples 631
Example One 632
Example Two 633
An Exception to the Application of the Penalty 633
Statute of Limitations 634
Penalty Case File 634
Conclusion § 6695A 635
Valuation Penalties on the Taxpayer and/or Appraiser 635
Summary 635
References for Valuation and Appraiser Penalties 636

Chapter 39
Alternative Dispute Resolution 637

Eric Rowen, JD, and Neil Beaton, ASA, CFA, CPA/ABV/CFF

Introduction 637
Alternative Dispute Resolution Act of 1998 639
Advantages of Arbitration versus Litigation 640
Choosing Arbitrators or Mediators 641
Arbitrators 641
Mediators 641
Process for Selecting Arbitrators 642
Instructions to Arbitrators 642
Communications with Parties and Attorneys 643
Site Visit 643
Hearings 643
Reporting an Arbitration Conclusion 643
Alternative Dispute Resolution in Marital Dissolutions 644
Alternative Dispute Resolution in Federal Tax Disputes 645
Summary 646
References for Alternative Dispute Resolution 647
Books and Publications 647
Professional Arbitration and Mediation Organizations 648

Chapter 40
Examining a Business Valuation Expert in Depositions and at Trials 649
Anita M. Ventrelli, JD

Introduction 649
Trial Testimony Considerations 650
Background and Qualifications (Chapter 37) 652
Education 652
Professional Credentials and What the Expert Did to Attain the Credential 652
Experience 653
Assignment (Chapters 1 and 2) 654
Work Done 654
Sources of Information 654
Economic and Industry Information (Chapter 17) 654
Company Information (Chapter 5) 655
Financial Statement Adjustments (Chapter 15) 655
Comparative Financial Statement Analysis (Chapter 16) 656
Overall Valuation Methodology (Chapter 3) 656
Income Approach (Chapter 6) 657
Developing a Discount Rate (Chapter 7) 657
Market Approach (Chapter 8) 658
The Asset-Based Approach (Chapter 9) 659
Discounts and/or Premiums (Chapter 18) 660
Reconciliation of Value Indications (Chapter 19) 660
Concluding Inquiries and Principles 660
Common Errors 660
Summary 661
Reference for Cross-Examining Business Valuation Expert 662

Appendix A: Glossary of Business Valuation Terms 663

Appendix B: Fair Value in Dissent and Oppression 683
Gilbert E. Matthews, CFA

Appendix C: Terms of the Market Exception 721
Gilbert E. Matthews, CFA

Index of Court Decisions 731
Subject Index 749

Table of Exhibits

Exhibit 2-1: Levels of Value	20
Exhibit 3-1: Schematic Diagram of Business Valuation Approaches and Methods	28
Exhibit 3-2: Value of Invested Capital and Direct Valuation of Equity Procedures	29
Exhibit 4-1: Widget Corporation Financial Data	34
Exhibit 4-2: Levels of Financial Statement Preparation	35
Exhibit 5-1: Preliminary Documents and Information Checklist for Business Valuation of Typical Business	46
Exhibit 5-2: Description of the Business	54
Exhibit 5-3: Markets and Marketing	55
Exhibit 6-1: Terms and Notations Commonly Used in the Income Approach	61
Exhibit 6-2: Discounted Present Value of an Annuity	62
Exhibit 6-3: Schematic Showing Timeline of Receipt of Economic Income Equivalent to Formula 6-5	66
Exhibit 6-4: Schematic Showing Timeline of Receipt of Economic Income under the Midyear Discounting Convention	74
Exhibit 6-5: The Midyear Convention in the Capitalization Method	76
Exhibit 6-6: The Midyear Convention in the Discounting Method	78
Exhibit 7-1: Schematic Diagram Illustrating Beta	88
Exhibit 8-1: Major Market Approach Business Valuation Scenarios	104
Exhibit 8-2: Marvel Corporation Financial Data	112
Exhibit 8-3: Marvel Corporation Invested Capital Valuation Multiples	113
Exhibit 8-4: Marvel Corporation Common Equity Valuation Multiples	114
Exhibit 8-5: Widget Corporation and Guideline Companies Comparative Financial Analysis	118
Exhibit 8-6: Widget Corporation Guideline Company Invested Capital Multiples	119
Exhibit 8-7: Widget Corporation Valuation Using Invested Capital Multiples	121
Exhibit 8-8: Widget Corporation Guideline Company Equity Multiples	122
Exhibit 8-9: Widget Corporation Valuation Using Equity Multiples	123
Exhibit 9-1: Alpha Company Adjusted Net Asset Value	131
Exhibit 10-1: Illustration of Excess Earnings Method	139
Exhibit 10-2: Definitions of Goodwill	141

Exhibit 10-3: A "Sanity Check" for a Value Indicated by the Excess Earnings Method 142
Exhibit 10-4: Revenue Ruling 68–609 142
Exhibit 11-1: Rules of Thumb for Valuation 151
Exhibit 12–1: Personal versus Enterprise Goodwill in Divorce 158
Exhibit 13-1: Compensation Ratios from Dunn & Bradstreet—Example Machine Shops 171
Exhibit 13-2: Compensation Ratios from IBIS*World*—Example Machine Shops 172
Exhibit 13-3: Compensation Ratios from ERI's Executive Compensation Assessor®—Example Machine Shops 173
Exhibit 13-4: Clary Hood Compensation, Deficiency, and Penalty 178
Exhibit 14-1: Tables 1, 2, and 3—"With Model" 190
Exhibit 14-2: Measuring Impact on Gross Profit from Competition by Key Person 192
Exhibit 14-3: Tables 1, 2, and 3—"Without Model" 194
Exhibit 15-1: Meteor Manufacturing, Inc.: Adjustments to Income Statement 211
Exhibit 15-2: Meteor Manufacturing, Inc.: Adjustments to Balance Sheet 212
Exhibit 16-1: Jasper Steel: Two-Year Balance Sheet and Income Statement 218
Exhibit 16-2: Jasper Steel: Horizontal Analysis of Balance Sheet and Income Statement 219
Exhibit 16-3: Omega Steel Mills and Jasper Steel: Sales Figures in Dollars 220
Exhibit 16-4: Omega Steel Mills and Jasper Steel: Sales Figures in Percentages 220
Exhibit 16-5: Omega Steel Mills Sales Figures 221
Exhibit 16-6: Trend of Omega Steel Mills Sales 221
Exhibit 16-7: Growth of Omega Steel Mills Sales 222
Exhibit 16-8: Trend and Growth of Omega Steel Mills Sales 223
Exhibit 16-9: L.M. Shaw, Omega Steel Mills, and Jasper Steel: 2021 Balance Sheet and Income Statement 223
Exhibit 16-10: L.M. Shaw, Omega Steel Mills, and Jasper Steel: Common-Size Balance Sheet and Income Statement 225
Exhibit 16-11: L.M. Shaw, Omega Steel Mills, and Jasper Steel: Common-Size Balance Sheet and Income Statement with Industry Statistics 226
Exhibit 16-12: Selected Jasper Steel Financial Information 228
Exhibit 16-13: Jasper Steel Return on Assets 228
Exhibit 16-14: Hypothetical Return on Assets 228
Exhibit 16-15: Effects of Asset Levels 229
Exhibit 16-16: Jasper Steel Profit Margin, Turnover, and Return on Assets 2017–2021 230
Exhibit 16-17: Jasper Steel Common-Size Income Statement 2017–2021 230
Exhibit 16-18: Jasper Steel Common-Size Balance Sheet 2017–2021 231

Exhibit 16-19: Jasper Steel Turnover Ratios 2017–2021 232
Exhibit 16-20: Return on Equity and Debt-to-Equity 232
Exhibit 16-21: Effect of Debt-to-Equity Ratio 233
Exhibit 16-22: Jasper Steel Liquidity Ratios 2017–2021 234
Exhibit 16-23: Jasper Steel Solvency Ratios 2017–2021 236
Exhibit 17-1: 2022 GDP in Billions of Current Dollars 241
Exhibit 17-2: All-Urban Consumer Price Index 1982–84 = 100 242
Exhibit 17-3: Impact from Variable versus Fixed Costs 243
Exhibit 17-4: 2022 GDP by State Current Dollar 244
Exhibit 17-5: 2022 Per Capita and Total Personal Income by State 245
Exhibit 17-6: Selected Historical and Forecasted Revenue Growth Rates 246
Exhibit 17-7: Selected Industry Common-Size Financial Statements and Ratios 248
Exhibit 18-1: Levels of Value 252
Exhibit 18-2: Variations in Initial Value Dependent on Valuation Approach 261
Exhibit 18-3: Summary of Restricted Stock Studies 267
Exhibit 18-4: Implied DLOM on LEAPS Stratified by Revenue 271
Exhibit 18-5: Johnson/Park Empirical Method Summarized 272
Exhibit 19-1: Example of Explicit Weighting of Value Indications 287
Exhibit 19-2: Illustrative Business Enterprise, Inc. Business Valuation Methods and Value Estimates: Valuation Analysis and Conclusion 288
Exhibit 21-1: Taxable Transactions Requiring Valuations 330
Exhibit 23-1: Dissenting Shareholders—Fair Value Definition by State 375
Exhibit 23-2: Selected Chancery Court Decisions Relying on Valuation Methods from 2010 to 2023 393
Exhibit 24-1: Simplified Steps to an Initial Leveraged ESOP Transaction 407
Exhibit 24-2: Simplified Steps Subsequent to the Initial Stock Purchase Transaction 408
Exhibit 25-1: Present Value of $1,000 at Various Market Rates of Interest 428
Exhibit 26-1: Traditional Corporate Valuation Model for Identical C and S Corps 434
Exhibit 26-2: Significant Cases Related to Pass-through Entity Valuations 436
Exhibit 28-1: Economic Damages Categories by Intellectual Property (IP) Type 460
Exhibit 28-2: Summary of the *Georgia-Pacific* Factors 462
Exhibit 29-1: Levels of Value 484
Exhibit 29-2: Proceeds Are NOT a Corporate Asset 488
Exhibit 29-3: Proceeds Are a Corporate Asset 489
Exhibit 30-1: Implied Target Company per Share Reference Ranges 508
Exhibit 32-1: Ex Ante Damages Calculation Example 522
Exhibit 32-2: Ex Post Damages Calculation Example 523

Exhibit 32-3: Damage Calculation: Finite Loss Period 526
Exhibit 32-4: Damage Calculation: Permanent Loss (Business Still Operational) 526
Exhibit 32-5: Damage Calculation: Permanent Loss (Business Destroyed) 527
Exhibit 32-6: Damage Calculation: Permanent Loss (Business Destroyed—"Slow Death") 528
Exhibit 32-7: Summary of Key Differences between Lost Profits and Lost Business Value Damage Calculations 530
Exhibit 36-1: Summary of Discovery Rules 586
Exhibit 37-1: Professional Accreditation Quick Reference List 621

Foreword—Perspective from the Bench

Judge Steven I. Platt (Ret.)

The Platt Group, Inc., Annapolis, Maryland

In my over 35 years serving as a judge on three different Maryland courts, cases where valuation was an important component were among the most challenging. Valuation is not an area where law schools provide much background for what's ahead. The terminology and theories can be challenging even for experienced attorneys. The third edition of *The Lawyer's Business Valuation Handbook* provides the attorney first confronted with valuation issues with a thorough understanding of the techniques for valuing used by "experts" for closely held businesses and interests in closely held businesses.

The beginning chapters cover the terminology and theories of appraisal employed by valuation practitioners. For example, disputes arise over the meaning of *fair market value*, often used as the default definition of value in contracts, such as buy-sell agreements. But the value of partial interests in businesses most often requires analysis of whether a discount needs to be applied to a proportionate interest in the entity owning the business in order to correctly value it. The chapter "Discounts and Premiums" provides the attorney with a thorough understanding of the theory and the different methodologies used to estimate appropriate partial interest discounts in business entities.

That chapter is followed up with a chapter "Valuing Interests in Real Property Holding Entities" that deals specifically with the nuances of differences between the real estate appraisal that may be used in valuing the underlying real property and the valuation of a partial interest in an entity owning the real property.

Many chapters deal with specific areas of controversy. For example, the chapter "Employment and Noncompetition Agreements" walks the reader through the legal and valuation aspects of this often contentious and evolving area of the law, and includes an example that helps the attorney understand the intricacies that surround quantifying the damages resulting from a breach of contract.

The chapter "Valuing Intellectual Property and Intangible Assets" provides a good overview of an area where infringement disputes can arise, and the chapter "Valuation in Lost Profits Damages Matters" lays out the concepts and process of quantifying damages from such infringements.

The series of chapters "Admissibility and Impact of Expert Business Valuation Evidence," "Discovery and the Business Valuation Expert," and "Examining a Business Valuation Expert in Depositions and at Trials," contributed by a noted litigator, can prepare an attorney for litigation of valuation disputes, from screening and selecting an appropriate, qualified expert to understanding the discovery process to effectively preparing your witness for deposition and trial and finally to delving into the positions taken by an opposing expert at deposition and at trial.

Since leaving the bench, I have been focused on resolving disputes through mediation and arbitration. These paths are often preferable to the courtroom because they are private venues, keeping confidential information and the "dirty laundry" out of the public eye. The chapter "Alternative Dispute Resolution" provides a good primer on the value of such procedures and the process, so an attorney can explain these alternative methods of dispute resolution, which often are more efficient and more economical than litigation to the attorneys' client.

I therefore highly recommend the third edition to any attorney first confronted with a valuation dispute and even to an experienced attorney as a refresher. Judges confronted with hearing a valuation dispute will also benefit from the easy-to-read style of the third edition and its thorough content focused on giving an attorney what he or she needs to effectively represent clients, while at the same time assist the court or the ADR tribunal in reaching a fair and evidence-based resolution of the dispute presented to it for disposition.

Note: Upon "retirement" from the bench, Judge Platt is currently engaged in mediation, arbitration, and neutral case evaluation of complex civil litigation. He is a Neutral and member of the Maryland Board of Directors of The National Academy of Distinguished Neutrals, which, after a thorough peer review by the board of directors, selects only the top 10% of Neutrals in the country. Judge Platt is the author of *Lessons Lived and Learned—My Life On and Off The Bench*, available at www.judgestevenplatt.com.

Foreword—Tax Law Perspective

Stephanie Loomis-Price

Partner, Perkins Coie, LLP, Seattle, Washington, and Austin, Texas

Fellow, American College of Trust and Estate Counsel, and Fellow, American College of Tax Counsel

Valuation controversies in federal tax issues are frequent and complicated. The third edition of *The Lawyer's Business Valuation Handbook* introduces the reader—often an attorney—to valuation theory in straightforward terms, providing knowledge necessary to work with sophisticated business appraisers, zealous IRS representatives, and thoughtful judges. The contributing authors provide a thorough background on valuation theory, highlighting the major areas of which attorneys should be aware.

For example, the chapters on "Employment and Non-Competition Agreements" (an expanded and updated chapter in this third edition) and "Valuation of Stock of S-Corporations and Interests in Other Pass-through Entities" provide attorneys with straightforward explanations of the complexities of these often controversial topics in such a way that the reader comes away with an understanding difficult to find elsewhere and armed with convincing arguments as a result.

The chapters "Financial Statement Terminology" and "Financial Statement Adjustments" provide important background in the process of converting basic financial statement information to information used in valuing closely held businesses and interests in such businesses.

The chapters covering "Discounts and Premiums," "Valuations for Gift, Estate, and Charitable Contribution Matters" (two chapters that have been updated in the third edition) and "Valuing Interests in Real Property Holding Entities" (a new chapter in this edition) are contributed by noted practitioners, providing not just the background for, but also insights into, what are most likely the most controversial areas in federal gift, estate tax, and charitable contribution litigation—the valuation of interests in closely held businesses.

The third edition also provides a good introduction into other areas of federal income tax controversies in the chapter "Valuations for Federal Income Tax Matters" (another new chapter in the third edition), including a good primer on related party transfer pricing issues.

The chapter "Appraisal Reports" will assist the attorney in understanding the content that should be included in a thorough appraisal report, and the chapter "Checklists for Reviewing Valuation Reports" provides invaluable resources to assist in the appraisal review process.

The chapters "Admissibility and Impact of Business Valuation Evidence," contributed by a noted litigator, and "Business Valuation Standards and Credentials" provide insights into screening and selecting business valuation experts.

The chapters "Discovery and the Business Valuation Expert" and "Examining a Business Valuation Expert in Depositions and at Trials," both contributed by a noted litigator, will help the attorney understand the processes, and how to avoid the pitfalls, of taking a dispute to court.

The chapter "Alternative Dispute Resolution" explains alternative avenues of settling a dispute in the valuation and tax contexts.

Finally, the chapter "Valuation and Appraiser Penalties" (another new chapter in the third edition) explains the ins and outs of dealing with the Internal Revenue Service when the differences between the taxpayer's and IRS's positions are significant.

I recommend the third edition to any attorney involved in tax controversy work (and to CPAs and other tax professionals as well). Our highly charged environment of increased scrutiny by the IRS at the audit level only increases the need for tax practitioners' preparedness to assist in obtaining the best supportable and defensible appraisal report against often ill-founded positions of the IRS.

The third edition stands ready to equip you with the tools you are likely to need in guiding our colleagues at the IRS as to valuation methodologies and approaches that they need to consider.

Background: Ms. Price has assisted clients in numerous federal tax cases in U.S. Tax Court, the U.S. Court of Claims, and the U.S. Courts of Appeals for the Fifth, Eighth, and Eleventh Circuits. Named *Lawyer of the Year*—Trust and Estates in Austin by *Best Lawyers in America®*, 2020 and 2024.

Foreword—Family Law Perspective

Thomas J. Sasser

Managing Partner with Sasser, Cestero & Roy, PA, West Palm Beach, Florida

Fellow and National Vice President of the American Academy of Matrimonial Lawyers and Fellow and President of the International Academy of Matrimonial Lawyers

Family law practitioners are confronted with valuation issues every day. Among the most difficult issues that family lawyers confront is the valuation of interests in closely held businesses. The third edition will provide counsel who is first confronted with such a valuation issue with the background necessary to understand valuation theory and the basics of conducting an appraisal. The third edition will also prepare you for discussing valuation issues with the business appraiser and, more importantly, with your clients.

The beginning chapters walk through the basics of valuing a closely held business and partial interests in closely held entities, the appraisal process, and the more difficult areas that can lead to disagreement. For example, partial interests in closely held entities require an understanding of discounts that may be applicable in arriving at a valuation conclusion. The chapters "Discounts and Premiums" (a completely updated chapter in the third edition) and "Valuing Interests in Real Property Holding Entities" (a new chapter in the third edition) walk you through the reasons for discounts and the current methodologies used in estimating supportable discounts and when they are applicable.

The chapters "Personal versus Enterprise Goodwill" and "Marital Dissolution Valuations" (both completely updated chapters in the third edition), contributed by two noted experts in marital valuations, go deep into the controversies that confront the family law practitioner. The chapters provide the insights into the theories and some of the most important court decisions with which you need to be familiar.

The chapters "Admissibility and Impact of Business Valuation Evidence," contributed by a noted family law litigator, and "Business Valuation Standards and Credentials" provide invaluable insight into screening and selecting business valuation experts.

The chapters "Discovery and the Business Valuation Expert" and "Examining a Business Valuation Expert in Depositions and at Trials," both contributed by that noted litigator, will help you understand the processes and the pitfalls of taking a dispute to court.

Finally, the chapter "Alternative Dispute Resolution" explains viable alternative avenues of settling a dispute.

I highly recommend the third edition to all family law practitioners. For the novice, it is a valuable primer that will help get you up to speed in the most important areas of valuing closely held businesses and interests in closely held entities. For the experienced practitioner, the third edition will be a valuable refresher and will provide you with important references to some of the best resources that go deeper into valuation theory and controversies. The third edition will provide both the novice and experienced practitioner with the key terminology and an understanding of the logic used in the valuation process so that you can better communicate with your clients and help them select the best business valuation expert to deal with the business valuation issues that are a part of the dissolution of their marriage.

Background: Mr. Sasser is past chair of the Family Law Section of The Florida Bar and four-time past chair of the Florida Bar Marital and Family Law Board Certification Review Course and was selected to *Super Lawyers*®, 2006–2024.

Foreword—Corporate Law Perspective

Lewis H. Lazarus and K. Tyler O'Connell

Partners with Morris James LLP, Wilmington, Delaware

Valuation issues are ubiquitous for lawyers working in sophisticated practices with corporations, limited liability companies, or other business entity forms. Whether in advising a client concerning a potential transaction, or in assessing how a reviewing court may assess valuation issues after the fact, *The Lawyer's Business Valuation Handbook* has been a key resource for transactional attorneys and business litigators alike since its initial publication in 2000. Reflecting its importance, this Handbook is frequently cited by courts in Delaware and elsewhere in addressing valuation issues involving business entities.

The third edition provides the attorney confronted with valuation issues, whether tax-related or dispute-related, with a thorough understanding of the theory of valuing businesses and interests in business entities. The chapters reflect updates or contributions by noted valuation practitioners who are steeped in the theory and well-experienced in the controversies that can develop. Like prior editions, the third edition provides business lawyers with critical information and perspective in considering the various areas in which valuation issues may arise.

For example, for those lawyers whose clients are confronted with owner disputes, the chapter "Shareholder and Partner Disputes" provides an overview of the current state of the law and theory concerning valuation in disputes involving the exercise of dissenters' rights and actions involving alleged breaches of fiduciary duties. The chapters "Reasonable Compensation," "Employment and Noncompetition Agreements" (a newly updated and expanded chapter in the third edition), and "Valuation Provisions in Buy-Sell Agreements" each provide background in these specialized areas that will help practitioners explain them to clients to minimize potential problems in the future. The Handbook also includes new chapters on "Valuing Intellectual Property and Intangible Assets" and "Valuation in Lost Profits Damages Matters," recurring issues specifically addressed in the Handbook.

Employee stock ownership plans (ESOPs) are often discussed among business owners. The chapter "Valuations for Employee Stock Ownership Plans" (a new chapter in the third edition) explains the intricacies of ESOPs and the valuation issues that result.

For those whose areas of practice include federal taxation, the chapter "Valuations for Federal Income Tax Matters" will serve as a valuable primer or refresher into some of the more controversial areas, including related-party transfer pricing.

A new chapter "Valuation in Fairness Matters" addresses the law and valuation theory pertinent to financial advisors' fairness opinions—that is, assessing whether a transaction is financially fair to the business entity, its owners, or some subset thereof. Similarly, the new chapter "Valuation in Solvency Matters" discusses the legal standards and analytical approach to assess whether an entity is solvent and expected to remain so following an anticipated transaction. These are critical issues to owners, members of management, and their legal counsel to help ensure legal compliance, to minimize risk to important transactions, and to appropriately present disputes when they arise.

We highly recommend the third edition to any business lawyer as an important resource for advising clients concerning recurring valuation issues, whether ex ante when considering a potential transaction, or ex post in ensuring the merits of any valuation disputes are presented appropriately to a reviewing court. Whether practitioners find it on a bookshelf or in digital form, business lawyers and their advisors working on important matters for sophisticated clients should have this excellent treatise at the ready.

Background: For almost 40 years, Lewis Lazarus's practice has focused on representing parties in disputes concerning the governance of Delaware corporations and other business entities. He has served as counsel in seminal cases that have helped shape the contours of Delaware corporate law. He has been recognized by *Chambers and Partners*, *Best Lawyers in America*®, and *Super Lawyers*®, among other publications.

Tyler O'Connell has more than 20 years' experience representing directors, officers, members of management, and significant investors in litigation involving Delaware business entities, as well as transactions that may present litigation risk. His work has been recognized by *Chambers and Partners*, *Best Lawyers in America*®, and *Super Lawyers*®, among other publications.

About Shannon Pratt

Shannon P. Pratt, DBA, CFA, FASA, ARM–BV, MCBA, MCBC, CM&AA, was recognized as the foremost authority in the field of business valuation and was a legendary author and teacher of the many concepts used today throughout the world.

He was a graduate of the University of Washington, where he studied journalism and business administration, and Indiana University, where he earned his doctorate in business administration/finance.

Shannon founded Willamette Management Associates in 1969, which set him upon a journey of providing valuations and expert testimony for the next 50 years. He authored his first valuation book, *Valuing a Business: The Analysis and Appraisal of Closely Held Companies*, in 1981. This book has served as the basis for educating thousands of business valuation consultants.

Shannon developed and taught business valuation courses for the American Society of Appraisers (ASA) and taught business valuation courses for accounting and appraisal organizations around the world. He later founded Business Valuation Resources and Shannon Pratt Valuations.

Shannon's professional recognitions include being conferred the designation of Fellow (FASA) by his peers for contributions to ASA and the appraisal profession—the highest honor ASA bestows. He held a specialty designation in Appraisal Review and Management for Business Valuation; a Master Certified Business Appraiser; a Chartered Financial Analyst; a Master Certified Business Counselor; and Certified in Mergers and Acquisitions.

Dr. Pratt's professional recognitions included being awarded a life member of the Business Valuation Committee of the ASA, a life member of the ASA, past chair and a life member of the ESOP Association Advisory Committee on Valuation, a life member of the Institute of Business Appraisers, the Magna Cum Laude in Business Appraisal award from the National Association of Certified Valuation Analysts, and the distinguished service award of the Portland Society of Financial Analysts. He was also a past trustee of the Appraisal Foundation.

Dr. Pratt authored or coauthored the following McGraw-Hill books: *Valuing a Business: The Analysis and Appraisal of Closely Held Companies*, 5th ed. (2008); *Analyzing Complex Appraisals for Business Professionals* with John Lifflander (2016); and *Valuing Small Businesses and Professional Practices*, 3rd ed. (1998). He is coauthor of the following Wiley books: *Cost of Capital: Applications and Examples*, 5th ed. with Roger J. Grabowski (2014); *Standards of Value*, 2nd ed. with Jay Fishman and William Morrison (2013); *Cost of Capital in Litigation: Applications and Examples* with Roger J. Grabowski (2011); and *Business Valuation and Taxes: Procedure, Law and Perspective*, 2nd ed. with the late Honorable David Laro (2011). He is the author of the following Wiley books: *Business Valuation Discounts and Premiums*, 2nd ed. (2008); *The Market Approach to Valuing Businesses*, 2nd ed. (2005); and the *Business Valuation Body of Knowledge: Exam Review and Professional Reference*, 2nd ed. (2003). He is coauthor of the following American Bar Association books: *The Lawyer's Guide to the Cost of Capital* with Roger J. Grabowski (2014) and *The Lawyer's Business Valuation Handbook*, 2nd ed. with Alina V. Niculita (2013). He was also coauthor of the annual PPC's *Guide to Business Valuations* (Thomson Reuters) and *A Consensus View: Q&A Guide to Financial Valuation* with James Hitchner and Jay Fishman (Valuation Products and Services, 2016).

Shannon Pease Pratt passed away in his sleep on the morning of November 26, 2021, at his home in Portland.

About the Editors

Roger J. Grabowski, FASA, has had a career of more than 50 years in valuation and headed the editorial team for this third edition.

Mr. Grabowski has testified in court as an expert witness on various valuation matters. For example, his testimony in the U.S. District Court was referenced in the U.S. Supreme Court's landmark *Newark Morning Ledger* opinion (allowing amortization of customer-based intangible assets). His use of the discounted cash flow (DCF) method and the modified capital asset pricing model (MCAPM) for estimating the cost of capital for operating businesses was accepted by the U.S. Tax Court in the Northern Trust Company decision (the first time that the U.S. Tax Court accepted the DCF method and the MCAPM in valuing a closely held business).

Mr. Grabowski is co-developer of the annual *Risk Premium Report—Size and Risk Studies* for estimating cost of equity capital (available via the Kroll Cost of Capital Navigator) and has coauthored several books, contributed to other books, and authored and coauthored numerous papers.

He is the contributing author to *The Art of Valuation: Reflections, Stories and Strategies from Business Appraisal* (The Appraisal Institute, 2023); coauthor of the chapters "Case Study on Cost of Capital," in *Cases in Financial Management: Applications for Financial Analysis* (World Scientific Publishing, 2023), and "Discounts Rates in Theory," in *Lost Profits Damages: Principles, Methods and Applications* 2nd ed. (Valuation Products and Services, 2022); contributing author and co-editor of *Shannon Pratt's Valuing a Business: The Analysis and Appraisal of Closely Held Companies* 6th ed. (McGraw-Hill, 2022); coauthor of *Valuation Handbook-International Guide to Cost of Capital: 2021 Summary Edition* (CFA Institute Research Foundation, 2021), coauthor with Shannon Pratt of *The Lawyer's Guide to Cost of Capital* (American Bar Association, 2014), *Cost of Capital: Applications and Examples* 5th ed. (Wiley, 2014); *Cost of Capital: Workbook and Technical Supplement,* 4th ed. (Wiley, 2011), and author of *Closely Held Corporations: Valuations* (Steven C. Dilley's Federal Tax Workshops, 1983).

Among the papers he authored are "Cost of Capital Estimation in the Current Distressed Environment" in *The Journal of Applied Research in Accounting and Finance* (July 2009) and "Comparing Growth Rates Used in Discounted Cash Flow Valuations" in *Business Valuation Review* (2021). He is a former editor of the ASA's *Business Valuation Review*.

Mr. Grabowski served on The Appraisal Foundation's Working Group that developed the advisory Valuation in Financial Reporting #5–The Company-Specific Risk Premium.

Most recently he was managing director with Kroll's (formerly Duff & Phelps) Valuation Advisory Services practice. Previously he was managing director with Standard & Poor's Corporate Value Consulting practice, a partner with PricewaterhouseCoopers LLP, and a partner with one of its predecessor firms, Price Waterhouse, where he founded its U.S. Valuation practice and managed the Real Estate Appraisal practice. Before that, he was one of the founders of the valuation firm, Valtec Associates, and started his valuation career with American Valuation Consultants. Mr. Grabowski is an Accredited Senior Appraiser, accredited in business valuation, and a Fellow of the ASA (FASA), the ASA's highest distinction. In 2022, the ASA awarded Mr. Grabowski the Special Recognition Award in memory of Shannon Pratt and, in 2023, the ASA awarded him their Lifetime Achievement Award. He received his BBA from Loyola University of Chicago and did his doctoral studies in finance at Northwestern University.

Alina V. Niculita, ASA, ARM-BV, CFA, MBA, is director of Valuation Services at Morones Analytics, LLC., and previously was president and chief operating officer of Shannon Pratt Valuations. She was previously managing editor of Shannon Pratt's Business Valuation Update and Economic Outlook Update.

Over the past 20 years, she has served as an author, coauthor, and contributing author of business valuation articles, book chapters, and books, several with Dr. Pratt. She was assistant author of *Valuing a Business: The Analysis and Appraisal of Closely Held Companies*, 5th ed. (Wiley, 2008); coauthor of *Business Valuation Body of Knowledge Workbook*, 2nd ed. (Wiley, 2003); *Cost of Capital Workbook*, 2nd ed. (Wiley, 2002); *The Market Approach to Valuing Businesses Workbook*, 2nd ed. (Wiley, 2006); and *Closely Held Business Valuation* (Bloomberg Tax Portfolio 5147). She is also a contributor to BVR's *Guide to Personal v. Enterprise Goodwill* (2009), *The Comprehensive Guide to the Use and Application of Transaction Databases*, 4th ed. (2020), *Valuing a Business*, 6th ed. (2022), *Lawyers Guide to Cost of Capital* (2014); *Cost of Capital Applications and Examples*, 5th ed. (2014); and *Financial Valuations: Applications and Models*, 5th ed. (2024).

Ms. Niculita has been a designated member of the American Society of Appraisers (ASA) for 18 years, and an active volunteer, including serving as treasurer of ASA's Portland Chapter Committee, a current member of ASA's Business Valuation Discipline Committee, and a member of the Editorial Review Board of the Business Valuation Review, the official publication of the Business Valuation Committee of the ASA. Ms. Niculita holds the Business Valuation credential and the Accredited in Review Management in Business Valuation credential from the ASA, and the certified financial analyst credential from the CFA Society.

Ms. Niculita received her MBA from the Joseph M. Katz Graduate School of Business at the University of Pittsburgh and a bachelor degree in economics, banking, and finance from the Academy of Economic Studies in Bucharest, Romania.

About the Editorial Advisory Board

This book has benefited immeasurably from an extraordinary amount of peer review from a blue-ribbon Editorial Advisory Board that provided valuable guidance, comments, and suggestions through the entire updating process, as well as contributing chapters to the third edition.

Jay E. Fishman, FASA, FRICS

Stout, Managing Director

Bala Cynwyd, PA

Erin D. Hollis, ASA, CDBV

AIW, LLC, Managing Member

Chicago

Kenneth J. Pia, Jr., ASA, CPA/ABV, MCBA

Marcum, LLP, Partner

New York

Jeffrey S. Tarbell, ASA, CFA

Houlihan Lokey, Director

San Francisco

Anita Ventrelli, JD

Schiller DuCanto & Fleck, LLP, Senior Partner

Chicago

About the Authors

Arlene L. Ashcraft, MBA, ASA, CFA, contributed to the chapter "Valuation for Employee Stock Ownership Plans." She is a partner at Weaver and Tidwell, LLP. She is vice president of the ASA Business Valuation Committee, past vice chair of the board of examiners of the ASA Business Valuation Committee, and a member of the ESOP Association's Advisory Committee on Valuation.

Christopher Bakewell, MBA, ASA, CLP, contributed to the chapter "Valuing Intellectual Property and Intangible Assets." Mr. Bakewell is a vice president and an officer of Charles River Associates where he specializes in valuation and licensing in issues involving technology-rich businesses and intellectual property rights. Mr. Bakewell is the author or coauthor of several publications on the subjects of valuation and licensing, and often speaks on these subjects. He also holds the designations of accredited senior appraiser from the ASA and certified licensing professional from the Licensing Executives Society. He has been qualified and testified as an expert witness in federal court, various state courts, and in domestic and international arbitration panels. Mr. Bakewell earned an MBA in finance from the Robert H. Smith School of Business at the University of Maryland at College Park, where he was a graduate fellow.

Bob Bartell, CFA, authored the chapter "Valuation in Solvency Matters." He is president of the corporate finance unit of Kroll, LLC, and CEO of Kroll Securities, LLC. Mr. Bartell has specialized in a broad array of corporate finance engagements, including fairness and solvency opinions and financial restructuring.

Neil Beaton, ASA, CFA, CPA/ABV, CFF, contributed to the chapter "Alternative Dispute Resolution." He is a managing director with Alvarez & Marsal Valuation Services, LLC. Mr. Beaton has authored two books on early-stage company valuation. He is former co-chair of the AICPA's Valuation of Private Equity Securities Task Force, and a former member of its ABV Exam Committee and its Mergers & Acquisitions Disputes Task Force.

David G. Clarke, ASA, contributed to the chapter "Shareholder and Partner Disputes." Mr. Clarke is managing principal at The Griffing Group, and serves as the leader of the firm's Valuation Litigation Practice. He has 40 years of experience in providing valuation opinions and expert witness testimony in a broad range of industries for a variety of purposes, including commercial litigation, corporate transactions, estate and gift taxation, intellectual property valuation, employee stock ownership plan compliance, purchase price allocation, and impairment testing. Mr. Clarke has provided expert valuation services, opinions, and testimony for plaintiffs and defendants in a number of jurisdictions, including the Delaware Court of Chancery and the U.S. District Court. His testifying experience includes providing opinions of fair value for shareholder appraisal actions and fiduciary cases (including entire fairness and derivative shareholder actions) and opinions of economic damages related to intellectual property infringement and contract disputes. He has also provided expert consulting and testimony in preliminary injunction matters.

Jay E. Fishman, FASA, FRICS, contributed to the chapters "Personal versus Enterprise Goodwill," "Marital Dissolution Valuations," "Appraisal Reports," and "Business Valuation Standards and Credentials." He is a managing director of Stout, formerly with Financial Research Associates, a firm he founded 40 years ago. Mr. Fishman has coauthored several books: PPC's *Guide to Business Valuations* with Shannon Pratt, and *Standards of Value* with Shannon Pratt and William Morrison. He has been qualified as an expert witness and provided testimony in various courts and has taught courses on business valuation for the Internal Revenue Service, the National Judicial College, the Hong Kong Society of Accountants and on behalf of the World Bank in St. Petersburg, Russia. Mr. Fishman is former chair and current member emeritus of the Business Valuation Committee of the ASA, former editor of the *Business Valuation Review*, former chair of the ASA's Government Relations Committee, former trustee of The Appraisal Foundation, a former member of its Appraisal Standards Board and Appraisal Practice Board and former member of the Board of Trustees of the International Valuation Standards Council. In 2020, the ASA awarded Mr. Fishman their Lifetime Achievement Award and in 2023 awarded Mr. Fishman the Special Recognition Award in memory of Shannon Pratt.

William H. Frazier, ASA, contributed to the chapter "Discounts and Premiums." He is managing director at Weaver and Tidwell, LLP. Mr. Frazier has testified as an expert in U.S. Tax Court, developed the Nonmarketable Investment Company Evaluation method, authored the paper "The NICE Method Theory and Application" and was a contributing author for *Shannon Pratt's Valuing a Business*, 6th ed. Mr. Frazier has served as chair on the ASA Government Relations Committee, Business Valuation Committee (treasurer and secretary), Standards Sub-committee of Business Valuations Committee, and Educational Foundation. Mr. Frazier previously was a member of the IRS Advisory Council.

Roger J. Grabowski, FASA, updated the chapters "Defining Value in the Relevant Context: Standards of Value," "Value to Whom? Levels and Premises of Value," "Overview of Business Valuation Approaches, Methods, and Procedures," "The Income Approach," "Developing a Discount Rate," "The Asset-Based Approach," "The Excess Earnings Method," and "Valuing Stock of S Corporations and Interests in Other Pass-through Entities"; contributed to the chapters "Reconciliation of Value Indications," and "Valuing Interests in Real Property Holding Entities"; and authored the chapter "Valuations for Federal Income Tax Matters." See his bio in About the Editors.

Travis W. Harms, CFA, CPA/ABV, contributed to the chapter "Valuations for Gift, Estate, Charitable Contribution Matters." He is a senior vice president at Mercer Capital and leads the firm's Family Business Advisory Services group. Mr. Harms has been active in the field of business valuation for more than 20 years. Mr. Harms is the author of *The*

12 Questions That Keep Family Business Directors Awake at Night and coauthor of *Business Valuation: An Integrated Theory*, 3rd ed.

Paul Heidt, ASA, CPA/ABV, contributed to the chapters "Financial Statement Adjustments" and "Comparative Financial Statement Analysis." He is with Morones Analytics and has 20 years of specialized experience in financial analysis and research, business appraisals, lost earnings analyses, and litigation research. Mr. Heidt has authored several articles and headed the development of a widely used valuation database. He received a post baccalaureate in accounting from Portland State University and a BS in finance from the University of Portland.

Erin D. Hollis, ASA, CDBV, updated the chapter "Reasonable Compensation." She is the managing member of AIW, LLC, and has provided expert witness testimony services since 2000. Ms. Hollis is a former chair of the ASA Business Valuation Committee, former member of the Valuation Advisory Committee for the ESOP Association and a member of the Association of Insolvency & Restructuring Advisors.

Bruce A. Johnson, ASA, contributed to the chapters "Discounts and Premiums" and "Valuing Interests in Real Property Holding Entities." Mr. Johnson is managing partner of MPJ Business Valuations and a member of the Corporate Finance Advisory Board for Texas A&M University. He is the author of the Johnson Restricted Stock Study and Johnson/Park Empirical Method for discounts for lack of marketability, developer for the ASA's course on discounts and premiums, and a contributing author for *Guide to Business Valuation, Shannon Pratt's Valuing a Business*, 6th ed. and the *Comprehensive Guide for the Valuation of Family Limited Partnerships.*

Michael Gregory, ASA, CVA, authored the chapter "Valuation and Appraiser Penalties." He had 32 years of experience at the IRS where he headed up business valuation nationally for 11 of those years. Mr. Gregory has authored 12 books, including *Business Valuations and the IRS*, contributed to three other books, and written over 55 articles. He has testified in U.S. Tax Court and managed an expert witness group with up to 21 experts. He is a qualified mediator with the Minnesota Supreme Court. He received his MS from the University of Wisconsin-Madison, and his MBA in finance from DePaul University.

Jill Kosonen, BS, contributed to the chapter "Valuing Intellectual Property and Intangible Assets." She is a director in the transfer pricing practice with Kroll LLC. Ms. Kosonen has over 20 years of experience in designing, documenting, and resolving a wide range of transfer pricing matters. She is a director, International Committee co-chair, a member of the Chicago Tax Club, and a member of the National Association of Business Economics. Ms. Kosonen earned a BS in business economics from Miami University where she currently advises the Economics Department as the chair of the Economic Advisory Board.

Timothy R. Lee, ASA, contributed to the chapter "Checklists for Reviewing a Business Valuation Report." Mr. Lee is the managing director of Corporate Valuation Services at Mercer Capital and is a member of the firm's board of directors. He has contributed valuation articles, advisory briefs, and other content to numerous valuation and ESOP-related organizations. Mr. Lee is coauthor of A *Reviewer's Handbook to Business Valuation: Practical Guidance to the Use and Abuse of a Business Appraisal.*

Kimberly Linebarger, CPA, CFA, ASA, ABV, CVA, updated the chapter "Economic and Industry Analysis." She is a director with Moss Adams, LLP, in Portland, Oregon, where she focuses on valuations for litigation support, estate and gift, and buy/sell purposes of businesses, with an emphasis in the automotive and dealer industry. She previously was with Shannon Pratt Valuations and has been a contributing author to multiple publications, including *A Dealer Guide to Dealership Valuation*, National Automobile Dealers Association and *Cost of Capital: Applications and Examples*, 5th ed. Ms. Linebarger is a member of the Estate Planning Council of Portland and has served on the Valuation Credentialing Board and Executive Advisory Board of the National Association of Certified Valuators and Analysts.

William P. McInerney, ASA, contributed to the chapter "Shareholder and Partner Disputes." He is a Manager at the Griffing Group where he provides expert reports and litigation support for matters heard in a variety of jurisdictions, including U.S. District Court, U.S. Tax Court, the Delaware Court of Chancery, New York State Supreme Court, the Superior Court of New Jersey, and other state, district, and county courts in California, Illinois, Oklahoma, Texas, and Wisconsin. Mr. McInerney has coauthored several articles and holds a BS from Purdue University.

Z. Christopher Mercer, FASA, CFA, ABAR, contributed to the chapter "Valuation Provisions in Buy-Sell Agreements" He is the founder and chair of Mercer Capital with 40 years of experience. Mr. Mercer is the author or coauthor of ten books, including *Business Valuation: An Integrated Theory*, 3rd ed., and *Unlocking Private Company Wealth, Buy-Sell Agreements for Closely Held and Family Business Owners.* He has served as an expert witness.

Ryan Montgomery, J.D., LLM, contributed to the chapter "Valuations for Gift, Estate, Charitable Contribution Matters." He is a member in Montgomery Purdue PLLC in Seattle, Washington. His areas of practice are business, probate and estate administration, real estate, estate planning, and trusts. He received his undergraduate, JD, and LLM degrees from the University of Washington. Ryan is a frequent author on tax and estate administration topics and is a past executive committee member of the Washington State Bar Association, Real Property Probate and Trust council.

Serena Morones, ASA, CPA/ABV, CFE, contributed to the chapters "Financial Statement Adjustments" and "Comparative Financial Statement Analysis." She is a damages expert with Morones Analytics, with 20 years of experience in forensic accounting. She previously served as controller at both public and private companies and on the audit staff at one of the Big Four accounting firms. She has served as an expert witness in numerous matters and has authored several articles. Ms. Morones received a master of taxation degree from Portland State University and a BA in accounting from the University of Oregon.

Robert B. Morrison, FASA BV/IA, authored the chapter "Employment and Noncompetition Agreements." After a long career, he retired from Rosenfield & Company, PLLC where he was a partner and led the firm's valuation practice. A former international president of the ASA, he also served as the chair of the ASA Business Valuation Committee, chair of the International Institute of Business Valuers, and as a member of the Business Valuation Resource Panel and the Board of Trustees of The Appraisal Foundation.

Alina V. Niculita, ASA, ARM-BV, CFA, MBA, updated the chapters "Financial Statement Terminology Used in Business Appraisal," "The Market Approach," "Rules of Thumb," and "Valuing Professional Practices and Small Service Businesses"; authored the chapter "Company Data, Site Visits, and Interviews" and contributed to the chapter "Reconciliation of Value Indications." See her bio under About the Editors.

Lucas M. Parris, ASA, CFA, CEIV™, contributed to the chapter "Checklists for Reviewing a Business Valuation Report." Mr. Parris is a senior vice president at Mercer Capital, where he leads that firm's Financial Reporting Valuation Group as well as the firm's insurance industry team. He is a frequent speaker and author on valuation-related topics.

Kenneth J. Pia, Jr., ASA, CPA/ABV, MCBA, contributed to the chapters "Personal versus Enterprise Goodwill," "Marital Dissolution Valuations," and "Business Valuation Standards and Credentials." He is a partner and the leader of the Business Valuation Industry group at Marcum, LLP, with more than 30 years of experience. Mr. Pia is past chair of the ASA Business Valuation Committee, a member of the National Business Valuation Education Sub-Committee, and teaches nationally for the ASA accreditation program. Mr. Pia is also a charter member of the American Academy of Matrimonial Lawyers Foundation's Forensic & Business Valuation Division and was recently named to the American Academy for Certified Financial Litigators Advisory Board for New York and Connecticut. He has testified in federal and state courts and in arbitration proceedings.

Julia Rowe, MA, CPA, contributed to the chapter "Valuing Intellectual Property and Intangible Assets." She is a vice president of Charles River Associates. Ms. Rowe has served as an expert witness through deposition and trial. Ms. Rowe has testified regarding the calculation of damages in patent infringement cases, as well as breach of contract, trademark infringement, copyright infringement, and theft of trade secrets. She has authored several publications and has been an invited speaker on the subjects of valuation and licensing. Ms. Rowe holds a master of accountancy degree from the Kellstadt Graduate School of Business at DePaul University.

Eric Rowen, JD, contributed to the chapter "Alternative Dispute Resolution." He is a shareholder in Greenberg Traurig, LLP, in Las Vegas and Los Angeles where he is co-chair of the real estate litigation practice and chair of the Western Region real estate litigation group where he concentrates on litigation, real estate, real estate financing, commercial leasing, workouts, bankruptcy, and trust and estate litigation. He received his JD from Loyola Law School, Los Angeles, and his BA from the University of California at Irvine.

Elise Scoles contributed to the chapter "Shareholder and Partner Disputes." She is a manager at the Griffing Group where she provides support for valuation matters, including litigation in the Delaware Court of Chancery, U.S. District Court, and other state courts. Ms. Scoles holds a BS from DePaul University.

Jeffrey S. Tarbell, ASA, CFA, contributed to the chapters "Valuation for Employee Stock Ownership Plans," "Valuation Provisions in Buy-Sell Agreements," and "Appraisal Reports" and authored the chapter "Valuation in Fairness Matters." He has more than 30 years of valuation experience. He is a member of Houlihan Lokey's Financial and Valuation Advisory business where he leads that firm's Estate and Gift Tax Valuation practice, co-leads the ESOP Valuation practice, and is a member of the Technical Standards Committee. He is member of the ASA Board of Governors, a former chair of the ASA Business Valuation Committee, and a former chair of the Valuation Advisory Committee of the ESOP Association. He has testified in various state and federal courts and before hearings of the U.S. Congress and U.S. Department of Labor.

William W. Thomsen, MBA, ASA, CFA, authored the chapter "Valuation in Lost Profits Damages Matters." He has over 20 years' experience providing business valuations and economic analysis across a broad range of industries. Mr. Thomsen has testified on numerous occasions as an expert witness on valuation and economic damage issues and has qualified as an expert witness in U.S. District Court and a number of county superior courts. He holds an MBA in finance from Columbia University.

Terry G. Whitehead, ASA, CPA, contributed to the chapters "Financial Statement Adjustments" and "Comparative Financial Statement Analysis." He is with Morones Analytics and has 25 years of experience providing business valuations, financial analysis, and lost profits damage analysis. Mr. Whitehead received a BS in business administration from Warner Pacific College.

Anita Ventrelli, JD, authored the chapters "Admissibility and Impact of Expert Business Valuation Evidence," "Discovery and the Business Valuation Expert," and "Examining a Business Valuation Expert in Depositions and at Trials." She is senior partner with Schiller DuCanto & Fleck, LLP, where she serves on the Executive Committee. Ms. Ventrelli currently serves on the board of the ABA/NITA Trial Advocacy Institute, as a Family Law section delegate to the ABA House of Delegates, and on the board of the Schiller DuCanto and Fleck Family Law Center at DePaul University. She received her JD from the College of Law at DePaul University and her undergraduate degree from the University of Michigan.

Preface

This third edition is designed for attorneys and judges who frequently, occasionally, or even for the first time encounter disputed (or potentially disputed) business valuation issues. It serves all of the above because it is written and organized both as a tutorial and a reference manual.

The authors have extensive experience in business valuation matters for a wide variety of purposes, including tax matters (e.g., estate, gift, charitable contributions), transactional matters (e.g., mergers and acquisitions, going public, going private), and litigation or potential litigation (e.g., tax matters, shareholder disputes, marital dissolutions). All of these have elements in common, and many have specialized elements, thus requiring generalized chapters and also chapters addressing a particular valuation purpose.

EVOLUTION OF *THE LAWYER'S BUSINESS VALUATION HANDBOOK*

The first edition was published in 2000. Before Shannon Pratt retired, planning had begun for updating both his *Valuing a Business: The Analysis and Appraisal of Closely Held Business, the* primary source for educating business appraisers in valuing closely held businesses since it was first published in 2001, and this book. After he retired, the ASA Educational Foundation took leadership in maintaining Shannon's legacy. First, a group of some of the foremost valuation practitioners updated *Valuing a Business*, with the sixth edition being released in 2022. Now a group of renowned attorneys and valuation practitioners have updated this book, working to maintain the style of the book as established by Shannon while updating the content to 2024.

SAME SHARES MAY HAVE DIFFERENT VALUES

It is important to recognize that the same block of shares may have different values—even on the same day—depending on the statute and the case law governing the transaction. For example, a number of states do not allow discounts for lack of control and/or lack of marketability in dissenting stockholder suits, whereas federal, gift, estate, and income tax statutes universally use the standard of *fair market value*, which the courts have interpreted to allow such discounts.

UPDATED CHAPTERS

Much has happened since the last edition and most chapters have been expanded and all have been updated to reflect the changes. For example, we updated the discussion on *levels of value*, reflecting the current thinking on explaining differences in value conclusions.

Valuation discounts and premiums continue to be a prime area of controversy. The chapter "Discounts and Premiums" reflects the most current thinking on estimating appropriate discounts. A separate chapter, "Valuations of Gift, Estate, and Charitable Contribution Matters" highlights the decisions that have come down where discounts have been a major issue and discusses the conflicting *Blount* and *Connelly* decisions; in early 2024, the U.S. Supreme Court issued its opinion in *Connelly v. U.S.*, and the chapter discusses that opinion.

When originally written, the chapter on "Examining Business Valuation Experts at Deposition and at Trial" was not designed to distinguish between taking discovery deposition testimony and eliciting trial testimony from expert witnesses. This updated chapter differentiates between the two to illustrate how treating each differently aids discovery and structuring trial testimony.

We added a discussion on appraiser's reliance on other experts in the chapter "The Asset-Based Approach."

References at the end of each chapter are updated, providing the reader with resources that go even deeper into the chapter topics. Appendix A, Glossary of Business Valuation Terms, has been updated to provide the reader with updated references.

HIGHLIGHTS OF WHAT'S NEW IN THIS EDITION

We added a brief outline at the beginning of each chapter, highlighting topics covered in the chapter.

We have added the following new chapters:

- **Company Information, Site Visits, and Interviews:** due diligence that should be taken in preparing a business valuation
- **Developing a Discount Rate:** expanded discussion in a separate chapter on this integral component of any income approach valuation including new material on discount rates for small closely held businesses
- **Employment and Noncompetition Agreements:** expanded discussion, moved to a separate chapter
- **Valuations for Federal Income Tax Matters:** separate chapter covering federal tax valuation issues (other than gift, estate, and charitable contribution matters), including an introduction to transfer pricing
- **Shareholder and Partner Disputes:** new Appendix B, Fair Value in Dissent and Oppression, with state-by-state definitions of value in dissent and oppression matters and new Appendix C, Terms of the Market Exception, with state-by-state restrictions on appraisal rights for publicly held shares
- **Valuing Interests in Real Property Holding Entities:** covering partial interest discounts and the relationship between entities owning the real property and those owning a related operating business
- **Valuing Intellectual Property and Intangible Assets:** covering legally protected intellectual property, rights of publicity, income tax and transfer pricing considerations, and differences in valuing such assets for financial reporting purposes
- **Valuation in Fairness Matters:** introduction to principles of corporate law relevant to fairness opinions, role of corporate directors and their fiduciary duties, and directors' responsibilities and decision-making in a transactional context
- **Valuation in Solvency Matters:** introduction to claims of fraudulent conveyance/transfers, *reasonably equivalent value*, solvency opinions, director duties as a company approaches insolvency

- **Valuation in Lost Profits Damages Matters:** estimation of lost profits or lost business value, prerequisites to damage recovery, and key concepts in damage calculations
- **Valuation and Appraiser Penalties:** relationship of standards and valuation penalties at the federal level, history and definitions, qualified appraiser and appraisal, and examples of penalty calculations

An Index of Court Decisions complements the Subject Index.

DISCOUNTS AND PREMIUMS

This chapter has been greatly expanded and updated as a major issue in many cases is premiums and discounts, especially discounts for lack of marketability (DLOM). As empirical DLOM databases have expanded, courts prefer that the business appraiser access the databases and select the transactions most resembling the subject company rather than just use the average discounts. Further, current valuation practice has evolved to encompass greater application of quantitative methods in measuring discounts for lack of control (i.e., discounts applicable to minority interest) and lack of marketability. The chapter covers developments in discounts for tax on trapped-in capital gains, voting versus nonvoting stock, key person discounts, and discounts for environmental litigation and other contingent liabilities.

VALUING STOCK IN S CORPORATIONS AND INTERESTS IN OTHER PASS-THROUGH ENTITIES

Pass-through entities have become the predominant form of closely held business organization. We updated this chapter to reflect recent valuation-related developments. We have also updated the chapter on valuing professional practices and small service businesses.

BUY-SELL AGREEMENTS

In the course of reviewing valuation reports pursuant to buy-sell agreements, we see many ambiguous valuation provisions in buy-sell agreements. Many even omit the applicable definition of value (the subject of Chapter 1). To assist attorneys in drafting unambiguous valuation provisions in such agreements, we have updated and expanded the chapter on buy-sell agreements.

REPORT REVIEWS

One of the most frequent (and hard to catch) categories of errors in business valuation reports is errors of omission. We've updated the two chapters on reports—a general chapter on appraisal reports (what a good report should have) and a "working chapter" with checklists for reviewing reports. The chapter "Checklist for Reviewing a Business Valuation Report" is free of copyright restrictions and is meant to be copied and the blanks filled in for each report. Two or more copies may be utilized for comparing your expert's report with that of the opposing expert and identifying the differences.

COURT POSITIONS CITED, SOMETIMES CHALLENGED

Court decisions are cited throughout to illustrate courts' positions on many issues. On some issues, various courts are unanimous in their positions, but on other issues courts' positions vary according to jurisdiction. For those that vary, we cite from decisions on either side of an issue. Occasionally, when we feel that one court's treatment of an issue is sounder than another, we say so, and tell you why. We believe that attorneys should know court precedents and usually should follow them, but sometimes it pays to challenge an unsound precedent and make new law.

We welcome questions and comments: please send to Roger J. Grabowski at rjg264@comcast.net.

Acknowledgments

This edition would not have been possible without the generous support of the ASA Educational Foundation, Carol Akers Klug, Chair, Board of Directors.

The third edition is far richer as a result of the contributions of the following reviewers:

Bruce Bingham, FASA

Berkeley Research Group, Managing Director

New York

Elizabeth I. Ciccone, ASA, Esq.

Marcum LLP, Partner

New Haven, CT 06511

Steven R. Dixon, JD

Steptoe & Johnson, LLP, Partner, Tax Litigation and Controversy

Washington, DC

Carla G. Glass, FASA, IA, CFA

Marcum, LLP, Managing Director (ret.)

New Haven, CT

Gary C. Karch, JD

McDermott Will & Emery, LLP, Partner, Tax

Chicago

Terri A. Lastovka, ASA, CPA, JD, ARM

Valuation & Litigation Consulting, LLC

Cleveland, OH

Gilbert E. Matthews, CFA

Sutter Securities Inc.

San Francisco

Penelope Pentzas
Schiller DuCanto & Fleck, LLP, Law Clerk
Chicago

David Ptashne, ASA, CFA
Kroll, LLC, Transfer Pricing
Chicago

Brady Sweet
Schiller DuCanto & Fleck, LLP, Law Clerk
Chicago

Marianna Todorova, CFA, CPA/ABV
Kroll, LLC, Office of Professional Practice
New York

Grant Zindel served as project manager for this edition. He acted as a liaison and coordinated with the contributing authors, the publisher, and the outside reviewers, assisted with obtaining permission to use material reprinted in this book from other sources, and edited the manuscript. Grant Zindel also assisted in creating the index for this edition. Thanks to his dedication and professionalism, the index is comprehensive and user friendly. This book would simply not have been completed without Grant's dedication.

We also would like to thank the editorial and production staffs at Lachina Creative, especially Molly Montanaro, and at the American Bar Association for their assistance with this third edition.

CHAPTER 1

Defining Value in the Relevant Context: Standards of Value

Roger J. Grabowski, FASA

INTRODUCTION

In this chapter you will learn about:

- Standards of "value" (also commonly referred to as Definitions of Value) based on the laws and common usages in valuation and other matters:
  - Fair market value
  - Fair value under state statutes
  - Fair value for financial reporting
  - Investment value (commonly referred to as "strategic" or "synergistic" value)
  - Intrinsic or fundamental value
- Sources for authority as to the appropriate standard of value and its meaning
- Appropriate standard of value in a specific situation as a legal matter

The goal of this book is for the attorney/reader to understand what a business valuation/appraisal entails in order to be in a better position to discuss the appraisal process and report with the appraiser and with the attorney's client.

What is a valuation/appraisal of a business or an interest in a business? *Black's Law Dictionary* defines *valuation* as:

> The act of ascertaining the worth of a thing. The estimated worth of a thing.[1]

Valuation is defined in the *International Valuation Glossary—Business Valuation* (Glossary) as:

> The act or process of developing an opinion or conclusion of value at a **Valuation Date**, using a **Premise of Value**, a **Standard of Value** and one or more **Valuation Approaches**. Also, known as **Appraisal.**[2]

---

1. Brian A. Garner, Black's Law Dictionary 1551 (11th ed.). Some mistakenly refer to the process as *evaluation*, defined in the Oxford dictionary as "the making of a judgment about the amount, number or value of something; assessment."

2. *International Valuation Glossary—Business Valuation* 11 (jointly published by the ASA, CBV Institute Royal Institute of Chartered Surveyors, and Saudi Authority of Accredited Valuers, Feb. 24, 2022).

The Appraisal Foundation in its *Uniform Standards of Professional Appraisal Practice* (USPAP) specifies that the process of forming an opinion of value is *appraisal*, defined as "the act or process of developing an opinion of value; an opinion of value."[3]

In discussing the terms *valuation* or *appraisal* with some clients, they may be surprised to learn that there may be more than one definition of value for the same property at the same time. Furthermore, one definition may legitimately lead to an amount that is more than twice the amount from another definition.

For example, the phrase "fair market value of these shares" is frequently found in buy-sell agreements. Often the noncontrolling (i.e., minority) parties to the agreements just assume that "fair market value" means a proportionate share of the value of the enterprise as a whole. When the triggering event occurs, they are shocked to find out that the term implies discounts should be applied for lack of control and lack of marketability, sometimes totaling as much as 50%!

The oft-quoted expression "value lies in the eye of the beholder" is not very helpful when there is a legal need for a definition of value. Unquestionably, value is defined differently in different legal contexts. Unfortunately, the quest for the appropriate definition in any particular legal context is often a very difficult one. Therefore, identifying the correct definition of value in the legal context is a crucial beginning step in an appraisal.

> It is impossible to intelligently discuss methods of valuation without reference to some assumed definition of value. . . .[4]

The appraiser and the attorney should agree on the definition of value at the outset, and the definition should be included in the written assignment. It is best to define and cite the source of the definition and, if appropriate, to include such details in a buy-sell or operating agreement.

The valuation practitioner can bring experience to bear in helping the attorney at this step. However, the appropriate definition of value to be used in a specific circumstance is, ultimately, a legal question and therefore is the responsibility of the attorney.

If an expert's procedures do not follow the pertinent legal definition of value, the judge may disallow the entire testimony.[5]

COMMONLY USED DEFINITIONS OF VALUE[6]

The two most common expressions indicating definitions of value found in U.S. statutes are:

- Fair market value
- Fair value

---

3. The Appraisal Foundation, *Definitions*, *in* UNIFORM STANDARDS OF PROFESSIONAL APPRAISAL PRACTICE (USPAP) 3 (2024). These principles are applicable to valuation services in general, defined by USPAP as "a service pertaining to an aspect of property value, regardless of the type of service and whether it is performed by appraisers or by others."

4. JAMES C. BONBRIGHT, VALUATION OF PROPERTY, Vol. I, at 128 (The Michie Company, 1965 [reprint of 1937 ed.]).

5. *See, e.g.*, Matter of Slant/Fin. Corp. v. The Chicago Corp. (N.Y. Sup. Ct. Oct. 5, 1995), *aff'd*, 236 A.D.2d 547, 654 N.Y.S.2d 627 (N.Y. App. Div. Feb. 18, 1997); Le Beau v. M.G. Bancorporation, Inc., 1998 Del. Ch. Lexis 9, 1998 WL 44993 (Del. Ch. Jan. 29, 1998).

6. For a thorough discussion of definitions of value, *see* Chapter 2 in JAY FISHMAN ET AL., STANDARDS OF VALUE: THEORY AND APPLICATIONS (2d ed. 2013).

There are other significant terms that appear in court case opinions, such as market value, true value, true cash value, intrinsic value, investment value, marital value, and more. These opinions rarely explain the meaning of the term or include authority or precedent for its use.

Other than fair market value and fair value, business appraisers and investment bankers will also frequently use investment value, intrinsic value, or fundamental value. These three terms are often found in court opinions, but again, usually without definition.

Fair Market Value

In North America, the most widely recognized and accepted standard of value is fair market value. It is the standard that applies to most U.S. federal and state tax matters, such as estate taxes, gift taxes, inheritance taxes, income taxes, and ad valorem taxes. It is also the legal standard of value in some other valuation situations, primarily those involving taxes.

Fair market value is defined in the Glossary as:

> A Standard of Value considered to represent the price, expressed in terms of cash equivalents, at which property would change hands between a hypothetical willing and able buyer and a hypothetical willing and able seller, each acting at arm's length in an open and unrestricted market, when neither is under compulsion to buy or sell and when both have reasonable knowledge of the relevant facts.[7]

The U.S. Treasury Regulations define the fair market value of a business interest as:

> The net amount which a willing purchaser, whether an individual or a corporation, would pay for the interest to a willing seller, neither being under any compulsion to buy or to sell and both having reasonable knowledge of relevant facts.[8]

There is general agreement that the definition implies that the parties have the ability—as well as the willingness—to effectuate this hypothetical cash transaction. The "market" in this definition can be thought of as all the potential buyers and sellers of like businesses or professional practices.

In the legal interpretations of fair market value, the willing buyer and the willing seller are hypothetical persons, dealing at arm's length, rather than any particular parties. In other words, a price would not be considered representative of fair market value if it is influenced by special motivations not characteristic of a typical buyer or seller.

In Canada, however, fair market value may include the value of synergies with a particular buyer.[9]

The fair market value concept, however, which assumes an open and unrestricted market, does not preclude identifying groups of willing participants. Quite the contrary, the business appraiser should be able to identify categories of willing purchasers. Furthermore, the appraiser cannot ignore the position of the seller. However, the seller is assumed to be willing to sell under conditions that exist as of the valuation date.

The concept of fair market value also assumes prevalent economic and market conditions at the date of the particular valuation. You have probably heard it said many times: "I couldn't get anywhere near the value of my house if I put it on the market

7. *International Valuation Glossary—Business Valuation*, *supra* note 2, at 5.

8. 26 C.F.R. 20.2031–.2033, Valuation of Property in General. *See also* Rev. Rul. 59-60.

9. For a thorough discussion of the issue, *see* Richard M. Wise, *The Effect of Special Interest Purchases on Fair Market Value in Canada*, 22(4) Bus. Valuation Rev. 196–202 (2003).

today," or "The value of XYZ Company stock is really much more (or less) than the price it's selling for on the New York Stock Exchange today." The standard of value that those people have in mind is some standard other than fair market value because the concept of fair market value means the price, in terms of cash or cash equivalents, at which a transaction could be expected to take place under conditions existing at the valuation date. The terms *market value* and *cash value* are sometimes used interchangeably with *fair market value.*

Real estate appraisers generally use the term *market value* rather than *fair market value,* defined in USPAP as follows:

> A type of value, stated as an opinion, that presumes the transfer of a property (i.e., a right of ownership or a bundle of such rights), as of a certain date, under specific conditions set forth in the definition of the term identified by the appraiser as applicable in an appraisal.[10]

Comment: Forming an opinion of market value is the purpose of many real property appraisal assignments, particularly when the client's intended use includes more than one intended user. The conditions included in market value definitions establish market perspectives for development of the opinion. These conditions may vary from definition to definition but generally fall into three categories:

1. The relationship, knowledge, and motivation of the parties (i.e., seller and buyer)
2. The terms of sale (e.g., cash, cash equivalent, or other terms)
3. The conditions of sale (e.g., exposure in a competitive market for a reasonable time prior to sale)

Appraisers are cautioned to identify the exact definition of market value, and its authority, applicable in each appraisal completed for the purpose of determining market value.[11]

As one can see from the preceding, market value as defined by USPAP is virtually synonymous with fair market value as defined in the U.S. Treasury Regulations.[12]

The U.S. Tax Court articulated the following as some guiding principles regarding the estimation of fair market value:

1. The willing buyer and the willing seller are hypothetical persons, rather than specific individuals or entities, and the characteristics of these hypothetical persons are not necessarily the same as the personal characteristics of the actual seller or a particular buyer.

2. Fair market value is determined as of the valuation date, and no knowledge of unforeseeable future events, which may have affected the value is given to the hypothetical persons.

3. Fair market value equals the highest and best use to which the property could be put on the valuation date, and fair market value takes into account special uses that are

10. USPAP, *supra* note 3, *Definitions* at 5.
11. *Id. See also* Chapter 27, "Valuing Interests in Real Property Holding Entities."
12. For a discussion of the differences, *see* Michael V. Sanders, *Market Value: What Does It Really Mean?*, Appraisal J. 206–18 (Summer 2018).

> realistically available due to the property's adaptability to a particular business. Fair market value is not affected by whether the owner has actually put the property to its highest and best use. The reasonable, realistic, and objective possible uses for the property in the near future control the valuation thereof. Elements affecting value that depend upon events or a combination of occurrences which, while within the realm of possibility, are not reasonably probable, are excluded from this consideration.[13]

It is generally understood that fair market value means a value in cash or cash equivalents (as indicated in the USPAP definition of market value) unless otherwise stated.

It is important to recognize that the fair market value of an equity interest in a business is not necessarily the pro rata share of the fair market value of the equity of the entire business.[14] The value of fractional equity interests can be impacted by such factors as discounts for lack of control, illiquidity and blockage discounts (i.e., large size of block relative to normal trading volume), and discounts for restrictions on marketability (these discounts are discussed in Chapter 18, "Discounts and Premiums").

Fair Value under State Statutes

The expression *fair value* is an excellent example of ambiguous terminology used in the field of business appraisal. To understand the meaning of this expression, one must know the context of its use. In the context of a standard of value in business valuation, the term *fair value* is a term found in state statutes governing dissenting stockholder and minority oppression actions. Such meaning is quite different from the term *fair value* as used in Generally Accepted Accounting Principles (GAAP) (as discussed later in the section "Fair Value for Financial Reporting"). Courts have given very different interpretations to the term *fair value* as a statutory business value standard.

Presently, fair value is the statutory standard of value provided for in most states. Courts will apply this statutory standard in cases involving dissenting stockholders' appraisal rights. These rights of action arise where the aggrieved party alleges that they are being forced to accept less than adequate consideration for their stock following a merger or sale of the business. Here, the aggrieved party seeks to enforce their right to have their shares appraised and to receive fair value in cash.[15]

In the jurisdictions that have adopted the Model Business Corporation Act, the definition of fair value is as follows:

> Fair value means the value of the corporation's shares determined:
>
> (i) immediately before the effectiveness of the corporate action to which the shareholder objects;
>
> (ii) using customary and current valuation concepts and techniques generally employed for similar businesses in the context of the transaction requiring appraisal; and
>
> (iii) without discounting for lack of marketability or minority status except, if appropriate, for amendments to the articles of incorporation pursuant to section 13.02(a)(4).[16]

---

13. Pabst Brewing Co. v. Comm'r, T.C. Memo. 1996-506 (1996). *See also* Standard of Value in Chapter 21.
14. Pro-rata share meaning its proportionate share of the whole enterprise (100%).
15. For a complete listing of states' dissenters' rights statutes, *see* Exhibit 23-1 in Chapter 23.
16. Model Business Corporation Act (updated through May 2019), Section 13.01 Definitions (American Bar Association, Business Law Section, Corporate Laws Committee). *See* Chapter 23.

Even in states that have adopted the Model Business Corporation Act, there are differences in the definition of fair value and in the interpretation of fair value. In some states, the statutory definition of fair value does not include the prohibition against adjusting value to reflect either lack of marketability or noncontrolling status. When a situation arises of actual or potential stockholder dissent or dissolution action, it is necessary to carefully research the legal precedents applicable to each case.

The term *fair value* is also found in the dissolution statutes of those states in which noncontrolling stockholders can trigger a corporate dissolution under certain circumstances (e.g., Florida Statutes § 607.1340; California Corporations Code § 2000). Even within the same state, however, a study of case law precedents does not necessarily lead one to the same definition of fair value under a dissolution statute as under that state's dissenting stockholder statute (note: dissolution versus dissenting).

The term *fair value* in the context of state statutes is more extensively discussed in Chapter 23, "Shareholder and Partner Disputes," and Chapter 30, "Valuation in Fairness Matters."

In summary, *fair market value* is a willing buyer/willing seller standard, whereas *fair value* does not necessarily assume a "willing" seller and/or a "willing" buyer.

Fair Value for Financial Reporting

It is important to understand the basics of the definition of fair value as used for financial reporting in that the amounts carried for assets and liabilities in the financial statements may be stated at fair value instead of historical cost. For example, assets reported on the balance sheet that were acquired in an acquisition are typically stated at fair value. Longer-term liabilities are typically restated at their fair values.

The Financial Accounting Standards Board (FASB) has codified its fair value measurement guidance in Accounting Standards Codification Topic 820, *Fair Value Measurement* (ASC 820), effective for financial statements issued for fiscal years beginning after November 15, 2007. Since becoming effective, ASC 820 has been amended multiple times, and certain aspects of the standard may continue to be revised. ASC 820 does not itself require or permit fair value measurements—this is done by other ASC Topics. Rather, ASC 820 defines fair value, establishes a framework for measuring fair value, and expands related disclosures.

ASC 820 defines fair value as:

> The price that would be received to sell an asset or paid to transfer a liability in an orderly transaction between market participants at the measurement date.[17]

The important feature of this definition is that fair value is an *exit price*, not the price that would be paid to acquire the asset or to assume the liability (an entry price). Furthermore, it is not the price to settle or extinguish the liability, as the liability is assumed to remain outstanding as of the measurement date. Fair value is not adjusted for transaction costs.

---

17. ASC 820-10-20. The International Accounting Standards Board (IASB) uses the same definition in the International Financial Reporting Standards (IFRS). *See* IFRS 13: *Fair Value Measurement*. The fair value guidance in ASC 820 and IFRS 13 is substantially converged, but not identical.

A fair value measurement should consider the characteristics of the asset or liability that a *market participant* would consider. Market participants are buyers and sellers in the principal (or the most advantageous) market for the asset or liability, acting in their economic best interest. These market participants are (1) independent of each other, (2) knowledgeable about factors relevant to the asset or liability and the transaction (including having information that might be obtained through usual and customary due diligence efforts), (3) able to transact (i.e., have the legal and financial ability to do so), and (4) willing to transact (i.e., motivated but not forced or otherwise compelled to transact). Market participants need not be identified specifically; it is sufficient to describe their general characteristics.

With regard to the characteristics of the asset or liability, a key ASC 820 concept to keep in mind is that a fair value measurement is for a particular *unit of account* (i.e., the level of aggregation or disaggregation of the item for the purpose of recognizing it in the financial statements). How the unit of account is specified is critical to the fair value measurement. For example, consider the difference between a single share of stock and a controlling interest; or a liability with a third-party credit enhancement—depending on whether the unit of account includes or excludes the credit enhancement, the fair value conclusions can be vastly different. But for a few exceptions, ASC 820 does not itself provide unit of account guidance; rather, this is addressed by other ASC Topics that call for fair value measurements (e.g., when accounting for a business acquisition).

ASC 820 assumes the orderly transaction takes place in the principal market (the market with the greatest volume and level of activity for the asset or liability), or, in the absence of a principal market, in the most advantageous market for the asset and liability. The most advantageous market maximizes the amount that would be received to sell the asset (and, respectively, minimizes the amount that would be paid to transfer the liability), after considering transaction and transportation costs (for market identification purposes). The market that the company normally would access to complete an exit transaction, given its business activities, is presumed to be the principal or most advantageous market, absent evidence to the contrary.

ASC 820 clarifies that the term *fair value* is intended to mean a market-based measure, not an entity-specific measure (i.e., entity-specific synergies do not belong in measuring fair value).

Although the FASB emphasizes "market participant assumptions at the measurement date," there are differences between "fair value" for financial reporting purposes and "fair market value." This is largely due to the unique fair value measurement framework of ASC 820 and its key concepts. For example, while *premiums and discounts* may be applied in a fair value measurement where they (1) are consistent with the characteristics of the asset or liability, (2) would be considered by market participants in their pricing analyses, and (3) cannot be inconsistent with the unit of account for the asset or liability specified by the relevant ASC Topic. As such, a discount is not applied for a *contractual restriction* on the sale of an equity security (e.g., an underwriter lock-up agreement), because the restriction is not considered to be part of the unit of account of the security (per ASC 820). Similarly, premiums or discounts that reflect *the size of the holding* (a block of stock) are a characteristic of the company's position, and not the asset or liability itself; thus, no "blockage discount" (discussed in Chapter 18, "Discounts and Premiums") can be applied in the fair value measurement because the size of the holding cannot be absorbed given normal daily trading volume. However, if the unit of account is stipulated to be either a controlling or a noncontrolling (minority) interest by the relevant ASC Topic that calls for the fair value measurement, a premium or a discount may be appropriate if market participants would consider it in their pricing analysis (e.g., a discount for lack of control or a discount for lack of marketability for a noncontrolling interest as the unit of account). In another specific example, a *legal restriction preventing the sale of shares* on a national securities exchange or an over-the-counter market until the shares are registered or certain conditions are met is deemed included in the unit of account of the equity security and is a characteristic of the asset that would be considered by a market participant; thus, it would lead to an adjustment in the fair value measurement.

The FASB did not adopt the definition of fair market value because it did not want the definition of fair value to be saddled with the nuances of court interpretations of fair market value.

Investment Value

Investment value is defined in the Glossary as:

> A **Standard of Value** considered to represent the value of an asset or business to a particular owner or prospective owner for individual investment or operational objectives. Also known as value to the owner.[18]

The primary distinguishing characteristic of investment value is that it denotes *value to a particular owner or investor* (in Canada, the term used is "value to the owner"). This is in contrast to fair market value, which is a concept of value in exchange, assuming hypothetical, typically motivated buyers and sellers. In other words, investment value is the value to a particular individual or entity, considering that individual's or entity's situation, perceptions, and motivation, not necessarily value in the marketplace. This is also essentially the same way that investment value is defined in the context of real estate appraisal.[19]

Investment value is generally a "subjective" value, whereas *fair market value* is an "objective" value.

There are many valid reasons for the investment value to one particular owner or prospective owner to differ from the fair market value. Investment value considers the following unique factors:

1. Synergies with other operations owned or controlled—for example, buyer has a particular use for the particular property
2. Relationships with other owners
3. Differences in estimates of future earning power and/or perception of degree of risk
4. Differences in aversion to or willingness to accept degrees of risk
5. Differences in income tax status

Many of the these factors are embedded in strategic merger and acquisition transactions and are commonly referred to as strategic (or synergistic) value. Whether or not the term *investment value* is actually used, the concept is sometimes found in business

18. *International Valuation Glossary—Business Valuation*, *supra* note 2, at 7.
19. *See* Appraisal Inst., The Appraisal of Real Estate 54–55 (15th ed. 2020).

valuations for marital dissolution. That is, the courts often focus on value to the spouse who operates the business as opposed to value that could be realized in the market.

Finally, investment value has a slightly different meaning when used in the context of dissenting stockholder lawsuits. In this context, it means a value based on *earning power* (i.e., economic income, a concept discussed in Chapter 6, "The Income Approach"). However, in measuring the value of earning power when applying the income approach, the appropriate present value discount rate or the direct capitalization rate is usually considered to be a consensus rate rather than a rate particularly appropriate for any specific investor.

Intrinsic or Fundamental Value

Intrinsic value is defined in the Glossary as:

> The value that an investor considers, on the basis of available facts, to be the "true," "real," or fundamental value that will become the **Market Value** when other investors reach the same conclusion.[20]

Financial analysts that follow and report on publicly traded stock commonly use *intrinsic value* (sometimes called *fundamental value*) to estimate value. Intrinsic value differs from investment value in that it represents an analytical judgment of value based on the investment characteristics perceived by a financial analyst rather than on how the characteristics comport to the circumstances of a particular investor.

Concurrence on the meanings of intrinsic value and fundamental value is found in the following definitions from an authoritative reference in the accounting field.

- Intrinsic value: The amount that an investor considers, on the basis of an evaluation of available facts, to be the "true" or "real" worth of an item, usually an *equity security*. The value that will become the market value when other investors reach the same conclusions. The various approaches to determining intrinsic value in the finance literature are based on expectations and discounted cash flows. *See expected value; fundamental analysis; discounted cash flow method.*[21]
- Fundamental analysis: An approach in security analysis which assumes that a security has an "intrinsic value" that can be determined through a rigorous evaluation of relevant variables. Expected earnings is usually the most important variable in this analysis, but many other variables, such as dividends, capital structure, management quality, and so on, may also be studied. An analyst estimates the "intrinsic value" of a security on the basis of those fundamental variables and compares this value with the current market price of this security to arrive at an investment decision.[22]

In the analysis of securities, intrinsic value is generally considered the appropriate price for a stock according to a financial analyst who has completed a fundamental analysis of the company's assets, earning power, and other factors. The authors of one book comment on the notion of intrinsic value as follows:

> The purpose of security analysis is to detect differences between the value of a security as determined by the market and a security's "intrinsic value"—that is, the value that

---

20. *International Valuation Glossary—Business Valuation, supra* note 2, at 6.

21. Kohler's Dictionary for Accountants 285 (W.W. Cooper & Yuri Ijiri eds., 6th ed. 1983), reprinted with permission.

22. *Id.* at 228.

> the security ought to have and will have when other investors have the same insight and knowledge as the analyst.[23]

If the market value is below what the analyst concludes is the intrinsic value, then the analyst considers the stock a "buy." If the market value is above the assumed intrinsic value, the analyst suggests selling the stock.

It is important to note that the concept of intrinsic value cannot be entirely disassociated from the concept of fair market value because the actions of buyers and sellers based on their specific perceptions of intrinsic value eventually lead to the consensus market value and the constant and dynamic changes in market value over time.

Case law often refers to intrinsic value. However, almost universally, such references do not define the term other than by reference to the language in the context in which it appears. Such references to intrinsic value can be found both in case opinions where there is no statutory standard of value and also in case decisions where the statutory standard of value is specified as fair value under state statutes or even fair market value. When references to intrinsic value appear in the relevant case law, the court usually is referring to notions such as those discussed in this section. It is also common to find court cases that use the term *intrinsic value* to mean the inherent worth of the stock to the owner—in other words, to equate the term to investment value, as defined earlier.

OTHER TERMS REFERRING TO VALUE

Acquisition Value

The term *acquisition value* means the value to a particular acquirer. It is a term that is very similar to strategic value (defined later in this chapter). In this sense, the term falls within the concept of investment value, as described in the previous section.

The term may also be used to denote the actual price at which a transaction occurred. In this sense, it would be the same as transaction value, described more fully later in the chapter.

Book Value

The term *book value* is an accounting term, not a financial valuation term, and is not necessarily, or even usually, indicative of any of the definitions of value discussed in the previous section. It is not related to any concept of economic value.

The term represents historical costs of assets owned by the entity, minus any depreciation, amortization, or liabilities deducted in the accounting system used by that entity (i.e., net book value).

The Glossary defines *net book value* as follows:

> The difference between a business' total assets and liabilities at accounting book values (synonymous with book equity). With respect to a specific asset, this is the original capitalized cost less accumulated amortization, depreciation, depletion, allowances, or impairment.[24]

23. James H. Lorie et al., The Stock Market: Theories and Evidence (2d ed. 1985).
24. *International Valuation Glossary—Business Valuation*, *supra* note 2, at 8.

It is noteworthy that many of a company's most valuable assets, especially if goodwill and other intangible assets are internally developed rather than purchased,[25] may not appear on the balance sheet at all. Similarly, there may be liabilities, especially those of a contingent nature, that do not appear on the balance sheet.

Going-Concern Value

The term *going-concern value* has two separate and distinct meanings, depending on the context in which it is used.

In one sense, it refers to the premise of the total value of the operations of the company on an ongoing basis. The Glossary defines *going-concern value* as follows:

> A **Premise of Value** that assumes the business is an ongoing commercial enterprise with a reasonable expectation of future earning power.[26]

In this context, going-concern value means the value of the business having a system of operating assets, personnel in place, an operational plant, and the necessary licenses, systems, and procedures in place allowing the business the ability to operate. This concept is discussed in more detail in the section on "Premises of Value" in Chapter 2.

The other concept of going-concern value is that of an intangible asset. It can be thought of as the difference between merely a set of physical assets and a "turnkey" operation ready to do business.

For example, some courts, in addressing the value of a professional practice for marital dissolution purposes, have distinguished between the personal goodwill of the professional (not part of the marital estate) and the value of having support staff, systems, and other operating systems in place (the "going-concern value," to be valued and included as part of the marital estate). Other courts, however, consider "going-concern value" as "the ability to generate income without interruption, even when there has been a change in ownership," and find that goodwill value is a component of the going-concern value of a business.[27]

Enterprise Value

A term that causes much confusion is *enterprise value*. Frequently, it is used to refer to the market value of the company's entire capital structure (all equity plus long-term debt, minus excess cash). Less often, it is used to describe market capitalization (total shares outstanding multiplied by the share price) plus interest-bearing debt plus preferred stock minus total cash and cash equivalents. At other times, it refers to the total value of the company's common stock on a controlling interest basis.

Enterprise value is defined in the Glossary as follows:

> The **Market Value of Invested Capital**, typically adjusted to remove all or a portion of cash and cash equivalents, and other **Non-Operating Assets**.[28]

---

25. For example, in-process research and development (IPR&D) generally refers to R&D acquired in an acquisition.

26. *International Valuation Glossary—Business Valuation*, *supra* note 2, at 5.

27. *See, e.g.*, Miami Valley Broadcasting Corporation and Carolina Broadcasting Company v. United States, 204 Ct. Cl. 592 (1974), 499 F.2d 677; Black Industries, Inc. v. Comm'r, 1979 T.C. Memo. 61. In VGS Corp. v. Comm'r, 68 T.C. 563 (1977), the Tax Court found that there were no excess earnings and, therefore, no goodwill; but the court ruled that there was going-concern value.

28. *International Valuation Glossary—Business Valuation*, *supra* note 2, at 4.

When this term is encountered, one should carefully try to interpret its meaning from the context in which it is used.

Liquidation Value

Liquidation value is defined in the Glossary as follows:

> The amount, net of relevant costs (e.g., preparation and disposal), that would be realized if the business is terminated, and the assets are sold.[29]

It is the net amount that can be realized (after liquidation expenses) in either an orderly or a forced sale of the business assets or some portion of them. Variations of liquidation value are discussed in Chapter 2 under the section on "Premises of Value."

Strategic Value (Synergistic Value)

A *strategic* or *synergistic value* reflects added benefits to a particular acquirer because of synergies with the acquiree. The Glossary defines *synergistic value* as follows:

> The expected value resulting from a combination of two or more assets or businesses, which is greater than the sum of the separate individual parts.[30]

That is, it is a price or potential price reflecting all or some portion of the value of synergistic benefits created through the combination of the respective entities for which a buyer might be willing to pay. Such benefits could include, for example, increasing market share, adding new strategic alliances, reducing costs by combining operations (particularly in the form of either staff reductions, sale of redundant assets, or economies of scale), and/or raising prices by eliminating a competitor, to name a few. In Exhibit 2-1, it is termed "Strategic Control Value."

Synergistic value generally reflects some added value above fair market value. Because it reflects the value of benefits available to a particular buyer, it is usually considered to fall within the concept of investment value, as discussed previously.

Transaction Value

Transaction value is the price at which a transaction occurs. The transaction could be either in the form of an asset sale or a stock sale. The International Business Brokers Association (Business Brokers Glossary) defines the term as follows:

> The total of all consideration passed at any time between the buyer and seller for an ownership interest in a business enterprise and may include, but is not limited to, all remuneration for tangible and intangible assets such as furniture, equipment, supplies, inventory, working capital, non-competition agreements, employment, and/or consultation agreements, licenses, customer lists, franchise fees, assumed liabilities, stock options, stock or stock redemptions, real estate, leases, royalties, earn-outs, and future considerations.

Some definitions exclude the value of noncompetition agreements and/or employment agreements on the basis that payments for these intangibles often are contingent on the owner's future personal performance.

Transaction value specifically refers to price as opposed to value. It is empirical (historical) in nature, not a legal standard of value. Price is the face value (the amount shown on the transaction documents) at which a specific transaction occurred, without

---

29. *International Valuation Glossary—Business Valuation*, *supra* note 2, at 7.
30. *International Valuation Glossary—Business Valuation*, *supra* note 2, at 11.

any adjustment to cash-equivalent value to reflect special terms. The price may or may not be the result of an arm's-length negotiation. It may be arrived at by negotiation, by contract, by court order, or by some other means. It may or may not comport to any of the definitions of value discussed in the previous section. The use of transaction prices in the market approach to appraisal is further discussed in Chapter 8.

SOURCES OF AUTHORITY FOR DEFINITION OF VALUE

The search for the appropriate definition of value usually proceeds in approximately the following hierarchy:

- Statutory law
- Legally binding rules and regulations
- Contractual definitions of value
- Non–legally binding administrative rules
- Prior court decisions
- Direction from the court
- Direction from the attorney
- Use of Internal Revenue Service (IRS) authority in non-tax situations
- Opinions of other attorneys and appraisers

Statutory Law

Generally, statutes have the advantage of having the greatest force of law and the disadvantage of being the least explicit of all sources in defining value. The relevant statutes may be either federal or state. For example, federal statutes require that valuations for tax purposes will be at fair market value.[31] Most state statutes governing dissenting stockholders require that valuations will be at fair value and most (if using the Revised Model Business Corporation Act or a close variation of it) add that the valuation date will be the day before the event to which the shareholder dissents, without considering the effect of that event. Most state statutes governing marital dissolution are silent about definitions of value other than some language about valuation dates.

Specifics of statutory law are discussed in considerable detail in the various chapters relating to the purposes of the valuation, such as gift and estate tax, shareholder disputes, marital dissolution, and so on. The purpose of this chapter is simply to make the point that statutory law usually is the first stop in the quest for the proper legal definition of value. Some examples of statutory law include the following.

Federal Statutes

- The Internal Revenue Code (I.R.C.), especially § 2031 on estate taxes and § 2512 for gift taxes
- Employee Retirement Income Security Act (ERISA) (29 U.S.C. § 1002(26))
- The U.S. Bankruptcy Code (11 U.S.C. § 522(a)(2) "value" means fair market value as of the date of filing the petition)[32]
- The Securities and Exchange Act

31. I.R.C. § 2031. An exception are certain related party transactions under I.R.C. § 482, discussed in Chapter 21, "Valuations for Federal Income Tax Matters."

32. *See, e.g.*, Active Wear, Inc. v. Parkdale Mills, Inc., 331 B.R. 669 (W.D. Va. 2005) (elaborates on the statutory definition and defines fair market value as the "value the debtor/bankrupt could receive for the property in a liquidation sale").

State Statutes

- State revenue codes
- State securities codes
- Business Corporations Act (often the Uniform Business Corporation Act), usually addressing dissenting stockholder valuations
- Statutes granting oppressed minority shareholder relief, including an appraisal option (in a growing number of states)
- Marital dissolution statutes, which generally do not address valuation matters

Legally Binding Rules and Regulations

Many legislative bills authorize rules and regulations that have the force of law, with implementation delegated to an administrative authority. Examples include:

- U.S. Treasury Regulations
- Federal and State Rules of Evidence and Civil Procedure
- Various state revenue regulations
- Department of Labor (DOL) Proposed Regulation Relating to the Definition of Adequate Consideration for ESOP (Employee Stock Ownership Plan) stock[33]

Comment: The DOL never finalized or issued the 1988 proposed regulation. Following a petition by The ESOP Association, the DOL announced in April 2023 that it would move forward with a public notice and comment rulemaking on a regulation to clearly define Adequate Consideration under ERISA, § 408(e), 29 U.S.C. § 1108(e).

Contractual Definitions of Value

Parties sometimes are bound by contractual definitions of value in documents governing certain types of transactions. Such documents may include:

- Articles of organization
- Articles of incorporation or partnership
- Bylaws
- Shareholder, close-corporation operating or partnership agreements with "buy/sell" provisions
- Prenuptial/postnuptial agreements
- Agreements made specifically for the purpose of settlement of the instant dispute, such as arbitration agreements

Such agreements may be very helpful in defining value for the purpose at hand, or they may be the source of another element of controversy.

Is the definition of value legally binding in the instant case? Even if it is not, it may be accorded some weight, especially if it has been used in other transactions with some similar characteristics.

Is the definition of value clear and unambiguous? Unfortunately, documents intended to provide guidance all too often are drafted with ambiguous language that leaves the interpretation subject to controversy in itself. It is recommend that an appraiser

33. 53 Fed. Reg. 17,632, 17,633 (May 17, 1988).

be consulted to review draft language relating to value to be sure that the attorneys and all parties to the agreement understand the value implications in the document.

Non–Legally Binding Administrative Rulings

Many government agencies issue rulings containing their interpretations of definitions of value. Courts usually give consideration to such rulings, but a court will not necessarily accept them if it feels that they are not consistent with the law.

For example, the IRS issued Revenue Ruling 81–253, which said that a discount for lack of control (i.e., minority interest) should not be applied to gifts of noncontrolling interest of shares of stock if other members of the family controlled the company. IRS Revenue Rulings represent the position of the IRS; they are not the law. The position taken in Revenue Ruling 81–253 lost every time it was challenged in court,[34] and finally (after 12 years) the IRS reversed its position with Revenue Ruling 93–12, recognizing that shares were to be valued based on the size of the block transferred, irrespective of attribution of family control value.

Prior Court Decisions (i.e., Precedence)

By far the richest source of specific guidance as to definitions of value in almost any legal context is interpretation found in prior case decisions. This book contains many annotations to decisions on valuation issues in many legal contexts (e.g., income tax, dissent, divorce) and in many jurisdictions. Careful study of prior case law is an important step in understanding the relevant legal definition of value.

Having made that point, again, it is also important to examine many challenges and pitfalls inherent in using prior case law as a source of guidance for definitions of value and to understand the context.

Lack of precedent. There are valuation issues for which no precedent exists in many state jurisdictions. In such cases, courts tend to cite precedent from other states that have similar statutes governing the issue. Each attorney, of course, seeks out precedent in other jurisdictions that support his or her position.

Ambiguous language. Most judges are not experts in financial language, and financial language itself has many ambiguities. For example, an opinion may use the term *fair market value* and then accept valuation methods that reflect factors that are not consistent with the common understanding of the definition.

Distinguishable facts and circumstances. Attorneys, and sometimes appraisers, may identify facts and circumstances in the case at bar that may lead to an interpretation of the definition of value that is different from that found in a seemingly on-point prior decision.

Sweeping generalizations. Opinions sometimes contain broad statements that, if read literally, would apply to a broader set of cases or circumstances than the court may have intended. Here the solution would be to carefully distinguish the facts and circumstances of the instant case from those of the case with the over-sweeping statement. It usually is preferable that the attorney, rather than the appraiser, originate the discussion of such distinctions in court.

34. *See, e.g.*, Est. of Andrews v. Comm'r, 79 T.C. 938 (1982).

Changing and contradictory precedent. Judicial positions on issues sometimes change as a result of revisiting an issue. Be sure to rely on the latest case decisions. Precedents within a jurisdiction sometimes seem to contradict each other. In that case, one might look for possible differentiation in facts and circumstances between the seemingly contradictory precedents. When relying on a U.S. Court of Appeals decision, remember that it is only controlling in the circuit that issued the opinion, and it is not uncommon to find different circuits holding contradictory opinions.

Direction from the Court

Sometimes, especially in a case of first impression on an issue, it is possible for the attorney to request and get a ruling from the court on the definition of value and/or the applicable valuation date before the appraiser prepares the report. This can save a great deal of expense in preparing reports under different definitions of value and/or two or more different valuation dates.

Direction from the Attorney

Sometimes the attorney has a clear-cut concept of the legal theory of the case, and that theory dictates a definition of value that the attorney directs the appraiser to use. If the source of the definition of value is the attorney rather than some quotable statutory or regulatory language, the appraiser usually will state this in the discussion of the definition of value in the introductory portion of the report.

Use of IRS Authority in Non-Tax Situations

It is not uncommon for appraisers to cite IRS authority, such as Revenue Rulings, when describing the nuances of the definition of fair market value. If this is done for a valuation other than for federal taxes, counsel should make sure that the legal standard of value is fair market value, and that the legal context has not created any nuances of the definition different from those for federal tax purposes.

Opinions of Other Attorneys and Appraisers

From time to time, one may obtain points of view on definitions of value from experienced attorneys or appraisers. These may come from either writings or discussions.

For example, one leading California corporate attorney has published clear-cut ideas about the definition of fair value under California Corporations Code § 2000. This attorney adds that "the cases provide only a patchwork of insights, only some of which are consistent with the basic purpose of § 2000."[35]

SUMMARY

Value is defined differently in different legal contexts. Unfortunately, the quest for the appropriate definition in any particular legal context is often a very difficult one.

35. Arthur J. Shartsis, *Dissolution Actions Yield Less than Fair Market Value* (*Appraising for 'Fair Value' under California Corporations Code Section 2000*) (Jan. 1, 2000), https://www.sflaw.com/dissolution-actions-yield-less-than-fair-market-enterprise-value-appraising-for-fair-value-under-california-corporations-code-section-2000/.

Therefore, identifying the correct standard and definition of value in the proper legal context is a crucial beginning step in an appraisal.

This chapter introduced commonly used definitions of *value*, defined other often-used terms referring to value, and, finally, reviewed sources of authority for the definition of value.

The standard or definition of value appropriate in a particular matter is, ultimately, a legal question and therefore is the responsibility of the attorney.

REFERENCES FOR DEFINING VALUE IN THE RELEVANT CONTEXT

American Society of Appraisers Business Valuation Committee Special Topics #4, "The 'Willing Buyer' and 'Willing Seller' in Fair Market Value." *Business Valuation Review* 36 (2) (Summer 2017), 44–47.

Fishman, Jay E., Bruce Johnson, Kent Pummel, et al., 2023. "What Is Value." In PPC's *Guide to Business Valuations*. 201.3 to 201.21 (Carrolton, TX: Thomson Reuters).

Fishman, Jay E., Shannon P. Pratt, and William J. Morrison. 2013. "Common Standards and Premises of Value." In *Standards of Value: Theory and Applications*, 2nd ed. Chap. 1, 17–27 (Hoboken, NJ: John Wiley & Sons).

Mercer, Z. Christopher. 2022. *Fair Market Value—Analysis and Review of This Seminal Ruling from Business and Valuation Perspectives*, available at https://chrismercer.net.

Morrison, William J. and Jay E. Fishman. 2017. "Business Valuation Concepts." In *The Business Valuation Bench Book*. 5–7 (Portland, OR: Business Valuation Resources).

Pratt, Shannon P. and ASA Educational Foundation. 2022. "Standards of Value." In *Shannon Pratt's Valuing a Business: The Analysis and Appraisal of Closely Held Businesses*, 6th ed. Chap. 2, 28–35 (New York: McGraw-Hill).

CHAPTER 2

Value to Whom?

Levels and Premises of Value

Roger J. Grabowski, FASA

INTRODUCTION

In this chapter you will learn about:

- *Levels of value*—the degree of control and liquidity of the ownership interest (e.g., shares)
- *Premises of value*—the assumed status of the business under which a transaction would be expected to take place, such as a going concern or in liquidation

Levels of value refers to the degree of control and the ease with which the holder can convert the shares into cash. The greater the control and the faster a holder can convert the shares to cash, the greater the value. Discounts for lack of control usually are taken before discounts for lack of marketability and the discount for lack of marketability usually is applied to whatever level of control is determined. In other words, the discounts for lack of control and lack of marketability are taken sequentially not additively.

Premises of value in this context refers to the state of the company at the valuation date; that is, is it a going-concern value or a value in liquidation?

LEVELS OF VALUE

The attorney and the appraiser should decide at the outset what level of value is appropriate for the subject interest that is being valued.

Business appraisers have traditionally referred to the available perspectives as levels of value. For example, is the subject interest a controlling interest or a noncontrolling interest? Is it easier for a holder of the interest to convert the interest to cash (e.g., the interest is publicly traded stock) or more difficult (e.g., noncontrolling interest with transfer restriction in a closely held business)? While a variety of charts have been offered by appraisers and observers over the years, Exhibit 2-1 includes the primary components that are common to all such charts.[1]

1. This section and Exhibit 2-1 are adapted from Shannon P. Pratt & ASA Educ. Found., Shannon Pratt's Valuing a Business: The Analysis and Appraisal of Closely Held Businesses 54–55 (6th ed. 2022). Used with permission.

Exhibit 2-1 Levels of Value

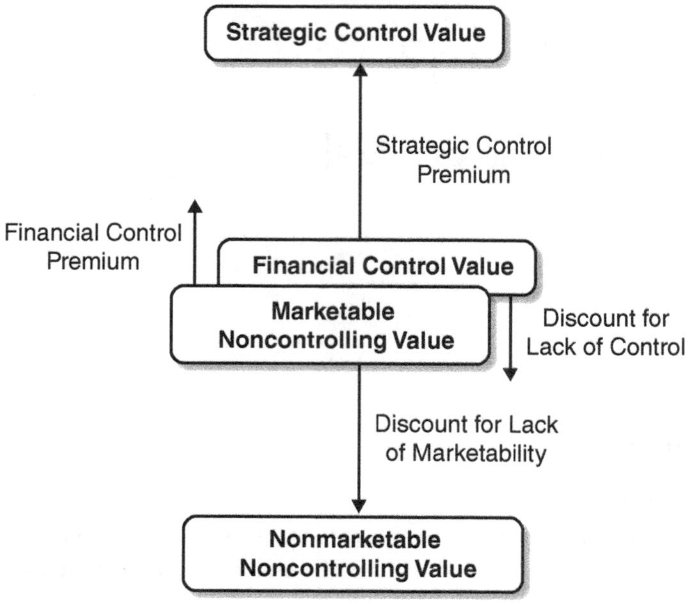

Source: SHANNON PRATT'S VALUING A BUSINESS: THE ANALYSIS AND APPRAISAL OF CLOSELY HELD BUSINESSES 55 (6th ed.); adapted from Z. CHRISTOPHER MERCER & TRAVIS W. HARMS, BUSINESS VALUATION—AN INTEGRATED THEORY 37 (3d ed.). Used with permission.

Exhibit 2-1 identifies four distinct levels of value and four discounts or premiums that relate the levels to one another. The different levels of value, and the corresponding discounts or premiums, are rooted in differences in economic income (discussed in Chapter 4) and differences in risk brought about from the typical differences in rights that the holders have given the levels of value represented in the exhibit.

Referring to Exhibit 2-1, the top level is strategic control value (sometimes termed synergistic value). This level reflects the value that a strategic buyer might pay recognizing the perceived synergies between the selling company and the buying company. This level could be appropriate if the purpose of the appraisal was to estimate a price that a synergistic buyer might pay. However, unless there is a group of synergistic buyers who create a market, fair market value generally reflects the value of the company on a stand-alone basis and does not include possible synergies with other companies (i.e., financial control value).

The line below financial control value, "marketable noncontrolling (often termed marketable minority) value," reflects an estimate of what the noncontrolling shares might trade for in a public market. Marketable is usually defined as the ability to convert the asset to cash very quickly, at minimal costs, with a high degree of certainty of realizing the anticipated amount of proceeds. If the company is run at maximum efficiency and noncontrolling shareholders are treated equally with control shareholders, there may be no basis for a control premium.

The typical levels of value to be appraised in a closely held company are either control or nonmarketable noncontrolling. "Nonmarketable" generally means that the shares cannot be sold to the general public because they have not been registered with the Securities and Exchange Commission (SEC). The shares may be legally saleable in a private sale, but they are not liquid. As such, nonmarketable is sometimes referred to as illiquid.

Chapter 18, "Discounts and Premiums," further elaborates on the levels of value and discusses premiums for control and discounts for lack of control and lack of marketability as well as discounts for other characteristics of an equity ownership interest.

PREMISES OF VALUE

A *premise of value* is an assumption about the status of the business under which a transaction would be expected to take place, that is, as a going concern or in liquidation, or some variation or combination of going-concern or liquidation value (e.g., some operating assets and some excess assets). The selection among alternative possible premises of value obviously can have a major impact on value.

In some situations, the premise of value is mandated as part of the definition of value by controlling documents or the purpose of the valuation. In other situations, the premise of value is left to the appraiser's judgment. For example, it may be left to the appraiser to determine what premise of value represents the highest and best use of the business or property.

Virtually all businesses or interests in businesses may be appraised under any of the following four alternative premises of value:

1. *Value in continued use as part of a going concern.* Value in continued use, as a mass assemblage of income-producing assets,[2] and as a going-concern business enterprise.
2. *Value in place, as part of a mass assemblage of assets.* Value in place, as part of a mass assemblage of assets, but not in current use in the production of income and not as a going concern business enterprise.
3. *Value in exchange, in an orderly liquidation.* Value in exchange, on a piecemeal basis (not part of a mass assemblage of assets), as part of an orderly disposition; this premise contemplates that all the assets of the business enterprise will be sold individually and that they will enjoy normal exposure to their appropriate secondary market.
4. *Value in exchange, in a forced liquidation.* Value in exchange, on a piecemeal basis (not part of a mass assemblage of assets), as part of a forced liquidation; this premise contemplates that the assets of the business enterprise will be sold individually and that they will experience less than normal exposure to their appropriate secondary market (i.e., the assets are "rushed" to the market).[3]

Each of these alternative premises of value may apply under the same standard, or definition, of value. For example, the fair market value standard calls for a "willing buyer" and a "willing seller." Yet the willing buyer and seller have to make an informed economic decision about how they will transact with each other with regard to the subject business. In other words, is the subject business worth more to the buyer and the seller as a going concern that will continue to operate as such, or as a collection of individual assets to be put to separate uses? In either case, the buyer and seller are still "willing."

---

2. That is, the value of the business having a system of operating assets, systems, and personnel in place, an operational plant, and the necessary licenses, systems, and procedures in place allowing the business the ability to operate.

3. Pratt & ASA Educ. Found., *supra* note 1, at 34.

And, in both cases, they have concluded a set of transactional circumstances that will maximize the value of the collective assets of the subject business enterprise.[4]

If left to the judgment of the appraiser, the premise of value selected may depend on whether the interest is being valued on a controlling interest or noncontrolling interest basis. In a controlling interest valuation, the selection of the appropriate premise of value typically is a function of the highest and best use of the collective assets of the subject business enterprise. The appraiser might value the operations of the business on a going-concern basis and the assets not necessary to operations valued on a liquidation basis.

If valuing on a noncontrolling interest basis, the appraiser is more likely to value the interest on the basis of its "operative reality," that is, assuming "business as usual." For instance, a profitable operating business would be valued as a going concern. In other words, the appraiser normally would not assume a liquidation of any assets unless there was an indication that such a liquidation was imminent. This treatment has been accepted by the courts.[5]

MATCHING THE VALUATION METHODOLOGY WITH THE STANDARD AND PREMISES OF VALUE

Perhaps the single, most prevalent broad reason many valuations miss the mark is failure to use valuation approaches and methods that are consistent with the definition of value being adopted.

In Chapter 1 standards of value are presented and discussed, and in this chapter premises of value and ownership characteristics are discussed and presented. Exhibit 2-1 puts the premises and ownership characteristics in perspective. This chapter, at least broadly, introduces the topic of approaches to value and elaborates a bit further on two of the most important ownership characteristics to consider: controlling versus noncontrolling ownership interests and degree of marketability. *All these concepts must be taken into consideration together in deciding exactly which valuation methods to use and what assumptions and data will go into the implementation of those methods.*[6]

SUM OF PARTS NOT NECESSARILY EQUAL TO WHOLE

Since partial ownership interests in a business are impacted by appropriate discounts and premiums differently than controlling ownership interests, the sum of the values of the individual ownership positions may be less than the overall business enterprise value. In most cases, when dealing with noncontrolling shares of a closely held company, the sum of the values of the partial ownership interests taken individually is less than what might be received if a single buyer purchased the entire entity. The company in its entirety has a different value because it conveys different rights and interests than the sum of all the interests taken on a noncontrolling ownership interest basis.

---

4. *Id.*

5. *See, e.g.*, Foltz v. U.S. News & World Report, Inc., 106 F.R.D. 338 (D.C. Cir. 1984), *appealed and affirmed.*

6. Pratt & ASA Educ. Found., *supra* note 1, at 58.

This economic fact, of course, is a catalyst for both merger and acquisition activity and dissenting shareholder lawsuits.

It is also important for attorneys and other advisors to alert clients entering into buy-sell agreements at *fair market value* that this term usually means something less than a pro rata proportion of the total enterprise value, unless other provisions are specified.[7]

SUMMARY

Shareholders have no direct claim on a corporation's assets because a corporate or partnership entity intervenes between the assets and the shareholder or partner. Therefore, the value of a share of stock or a partnership interest can be more than or less than a proportionate share of the underlying net asset value and sometimes bears little relationship to the underlying net asset value.

Lack of control and lack of marketability are distinct concepts, yet they are related. Both controlling and noncontrolling ownership interests in closely held companies may suffer somewhat from lack of marketability due to the inability to convert the asset to cash very quickly, at minimal costs, with a high degree of certainty of realizing the anticipated amount of proceeds.

Noncontrolling owners lack control over various decisions affecting the business enterprise, depending on the degree of control. Noncontrolling ownership interests may be worth considerably less than a pro rata portion of the business valued as a single, 100% ownership interest.

The market pays a premium for liquidity as compared with an illiquid asset, or, conversely, demands a discount for lack of liquidity as compared with a liquid asset. Business interests that lack ready marketability generally are worth less than otherwise comparable business interests that are readily marketable.

The sum of the values of individual fractional interests in a business is not necessarily, or even usually, equal to the value of a 100% ownership interest in the business. Think of it as 2 plus 2 equals something greater than 4.

REFERENCES FOR LEVELS AND PREMISES OF VALUE

Fishman, Jay E., Bruce Johnson, Kent Pummel, et al. 2023. "Defining the Subject Being Valued" and "Defining Future Benefits." In PPC's *Guide to Business Valuations*, 202.5 to 202.7 (Carrollton, TX: Thomson Reuters).

Fishman, Jay E., Shannon P. Pratt, and William J. Morrison. 2013. "Common Standards and Premises of Value." In *Standards of Value: Theory and Applications*, 2nd ed. Chap. 1, 28–32 (Hoboken, NJ: John Wiley & Sons).

Morrison, William J. and Jay E. Fishman. 2017. "Business Valuation Concepts." In *The Business Valuation Bench Book*, 5–7 (Portland, OR: Business Valuation Resources).

Pratt, Shannon P. and ASA Educational Foundation. 2022. "Levels of Value." In *Shannon Pratt's Valuing a Business: The Analysis and Appraisal of Closely Held Businesses*, 6th ed., 54–59 (New York: McGraw-Hill).

7. *Id.* at 59.

CHAPTER 3

Overview of Business Valuation Approaches, Methods, and Procedures

Roger J. Grabowski, FASA

INTRODUCTION

In this chapter you will learn about:

- Basic business valuation approaches
- Methods used within each approach
- Business appraisal procedures
- Valuing a business interest based on the invested capital procedure or the direct equity procedure
- Approaches and methods that are not totally discrete
- Ambiguities in business valuation terminology

The classification of business valuation methodology, in general, and, more specifically, its applications in business appraisal is somewhat arbitrary because the methods are not totally discrete. Nevertheless, classification of methodologies helps bring some organization, which aids in both implementing and reviewing the appraisal process. The classification of methodology as presented in this chapter, while not followed universally, represents a growing consensus on the taxonomy of business appraisal. The organization of the remainder of the book generally follows this classification.

HIERARCHY OF APPROACHES, METHODS, AND PROCEDURES

The business valuation and appraisal communities generally have adopted a hierarchy of the terms *approach*, *method*, and *procedure*:

- *Approach* is the broadest of the three terms
- *Method* refers to general ways of implementing the approaches
- *Procedure* means the specific calculations, data used, and other details involved in a specific method

Basic Appraisal Approaches

The three generally accepted approaches in business valuation essentially are analogous to the three approaches used in real estate appraisal:

1. **Income approach**—valuing the business or business interest based on some form of expected economic income stream; in real estate appraisal usually called "capitalization"
2. **Market approach**—valuation of the business or business interest by reference to other transactions; in real estate appraisal usually called the "comparable sales approach"
3. **Asset-based approach**—valuation of the business based on its assets and liabilities; somewhat analogous to the "cost approach" in real estate appraisal[1]

METHODS USED WITHIN APPRAISAL APPROACHES

Within each of the three approaches, there is reasonably wide consensus on the terminology used to denote the methods employed:

Income Approach Methods

Discounting—forecasting the expected economic income over the life of the investment and discounting each increment of that expected income back to a present value at a rate of return known as a *discount rate.* This method is also known as the discounted cash flow (DCF) method when economic income has been defined as net cash flow. (The procedures are similar to the method known as "yield capitalization" in real estate appraisal.)

Capitalizing—observing or estimating a single period's economic income and dividing it by a rate of return adjusted for expected growth known as a *capitalization rate.* This method is also known as the capitalization method. (It is analogous to "direct capitalization" in real estate appraisal.)

Market Approach Methods

Guideline public company method (sometimes called the "comparable company method")—derives valuation multiples from prices and financial data of common stock traded in the public market and applies the multiples to the appropriate financial data of the subject company. No counterpart exists in real estate appraisal because there is no organized market for fractional interests in real estate; any markets that might exist for fractional interests in real estate are likely to be very small and ad hoc.

Guideline transaction method—derives valuation multiples from prices and financial data of public or private companies that have been sold and applies the multiples to the appropriate financial data of the subject company. This method is analogous to the "comparable sales approach" in real estate appraisal. (Some might further subdivide this method based on whether the guideline company was public or private before the sale.)

Past transactions method—uses multiples of financial data from the company's own past transactions:

- Past change of ownership of 100% or a controlling interest in the subject company
- Past transactions of minority interests in the subject company
- Past acquisitions made by the subject company
- Past firm offers (but must examine whether bona fide and arm's length)

1. The Asset Approach (term used in the Glossary) is synonymous with the Asset-based Approach.

Buy-sell agreements—placed arbitrarily under the market approach with the idea that someone negotiated and agreed to the buy-sell terms at some point in the past. Depending on the purpose of the valuation and the terms of the buy-sell agreement, its valuation provisions may range from defining how value is measured to irrelevant. The weight, if any, to be accorded to the valuation terms of the agreement is often a critical decision. The agreement may be binding for some valuation purposes and not for others. Sometimes the degree of weight may depend on the extent to which the agreement was arm's length when negotiated. Often the appraiser and/or the court decides that the terms of the buy-sell agreement are a factor to be considered but are not binding. One reason is because these agreements can be, and often are, changed.

Rules of thumb—employs "ballpark" ranges of possible values derived from simple formulas used in a particular industry. It is sometimes classified under the market approach, because the rules are allegedly market-derived averages, but generally without any support derived from underlying market data. Rules of thumb are discussed in detail in Chapter 11.

Asset-Based Approach Methods

Asset accumulation (adjusted net asset value) method—adjusts all the company's assets (both tangible and intangible) and liabilities to current value, usually fair market value, and subtracts the liabilities from the total value of the assets in order to derive the overall value of equity.

- *Going-concern premise*: adjusts all assets and liabilities to current fair market value in continued use and subtracts the liabilities from the assets.
- *Liquidation premise*: adjusts all assets and liabilities to fair market value on a liquidation premise of value and subtracts all the liabilities and liquidation costs from the assets.
- *Hybrid premise*: values assets expected to be in continuing operation on a going-concern basis and nonoperating assets on a liquidation basis. This could involve more than one operating unit of the business, where each operating unit is valued on a going-concern basis and nonoperating assets on a liquidation basis. This latter version sometimes is called a "breakup method" or "disaggregation method."

Excess earnings method—adjusts only the company's tangible assets to current value—again, usually fair market value in continued use—and subtracts the liabilities to obtain a net tangible asset value. Estimates the amount of income needed to support the net tangible assets. If there is income over and above that amount, the excess income is divided by a capitalization rate to estimate the value of the company's intangible assets. Adds the estimated value of the intangibles to the value of the tangible assets.

This method is classified under the asset-based approach because, in theory, it adds the values of the tangible and intangible assets. Because it involves the capitalization of excess income, some appraisers prefer to call it a "hybrid method," and some may even classify it under the income approach. In this book, it is discussed separately in Chapter 10.

SUMMARY OF BUSINESS APPRAISAL APPROACHES AND METHODS

A schematic diagram of this classification of business valuation approaches and methods is presented in Exhibit 3-1.

Exhibit 3-1 Schematic Diagram of Business Valuation Approaches and Methods

Approaches	Methods
Income	Discounting (discounted cash flow—DCF) Capitalizing (capitalization)
Market	Guideline public companies Guideline transactions Past transactions Buy-sell agreement Rules of thumb
Asset-based	Adjusted net asset value • Going-concern basis • Liquidation basis • Hybrid basis Excess earnings (sometimes classified as "hybrid")

BUSINESS APPRAISAL PROCEDURES

A "procedure" is a more detailed step used in implementing an appraisal method. For example, as we will see in Chapter 7, several accepted procedures can be employed to develop discount and capitalization rates within the discounting and capitalizing methods. These procedures are often referred to as "methods" and can be considered as methods within methods or as the different ways that a method can be carried out.

For example, the "DCF method" is a good example of ambiguous terminology. The discounted cash flow method, or the discounting method, is a major valuation method within the income approach. However, that same term is commonly used to describe a procedure for estimating the discount or capitalization rate to be used within either the discounting or the capitalization method in the income approach.

Invested Capital versus Equity

Another important example of different procedures is the choice of either valuing the equity directly or valuing the firm's total invested capital (common stock [common equity] plus any preferred stock and interest-bearing debt, including current maturities) and then subtracting the debt to arrive at a value for the common equity.

This choice of procedures can be available within most of the valuation methods. For example, within the market approach, using either the guideline public company or the guideline transaction method, one could value the equity directly by using a price-to-earnings multiple. Alternatively, one could use the multiple of market value of invested capital to earnings before interest, taxes, and depreciation (MVIC-to-EBITDA) to estimate the value of the firm's invested capital and then subtract the debt from that value to estimate the value of equity.

Some businesses have more than one class of equity, usually preferred equity and common equity. The preferred equity is senior to the common equity and, from a financial analysis point of view, usually has more of the characteristics of debt than equity. Therefore, the term *equity* typically is used to mean only the common equity, and the value of preferred equity would be subtracted along with the debt in the invested capital procedures to arrive at the common (or residual) equity value. This may require the preferred stock to be valued as well.[2]

Exhibit 3-2 summarizes procedures commonly used within various valuation methods.

Exhibit 3-2 Value of Invested Capital and Direct Valuation of Equity Procedures

Valuation Method	Valuation Procedures
Income approach: either discounting or capitalizing	*Invested capital procedure*: discount or capitalize the expected returns (usually measured as cash flows) available to holders of all components of invested capital and then subtract the debt to obtain value of common equity. *Direct equity procedure*: discount or capitalize only those returns available to equity (e.g., common equity).
Market approach: using either guideline public companies, guideline transactions, or other market approach methods	*Invested capital procedure*: use market value of invested capital in the numerator of the ratio used to compute the multiple, returns available to all invested capital in the denominator; apply the multiple to the returns available to all invested capital and subtract the debt to obtain the value of common equity. *Direct equity procedure*: use only value of equity in the numerator of the ratio used to compute the multiple, returns available to common equity in the denominator.
Asset-based approach: asset accumulation method (adjusted net asset value)	By definition, the assets on which all invested capital has claims are valued and the debt subtracted to obtain net asset value (value of common equity).
Excess earnings method	This method values common equity directly, because the method requires subtracting the debt to obtain the net tangible asset value.
Rules of thumb	Rules of thumb generally are intended to value all the invested capital. An example is the price-to-sales multiple. Therefore, the debt, if any, would have to be subtracted to obtain the common equity value (although the exact procedure may vary from one rule of thumb to another).

APPROACHES AND METHODS NOT TOTALLY DISCRETE

Business appraisers usually try to use two or more appraisal methods to maximize the reliability of the appraiser's concluded value. Appraisers may give different relative weights to different methods or conclude that one appraisal method is dominant in a given situation. The reconciliation of results from different methods to reach a final conclusion is discussed in Chapter 19, "Reconciliation of Value Indications."

When business appraisers apply different methods, they generally try to make the data and procedures used in each method as discrete as possible from those used in the other methods to reach the different indications of value as independently as possible.

2. *See* Rev. Rul. 83–120, issued to enhance guidance from Rev. Rul. 59–60.

For example, net cash flow usually is used in the income approach, while other income measures (e.g., sales or net income) are typically employed in the market approach.

However, there is necessarily some interrelationship among the methods. All methods are based on some form of economic income (the meaning of economic income is discussed in Chapter 4) and/or asset values, and all depend to some extent on market data.

Both the income approach and market approach may use historical economic income, expected economic income, or a combination. The asset-based approach uses adjusted asset values for all assets, while the income and market approaches may use asset values for excess or nonoperating assets. The income approach derives its discount and capitalization rates from data extracted from the market. The market approach uses market-derived multiples of some form of economic income variables and/or asset values.

Business appraisers capitalize income in both the market and income approaches; they just develop their capitalization rates in different ways. In the market approach, capitalization rates (typically expressed as a market multiple) come from direct observation of specific market transactions. In the income approach, on the other hand, capitalization rates are developed through applying formulas using broad market rate of return data. The asset-based approach develops its adjusted asset values from market data.

In reviewing descriptions of different appraisal methods used in an appraisal report, the reader should think about the extent to which each method is really an indication of value independent of another method, or whether the appraiser is simply presenting the same data in different formats. For instance, the use of a market multiple of book value of equity in the market approach and the use of the book value of equity in the asset-based approach as separate indications of value are actually one and the same method.

Another common misconception is the use of both a single-year capitalization of cash flow method and a multiyear discounted cash flow method. These two methods should not be used to produce two separate value indications within the same valuation assignment. As will be seen later, theoretically these methods should produce the same value. Rather, the appraiser should determine if cash flow is sustainable and/or consistent (use a single-year capitalization) or not (use a multiyear forecast for the discounted cash flow).

The appraiser should also consider adjustments consistently. For example, if in the income approach the appraiser has increased the discount rate (or decreased the capitalization rate) for increased risks of the subject business, then an adjustment downwards in the market approach should also be considered.

AMBIGUITIES OF BUSINESS VALUATION TERMINOLOGY

Unfortunately, the terminology found in the literature of financial theory and corporate finance is loaded with ambiguities, and these carry over into the literature of business appraisal and business appraisal reports. It is very important for business appraisers to properly define all approaches, methods, and procedures used in their analysis, in order to present a clear understanding.

In this book, terminology is defined within the context of the discussion where it is used, as well as in Chapter 4, and a glossary is provided in Appendix A.

Many appraisal reports contain definitions of terms. These definitions should be read carefully, because different appraisers may use the same term differently. If definitions are not included, consult the index of this book or the glossary for common uses. Some appraisers may not always use terms as they are commonly defined, and the reader may have to figure out the intended definition. Reading and trying to interpret court case decisions is also a huge problem when the author of the opinion has not had a technical education in the esoteric terminology of finance.

The following chapter is a primer on terminology commonly found in financial statements and business appraisal.

SUMMARY

While business valuation approaches and methods are not totally discrete, there is broad consensus on three generally accepted approaches: the income approach, the market approach, and the asset-based approach.

Within each approach, there are two or more generally accepted methods. For example, within the income approach, the basic methods are *discounting* and *capitalizing.* Within the market approach, there is the *guideline public company* method, the *guideline transaction* method, the *past transactions and/or offers* method, *buy-sell agreements*, and *rules of thumb* (used in some industries). Within the asset-based approach, there is the *asset accumulation* (*adjusted net asset value*) method and the *excess earnings* method.

Within each method there is a variety of accepted procedures for its implementation. Two of the most important are the *invested capital procedure* (valuing the entire capital structure and subtracting the senior obligations to arrive at the residual common equity value) and the *direct equity valuation procedure* (using techniques that value the common equity directly); either procedure may be used with most methods.

Business valuation can include some ambiguous terminology. This book defines each term in the context in which it is used, and a general glossary is included in Appendix A. Chapter 4 also discusses common terminology found in business appraisal.

REFERENCES FOR OVERVIEW OF BUSINESS VALUATION APPROACHES, METHODS, AND PROCEDURES

Fishman, Jay E., Bruce Johnson, Kent Pummel, et al. 2023. "Valuation Approaches and Methods." In PPC's *Guide to Business Valuations*, 203.3 (Carrollton, TX: Thomson Reuters).

Morrison, William J. and Jay E. Fishman. 2017. "Approaches to Value." In *The Business Valuation Bench Book*, 9–13 (Portland, OR: Business Valuation Resources).

Pratt, Shannon P. and ASA Educational Foundation. 2022. "Accepted Business Valuation Approaches and Methods." In *Shannon Pratt's Valuing a Business: The Analysis and Appraisal of Closely Held Businesses*, 6th ed., 50–54 (New York: McGraw-Hill).

CHAPTER 4

Financial Statement Terminology Used in Business Appraisal

Alina Niculita, ASA, ARM, CFA

INTRODUCTION

In this chapter you will learn about:

- Basics of the balance sheet
- Basics of the income statement
- Commonly used measures of economic income
- Methods of accounting—accrual basis versus cash basis

Because virtually all business appraisal approaches, methods, and procedures use either actual or estimated numbers extracted or computed from financial statements, this chapter provides a road map to the terminology and meanings of those numbers as they are used in business appraisal.

This chapter includes both accounting and financial terms. Many of the numbers represented by the accounting terms can be read directly from financial statements. Yet, other numbers representing other accounting terms or financial terms must be computed. This chapter will define the terms and, where necessary, illustrate how to compute amounts for each. However, readers should understand that this is only the most perfunctory primer and that they will need to refer to other sources, such as those shown at the end of Chapter 15, for illustrations of more complex financial statements.

With the information shown in Exhibit 4-1, it is possible to extract or compute most of the financial variables that typically are used in the various approaches to business valuation. This chapter necessarily involves numbers and computations. However, it would be impossible to simplify it much more without omitting concepts that one is almost certain to encounter within the scope of reviewing valuation reports. Therefore, it is suggested that the reader peruse it quickly the first time through and thereafter use it as a reference.

THE BASIC FINANCIAL STATEMENTS

The two most commonly used financial statements are the *balance sheet* and the *income statement.* The balance sheet presents assets, liabilities, and owner's equity at a point in time, generally all at *book value.* Book value generally represents original historical cost and may be reduced by depreciation and other noncash charges in accordance with accounting principles. Adjustments to bring these figures to market value are discussed in Chapter 15. The income statement presents revenues, expenses, and net income over a specific reporting period, such as a month, quarter, or entire fiscal year. Sometimes, if the valuation date is not close to the end of a company's fiscal year, it may be necessary to use *interim financial statements*, that is, those prepared at a time other than the company's fiscal year-end. An example balance sheet and income statement and other financial data for Widget Corporation are shown in Exhibit 4-1.

Exhibit 4-1 Widget Corporation Financial Data

Widget Corporation Balance Sheet
Assets

Current Assets	
Cash	$500,000
Accounts Receivable	1,000,000
Inventory	1,500,000
Total Current Assets	$3,000,000
Plant & Equipment	
At Cost	$5,000,000
Less: Accumulated Depreciation	3,000,000
Net Plant & Equipment	$2,000,000
Total Assets	$5,000,000

Liabilities and Equity

Current Liabilities	
Accounts Payable	$500,000
Accrued Expenses	$500,000
Total Current Liabilities	$1,000,000
Long-Term Interest-Bearing Debt	3,000,000
Total Liabilities	$4,000,000
Preferred Stock	$0
Common Equity (1,000 shares outstanding)	1,000,000
Total Liabilities and Equity	$5,000,000

Widget Corporation Income Statement

Sales	$10,000,000
Cost of Goods Sold	6,000,000
Gross Margin	$4,000,000
Selling, General, and Administrative Expenses	2,700,000
Operating Income, before Interest and Taxes	$1,300,000
Interest Expense	300,000
Income before Taxes	$1,000,000
Income Taxes	300,000
Net Income	$700,000

Widget Corporation Other Financial Data

The following data are derived from Statement of Cash Flows, footnotes to financial statements, and company books and records:

1. Interest rate on the long-term debt is 10%.
2. The selling, general, and administrative expenses include depreciation of $250,000.
3. The selling, general, and administrative expenses include compensation for the president (who owns 100% of the stock and both manages the company and maintains all the key customer contacts) as follows:

Salary	$500,000
Bonus	200,000
Retirement Plan Contribution	100,000
Health and Life Insurance	50,000
Discretionary Entertainment Expenses (golf club, yacht, etc.)	100,000
Total Owner's Compensation	$950,000

4. Capital expenditures average about $300,000 per year.
5. The company's sales are growing at about 10% per year.
6. The company maintains net working capital at about 20% of sales, typical for its industry.
7. No changes in the level of long-term debt are contemplated in the foreseeable future.

The three levels of attestation of financial statements, in descending order of their degree of detail (and, oftentimes, their reliability), are Audited, Reviewed, and Compiled. Definitions of each are shown in Exhibit 4-2. The appraiser's report will typically indicate which level of financial statement preparation was used and who prepared the statements. This may be different for different time periods, and, if so, this information should be listed for each.

The balance of this chapter defines the terms used to describe the most important components of these statements. Analysis of the financial statements is covered in Chapters 15 and 16.

Exhibit 4-2 Levels of Financial Statement Preparation

1. Audited Statements. In audited statements, the independent auditor expresses an opinion or, if circumstances require, disclaims an opinion, regarding the fairness with which the financial statements present the financial position, the results of operations, and the changes in financial position, in accordance with generally accepted accounting principles.
2. Reviewed Statements. The independent accountant expresses limited assurance in reviewed statements that there are no material modifications that should be made to the statements in order for them to be in conformity with generally accepted accounting principles. A review does not provide assurance that the accountant will become aware of all the significant matters that would be disclosed in an audit.
3. Compiled Statements. Finally, the compiled statements are management's representations presented in the form of financial statements, but the accountant has not undertaken any efforts to express assurance on the statements. Sometimes statements are prepared internally by management without the services of an outside accountant.

BALANCE SHEET CONCEPTS

Common Equity

Common equity (at book value) consists of paid in capital plus retained earnings. In Widget Corporation, common equity at book value is

$1,000,000 from the Balance Sheet

Invested Capital

Invested capital consists of equity plus interest-bearing debt. For Widget Corporation, invested capital at book value is:

Interest-bearing debt	$3,000,000
Common equity	1,000,000
Book value of invested capital[1]	$4,000,000

If the company had preferred stock, this would be shown as an additional item in the capital structure and included as part of the market value of invested capital (MVIC).

Capital Structure

Capital structure is the relative proportions of the various elements of invested capital. In this case, at book value:

Interest-bearing debt	$3,000,000	75%
Equity	1,000,000	25%
	$4,000,000	100%

Book Value

With respect to assets, the book value of the plant and equipment is the capitalized (original) cost minus the accumulated depreciation. For Widget Corporation, for example:

Plant and equipment	$5,000,000
Less: Accumulated depreciation	3,000,000
Net book value of plant and equipment	$2,000,000

With respect to the whole business, the book value is the difference between the total assets (net of depreciation, depletion, and amortization) and the total liabilities.

1. Some financial analysts and appraisers deduct cash when computing invested capital. Alternatively, some deduct cash that they consider to be in excess of the company's cash requirements for operations. The important thing is that the analyst or appraiser be consistent. For example, if cash is deducted when computing invested capital for the subject company in the market approach, it must be deducted when computing invested capital for the guideline companies as well.

This is also called *net book value* and equals the book value of equity. For Widget Corporation, this is:

Total assets	$5,000,000
Less: Total liabilities	4,000,000
Book value of equity	$1,000,000

Book Value per Share

On a per-share basis, the book value is the value of common equity divided by the number of shares outstanding. For Widget Corporation, it is:

$$\frac{\$1{,}000{,}000}{1{,}000 \text{ Shares}} = \$1{,}000 \text{ per share}$$

Tangible Book Value versus Total Book Value

Tangible book value reflects only the company's tangible assets (e.g., current assets, plant and equipment) minus liabilities. Total book value reflects both tangible and intangible assets. Examples of intangible assets include copyrights, patents, goodwill, and the like. If a company acquires its intangible assets, they generally are listed on the balance sheet and are part of the book value. On the other hand, if the company creates its own intangible assets, the costs to create may have been expensed in the income statement and, therefore, the resulting intangible assets do not appear on the balance sheet. As such, for comparative consistency, business appraisers usually prefer to work with only the tangible book value rather than the total book value. In any case, to completely understand the financial statements being analyzed, the reader of the report should know whether there are any intangible assets included in the book value and if that figure is used for any computations in the valuation report.

Net Working Capital

Net working capital is defined as the current assets minus the current liabilities held in a business for its day-to-day operational needs of meeting its obligations. Current assets are those that are expected to generate cash within one year, and current liabilities are obligations due to mature within one year. For Widget Corporation, it is:

Current assets	$3,000,000
Less: Current liabilities	1,000,000
Net working capital	$2,000,000

MISCELLANEOUS EXPENSE CONCEPTS

Noncash Charges

Noncash charges are items that are recorded as expenses on the income statement but do not require a cash outlay. Examples include depreciation, depletion, amortization, and deferred taxes.

For Widget Corporation, the only noncash charge is:

Depreciation: $250,000 from Other Financial Data

Noncash charges are added back to the net income to arrive at net cash flow, and are added back to the operating income to arrive at the earnings before interest, taxes, depreciation, and amortization (EBITDA).

Owners' Compensation (Including Disclosed or Hidden Perks)

Owners' compensation includes all elements of compensation, including salary, bonuses, retirement benefits, life and health insurance benefits, discretionary expenses, and value of stock options. For Widget Corporation, reported owner's compensation is:

$950,000 from Other Financial Data

LEVELS OF ECONOMIC INCOME

One of the most crucial and yet highly ambiguous concepts used in business valuation is that of income, sometimes referred to as *earnings*. It is common to see one or the other of these two terms used without further definition. So many different levels of income are employed in various business valuation methods and procedures that the term *income* is virtually meaningless until the level of income intended is clearly specified.

In recent years, the business appraisal profession has embraced the broad term *economic income* to mean some level of income (any level) that needs further specific definition before it can be used meaningfully in a business valuation method or procedure. All the following levels of economic income are commonly used in business appraisal practice:

- Sales (revenues, net of returns and allowances)
- Earnings before interest and taxes (EBIT)
- Earnings before interest, income taxes, depreciation, and amortization (EBITDA)
- Owners' (or sellers') discretionary earnings (or cash flow)
- Gross cash flow (net income plus noncash charges)
- Debt-free net income
- Debt-free cash flow
- Pretax income
- Net income
- Net cash flow to invested capital
- Net cash flow to equity

Sales (Net Revenues)

The terms *sales* and *net revenues* generally are used interchangeably.[2] For Widget Corporation, it is:

$10,000,000 from the Income Statement

A multiple of sales is often used in the market approach when valuing invested capital. It is less frequently used (and potentially very misleading) when valuing equity directly, because sales are based on the assets supported by the entire capital structure.

---

2. Also used are *net sales* and *revenues.*

EBIT (Also Called *Operating Income*)

For Widget Corporation, EBIT is:

$1,300,000 from the Income Statement

EBIT is one of the most used variables in the market approach *when valuing invested capital.*

EBITDA

EBITDA is computed as earnings before interest, income taxes, and *all* noncash charges, including depreciation, amortization, depletion, and deferred taxes. Widget Corporation's EBITDA is:

EBIT (operating income)	$1,300,000
Plus: Depreciation	250,000
EBITDA	$1,550,000

EBITDA is also a commonly used variable in the market approach *when valuing invested capital.*

Discretionary Earnings

Discretionary earnings (also called *sellers' discretionary cash flow* (SDCF), *sellers' discretionary earnings* (SDE), or *owners' discretionary cash flow* (ODCF)) may be defined, in certain applications, to reflect earnings of a business enterprise prior to adjustment for the following items: income taxes, depreciation and amortization, interest expense or income, and owner's total compensation for those services, which could be provided by a sole owner/manager. For Widget Corporation, discretionary earnings are:

EBIT (operating income)	$1,300,000
Plus: Depreciation	250,000
Plus: Owners' compensation	950,000
Discretionary earnings	$2,500,000

Discretionary earnings are used in the transaction method in the market approach usually only when valuing small businesses.

Gross Cash Flow

When the term *gross cash flow* is used, it almost always means *gross cash flow to equity,* sometimes just called *cash flow.* It is defined as net income plus noncash charges. For Widget Corporation, gross cash flow is:

Net income	$700,000
Plus: Depreciation	250,000
Gross cash flow	$950,000

Debt-Free Net Income (DFNI), Also Called *NOPAT* (Net Operating Profit After Income Taxes)

Debt-free net income means what the net income would be if there were no debt. It is computed by adding the interest expense, net of the tax effect (income taxes saved because the interest is a tax-deductible expense) to the net income. For Widget Corporation, debt-free net income is:

Net income	$700,000
+ Interest expense, net of pro forma income taxes: $300,000 × (1 − 0.30)	210,000
[Taxes of $300,000 on $1,000,000 pretax income, or 30%]	$910,000

The same result is obtained by tax-affecting EBIT, or the operating income:

EBIT (operating income)	$1,300,000
Less income taxes (30% tax rate)	390,000
Debt-free net income	$910,000

When DFNI or NOPAT is used, it is often in the context of the market approach *when valuing invested capital.* Use of the term does not mean that the business has no debt; rather, the cost of debt financing is reflected in the discount rate or capitalization rate.

Debt-Free Gross Cash Flow (DFCF)

Debt-free gross cash flow means what the gross cash flow would be if there were no debt. It is debt-free net income plus noncash charges. For Widget Corporation, debt-free cash flow is:

Debt-free net income	$910,000
Plus: Depreciation	250,000
Debt-free cash flow	$1,160,000

When debt-free cash flow is used, it is in the context of the market approach *when valuing invested capital.*

The "debt-free" measures are used to make companies with significantly different capital structures more comparable to each other. Debt-free net income and debt-free gross cash flow are hypothetical numbers, representing the amounts as if the business had no debt. Because they are hypothetical, they are not as widely used. As such, many financial analysts and business appraisers prefer using multiples of EBITDA and EBIT when valuing invested capital.

Pretax Income

Pretax income is income after all expenses except income taxes. For Widget Corporation, pretax income is:

$1,000,000 from the Income Statement

Pretax income often is used in the market approach when valuing equity directly. It is sometimes used in the excess earnings method and sometimes as a proxy for net income in a small company, sole proprietorship, subchapter S corporation, limited liability company, or partnership where the entity does not pay any income taxes, but the taxable income is "passed through" to the owners who are liable for income taxes due.

Net Income

Net income is income after all expenses, including interest, owner's compensation, noncash charges, and income taxes paid by the entity. For Widget Corporation, net income is:

$700,000 from the Income Statement

Net income is used in the market approach when valuing equity directly, and sometimes used in the excess earnings method. In some circumstances, net income may be used in the income approach, but, more frequently, net cash flow is used in the income approach.

Primary versus Diluted Net Income per Share

On a per-share basis, net income can be stated as either primarily *net income per share* or *diluted net income per share.* "Primary" is computed based on the number of shares outstanding. "Diluted" is computed on the assumption of convertible debt being converted to common stock, preferred stock being converted to common stock, and warrants and options to buy stock being exercised. When performing comparative analysis, it is important to be sure that any figures used for comparison are computed on the same basis.

Net Cash Flow to Invested Capital

Net cash flow to invested capital is the amount of cash available to distribute to owners and stakeholders of all components of the capital structure (preferred and common equity and interest-bearing debt) after leaving enough for the capital expenditures and working capital necessary to sustain projected operations. The computation is as follows:

Net income (after taxes) to common equity
\+ Noncash charges (depreciation, amortization, deferred taxes, etc.)
− Capital expenditures[3]
± Changes in net working capital[4]
\+ Interest expense, net of the income tax effect (interest expense x [1 – income tax rate])
\+ Preferred dividends, if any
= Net cash flow to overall invested capital

3. Assumes that these amounts are those necessary to support projected business operations.
4. *Id.*

For Widget Corporation, net cash flow to invested capital is:

Net Income		$700,000
+	Depreciation	250,000
–	Capital expenditures	(300,000)
–	Additions to net working capital	(200,000)
+	Interest expenses, net of pro forma income taxes[5]	
	$300,000 x (1 – 0.30)	210,000
	Net cash flow to invested capital	$ 660,000

This is the measure of economic income that is preferred by business appraisers and the professional financial community when using the income approach to value a company's invested capital. From the valuation of invested capital, the debt and preferred equity are subtracted to obtain the value of common equity.

Net Cash Flow to Equity

Net cash flow to equity (sometimes called *free cash flow to equity* or *net free cash flow to equity*) is the amount of cash available to equity owners to withdraw from or distribute from the business after leaving enough for the capital expenditures and working capital necessary to sustain projected operations. The computation is as follows:

Net income (after taxes)	
+	Noncash charges (e.g., depreciation, amortization, deferred income taxes)
–	Capital expenditures[6]
±	Changes in net working capital[7]
±	Net changes in interest-bearing debt
=	Net cash flow to equity

If there are preferred dividends, they must also be subtracted. The objective is to estimate the net cash flow available to common equity holders. For Widget Corporation, net cash flow to equity is:

	Net income	$ 700,000
+	Depreciation	250,000
–	Capital expenditures	(300,000)
–	Additions to net working capital	(200,000)
Net cash flow to equity[8]		$ 450,000

This is the measure of economic income that is most preferred by the corporate financial community when using the income approach to value equity. The net cash flow to equity is also used as the economic income variable in the excess earnings method.

5. Income taxes of $300,000 on $1 million pretax income, or 30%.

6. Assumes that these amounts are the levels necessary to support projected business operations.

7. *Id.*

8. If the company is growing, it may increase long-term debt; if highly leveraged, it may decrease long-term debt. An increase in long-term debt would increase net cash flow to equity, and paydown of long-term debt would decrease net cash flow to equity. Widget Corporation does not anticipate any changes in the level of long-term debt per Other Financial Data.

VARIABLES AFFECTING NET CASH FLOW

Capital Expenditures

Capital expenditures are the amounts paid for assets expected to have a long-term economic life (usually more than one year), recorded on the balance sheet at the amount paid, and then depreciated (or depleted or amortized) over time as expenses on the income statement, which reduces book value on the balance sheet. For Widget Corporation, capital expenditures are:

Approximately $300,000 per year from Other Financial Data

Normalized expected capital expenditures must be estimated as a component in computing the net cash flow in the income approach, because the capital expenditure requirements represent a portion of the gross cash flow that must remain in the business to support projected operations.

Changes in Net Working Capital

Changes in the net working capital are the amounts added to or subtracted from the net working capital needed to support the operations and growth of the business.

Expected sales growth:	
10% x $10,000,000	$1,000,000
Percentage of sales needed as additional net working capital (the percentage of incremental sales, from Other Financial Data)	20%
Expected additional need of net working capital	$ 200,000

Similar to capital expenditures, changes in the net working capital must also be estimated as one of the components in computing the net cash flow in the income approach, because it represents an amount of cash flow that must remain in the business to support projected operations and growth.

Changes in Debt

If the company increases its debt, the increase is an addition to the net cash flow to equity. Conversely, repayments of the debt are a reduction of net cash flow to equity.[9] For Widget Corporation, the expected changes in debt are:

$0 per year from Other Financial Data

CASH VERSUS ACCRUAL BASIS ACCOUNTING

Most companies record their accounting on an *accrual basis* in accordance with Generally Accepted Accounting Principles (GAAP). However, some companies, especially smaller ones, prepare their financial statements on a *cash basis*. Some companies prepare financial statements on an accrual basis, and income tax returns on a cash basis. Other

9. Some businesses are able to use short-term debt as being equivalent to long-term financing, generally during periods of relatively low, stable interest rates.

companies do not prepare financial statements separate from the income tax returns, in which case it should be ascertained whether the tax returns are on a cash or accrual basis (this is noted on the income tax return itself).

Accrual Basis Accounting

In *accrual basis accounting*, revenues and expenses are recorded when they are earned or incurred. For example, when a company renders services (or sells a product) and bills/invoices the customer for later payment, the revenue is shown on the income statement when the invoice is issued, and the account receivable becomes an asset on the balance sheet. Conversely, when this same company purchases materials and receives a bill from its vendor to pay, the expense is shown on the income statement when the bill is received, and the account payable becomes a liability on the balance sheet. This is based on the accounting principle of matching costs with related revenues.

Cash Basis Accounting

In *cash basis accounting*, revenues and expenses are recorded when they are received or paid. For example, if a company renders services (or sells a product) and bills the customer for later payment, the revenue is not shown on the income statement until it is collected, and the account receivable is never shown on the balance sheet. And, when this same company purchases materials, the expense is not recorded on the income statement until the vendor is paid. In a cash basis accounting financial statement, one does not see accounts receivable or accounts payable.

Conversion from Cash to Accrual Basis

Valuations are usually performed on accrual basis data. For example, once a service has been performed, the revenue and profit generally are considered part of the income stream, and the related receivable usually is considered an asset of the company.

Therefore, if the subject company accounts on a cash basis, the business appraiser usually adjusts the financial statements from a cash basis to an accrual basis for the purpose of valuation. Of course, there can be exceptions depending on the specific facts of the situation (e.g., when a buy-sell agreement requires valuation using cash basis accounting data is determined to be controlling for the valuation purpose at hand).

All data that has been presented in this chapter has been assumed to be on an accrual basis.

SUMMARY

This chapter has provided a rudimentary guide to the terms most often encountered with respect to financial statements as they are used in business valuation. It is a handy reference for any term the reader is unfamiliar with or unsure of the definition commonly used in the context of valuation.

CHAPTER 5

Company Information, Site Visits, and Interviews

Alina Niculita, ASA, ARM, CFA

INTRODUCTION

In this chapter you will learn about:

- Types of company information that are typically collected in the valuation process
- Best practices for conducting site visits and management interviews
- Selected topics of inquiry and their purpose during management interviews
- A Tax Court case where superior knowledge of the business resulted in a victory for the taxpayer

After defining the valuation assignment (discussed in Chapters 1 and 2), the business appraiser moves on to the next steps of the valuation process, which include gathering company information, conducting site visits, and interviewing the management. At the onset of the valuation process, the appraiser typically sends a list of requested documents to the client. An example of such a list is included in Exhibit 5-1. This list is generic and preliminary, as not all documents will be needed in every valuation, and more documents will need to be added to the list as the engagement progresses.

GATHERING COMPANY INFORMATION

To conduct a business valuation, the business appraiser typically collects two types of information: (1) information about the internal environment of the subject company, or company specific data, and (2) information about the external environment of the company. External information includes information about the broad economic environment and the company's industry, as well as market data or transaction data relevant to the subject company.

Company-Specific Information

The appraiser's purpose in gathering and reviewing company-specific information is to obtain an understanding of the business. Understanding the business helps the appraiser choose the most appropriate valuation approaches, methods, and procedures (discussed in Chapter 3). Here the appraiser will request information about all aspects of the business, as the appraiser is trying to learn as much as possible about the operations, markets, finances, and past and future expected financial performance of the business. Some company-specific information is gathered in the form of written documents, and some is gathered during management interviews and site visits. Examples of written documents include items such as financial statements and reports, income tax returns, contracts, and shareholder agreements, to name a few.

External Information—Impact on the Subject Company

The purpose of gathering and analyzing external information is to obtain an understanding of the industry and the broad economic environment in which the business operates as of the valuation date, which is useful in assessing the risk profile and the prospects for growth of the business. Market data and transaction data include rate of return data (for use in developing discount rates and capitalization rates), valuation multiples, and data on valuation discounts and premiums, which is used in the various valuation methods applied. Industry and economic data may be provided by the business, but more commonly is gathered from publicly available sources. Market data and transaction data is usually gathered from databases to which business appraisers maintain paid subscriptions.

Exhibit 5-1 Preliminary Documents and Information Checklist for Business Valuation of Typical Business[1]

Financial Statements for Typical Business

- Balance sheets, income statements, statements of changes in cash flow, and statements of stockholders' equity for the last five fiscal years or economic cycle
- Income tax returns for the same years
- Latest interim statements and interim statements for comparable period(s) of previous year

Other Financial Information

- Summary property, plant, and equipment list; depreciation schedule; and capital budget
- Aged accounts receivable summary
- Aged accounts payable summary
- List of marketable securities and prepaid expenses
- Inventory summary, with any necessary information on inventory accounting policies
- Synopsis of leases for facilities or equipment lease or rental contracts
- Any other existing contracts (employment agreements, covenants not to compete, supplier agreements, customer agreements, royalty agreements, loan agreements, labor contracts, employee benefit plans, and so on)
- List of stockholders, with number of shares owned by each
- Schedule of insurance in force (key person life, property and casualty, liability)
- Budgets or forecasts, for a minimum of five years
- Business or strategic plan, if available

1. Shannon Pratt, Valuing a Business: The Analysis and Appraisal of Closely Held Businesses 68 (6th ed. 2022). Used with permission.

- List of subsidiaries and/or financial interests in other companies
- Key personnel compensation schedule, including benefits and personal expenses
- Details of any transactions with related parties

Company Documents

- Articles of incorporation, bylaws, and any amendments to either (or equivalent documents for a limited liability company or partnership)
- Any existing buy-sell agreements, options to purchase stock, or rights of first refusal
- Franchise or operating agreements, if any

Other Information

- Brief history, including how long in business and details of any changes in ownership and/or any bona fide offers received
- Brief description of the business, including position relative to competition and any factors that make the business unique
- Marketing literature (catalogs, brochures, advertisements, and so on)
- List of locations where company operates, with size and recent appraisals
- List of competitors, with location, relative size, and any relevant factors
- Organization chart
- Résumés of key personnel, with age, position, compensation, length of service, education, and prior experience
- Personnel profile: number of employees by functional groupings, such as production, sales, engineering/R&D, personnel and accounting, customer service/field support, and so forth
- Trade associations to which the company belongs or would be eligible for membership
- Relevant trade or government publications (especially market forecasts)
- Any existing indicators of asset values, including latest property tax assessments and any appraisals that have been performed
- Lists of customer relationships, supplier relationships, contracts, patents, copyrights, trademarks, and other intangible assets
- Any contingent or off-balance sheet liabilities (pending lawsuits, compliance requirements, warranty or other product liabilities, estimate of medical benefits for retirees, and so on)
- Any filings or correspondence with regulatory agencies
- Information on prior transactions in the stock or any related party transactions

The discussion that follows expands on the various types of company-specific information used in a valuation engagement, as listed in Exhibit 5-1.

Financial Statements

There are typically four components of financial statements, as follows:

- Income statement
- Balance sheet
- Statement of cash flows
- Statement of stockholders' equity

The income statement presents a summary of the company's revenues, expenses, and profits (or losses) for a specific reporting period such as a month, a quarter, or a year. The balance sheet presents the company's assets, liabilities, and equity as of a given point in time such as the end of a reporting period. It is important to realize that the amounts listed on a company's balance sheet are supposed to be presented in accordance with Generally Accepted Accounting Principles (GAAP), but do not necessarily represent the fair market value of those accounts. The cash flow statement shows the changes in financial position (cash balance as well as the sources and uses of cash) during the reporting period and presents changes in balance sheet accounts as of two points in time. Appraisers use the cash flow statement as a source of information on noncash charges such as depreciation and amortization, capital expenditures, and changes in working capital. The statement of stockholders' equity reports all the changes during the reporting period and the value of the equity at the end of the reporting period in accordance with GAAP.

As discussed in Chapter 4, there are three levels of scrutiny in the preparation of financial statements when an independent accounting firm has prepared the financials:

- Audited financial statements
- Reviewed financial statements
- Compiled financial statements

Audited financial statements present the highest level of outside examination by an independent Certified Public Accounting (CPA) firm. Reviewed financial statements present a lesser level of assurance by way of analytical procedures performed by the CPA firm. Compiled financial statements are simply management's representation of the financial results without any assurance from an outside accounting firm. While appraisers would ideally prefer to work with audited financial statements, the reality is that most businesses do not have their financial statements audited or reviewed, or even compiled by an outside firm. Frequently, especially for smaller businesses, financial statements are prepared internally, without the involvement and review of an outside accountant.

When requesting financial statements, a typical look-back period is five years leading up to the valuation date, but this may change depending on the circumstances of each case. For example, the relevant period may be the length of a business cycle, while, for other businesses, the relevant period may be a shorter period of time if business operations have changed recently.

When the valuation date is different than the date of a fiscal year-end, the appraiser may need to request interim financial statements. For instance, if the valuation date is March 31, and the business's fiscal year end is December 31, the appraiser would likely request financial statements for the three months ended March 31 for both the current year and the prior year,[2] in addition to the financial statements for the five or so prior fiscal years. In this case, the appraiser may also calculate the company's financial statements for the latest 12 months (LTM) of operations to be able to compare the LTM results with the prior fiscal years' results. Another term used for LTM is trailing 12 months (TTM). Because the interim financial statements typically would not include certain year-end

2. If the engagement is in a litigation context and the valuation date is March 31, depending on the circumstances, the appraiser may request the most recent financial statements available as of March 31 (knowing that the actual March 31 statements may not be available until several weeks later) plus other interim financial information.

adjustments such as for inventory, depreciation, fixed assets, and accrued and prepaid expenses, the business appraiser may need to request input for such adjustments from the company's accountant.

Income Tax Returns

It is common to find discrepancies between the amounts presented in the company financial statements and on the income tax returns. The reasons for the discrepancies may include temporary timing differences. To value large companies with formalized financial statements, business appraisers commonly use financial statements of varying levels of assurance as discussed earlier, with income tax returns being of lesser importance. For small businesses with only internal financial statements, or no formally prepared financial statements, income tax returns may be the most reliable source of financial information. In this case, the appraiser may use the information in the income tax returns as a basis for financial statements, as this is the best information available.

Other Financial Information

Several financial schedules may be helpful in understanding the company's assets, excess assets, and working capital needs, including the following:

- Aged receivables and payables schedules
- Marketable securities statement from brokerage firm
- Prepaid expenses list
- Inventory list
- Property, plant, and equipment list (with evidence of property values, i.e., detailed depreciation schedule typically prepared by the income tax return preparer and/or fixed asset appraisals)

Depending on the size and sophistication of the business, some of these items may not be available, in which case, the appraiser can discuss these items during a management interview. Some items, such as the inventory list, may not be relevant in, say, a professional services firm. For smaller companies, the depreciation schedule in the income tax return may be provided in lieu of the property, plant, and equipment list. Evidence of property values can be obtained from qualified appraisers, if available, or may come from tax assessments of real property or from insurance appraisals. However, the source of these indications of value should be identified because those may use a different standard of value than that for the subject valuation.

One item commonly requiring adjustment in a business valuation is the owners' compensation. Owner and related party compensation often needs to be adjusted to a market level. Owners of closely held businesses often pay themselves based on either available cash flow or based on tax planning considerations. This needs to be adjusted to a market rate compensation for the job responsibilities of the position, actual hours worked, and value to the company (e.g., based on amount of revenue brought in), as if an unrelated party was being paid to do his job. Documents that help with the assessment of this adjustment include the following:

- Schedule of officers' and directors' compensation schedule for the same number of years as the financial statements analyzed
- Detail of titles, roles, responsibilities, and hours worked
- Payroll data of non-family, highly compensated employees

Another document related to owner benefits is a schedule of dividends or distributions. This would typically address the same years as the financial statements analyzed and would show the dividends and distributions received by owners. Alternatively, this information can be found (if the company is a Subchapter S corporation, Limited Liability Company, or partnership) on each Schedule K-1 attached to the company's income tax returns.

Other items that may require adjustments include the company's transactions with related parties. A common example of related party adjustment is rent expense paid to the equity owners or to an entity that is owned by the same individuals as the subject company. In this situation, say, Mr. Smith owns 100% of XYZ Inc. and XYZ rents the facility out of which it operates from ABC, LLC, owned 100% by Mr. Smith and his family. In this situation, the rent paid is often simply equal to the cash flow required to service the mortgage and is not market rate (therefore, needing adjustment). Another common example is compensation paid to other family members who work in the business, oftentimes being paid much more than the market rate for the work done. These items should be discussed at the management interviews.

Past transactions in the stock of the company or past bona fide offers to buy the subject company may provide insights into value if the transactions or negotiations were at arm's length. As a result, underlying documents such as purchase agreements or letters of intent are often requested. The appraiser then reads and analyzes these documents and decides to what extent they are relevant to the current valuation.

Another important category of requested financial information is the company's forward-looking budgets, forecasts, and projections. Since, theoretically, business value is based on the future expected results, the company's reasonable estimates of the future expected results are relevant for the appraiser to consider and review. Just as with past transactions in company stock, the appraiser needs to determine to what extent the company's estimates for the future are reasonable and should be used in the current valuation. One useful way the appraiser can gauge the accuracy of the company at forecasting is to compare past budgets with actual results. The availability of forward-looking information varies greatly from none at all to multiyear projections. Generally, the smaller and less sophisticated the business, the lower the likelihood that the company will have any reliable forward-looking information. Larger companies often have at least a one-year budget and may regularly prepare long-term projections. It is important to note that if budgets or forecasts have never been prepared previously, any done for the current valuation require scrutiny as they may represent a biased view of the company. Further, if past budgets/forecasts have not been met, that may indicate that the current ones are unreliable.

Off–balance sheet assets or liabilities are another category of information and documents that the appraiser needs to consider. Off–balance sheet assets include expected awards from lawsuits and intangible assets such as patents, copyrights, and trademarks. Off–balance sheet liabilities include expected payments due to lawsuits, obligations related to leases, potential lawsuit claims, unrecorded warranty liabilities, unfunded pension liabilities, or environmental contamination liabilities. An analysis of off–balance sheet assets and liabilities may lead the appraiser to add assets and liabilities to the company's balance sheet, contributing to an increase or decrease in the concluded value.

Future capital expenditures represent future outflows of cash, which, everything else held constant, potentially could result in a decrease in the value of the business. Future capital expenditures should be matched with anticipated growth in the business. For example, if the subject manufacturing company has no available space to expand and its workforce is working three shifts, any forecast increases in revenues will require investments in expanded property and equipment (i.e., increased capital expenditures). The company may or may not have a long-term plan to invest in property, plant, and equipment and deferred maintenance projects that the appraiser can request and analyze to assess its impact on the current value. Potential deferred maintenance should be investigated by the appraiser.

Operating Information

Several types of documents and information help the appraiser understand the operations of the business, as discussed here.

- **Company history.** The appraiser may request a summary written history of the business that includes the key dates in the company's history; alternatively, this may be better addressed in person at the management interviews.
- **Marketing materials.** This may include websites, social media sites, brochures, or price lists that help the appraiser become familiar with the company's offerings and prepare follow-up questions for the management interviews.
- **Key personnel.** This is a list of personnel that play an important role in the company and ideally includes information such as position, tenure, age, and compensation. Ideally, an organizational chart would have been provided.
- **Schedule of key person life insurance.** This document identifies the key persons covered, whether it is a cross-purchase policy to buy out a deceased owner's interest or provide cash flow to the business in the unfortunate event that an owner dies, and amount of coverage.
- **Customer and supplier base.** This list identifies the company's top customers by revenues and suppliers by expenses from recent years. The fewer customers and/or suppliers, typically the greater the risk the company has of losing any of them. For example, if 90% of the revenues come from one customer, the loss of that customer would have a significant detrimental effect on the company's future prospects. The appraiser should also investigate the financial stability of such a customer, as a financially weak or struggling customer increases the risk to the subject company. Also, does the subject company provide a relatively unique product or service such that the customer would have a difficult time replacing the company as a supplier? Or is the product or service provided a "commodity"? If so, the customer will often continually ask for price decreases. The order backlog is another document that can be relevant; it helps the appraiser better measure the likelihood of realizing budgeted revenues in upcoming periods.
- **List of competitors.** This list may be helpful in assessing the level of competition in the company's market and in identifying potential comparable companies for the business.
- **Contracts.** If relevant to the company's business, the appraiser may want to request the company's main contracts and assess their impact on the value of the business. Aspects to review include the length of contracts and whether the contracts are easily cancelable.
- **Industry and trade associations.** The appraiser may wish to request a list of trade associations the company belongs to or with relevant publications that can deepen the appraiser's understanding of the industry and business.

Company Documents Relating to Owners' Rights

Several documents include important information regarding the rights of owners and potential impact to the valuation of specific business interests, as follows:

- **Articles of incorporation, partnership or stockholder agreement, or Limited Liability Company operating agreement.** These organizational documents are important because they describe the rights, privileges, and restrictions affecting the equity holders, which can affect the valuation of the entity or a specific interest in the entity.

- **Buy-sell agreements and employee stock ownership plans agreements.** These agreements often contain provisions that restrict the marketability of the subject interest and affect its value.
- **Employment and noncompete agreements.** These agreements may affect the value of the entity and the subject interest. For example, if a key salesperson does not have a noncompete agreement and were to leave the company, that person may be able to take a significant portion of the sales away from the company; that is a significant risk.

Site Visits and Interviews

The purpose of the site visit and management interviews is to further the understanding of the business and to enhance and complement the information that was received in written form. Some of the requested information may not have been available; in that case, the appraiser can plan on discussing the missing information with management. The appraiser can also ask clarifying questions about the documents received and ask follow-up questions. By meeting the management team, the appraiser can form his or her opinion about the effectiveness and competency of its members. By seeing the company's site, the appraiser can get a better understanding of the size and operations of the business and observe firsthand the condition of the company's assets and facilities, as well as its capacity. Another topic for the management interviews is the current and potential changes in the business that might make the future different from a simple extrapolation of historical data. Finally, it is useful for the appraiser to meet and develop some level of rapport with the individuals being interviewed so that when additional information is needed after the management interviews, it can be more easily obtained.[3]

After obtaining the requested documents, but before the interviews and site visit, the appraiser typically performs various preliminary financial analyses, such as:

- Create comparative schedules of the company's financial statements over several years displaying the annual trends
- Calculate common size financial statements, where all the amounts in the income statement are expressed as a percentage of total revenues and all amounts in the balance sheet are expressed as a percentage of total assets, to look for trends and anomalies
- Compare the company's performance with its peers
- Analyze working capital and capital expenditure needs
- Calculate preliminary inputs for estimating the appropriate discount rate (discussed in Chapter 7)

At this stage, the business appraiser (or a member of the appraiser's staff) will gather external information such as industry and economic data and market and transaction data. During this preliminary review and analysis of company internal and external information, the appraiser can highlight areas of inquiry before the management interviews and site visit. For instance, if a decrease or increase in revenues and profitability is apparent in the financial statements, the appraiser can plan to ask about the reasons for the trends observed. If the reasons for the trends observed are expected to continue, there could be a reasonable expectation that the trends observed will also continue. If

3. *See* Chapter 36, "Discovery and the Business Valuation Expert," for a discussion of site visits and management interviews as part of the discovery process.

there was recent transaction in the company stock, the appraiser will want to discuss the transaction during the interviews to assess the degree to which the past transaction may be indicative of the stock's current value. If the company provided a budget or financial forecasts, the appraiser can ask questions about the underlying assumptions in order to assess their reasonableness and relevance in the valuation. If a review of the company external information reveals that changes are expected in the company's industry, that topic can be earmarked as an area of inquiry. While reading and analyzing the documents produced and conducting the preliminary financial analysis, it is advisable to prepare a comprehensive list of questions in advance of the management interviews and site visit. At the time of the interviews, there will likely be more follow-up questions, but having a preliminary list of questions prepared in advance will greatly aid in conducting the interviews in an efficient and productive manner.

Interviews

While interviewing management and other individuals knowledgeable about the business is always advisable, conducting a site visit is not always possible or required. The need for a site visit depends on many things: the purpose of the valuation, the nature of the business, the size and complexity of the business, and, on a practical note, the budget for the project. For instance, the valuation of a large manufacturing enterprise for income tax purposes may warrant a site visit, whereas the valuation of certain professional practices or other asset-light service businesses for divorce purposes may not benefit to the same extent from a site visit. In the post Covid-19 era, video teleconferencing platforms (such as Zoom, Teams, Webex, etc.) present an opportunity for the business appraiser to more easily conduct management interviews, reducing the need and expense to travel to the site. Experienced business appraisers, however, understand that in-person meetings are generally preferable.

When identifying which individuals should be interviewed, the appraiser needs to consider the types of topics to be discussed, and the size and complexity of the business. For a large complex company, several individuals may need to be interviewed, such as the company's president, chief operating officer, marketing or sales manager, and chief financial officer. For a small company, all of these titles could be the responsibility of only one or two persons. The number of individuals to be interviewed and the breadth of the interviews also depends on the purpose of the valuation. For litigation matters, the appraiser may need to interview a dozen individuals, whereas for valuations for internal purposes, such as estate or sale planning, the breadth of the investigation may be narrower. Sometimes, individuals outside the company may need to be interviewed; these may include professionals related to the company (e.g., the company's attorney, independent accountant, tax advisor, banker) or other outsiders (with the company's permission) (e.g., customers, suppliers, competitors, and former employees).

It is generally advisable to conduct the management interviews and the site visit early in the valuation process. This way, the appraiser makes sure to find out important information that was not apparent from the initial review of documents and allows for the next steps in the valuation process to be planned accordingly. An almost limitless number of topics could be discussed at the management interview, but the appraiser should focus the discussion on the key drivers that affect the value of the subject company in order to make the site visit and management interviews as efficient and productive as possible. Because the management interviews are generally important to better understand the documents previously discussed, the following are some generic topics that may be discussed at the management interviews.[4]

- **Company history.** The focus here is usually to identify the relevant look-back period for the business, and what changes have occurred in the recent past. The appraiser can decide the number of years of financial statements on which to base the valuation. This can also help the appraiser identify any nonrecurring events in the company's history.
- **Description of the business.** The purpose of this topic is to find out how the company perceives itself and the industry it operates in. Exhibit 5-2 is an example of a series of questions designed to facilitate this discussion.

Exhibit 5-2 Description of the Business[5]

The analyst should try to gain an understanding of how the company perceives itself:

- What is the history of the company and what does the company do?
- What drives demand for the company's products or services?
- What makes this company particularly well qualified to do it?
- What is the company's perception of the economic niche into which it fits?
- How does the company try to do the best job of fitting in its niche?
- What are the company's major strengths and weaknesses?
- What are the company's major threats and opportunities?
- What are the key factors that enable the company to operate profitably?
- How does the company differentiate itself from its competition?
- What is the company's market share, and how has it changed over time?
- What is the company doing that is expected to cause its future to differ from recent history?

The analyst should try to gain an understanding of how the company perceives the industry within which it operates:

- What are the nature and rate of technological changes affecting the industry?
- What developments or trends are expected in the industry in the foreseeable future?
- What special industry factors have a bearing on this company?
- To what extent are the company's fortunes subject to outside forces over which it has no control?
- What is the progress and prognosis for new products or services, locations, channels of distribution, etc.?
- What other aspects of the operation and of the industry are in a developmental or transitional stage?
- Is the industry in a period of consolidation (i.e., are companies acquiring each other)?
- Is the industry in a growth phase or in a construction phase?
- What are the expectations regarding future growth in the industry?
- How will all these forces impact the future compared with the recent history?

---

4. For an in-depth discussion of these topics, *see* Chapter 5, "Site Visits and Interviews" in Shannon P. Pratt & ASA Educ. Found., Shannon P. Pratt's Valuing a Business: The Analysis and Appraisal of Closely Held Businesses (6th ed. 2022).

5. *Id.* at 86. Used with permission.

- **Operations.** A discussion of company operations will include suppliers, labor force, plant and equipment, and inventory. The purpose is to understand what the operations of the business are and to assess the risk of the business stemming from the various aspects of its operations.
- **Markets and marketing.** The purpose of this topic is to understand the company's markets, its customers, and its prospects for future growth. Exhibit 5-3 presents examples of questions that would help the appraiser with focusing the discussion.

Exhibit 5-3 Markets and Marketing[6]

- Who are its customers?
- Why do customers buy from this company instead of from the competition?
- Is its target market growing or shrinking?
- Overall, what are the company's prospects for the future?
- What are the forces that determine the demand and changes in demand for the company's products or services?
- To what extent can the company rely on repeat business and customer continuity?
- Does the market have identifiable seasonal, cyclical, or secular characteristics?
- Are there technological changes in progress or in prospect that will alter its share of the market?
- Are delivery channels stable or evolving?
- What is this business planning to do in order to remain competitive?
- What does the company do to anticipate and cope with market changes, and how effective are its efforts?
- What is the economic outlook for these markets, and what are the competitors' likely actions?
- Does the company have its own direct sales force, or do they rely on dealers or distributors?
- What is the degree of turnover?
- How are new sales and marketing people identified, and where do terminated employees go?
- What are the structure and level of compensation for marketing people, and how do they compare with the competition?
- With respect to the order backlog, how does this year's backlog compare with last year's backlog, as well as expectations for next year's backlog?
- What is the customer turnover rate?
- To what extent is the company dependent on one or a few key customers?
- What are the customers' motivations in choosing to do business with this company or its competitors, and how is the company addressing those motivations?
- What changes are anticipated for the marketing program?
- How does the company plan to capitalize on future opportunities?
- If competitive forces or other problems are building up, what is the company doing to protect itself?

6. *Id.* excerpted at 90. Used with permission.

- **Finance.** The purpose here is to increase the appraiser's understanding of the financial aspects of the business beyond what the documents show. Specific topics here include current assets, fixed assets, intangible assets, current liabilities, capital structure, off-balance sheet items, insurance, and dividends.
- **Prior arm's-length transactions or offers.** If there were prior transactions or firm offers, the management interviews are a good opportunity to determine if they were arm's length and if the offers were bona fide. Details not otherwise present in the documents received may surface that change the appraiser's perspective on the usefulness of the data.
- **Management compensation.** Business owners who work in the business can decide to pay themselves an amount that is different from the amount they would pay a non-owner employee. The appraiser needs to understand if key management are paid at a market rate, and if not, what adjustments are necessary (see preceding discussion).
- **Intangible assets and goodwill.** Management may discuss intangible assets and indications of goodwill of the business such as brand names, trademarks, favorable contracts, highly qualified workforce, loyal customer base, or favorable location. This is an indication that the company may have value in excess of its tangible assets.
- **Future plans.** This is where the appraiser learns about plans for new products or services, new locations, new personnel, as well as the means of financing any future growth. This will help in assessing future growth prospects and risk profile for the business. This discussion may also include the company's forward-looking forecasts if they were provided to the appraiser. With this, the appraiser can better understand the assumptions that underly the forecasts, assess the reasonableness and accuracy of the forecasts, and understand investments needed in fixed assets and human resources if the company is to meet the forecasts.
- **Catch-all questions.** It is good practice at the end of a management interview to ask a catch-all question such as: "Are there any items that are of importance to the value of the business that were not discussed?"

COURT'S VIEW ON COMPANY INFORMATION

In *Kohler*,[7] the Tax Court sided completely with the taxpayer, and the favorable decision was due in part to the failure of the IRS's expert to adequately consider specific company information in the valuation process. Furthermore, the taxpayer's experts reasonably relied on information received from the company and information they learned during the site visit and management interviews. The Tax Court emphasized that the taxpayer's experts were very familiar with the business and called their reports "thoughtful and credible." The opinion noted that one of the taxpayer's experts spent three and a half days at the company interviewing 12 employees, including considerable time with the president and the general counsel/executor of the estate. On the other hand, the opinion specified that the IRS expert met with Kohler management "once, for about two and a half hours."[8]

---

7. Kohler v. Comm'r, U.S. Tax Court, July 25, 2006.
8. *Id.*

Kohler, a large private company and one of the leading manufacturers of kitchen and bath products, issued two business plans: a management plan (which was a realistic forecast of achievable targets) and an operations plan (which was a theoretical, aspirational projection). Kohler regularly updated its management plan for outside stakeholders, while its "perfect environment, aspirational" operations plan was for internal use only. Kohler paid annual dividends since 1900 and its stated policy was to pay out 7% to 10% as dividends, even during recessions, and reinvest at least 90% of its annual earnings in the business.

In his valuation, the IRS expert ignored the company's long-term and consistent practice of paying dividends and chose not to apply a dividend-based income approach. The taxpayer's experts applied a discounted dividend method. Similarly, to forecast revenues in his discounted cash flow method, the IRS's expert relied primarily on the aspirational operations plan, "because he thought the aspirational operations plan was a more likely scenario,"[9] contrary to Kohler's view and usage of the two business plans. The court disagreed, saying he weighted the results in a manner "inconsistent with the reality of the business."[10] Finally, the IRS's expert did not use the company's expense forecasts, but instead made his own "without first discussing them with anyone at Kohler."[11] The taxpayer's experts reasonably relied on the company's more realistic management plan and expense forecasts.

This decision highlights the importance of comprehensive information gathering, data collection, analysis, and understanding the business in order to adequately reflect that information in the valuation approaches, methods, and procedures applied in the valuation.

SUMMARY

Appraisers will collect internal and external information about the company. Company-specific information gathering takes place either in the form of written documents or during management interviews and site visits. While management interviews and site visits are recommended, they are not always practical or necessary. There are numerous types of documents that are required in the valuation process, including financial, operational, marketing, governance, to name a few. The purpose of the management interviews is to complement and enhance the appraiser's understanding of the documents received. Conducting a diligent information-gathering process and effectively interviewing management helps the appraiser understand the business better and apply that knowledge in the valuation process, which results in more accurate valuations, as this has been recognized by the courts.

9. *Id.*
10. *Id.*
11. *Id.*

REFERENCES FOR COMPANY INFORMATION, SITE VISITS, AND INTERVIEWS

Fishman, Jay E., Bruce Johnson, Kent Pummel, et al. 2022. *PPC's Guide to Business Valuations*, 400 (Carrollton, TX: Thomson Reuters).

Laro, David, and Shannon P. Pratt. 2011. "Site Visits and Interviews." In *Business Valuation and Federal Taxes: Procedures, Law and Perspective*, 2nd ed. Chap. 14, 158–61 (Hoboken, NJ: John Wiley & Sons).

Pratt, Shannon P., and ASA Educational Foundation. 2022. "Gathering Company Data" and "Site Visits and Interviews." In *Shannon Pratt's Valuing a Business: The Analysis and Appraisal of Closely Held Businesses*, 6th ed., Chap. 4, 65–81; Chap. 5, 83–95 (New York: McGraw-Hill).

Trugman, Gary. 2022. "Data Gathering." In *Understanding Business Valuation*, 6th ed., Chap. 5, 121–151 (Portland, OR: Business Valuation Resources).

CHAPTER 6

The Income Approach

Roger J. Grabowski, FASA

INTRODUCTION

In this chapter you will learn about:

- Theory of the income approach
- Concept of discounting economic income
- Concept of capitalizing economic income
- Basic methods for discounting economic income
- Basic methods for capitalizing economic income
- Why there is a preference for measuring economic income by net cash flow
- Adjusting the capitalization and discounting formulas to account for when economic income is received
- Common errors

The basic theory of the income approach is that the value of a business is the present value of the expected future income streams that the business will generate. Therefore, to value a business under the income approach, the appraiser must first

- Estimate the business's future economic income, and then
- Discount this estimated economic income stream to a present value at a discount rate that properly accounts for the risk of that prospective income stream.

The appraiser can use the income approach to value a wide range of valuation subjects, such as a business, an interest in a business, or even an intangible asset. The appraiser can also use the income approach to quantify lost profits in a claim of damages, provided that (1) the prospective economic income stream is consistent with the subject of the valuation, and (2) the discount rate is appropriate for that measure of economic income for the valuation subject.

This book tackles the income approach first because it is typically considered the dominant approach in business valuation.[1]

The underlying concepts of the income approach are understandable even for those unfamiliar with the arithmetic formulas and notations used in business valuation.

The starting point for the income approach is estimating future economic income. As used herein, *economic income* is any inflow into an economic unit in exchange for

1. Although, as discussed in Chapter 8, Revenue Ruling 59-60 and many investment bankers also place heavy emphasis on the market approach.

goods, services, or capital. In this definition, the *economic unit* can be either a business entity (like a corporation, partnership, or professional practice) or an interest in a business. And the inflow can be gross (before recognition of any outflows) or net (after recognition of certain outflows). From the perspective of a business entity, the term *economic income* could mean gross revenues, gross profits, net operating profits, net income before tax, net income after tax, operating cash flow, net cash flow before tax, net cash flow after tax, net cash flow available for distribution to owners (e.g., dividends), or net cash flow available for distribution to the suppliers of investment capital (e.g., interest to providers of debt capital and dividends to providers of equity capital), among other definitions of economic income. The appraiser can use any of these measures of economic income to determine value under the income approach. Industry analysts often focus on a particular measure of economic income when analyzing a business in that industry.

Estimating future economic income is only the first step; the appraiser must then discount that estimated future economic income to present value. In doing so, the appraiser must account for the risk of realizing the expected economic benefits from the investment. This means estimating an appropriate expected return; this estimate is called the *discount rate* (alternatively referred to as the *cost of capital*, the *expected return*, the *required return*, the *hurdle rate*, or the *opportunity cost of capital*). As the term is used in this context, *risk* is defined as *the degree of uncertainty about the realization of the expected future benefits* (as measured by expected *economic income*). The essence of risk is the potential that actual benefits will vary from the expected benefits. For a given level of expected future economic income, an investment is *more* (*less*) valuable if the expected economic income associated with it is *more* (*less*) certain, everything else held constant. In other words, for a given level of expected prospective economic income (e.g., cash flow, dividends, accounting earnings), the *lower* the risk, the *greater* the present value, and vice versa.

The *discounted cash flow* (DCF) form of the discounted economic income method is the most conceptually correct method because it captures the driving principle of valuation: value is the present worth of future benefits and the best measure of future benefits from a business is net cash flow that an entity generates that can be distributed to the investors or reinvested in the business.

Not only is the DCF the most theoretically correct valuation method, it is also the most widely practiced valuation method in the world of corporate finance. Furthermore, valuation experts increasingly use this method, and more courts are adopting it. For example, the U.S. Tax Court regularly accepts the DCF method for valuing operating businesses of a closely held company.[2] In the family law area, some courts have blessed the DCF method.[3] Other courts have rejected the method when the supporting data was insufficient.[4]

An alternative method of measuring the present value of the estimated future economic income is *capitalizing*. As will be discussed, capitalizing is a shortcut to the DCF method that hopes to produce a similar result.

---

2. *See, e.g.*, The Northern Trust Co., Arthur L. Simon, Jeffery J. Simon, Transferees and Trustees, et al. v. Comm'r, 87 T.C. 349 (U.S.T.C. 1986).

3. *See, e.g.*, Guiffre v. Baker, 1996 WL 535254, 1996 Ohio App. LEXIS 3673 (Ohio Ct. App. 1996) and Sergi v. Sergi, 1996 WL 425914, 1996 Ohio App. LEXIS 3241 (Ohio Ct. App. 1996) (the courts in those cases accepted the DCF method over the excess earnings method); Howell v. Howell, 523 S.E.2d 514 (Va. Ct. App. 2000).

4. *See, e.g.*, Shooltz v. Shooltz, 498 S.E.2d 437 (Va. Ct. App. 1998).

In both *discounting* and *capitalizing*, an expected stream of economic income is converted into a present value. In other words, the process estimates what an investor would pay today (or as of the effective valuation date) for an expected economic income stream in the future.

Exhibit 6-1 contains the most commonly used terminology and notations that should be of some assistance.

Exhibit 6-1 Terms and Notations Commonly Used in the Income Approach

The notation system used in this book is the Pratt notation system, which is used in the courses of the ASA, in *Shannon Pratt's Valuing a Business—The Analysis and Appraisal of Closely Held Companies* 6th ed. (McGraw Hill, 2022) and in Shannon P. Pratt and Roger J. Grabowski, *Cost of Capital: Applications and Examples* 5th ed. (John Wiley & Sons, Inc., 2014). No matter what notation system is used in an appraisal report, each term should be defined.

PV	=	Present Value In appraisal terms, this is the estimated value as of the specified appraisal date.
D	=	Dividend This is usually the expected annual dividend, although it could be the actual dividend for the past 12 months or some other time period.
c	=	Capitalization rate A percentage, expressed as a decimal (for example, 20% = .20), which is used as a denominator to divide into some amount of income (for example, dividends, earnings, cash flow) to arrive at an indication of value.
k	=	Discount rate (cost of capital) The total expected rate of return that the market requires to attract investment into the business or securities of the type being valued, reflecting investment risk and other characteristics of the investment.
g	=	Growth The average compound annual rate at which a financial variable (for example, dollar amount of dividends, earnings, cash flow) is expected to increase in the future. As used in the income approach formulas, this usually is a long-term rate, technically in perpetuity.
E	=	Expected economic income This is a generalized variable used in an income formula without specifying the definition of income. Income in this formula could be dividends, earnings cash flow, or some other income variable.
WACC	=	Weighted Average Cost of Capital The weighted discount rate for each type of security in the company's capital structure (for example, common stock, preferred stock, long-term debt), each component weighted by its percentage of the market value of the company's total invested capital that is represented by the respective capital component.
W	=	Weight The percentage of each component of the capital structure out of the total, with each measured at market value.
t	=	Income tax rate The company's combined federal and state corporate tax rate.

THE CONCEPT OF DISCOUNTING

The process of discounting involves converting the economic income expected to be received in a future period into its present value through the application of a *discount rate*. That discount rate represents the market's required rate of return for investments of comparable risk. It is instructive to understand that *discounting* is exactly the inverse of *compounding*. In compounding, one invests a certain amount of money at some expected, annually compounded rate of return. Assuming that the expected rate of return is achieved, and that each year's return is added to the principal to continue to compound, one can compute what that investment will be worth at a future date. In discounting, one starts with a payment expected to be received at some specified point in the future, and then discounts that value from that future point back to the time one expects to pay for that future economic income, using the required rate of return reflecting the risk (degree of uncertainty) of realizing the payment at the future date and in the amount expected.

The essence of the DCF method is discounting the amount of each discrete increment of expected future economic income to a present value and then adding the present values of each increment to obtain the present value of the investment. Exhibit 6-2 shows a schematic example.

Exhibit 6-2 Discounted Present Value of an Annuity

Amount to be received at end of each year			**Today's value (present value)**
Year 1	$1,000	1 year @ 8%	$925.93
Year 2	$1,000	2 years @ 8%	$857.34
Year 3	$1,000	3 years @ 8%	$793.83
Total			$2,577.10
			Total present value of three-year annuity of $1,000 per year with a compound rate of return of 8% per year.

Note how this is just the opposite of compounding. If you invested $925.93 for a year at 8%, it would be worth $1,000 at the end of the year. If you invested $857.34 for two years at 8% compounded annually, it would be worth $1,000 at the end of two years, and so forth.

$925.93 x 1.08 = $1,000
$857.34 x 1.08 x 1.08 = $1,000
$793.83 x 1.08 x 1.08 x 1.08 = $1,000

THE CONCEPT OF CAPITALIZING

In capitalizing, instead of estimating each future increment of economic income and discounting it to present value, one selects a single expected number and simply divides that number by a rate of return adjusted for the long-term expected rate of growth in the economic income. This divisor is called a *capitalization rate*. As mentioned, capitalizing is a shortcut form of discounting. It has the same objective—to estimate the present value of an expected future income stream. But with capitalization, some implicit assumptions are made to simplify the procedure.

One of two assumptions is implicit in the capitalization method. Either:

1. The amount of income being capitalized will remain constant each year into perpetuity, or
2. The amount of income being capitalized will either increase or decrease at some constant annually compounded rate into perpetuity.

In capitalizing, as in discounting, one is converting expected future economic income into a value. In capitalizing, however, one is using only a single period's expected benefit (instead of estimating all the future expected benefits for each period separately like done when discounting). That single period benefit is usually next year's expected economic income. That single period benefit is divided by a *capitalization rate.*

As explained in more detail later, the capitalization rate, as used in the income approach, typically builds on a combination of the long-term expected growth rate in economic income and the discount rate. In the unique situation of assumption 1 (constant income), the capitalization rate and the discount rate will be equal (long-term growth rate is zero). Under assumption 2 (reasonably constant growth or decline in the income stream), the capitalization rate will equal the discount rate minus (or plus) the long-term sustainable rate of growth (or decline). Essentially, capitalization is capturing the value of an indefinite income stream while factoring in the long-term rate of growth or decline.

Appraisers can use the capitalization method in the context of a market approach (in either the guideline public company or the transaction method). In the market approach, however, the appraiser derives the capitalization rates by direct observation in the market rather than as a function of the discount rate, and implied assumptions 1 and 2 do not necessarily apply. Also, for the capitalization method in the income approach, the preferred income variable is *net cash flow*, as discussed later. Appraisers rarely use net cash flow in the market approach. Instead, the appraiser capitalizes other economic income measures, such as net income and earnings before interest and taxes. For example, appraisers use the inverse of the price-to-earnings multiple (i.e., ratio of earnings-to-price) to capitalize earnings.

THE BASIC CAPITALIZED ECONOMIC INCOME MODEL

The Constant Income Capitalization Model

The simplest form of the constant income capitalization model found in the market, and familiar to most people, is the perpetual life (noncallable) preferred stock.

Preferred stock is technically classified as equity, but from a valuation standpoint, it is more like debt in some important ways. The dividends normally are at a fixed-dollar amount for the life of the stock, which in many cases is into perpetuity. Corporations pay preferred stock dividends before any dividends on common stock but after debt service requirements. If, as in the case of the perpetual life preferred stock, the expected income stream is the same every year and expected to last forever, the procedure is simply to divide the amount of annual dividend or cash distribution by the capitalization rate.

The constant income capitalization formula is:

Formula 6-1

$$PV = \frac{D}{c}$$

Where:

PV = Present Value
D = Dividend (or distributions, in case of a partnership or Limited Liability Company)
c = Capitalization rate

For example, assume:

Dividend	$5 per year
Discount rate	10%
Expected growth rate	0%
Equals capitalization rate	10%

Inserting these numbers in Formula 6-1 gives us:

Formula 6-2

$$PV = \frac{\$5}{0.10}$$
$$PV = \$50$$

Thus, a preferred stock that pays $5 per year indefinitely and has a capitalization rate of 10% has a present value of $50.

Note: The choice of the capitalization rate is just as important as the amount of income being capitalized. Chapter 7 explains the proper procedures for developing capitalization rates.

The Constant Growth Income Capitalization Model

In many business enterprises, appraisers expect the net cash flow or other income stream to increase over time. If the appraiser can estimate expected growth in the income stream at a reasonably steady rate and for a very long period, then it is possible to include the expected growth rate of the returns into a capitalization model that takes into account that expected growth.

The procedure for the capitalization growth model is:

1. In the numerator of the capitalization equation, multiply last year's normalized economic income by a growth factor.
2. In the denominator, subtract the rate of growth from the discount rate.

The capitalized income formula under the assumption of a constant rate of growth is:

Formula 6-3

$$PV = \frac{E_0(1 + g)}{k - g}$$

Where:

PV = Present value

E = Economic income in the year immediately preceding the effective valuation date

g = Growth rate in expected income level, sustainable into the indefinite future (theoretically in perpetuity)

k = Discount rate (often called the cost of capital)

This formulation of the constant growth model is commonly referred to as the *Gordon Growth Model.*[5] The discount rate represents the *total* required rate of return (dividends or distributions plus capital appreciation). Chapter 7 discusses how to develop discount rates.

Look at an example applying this formula. Assume:

Last year's payout	$10
Expected annually compounded growth in amount of payout	3%
Discount rate	13%

Inserting those numbers in Formula 6-3 gives us:

Formula 6-4

$$PV = \frac{\$10(1 + 0.03)}{0.13 - 0.03}$$

$$= \frac{\$10.30}{0.10}$$

$$= \$103$$

Of course, if the starting point were next year's expected return (E_1 instead of E_0), then one does not need to multiply by the growth factor in the numerator. But one would still subtract the growth rate from the discount rate (total required rate of return) to obtain the capitalization rate in the denominator.

When using the constant growth model, it is important to select a realistic long-term sustainable growth estimate.

5. The Gordon Growth Model is named after Professor Myron Gordon, who popularized use of this model.

THE BASIC DISCOUNTED ECONOMIC INCOME MODEL

The Discounted Economic Income Model for a Limited Life Investment

The simplest and most familiar instance of a limited-life investment model is a bond with no special features. Such a bond pays a fixed amount of interest each year and the holder expects to receive a fixed amount when the bond matures.

The discounted economic income formula for the value of a limited-life investment is:

Formula 6-5

$$PV = \frac{E_1}{(1 + k)} + \frac{E_2}{(1 + k)} + \ldots + \frac{En}{(1 + k)}$$

Where:

PV = Present value

$E_1 \ldots En$ = Expected economic income in each of periods 1 through n

k = Discount rate (cost of capital)

Exhibit 6-3 presents the timeline of economic income estimates valued in Formula 6-5 (economic income assumed to be realized at the end of each of the future years).

Exhibit 6-3 Schematic Showing Timeline of Receipt of Economic Income Equivalent to Formula 6-5

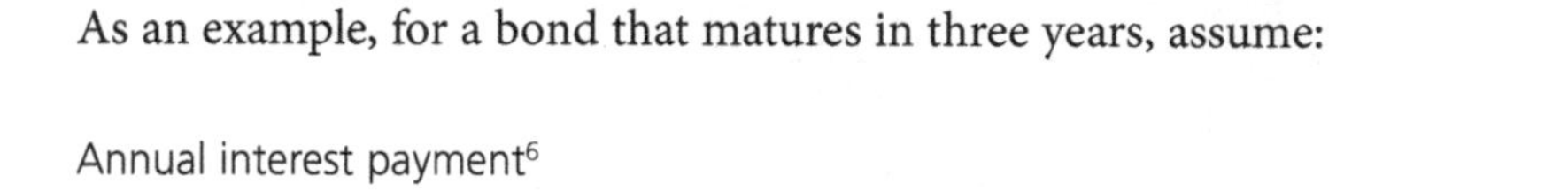

Where:
0 = Valuation date
^ = Point in year where economic income assumed to be realized

As an example, for a bond that matures in three years, assume:

Annual interest payment[6]	\$80
Value at maturity (\$1,000 plus the last year's \$80 interest payment)	\$1,080
Yield to maturity on bonds of comparable risk as of the effective valuation date	10%
n, the number of years to maturity	3

6. Most bonds pay interest semiannually, but for the sake of simplifying the illustration, assume that this bond pays interest only at the end of each year.

In other words, the yield to maturity available on comparable bonds today (in the preceding example) is greater than the rate of interest on the face value of the subject bond (8% = \$80/\$1,000). In this case, the value of the bond is less than its face value.

Inserting these numbers in Formula 6-5 gives us:

Formula 6-6

$$PV = \frac{\$80}{(1 + 0.10)} + \frac{\$80}{(1 + 0.10)^2} + \frac{\$1080}{(1 + 0.10)^3}$$

$$= \frac{\$80}{1.100} + \frac{\$80}{1.210} + \frac{\$1080}{1.331}$$

$$= \$72.73 + \$66.12 + \$811.42$$

$$= \$950.27$$

Note: In these computations, each year's return has been reduced to its present value by a divisor. This divisor can be converted into a multiplier by dividing each divisor into 1. For example, the divisor for the first year's payment is 1.100. Dividing that into 1 (1÷1.100) results in a multiplier of 0.909. Similarly, the multipliers for years 2 and 3 are 0.826 and 0.751, respectively.

It is common to see these multipliers presented as "discounting factors." Here is how that data would typically appear:

Year	Amount	Discounting Factor	Present Value
1	\$ 80	0.909	\$ 72.72
2	\$ 80	0.826	\$ 66.08
3	\$ 1,080	0.751	\$811.08
			\$949.88

(The figures between this tabular presentation and the formula presentation differ slightly because of rounding.)

The Discounted Economic Income Method Using a "Terminal Value"

Most businesses are expected to have a long and potentially indefinite life. It is not, however, usually possible to make reasonably accurate estimates of expected economic income on a year-by-year basis for many years into the future.

Appraisers deal with this dilemma by using specific estimates as far into the future as those estimates are reasonably reliable (termed the *discrete period*), and then calculate a value for the business at the end of the discrete period. This value beyond the discrete period is called a *terminal value* (or *residual value* or *continuing value*). There are two valid methods for estimating the terminal value: (1) the capitalization model and, more specifically, the constant growth capitalization model; and (2) an exit multiple method.

The formula for the discounted economic income model, using a terminal value calculated by the constant growth capitalization model, is as follows:

Formula 6-7

$$PV = \frac{E_1}{(1+k)} + \frac{E_2}{(1+k)^2} + \frac{E_n}{(1+k)^n} + \frac{\frac{E_n(1+g)}{k-g}}{(1+k)^n}$$

Where:

PV	=	Present value
$E_1 \ldots E_n$	=	Expected economic income in each of the periods 1 through n
k	=	Discount rate (cost of capital)
g	=	Growth rate in economic income beyond year n (expected sustainable annually compounded rate)

Note: The preceding formula is an exact combination of Formula 6-5, the limited life discounted economic income model, and Formula 6-3, the constant growth income capitalization model. In Formula 6-7, the terminal value is $E_n (1 + g)/(k - g)$ and is estimated using the Gordon Growth Model just discussed.

What discrete estimation period should appraisers use (i.e., how many years) before using the terminal value factor? The analytically correct answer is that the appraiser should use specific estimates until the company is expected to reach a steady growth state. The discrete estimation period typically runs from three to ten years, with five years being commonly used.

To make our example as simple as possible, assume only a three-year discrete estimation period and the following estimates:

Net cash flow Year 1:	\$100
Net cash flow Year 2:	\$130
Net cash flow Year 3:	\$150
Required rate of return (discount rate):	20%
Annually compounded growth in net cash flow beyond Year 3:	5%

Inserting these numbers in Formula 6-7 gives us:

Formula 6-8

$$PV = \frac{\$100}{(1+0.20)} + \frac{\$130}{(1+0.20)^2} + \frac{\$150}{(1+0.20)^3} + \frac{\frac{\$150(1+0.05)}{0.20-0.05}}{(1+0.20)^3}$$

$$= \frac{\$100}{1.200} + \frac{\$130}{1.440} + \frac{\$150}{1.728} + \frac{\$157.50(1/.15)}{1.728}$$

$$= \$83.33 + \$90.28 + \$86.81 + 607.64$$

$$= \$868.06$$

Again, each year's expected economic income and the terminal value is reduced to present value using a divisor.

Note: The terminal value divisor uses the same number of years into the future as the expected return in the last year's discrete estimation period because the last discrete period's return is expected to be received at the *end* of Year 3; and the capitalized value in the terminal value calculation represents the value as of the *beginning* of Year 4, which is essentially the same moment as the end of Year 3.

One can convert the divisors used in Formula 6-8 to multipliers (discounting factors) and present the results in tabular form as follows:

Year	Amount	Discounting Factor	Present Value
1	$ 100	0.833	$ 83.30
2	$ 130	0.694	$ 90.22
3	$ 150	0.579	$ 86.85
Terminal Value	$ 1,050	0.579	$ 607.95
Total Present Value			$ 868.32

(The figures differ slightly because of rounding.)

Another important item to note is that the shorter the specific estimation (discrete) period, the greater the effect of the terminal value on the indicated present value. In other words, the shorter the specific estimation period, the more the discounting method begins to look like the capitalizing method. Because of this, the assumed long-term growth rate following the specific estimation period takes on great significance and a reader should consider whether the growth rate into the long-term future seems reasonable. As a result, the shorter the specific estimation period, the larger the terminal value becomes as a percentage of the total present value. To illustrate this point, in the preceding example, the terminal value represents 70% of the total present value. Now assume in the example varying growth rates in income beyond Year 3 from zero to 15%, still assuming a discount rate (total cost of capital) of 20%. These varying assumptions would have the following effect on the example:

Assumed Growth Rate after Year 3 (%)	Terminal Value (TV)	Present Value of Terminal Value (PVTV)	Total Present Value (TPV)	PVTV as a % of TPV
0	$ 750[a]	$ 434	$ 694	63%
1	$ 797[b]	$ 461	$ 721	64%
2	$ 850[c]	$ 492	$ 752	65%
3	$ 909	$ 526	$ 786	67%
4	$ 975	$ 564	$ 824	68%
5	$ 1,050[d]	$ 608	$ 868	70%
6	$ 1,136	$ 657	$ 917	72%
7	$ 1,235	$ 715	$ 975	73%
8	$ 1,350	$ 781	$ 1,041	75%
9	$ 1,486	$ 860	$ 1,120	77%
10	$ 1,650	$ 955	$ 1,215	79%
11	$ 1,850	$ 1,070	$ 1,330	80%
12	$ 2,100	$ 1,215	$ 1,475	82%
13	$ 2,421	$ 1,401	$ 1,661	84%
14	$ 2,850	$ 1,649	$ 1,909	86%
15	$ 3,450[e]	$ 1,996	$ 2,256	88%

a = ($150 × (1+0)) / (0.20 – 0)
b = ($150 × (1+0.01)) / (0.20 – 0.01)
c = ($150 × (1+0.02)) / (0.20 – 0.02)
d Same as preceding example
e = ($150 × 1+0.15) / (0.20 – 0.15)

As already shown, the greater the growth rate assumed in the terminal value calculation, all else constant, the greater the present value of the terminal value is as a percentage of total present value. The greater the percentage of the total value represented by the terminal value, the more support for the underlying assumptions should be provided by the appraiser.

The discounted economic income model is obviously sensitive to the amounts of income estimated during the discrete period and the long-term growth expected beyond the discrete period. The reader should inquire whether the estimates used were prepared during the normal course of business or were prepared in connection with a transaction for buyers or lenders (which estimates tend to often be optimistic), or for justifying the price to be paid (which estimates are perhaps pessimistic).[7]

If the estimates are forecasts prepared by management in the normal course of business, the reader might inquire into the company's "track record" of meeting, failing to meet, or exceeding its prior forecasts. The reader also might inquire if any "sensitivity analysis" was conducted in which the business computed the impact of changing certain variables in the assumptions.[8]

It is important to consider whether the different components of the estimated economic income during the discrete period or during the long-term growth estimate are reasonable. For example, appraisers often make the simplifying assumption that expected long-term growth of a mature business should equal real growth (i.e., inflation removed) in the widely published Gross Domestic Product (GDP) plus expected inflation. This assumption is likely faulty because growth in real GDP is largely fueled by new businesses and technologies. That is, the impact of new firms on GDP is approximately two-thirds of the real GDP growth over time, while the real growth rate of existing businesses is considerably less than real GDP (approximately one-third of the real GDP growth over time).[9]

Although annual depreciation can exceed capital expenditures in some years, over the long term, capital expenditures must exceed depreciation for a company to grow.[10]

Capitalization Model versus Market Multiples for Estimating Terminal Value

An alternative procedure to estimate the terminal value is to apply estimated market multiples to some measure of the company's economic income projected for the year following the end of the discrete estimation period. For example, the appraiser could

---

7. The terms "forecast" and "projection" are often used interchangeably to refer collectively to two different categories of prospective financial information. *Forecasts* are defined as prospective financial information based on the conditions and course of actions that are expected to exist during the forecast period. *Projections* reflect expected future conditions given one or more hypothetical conditions, answering the question "what would happen if…?" *See* AICPA Guide for Prospective Financial Information, AT-C Section 305.09, for formal definitions of forecasts and projections.

8. For useful guidance in evaluating forecasts, see AICPA Guide, *supra* note 7, and Mandatory Performance Framework for the Certified in Entity and Intangible Valuations Credential (2017), appraisers.org. While the CEIV Credential is no longer issued, the Performance Framework continues to be referenced.

9. Bradford Cornell & Richard Gerger, *Long-run Growth Rates in Discounted Cash Flow Models*, Bus. Valuation Rev. 41(3) 91–94 (Fall 2022). *See also* Shannon P. Pratt & ASA Educ. Found., Shannon Pratt's Valuing a Business: The Analysis and Appraisal of Closely Held Businesses 275–79 (6th ed. 2022).

10. *See* M. Mark Lee, *The Ratio of Depreciation and Capital Expenditures in DCF Terminal Values*, Financial Valuation and Litigation Expert 7–8 (Aug.–Sept. 2007); Brant H. Armentrout, *A Sanity Test When Estimating Capital Expenditures in Excess of Depreciation*, Bus. Valuation Rev. 136–41 (Sept. 2003); Dan McConaughy & Lorena Bordi, *The Long-Term Relationships between Capital Expenditures and Depreciation across Industries: Important Data for Capitalized Income Based Valuation*, Bus. Valuation Rev. 14–18 (Mar. 2004); Brian Lee, Dan McConaughy, Mary Ann Travers & Steven Whitehead, *The Long-Term Relationships between Capital Expenditures and Depreciation and Long-term Net Working Capital to Sales Across Industries*, Bus. Valuation Rev. 87–125 (Summer/Fall 2012); Gilbert E. Matthews, *CapX = Depreciation Is Unrealistic Assumption for Most Terminal Values*, Bus. Valuation Update 1–3 (Mar. 2002).

estimate net income for the year following the discrete estimation period and apply a price-to-earnings ratio to estimate the terminal value. While both of these procedures are theoretically valid and can produce reasonable terminal values, many business appraisers prefer the capitalized economic income method.

If the appraiser is valuing the entire invested capital rather than just the common equity (as discussed in Chapter 3), then the appraiser might use a multiple of earnings before interest and taxes (EBIT) or a multiple of earnings before interest, taxes, depreciation, and amortization (EBITDA) derived from prior transactions in the marketplace and based on historical or estimated EBIT or EBITDA in those transactions. Investment bankers and others valuing companies in a transaction context often follow this approach because they are typically pricing the acquisition of the entire business (i.e., value of equity plus assumption of debt).

Although financial analysts may use the market multiples procedure to estimate terminal value, many in the business valuation community tend to prefer the income capitalization growth model. A frequently used assumption is that future market multiples will not change from those at the effective valuation date. This is not, however, necessarily a sound assumption because markets do change at times. For example, if an industry is in a high-growth stage now, that usually is reflected in high market multiples. When the industry reaches more of a steady state, it is unlikely that market multiples will remain so high. Even if the financial analyst assumes that multiples in a high-growth industry will moderate, the level of multiples at any future date is hard to predict. If the appraiser is applying the market multiple method to estimate the terminal value, that multiple needs to reflect an expected long-term growth for periods after the discrete period. The relationship between growth rates and market multiples is discussed in Chapter 8.

The terminal value issue is critically important in the discounting method because it often accounts for more than half the total value in the discounted cash flow method. Therefore, it is typically appropriate to conduct some sort of reasonableness check on the terminal value. If the appraiser uses the constant growth model to estimate the terminal value, the reader can check to see whether the market multiples implied by the terminal value are reasonable. If the appraiser uses market multiples to estimate the terminal value, the reader can check to see whether the capitalization rate and the imbedded long-term growth rate implied by the terminal value are reasonable.

PREFERENCE FOR NET CASH FLOW IN INCOME APPROACH

The consensus among business appraisers and the corporate finance community is that net cash flow is the preferred measure of economic income to use in the income approach. Each of these reasons are discussed in turn.

- Net cash flow represents what the owner can take out and still expect to achieve the projected returns.
- Net cash flow matches with empirical data supporting the discount rate.
- Net cash flow keeps results of the income approach independent from results of the market approach (because the latter usually uses other income variables and generally not net cash flow) and therefore strengthens the extent to which the results under one method reliably corroborate the results under the other.

The following discusses each of these reasons in turn.

Net Cash Flow Is What You Get

Net cash flow as defined in Chapter 4 is cash flow remaining *after* allowing for necessary capital expenditures and the net working capital needed to support the forecasted sales growth. In other words, net cash flow is what the controlling owner can take out of the company without impairing the company's operations. This is the economic income variable that ultimately is of greatest importance to most investors.

Public companies tend to put more emphasis on net income than private companies do, but in the long run, net cash flow is the most essential ingredient to the success of any company. This is an important conceptual reason for focusing on net cash flow in estimating value.

Net Cash Flow Matches Empirical Data

Rate of return data (e.g., data provided in Kroll's *Cost of Capital Navigator*, discussed in Chapter 7) commonly used for developing discount rates reflects *total stock returns*, that is, dividends plus or minus capital appreciation or depreciation. (The data is based on public stocks for which the dividends are distributed, and the stock is in a liquid market, so the investor can sell the stock and realize the appreciation or depreciation.) This is tantamount to the appraiser's definition of *net cash flow to equity capital*.

Use of Net Cash Flow Strengthens the Corroborative Power of the Income Approach

Ideally, appraisers can use two or more valuation approaches to enhance the reliability of their valuation conclusions. To the extent that components of the different methods they use in this corroboration do not overlap, this increases the extent to which the conclusion under one method reliably corroborates the conclusion under another.

Despite the preference for using net cash flow in the income approach, appraisers rarely use net cash flow in the market approach. This is because, for the comparative companies, one does not know whether two of the components of net cash flow—capital expenditures and additions to net working capital for any year—represent normalized amounts for those companies. If the amounts do not, the appraiser would be capitalizing abnormal figures and thus deriving a distorted indication of value. Therefore, in the market approach, appraisers generally use many measures of economic income *except* net cash flow (for example, net income, pretax income, gross cash flow, EBIT, EBITDA, "discretionary earnings," all defined in Chapter 4).

Thus, using net cash flow as the economic income variable in the income approach is a way to strengthen the extent to which the income approach can reliably corroborate the results from other valuation approaches.

ADJUSTING FORMULAS TO ACCOUNT FOR WHEN ECONOMIC INCOME IS RECEIVED

The income approach procedures shown in previous sections implicitly assume that all the proceeds are received or distributed at the end of each year (as displayed in the timeline in Exhibit 6-3). Indeed, many businesses wait until the end of the year to assess their cash needs and availability before deciding what to distribute to owners. Also, many have seasonal cash flow patterns. However, it is reasonable to assume that proceeds are received more or less evenly throughout the year, appraisers reflect this assumption with a mathematical procedure called the *midyear discounting convention.* Exhibit 6-4 shows the timeline assumed in the *midyear discounting convention.*[11]

Exhibit 6-4 Schematic Showing Timeline of Receipt of Economic Income under the Midyear Discounting Convention

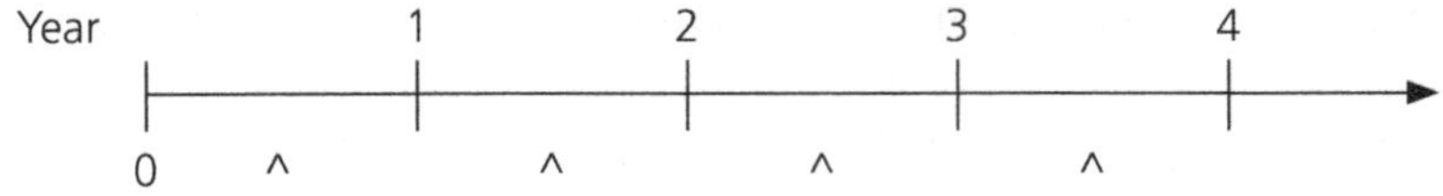

Where:
0 = Valuation date
^ = Point in year where economic income assumed to be realized

The idea behind this convention is that the appraiser can reasonably approximate the effect of receiving proceeds more or less evenly throughout the year by assuming that all the proceeds are received in the middle of each year (thus the term *midyear convention*). Because it assumes that the net cash flows will be realized earlier, the midyear convention procedure will always produce a greater value indication than assuming the net cash flows are received at the end of each year. The greater the discount or capitalization rate, the greater the difference will be between the values indicated by these two alternative assumptions.

Exhibit 6-5 (at the end of this chapter) illustrates an example of applying the midyear convention in the capitalization method. Exhibit 6-6 (at the end of this chapter) illustrates an example of applying the midyear convention in the discounting method.

COMMON ERRORS

While simple in basic concept, the application of the discounted economic income method provides many opportunities for errors. The following are a few of the common errors that can be made.[12]

- **Extrapolation of the recent past and assuming that such estimate represents the best estimate of future results.** All valuation is a function of expected prospective economic income. History is relevant only to the extent that it may provide useful guidance in estimating future economic income. Nevertheless, it is not as uncommon as one might think to see forecasts (even those prepared by management) that are nothing more than a statistical extrapolation of past results, with no analysis of the extent to which the forces generating future economic income will or will not duplicate the recent past. Often, they will not, and valuations using such forecasts are typically unreliable.
- **Assumptions that produce a standard or premise of value other than that called for in the valuation engagement.** A common example of this type of error is making unsupported adjustments to estimated future economic income that only a control

11. The formulas and examples are described in Shannon P. Pratt & Roger J. Grabowski, Cost of Capital: Applications and Examples 60–67 (5th ed. 2014).

12. This list is adapted from Pratt & ASA Educ. Found., *supra* note 8, at 177–80, 204–05.

owner could cause to happen (e.g., lowering the control owner's salary) when valuing a noncontrolling ownership interest (e.g., it is likely that the owner's salary will continue).

- **Relying on an excessive growth rate.** Relying on a high, near-term growth rate may lead to an overvaluation if that growth is not sustainable over the long term. The appraiser must determine the appropriate long-term growth rate by considering the characteristics of the subject company and the industry and economy in which it operates.

  Financial analysts often consider the consensus long-term nominal growth rate for GDP in evaluating the reasonableness of the long-term growth rate. There are, however, certain characteristics of a company or industry that lend themselves to higher growth rates for limited periods of time. GDP growth results from growth of both old and new businesses. Research has shown that only about one-third of the growth in GDP comes from older existing businesses. In a normalized state of operations, long-term inflation is often a useful indicator of expected long-term growth.[13]

SUMMARY

The income approach is the most widely used method of valuation because it can be tailored to the specific facts of a subject investment.

The discounted economic income method can be used in conjunction with almost any combination of standards of value and ownership characteristics, as long as the estimates of future economic income underlying the valuation variables used in the calculation are consistent with the definition of value being sought.

The capitalized economic income method is essentially an abridged version of the discounted economic income method. The primary difference is in the treatment of future changes in the expected economic income. In the discounted economic income method, future changes in economic income are specifically reflected in the discrete period economic income estimates in the numerator of the arithmetic equation. In the capitalized economic income method, future changes in economic income are combined into a single growth rate. This single growth rate is subtracted from the present value discount rate in the denominator of the arithmetic equation.

Like the discounted economic income method, the capitalized economic income method is a forward-looking exercise. Using an average of actual past economic income is appropriate only if that average represents the expected level of sustainable economic income in the future.

There are a variety of valid ways to develop a terminal value, although many appraisers prefer the capitalized economic income method. The greater the percentage of total value represented by the terminal value, the more support the appraiser should provide for the underlying assumptions. In such cases, the reader may consider applying increased scrutiny to those assumptions.

13. Cornell & Gerger, *supra* note 9.

Exhibit 6-5 The Midyear Convention in the Capitalization Method

The midyear convention is accomplished in the capitalization method by a minor variation in the capitalization formula presented in Formula 6-1.

The modification is made in the numerator of the capitalization formula. In Formula 6-1, we capitalize next year's economic income (which in that formula is presented as next year's dividend or distribution) as follows:

$$PV = \frac{E_1}{c}$$

Where:

PV = Present value

E_1 = Expected economic income in the next full period immediately following the effective valuation date

c = Capitalization rate (as defined previously)

To introduce the midyear convention assumption, we multiply the above by 1 plus the discount rate (k), raised to the power of 0.5 (to reflect a half year). In other words, the expected income is multiplied by $(1 + k)^{0.5}$ resulting in the following formula:

Formula 6-9[1]

$$PV = \frac{E_1(1 + k)^{0.5}}{c}$$

Where:

PV = Present value

E = Expected economic income in the full period immediately following the effective valuation date

k = Present value discount rate (cost of capital)

c = Capitalization rate (as defined previously)

To illustrate with an example, assume:

E_1 = \$105

k = 20%

c = 15% (20% less growth rate of 5%)

[1] Proof of the accuracy of this method is presented in Todd A. Kaltman, *Capitalization Using a Mid-Year Convention*, Bus. Valuation Rev. 178–82 (Dec. 1995).

Inserting these numbers in Formula 6-9 gives us the following:

Formula 6-10

$$PV = \frac{\$105(1 + 0.20)^{0.5}}{0.15}$$

$$PV = \frac{\$105(1 + 1.09545)}{0.15}$$

$$= \frac{\$115.02}{0.15}$$

$$= \$766.82$$

Similarly, the Gordon Growth Model (Formula 6-3) can be modified to reflect the midyear convention by adding the same term in the numerator:

Formula 6-11

$$PV = \frac{E_0(1 + g)(1 + k)^{.05}}{k - g}$$

Where:

PV = Present value

E_0 = Expected economic income in the full period immediately preceding the effective valuation date

g = Expected long-term sustainable rate of growth in the economic income from the year immediately preceding the effective valuation date

k = Present value discount rate (cost of capital)

To illustrate with an example, assume:

E_0 = \$100

g = 5%

k = 20%

Inserting these numbers in Formula 6-11 gives us the following:

Formula 6-12

$$PV = \frac{\$100(1 + 0.05)(1 + 0.20)^{00.5}}{0.20 - 0.05}$$

$$PV = \frac{\$100(1.05)(1.09545)}{0.15}$$

$$PV = 766.82$$

Exhibit 6-6 The Midyear Convention in the Discounting Method

To reflect the midyear convention in the discounting method, the number of periods by which each year's proceeds is discounted is reduced by a half year. In other words, each exponent in the denominator, n, is reduced by 0.5. The modified formula (modified from Formula 6-7) is as follows:

Formula 6-13

$$PV = \frac{E_1}{(1+k)^{0.5}} + \frac{E_2}{(1+k)^{1.5}} + \ldots + \frac{E_n}{(1+k)^{n-0.5}} + \frac{\dfrac{E_n(1+g)}{k-g}}{(1+k)^{n-0.5}}$$

where the variables are defined the same as in Formula 6-7.

For simplicity in an example, we will use only a three-year specific forecast period and will use the same assumed figures as in Formula 6-8:

Net cash flow Year 1	\$100
Net cash flow Year 2	\$130
Net cash flow Year 3	\$150
Required rate of return (discount rate):	20%
Annually compounded growth in net cash flow beyond Year 3	5%

Inserting these numbers in Formula 6-13 gives us:

Formula 6-14

$$PV = \frac{\$100}{(1+0.20)} + \frac{\$130}{(1+0.20)} + \ldots + \frac{\$150}{(1+0.20)^{2.5}} + \frac{\dfrac{\$150(1+0.05)}{0.20-0.5}}{(1+0.20)^{2.5}}$$

$$= \frac{\$100}{1.10} + \frac{\$130}{1.31} + \ldots + \frac{\$150}{1.58} + \frac{\dfrac{\$157.50}{0.15}}{1.58}$$

$$= \$90.91 + \$99.24 + \$94.94 + \$664.56$$

$$= \$949.65$$

Note that the preceding value is greater than the value from the year-end assumption—in this case \$949.65 compared with \$868.06 from Formula 6-8.

An alternative procedure is to reflect the midyear convention in the terminal value using the modified Gordon Growth Model (Formula 6-11), in which case the terminal value is discounted by n years instead of n–0.5 years. This formula is written as follows:

Formula 6-15

$$PV = \frac{E_1}{(1+k)^{0.5}} + \frac{E_2}{(1+k)^{1.5}} + \ldots + \frac{E_n}{(1+k)^{n-0.5}} + \frac{\dfrac{E_n(1+g)(1+k)^{.5}}{k-g}}{(1+k)^{n}}$$

Where the variables are defined the same as in Formula 6-7. This will produce exactly the same result as Formula 6-13.

The difference in value between the year-end and the midyear conventions is equal to $(1+k)^{0.5}$.

REFERENCES FOR INCOME APPROACH

Basic Income Approach References

Fishman, Jay E., Bruce Johnson, Kent Pummel, et al. 2022. "Capitalized and Discounted Cash Flow Methods." In *PPC's Guide to Business Valuations*, 5–1 to 5–90 (Carrollton, TX: Thomson Reuters).

Hitchner, James R. 2017. "Income Approach." In *Financial Valuation: Applications and Models*, 4th ed., Chap. 5, 117–83 (Hoboken NJ: John Wiley & Sons, Inc.).

Hitchner, James, Shannon P. Pratt, and Jay E. Fishman. 2016. "Income Approach." In *A Consensus View: Q&A Guide to Financial Valuation*, Chap. 1, 1–63 (Ventnor City, NJ: Valuation Products and Services, LLC).

Laro, David, and Shannon P. Pratt, 2011. "The Income Approach." In *Business Valuation and Federal Taxes: Procedures, Law and Perspective*, 2nd ed. Chap. 15, 162–94 (Hoboken, NJ: John Wiley & Sons).

Morrison, William J., and Jay E. Fishman. 2017. "Income Approach." In *The Business Valuation Bench Book*, Chap. 3, 15–54 (Portland, OR: Business Valuation Resources).

Pratt, Shannon P., and ASA Educational Foundation. 2022. "Income Approach: Discounted Economic Income Method," "Income Approach: Capitalized Economic Income Method," and "Income Approach: Forecasting Economic Income." In *Valuing a Business: The Analysis and Appraisal of Closely Held Businesses*, 6th ed., Chap. 9, 155–80; Chap. 10, 181–206; Chap. 12, 257–81 (New York: McGraw-Hill). Includes extensive bibliography and data references in online appendix.

Pratt, Shannon P., and Roger J. Grabowski. 2014. *Cost of Capital: Applications and Examples*, 5th ed. (Hoboken, NJ: John Wiley & Sons, Inc.).

Pratt, Shannon P., and Roger J. Grabowski. 2011. *Cost of Capital in Litigation: Applications and Examples* (Hoboken, NJ: John Wiley & Sons, Inc.).

Pratt, Shannon P., and Roger J. Grabowski. 2014. *The Lawyer's Guide to Cost of Capital: Understanding Risk and Return for Valuing Businesses and Other Investments.* (Chicago: American Bar Association).

Trugman, Gary. 2022. "The Income Approach." In *Understanding Business Valuations*, 6th ed., Chap. 12, 441–77 (Portland, OR: Business Valuation Resources).

Articles and Research Papers

Grabowski, Roger J., "Comparing Growth Rates Used in Discounted Cash Flow Valuations," *Business Valuation Review* 40:1 (Winter 2021): 2–12.

Greer, Willis R. Jr., "The Growth Rate Term in the Capitalization Model," *Business Valuation Review* (June 1996): 72–9.

CHAPTER 7

Developing a Discount Rate

Roger J. Grabowski, FASA

INTRODUCTION

In this chapter you will learn about:

- Concept of a discount rate
- Appropriate ways to develop a discount rate
- Concept of a capitalization rate
- Appropriate ways to develop a capitalization rate
- Matching the discount rate with the definition of economic income

Chapter 6 demonstrated that the discount rate estimate has a significant impact on the indicated present value. Appraisals that fail to provide careful attention and rationale to the determination of the discount rate estimates may result in unsupportable value conclusions. This chapter explains the concept of the discount rate and accepted procedures for its estimation.

CONCEPT OF THE DISCOUNT RATE

The discount rate is the expected *total rate of return* that an investor would demand in order to commit funds to a particular investment. It is market driven and forward looking; it represents the expected rates of return available in the market on other investments with comparable risk. The discount rate is commonly referred to as the *cost of capital*, the *expected return*, the *required return*, the *hurdle rate*, or the *opportunity cost of capital*.

The expected total rate of return includes two elements:

- Cash payouts (distributions)
- Capital appreciation (or capital depreciation) (i.e., the increase or decrease in the value of the underlying investment)

For example, consider a stock market investment opportunity for which the investor has the following expectations:

Stock price	\$50
Annual dividend	\$2
Expected annual price increase	10%

The expected appreciation would be \$5 per share (0.10 × \$50). Add that \$5 to the dividend of \$2 and the total expected return is \$7. On an investment of \$50, the total expected return is 14% (\$7 total return divided by \$50 purchase price = 0.14).

These observed or expected market rates of return for various components provide an empirical basis for estimating market-required total rates of return (discount rates) for different types of investments.

Elements of the Discount Rate: Risk-Free Rate and a Premium for Risk

From a financial analysis perspective, the methods commonly used to estimate the discount rate typically have the same basic framework:

Discount rate = Risk-free interest rate + Premium for risk

These methods generally include the following elements:

- A "real rate of return" for foregoing the use of money for some period of time *plus* an expected rate of inflation over the life of the investment (typically, the yield to maturity on U.S. government securities is used as a proxy for the risk-free rate; the implied assumption is that the U.S. government will not default on these obligations and that interest rates reflect inflation).
- A premium for risk where *risk* is defined as *the degree of certainty or uncertainty of actually realizing the expected returns at the times and in the amounts expected.* Because risk lies in the "eye of the beholder" and is not directly observable in the marketplace, financial analysts have developed various ways to use market data to quantify the element of risk in the discount rate. This quantification is arguably the single most challenging exercise in the discipline of valuation analysis. The next sections explain procedures used for quantifying risk in deriving the discount rate.

ESTIMATING DISCOUNT RATES FOR FIXED-INCOME SECURITIES

Unlike discount rates for equities, estimating discount rates for fixed-income securities is relatively easy because financial websites provide the expected returns (yield to maturity) for publicly traded bonds, and rating services provide guidelines for categorizing bonds and preferred stocks by their degree of risk. The difference between the yield to maturity for any given corporate bond (for example, a corporate bond rated "BB") and a U.S. government bond of the same maturity represents the risk premium impounded into the market's required rate of return for the corporate bond. Rating agencies (e.g., S&P Global and Moody's) publish risk ratings for most publicly traded bonds and the general criteria for each level of risk range. If the appraisal requires the business appraiser to estimate the risk for the debt or preferred stock of a closely held company, the appraiser compares the closely held company risk factors with one of the rating service's criteria for risk grades, estimates the risk grade for the closely held company, and observes the market's required rates of return for the securities of companies with that risk grade.[1]

1. For detailed procedures for analyzing and valuing debt instruments and preferred stock, *see* Shannon P. Pratt & ASA Educ. Found., Shannon Pratt's Valuing a Business: The Analysis and Appraisal of Closely Held Businesses 589–614, 615–31 (6th ed. 2022).

ESTIMATING DISCOUNT RATES FOR EQUITY

The two most commonly applied methods for estimating the discount rate used for discounting economic income to equity capital are:

- The build-up method
- The capital asset pricing model (CAPM) or an expanded form of CAPM, the modified capital asset pricing model (MCAPM).

Both methods start with a risk-free rate and then add incremental measures of risk in building-block fashion to account for the fact that investors demand *additional* return to induce them to invest in assets considered to be riskier than risk-free assets such as Treasury securities. The build-up method is presented before presenting the CAPM and MCAPM only because the build-up method is actually a simplified version of the MCAPM. The build-up method implicitly reflects the simplifying assumption that the sensitivity of returns for the subject company relative to returns for the market as a whole are about the same as for the typical public company in the market.

Build-up Method

As its name suggests, the build-up method for estimating equity discount rates consists of a series of building blocks. The foundation is the risk-free interest rate; appraisers then add some or all of the following risk premiums:

- General equity risk premium
- Industry risk premium
- Size premium
- Company-specific risk adjustment (which is usually an addition, but could be a subtraction)

Each subcomponent of the risk premium represents the "reward" (in the form of an incremental rate of return) to an investor for taking on a specific risk. The risk-free rate is the rate of return available on a risk-free security as of the valuation date. The general equity risk premium is the reward for investing in the stock market as opposed to the risk-free nature of a government security. The industry risk premium accounts for the relative risk of the specific industry in which the subject business operates. The size premium is an adjustment to the general equity risk premium to account for the fact that smaller companies tend to be riskier than the larger companies on the stock market. The company-specific risk adjustment reflects the reward for investing in a specific company with risks for which the other factors do not account. Because the build-up method estimates the discount rate as the sum of the risk-free rate and various risk premiums, the method is called an *additive* model and the method's components are referred to as *building blocks.*

Risk-Free Rate

As noted earlier, the risk-free rate usually is the yield-to-maturity available on U.S. government securities as of the valuation date. The short-term U.S. Treasury bill is considered to be the ultimate risk-free security. In estimating the discount rate appropriate for equity investments, however, the short-term Treasury bill has an important shortcoming: its maturity does not match the anticipated investment horizon (or holding period) of most equity investors. The Treasury bill rate is much more volatile than longer-term U.S. government bond yields, and the Treasury bill yield may not reflect longer-term inflation expectations. Therefore, most business appraisers prefer to use the yield on a long-term U.S. government bond—such as the 20-year Treasury bond—as the risk-free component for estimating the discount rate for equity capital.[2]

Investors recognize that the 20-year U.S. government bond has an element of risk called *horizon risk* (or *interest rate risk*), meaning that the value of the principal will fluctuate with future changing levels of interest rates during the term of the bond, and the current yield-to-maturity reflects compensation for this risk. The longer rates are preferable, in part because they are more stable over time and less subject to short-term influences. Also, the longer maturity more closely matches the assumed long life of most businesses.[3]

Equity Risk Premium

The next building block is a general equity risk premium (ERP). This represents the rate of return that investors expect from a portfolio of large public stocks (such as the Standard & Poor's 500 (S&P 500)) in excess of the rate available on U.S. government securities.

Like all discount rate components, the ERP is a forward-looking concept. It reflects an expectation as of the valuation date. The ERP is a function of expected returns on a diversified portfolio of equities minus an expected yield on a risk-free security to which it is compared over a specified period. There is no universally accepted method for estimating the equity risk premium and in practice, academics and financial advisors use a wide variety of equity risk premium estimates.

The *U.S. Cost of Capital Module* provides analysts with two long-term equity risk premium series based upon realized returns: (1) the historical long-horizon expected equity risk premium and (2) the supply-side long-horizon expected equity risk premium.[4] Data from these risk premiums is based on historical stock market returns compared with historical U.S. government security yields. These represent long-term average equity risk premiums through the business cycles. There are some significant disagreements about how appraisers should use this data to estimate a general equity risk premium as of any given date, but the technical details of these disagreements are beyond the scope of this book.[5]

---

2. Ibbotson & Kroll, LLC, Stocks, Bonds, Bills, and Inflation (SBBI) Yearbook includes equity risk premium data measured relative to 20-year U.S. government bond yields. Online sources include FRED Economic Data, Federal Reserve Bank of St. Louis, https://fred.stlouisfed.org/series/GS20.

3. For more detail about these arguments and estimating the risk-free rate during times of economic crisis and actions of the Federal Reserve to reduce interest rates, *see* Pratt & ASA Educ. Found., *supra* note 1, at 213–16.

4. The supply-side ERP removes the effect on historical ERPs due to increases in stock market multiples over time. The supply-side ERP is published in the Kroll (formerly Duff & Phelps) Cost of Capital Navigator–U.S. Cost of Capital Module, available by subscription at https://www.kroll.com/en/cost-of-capital.

5. For more detail about these and other data and arguments regarding their use, *see* Pratt & ASA Educ. Found., *supra* note 1, at 216–21. The Delaware Court of Chancery has generally accepted use of the supply-side long-horizon equity risk premium for developing discount rates; *see, e.g.*, Shannon P. Pratt & Roger J. Grabowski, Cost of Capital: Applications and Examples 904–08 (5th ed. 2014).

The *U.S. Cost of Capital Module* also provides analysts with a *conditional* equity risk premium, which reflects current market conditions. Another important source of risk premiums is the Kroll *Risk Premium Report*.[6]

Industry Risk Premium in Build-up Method

The *industry risk premium* (IRP) used in the build-up method accounts for the market risk differences among industries. Industry risk premiums are calculated using an average risk measure for an industry from the risk measures for companies that contribute substantial sales to the respective industry.[7]

Size Premium in Build-up Method

Extensive empirical studies have shown that over time smaller companies tend to have greater risk than larger companies, even after accounting for differences in company risks (as quantified by beta, discussed later in the section on MCAPM). Although some commentators disagree with applying a size premium, most appraisers believe that a size premium is an appropriate component of the MCAPM. Because of this greater risk, smaller companies have a greater required rate of return. The incremental addition to the discount rate to reflect the company size component of risk is called the *size premium*.

There is also data on the historical magnitudes of the size effect. The *U.S. Cost of Capital Module* includes two U.S. size premium datasets:

- The ***Risk Premium Report—Size Study*** provides risk premiums for use in the build-up method that combine the ERP and the size premiums based on eight different measures of size.[8]
- The ***CRSP Deciles Size Study***[9] provides size premiums based on just one measure of size: market value of common equity.[10]

Company-Specific Risk Adjustment in Build-up Method

If and to the extent that the risk of the subject company differs from the average of the companies from which the appraiser derived the size adjustment, the build-up method discount rate applies a company-specific risk adjustment. Estimating this adjustment necessarily requires some subjective judgment on the part of the appraiser. The more

6. The Risk Premium Report, published since 2000, is available exclusively in the online Cost of Capital Navigator–U.S. Cost of Capital Module.

7. The risk measure used is known as *beta*, which is discussed later. The U.S. Cost of Capital Module publishes alternative measures of IRP using broad measures of industry risk with the weighting for each company's risk measure based on the sales of the industry as a whole. The Module also provides analysts with a spreadsheet tool to build a customized measure of industry risk based on companies with characteristics most like those of the subject business.

8. Two measures based on market values as a measure of size (market value of common equity, market value of invested capital) and six based on fundamental measures of size (book value of common equity, five-year average net income, total assets, five-year average EBITDA, sales, and number of employees).

9. The CRSP Deciles Size Study was published through 2017 in the Ibbotson Associates Stocks, Bonds, Bills, and Inflation (SBBI) Valuation Yearbook and, since 2018, is available in the online Cost of Capital Navigator–U.S. Cost of Capital Module.

10. Another source of historical ERP data and size premiums is the Cost of Capital Professional, available by subscription at https://www.bvresources.com/products/cost-of-capital-professional.

that the appraiser's judgment is based on rigorous financial analysis, the more reliable the result is likely to be.

Chapter 16 discusses financial statement analysis in more detail. The appraiser can use many of the ratios from that chapter to compare the subject company to industry averages. If the appraiser has used the market approach, the subject company's financial ratios can be compared with those of the guideline companies identified in the market approach.

There are many qualitative factors that also might have an impact, such as recent actual or potential competition, quality and depth of management, concentration of customers, condition of facilities, and many others. It is important, however, to avoid double counting any company-specific risk premium factors that may have already been reflected in the size premium or at any other point in the estimation of the discount rate.

Summary Illustration of the Equity Discount Rate Using the Build-up Method

Here is a typical presentation of the estimation of an equity discount rate by the build-up method (using Kroll data):

Risk-free rate	3.79%[a]
Equity risk premium	6.35%[b]
Size premium	2.14%[c]
Company-specific risk adjustment	2.0%[d]
Equity discount rate	14.28%
Rounded to	14.3%

a. Yield on 20-year U.S. Treasury bonds as of valuation date, January 30, 2023.
b. Supply-side equity risk premium for full period 1926–2022, from the Kroll U.S. Cost of Capital Module.
c. Kroll CRSP Decile Size Study (9th decile).
d. See pp. xx of appraiser's valuation report for supporting analysis.

Here is another example illustrating the use of an industry risk premium when calculating an equity discount rate (using Kroll data):

Risk-free rate	3.79%[a]
Equity risk premium	6.35%[b]
Size premium	2.14%[c]
Industry risk premium	1.33%[d]
Company-specific risk adjustment	2.0%[e]
Equity discount rate	15.61%
Rounded to	15.6%

a. Yield on 20-year U.S. Treasury bonds as of valuation date, January 30, 2023.
b. Supply-side equity risk premium for full period 1926–2022, from the Kroll U.S. Cost of Capital Module.
c. Kroll CRSP Decile Size Study (9th decile).
d. Kroll U.S. Cost of Capital Module (Information Technology, GICS 45).
e. See pp. xx of analyst's valuation report for supporting analysis.

The following is a typical presentation of how an appraiser might estimate an equity discount rate with the build-up method (using Risk Premium Report data):

Risk-free rate	3.79%[a]
Equity risk premium (including size premium)	14.14%[b]
Company-specific risk adjustment	2.0%[c]
Equity discount rate	19.93%
Rounded to	19.9%

a. Yield on 20-year U.S. Treasury bonds as of valuation date, January 30, 2023.
b. Risk Premium Report—Size Study 2023, smoothed equity risk premium for portfolio 25 = 13.38%, size measured by market value of equity plus equity risk premium adjustment for difference between the ERP reported for 1963–2022 and supply-side ERP = 0.76%.
c. See pp. xx of appraiser's valuation report for supporting analysis.

Capital Asset Pricing Model and Modified Capital Asset Pricing Model

Many consider the CAPM to be the most theoretically correct method for estimating an equity discount rate. Despite some theoretical and empirical challenges, the CAPM (or, alternatively, the MCAPM) remains the most commonly used method by corporate finance practitioners.

The only difference between the CAPM and the build-up method is a modifier (coefficient) applied to the general equity risk premium. This modifier is called beta. MCAPM is typically used by appraisers and incorporates a size premium and company-specific risk adjustments.

Definition of Beta

Beta is a measure of *market risk* (that is, how returns of a specific investment are expected to vary compared to returns in the overall market change over time). In theory, beta is a forward-looking risk measure. It measures the sensitivity of returns in an individual security (or portfolio of securities) relative to returns in the market. The most commonly used benchmark for returns on the market is the total return (dividends and capital appreciation) realized over time for the S&P 500 stock composite average.

The risk that beta measures is called *systematic risk* because it is a stock's risk tied to the risk of the overall market. The theory is that market risk cannot be removed by holding a fully diversified portfolio of securities and this market risk is part of the risk of every equity investment. The CAPM assumes that the risk premium portion of a security's expected total return is a function of that security's systematic risk. (The other portion of the total risk that is not related to changes in the market is called *unsystematic* risk and is captured in the MCAPM by the company-specific risk adjustment.)

Estimating Beta

Theoretically, market beta is a forward-looking concept because it measures the sensitivity or volatility of a security in comparison to the market as a whole. It is used to evaluate the expected risks and returns of a specific investment. The theory is silent on how to estimate market beta.

For a publicly traded security (or a portfolio of such securities), beta is typically measured from market data, usually for a two- to five-year look-back period. This approach assumes that the observed past beta is the best predictor of the future beta. Beta measures the relative movement (i.e., covariance) of a security's returns with changes in market returns.

Covariance measures the degree to which the return on a particular security and the overall market's return move together. Covariance is not volatility. Rather it is a measure of the relationship between two variables, evaluating how much and to what extent the variables change together.[11]

A security with a high level of covariance means that a large change in the returns of the market tends to be associated with a large change in the security's returns. If returns for the subject security or portfolio go up and down at the same degree as the market, then the subject beta equals 1.0. If the returns tend to be more volatile in response to market moves (i.e., go up more than the market when the market goes up and go down more than the market when the market goes down), then beta will be greater than 1.0. Conversely, if the returns tend to be less volatile in response to changes in market returns, then beta will be less than 1.0.

Exhibit 7-1 shows schematically how the market-required rate of return increases as beta increases.

Exhibit 7-1 Schematic Diagram Illustrating Beta

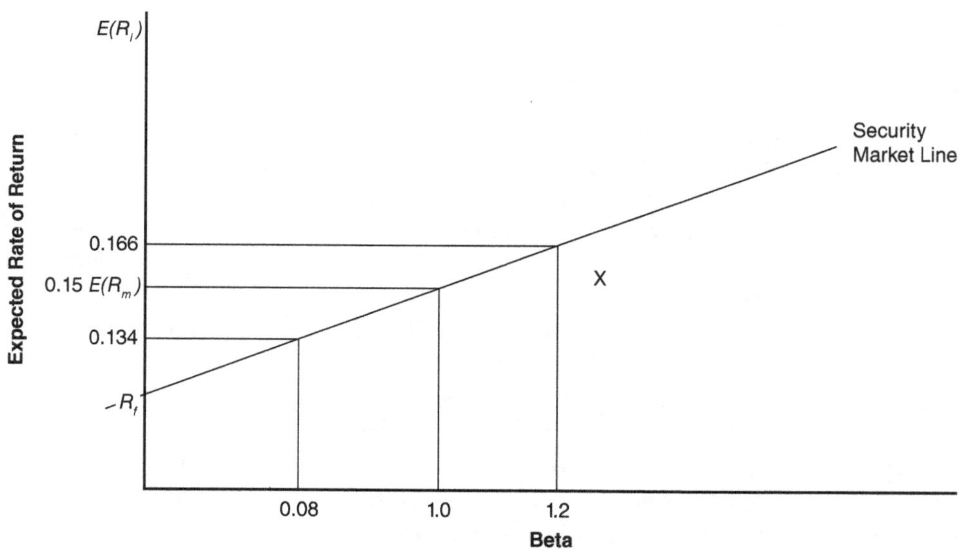

11. A *positive* covariance indicates that the two variables tend to move in the same direction. A *negative* covariance indicates that the variables tend to move in the opposite direction.

In this diagram:

E(Ri)	=	Expected return for the individual security
E(Rm)	=	Expected return on the market
Rf	=	Risk-free rate available as of the valuation date
X	=	Risk and return profile for a particular company

In a market in perfect equilibrium, all securities would fall on the security market line. If security X has a high beta (as shown in the diagram) and a security analyst expects the returns for that security to be as shown, the analyst would consider the security overpriced.

As this exhibit shows, the beta for the market as a whole is 1.0. Therefore, from a numerical standpoint, the beta has the following interpretations:

Beta > 1.0	When market rates of return move up or down, the rates of return for the subject tend to move in the same direction and with greater magnitude. For example, for a stock with no dividend, if the market is up 10%, the price of a stock with a beta of 1.2 would be expected to be up 12%. If the market is down 10%, the price of the same stock would be expected to be down 12%. Many high-tech companies are good examples of stocks with high betas.
Beta = 1.0	Fluctuations in rates of return for the subject tend to equal fluctuations in rates of return for the market.
Beta < 1.0	When market rates of return move up or down, rates of return for the subject tend to move up or down, but to a lesser extent. For example, for a stock with no dividend, if the market is up 10%, the price of a stock with a beta of .8 would be expected to be up 8%. The classic example of a low-beta stock would be a utility that has not diversified into more risky activities.
Negative beta (Rare)	Rates of return for the subject tend to move in the opposite direction from changes in rates of return for the market. Stocks with negative betas are rare. A few gold-mining companies have had negative betas in the past.

Source: Shannon Pratt & Roger Grabowski, Cost of Capital: Applications and Examples 193–94 (5th ed.).

Betas for Closely Held Companies

Because a closely held company by definition does not have regular daily, weekly, or monthly public market trading prices, the business appraiser cannot measure the volatility in daily, weekly, or monthly returns the way a financial analyst does for publicly traded stocks. Therefore, appraisers who aim to use the CAPM or MCAPM to estimate an equity discount rate for a closely held company must develop a proxy for the closely held company's beta.

The most common way of doing this is to observe the betas of a sample of public companies in the same industry and match the characteristics of the subject company to the sample. The appraiser then can use some measure of central tendency (e.g., the average or median) of the betas of those companies as a proxy for the beta of the subject business. Ideally, the appraiser would develop a proxy using beta estimates of specific companies with characteristics best matching those of the subject company.[12] If the

12. Factors that have been shown to impact differences in betas include (1) diversification (contrary to the conventional view, research finds that diversified firms generally have a lower cost of capital than comparable

appraiser has used a guideline public company valuation method, the list of guideline companies used in the market approach is a good source of specific public companies for deriving a beta. The appraiser may obtain beta estimates for individual companies from published sources or compute their own beta estimates. Or the appraiser might use industry average betas from the Kroll *U.S. Industry Benchmarking* dataset.[13]

Incorporating Beta into the Equity Risk Premium

To incorporate beta into the equity risk premium, the appraiser multiplies the general equity risk premium by the beta. The following illustration uses the general equity risk premium of 6.35% from the preceding illustration.

First, consider company *i*, whose returns are assumed to be *less* sensitive to changes in overall market returns than those of the average company, and for which the appraiser assigned a beta of 0.75:

$$0.75 \times 6.35\% = 4.76\% \text{ equity risk premium for company } i.$$

Next, consider company *j*, whose systematic risk is estimated to be equal to the market as a whole and is therefore assigned a beta of 1.0:

$$1.0 \times 6.35\% = 6.35\% \text{ equity risk premium for company } j.$$

Finally, consider company *k*, whose returns are assumed to be *more* sensitive to changes in overall market returns than those of the average company, and for which the appraiser assigned a beta of 1.2:

$$1.2 \times 6.35\% = 7.62\% \text{ equity risk premium for company } k.$$

Size Premium in MCAPM

Many empirical studies performed since the advent of CAPM have found that realized total returns on smaller companies have been substantially greater over a long period of time than predicted by pure CAPM (where beta is the only measure of risk). The original size effect studies measured size based on market capitalization of equity (e.g., the CRSP Decile Size Study). Later studies were expanded to include accounting measures of size (e.g., net income in the Risk Premium Report—Size Study).

---

portfolios of stand-alone firms); (2) customer concentration (research has shown that a more concentrated customer base increases the supplier firm's risks, resulting in a greater beta and that this relation is more pronounced for supplier firms that are more likely to lose major customers, or that are more prone to large losses if they lose such customers); (3) differences in growth expectations account for differences in risk and betas (research has shown that the expectation of keeping up high growth is risky); (4) firm age (research has shown that betas decline, on the average, as the age of firms increase (even within an industry) due to the increased familiarity of analysts as firms age and firm managements have demonstrated their ability to meet prior expectations). *See* article references to this chapter for papers providing this information.

13. Company-level beta estimates and industry-level beta and industry-level cost of equity capital estimates (derived from applying various methods) are presented in the Cost of Capital Navigator–U.S. Company-level Betas dataset and the U.S. Industry Benchmarking dataset, available by subscription at https://www.kroll.com/en/cost-of-capital.

The notion in the pure CAPM that investors only care about market risk (systematic risk) assumes that all unique or unsystematic risk can be eliminated by holding a perfectly diversified portfolio of risky assets that will, by definition, have a beta of 1.0. But research has shown that many investors do not hold perfectly diversified portfolios, and other risk factors are priced by the market. Expanding the pure CAPM to reflect the size effect and company-specific risk results in a modified CAPM (MCAPM).

The *Risk Premium Report—Size Study* and the *CRSP Decile Size Study* detail size premiums that are called *size premiums in excess of CAPM* (i.e., returns observed in excess of the returns predicted by beta). Appraisers can use these size premiums to incorporate the size effect into the equity discount rate when using the MCAPM.

Company-Specific Risk Adjustment in MCAPM

To the extent that the company has risk factors that have not already been reflected in the general equity risk premium as modified by beta and reflected in the size premium, it is possible that a further risk adjustment is warranted. Again, care is required to ensure that the appraiser is not double-counting risk factors already captured by beta or the size premium. For example, the subject company's geographical and product diversification may be captured by beta if the public companies used in developing the proxy beta have similar risks. The appraiser should also consider whether the subject company's weaknesses in management depth (i.e., key personnel dependence) or other such elements (e.g., very small market share) are any more limited than those of the companies the appraiser used to estimate the size factor.

Summary Illustration of the Equity Discount Rate Using MCAPM

The following is a typical presentation of the estimation of an equity discount rate using the MCAPM (using CRSP Decile Size Study data):

Risk-free rate		3.79%[a]
General equity risk premium	6.35%[b]	
Beta	× 1.21[c]	
Beta-adjusted ERP		7.68%
Size premium in excess of CAPM		2.15%[d]
Company-specific risk adjustment		1.00%[e]
Equity discount rate		14.62%
Rounded		14.6%

a. Yield on 20-year U.S. Treasury bonds as of valuation date, January 30, 2023.
b. Supply-side equity risk premium for full period 1926–2022, from Kroll U.S. Cost of Capital Module.
c. Median beta for the group of guideline public companies to be most comparable to the subject company.
d. Kroll CRSP Decile Size Study (9th decile).
e. See pp. xx of appraiser's valuation report for supporting analysis.

The following is a typical presentation of the estimation of an equity discount rate using the MCAPM (using Risk Premium Report data):

Risk-free rate		3.79%[a]
Equity risk premium	6.35%[b]	
Beta	× 1.21[c]	
Beta-adjusted ERP		7.68%
Size premium in excess of CAPM		5.93%[d]
Company-specific risk adjustment		1.00%[e]
Equity discount rate		18.40%

a. Yield on 20-year U.S. Treasury bonds as of valuation date, January 30, 2023.
b. Supply-side equity risk premium for period 1963–2022 as reported in Risk Premium Report.
c. Median beta for the group of guideline public companies as determined for the subject company.
d. Risk Premium Report—Size Study 2023, smoothed premium over CAPM for portfolio 25, size measured by market value of equity.
e. See pp. xx of analyst's valuation report for supporting analysis.

Although the CAPM and MCAPM are probably the most widely used methods used in corporate finance today for estimating the discount rate appropriate for valuing equity capital, there is some controversy about relying on the beta factor as a measure of risk. There are alternative methods that purport to capture the risk associated with an equity as well or better than CAPM and MCAPM, although some are relatively untested, and others have not been adopted widely.

CONCEPT AND ESTIMATION OF CAPITALIZATION RATES

Concept of a Capitalization Rate

As noted earlier in this chapter, a *capitalization rate* is a divisor applied to a single number representing some type of economic income to derive an estimate of value. In the discounting method, the numerator of the discounting formula fully accounts for all the changes in future expected returns. In capitalizing, only a single number is used in the numerator and *all future changes in the expected income are incorporated into the capitalization rate*; that is, subtracting the growth rate from the discount rate reflects the future changes in expected income.

Elements of the Capitalization Rate

There are two basic elements that make up a capitalization rate:

1. A discount rate, which represents the total annually compounded rate of return the investor requires over the life of the investment, reflecting the risk of the investment
2. An annualized expected rate of growth or decline in the amount of the economic income variable being capitalized

In the context of the income approach, one specifically quantifies each of these two elements. In the context of the market approach (see Chapter 8), one simply observes the total capitalization rate for each of several possible measures of economic income (i.e., the inverse of observed multiples); but the appraiser has no way of knowing for sure which portion of any observed capitalization rate represents the required total rate of return and which portion represents the expected changes in the variable being capitalized.

Estimating Equity Capitalization Rates

As suggested in the preceding section, the capitalization rate is simply the discount rate plus or minus the expected annually compounded rate of change in the variable being capitalized. In terms of a formula, this computation is:

Formula 7-1

$$PV = E_0 \frac{(1 + g)}{c}$$

Where:

c = Capitalization rate = $k - g$
k = Discount rate (cost of capital or total required rate of return)
g = Growth rate (in the variable being capitalized)

For an example, assume:

Discount rate:	20%
Long-term sustainable growth rate	5%

Inserting these numbers in Formula 7-1 gives us:

Formula 7-2

$$20.0\% - 5.0\% = 15.0\%$$

It is important to note that the g, the *growth rate* in the economic income being capitalized (e.g., in the discounted net cash flow method the economic income is net cash flow), is assumed to be an expected long-term annualized rate into perpetuity and typically includes expected long-term inflation. The reader must keep this requirement in mind when assessing whether the rate used is reasonable. If the growth rate is overestimated, then the capitalization rate will be too low and ultimately overestimate the resulting value, and vice versa.

DISCOUNT RATES FOR SMALLER CLOSELY HELD BUSINESSES

The data used in the build-up method, CAPM and MCAPM, for the equity risk premium and size premiums are derived from returns on publicly traded companies. Some authors have postulated that there is a difference in the private capital market confronting small and medium sized businesses (SMEs) and the public capital market for public companies.[14] Specifically, factors that may differentiate the private capital market from the public capital market include:

14. *See* Robert T. Slee, Private Capital Markets: Valuation, Capitalization and Transfer of Private Business Interests 1–15 (2d ed. 2011).

- Risk and return (appropriate discount rate) are relatively unique to each market given the characteristics of each market.
- The expected holding period for investors in SMEs is generally different from that of investors in public companies, and the liquidity of their investments is quite different within each market.
- Motives of owners of SMEs are oftentimes different from those of professional managers of and investors in public companies.
- SMEs are priced at specific points in time, while public companies are priced continuously.
- Public markets allow relatively easy access to capital, while private capital investment is more difficult to arrange; while public companies typically have ready access to capital, smaller SMEs must create capital solutions one deal at a time with uncertainty as to success.
- Public markets are relatively efficient because of the availability, accuracy, and completeness of information published by public companies; private markets are relatively inefficient because many SMEs do not prepare audited financial statements and, even if they do, they are typically not prepared in a timely fashion nor to the level of detail compared to public companies.

The goal of the appraiser is to evaluate the risk of the business and estimate the appropriate rate of return (discount rate) given the risk or likelihood of achieving a certain level of economic income. Risk and expected return are viewed and defined differently by owners and managers in each SME segment (i.e., small-market owners, lower-middle-market owners, middle-middle-market-and-up owners). For example, owners of small-market SMEs view risk/return more from a personal perspective, whereas owners of middle-middle-market SMEs view risk/return more by comparison to investment markets. While both capital markets, the private and public capital markets, treat risk similarly (i.e., the greater the risk, the greater the return to compensate for the added risk), the returns for small-market SMEs are often measured in both personal and financial terms while the returns for middle-middle-market SMEs are measured almost exclusively in financial terms (as discussed in preceding sections of this chapter).

Risk of an investment and its value must be developed based on the risks (and pricing) perceived by investors that comprise the pools of market participants for the subject asset, as marginal investors in these pools set the market price.

Measuring Equity Discount Rates for SMEs

Risk Premium Report. For companies categorized as middle-middle-market-and-up and companies in the upper end of the lower-middle-market, the Risk Premium Report—Size Study provides data on rates of return realized from investments in smaller public companies and size premiums for use in developing discount rates.[15] The Report provides information about select financial information for the companies that form the basis for the returns and size premiums of the company groupings (called portfolios) of the smallest of the companies reported (i.e., book value of equity, five-year average net income, total assets, five-year average earnings before interest, income taxes, depreciation and amortization, sales), reporting the information segregated from the largest to smallest companies. This data can then be used to compare the companies comprising that portfolio to the characteristics of the subject company.

15. Risk Premium Report, *supra* note 6.

Private Capital Markets Report (PCMR). The PCMR is an extensive annual survey covering different types of investors within the private capital markets, including both debt and equity investors.[16] The project also presents owner data via the inclusion of a business owner survey. The survey is unique in that it provides a wealth of current forward-looking data that can be very useful to an analyst in the private equity markets. The PCMR outlines expected rates of return within the closely held markets. This is a key benefit of the survey, as valuation is a forward-looking concept.

Total Beta. Some authors have postulated that it is appropriate to adjust pure CAPM or MCAPM when considering the rate of return appropriate for the owner of closely held businesses because the owners are typically undiversified as already discussed. Proponents of the use of total beta (TB) (instead of beta) recognize that the risk of being undiversified is an extra risk confronting the investor in the subject company stock if the investor is not diversified or cannot diversify his or her holdings. TB is one method for quantifying the risk taken on by that undiversified investor. TB is a risk measure equal to the standard deviation of total returns expected for a publicly traded stock divided by the standard deviation of total returns expected for the market portfolio. Practitioners promulgating TB generally use realized returns and the standard deviation of realized returns over a look-back period as an estimate of expected future returns for a subject publicly traded stock and the market portfolio. The TB is therefore a proxy for the risk of a closely held company.

The market for closely held businesses is not necessarily comprised of nondiversified buyers and sellers since there are many market participants who are active buyers and sellers and are relatively diversified. Generally, markets, other than possibly for the pool of buyers for small-market businesses, are comprised of well-diversified investors. For example, private equity (PE) investors have expanded the market of likely buyers for closely held businesses. Further, PE investors often acquire smaller businesses to add onto other businesses they own. Their goal is often to take a *platform* business and grow that business through acquiring synergistic businesses to add on to (or tuck into) the platform. That is, they also consider the synergies that they may be able to obtain in making an offer for a closely held business.[17]

Proponents of TB assert that using TB as the risk measure is applicable where the market is determined by nondiversified investors; as such, using TB for any company other than small-market companies may not meet the fair market value standard. The proponents' interpretation of TB as the risk measure in estimating total returns is based on the premise that most owners of small, closely held businesses are completely undiversified and, therefore, the discount rate appropriate for the closely held business should include that extra amount due to the owner being undiversified.

One cannot make any assumption about the market for the subject interest or business by simply looking to the current owner of the subject interest or company. Before using TB, the appraiser must examine the market for the subject interest or company and determine if the willing buyers are predominantly or exclusively comprised of

---

16. Craig R. Everett, *2023 Private Capital Markets Report*, Pepperdine Digital Commons (May 4, 2023), http://digitalcommons.pepperdine.edu/gsbm_pcm_pcmr/16.

17. *Id.* at 45. Investment bankers reported that 48% of closed business transactions involved platform investments, while 52% involved add-on investments.

nondiversified investors. Remember, fair market value is not based on the characteristics of the current holder.

Also, given the differences in the market characteristics of investors in small-market and publicly traded companies, does it make any sense to extrapolate risk measures for investments in large, publicly traded companies, as one does in estimating TB, to measure the risks of investing in small-market companies?[18]

VALUING INVESTED CAPITAL VERSUS VALUING EQUITY

Chapter 3 explained that an accepted procedure in any of the valuation approaches is to value all the *invested capital* and then subtract the value of the debt (and preferred stock, if any) to obtain the value of the common equity.

To use this procedure in the income approach, the numerator of the equation (the dollar amounts of expected returns) must include the returns available to all the invested capital, which includes *both* the debt holders and the equity holders (adjusted for risk given the debt in the capital structure). The denominator (the discount or capitalization rate) must reflect a blending of the costs of each of the component costs of capital on the basis of their proportions of the capital structure, measured at market values.[19] This blended rate is called the *weighted average cost of capital* (WACC). The numerator is often termed *debt free* (or unleveraged) because it does not reflect a reduction for interest expense; that expense is reflected in the WACC used in the denominator.

Concept of Weighted Average Cost of Capital

The weighted average cost of capital (WACC) is the blended discount rate of all the capital structure components, each weighted at its pro rata portion of the total capital structure. It is also termed a business's *overall cost of capital*. It is critical that the appraiser assign weight to each component at market value and *not* at book value. (Weighting the components at book value rather than at market value is a common mistake that can result in a significant error.)

Basic WACC Computation Model

The formula for the weighted average cost of capital where the entity only has equity capital and debt capital is:

Formula 7-3

$$WACC = (k_e \times W_e) + (k_{d(pt)}[1 - t] \times W_d)$$

18. *See* Pratt & ASA Educ. Found., *Estimating the Discount Rate for Smaller Closely Held Businesses*, Appendix to Chapter 11, *supra* note 1, for a more extensive discussion, https://www.appraisers.org/docs/default-source/6.-publications/vab6/ch-11-estimating-the-discount-rate-for-smaller-closely-held-businesses.pdf.

19. Debt capital is often measured at book value because book values often approximate market values.

Where:

$WACC$	=	Weighted average cost of capital
W	=	Weight (the percentage of each component of the company's total capital structure, measured at market value)
k_e	=	Equity discount rate (i.e., cost of equity capital)
$k_{d(pt)}$	=	Discount rate on debt capital (i.e., cost of debt capital) before income taxes (that is, before adjusting the discount rate for the tax deductibility of interest expense)
t	=	Income tax rate

Of course, if there is preferred stock or other components of the capital structure, there would need to be additional components in the formula to accommodate additional components of the capital structure.

For an example of application of the preceding formula, assume:

Equity discount rate:	20%
Percentage of equity in the capital structure (at market value)	60%
Discount rate on debt (pretax)	10%
Income tax rate	30%
Percentage of debt in the capital structure	40%

Inserting these numbers in Formula 7-3 gives us:

Formula 7-4

$$
\begin{aligned}
WACC &= (20\% \times 60\%) + (10\% \, [1 - 30\%] \times 40\%) \\
&= 0.12 + (0.07 \times 0.40) \\
&= 0.12 + 0.028 \\
&= 0.148 \text{ or } 14.8\%
\end{aligned}
$$

The preceding is often presented in tabular form:

Component	**Discount Rate**	**Weight**	**Weighted Discount Rate**
Equity	20%	60%	0.12
Debt	10% (1 – 30%)	40%	0.028
Weighted average cost of capital			0.148

Derivation of Weights for WACC

In the preceding example, the discount rate for equity capital (i.e., the cost of equity) is 20% and the discount rate on debt capital (after the income tax effect) is only 7%. Such a large difference is not uncommon. Consequently, the weights used in the WACC can dramatically affect the overall discount rate on invested capital (i.e., weighted average) discount rate and thus the indicated value. The appropriate weighting is often a major area of disagreement among appraisers.

The choice of weights may differ when an appraiser is valuing a controlling interest versus a noncontrolling interest. They also may be different under different standards of value.

Controlling interests. Some appraisers may use the company's actual capital structure to estimate the fair market value of controlling interests. There is, however, a good case for using an alternative capital structure because one of the perquisites of control ownership is the power to change the capital structure. One might assume that a new investor would employ the most optimal capital structure possible in order to minimize the company's overall cost of capital. Appraisers sometimes use the industry average capital structure as a proxy for the optimal capital structure.[20] Appraisers may also develop an estimate of the industry average (optimal) capital structure by examining the capital structures of their selected guideline public companies.

A common error by appraisers is using industry average capital structures measured at book value. Using book values for debt is reasonable if the value for debt is close to market value. But reflecting a value for equity (based on depreciated historical costs) that is considerably less than market value distorts the weights by overstating the debt proportion and understating the equity proportion, thereby understating the invested capital discount rate, and overstating the indicated business value.

The data in the *U.S. Industry Benchmarking* dataset is from only public companies. Closely held companies typically have less access to the debt markets for financing than public companies. As such, it may be appropriate to assume a marginally higher proportion of equity for a closely held company.

Changing the capital structure weights significantly can also change the cost of each component of the capital structure. As leverage (percentage of debt) is increased, risk increases for both the debt and the equity, consequently increasing the cost of each component. A common error is to hypothesize a much greater percentage of debt with no increase in the discount rate on debt capital or equity capital (as the risks increase with increases in debt), thereby lowering the computed WACC and reaching an unattainably inflated value for the company.

Noncontrolling interests. When valuing a noncontrolling interest at fair market value or in a fair value calculation when the legal standard assumes no change in management (such as in a Delaware Statutory Appraisal matter), the appraiser almost always uses the company's actual capital structure because the owner of a noncontrolling interest lacks the ability to change the capital structure. At first glance, this may seem like a dilemma because the appraiser needs to weigh the capital structure components at market value, which are not yet known because that is what the appraiser is trying to determine. However, the dilemma is easily solved with a spreadsheet such as Microsoft Excel using an *iterative process*, which tests different capital structures until one works.[21]

Another source of weights for the capital structure (for use in the market approach or in the income approach) begins with observing the capital structures of the guideline public companies. If the observed capital structures among the guideline public companies vary a great deal, the appraiser can remove the impact of financing differences

---

20. The Kroll U.S. Industry Benchmarking dataset, *supra* note 13, provides industry average capital structures measured using market value.

21. The iterative process is described in Cost of Capital, *supra* note 5, at 562–64.

by a procedure called "unlevering" the observed betas. The unlevered betas (sometimes called asset betas) measure the operating risks of the companies. After assessing the appropriate operating risk for the subject company, the appraiser then adjusts the operating beta estimate for the appropriate financing risk of the subject business (a process called "levering" the operating beta). This topic is beyond the scope of this book.[22]

MATCHING THE DISCOUNT RATE WITH THE DEFINITION OF ECONOMIC INCOME

In some situations (e.g., before some courts, valuing nontaxable investments, valuing a pass-through entity, or discounting economic income for unitary business property tax assessments), appraisers may use a different measure of economic income. Suppose the appraiser needs to convert the discount rate to an equivalent discount rate commensurate with another measure of economic income (e.g., pretax income). If the appraiser can reasonably assume that the relationship (ratio) of pretax net income to net cash flow is constant over time, then the formula for converting a net cash flow discount rate to a pretax net income discount rate for use in the discounted economic income method is as follows:[23]

Formula 7-5

$$k_{pti} = \left[\frac{\text{Pretax Income}}{NCF_e}(k_e - g)\right] + g$$

Where:

k_{pti} = Discount rate applicable to pretax income

$\frac{\text{Pretax Income}}{NCF_e}$ = Assumed constant ratio of pretax income to net cash flow to equity

k_e = Discount rate applicable to net cash flow

g = Annual compound growth rate in perpetuity for both pretax income and net cash flow

Note the *critical assumptions* inherent in this formula:

1. Pretax income and net cash flow bear a constant relationship to each other over time.
2. Both grow at the same constant annual compound rate into perpetuity.

It should be noted that a similar formula can give discount rates appropriate for earnings streams other than pretax income, such as net income.[24] The conversion procedure described in Formula 7–5 is appropriate for the capitalization of economic income

22. *Id.* at 234–68. This process adjusts for differences in equity risk due to differences in debt financing in the capital structure.

23. For a discussion of the limitations of this formula, *see* Pratt & ASA Educ. Found., *supra* note 1, at 213–16. For a more extensive discussion, *see Adjusting the Discount Rate to Alternative Economic Income Measures* in Cost of Capital, *supra* note 5, at 881–95.

24. Substituting net income for pretax income in Formula 7-5.

method and not necessarily appropriate for the discounted economic income method (where growth rates may change over time).[25]

COMMON ERRORS

While the basic theory behind estimating a discount rate is simple, applying that theory provides ample opportunities for errors. The following are a few of the most common errors.[26]

- **Confusing discount rates with capitalization rates.** The discount rate is the cost of capital and applies to all future economic income. The capitalization rate (as discussed in the previous chapter) is a divisor applied to some historical economic income (e.g., latest 12 months' earnings, cash flow). Generally, these two rates are equal only when the expected level of economic income is constant (no growth) into perpetuity.
- **Mismatching the discount rate with the economic income measure.** Perhaps the most common error in estimating a discount rate is using a discount or capitalization rate that is inappropriate for the type of economic income being discounted or capitalized. This general category of error has innumerable variations. Only a few are listed here.
    - Using a safe rate to discount or capitalize a risky return. While not the most common error, this is one of the most egregious. Some analysts and appraisers have even made the mistake of discounting a highly risky series of projected economic income figures using the Treasury bill rate.
    - Applying a discount rate to an income variable defined differently from that to which the discount rate is applicable. This general error has many variations. As discussed earlier, most of the methods and sources for developing discount rates (both used in the practical application of contemporary financial theory and discussed in this book) produce a discount rate that applies to net cash flow. A common error in adjusting an after-tax discount rate to its pretax equivalent is to divide the after-tax discount rate by one minus the tax rate.
    - Applying a discount rate in real terms to an estimated economic income in nominal (current) terms. Some analysts and appraisers erroneously subtract the anticipated inflation rate from the discount rate and then apply the adjusted discount rate to economic income estimates that includes inflation (and vice versa). This is a common way to double-count inflation.
- **Applying a WACC to an equity cash flow.** As discussed previously in this chapter, net cash flow to equity (after interest is deducted) should be discounted at the cost of equity and net cash flow to invested capital (debt free) should be discounted at WACC. This error mismatches the cash flows and the discount rates.
- **Estimating a capital structure for the subject company different than the company's actual capital structure (and thereby deriving a WACC different from the company's actual WACC) when the standard of value is fair market value on a noncontrolling basis.** If an acquirer were to use its own WACC, the implied result would be *investment value* to that acquirer instead of fair market value. Moreover, if the interest is a noncontrolling interest, the holder of the interest could not force a change in capital structure.
- **Using a discount rate as a capitalization rate.** Some appraisers fall into the trap of using the discount rate (i.e., the cost of capital) as a capitalization rate. One may see the

---

25. For derivation of an equivalent discount rate for use in the discounted economic income method, *see* COST OF CAPITAL, *supra* note 5, at 891–94.

26. This list is adapted from PRATT & ASA EDUC. FOUND., *supra* note 1, at 177–80, 254–55.

opposite from time to time where the appraiser uses a capitalization rate to discount prospective cash flow or other expected economic income to a present value.

SUMMARY

The discount rate is the expected rate of return that market participants (i.e., the pool of likely willing buyers) require to attract funds to a particular investment. The discount rate (also commonly referred to as the *cost of capital*, the *expected return*, the *required return*, the *hurdle rate*, or the *opportunity cost of capital*) is always an *expected* (or forward-looking) return.

The appraiser should derive the present value discount rate in the same manner for both the discounted economic income method and the capitalized economic income method. Whether the appraiser uses a build-up method, CAPM, or MCAPM, that discount rate includes expected inflation. Therefore, the appraiser should use a growth rate that also reflects inflation.

In applying either the build-up method or the MCAPM to estimate a discount rate when valuing closely held businesses, appraisers have typically had to rely on data derived from public companies to obtain an *as-if-freely-traded* discount rate. This results in an *as-if-freely-traded* indication of value in applying the discounted economic income or capitalization of economic income methods. The business appraiser then may apply appropriate discounts for lack of control and discounts for lack of liquidity and/or marketability (discussed in Chapter 18) to arrive at an indication of value for a closely held business or closely held business interest.

REFERENCES FOR DEVELOPING DISCOUNT RATES

Basic Discount Rate References

Fishman, Jay E., Bruce Johnson, Kent Pummel, et al. 2022. "Capitalized and Discounted Cash Flow Methods." In PPC's *Guide to Business Valuations*, 5–1 to 5–90 (Carrollton, TX: Thomson Reuters).

Hitchner, James R. 2017. "Cost of Capital/Rates of Return." In *Financial Valuation: Applications and Models*, 4th ed., Chap. 6, 185–269 (Hoboken, NJ: John Wiley & Sons, Inc.).

Hitchner, James, Shannon P. Pratt, and Jay E. Fishman. 2016. "Cost of Capital/Rates of Return." In *A Consensus View: Q&A Guide to Financial Valuation*, Chap. 2, 65–191 (Ventnor City, NJ: Valuation Products and Services, LLC).

Pratt, Shannon P. and ASA Educational Foundation. 2022. "Income Approach: Developing the Discount Rate." In *Shannon Pratt's Valuing a Business: The Analysis and Appraisal of Closely Held Businesses*, 6th ed., Chap. 11, 207–56 (New York: McGraw-Hill). Includes extensive bibliography and data references in online appendix.

Pratt, Shannon P., and Roger J. Grabowski. 2014. *Cost of Capital: Applications and Examples*, 5th ed. (Hoboken, NJ: John Wiley & Sons, Inc.).

Pratt, Shannon P., and Roger J. Grabowski. 2011. *Cost of Capital in Litigation: Applications and Examples* (Hoboken, NJ: John Wiley & Sons, Inc.).

Pratt, Shannon P., and Roger J. Grabowski. 2014. *The Lawyer's Guide to Cost of Capital: Understanding Risk and Return for Valuing Businesses and Other Investments* (Chicago: American Bar Association).

Trugman, Gary. 2022. "Discount Rates and Capitalization Rates." In *Understanding Business Valuations*, 6th ed., Chap. 13, 479–522 (Portland, OR: Business Valuation Resources).

Articles and Research Papers

Chincarini, Ludwig B., Daehwan Kim, and Fabio Moneta, "Beta and Firm Age," *Journal of Empirical Finance* 58 (2020): 50–74.

Dhaliwal, Dan S., Joshua Judd, Matthew Serfling, and Sarah Shaikh, "Customer Concentration Risk and the Cost of Equity Capital," *Journal of Accounting & Economics* 61:1 (February 2016): 23–48.

Ellis, J., E.C. Fee, and S. Thomas, "Proprietary Costs and the Disclosure of Information About Customers," *Journal of Accounting Research* 50 (2012): 685–727.

Hann, Rebecca N., Maria Ogneva, and Oguzhan Ozbas, "Corporate Diversification and the Cost of Capital," *The Journal of Finance* 68:5 (May 2013): 1961–99.

Solo, David, Didier Sornette, and Florian Ulmann, "Dynamical Internal Cost of Capital Driven by Cash Flow Growth," (March 11, 2021). Swiss Finance Institute Research Paper No. 21-24; available at https://ssrn.com/abstract=3803164.

Cost of Capital Data References

Cost of Capital Navigator: U.S. Cost of Capital Module (Kroll, LLC). Size premiums, risk premiums (*Risk Premium Report*), equity risk premiums, risk-free rates, and industry risk premiums, updated annually. U.S. Industry Benchmarking dataset with U.S. industry-level inputs used to estimate cost of capital and industry-level benchmarks used to augment and support custom analyses, updated quarterly. U.S. Company-level Beta dataset provides individual company beta estimates. Available by subscription at https://www.kroll.com/en/cost-of-capital.

Everett, Craig R. 2023, *Private Capital Markets Report*. (Malibu, CA: Pepperdine Grazia Dio Business School). http://digitalcommons.pepperdine.edu/gsbm_pcm_pcmr/16.

Ibbotson, Roger, and Kroll, LLC (formerly Duff & Phelps). U.S. capital markets performance statistics and data for seven assets classes published annually. In *Stocks, Bonds, Bills, and Inflation® (SBBI®) Yearbook*. Available for purchase at https://www.kroll.com/en/cost-of-capital/stocks-bonds-bills-inflation-sbbi-yearbook.

CHAPTER 8

The Market Approach

Alina Niculita, ASA, ARM, CFA

INTRODUCTION

In this chapter, you will learn about:

- Market approach to valuation: concept and overview
- Valuing controlling versus noncontrolling interests
- Valuing invested capital versus equity
- Sources of market approach data, including guideline transaction data and guideline public company data
- Developing market multiples for valuation of invested capital and equity
- Criteria for selecting guideline companies, including the number of guideline companies
- Other methods under the market approach

In this chapter, the calculation of invested capital and equity valuation multiples are illustrated. Additionally, a case study valuing a hypothetical business using the market approach is presented.

MARKET APPROACH CONCEPT AND OVERVIEW

The concept of the market approach is based on the principle of substitution whereby valuation guidance can be found in transactions involving similar companies. In a way, this is like appraising a house by analyzing sales of similar houses. However, "similar" businesses have far more differences than similar houses, creating a need to carefully analyze the similarities and differences. The market approach to business appraisal also has several dimensions that must be considered that are either not found at all or are treated differently in the real estate appraisal sales comparison approach, including:

- Valuing controlling versus noncontrolling interests
- Valuing total invested capital versus direct valuation of equity
- Whether guideline transactions are sales of entire businesses or publicly traded minority interest stock market transactions

These possibilities are shown schematically in Exhibit 8-1.

Exhibit 8-1 Major Market Approach Business Valuation Scenarios

Valuing Controlling Interest		
	Valuing Total Invested Capital	Using sales of entire companies
		Using publicly traded guideline companies
	Direct Valuation of Equity	Using sales of entire companies
		Using publicly traded guideline companies
Valuing Minority Interest		
	Valuing Total Invested Capital	Using sales of entire companies
		Using publicly traded guideline companies
	Direct Valuation of Equity	Using sales of entire companies
		Using publicly traded guideline companies

Valuing Controlling versus Noncontrolling Interests

In real estate appraisal, valuations are virtually always of a 100% controlling (fee-simple) interest or a leased fee interest (value of the real property subject to existing leases) in the real property itself, as if there is no outstanding debt. After that, if one is valuing a partial interest in the property, some lack of control discount may be applied to the fractional interest's pro rata portion of the fee-simple interest value.

In business appraisal, noncontrolling interests often can be valued directly, that is, without ever addressing the question of what the company as a whole, on a controlling interest basis, might be worth. This is possible because appraisers can base their market approach valuation on cash flows that are on a noncontrolling basis. This is discussed more fully in Chapter 18, "Discounts and Premiums."

The differences between noncontrolling and control value usually are considerably greater for businesses than for real estate because owners of a fractional interest in real estate may have the right to demand partition, thus converting their ownership interest to a pro rata controlling interest or fee-simple interest.

Owners of stock or partnership interests generally have no such right, leaving them at the mercy of policy decisions of the control owners.

Assume that the appraiser is beginning the valuation of a noncontrolling interest with data on sales of entire companies (merger and acquisition transactions) in the market approach (called the *guideline transaction* method). Because the transactions represent prices paid for controlling interests, it usually would be appropriate to make both a lack of control and lack of marketability adjustment to the indicated control value.

Similarly, if the appraiser is beginning the valuation of a controlling interest with data on sales of publicly traded minority interest transactions (i.e., stock prices guideline public companies) in the market approach (called the *guideline public company* method), it may be appropriate to adjust cash flows to the level that a controlling owner could achieve (controlling adjustments). The appraiser might then consider applying a discount for lack of marketability.

Appraisers disagree about what type of adjustments are considered controlling, and about whether a discount for lack of marketability is applicable to a controlling interest. Some appraisers consider an adjustment for owner's reasonable compensation to be appropriate in a noncontrolling interest valuation, while others view this type of adjustment to be a controlling adjustment. Similarly, there is no consensus in the valuation community about the appropriateness of applying a discount for lack of marketability to a controlling interest. This is discussed more fully in Chapter 18.

Valuing Total Invested Capital versus Direct Valuation of Equity

In real estate appraisal, property is typically appraised without regard to how much debt or other claims there may be against it. In business appraisal, if all components of the capital structure are appraised, it usually is called *value of invested capital* or *market value of invested capital* (MVIC). However, in business appraisal, the equity interest sometimes is valued directly without going through the step of estimating the value of the entire company, including debt and equity interests combined.

To obtain the equity value directly, one can use market multiples of various levels of income available to equity owners (for example, price-to-earnings ratios, etc.). Alternatively, one can value the entire invested capital, including returns available to holders of interest-bearing debt and preferred stock, and then subtract the value of the *senior* securities (holders of interest-bearing debt and preferred stock receive payments before those to common equity, as they have a senior claim on the cash flow) to obtain the value of the common equity.

Either procedure can be used for valuing controlling or noncontrolling interests. However, the invested capital procedure tends to be preferred for valuing controlling interests and the direct valuation of equity tends to be preferred for valuing noncontrolling interests.

The reason that the invested capital procedure is preferred when valuing a controlling interest is that the owner of the controlling interest has the ability (i.e., control) to change the capital structure if that may enhance the value of the equity. On the other hand, the noncontrolling interest owner does not have that option. If the subject and guideline public companies have considerably different capital structures, however, eliminating the potential effects of that difference sometimes is a reason (sometimes a compelling reason) to use the invested capital procedure even when valuing noncontrolling interests.

Using Sales of Entire Companies or Guideline Public Companies

As noted in Chapter 3, there are two commonly used types of market transactions:

1. Sales of entire companies or possibly controlling interests in companies. Some would divide this into two subcategories: companies that were publicly traded before the transaction and companies that were closely held before the transaction.
2. Publicly traded company transactions (day-to-day transactions of noncontrolling interests in companies in the public stock markets)

Unfortunately, practically no reliable data is available on noncontrolling interest transactions in closely held companies. Therefore, if the appraiser is using the market approach to value a noncontrolling interest in a closely held business, he or she may be forced to start with the available data on sales of entire closely held businesses and adjust for the lack of control and marketability factors.

Fortunately, however, there have been significant improvements in recent years in the amount, quality, and ease of access to both public market transaction data and data on sales of entire companies, both public and closely held. This makes a good market approach valuation much more feasible today for many companies.

SOURCES OF MARKET APPROACH DATA

As noted earlier, market data can be classified in two groups: (1) sales of entire companies and (2) market prices of stock of publicly traded companies. Public company data usually has the advantages of being more complete and more verifiable.

On the other hand, if one is valuing a controlling interest, it may be preferable to start the valuation with data on controlling interest guideline transactions (where controlling income stream adjustments are disclosed). One then does not need to deal with the issue of adjusting the income streams of guideline public companies for control. Most appraisers consider a control-adjusted income stream to be the starting point in arriving at a "control" value. Another reason to use transactions of controlling interests in closely held businesses in some cases is because many industries and professional practices have few or no public companies and, even in industries where one can locate public companies, they are rarely comparable to smaller closely held companies, which are broadly categorized in the same industry due to size, geographic breadth, and product/service diversification. For example, the local contractor doing home remodeling or constructing one home at a time cannot be compared to a national homebuilder, even though they are classified as being in the same industry.

Sales of Public Companies

If a public company is sold, required filings with the Securities and Exchange Commission (SEC) provide excellent data for implementing a market approach valuation. Because the transactions are not likely to be on the effective valuation date for the subject, the appraiser needs to consider the differences in market conditions between the transaction date and the subject valuation effective date and make any adjustments deemed appropriate.

Business appraisers use many sources to locate sales of public companies. Unlike with currently traded stocks, however, there is no single source that is totally comprehensive as to the terms of the transaction, so appraisers often use several sources to search for transactions.

If one is relying on public company data, the most reliable source will always be pulling information directly from SEC filings. However, this process can be time-consuming and inefficient since collecting multiple years of data from SEC filings may take several days to complete. For these reasons, many business appraisers use a database to obtain financial data for guideline public companies. Such databases often include a link to the actual SEC filing, giving business appraisers the ability to check the accuracy of the data.

Sales of Closely Held Companies

Data on sales of closely held companies is usually considerably more limited than data on sales of public companies. Unlike real estate transactions, for which data generally is required to be filed at the relevant government agency and made publicly available, there is no requirement for releasing any data on sales of closely held companies. Therefore, unless the buyer is a public company and the purchase is of a sufficient size to require an SEC filing, the data services that collect closely held company transaction data usually gather it from the transaction intermediaries (i.e., business brokers) rather than directly from the companies sold. This generally means that the data for each individual transaction may not be able to be independently verified. While this is a limitation, the services have no reason to be biased. Furthermore, if valuing an interest in a closely held company, some business appraisers prefer to use closely held company transactions rather than public company transactions as a starting point.

There are several closely held sale transaction databases, all greatly expanded in recent years. These are listed and described briefly in the References at the end of this chapter.

Guideline Public Company Data

More than 12,000 operating companies are required to file financial data with the SEC. The major reports are:

- Annual report, on Form 10-K
- Quarterly report, on Form 10-Q
- Special events report, on Form 8-K
- Registration statement for initial public offering, on Form S-1
- Registration statement and proxy statement for merger in which securities are issued, on Form S-4
- Information with respect to company being acquired, on Form 14D9

There are also thousands of public companies that are not required to file with the SEC, because either their number of stockholders or the amount of their assets falls below the SEC levels that require filing.

Since May 1996, all companies required to file with the SEC must do so electronically on the Electronic Data Gathering and Retrieval system, commonly known as EDGAR. All documents filed on EDGAR are in the public domain and may be retrieved at no charge through the internet. Various commercial systems also are available and provide enhanced capabilities to manipulate public company filing data. The data provides the information the business appraiser or financial analyst needs to perform all the market multiple calculations discussed in this chapter. Since 2009, the SEC has required all public companies to tag their financial statements and footnotes with *eXtensible Business Reporting Language* (XBRL). Databases that use this tagged financial statement data pull directly from the SEC filings, and they offer auditable data so that a business appraiser or financial analysts can see how the figure was calculated (often including the link to the actual SEC filing). Because trading in public securities occurs each business day, the price information for public company securities should be as of, or within a day or two of the effective date of the valuation. Usually, the public company fundamental data (e.g., sales, earnings) should be as close to the valuation date as possible or as close to the latest date available for the subject company as possible.

DEVELOPING MARKET MULTIPLES FOR VALUATION

Similar to real estate appraisal, the market approach in business appraisal requires some "units of comparison." In real estate, for example, price per square foot is a common unit of comparison. In business valuation, however, physical units of comparison (for example, number of board feet per year of manufacturing capacity) are much less common. The units of comparison usually are in some form of dollar measurement of various levels of income-producing capacity or asset values. In other words, the objective is to observe the transaction price and compute the multiple of that price times some relevant fundamental variables, such as sales, earnings, gross cash flow, net asset value, and so on. The fundamental variables used in the market approach are defined and illustrated in Chapter 4. This chapter will present an example of the market approach using some of the most commonly encountered market multiples.

Invested Capital Multiples

When valuing the entire invested capital of a company (i.e., equity and debt), the numerator of the market multiple is the market value of invested capital (MVIC). This is defined as the market value of all the common and preferred stock and interest-bearing debt.

Technically, invested capital is "long term" and would include only long-term debt, excluding the portion classified as current. However, more often than not, short-term interest-bearing debt also is included. One reason for this is that it often is difficult or even impossible, at least for the guideline public companies, to determine how much of the interest expense is attributable to long-term versus short-term debt.

Many business appraisers and valuation analysts, and almost all investment bankers, subtract out excess cash and cash equivalents when they are defining and computing MVIC (and typically refer to the resulting figure as enterprise value rather than MVIC). This is to focus on the value of the company's operations without distortions of cash-rich versus cash-poor companies. If this is done for the guideline public companies, then, to be consistent, excess cash and equivalents for the subject company must be added back after the multiples have been applied to estimate the company's value. Because of these two ambiguities in computing MVIC, it is essential that the appraiser preparing the report define how MVIC is computed.

Because the numerator includes the market value of all invested capital, the denominator used to create the multiple must include all the returns available to all the invested capital. Usually this means adding all the interest paid in addition to all the returns available to common equity. If there is preferred stock, the dividends on the preferred stock also must be included.

To recap from Chapter 4, the denominators typically used for invested capital multiples include the following:

- **Sales.** This is the only income statement denominator that can logically be used in either invested capital or equity market multiples. However, it is a more relevant multiple for invested capital than for equity because the multiples of market value of equity-to-sales can be significantly distorted by differences in capital structures among the companies.
- **Discretionary earnings.** Discretionary earnings include gross cash flow before interest, taxes, depreciation and amortization, and all compensation to one owner/manager. Typically, this level of earnings is used only for small businesses and professional practices with one key owner/operator.

- **Earnings before interest, income taxes, depreciation, and amortization (EBITDA).** A multiple of EBITDA is the market multiple most preferred by acquirers for valuing companies under the market approach. It represents gross cash flow before taxes and eliminates the possibly distorting effect of differing depreciation policies and capital expenditures among companies.
- **Earnings before interest and income taxes (EBIT).** This is the second most preferred invested capital market multiple.
- **Debt-free net income (DFNI).** A multiple based on an estimation of what after-tax net income to invested capital would be if there were no interest-bearing debt.
- **Debt-free cash flow (DFCF).** A multiple based on an estimate of what after-tax gross cash flow available to invested capital would be if there were no interest-bearing debt.
- **Book value of invested capital.** When this multiple is used, it may refer to total book value or only include tangible book value. Intangibles assets are usually eliminated because the different methods of acquiring intangibles and accounting for them can distort comparisons between companies.
- **Adjusted book value of invested capital.** In some cases, this multiple can be used if it is possible to adjust values of major assets to market value for both the subject and guideline public companies. Ideally, one would adjust all assets and liabilities to market value, but this may be impractical in some cases.

Equity Multiples

When valuing equity directly, the numerator of the market multiple is the market value of common equity, often simply referred to as "price." This may be expressed on either the basis of the aggregate value of common stock outstanding or on a per-share basis. Of course, the financial fundamental in the denominator must be expressed on the same basis.

Because the numerator is the market value of common equity, the denominator used to create the multiple must consist of returns at the common equity level (after deductions for interest and preferred dividends). To recap from Chapter 4, the denominators typically used for equity valuation multiples include:

- **Sales.** One should be careful using a multiple of sales for an equity valuation because:
  - It may be distorted because of different degrees of leverage among companies.
  - Using sales by itself, there is an implicit assumption that the subject and guideline public companies have similar cost structures, which may or may not be true. (If detailed expense data is available for the guideline public companies, the price-to-sales multiple can be adjusted to reflect differences in the companies' cost structures.)
  - It may be more appropriate for a control-basis valuation than for a noncontrolling valuation on the theory that a control buyer may be able to bring the cost structure into line with industry averages after acquiring the customer base.
- **Gross cash flow (often just called cash flow).** Net income plus noncash charges; particularly helpful if the subject and guideline public companies have significantly different depreciation accounting policies.
- **Pretax income (net income before taxes).** Price-to-earnings (P/E) ratios for public companies are reported on an after-tax basis (i.e., after income taxes are paid by the entity). Be careful that the appraiser has not used an after-tax P/E ratio and applied it to pretax earnings (a common error).
- **Dividends or withdrawals.** When valuing a controlling interest, the focus usually is on the capacity to pay dividends or withdrawals. However, when valuing a noncontrolling interest, the focus generally is on actual dividends or withdrawals, because the noncontrolling owner cannot cause more to be paid.

- **Book value of equity.** Same comments apply as for book value of invested capital.
- **Adjusted book value.** Same comments apply as for adjusted book value of invested capital.

Time Periods for Company Financial Statement Data

Unless there is some special reason, balance sheet data should be the most recent available data as of the valuation date. As for the income statement data, several different time periods can be derived from the guideline public company data, such as:

- Latest fiscal year
- Latest 12 months (sometimes called trailing 12 months)
- Some number of years' simple average (such as three, five, seven, or ten years, with five years being the most common)
- Some number of years' weighted average (typically placing the greatest weight on the latest years based on the theory that most recent results should be most representative of future expectations)
- Estimates for the coming year
- Estimates for additional future years beyond the coming year, if available

It is important that the time periods for which the guideline public company data is computed are similar to those used for the subject company. If the subject company had drastic changes in its operations (such as major new or discontinued product lines), it may be appropriate to go back only as far as the latest major change. The reader should be satisfied that the rationale for the period or periods chosen makes sense in terms of developing a reasonable value for the subject by reference to the guideline public companies. In addition, if the appraiser develops "forward multiples" from estimates of the coming year and beyond, such multiples are only estimates and not fact; they are only as good as the estimators.

If one is using sales of closely held companies for guideline company multiples, usually only the latest year's data prior to the closely held company transaction is available. While this is a limitation, it is often the case that the closely held companies sold were much more comparable to the subject than any public companies due to size and diversification issue.

CRITERIA FOR SELECTING GUIDELINE COMPANIES

One succinct quote summarizes the essence of the key characteristic that should be present in a guideline company: "Do the underlying economics driving this comparable company match those that drive our company?"[1]

In Revenue Ruling 59-60, the Internal Revenue Service, one of the strongest proponents of the guideline public company method, makes the following observation:

> Although the only restrictive requirement as to comparable corporations specified in the statute is that their lines of business be the same or similar, yet it is obvious that

1. Daniel W. Bielinski, *The Comparable Company Approach: Measuring the True Value of Privately Held Firms*, CORP. CASHFLOW MAG. 64-66 (Oct. 1990).

consideration must be given to other relevant factors in order that the most valid comparison possible will be obtained.[2]

The most obvious criterion for comparability is line of business. The next most important criterion probably is markets served. For example, in valuing a manufacturer of electrical controls for sawmills, the most important criterion might not be manufacturers of electrical controls, but manufacturers of equipment used in the forest products industry. In *Estate of Gallo*[3] (Gallo Wine Co.), faced with an absence of publicly traded wine producers, appraisers on both sides expanded the line of business criteria to include brewers, distillers, soft-drink bottlers, and major consumer brand agricultural food producers. The Tax Court accepted this procedure.

Other criteria may include:

- Size
- Comparability of earnings and earnings trends
- Position in industry
- Capital structure
- Maturity of company and growth
- Liquidity

One thing that all the selection criteria have in common is that they attempt to identify companies that are subject to the same risk factors as the subject company.

Occasionally, the appraiser has the luxury of many available guideline public companies and can narrow the selection down to those that are highly similar. More often it is necessary to broaden the criteria.

As noted earlier, it is useful to the reader of the valuation report if the appraiser states the criteria used and demonstrates that all companies that met the criteria were used or, if not, why certain ones that would appear to meet the criteria were rejected.

HOW MANY GUIDELINE COMPANIES?

The more detailed and reliable the data for each company and the more similar the guideline companies to the subject company, the fewer companies are needed. With public company data, or with detailed closely held company data, business appraisers usually are comfortable with five to seven companies, sometimes as few as three. However, in *Estate of Hall*[4] (Hallmark Greeting Cards, itself a public company), the Tax Court rejected a valuation that was based entirely on the only other publicly traded greeting card company at the time, American Greetings; and it accepted the analysis of a broad group of high market share consumer goods, such as Parker Pens. If there is only one excellent guideline company, the appraiser certainly should use it but generally should not rely on it entirely.

---

2. Rev. Rul. 59-60, 1959-1 C.B. 237, § 4(h).
3. Est. of Gallo v. Comm'r, 50 T.C.M. 470 (1985).
4. Est. of Hall v. Comm'r, 92 T.C. 312 (1989).

ILLUSTRATION OF DEVELOPING GUIDELINE COMPANY MULTIPLES

Exhibit 8-2 is financial data for Marvel Corporation, selected as a guideline public company, in the same format as the data for Widget Corporation in Exhibit 4-1. Exhibit 8-3 develops four invested capital multiples for Marvel Corporation, using the information from Exhibit 8-2. Exhibit 8-4 develops five equity valuation multiples for Marvel Corporation, also using the information from Exhibit 8-2.

Exhibit 8-2 Marvel Corporation Financial Data

Marvel Corporation Balance Sheet

Assets

Current Assets		
Cash		$1,500,000
Accounts Receivable		2,500,000
Inventory		5,000,000
Total Current Assets		$9,000,000
Plant & Equipment		
At Cost	$24,000,000	
Less: Accumulated Depreciation	$20,000,000	
Net Plant & Equipment		4,000,000
Total Assets		$13,000,000

Liabilities and Equity

Current Liabilities	
Accounts Payable	$3,000,000
Long-Term Debt (including current portion)	6,000,000
Total Liabilities	$9,000,000
Common Equity (4,000,000 shares outstanding)	4,000,000
Total Liabilities and Equity	$13,000,000

Marvel Corporation Income Statement

Sales	$40,000,000
Cost of Goods Sold	26,000,000
Gross Margin	$14,000,000
Selling, General and Administrative Expenses	10,000,000
Operating Income, Before Taxes	$4,000,000
Interest Expense	480,000
Income Before Taxes	$3,520,000
Income Taxes	1,408,000
Net Income	$2,112,000

Marvel Corporation Other Financial Data

The following data is derived from Statement of Cash Flows, footnotes to financial statements, and other available data:

1. Interest rate on the long-term debt is 8%.
2. The selling, general, and administrative expenses include depreciation of $1,000,000.
3. Market value of debt is about the same as book value of debt.
4. Market price of stock as of valuation date is $6 per share.
5. Consensus forecast is that sales and earnings will grow at about 12% per year.

Exhibit 8-3 Marvel Corporation Invested Capital Valuation Multiples

Market Value of Invested Capital (MVIC)

Long-Term Debt:	$6,000,000	20%
Equity: 4,000,000 shares @ $6	24,000,000	80%
Market Value of Invested Capital	$30,000,000	100%

MVIC/Sales:

$$\frac{\text{MVIC}}{\text{Sales}} = \frac{\$30{,}000{,}000}{\$40{,}000{,}000} = 0.75$$

MVIC/EBITDA:

Operating Income Before Taxes (pretax income plus interest expense)	$4,000,000
Plus: Depreciation	1,000,000
Earnings Before Interest, Taxes, Depreciation and Amortization	$5,000,000

$$\frac{\text{MVIC}}{\text{EBITDA}} = \frac{\$30{,}000{,}000}{\$5{,}000{,}000} = 6.00$$

MVIC/EBIT:

Operating Income Before Taxes (pretax income plus interest expense)	$4,000,000

$$\frac{\text{MVIC}}{\text{EBIT}} = \frac{\$30{,}000{,}000}{\$4{,}000{,}000} = 7.50$$

MVIC/Book Value of Invested Capital:

Book Value of Long-Term Debt	$ 6,000,000
Book Value of Equity	4,000,000
Book Value of Invested Capital	$10,000,000

$$\frac{\text{MVIC}}{\text{BV of Invested Capital}} = \frac{\$30{,}000{,}000}{\$10{,}000{,}000} = 3.00$$

Exhibit 8-4 Marvel Corporation Common Equity Valuation Multiples

Note: When valuing equity directly, these multiples often are presented on a per-share basis. The multiple should be exactly the same whether computed on a per-share or aggregate common equity basis.

Market Value of Equity ("Price")

4,000,000 shares × $6 per share = $24,000,000

Price/Sales (Price/Revenue)

$$\frac{\text{Price}}{\text{Sales}} = \frac{\$24{,}000{,}000}{\$40{,}000{,}000} = 0.60$$

Price/Cash Flow (Price/Gross Cash Flow)

Net Income	$2,112,000
Plus: Depreciation	1,000,000
Cash Flow (gross)	$3,112,000

$$\frac{\text{Price}}{\text{Cash Flow}} = \frac{\$24{,}000{,}000}{\$3{,}112{,}000} = 7.71$$

Price/Pretax Income (Price/Pretax Earnings)

$$\frac{\text{Price}}{\text{Pretax Income}} = \frac{\$24{,}000{,}000}{\$3{,}520{,}000} = 6.82$$

Price/Earnings (Price/Net Income)

$$\frac{\text{Price}}{\text{Net Income}} = \frac{\$24{,}000{,}000}{\$2{,}112{,}000} = 11.36$$

Note: The term price/earnings (P/E), as used in the daily financial press, stock reporting services, and corporate finance, means price to net income after taxes. A common error is to apply the P/E ratio to pretax income. The only condition under which this is justifiable is where it can be assumed that the effective tax rate is zero.

Price/Book Value

$$\frac{\text{Price}}{\text{Book Value of Equity}} = \frac{\$24{,}000{,}000}{\$4{,}000{,}000} = 6.00$$

DECIDING WHERE SUBJECT COMPANY MULTIPLES SHOULD FALL RELATIVE TO OBSERVED GUIDELINE PUBLIC COMPANY MULTIPLES

The appraiser will have developed valuation multiples for several guideline public companies in the same manner as illustrated previously for Marvel Corporation which results in a range for each calculated multiple. For each multiple calculated, the appraiser must select one multiple from the range to apply to the subject company's counterpart financial variable. An important step in evaluating the work of the appraiser is to evaluate how the multiple to be applied to each subject company financial variable was selected.

Relationship between Market Multiples and Capitalization Rates

A *multiple* in the market approach is comparable to a *capitalization rate* in the income approach. A multiple is actually the reciprocal of a capitalization rate; that is, 1 divided by the multiple equals the capitalization rate. Conversely, 1 divided by the capitalization rate equals the multiple.

To illustrate, assume the following:

Guideline company price:	\$20 per share
Guideline company earnings:	\$1 per share

To compute the guideline public company price-to-earnings multiple, divide the price by the earnings:

Formula 8-1

$$\text{P/E Multiple} = \frac{\text{Price}}{\text{Earnings}} = \frac{\$20}{\$1} = 20x$$

To convert the P/E multiple to a capitalization rate, applicable to net income, divide 1 by the P/E multiple:

Formula 8-2

$$\text{Capitalization Rate} = \frac{1}{20} = 0.05$$

To convert the capitalization rate to a multiple, divide 1 by the capitalization rate:

$$\text{P/E Multiple} = \frac{1}{0.05} = 20x$$

Multiplying by the P/E multiple or dividing by the capitalization rate should lead to the same result. For instance, if earnings equal \$10 million, the value of the company will be \$10 × 20 = \$200 million or \$10/0.05 = \$200 million.

The magnitude of the multiple depends largely on two factors: expected growth rate and risk. We know this to be true because growth and risk are two of the inputs that constitute a capitalization rate, which is the inverse of the multiple. With the income approach, the respective factors of risk and expected growth are quantified individually. However, in the market approach, multiples for company variables are observed in the market (i.e., computed from market transaction data), and therefore it is not possible to determine exactly how much any given company's multiple was influenced by expected growth versus perceived risk.

Multiples Selected Based on Comparative Analysis

Analysts typically base the selection of valuation multiples on a comparative analysis between the subject company and the guideline public companies. This usually involves some combination of quantitative and qualitative analysis.

- **Quantitative analysis.** Quantitative data is anything that can be counted or measured and refers to numeric data, telling us how many, how much, or how often in calculations. Exhibit 8-5 is a somewhat abbreviated example of a typical comparative quantitative analysis, using the selected ratios discussed in Chapter 16.
- **Qualitative analysis.** Qualitative data is descriptive, referring to things that can be observed but not measured, helping us to understand why or how. Most of the qualitative factors that the appraiser would consider are those that impact risk. Just as higher risk requires a higher discount rate or capitalization rate in the income approach, higher risk produces lower multiples in the market approach. Some of the common comparative qualitative factors to consider include:
  - Depth of management
  - Concentration versus breadth of customer base
  - Concentration versus breadth of product/service base
  - Concentration versus breadth of geographical operations
  - Comparative cost structure (make sure, however, that the appraiser has not double-counted this both here and in the quantitative analysis)
  - Other effects of size differences, such as buying power, supplier dependence, affordability of advertising, etc.
  - Growth (recently realized and expected) or lack thereof
  - Profitability
  - Audited financial statements of the subject business or not
  - Makeup of board of directors—all internal or external members also

Having conducted a careful comparative analysis, the appraiser may conclude[5] that the characteristics of the subject company are so comparable to the selected guideline public companies that every multiple for every variable should be the median as observed among the guideline public companies. More often than not, however, based on the comparative analysis, the expert will differentiate the subject company from the guideline public companies, resulting in a departure from the median multiples for one or more variables. Some appraisers will remove outlier pricing multiples. In some cases, the comparative financial analysis may indicate that the subject company is most like one, two, or a few of the guideline public companies. In that case, the appraiser may choose multiples close to those of the companies that appear to be more comparable to the subject than others. Some appraisers try to stay away from saying one guideline public company is "most" like the subject company. Some appraisers prefer to show percentiles—10%, 25%, median, 75%, 90%—and then decide on which percentile to use. No matter what quantitative analysis is used to select the appropriate multiples for the subject company, there will always be a degree of professional judgment involved in the selection.

Different Multiples May Be Higher or Lower Relative to Guideline Companies

As noted earlier, expected growth and risk are the two most important determinants of what multiple should be chosen for the subject company relative to the guideline companies. For example, higher leverage and lower coverage of interest obligations would be indications of higher risk.

---

5. In *Bridging the Gap between Public and Private Market Multiples*, Bus. Valuation Rev. 95–101 (Sept. 1998), Richard W. Goeldner II suggests going as far as quantifying all these factors in terms of their impact on risk and potential future growth and suggests that it is not unreasonable for private company multiples to be half of observed public company multiples, or even less.

These differences between subject and guideline public companies may lead to reductions of average multiples, sometimes referred to as a "fundamental discount."

However, criteria for selection of multiples may be influenced by factors other than just expected growth and risk. For example, price-to-sales multiples are heavily influenced by return on sales. This is logical because a company that earns more per dollar of sales (has higher profit margins) is likely to sell for a higher value per dollar of sales. Similarly, return on invested capital will influence the MVIC-to-book value of invested capital multiples, and return on equity will influence the price-to-book value of equity multiples. Similarly, a company that earns more per dollar of book value is likely to sell for a higher value per dollar of book value. For example, a company with a very low return on equity may be operating very conservatively with a low degree of risk and deserve higher than average multiples for some or all income variables, but a below average price-to-book value multiple. Comparing the long-term growth performance of guideline public companies to the subject company may be helpful when deciding on what pricing multiples to use.

RELATIVE WEIGHTS TO ACCORD VARIOUS MULTIPLES

Some valuation multiples are clearly more important for some industries than for others. For example, values of financial assets are very important for valuing financial institutions, while asset values may have very little relevance for most service businesses and professional practices.

One clue to the relative importance of different valuation multiples in any given industry is the degree of central tendency versus dispersion of the multiples observed in the market for that industry. If multiples for a certain variable cluster in a narrow range, that tends to indicate that pricing of companies in that industry tends to depend more on that financial variable than on others. On the other hand, a very wide dispersion among observed multiples suggests that the particular multiple is not very important in that industry.

Another factor to consider is the available data. If data that is needed to compute certain multiples is not available for several of the chosen companies, the appraiser may choose to put less weight on that multiple, even if it might have been considered more important if it were available for more companies.

Also, multiples for certain variables may be accorded little or no weight if they appear to be not very meaningful. For example, if an industry had such a bad year that earnings were minimal (e.g., night clubs and hotels during the Covid-19 pandemic of 2020), resulting in atypical price-to-earnings multiples, the P/E multiple on that year's earnings may be accorded no weight.

ILLUSTRATION OF VALUATION BY MARKET APPROACH

Using the data from Exhibits 8-3 through 8-5, Exhibit 8-6 develops invested capital multiples to apply to Widget Corporation. Exhibit 8-7 develops an indicated value for Widget Corporation using the invested capital procedure. Exhibit 8-8 develops equity multiples to apply to Widget Corporation. Exhibit 8-9 develops an indicated value directly for Widget Corporation's equity. In this illustration, the rationale for the appraiser's various choices is indicated briefly in the footnotes to the tables. In most reports, the rationale would be explained more fully in the text, exploring underlying relationships

Exhibit 8-5 Widget Corporation and Guideline Companies Comparative Financial Analysis

	Guideline Company								
Ratio	**Marvel**	**Neon**	**Optimal**	**Premier**	**Quartz**	**Range**	**Median**	**Widget**	**Comment**
Return on Equity	0.528	0.150	0.700	0.300	0.900	0.150–0.900	0.528	0.700	Above median, but range very wide
Return on Invested Capital	0.240	0.100	0.400	0.200	0.500	0.100–0.500	0.240	0.228	Near median, but range very wide
Return on Sales	0.053	0.030	0.080	0.090	0.040	0.030–0.090	0.053	0.070	Above median
Long-term Debt to Total Capital (at book value)	0.60	0.67	0.32	0.40	0.50	0.32–0.67	0.50	0.75	Highly leveraged, above top of range
Current Ratio	3.0	4.0	3.5	2.5	2.0	2.0–4.0	3.0	3.0	At median
Quick Ratio	1.3	2.0	1.8	1.0	0.8	0.8–2.0	1.3	1.5	Near median
Times Interest Earned (EBIT/Interest Expense)	8.3	2.0	9.8	5.0	4.0	2.0–9.8	5.0	2.3	Near bottom of range

and explaining reasons for the appraiser's judgment. For example, while dispersion of observed multiples for the guideline public companies is a useful quantitative observation, the analytical reasoning and judgment applied may be more important in assigning weights to variables in many cases.

The various multiples within each group (invested capital and equity) produced similar results, but the direct equity procedure produced significantly higher values. The reason is that the company has benefited from a considerably greater degree of leverage than the guideline public companies have. Perhaps this risk should be reflected by equity multiples having greater discounts from the guideline public company median multiples than were actually used. The appraiser in this case was cautiously optimistic and valued the equity at $5.7 million on the basis of a continued good outlook for the company. This value was based on an equal weighting of the two indications of value from the equity and the invested capital procedures. However, most appraisers would choose either an invested capital multiple or equity multiple, but not both.

Exhibit 8-6 Widget Corporation Guideline Company Invested Capital Multiples

	Market Value of Invested Capital (MVIC) to			
	Sales	**EBITDA**	**EBIT**	**Book Value**
Marvel	0.75	4.68	5.55	3.00
Neon	0.40	5.00	6.20	1.50
Optimal	0.80	5.50	6.90	6.00
Premier	0.90	6.00	8.00	2.00
Quartz	0.60	4.80	6.20	3.00
Mean	0.67	5.20	6.33	3.90
Median	0.75	4.80	6.20	3.00
Range	0.40–0.90	4.68–6.00	5.00–8.00	1.50–7.00
Coefficient of Variation	0.263	0.102	0.175	0.631
Multiple Selected	0.80(a)	5.50(b)	6.90(c)	3.00(d)

a. Above median because Widget return on sales above median (Exhibit 8-5).
b. Near median—Widget reasonably comparable to group.
c. Near median—Widget quite comparable to group.
d. At median because Widget return on invested capital near median (Exhibit 8-5).

VARIATIONS FOR SMALLER COMPANIES AND PROFESSIONAL PRACTICE VALUATIONS

Smaller businesses and professional practices have certain characteristics that generally lead to more emphasis on specific variables than might be inappropriate for larger companies. Among the most important of these characteristics are:

- Involvement of the owner
- Lack of good accounting data

Such companies are regularly the subject of valuation disputes in marital dissolution and shareholder disputes. The smaller the company and the greater the role of the owner, the more difficult it often becomes to estimate the economic income of the business. Generally, because of the owner involvement and limited reliable accounting data, more emphasis is often placed on variables toward the "top line" of the income statement (e.g., sales or revenues) versus the "bottom line" of the income statement (e.g., pretax income) in assessing the value of the business. In other words, in valuations of smaller companies and professional practices, price-to-sales multiples become relatively more important than in valuations of larger companies.

Involvement of the Owner

Typically, owners of small businesses and professional practices withdraw enough in compensation that there are no "earnings" left to capitalize. Therefore, using valuation measures that are before owner's compensation avoids the argument about how much is reasonable compensation. Of course, Subchapter S corporations tend to have the opposite issue—officers' compensation is often below market in order to reduce payroll taxes. And owners of single-member limited liability companies do not take W-2 wages at all pursuant to income tax law.

For marital dissolution valuations, ignoring reasonable compensation is fine for states in which any personal goodwill is included in the marital estate. However, in states where only "practice" or "entity" goodwill is included in the marital estate, the issue of reasonable compensation cannot be avoided just by using price-to-sales and price-to-discretionary earnings multiples.

Availability of Comparative Accounting Data

For very small businesses and professional practices, there may be few or no truly comparable guideline public companies to use to develop valuation multiples. The three data sources that provide multiples for smaller businesses and professional practices (*BIZCOMPS*, *ValuSource Market Comps* (previously the IBA Market Database), and *DealStats*) provide a variety of valuation multiples from mostly smaller closely held companies. The three databases that provide data on such small businesses and professional practices have expanded in recent years and now collectively encompass many thousands of transactions, making the market approach for valuing such companies and practices much more feasible than it was in the past.

Exhibit 8-7 Widget Corporation Valuation Using Invested Capital Multiples

	Sales		EBITDA		EBIT	Book Value		Weighted Value of Invested Capital
Widget Corporation Fundamental (as computed for Widget Corporation in Chapter 4)	$10,000,000		$1,550,000		$1,300,000	$4,000,000		
Selected Multiple (from Exhibit 8-6)	× 0.80		× 5.50		× 6.90	× 3.00		
Indicated Value	$8,000,000		$8,525,000		$8,970,000	$12,000,000		
Weight	× 0.20 (a)		0.50 (b)		0.30 (c)	0 (d)		
Weighted Value	$1,600,000	+	$4,262,500	+	$2,691,000		=	$8,553,000
Less: Long-Term Debt								3,000,000
Indicated Value of Common Equity								$5,553,500

a. Deserves some consideration, but profitability ratios more important.
b. Lowest coefficient of variation (Exhibit 8-6)—the variable the industry considers most important.
c. Next lowest coefficient of variation (Exhibit 8-6).
d. No weight. Coefficient of variation very wide, likely because of differences in historical costs and depreciation. Most analysts would not show computations to which they gave no weight, but we show this for illustration only.

Exhibit 8-8 Widget Corporation Guideline Company Equity Multiples

	Market Value of Equity to				
	Sales	**Cash Flow**	**Pretax Income**	**Net Income**	**Book Value**
Marvel	0.60	7.71	6.82	11.36	6.00
Neon	0.30	6.20	5.52	7.78	2.50
Optimal	0.70	7.29	6.21	8.63	7.21
Premier	0.75	8.13	7.04	9.86	2.92
Quartz	0.50	6.83	4.55	6.28	7.50
Mean	0.57	7.23	6.03	8.78	5.23
Median	0.60	7.29	6.03	8.63	6.0
Range	0.30-0.75	6.2-8.13	4.55-7.04	6.28-11.36	2.5-7.5
Coefficient of Variation	0.314	0.104	0.169	0.221	0.543
Multiple Selected	0.65(a)	7.0(b)	5.8(b)	7.5(b)	7.0(c)

a. Above median because Widget return on sales above median (Exhibit 8-5).
b. Slightly below median because of slightly higher risk (Exhibit 8-5).
c. Above median because of above-average return on equity (Exhibit 8-5).

In any case, it often is somewhere between difficult and impossible to develop reliable income data for such subject entities beyond sales, so it may be necessary to limit the market approach multiples to this variable.

PRIOR TRANSACTIONS, OFFERS, AND BUY-SELL AGREEMENTS

One must consider any prior transactions, offers to buy, and buy-sell agreements of the subject company because they sometimes provide some level of market evidence of value and, to some extent, may be utilized in the market approach.

Arm's-Length Negotiations

When considering a prior transaction, an offer, or an agreement, the first question to ask is whether it was negotiated on an arm's-length basis.

If it was between unrelated parties, it is usually assumed to have been negotiated at arm's length. Even among related parties, investigation may lead to the conclusion that there was an arm's-length negotiation. If the degree of arm's-length negotiation cannot be ascertained, an appraiser may make a judgment call about whether it represented fair market value at the time; in which case one can conclude that the parameters are controlling (or at least useful guidance for valuation in the current transaction).

Prior Transactions

If the transactions were reasonably arm's length, prior transactions may be one of the best guides to market value. Such transactions may include:

- Prior purchase or sale of the entire company
- Sales of noncontrolling ownership interests
- Acquisitions of other companies by the subject company

Exhibit 8-9 Widget Corporation Valuation Using Equity Multiples

	Sales	Cash Flow	Pretax Income	Net Income	Book Value	Weighted Value
Widget Corporation Fundamental (as computed for Widget in Chapter 4)	$10,000,000	$ 950,000	$1,000,000	$ 700,000	$1,000,000	
Selected Multiple (from Exhibit 8-8)	× 0.65	× 7.0	× 5.8	× 7.5	× 7.0	
Indicated Value	$6,500,000	$6,650,000	$5,800,000	$5,250,000	$7,000,000	
Weight	× 0.20(a)	× 0.50(b)	× 0.15(c)	× 0.15(d)	× 0(e)	
Weighted Value	$1,300,000	+ $3,325,000	+ $ 870,000	+ $ 787,500		= $6,282,500

a. Deserves some consideration, but profitability ratios more important (also, multiple of sales considered in invested capital ratios, where it may be a more meaningful multiple).
b. Lowest coefficient of variation, clearly the variable the industry considers most important; similar to EBITDA in invested capital ratios.
c.,d. Approximately the industry average effective tax rates and equal coefficients of variation, so equal weight to each but combined, less than cash flow.
e. Very wide coefficient of variation reflecting greatly different leverage and historical cost bases—not a good comparison with guideline companies. Most analysts would not show computations to which they gave no weight, but we show this for illustration only.

These transactions can be analyzed to determine the valuation multiples that the transactions represented at the time. The relevance of the actual prior transaction can be judged based on (1) the time since the transaction; (2) the changes to the company, industry, and economy since that time; and (3) changes in noncash components of the transaction (i.e., change in value over time of real estate component of the value). Adjustments to the actual multiples may be appropriate based on changes in market conditions.

Offers to Buy

If the company received a bona fide firm offer to buy, that offer can be analyzed in the same way as a prior transaction. Such offers should be arm's length, documentable, and have financing in place for the offer. Such bona fide offers that can be used in this manner do occur and the possibility merits an investigation, but they are rare.

Even if an offer appears bona fide on the surface, an investigation of escape clauses and prospective price changes based on due diligence and whether the buyer was legitimately willing and able to complete the transaction may lead to a different conclusion.

Buy-Sell Agreements

A common controversy is the extent to which an existing buy-sell agreement should control or influence the value of any given transaction. This may ultimately be a legal determination, based on the purpose of the appraisal. For example, the buy-sell value may not be controlling for estate tax reporting if it fails to meet certain criteria (see Chapter 20, "Valuations for Gift, Estate, and Charitable Contribution Matters"), even though the buy-sell value is binding on the estate. In marital dissolutions, most courts have great discretion as to how much weight, if any, to accord the buy-sell agreement. One needs to refer to the case law.

DEFINITION OF MARKET VALUE IN SOME FAIR VALUE CASES

In cases where the issue is the fair value in a dissenting stockholder or minority oppression suits, courts tend to look at income value, asset value, and market value. And, in some jurisdictions, the indication of market value may only be based on past transactions.

If this is the precedent in the particular jurisdiction in which the matter is being heard, the multiples of income statement variables derived from the guideline public company method would best be subsumed in the income approach value, and market multiples of asset variables may be considered under an asset-based approach.

SUMMARY

The market approach to business valuation is similar to the sales comparison approach in real estate appraisal where houses are valued by comparing them with other houses that have been sold. Unlike real estate appraisal, business valuation presents unique challenges. These challenges include the valuation of controlling versus noncontrolling interests and the availability of market data. Because reliable market data on noncontrolling interest transactions in closely held companies is not available, the appraiser must use the best data available and make appropriate adjustments accordingly. Such adjustments may include discounts for lack of control and lack of marketability, and their application is dependent on the circumstances of each valuation. The two main valuation methods under the market approach are the guideline transaction method and the guideline public company method. Other less common methods include the prior transaction method, and methods based on bona fide offers and buy-sell agreements.

REFERENCES FOR THE MARKET APPROACH

Basic Market Approach References

Crow, Matthew R. 1999. "Developing Valuation Multiples Using Guideline Companies." In *CPA Litigation Service Counselor* (September): 8–9.

Fishman, Jay E., Bruce A. Johnson, Kent Pummel, et al. 2023. "Valuation Methods Based on Guideline Company Data." In *PPC's Guide to Business Valuations*, 600 (Carrollton, TX: Thomson Reuters).

Fowler, Bradley, A. 1996. "How Do You Handle It?" In *Business Valuation Review* (September): 136–7.

Goeldner, Richard W. 1998. "Bridging the Gap between Public and Private Market Multiples." In *Business Valuation Review* (September): 97–101.

Hitchner, James R. 2017. "Market Approach." In *Financial Valuation: Applications and Models*, 4th ed., Chap. 8, 291–342 (Hoboken, NJ: John Wiley & Sons).

Laro, David and Shannon P. Pratt, 2011. "The Market Approach." In *Business Valuation and Federal Taxes: Procedures, Law and Perspective*, 2nd ed. Chap. 16, 195–242 (Hoboken, NJ: John Wiley & Sons).

Matthews, Gilbert E. 2006. "When Averaging Multiples, Apply the Harmonic Mean." In *Business Valuation Update* 1–4 (June).

Morrison, William J. and Jay E. Fishman. 2017. "Market Approach." In *The Business Valuation Bench Book*, Chap. 6, 69–74 (Portland, OR: Business Valuation Resources).

Nath, Eric W. 1997. "How Public Guideline Companies Represent 'Control' Value for a Private Company." In *Business Valuation Review* (December): 167–71.

Peters, Jerry O. 1999. "Adjusting Price/Earnings Ratios for Differences in Company Size." In *Business Valuation Review* (June): 71–85.

Pratt, Shannon P. and ASA Educational Foundation. 2022. "Guideline Public Company Method," and "Guideline Transaction Method." In *Shannon Pratt's Valuing a Business: The Analysis and Appraisal of Closely Held Businesses*, 6th ed., Chap. 13, 283–323; Chap. 14, 325–41 (Hoboken, NJ: John Wiley & Sons).

Pratt, Shannon P. 2000. "Controversies Involving the Market Approach to Business Valuation; Raising the Issues, Soliciting Feedback." *In Shannon Pratt's Business Valuation Update* (November).

—. 2005. The *Market Approach to Valuing Business*, 2nd ed. (Hoboken, NJ: John Wiley & Sons).

Pratt, Shannon P. and Alina V. Niculita. 2006. *The Market Approach to Valuing Businesses Workbook*, 2nd ed. (New York: John Wiley & Sons).

Ross, Franz. 2004. "'Just One Thing': The Most Reliable Variable for Use in the Market Approach." In *Shannon Pratt's Business Valuation Update* (August).

Sheeler, Carl L. 2004. "The Market Approach: A Neglected and Misunderstood Aspect of Business Value." In *Journal of Financial Planning* (May): Article 7.

—. 2004. "A Misunderstood Aspect of Business Value: The Market Approach." In *The CPA Journal* (October).
Trugman, Gary. 2022. "The Market Approach—Part I," and "The Market Approach—Part II." In *Understanding Business Valuation*, 6th ed., Chap. 9, 297–362; Chap. 10, 363–401 (Portland, OR: Business Valuation Resources).
—. 2003. "Guideline Public Company Method-Control or Minority Value?" *Shannon Pratt's Business Valuation Update* (December).
Wise, Richard. 2003. "Application of the Market Approach in Valuing a Canadian Business." Presentation to the 22nd Annual Advanced Business Valuation Conference of the American Society of Appraisers, (October).
—. 2004. "Caveats for Market Approach." In *CA Magazine* (January-February).
—. 1996. "Multiple-of-Revenues as a Valuation Method." In *Business Valuation Digest* (October): 1–4.

Private and Public Company Sale Databases

S&P Capital IQ®, www.spglobal.com. Capital IQ provides information on both public and private companies, in the USA and internationally sourced from SEC filings.

ValuSource M&A Comps, www.valusource.com. Previously named *DoneDeals*, this database includes middle-market transactions consisting of private companies acquired by public companies collected from SEC filings.

Pitchbook™, www.pitchbook.com. This is an online searchable database of public and private equity transactions, including deal structure and history and pricing information.

FactSet Mergerstat/BVR Control Premium Study, www.bvresources.com. FactSet Mergerstat/BVR Control Premium Study compiles information on publicly announced mergers, acquisitions, and divestitures involving operating entities. In addition, this database tracks acquisition premiums for completed transactions involving public target companies where a controlling interest was acquired.

BIZCOMPS, www.bizcomps.com. This database provides data for small, Main Street-type businesses in the United States that it sources from business brokers. It provides price to sales and price to discretionary earnings ratios.

ValuSource Market Comps (previously the IBA Market Database), www.valusource.com. This database consists of mainly small, private company transactions in the United States sourced from the business intermediaries community. It provides price to sales and price to discretionary earnings ratios, mostly small businesses and professional practices.

DealStats, www.bvresources.com. This database combined two databases previously named Pratt's Stats and Public Stats and it consists of both private and public company transactions sourced from business intermediaries and from SEC filings. It provides six invested capital valuation multiples already computed, and information for most companies to compute all market valuation ratios discussed in this chapter.

Peercomps, peercomps.gvalue.com. This database includes private business transactions compiled from Small Business Administration (SBA) lenders curated to exclude distressed businesses and investment value transactions. As of this writing, the database includes more than 14,000 transactions adjusted to reflect an asset sale structure. Multiples available include Price/EBITDA, Price/SDE, and Price/Revenues.[6]

---

6. Jim Turner, *Peercomps: One of the Most Reliable Guideline Company Transaction Databases*, The Value Examiner 20–23 (Nov./Dec. 2023).

Public Company Data

EDGAR (Electronic Data Gathering, Analysis, and Retrieval), www.sec.gov/edgar. There are more than 20,000 publicly traded operating companies, all of which report data electronically to the Securities and Exchange Commission on a system called EDGAR. This data is free to the public.

Yahoo Finance, www.finance.yahoo.com. Yahoo finance offers an equity screening tool. The analyst can search stocks by industry, market capitalization, size, growth, and other criteria.

TagniFi, www.tagnifi.com. You can use TagniFi to search for guideline public companies by industry, market capitalization, size, business description, and other criteria. TagniFi also offers earnings consensus estimates. The database links to the original reported financial statement line items in the SEC source document. TagniFi offers an Excel plugin that helps develop public company data tables.

Pitchbook™, www.pitchbook.com. This is an online searchable database of public and private equity transactions, including deal structure and history and pricing information. Analysts can screen for public companies using several search criteria and the platform offers an excel plugin tool to help create spreadsheets. The platform offers financial details sourced from SEC filings and financial analyst estimates.

Business Valuation Resources: Guideline Public Company Comps Tool, www.bvresources.com/products/guideline-public-company-comps-tool. The analysts have access to financial statements, financial ratios, and multiples for guideline public companies. The database allows for screening using several search criteria. The tool includes an Excel plugin and provides suggested public company peer sets based upon guideline public companies used in SEC fairness opinions.

Other Resources: See Chapter 17, "Economic and Industry Analysis."

CHAPTER 9

The Asset-Based Approach

Roger J. Grabowski, FASA

INTRODUCTION

In this chapter you will learn about:

- Basic concepts of the asset-based approach
- Procedure for implementing the asset-based approach
- An illustration of applying the asset accumulation method
- Reliance on experts providing input into asset-based approach
- When using an asset-based approach is useful

The basic concept of the asset-based approach is that if all the company's assets and liabilities are revalued to current values, then the difference between the assets and the liabilities should equal the value of the equity.[1]

The asset-based approach generally is assumed to produce a control basis value because only a control owner has the prerogative of accessing the value of the company's underlying assets. From this value, if one is valuing a noncontrolling interest, it may be appropriate to adjust for factors such as a discount for lack of control and a discount for lack of marketability, as discussed in Chapter 18, "Discounts and Premiums." If one is valuing a controlling interest, it may or may not be appropriate to deduct a discount for lack of liquidity, although it would be a smaller discount than a discount for lack of marketability for a noncontrolling interest, as discussed in Chapter 18.

DISCRETE VERSUS COLLECTIVE REVALUATION

If each asset and liability is individually identified and valued, that method may be called, for instance, the *net asset value method*, the *adjusted net asset value method*, the *adjusted net worth method*, the *adjusted book value method*, the *asset build-up method*, the *asset accumulation method*, or some similar method.[2] For the purpose of this chapter, we will refer to the discrete revaluation of all assets as the *asset accumulation method*. The premise of value may be either going concern or liquidation.

---

1. The terms *asset-based approach* and *asset approach* are synonymous.

2. For a more extensive discussion, *see* Chapter 16, "Asset-Based Approach: Asset Accumulation Method," in Shannon P. Pratt & ASA Educ. Found., Shannon Pratt's Valuing a Business: The Analysis and Appraisal of Closely Held Businesses (6th ed. 2022).

In collective revaluation of assets, the tangible assets (or at least the preponderance of them) usually are adjusted to current values, as discussed in subsequent sections of this chapter. The intangibles then are valued collectively by capitalizing any amount of return that the company achieves over and above a fair return on its tangible assets at their current values. This method is called the *excess earnings method,* which assumes a going-concern premise of value and is discussed separately as the subject of the next chapter.

In some cases, only a partial revaluation of assets is practical. There are too many variations on this possibility to go into details and the reviewer is left to judge whether the conclusions reached are adequately supported.

STEPS IN THE ASSET ACCUMULATION METHOD

The six basic steps are as follows:

1. **Obtain or develop an accrual basis balance sheet.** If the entity maintains its accounting on a Generally Accepted Accounting Principles (GAAP) basis, no adjustments are necessary to conform to GAAP. If the company maintains its accounting on a cash basis, then adjustments to the accrual basis are necessary.
2. **Determine which assets and liabilities on the GAAP-basis balance sheet require revaluation.** Assets with no realizable value, such as deferred finance points that were capitalized and are being amortized over the life of the loan, typically have a value equal to zero. Other assets that are being amortized for income tax purposes should be included as the future amortization will result in actual income tax savings.
3. **Identify any off-balance sheet actual or contingent assets or liabilities. This could be an unlimited list, but some of the more common items include:**
    - Assets fully depreciated but still in service
    - Inventory or accounts receivable written off by accounting policy but still salable or collectible; alternatively unsaleable inventory and uncollectible accounts receivable that are still on the books
    - Intellectual property developed internally and therefore expensed instead of capitalized
    - Workforce in place, systems, and similar elements of "going-concern value"
    - Goodwill
    - Expected proceeds or costs related to existing or potential lawsuits
    - Environmental liabilities
    - Warranty liabilities
    - Deferred compensation agreements
    - Liability for corporate capital gains taxes on appreciated assets[3]
4. **Value the items identified in Steps 2 and 3.** This may require appraisals by asset appraisers, for appraisal of real estate and/or machinery and equipment would not be a skill possessed by most business appraisers. Later we discuss steps that should be taken by the business appraiser when relying on reports prepared by others.

---

3. U.S. income tax cases have begun to recognize all or some portion of this liability. *See, e.g.*, Est. of Jelke v. Comm'r, 507 F.3d 1317 (11th Cir. 2007); Est. of Davis v. Comm'r, 110 T.C. 530 (1998); Eisenberg v. Comm'r, T.C.M. 1997-483, 74 T.C.M. (CCH) 1046 (1997); Est. of Simplot v. Comm'r, 112 T.C. No. 13, 1999 WL 152610 (1999). Family law courts have been reluctant to recognize this liability unless sale is imminent. *See, e.g.*, Granger v. Granger, 579 N.E.2d 1319 (Ind. Ct. App. 1991); *In re* Marriage of Hay, 907 P.2d 334 (Wash. Ct. App. 1995); Crooker v. Crooker, 432 A.2d 1293 (Me. 1981).

5. **Include a deferred tax liability for appreciated assets that will be liquidated.**
6. **Construct a market value–based balance sheet using the adjusted values.** The net result of this should be the market value of the equity. In other words, the difference between the market value of assets and the market value of liabilities equals the market value of equity.

VALUATION PREMISES FOR ADJUSTING BALANCE SHEET VALUES

Generally speaking, each item will be valued on one of the following four premises of value:

1. **Value in continued use, as part of a going concern.** This usually means either *used replacement cost*, including installation, or *replacement cost new* less depreciation, amortization, and/or adjustments for obsolescence.
2. **Value in place, as part of a mass assemblage of assets.** This generally would be used for a manufacturing plant in working order but not currently operating because of market conditions, bankruptcy, or other various reasons.
3. **Value in exchange, in an orderly liquidation.** This may be appropriate for all assets if an orderly liquidation is contemplated for the entire company. If the company is being valued as a going concern, an orderly liquidation premise may be appropriate for nonoperating or excess assets.
4. **Value in exchange, in a forced liquidation.** This may be appropriate if, for example, it was assumed that the assets would be sold piecemeal at auction.

ILLUSTRATIVE ASSET ACCUMULATION METHOD

Exhibit 9-1 shows an example of an asset accumulation method, adjusting the balance sheet resulting in an adjusted net asset value. There would be an explanation in either the text or footnotes for each item added to the balance sheet or adjusted from its original balance sheet value.

Exhibit 9-1 Alpha Company Adjusted Net Asset Value

Assets	As Reported	Adjustments	As Adjusted
Cash & Marketable Securities	$100,000	$30,000(a)	$130,000
Inventory	200,000	50,000(b)	250,000
Total Current Assets	$300,000		$380,000
Property & Equipment	70,000		70,000
Land Held for Expansion	150,000	100,000(c)	250,000
Total Assets	$520,000		$700,000
Liabilities & Equity			
Accounts Payable	$50,000		$50,000
Long-Term Debt	200,000	−20,000(d)	180,000
Corporate Taxes		30,000(e)	30,000

Assets	As Reported	Adjustments	As Adjusted
Total Liabilities	$250,000		$260,000
Stockholders' Equity	270,000		440,000
Total Liabilities	$520,000		$700,000

a. To adjust to market prices as of the effective valuation date
b. To adjust from LIFO to FIFO cost basis as of the effective valuation date
c. To adjust land to appraised market value as of the effective valuation date
d. To reduce the value of the long-term debt (with interest rate of 8%) to current market value (in light of current market interest rate of 10% on other comparable debt)
e. To record the corporate tax liability on the difference between the assets' cost basis and current market value

BREAKUP VALUE

Some companies may have two or more operating entities and possibly some nonoperating assets. The stock market tends to value such public companies at less than the collective value of each operating company plus the nonoperating assets.

In considering a possible acquisition of such a company, the acquirer might like to estimate what could be realized by selling each of the operating companies and the nonoperating assets separately. This is called the breakup value.

Studies have shown that conglomerates tend to sell at a discount from their breakup values. Investors seem to prefer a "pure play" in an industry over a package of dissimilar companies or assets. One variation on the asset approach is to estimate a company's breakup value.

RELIANCE ON EXPERTS

In preparing an adjusted balance sheet for use in the asset accumulation method of the asset-based approach, the business appraiser often needs to rely on current estimates of the value of the underlying assets provided by others (e.g., real property, machinery, and equipment). Another source of valuation estimates may be from the disclosures of fair values for tangible and intangible assets in the financial statements.[4]

In relying on current valuations or fair value disclosures, the appraiser is placing reliance on the opinions of other valuation specialists (appraisers from other disciplines). The *Uniform Standards of Professional Appraisal Practice* (USPAP) Standards Rule 10-3(c) provides guidance to the business appraiser to assist in determining the competence of other valuation specialists.[5]

Among the factors the business appraiser must consider before relying upon reports prepared by others, are the following:

4. Fair values for financial reporting purposes was discussed in Chapter 1 and in the next section of this chapter.

5. *See* Chapter 37, "Business Valuation Standards and Credentials," for a discussion of USPAP; *see also* The Appraisal Found., 2024 USPAP Guidance and Reference Manual 252, *Frequently Asked Question 271, Replying on Reports of Others.*

- Is there a reasonable basis for believing the specialist(s) preparing the report(s) are competent to value the subject assets?
- Is there any reason to doubt the credibility of the specialist's report being relied upon?

In assessing the competence of another specialist, the business appraiser relies on such factors as the specialist's credentials, education, and/or experience. Additionally, in assessing whether to rely on the specialist's report, the business appraiser may inquire about instructions provided to the specialist by the client and whether there were any restrictions on the scope of work performed by the specialist that the business appraiser does not find reasonable for the business appraiser's use. Finally, the business appraiser might become aware of reasons to doubt the credibility of the specialist, whether due to bias on the part of the specialist or the specialist lacking expertise.

When a business appraiser relies on reports prepared by others, the business appraiser's report is likely to include a statement that they have done so, that they are not opining on the value of those particular subject assets, and that if the value of those assets were different, the business appraisal conclusion might be different. The business appraiser's report may refer to this as an "extraordinary assumption," which is a term with specific meaning within business appraisal professional standards.

Furthermore, the business appraiser may need to perform additional procedures to evaluate the information drawn from reports prepared by others. For example, if the business appraiser is using fair value disclosures in the asset accumulation method, the business appraiser may look back at prior financial statements to determine when the fair value disclosures were prepared to determine whether they likely represent reasonable estimates of current values. When the business appraiser relies on fair value disclosures in audited financial statements, the business appraiser still needs to apply a degree of professional skepticism before using the reported values. Inclusion of such values in audited financial statements might not guarantee that the fair values are correct as evidenced by reports of the Public Company Accounting Oversight Board (PCAOB).[6]

When Are Asset-Based Methods Used?

There are numerous reasons why application of the asset-based method may be required. They are generally related to financial reporting, tax reporting, litigation, or advisory.[7]

Financial Reporting

The issuance of Accounting Standards Codification (ASC) ASC 805 *Business Combinations*[8] expanded financial reporting requirements for measuring assets of acquired businesses at fair value (as defining for financial reporting).[9] Buyers are generally required

6. The PCAOB oversees the audit quality of public companies. In their reports, fair value disclosures have often been cited by PCAOB as an area of audit failure. The most recent report was published in December 2023, available at https://pcaobus.org; under Resources—staff publications "Spotlight: Observations from Target Team's 2022 Inspections." Such failures might occur more often in audits of closely held companies that lack PCAOB oversight.

7. This section is adapted from Pratt & ASA Educ. Found., *supra* note 2, at 676–77. Used with permission.

8. Accounting Standards Update *Business Combinations* (Topic 805); requirements parallel those of International Financial Reporting Standards 13 *Fair Value Measurement* (International Accounting Standards Board, May 2011).

9. As defined in Accounting Standards Codification Topic 820, *Fair Value Measurement* (ASC 820), discussed in Chapter 1.

to value all assets including identifiable intangible assets when they are acquired.[10] The buyer determines the fair value of the purchase consideration for the business, then allocates that value among the acquired tangible and intangible assets for recognition on its opening balance sheet. This type of valuation is often referred to as a purchase price allocation.

The costs of compliance with ASC 805 may be significant for closely held (private) companies. Given these cost concerns, ASC 805-20-25-30 (June 15, 2023) allows closely held companies to elect an accounting alternative for the recognition of identifiable intangible assets acquired in a business combination. Closely held companies that make this election are not required to value customer-related intangible assets as well as other identifiable intangible assets (unless they are capable of being sold or licensed independent from the other assets of the acquired business; e.g., trade names) or noncompete agreements as a part of business combination accounting.

Income Tax Reporting

U.S. tax laws give rise to several situations where valuations of tangible and intangible assets may be required.

Internal Revenue Code (I.R.C.) § 482 provides rules regarding transfer pricing. Section 482 requires that related-party transactions involving the transfer of intangible assets "yield results that are consistent with the results that would have been realized if uncontrolled taxpayers had engaged in the same transaction under the same circumstances."[11] Therefore, in related-party transactions, intangible assets may need to be valued for transfer-pricing purposes. See discussion in Chapter 21, "Valuations for Federal Income Tax Matters."

Unlike the requirements for amortization of intangible assets for financial reporting purposes, which lead to differing amortization periods for different intangible assets, I.R.C. § 197 specifies that taxpayers may amortize the tax basis of acquired intangible assets and goodwill ratably over a 15-year period. Even if their economic lives are different, the tax treatment of different types of intangible assets is generally the same under § 197. The taxpayer's calculation of the § 197 basis of its intangible assets and goodwill is also a residual calculation. As all intangibles have a 15-year amortization period, measurement of the economic life and value of specific intangible assets is not necessary.

Litigation

The asset accumulation method is not used very often for valuation of operating entities, particularly in noncontrolling interest appraisals. The focus for operating entities tends to be more on the income approach, the market approach, or the excess earnings method (discussed in Chapter 10).

However, in a number of situations, the courts do reach a valuation conclusion either entirely or partially on valuation by the asset-based approach. These may include but are not limited to:

---

10. Intangible assets are said to be identifiable if they arise out of contractual or legal rights or if they are separable from the business and capable of being sold, licensed, transferred, rented, or exchanged. *See* ASC 805-20-20 under *Identifiable*.

11. www.irs.gov/businesses/international-businesses/transfer-pricing

- Start-up companies
- Holding companies, financial institutions, agricultural businesses, and other asset-intensive businesses
- Marital estate valuations of companies or practices in which all goodwill is personal and the state's case law does not consider personal goodwill a marital asset
- Companies that may not be financially viable as operating companies

In one marital dissolution, for example, the husband owned two start-up companies. The husband's lawyer moved to strike the testimony of the wife's expert, who used the discounted cash flow method, even though the projections had been made by the husband. The trial court granted the motion and was upheld on appeal, "because the expert's projections and opinion were overly speculative and by implication, unreliable," leaving only the testimony on asset value on which the trial court had based its conclusion.[12]

Advisory and Consulting

Valuations of assets are also sometimes performed in an advisory or consulting capacity. For example, if a business is evaluating the purchase or sale of a self-created intangible asset or a group of intangible assets or even self-created equipment that embodies self-created intellectual property, the business may consult external professionals to support valuations.

SUMMARY

The asset accumulation method is a common method under the asset-based approach. The theoretical underpinning of this method is simple: the value of the business enterprise is the value of the business assets less the value of the business liabilities (both tangible and intangible, recorded and contingent).

Application of the asset accumulation method involves the separate identification and individual valuation of all business asset categories and the identification and valuation of all business liability categories. In these individual asset and liability valuations, it is important that the appraiser applies both (1) a standard of value and (2) a premise of value that are consistent with the purpose and objective of the business enterprise valuation.

It is conceptually incorrect to automatically conclude that the value of a business is based only on the value of its tangible assets. Likewise, it is also conceptually incorrect to conclude that the value of a business is equal to its accounting book value—without the use of generally accepted valuation procedures and rigorous fundamental analyses to support that conclusion.

REFERENCES FOR ASSET-BASED APPROACH

Fishman, Jay E., Bruce Johnson, Kent Pummel, et al. 2023. "Net Asset Value Method," and "Liquidation Value Method." In PPC's *Guide to Business Valuations*, 702, 703 (Carrollton, TX: Thomson Reuters).

12. Shooltz v. Shooltz, 27 Va. App. 264, 498 S.E.2d 437 (1998).

Hitchner, James R. 2017. "Asset Approach." In *Financial Valuation: Applications and Models*, 4th ed., Chap. 9, 343–89 (Hoboken, NJ: John Wiley & Sons, Inc.).

Laro, David and Shannon P. Pratt, 2011. "The Asset-Based Approach." In *Business Valuation and Federal Taxes: Procedures, Law and Perspective*, 2nd ed. Chap. 17, 243–8 (Hoboken, NJ: John Wiley & Sons).

Morrison, William J. and Jay E. Fishman. 2017. "Asset-Based Approach." In *The Business Valuation Bench Book*, Chap. 4, 55–9 (Portland, OR: Business Valuation Resources.

Pratt, Shannon P. and ASA Educational Foundation. 2022. "Asset-Based Approach: Asset Accumulation Method." In *Shannon Pratt's Valuing a Business: The Analysis and Appraisal of Closely Held Businesses*, 6th ed., Chap. 16, 361–81 (New York: McGraw-Hill).

Trugman, Gary. 2022. "The Asset-Based Approach." In *Understanding Business Valuation*, 6th ed., Chap. 11, 403–40 (Portland, OR: Business Valuation Resources).

CHAPTER 10

The Excess Earnings Method

Roger J. Grabowski, FASA

INTRODUCTION

In this chapter you will learn about:

- Background of the excess earnings method
- Procedures in implementing the excess earnings method
- A critique of Revenue Ruling 68–609
- Common errors in applying the excess earnings method

Even though the excess earnings method as specified in Revenue Ruling 68–609 is considered the valuation method of last resort by the Internal Revenue Service (IRS) and many in the business appraisal profession, it is one of the most widely used and abused of all business valuation methods because there are many components within its development that are subjective or misunderstood. It is used most often for valuing small businesses and professional practices and is especially popular among appraisers performing valuations for property settlements in marital dissolutions.

BACKGROUND OF THE EXCESS EARNINGS METHOD

The excess earnings method is sometimes called the Treasury method because this valuation method originally appeared in a 1920 publication by the U.S. Treasury Department, *Appeals and Review Memorandum Number 34* (ARM 34). It was adopted to estimate the intangible value of goodwill lost by breweries and distilleries forced out of business because of the legal imposition of prohibition in the United States. In 1968, the IRS updated and restated ARM 34 into Revenue Ruling 68–609, which is discussed in a subsequent section.

Keep in mind that the excess earnings method originally was created for the purpose of valuing intangible assets, not for valuing a company as a whole. Consequently, perhaps the most appropriate application of the excess earnings method is for allocating total value between tangible and intangible assets. Examples of this include:

- Divorce cases in jurisdictions where goodwill value is considered a separate, personal asset rather than a marital asset and therefore needs to be separated from the value of the business or practice
- Conversions from Subchapter C corporations to Subchapter S corporations

- Eminent domain cases, in which the tangible and intangible values need to be recognized separately
- Property tax cases, in which a company's tangible assets are subject to property tax but its intangible assets are not
- Damage cases, such as a breach of a patent or trademark

BASIC STEPS IN THE EXCESS EARNINGS METHOD

The basic steps in the excess earnings method are summarized as follows:

Step 1. Estimate a normalized level of earnings or cash flow.

Step 2. Estimate the net tangible asset value for the subject company as of the effective valuation date. (The net tangible asset value usually is defined as the fair market value of the tangible assets minus the liabilities.)

Step 3. Estimate a rate of return that would be required to support the tangible assets used in the business.

Step 4. Multiply the value of net tangible assets (from Step 2) by the required rate of return on net tangible assets (from Step 3). This is the dollar amount of return required to support the net tangible assets employed in the business.

Step 5. Subtract the required dollar amount of return on tangible assets (from Step 4) from the estimated normalized earnings (from Step 1). This is the "excess earnings" or the earnings attributable to the entity's intangible assets.

Step 6. Select a capitalization rate that is an appropriate required return on intangible assets (excess earnings).

Step 7. Divide the excess earnings by the excess earnings capitalization rate (from Step 6). This is the value of the excess earnings, thus the implied value of the entity's intangible assets.

Step 8. Add the entity's intangible value (from Step 7) to the entity's net tangible asset value (from Step 2). This is the total value of the business or professional practice, generally assumed to represent a 100% controlling ownership value.

Note: In a sense, the excess earnings method is viewed by many as a subset of the net asset value method, by adding the derived value of the intangible assets to the value of the net tangible assets. Most of the time, this method is regarded as a hybrid method.

APPLYING THE EXCESS EARNINGS METHOD

Exhibit 10-1 illustrates the estimation of the value of an entity by the excess earnings method.

Exhibit 10-1 Illustration of Excess Earnings Method

Step 1. Estimated normalized net cash flow		$ 25,000
Step 2. Estimated net tangible asset value	$100,000	
Step 3. Estimated required rate of return to support tangible assets	15%	
Step 4. Dollar amount of required rate of return on tangible assets		$15,000
Step 5. Dollar amount of excess earnings (Step 1 minus Step 4)		$10,000
Step 6. Capitalization rate applicable to excess earnings		25%
Step 7. Value of intangible assets, estimated as capitalized excess earnings (Step 5 amount divided by Step 6 rate—$10,000 divided by .25)		$40,000
Step 8. Total value of entity: valuation of intangible assets (capitalized excess earnings, from Step 7) plus value of net tangible assets (from Step 2)		100,000
Total value of entity		$140,000

Step 1. Estimate a normalized level of *economic income* (e.g., normalized net income as the measure of economic income, discussed in Chapter 6, "The Income Approach") that is expected to be sustainable into the future.[1] The analyst's report should show how the normalized economic income was estimated and what definition of economic income was used (for example, net income, net cash flow, etc.).

Step 2. Estimate the net tangible asset value, which means adjusting each tangible asset and each liability to its current value (as of the valuation date), usually fair market value on a going-concern basis, and then subtract the liabilities from the adjusted asset values. The analyst's report should show each adjustment that was made to the balance sheet and the basis for each adjustment.

Step 3. Estimate the rate of return that would be required to support the tangible assets. This rate normally would be higher than the company's bank borrowing rate. Banks will almost never lend 100% of the value of tangible assets. Therefore, the rate to support assets usually needs to be some blend (weighting) of the company's cost of debt and its higher cost of equity (as discussed in Chapter 7, "Developing a Discount Rate"). The appraiser's report should show the computations made to estimate the required rate of return on tangible assets. It is preferable that a rate of return for each discrete asset be selected to arrive at a weighted average rate of return for all net tangible assets.

1. IRS Revenue Ruling 68-609 describes economic income as "earnings" without defining the term. This is discussed later in this chapter.

Step 4. Multiply the required rate of return on net tangible assets from Step 3 times their net tangible asset value from Step 2.

Step 5. Subtract the dollar amount of the required return on net tangible assets from Step 4 from the estimated normalized economic income from Step 1.

Step 6. Develop a capitalization rate applicable to the excess earnings. This is the most subjective step in the process.

The capitalization rate usually will be at or above the high end of reasonable equity capitalization rates for the entire company, as discussed in Chapter 7. To put it in perspective, the reciprocal of the excess earnings capitalization rate is the number of years' worth of expected future excess earnings the buyer can be expected to pay to acquire the business or professional practice (sometimes called the *payback period*). For example, a capitalization rate of 25% (i.e., 0.25) means that a buyer would be willing to pay four years' worth of expected future excess earnings:

$$\frac{1}{0.25} = 4 \text{ years}$$

If a buyer would only be willing to pay for 90 days' worth of expected future excess earnings (perhaps typical for buying something such as a vending route), the capitalization rate would be 400%:

$$\frac{1}{0.25 \text{ years (1/4 of a year)}} = 4.0 = 400\%$$

An alternative method of estimating the capitalization rate for excess earnings is to use something above the normal equity capitalization rate, recognizing that the "excess" portion of the earnings is the riskiest part.

The appraiser's report should explain how the capitalization rate for excess earnings was developed.

Step 7. Divide the estimated dollar amount of excess earnings from Step 5 by the excess earnings capitalization rate from Step 6.

Note: The excess earning method represents the "big pot" theory of intangible value, that is, the values of individual intangible assets are not separately identified; instead, they are lumped into one figure.[2] This figure frequently is referred to as the entity's goodwill. However, more narrowly, goodwill is defined as the propensity of customers to return to the business, that is, the expectation of continued patronage. The value of excess earnings really is a somewhat broader concept, usually including other intangible assets besides goodwill in the more narrowly defined sense. Exhibit 10-2 shows a variety of definitions of goodwill.

Step 8. Add both the net tangible asset portion from Step 2 and the intangible asset portion of the value of the entity from Step 7.

2. Normally, this means all intangible assets. It is possible, however, that certain specific intangible assets may be identified and valued separately.

Exhibit 10-2 Definitions of Goodwill

Black's Law Dictionary shows a variety of definitions of goodwill:

Goodwill. The favor which the management of a business wins from the public. The favorable consideration shown by the purchasing public to goods or services known to emanate from a particular source. White Tower System v. White Castle System of Eating Houses Corporation, C.C.A. Mich., 90 F 2d 67, 69. Property of an intangible nature, commonly defined as the expectation of continued public patronage. *In re* Marriage of Lukens, 16 Wash. App. 481, 558 P.2d 279, 280.

The custom of patronage of any established trade or business; the benefit or advantage of having established a business and secured its patronage by the public. And as property incident to business sold, favor vendor has won from public, and probability that all customers will continue their patronage. It means every positive advantage that has been acquired by a proprietor in carrying on his business, whether connected with the premises in which the business is conducted, or with the name under which it is managed, or with any other matter carrying with it the benefit of the business.

The excess of cost of an acquired firm or operating unit over the current or fair market value of net assets of the acquired unit. Informally used to indicate the value of good customer relations, high employee morale, a well-respected business name, etc., which are expected to result in greater than normal earning power.

The ability of a business to generate income in excess of normal rate on assets, due to superior managerial skills, market position, new product technology, etc. The capacity to earn profits in excess of a normal rate of return due to establishment of favorable community reputation and consumer identification of the business name. North Clackamas Community Hospital v. Harris, C.A. Or., 664 F 2d 701, 706.

As applied to law firms, term refers to ability to attract clients as result of firm's name, location, or the reputation of lawyers. Bump v. Stewart, Wimer & Bump, P.C., Iowa, 336 NW 2d 731, 736.

For accounting purposes, goodwill has no basis unless it is purchased. In the purchase of a business, goodwill generally is the difference between the purchase price and the value of the assets acquired.[3]

A "SANITY CHECK" FOR VALIDITY OF AN EXCESS EARNINGS METHOD VALUE

The overall company capitalization rate implied by the value indicated by the excess earnings method should, theoretically, equal the company's overall capitalization rate (i.e., incorporating a weighted-average cost of capital as the discount rate in developing the capitalization rate, as described in Chapter 7). If the implied overall capitalization rate is greater than what would be indicated by conventional income approach methods, the excess earnings method indication of value may be too low. Conversely, if the implied overall capitalization rate is less than what would be indicated by conventional

3. Goodwill, Black's Law Dictionary (6th ed. 1991).

income approach methods, the excess earnings method indication of value may be too high. An illustration of applying this test for reasonableness is shown in Exhibit 10-3.

Exhibit 10-3 A "Sanity Check" for a Value Indicated by the Excess Earnings Method

Company overall capitalization rate implied by the excess earnings method valuation shown in Exhibit 10-1:

$$\frac{\text{Estimated normalized net cash flow}}{\text{Indicated entity value}} = \frac{\$25{,}000}{\$140{,}000} = 0.179$$

The "sanity check" would be to develop a capitalization rate by the build-up method or MCAPM procedures shown in Chapter 7. Then, for example, if the capitalization rate were 19.0 percent, this would be only 1.1 percentage points above the rate implied in the excess earnings method valuation. This is very close. If one were to capitalize the company's normalized net cash flow of $25,000 at 19.0 percent, the indicated value would be $131,579, very close to the $140,000 indicated by the excess earnings method. If, however, the results were significantly different (for example, several percentage points difference in the capitalization rate), then the assumptions supporting each step of the process should be examined carefully.

Alternatively, if one has developed the excess earnings capitalization rate by adding an additional risk premium to the equity capitalization rate developed by the build-up method, CAPM or MCAPM procedure, then the payback period might be used as the reasonableness check. (The payback period was discussed in conjunction with Step 6 of the excess earnings method.)

Critique of Excess Earnings Method in Revenue Ruling 68–609

In 1968, the IRS updated and restated the ARM 34 valuation method. This occurred with the publication of IRS Revenue Ruling 68–609, which is reproduced as Exhibit 10-4. Revenue Ruling 68–609 is still in effect today.

Exhibit 10-4 Revenue Ruling 68–609

SECTION 1001. - DETERMINATION OF AMOUNT OF AND RECOGNITION OF GAIN OR LOSS

26 CFR 1.1001-1: Computation of gain or loss. (Also Section 167; 1.167(a)-3.)

1968-2 C.B. 327; 1968 IRB LEXIS 239; REV. RUL. 68-609 July, 1968

The "formula" approach may be used in determining the fair market value of intangible assets of a business only if there is no better basis available for making the determination; A.R.M. 34, A.R.M. 68, O.D. 937, and Revenue Ruling 65-192 superseded.

The purpose of this Revenue Ruling is to update and restate, under the current statute and regulations, the currently outstanding portions of A.R.M. 34, C.B. 2, 31 (1920),

A.R.M. 68, C.B. 3, 43 (1920), and O.D. 937, C.B. 4, 43 (1921).

The question presented is whether the "formula" approach, the capitalization of earnings in excess of a fair rate of return on net tangible assets, may be used to determine the fair market value of the intangible assets of a business.

The "formula" approach may be stated as follows:

A percentage return on the average annual value of the tangible assets used in a business is determined, using a period of years (preferably not less than five) immediately prior to the valuation date. The amount of the percentage return on tangible assets, thus determined, is deducted from the average earnings of the business for such period and the remainder, if any, is considered to be the amount of the average annual earnings from the intangible assets of the business for the period. This amount (considered as the average annual earnings from intangibles), capitalized at a percentage of, say, 15 to 20 percent, is the value of the intangible assets of the business determined under the "formula" approach.

The percentage of return on the average annual value of the tangible assets used should be the percentage prevailing in the industry involved at the date of valuation, or (when the industry percentage is not available) a percentage of 8 to 10 percent may be used.

The 8 percent rate of return and the 15 percent rate of capitalization are applied to tangibles and intangibles, respectively, of businesses with a small risk factor and stable and regular earnings; the 10 percent rate of return and 20 percent rate of capitalization are applied to businesses in which the hazards of business are relatively high.

The above rates are used as examples and are not appropriate in all cases. In applying the "formula" approach, the average earnings period and the capitalization rates are dependent upon the facts pertinent thereto in each case.

The past earnings to which the formula is applied should fairly reflect the probable future earnings. Ordinarily, the period should not be less than five years, and abnormal years, whether above or below the average, should be eliminated. If the business is a sole proprietorship or partnership, there should be deducted from the earnings of the business a reasonable amount for services performed by the owner or partners engaged in the business. See Lloyd B. Sanderson Estate v. Commissioner, 42 F.2d 160 (1930). Further, only the tangible assets entering into net worth, including accounts and bills receivable in excess of accounts and bills payable, are used for determining earnings on the tangible assets. Factors that influence the capitalization rate include (1) the nature of the business, (2) the risk involved, and (3) the stability or irregularity of earnings.

The "formula" approach should not be used if there is better evidence available from which the value of intangibles can be determined. If the assets of a going business are sold upon the basis of a rate of capitalization that can be substantiated as being realistic, though it is not within the range of figures indicated here as the ones ordinarily to be adopted, the same rate of capitalization should be used in determining the value of intangibles.

Accordingly, the "formula" approach may be used for determining the fair market value of intangible assets of a business only if there is no better basis therefore available.

See also Revenue Ruling 59-60, C.B. 1959-1, 237, as modified by Revenue Ruling 65-193, C.B. 1965-2, 370, which sets forth the proper approach to use in the valuation of closely-held corporate stocks for estate and gift tax purposes. The general approach, methods, and factors, outlined in Revenue Ruling 59-60, as modified, are equally applicable to valuations of corporate stocks for income and other tax purposes as well as for estate and gift tax purposes. They apply also to problems involving the determination of the fair market value of business interests of any type, including partnerships and proprietorships, and of intangible assets for all tax purposes.

A.R.M. 34, A.R.M. 68, and O.D. 937 are superseded, since the positions set forth therein are restated to the extent applicable under current law in this Revenue Ruling. Revenue Ruling 65-192, C.B. 1965-2, 259, which contained restatements of A.R.M. 34 and A.R.M. 68, is also superseded.

Use of Historical Averages Impractical

The ruling refers to using an average of five or more years' values of the tangible assets and average earnings over a similar period. This does not really make economic sense from a valuation viewpoint, recognizing that, as stated in Revenue Ruling 59–60, "Valuation is a prophesy as to the future." What really matters is the fair market value in continued use of tangible assets employed as of the effective valuation date and the best estimate of earning power as of that date. Most appraisers agree with this.

"Required Return on Tangible Assets" Is Ambiguous

The statement in Revenue Ruling 68–609, "*The percentage of return on the . . . value of the tangible assets used should be the percentage prevailing in the industry involved at the date of valuation . . .*" is ambiguous. It should be made clear that it means the rate of return an investor would have to expect to receive to supply capital for net tangible assets in that industry as of the effective valuation date.

No Definition of "Earnings"

Probably the biggest shortfall in Revenue Ruling 68–609 is the lack of a definition of "earnings." Analysts use a variety of "earnings" measures, including net income, pretax income, gross cash flow, net cash flow, or a variety of other economic income variables.

The required rates of return on both tangible and intangible assets are quite different from one definition of earnings to another. As discussed in Chapter 6, "The Income Approach," analysts today tend to lean toward net cash flow as the measure of economic income to be capitalized. However, little, if anything, had been written about the advantage of net cash flow as a measure of economic income for valuation purposes when the ruling was written in 1968.

No Guidance for Intangibles Capitalization Rate

The Ruling offers no guidance for developing a capitalization rate applicable to the excess earnings. Furthermore, the financial community has not developed any satisfactory empirical means of supporting such a rate with market data. Therefore, the rate used represents a major subjective judgment on the part of the analyst about the expected rate that an investor would require to obtain the company's expected stream of "excess earnings." This allows for a high level of manipulation in the value and therefore demonstrates the extreme need for some type of a "sanity check," as discussed earlier. It is this lack of an empirically supported basis for the capitalization rate applied to excess earnings that many consider the weakest link in the excess earnings method.

COMMON ERRORS IN APPLYING THE EXCESS EARNINGS METHOD

The most common errors to look for in a valuation of a business or professional practice using the excess earnings method are:

- Not properly defining the earnings stream
- Using an unrealistic amount of earnings
- Failing to allow for reasonable owner's compensation
- Not properly arriving at a fair market basis of net tangible asset value
- Using an unsupported and/or unrealistic rate of return on net tangible assets

- Using an unsupported or unrealistic capitalization rate for excess earnings
- Using IRS illustrative rates instead of currently applicable rates
- Representing that the IRS claims that excess earnings is a preferred valuation method: "*The 'formula' approach should not be used if there is better evidence available from which the value of intangible assets can be determined.*" See Rev. Rul. 68–609, fourth paragraph from the end.

Undefined Earnings Stream

As noted earlier, there can be many different levels of economic earnings, such as net income, pretax income, gross cash flow, net cash flow, and others (see Chapter 4, "Financial Statement Terminology Used in Business Appraisal"). The capitalization rate must be one that is appropriate for the level of earnings capitalized. Unless the level of earnings used is properly defined, it is hard, if not impossible, to evaluate whether the support provided for it is reasonable or whether the capitalization rate applied to it is appropriate.

Unsupported Normalized Earnings Stream

The critical concept about the earnings stream is that it is expected to be sustainable into the foreseeable future. If past earnings are being used as a guide, Revenue Ruling 68–609 states, "The past earnings to which the formula is applied should fairly reflect the probable future earnings." All too often reports contain mechanical compilations of past earnings with no analysis to support any judgment about whether the level of earnings capitalized represents reasonable future expectations.

Failure to Allow for Owner's Compensation

Revenue Ruling 68–609 clearly states, and the valuation profession agrees, that "*there should be deducted from the earnings of the business a reasonable amount for the services performed by the owner or partners engaged in the business*" (discussed in Chapter 13, "Reasonable Compensation"). Yet analysts often capitalize earnings before taking into account any compensation for the services of the owner(s).

Unsupported Net Tangible Asset Value

This is a common problem, because most business appraisers are not appraisers of tangible assets, such as real estate or machinery and equipment. If the company has such assets but does not have appraisals of them, business appraisers often just use book value, which may bear little relationship to current value. If there is no carefully analyzed and supported net tangible asset value, then the validity of the excess earnings method may be highly questionable.

Unsupported or Unrealistic Required Rate of Return on Tangible Assets

Employing tangible assets in a business certainly is not without risk. The required return on tangibles must reflect the degree of risk involved. This rate should reflect some blending of the company's cost of debt and cost of equity, and the details of estimating this rate should be disclosed. Mis-estimation of the required rate of return on tangibles might be brought to light, or at least suspected, after a "sanity check."

Unsupported or Unrealistic Capitalization Rate for Excess Earnings

The appropriate capitalization rate for excess earnings depends on two factors:

- The expected persistence of the excess earnings (how long into the future the excess earnings are reasonably expected to continue)
- The risk (how certain a reasonable person would be about whether the expected persistence of the excess earnings actually will be achieved and the potential volatility of expected returns)

As noted earlier, the capitalization rate applied to excess earnings implies a number of years' worth of expected future earnings impounded into the value of the business (for example, a 20% capitalization rate implies that the buyer would pay for five years of expected future excess earnings [1/.20 = 5 years], as shown earlier in the chapter). This number of years is sometimes called the payback period. This is a subjective, yet crucial element, of the excess earnings method and the choice of capitalization rate should have some reasonable basis. No matter how carefully it is supported, many still would consider it a "guesstimate."

Using Rates in the Revenue Ruling 68–609 Illustration Instead of Currently Supportable Rates

Revenue Ruling 68–609 uses, for the purpose of illustration, rates of 8% to 10% on tangible assets and 15% to 20% for the excess earnings capitalization rate. The Ruling states, "*The percentage of return . . . should be the percentage prevailing in the industry involved at the date of valuation. The above rates are used as examples.*" Despite this, appraiser reports continue using the 8% to 10% on tangibles and 15% to 20% on excess earnings "because the IRS recommends these rates."

Claiming That the IRS Recommends Use of the Excess Earnings Method

Revenue Ruling 68–609 clearly states: "The 'formula' approach should not be used if there is better guidance available from which the value of intangibles can be determined. Accordingly, the 'formula' approach may be used for determining the fair market value of intangible assets *only if there is no better basis therefore available.*" [Emphasis added.] Yet many reports imply that the excess earnings method is recommended by the IRS.

SUMMARY

The excess earnings method continues to be a widely used method to derive a value indication, particularly for smaller businesses and professional practices, and also when separating the value of tangible and intangible assets. If this method is used, the reviewer of such an appraisal will want to make sure that all the method's components are thoroughly supportable. In the end, the value indication should be based on a reasonable weighted average rate of return that can be reconciled with the income approach method used.

This chapter discussed the background of the excess earnings method and the basic steps involved in the excess earnings method; it showed a basic illustration of applying the excess earnings method and a "sanity check" for the validity of the value developed by the excess earnings method. The chapter also discussed a critique of Revenue Ruling 68–609 demonstrating the origin of much of the confusion in applying the excess earnings method and common errors in applying the excess earnings method.

REFERENCES FOR EXCESS EARNINGS METHOD

Feder, Robert T., et al. 2019. "Valuation of Closely Held Businesses." In *Valuation Strategies in Divorce*, 5th ed., Chap. 3 (Philadelphia: Wolters Kluwer Legal & Regulatory U.S.).

Fishman, Jay E., Bruce Johnson, Kent Pummel, et al. 2023. "Excess Earnings Method." In PPC's *Guide to Business Valuations*, 704 (Carrollton, TX: Thomson Reuters).

Hitchner, James R. 2017. "Excess Cash Flow Method." In *Financial Valuation: Applications and Models*, 4th ed., Chap. 5, 153–62 (Hoboken, NJ: John Wiley & Sons, Inc.).

Internal Revenue Service. *IRS Appeals Officer Valuation Training Course*, 1997 ed., 7-15 to 7-16.

Morrison, William J. and Jay E. Fishman. 2017. "Hybrid-Excess Earnings Method." In *The Business Valuation Bench Book*, Chap. 5, 61–7 (Portland, OR: Business Valuation Resources).

Pratt, Shannon P. and ASA Educational Foundation. 2022. "The Capitalized Excess Earnings Method." In *Shannon Pratt's Valuing a Business: The Analysis and Appraisal of Closely Held Businesses*, 6th ed., Chap. 15, 343–59 (New York: McGraw-Hill).

—, and Roger J. Grabowski. 2014. "How Cost of Capital Relates to the Excess Earnings Method of Valuation." In *Cost of Capital: Applications and Examples*, 5th ed., Chap. 36, 873–80 (Hoboken, NJ: John Wiley & Sons, Inc.).

—. 1997. "Practitioners disagree strongly on excess earnings methodology" (results of a survey of business appraisers). In *Shannon Pratt's Business Valuation Update* (April): 1–3.

Trugman, Gary. 2022. "The Excess Earnings (formula) Method." In *Understanding Business Valuations*, 6th ed., Chap. 12, 469–77 (Portland, OR: Business Valuation Resources).

CHAPTER 11

Rules of Thumb

Alina Niculita, ASA, ARM, CFA

INTRODUCTION

In this chapter you will learn about:

- Issues with using rules of thumb
- Data reported in the sources of rules of thumb
- Example calculations of rules of thumb
- Courts' reactions to using rules of thumb in a valuation

The first thing to say about rules of thumb is that they are practically never relied on as a primary appraisal method. Having said that, if there are valuation rules of thumb for a particular industry, especially if widely recognized, they can be useful to estimate a "ballpark" range of value or to possibly be used as a sanity check against other methods.

Rules of thumb often are classified within the market approach to business valuation because they are thought to have their origins in transactions in the industry. However, their actual origins can vary greatly from pure folklore to actual transaction studies.

RULES OF THUMB DISCLAIMERS

Two books provide extensive listings of business pricing rules of thumb and express strong warnings against relying on rules of thumb for business appraisal.

According to the *Business Reference Guide* (Guide):

> [R]ules of thumb are just that—they are guesses. They can make great sanity checks, "ballparks" for pricing, but they should not be used for valuing or anything that is even close to a valuation or an appraisal.[1]

Another text offers a variety of caveats about rules of thumb:

> Formulas are general in nature. Adjustments must be made to account for variations in revenue and cash flow trends; location; lease; condition of the plant, fixtures, and equipment; reputation with customers, suppliers, bankers, and others; special skills required; difficulty in starting the business; and so forth. [. . .]

1. Tom West, The 2008 Business Reference Guide: The Essential Guide to Pricing a Business (18th ed. 2008).

> There is no single formula that will work for every business. Formula multipliers offer ease of calculation, but they also obscure details. This can be misleading. Net revenue multipliers are particularly troublesome because they are blind to the business's expense and profit history. It is easy to see how two businesses in any given industry group might have the same annual net revenue (ANR), yet show very different cash flows. A proper valuation will go beyond formulas and include a full financial analysis whenever possible.[2]

Both texts caution that valuations change over time in response to changing economic and industry conditions. Furthermore, at any given time, valuations may vary considerably from one locale to another. According to the Guide:

> Also, keep in mind that rules of thumb can vary by area and even by location.[3]

General Nature of Rules of Thumb

Rules of thumb usually are expressed as multipliers. The most common is a multiple of revenues, such as "Many accounting practices sell for 0.75x to 1.25x annual revenues." The other popular multiple for rules of thumb is a multiple of "discretionary earnings," also called Sellers Discretionary Cash Flow (SDCF), Owner's Cash Flow (OCF), or Sellers Discretionary Earnings (SDE). SDE is a calculation of the total financial benefit that a full-time owner/operator would derive from the business on an annual basis. This calculation starts with EBITDA (as described in Chapter 4) and then is adjusted for discretionary and nonrecurring items. Finally, the single owner's compensation is added to arrive at SDE.

Occasionally, rules of thumb can relate to some measure of physical volume. For example, one rule of thumb for barbershops is a multiple of SDE plus inventory plus xx dollars per chair. Other examples include both the cable and cellular phone industries, which have been valued at x dollars per actual and/or potential subscriber. The Delaware Court of Chancery in one decision used dollars per recoverable ton of coal reserves as a valuation method.[4]

To the extent that rules of thumb are used, they are usually applied to smaller businesses and professional practices. They generally assume that the sale of the business would be on an asset basis rather than on a stock basis. And it is usually assumed that the rule of thumb represents the transfer of the operating tangible and intangible assets but not real estate or current assets or liabilities (for example, cash, accounts receivable, inventory, accounts payable). Often a covenant not to compete and/or an employment or consulting agreement is included in the transaction. A major problem with rules of thumb is that they are not clear about exactly what business assets they purport to represent. Furthermore, they do nothing to deal with the essential valuation factors of relative risk and growth prospects.

---

2. Glenn Desmond, Handbook of Small Business Valuation Formulas and Rules of Thumb 12 (3d ed. 1993).

3. Business Brokerage Press, The 2023 Business Reference Guide: The Essential Guide to Pricing a Business xi (33th ed.).

4. Neal v. Ala. By-Products Corp., 1990 Del. Ch. LEXIS 127 (Aug. 1, 1990), *aff'd*, Ala. By-Products Corp. v. Neal, 588 A.2d 255 (Del. 1991).

RULES OF THUMB ARE NOT CASH-EQUIVALENT PRICES

Rule of thumb values are intended to indicate face values of transactions, not necessarily cash-equivalent values; most businesses are sold on terms and not for cash. Frequently, transactions are partially seller-financed with favorable interest rates, and sometimes include consulting or employment agreements, which are additional components of the sale price. Thus, if such rules of thumb or comparable transactions are used to develop fair market value (which assumes cash equivalency, as discussed in Chapter 1), adjustments must be made accordingly.

RULE OF THUMB EXAMPLES

The *Business Reference Guide* provides rules of thumb for more than 600 industries and business types, along with benchmark data, industry trends, pricing tips, and expert comments. A sampling of various rules of thumb are shown in Exhibit 11-1. Although many multiples are stated in terms of revenue, the Guide also includes rules based on other parameters, such as EBITDA and SDE (see Chapter 8, "The Market Approach").

CHECKING ALLEGED RULES OF THUMB AGAINST ACTUAL TRANSACTIONS

How close are the rules of thumb to what actually happens in the marketplace? There are three databases available that report various market multiples for actual completed sales of businesses. These are *BIZCOMPS*, the *ValuSource Market Comps* (previously the IBA Market Database), and *DealStats* (formerly Pratt's Stats). *DealStats* also indicates whether a covenant not to compete or an employment agreement was involved and, if so, how much value was allocated to it.

Exhibit 11-1 includes data on multiples of revenue derived from actual transactions from the *DealStats* and *BIZCOMPS* databases. You can see from the exhibit that the multiples from actual transactions diverge quite a bit from the rules of thumb, proving that rules of thumb are not very reliable.

Exhibit 11-1 Rules of Thumb for Valuation

Occupation	2023 Business Reference Guide[5]	Actual Transactions from *DealStats*[6]	Actual Transactions from *BIZCOMPS*[7]
Accounting Firms	100 to 135% of annual revenues plus inventory	Range: 24–172% m=0.93 me=0.96	Range: 8–126% m=0.92 me=0.96
Auto Repair Shops	30 to 40% of annual sales plus inventory	Range: 8–291% m=0.43 me=0.37	Range: 3–168% m=0.42 me=0.37

5. The 2023 Business Reference Guide, *supra* note 3.
6. From *DealStats*, compiled by Morones Analytics.
7. From *BIZCOMPS*, compiled by Morones Analytics.

Occupation	2023 Business Reference Guide[5]	Actual Transactions from *DealStats*[6]	Actual Transactions from *BIZCOMPS*[7]
Beauty Salons	35% of annual revenues plus inventory, fixtures and equipment	Range: 4–249% m = 0.38 me = 0.33	Range: 3–120% m=0.36 me=0.31
Dental Practices	65 to 85% of annual sales, includes inventory	Range: 8–269% m=0.65 me=0.63	Range: 19–112% m=0.61 me=0.60
Dry Cleaners	80 to 100% of annual sales plus inventory	Range: 11–98% m=0.56 me=0.71	Range: 26–106% m=0.65 me=0.67
Fast-Food Franchises	30 to 40% of annual sales	Range: 5–161% m=0.40 me=0.36	Range: 3–260% m=0.39 me=0.34
Insurance Agencies	200 to 275% of annual sales, includes inventory	Range: 1–872% m=0.79 me=0.38	Range: 8–310% m=1.49 me=1.55
Medical Practices (Physicians)	40 to 60% of annual sales includes inventory	Range: 14–170% m=0.60 me=0.38	Range: 5–171% m=0.55 me=0.46
Restaurants	30 to 40% of annual sales	Range: 7–250% m=0.61 me=0.50	Range: 2–190% m=0.35 me=0.30
Travel Agencies	1.8-3 times SDE plus inventory	Range: 100-370% m=2.2 me=2.2	Range: 70–222% m=1.63 me=1.48
Veterinary Practices	70 to 75% of annual sales, includes inventory	Range: 26–131% m=0.70 me=0.71	Range: 15–143% m=0.70 me=0.70

m=mean; me=median; n/a=insufficient transactions for meaningful results

It is important to recognize that the transaction prices shown in both *DealStats* and *BIZCOMPS* represent face values of transactions, not cash-equivalent values. They can include seller financing, which in some cases is at below market rates, and often include future payments that are contingent on future performance (frequently referred to as earn-out provisions). Additionally, these market multiples may include values of noncompete covenants and employment agreements, which may or may not be appropriately considered part of the overall value, depending on the purpose of the valuation.

Also, most rules of thumb reflect the assumption that the seller will stay with the business for some period of time to assist in the transition from the old owner to the new owner. To this extent, they implicitly imply some level of personal goodwill. Some states tax personal goodwill separately. And in divorce matters, some states exclude personal goodwill from the marital estate. (See Chapter 12, "Personal versus Enterprise Goodwill.")

COURT REACTION TO RULES OF THUMB

Courts generally have been inclined to reject valuation opinions based on rules of thumb. One opinion, for example, contained the following language:

> [These] formulas [...] "are in reality the starting point of negotiation; and should not be confused with a valuation procedure." [...] Formulas based on gross billings are usually converted to a time pay-out of the purchase price and, as such, can be misleading because they are often negotiated more over the terms of payment than over the actual value of the business being acquired. [...] While "rules of thumb may be helpful to accountants or business people to gauge the overall fairness of a particular transaction," i.e., whether it is "in the ballpark," they are not at all helpful to the Court in fixing a specific value on a specific economic enterprise in an ancillary proceeding. A rule of thumb by definition provides no theory. At best it is a guide or points out direction. At worst, it is nothing.[8]

In one California case,[9] a court-appointed expert valued the husband's physical therapy practice between $450,000 and $547,000 but did not testify at trial. The wife called two witnesses, a physical therapist (a former partner of the practice who had purchased five physical therapy practices) and an expert accountant. Ultimately, the trial court valued the business using a multiplier of one times the business's four-year average gross profit of $1,015,779. The trial court supported its chosen multiple of 1 by starting with the rule of thumb in the Guide that was referenced in the court appointed expert's report, and then considered factors specific to the husband's physical therapy practice, as follows:

> Next, the court cited to a publication quoted in and attached to [the joint expert's] report, called the "Business Reference Guide: The Essential Guide to Pricing a Business" (hereafter the Guide) written by Tom West stating that as a rule of thumb the value of a physical therapy businesses may be determined by using a multiplier of 60% to 100% of annual collected fees. Applying this rule of thumb the court explained, "In this case the court has considered that the business is in a good location, is established in the medical community with a broad referral base, has an established core of professional employees, has the owners as a 'hands on' presence, has been in business for a lengthy period, has reoccurring patronage, and has a history of growth in income, and so finds that a multiple of 100 [percent] is appropriate."[10]

On appeal, the husband challenged the trial court's use of the Guide because of (1) lack of foundation for the author's expertise, (2) lack of evidence that the joint expert included the rule of thumb from the Guide in his appraisal or that the court understood it, (3) lack of support that the rule of thumb method was "reasonable," and (4) the rule of thumb method did not take into account the list of negative factors in the court-appointed expert's report.

---

8. Bostwick v. Bostwick, 1991 WL 42628 (Del. Fam. Ct. 1991), *quoted in* Robert D. Feder, Valuation Strategies in Divorce 451 (4th ed. 1997). *See also, e.g.*, Bolan v. Bolan, 32 Ark. App. 65, 796 S.W.2d 358 (1990) and Young v. Young, 600 So. 2d 1140 (Fla. Dist. Ct. App. 1992).

9. *In re* Marriage of Bauer, 2011 WL 4337093 (Cal. App. 4 Dist.), Sept. 16, 2011. Also summarized in *Tom West's Legacy to Appraisers: The Business Reference Guide*, Business Valuation Update (Feb. 2023).

10. *Id.* at 10.

> The appellate court admitted that the court-appointed expert used a different valuation method, but that did not mean that "there is no foundation for the Guide's method, or that it was incomplete, or that the court applied incorrectly."[11]

The appellate court cites other evidence considered by the trial court when it reached the conclusion of a one times gross earnings multiple including the testimonies of the wife's physical therapist and expert witnesses:

> [Wife's expert's] "market comparable approach" using the listing prices of other businesses is essentially identical to [court appointed expert's] approach of using a multiplier of gross income. The experts' opinions differed only with respect to the appropriate multiplier to use. [Wife's expert] opined one times gross income should be the multiplier based on what other physical therapy practices were selling for. [The court appointed expert] used a lower multiplier of .42. The Guide gave a range of .75 to 1.0. [Physical therapist] gave a range of between 1.0- and 1.5-times gross sales. All the witnesses who testified explained the multiplier depending on various marketability factors and [husband's] practice had many positive factors favoring a higher multiple. The court's use of 100% (the equivalent of using a multiplier of one) was well within the range of the evidence presented.[12]

It is important to note that both the testifying witnesses and the court-appointed expert all utilized the Guide, and no other methodology. Hence the Guide was the only evidence provided to the Court. As such, the Guide was the best evidence available to the Court to make a determination.

SUMMARY

This chapter has provided a discussion of business pricing rules of thumb that have their origins in business brokerage. While use of pricing rules of thumb is not recommended for business valuation, if there are widely used and recognized pricing rules of thumb for an industry, they can be useful to estimate a "ballpark" range of value, or as a "check" on values obtained from traditional business valuation methods.

REFERENCES FOR RULES OF THUMB

Desmond, Glenn. 1993. *Handbook of Small Business Valuation Formulas and Rules of Thumb*, 3rd ed. (Camden, ME: Valuation Press).

Feder, Robert, Ed. 1997. "Courts' Use of Rules of Thumb to Value Assets." In *Valuation Strategies in Divorce*, 4th ed., 450–3 (Hoboken, NJ: John Wiley & Sons, Inc.).

Fishman, Jay E. 1984. "The Problem with Rules of Thumb in the Valuation of Closely Held Entities." In *Fair$hare: The Matrimonial Law Monthly* (December): 13. Reprinted in Fishman, Jay E., Bruce A. Johnson, Kent Pummel, et al. 2022., PPC's *Guide to Business Valuations*, 7-53 to 7-54 (Carrollton, TX: Thomson Reuters).

Herman, Gregg. 2019. *101+ Practical Solutions for The Family Lawyer*, 4th ed., Chap. 95. (Chicago: American Bar Association).

11. *Id.* at 11.
12. *Id.* at 12.

Pratt, Shannon P. and ASA Educational Foundation. 2022. "Market Approach: Guideline Transaction Method." In *Shannon Pratt's Valuing a Business: The Analysis and Appraisal of Closely Held Businesses*, 6th ed., Chap. 14, 336–7 (New York: McGraw-Hill).

The 2023 Business Reference Guide: The Essential Guide to Pricing a Business 33rd ed. (Wilmington, NC: Business Brokerage Press).

Transaction Databases with Price/Revenue and Price/Discretionary Earnings Ratios

*BIZCOMPS**

P.O. Box 97757
Las Vegas, NV 89193
(702) 454-0072

*DealStats**

Business Valuation Resources
111 S.W. Columbia St., Ste. 750
Portland, OR 97201
(503) 479-8200

ValuSource Market Comps

ValuSource
4575 Galley Road, Ste. 200E
Colorado Springs, CO 80915
(800) 825-8763

* These databases can be accessed through BVResources.com.

CHAPTER 12

Personal versus Enterprise Goodwill

Jay E. Fishman, FASA, FRICS, and Kenneth J. Pia, Jr., ASA, CPA/ABV, MCBA

INTRODUCTION

In this chapter, you will learn about:

- Differences in characteristics between personal (professional) and enterprise (entity) goodwill
- How personal goodwill can impact a divorce case
- Relevant case law decisions on the issue of personal goodwill

The distinction between personal and enterprise goodwill is becoming an increasingly important aspect of business valuation.[1] This is primarily true in conjunction with marital dissolution matters, where an increasing number of states are requiring a separation of personal goodwill from enterprise goodwill, with many excluding personal goodwill from the marital estate. The distinction can also be a significant factor in corporate taxation, where the source of proceeds from a sale can be considered personal goodwill and therefore not typically subject to taxation.

At last count prior to publication, the latest court cases in 30 states and the District of Columbia now include enterprise goodwill as part of the marital estate in a dissolution but exclude personal goodwill. Louisiana has even passed a statute to that effect.[2]

The number of states whose recent court case rulings included both enterprise and personal goodwill as part of the marital estate has shrunk to 13. The remaining states have more complex components in determining whether goodwill should be included in the marital estate; with some factors including marketability or salability, whether the business is a professional practice, or whether the professional will continue to practice.[3]

Exhibit 12-1 indicates the latest position of those states that have taken a stance on the issue of personal and enterprise goodwill.

---

1. *See* Exhibit 10-2 for various views as to the definition of goodwill.
2. La. Rev. Stat. § 9:2801.2 (2009).
3. Business Valuation Resources, Charting Goodwill Jurisprudence + Map (as of April 2019).

Exhibit 12–1 Personal versus Enterprise Goodwill in Divorce

State	Position	Case	Type of Practice
Alabama	No decision		
Alaska	Enterprise goodwill is marital, personal goodwill is not.	*Richmond v. Richmond*, 779 P.2d 1211 (Alaska 1989)	Law practice
Arizona	No distinction; personal and enterprise goodwill are marital.	*Mitchell v. Mitchell*, 732 P.2d 208 (Ariz. 1987)	Accounting practice
Arkansas	Enterprise goodwill is marital, personal goodwill is not.	*Tortorich v. Tortorich*, 902 S.W. 2d 247 (Ark. App. 1995)	Dental practice (oral surgery)
California	No distinction; personal and enterprise goodwill are marital.	*In re Marriage of Lopez*, 38 Cal. App. 3d 93 (1974)	Law practice
Colorado	No distinction; personal and enterprise goodwill are marital.	*In re Marriage of Huff*, 834 P.2d 244 (Colo. 1992)	Law practice
Connecticut	Enterprise goodwill is marital, personal goodwill is not.	*Eslami v. Eslami*, 591 A.2d. 411 (Conn. 1991)	Medical practice
Delaware	Enterprise goodwill is marital, personal goodwill is not.	*E.E.C. v. E.J.C.*, 457 A.2d 688 (Del. 1983)	Law practice
District of Columbia	Enterprise goodwill is marital, personal goodwill is not.	*McDiarmid v. McDiarmid*, 649 A.2d 810 (D.C. App. 1994)	Law practice
Florida	Enterprise goodwill is marital, personal goodwill is not.	*Thompson v. Thompson*, 576 So. 2d 267 (Fla. 1991)	Law practice
Georgia	Enterprise goodwill is marital; personal goodwill is not.	*Miller v. Miller*, 288 Ga. 274;05 S.E.2d 839 (Nov 22,2010	Medical Practice
Hawaii	Enterprise goodwill is marital, personal goodwill is not.	*Antolik v. Harvey*, 761 P.2d 305 (Haw. App. 1988)	Chiropractic business
Idaho	Majority declines to distinguish personal and business goodwill; dissent strongly disagrees.	*Stewart v. Stewart*, 2007 Ida. LEXIS 17 (Jan. 26, 2007)	Dermatology practice
Illinois	Enterprise goodwill is marital, personal is not.	*In re Marriage of Head*, 652 N.E. 2d 1246 (Ill. App. 1995)	Medical practice

State	Position	Case	Type of Practice
Indiana	Enterprise goodwill is marital; personal goodwill MAY BE (a party wishing to exclude personal goodwill must submit evidence of its value to the trial court).	*Balicki v. Balicki*, 837 N.E.2d 532 (Ind. App. 2005)	Mechanical/ Construction
Iowa	Not clear; recognizes goodwill is dependent on the professional continuing in practice, and is a factor bearing on his/her future earning potential.	*In re Marriage of Hogeland*, 448 N.W.2d 678 (Iowa App. 1989)	Dental practice
Kansas	After July 1, 1998 professional goodwill to the extent it is marketable for that particular professional shall become marital property	KAN. STAT. ANN. § 23-2801(a)	
Kentucky	Enterprise goodwill is marital; personal goodwill is not.	*Gaskill v. Robbins*, 2009 WL 425619 (Ky.) (Feb. 19, 2009)	Accounting practice
Louisiana	Enterprise goodwill is marital, personal goodwill is not.	Statute: La. R.S. 9:2801.2 added by Acts 2003, No. 837 ß 1 and amended by Acts 2004, No. 177 ß 1	
Maine	Enterprise goodwill is marital; personal goodwill is not.	*Ahern v. Ahern*, 2008, 2008 Me. LEXIS 1 (Jan 3, 2008)	Dental practice
Maryland	Enterprise goodwill is marital, personal is not.	*Prahinski v. Prahinski (II)*, 75 Md. 227 (1990)	Law practice
Massachusetts	Enterprise goodwill is marital, personal goodwill is not.	*Goldman v. Goldman*, 554 N.E.2d 860 (Mass. App. 1990)	Medical practice
Michigan	No distinction; personal and enterprise goodwill are marital.	*Brusach v. Brusach*, 2017, Mich. App. LEXIS 1619	Veterinary practice
Minnesota	Enterprise goodwill is marital, personal goodwill is not.	*Roth v. Roth*, 406 N.W.2d 77 (Minn. App. 1987)	Chiropractic business
Mississippi	Neither personal nor enterprise goodwill is marital.	*Watson v. Watson*, 882 So. 2d 95 (Miss. 2004)	Veterinary clinic

State	Position	Case	Type of Practice
Missouri	Enterprise goodwill is marital, personal goodwill is not.	*Hanson v. Hanson*, 738 S.W.2d 429 (Mo. 1987)	Medical practice
Montana	No distinction; personal and enterprise goodwill are marital.	*In re Marriage of Hull*, 219 Mont. 480 (1986) 950 P.2d 1373 (Mont. 1997)	Medical practice
Nebraska	Enterprise goodwill is marital, personal goodwill is not.	*Taylor v. Taylor*, 386 N.W.2d 851 (Neb. 1986)	Medical practice
Nevada	No distinction; personal and enterprise goodwill are marital.	*Ford v. Ford*, 782 P.2d 1304 (Nev. 1989)	Medical practice
New Hampshire	Enterprise goodwill is marital, personal goodwill is not.	*In re Watterworth*, 821 A. 2d 1107 (N.H. 2003)	Medical practice
New Jersey	No distinction; personal and enterprise goodwill are marital.	*Dugan v. Dugan*, 457 A.2d 1 (N.J. 1983)	Law practice
New Mexico	No distinction; personal and enterprise goodwill are marital.	*Mitchell v. Mitchell*, 719 P.2d 432 (N.M. App. 1986)	Accounting practice
New York	No distinction; personal and enterprise goodwill are marital.	*Moll v. Moll*, 722 N.Y.S.2d 732 (2001)	Stockbroker
North Carolina	No distinction; personal and enterprise goodwill are marital.	*Poore v. Poore*, 7331 S.E.2d 266 (N.C. App. 1985)	Dental practice
North Dakota	No distinction; personal and enterprise goodwill are marital.	*Sommers v. Sommers*, 660 N.W.2d 586 (N.D. 2003)	Medical practice
Ohio	Personal and enterprise goodwill in professional practice is marital.	*Kahn v. Kahn*, 536 N.E.2d 678 (Ohio 1987)	Medical practice
Oklahoma	Enterprise goodwill is marital, personal is not.	*Traczyk v. Traczyk*, 891 P.2d 1277 (Okla. 1995)	Medical practice/foot clinic
Oregon	Enterprise goodwill is marital, personal is not.	*Slater v. Slater*, 245 P.3d 676 (Ore. Ct.App.2010)	Chiropractic clinic
Pennsylvania	Enterprise goodwill is marital, personal goodwill is not.	*Butler v. Butler*, 63 A.2d 148 (Pa. 1995)	Accounting firm
Rhode Island	Enterprise goodwill is marital, personal goodwill is not.	*Moretti v. Moretti*, 766 A.2d 925 (R.I. 2001)	Professional landscaper

State	Position	Case	Type of Practice
South Carolina	Neither personal nor enterprise goodwill is marital.	*Moore v. Moore*, 2015 S.C. LEXIS 343	Retail store (lighting fixtures, home furnishings)
South Dakota	Enterprise goodwill in professional practice is marital; expressly declined to decide whether personal goodwill in professional practice is marital.	*Endres v. Endres*, 532 N.W.2d 65 (S.D. 1995)	Dairy and concrete business
Tennessee	Neither personal nor enterprise goodwill is marital.	*Smith v. Smith*, 709 S.W.2d 558 (Tenn. App. 1985)	Law firm
Texas	Enterprise goodwill is marital, personal goodwill is not.	*Nail v. Nail*, 486 S.W.2d 761 (Tex. 1972)	Medical practice
Utah	Enterprise goodwill is marital, personal goodwill is not.	*Sorensen v. Sorensen*, 839 P.2d 774 (Utah 1992)	Law practice
Vermont	Enterprise goodwill is marital, personal goodwill is not.	*Mills v. Mills*, 167 Vt. 567 (1997)	Law practice
Virginia	Enterprise goodwill is marital, personal goodwill is not.	*Howell v. Howell*, 31 Va. App. 332 (2000)	Law practice
Washington	No distinction; personal and enterprise goodwill are marital.	*In re Marriage of Hall*, 692 P.2d 175 (Wash. 1984)	Medical practice
West Virginia	Enterprise goodwill is marital, personal goodwill is not.	*May v. May*, 214 W. Va 394 (2003)	Dental practice
Wisconsin	Distinguishing salable from nonsalable goodwill finding salable professional goodwill is divisible and includable in the marital estate.	*McReath v. McReath*, 2011 Wisc. LEXIS 354 (July 12,2011)	Dental practice
Wyoming	Enterprise goodwill is marital, personal goodwill is not.	*Root v. Root*, 65 P.3d 41 (Wyo. 2003)	Medical practice

Source: Adapted and updated from "*Charting Goodwill Jurisprudence + Map*," by Business Valuation Resources. ©2019. Reprinted with permission of Business Valuation Resources, Portland, Oregon. www.bvesources.com.

The valuation of noncompete agreements, which many consider an indicium of personal goodwill in the context of marital dissolution, is discussed in more detail in Chapter 14, "Employment and Noncompetition Agreements."

Similarly, covenants not to compete are categorized by most, but not all, states as a personal asset not subject to distribution, due to their restrictions on the future activities of the spouse.[4] Arguably, a covenant not to compete can be a mechanism for buyers to contractually effectuate the transfer of an individual's personal goodwill.

DISTINCTION BETWEEN ENTERPRISE AND PERSONAL GOODWILL

Goodwill is an intangible asset that contributes to earnings as a result of name, reputation, customer and employee loyalty, location, products, and similar factors not separately identified. It is the expectancy of repeat patronage. The issue in distinguishing enterprise from personal goodwill is what or who is generating that expectancy of repeat patronage.

Enterprise (business or entity) goodwill is the part of goodwill that is attributable to the entity as opposed to the individual. Goodwill is the total value of an enterprise, less its tangible and identifiable intangible value. Enterprise goodwill is an intangible asset owned by and associated with the operation of the business entity and can include the business's locations, customer base, trained workforce, reputation, product brands, and name.

Personal goodwill is the part of goodwill that is attributable to the individual as opposed to the entity. Personal goodwill is owned by a shareholder or employee and exists when that person's skills, reputation, expertise, knowledge, and relationships with customers, suppliers, vendors, employees, and so on, directly contribute to the company's success. Personal goodwill is associated with specialized skills, personal relationships, and reputation of the owners as opposed to the name and reputation of the organization itself.

Simply stated, for enterprise goodwill to exist, it must be institutionalized with recognition of the business and not be primarily attributable to any individual(s). In practice, it is not unusual for a business to have elements of both enterprise and personal goodwill. In those instances, an allocation is usually made between both elements. Other identifiable intangible assets like trademarks, patents, assembled workforce, and favorable contracts should also be considered.

An analysis of whether the goodwill of a business is enterprise or personal or some combination of both begins with a thorough understanding of the business. This includes reviewing detailed job descriptions for management, and an analysis of customer relationships and the level of competition.

Enterprise Goodwill Characteristics

The following characteristics are generally indicative of enterprise goodwill:

- Company has written contracts with major customers
- Company has written contracts with major suppliers
- Company has written employment and/or noncompete agreements with key employees
- Large business with formalized organizational structure, systems, and controls
- Company has formalized production methods and business systems
- Business or practice is not heavily dependent on personal service performed by the owner(s)

---

4. *See, e.g.*, Kricsfeld v. Kricsfeld, 588 N.W.2d 210, 1999 Neb. App. LEXIS 1 (Neb. Ct. App. 1999) (Nebraska's court of appeals looked to other jurisdictions and concluded that the covenant not to compete is not a marital asset.); *also see* Chapter 14, "Employment and Noncompetition Agreements."

- Company sales result from company name recognition and/or salesforce as opposed to name and reputation of key individuals
- Company has an advantageous location(s)
- Company itself has brand recognition

Personal Goodwill Characteristics

As implied by the word "personal," this intangible asset is the capitalized income stream or cost savings generated by a key employee who lacks an employment contract and/or noncompete agreement. Personal goodwill exists if the loss of that key person would reduce the future revenue and/or profits of the business for some period. This is referred to as a valuation "with and without" the key person.

The following characteristics are generally indicative of personal goodwill:

- Entrepreneurial business highly dependent on owner's personal skills, knowledge, reputation, personality, expertise, and relationships
- No noncompete or employment agreements
- Personal services provided by the owner(s) are an important feature in the company's products or services
- Personal know-how
- Sales and performance largely dependent on owner's personal relationship with customers and reputation
- Product and/or services know-how and supplier relationships rest primarily with the owner(s)

CASE EXAMPLES

Divorce Cases[5]

By way of example, the following are two cases in which personal goodwill was at issue.

In a large neuropsychiatry practice, the doctor, who owned 100% of the stock, had largely institutionalized (enterprise) the goodwill. The company had a staff of about 60 doctors and therapists, some as employees, and some as independent contractors. It had employment and noncompete agreements with all the department heads and key doctors. It also had contracts with all the hospitals it serviced, and most of the doctors had their own patient relationships. The doctor/owner personally saw few patients, but he negotiated the contracts with the hospitals and hired all the key professionals. The court concluded that the goodwill was 70% institutional (i.e., enterprise) and 30% personal.

A specialized niche insurance agency was the opposite. The president had personal relationships with all the underwriters and most of the larger customers. He had also developed very loyal relationships with all the largest producing agents. The agency had no contracts with any customers and no employment or noncompete agreements. In this case, most of the goodwill was found to be personal.

5. Shannon P. Pratt & Alina V. Niculita, *The Distinction between Personal and Enterprise Goodwill* (June 17, 2022), www.familylawyermagazine.com.

Income Tax Cases

In the landmark *Martin Ice Cream* decision,[6] an individual named Strassberg was the first distributor of Häagen-Dazs ice cream. He had successfully placed Häagen-Dazs ice cream in a significant number of large grocery chains. When Pillsbury acquired Häagen-Dazs, the acquisition included all distributor rights. The Internal Revenue Service (IRS) determined there was a large enterprise-level intangible asset related to the distributor rights. However, the court ruled that most of the value of the distributorship was personal to Strassberg, the stockholder, which saved a large amount of tax at the corporate level.

In *Norwalk*,[7] another landmark decision, an accounting firm liquidated, and an IRS agent determined there had been a liquidating distribution of enterprise-level intangible assets, and so the IRS agent assessed a tax on approximately $600,000 of corporate gain on the distribution. However, because there was no noncompete agreement between the shareholders and the accounting firm, the court ruled that all the otherwise enterprise-level intangibles that the IRS had deemed distributed at the time of the liquidation were, in fact, personal goodwill. The court stated,

> We find no authority which holds that an individual's ability is part of the assets of a corporation by which he is employed where, as in the instant case, the corporation does not have a right by contract or otherwise to the future services of the individuals.

These are only two examples of many cases that include the issue of personal goodwill. Counsel should be familiar with the qualitative factors included in case law applicable to the jurisdiction in which the matter is filed.

SUMMARY

The classification of an intangible asset as personal goodwill could have a material impact on the financial outcome of a divorce or the taxation of the sale of a business. First, knowledge of the applicable statutes and case law is necessary to determine whether personal goodwill is a marital asset or not, or taxable as a separate asset. Next, if personal goodwill is to be carved out of the marital estate or purchase price allocation, the valuation expert needs to perform a credible analysis in order to present persuasive testimony and valuable evidence to the court or IRS.

REFERENCES FOR PERSONAL VERSUS ENTERPRISE GOODWILL

Business Valuation Resources. 2020. *Business Valuation in Divorce Case Law Compendium*, 5th ed.

Business Valuation Resources. 2012. BVR's *Guide to Personal v. Enterprise Goodwill*, 5th ed.

Business Valuation Resources. 2011. *Valuing Goodwill in Divorce.*

Hitchner, James R. 2017. "Trifurcation of Goodwill and the Concept of Tradeable Personal Goodwill," and "Personal Goodwill in Commercial Businesses." In *Financial*

6. Martin Ice Cream, Co. v. Comm'r, 110 T.C. 189, 1998 U.S. Tax. Ct. LEXIS 17 (1998).
7. Norwalk v. Comm'r, T.C. Memo. 1998-279 (1998).

Valuation: Applications and Models, 4th ed., Chap. 19, 843–5 (Hoboken, NJ: John Wiley and Sons, Inc.).
Laro, David and Shannon P. Pratt, 2011. "Personal versus Enterprise Goodwill." In *Business Valuation and Federal Taxes: Procedures, Law and Perspective*, 2nd ed. Chap. 22, 333–42 (Hoboken, NJ: John Wiley & Sons).
Pratt, Shannon P. and ASA Educational Foundation. 2022. "Goodwill and Going-Concern Value" and "Goodwill." In *Shannon Pratt's Valuing a Business: The Analysis and Appraisal of Closely Held Businesses*, 6th ed., Chap. 25, 572–6; Chap. 44, 1036–46. Includes extensive bibliography and data references in online appendix.
Trugman, Gary. 2022. "Professional versus Practice Goodwill." In *Understanding Business Valuations*, 6th ed., Chap. 22, 817–43 (Portland, OR: Business Valuation Resources).
Wood, David, "'MUM's the Word': A Formal Method to Allocate Blue Sky Value in Divorce." *Business Valuation Update* (March 2007).

CHAPTER 13

Reasonable Compensation

Erin Hollis, ASA

INTRODUCTION[1]

In this chapter you will learn:

- Key variables to consider when assessing reasonable compensation
- Adjustments to owner-employee compensation
- Approaches to determine reasonable compensation
- Equity incentives
- Common errors when estimating reasonable compensation

Compensation taken by owner-employees[2] in a business is often a contentious topic in valuation and litigation matters. Those shareholders who hold a controlling ownership position ultimately determine the level of wages paid to the firm's employees, which can impact the value of a closely held business or professional practice. Compensation that is in excess of market value for services provided diminishes enterprise value and, likewise, compensation that is below market value overstates a company's worth. Therein lies the concern of what is "reasonable compensation," how is it determined, and when should it be adjusted?

WHAT IS REASONABLE COMPENSATION?

Reasonable compensation, also referred to as "replacement compensation," can be defined simply as "*what would an unrelated third party pay someone to do the same task?*" Treas. Reg. § 1.162-7(b)(3) defines reasonable compensation as the amount that would ordinarily be paid for like services by like organizations in like circumstances. Regulation § 1.162-7 specifies the requirements of reasonable compensation as "ordinary and necessary expenses paid or incurred in carrying on any trade or business, a reasonable allowance for salaries or other compensation for personal services actually rendered. The test of deductibility in the case of compensation payments is whether they are reasonable and are in fact payments purely for services."

---

1. The author thanks Kimberly Linebarger CFA, CPA, for her contribution to the chapter's content in the prior edition.

2. An owner-employee, for purposes of this chapter, is defined as an individual who has ownership, rights and privileges in a closely held business or professional practice and also provides some level of services.

When dealing with owner-employees, compensation may be paid in various forms of economic benefit (either fixed or variable) and for more than just one service or duty. The appraiser must identify the total economic consideration being paid for the services performed by the employee in question and compare that to the compensation that would be needed to attract an employee (or in some cases *employees*) of similar skill in the same or similar industry to perform the same task(s).

Before determining reasonable compensation for a business owner, a business appraiser should review, analyze, and understand the company's financial performance and competitive landscape. They can use that knowledge to spot trends and differences between the subject company and comparable businesses, as well as draw inferences from industry metrics and norms.

For example, if a company has a bookkeeper who is a sibling of one of the company's owners and is receiving a wage that appears to be reasonable for a full-time employee, the appraiser should inquire as to whether this employee is legitimately fulfilling the role of a full-time bookkeeper. If during interviews it is determined that the owner's relative works only ten hours per week, an adjustment to the employee's wages to that of a part-time bookkeeper should be made. If the appraiser fails to identify this adjustment, it may be detrimental to the validity of the valuation conclusion.

When assessing reasonable compensation, salary increases must also be considered, if applicable. The three most common determinants of salary increases are the state of the economy and labor market; the pay rate relative to the market; and employee performance. Other factors that may contribute to salary increases include acquired skills or knowledge and longevity. Salary increases allow a company to remain competitive in the marketplace, attract talent, and retain employees.

There are key variables to consider when assessing owner-employee compensation. Generally, these factors include the type of position, complexity of the job and effort committed, size and location of the company, employee qualifications, as well as the total compensation being paid. In addition to wages, total compensation may also include:

- Stock option plans[3]
- Long-term incentive plans
- Profit sharing
- Bonuses
- Commissions and draws
- Carried interest or profits interest[4]
- Pensions
- Benefits (e.g., health and life insurance)
- Perquisites (e.g., use of a company-owned automobile, hunting cabin, etc.)

3. The income tax treatment of options is discussed in Chapter 21, "Valuations for Federal Income Tax Matters."

4. Carried interest is a contractual right that entitles the investment manager (e.g., general partner) to share in the profits of an investment in excess of the amount contributed to the investment. Discussed in Chapter 21, "Valuations for Federal Income Tax Matters."

Additionally, there may be other obligations an owner-employee is responsible for and may be compensated accordingly, including:

- Personal guaranteeing of company debt, leases, or contracts
- Serving on the board of directors
- Serving as trustee for the company retirement plan or other employee benefit plan

TAX COURT AND REASONABLE COMPENSATION

As reasonable compensation has become more of an issue, significant guidance has come out of the U.S. Tax Court. There are two main tests the Tax Court has used to determine reasonable compensation: the Multifactor Test and the Independent Investor Test.

The Multifactor Test is essentially a list of factors the Tax Court examines. This analysis produces a conclusion about the reasonableness of an employee's compensation. While the factors looked at are not always consistent among courts or cases, many of them follow some of the same underlying ideas. Courts have applied a variety of multifactor tests.

U.S. Tax Court's Five-Factor Test

In *LabelGraphics*,[5] the Tax Court uses a five-factor test for assessing the reasonableness of the executive compensation income tax deduction related to employees/owners of closely held corporations. Those factors include:

Factor One: The employee's role in the company

Factor Two: A comparison of the compensation paid to similarly situated employees in similar companies

Factor Three: The character and condition of the company

Factor Four: Whether a relationship existed between the company and employee that may permit the company to disguise nondeductible corporate distributions as deductible compensation

Factor Five: Whether the compensation was paid pursuant to a structured, formal, and consistently applied program

Criticism concerning the Multifactor Test has led to an increase in the use of the Independent Investor Test. The Independent Investor Test, as outlined in the opinion of *Exacto Spring Corp.*,[6] examines whether, given the company's current dividends and return on equity, a neutral stockholder would approve the employee's level of compensation. This test allows for a more unbiased and quantitative analysis versus the Multifactor Test. Often the Tax Court will use both tests to reach a decision on reasonable compensation.

Critics of the Multifactor Test consider it unworkable, vague, and subjective. Such is the case with the *Exacto* opinion, which used a seven-factor analysis, as it was overruled

---

5. LabelGraphics, Inc. v. Comm'r, T.C. Memo 1998-343 (Sept. 28, 1998), *aff'd*, 221 F.3d 1091 (9th Cir. 2000).

6. Exacto Spring Corp. v. Comm'r (196 F.3d 833 (7th Cir. 1999)).

in favor of the taxpayer upon appeal. Further, on appeal, *Menard*[7] also used the Independent Investor Test, and the original decision was overturned in favor of the taxpayer.

IRS JOB AID

The *Reasonable Compensation Job Aid for IRS Valuation Professionals* discusses three approaches to determine reasonable compensation: income, market, and cost (essentially analogous to the three approaches used in real estate appraisal); and the usage of each depends on the information utilized, resources available, and facts ascertained from management interviews.

The **income approach** (aka Independent Investor Test) considers whether a hypothetical investor would be satisfied with their return on investment when looking at the financial performance of the business in conjunction with the compensation level of the owner. The rationale behind this approach is that investors pay employees to work to increase the value of the business. This approach can only be correctly applied when the fair market value of the company is available for each year that compensation is examined. As the fair market value of the business is not always available, the market approach might be more readily employed. However, the income approach is generally used when no comparable data is available. This approach tends to work best for outliers, or business owners who have a unique occupation or who are achieving results significantly better than their peers. In those situations, comparable data is not available or appropriate to use.

A high rate of return indicates that the business's value increased due to the employee's valuable services. Therefore, if investors obtain returns above what they should reasonably expect, an employee's salary is presumptively reasonable.

The mechanics of assessing rates of return to compensation are similar to *Label-Graphics'* third factor, where the character and condition of the company are analyzed based on its financial condition, financial performance, and rates of return that enhance shareholder value. How well the company has been managed and grown is a critical element of assessing the reasonableness of compensation paid to the owner-employee.

It should be noted that the seminal case employing the Independent Investor Test is the 1983 decision by the Ninth Circuit Court of Appeals in *Elliotts*.[8] In *Elliotts*, although none of the factors were weighted, all five factors were considered and all were persuasive in favor of the taxpayer. The nature and quality of the services performed by the owner-employee is an overreaching principle. However, other courts have given the Independent Investor Test a greater, if not a commanding, role in their decisions. In general, the Independent Investor Test requires reference to an acceptable level of return, which is difficult to assess due to its subjectivity; and the level of return varies by industry, company, and other considerations.

The **market approach** (aka Industry Comparison Approach), commonly used by business valuation experts, compares the business owner's compensation to compensation within the same industry. Industry or market databases are utilized. The Industry

7. Menard Inc. v. Comm'r (No. 08-2125, 7th Cir. 2009).
8. Elliotts Inc. v. Comm'r (716 F.2d 1241).

Comparison Approach is generally used for mature medium and large businesses where the business owner provides only one duty: managing the business. Basically, the question being answered is: *How much would a third party pay a qualified non-owner employee for the same position in the subject company?*[9]

The following exhibits display a sample of ratios available from the industry databases First Research—Dun & Bradstreet (shown in Exhibit 13-1), IBIS*World* (shown in Exhibit 13-2), and ERI Executive Compensation Assessor® (shown in Exhibit 13-3). Databases may break data down by company size and by year. Typically, the more detailed the information, the better the results. Although the benchmark data may not be as statistically sound as desired, the onus falls on the appraiser to apply the information correctly to derive a reliable outcome. Therefore, it is imperative the structure and application of the data be understood. For example, total "officer's compensation" may or may not include employee benefits or bonuses, and the compilation may differ from one database to another.

Exhibit 13-1 Compensation Ratios from Dunn & Bradstreet—Example Machine Shops

First Research—Dun & Bradstreet				**Machine Shops**
NAICS	**33271**			
Data Period: 2021				Last Update Dec. 2022
Table Data Format: Mean				
Company Size	All	Large	Medium	Small
Size by Revenue		Over $50M	$5M–$50M	Under $5M
Company Count	13,514	59	544	12,911
Income Statement				
Net Sales	100%	100%	100%	100%
Gross Margin	33.2%	31.2%	34.1%	35.2%
Officer Compensation	2.2%	1.9%	2.0%	2.6%
Advertising & Sales	0.6%	0.5%	0.6%	0.6%
Other Operating Expenses	25.3%	24.2%	26.0%	26.3%
Operating Income	5.2%	4.6%	5.4%	5.7%
Net Income	2.7%	2.5%	2.8%	2.9%

9. For a list of resources on reasonable compensation, see Compensation Resources section at the end of this chapter.

Exhibit 13-2 Compensation Ratios from IBIS*World*—Example Machine Shops

Ratio	2017	2018	2019	2020	2021	3-Year	5-Year	10-Year
EBIT/Revenue	5.7	6.7	9.1	12.4	7.5	9.7	8.3	7.0
EBITDA/Revenue	9.2	11.0	15.5	21.4	13.3	16.8	14.1	11.4
Leverage Ratio	29.6	9.8	7.1	5.6	9.2	7.3	12.3	19.9
Taxes Paid/Revenue	1.5	1.4	1.2	1.2	1.1	1.2	1.3	1.4
Total Revenue	100.0	100.0	100.0	100.0	100.0	100.0	100.0	100.0
Business receipts	96.1	95.7	97.2	96.4	96.4	96.7	96.4	96.5
Cost of goods	66.7	65.9	66.1	66.1	66.3	66.2	66.2	66.6
Gross Profit	33.3	34.1	33.9	33.9	33.7	33.8	33.8	33.4
Salaries and wages	8.9	8.8	9.4	9.7	9.5	9.5	9.2	9.0
Advertising	1.1	1.2	1.3	1.4	1.3	1.3	1.2	1.2
Depreciation	2.8	2.6	2.6	2.8	2.6	2.6	2.7	2.6
Depletion	0.0	0.0	0.1	0.3	0.1	0.2	0.1	0.1
Amortization	0.7	1.7	3.7	6.0	3.1	4.3	3.1	1.8
Rent paid	1.4	1.5	1.6	1.5	1.6	1.6	1.5	1.6
Repairs	0.9	0.8	0.5	0.3	0.2	0.3	0.5	0.6
Bad debts	0.4	0.4	0.2	0.2	11.5	4.0	2.5	1.4
Employee benefit programs	1.9	2.7	4.3	5.9	6.6	5.6	4.3	2.9
Compensation of officers	1.8	2.9	7.1	16.5	18.4	14.0	9.3	5.5
Taxes paid	1.5	1.4	1.2	1.2	1.1	1.2	1.3	1.4
Interest Income	0.4	0.7	1.2	0.6	0.4	0.7	0.6	0.5
Royalties	0.8	1.5	2.6	3.4	1.7	2.6	2.0	1.2
Rent Income	0.4	0.6	0.6	0.3	0.2	0.3	0.4	0.3
Net Income	2.0	1.5	1.1	1.6	1.2	1.3	1.5	1.9

Exhibit 13-3 Compensation Ratios from ERI's Executive Compensation Assessor®—Example Machine Shops

Individual Profile
Today's Date: 10/27/2023
Data as of: 7/1/2023

Chief Executive Officer
eDOT: 189117026
SOC: 111011
Pay Period: Annual

	Base Salaries					Incentive					Total Cash				
Revenue	10th Percentile	25th Percentile	Median	75th Percentile	90th Percentile	10th Percentile	25th Percentile	Median	75th Percentile	90th Percentile	10th Percentile	25th Percentile	Median	75th Percentile	90th Percentile
1,000,000,000	323,302	481,018	659,800	892,215	1,097,247	381,412	567,477	778,392	1,052,583	1,294,467	704,714	1,048,495	1,438,192	1,944,798	2,391,713
500,000,000	288,156	428,727	588,073	795,223	977,966	296,406	441,002	604,911	817,992	1,005,967	584,562	869,729	1,192,984	1,613,215	1,983,932
100,000,000	228,080	339,344	465,468	629,431	774,074	142,277	211,685	290,362	392,643	482,872	370,357	551,028	755,831	1,022,073	1,256,946
50,000,000	205,797	306,191	419,994	567,938	698,451	93,696	139,404	191,217	258,574	317,994	299,494	445,596	611,212	826,512	1,016,445
10,000,000	148,585	221,069	303,234	410,049	504,278	35,708	53,127	72,873	98,543	121,188	184,292	274,196	376,107	508,592	625,466
5,000,000	121,041	180,089	247,023	334,038	410,800	26,567	39,527	54,218	73,316	90,164	147,608	219,616	301,241	407,354	500,964
1,000,000	67,750	100,800	138,265	186,968	229,934	16,821	25,027	34,329	46,422	57,090	84,571	125,827	172,594	233,390	287,023

All Values in United States Dollars

Organization Data:

Area: United States Average
Industry: Machine Shops, Turned Products and Screw, Nut and Bolt Manufacturing
Codes: eSIC: 3450, NAICS: 332710, usSEC: 3451
Revenue: 1,000,000
Planning Date: 10/27/2023
Annualized Salary Trend: Data Driven

ERI's Executive Compensation Assessor®
Individual Profile
Job Description
Today's Date: 10/27/2023
Data as of: 7/1/2023

Job Number	ERI Job Title	Description
1	Chief Executive Officer	Plans, develops, establishes, and oversees interpretation and implementation of policies and objectives of organization in accordance with board directives and corporation charter. Responsible for the profitability of the entire organization. Holds position of the top executive and principal organization leader in the organization. This position is distinguished from others in that it is the top ranking executive and, in most cases, is the highest paid executive in the organization. Confers with organization officials to plan business objectives, to develop organizational policies to coordinate functions and operations between divisions and departments, and to establish responsibilities and procedures for attaining objectives. Reviews activity reports and financial statements to determine progress and status in attaining objectives and revises objectives and plans in accordance with current conditions. Directs and coordinates formulation of financial programs to provide funding for new or continuing operations to maximize returns on investments, and to increase productivity. Plans and develops industrial, labor, and public relations policies designed to improve company's image and relations with customers, employees, stockholders, and public. Evaluates performance of executives for compliance with established policies and objectives of firm and contributions in attaining objectives. May preside over board of directors. May serve as chairman of committees, such as management, executive, engineering, and sales.
Organization Data:		
Area: United States Average Industry: Machine Shops, Turned Products and Screw, Nut and Bolt Manufacturing Codes: eSIC: 3450, NAICS: 332710, usSEC: 3451 Revenue: 1,000,000 Planning Date: 10/27/2023 Annualized Salary Trend: Data Driven		

The **cost approach** (aka the Many Hats Approach) is typically utilized for small businesses when an owner provides more than one service for the company or wears many hats. The services are segregated by duty and percentage of time spent. For example, a business owner may provide company administration, accounting, marketing, engineering, purchasing services, and human resources.

The cost approach quantifies the amount of time devoted to the different duties and determines a comparable wage for each job duty performed by the business owner. The services and allocation of time are added to arrive at a total "cost" to replace the services of the business owner. A weakness of the Many Hats Approach is that it is often difficult to accurately allocate the percentage of time and find market salaries for each position, especially if the services are niche services. Also, a business owner may provide several services only to a small degree, which makes quantifying difficult.

ADJUSTING COMPENSATION

Some situations where the issue of adjusting compensation may be considered are when the key person is also a shareholder, when there is a family relationship between the employee and the owner(s), and when personal versus enterprise goodwill is a concern.

Typically, reasonable compensation is adjusted (i.e., normalized) when an owner-employee (or family member of the owner) is found to be underpaid or overpaid. Reasonable compensation adjustments are most frequently made when a controlling interest is being valued. The underlying idea behind the adjustment is that a controlling owner would be able to adjust the owner's compensation to reflect current market rates.

If valuing a noncontrolling ownership position, an adjustment may not always be appropriate as the noncontrolling shareholder may not have the ability to dictate compensation rates unless otherwise stated as part of an equity position. An example where an adjustment might take place in a noncontrolling valuation is if the issue being litigated deals with shareholder oppression by the controlling shareholder over the noncontrolling shareholder.

Keep in mind that any adjustment to compensation may have a compounding effect on the enterprise value of a business. This is especially true if applying a methodology utilizing historical cash flows. As such, correctly identifying and addressing reasonable compensation issues are important in the valuation process. When utilizing the discounted cash flow method of the income approach, for example, the value of a company is based on discounted future returns and often based on company management's forecasts. When applying the discounted cash flow method, normalization of historical compensation is less important than would be in a capitalization of historical cash flows method. However, it is important for the appraiser to consider the adjustment of projected cash flows that include compensation that may not be in alignment with market rates.

When reasonable compensation is a key issue in the valuation of a closely held business or professional practice, an independent compensation expert may be consulted. More often, however, the business appraiser is responsible for determining if and to what extent any reasonable compensation adjustments should be made. The appraiser will then use one of the earlier described approaches while considering one or more of the factors as outlined in the Multifactor Test or other tests.

REASONABLE COMPENSATION IN CORPORATIONS

In matters involving shareholder litigation, such as shareholder oppression, excess compensation taken by a controlling shareholder can result in reduced available cash flows and understated dividends. Further, excess compensation likely results in an understatement of the fair value of the stock.

Employee Stock Ownership Plan (ESOP) participants are damaged by excessive executive compensation payments as they decrease the fair market value of the ESOP-owned sponsor company. Claims can be brought against the plan trustee for allowing excess compensation.

In family law matters, the level of compensation affects both the value of the business held in the marital estate, which is subject to property division, and the level of spousal support paid by the business-owner spouse. If a controlling shareholder receives a high level of executive compensation, and the company reports a return on equity below its peers, this may indicate the owner-spouse may be taking above-market compensation. If the owner-spouse's compensation is below a reasonable level, this can lead to an overstatement of the business enterprise value.

The appraiser should conduct a management interview with the business owner-spouse to ascertain the specifics of the level of compensation. The owner may be taking compensation at a rate below market value if the owner is attempting to grow the company by reinvesting cash flow. Alternatively, there may be plans to sell the company and lower owner compensation will improve the appearance of the income statement and cash flow. Nevertheless, compensation at a rate too high can result in an understated business value, and compensation too low can result in understated spousal support. In all cases, it is important to examine compensation over a period of years, possibly five, to determine a reasonable level of compensation.

Furthermore, if not careful, the concern of double-dipping may arise. Once excess income is added back to the income stream in the business valuation it should no longer be considered for determining future personal income in the spousal support calculation. In *Grunfeld v. Grunfeld*,[10] the New York Court of Appeals stated, "Once a court converts a specific stream of income to an asset, that income may no longer be calculated into the maintenance formula and payout." The concept and treatment of double-dipping varies by jurisdiction.

Determining whether shareholder compensation is reasonable in a family law dispute is similar to determining whether executive compensation is reasonable in U.S. Tax Court cases. For example, in *H.W. Johnson, Inc.*,[11] the corporation was deemed to have declared deductions that exceeded what the IRS considered reasonable compensation, under § 162(a)(1), for its two shareholders for the filing years 2003 and 2004. A five-factor test and the Independent ("Hypothetical," as it is called in this decision) Investor Test was employed to determine reasonable compensation. The courts have consistently ruled that no one factor is determinative in decision-making and this case upholds that stance. The Ninth Circuit ruled that a hypothetical investor would accept pretax equity returns of 10% and ruled that four of the five factors were met.

10. Grunfeld v. Grunfeld, 94 N.Y.2d 696 (2000).
11. H.W. Johnson, Inc. v. Comm'r, T.C. Memo 2016-95 (U.S.T.C. May 11, 2016).

A Subchapter C corporation (C corp) shareholder may structure compensation to minimize taxes and avoid double taxation. Maximizing shareholder compensation increases corporate income tax deductions and decreases the apparent taxable income of the company. Furthermore, by taking a higher compensation, the owner avoids taking dividends (which are not deductible to the corporation) and avoids double taxation (corporate tax on profits plus individual tax on dividends). An appraiser may measure executive compensation as a percentage of gross sales; however, an analysis of net income is typically considered of higher importance, as it more accurately gauges whether a closely held company is disguising the issuance of dividends as shareholder compensation.

Conversely, for pass-through entity shareholders or members, not taking compensation avoids certain taxes, such as payroll taxes, as compensation is derived from Subchapter S corporation (S corp) income distributions. As one can see, the C corp owner and S corp owner have competing issues. The C corp owner desires higher compensation to avoid double taxation, while the S corp owner desires lower compensation to avoid payroll taxes. Either way, it is all about questionable tax planning, which the IRS may take issue with.

Case Example: *Clary Hood, Inc. v. Commissioner*

Clary Hood, Inc. (CHI), an excavation subcontractor, was a closely held C corp taxpayer that was started by Mr. Hood and his wife in 1980. The issues to be decided by the Tax Court were (1) the amount that CHI could deduct under § 162(a)(1) as reasonable compensation paid to its chief executive officer/shareholder during the tax years at issue; and (2) whether CHI was liable for the substantial understatement accuracy-related penalties under §§ 6662(a) and (b)(2) for the tax years at issue.

CHI had grown substantially from 2012 to 2016, and Mr. Hood had contributed largely to that growth through his own personal oversight, strategic decision-making, and industry contacts. Hood rarely took vacations, worked 60 to 70 hours a week, and wore many hats in the business. Under his direction, the company grew revenues from $23 million in 2012 to almost $69 million in 2016. The Tax Court considered other factors, too, including: CHI never declared or paid cash dividends to its shareholder; Mr. Hood had no written employment agreement; the company board of directors was comprised solely of Mr. and Mrs. Hood, who set the amount of compensation and bonuses; and the Hoods personally guaranteed bonding, loans, credit lines, and capital leases, but were never compensated for these guarantees.

The company's financial officer believed that Mr. Hood was undercompensated in prior years and consulted with an accounting firm to determine a reasonable compensation with a $5 million catch-up bonus for 2015 and another $5 million for 2016. The accountants also calculated the "Return on Equity for the Year." The "Clary Hood Calculated Compensation" items included the following: (1) a base salary beginning with $200,000 for the tax year ending May 31, 2000, then increasing 5% annually; (2) an annual bonus amount of 20% of profits before taxes; (3) an annual fee of $100,000 for bonding guarantees; and (4) an annual debt guaranty fee equal to approximately 1% of the debt and capital leases personally guaranteed by Hood.

Following an audit of CHI's federal returns, the IRS issued a notice of deficiency and disallowed the alleged excess compensation and also assessed understatement penalties. CHI hired two experts to support their claim of compensation. One expert compared CHI to multinational public companies and used the Independent Investor Test; both methods were deemed not appropriate by the court. The other expert produced a report that was found by the court to be "materially lacking." The government's expert used RMA (Risk Management Association) data, PAS survey data (executive compensation for contractors compiled by PAS, Inc.), and applied the multifactor approach. He also offered two opinions—one excluding compensation for the surety bond guarantees, and one including the guarantees. Although one of the other experts also used RMA data, it was the interpretation and application of the data that also made the difference in the opinion of the court. The decision of the court is summarized in Exhibit 13-4.

Although only a memorandum decision, the opinion is a representative example of what is thought to be justified compensation from the viewpoint of an employee-owner versus what is reasonable to an independent investor or a third-party, such as the IRS.

Exhibit 13-4 Clary Hood Compensation, Deficiency, and Penalty

Year End	CHI Revenue	CHI Shareholder's Equity	Mr. Hood's Comp. (Including Bonus)	Tax Court Reasonable Compensation	Assessed Tax Deficiency	Penalty § 6662
2016	$68,834,166	$31,262,166	$5,196,500	$1,362,831	$1,613,308	$322,662
2015	$44,111,646	$21,742,422	$5,168,559	$3,681,269	$1,581,202	$316,240
2014	$34,074,836	$17,419,060	$1,681,538			
2013	$42,830,999	$11,965,811	$1,381,707			
2012	$23,680,476	$7,112,009	$221,100			

EQUITY INCENTIVES IN LLCS

Owners of a Limited Liability Company (LLC) may want to reward employees, but since LLCs do not have stock they cannot participate in some common employee benefit programs, such as awarding stock options or giving employees actual rights to company stock. LLCs also cannot sponsor employee stock ownership plans (ESOPs).

A common approach to granting equity interest in an LLC is to share "profits interest," which is akin to stock appreciation rights (SARs) in a corporation.[12] Like SARs, there is a shared interest in the increase of the value of the LLC over a specified period of time.

Another type of incentive for LLC employees is a capital interest, which is equivalent to restricted stock. The employee receives the full value of the membership units versus just the increase in value. However, the use of capital interests is not as popular due to potentially unfavorable tax consequences for the employee.

A simpler approach may be to issue the equivalent of phantom shares in the form of a unit rights plan or unit appreciation rights plan. Similar to stock options, these plans are subject to time-based vesting. In a unit rights plan, the employee is paid in cash when the units vest. In a unit appreciation rights plan, only the increase in value is paid. Tax treatment is similar to a cash bonus. As with a phantom stock plan, the employee is not an LLC member and does not receive a schedule K-1.

12. The tax treatment is discussed in Chapter 21, "Valuations for Federal Income Tax Matters."

While many of these incentives are contingent upon performance of the entity, they should, nonetheless, be considered as part of evaluating reasonable compensation.

COMMON ERRORS

The following are some common errors encountered when calculating reasonable replacement compensation:

- **Inappropriate application of data.** If using a database or survey, not understanding the data or misapplying the data. RMA data, for example, includes other sources of income, such as bonuses and fringe benefits, and may also include more than one officer.
- **Not considering specific attributes.** The owner-spouse's position must be consistent with the data provided in the survey or database.
- **Not using relevant data, such as timely or geographic consideration.** Finding usable and relevant data is the biggest problem when determining reasonable compensation. This is especially true for niche industries, uncommon positions, or unique expertise.
- **In family law matters, double-dipping.** If excess income is added back in the business valuation process, it is converted to an asset, and should no longer be considered for determining spousal support. When calculating spousal-support payments, it is important to understand the relationship between the community property asset value and future income to the owner-spouse. Although this is a legal issue for counsel to address, it is important for the business appraiser to understand the nuance.
- **Maintaining compensation at a fixed rate over time.** This is not only unrealistic, but it is also contrary to economic reality and can skew a company's value.
- **Independent Investor Test.** It is incorrect to use the book value of equity when no business valuation is available, as there may be unrecorded intangibles or excess compensation or accelerated depreciation taken that may have lowered the book value.
- **Many Hats Approach.** Adding up market salaries of full-time positions on a full-time basis, as it will distort the amount of time actually worked. Each position must be allocated a percent of "full time."
- **Inserting sentiment into the equation.** The business appraiser should keep in mind that he or she is not giving an opinion about whether the specific person is overcompensated or undercompensated based on how well the person performs his or her duties. The adjustment is not determinative of whether the specific individual is worth more or less to the subject company. Rather it is based on the principle of substitution.

COMPENSATION RESOURCES

To verify the compensation needed to attract an executive of similar skills, many appraisers will consult a database or a trade association survey. The availability of faultless data is scarce; therefore, the business appraiser must utilize common sense and logic when deciding which information should be used. When available, the business appraiser should examine more than one source of data and use his or her best judgment to determine the reasonableness of the data for the position in question.

The following is a list of resources often consulted:

- American Salaries and Wages Survey, Gale Research
- America's Career InfoNet, sponsored by the U.S. Department of Labor
- Compdata Surveys, Dolan Technologies, Corp.
- Compensation.BLR.com, Business & Legal Resources

- CompQuest Online, Towers Watson Data Sources
- EquilarInsight, Equilar, Inc.
- Executive Compensation Assessor, Economic Research Institute (ERI)
- First Research Dun & Bradstreet
- IBIS*World*
- IRS Ratios
- Kenexa CompAnalyst Executive, Kenexa, Inc.
- Occupational Employment Statistics, Bureau of Labor Statistics (BLS), U.S. Department of Labor
- Officer Compensation Data, Integra Information
- RCReports
- RMA *Annual Statement Studies*, Risk Management Associates
- Robert Half
- Salary.com for Businesses
- Specific industry or trade organization databases and surveys

Many of these resources provide data by company size, industry, and location. While it is easy to simply use a number given by one of these sources, it is critical that the appraiser be aware of the assumptions and limitations of the data and, thus, the defensibility of the number utilized. The appraiser needs to look at the job position and consider all compensation elements to be sure that the entire compensation package is accounted for.

When determining adjustments to compensation, the following items need to be identified:

- Pay scales of comparable employees in comparison to the financial performance and condition of the company
- Sources of salary information for the identified job position
- Relevancy and shortcomings of the compensation data utilized

The following is the "12-Point Checklist for Business Valuation Appraisers":[13]

1. Is the data collected on a national or regional basis?
2. Does the data include owner/employees where the amount of compensation reported may also include business profits as compensation (i.e., partners in professions and businesses)?
3. Concerning data from business and professional associations, what are the sampling sizes that relate to the subject valuation?
4. When using SIC/NAICS codes in identifying comparable companies, how do the characteristics of the subject company compare with the broader range of companies covered by the SIC/NAICS code?
5. How does the data use/define the job titles, and are the actual duties comparable to the duties/hours of the subject owner/employee?
6. Does the data survey reflect averages? Medians? Quartiles?
7. Does the survey fairly reflect compensation for people with particular niches and subspecialties (e.g., matrimonial attorneys, forensic accountants, etc.)?
8. Does the valuator need to include multiple job titles from the survey data to cover the owner/employee's duties?
9. What is the reliability of the statistics and sources that the survey uses?

---

13. For a more extensive discussion on the checklist, *see Reasonable Compensation: Can Your Opinion Survive This 12-point Checklist?* Business Valuation Update (July 2006).

10. Where applicable, are stock options, restricted stock, phantom stock compensation, as well as other perks reflected in the data survey, and comparable to the owner/employee in question?
11. Were all companies in the database consistent in having/not having retirement plans separate from salary?
12. Is the owner a "key person" in the business or a top performer/sales generator?

SUMMARY

What constitutes reasonable compensation can be interpreted differently by different people. It is the appraiser's duty to analyze the deduction taken for reasonableness in consideration of the duties performed, the size of the company, and the employee's experience. An owner's compensation can be a focus of contention in litigation matters or an expense that must be normalized for taxation or transactions. The appraiser must utilize the most appropriate methodology, approaches, and data to make normalizing adjustments. Compensation that is in excess of market value diminishes business value and, likewise, compensation that is below market value overstates a company's value.

By understanding and identifying key personnel and job responsibilities, the appraiser can determine whether a compensation adjustment is appropriate and to what degree. If a compensation adjustment is deemed appropriate, the appraiser needs to conduct comprehensive research of relevant data sources for the particular industry and job responsibilities. Knowledge of both the pros and cons of the data utilized will assist in justification of the adjustment. Considering these criteria can lead to more reasonable compensation adjustments. Finally, it is critical the appraiser be aware of the assumptions and limitations of the data and, thus, the defensibility of the number utilized.

REFERENCES FOR REASONABLE COMPENSATION

Hitchner, James R. 2017. "Reasonable Compensation." In *Financial Valuation: Applications and Models*, 4th ed., Chap. 22, 889–910 (Hoboken NJ: John Wiley & Sons, Inc.).

Miller, Scott R. and Clarlene M. Blalock. 2017. "Compensation Adjustments in Business Valuations for Family Law Disputes" In *American Journal of Family Law* 31:1 (Spring): 3–13.

Panitz, Philip Garrett and Paul Bonner. 2009. "Executive Compensation: What's Reasonable?" In *Journal of Accountancy* 207:6 (June): 56–61.

Pratt, Shannon P. and ASA Educational Foundation. 2022. "Valuing Employee Stock Option." In *Valuing a Business: Analysis and Appraisal of Closely Held Businesses*, Chap. 29, 661–9 (New York: McGraw-Hill).

Reasonable Compensation Job Aid for IRS Valuation Professionals (October 29, 2014), available at https://www.irs.gov/pub/irs-lbi/Appendix%20to%20Reasonable%20Compensation%20Job%20Aid%20for%20IRS%20Valuation%20Professionals.pdf.

Reilly, Robert F. 2023. "Best Practices for Reasonableness of Executive Compensation Analysis," *Insights* (Winter).

Seigneur, Ronald and Kevin Yeanoplos. 2010. *Reasonable Compensation: Application and Analysis for Appraisal, Tax and Management Purposes* (Portland, OR: Business Valuation Resources).

CHAPTER 14

Employment and Noncompetition Agreements

Robert B. Morrison, FASA, BV/IA

INTRODUCTION

In this chapter you will learn about:

- Recognition of employment, noncompetition, and nonsolicitation agreements as intangible assets
- Current state of and pending changes to enforceability of noncompetition agreements
- Income tax treatment of noncompetition agreements
- Considerations in valuing a noncompetition agreement
- Considerations in valuing employment agreements

This chapter addresses two commonly found intangible assets resulting from contracts and agreements "owned" by the business: (1) noncompetition and nonsolicitation agreements, and (2) employment agreements.

NONCOMPETITION AND NONSOLICITATION AGREEMENTS

Employment, noncompetition, nonsolicitation, and other agreements restricting a business owner, officer, or key employee ("key person"; sometimes referred to as "covenantor") from competing with a business entity and/or soliciting customers and employees of that entity are critical to the protection and preservation of the value of the company. For purposes of this chapter, the term *noncompete agreement* (NCA) will be used interchangeably for any such agreements or clauses in agreements.

The typical noncompete agreement is between a business entity and key persons. An employer may require that key persons execute a noncompete agreement as a precondition to employment. Buyers of companies overwhelmingly require noncompete agreements from the target company's key persons.[1] If not already subject to restrictions, buyers will require those key persons to enter into noncompete agreements as a condition of closing a transaction.

---

1. Business Valuation Resources, LLC compiles and maintains a database of information from actual business transactions (*DealStats*®), available at www.bvresources.com. Information captured includes whether or not a noncompete agreement was included in the transaction, and, if so, terms of the agreement. Only 0.5% of the transactions reported no noncompete agreement.

NONCOMPETE AGREEMENTS, TANGIBLE AND INTANGIBLE ASSETS

Operating business enterprises consist of a portfolio of tangible and intangible assets that are deployed in a manner that will hopefully generate revenues, profits, cash flows, and economic returns to the business owners. Each asset of the business contributes to the overall economic returns and value of the business enterprise.

Business value is the present value of expected future profits and cash flows. Buyers will place a lower value (if any value at all) on a business where key persons are free to exit the business to compete and free to take customers, employees, trade secrets, and know-how with them.

Over the past 50 years, corporate value has transitioned from value embedded in tangible assets to that imbedded in intangible assets. With that transition, increasing focus is placed on, and investment made in, the more portable intangible assets. Identifiable intangible assets (e.g., employees, customer relationships, trade secrets, intellectual property, know-how) may have greater value, and generally have substantially more portability than tangible assets. A departing key person would be hard-pressed to take a piece of machinery with them to a new employer. However, that same departing key person could easily take with them employees, trade secrets, know-how, and customer relationships. Herein lies the value of the noncompete agreement to a business: a mechanism used to protect and preserve the intangible assets and business value.

Covenants restricting competition and solicitation may be found in several forms. The most obvious is a noncompetition and/or nonsolicitation agreement. Covenants restricting competition and solicitation may also be found in employment agreements, ownership agreements (e.g., shareholder agreement, operating agreement, partnership agreement), and stock or asset purchase agreements.

NONCOMPETE AGREEMENTS AND ENFORCEABILITY

The enforceability of noncompete agreements varies by jurisdiction and is subject to state statutes and case law. Currently, California, North Dakota, Oklahoma, and Washington, D.C., ban noncompete agreements with a few narrow exceptions.[2] Other states have discussed adopting restrictions.[3]

In those states where noncompete agreements are not banned, to be enforceable, the noncompete agreement generally must (1) be needed to protect an employer's legitimate business interest; (2) state the nature of the business, products, or services in which the key person may not participate; (3) state a finite, reasonable time period during which the restriction applies; (4) state a reasonable geographical boundary in which the restriction applies; and (5) result in some economic benefit to the key person for entering into the noncompete agreement. Noncompete agreements are frequently challenged by the key person for an overly broad or vague business definition or unreasonable length of the restriction and size of the restriction area.

2. Leah Shepherd, *More States Block Noncompete Agreements*, Soc'y for Hum. Res. Mgmt. (Sept. 15, 2022), https://www.shrm.org/topics-tools/employment-law-compliance/states-block-noncompete-agreements.

3. *See New York State Legislature Passes Prohibition on Employer Noncompete Agreements* (June 21, 2012), https://www.morganlewis.com/pubs/2023/06/new-york-state-legislature-passes-prohibition-on-employer-noncompete-agreements. Governor Hochul vetoed the ban because it included a ban on high-paid workers.

The appraiser should be directed by counsel as to the appropriate law before any valuation of a noncompete agreement is made.

NONCOMPETITION AGREEMENTS AND PUBLIC POLICY

There are opposing views as to whether noncompetition agreements are beneficial as a matter of public policy. Proponents argue that noncompete agreements are necessary to retain key persons and to protect the company's value and investment in intangible assets. Opponents argue that noncompete agreements inhibit innovation by restricting the mobility of the workforce and that they suppress wages and benefits. Opponents also argue that employee retention is forced through contract rather than through enhancement of compensation and benefits packages.

Federal regulation of noncompete agreements has been discussed for years[4] and, as a result of a 2021 Executive Order,[5] on April 23, 2024, the Federal Trade Commission (FTC) issued a new rule banning noncompete clauses, which the FTC asserts hurt workers and harm competition. The rule exempts a noncompete clause entered into by a key person who is selling a business or otherwise selling all or a substantial portion of that person's interest in the company.[6]

In response to the new rule, the U.S. Chamber of Commerce President and CEO stated, "The [FTC]'s decision to ban employer noncompete agreements across the economy is not only unlawful but also a power grab that will undermine businesses' ability to remain competitive" and that the organization intended to file suit "as soon as possible."[7]

NONCOMPETITION AGREEMENTS AND TAXES

The controlling owners of closely held businesses typically do not have noncompete agreements between themselves and the company they own. However, buyers of closely held businesses typically require noncompete agreements from the selling owners and other key persons. The tax treatment for amounts paid for the noncompete agreement depends on how the buy/sell transaction is structured and completed.

If the noncompete agreement is "merely a protective device to insure the conveyance of goodwill [and/or other assets]," the noncompete agreement will likely be considered a capital asset. As a capital asset, for income tax reporting purposes, the price paid for or the value of the noncompete agreement is amortized by the buyer and considered in the seller's gain on sale.[8]

---

4. Office of Economic Policy, U.S. Dep't of the Treasury, Non-Compete Contracts: Economic Effects and Policy Limitations (Mar. 2016).

5. The White House, Executive Order on Promoting Competition in the American Economy (July 9, 2021), https://www.whitehouse.gov/briefing-room/presidential-actions/2021/07/09/executive-order-on-promoting-competition-in-the-american-economy/.

6. U.S. Fed. Trade Comm'n, FTC Announces Rule Banning Noncompetes (Apr. 23, 2024), https://www.ftc.gov/news-events/news/press-releases/2024/04/ftc-announces-rule-banning-noncompetes.

7. Brett Rowland, *Business Group Plans to Sue after FTC Bans Noncompete Contracts*, The Center Square (Apr. 23, 2024), https://www.thecentersquare.com/national/article_94afe118-01b6-11ef-b226-f32f03c5526b.html.

8. Forward Commc'ns Corp. v. United States, 608 F.2d 485 (Ct. Cl. 1979).

However, "where the parties agree that the seller should be separately compensated for his loss of earnings (not from the transferred business but from other sources) . . . [t]he seller may be required to treat the substituted earnings as ordinary income [taxed at a higher rate], and correspondingly the buyer may become entitled to deduct them from ordinary income as business expenses."[9]

There is a built-in conflict between the buyer and seller as a result. The buyer wants to characterize the price or value of the noncompete agreement as a separate payment for the key person's loss of future income, thereby allowing the buyer to fully deduct the payment for the noncompete agreement when paid (as opposed to amortizing it over time). However, the seller wants to characterize the price or value of the noncompete agreement as a device to protect the goodwill so that it becomes part of the seller's gain on sale and taxed at rates lower than ordinary income.

At the time of the *Forward Communications Corp.* decision, if the noncompete agreement was determined to be a capital asset (i.e., part of goodwill), goodwill was not amortized. Therefore, the buyer (at the time) was unable to take noncash amortization expense deductions. However, if the noncompete agreement was determined to be compensation to the key person for lost future earnings, the value or cost of the noncompete agreement was fully deductible as an operating expense.

Subsequent to the decision in *Forward Communications Corp.*, the income tax code changed to allow amortization of all intangible assets, including goodwill and NCAs, over 15 years.[10] While more favorable to the buyer than no amortization, it is still less advantageous (to the buyer) than a deduction as an operating expense.

The courts have applied four tests to determine whether the price paid or value of the noncompete agreement should be treated as a capital asset to be considered in the seller's capital gain determination and amortized over 15 years by the buyer, or as ordinary income to the seller and an expense deduction to the buyer. These tests are:[11]

1. Whether compensation paid for the noncompete agreement is separable from the price paid for the goodwill: if the price paid is closely related to the goodwill, it will be treated as part of the capital transaction and, therefore, a capital asset (i.e., not ordinary income to the key person and operating expense to the covenantee).
2. Whether either party is attempting to repudiate an amount knowingly fixed (agreed to) by both parties as the amount allocable to the noncompetition agreement: the calculable tax effect may fairly be assumed to have been a factor in determining the final transaction price.
3. Whether there was mutual intent: even in the absence of a specific allocation of purchase price to a noncompete agreement, if both parties intended that some amount of the purchase price would be allocated to the noncompete agreement (as a separable price paid for the noncompete agreement), it will be treated as ordinary income to the key person and as an operating expense to the covenantee.
4. Whether the noncompete agreement was economically real: "[T]he covenant must have some independent basis in fact or some arguable relationship with business reality such

9. *Id.*
10. 26 U.S.C. § 197 – Amortization of goodwill and certain other intangibles.
11. *Forward Commc'ns*, 608 F.2d 485.

that reasonable men, genuinely concerned with their economic future, might bargain for such an agreement."[12]

The courts set forth an 11-factor test to assess the economic reality of a noncompete agreement. The noncompete agreement may not be considered economically "real" if:[13]

- The key person does not have the industry knowledge and business expertise to realistically compete
- The key person has no intention to return to the market to compete
- The key person does not have the financial capacity and economic resources to compete
- There is no real economic threat to the company from competition from the key person
- The key person has no proprietary relationship/does not have the primary contact with customers, suppliers, and other business contacts
- The duration and geographic scope of the noncompete is not sufficient to preclude the key person from competing
- The noncompete is unenforceable or has a high risk of being determined to be so
- The key person is of an age or health such that competition is unlikely or likely to be ineffectual
- Payment to the key person for the noncompete agreement is pro rata based on their ownership in the business (i.e., a disguised dividend)
- Payments under the noncompete agreement survive the death of the key person
- There is no evidence of active negotiation over the terms and value of the noncompete

The disparate tax treatment of a noncompete agreement has material economic consequences for the buyer and seller. It is in the best interest of both parties to knowledgably negotiate the amount and nature of the noncompete such that the intent of the parties is clear.

NONCOMPETITION AGREEMENTS AND VALUE

The value of a business and of the assets that make up a business is the present value of all future benefits of ownership. When considering the value of a noncompete agreement, the future benefits of ownership are the future cash flows of the company that would disappear from competition by the key person due to the absence of a noncompete agreement. Therefore, the value of a noncompete agreement is a function of the estimated cash flows saved or protected by virtue of the noncompete agreement's existence.

Prior to valuing a noncompete agreement, the appraiser must determine whether the agreement is legal and/or enforceable. Obviously, an illegal or unenforceable noncompete agreement has little or no value. The mere fact that there exists uncertainty whether a particular noncompete agreement is enforceable also impacts value. The greater the uncertainty, the lower the value. Generally, appraisers are not trained in law and are not qualified to determine the enforceability of the noncompete agreement provisions and therefore should rely on legal counsel for that determination.

---

12. Schulz v. Comm'r, 294 F.2d. 52, 55 (9th Cir. 1961).

13. In *Valuing Covenants Not-to-Compete: An 11-Factor Checklist.* 18(2) Bus. Valuation Update (Feb. 2012), Gary Trugman summarized the 11-factor test as enumerated in the Thompson decision.

IRS Weighs In

The Internal Revenue Service (IRS) issued guidance for the valuation of noncompete agreements for income tax purposes.[14] In particular, the IRS cited three relevant factors that impact the value of the noncompete agreement:

1. **Ability of the key person to compete effectively with the covenantee.** The courts have ruled that the ability of a key person to compete effectively is evidenced by their experience in, and knowledge of, the transferred business.
2. **Feasibility of effective competition by the key person within the time and area specified by the covenant, in view of the activity and market.** Presenting the approaches by which the key person may compete within the period of the covenant satisfies this requirement. Unlike the question of ability, which focuses on factors specific to the key person, the question of feasibility is normally associated with outside factors such as barriers to entry. Such barriers might include time to start a competing business, regulatory environment, availability of viable competitive facilities, competitive response to a new market entrant, and the amount of capital investment required in light of anticipated profits and returns to owners.
3. **Desirability of the key person to compete with the covenantee.** The courts, in the context of an interrogative, have usually examined this motive. The desire to compete can be demonstrated by showing that there are no factors that would inhibit the key person's desire to compete, and by his or her indication that he or she would want to stay in this market and business. In other words, the analysis should consider whether there is anything that would reduce the desirability of competition by the key person.

Valuation of a Noncompetition Agreement

Neither the market approach nor the cost approach lends itself to the valuation of a noncompete agreement. It is virtually impossible to obtain the necessary information regarding a meaningful number of sufficiently similar noncompete agreements in the marketplace to use a market approach. The cost of negotiating and preparing a noncompete agreement may be rather de minimis and, as such, may not be a reliable measure of the value of a noncompete agreement.

The value of a noncompete agreement is in the protection of future income and cash flow. Therefore, the income approach is most commonly used in the valuation of a noncompete agreement. The most common method to valuing a noncompete agreement is the *with and without method* (the WWO method) or a variation thereof. The WWO method is a qualitative and quantitative exercise that involves application of professional judgment by the appraiser. The appraiser must assess and measure factors that affect the financial impact should a key person engage in competition, and the probability of competition absent the noncompete agreement. Specific consideration is given to the financial impact of competition from the key person, the feasibility of competition from

14. Rev. Rul. 77–403, 1977-2 C.B. 302.

the key person, the desirability of the key person to compete, and the ability of the key person to compete.

The general steps of the WWO method are as follows:

1. Develop a forecast of future annual cash flows for the duration of the covenant period, assuming the covenant is in place. Discount the cash flows to present value (With model).
2. Develop a hypothetical forecast of future annual cash flows for the duration of the covenant period assuming (i) there is no restriction on the key person against competition, (ii) competition is feasible, (iii) the key person has the ability and desire to compete, and (iv) the key person would choose to compete absent the NCA. Discount the cash flows to present value (Without model).
3. Subtract the present value of cash flows from the Without model from those of the With model.

The result of the first three steps is the present value of the financial impact on the cash flows of the company during the restriction period, assuming the key person has the ability and desire to compete, that it is feasible for the key person to compete, and that the key person does compete.

The next step is to determine the probability that the key person would compete. This requires an evaluation of the three factors defined in IRS Revenue Ruling 77–403: ability, feasibility, and desire.

1. Evaluate the ability and the desire of the key person to compete even without the covenant, and the feasibility of competition.
2. Develop the probability of competition from the analysis of feasibility, ability, and desire and apply the probability to the present value of the difference in cash flows between the With model and the Without model.

With Model

The primary drivers of business value are growth (revenues and profits), profitability, and risk. Everything else being equal, companies with greater expected growth are more valuable; companies that are more profitable are more valuable; and companies with lower perceived risk to their future economic returns (profits and cash flows) are more valuable.

The With model forecast is the same as that which would be used in the valuation of the company assuming NCAs exist with the key persons. That forecast is typically developed based upon the appraiser's research and analysis of the industry and the subject company's historical performance, and by management's and others' expectations of future revenues, profits, and cash flows.

For illustration purposes, assume the subject noncompete agreement has a five-year restriction period. Exhibit 14-1, Tables 1, 2, and 3, present an example of the With model.

Exhibit 14-1 Tables 1, 2, and 3—"With Model"

TABLE 1
XYZ CORP.
Forward Annual Net Income—With Model
2xx1–2xx5

	$ in thousands; for the 12 months ending				
	2xx1	2xx2	2xx3	2xx4	2xx5
Revenues	$ 12,345	$ 14,814	$ 16,666	$ 17,916	$ 18,722
Annual growth	*20.00%*	*20.00%*	*12.50%*	*7.50%*	*4.50%*
Gross profit margin	35.00%	36.00%	37.00%	38.00%	38.00%
Gross profit	$ 4,321	$ 5,333	$ 6,166	$ 6,808	$ 7,114
Operating expense	$ (3,086)	$ (3,240)	$ (3,370)	$ (3,488)	$ (3,610)
Annual growth	*5.00%*	*5.00%*	*4.00%*	*3.50%*	*3.50%*
Net operating income	$ 1,235	$ 2,093	$ 2,796	$ 3,320	$ 3,504
Other income or expense	–	–	–	–	–
Net pretax income	$ 1,235	$ 2,093	$ 2,796	$ 3,320	$ 3,504
State federal taxes	$ (309)	$ (523)	$ (699)	$ (830)	$ (876)
Net income	$ 926	$ 1,570	$ 2,097	$ 2,490	$ 2,628

TABLE 2
XYZ CORP.
Forecasted Annual Cash Flows to Invested Capital—With Model
2xx1–2xx5

	$ in thousands; for the 12 months ending				
	2xx1	2xx2	2xx3	2xx4	2xx5
Net income	$ 926	$ 1,570	$ 2,097	$ 2,490	$ 2,628
=+ After-tax interest	$ –	$ –	$ –	$ –	$ –
= + Depreciation	$ 123	$ 148	$ 167	$ 179	$ 187
= - Capital expenditure	$ (129)	$ (155)	$ (174)	$ (187)	$ (196)
= - Δ Working capital	$ (275)	$ (247)	$ (185)	$ (125)	$ (81)
Net cash flow to invested capital *(Net "debt-free" cash flow)*	$ 645	$ 1,316	$ 19,052	$ 2,357	$ 2,518

TABLE 3
XYZ CORP.
Present Value of Cash Flows—With Model
as of 12/31/2xx5

	$ in thousands		
	Net Cash Flow	Present Value Factor*	Present Value
2xx1	$ 645	0.9225	$ 595
2xx2	$ 1,316	0.7851	$ 1,033
2xx3	$ 1,905	0.6682	$ 1,273
2xx4	$ 2,357	0.5687	$ 1,341
2xx5	$ 2,538	0.4840	$ 1,228
Present Value of Cash Flows			$ 5,470

*Based on Discount rate of 17.5%

As presented in Exhibit 14-1, Table 3, the present value of XYZ Corp.'s unaffected (i.e., With model) cash flows during the five-year noncompetition restriction period is $5,470,000.[15]

Without Model

The Without model is based on an analysis of the effect competition, if exercised, would have on the subject company's future growth and profitability, and on the perceived risk of future economic benefits. This is often the most difficult part of the analysis.

- **Growth.** Competition from a former owner, officer, or key person may result in the direct loss of customers and business initially, and slower future growth.

  Evaluation of the growth impact from competition involves critical analysis of the source and trending of revenues of the company and of the industry. In some circumstances, the loss of revenues from specific customers or clients for which the key person has the primary direct relationship may be identified and quantified. In this assessment, consideration is given to any contractual restrictions between the company and the customer. Additional consideration is given to the ease with which those customers or clients may switch providers. Difficult or complex logistics, and/or excessive costs necessary to change providers may dissuade customers and clients from following the key person.

  A key aspect in evaluating growth in the Without model is an evaluation of the role the key person had with historic organic growth. If the key person was the company's primary rainmaker, this would have a chilling effect on the company's expectations of future growth if the key person were to compete, at least until the company would be able to replace that person.

  Another factor that impacts the growth of the company in the Without model is the logistics required for the key person to compete. There may be a start-up period during which the key person would need to obtain necessary licenses and approvals to operate; acquire facilities, inventory, and capital equipment; and attract and hire personnel. During this start-up period it would be likely that the subject company would retain most,

15. This is the value of the "invested capital": total assets minus non-interest-bearing liabilities.

if not all, of its revenues. The longer the start-up period, the less impact the competition will have on the subject company's revenues.

Finally, the impact of another competitor in the market is considered. New entrants to a market develop revenues by taking market share away from existing participants and/or by attracting a share of a growing market. A high-growth industry or market may well be able to absorb a new entrant without material impact to the legacy providers. However, if the company operates in a more mature industry where growth of the size of the overall market is limited, the addition of another competitor could negatively impact the growth prospects for all market participants as that new competitor attempts to attract market share.

- **Profitability.** Competition from a key person may result in price competition and may require expensive defensive tactics on the part of the company, both of which erode profitability.

  The concept of profitability in the context of valuing a noncompete agreement relates to what percent of each dollar of revenue is turned into profits and incremental cash flow. The analysis of the impact competition from the key person would have on profitability is performed at three levels: (1) *gross profit* (profit after costs of sales), (2) *net operating profit* (gross profit minus operating profits), and (3) *net cash flow*.

  - *Gross profit* equals revenues minus cost of sales or cost of goods sold. Generally speaking, cost of sales and cost of goods sold have a direct relationship with revenues. This means that everything else being equal, a certain percentage change in revenues will be accompanied by the same percentage change in cost of sales. Because of this, the gross profit margin percentage (gross profit divided by revenue) will remain fairly constant as revenues change, unless sales prices change at a different rate than costs of sales, or vice versa. Exhibit 14-2 provides an example of changes in gross profit as revenues change.

Exhibit 14-2 Measuring Impact on Gross Profit from Competition by Key Person

Assume that XYZ, Inc. sells its product for $100 per unit. It costs XYZ $40 per unit in direct materials and direct labor to make. The gross profit is $60 ($100 – $40), or 60% of revenue. The following illustrates the sale of 1,000 units:

		% of Revenue
Revenues (1,000 units at $100)	$100,000	100%
Cost of goods sold (1,000 units at $40)	$(40,000)	−40%
Gross profit	$ 60,000	60%

If XYZ experiences a decline in revenue due to the loss of a customer to the departed key person, the gross profit per unit will still be $60 (60% of revenues), illustrated as follows:

		% of Revenue
Revenues (800 units at $100)	$ 80,000	100%
Cost of goods sold (800 units at $40)	$(32,000)	−40%
Gross profit	$ 48,000	60%

While total gross profits may decline because fewer units are sold, the gross profit margin (profitability) remains the same: 60%.

New competition from an exited key person without an NCA may force XYZ to lower its price on the product to $90 to try and maintain market share. It still costs $40 to produce. The gross profit is lowered to $50 ($90 – $40), or 55.6% or revenue as illustrated here:

		% of Revenue
Revenues (1,000 units at $90)	$ 90,000	100%
Cost of goods sold (800 units at $40)	$(40,000)	−44.4%
Gross profit	$ 50,000	55.6%

On the other hand, assume that the cost of direct labor goes up $10 per unit while the selling price remains at $100. The gross profit declines to $50 ($100 – $50), or 50% of revenues as illustrated here:

		% of Revenue
Revenues (1,000 units at $100)	$100,000	100%
Cost of goods sold (1,000 units at $50)	$(50,000)	50%
Gross profit	$50,000	50%

The departure of a key person without an NCA may result in the need to lower prices to compete and maintain market share. A new competitor may also increase demand and competition for resources such as labor and materials, thereby increasing costs. These factors are all analyzed in assessing the impact of competition from a former key person not held to an NCA.

- *Net operating profit* equals gross profit minus operating expenses. Operating expenses include advertising, rent, office staff, and other nondirect salaries and wages, insurance, office supplies, overhead, and so on. Basic categories of operating expenses are:
  - *Fixed.* Changes in revenue have little or no impact on fixed expenses. Fixed expenses as a percent of revenue will increase as revenues decrease (same level of fixed expenses divided by lower revenues). Fixed expenses as a percentage of revenue will decrease as revenues increase (same level of fixed expenses divided by higher revenues). Rent is generally a good example of a fixed cost. However, conceivably, a business that loses a material amount of business to a competing key person could, subject to contractual obligations, reduce rent by downsizing facilities. Fixed costs are reviewed in the context of the magnitude of the forecasted loss of revenues from competition by the key person.
  - *Semi-fixed.* Smaller changes in revenue may have little or no impact on semi-fixed expenses, whereas greater changes in revenue may have an impact. Semi-fixed expenses as a percent of revenue will increase as revenues decrease, but not as much as fixed expenses. Semi-fixed expenses as a percent of revenue will decrease as revenues increase but not as much as fixed expenses. As an example, and depending on the subject business's office staff capacity, reductions in revenue due to competition from the key person may at some point warrant a reduction in office work staff, thereby lowering nondirect salary and wage expenses.
  - *Variable.* Variable expenses, such as direct labor and direct materials, change in lock-step with revenues. Variable expenses *as a percentage of revenue* will remain relatively flat in response to increases and decreases in revenues. Analysis is undertaken to determine if there are any variable expenses categorized in *operating expenses* (e.g., advertising or commissions). The entry of a new competitor may require the company to increase its advertising budget.

- *Net cash flow* is the profit remaining after all cash expenses are paid and investments have been made in working capital, fixed assets, and other capital assets.[16] In addition to consideration of all expenses, the analysis of the value of a noncompete agreement also involves an analysis of what impact, if any, competition from a departed key person might have on working capital and capital asset investment requirements.

- **Risk.** Competition from a former owner, officer, or key person may increase the uncertainty of the subject company's future. Uncertainty equals risk. Investors and owners will require greater rates of returns to compensate for greater risk. Banks and other lenders will require higher interest rates to compensate for greater risk. The consequence of greater risk to the business owner's future returns due to competition from the key person equates to greater value of the noncompete agreement.

  Valuation of a noncompete agreement involves an assessment of any change in the perceived risk of the company's future benefits of ownership (cash flows) due to the possibility that a key person may depart and compete. Risk is typically accounted for in the selection of discount rates to use in the With and Without method. However, care is taken to not overlap concepts and double count the impact of expected increased risk.

  As previously discussed, development of the Without model requires the appraiser to estimate the reduction in revenue from the key person's departure and competition. Selection of the discount rate should exclude any consideration of the risk of loss of revenues already accounted for.

Exhibit 14-3, Tables 1, 2, and 3, present an example of the Without model.

Exhibit 14-3 Tables 1, 2, and 3—"Without Model"

TABLE 1
XYZ CORP.
Forecasted Annual Net Income—Without Model
2xx1–2xx5

	$ in thousands; for the 12 months ending				
	2xx1	2xx2	2xx3	2xx4	2xx5
Revenues—With Scenario	$ 12,345	$ 14,814	$ 16,666	$ 17,916	$ 18,722
Revenues lost to competition	0.0%	5.0%	10.0%	10.0%	10.0%
Revenues—Without Scenario	$ 12,345	$ 14,073	$ 14,999	$ 16,124	$ 16,850
Annual growth	*20.00%*	*14.00%*	*6.60%*	*7.50%*	*4.50%*
Gross profit margin	35.0%	33.0%	33.0%	34.0%	35.0%
Gross profit	$ 4,321	$ 4,644	$ 4,950	$ 5,482	$ 5,898
Operating expense	$ (3,086)	$ (3,240)	$ (3,370)	$ (3,488)	$ (3,610)
Annual growth	*5.0%*	*5.0%*	*4.0%*	*3.5%*	*3.5%*

16. This is invested capital (debt-free or before-debt) net cash flow: cash flow before considering debt interest and principal payments or equity dividends or capital distributions. Equity net cash flow is that cash flow remaining after payment of debt interest and principal, too.

Net operating income	$1,235	$1,404	$1,580	$1,994	$2,288
Other income or expense	–	–	–	–	–
Net pretax income	1,235	1,404	1,580	1,994	2,288
State and federal taxes	(309)	(351)	(395)	(499)	(572)
Net income	$ 926	$1,053	$1,185	$1,495	$1,716

The Without model forecasted net income reflects the following assumptions:

Revenue/growth:

- It would take the covenantor a year to obtain the necessary licenses and permits, to acquire facilities, to hire a workforce, to acquire inventory, and to complete any other logistics before actually being able to take and fulfill orders. There would be immaterial, if any, impact on revenues in 2xx1. (With revenue growth and Without revenue growth = 20%)
- It would take the covenantor another year to achieve full market penetration.
- At full penetration, competition from the covenantor would result in a 10% annual loss in revenues.

Profitability:

- The loss of 5% to 10% of revenues in 2xx2 and 2xx3 would require the company to lower prices in an attempt to minimize the loss of clients and revenues, resulting in lower gross profit margin.
- The loss of revenues and customers would not materially affect operating expenses with the possible exception of temporary relief in the form of salaries, wages, and benefits of the covenantor until they are replaced. Offsetting that would be costs to recruit that replacement.

Risk:

- A company is a portfolio of tangible and intangible assets that provide economic returns and help the company pay its costs of capital. Typically, as one moves down the asset side of the balance sheet, the perceived risk of the asset increases. For example, cash, at the top of the asset side of the balance sheet, is the least risky asset in a company while the intangible "goodwill," at the bottom of the asset side of the balance sheet, is the riskiest. Each individual asset is expected to provide an economic return for the business operation. The riskier assets are expected to generate a greater return than the less risky assets. However, the weighted average return on assets must equal or exceed the weighted average cost of capital in order for the company to prevent a decline in value.
- Noncompete agreement asset is considered riskier than the overall risk of the company. Even though the estimated impact on revenue and profitability is based on a thorough analysis, it is not certain. Further, especially given the labor markets, it is not certain when or if the covenantor would be replaced. Therefore a 20% discount rate is used in the Without model while 17.5% was used in the With model.

Exhibit 14-3 Tables 1, 2 and 3 Without Model (*continued*)

TABLE 2
XYZ CORP
Forecasted Annual Cash Flows to Invested Capital—Without Model
2xx1–2xx5

	$ in thousands; for the 12 months ending				
	2xx1	2xx2	2xx3	2xx4	2xx5
Net income	$ 926	$1,404	$1,580	$1,994	$2,288
= + After-tax interest	–	–	–	–	–
= + Depreciation	123	141	150	161	169
= - Capital expenditures	(129)	(147)	(157)	(168)	(176)
= - Δ Working capital	(275)	(247)	(185)	(125)	(81)
Net cash flow to invested capital	$ 645	$1,151	$1,388	$1,862	$2,200
(Net "debt-free" cash flow)					

TABLE 3
XYZ CORP.
Present Value of Cash Flows—Without Model
as of 12/31/2xx5

	$ in thousands		
	Net Cash Flow	Present Value Factor*	Present Value
2xx1	$ 645	0.9129	$ 589
2xx2	$ 1,151	0.7851	$ 875
2xx3	$ 1,905	0.6682	$ 880
2xx4	$ 2,357	0.5687	$ 984
2xx5	$ 2,538	0.4840	$ 968
Present value of cash flows			$ 4,296

*Based on Discount rate of 20.0%

The following table summarizes the difference in present value of the cash flows:

With Model (Exhibit 14-1, Table 3)	$5,470,000
minus Without Model (Exhibit 14-3, Table 3)	4,296,000
Present value of cash flows attributable to noncompete	$1,174,000

The probability of competition from the key person now needs to be evaluated. The ability, feasibility, and desirability are each assessed in percentage format. This is largely a qualitative analysis by the appraiser. If possible, the buyer, seller, and/or key persons are interviewed. While logistically difficult, and frequently not feasible, interviews with key customers can be beneficial. Inquiry is made and research is conducted to determine the ease or difficulty of obtaining necessary permits, approvals, capital equipment, facilities, and a workforce. Inquiry is made and research is also conducted related to the market and industry: can the market absorb another provider and how will the market react to additional competition?

For example, based on interviews of the company's officers and of the departing key person, and research of the industry's competitive environment, the appraiser of the noncompete agreement in the illustration made the following determinations:

Ability. The departing key person has been in the industry for decades and is highly regarded. However, the person is 70 years old and has experienced some health issues recently. A 90% factor is assigned to the person's ability to compete.

Feasibility. There are significant barriers to entry to this industry including heavy regulation and a significant start-up capital requirement. Labor markets are tight and there is a material cost for customers to change providers. Finally, there have been numerous failures of competing start-ups recently. A 50% factor is assigned to the feasibility of competition.

Desirability. The key person has been in the business all of his or her professional life and previously expressed an intention to work until no longer possible. Even with the aforementioned health issues, the key person expressed a desire to stay in the business regardless of who the employer might be. A 100% factor was assigned for their desire to compete.

The difference in present value of the cash flows is $1,174,000. That would be the value of the noncompete agreement if the ability, feasibility, and desirability were each 100%. However, they were not. The three percentages are multiplied together, resulting in a cumulative factor of 45%: 90% × 50% × 100% = 45%. Therefore, the value of the noncompete agreement adjusted for (1) the ability of the key person to compete, (2) the feasibility of the key person to compete, and (3) the desirability of the key person to compete is $1,174,000 × 45% = $528,300.

Noncompetition Agreements and Personal Goodwill

It is generally understood that a company's goodwill is its reputation, customer loyalty, and the propensity for repeat business. As an asset, business or enterprise goodwill contributes to the overall value of the business enterprise. A business owns its goodwill and can transfer the goodwill asset and its contributory value to a buyer.

While business or enterprise goodwill is owned and may be transferrable by the business, "personal goodwill" may not. Personal goodwill is the reputation, personal relationships, and individualistic qualities of an individual. While personal goodwill asset(s) may have value by creating cash flows and returns for the business, the business cannot transfer that personal goodwill as it is not the owner.

The issue of enterprise goodwill value versus personal goodwill value typically arises in two areas: federal income tax implications from the sale of a business and distribution of assets in marital dissolution matters.

Federal Income Tax Implications

Some companies elect, and others are required to file federal income tax returns and pay federal income taxes as a Subchapter C corporation (C corp). The net income and the gains from the sale of assets by a C corp are taxed at the corporate level (versus a Subchapter S corporation where the company is not taxed; rather, income and gains are passed through to the shareholders to be included in their personal taxable income). Furthermore, distributions (i.e., dividends) from a C corp are taxed at the individual shareholder level (versus an S corp where distributions to shareholders are deemed a nontaxable return on investment).

The C corp sale of goodwill and resulting dividend to shareholders is taxed twice: once at the corporate level and once at the shareholder level. Tax courts have ruled that personal goodwill is not a corporate asset and cannot be transferred by the corporation. As such, the personal goodwill should not be included in the determination of the tax on the company's capital gain. The gain on the sale of personal goodwill is taxed only once—at the shareholder level.

Personal goodwill may be transferred to the company through a noncompete agreement. In *Martin Ice Cream*,[17] the Tax Court held that personal goodwill is transferred to the corporation when the holder of the personal goodwill can no longer benefit from it without the employer (e.g., through a noncompete agreement). In *Martin*, the court held that customer relationships of the shareholder-employee were not corporate assets when the employee was not party to a noncompete agreement (or employment agreement). A tax position that the seller's gain includes personal goodwill will likely fail if a noncompete agreement exists.[18]

Once it is determined that personal goodwill does exist, it must be valued independent of the business enterprise. A common method for valuing personal goodwill is to value a hypothetical noncompete agreement between the company and the individual with the personal goodwill. The premise is that the value of the noncompete agreement represents the difference between what a buyer would pay for a company with and without protection from and/or continued participation by the subject employee.

Logically, the With and Without method described earlier is often used for this purpose.

Marital Dissolution Implications

In many states, personal goodwill of a spouse in a business is not a marital asset and, therefore, not subject to equitable distribution. As a simple example, the profits and returns enjoyed by a dentist (or CPA or attorney) are returns on their personal goodwill. Patient loyalty is based on that dentist's personal reputation and achievements. As presented earlier, the value of personal goodwill may be measured using the With and Without method.

Personal goodwill in the context of marital dissolution is discussed in more detail in Chapter 12, "Personal versus Enterprise Goodwill."

17. Martin Ice Cream Co., 110 T.C. 189 (1998).

18. *See also* Chapter 12, "Personal versus Enterprise Goodwill."

EMPLOYMENT AGREEMENTS

Employment agreements are legally binding agreements (i.e., contracts) between an employer and employee(s). Employment agreements outline the rights, responsibilities, and obligations of both parties during the course of (and sometimes beyond) the employee's employment. Employment agreements often include clauses that restrict the employee's ability to compete with the company, and/or solicit customers/clients and employees for a certain duration after employment ends.

Employment Agreements and Value

A company's assembled and trained workforce by and of itself has additive value to a business enterprise. Value lies in the economic benefit a buyer receives in the relief from the time and expense of having to recruit, hire, and train a comparable workforce. The value of the assembled, trained workforce is determined using a replacement cost approach: what would a buyer incur in terms of recruiting, hiring, and training costs (including inefficiencies due to learning curves) to replace the assembled workforce? Naturally, a workforce of highly skilled and experienced and/or highly compensated employees such as a professional services firm will be more valuable than a workforce of minimum-wage employees such as a retail operation.

Some members of a workforce may also be subject to an employment agreement. Employment agreements are assets of the employer-enterprise. The value of any particular employment agreement is imputed from one or more of three primary components:

1. Employment agreements frequently include clauses restricting the employee's ability to compete or solicit customers, clients, or employees upon expiration of the employment agreement or upon the employee's departure from the employer. Similar to noncompete agreements, the restrictions of these clauses may survive expiration of an employment agreement or termination of employment for a stated period of time. The With and Without method discussed earlier is used to value this feature of the employment agreement.

   When key persons are subject to both noncompete and employment agreements, care must be taken to not "double count" the value of the noncompete agreement and the value of the noncompete clause(s) of the employment agreement.
2. Employment agreements set forth the compensation to be paid to the employee. Although not frequent and perhaps even theoretical, an employment agreement with contractual compensation for the remaining term of the employment agreement that will be less than the expected future market compensation for a comparably qualified and situated candidate may have value resulting from that differential. The company is receiving employee services at a cost less than the market. The present value of the after-tax differential (using an appropriate risk-adjusted discount rate) equates to the value of this component.
3. Employment agreements are reserved for key employees. Similar to the workforce asset, the employment agreement also has value in the relief from costs to recruit, hire, and train comparable personnel. Again, care should be taken to prevent "double counting" for this in the employment agreement and in the workforce in place.

Employment Agreements and Litigation

Employment agreements are contracts. The employer or the employee may make a claim for an alleged breach by the other party of their responsibilities under the agreement and seek damages.

- **Employee breach.** Monetary damages sought by an employer for an alleged breach by the employee will be related to the three components of the employment agreement value just discussed. An employee breach is an impairment of the value of that asset. The damages will relate to the economic losses from competition and solicitation of customers and employees by the former employee (which may include theft of trade secrets and know-how) and the cost of recruiting, hiring, and training a replacement, perhaps at higher compensation.
- **Employer breach.** Claims for damages by employees for the employer's breach may include a wrongful termination action. The employee-plaintiff claims that they and the employment agreement were wrongfully terminated and that they, therefore, are entitled to recover economic benefits of the employment agreement not yet received. Alternatively, the claim may be that a portion of the employment agreement (i.e., not the entire agreement) was breached.

In either case, the economic benefits for which recovery is sought will depend on the facts and circumstances and the specific terms of the employment agreement. Those economic benefits may include:

- Salary and bonuses
- Employee benefits (health insurance, life insurance, 401(k) match, etc.)
- Vehicle allowance
- Club membership
- Deferred compensation
- Profit sharing
- Stock options

The magnitude of the damages will depend on several factors, including:

- Remaining term of the agreement
- Ability of the employee-plaintiff to uphold their obligations under the agreement for the remaining term
- Ability of either party to terminate the agreement early
- Economic value of the employee-plaintiff's compensation and benefits package
- Ability of the employee-plaintiff to find new, comparable employment (referred to as mitigation of damages)
- Economic terms of the new employment

Some economic benefits of an employment agreement may not be fixed, but rather may be contingent and/or dependent on factors that are not controllable by the employee. For example, the amount of bonus, profit share, or deferred compensation may depend on the financial performance and financial condition of the company and may be difficult to estimate. Claims for those types of contingent compensation damages must be accompanied by objective support for the estimates.

Employment agreements are assets of the company. Depending on the facts and circumstances, and the actual terms of the specific agreements, they may have value independent of noncompete and nonsolicitation clauses. The value of employment agreements and the economic benefits therein become the issue in litigation over the agreements.

SUMMARY

A significant amount of business value can be tied up in a company's intangible assets. Intangible assets such as customer relationships, trade secrets, know-how, and other intellectual property frequently are easily transported from one business owner to another. Prudent business owners and buyers of businesses protect these assets by requiring that key persons enter into noncompete agreements with the company. Because of this, noncompete agreements may have material value generated from the protection and preservation of revenues, profits, and cash flows.

Enforcement of noncompete agreements varies by jurisdiction based on state statutes and case law. In those states where such agreements are allowed, certain criteria must be met in order for the noncompete to be valid and enforceable.

Appraiser's judgment is required in the valuation of the noncompete agreement. The preferred method for valuing a noncompete agreement is the With and Without method. First, the present value of the expected impacts on the cash flows of the business are forecasted for the restriction period. Then, the probability of competition from the key person (covenantor) is assigned based on an assessment of the key person's ability and desire to compete, and the feasibility of them successfully competing.

Employment agreements between the company and key personnel are also intangible assets with contributing value to the business enterprise. Employment agreements may have value beyond the noncompete and nonsolicitation clauses of those agreements. This is proven by the vigorous legal battles that result from claims by employers and/or employees due to claimed breach of those agreements by the other party.

REFERENCES FOR EMPLOYMENT AND NONCOMPETITION AGREEMENTS

American Bankruptcy Institute. 2006. "A Guide to Valuation of the Assembled Workforce Intangible Asset." *ABI Institute Journal* (October 2006).

Reilly, Robert F. and Robert P. Schweihs. 2013. "Human Capital Intangible Assets." In *Guide to Intangible Asset Valuation*, Chap. 29, 611–26 (New York: American Institute of Certified Public Accountants, Inc.)

Trugman, Gary. 2022. "Noncompete Agreements." In *Understanding Business Valuations*, 6th ed., Chap. 22, 844–72 (Portland OR: Business Valuation Resources).

CHAPTER 15

Financial Statement Adjustments

Serena Morones, ASA, CPA/ABV, CFE, Paul Heidt, ASA, CPA/ABV, and Terry G. Whitehead, ASA, CPA/ABV

INTRODUCTION

In this chapter you will learn about:

- Reasons appraisers make financial statement adjustments
- Common types of financial statement adjustments
- Adjustments for controlling owner expenses
- Separating nonoperating and excess assets
- Differences in methods of accounting

One of the more frequent sources of controversy in business valuation is adjustments to financial statements made for the purpose of valuation. When reviewing a business valuation, one should ask the following questions:

- Were adjustments made that should not have been made for the purpose of this valuation?
- Are there adjustments that should have been made but were not?
- For the adjustments made, is there adequate support for the amount of each?

REASONS FOR FINANCIAL STATEMENT ADJUSTMENTS

There are several reasons to make financial statement adjustments, and the reviewer can best assess the propriety of each adjustment with these reasons in mind. A certain adjustment may be appropriate for one valuation but not another.

One of the reasons for financial statement adjustments is to make the historical results reflect amounts closer to economic reality for valuation purposes. Another reason, if a market approach is used, is to align the subject company's and guideline public companies' operating results on a more consistent accounting basis for comparative purposes. Similarly, if the subject company's financial ratios are being compared to "industry averages" from an available independent data source, the financial statement adjustments should put the subject company's figures on a basis consistent with the industry-average figures for comparative purposes.

In a somewhat broad sense, it may be helpful to consider financial statement adjustments within the following five categories:

- **Normalization adjustments.** These adjustments reflect unusual or nonrecurring items, which would generally be made for all valuation purposes. While this chapter focuses on the subject company, these adjustments should also be considered for guideline public companies used in the market approach.[1]
- **Personal expenses and related-party transactions.** Transactions between the owners and the company may not be at arm's length (i.e., do not reflect market rates). To the extent that they are not and can be changed by the interest being valued, they should be adjusted.
- **Control adjustments.** These are adjustments that a typical control owner could influence, usually to assess the economic income that would potentially be available to a controlling ownership interest. These typically would be made if valuing a controlling ownership interest but not a noncontrolling ownership interest.
- **Nonoperating adjustments.** In most instances, nonoperating items should be adjusted from the balance sheet and/or income statement and treated separately for valuation purposes. A primary reason for doing this is to value the subject company's operations independently. Any nonoperating assets would then be considered separately and added to the operating value of the subject company, if appropriate. In some cases, these adjustments may be highly controversial, which will be discussed later in this chapter.
- **Accounting basis adjustments.** For valuation purposes, accrual basis financial statements are generally considered to be most appropriate. As a result, adjustments that convert the subject company's financial data from a cash basis to an accrual basis may be necessary, including the recognition of accounts receivable and accounts payable. Additionally, financial statements prepared in accordance with Generally Accepted Accounting Principles (GAAP) are generally considered preferable to tax-basis financial statements. GAAP financial statements follow the matching principle regarding the timing recognition of revenue and expenses, which may differ from tax-basis reporting. These adjustments are intended to result in comparability between the guideline companies and the subject company and the expected economic reality of long-term normalized operating results.

Some adjustments may affect both the income statement and the balance sheet, while others may only affect one or the other. Destruction of a building by fire, for example, ordinarily would result in a lower-than-normal reported net income and removal of the building from the company's balance sheet. In this circumstance, the income statement might be adjusted to eliminate the effects of this nonrecurring event. However, there would be no need to adjust the balance sheet because the building no longer exists (and has presumably already been written off). If the market approach has been used in the valuation, it is appropriate to make similar adjustments to the guideline companies' financial statements, as discussed in Chapter 8, "The Market Approach."

While the potential variety of financial statement adjustments is extensive, this chapter specifically discusses those most commonly encountered by an appraiser. References to more extended discussions of financial statement adjustments are included at the end of this chapter. There are available alternatives in acceptable accounting policies, even within the constraints of GAAP. To the extent that the subject company's accounting policies differ from typical industry or guideline company policies, it may be appropriate to make adjustments to align the subject company's reported results for comparability purposes.

---

1. For example, a guideline public company may report discontinued operations for which the analyst would adjust when computing market multiples.

NORMALIZING ADJUSTMENTS

The basic concept of normalizing adjustments is to present data so that it represents the economic reality of an ongoing business or of accounting conventions customarily used in a particular industry for comparative purposes. If the historical financial statements are to be used as guidance for estimating future economic income, then the effect of unusual or nonrecurring items should be adjusted (i.e., eliminated). If the subject company's financial statements are to be compared with other specific companies or industry averages, they should be aligned on a comparable accounting basis. This section briefly discusses the most commonly encountered normalizing adjustments and identifies others that, although less frequent, are still considered valid for valuation purposes.

It is not necessary for accounting entries to be classified as "extraordinary" under GAAP to qualify as nonrecurring for valuation purposes. There are many items, such as gains or losses on sales of major assets, that are unusual or nonrecurring for the subject company but would not necessarily be identified as extraordinary under GAAP.

Nonrecurring Items

The effect of nonrecurring items should be adjusted from the subject company's financial statements to make them more representative of ongoing operations. Such adjustments also usually make the financial statements more comparable to industry averages or to guideline public companies. Also note that similar adjustments may be necessary for the guideline companies.

Some examples of nonrecurring items include:

- Gains or losses from the sale of major assets
- Gains or losses from litigation
- Unusual level of bad debts
- Net casualty losses (after insurance recovery)
- Effects of labor strikes or other business disruptions

While this list is brief, it conveys the general idea. These items are adjusted so that historical financial statements are more representative of the subject company's ongoing operations.

Sometimes an appraiser may regard an item (such as a labor strike) as *infrequent* although not absolutely *nonrecurring*. A reasonable treatment in that case may be to allocate the adjustment over several years of income statements instead of eliminating it entirely. The same may apply to write-downs, which typically should be charged to a series of prior periods.

When the appraiser adjusts the income or expense, it is important that the adjustment nets out any related income or potential capital gains tax effect, as discussed later in this chapter (that is, the adjustment should be net of any income tax consequences).

PERSONAL EXPENSES

Personal expenses recorded in the books of a company can overstate operating expenses and understate the profitability of a company. Some common examples of personal or discretionary expenses reported in the financial statements include:

- Automobile expenses for personal use
- Credit card charges for personal items paid by the company
- Meals and travel expenses unrelated to the business
- Fitness or country club dues
- Personal telephone or utilities
- Professional services, such as a divorce attorney or other personal contractors
- Expenses related to children, such as wages above the market value of work performed or college tuition

An appraiser or forensic accountant may be engaged to analyze expenses recorded in the accounting records of a business and determine if a business owner included personal expenses. Sometimes the personal expenses are obvious; other times they may fall into a gray area considered "discretionary expenses." These discretionary expenses are expenses that may be common but are neither distinguished as *clearly necessary* nor *potentially unnecessary*. One business owner may ultimately spend more money on this category of expense than another business owner in the same line of business.

Meals and entertainment are examples of discretionary expenses. Some business owners may feel a need to frequently entertain clients, while another owner in the same line of business does not spend as much money on meals and entertainment. Another example may be a higher level of compensation and benefits paid to employees.

The process of analyzing whether these discretionary expenses are ordinary and necessary or personal in nature is often subjective. However, an experienced appraiser can typically identify the patterns in business expenses that emerge over time. Through exposure to a wide variety of businesses, an appraiser may form a reasoned opinion about what types of expenses qualify as an ordinary and necessary business expenses rather than personal expenses.

The effect of personal expenses should be adjusted in the subject company's financial statements to make them more representative of ongoing operations and to make them more comparable to industry averages or to other guideline companies.

Discontinued Operations

If a company has discontinued a line of business that previously reported income or losses that have not been (or would not be) replaced by alternative uses of the company's resources with comparable returns, then the effects of those discontinued operations typically should be adjusted. If an alternative line of business is being consummated, the financial statements should be adjusted for any abnormalities that might result during the start-up phase.

If it is difficult or impossible to sort out the effects of the discontinued operation(s) in the company data, then a reasonable alternative may be to consider financial statements only for the periods subsequent to the discontinued operations. If using a market approach, averages of financial data for the guideline companies should be compared only for periods similar to those used for the subject company.

Inventory Accounting Methods

Two basic categories of inventory adjustments often are encountered: (1) first-in, first-out (FIFO) versus last-in, first-out (LIFO) accounting policies and (2) write-down and write-off policies.

- **FIFO versus LIFO accounting policies.** Both GAAP and the IRS (tax law) allow accounting for inventory on either a FIFO basis or a LIFO basis. The FIFO inventory accounting method assumes, for accounting purposes, that the oldest unit of an inventory item purchased is the next unit sold. The LIFO method assumes that the most recently purchased unit of an inventory item purchased is the next unit sold. To the extent that inventory prices go up, LIFO produces lower figures for earnings and inventory than does FIFO.

  If using the market approach, all of the companies' data should be stated on a comparable basis, either all LIFO or all FIFO (unless the difference is immaterial). If a company accounts on a FIFO basis, the financial statements do not contain the data that would be needed to convert to a LIFO basis. Therefore, if some companies are on a LIFO basis and others are on a FIFO basis, the only practical adjustment available is to convert all companies to a FIFO basis.

  There are also some other methods of inventory accounting that are acceptable under GAAP that should be adjusted for valuation purposes, but they are encountered infrequently and thus beyond the scope of this chapter.
- **Write-down and write-off policies.** Companies may be very aggressive or very conservative in their periodic inventory adjustments. Some companies may write off anything that has not sold in a certain number of months, resulting in tens or hundreds of thousands of dollars of salable inventory adjusted from the balance sheet and expensed through cost of goods sold. Others may hold obsolete inventory that should have been previously written off the balance sheet and charged to cost of goods sold. This is a subject that appraisers typically address during a site visit and management interviews if they believe it may be a material item.

Depreciation and Depletion Methods and Schedules

There is wide latitude within GAAP regarding methods of accounting for depreciation and depletion. There is also considerable latitude regarding the length of the time over which various assets may be depreciated. While the methods used for income tax reporting are prescribed, those methods often differ from those methods used for financial reporting.

Again, the general goals of adjustments are to approximate economic reality and to conform to industry practices if comparisons are to be made either to industry averages or to individual guideline companies.

Net Operating Losses Carried Forward

If a company is allocating a prior period's net operating loss (NOL) to current or future period earnings, the effect of that normally would be adjusted from the income statement, since it would not represent ongoing operations and because guideline companies and industry averages would not be expected to reflect such NOLs.

Whether the present value of such NOLs is a proper addition to the balance sheet for valuation purposes is based on the facts and circumstances and may become an issue. The main criterion for deciding whether to recognize NOLs as assets is the degree of certainty and timing of the company's ability to deduct them against future taxable income (or the potential for a buyer of the company to do so). In most transactions of companies with NOLs, some compromise about their value is reached if they are transferable, although some buyers may not accord them any value at all. In any event, the value of NOLs projected to be used in the future should be converted to a present value, with an appropriate discount rate typically being the subject company's cost of capital.

Reserve and Allowance Accounts

Many reserve and allowance expense items may appear on the income statement, and related reserve accounts may appear on the balance sheet.

- **Allowance for doubtful accounts—accounts receivable.** Many companies reporting accounts receivable deduct some allowance for potentially uncollectible accounts. As with inventory, some companies are aggressive and others conservative in writing off or establishing valuation reserves for potentially uncollectible accounts. Some companies may have written substantial amounts of receivables off their books that eventually may be collected, while other companies may show no allowance for doubtful accounts and no related bad-debt expense, even though their receivables may include substantial uncollectible accounts. Analysts can vary considerably in their degree of thoroughness in investigating these items and in their aggressiveness or conservatism in adjusting the figures presented on the financial statements.
- **Pension liabilities.** Underfunded or overfunded pensions can be another area of adjustment and, in some cases, controversy. If a company's pension trust is underfunded, the company typically shows a liability account, which it reduces with annual contributions. Amounts can be highly controversial, depending on actuarial assumptions. If a company's pension trust is overfunded, the company rarely shows the surplus as an asset, but some would argue that the company should do so for valuation purposes. In some cases, if a discounted cash flow method is used, the recognition of overfunding may be reflected through a lower level of contributions in the future.

Other Normalizing Adjustments

Many other adjustments may be encountered either to approximate economic reality or to adjust accounting figures for comparative purposes. If any of them become a controversy over which the court or the attorney desires insight beyond what is presented in the evidence or in this chapter, the references at the end of this chapter should be helpful. The following are some other subjects that may give rise to normalization adjustments:

- Treatment of intangible assets, including leaseholds and other intangibles
- Capitalization versus expensing of various costs
  - Usually, a sizable current expenditure that is expected to produce benefits in future periods is recorded as an asset (i.e., capitalized). Later, as the asset is disposed of or used up, its balance is reduced, and an expense recorded. If the expenditure is inconsequential or if no future benefits are apparent, the current expenditure might be immediately recorded as an expense. Obviously, judgments regarding the materiality of or the future benefits associated with the current expenditures can differ across entities, resulting in inconsistent accounting treatments.
- Timing of the recognition of revenues and expenses
  - Contract work (e.g., work in progress, contingent fee work, percentage of completion or completed contract terms)
  - Installment sales
  - Actual or contingent liabilities (e.g., guarantees, warranties)
  - Prior-period adjustments
- Deferred maintenance (e.g., routine maintenance neglected)
- Treatment of interests in affiliates
- Adequacy or deficiency of liabilities

All these normalizing adjustments and many others are discussed in the "References for Financial Statement Adjustments" at the end of this chapter.

CONTROL ADJUSTMENTS

Control adjustments reflect changes that only a control owner would have the ability to make in the operation of the company, as opposed to adjustments in the presentation of actual operations or conditions. For the most part, this category of adjustments deals with financial relationships with insiders or members of a control group. To some extent, this category could include adjustments for perceived inefficiencies or excess costs.

Reasonable Compensation

The most frequent financial statement adjustment issue is reasonable compensation to control parties. "Compensation" in this context includes all payments and perquisites—salary, bonuses (or other forms of incentive compensation), stock and stock options, retirement plans, medical benefits, and expenses—that could be construed as personal benefits. Chapter 13, "Reasonable Compensation," covers in more detail the adjustments for reasonable compensation.

Related-Party Transactions

Related-party (insider) transactions that might be adjusted usually are payments for services at other than market rates or of dubious value. The most common of these are:

- **Nonmarket rate rents or leases.** If the related parties lease premises to the operating company, such leases may not be at market rates. This adjustment would involve restating the expense on the income statement at an estimated market rent, which is often provided by a real estate appraiser or other qualified specialist.
- **Employment payments.** If relatives or friends are on the payroll at more than the value of services rendered, an adjustment to eliminate or reduce that expense may be warranted.
- **Planes, trains, and automobiles (not to mention boats).** It is common to question the company's need for one or more airplanes, luxury automobiles, yachts, sailboats, condominiums, hunting lodges, and other retreats, although there are situations in which they are legitimate expenses. If these items are adjusted, this typically involves reducing or eliminating the income statement expenses and sometimes reclassifying the assets to other (nonoperating) assets rather than operating assets.

Note: There exists a minority (but legitimate) school of thought that considers what was just classified as control adjustments to be normalizing adjustments, even in a noncontrolling interest valuation where the noncontrolling interest holder cannot force the company policy to change. The reason for this is to align the subject company on a basis comparable to the guideline companies. A discount for lack of control may then be required at the end of the valuation.[2]

SEPARATING OPERATING ASSETS FROM NONOPERATING AND EXCESS ASSETS

Two primary reasons to separate operating assets from nonoperating and excess assets are:

- To make comparisons with other entities
- To consider adding some value for nonoperating or excess assets to the going-concern value of the subject company as an operating entity. (If one is valuing a company on a noncontrolling interest basis because the noncontrolling owner cannot control the disposal of the assets, there may be little or no adjustment.)

2. David Laro & Shannon Pratt, Business Valuation and Taxes: Procedure, Law, and Perspective 138 (2d ed. 2011).

Comparisons with Other Entities

If the analyst is using a market approach, the guideline companies and the subject company should be as comparable as possible to make the comparison of derived financial ratios as valid as possible. Thus, valuation multiples derived from guideline companies can be applied to the operations of the subject company to derive a value as an operating company.

If the analyst is using an income approach, the operations should be valued separately from the nonoperating assets, using comparative industry data to help develop appropriate discount and/or capitalization rates for a well-defined industry operation comparable to others.

Similarly, if comparing various financial ratios with industry averages and guideline companies, the comparisons are most meaningful if the companies are similar operationally.

While this separation is desired for purity in comparisons, it leaves the sticky problem of how to treat the nonoperating or excess assets separated from the operating assets.

Treatment of Nonoperating and Excess Assets

If nonoperating or excess assets are separated from the operating assets, then the question arises about how to treat them for valuation purposes. Even the question about whether something should be classified as a nonoperating or excess asset may be controversial. It may be possible to find public companies whose major assets are similar to the nonoperating assets of the subject company. In this event, relevant valuation multiples derived from the public guideline companies may be used to value the nonoperating assets of the subject company.

However, much of the answer to the appropriate treatment of nonoperating or excess assets depends on whether the valuation is carried out on a controlling or noncontrolling interest basis. If the valuation is performed on a controlling basis, each asset may be valued assuming its highest and best use. Therefore, if it is worth more in liquidation than in use, the estimated net proceeds from liquidation may be added to the value as an operating company.

But even on a controlling basis, if valuing the subject company as a going concern, some policies that the control owners follow might not be followed by others, and there may be a debate about the existing control owners' policies. Treatment then becomes a matter of negotiation. There are no hard-and-fast rules.

If valuing on a noncontrolling interest basis, the noncontrolling interest holder likely has little or no influence over devoting the assets to their highest and best use. In this case, additional consideration may be necessary in order to identify potential value attributable to a noncontrolling interest holder.

CASH VERSUS ACCRUAL ACCOUNTING

Cash accounting means that both revenues and expenses are recognized when they are received or paid. Accrual accounting means that revenues are recognized when they are earned (as opposed to received), and expenses are recognized when they are incurred (as opposed to paid). For example, under accrual accounting, a legal fee is recorded as revenue when it is earned, even though it may not be collected until a year later. Under cash accounting, the revenue would not be recognized until the cash was in hand.

Valuation is based primarily on accrual accounting, reflecting revenues earned and expenses incurred. Certain closely held businesses, including many professional practices, report their financial statements on a cash basis. If so, for valuation purposes, it usually is necessary to convert the cash basis financial statements to accrual basis financial statements before proceeding with the valuation process.

If there is a buy-sell agreement tied to cash-basis accounting, then there may be an issue about whether or not to convert to an accrual basis for valuation purposes. This controversy often arises in marital dissolutions (see Chapter 22, "Marital Dissolution Valuations"). In this case, it generally is necessary to consult precedential case law in the relevant jurisdiction to assess whether the court will consider the buy-sell agreement to be controlling, or what impact it might have, if any.

ILLUSTRATIVE FINANCIAL STATEMENT ADJUSTMENTS

Exhibits 15-1 and 15-2 show typical presentations reflecting a few examples of financial statement adjustments discussed in this chapter. In some cases, the text of the report may contain more explanation of each adjustment than the brief footnote in the exhibit, especially if the adjustment is significant. In other cases, it may be necessary to obtain the analyst's working papers or to question the analyst to gain a more complete explanation.

Exhibit 15-1 Meteor Manufacturing, Inc.: Adjustments to Income Statement

	20X3	20X4	20X5	20X6	20X7
Net Income as Reported	$240,000	$250,000	$150,000	$280,000	$300,000
Plus: Loss from Fire[a]			80,000		
Plus (Minus): Adjustments to Costs of Goods Sold	15,000	(10,000)	10,000	20,000	30,000
to Convert from LIFO to FIFO[b]					
Plus: Adjustments to Widget Machines' Depreciation[c]	7,000	7,000	8,000	10,000	
Plus: Compensation Adjustment[d]	60,000	70,000	75,000	80,000	100,000
Adjusted Net Income	$322,000	$317,000	$323,000	$390,000	$430,000

a. Physical damage was $250,000 and business interruption loss estimated at $150,000, totaling $400,000, offset by $300,000 of insurance. Loss of $100,000 less $20,000 tax effect (at 20% effective tax rate) equals $80,000.

b. Convert Meteor and guideline companies from LIFO to FIFO inventory basis, net of related tax effect.

c. To convert Meteor depreciation from five-year straight line to seven-year straight line (net of related tax effect) to conform to average industry practice.

d. To adjust CEO compensation to level typical for similar executives, net of 20% effective tax rate.

Exhibit 15-2 Meteor Manufacturing, Inc.: Adjustments to Balance Sheet

	As Reported	Adjustments	As Adjusted
Assets			
Cash	$ 50,000		$ 50,000
Accounts Receivable	30,000		30,000
Inventory[a]	200,000	100,000	300,000
Total Current Assets	280,000	100,000	380,000
Plant and Equipment	200,000		200,000
Less: Accumulated Depreciation[b]	(100,000)	30,000	(70,000)
Net Plant and Equipment	100,000	30,000	130,000
Total Assets	$ 380,000	$130,000	$510,000
Liabilities and Equity			
Accounts Payable	$ 60,000		$ 60,000
Long-term Debt	200,000		200,000
Total Liabilities	260,000		260,000
Stockholders' Equity	120,000	130,000	250,000
Total Liabilities and Equity	$ 380,000		$510,000

a. To adjust inventory from LIFO to FIFO basis to put book value on a basis comparable to guideline companies.

b. To convert Meteor portion of accumulated depreciation from a five-year life to a seven-year life to put book value of plant and equipment on an accounting basis comparable to guideline companies.

In the example of income statement adjustments, the tax effect (the effective cost is reduced due to the tax deductibility of the item) is accounted for in each individual line item; another acceptable treatment is to adjust the pretax income and take the tax adjustment as an additional line item.

Income Statement Adjustments

The following adjustments, presented in Exhibit 15-1, are examples of some common adjustments typically made by appraisers to the income statement:

- **Nonrecurring event adjustment.** Adjustment (a) for the fire is an example of an adjustment for a nonrecurring event. This adjustment would be made whether valuing a controlling or noncontrolling interest, to make the financial statements more representative of ongoing earning power and more directly comparable to industry averages and guideline companies.
- **Inventory adjustment.** Adjustment (b) is to adjust the subject company to a FIFO inventory basis for direct comparison with guideline companies (those that were on LIFO also were adjusted). This adjustment would be made whether valuing a controlling or noncontrolling interest if necessary for comparative purposes.
- **Depreciation adjustment.** Adjustment (c) decreases the annual depreciation charged to one-seventh of the purchase cost per year from one-fifth of the purchase cost per

year (thus increasing adjusted net income) to conform to the typical guideline company depreciation policies for comparative purposes. This adjustment would be made whether valuing a controlling or noncontrolling interest if appropriate for comparative purposes.

- **Compensation adjustment.** Adjustment (d) removes compensation that is above industry averages for comparable executives from expenses, thus increasing the adjusted net income (net of the income tax effect of the lower expense). This adjustment would be typical when valuing a controlling interest on the assumption that a control owner could replace the Chief Executive Officer with an equally competent executive for the amount of compensation substituted on the income statement. This adjustment may also be warranted in valuing a noncontrolling interest; however, consideration should be given to the fact that the noncontrolling interest holder could not cause this expense reduction to occur.[3]

Balance Sheet Adjustments

The following adjustments, shown in Exhibit 15-2, are two examples of adjustments made by appraisers to the balance sheet:

- **Inventory adjustment.** Adjustment (a) adds the LIFO reserve shown on the company's financial statement footnotes back to the inventory account so that it is reflected as if on a FIFO basis. This adjustment would be made for comparative purposes whether valuing on a controlling or noncontrolling interest basis.
- **Depreciation adjustment.** Adjustment (b) decreases the accumulated depreciation, thus increasing the net plant and equipment to a seven-year depreciation schedule for Meteor Manufacturing. The purpose is to adjust the book value for comparative purposes to the same basis as guideline companies and industry averages.

Note: Although these adjustments may bring the asset accounts closer to the fair market value, this is *not* their purpose. The assets normally would be further analyzed if an asset approach were to be used. These adjustments are for comparative purposes, to make meaningful financial ratio comparisons between the subject company and guideline companies or industry averages and to make it possible to use meaningful valuation multiples in the market approach.

For example, note that the adjustments more than doubled the book value of the stockholders' equity. If the industry average price-to-book value ratio were 2.0, applying that ratio to the unadjusted book value would give a misleading indication of value for the equity of less than half of what it should be based on the adjusted balance sheet.

SUMMARY

In valuation, financial statement adjustments are made to reflect a company's historical results closer to economic reality, align the subject company's operating results with those of guideline companies, and to allow for more direct comparisons to industry averages. Financial statement adjustments include normalization adjustments, control adjustments, separation of nonoperating items from operating items, and adjusting for

3. Some analysts would make this adjustment for comparability even when valuing a noncontrolling interest, and then reflect the compensation disparity in a discount for lack of control.

differing accounting policies. Common income statement adjustments to consider include the removal of nonrecurring events and adjustments to inventory, depreciation, and compensation, while common balance sheet adjustments include inventory and depreciation adjustments.

REFERENCES FOR FINANCIAL STATEMENT ADJUSTMENTS

Books

Fishman, Jay, Bruce A. Johnson, and Kent Pummel. 2023. "Review and Adjustment of the Financial Statements." In PPC's *Guide to Business Valuations*, 404 (Carrollton, TX: Thomson Reuters).

Laro, David and Shannon P. Pratt. 2011. "Adjustments to Financial Statements." In *Business Valuation and Federal Taxes: Procedures, Law and Perspective*, 2nd ed. Chap. 11, 133–39 (Hoboken, NJ: John Wiley & Sons).

Penman, Stephen H. 2012. *Financial Statement Analysis & Security Valuation*, 5th ed. (New York: McGraw-Hill).

Pratt, Shannon P. and ASA Educational Foundation. 2022. "Analyzing Financial Statements" and "Financial Statement Ratio Analysis." In *Shannon Pratt's Valuing a Business: The Analysis and Appraisal of Closely Held Businesses*, 6th ed. Chap. 7, 107–32; Chap. 8, 133–54 (New York: McGraw-Hill).

Subramanyam, K.R. 2014. *Financial Statement Analysis*, 11th ed. (New York: McGraw-Hill).

Article

Morones, Serena and Murphy, Jennifer. 2014. "Is This Business or Personal? Identifying Personal Expenses Run through a Business." Morones Analytics.

CHAPTER 16

Comparative Financial Statement Analysis

Serena Morones, ASA, CPA/ABV, CFE, Paul Heidt, ASA, CPA/ABV, and Terry G. Whitehead, ASA, CPA/ABV

INTRODUCTION[1]

In this chapter you will learn about:

- Reasons for comparative financial statement analysis
- Tools of financial statement analysis
    - Horizontal analysis
    - Trend analysis
    - Vertical analysis
- Analysis of profitability
- Analysis of liquidity
- Analysis of risk
- Industry data resources

The chapter provides a useful reference for those seeking some insight into the calculation and interpretation of financial statement analysis techniques commonly used in business valuation.

While financial statement analysis is an exercise based on historical data, it can help in formulating expectations about the future. These expectations are the basis for valuation, and they fall largely into two categories: **levels of operating performance** (for example, various measures of profitability) and **risk** (the certainty or uncertainty of achieving expected results).

The valuation analyst should use financial statement analysis as a guide when formulating or reviewing future expectations of a subject company's financial performance. In the income approach, for example, the financial statement analysis should assist with the formulation or review of both the future operating results (i.e., forecasts) and the degree of risk in achieving the forecasted results, which affects the discount or capitalization rate to be applied to those forecasts. In the market approach, the financial statement

---

1. The authors thank the late Dr. Donald S. Shannon, former esteemed professor of accountancy at DePaul University and practicing business valuation analyst who served as founding president of the Business Valuation Association of Chicago and contributed the chapter in the first edition. The authors would also like to thank Angelina McKedy who updated the chapter in the second edition.

analysis should provide a reasonable level of comparability for both the expected growth and risk with the selected guideline public companies, both of which may have an impact on the selected multiples to be applied to the subject company's fundamental data.

Readers should keep in mind that all financial statement analysis discussed in this chapter is **based on book values after normalizing adjustments and not on market values.** Thus, to the extent that companies in an industry are more homogenous with respect to factors such as the age of their assets and their accounting practices, the more meaningful the comparative financial analysis will be.

Finally, every financial ratio may not provide a similar level of significance in any given valuation. The nature of the industry and/or the subject company may indicate certain ratios are particularly relevant to the valuation at hand. Some ratios, although computed in a standardized ratio template, may be irrelevant for a particular valuation and require no discussion at all. Ideally, the analyst will identify those financial factors that are significant to the valuation of the subject company and explain how those factors affect the inputs or assumptions (e.g., forecasts, discount and capitalization rates, valuation multiples) that lead to the valuation conclusion. If the financial statement analysis is not connected, at some point in the report, to the steps leading to the value conclusion, it is a rather empty exercise.

Most readers have likely analyzed and compared products such as homes, automobiles, or major appliances and identified relevant comparisons between models or brands. In financial markets, ownership interests are the "products," and their financial reports can be considered the brochures used to describe those products. Financial statement analysis, or ratio analysis, simply provides a means of organizing the relevant financial information to facilitate an orderly comparison. While a number of useful ratios are a natural byproduct of this analysis, the analyst is primarily concerned with identifying future expected entity performance or comparing the subject company to industry benchmarks. Hopefully, a critical review of a company's past performance will highlight its relevant characteristics, resulting in more insightful analysis and interpretation of a company's forecasts, to the extent that the company prepares forecasts, and expectations.

Financial statement or ratio analysis involves comparison. Seldom is the result of an individual ratio conclusive on its own. However, changes in financial ratios from one period to another, or over a succession of periods, can be very informative. Likewise, the comparison of the subject company's ratios to the ratios of its competitors or to industry benchmarks can also be very informative.

The financial information used in this chapter represents three hypothetical steel companies.

TOOLS OF COMPARATIVE FINANCIAL STATEMENT ANALYSIS

Analysts use several types of financial tools to make meaningful comparisons, for the subject company over time and against other benchmark companies and/or industry averages. These financial tools are discussed in this chapter in the following order:

- **Horizontal analysis.** Comparison of a subject company's operating results between one year and the next.
- **Trend analysis.** Comparison of changes in a subject company's trends or results over several successive years.

- **Vertical analysis.** Comparisons among specific companies and/or between the subject company and industry averages for the same period. Vertical analysis employs the financial tool referred to as common-size statements:
  - **Common-size income statements.** Every line item is expressed as a percentage of sales.
  - **Common-size balance sheets.** Every line item is expressed as a percentage of total assets.
- **Profitability ratios.** Various measures of profitability expressed as a percentage of a selected financial statement benchmark.
- **Liquidity measures.** Ratios among various financial statement items indicative of the subject company's short-term liquidity.
- **Risk measures.** Ratios indicating a company's financial risk.

Various authors and analysts may classify these financial tools by different categories or different names, but the essence of the idea is quite consistent from one author or analyst to another.

One caveat is worth mentioning at the outset. There is no single set of ratios published by reporting services or used by analysts that establishes a universally accepted convention. Different reporting services furnish different ratios, although they may have the same name, such as "profit divided by total assets." For example, Risk Management Association (RMA) provides the ratio "profit *before* taxes divided by total assets," while Dun & Bradstreet provides "profit *after* taxes divided by total assets." Furthermore, a ratio bearing the same name may be calculated in a slightly different way by different services or analysts. Also, the different services may furnish information for different time periods or intervals.

For the comparisons to be meaningful, they should be computed the same way for the subject company as for the companies used for comparison. For clarity, the valuation report should include a definition of each ratio used, either in the text or in an exhibit or appendix.

HORIZONTAL ANALYSIS

Exhibit 16-1 shows the balance sheets and income statements for Jasper Steel for two years. An analyst could likely spot some interesting changes in the amounts, as reported, from 2020 to 2021. However, Exhibit 16-2 shows that after applying horizontal analysis, the significant changes in the information become even more apparent.

Horizontal analysis involves displaying the amounts and percentages of the changes in the operating results from one year to the next. For example, accounts receivable decreased by $87,108, which represents a decrease of 22.5%.

Notice in the balance sheet that total assets increased by $242,162, or 8.1%. There was a nearly proportional increase in inventory. However, other current assets and net plant and equipment increased proportionately more than the total assets. These increases were partially offset by the significant drop in accounts receivable.

In the income statement, net income decreased by $30,774, or 10.5%. This was due in part to the 0.8% decline in sales accompanied by the 0.4% increase in cost of goods sold and the 1.8% increase in selling, general, and administrative expenses. These three shifts were responsible for a decrease in the operating income of $48,671. This decline was partially offset by a significant increase in the nonoperating income and lower income tax expense.

The analyst might have gleaned these observations from the presentations in Exhibit 16-1. However, showing the percentages of the change together with the respective dollar amounts (as in Exhibit 16-2) makes it easier to identify what has happened over the interval.

Of course, these observations, per se, are not answers; they simply raise questions to be answered. Why did these changes take place? What might the underlying causes for these current changes imply about future expectations? Are these transient changes or are similar changes likely to persist?

Exhibit 16-1 Jasper Steel: Two-Year Balance Sheet and Income Statement

	Jasper Steel	
Balance Sheet (000$)	**12/31/2021**	**12/31/2020**
Cash and Marketable Securities	$308,696	$283,381
Accounts Receivable	299,244	386,352
Inventory	435,884	397,048
Other Current Assets	85,643	58,727
Total Current Assets	1,129,467	1,125,508
Net Plant and Equipment	2,097,078	1,858,875
Total Assets	$3,226,545	$2,984,383
Total Current Liabilities	$486,897	$524,453
Long-Term Debt	215,450	167,950
Other Liabilities	169,250	139,362
Total Liabilities	871,597	831,765
Retained Earnings	2,016,856	1,795,276
Other Equity	338,092	357,342
Shareholders' Equity	2,354,948	2,152,618
Total Liabilities and Equity	$3,226,545	$2,984,383

	Jasper Steel	
Income Statement (000$)	**12/31/2021**	**12/31/2020**
Sales	$4,151,232	$4,184,497
Cost of Goods Sold	3,591,783	3,578,941
Gross Margin	559,449	605,556
Selling, General, and Administrative Expenses	147,973	145,409
Operating Income	411,476	460,147
Nonoperating Income	3,832	35
Income Before Taxes	415,308	460,182
Income Taxes	151,600	165,700
Net Income	$263,708	$294,482

Exhibit 16-2 Jasper Steel: Horizontal Analysis of Balance Sheet and Income Statement

	Jasper Steel	
Balance Sheet (000$)	**Amount of Change**	**% Change**
Cash and Marketable Securities	$25,315	8.9%
Accounts Receivable	(87,108)	- 22.5%
Inventory	38,836	9.8%
Other Current Assets	26,916	45.8%
Total Current Assets	3,959	0.4%
Net Plant and Equipment	238,203	12.8%
Total Assets	$242,162	8.1%
Total Current Liabilities	($37,556)	-7.2%
Long-Term Debt	47,500	28.3%
Other Liabilities	29,888	21.4%
Total Liabilities	39,832	4.8%
Retained Earnings	221,580	12.3%
Other Equity	(19,250)	- 5.4%
Shareholders' Equity	202,330	9.4%
Total Liabilities and Equity	$242,162	8.1%

	Jasper Steel	
Income Statement (000$)	**12/31/2021**	**12/31/2020**
Sales	($33,265)	- 0.8%
Cost of Goods Sold	12,842	0.4%
Gross Margin	(46,107)	- 7.6%
Selling, General, and Administrative Expenses	2,564	1.8%
Operating Income	(48,671)	- 10.6%
Nonoperating Income	3,797	10848.60%
Income Before Taxes	(44,874)	- 9.8%
Income Taxes	(14,100)	- 8.5%
Net Income	($30,774)	- 10.5%

Horizontal analysis does not provide all the answers. However, it does help the analyst identify important questions to consider.

TREND ANALYSIS

Trend analysis is a variation of horizontal analysis. Instead of focusing on changes from one year to the next, trend analysis describes changes over several successive years using one of three popular methods. Trends can be analyzed on the basis of ratios (as in Exhibit 16-4) or as absolute amounts (as in Exhibit 16-5).

Exhibit 16-3 shows the sales for Omega Steel Mills and Jasper Steel for four years.

Jasper's sales are 4.5 to 5.5 times greater than Omega's sales. This difference in magnitude makes it difficult to determine which company has experienced the greater sales growth over the entire interval, each year relative to the base year, by simply reviewing the dollar amounts.

The first method is demonstrated in Exhibit 16-4. This exhibit shows the data from Exhibit 16-3 expressed as percentages of the base year, 2018. For example, Omega's figure of 125.5% for 2021 is calculated by dividing $892,583 by $710,971 and multiplying by 100.

Exhibit 16-3 Omega Steel Mills and Jasper Steel: Sales Figures in Dollars

SALES (000$)	12/31/2021	12/31/2020	12/31/2019	12/31/2018
Omega Steel Mills	892,583	768,558	772,815	710,971
Jasper Steel	4,151,232	4,184,497	3,647,030	3,462,045

Exhibit 16-4 Omega Steel Mills and Jasper Steel: Sales Figures in Percentages

SALES (Base = 2018)	12/31/2021	12/31/2020	12/31/2019	12/31/2018
Omega Steel Mills	125.5%	108.1%	108.7%	100.0%
Jasper Steel	119.9%	120.9%	105.3%	100.0%

Once the figures have been converted in this fashion, it becomes apparent that Omega's sales growth exceeded that of Jasper (although in 2020, the reverse was true).

The second and third methods for describing trends will be illustrated using Omega's sales figures from 2012 through 2021 as shown in the first three columns of Exhibit 16-5. (The "period" is simply an alternative way to identify the year. Zero is the earliest year and nine is the most recent year.)

The second method is to fit a trend line to the data. The points in Exhibit 16-6 represent Omega's sales by period. The dotted line has been fitted through these points (using regression analysis, a statistical technique). The numerical values associated with the line are shown in the fourth column of Exhibit 16-5. The important thing to recognize about this method is that it presumes sales are increasing by a constant amount each period.

The third method is to calculate a growth rate. In Exhibit 16-5, the initial sales figure (for period zero) is $230,192, and the final figure (for period nine) is $892,583. Mathematically, it is easy to find the percentage increase that, if applied period by period, will cause the initial amount to grow to the final amount. In this example, this percentage, or annual growth rate, is 16.25%.

The fifth column of Exhibit 16-5 shows the numerical values associated with the "smooth" transition from the initial figure to the final figure. Exhibit 16-7 is identical to

Exhibit 16-6 with the addition of a solid line representing this "smooth" transition. The important thing to recognize about this method is that it presumes sales are increasing by a constant percentage each period.

Exhibit 16-5 Omega Steel Mills Sales Figures

(1)	(2)	(3)	(4)	(5)
Year	**Period**	**Omega's Sales**	**Adding the Constant Amount of 69,928.9**	**Applying the Growth Rate of 16.25%**
2012	0	**230,192**	296,472	**230,192**
2013	1	331,234	366,401	267,600
2014	2	489,357	436,330	311,086
2015	3	397,722	506,259	361,640
2016	4	679,823	576,188	420,409
2017	5	838,268	646,117	488,728
2018	6	710,971	716,046	568,149
2019	7	772,815	785,975	660,477
2020	8	768,558	855,903	767,809
2021	9	**892,583**	925,832	**892,583**

Exhibit 16-6 Trend of Omega Steel Mills Sales

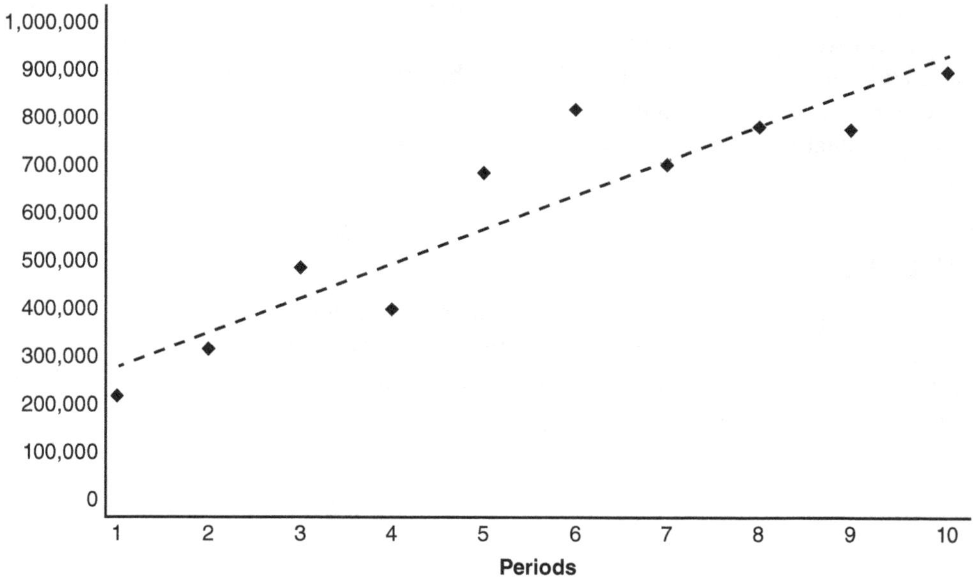

Exhibit 16-7 Growth of Omega Steel Mills Sales

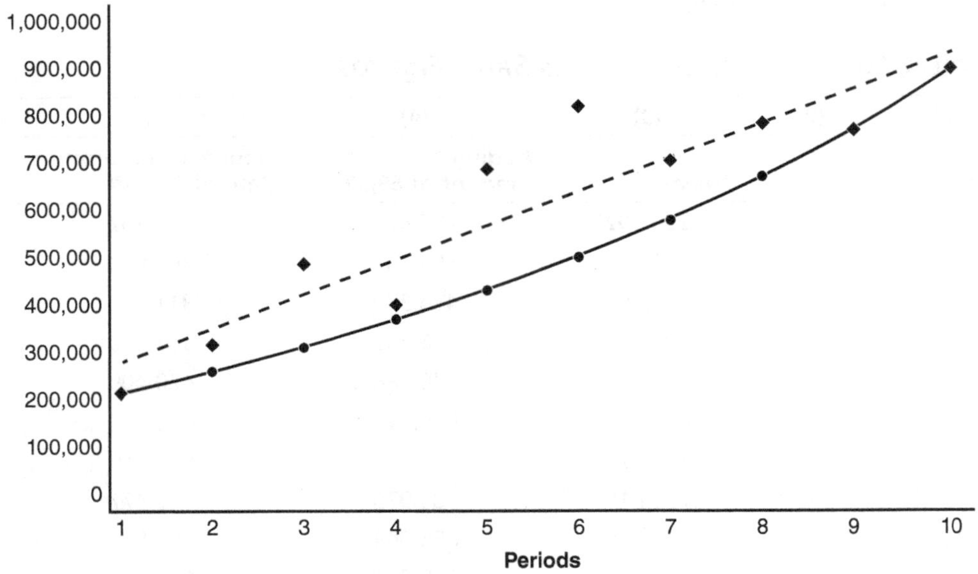

It is worth noting that trend lines and growth rates are calculated from historical data. Care should be exercised when using these trends based on historical information to project future performance, as very different inferences can result.

Exhibit 16-8 shows the results of carrying the trend line and the growth path out to the 15th period. As shown in the exhibit, the pattern of sales after period ten implied by using the constant percentage growth rate exceeds that implied by using the constant dollar trend line. This trend line technique can be used to analyze changes over time in many different financial variables.

For presentation purposes, trends can be presented either graphically or in tabular form.

VERTICAL ANALYSIS

Exhibit 16-9 shows the balance sheets and income statements for L.M. Shaw, Omega, and Jasper for 2021. Again, due to differences in the size of these companies, it is not particularly easy to identify similarities or differences in their financial profiles simply by looking at the dollar amounts.

Exhibit 16-8 Trend and Growth of Omega Steel Mills Sales

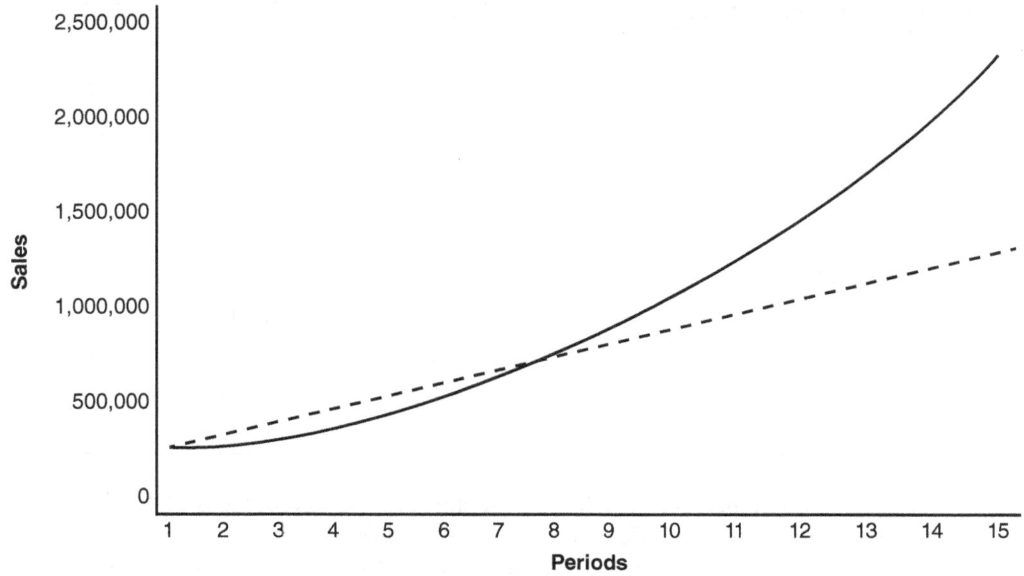

Exhibit 16-9 L.M. Shaw, Omega Steel Mills, and Jasper Steel: 2021 Balance Sheet and Income Statement

	L.M. Shaw	Omega	Jasper
Balance Sheet (000$)	**12/31/2021**	**12/31/2021**	**12/31/2021**
Cash and Marketable Securities	$874	$9,044	$308,696
Accounts Receivable	47,311	67,254	299,244
Inventory	36,418	196,279	435,884
Other Current Assets	614	20,188	85,643
Total Current Assets	85,217	292,765	1,129,467
Net Plant and Equipment	21,060	638,609	2,097,078
Other Assets	13,157	62,596	-
Total Assets	$119,434	$993,970	$3,226,545
Total Current Liabilities	$30,326	$252,516	$486,897
Long-Term Debt	13,829	270,440	215,450
Other Liabilities	1,785	89,607	169,250
Total Liabilities	45,940	612,563	871,597
Retained Earnings	40,002	125,479	2,016,856
Other Equity	33,492	255,928	338,092
Shareholders' Equity	73,494	381,407	2,354,948
Total Liabilities and Equity	$119,434	$993,970	$3,226,545

	L.M. Shaw	Omega	Jasper
Income Statement (000$)	**12/31/2021**	**12/31/2021**	**12/31/2021**
Sales	$219,475	$892,583	$4,151,232
Cost of Goods Sold	187,222	781,789	3,591,783
Gross Margin	32,253	110,794	559,449
Selling, General, and Administrative Expenses	24,940	56,189	147,973
Operating Income	7,313	54,605	411,476
Nonoperating Income	1,731	4,196	3,832
Interest Expense	1,631	38,485	–
Income Before Taxes	7,413	20,316	415,308
Income Taxes	3,036	8,387	151,600
Net Income	$4,377	$11,929	$263,708

Vertical analysis involves displaying the amounts as percentages of total assets, or total sales, to eliminate the effects of size. The resulting financial statement ratios are frequently referred to as "common-size" statements. Exhibit 16-10 restates the financial statements in terms of these percentages. For example, L.M. Shaw's accounts receivable were 39.6% of its total assets ($47,311 ÷ $119,434) and its cost of goods sold was 85.3% of its sales ($187,222 ÷ $219,475).

Given this common-size perspective, one might immediately notice a number of items that require further investigation. In the balance sheets, while plant and equipment make up approximately 65% of Omega's and Jasper's total assets, Shaw's plant and equipment represent only 17.6% of its total assets. This could indicate that Shaw's assets are older and more fully depreciated, but other explanations might be plausible. Omega also relies more heavily on debt financing than do either Shaw or Jasper.

In the income statements, the cost of goods sold percentages do vary somewhat across the companies, but the relatively large differences in operating income percentages are explained, for the most part, by selling, general, and administrative expenses.

Exhibit 16-11 is the same as Exhibit 16-10 except that industry statistics have been added for the Standard Industrial Classification (SIC) code 3312 (Steel Mills), in which Shaw, Omega, and Jasper all belong. RMA and Integra Information (Integra) (see Industry Data Sources below) compile industry statistics. At the end of this chapter is a brief listing of commonly used industry resources and the strengths and weaknesses of each. This additional industry information confirms some of the prior observations and mitigates others. For example, Shaw's plant and equipment percentage is still low relative to the industry statistics displayed. On the other hand, Omega's and Jasper's plant and equipment appear to be somewhat above average. This last fact would not have been evident without the industry comparison.

Exhibit 16-10 L.M. Shaw, Omega Steel Mills, and Jasper Steel: Common-Size Balance Sheet and Income Statement

	L.M. Shaw	Omega	Jasper
Balance Sheet (000$)	**12/31/2021**	**12/31/2021**	**12/31/2021**
Cash and Marketable Securities	0.7%	0.9%	9.6%
Accounts Receivable	39.6%	6.8%	9.3%
Inventory	30.5%	19.7%	13.5%
Other Current Assets	0.5%	2.0%	2.7%
Total Current Assets	71.4%	29.5%	35.0%
Net Plant and Equipment	17.6%	64.2%	65.0%
Other Assets	11.0%	6.3%	0.0%
Total Assets	100.0%	100.0%	100.0%
Total Current Liabilities	25.4%	25.4%	15.1%
Long-Term Debt	11.6%	27.2%	6.7%
Other Liabilities	1.5%	9.0%	5.2%
Total Liabilities	38.5%	61.6%	27.0%
Retained Earnings	33.5%	12.6%	62.5%
Other Equity	28.0%	25.7%	10.5%
Shareholders' Equity	61.5%	38.4%	73.0%
Total Liabilities and Equity	100.0%	100.0%	100.0%

	L.M. Shaw	Omega	Jasper
Income Statement (000$)	**12/31/2021**	**12/31/2021**	**12/31/2021**
Sales	100.0%	100.0%	100.0%
Cost of Goods Sold	85.3%	87.6%	86.5%
Gross Margin	14.7%	12.4%	13.5%
Selling, General, and Administrative Expenses	11.4%	6.3%	3.6%
Operating Income	3.3%	6.1%	9.9%
Nonoperating Income	0.8%	0.5%	0.1%
Interest Expense	0.7%	4.3%	0.0%
Income Before Taxes	3.4%	2.3%	10.0%
Income Taxes	1.4%	0.9%	3.7%
Net Income	2.0%	1.3%	6.4%

Exhibit 16-11 L.M. Shaw, Omega Steel Mills, and Jasper Steel: Common-Size Balance Sheet and Income Statement with Industry Statistics

Balance Sheet (000$)	L.M. Shaw	Omega	Jasper	RMA*	Integra*
Cash and Marketable Securities	0.7%	0.9%	9.6%	6.7%	8.7%
Accounts Receivable	39.6%	6.8%	9.3%	30.9%	23.9%
Inventory	30.5%	19.7%	13.5%	25.1%	16.2%
Other Current Assets	0.5%	2.0%	2.7%	3.3%	3.6%
Total Current Assets	71.4%	29.5%	35.0%	65.9%	52.4%
Net Plant and Equipment	17.6%	64.2%	65.0%	25.6%	33.1%
Other Assets	11.0%	6.3%	0.0%	8.4%	14.5%
Total Assets	100.0%	100.0%	100.0%	100.0%	100.0%
Total Current Liabilities	25.4%	25.4%	15.1%	43.0%	27.1%
Long-Term Debt	11.6%	27.2%	6.7%	17.4%	25.9%
Other Liabilities	1.5%	9.0%	5.2%	7.2%	7.1%
Total Liabilities	38.5%	61.6%	27.0%	67.6%	60.1%
Retained Earnings	33.5%	12.6%	62.5%		
Other Equity	28.0%	25.7%	10.5%		
Shareholders' Equity	61.5%	38.4%	73.0%	32.4%	39.9%
Total Liabilities and Equity	100.0%	100.0%	100.0%	100.0%	100.0%

Income Statement (000$)	L.M. Shaw	Omega	Jasper	RMA*	Integra*
Sales	100.0%	100.0%	100.0%	100.0%	100.0%
Cost of Goods Sold	85.3%	87.6%	86.5%	76.5%	78.2%
Gross Margin	14.7%	12.4%	13.5%	23.5%	21.8%
Selling, General, and Administrative Expenses	11.4%	6.3%	3.6%	17.5%	18.9%
Operating Income	3.3%	6.1%	9.9%	6.0%	2.9%
Nonoperating Income	0.8%	0.5%	0.1%		0.1%
Interest Expense	0.7%	4.3%	0.0%		1.7%
Income Before Taxes	3.4%	2.3%	10.0%	4.7%	1.3%
Income Taxes	1.4%	1.0%	3.6%		0.5%
Net Income	2.0%	1.3%	6.4%		0.8%

*RMA and Integra statistics based on previous editions of this chapter for illustrative purposes.

Omega's debt and equity ratios appear to be in line with those of the industry indications. Both Shaw and Jasper appear to rely less heavily on debt and more heavily on equity than the industry does as a whole. Again, this fact would not have been evident without the industry comparison.

In the income statements, all three companies show higher percentages for cost of goods sold than do the industry aggregates.

In addition, all the companies' selling, general, and administrative expenses are lower than the industry's comparable data. Shaw's operating income percentage is only about half that of the industry information provided by RMA and in line with the industry information provided by Integra as a whole. An analyst likely needs to ask some additional questions concerning this situation for Shaw and the differences in the industry information being reported.

For Omega, its operating profits seem to be roughly in line with the RMA statistics (which include only the larger firms) and double the industry average as reported by Integra. Once again, an analyst should dive deeper into the data being reported and the possible differences. Part of the reason Omega may be in line with the RMA data may be that Omega includes some expenses in its cost of goods sold that other industry participants tend to include in their selling, general, and administrative expenses.

This briefly sums up the horizontal, trend, and vertical analyses, which allows for comparisons over time, across firms, or against industry standards. While doing so, we have briefly suggested the types of insights that might result while using these financial tools in a particular context.

Most valuation reports will include some explicit or implicit form of trend analysis of sales, other major expenses, capital expenditures, working capital requirements, and so forth. Also, many reports will include vertical analysis as the analyst attempts to compare the subject company to comparable public companies of different sizes or to industry norms. Horizontal analysis from one year to the next may not be formally presented in the report, but it should be observed by the analyst or included in the working papers, since the analyst should be cognizant of all significant changes that have taken place in the subject company over the recent past.

Perhaps the "art" of financial statement analysis is becoming apparent. In a practical context, there is no clear stopping point. The analyst can always continue to probe and search for explanation. No doubt the reader could find other issues worthy of comment that were not covered here. There are virtually endless calculations that can be made. Perhaps the ultimate judgment is to identify the point at which an appropriate level of analysis has been completed to form an accurate financial picture of the subject company.

With this in mind, we turn to the analysis of a subject company's profitability.

ANALYSIS OF PROFITABILITY

Information from Jasper Steel will be used to illustrate the analysis of profitability. Selected information from Exhibit 16-9 is repeated as Exhibit 16-12 for this purpose.

Exhibit 16-12 Selected Jasper Steel Financial Information

Jasper Steel	12/31/2021
Total Assets	$3,226,545
Total Liabilities	$871,597
Equity	$2,354,948
Sales	$4,151,232
Net Income	$263,708

This limited amount of information is sufficient to begin to analyze Jasper's performance. One popular measure for gauging a company's profitability is its return on assets (ROA), which is the amount of income it generates compared to the amount invested in its total assets. As shown in Exhibit 16-13, Jasper's return on assets was 8.17%.

Exhibit 16-13 Jasper Steel Return on Assets

RETURN ON ASSETS	=	TURNOVER	×	PROFIT MARGIN
$\frac{\text{Net Income}}{\text{Total Assets}}$	=	$\frac{\text{Sales}}{\text{Total Assets}}$	×	$\frac{\text{Net Income}}{\text{Sales}}$
$\frac{263{,}708}{3{,}226{,}545}$	=	$\frac{4{,}151{,}232}{3{,}226{,}545}$	×	$\frac{263{,}708}{4{,}151{,}232}$
8.17%	=	1.29 times	×	6.35%

Return on assets can easily be broken down into two separate factors: turnover and profit margin. *Turnover* is simply a measure of how efficiently the company can generate sales with the assets under its stewardship. *Profit margin* is the amount of income or profit per dollar of sales.

Jasper's profit margin per dollar of sales was 6.35%. Since Jasper's sales were 1.29 times larger than its total assets, its return on assets was 8.17%, which is 1.29 times as large as its profit margin of 6.35%.

It is important to note that companies can control the amount of assets they utilize, as well as their profit margin. They cannot control sales. No doubt they can take steps to influence the amount of their sales—for example, by modifying their selling, advertising, and promotion strategies. In the final analysis, however, the consumers or the marketplace will determine the level of sales.

The implications of the potential market reaction can easily be illustrated. Assume the starting point is shown in Exhibit 16-14, which has the same structure as Exhibit 16-13 but uses simpler, *hypothetical* amounts.

Exhibit 16-14 Hypothetical Return on Assets

RETURN ON ASSETS	=	TURNOVER	×	PROFIT MARGIN
$\frac{\text{Net Income}}{\text{Total Assets}}$	=	$\frac{\text{Sales}}{\text{Total Assets}}$	×	$\frac{\text{Net Income}}{\text{Sales}}$
$\frac{240}{2{,}400}$	=	$\frac{3{,}600}{2{,}400}$	×	$\frac{240}{3{,}600}$
10.0%	=	1.5 times	×	6.67%

At this point, management might attempt to improve its return on assets by reducing its level of total assets (see Exhibit 16-15, left side). Initially, the return on assets may increase. However, the market may react. The company may have to cut its assets by granting less credit and reducing its receivables, holding less inventory, cutting back on the number of its delivery trucks, or eliminating a warehouse or distribution facility. Any one of these could potentially produce market dissatisfaction and sales could decrease as a result.

Alternatively, management might attempt to increase its profit margin (see Exhibit 16-15, right side). Again, the return on assets initially may increase and, again, the market may react. The company may have increased its profit margin by increasing the price of its products or lowering their quality, which could result in decreasing sales.

The purpose of this discussion is to show that the ideal or optimal levels of these two principal ratios (turnover and profit margin) are not easy to discern. Predicting market reaction is a tricky proposition. For this reason, industry norms or aggregates are frequently considered. Analysts want to understand where a company stands relative to its peers. If the company in question has deviated too far from standard industry practice with respect to either of these two measures, then some explanation is in order. What caused the deviation? What are its likely consequences? Will it persist?

Exhibit 16-15 Effects of Asset Levels

		USE FEWER ASSETS MAINTAIN PROFIT MARGIN					MAINTAIN ASSET LEVELS INCREASE PROFIT MARGINS		
240	=	3,600	×	240	320	=	3,600	×	320
1,800		1,800		3,600	2,400		2,400		3,600
13.3%	=	2.0	×	6.67%	13.3%	=	1.5	×	8.88%
		SALES MIGHT FALL					SALES MIGHT FALL		
180	=	2,700	×	180	240	=	2,700	×	240
1,800		1,800		2,700	2,400		2,400		2,700
10.0%	=	1.5	×	6.67%	10.0%	=	1.125	×	8.88%
		SALES MIGHT FALL EVEN FURTHER					SALES MIGHT FALL EVEN FURTHER		
160	=	2,400	×	160	213.3	=	2,400	×	213.3
1,800		1,800		2,400	2,400		2,400		2,400
8.88%	=	1.33	×	6.67%	8.88%	=	1.0	×	8.88%

Returning to the Jasper case, recall that its return on assets was 8.17% in 2021. How does this compare with Jasper's past experience and how does it compare to industry benchmarks? Exhibit 16-16 summarizes information that can be used to answer these questions.

It appears that Jasper's 2021 return on assets of 8.17% is the result of a gradual deterioration in the firm's profitability. Both its profit margin and its turnover ratio (ratio of sales or revenues to assets is an indicator of the efficiency of a company in using its assets to generate revenue) have declined somewhat since 2017. However, Jasper appears to have a much higher return on assets than the current industry benchmarks. Its profit margin is also higher than the industry indications, but its turnover ratio is in line with industry benchmarks.

The analyst might consider further investigation of the return on assets. Starting with the profit margin, the analyst might review common-size income statements over a series of years and compare these to industry norms. The relevant data for such comparisons is given in Exhibit 16-17.

Exhibit 16-16 Jasper Steel Profit Margin, Turnover, and Return on Assets 2017–2021

Return on Assets	12/31/2021	12/31/2020	12/31/2019	12/31/2018	12/31/2017	RMA*	Integra*
Profit Margin (%)	6.35%	7.04%	6.80%	7.93%	7.62%		0.80%
Turnover (times)	1.29	1.40	1.39	1.51	1.49	1.50	1.54
Return on Assets (%)	8.17%	9.87%	9.47%	11.96%	11.32%		1.20%

* RMA and Integra statistics based on previous editions of this chapter for illustrative purposes.

Exhibit 16-17 Jasper Steel Common-Size Income Statement 2017–2021

Income Statement (%)	12/31/2021	12/31/2020	12/31/2019	12/31/2018	12/31/2017	RMA*	Integra*
Sales	100.00%	100.00%	100.00%	100.00%	100.00%	100.00%	100.00%
Cost of Goods Sold	86.52%	85.53%	86.07%	83.77%	83.74%	76.50%	78.20%
Gross Margin	13.48%	14.47%	13.93%	16.23%	16.26%	23.50%	21.80%
Selling, General, and Administrative Expenses	3.57%	3.47%	3.31%	3.77%	3.81%	17.50%	18.90%
Operating Income	9.91%	11.00%	10.62%	12.46%	12.45%	6.00%	2.90%
Nonoperating Income	0.09%	0.00%	0.01%	0.03%	–0.45%		
Income Before Taxes	10.00%	11.00%	10.63%	12.49%	12.00%	4.70%	1.30%
Income Taxes	3.65%	3.96%	3.83%	4.56%	4.38%		0.50%
Net Income	6.35%	7.04%	6.80%	7.93%	7.62%		0.80%

* RMA and Integra statistics based on previous editions of this chapter for illustrative purposes.

Over the past five years, Jasper's cost of goods sold has increased somewhat. It appears this increase is the principal reason for the decline in the profit margin. Additional effort would be required to ascertain whether this tendency is likely to continue or possibly reverse.

Had there been erratic shifts in the firm's profit margins or any of its components, this type of analysis would have brought them to light.

Comparing Jasper's 2021 experience to the industry benchmarks shows that it is doing quite well, comparatively. Its net income before taxes is a higher percentage of its sales than the industry. As mentioned previously, the fact that its cost of goods sold is a higher percentage of sales and its selling, general, and administrative expense is a lower percentage of sales compared to the industry, may be related to how Jasper classifies certain expenses. It would require further and perhaps more detailed investigation on the part of the analyst to ascertain why these differences exist.

The purpose of reviewing the common-size balance sheets over a series of years and the relevant industry benchmarks is to begin to ascertain which level of assets, if any, might be too high or too low. The relevant data for such comparisons is given in Exhibit 16-18.

As was identified in the common-size income statements, Jasper's common-size balance sheets have remained fairly stable over time. Focusing on total current assets and net plant and equipment, it seems that Jasper maintains a smaller percentage of its total assets in current assets and a much larger percentage in net plant and equipment than is true for the rest of the industry. This observation, made for the year 2021 during the initial discussion of vertical analysis, seems to be applicable since at least 2017.

One limitation of the common-size balance sheets is that they simply relate assets to assets, that is, they relate each asset component to total assets. The concern here is with the relationship between assets and sales. Therefore, the analyst may refer to the component turnover measures that relate the asset components to sales, as shown in Exhibit 16-19.

Overall, Jasper is generating lower sales per dollar of total assets than the rest of the industry. Its sales are 1.3 times its total assets (its total asset turnover), which is less than the RMA and Integra benchmarks. The receivable turnover measures are higher than the industry benchmarks, which indicates that these assets are smaller than assets that might be found for other companies in the industry, relative to their sales.

The opposite is true for the fixed-asset turnover measure. Jasper's fixed-asset turnover of 1.98 is significantly less than the RMA and Integra industry benchmarks. Again, it would appear that Jasper's fixed assets are excessive. In other words, Jasper appears to be making less efficient use of its assets than its competitors.

Exhibit 16-18 Jasper Steel Common-Size Balance Sheet 2017–2021

Balance Sheet (%)	12/31/2021	12/31/2020	12/31/2019	12/31/2018	12/31/2017	RMA*	Integra*
Cash and Marketable Securities	9.57%	9.50%	3.99%	8.79%	5.09%	6.70%	8.70%
Accounts Receivable	9.27%	12.95%	11.17%	12.33%	12.89%	30.90%	23.90%
Inventory	13.51%	13.30%	14.73%	13.36%	12.14%	25.10%	16.20%
Other Current Assets	2.66%	1.96%	1.73%	1.70%	1.78%	3.20%	3.60%
Total Current Assets	35.01%	37.71%	31.62%	36.18%	31.90%	65.90%	52.40%
Net Plant and Equipment	64.99%	62.29%	68.38%	63.82%	68.10%	25.60%	33.10%
Other Assets	0.00%	0.00%	0.00%	0.00%	0.00%	8.50%	14.50%
Total Assets	100.00%	100.00%	100.00%	100.00%	100.00%	100.00%	100.00%

* RMA and Integra statistics based on previous editions of this chapter for illustrative purposes.

Exhibit 16-19 Jasper Steel Turnover Ratios 2017–2021

Turnover Ratios (%)	12/31/2021	12/31/2020	12/31/2019	12/31/2018	12/31/2017	RMA*	Integra*
Sales/ Receivables (times)	13.87	10.83	12.46	12.22	11.53	7.10	6.48
Sales/Fixed Assets (times)	1.98	2.25	2.04	2.36	2.18	3.80	4.62
Total Asset Turnover (times)	**1.3**	**1.4**	**1.4**	**1.5**	**1.5**	**1.5**	**1.5**

* RMA and Integra statistics based on previous editions of this chapter for illustrative purposes.

This point has purposely been emphasized to encourage cautious interpretations of the numbers. Jasper's fixed assets indeed are high relative to its sales. Every measure previously discussed has indicated this. However, are these assets excessive? Perhaps not.

There is an alternative explanation. Perhaps Jasper's fixed assets are relatively new and have been used and depreciated less than the fixed assets of other firms in the industry. In this event, the low fixed-asset turnover measure probably should not be interpreted as a sign of too many fixed assets that simply are being used inefficiently, but rather as a potential competitive advantage for Jasper.

To summarize, Jasper's return on assets fell from nearly 12% in 2018 to a little more than 8% in 2021. This decline in Jasper's profitability for the most part was caused by a rising cost of goods sold and a slight decline in the total asset turnover. Despite this, in 2021, the company was very much in line with and slightly higher than its industry's profitability benchmarks.

So far, in the discussion of a firm's profitability, the focus has been on the return on total assets. Before leaving the analysis of profitability, some attention should be given to return on equity (i.e., the net amount of total assets minus total liabilities). A firm's return on equity (ROE) is the amount of income it generates relative to its equity. As shown in Exhibit 16-20, Jasper's return on equity was 11.20%.

Exhibit 16-20 Return on Equity and Debt-to-Equity

RETURN ON EQUITY	DEBT-TO-EQUITY
Net Income / Equity	Total Liabilities / Equity
263,708 / 2,354,948	871,597 / 2,354,948
11.20%	**0.37**

The debt-to-equity ratio has also been calculated. The reason it has been calculated is because this ratio provides an important link between return on equity and return on assets. The simple formula in Exhibit 16-21 shows that for a given return on assets, the larger the debt-to-equity ratio, the larger the return on equity will be. In Jasper's case, its 2021 return on equity of 11.20% can be explained by multiplying its return on assets of 8.17% times one plus its debt-to-equity ratio of 0.37.

Exhibit 16-21 Effect of Debt-to-Equity Ratio

$$\text{Return on Equity} = \text{Return on Assets} \times 1 + \frac{\text{Total Liabilities}}{\text{Equity}}$$

$$\mathbf{11.20\% = 8.17\% \times 1.37}$$

There are several reasons why the analyst should be concerned with the return on equity. First, it is the rate of return relevant to the owners, buyers, and sellers of firms. However, there is another important reason.

A company's growth rate is influenced by how much it earns on its equity and how much it reinvests. Firms with higher returns on equity that reinvest a larger proportion of their earnings in income-producing assets or initiatives will have higher growth rates, other things being equal.

Generally, a company's projected future growth is likely to have a positive influence on its business value. Possible indicators of future growth can be:

- Return on assets as measured by (1) turnover and (2) profit margin
- Return on equity as measured by the return on assets and (3) the debt-to-equity ratio
- Growth in net income as measured by return on equity (which is affected by many factors) and (4) how much the firm reinvests

The analyst should have a clear understanding of how these four factors have behaved in the past and whether they are likely to be sustained over future periods.

ANALYSIS OF LIQUIDITY

The analysis of a firm's profitability is critical in determining its value. However, the analyst also should assess the firm's liquidity. Liquidity refers to a firm's ability to pay its bills on a timely basis and to meet unexpected needs for cash. Exhibit 16-22 includes some of the more popular ratios used to make this assessment for Jasper.

As shown in Exhibit 16-22, the numerator of the quick ratio includes cash, marketable securities, and accounts receivable. These items are cash or investments that can be converted into cash quickly. These near-cash assets are compared to the firm's current or short-term liabilities. When the value of the ratio is large, more near-cash assets are available to meet the firm's short-term obligations. By this measure, in 2021, Jasper was slightly more liquid than the RMA benchmark and in line with Integra benchmark measures of other firms in the industry.

Exhibit 16-22 Jasper Steel Liquidity Ratios 2017–2021

Liquidity Ratios (%)	12/31/2021	12/31/2020	12/31/2019	12/31/2018	12/31/2017	RMA*	Integra*
Quick (times)	1.2	1.3	0.9	1.1	0.9	0.8	1.2
Current (times)	2.3	2.1	1.8	1.9	1.7	1.7	1.9
Sales/Inventory (times)	9.5	10.5	9.5	11.3	12.2		
Cost of Goods Sold/Inventory (times)	8.2	9.0	8.1	9.5	10.3	4.7	7.4

* RMA and Integra statistics based on previous editions of this chapter for illustrative purposes.

QUICK RATIO

$$\frac{\text{Cash \& Securities + Receivables}}{\text{Current Liabilities}}$$

$$\frac{308{,}696 + 299{,}244}{486{,}897}$$

1.2

RECEIVABLE TURNOVER

$$\frac{\text{Sales}}{\text{Accounts Receivable}}$$

$$\frac{4{,}151{,}232}{292{,}244}$$

14.2

CURRENT RATIO

$$\frac{\text{Current Assets}}{\text{Current Liabilities}}$$

$$\frac{1{,}129{,}467}{486{,}897}$$

2.3

The current ratio is similar to the quick ratio except that the numerator includes all current assets and not just the near-cash assets. This means inventory is included as one of the assets that can be utilized to meet current obligations. Since inventory takes longer to convert into cash than cash, marketable securities, or accounts receivable, the current ratio is viewed as a "softer" measure of a firm's ability to meet its short-term obligations. Again, by this measure, in 2021, Jasper was more liquid than other firms included in the industry benchmarks.

To take the analysis of liquidity a step further, the accounts receivable should be analyzed more closely. Small turnover ratios (sales/receivables) indicate large receivable balances. Unduly large balances in this account may signal problems such as uncollectible accounts.

In Exhibit 16-22, another modification of the component turnover measures involves the inventory turnover. The inventory turnover measure is typically calculated with cost of goods sold in the numerator and dividing this by the average inventory balance. In Exhibit 16-22, it was shown that Jasper's cost of goods sold to inventory measure was slightly higher than the industry indications.

ANALYSIS OF RISK

Risk refers to a firm's ability to survive over an extended period. Declining profitability and liquidity measures may be signals of a company's financial distress and potential bankruptcy. Analysts often look at two other ratios as well when analyzing risk and issues with solvency. These ratios are the debt-to-equity ratio and interest coverage. Exhibit 16-23 shows Jasper's values for these ratios.

The debt-to-equity ratio was described earlier in this chapter when discussing the link between the return on assets and the return on equity. It expresses the relationship between capital contributed by creditors and that contributed by owners. A large value for this ratio signals a firm's increasing principal and interest obligations and a corresponding increasing risk to creditors. A lower ratio generally indicates greater long-term financial security. Jasper has a much lower debt to equity ratio than the industry indications based on its minimal reliance on debt. This may or may not be ideal and the analyst needs to understand what the optimal capital structure for a company in this industry might be.

The interest coverage ratio indicates how easily a company is able to pay interest on its outstanding debt. A large ratio indicates that a borrower should have little difficulty meeting its interest obligations. For 2017 through 2021, Jasper had little or negligible interest expense. Apparently, the bulk of its liabilities were non-interest bearing. The interest coverage ratio calculation in Exhibit 16-23 uses information taken from Jasper's 2021 financial statements.

Exhibit 16-23 Jasper Steel Solvency Ratios 2017–2021

Solvency Ratios	12/31/2021	12/31/2020	12/31/2019	12/31/2018	12/31/2017	RMA*	Integra*
Debt/Equity (times)	0.37	0.39	0.40	0.43	0.54	1.90	1.50
EBIT/Interest (times)	**na**	**na**	**na**	**na**	27.40	5.70	1.69

* RMA and Integra statistics based on previous editions of this chapter for illustrative purposes.

INTEREST COVERAGE

$$\frac{\text{Earnings Before Interest and Taxes}}{\text{Interest Expense}}$$

$$\frac{370{,}447}{13{,}515}$$

27.4

Jasper relies very little on debt financing. Barring some unforeseen deterioration in its profitability or liquidity or a major change in its capital structure, this company is at very little risk of becoming insolvent. For a further discussion of the risk of insolvency, see Chapter 31, "Valuation in Solvency Matters."

INDUSTRY DATA RESOURCES

Comparing subject companies and comparable companies to industry statistics is highly useful in analyzing financial statements. The following is a sample of several data resources that appraisers might use to make such comparisons and the strength and weaknesses of each resource:

Integra Three-Year and Five-Year Industry Reports. MicroBilt.

Strengths: Integra offers benchmarking reports based on three years of data and five years of data. The three-year report provides a summary of income, assets, and liabilities for each industry, eight key financial ratios, and four graphs of key operating trends. The five-year report provides an industry overview summary, 60 key financial ratios, detailed income statements and balances, and cash flow charts.

Weaknesses: Integra information is based on annual information, which at times can take several months to be added to these databases.

RMA Annual Statement Studies. Philadelphia: Risk Management Association, annual.

Strengths: RMA data covers more than 750 different industries, both nationally and regionally, based on the North American Industry Classification System codes; its company data includes privately owned company data submitted to banks by businesses. RMA also breaks out companies by sales and asset size ranges. The data includes more than 20 key financial ratios (including the recently added EBITDA to sales ratio), as well as common-sized balance sheet and income statement line items. A new RMA valuation edition, only available through the *ValuSource Valuation Edition*, sorts each data element into an array and calculates percentiles at every tenth allowing for better analysis of the subject company.

Weaknesses: RMA data comes from member institutions (typically banks). Some of the industry groups may report only a small number of companies and one needs to determine if that truly captures an industry. The data also is based on companies applying for credit, which may indicate some financial need or distress.

A wide range of industry sources is available, including trade associations, and it is prudent to recognize the strengths and weaknesses of the resources that an appraiser chooses; it also may be fruitful to explore industry sources that were not utilized by an appraiser.

SUMMARY

This chapter has examined three forms of comparative financial statement analysis: horizontal, trend, and vertical analysis. The discussion in this chapter covered assessing the profitability, liquidity, and long-term solvency of an enterprise. Hopefully, the artful nature of this type of analysis and the judgment required in its execution have been satisfactorily communicated.

Again, the purpose of the analysis of historical financial statements is to call attention, in an organized manner, to questions whose resolution will assist the analyst in making reasonable determinations about the financial *future* activity of an enterprise. Appraisers analyze the past and present to gain a better understanding of the future. Value is all about future returns and related risk. The word *future* is used in Revenue Ruling 59-60 fifteen times!

REFERENCES FOR COMPARATIVE FINANCIAL STATEMENTS

Fishman, Jay E., Bruce Johnson, Kent Pummel et al. 2022. "Review and Adjustment of the Financial Statements," and "Financial Statement Analysis." In PPC's *Guide to Business Valuations*, 404, 405 (Carrollton, TX: Thomson Reuters).

Hitchner, James R. 2017. "Financial Statement and Company Risk Analysis." In *Financial Valuation: Applications and Models,* 4th ed., Chap. 54, 77–115 (Hoboken NJ: John Wiley & Sons, Inc.).

Laro, David and Shannon P. Pratt, 2011. "Comparative Financial Statements." In *Business Valuation and Federal Taxes: Procedures, Law and Perspective*, 2nd ed. Chap. 12, 140–48 (Hoboken, NJ: John Wiley & Sons).

Pratt, Shannon P. and ASA Educational Foundation. 2022. "Analyzing Financial Statements," and "Financial Statement Ratio Analysis." In *Valuing a Business: The Analysis and Appraisal of Closely Held Businesses,* 6th ed., Chap. 7, 107–31; Chap. 8, 133–51 (New York: McGraw-Hill). Includes extensive bibliography and data references in online Appendix.

Trugman, Gary. 2022. "Data Analysis." In *Understanding Business Valuations*, 6th ed., Chap. 6, 153–214 (Portland OR: Business Valuation Resources).

CHAPTER 17

Economic and Industry Analysis

Kimberly Linebarger, ASA, CPA/ABV, CFA, CVA

INTRODUCTION[1]

In this chapter you will learn about:

- Purpose of examining the economy and industry data as part of the appraisal process
- Sources of data about the overall state of the economy and insights that can be learned
- Sources of data about differences in regional economic conditions and insights that can be learned
- Sources of data about international economic conditions and insights that can be learned
- Sources of data about industries and insights that can be learned

Economic and industry analysis is a vital part of a business valuation, as a company cannot be analyzed in a vacuum. The focus of the economic and industry sections of a business valuation report is on the economic environment in which the subject company operates and in which it intends to continue to operate. The Internal Revenue Service recognizes the importance of this broader context. Revenue Ruling 59–60 recommends consideration of "the economic outlook in general and the condition and outlook of the specific industry in particular" when the fair market value of a business is being determined. The purpose of examining the economy, in general, and the industry, in particular, is to temper or supplement the conclusions that might be reached from the analysis of financial statements alone.

The value of a company should generally benefit from the current perception that the industry or economy will be prosperous, while the value of a company likely will be impaired if expectations are that an industry is in decline or that the economy is suffering. But there can be exceptions. For example, a particular company may have been enjoying increasing sales in an industry that is expected to experience decline in the near future. The prospects for the relevant industry, its anticipated growth rate, and current opinions about the factors that might promote or impede this growth need to be understood by the analyst.

As is true with the analysis of financial statements, economic and industry analysis requires the analyst to make a vast array of choices about which factors to review, emphasize, pursue in greater detail, and find relevant to the case under consideration. The methodologies

---

1. The authors thank the late Dr. Donald S. Shannon, former esteemed professor of accountancy at DePaul University and practicing business valuation analyst who served as founding president of the Business Valuation Association of Chicago and contributed the chapter in the first edition.

used in such an analysis and the structure for the economic and industry analysis segment of a valuation report will vary depending on the nature of the subject company.

The analyst must be able to present the relevant factors that will logically impact the subject company. With the analysis of economic and industry conditions, the analyst must often interpret and summarize analyses that have been prepared by others. This chapter will outline some of the basic components found, in some form, in the typical economic and industry analysis.

The sources of information used often in this segment will be broadly described and a few specifically identified. The intent is to be illustrative rather than comprehensive.

From the valuation perspective, it is important to understand first the recent history and current state of the economy and industry at the valuation date, and then the current perception of their probable prospects.

NATIONAL ECONOMY—RECENT STATUS

The revenues of all firms depend to a greater or lesser extent on the vigor of the overall economy. There is an enormous amount of readily available information concerning the U.S. economy. The Federal Reserve Bank of St. Louis is one of the most comprehensive sources of information. The St. Louis Fed offers three online databases that provide current and historical data on U.S. economic time series. The information is easily viewed and downloadable into commonly used applications. When used in conjunction, these three databases offer a wealth of information.

- Federal Reserve Economic Data (FRED) offers current and revised historical time series.
- Archival Federal Reserve Economic Data (ALFRED) offers economic time series available as of a specific date in history.
- Federal Reserve Archival System for Economic Research (FRASER) provides links to historical economic statistical publications.

The analyst must be able to identify relevant information that will clearly impact, whether positively or negatively, the subject company. The following is a sampling of key measures that might be referenced.

- **Gross Domestic Product (GDP).** Available from the Bureau of Economic Analysis. GDP represents the total output of goods and services produced by labor and property located in the United States.
- **Federal Reserve Board Index of Industrial Production.** This provides the current amount of industrial production relative to a base-year period. The index is presented for many component parts of the economy, giving the analyst a convenient measure of the relative growth for the specific element of interest.
- **Selected labor, personal income, and population statistics.** These explain the extent to which the nation's citizens are employed and provide the analyst with some insight into consumers' ability to purchase goods and services.
- **Consumer Price Index (CPI).** This shows the extent to which the nation's growth is the result of real increases in output (i.e., impact of inflation removed) rather than higher prices being paid for the same amount of goods.
- **Capacity utilization.** This explains the level of manufacturers' activity and may be used to detect inflationary pressure.
- **Key interest rates.** These provide the costs of borrowing funds for consumption and investment.

GDP is the broadest measure of economic activity used to determine where the economy has been, is, and is likely to go. It is calculated by summing the expenditures of the four major participants in the system—households (personal consumption expenditures), businesses (gross private domestic investment), the foreign sector (net exports of goods and services), and the government (government consumption expenditures and gross investment). These four major participants can be broken down further. Exhibit 17-1 shows GDP in billions of current dollars for the year 2022.

Exhibit 17-1 2022 GDP in Billions of Current Dollars

	Billions of Dollars	Percentage Change
Personal Consumption Expenditures	17,357.2	2.7%
Gross Private Domestic Investment	4,632.2	4.0%
Net Exports of Goods and Services	(975.0)	–
Government Consumption Expenditures and Gross Investment	4,448.1	−0.6%
Gross Domestic Product*	25,462.7	2.1%

Personal Consumption Expenditures		
Durable	2,185.50	−0.4%
Nondurable	3,755.90	−0.5%
Services	11,415.80	4.5%
Gross Private Domestic Investment		
Fixed Investment	4,473.60	−0.2%
Change in Private Inventories	158.9	–
Net Exports of Goods and Services		
Exports	2,975.80	7.1%
Imports	−3,950.90	8.1%
Government Consumption Expenditures and Gross Investment		
Federal	1,646.70	−2.5%
State and Local	2,801.40	0.7%
Gross Domestic Product	25,462.70	2.1%

*Does not add precisely because of rounding.
Source: Bureau of Economic Analysis, Survey of Current Business (May 25, 2023).

The CPI is an often-used measure of inflation. The index represents the goods and services purchased for consumption by a population. A rise in inflation indicates a general rise in the price and costs of a given good over time. For example, with all other things being equal, if the subject company experiences an inflationary increase in its product costs but does not increase its product prices at the general rate of inflation, this will negatively impact the subject company's gross margin and consequently its cash flows. Exhibit 17-2 presents information from the all-urban CPI.

Exhibit 17-2 All-Urban Consumer Price Index 1982–84 = 100

			Percentage Change	
Year	December	Annual Average	Dec-Dec	Ave-Ave
2012	231.2	229.6	1.8%	2.1%
2013	234.7	233	1.5%	1.5%
2014	236.3	236.7	0.7%	1.6%
2015	237.8	237	0.6%	0.1%
2016	242.6	240	2.1%	1.3%
2017	247.8	245.1	2.1%	2.1%
2018	252.8	251.1	2.0%	2.4%
2019	258.6	255.7	2.3%	1.8%
2020	262	258.9	1.3%	1.3%
2021	280.9	271	7.2%	4.7%
2022	299	292.6	6.4%	8.0%

Source: U.S. Bureau of Labor Statistics, U.S. Bureau of Labor Statistics, Consumer Price Index for All Urban Consumers: All Items in U.S. City [CPIAUCSL] & Annual Average [CPIAUCSL], retrieved from FRED, Federal Reserve Bank of St. Louis.

Using these and other measures, the analyst should be able to understand the national economy's recent performance and use that analysis as an introduction to projections of the economy's future performance.

NATIONAL ECONOMY—OUTLOOK

What is a reasonable estimate of the magnitude of change in the nation's economic activity that an analyst might expect? The average annual percentage change in real GDP (i.e., impacts of inflation removed) for the 20 years from 2003 through 2022 was 2.0%. The average annual percentage change in real GDP from 1953 through 2022 was 3.5%. During strong expansions, the pace of the growth may increase to 5% or more for brief periods. During severe recessions, real GDP can decline for an extended period.

This range of national economic activity may appear somewhat inconsequential and may seem to have only a relatively small impact on a company's sales. However, even small changes in sales can significantly impact a company's profits. As a preliminary matter, it is important to distinguish between two types of costs or expenses:

1. Fixed costs that remain constant over different levels of sales
2. Variable costs that tend to fluctuate, in total, with sales

Firms with larger proportions of fixed costs generally experience larger profit swings. The presence of fixed costs *amplifies* the impact a percentage change in sales will have on the percentage change in profits.

Exhibit 17-3 demonstrates this fact. All three firms initially have profits of $2. From this position, the effects of a 1% rise or fall in sales is shown. The profits of Firm A, with no fixed costs, also rise or fall by 1%. On the other hand, the profits of Firm C, with $25 of fixed costs, rise or fall by 13.5%. (Firm B is an intermediate case.)

Exhibit 17-3 Impact from Variable versus Fixed Costs

Firm A

	Initial	Up	Down
Sales	100.0	101.0	99.0
Variable Costs	98.0	99.0	97.0
Fixed Costs	0.0	0.0	0.0
Profit	2.0	2.0	2.0
Percentage Change		1.00%	−1.0%

Firm B

	Initial	Up	Down
Sales	100.0	101.0	99.0
Variable Costs	90.0	90.9	89.1
Fixed Costs	8.0	8.0	8.0
Profit	2.0	2.1	1.9
Percentage Change		5.00%	−5.0%

Firm C

	Initial	Up	Down
Sales	100.0	101.0	99.0
Variable Costs	73.0	73.7	72.3
Fixed Costs	25.0	25.0	25.0
Profit	2.0	2.3	1.7
Percentage Change		13.50%	−13.5%

Because most firms have substantial levels of fixed costs, the analyst needs to be alert to any potential change in overall economic activity and be aware of the likely impact this change may have on the sales and profits of the subject company.

One way to forecast economic fluctuations is to study leading indicators, which are a series of measurements that typically go down or up before the GDP does. Most often, the appraiser will defer to the judgment of economic analysts as to interpreting economic forecasts. Several publications provide forecasts for the U.S. economy. Among those are:

- *The Economic Report of the President*, prepared annually by the U.S. Council of Economic Advisors
- *Economic Indicators*, prepared monthly by the U.S. Council of Economic Advisors for the Congressional Joint Economic Committee
- *National Economic Trends*, prepared monthly by the Federal Reserve Bank of St. Louis
- *Livingston Survey*, published semi-annually by the Federal Reserve Bank of Philadelphia
- *Economic Outlook Update*, published monthly and quarterly by Business Valuation Resources

Also, news outlets, such as *Bloomberg, Financial Times, Reuters, Washington Post, New York Times*, and *The Wall Street Journal*, are good sources of timely information on the national economy.

After reading and analyzing the economic data (with, of course, selected emphasis) and reading informed forecast reports prepared by economic analysts (taking care to note any issues that are receiving special attention), the valuation analyst should be in a good position to give his or her synopsis of the prevailing assessment of the current state of the national economy and its prospects over the near future.

REGIONAL INFORMATION

In many cases, a company's operations may be significantly affected by the economies of one or more states or regions. In those instances, the analyst should acquire some knowledge of the economic climate within these areas.

Fortunately, the Bureau of Economic Analysis (BEA) offers access to many regional economic indicators called BEA's *Regional FACT Sheets* (BEARFACTS) on its website. In addition, several regional series related to employment, manufacturing, housing, consumption, income, and so on, can be accessed through FRED.

The GDP information shown in Exhibit 17-1 is provided for each state. Exhibit 17-4 shows the gross state product information for 10 of the 50 states in millions of current dollars for the year 2022.

Exhibit 17-4 2022 GDP by State Current Dollar*

	GDP millions	Annual Percentage Change	Percentage Change Rank
United States	25,462,722		
Idaho	109,546	4.9%	1
Tennessee	475,755	4.3%	2
Florida	1,389,070	4.0%	3
Nevada	215,918	3.7%	4
Texas	2,355,960	3.4%	5
...			
Oklahoma	240,534	−1.0%	46
North Dakota	73,267	−1.3%	47
Iowa	231,108	−1.5%	48
Louisiana	281,429	−1.8%	49
Alaska	63,618	−2.4%	50

*Preliminary
Source: U.S. Bureau of Economic Analysis

Another potential barometer of the relative well-being of a state is the total personal income earned by its residents. The national measure of personal income also is available for each state. Exhibit 17-5 shows the personal income of 10 of the 50 states for the year 2022. Again, the data shown in Exhibits 17-4 and 17-5 is available for many years and can be used by the analyst to detect trends in the state economies of interest.

Exhibit 17-5 2022 Per Capita and Total Personal Income by State*

	Per Capita	Total (Millions)
United States	$65,423	21,804,788
Connecticut	$84,972	308,126
Massachusetts	$84,945	593,083
New Jersey	$78,700	728,900
New York	$78,089	1,536,577
California	$77,339	3,018,471
...		
Arkansas	$51,787	157,725
New Mexico	$51,500	108,836
Alabama	$50,673	256,949
West Virginia	$49,169	87,282
Mississippi	$46,248	135,972

*Preliminary
Source: U.S. Bureau of Economic Analysis

Banks and universities frequently provide useful regional analyses and outlooks. For example, many of the regional Federal Reserve Banks prepare periodic analyses of business and economic trends for each district in their respective regions. In many cases, these appear in periodicals, such as the *Beige Book* (Board of Governors of the Federal Reserve System), *Regional Review* (Federal Reserve Bank of Boston), the *Quarterly Review* (Federal Reserve Bank of Minneapolis), and the *Chicago Fed Letter.*

INTERNATIONAL INFORMATION

Often a company will be affected by international economies. Even small companies may have some international operations. The amount of information concerning international operations is rapidly growing. The valuation professional should be aware of any international factors that may affect the subject company. The availability and sources of information will depend on the specific country. The following are broad sources of information:

- *Global Economic Prospects*, prepared by The World Bank
- *CountryData Online*, available from The PRS Group
- *WFE Statistics Database*, available from the World Federation of Exchanges
- *Economic Global Updates*, available from S&P Global

The analyst should be able to find more specific information through basic research concerning the specific country. That country's government offices and public firms operating within the country often will provide useful information.

INDUSTRY—GENERAL DATA

Having completed their analysis of the national economy, most analysts will turn their attention to providing an assessment of the recent status of, and forecast for, a particular industry. To obtain a deeper understanding of the factors facing the industry and a clearer sense of its prospects, the analyst will turn to sources designed to provide this type of information. Many of these sources are very extensive and very insightful. They usually provide a review of the industry's recent status before, or in conjunction with, making their forecasts. Some publications that provide industry forecasts are:

- *Industry Reports*, published by IBIS*World*
- *Industry Profiles*, published by Dun & Bradstreet—First Research
- *Industry Growth Outlook Report*, published by Microbilt—Integra

The analyst also should review business periodicals for relevant industry information. Trade associations can also be very important sources of information, which should be referenced when studying specific industries. Frequently, these associations collect financial information from their members and publish interesting composite financial data in their periodicals. Also, they publish general information about their industries and provide insiders' views on the issues that might impact their industries' outlook. Descriptions of these associations, their publications, and how to contact them can be found in the *Encyclopedia of Associations*, published by Gale.

Exhibit 17-6 has been included to show the differences in future growth rates that exist across industries. Four sets of industry composite data as well as the GDP and the Personal Consumption Deflator, an inflation indicator, are shown from Integra Information's *Industry Growth Outlook Report*. A review of this data shows the range of future growth differences that can exist across industries. The forecasted growth rate across the industries presented for 2022 ranges from –3.7% to 9.5%.

Exhibit 17-6 Selected Historical and Forecasted Revenue Growth Rates

	SIC# 4724	SIC# 3716	SIC# 1311	SIC# 3312		
	NAICS# 561510	NAICS# 336213	NAICS# 211111	NAICS # 324199 331111 331221 331112		
	Travel Agencies	Motor Homes Manufacturing	Crude Petroleum and Natural Gas Extraction	Blast Furnaces and Steel Mills	GDP	PCE Deflator
Historical						
2019	3.3%	−11.1%	−3.4%	−10.7%	4.1%	1.5%
2020	3.2%	−14.3%	−33.4%	−18.2%	−2.1%	1.2%
2021	4.1%	19.4%	100.0%	47.5%	10.1%	3.8%
Forecasted						
2022	4.2%	3.4%	−3.7%	9.5%	8.8%	6.1%

	SIC# 4724	SIC# 3716	SIC# 1311	SIC# 3312	GDP	PCE Deflator
2023	4.9%	3.1%	6.0%	6.2%	5.1%	3.4%
2024	0.7%	4.2%	4.7%	5.4%	4.6%	2.3%

Notes:
(a) Integra utilizes proprietary econometric models to deliver its industry-specific sales growth data, which is updated every six months. The sales growth rates are developed using (1) a historical database derived from government and private sources and (2) macroeconomic forecasts of the U.S. economy provided by INFORUM, a leader in forecasting and modeling. Depending on the level of detailed information available, aggregated sales growth rates may be applied to related industries.
(b) Gross Domestic Product (GDP) is a measure of the total production of goods and services in the U.S. economy. The GDP forecast information is provided by INFORUM.
(c) Personal Consumption Expenditure (PCE) Deflator. The PCE Deflator is an index of the prices of goods and services purchased by people resident in the United States. The PCE deflator information is provided by INFORUM.

Source: All Integra Information Reports are owned by MicroBilt Corporation and are protected by U.S. copyright laws. All rights reserved. Used with permission. Please visit www.microbilt.com for more information.

While studying a particular industry, the analyst should keep in mind the end objective of this effort. The analysis is being conducted to see how the subject company has been and will be affected by the various industry trends. For example, how would the subject company be affected by increases in the prices of the raw materials it uses, new technology, changes in population demographics, increased foreign competition, inflation, and so on?

The broader industry perspective should give the analyst a reasonable basis for answering questions of this nature. It should help the analyst see how to modify the conclusions reached from the analysis of the subjective company's financial statements, if any such modification is warranted.

INDUSTRY—COMPOSITE COMPANY DATA

In addition to studying the industry issues, trends, and prospects, the analyst should understand the industry profile. What are the typical patterns found in the financial statements of firms in the industry? What is the characteristic turnover ratio (measure of revenue to assets), profit margin, debt-to-equity ratio, current ratio, and so on? Some major sources of this type of composite data are:

- *Annual Statement Studies & Industry Reports*, published by The Risk Management Association (RMA)
- *Industry Key Statistics*, published by IBIS*World*
- Integra Information Industry Reports, published by Microbilt—Integra

Exhibit 17-7 has been included to show the differences that exist across industries. Four sets of industry composite data are shown from Integra Information's *Five-Year Industry Reports.* Even a cursory review of the common-size statements reveals major differences across these industry groupings. In the balance sheets, current assets range from 34.1% to 61.0%, fixed assets from 7.7% to 30.9%, and long-term debt from 4.5% to 21.7% of total assets. In the income statements, the gross margin percentages range from 22.9% to 66.3%, and the profit before taxes ranges from 0.5% to 3.8% of sales.

Exhibit 17-7 Selected Industry Common-Size Financial Statements and Ratios

	SIC# 4724	**SIC# 3716**	**SIC# 1311**	**SIC# 3312**
	NAICS#	NAICS#	NAICS#	NAICS#
	561510	336213	211111	324199 331111 331221 331112
	Travel Agencies	Motor Homes Manufacturing	Crude Petroleum and Natural Gas Extraction	Blast Furnaces and Steel Mills
Balance Sheet (%)				
Current Assets	52.5%	61.0%	34.1%	57.7%
Fixed Assets	7.7%	30.9%	14.5%	25.5%
Other Assets	4.4%	2.2%	3.5%	5.0%
Total Assets	100.0%	100.0%	100.0%	100.0%
Current Liabilities	43.5%	34.6%	20.6%	23.8%
Long-term Debt	4.5%	16.9%	18.4%	21.7%
Other Liabilities	11.4%	6.9%	7.7%	4.4%
Total Liabilities	59.9%	58.5%	47.0%	50.8%
Equity	40.1%	41.6%	53.1%	49.2%
Income Statement (%)				
Revenue	100.0%	100.0%	100.0%	100.0%
Gross Margin	61.9%	22.9%	66.3%	28.6%
Operating Expenses	61.1%	18.7%	65.1%	24.8%
Operating Income	0.8%	4.2%	1.2%	3.8%
Pretax Income	0.5%	2.8%	3.2%	3.8%
Net Income	0.3%	1.8%	2.0%	2.3%
Selected Ratios				
Return on Equity	1.2%	10.1%	1.8%	8.0%
Return on Assets	0.5%	4.2%	0.9%	4.0%
Current Ratio	1.21%	1.76	1.66	2.43
Quick Ratio	0.97%	0.74	1.35	1.34
Debt/Equity	1.49%	1.41	0.89	1.03

Notes:
Year Ending: 2021
Sales Range: All

After studying one or more reports on the industry outlook, relevant trade association publications, selected commentaries from business periodicals, and the industry composite data described in this section, the analyst should have a clear understanding of the measures that are considered important benchmarks for the industry under review.

It is important for the user of industry benchmarks to understand the following:

- The North American Industry Classification System (NAICS) replaced the Standard Industrial Classification (SIC) system in 1997 but both are typically used to determine a company's industry designation. At this time, many publications still present both SIC and NAICS codes.
- Many companies have varied product lines. Companies are sorted into industries according to their primary product lines. In many cases, the primary product line accounts for less than half of a company's sales.
- There is no central agency that assigns NAICS codes or SIC codes, but rather they are assigned based on information provided by the company itself.
- The benchmark may have been derived from a small selection of firms.
- The benchmark may include data from companies with extreme characteristics.

For these and similar reasons, composite industry measures should be used with some caution. When provided, statistics that reveal the ranges of these measures should be reviewed. Wide ranges may be the result of including dissimilar operations in the composite. Also, it is desirable (although not always possible) to study the changes in an industry's benchmarks over a full business cycle.

Additionally, to the extent possible, an industry composite should be calculated from the data of companies that are roughly the same size as the subject company.

SUMMARY

The analysis of the financial statements of a particular company tends to be somewhat introspective. Economic and industry analysis calls for a more encompassing point of view. Many complex relationships must be assessed simultaneously.

The analyst needs to understand the recent *past* performance of the national, regional, or international economy; how the industry under review has reacted to recent shifts in the economy; and how the subject company has reacted to recent shifts in the performance of that industry. Next, the analyst needs to understand the current perception of the probable future direction of the economy and how the industry will react to any future shifts. Then, the analyst must determine how the subject company may be affected by such industry reactions.

In the process of reviewing the appropriate data and reading relevant reports, the analyst should be able to discern which factors pertaining to the subject industry require emphasis. Focusing on these factors should result in more reliable statements about the outlook for the subject company.

REFERENCES FOR ECONOMIC AND INDUSTRY ANALYSIS

Fishman, Jay E., Bruce Johnson, Kent Pummel, et al. 2022. "Economic, Industry and Market Data." In PPC's *Guide to Business Valuations* 403 (Carrollton, TX: Thomson Reuters).

Laro, David and Shannon P. Pratt. 2011. "Economic and Industry Analysis." In *Business Valuation and Federal Taxes: Procedures, Law and Perspective*, 2nd ed. Chap. 13, 149–58 (Hoboken, NJ: John Wiley & Sons).

Pratt, Shannon P. and ASA Educational Foundation. 2022. "Researching Economic and Industry Information." In *Valuing a Business: The Analysis and Appraisal of Closely Held Businesses*, 6th ed., Chap. 6, 97–105 (New York: McGraw-Hill). Includes extensive bibliography and data references in online Appendix.

CHAPTER 18

Discounts and Premiums

William H. Frazier, ASA and Bruce A. Johnson, ASA

INTRODUCTION

In this chapter you will learn about:

- Premiums for control
- Discounts from the proportionate value of the overall business to account for the characteristics of the subject interests at the owner level relative to the degree of control (a shareholder level discount called discount for lack of control, sometimes referred to by the acronym DLOC)
- Discounts to account for the impaired marketability of a noncontrolling interest in a closely held business (a shareholder level discount called discount for lack of marketability, sometimes referred to by the acronym DLOM)
- Discounts to account for the relative illiquidity and/or impaired marketability of a controlling interest in closely held business (a shareholder level discount called discount for lack of liquidity and, in some circumstances, an additional discount for lack of marketability)
- Blockage discounts for large interests in public companies
- Discounts for risks that impact the overall entity valuation to account for specific risks that may not be accounted for in the application of the income, market, or the asset-based approaches used to value the entire entity (entity level discounts)

Very often, the biggest money issue in a valuation of an interest in a business or business interest is not the basic value of the overall entity, but what adjustments in the form of discounts and/or premiums should or should not be applied, at either the entity or the owner/shareholder level.[1]

Generally, the biggest issues are:

- **Lack of control/control.** Should there be a discount for lack of control or a control premium? If so, what magnitude?
- **Lack of marketability.** Should there be a discount for lack of marketability for noncontrolling ownership interests? If so, what magnitude?
- **Lack of liquidity and/or marketability.** Should there be a discount for lack of liquidity for controlling ownership interests? A discount for lack of marketability? If so, what magnitude?

---

1. In this chapter, examples discuss common stock issued by corporations. In almost all instances the same issues impact equity securities issued by other business forms such as limited partnerships and limited liability companies (LLCs).

These factors, when combined, can, at times, make the value of a noncontrolling ownership interest less than half the value of a proportionate share of the value of the business as a whole. Other discounts that sometimes come into play at the *owner/shareholder level* are discounts for nonvoting shares and blockage discounts for large blocks of public company shares. Other discounts that sometimes come into play at the *entity level* are discounts for key person dependence (risk) and discounts for the tax on built-in capital gains.

LEVELS OF VALUE

Shannon Pratt often emphasized that discounts and premiums have no meaning until the base to which they are applied is clearly defined. In business valuation, the various base values to which adjustments (discounts and premiums) may be applied are referred to as "levels of value." Different valuation methods result in different initial base levels of value. To assist the reader's conceptual thinking about the various base values to which premiums or discounts might be applied, Exhibit 18-1 presents one basic understanding of levels of value of a business, emphasizing the ownership characteristics of interests based on the amount of control of the subject interest (i.e., discount for lack of control or premium for control) and discount for lack of marketability for a noncontrolling interest.[2]

Exhibit 18-1 Levels of Value

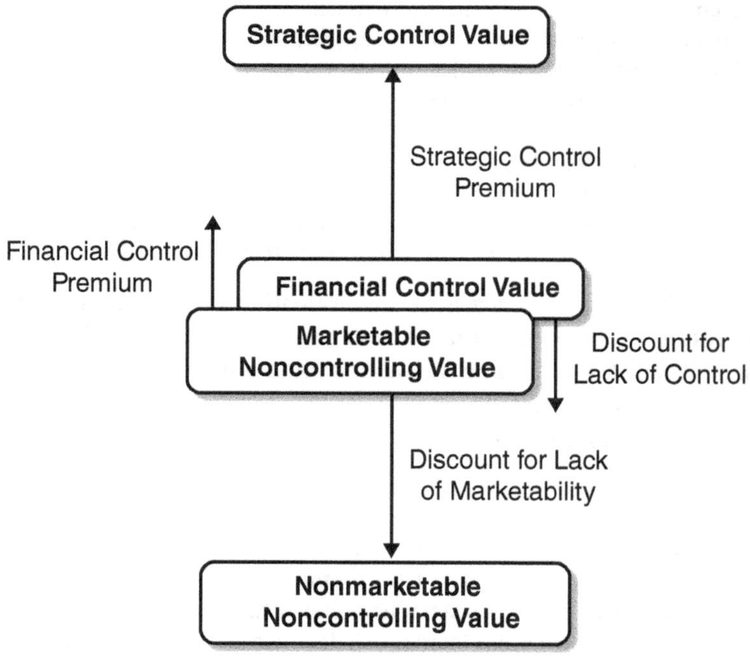

Source: Shannon P. Pratt & ASA Educ. Found., Shannon P. Pratt's Valuing a Business: The Analysis and Appraisal of Closely Held Businesses 55 (6th ed.); adapted from Z. Christopher Mercer & Travis W. Harms, Business Valuation—An Integrated Theory 37 (3d ed.). Used with permission.

2. Exhibit 18-1 is but one representation of levels of value; other authors have depicted levels of value in different ways. Exhibit 18-1 repeats Exhibit 2-1.

Financial control value and strategic control value are generally considered two distinct levels of value.

Financial control value involves the price paid to obtain control and be able to manage and oversee the financial resources of an organization and access the ability to manage income distribution (such as compensation, dividends, and distributions) and, most importantly, the ability to approve or reject matters submitted to a stockholder vote. The premium over a noncontrolling (minority) marketable value can be realized by many possible buyers who comprise the market of willing buyers.

Strategic control value (also termed synergistic value or investment value) involves the price paid to be able to combine the resources of two companies resulting in efficiencies or economies of scale. The magnitude of the difference between strategic control value and financial control value varies depending on the potential benefits of combining the two companies (e.g., at the most basic level, the benefits are simple cost savings (merging of accounting, legal and human resources), while at a more complex level, the benefits can be varied, such as, increased revenues due to complimentary nature of product offerings to customers). A value premium over the financial control level of value is available for synergistic buyers, with the buyer who successfully acquires a company typically being the bidder who hypothesizes that it can obtain the greatest potential for synergy with the subject company.

We specify distinct financial control and strategic control values because applicability of any premium over the noncontrolling, marketable level of value depends on the standard of value being applied. While often termed *control premiums* in the literature (i.e., premium paid over the noncontrolling, marketable level of value for financial control and the premium paid to gain synergistic benefits) and in court decisions, the commonly used source to measure this premium has been acquisition price premiums paid in the acquisition of publicly traded companies. These premiums are really acquisition premiums that often, depending on the buyer, combine a premium for control plus a strategic control premium. Some standards of value exclude strategic control premiums, which can only be realized by a unique buyer. These premiums may also reflect that the acquired company was undervalued by the public market prior to its acquisition, or the buyer overpaid for the acquisition.

MEASURING THE VALUE DIFFERENTIAL BETWEEN LEVELS OF VALUE

The separation between the various levels of value as shown in Exhibit 18-1 does not mean that there is always value associated with incremental elements of control. The right to exercise certain elements of control does not necessarily enable the holder of a controlling interest to create more economic value with that control. Rather, movement up or down the spectrum from one level of control to another provides the *potential* for more value or less value, respectively, but it is possible that no value change is associated with movement between any two levels for a specific ownership interest.

Value might not increase for a given step-up in level because, for instance, the noncontrolling owners may already have been sharing in the greater level of economic income without having control of them, or because there is no additional economic income to be derived from the element of control (see Chapter 4 for a discussion of measures of economic income).

For example, a publicly traded equivalent value always represents a noncontrolling value for an entity. But it might also represent a controlling value for that entity, whether stand-alone or in the hands of a hypothetical pool of buyers, if there are no additional benefits to be gained by the exercise of additional elements of control, or from economic benefits from synergies, at those levels.[3]

The noncontrolling, marketable level of value for a closely held company could be the same as the value to a financial control owner, if the subject company is already being operated in a way that maximizes the company's value and would not benefit from combination with a typical hypothetical buyer.

DISTINGUISHING THE CONTROL FACTOR FROM THE MARKETABILITY FACTOR

The discount for lack of control and the discount for lack of marketability are separate adjustments.[4] Depending on the methodology employed when valuing a noncontrolling ownership interest, the discount for lack of control may be implicitly included in the calculation and therefore an additional discount for lack of control will not need to be applied. For instance, if value is determined by capitalizing the cash flows of the business as it is operated by the controlling owner(s), then the resulting value is on a noncontrolling (minority) level of value, and no additional discount would be necessary or appropriate.

The discount for lack of control and discount for lack of marketability are "multiplicative" rather than "additive" discounts. For example, applying a 20% discount for lack of control and a 25% discount for lack of marketability results in a 40% effective discount, not a 45% discount as some might assume.

Controlling Value		$100.00
Minus: DLOC	20%	$(20.00)
Noncontrolling, Marketable Value		$ 80.00
Minus: DLOM	25%	$(20.00)
Noncontrolling, Nonmarketable Value		$ 60.00
Overall Discount		40%

The U.S. Tax Court in the *Andrews* decision articulated the distinction very clearly:

> In their arguments, neither petitioner nor respondent clearly focuses on the fact that two conceptually distinct discounts are involved here, one for lack of marketability and

3. In *Control Premiums and Minority Interest Discounts in Private Companies*, 14(3) Bus. Valuation Rev. 107–12 (Sept. 1994), Eric Nath argued that publicly traded share prices often represent control values or there would be more takeovers in the public markets.

4. *See, e.g.*, Hess v. Comm'r, T.C. Memo. 2003-251 (Aug. 20, 2003) (25% DLOM; 15% DLOC); Est. of Green v. Comm'r, T.C. Memo. 2003-348 (Dec. 29, 2003) (35% DLOM; 17% DLOC); Est. of Thompson v. Comm'r, T.C. Memo. 2004-174 (July 26, 2004) (30% DLOM; 15% DLOC).

> the other for lack of control. The minority shareholder discount is designed to reflect the decreased value of shares that do not convey control of a closely held corporation. The discount for lack of marketability, on the other hand, is designed to reflect the fact that there is no ready market for shares in a closely held corporation. Although there may be some overlap between these two discounts in that lack of control may reduce marketability, it should be borne in mind that even controlling shares in a nonpublic corporation suffer from lack of marketability because of the absence of a ready private placement market and the fact that flotation costs would have to be incurred if the corporation were to publicly offer its stock.[5]

Significantly, the court in this opinion recognized that even controlling interests may have some degree of lack of liquidity and/or lack of marketability.

LACK OF CONTROL VERSUS CONTROL

The Noncontrolling Owner's Situation

Following are some prerogatives of control that a control owner enjoys but a noncontrolling owner does not. Some control owners may exercise the prerogatives through control of the board of directors, leaving others to the board and the management selected by the board (e.g., a private equity fund or an Employee Stock Ownership Plan); while in other cases, the control owner(s) through both control of the board and through control of management of the business (i.e., a control owner who controls the selection of the board of directors and who is appointed president and chief executive officer) may more directly exercise such prerogatives as:

1. Select or remove the company's directors, officers, and employees
2. Determine compensation and benefits/perquisites for directors, officers, and employees
3. Determine operational and strategic policy, including the direction of the business
4. Buy, sell, lease, or hypothecate company assets
5. Select those with whom to do business and enter into binding contracts
6. Consummate mergers, acquisitions, and divestitures
7. Sell a controlling interest in the company, with or without participation by the noncontrolling owners
8. Change the capital structure
9. Register the company's stock or debt for public offering
10. Determine the amount and timing of dividends/distributions
11. Amend many governing documents[6]
12. Block any of the preceding actions

Degrees of Control versus Lack of Control

The matter of lack of control versus control is not simply a "one or the other" matter but rather one of degree. When valuing voting stock issued by corporations, this spectrum can be summarized generally as follows:

- **100% control.**

---

5. Est. of Andrews v. Comm'r, 79 T.C. 938 (1982).

6. A requirement for unanimous consent or consent of certain noncontrolling owners may be embodied in certain governing documents (e.g., an agreement among all of a company's shareholders).

- **Slightly less than 100% control.** Noncontrolling interest might be a nuisance; any shareholder, no matter how small the ownership interest, has shareholder rights that can be exacted on the majority.
- **Less than 80% control.** Controlling owner cannot consolidate financial statements for tax purposes.
- **Less than a supermajority where a supermajority is required for certain corporate actions.** About half the states require a supermajority vote (often two-thirds, but some states have different requirements) to effect certain corporate actions, such as merger or liquidation. Some articles of incorporation and bylaws contain such requirements, even if they are not mandated by state law. Supermajority voting requirements also may be imposed contractually in a stockholders' agreement, debt instrument, or other contract. This can be a very significant factor when valuing either a noncontrolling interest large enough to block a corporate action (often referred to as "blocking control") or a majority not large enough to control all corporate actions.
- **50% interest of a closely held company.** Has blocking power but cannot force things to happen (except when one party is accorded certain control prerogatives by contract). It is not a controlling interest, and there exists a very real potential for deadlock. (For a public company, 30% to 40% interest often represents working control, and may be true for a closely held company depending on the size of the interests held by the other owners.)
- **"Swing vote" minority block.** Whether a minority block constitutes a "swing block" depends on the distribution of ownership of the other stock. If it is likely that the block can be combined with another block to effect a corporate action, it usually is considered a swing block. Of course, the relationships between the parties owning the other stock may have a bearing on the value of the swing block as a practical matter.[7]
- **Enough votes to elect a director under cumulative voting.** There may be some element of control value to the ability to elect one or more directors.[8] However, the cumulative voting provision has become less frequent in recent years.
- **Sufficient percentage to bring an oppression dissolution action.** As further discussed in Chapter 23, "Shareholder and Partner Disputes," some states have provisions that require a minimum percentage of the outstanding stock to be involved to commence a dissolution action under the state's oppression statute. For example, whether such a right adds any value to the stock depends not only on whether the size of the block is sufficient but also on whether the company has created whatever conditions are required to institute such an action.[9]

Other Forms of Noncontrolling Interests

For nonvoting stock, limited partner interests in limited partnerships, member interests in limited liability companies, and assignee interests, the recognition of the interest as

---

7. However, this is not taken into account in gift and estate tax transactions due to the definition of fair market value; *see* Chapter 20, "Valuations for Gift, Estate, and Charitable Contribution Matters."

8. State statutes and a company's governing documents may provide for cumulative voting. Under noncumulative voting, a simple majority of the voting interests can elect all the directors. Under cumulative voting, votes may be combined for a single director.

9. For example, under California Corporation Code § 2000, such an action requires 33 1/3% of the stock. In *Howard v. Shay*, 100 F.3d 1484 (9th Cir. 1996), the plaintiff claimed inadequate consideration was paid in buying out a 40% ESOP owned interest, the court determined that the block size added no value pursuant to this provision because the corporation had not conducted any actions sufficient to trigger a dissolution suit by the minority.

"noncontrolling" or "controlling" in terms of percentage ownership is largely irrelevant. The issue, from a valuation standpoint, is whether the subject interest enjoys any elements of control and, if so, how much?

In numerous Tax Court decisions, significant discounts for lack of control have been recognized for equity interests with limited or no voting rights wherein the size of the block being valued constituted a majority ownership interest in the entity. For example, in the 2020 *Grieve* decision, a discount for lack of control was permitted for a 99.8% nonvoting member interest in a limited liability company.[10]

Quantifying Lack of Control (Minority) Discounts

As already enumerated, there may be some reason to take some discount from a proportionate 100% control value even if the interest being valued is more than strictly 50%. Similarly, a noncontrolling interest that enjoys some elements of control may be accorded something less than the full discount for lack of control that might be accorded absent such factors.

Even apart from these complications, mustering empirical evidence to support a discount for lack of control is not an easy task. Almost certainly some element of subjectivity is involved, because much of the empirical data on which business appraisers rely are acquisition prices and premiums paid from which implied discounts are derived. Thus, the universe from which to derive the discount is often limited in terms of the comparability of the companies and the amount of information disclosed about the transactions and companies acquired.

There are two procedures used in practice when valuing a noncontrolling ownership interest: the indirect and direct procedures.

Many appraisers use an indirect procedure whereby they value the equity of the entire entity on a controlling basis, multiply by the proportionate ownership represented by the interest, and then apply a discount for lack of control (discussed later) to account for the noncontrolling nature of the subject interest.

Other appraisers prefer a direct procedure of valuing the subject interest. In the direct procedure, the appraiser uses measures of economic income that are expected by the noncontrolling owner (e.g., cash flows) when applying the income approach and the guideline public company method of the market approach in valuing the equity interest,[11] rather than applying discounts to a proportionate interest of the entire equity.[12]

Appraisers who prefer the direct procedure contend that developing a discount for lack of control using acquisition premium data can introduce error. Acquisition premiums generally reflect an increase in economic benefits the new owner can derive, either because of those things a controlling owner can do that were listed previously or because of potential synergies. Information is often limited or not available on any of those economic benefits reflected in acquisition prices/premiums and whether they were paid simply for control or for being in a position to benefit from potential synergies.

When using the direct procedure to value interests, the resulting level of indicated value (controlling or noncontrolling) depends on whether a controlling or noncontrolling

10. Grieve v. Comm'r, T.C. Memo. 2020-28.
11. *See* Chapter 3, "Overview of Business Valuation Approaches, Methods, and Procedures" and Exhibit 3-2.
12. Often referred to as pro rata share of the enterprise.

measure of economic income is used in the calculation of value in the income and market approaches. For example, if an appraiser makes adjustments to the reported economic income such as reducing excess compensation, adjusting for market level of rent or capital structure modifications, the resulting the economic income (either because of control or the economic benefit of synergies) is that which a controlling owner could realize, and valuing that income results in an indicated controlling interest value.[13] Alternatively, if no adjustments that a controlling owner could implement are made, the resulting value indication is a noncontrolling value.

However, there may be times when the history of how the subject entity has been governed by controlling owners indicates that they have been taking advantage of their control position at the expense of noncontrolling owners.

Data used to develop discount or capitalization rates in the income approach are typically derived from data drawn from the public company marketplace representing the risks of public companies. Similarly, market multiples used in the guideline public company method of the market approach are drawn from public company data. While public companies generally have a higher standard of governance and are, in theory, typically governed for the benefit of the shareholders, the subject interest in the closely held company may be subject to greater governance risks, and an added discount for lack of control may be warranted even though the direct methodology is being used to account for greater risk that controlling owners may take advantage of their position vis-à-vis the noncontrolling owners.

At the entity level, the asset-based approach (see Chapters 9 and 10) always results in a controlling value since it is based on the value of the entirety of the underlying net assets. At the 100% ownership level, the value of the entities' assets minus its liabilities is referred to as net asset value (sometimes referred to as NAV). The value of a noncontrolling interest may be derived by applying both discount for lack of control and discount for lack of marketability to the implied proportionate equity interest. However, since the noncontrolling equity holder does not possess the ability to control compensation, distributions, or liquidation, and, if the entity generates positive cash flows, the income and market approaches may be preferable approaches when valuing a noncontrolling interest. This point has been established in three recent Tax Court decisions.[14]

ESTIMATING CONTROL PREMIUMS

Control premium data is derived from acquisition premiums paid for publicly traded stocks. Every year, there are companies whose stock has traded in public markets acquired in some form of buyout or merger. Studies are published regularly comparing public market trading prices before the announcement of an acquisition or merger to the price paid to stockholders (or value received) in the acquisition or merger. The percentage difference between the takeover price and the previous market trading price may be

13. There are differences of opinion in valuation literature about what constitutes a controlling adjustment. Some appraisers make compensation adjustments for noncontrolling valuations. For example, when the majority shareholder may be paid excess compensation which is really a dividend. *See* Chapter 13, "Reasonable Compensation," and Chapter 15, "Financial Statement Adjustments."

14. Est. of Giustina v. Comm'r, T.C. Memo. 2011-141, *aff'd*, 1586 F. App'x 417 (9th Cir. 2014); Est. of Jones v. Comm'r, T.C. Memo. 2019-101; Cecil v. Comm'r, T.C. Memo. 2023-24.

viewed as a measure of a control premium. Acquisition data provides a snapshot of the result of historical transactions that is based on a number of factors.

In the investment world, acquirors do not use control premiums to price acquisitions. Rather, acquirors estimate the increased economic income that might be realized from making the acquisition. Based on that increased economic income, they estimate the value to the acquiror from the acquisition and then determine an offering price. While acquirors desire to retain all value increase resulting from the acquisition for themselves, in order to be the successful bidder they typically must share the estimated increased value between the seller and the acquiror.[15]

DISCOUNTS FOR LACK OF CONTROL

Indirect Methodology

When valuing a noncontrolling interest using the indirect methodology, the appraiser starts with the value of a controlling interest (i.e., value of a proportionate interest in the entire business) and then subtracts (1) a discount for lack of control and then (2) a discount for lack of marketability.[16] The appraiser must estimate the discount for lack of control. The following discusses the most common methods of estimating a discount for lack of control for use in the indirect methodology.

Discount for Lack of Control Estimated from Acquisition Premiums for Publicly Traded Stocks

Those same studies comparing public market trading prices before the announcement of an acquisition or merger to the price paid to stockholders (or value received) in the acquisition or merger can be used to estimate a discount for lack of control. The percentage difference between the acquisition price and the previous market trading price may be viewed as a proxy for the noncontrolling interest discount. For example, if the takeover price was $10 per share and the public market trading price had been $8 per share, the difference of $2 per share as a percentage of the $10 control acquisition price would suggest a 20% discount for lack of control. (In this sense, the implied discount for lack of control is the "other side of the coin" of the control premium, that is, the control premium would be $2 divided by $8, or 25%; the implied discount for lack of control would be $2 divided by $10, or 20%.) Valuation analysts have many sources available for such data. A few of the most common are listed in the references at the end of this chapter. No single source is totally comprehensive.

The strengths of such data are that they are readily available, easily verifiable, and almost always representative of arm's-length negotiated transactions. However, certain issues also should be recognized:

- Acquisition prices often reflect elements of strategic or synergistic value and, therefore, the premiums paid may reflect some elements in addition to control; if the successful

15. The Appraisal Foundation. Valuations in Financial Reporting Valuation Advisory 3: The Measurement and Application of Market Participant Acquisition Premiums (Dec. 2017).

16. Many question the order of the application of these discounts; but since they are multiplicative, the order really does not matter. Many appraisers apply the discount for lack of control first because the data used to estimate the discount for lack of marketability comes from minority interest transactions as discussed later.

acquiror has unique synergies not generally available to other bidders, the resulting premium will result in overstating the implied discount for lack of control.

- Because these companies are being acquired, they are considered to be subject to selection bias in that (1) only the best, most profitable companies; (2) companies that are undervalued in the public market; or (3) companies that are not performing at their best are being acquired; this may overstate the premium and implied discount for lack of control.[17]
- Some of these transactions result in negative premiums. Typically, this issue is overlooked or these transactions are not included when they may well should be.
- Instead of merely using averages or medians of the whole dataset, it is a best practice for the appraiser to attempt to select transactions that are of similar companies and adjust the observed control premium based on the ability of the acquiror of the subject company to enhance cash flows or lower the risk of the acquiror. Selecting specific transactions assumes a sufficient number of those types of transaction exist and that the analyst has adequate information to estimate synergistic benefits.

Discount for Lack of Control Estimated from Secondary Market Prices

In estimating the discount for lack of control for asset holding companies (e.g., entities holding interests in real estate, oil and gas, etc.) from the estimated net asset values of those entities, the appraiser often looks to different sources of market evidence to estimate a discount for lack of control.

Data on transaction prices of noncontrolling interests in asset holding companies compared to underlying net asset values demonstrates the discounts at which these transactions take place relative to underlying net asset values and provide evidence that discounts for lack of control occur in arm's-length transactions.[18] Studies indicate that the portion of the total discount from net asset value is 90% to 95% due to lack of control (with the remaining difference attributable to the lack of marketability).[19] Further research has indicated that the discount for lack of control observed in the data is based on investors seeking a certain level of return and the discount for lack of control is the result of paying less than pro rata the net asset value.[20]

Discounts for Lack of Control Estimated from Closed-End Funds

Closed-end funds are portfolios of pooled assets (typically pools of marketable or other securities) that sell only a limited number of units and invest the proceeds in securities. Unlike open-end mutual funds, closed-end funds generally do not continue to issue additional units and do not buy their own shares back from investors who wish to cash in their holdings. Instead, the funds trade on an exchange like corporate shares. The fund's shares often transact at a discount from the fund's net asset value per share, although they may trade at a premium at times. The discount from the net asset value at which the units trade is viewed as primarily reflecting the lack of control holders of the units have over investment and operating decisions made by the managers of the funds.

---

17. Nath, *supra* note 3.

18. Bruce A. Johnson & James R. Park, *Study of Discounts of Limited Partnership Units Traded in a Secondary Market*, 14(3) Bus. Valuation Rev. 99–101 (Sept. 1995).

19. Partnership Profiles, Inc., 2022 Rate of Return Study.

20. Bruce A. Johnson et al., Comprehensive Guide for the Valuation of Family Limited Partnerships 35–36 (2021).

Such discounts can also be affected by tax considerations (e.g., built-in capital gains on the investments) and the extent and regularity of distributions. Also, closed-end funds are professionally managed and are subject to oversight and reporting requirements by the Securities and Exchange Commission (SEC).

Appraisers have used observed discounts as a measure of discount for lack of control for investment companies like family limited partnerships and LLCs that own marketable securities and other investments. It is important to closely examine which closed-end funds are included in any estimate of discount for lack of control. For example, closed-end funds often focus on stocks of certain industries (e.g., real estate). One needs to compare the focus of the closed-end funds to the business of the subject closely held investment company. For example, if the subject closely held investment company is invested primarily in direct ownership of real estate, closed-end funds that invest in real estate investment trusts and real estate operating companies are not comparable to investment companies that invest directly in real estate.[21] One needs to adjust the discount for lack of control implied from the closed-end funds for differences between the subject closely held investment company and the closed-end funds. Typical differences that would cause one to conclude a greater discount for lack of control than that implied by closed-end funds are differences in distribution policy, differences in depth of management, unaudited versus audited financial statements, diversification, and compliance with SEC regulations.

Direct Procedure

Exhibit 18-2 illustrates the relationship when applying the various valuation approaches and the resulting initial values, either noncontrolling or controlling. Again, when using the income approach or the guideline public company method, the economic income used determines whether the resulting initial value of an interest is controlling or noncontrolling. Alternatively, if no adjustments that a controlling owner could implement are made, the resulting value indication is a noncontrolling value.

Exhibit 18-2 Variations in Initial Value Dependent on Valuation Approach

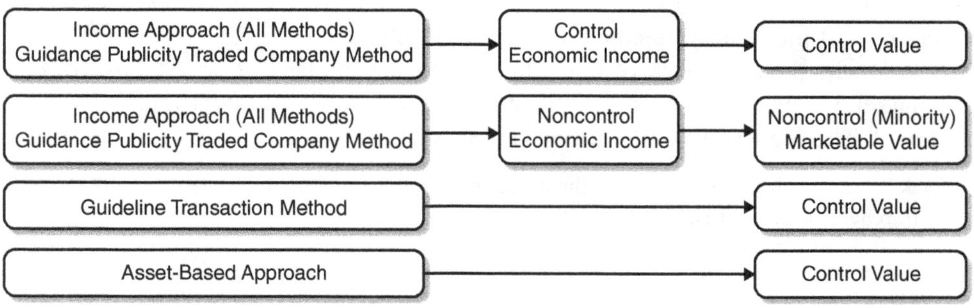

21. Partnership Profiles, Inc., 2023 Closed-End Fund Report 20 (May 2023).

The direct procedure avoids the subjectivity of measuring the appropriate discount for lack of control so the reduction in value (typically present in a noncontrolling, marketable value) is quantitatively determined based on the specific economic income available to the subject interest.

It is often preferable to directly value a noncontrolling interest for operating companies.[22] In the financial markets, investors determine how much they will pay for an investment based on their expected future benefit and a desired rate of return that reflects the risk of the investment. Investors do not apply discounts to determine market value. Any implied discount from pro rata value of the entire entity is simply the result of an investor seeking a rate of return based on their evaluation of the risk of the investment in that entity.

DISCOUNTS FOR LACK OF MARKETABILITY

The Concept of Marketability

The *International Valuation Glossary—Business Valuation* (Glossary) defines marketability as "the ability to quickly convert property to cash at minimal cost."[23] This definition is consistent with the definition of marketability in the *Encyclopedia of Banking and Finance*:

> MARKETABILITY. The relative ease and promptness with which a security or commodity may be sold when desired, at a representative current price, without material concession in price merely because of the necessity of sale. Marketability connotes the existence of current buying interest as well as selling interest and is usually indicated by the volume of current transactions and the spread between the bid and asked price for a security—the closer the spread, the closer are the buying and selling interests to agreement on price resulting in actual transactions. To look at it from the standpoint of a dealer maintaining the MARKET, the closer his bid to current transactions and the smaller his markup as to asking prices, the larger the volume will be. By contrast, inactive securities that rarely trade or for which buyers have to be located or sales negotiated are characterized by large spreads between the bid and asked prices.[24]

It is apparent from these definitions that marketability means much more than just lack of restrictions against a sale; it means, in a very positive sense, the existence of an efficient market mechanism to convert the interest into cash.

Conversely, then, the lack of marketability means the lack of an established, efficient market or some contractual or practical limitation on an investors ability to sell the investment. The Internal Revenue Service (IRS) states:

> Lack of marketability is defined as the absence of a ready or existing market for the sale or purchase of the securities being valued.[25]

---

22. Jay E. Fishman et al., Guide to Business Valuation 8–38 (2022).

23. *See, e.g.*, Matter of Slant/Fin. Corp. v. The Chicago Corp. (N.Y. Sup. Ct. Oct. 5, 1995), *aff'd*, 236 A.D.2d 547, 654 N.Y.S.2d 627 (N.Y. App. Div. Feb. 18, 1997); Le Beau v. M.G. Bancorporation, Inc., 1998 Del. Ch. Lexis 9, 1998 WL 44993 (Del. Ch. Jan. 29, 1998).

24. Charles J. Woefel, Encyclopedia of Banking & Finance 729 (10th ed. 1994).

25. IRS Valuation Guide for Income, Estate and Gift Taxes 9-3 (May 1997).

Degrees of Marketability or Lack Thereof

As with the minority versus control factor, an interest is not necessarily fully marketable or fully nonmarketable. The marketability or lack thereof usually is a matter of degree. Without attempting to address every conceivable situation, the following gives a general idea of the spectrum of marketability or lack thereof:

- **Registered with the Securities and Exchange Commission and with an active trading market** (the benchmark from which some lack of marketability discount usually is indicated).
- **Registered with the SEC and fully reporting, but with a somewhat thin trading market.**
- **A nonregistered stock with contractual liquidity rights** (right of the owner to sell, usually to the issuing company, under specified circumstances and terms). The most common example is Employee Stock Ownership Plan (ESOP) stock, where the plan includes a "put" option to sell the stock at the employee's retirement or certain other times (see discussion in Chapter 24).
- **Registered with the SEC, but not required to file 10-K and other reports**[26] (a "nonreporting company").
- **Closely held company with an imminent (or likely) initial public offering (IPO)** (but note that (1) the pricing is uncertain, (2) the IPO may not occur, and (3) the interest being valued may be subject to restrictions as to sale).
- **Closely held company with frequent private transactions.**
- **Closely held company with few or no transactions.**
- **Closely held company with interests subject to restrictive transfer provisions.**
- **Closely held company with ownership interests contractually prohibited from transfer** (for example, tied up in a trust for some period of time).

Other Factors Affecting Discounts for Lack of Marketability

Besides the factors implied in the preceding "Degrees of Marketability" section, certain other factors influence the size of the discount for lack of marketability:

- **Dividends or partner distributions.** These are probably most important. This makes sense, because stockholders or partners who receive a good cash return on their investment on a regular basis do not depend so much on their ability to sell to realize cash proceeds.
- **Pool of potential buyers.** The more potential buyers there are, the greater the likelihood of being able to sell; the fewer the potential buyers, usually the harder it is to sell. Small blocks are often easier to sell than larger blocks as the amount of the investment for such a block is less.
- **Information access and reliability.** The degree to which information is or is not made available to noncontrolling owners and the reliability of that information affects the discount for lack of marketability. For example, an article on partnership interest valuations states, "An important basis for illiquidity discounts is the difficulty faced by prospective

---

26. Many companies are registered with the SEC for public trading of their stock, but are exempt from filing 10-K, 10-Q, 8-K, and similar reports because of either a small asset size or a limited number of stockholders. Details of such exemptions are beyond the scope of this book, but such companies usually have very limited trading markets.

purchasers in obtaining information."[27] One closely held company discount study concluded that companies with audited financial statements have lower marketability discounts than do companies with unaudited financial statements.[28]

Benchmark for Marketability

As noted earlier, for a discount to have a precise meaning, there must be a precise definition of the benchmark value to which the discount is to be applied. In the U.S. public markets, a security holder can sell a security online in seconds, usually at or within a small fraction of a percent of the last price at which the security traded, with no commission cost, and receive the cash proceeds within two business days.

The market for publicly traded securities in the United States is the most liquid market for any kind of property anywhere in the world. This is one of the major reasons companies are able to raise investment capital from both institutional and individual investors—the ability to liquidate the investment immediately, at little cost, and with virtual certainty about the realization of the widely publicized market price.

The equity securities of closely held entities are, by definition, nonmarketable, that is, there is no readily available market into which such securities might be sold.[29] They can be sold privately in negotiated transactions that utilize available exemptions from registration. This can be a lengthy, laborious process that ordinarily requires an investment banker or other financial intermediary be brought in to facilitate and execute the transaction. Besides the problems of actually trying to sell the stock (and because of them), the liquidity of closely held stock is further impaired by banks and other lending institutions' unwillingness to accept it as loan collateral, as they would accept public stock.

The basis for most of the inputs that are used in a business appraisal (e.g., data used in developing discount rates, multiples derived from guideline public companies) come from the public market. Therefore, it is necessary to deduct a discount for lack of marketability and this may be the largest adjustment that occurs in the valuation. This is especially true for noncontrolling interests, but also can apply to controlling interests. Discounts for lack of marketability may range from as little as 15% to as much as 50% or more for noncontrolling interests. As for controlling interests, discounts for lack of liquidity and/or marketability, when applied at all, may range from as little as 5% to as much as 20%.

However, it is critical to realize that discounts are the result of observing the pricing of transactions. Investors do not incorporate discounts into their acquisition pricing proposals when acquiring such interests. Rather, investors pay less for a nonmarketable interest because paying less increases the rate of return on the investment. Investors base

27. Mark S. Thompson & Eric S. Spunt, *The Widespread Overvaluation of Fractional Ownership Positions*, Trusts & Estates 62–66 (June 1993). *See also* Michael J. Bolotsky, *Adjustments for Differences in Ownership Rights, Liquidity, Information Access, and Information Reliability: An Assessment of "Prevailing Wisdom" versus the "Nath Hypotheses,"* 10(3) Bus. Valuation Rev. 94–110 (Sept. 1991). Bolotsky's position is that conceptually, this is a factor separate from marketability, but he recognizes the reality that there is no good way to measure this factor separately.

28. Gus De Franco et al., *Do Private Company Targets That Hire Big 4 Auditors Receive Higher Proceeds*, 28(1) Contemporary Acct. Rsch. 215–62 (Spring 2011).

29. Rev. Rul. 59-60, 1959-1 CB 237.

their investment decision on their required rates of return for the risks taken and the increased rate of return offsets the risk associated with the lack of marketability. There is quite a bit of empirical evidence showing that prices are paid that result in discounts for lack of marketability in arm's length transactions. However, it is the application and understanding of this information that is important as to whether the discount for lack of marketability can be supported when scrutinized.[30]

Quantifying Lack of Marketability Discounts

There are multiple techniques that have been developed to determine a discount for lack of marketability. These techniques can be divided into two areas to examine when determining a discount for lack of marketability:

1. Qualitative-based methods
2. Analytical-based methods

Qualitative-Based Methods

These techniques are based on analyzing data from restricted stocks and initial public offerings (IPOs). Applying either dataset requires judgment, but the data from both is important because it shows that discounts do occur in arm's-length transactions. These qualitative methods are helpful for determining a range for the discount for lack of marketability. Analytical techniques, on the other hand, are calculation-based and typically use the impact on the rate of return to objectively compute a discount for lack of marketability. These techniques incorporate the ability to model holding periods and the risk that comes from lack of marketability to determine the discount for lack of marketability.

Using Restricted Stock Studies[31]

Typically, something less than 100% of the shares of a "publicly traded company" are registered with the SEC. Shares that are not so registered cannot be sold via a public market or exchange without an appropriate registration or exemption from the regulations. These shares are called "restricted stock" or "letter stock" (the latter term because sometimes a legend or letter is frequently attached to the stock certificate explaining the limitations on its transferability). The unregistered or restricted shares may be founders' or insiders' stock that has never been registered, or may be stock issued in an acquisition or to raise capital.[32]

Although such shares may not be sold on the open market, they may be sold in a private transaction with institutions or other sophisticated investors. Following such a private sale, the restrictions continue. However, there exists a "safe harbor" in SEC Rule 144, which generally permits resale of the restricted stock after an initial holding period, and subject to restrictions on the volume of shares that can be sold into the public markets.

Primarily because of these restrictions on marketability, such transactions usually are at a discounted price compared to the same day's public market price. Because the restricted stocks are identical to the stocks sold in the public market in every respect

---

30. Johnson et al., *supra* note 20, at 151–52.

31. For a more detailed discussion, *see* James R. Hitcher et al. Discount for Lack of Marketability: Guide and Toolkit (2017).

32. These may be exempt from registration under SEC Rule 144.

except for their impaired marketability, differences in the prices of these restricted stock transactions and the same day's public market price are widely considered to isolate the discount attributable to lack of marketability.

To help quantify the marketability factor, studies have been conducted over the last 50 years in an effort to quantify the price differential between public company stock that is freely traded and restricted stock of the same company. These studies have been conducted by many different independent parties and encompass hundreds of transactions. Until the SEC lowered the required Rule 144 holding period from two years to one year in 1997, the average discounts ranged from 22% to 45%, with the majority clustering around 35% when the holding period is the longest (two years). Exhibit 18-3 presents a summary of the results of these studies. Over the years, the required holding period has been reduced to six months, and the observed discount for lack of marketability has declined because the holding period has declined accordingly.

While the observed discounts have declined, these stocks will become freely traded simply with the passage of time. This is not true with interests in closely held businesses.

Analysts have tried to identify factors that affect the percentage of discount for lack of marketability. Apart from the amounts of dividends or withdrawals, the factor that seems to stand out most clearly is the size of the company. For example, the Management Planning study,[33] reviewing transactions from 1980 to 1996, found the following differences in average discounts based on the size of the company as measured by revenues:

Revenues	**Average Discount**
Under $10 million	32.9%
$10 million to $30 million	30.8%
$30 million to $50 million	25.2%
$50 million to $100 million	19.4%
Over $100 million	14.9%

Both the SEC[34] and the Johnson[35] studies also show that the marketability discounts are greater, on average, for smaller companies.

33. *See* Exhibit 18–3.
34. *Id.*
35. *See* Bruce A. Johnson, *Quantitative Support for Discounts for Lack of Marketability*, *in* SHANNON PRATT'S BUSINESS VALUATION UPDATE 1–3 (Dec. 1999).

Exhibit 18-3 Summary of Restricted Stock Studies

Empirical Study	Years Covered in Study	Average Price Discount
SEC overall average [a]	1966–1969	25.8%
SEC nonreporting OTC companies [a]	1966–1969	32.6%
Gelman [b]	1968–1970	33.0%
Trout [c]	1968–1972	33.5%
Moroney [d]	[k]	35.6%
Maher [e]	1969–1973	35.4%
Standard Research Consultants [f]	1978–1982	45.0% [l]
Willamette Management Associates [g]	1981–1984	31.2% [l]
Silber [h]	1981–1988	33.8%
FMV Opinions, Inc. [i]	1980–1992	23.0%
Management Planning, Inc. [j]	1980–1996	27.1%
Johnson [m]	1991–1995	20.0%
Columbia Financial Advisors [n]	1996–April 1997	21.0%
Columbia Financial Advisors [n]	May 1997–1998	13.0%
Pluris Valuation Advisors (Liquistat) [o]	2005–2006	32.8%
Trugman Valuation Associates, Inc. [p]	2007–2008	18.1%
Management Planning, Inc. (Update) [q]	2000–2007	14.6%
Management Planning, Inc. (Update) [r]	1980–2009	15.9%
Stout Risius Ross, LLC [s]	2005–2010	10.9%
Trugman Valuation Associates (Update) [t]	2009–2010	15.9%
Stout Risius Ross, LLC [u]	1980–2018	15.8%

a. "Discounts Involved in Purchases of Common Stock (1966–1969)," *Institutional Investor Study Report of the Securities and Exchange Commission*, H.R. Doc. No. 64, Part 5, 92nd Congress, 1st Session, 1971, pp. 2444–56.
b. Milton Gelman, "An Economist-Financial Analyst's Approach to Valuing Stock in a Closely Held Company," *Journal of Taxation* (June 1972), p. 353.
c. Robert R. Trout, "Estimation of the Discount Associated with the Transfer of Restricted Securities," *Taxes* (June 1977), pp. 381–85.
d. Robert E. Moroney, "Most Courts Overvalue Closely Held Stocks," *Taxes* (March 1973), pp. 144–55.
e. J. Michael Maher, "Discounts for Lack of Marketability for Closely Held Business Interests," *Taxes* (September 1976), pp. 562–71.
f. William F. Pittock and Charles H. Stryker, "Revenue Ruling 77–276 Revisited," *SRC Quarterly Reports* (Spring 1983), pp. 1–3.
g. Willamette Management Associates study (unpublished).
h. William L. Silber, "Discounts on Restricted Stock: The Impact of Illiquidity on Stock Prices," *Financial Analysts Journal* (July–August 1991), pp. 60–64.
i. Lance S. Hall and Timothy C. Polacek, "Strategies for Obtaining the Largest Valuation Discounts," *Estate Planning* (January–February 1994), pp. 38–44.
j. Robert P. Oliver and Roy H. Meyers, "Discounts Seen in Private Placements of Restricted Stock: The Management Planning, Inc., Long-Term Study (1980–1996)" (Chapter 5) in Robert F. Reilly and Robert P. Schweihs, eds., *The Handbook of Advanced Business Valuation* (New York: McGraw-Hill, 2000).
k. Although the years covered in this study the likely to be 1969–1972, no specific years were given in the published account.
l. Median discounts.

m. Bruce Johnson, "Restricted Stock Discounts, 1991–95," *Shannon Pratt's Business Valuation Update* (March 1999), p. 1–3; "Quantitative Support for Discounts for Lack of Marketability," *Business Valuation Review* (December 1999), pp. 152–155.
n. Kathryn, F. Aschwald, "Restricted Stock Discounts Decline as Result of 1-Year Holding Period," *Shannon Pratt's Business Valuation Update* (May 2000), p. 1–5.
o. Espen Robak, "Discounts for Illiquid Shares and Warrants: The Liquistat Database of Transactions on the Restricted Securities Trading Network," Pluris Valuation Advisors White Paper Draft (January 22, 2007), pp. 26–27. www.plurisvaluation.com.
p. William Harris, "Trugman Valuation Associates, Inc. Restricted Stock Study," *Business Valuation Review* (Fall 2009), pp. 128–139. Also see "Gary R. Trugman, "Premiums and Discounts (Valuation Adjustments)—Part II" in *Understanding Business Valuation: A Practical Guide to Valuing Small to Medium Sized Businesses*, 5th ed. (New York: American Institute of Certified Public Accountants, Inc., 2017), pp. 597–692.
q. Management Planning, Inc. *Perspectives* (Winter 2009), pp. 1, 11. www.mpival.com.
r. Ezra Angrist, Harry Curtis, III, Daniel Kerrigan, "Regression Analysis and Discounts for Lack of Marketability," *Business Valuation Review* Vol. 30 (1) (Spring 2011), pp. 36–48.
s. Aaron M. Stumpf, Robert L. Martinez, and Christopher T. Stallman, "The Stout Risius Ross Restricted Stock Study: A Recent Examination of Private Placement Transactions from September 2005 through May 2010," *Business Valuation Review* Vol. 30 (1) (Spring 2011), pp. 7–19.
t. William Harris, "Trugman Valuation Associates (TVA) Restricted Stock Study—An Update," *Business Valuation Review* Vol. 30 (4) (Winter 2011), pp. 132–139.
u. 2020 Edition of the Stout Restricted Stock Study Companion Guide, www.bvresources.com/stout.

Source: Shannon Pratt's *Valuing a Business: The Analysis and Appraisal of Closely Held Businesses* 428 (6th ed.). Used with Permission.

In 1977, the IRS issued Revenue Ruling 77–287, recognized restricted stock transaction data as relevant evidence for quantification of the discount for lack of marketability. However, its application remains subjective. In *Mandelbaum*[36] the U.S. Tax Court found that restricted stock studies are a starting place for an appraiser to estimate a discount for lack of marketability. The discount for lack of marketability should be adjusted upward or downward for the subject company's specific factors and characteristics.[37] In *Weinberg*,[38] Judge Whalen did not agree with the taxpayer's use of the standard restricted stock studies, indicating that the taxpayer's expert "failed to adequately take into account certain characteristics of the subject limited partnership interest." In *Perrachio*,[39] the judge ruled that the taxpayer's expert . . .

> makes no attempt whatsoever to analyze the data from those [restricted stock] studies as they relate to the transferred interests. Rather, he simply lists the average discounts observed in several such studies, effectively asking us to accept on faith the premise that the approximate average of those results provides a reliable benchmark for the transferred interests. Absent any analytical support, we are unable to accept that premise.[40]

Restricted stocks generally are restricted only for a limited period (as discussed earlier), after which they can be sold in an active public market, which already exists. That is, the stocks studied became fully marketable only through the passage of time with the

36. Bernard Mandelbaum et al. v. Comm'r, T.C. Memo. 1995-255 (1995).
37. Many of these factors are enumerated in the decision itself and are often referred to as the "Mandelbaum Factors." For insights into this often-cited decision, *see Do Not Assume, Just Know the Rules, in* THE ART OF VALUATION: REFLECTIONS, STORIES, AND STRATEGIES FROM BUSINESS APPRAISAL 157–59 (Sarah von Helfenstein ed., The Appraisal Found., 2023).
38. Est. of Etta H. Weinberg et al. v. Comm'r, T.C. Memo. 2000-51 (2001).
39. Est. of Peter S. Perrachio v. IRS, T.C. Memo. 2008-280.
40. *Id.*

owner not having to take any direct action. The studies discussed earlier did not seek to determine whether the discount would be greater if the stock were of a closely held company, which has no public market and may not ever have a public market.

Using Pre-IPO Studies

When a company goes public for the first time, that is, undertakes an initial public offering (IPO), it is required to file a registration statement with the SEC. One of the disclosures required, along with financial statement information, is details of all transactions in the company's stock during the three years prior to filing. These details include transaction date, transaction price, number of shares, and identities of buyers and sellers. From these and the financial statement data, it is possible to compute price-to-earnings ratios, transaction size as a percent of shares outstanding, and other analytical details. The pre-IPO studies compute the discount observed from pre-IPO transactions compared to the IPO price and impute a discount (pre-IPO discount).

There have been three primary studies that are cited that tracked pre-IPO transactions relative to public offering prices: (1) Emory & Co. Pre-IPO Studies (transactions from 1981 through 2000); (2) Willamette Management Associates Studies (transactions from 1975 through 2002); and (3) Valuation Advisors Discount for Lack of Marketability Studies (online database of transactions that is kept current).[41]

While used successfully in Tax Court in some matters, courts have, just as often, rejected the use of pre-IPO studies for determining discounts for lack of marketability. One court noted that it is difficult to verify the underlying data from the transactions and there is selection bias in only looking at companies that were IPO-worthy and succeeded in going public. Also, the holding periods significantly impact the magnitude of the discount while there are other factors to consider. Another criticism is that IPO prices are often high (or low) relative to where the price settles in the weeks after the offering. This may overstate the discount for lack of marketability due to the buildup and excitement of the IPO; these factors are typically not present in a noncontrolling interest of a closely held company. The studies have been criticized as conceptually unsound because the pre-IPO transactions and the subsequent IPO are priced at materially different dates and because the IPO price is not knowable at the earlier date.[42]

In two recent court cases, *Giustina*[43] and *Cecil*,[44] the Tax Court held that the pre-IPO method overstated the discount for lack of marketability. In two other recent cases, *Jones*[45] and *Nelson*,[46] the pre-IPO method was cited as one of three or four methods used by a testifying expert to estimate the discount for lack of marketability.

---

41. These studies are summarized in the online appendix to Shannon P. Pratt & ASA Educ. Found., Shannon P. Pratt's Valuing a Business (6th ed. 2022), https://www.appraisers.org/shop/publications-and-subscriptions/books/valuing-a-business/appendix.

42. *See* Gilbert E. Matthews, *Why Pre-IPO Studies Are Unsound in Concept and in Practice*, 40(3) Bus. Valuation Rev. 97–103 (Fall 2022).

43. Est. of Giustina v. Comm'r, T.C. Memo. 2011-141, *aff'd*, 1586 F. App'x 417 (9th Cir. 2014).

44. Cecil v. Comm'r, T.C. Memo. 2023-24.

45. Est. of Jones v. Comm'r, T.C. Memo. 2019-101.

46. Nelson v. Comm'r, T.C. Memo. 2020-8.

Analytical Techniques

Restricted stock and IPO data illustrates that discounts for lack of marketability occur in arm's length transactions. These data are useful for establishing a range for the discount for lack of marketability. However, the quantification of the discount for lack of marketability can be estimated using certain analytical techniques. In one source, the authors state:

> The primary objection of the Tax Court has been the lack of rationale used to support discounts for lack of control and lack of marketability. It is not a question of whether discounts . . . are appropriate. It is how the amounts of these discounts have been determined that has raised concerns.[47]

Analytical techniques primarily use risk and return analyses to objectively determine a discount for lack of marketability. Commonly used techniques are (1) option pricing models for estimating a discount for lack of marketability; (2) Johnson/Park Empirical Method for estimating a discount for lack of marketability; and (3) hybrid methods—the Nonmarketable Investment Company Evaluation Method (NICE) and Quantitative Marketability Discount Model (QMDM)—two methods that directly estimate a combined discount for lack of control and discount for lack of marketability.

A discount for lack of marketability reflects the risk of owning a financial security that cannot be quickly converted to cash. Because the risk is greater, the expected rate of return is greater. Analytical techniques are based on this basic financial theory to determine the discount for lack of marketability. A brief discussion of each analytical method follows.

Option Pricing Models

A put option is a financial instrument used in the public market to give an owner the capacity to protect against a decline in value of a financial asset. A put option is a contract that gives the holder the right, but not the obligation, to sell an underlying security at a predefined price within a certain timeframe. This right to sell at a fixed price reduces the risk of loss, as the investor cannot lose more than the cost of the put option (premium). The cost of a put option, therefore, is a proxy for the discount for lack of marketability in that the option protects the holder of the stock until cash from a sale is realized.

In order to determine the option's value, three inputs are required: (1) risk-free rate of interest, (2) term of the option, and (3) expected volatility of the returns on the stock.

The option value is only a proxy for such an option for a closely held interest as there are no options traded for such interests. For an interest in a closely held company, the term and volatility factor must be estimated from guideline public company data. Any variability in these inputs can cause a wide dispersion of results.

There are a number of commonly cited option models and methods for estimating discount for lack of marketability that are commonly cited in the literature: (1) Chaffe Model, (2) Longstaff Model, (3) Finnerty Model, and (4) the Binomial Model.[48] Analysts

47. Bruce A. Johnson et al., *supra* note 20, at 4.

48. Pratt & ASA Educ. Found., *supra* note 41, at 443–45.

disagree about whether the option pricing models determine reasonable estimates of discounts for lack of marketability for stock of closely held companies.[49]

Depending on the option method used, an appraiser can get different results using the same inputs. Besides the variability of the results based on the inputs and method chosen, a criticism of using option methods to estimate a discount for lack of marketability is the fact that option methods only address the downside risk, which is not lack of marketability. Also, options pricing models are short-term financial instruments.

Options contracts with expiration dates that go beyond one year, known as LEAPS (Long-term Equity Anticipation Securities), are similar to short-term options in that they are publicly traded, except they are longer-term. One study examined LEAPS with various holding periods and published information on the impact on the implied discount for lack of marketability of the magnitude of sales, assets, beta, industry, profitability and leverage as shown in Exhibit 18-4.[50]

Exhibit 18-4 Implied DLOM on LEAPS Stratified by Revenue

Company Size in Revenue	Average	Median
$10 Billion plus	14.6%	13.4%
$1 Billion to $10 Billion	18.5%	16.6%
$500 Million to $1 Billion	24.8%	21.0%
Under $500 Million	31.2%	28.6%
Under $100 Million	38.1%	35.0%

Source: Ronald M. Seaman, *Minimum Marketability Discounts,* 3d ed., 27(1) Bus. Valuation Rev. 18–22 (Spring 2008).

It should be noted that if LEAPS are used as a comparison to estimate discounts for lack of marketability that LEAPS have a known expiration date and typically represent a minimum discount.

Johnson/Park Empirical Method

The Johnson/Park Empirical Method estimates the discount for lack of marketability based on the increase in the effective rate of return that results from the application of an adjustment for lack of marketability. The amount of the increase in the rate of return to account for the increased risk of lack of marketability is supported by three research studies indicating that investors generally require a 30% to 45% increase in the rate of return when comparing a nonmarketable interest to an equivalent marketable interest. These studies are updated annually. The latest information is summarized in Exhibit 18-5.

49. Ashok Abbott, *Discounts for Lack of Liquidity: Understanding and Interpreting Option Models,* 28(3) Bus. Valuation Rev. 144–48 (Fall 2009).

50. Ronald M. Seaman, *Minimum Marketability Discounts, 3d ed.,* 27(1) Bus. Valuation Rev. 18–22 (Spring 2008).

Exhibit 18-5 Johnson/Park Empirical Method Summarized

	Increase in Rate of Return					
Studies	**2018**	**2019**	**2020**	**2021**	**2022**	**AVG**
Private Equity vs. Public Equity Returns	36.4%	37.6%	35.7%	43.6%	44.8%	39.6%
Restricted Stock Transactions	29.5%	29.5%	29.5%	29.5%	29.5%	29.5%
LT vs. ST Bond Horizon Risk	43.5%	42.2%	46.5%	51.6%	43.1%	45.4%

Source: Partnership Profiles, Inc., 2022 Discount for Lack of Marketability Study 5–6.

The Johnson/Park Empirical Method[51] was used by the taxpayer's expert in the *Estate of Elsie Church*[52] and the *Estate of Emily Klauss*.[53]

Nonmarketable Investment Company Evaluation Method (NICE)

The NICE method is designed to estimate the fair market value of equity interests in family holding companies by estimating the discount rate that reflects the incremental risk of the subject holding company compared to the portfolio of its holdings. Such holding companies are usually closely held, family-owned investment entities (e.g., family limited partnerships (FLPs) and LLCs) that hold investment assets such as stocks, bonds, and real estate.[54]

NICE is confined to investment holding entities since the methodology is designed to provide the valuation analyst with significant guidance on the appropriate incremental required rate of return. That guidance is based on empirical research of the cost of illiquidity of various asset classes. Since such investment holding entities pay out little in the form of current returns, the primary economic return will come from the eventual liquidation of the investment holding entity.

The NICE method addresses the risks of both a lack of control and lack of marketability. The method estimates the price at which a transaction between a hypothetical willing seller and a hypothetical willing buyer would transpire based upon an entity's rate of return expectations given the assets the entity holds plus the additional rate of return requirements due to both the risks of lack of control and illiquidity and lack of marketability of the interest being valued. The component of the NICE method that accounts for the risks of holding a noncontrolling interest is referred to as the incremental required rate of return for lack of control (IROC), and the component of the NICE method that accounts for the added risk of illiquidity due to lack of marketability is referred to as the incremental required rate of return for lack of marketability (IROM).

Generally, the NICE method is intended to be used to estimate the value of equity interests that have very limited voting rights and poor access to information (i.e., lack of control); the incremental required rate of return for lack of control is estimated by an

51. Bruce A. Johnson, *The Empirical Method for Determining DLOM*, 19(3) Bus. Valution Update 1–6 (2013). The method was introduced in 1995.

52. Est. of Elsie Church v. United States (Cause No. SA-97-CA-0774-OG).

53. Est. of Emily Klauss, T.C. Memo. 2000-191.

54. William H. Frazier, *The NICE Method Theory and Application*, 41(2) Bus. Valuation Rev. 53–66 (Summer 2022).

analysis of academic research and empirical studies. The incremental required rate of return for lack of marketability is derived from empirical studies of publicly traded securities that represent noncontrolling interest pricing considerations.

The NICE method was used by the taxpayer's expert in the Tax Court case *Grieve*.[55]

Quantitative Marketability Discount Model (QMDM)

QMDM is a shareholder-level discounted cash flow model developed to help valuation analysts determine the value of noncontrolling, illiquid interests of businesses (see Exhibit 18-1). QMDM requires several inputs, such as the rate of appreciation of the business' expected cash flows, the investor's expected holding period, and the investor's required rate of return. It should be noted that this model is not designed to be used in isolation to only determine a discount for lack of marketability. Applying the QMDM results in a combined discount for lack of control and discount for lack of marketability because the shareholder level expectations regarding cash flows, risk, and growth are linked to corresponding expectations with respect to the business.

In *Janda*,[56] the Tax Court criticized the QMDM because small changes in the inputs can result in big differences in the outcome.

Comment: However, that is the case with most economic models whether it be the discounted cash flow method of the income approach or an option pricing model.

Discounts for Lack of Liquidity and Lack of Marketability for Controlling Interests

If the standard of value is fair market value, then a cash-equivalent value as of a certain date is required to be estimated. The choice of date may be one over which the owner has little or no control (for example, either date of death or the six-months-later alternative date for estate tax valuations or the date a transaction closed).

Often it usually takes months, even years, to prepare a business for a planned change in control ownership. There typically are significant accounting, legal, and management costs. There is a considerable degree of risk regarding whether the eventual sale of the business will result in the expected proceeds. For these and other reasons, it may be appropriate to apply a discount for lack of liquidity when valuing a controlling interest.

Business appraisers disagree on the need to apply a discount for lack of liquidity (though court decisions typically call the discount a discount for lack of marketability) when valuing a controlling interest of a closely held entity. Some believe that the ability to control a company provides some liquidity in that the controlling owner can undertake and approve a sale of the business and thus there is no need for a discount. Others argue that a lack of marketability should still be taken into consideration since the controlling interest cannot be assured that an offer to purchase will occur, and a sale may take 6 to 12 months to complete, creating illiquidity as of the valuation date. Regardless, it is widely accepted that noncontrolling positions are much more difficult to sell than

55. Grieve v. Comm'r, T.C. Memo. 2020-28.
56. Janda v. Comm'r, T.C. Memo. 2001-24.

controlling interests and that discounts for lack of liquidity for controlling interests are less than discounts for lack of marketability for noncontrolling interests.

However, the ability to transfer ownership of a controlling interest may also be restricted because of contractual restrictions (e.g., franchise agreement restrictions requiring approval of the franchisor before a transfer of ownership can take place) or governmental regulations (e.g., approval of the U.S. Department of Education must be received before transfer of ownership of a school that provides tuition assistance using federal funds can be effectuated). Thus, even ownership of 100% of an entity may be subject to a discount for lack of marketability because these types of restrictions impact the cash-equivalent value.

Merger arbitrage transactions can be used to quantify a discount for lack of liquidity/marketability for controlling interests since it provides insight into the risk that investors are willing to accept when investing in a controlling interest before the transaction consummates. The gap in price between the acquisition and the closing price of the target company serves as a proxy for the lack of liquidity/marketability of controlling interests.[57]

The U.S. Tax Court has been inconsistent about allowing a discount for lack of liquidity and/or discount for lack of marketability for controlling interests. Some cases have allowed up to 30%, while others have denied the discount entirely.

HOW THE APPLICABLE DEFINITION OF VALUE AFFECTS THE DISCOUNTS FOR LACK OF CONTROL AND LACK OF MARKETABILITY

Fair Market Value

As discussed in Chapter 1, the fair market value standard implies the most likely price at which an arm's-length transaction would be expected to take place between normally motivated investors in open market conditions. In cases of closely held noncontrolling ownership interests, the value usually would fully reflect both noncontrolling and marketability discounts compared with the value of a 100% interest. When valuing controlling interests, discounts for lack of liquidity and/or lack of marketability are sometimes applied.

Fair Value under State Statute

Under the standard of fair value, which is the statutory standard of value for most dissenting stockholder and oppression actions, discounts for lack of control are generally not permitted and discounts for lack of marketability are barred in many states and seldom used in most states other than in New York. Treatment of discounts and premiums under the fair value standard is discussed in some detail in Chapter 23, "Shareholder and Partner Disputes."[58] Although never statutorily mandated and rarely found in case opinions, it is conceivable that fair value may be considered as a standard of value in marital dissolutions. Indeed, New Jersey courts have applied the fair value standard in divorce cases.[59]

57. Ronald D. DiMattia, *Marketability Discounts for Controlling Interests Empirical Evidence*, CPA Expert (Summer 2008).

58. *See also* Gilbert E. Matthews, *Most States Reject Discounts in Appraisal and Oppression Cases–But There Are Some Exceptions*, 41(2) Bus. Valuation Rev. 67–80 (Summer 2022).

59. Brown v. Brown, 348 N.J. Super. 466, 792 A.2d 463 (N.J. App. Div. 2002).

OTHER DISCOUNTS

Key Person Discount

Some businesses are so dependent on a few key people or a single key person that a discount is warranted to reflect the potential impact of the loss of their services. This may be the case in an estate where the key person has died or when there is cause for concern about a key person's health or continued availability for whatever reasons.

The appropriate amount of a key person discount is not something that can be estimated with precision and may best be handled by increasing the rate of return in the income approach or reducing the pricing multiple used in the market approach to account for this risk. Some factors to consider are:

- **Services rendered** and the cost to the company of losing those services
- **Potential for replacement**, including the ability of others to take over and the costs of replacement
- **Risks** associated with disruption and replacement. There are two potential offsets to the possible costs:
    - **Compensation saved** (after any continuing obligations)
    - **Key person insurance**
- **Personal goodwill** associated with the relationships cultivated by a key member of management that may be hard to duplicate.

The U.S. Tax Court has recognized key person discounts. Amounts have generally ranged from 10% to 25% of the value of the business before other adjustments such as minority and marketability.[60] Alternatively, key person risk can be included in the company specific premium of the discount rate.[61]

Tax on Built-In Capital Gains Adjustment

An entity holds that assets with a fair market value substantially greater than the amounts at which those assets are carried on the books is said to have a "built-in capital gain" and thus carries an implicit liability for capital gain tax at the entity level when and if the assets were to be sold. Until 1986, tax law embraced what was called the General Utilities Doctrine, which allowed a Subchapter C corporation to liquidate and distribute proceeds to shareholders within one year and by so doing avoid paying capital gains tax at the corporate level. Changes brought about by the Tax Reform Act of 1986 eliminated the General Utilities Doctrine, thus leaving no practical method to avoid paying a corporate-level capital gains tax on the sale of appreciated assets.[62] Thereafter, the IRS resisted allowing any discount for built-in capital gains tax liability unless a sale of the assets was clearly imminent.

In *Davis*,[63] the Tax Court, for the first time, clearly articulated that a discount for the built-in capital gains tax should be recognized. Despite the favorable ruling, its recognition was relegated to only a small increase in the allowed discount for lack of

---

60. *See, e.g.*, Est. of Furman v. Comm'r, T.C. Memo. 1998-157 (1998); Est. of Mitchell v. Comm'r, T.C. Memo. 2002-98; Est. of Feldmar v. Comm'r, T.C. Memo. 1988-429 (1988).

61. Koffler v. Comm'r, 1978 T.C. Memo. 159.

62. *See* Chapter 26, "Valuing Stock of S Corporations and Interests in Other Pass-through Entities," for how the built-in capital gains liability is handled when a corporation elects to be taxed as a Subchapter S corporation.

63. Est. of Davis v. Comm'r, 86 T.C. 1156 (U.S.T.C. 1986).

marketability, which, monetarily, represented only a small fraction of the liability.[64] In 2000, in *Dunn*, the Tax Court echoed the Davis decision by, once again, recognizing the liability in the form of a small increase to the discount for lack of marketability.[65] The taxpayers, however, appealed to the U.S. Court of Appeals for the Fifth Circuit, which held that the liability should be recognized on a dollar-for-dollar basis.[66] Close to a decade later, overturning the Tax Court, the Eleventh Circuit held in *Frazier Jelke III*[67] that dollar-for-dollar discounts for built-in capital gains tax should be granted.

Thus, for appraisals where the subject entities are domiciled in the states of the Fifth and Eleventh Circuits, valuations for tax purposes recognize a dollar-for-dollar discount as the prevailing law. Outside of these states, however, the issue remains unclear. The Tax Court in *Richmond* refused to recognize the dollar-for-dollar deduction espoused in *Dunn* and *Jelke* and opted for a methodology that recognized the built-in gains tax liability but at an amount that was about one-third of the total liability.[68]

Family law courts generally have denied any adjustments to values to recognize potential trapped-in capital gains tax liability unless sale of the assets is imminent, and the operating spouse usually is left with no adjustment to the value of the company for this contingent liability. Of course, as with most rules, there are some exceptions.[69]

Voting versus Nonvoting Shares

The difference in value between voting and nonvoting minority shares depends largely on the size of the block and the distribution of ownership. In general, the greater the extent to which control is involved, the greater the impact of voting rights on the stock's value. If one stockholder has total control and there is no cumulative voting,[70] the question of whether the noncontrolling shares are voting or nonvoting is academic unless a split of the control block is foreseeable.

Empirical studies on the price differentials between voting and nonvoting publicly traded stocks indicate that for small noncontrolling interests, the market generally accords very little or no value to voting rights.[71] However, there is one situation in which a discount for lack of voting rights may be applicable. When voting power is concentrated with one shareholder, or a group of shareholders, it is logical that a notable difference in value between the voting and nonvoting stock would exist. However, empirical evidence based on acquisitions and recapitalizations of public companies with a dual class show that this premium is small.[72] In the recent *Cecil* decision, the court disallowed even a 2% discount for the nonvoting nature of the Class B shares, stating that (1) this

64. *Id.*

65. Est. of Dunn v. Comm'r, T.C. Memo. 2000-12.

66. Est. of Dunn v. Comm'r, 301 F.3d 339 (5th Cir. 2002).

67. Est. of Frazier Jelke III v. Comm'r, 507 F.3d 1317 (11th Cir. 2007).

68. Est. of Richmond v. Comm'r, T.C. Memo. 2014-26.

69. *See, e.g.*, Hamilton v. Hamilton, 2002 Ohio 2417 (Ohio App. 2002) (the court permitted a deduction for capital gains taxes, even though a sale was not imminent, where the husband would effectively have been forced to purchase the wife's shares in a company).

70. State statutes and a company's governing documents may provide for cumulative voting. Under noncumulative voting, a simple majority of the voting interests can elect all the directors. Under cumulative voting, votes may be combined for a single director.

71. When they are applied the differential is usually small, often no more than 5%.

72. Gilbert E. Matthews, *Valuation of Dual Class Shares*, Bus. Valuation Update 7–12 (Oct. 2017).

factor was already considered in the discount for lack of marketability, and (2) the two studies being used as support were more than ten years old.[73]

Blockage

The concept of blockage is that the quantity of individual units of something held would take a long time for the market to absorb under normal market conditions without a significant discount. Therefore, to sell all the units as one block, one would have to accept a discount from the aggregate value of the units if sold separately. The concept often is applied to real estate, where it might take a long time to sell off the individual lots in a subdivision.

A blockage discount is only applied to blocks of public stock when the size of the block might take several weeks or months to liquidate without affecting the share price under normal trading conditions. The concept is recognized by the courts,[74] but careful empirical evidence of trading must be presented to support it in each case.[75] Most blockage discounts are relatively small.

The concept of blockage usually is not applied directly in the case of closely held stocks, for there is no record of average trading volume with which to compare the size of the block.

SUMMARY

Discounts are adjustments made during the appraisal process that are necessary because business appraisers must rely on similar but different types of transactional data to value closely held interests. When it comes to control issues, a noncontrolling interest is worth less than a proportionate share of the controlling interest, so using the proper methodology and supporting the adjustment for lack of control is crucial. Many times, the inputs and data used in business appraisals are obtained from the public market. Accordingly, adjustments referred to as a discount for lack of marketability must be made to account for the risk and time it takes to convert a nonmarketable interest to cash.

When it comes to valuing family limited partnerships and LLCs, there is an abundance of transactional information to support discounts when valuing a noncontrolling interest. There are other less common discounts that are sometimes considered, like key person, tax on built-in capital gains, lack of voting rights, and blockage discounts. These adjustments, like discount for lack of control and discount for lack of marketability, must be determined in an objective manner that can withstand the scrutiny of audits, Tax Court, and other challenges.

---

73. Cecil v. Comm'r, T.C. Memo. 2023-24.

74. *See, e.g.*, Gallun v. Comm'r, T.C. Memo. 1974-284, 33 T.C. Memo. (CCH) 1316 (1974), in which the experts agreed that blockage reduced the value of an investment portfolio from $18,087,263 to $16,204,439, a difference of over 10%. *See also, e.g.*, Est. of Foote v. Comm'r, T.C. Memo. 1999-37 (3.3% blockage discount permitted where the block constituted 2.2% of the stock outstanding and was equal to 29 days of trading volume); Est. of Mellinger v. Comm'r, 112 T.C. 26 (1999) (25% blockage discount permitted); Est. of Gimbel v. Comm'r, 2006 Tax Ct. Memo. LEXIS 274 (Dec. 19, 2006) (effective 14.2% discount permitted on both restricted (14.4%) and nonrestricted stock (13.9%)).

75. William H. Frazier & Ronak P. Shah, *Determining the Cost of Blockage by the Market-Derived Blockage Model*, 37(2) Bus. Valuation Rev. 64–73 (Summer 2018).

Discounts often become the focus of the client or opposing party, including the IRS. It should be remembered that financial theory is based on risk versus return. Accordingly, any adjustment made in the appraisal process should examine the impact of that discount on the rate of return of the interest being valued in order to support the magnitude of the discount. The application and use of discounts requires knowledge, experience, and understanding of the complete appraisal process.

REFERENCES FOR DISCOUNTS AND PREMIUMS

Basic Discount and Premiums References

Bishop, David. 1999. "Trapped-in Capital Gains: Where Do We Go From Here?" *Business Valuation Review* (June): 64–68.

Feder, Robert D., Charles T. Rosoff, and Aleza Tadri. 2014. "Discounts and Premiums." In *Valuation Strategies in Divorce*, 5th ed. Chap. 3 (Wolters Kluwer).

Fishman, E. Jay, et al. 2023. "Application of Premiums and/or Discounts." In *PPC's Guide to Business Valuations*, 8-13 to 8-32 (Carrollton, TX: Thomson Reuters).

Hitchner, James R. 2017. "Valuation Discounts and Premiums." In *Financial Valuation: Applications and Models*, 4th ed., Chap. 10, 391–493. (Hoboken, NJ: John Wiley & Sons, Inc.).

Hitchner, James R., James Alerding, Joshua B. Angell, and Katherine E. Morris. 2017. *Discount for Lack of Marketability Guide and Toolkit* (Ventnor City, NJ: Valuation Products and Services LLC), available at www.valuationproducts.com/DLOM-Toolkit.

Hitchner, James, Shannon P. Pratt, and Jay E. Fishman. 2016. "Discounts and Premiums." In *A Consensus View: Q&A Guide to Financial Valuation*, Chap. 3, 193–255 (Ventnor City, NJ: Valuation Products and Services, LLC).

Internal Revenue Service. *IRS Appeals Officer Valuation Training Course*, 9-1 to 9-60.

Internal Revenue Service Engineering Valuation Program DLOM Team. 2009. *Discount for Lack of Marketability, Job Aid for IRS Valuation Professionals* (Washington, DC), available at irs.gov.

Johnson, Bruce A. 2021. *Comprehensive Guide for the Valuation of Family Limited Partnerships and LLCs*, 6th ed. (Portland, OR: Business Valuation Resources).

Laro, David and Shannon P. Pratt, 2011. "Entity-Level Discounts," "Minority Discounts/Control Premiums," "Discounts for Lack of Marketability," and "Other Shareholder-Level Discounts." "Economic and Industry Analysis." In *Business Valuation and Federal Taxes: Procedures, Law and Perspective*, 2nd ed. Chap. 18, 249–70; Chap. 19, 271–8; Chap. 20, 279–320 Chap. 21, 331–32 (Hoboken, NJ: John Wiley & Sons).

Lee, M. Mark. 2001. "Control Premiums and Minority Discounts: The Need for Economic Analysis." *Shannon Pratt's Business Valuation Update* (August 2001).

Lee, M. Mark. 2004. "The Discount for Lack of Control and the Ownership Control Premium." In R. Reilly and R. Schweihs, Eds. *The Handbook of Business Valuation and Intellectual Property Analysis.* (New York: McGraw-Hill).

Matthews, Gilbert E. 2022. "Most States Reject Discounts in Appraisal and Oppression Cases–But There Are Some Exceptions." *Business Valuation Review* 41:2 (Summer 2022): 67–80.

Mercer, Z. Christopher. 2005. *Valuing Shareholder Cash Flows: Quantifying Marketability Discounts.* E-Book. (Memphis: Peabody Publishing).

Mercer Z. Christopher and Travis W. Harms. 2020. "Introduction to QMDM," "The QMDM Assumptions in Detail," and "Applying the QMDM." In *Business Valuation: An Integrated Theory*, 3rd ed., Chap 9, 327–38; Chap. 10, 359–400; Chap. 11, 401–433 (Hoboken, NJ, John Wiley & Sons, Inc.).

Morrison, William J. and Jay E. Fishman. 2017. "The Basics of Discounts." In *The Business Valuation Bench Book,* Appendix 9, 99–106 (Portland, OR: Business Valuation Resources).

Pratt, Shannon P. *Discounts and Premiums* 2nd ed. 2009. (Hoboken, NJ: John Wiley and Sons, Inc.).

Pratt, Shannon P. and ASA Educational Foundation. 2022. "Control versus Lack of Control," "Market Evidence of Acquisition Premiums and Discounts for Lack of Control," "Discounts for Lack of Liquidity and Lack of Marketability," "Other Valuation Discounts." In *Valuing a Business: The Analysis and Appraisal of Closely Held Businesses*, 6th ed., Chap. 17, 385–407; Chap. 18, 409–418; Chap. 19, 419–463; Chap. 20, 465–479 (New York: McGraw-Hill). Includes extensive bibliography and data references in online Appendix.

Trugman, Gary R. 2022. "Premiums and Discounts (Valuation Adjustments)–Part I," "Premiums and Discounts (Valuation Adjustments)–Part II." In *Understanding Business Valuations*, 6th ed., Chap. 15, 523–47; Chap. 16, 549–623 (Portland, OR: Business Valuation Resources).

References for Premium and Discount Court Cases

BVUpdate™, *Deluxe BVUpdate*™, and *BVLaw*™ are available online at www.BVLibrary.com. (Portland, OR: Business Valuation Resources, LLC.). The online service can be searched by key word, such as marketability, minority, key person, etc.

U.S. Master Estate and Gift Tax Guide. 2023 (Riverwoods, IL: CCH Inc.).

Premium and Discount Data References

Mergerstat Review is published annually in print and digital forms, and monthly PDF updates provide summary information regarding an overview of the corporate transaction market. Available at www.bvresources.com/mergerstat.

FactSet Mergerstat/BVR Control Premium Study is an online database consisting of all takeovers of public companies since 1998. Available at www.bvresources.com/cps. Separate annual Control Premium Study published in four quarterly installments. The quarterly Control Premium Study is available complimentary to subscribers to the *FactSet Mergerstat/BVR Control Premium Study.*

Minority Interest Discount Database. Partnership Profiles, Inc. Several additional publications are available: Annual Rate of Return Study, Guideline Partnership Reports, Closed-End Fund Guideline Reports and Discount for Lack of Marketability Study. Available at www.partnershipprofiles.com.

LiquiStat™ *Database.* Pluris Valuation Advisors LLC, (212) 248-4500, www.pluris.com.

Stout Restricted Stock Study Database and DLOM Calculator. Business Valuation Resources, LLC, (888) 287-8258. Available by subscription at www.bvresources.com/stout.

Valuation Advisors' Lack of Marketability Discount Study™ (888) 287-8258. Available at www.bvmarketdata.com.

CHAPTER 19

Reconciliation of Value Indications

Roger J. Grabowski, FASA and Alina Niculita, ASA, ARM, CFA

INTRODUCTION

In this chapter you will learn about:

- Overall considerations in the reconciliation process
- How the appraiser should evaluate each indication of value
- How the appraiser should treat divergent results among business valuation methods
- If the appraiser should weigh or not weigh the various indications of value
- How the appraiser should support the value conclusion
- How a reader should scrutinize each individual indication of value and, collectively, the value conclusion
- The nuances of the value conclusion a reader should scrutinize

This chapter will focus on the reconciliation process from two perspectives: (1) the appraiser and (2) the reader who is looking to gain a thorough understanding of an appraisal conclusion.

As discussed in previous chapters, there are three generally accepted approaches to the valuation of businesses, business interests, and professional practices: the income approach, the market approach, and the asset-based approach. Within each approach there are a number of generally accepted valuation methods. Within each method there are a number of generally accepted procedures. Accordingly, valuation analyses progress from the more general to the more specific. First, the appraiser selects the appropriate approaches. Second, within each approach, the appraiser selects and applies the appropriate methods. And, finally, within each method, the appraiser performs the appropriate procedures.

OVERVIEW OF THE RECONCILIATION PROCESS

When reaching a business valuation conclusion, the analyses must undergo a reconciliation process. During the reconciliation process, it is important that the appraiser review all steps taken in the business valuation analysis while keeping in mind the valuation assignment. The purpose of the valuation assignment will determine the approaches, methods, and nuances of the valuation analysis.

Before a reader can assess the reasonability of the valuation conclusion, the reader must also understand the scope of work called for in the engagement. As a reader, two important questions must be answered:

- Did the appraiser appraise the correct property?
- Did the appraiser appraise the correct property the right way?

In other words, from an overall engagement perspective, the reader should consider the question, "Did the appraiser accomplish what he or she was engaged to do?"

A review of the business valuation assignment should consider the following:

- The purpose and objective of the appraisal
- The business enterprise ownership interest subject to appraisal
- The bundle of legal rights subject to appraisal

DID THE APPRAISER APPRAISE THE CORRECT PROPERTY?

As a reader, the question must be asked: Did the appraiser appraise the correct property? It is surprising how often appraisals are performed on something other than the specific property (e.g., interest in the business) at issue. The nature of the property has a bearing on appraisal methods and also on premiums and/or discounts.

A common error is to ignore the existence of a corporate or partnership entity and simply appraise the assets owned by the entity. This can result in an entirely asset-based appraisal, when an appraisal of a going-concern with the weight primarily (or even entirely) on an income approach would be more appropriate. The error also can result in ignoring valuable intangible assets, including goodwill.

A classic example of this occurred in *Sommers Drug Stores Co. v. Corrigan Enterprises, Inc.*,[1] an Employee Stock Ownership Plan (ESOP) valuation case, in which the plaintiff's expert used an asset liquidation method to determine fair market value. The court soundly rejected this approach, indicating that the "other relevant factors" that the expert should have considered included:

> The goodwill of the business; the economic outlook in the particular industry; the company's position in the industry and its management; the degree of control of the business represented by the block of stock to be valued; and the values of securities of corporations engaged in the same or similar lines of business which are listed on a stock exchange.

The court summed up its disapproval by saying, "[the expert's] utter failure to consider other relevant factors, or to explain his reasons for disregarding them, renders his testimony unworthy of credit."[2]

In another example discussed in Chapter 27, "Valuing Interests in Real Property Holding Entities," the Tax Court found that submitting real property appraisals, when the subject of the valuation was 72% of the stock of the entity that owned the real property,

1. Sommers Drug Stores Co. v. Corrigan Enters., Inc., 793 F.2d 1456 (5th Cir. 1986).
2. *Id.*

was not a proper appraisal of the subject stock and denied the entirety of the charitable contribution deduction.[3]

In the same vein, courts have observed that an asset-based approach alone usually is inappropriate to value operating companies, which generally are valued based on earnings, as an asset valuation tends to undervalue such companies.[4] Additionally, in a valuation of a noncontrolling ownership interest, assets may or may not play an important role in arriving at a per-share figure, as owners of noncontrolling interests cannot reach those assets.[5] Courts also have ruled that the exclusive use of an asset-based approach in a fair value appraisal action is erroneous because it is akin to determining the company's theoretical liquidation value.[6]

More important, a corporate or partnership structure standing between the owner and the assets usually calls for some discounts from the total fair market value of the net assets. Even if valuing on a control basis, discounts to consider would include, for example, unrealized taxes on trapped-in capital gains (if not already recognized as a deferred liability), contingent liabilities, and a discount for lack of liquidity (and, in certain cases, an additional discount for lack of marketability). If valuing on a noncontrolling interest basis, typically there would be discounts for both lack of control and lack of marketability.

Another problem regarding valuing the correct property can arise when there are two or more classes of stock. The appraiser must identify which class is being valued and how its features differ from the other.[7] If valuing a noncontrolling ownership interest, discounts may differ among classes. Indeed, even within a class, some shares may be subject to transfer restrictions that affect value.

Still another problem related to valuing the correct property may arise when the appraiser has not inquired into the purpose of the valuation. In *Chao v. Hall Holding Co., Inc.*,[8] the appraiser was hired to value a subsidiary of a holding company but was never informed and never knew that the purpose of the valuation was to determine how much an ESOP should pay for the holding company's stock. The court concluded that the appraiser had valued the wrong company and should have valued the holding company. Accordingly, the court concluded that the valuation could not be relied on.

---

3. Est. of Harvey Evenchick, Gregory V. Gadarian, Personal Representative, & Deanna Evenchick, Petitioners, v. Comm'r, T.C. Memo. 2013-34 (U.S.T.C. Feb. 4, 2013).

4. BTR Dunlop Holdings, Inc. v. Comm'r, T.C. Memo. 1999-377, 1999 Tax Ct. Memo. LEXIS 432 (Nov. 15, 1999); Foltz v. U.S. News & World Report, Inc., 663 F. Supp. 1494, 1987 U.S. Dist. LEXIS 5592 (D.D.C. 1987).

5. Foltz v. U.S. News & World Report, Inc., 663 F. Supp. 1494, 1987 U.S. Dist. LEXIS 5592 (D.D.C. 1987); Gibbons v. Gibbons, 94 P.3d 879, 194 Or. App. 257 (Or. Ct. App. 2004).

6. *See, e.g.*, Paskill Corp. v. Algoma Corp., 747 A.2d 549 (Del. 2000) (under Delaware law, the company's fair value must be determined on a going-concern basis, and a determination on a theoretical liquidation basis is proscribed).

7. For example, in rejecting an expert's report, "[the expert] did not address the nature of the two classes of stock issued by the corporation, whether they had cumulative voting rights or what differences existed between the two classes of stock." Est. of Kaufman v. Comm'r, T.C. Memo. 1999-119 (1999).

8. Chao v. Hall Holding Co. Inc., 285 F.3d 415, 2002 U.S. App. LEXIS 5929 (6th Cir. 2002).

DID THE APPRAISER APPRAISE THE CORRECT PROPERTY THE RIGHT WAY?

Once the appraiser has identified and valued the correct property, the valuation process will include a reconciliation of the methods, weighting of methodologies, attributes of ownership, and application of the correct standard of value. At this point in the review, the reader will look to answer the question: Did the appraiser appraise the correct property the right way? The reader will scrutinize the reconciliation of values and nuances of control and marketability that will result in the value conclusion.

MAJOR CONSIDERATIONS IN THE RECONCILIATION PROCESS

After the appraiser has developed different indications of values from the methods used, the appraiser must reconcile these into a final opinion of value. That final opinion may validly be a range of values, although for some appraisal purposes a single point estimate of value is required.

The reconciliation process is one in which the appraiser reconsiders each of the methods employed in the context of his or her level of confidence in each method. For both the appraiser and the reader, questions to consider in the reconciliation include:

- What was the quality and quantity of the data in each of the methods?
- What was the degree of reliability of the data in each of the methods?
- How appropriate was each of the methods for the specific valuation purpose?
- What was the spread (dispersion) of the value indications obtained from the employed methods?

It is reasonable to expect that various valuation methods will produce different values, as each approach takes a different perspective, based on either the subject company's income, the market, or the subject company's assets. At the same time, the subject company under each method is the same company, and its degree of risk, competence of management, degree of competition, financial structure, and so on, remain the same. This suggests that if all the methods employed are appropriate, each uses reasonably reliable data, and each is developed correctly, the indications of value obtained should be reasonably in close relation to one another.

Values should be compared after they are on an equivalent basis, that is, after premiums or discounts are applied to reach the level of value being sought. In other words, the values to be reconciled should all be on the same basis (e.g., control basis, nonmarketable noncontrolling basis, or whatever is appropriate).

A common error is the application of a single premium or discount to an indication of value developed from two or more valuation methods that imply dissimilar ownership characteristics. This can produce a conclusion that is not clearly fish nor fowl, that is, not clearly a noncontrolling or control value, nor clearly a fully marketable or nonmarketable value. In each situation, any discount or premium applied must be appropriate to adjust from the definition and level of value implied in the valuation method to the definition and level of value being sought in the appraisal.

As a reader, a good way to ensure the appropriateness of any control premium or discount to a particular valuation method (or "indication of value") is to ask: What type of value does this valuation method produce?

- Control marketable interest?
- Control illiquid interest?
- Marketable, noncontrolling interest?
- Nonmarketable, noncontrolling interest?

By answering this question, the reader will then know whether a control premium or discount is appropriate.

RECONCILING DIVERGENT RESULTS AMONG BUSINESS VALUATION METHODS

Ideally, the appraiser will use two or more approaches in the business valuation and these approaches will all yield virtually identical value conclusions. In practice, this rarely, if ever, happens.

Appraisers expect to estimate a range of valuation conclusions when several alternative valuation approaches are used. The normal situation occurs when several approaches result in a reasonably narrow dispersion of conclusions. These alternative conclusions, then, indicate the reasonable range of values for the subject business. They also provide mutually supportive evidence regarding the final valuation conclusion.

Occasionally, two or three valuation methods produce value indications within a reasonable range and then one method produces a clear and obvious value estimate far outside the range of the others (i.e., an outlier). For example, the value indication of the asset accumulation method under the asset-based approach (discussed in Chapter 9, "The Asset-Based Approach") may be a clear and obvious outlier compared to three other value estimates. Accordingly, the appraisal requires further analysis and consideration before a valuation conclusion can be reached.

What should the appraiser do regarding such an outlier value estimate? The appraiser could discard the valuation method that yields the outlier value estimate. This action is based on the rationale that the outlier valuation method simply is not reasonable given the subject set of facts and circumstances, or that, on careful consideration, the method is not appropriate for the type of company being valued (for example, the asset value of a high-tech company is very unlikely to be a meaningful measure of the company's fair market value).

If, after careful review, one of the appraisal methods that appears to have merit still produces an outlier, then it becomes a matter of appraisal judgment as to the extent to which the factors reflected in the valuation method actually contribute to the value of the business or interest being appraised, with weight accorded commensurately to the method in the final value estimate.

WEIGHTING OF VALUATION METHODS RESULTS

As with the selection of valuation methods, there are no scientific formulas or specific rules with regard to the weighting of the results of two or more business valuation methods. In fact, the same factors or guidelines that affect the selection of the valuation methods will influence the appraiser with regard to weighting the conclusions of these methods.

The chapters on the various approaches and methods contain more extensive discussion of the circumstances when each is most useful, and the reader is encouraged to read those chapters for guidance in weighting approaches and methods.

Keep in mind that different approaches to value are not discrete but have considerable overlap. For example, within the market approach, heavy emphasis may appropriately be placed on a multiple of an economic income figure, such as a price-to-earnings multiple. It could be argued that this is an alternate form of an income approach, thus lessening the need for separate weight on an income approach per se. Similarly, income approach methods depend on information about market conditions to estimate appropriate discount and capitalization rates. Thus, the better the job an income approach does on capturing and documenting market-required discount and/or capitalization rates, the less the need for separate weight on a market approach per se.

The appraiser must contemplate: "What attributes of ownership of this business or business interest give rise to the value of owning it?" If the income available for distribution to the owner is the primary value driver, then it may be appropriate that one or more methods within the income approach dominate the value conclusion. Of course, a capitalization of dividends (for a noncontrolling interest) or dividend-paying capacity (for a controlling interest) within the market approach based on guideline public companies could very well also capture the income-related value.

If the ability to sell the business or interest in the business is the primary value driver, then it may be appropriate that one or more methods within the market approach dominate the value conclusion.

If the value is derived primarily from the ownership of assets, then an asset-based approach may dominate. However, a market approach using a multiple of the market price of stock to underlying net asset value also may be a satisfactory way to capture asset-driven value (for example, in industries where asset value is correlated with fair market value of the stock, such as financial institutions and real estate investment trusts (REITs)). Generally, if asset value is high relative to other approaches, an asset-based approach tends to be more appropriate in valuing a controlling interest than a noncontrolling interest, for one of the important things that a control owner controls—and a noncontrolling owner does not—is utilization of the assets.

Hopefully, throughout the report, and at the point of reaching the final conclusion, the appraiser has provided clear explanations supporting the choice of approaches and methods and the weight accorded to each. The reader must then consider whether the methods used (and the weights accorded to each) are consistent with the appropriate definition of value in the specific legal context and are supported by the data available.

The reader must also keep in mind the court interpretations of the standard of value, if applicable. For example, family law courts in some states adhere to a strict definition of *fair market value* as "value in exchange." In some jurisdictions, personal goodwill that cannot be transferred may not be considered a marital asset, even though it may represent considerable value to the owner. However, it could be considered if *investment value* (value to the owner) were the applicable standard of value (see Chapter 12, "Personal versus Enterprise Goodwill").

The final value conclusion should be a number within the final range of values indicated by the various business valuation methods used in the analysis. The final value estimate may be a number indicated by one of the valuation methods; it may be heavily weighted to the result of the valuation method relied on most or it may be another number within the indicated range.

When an appraiser calculates a simple, unweighted arithmetic average to arrive at a final value estimate, this implies to the reader that all the valuation methods have equal validity and equal weight. While this may occur in certain instances, the reader should understand this is usually not the case and inspect the rationale behind the weighting.

EXPLICIT WEIGHTING

An intuitively appealing method of presenting the value conclusion is for the appraiser to:

1. Use subjective but informed judgment and decide on a percentage weight to assign the results of each relevant valuation approach or method used, and
2. Base the final valuation on a weighted average of the results of the various methods.

Suppose, for example, the appraiser is valuing a noncontrolling ownership interest in a closely held manufacturing company and ultimately relies on three valuation multiples developed through the guideline public company method. Because it is an operating company with a substantial asset base, the appraiser believes the appropriate price-to-earnings multiple should be accorded 60% of the total weight, the price-to-dividends ratio 10%, and the price-to-asset value multiple 30%. It can be assumed, in this case, the company has been unable to generate a good rate of return on its asset base; thus, the result would be as presented in Exhibit 19-1.

Exhibit 19-1 Example of Explicit Weighting of Value Indications

		Subject Company			
Multiple Name	**Multiple Amount**	**Fundamental Value per Share**	**Indicated Value per Share**	**Weight**	**Weighted Value Per Share**
Price/Earnings	5.0x	$2.00	$10.00	60%	$6.00
Price/Dividends	20.0x	$0.60	$12.00	10%	$1.20
Price/Net Asset Value	0.8x	$20.00	$16.00	30%	$4.80
					$12.00
Less: Discount for Lack of Marketability (35% × $12.00)				35%	−$4.20
		Concluded Value per Share			$7.80

In this case, although companies in the same industry generally are selling below their book value, the subject company is valued at a larger discount from book value than the average in its industry due to relatively poor earnings. However, the asset base is accorded some weight, and the company is valued at a lower discount from book value ($16 versus $20, a 20% discount) than it would be if it were valued strictly on a multiple of earnings basis ($10 versus $20, a 50% discount). As it turns out, in this case, the effect of the capitalization of dividends is neutral.

The main weakness of the preceding valuation analysis is that no generally accepted mathematical model is available for use in deriving the weights to assign to the results of each valuation procedure. The relative weights to assign each pricing multiple depend on the appraiser's judgment; however, this forces the appraiser to present his or her thinking in clearly quantified terms. The preceding narrative, coupled with the explicit weighting, provides important information about the appraiser's thought process. The procedure also has the appeal of being clear and easy to understand. If someone evaluating the results disagrees with some aspect of the appraiser's judgment, the point of departure is readily identifiable, and it is easy to apply an alternate set of numbers and quickly recompute the result.

The preceding example applies the weights to several variables within the market approach. It also is possible to apply specific weightings to the results of different approaches.

Court cases in which values of stock must be estimated under dissenting stockholders' appraisal rights have tended to rely on this weighting procedure. However, the wording of Revenue Ruling 59–60 does not embrace the method. The ruling states:

> Because the valuations cannot be made on the basis of a prescribed formula, there is no means whereby the various applicable factors in a particular case can be assigned mathematical weights in deriving the fair market value. For this reason, no useful purpose is served by taking an average of several factors (for example, book value, capitalized earnings, and capitalized dividends) and basing the valuation on the result. Such a process excludes active consideration of other pertinent factors, and the end result cannot be supported by a realistic application of the significant facts in the case except by mere chance.[9]

IMPLICIT WEIGHTING

Some appraisers use an implicit weighting scheme in their final valuation analysis and conclusion; that is, they present the valuation indications for each method performed and then simply present a final value estimate. They do not document or justify the thought process underlying their conclusion.

An example of this implicit weighting scheme is provided in Exhibit 19-2.

Exhibit 19-2 Illustrative Business Enterprise, Inc. Business Valuation Methods and Value Estimates: Valuation Analysis and Conclusion

Valuation Method	Value Estimate
Guideline Public Company Method	$18,000,000
Discounted Cash Flow Method	$20,000,000
Adjusted Net Asset Value Method	$24,000,000
Valuation Conclusion	**$22,000,000**

This analysis presents the final valuation conclusion. However, it is incomplete unless the appraiser explains and justifies the final value estimate concluded from this analysis. The explanation can cover both the conceptual preferability among the methods used as well as the degree of confidence in each method based on the relative quantity

9. Rev. Rul. 59–60, 1959-1 C.B. 237.

and quality of data available. When each method is performed properly, there probably will be little or no difference in the result between using an explicit or implicit weighting of value indications.

FINAL VALUE ESTIMATE

Any of the following types of final value estimates may be appropriate, given the purpose and objective of the business valuation:

- **A point estimate.** Usually the business valuation final value estimate is stated as a single figure or point estimate.
- **A range of value.** In this conclusion, the business valuation indicated value falls somewhere within a range of values. This may be reported solely as the conclusion of value or in conjunction with a point estimate.
- **A relationship value.** In this conclusion, the business valuation estimate is expressed as a relationship to a given value. For example, the value estimate is indicated to be "no less than $X million" or "no more than $Y million."

SUMMARY

In many appraisal reports, how the appraiser reaches a conclusion is often given short shrift with little information provided as to the thought process the appraiser employs in evaluating the value indications resulting from the various business valuation approaches and methods. Describing the reconciliation process can be as important as describing how the methods are employed.

Before a reader can assess the reasonability of the valuation conclusion, a reader must understand the nuances of each value indication. During the reconciliation process in the appraisal report, it is important for the appraiser to review all the steps of the business valuation.

As for the reader, one should answer the following two questions:

- Did the appraiser appraise the correct property?
- Did the appraiser appraise the correct property the right way?

In other words, from an overall engagement perspective, the reader should consider the question: Did the appraiser accomplish what he or she set out to accomplish?

The appraiser should not simply default to taking a measure of central tendency (i.e., the median or average) of the indicated values, unless the appraiser provides adequate support. Rather, the reconciliation process should provide the reader with a comprehensive understanding of the thought process employed in arriving at a valuation conclusion.

REFERENCES FOR RECONCILIATION OF VALUE INDICATIONS

Bishop, David M. 1998. "Reconciling the Indicated Values." In *Business Valuation Review* (March): 13–15.

Fishman, Jay E., Bruce Johnson, Kent Pummel, et al. 2023. "Selecting a Value from a Range of Values." In *PPC's Guide to Business Valuations* 8-2 to 8-10 (Carrollton, TX: Thomson Reuters).

Laro, David and Shannon P. Pratt, 2011. "Weighting of Approaches." In *Business Valuation and Federal Taxes: Procedures, Law and Perspective,* 2nd ed. Chap. 23, 343–7 (Hoboken, NJ: John Wiley & Sons).

Pratt, Shannon P. and ASA Educational Foundation. 2022. "Valuation Reconciliation and Conclusion." In *Shannon Pratt's Valuing a Business: The Analysis and Appraisal of Closely Held Businesses*, 6th ed. Chap. 21, 481–95 (New York: McGraw-Hill).

Salter, Roy, Vicentiu Covrig and Akanksha Bedi. 2022. "Reconciling Business Valuations from Multiple Valuation Methods." In *The Value Examiner* (March/April): 6–14.

The Appraisal Foundation. 2023. "Understanding the Differences: Conclusion of Value vs. Value Calculations." In *Valuation Brief 2023-1.* Available at The Appraisal Foundation Document Library (appraisalfoundation.sharefile.com).

CHAPTER 20

Valuations for Gift, Estate, and Charitable Contribution Matters

Ryan Montgomery, JD, LLM and Travis Harms, CFA, CPA/ABV

INTRODUCTION[1]

In this chapter you will learn about:

- The standard of value applied in most federal tax matters
- Nuances of the definition of fair market value
- Consideration of appraiser qualifications by the courts
- Which party has the burden of proof
- Adequate disclosure of taxable gifts
- Consideration by the courts of valuation procedures and methods
- Treatment of valuation discounts and premiums by the courts
- Who is a qualified appraiser for valuing charitable contributions
- How the courts have treated contingent liabilities
- How the courts have considered subsequent events
- Consideration of value stipulated in a buy-sell agreement
- Weighting of valuation methods in reaching a concluded value
- Courts' desire for litigants to settle valuation matters

There is more definitive precedential case law in the general area of valuations for federal tax purposes than for any other business valuation purpose. Some issues are well settled, but decisions on other issues continue to evolve. This chapter attempts to distinguish which issues are well settled, nearly settled, or still in some stage of evolution.

There also are issues about which decisions seem to be conflicting (for example, discounts for lack of marketability for controlling interests). However, as the late Judge David Laro had explained:

> Each valuation case is unique. Although guidance can be obtained from earlier cases, one case is rarely on point with another, and a significant differentiation of the facts can usually be made.[2]

Even among issues that are well settled in principle, there is still room for argument about magnitudes, especially in such areas as discounts for lack of control and discounts

---

1. The authors thank Noah Gordon, former legal counsel for Shannon Pratt Valuations, for his contribution to the prior edition.

2. Hon. David Laro, *A View from the Tax Court Bench: What Judges Want in Expert Records and Testimony*, 1(1) Shannon Pratt's Business Valuation Update 1–2 (Oct. 1995).

for lack of marketability for noncontrolling interests and discounts for lack of liquidity and marketability for controlling interests. Chapter 18, "Discounts and Premiums," addresses empirical data to support quantification of such discounts, and this chapter will discuss principles articulated by the courts regarding quantification of these factors and magnitudes of discounts ultimately decided.

An understanding of valuations for federal tax purposes is also important for valuations for many other purposes. Because of the extensive case law, Internal Revenue Service (IRS) Revenue Rulings, and other literature, valuation principles and decisions for tax purposes often are cited in valuation reports and court decisions for other purposes, including marital dissolution and bankruptcy.

Federal tax cases involving business valuations fall primarily into the following categories:

- Estate taxes
- Gift taxes
- Charitable contributions
- Ordinary income and capital gains taxes (discussed in Chapter 21)
- Transfer pricing (discussed in Chapter 21)

Although the standard of fair market value applies equally in all cases, the manner in which it applies can have extreme consequences for estate planning. Most important, for gift tax purposes each transfer is valued individually, while for estate tax purposes the entire amount in the estate is aggregated, regardless of how many different beneficiaries there may be. For example, if a 100% interest in a company is held in an estate, it will be valued as a 100% controlling interest, even if it is willed equally to three beneficiaries. But if three gifts of one-third interests are made, each will be valued as a distinct noncontrolling ownership interest, benefiting from the well-settled principle that the noncontrolling interest is discounted compared to a pro rata portion of the value of a 100% ownership interest in the business.

Also, if the estate holds more than one class of security, the combined effect of all may be aggregated for the purpose of valuation,[3] but in some cases it is more appropriate to value only the subject voting shares, rather than valuing all voting shares of the company and deriving a pro rata value from the whole.[4]

FAIR MARKET VALUE[5]

The standard of value for most federal tax cases is fair market value, defined by the IRS as:

> the price at which the property would change hands between a willing buyer and a willing seller, when the former is not under any compulsion to buy and the latter is not under any compulsion to sell, both parties having reasonable knowledge of the relevant facts.[6]

---

3. Ahmanson Found. v. United States, 674 F.2d 761 (9th Cir. 1981).

4. Est. of Simplot v. Comm'r, 249 F.3d 1191 (9th Cir. 2001).

5. An exception to this definition is in transfer pricing where the standard of value is "arm's length" pricing; *see* Chapter 21. For an extensive discussion available on the nuances of fair market value in the federal tax valuation context, *see* Jay E. Fishman, Shannon P. Pratt & William J. Morrison, Standards of Value: Theory and Applications 35–85 (2d ed. 2013).

6. Rev. Rul. 59–60. *See also* Treas. Reg. § 1.170A-1(c)(2) (Fair market value is "the price at which the property would change hands between a willing buyer and a willing seller, neither being under any compul-

There are many nuances to this definition, as discussed in a subsequent section. However, over several decades, the federal courts have developed seven standards that must be considered in determining fair market value. These are:

- Both the buyer and seller must be "willing."
- Neither buyer nor seller is under a compulsion to buy or sell the item in question.
- Both the buyer and seller are hypothetical persons.[7]
- Both the buyer and seller are aware of all facts and circumstances involving the item in question.
- The item in question is valued at its highest and best use, regardless of its current use (in the business valuation context, this usually means that investor value is maximized).
- The item is valued without regard to any event subsequent to the valuation date, unless such an event was reasonably foreseeable as of the valuation date or was relevant to the valuation.
- The transaction is for cash, is valued as of the transaction date, following a reasonable commercial process.[8]

To this day, one of the most instructive cases on fair market value of closely held stock for federal tax purposes is *Central Trust*,[9] which contains a lengthy, detailed discussion of valuation issues written more than 50 years ago. Although the reader must recognize that the structure of markets and financial theory and evidence have advanced since that decision, it is still the most comprehensive tax case discussion of basic valuation issues and remains well worth reading today. One other case of comparable instructive detail and quality on valuation under the fair market value standard is *Foltz*.[10] It involves a class-action suit alleging undervaluation of retiring employee stock under the fair market value standard.

One of the more lengthy discussions of the Tax Court's posture in determining fair market value is contained at the beginning of the opinion in *Furman*,[11] which we suggest is instructive reading in general.

Another case that is a good source for the modern history of fair market value is *Bank One*.[12]

---

sion to buy or sell and both having reasonable knowledge of relevant facts."). *See also* the Financial Institutions Reform, Recovery, and Enforcement Act of 1989, 12 C.F.R. § 34.42 (1994).

7. "What we will do is what we've always done—separate facts known or knowable at the date of death from those remoter in time or unforeseeable, and then ask what a hypothetical buyer in possession of these facts would offer for them in an arm's-length deal with a similarly knowledgeable hypothetical seller. And, we reiterate, we do not hypothesize a particular buyer or a particular seller with any particular skills or use for those assets." Jackson v. Comm'r, T.C. Memo. 2021–48, at 73 (2021), citing Est. of Giustina v. Comm'r, 586 F. App'x 417, 418–19 (9th Cir. 2014), *rev'g and remanding* T.C. Memo. 2011-141.

8. Hon. David Laro & Shannon P. Pratt, Business Valuation and Taxes: Procedure, Law, and Perspective 9 (2d ed. 2011).

9. Central Trust Co. v. United States, 305 F.2d 393 (Ct. Cl. 1962).

10. Foltz v. U.S. News & World Report, Inc., 106 F.R.D. 338 (D.C. Cir. 1984).

11. Est. of Furman v. Comm'r, T.C. Memo. 1998-157 (1998).

12. Bank One Corp. v. Comm'r, 120 T.C. 174, 2003 U.S. Tax Ct. LEXIS 13, 120 T.C. No. 11 (2003), *rev'd and remanded*, 2006 U.S. App. LEXIS 20430 (7th Cir. 2006).

Fair Market Value Assumes Adequate Knowledge

Central Trust makes the point that:

> [F]air market value presupposes not only hypothetical willing buyers and sellers, but buyers and sellers who are informed and have adequate knowledge of the material facts affecting value.[13]

In a 1999 case, for an example of this principle, Judge Laro rejected two sales proffered as evidence of fair market value, noting:

> Neither seller was reasonably informed regarding the value of their stock. . . . Both took the offer . . . because it sounded like a good amount of money. Their testimony revealed that they were not knowledgeable sellers who aimed to realize the fair market value of their stock.[14]

Must Consider Both Buyer and Seller—and Both Must Be Hypothetical

Quite a few Tax Court decisions have either modified or rejected an expert's opinion of value because the expert focused solely, or unduly, on the buyer, with no or inadequate consideration given to whether the value would be acceptable to a hypothetical willing seller. For example:

> (Petitioner's expert) seems to have focused too much on the willing buyer portion of the fair market value definition. He failed to consider whether a seller, under no compulsion to sell, would discount the pro rata value of his interest by 40 or 50 percent in order to consummate the sale. [FN: we note that petitioner . . . , a minority-interest holder under no compulsion to sell, testified that he would not sell his interest at the discount advocated by (petitioner's expert).][15]

Similarly, in another decision, the court stated:

> (Taxpayer's expert) focuses exclusively on the hypothetical willing buyer. (He) failed to consider whether a hypothetical seller would sell his or her interest in the partnership for $399,000. Ignoring the views of the willing seller is contrary to this well-established rule.[16]

Of course, a transaction cannot take place at more than the highest price that some willing buyer will pay. Fair market value assumes market conditions as they exist at the date of valuation. Therefore, if the seller is really willing, the implication would seem to be that he or she must accept what the market will bear at the valuation date. The existence of a market implies both buyers and sellers,[17] but it can be difficult to determine the market for a closely held company. For example, some buyers might be interested in continuing the business as their own, while others might be interested in the business as an investment. There also might be other buyers who see the business as offering synergies with other acquisitions or assets.[18] Addressing this issue, some tax regulations

---

13. 305 F.2d 393.
14. Est. of Kaufman v. Comm'r, T.C. Memo. 1999-119 (1999).
15. Moore v. Comm'r, T.C. Memo. 1991-546 (1991).
16. Est. of Lehmann v. Comm'r, T.C. Memo. 1997-392 (1997).
17. *See, e.g.*, Walter v. Duffy, 287 F.41 (3d Cir. 1923).
18. In *Identifying Pool of Willing Buyers May Introduce Synergy to Fair Market Value*, 7(4) Shannon Pratt's Business Valuation Update 1–3 (Apr. 2000), Roger J. Grabowski discusses the implications of the decision in *BTR Dunlop Holdings, Inc. v. Commissioner*, T.C. Memo 1999-377 (Nov. 15, 1999).

require that the value of the property at issue be measured in the market where it would most likely be sold.[19] To comply with this requirement, the attorney should instruct the business appraiser to analyze the marketplace to identify the most likely pool(s) of buyers. In any event, the "[s]election of the proper market for valuation purposes is a question of fact."[20]

In any case, the attorney would be well advised to be sure, in reviewing an appraisal report, that the perspective of the willing seller is not ignored.

Finally, both the seller and the buyer must be hypothetical. In one case, the Tax Court's decision was reversed because, according to the Court of Appeals, it based its ruling on speculation and imaginary scenarios that identified particular buyers, rather than hypothetical buyers.[21]

QUALIFICATIONS OF APPRAISERS

While the quality of evidence is of primary importance, the Tax Court also is very interested in appraisers' qualifications when deciding on the relative weight to accord the respective experts' testimony. For example, in *Berg*, the court's opinion included lengthy discussions of the experts' qualifications.

> (Taxpayer's first expert) is an experienced certified public accountant who has served on the faculty of several universities. He has also served as an expert witness in several cases that involved the determination of the effect of minority interest discount and lack of marketability discount. However, (he) has no formal education as an appraiser.
>
> (Taxpayer's second expert) is an experienced certified public accountant who has served as a professor at a university. (He) has no formal training as an appraiser, but has provided advisory services related to valuation of equity interest, mergers, acquisitions, leveraged buyouts, employee stock ownership plans, and litigation.
>
> (Internal Revenue Service's (IRS's) first expert), a professional appraiser, has completed courses sponsored by the American Society of Appraisers in research and analysis of business valuations, advanced valuation, and closely held business valuation. He is an associate member of the American Society of Appraisers, Business Valuation Section.
>
> (IRS's second expert), a professional appraiser, has completed an advanced business valuation seminar, a closely held corporations valuation seminar, four business valuation courses, and a business valuation strategy seminar. He is an associate member of the American Society of Appraisers, Business Valuation Section, and is a member of the Institute of Business Appraisers.
>
> (IRS's third expert), a professional appraiser, has completed courses in eminent domain valuation, going-concern valuation, and two courses in valuation of businesses and professional practices. He is a member of the American Institute of Real Estate Appraisers, an associate member in the American Society of Appraisers, Business Enterprise Section, and a member in the Institute of Business Appraisers.[22]

The Tax Court not only sustained the IRS's position, but also invoked the underpayment penalty:

---

19. *See, e.g.*, I.R.S. Treas. Reg., Estate Tax Reg. § 20.2031-1; I.R.S. Treas. Reg., Gift Tax Reg. § 25.2512-1.
20. Leibowitz v. Comm'r, T.C. Memo. 1997-243 (1997).
21. Est. of Simplot v. Comm'r, 249 F.3d 1191 (9th Cir. 2001).
22. Est. of Berg v. Comm'r, T.C. Memo. 1991-279 (1991).

> In addition, the expert reports submitted by petitioner were lacking in substance and analysis. The authors of the reports were not professional appraisers, had no formal education in the valuation of business enterprises, and were not members of any professional associations involved in the education and certification of appraisers.
>
> Petitioner has failed to carry its burden of showing that respondent abused his discretion in determining that petitioner failed to show a reasonable basis existed for the valuation on petitioner's 1986 estate tax return or that the claim was made in good faith. We therefore sustain respondent's determination with respect to the addition to tax pursuant to § 6660.[23]

In other cases, however, even though the reported amounts could trigger the § 6660 undervaluation penalty, the Tax Court has refused to impose the penalty on the grounds that the taxpayer retained a qualified appraiser and submitted the amount shown on the return in good faith.

With thousands of well-qualified business appraisers available and with recognized business valuation standards in place, as discussed in Chapter 37 on business valuation professional credentials and professional standards, it seems amazing that attorneys present so many unqualified "experts" with inadequate evidence and methodology before the U.S. Tax Court (or any court, for that matter). All too typical is this U.S. Court of Appeals opinion:

> The Tax Court rejected (taxpayer's expert's) entire opinion, emphasizing his lack of qualifications and the deficiencies in his methodology. We do not find the Tax Court clearly erred in rejecting (taxpayer's expert's) opinion.[24]

In *Kohler*,[25] the Tax Court gave no weight to the opinions of the IRS's expert who, although a chartered financial analyst (CFA) with a doctorate degree, was not credentialed in business valuation and did not follow The Appraisal Foundation's *Uniform Standards of Professional Appraisal Practice* (USPAP) standards. The court also looked unfavorably at the expert's innovative, but unsupported, financial model.

In *Thompson*,[26] the Tax Court criticized the experts for both parties, finding that they were inexperienced and that their valuations generally lacked credibility. Conversely, in *Caracci*,[27] the court rejected the taxpayer's attempt to challenge the IRS's expert's qualifications as "nonsensical and border[ing] on the frivolous" where the expert was a certified public accountant and a principal in a business valuation firm who had conducted numerous business valuations.[28]

In *Estate of Josephine Thompson*,[29] the Tax Court rejected both parties' valuations and, while declining to impose an underpayment penalty, criticized the estate's decision to hire an accountant and lawyer from Alaska (the estate was in New York) with relatively little valuation experience.

---

23. *Id. See also* Chapter 38, "Valuation and Appraiser Penalties."
24. Est. of Ford v. Comm'r, 53 F.3d 924 (8th Cir. 1995).
25. Kohler v. Comm'r, T.C. Memo. 2006-152, 2006 Tax Ct. Memo. LEXIS 156 (2006).
26. Est. of Thompson v. Comm'r, T.C. Memo. 2004-174 (2004).
27. Caracci v. Comm'r, 118 T.C. 379, 118 T.C. No. 25, 2002 U.S. Tax Ct. LEXIS 25 (2002).
28. *Id.* at 399.
29. Est. of Josephine Thompson v. Comm'r, T.C. Memo. 2004-174 (2004), *aff'd*, 499 F.3d 129 (2d Cir. 2007).

BURDEN OF PROOF

For examinations commencing before July 22, 1998, if the IRS issued a Notice of Deficiency, the burden of proof was on the taxpayer to prove that the value claimed by the IRS was wrong.[30] Since 1998, the burden of proof has shifted from the taxpayer to the IRS "[i]f, in any court proceeding, the taxpayer introduces credible evidence with respect to any factual issue relevant to ascertaining the liability of the taxpayer."[31]

In *Kohler*,[32] the estate/taxpayer successfully shifted the burden of proof to the IRS. In that case, at issue was a determination of the fair market value of stock of the company owned by the estate on the alternate valuation date. The estate elected the alternate valuation date and filed its return with a $47.01 million appraisal. The IRS determined the fair market value of the Kohler holdings on the alternate valuation date was $144.5 million. The parties stipulated that the value of the Kohler stock at issue in related gift tax cases would be calculated by reference to the value of the Kohler stock determined in the estate tax case. The parties also agreed that the per-share value for the different classes of Kohler stock in each case would be determined by reference to an agreed-on formula that would take into account the value of the Kohler stock determined in the estate tax case.

The Tax Court ruled that all the requirements for shifting the burden of proof were met. Although the IRS argued that the estate did not cooperate fully because it filed a motion to quash certain discovery requests, the court determined that the estate had legitimate concerns about providing confidential and proprietary business information that was possibly irrelevant absent a court order. Once the Tax Court denied the estate's motion to quash the summons, the estate provided the requested documents. Accordingly, the court found that the numerous exhibits that were part of the record belied the IRS argument. Accordingly, the burden shifted to the IRS.

In *Thompson*,[33] one issue the Second Circuit confronted was whether, once the taxpayer submitted a credible appraisal, the burden shifted to the IRS to prove valuation after the Tax Court rejected the IRS's values, and whether, as a result, the Tax Court should have adopted the taxpayer's values.

The taxpayer estate had included approximately 20% of the common shares of a closely held corporation. The estate calculated the value of the decedent's share of the company at $1.75 million, using the capitalization of income method. The IRS valued the estate's interest in the company at $32 million, using the guideline public company method and the discounted cash flow method.

The Second Circuit determined that the allocation of the burden of proof does not require the Tax Court to adopt the taxpayer's valuation, however erroneous, whenever the court rejects the IRS's proposed value; the burden of disproving the taxpayer's valuation can be satisfied by evidence in the record that impeaches, undermines, or indicates error in the taxpayer's valuation. In this case, the IRS not only presented evidence in support of its valuation, but also successfully rebutted the estate's valuation by identifying its

30. Tax Ct. Rule 142.
31. I.R.C. § 7491(a).
32. Kohler v. Comm'r, T.C. Memo. 2006-152, 2006 Tax Ct. Memo. LEXIS 156 (2006).
33. Est. of Josephine Thompson v. Comm'r, T.C. Memo. 2004-174 (2004), *aff'd*, 499 F.3d 129 (2d Cir. 2007).

errors and inconsistencies. The court reasoned that notwithstanding the allocation of the burden of proof in I.R.C. § 7491, the "Tax Court is not bound by the formulas and opinions proffered by expert witnesses. It may reach a determination of value based upon its own analysis of all the evidence in the record."[34]

ADEQUATE DISCLOSURE OF GIFTS

A gift and its value must be adequately disclosed on a gift tax return to start the three-year statute of limitations on the assessment of gift tax.[35] On December 3, 1999, the IRS published final regulations pertaining to the adequate disclosure of gifts.[36] The regulations contain a list of what information may be included with the gift tax return to ensure the gift will be deemed adequately disclosed. In response to extensive comments and concerns about the regulations as previously proposed, the IRS added a section to the regulations providing that a "qualified appraisal" may be submitted "in lieu of the information required" under one of the items in the list.[37]

ACCESS TO A BUSINESS'S SITES, MANAGEMENT, AND RECORDS

Clearly, the Tax Court expects experts to have access to site visits, management interviews, and company records to the extent necessary for a thorough appraisal. For example, a gift tax decision stated:

> It is also noted that petitioner's counsel refused to allow respondent's expert an opportunity to visit PCBCED's warehouse and bottling plant. To the extent that this reflects counsel's attitude and approach towards Tax Court litigation, the Court suggests that this is not the way we conduct proceedings.[38]

In *Kohler*,[39] the court discredited an opinion based on a site visit that lasted less than three hours because it did not provide the expert with adequate knowledge of the subject company, and the court lauded the detailed knowledge of the firm demonstrated by the opposing party's expert. In *Polack*,[40] the court credited the expert's appraisal because it was based on a thorough site visit, with interviews of individuals at the company who were key to an understanding of the company's value.

ARM'S-LENGTH TRANSACTIONS

The Tax Court will accord some weight to arm's-length sales of businesses or business interests, defined by *Black's Law Dictionary* as "a transaction negotiated by unrelated parties, each acting in his or her self-interest; the basis for fair market value determination."[41]

---

34. *Id.* at 10.
35. I.R.C. § 6501(c)(9).
36. 64 Fed. Reg. 67,767 (Dec. 3, 1999).
37. For a full discussion of the final regulations, see *IRS Adequate Disclosure Final Regulations Respond to Extensive Comments*, 1 Judges & Lawyers Business Valuation Update 4–5 (Jan. 2000).
38. Est. of Bruce v. Comm'r, T.C. Memo. 1993-244 (1993).
39. Kohler v. Comm'r, T.C. Memo. 2006-152, 2006 Tax Ct. Memo. LEXIS 156 (2006).
40. Polack v. Comm'r, T.C. Memo. 2002-145, *aff'd*, 366 F.3d 608 (8th Cir. 2004).
41. Black's Law Dictionary 71 (6th ed. 1990).

For example, in *Bennett*, the court said, "Usually, in determining the value of untraded stock, one would look at actual arm's-length sales of such stock in the normal course of business within a reasonable time before or after the valuation date."[42] (Although the decision clearly articulated the principle, there were no such transactions in the *Bennett* case.)

In *Morrissey*,[43] the Ninth Circuit reversed the Tax Court's rejection of the taxpayer's evidence of actual sales near the valuation date. The appellate court concluded that because those actual sales had been arm's length transactions, they presented the best evidence of fair market value.[44]

APPROACHES TO VALUE

The Tax Court expects all three valuation approaches to value—market, income, and asset-based—to be considered. The relative weight the court will accord to the various valuation approaches and methods generally depends on three factors:

- The type of company
- The quality of available data
- Whether the company might be liquidated or continue as a going concern

The Tax Court tends to rely more on an asset approach for holding companies and on a market or income approach for going concern operating companies. For hybrid companies, the court may weight the approaches to correspond to the degree to which the company has assets and earnings.[45]

A Tax Court opinion was even critical of an expert for not considering an asset approach for a company that most appraisers would have been very unlikely to have accorded the asset approach any weight.[46]

In *Hess*,[47] the court split the difference between the taxpayer's discounted cash flow (DCF) and the guideline public company methods and the IRS's DCF, net asset value, guideline transaction, and guideline public company methods.

In *Leichter*,[48] the issue of liquidation versus going concern was key. Here, the expert opined that the company was worth less on a going-concern basis than in liquidation, but the court criticized the expert for not explaining why a hypothetical seller would choose not to liquidate under such circumstances.

---

42. Est. of Bennett v. Comm'r, T.C. Memo. 1993-34 (1993).

43. Morrissey v. Comm'r, 243 F.3d 1145 (9th Cir. 2001).

44. *See also* Huber, Michael W. (2006) T.C. Memo. 2006-96 (actual "arms-length sales" of unlisted closely held stock (90 sales over a six-year period, including from sellers who were not former employees, directors, or their families) determines the fair market value of the stock for gift tax purposes). However, *cf.* Kosman, Jane O., TC Memo 1996-112 (Tax Court held that "a few sales" of closely held stock sold at per-share premium over a four-year period involving former employees, directors, or their families were not arm's-length sales for purposes of determining fair market value, because those premium prices were attributable to the sellers' association with the corporation).

45. Shannon P. Pratt & ASA Educ. Found., Shannon Pratt's Valuing a Business: The Analysis and Appraisal of Closely Held Companies 770–73 (6th ed. 2022).

46. Est. of Kaufman v. Comm'r, T.C. Memo. 1999-119 (1999).

47. Hess v. Comm'r, T.C. Memo. 2003-251 (2003).

48. Est. of Leichter v. Comm'r, T.C. Memo. 2003-66 (2003).

Market Approach

The IRS and the Tax Court look favorably on the market approach, which is heavily emphasized in Revenue Ruling 59–60. However, it is not uncommon for the court to reject an expert's utilization of the market approach if the court is not satisfied that the companies or transactions selected are sufficiently comparable to the subject company.

For example, in *Brookshire*, two experts for the taxpayer and the IRS's expert all used the guideline public company method, among others. However, the court rejected the IRS's version of the guideline company method:

> Respondent's expert overstates the value of the Brookshire common stock because of his use of three companies as comparable companies that have significant sales in markets other than retail grocery and that are not comparable to Brookshire. The use of these companies distorts each of the valuation methods used by respondent's expert.[49]

Note that this is *not* a rejection of the guideline company method; the court accepted the guideline companies used by the taxpayer's experts.

In should be borne in mind that Revenue Ruling 59–60 uses the language "the same or similar." Companies may be accepted as similar for reasons other than product or service line—for example, the markets into which they sell or their degree of brand dominance.

To illustrate, in both *Gallo*[50] (Gallo Wine) and *Hall*[51] (Hallmark Greeting Cards), the court relied entirely on the guideline publicly traded company method, even though there were no good public wine companies to use for Gallo Wine and only one public greeting card company to use for Hallmark. In *Gallo*, the experts used breweries, distilleries, soft-drink bottlers, and high brand recognition and market share food producers. In *Hall*, the analyst used high brand recognition and market share consumer nondurable products companies, such as Parker Pen. In both cases, the court arrived at a value as if the stock were publicly traded, then applied a 36% discount for lack of marketability based on restricted stock and pre-IPO transaction study data.

However, in *Heck*,[52] the court rejected the use of a single comparable company where it was insufficiently similar to the subject company. The court said, "As similarity to the company to be valued decreases, the number of required comparables increases." In *Cecil*,[53] the court rejected one expert's use of a single guideline public company.

In *Hess*,[54] the court upheld the comparison of the subject company to guideline companies solely based on price-to-earnings ratios where the guideline companies were similar to the subject company and the guideline companies were properly adjusted.

Watts[55] was a classic clash of opposing opinions on appropriate approaches to value—in that case, the taxpayer's reliance on the market approach and the IRS's reliance on the asset approach. The decedent's estate filed a valuation of $2,550,000 for a 15%

49. Est. of Brookshire v. Comm'r, T.C. Memo. 1998-365 (1998).
50. Est. of Gallo v. Comm'r, T.C. Memo. 1985-363 (1985).
51. Est. of Hall v. Comm'r, 92 T.C. 312 (1989).
52. Est. of Heck v. Comm'r, T.C. Memo. 2002-34 (2002).
53. Est. of William A.V. Cecil, Sr. v. Comm'r, T.C. Memo 2023-24 (Feb. 28, 2023).
54. Hess v. Comm'r, T.C. Memo. 2003-251 (2003).
55. Est. of Watts v. Comm'r, T.C. Memo. 1985-595 (1985), *aff'd*, 823 F.3d 483 (11th Cir. 1987).

interest in a timber-growing and timber-processing partnership. The notice of deficiency valued the interest at $20,006,000, based primarily on the liquidation value of the assets.

At trial, the taxpayers' experts based their valuations on publicly traded companies that processed timber and held timberlands. Based on these companies, they presented valuation parameters such as price-to-earnings multiples, multiples of partnership interest value to book value and to adjusted net asset value, and capitalization of partnership withdrawals. Because the Tax Court did not accept the respondent's liquidation value approach, it relied on values provided by the business valuation experts, including a 35% discount for lack of marketability, and ultimately confirmed the estate's value as originally filed at $2,550,000.[56]

Income Approach

Both the IRS and the U.S. Tax Court have traditionally leaned more toward the market approach than the income approach.[57] This is partly because of language in Revenue Ruling 59–60, written before the development of modern capital market theory, which evolved particularly in the 1960s and gave rise to the capital asset pricing model (CAPM) for developing discount rates (and extensive published data on rates of return for stocks). It also is partly because of concern about possible manipulation of both cash flow forecasts and discount rates in the discounted cash flow (DCF) method. Nonetheless, as the DCF method has achieved greater utilization in the professional financial community, it also has achieved greater acceptance in the Tax Court.

In a 1985 case, the IRS challenged income tax returns reflecting deductions for a company's contributions to an employee stock ownership trust at $61.35 per share, based on the fair market value arrived at by an independent appraisal firm. The IRS asserted that the value was between $5.36 and $8.00 per share. The independent appraisal gave heavy emphasis to earning power and dividend-paying capacity, while the IRS stressed net asset value (book value was $7.05 per share).

The court found itself in agreement with the emphasis placed on earning power and dividend-paying capacity. The court was somewhat concerned ". . . that the appraisals take into account a 20-year projection of earnings" but thought it was "not unreasonable in light of past earnings increases. . . ."[58] The court concluded that "the only reasonable appraisal presented to it was the one at $61.35 per share."[59]

In a 1986 decision, the Tax Court accepted the DCF method for valuing small, closely held operating businesses (having rejected the market approach due to lack of comparability between the selected guideline public companies and the subject operating businesses) and accepted use of the modified CAPM for estimating the discount rate.[60]

Yet the Tax Court has *rejected* the DCF method in cases where it believed that the model used by the expert was far too sensitive to minor changes in assumptions, such as the discount rate and/or the growth rate.[61] The court also rejected the income approach

---

56. *Id.*

57. Pratt & ASA Educ. Found., *supra* note 45, at 291.

58. Las Vegas Dodge v. United States, No. CV LV 79-7, RDF, 1985 WL 6366, at 18 (D. Nev. Mar. 20, 1985).

59. *Id.* at 25.

60. The Northern Trust Co., Arthur L. Simon, Jeffery J. Simon, Transferees & Trustees, et al. v. Comm'r, 87 T.C. 349 (U.S.T.C. 1986).

61. Morton v. Comm'r, T.C. Memo. 1997-166 (1997).

where the CAPM was used to value a small closely held company, as pure CAPM does not address unsystematic risk.[62]

The Tax Court also has been known to reach its conclusion by giving partial weight to a DCF method and partial weight to a market approach method. For example, one case gave 70% weight to the market method and 30% weight to the DCF method.[63]

In *Jung*, the Tax Court relied on the DCF approach because the publicly traded guideline companies available were not very good comparables to the subject. The court stated:

> In the instant case, we believe the DCF approach to valuing Jung Corp. is more reliable than the market comparable approach. The market comparable approach does not work well in the instant case because the comparable corporations do not have the same product mix (health and elastic textile) as Jung Corp. None of the experts relied exclusively on the market comparable approach.[64]

The Tax Court accepted the DCF method for valuing an interest in a real estate partnership that owned a property with a hotel. The court said:

> The value of any interest in real property that has an income stream can be estimated by the DCF method. See *Estate of Bennett v. Commissioner.*[65] The evidence before the Court shows that the property had a determinable income stream.[66]

The court then considered the noncontrolling (i.e., minority), nonmarketable status of the partnership interest.

In another case, the Tax Court accepted the DCF method over the market approach and applied a 31% discount for lack of control.[67]

Asset-Based Approach

Revenue Ruling 59-60 suggests that the asset-based approach should be accorded more weight for holding companies, while earnings-related methods should be accorded more weight for operating companies. For example, in *Jameson*,[68] which involved the valuation of a controlling interest in a holding company the primary asset of which was timber, the Tax Court determined the asset approach was appropriate because earnings were relatively low as compared to the fair market value of the assets. The IRS has tended to push this notion to the extreme in the case of family limited partnerships, where they often have used the asset approach exclusively.[69]

Until 1998, the IRS had been intransigent in its refusal to consider the tax on trapped-in capital gains liabilities. This would seem to be an internal contradiction.

---

62. Est. of Hendrickson v. Comm'r, T.C. Memo. 1999-278, 1999 Tax Ct. Memo. LEXIS 318 (1999).

63. Est. of Freeman v. Comm'r, T.C. Memo. 1996-372, 1996 WL 453872 (1996).

64. Est. of Jung v. Comm'r, 101 T.C. 412 (1993).

65. Est. of Bennett v. Comm'r, T.C. Memo. 1993-34 (1993); Est. of Hatchett v. Comm'r, T.C. Memo. 1989-637 (1989).

66. Est. of Lehmann v. Comm'r, T.C. Memo. 1997-392 (1997).

67. Rakow v. Comm'r, T.C. Memo. 1999-17.

68. Est. of Jameson v. Comm'r, T.C. Memo. 1999-43 (1999), *vacated and remanded*, 267 F.3d 366 (5th Cir. 2001).

69. For a discussion of valuation and tax issues related to family limited partnerships, *see* PRATT & ASA EDUC. FOUND., *supra* note 45, at 798–808.

Insistence on the asset approach to value an interest implies that value arises from potential proceeds from sale, which necessarily would be net of capital gains taxes. If one is not willing to recognize tax consequences in case of a sale, then it seems that one should value by other approaches, that is, the income and market approaches. As we will see in a subsequent section, the Tax Court has generally insisted on recognizing trapped-in capital gains tax liability as a valuation factor and the IRS has acquiesced.

DISCOUNTS

Discounts for Lack of Marketability (Noncontrolling Blocks)

The principle that, due to the lack of a ready market, noncontrolling (i.e., minority) blocks of closely held stock are worth less than otherwise similar publicly held stock is thoroughly entrenched in Tax Court rulings. The argument is not whether a discount is applicable, but rather, how much?

As discussed in more detail in Chapter 18, "Discounts and Premiums," the relevant empirical data has long been the Restricted Stock Studies (sales of blocks of nonregistered or restricted stock of public companies) and the Pre-IPO Studies (transactions in stock of closely held companies that subsequently had successful initial public offerings (IPOs)). With time, these studies have been criticized for various deficiencies, and other ways of arriving at discounts for lack of marketability (sometimes referred to as DLOM) have been employed, including the use of put options, put-call collars, regression analysis of the restricted stock studies, private placement studies, other analytical techniques (e.g., the Johnson/Park Empirical Method, the Nonmarketable Investment Company Evaluation Method (NICE), and the Quantitative Marketability Discount Model (QMDM)), and even analyses of stock illiquidity versus lack of marketability. All these alternatives have also been subject to criticism.

The Restricted Stock Studies were first published in the early 1970s and include data going back to the late 1960s. They were recognized as valid evidence supporting discounts for lack of marketability in Revenue Ruling 77–287. The Pre-IPO Studies first appeared in the early 1980s, with data back to 1975. They were first introduced in *Gallo*[70] and also used in *Hall*.[71]

In the late 1990s, the Tax Court explicitly directed attention to both these lines of studies in reaching discount for lack of marketability conclusions.[72] However, the court has not always accepted this data. Some criticisms of these studies are that they are dated, have limited sample sizes, are spread out over long periods of time, and may have substantial standard errors in their estimates. In *Jelke*,[73] for example, the court rejected the use of restricted stock studies, determining they were insufficiently similar to the

70. Est. of Gallo v. Comm'r, T.C. Memo. 1985-363 (1985).

71. Est. of Hall v. Comm'r, 92 T.C. 312 (1989).

72. *See, e.g.*, Mandelbaum v. Comm'r, T.C. Memo. 1995-255 (1995); Est. of Davis v. Comm'r, 110 T.C. 530 (1998); Est. of Williams v. Comm'r, T.C. Memo. 1998-59 (1998); Est. of Brookshire v. Comm'r, T.C. Memo. 1998-365 (1998); Okerlund v. United States, 53 Fed. Cl. 341 (Fed. Ct. Cl. 2002), *aff'd*, 365 F.3d 1044 (Fed. Cir. 2004).

73. Est. of Jelke v. Comm'r, T.C. Memo. 2005-131 (2005); affirmed as to the discount issue by 507 F.3d 1317 (11th Cir. 2007).

subject company as to size. In *McCord*,[74] the Tax Court preferred the data from a study of private placements (the "Bajaj" study) instead of data from pre-IPO studies (on appeal, the Fifth Circuit reversed on other grounds and did not address the discount for lack of marketability issue). In *Kelly*,[75] where interests in an investment limited partnership were being valued, the court rejected the use of restricted stock studies, finding that such studies examine mostly operating companies and that "there are fundamental differences between an investment company . . . and operating companies."[76] Instead, it used the Bajaj private placement study and adjusted the discount derived from this analysis by 3% to account for characteristics specific to the partnership.

The court in *Lappo*[77] had similarly preferred the private placement approach to what it characterized as the more "narrow" restricted stock approach in valuing an interest in a family limited partnership whose assets were marketable securities and real estate. The court in that case had also adjusted the discount by 3% to account for partnership-specific characteristics, such as the fact that it was closely held, relatively small, and unknown; there was no market for the interests; and the partnership had a right of first refusal to purchase the interests. In *Peracchio*,[78] rather than criticizing the restricted stock studies themselves, the court criticized the taxpayer's expert for failing to analyze and apply the data from these studies to the particular partnership interests being valued. In *Deputy*,[79] the IRS relied on restricted stock studies, while the taxpayer's expert applied a matrix his company had created to replicate an investor's decision process. The Tax Court preferred the taxpayer's matrix because it focused on the subject company's unique attributes. In *Janda*,[80] the court rejected the IRS's use of restricted stock studies as being too general, because it did not present evidence on the subject company's industry or companies with similar characteristics. However, the court also had "grave doubts" about the taxpayer's use of the QMDM, which the court found could produce dramatically different results based on slight variations in assumption inputs. Although *Litman*[81] rejected a generalized use of restricted stock studies, the Claims Court expressed a preference for using individual transactions from the restricted stock studies rather than averages.

In *Temple*,[82] the court rejected the taxpayer's exclusive reliance on restricted stock studies in preference for the IRS's "fuller" analysis that included academic research, the cost of going public, secondary market transactions, asset liquidity, partnership interest transferability, and historic distributions. Similarly, the court in *Robertson*[83] rejected a discount based on restricted stock studies that used subjective factors[84] in favor of a

---

74. McCord v. Comm'r, 120 T.C. 358 (2003), *rev'd*, 461 F.3d 614 (5th Cir. 2006).
75. Est. of Kelly v. Comm'r, T.C. Memo. 2005-235 (2005).
76. *Id.* at *7.
77. Lappo v. Comm'r, T.C. Memo. 2003-258 (2003).
78. Peracchio v. Comm'r, T.C. Memo. 2003-280 (2003).
79. Est. of Deputy v. Comm'r, T.C. Memo. 2003-176 (2003).
80. Janda v. Comm'r, T.C. Memo. 2001-24 (2001).
81. Litman v. United States, 78 Fed. Cl. 90 (Cl. Ct. 2007).
82. Temple v. United States, 2006 U.S. Dist. LEXIS 16171 (E.D. Tex. 2006).
83. Robertson v. United States, 2006 U.S. Dist. LEXIS 1167 (N.D. Tex. 2006).
84. *See also* James F. Kress, v. United States, 382 F. Supp. 3d 820 (E.D. Wis. 2019). In *Kress*, a family-only permitted transfer restriction was found to serve a bona fide purpose of maintaining family ownership and control and was not intended as a tax avoidance device. Nevertheless, the restriction was not given effect when determining the valuation of the company stock because the court found no evidence that unrelated

discount that also relied on restricted stock studies but supplemented the data from the studies with academic research. In *Green*,[85] the court accepted discount values from restricted stock studies but indicated that while pre-IPO studies were "entitled to some consideration," they did not justify a discount greater than 35%.[86]

A brief description of some of the other sources of empirical data supporting discount for lack of marketability follows.[87]

PUT OPTIONS

The put-option method estimates a discount for lack of marketability by calculating the cost of locking in the current price to protect the downside risk of price movements while the security is illiquid. The price of the put provides market evidence of the price investors will pay to ensure marketability. The formula for this model, as well as its key inputs (such as the risk-free rate and volatility) can be audited. The term of this model is more subjective. Potential criticisms of using this model are that it is a short-term, theoretical pricing model designed for liquid securities that is being applied to an illiquid security and that put options protect only against downside price movements, although the Black-Scholes model can be used to estimate the price of a theoretical put for stock that is not publicly traded. In *Gimbel*,[88] the court rejected the use of this method where the block was large and restricted, concluding that such options would have been unavailable for the estate's sizable block of restricted stock, which lacked both liquidity and marketability.

PUT-CALL COLLARS

A put-call collar locks in a security's price by selling away the upside while protecting against the downward price movements. This is done by buying a put option and selling a call option. Potential criticisms of this type of analysis to determining discounts for lack of marketability are that the lack of a derivatives market in the subject security results in significantly understating the cost to execute this strategy for a closely held security and that cost information is not available and can result in significant subjective judgment. Where this analysis is feasible for small blocks of publicly traded stock, it can be used to establish a floor for the discount. In *Litman*,[89] involving the valuation of a large block of restricted shares of stock, the court rejected the IRS's use of an option collar approach,

---

parties dealing at arm's length would agree to such an arrangement. The court ruled the restriction did not satisfy all of the requirements of I.R.C. § 2703(b), and that it should therefore be given no consideration in assessing the discount for lack of marketability.

85. Est. of Green v. Comm'r, T.C. Memo. 2003-384 (2003).

86. In *Est. of Davis v. Comm'r*, 110 T.C. 530 (1998), the Tax Court discussed the limitations of restricted stock studies and gave more weight to IPO studies. However, in *Zerbey v. Comm'r* (*In re* Estate of Richmond), T.C. Memo 2014-26, the court clarified that "there is no absolute rule that . . . IPO studies are superior to restricted stock studies, since in other circumstances we have preferred the latter. *See* Est. of Giustina v. Comm'r, T.C. Memo. 2011-141."

87. For a discussion of these sources of empirical data supporting a discount for lack of marketability, *see* PRATT & ASA EDUC. FOUND., *supra* note 45, at 419–63, ch. 19.

88. Est. of Gimbel v. Comm'r, 2006 Tax Ct. Memo. LEXIS 274 (2006).

89. Litman v. United States, 78 Fed. Cl. 90 (Cl. Ct. 2007).

finding that the size of the subject company's restricted stock, as compared to the public float, would render such a transaction impossible as a practical, real-world matter. Similarly, in *Gimbel*,[90] the court rejected the use of this method where the block was large and restricted, saying that "[c]ashless collars and prepaid variable forward contracts generally are used with blocks of stock that are highly liquid and marketable"; the court concluded that there would not have been a market for such hedging contracts in this instance.

REGRESSION ANALYSIS

Analysts have used regression analyses of restricted stock studies to provide a quantitative indication of the discount for lack of marketability for interests in a closely held company (using data on restricted stocks as a proxy for a discount on an interest in a closely held company). This is, therefore, a mathematical method that can be audited and, similar to the other approaches listed here, the inputs also can be audited.[91]

Combined Noncontrol (Minority) and Lack of Marketability Discounts

As discussed in Chapter 18, discounts for lack of control for noncontrolling interests and discounts for lack of marketability are two different concepts, although there may be some overlap. The Tax Court has clearly articulated this distinction:

> In their arguments, neither petitioner nor respondent clearly focuses on the fact that two conceptually distinct discounts are involved here, one for lack of marketability and the other for lack of control. The minority shareholder discount is designed to reflect the decreased value of shares that do not convey control of a closely held corporation. The lack of marketability discount, on the other hand, is designed to reflect the fact that there is no ready market for shares in a closely held corporation.[92]

In the majority of Tax Court cases in the 1980s and 1990s, lack of control (i.e., minority) and marketability factors were treated separately. Analytical methods that measure combined discounts have been introduced in some cases.[93] And some decisions have combined the two factors in the final decision.[94]

Discounts for 50% Interests

A 50% interest is neither a controlling interest nor a noncontrolling interest. While a 50% interest has blocking power, it cannot force things to happen (except when one party is accorded certain control prerogatives by contract), with a very real potential for deadlock. In most cases, the court will allow some discount for lack of control and also

---

90. *Est. of Gimbel*, 2006 Tax Ct. Memo. LEXIS 274.

91. John J. Stockdale, *A Test of DLOM Computational Models*, Bus. Valuation Rev. 131–37 (Fall 2008).

92. Est. of Andrews v. Comm'r, 79 T.C. 938 (1982).

93. *See, e.g.*, Est. of Elsie Church v. United States, Cause No. SA-97-CA-0774-OG and Est. of Emily Klauss, T.C. Memo. 2000-191 (the taxpayer's expert used the Johnson/Park Empirical Method); Pierson M. Grieve v. Comm'r, T.C. Memo. 2020-28, 2020 (the taxpayer's expert used the NICE method as one of methods supporting a discount for lack of marketability).

94. Est. of Furman v. Comm'r, T.C. Memo. 1998-157 (1998); Est. of Magnin v. Comm'r, T.C. Memo. 2001-31 (2001); Est. of Mitchell v. Comm'r, 250 F.3d 696 (9th Cir. 2001); Janda v. Comm'r, T.C. Memo. 2001-24 (2001); Est. of Deputy v. Comm'r, T.C. Memo. 2003-176 (2003); Temple v. United States, 2006 U.S. Dist. LEXIS 16171 (E.D. Tex. 2006).

some discount for lack of marketability.[95] For example, in one case of valuation of a 50% interest, the court stated, "We conclude that, in addition to a minority discount, some amount of lack of marketability discount should be applied."[96] In that case, the court was critical of the evidence offered by experts on both sides. The final value concluded by the court represented a combined discount of approximately 27% from the value arrived at by the comparative transaction method, although the court did not describe exactly how the final value was reached.

Discounts for Lack of Liquidity/Marketability (Controlling Interests)

In many reported decisions, the Tax Court has recognized that discounts for lack of liquidity (typically referred to as discounts for lack of marketability) for controlling interests in closely held companies are appropriate. The courts have used language such as the following:

> Even controlling shares in a nonpublic corporation suffer from lack of marketability because of the absence of a ready private placement market and the fact that flotation costs would have to be incurred if the corporation were to publicly offer its stock.[97]

The Tax Court has allowed discounts for lack of marketability for controlling interests up to at least 30%.[98]

In *Cloutier*,[99] the only issue was whether a discount for lack of marketability should be applied to a 100% ownership interest in a company whose primary asset was a television station. The taxpayer's expert argued for a 25% discount based on restricted stock and pre-IPO data, which apply to noncontrolling/minority interests. The Tax Court disallowed the discount entirely. The opinion concluded, "Because the stipulated value has not been shown to be representative of CGT's freely traded value, no discount for marketability is allowable."[100]

Cloutier is in sharp contrast to other cases. For example, in *Dougherty*,[101] the court found a 25% discount for lack of marketability applicable to a 100% controlling interest in the stock of an investment company where the base value was the value of the underlying assets. Another case that permitted a 25% discount for lack of marketability for a controlling interest was *Maggos*.[102]

In a 1999 case, the Tax Court determined a 20% discount for lack of marketability for an 81.93% interest in an S corporation selling industrial coatings.[103] There are many cases in the 10% to 15% range for discounts for lack of marketability for controlling

95. *See, e.g., In re* Est. of Propstra, 680 F.2d 1248 (9th Cir. 1982) (15 percent discount for undivided 50 percent interest).

96. Est. of Fleming v. Comm'r, T.C. Memo. 1997-484 (1997).

97. Est. of Andrews v. Comm'r, 79 T.C. 938 (1982).

98. Est. of Hendrickson v. Comm'r, T.C. Memo. 1999-278, 1999 Tax Ct. Memo. LEXIS 318 (1999).

99. Est. of Cloutier v. Comm'r, T.C. Memo. 1996-049 (1996).

100. *Id.*

101. Est. of Dougherty v. Comm'r, 59 T.C. 772 (1990).

102. Est. of Maggos v. Comm'r, T.C. Memo. 2000-129 (2000).

103. Est. of Desmond v. Comm'r, T.C. Memo. 1999-76 (1999).

interests.[104] A typical example is *Bennett*, where the Tax Court determined a 15% discount for a 100% interest in a real estate management and development company.[105]

Discounts for Lack of Control

As indicated in Chapter 18, discounts are applied to noncontrolling ownership interests. These discounts sometimes are referred to as discounts for lack of control (DLOCs). This discount may be granted independently of, or in addition to, the discount for lack of marketability.

In *Jelke*,[106] the taxpayer's expert discounted the subject minority interest by 25% for lack of control, while the IRS's expert discounted it by 5%. The taxpayer's expert assumed that the company was most like a closed-end, and not widely traded, investment fund holding publicly traded securities. Applying this assumption, the expert arrived at a 20% discount base and added an additional 5% discount because the subject company had fewer assets, paid fewer dividends, and posted lower short-term returns than did the comparable funds. The IRS expert's analysis began with an average discount (8.61%) for closed-end funds and reduced this on the basis that the company outperformed the guideline public companies used by the estate. The court adopted a 10% discount for lack of control, finding that although the company was smaller than some of the guideline public companies presented, it was well diversified, which reduced investment risk, and that investors in the company would base their investments on the company's history of good performance.

In *Green*,[107] the Tax Court determined a 17% discount for lack of control for a minority interest in a bank, rejecting a poorly explained 20% discount asserted by the taxpayer, but also not accepting the IRS's 15% discount, which it also found was not well supported.

In *Thompson*,[108] after adjusting the estate's expert's capitalization rate, the court applied a 15% minority discount to a 20% interest in a publishing company. The experts for both sides in *Hess*[109] agreed that a 15% discount for lack of control was applicable, but the court criticized the taxpayer's expert for using a discount under the guideline public company method, concluding that such a discount is already included and inherent in that method. The court in *Adams*[110] applied a 20% discount for lack of control to a 25% interest in a partnership because the taxpayer's expert provided "the lone specific analysis of the issues." In *Temple*,[111] the court determined a discount for lack of control in a range of 3.3% to 10.1% for limited partnerships holding publicly held marketable securities. The court arrived at this range by using closed-end funds data. The IRS's expert used all reporting closed-end funds and calculated the discount based on the mean of the reported discounts and premiums from net asset value. The taxpayer's expert used

---

104. *See, e.g.*, Est. of Dunn v. Comm'r, T.C. Memo. 2000-12 (2000), *rev'd on other grounds*, 201 F.3d 339 (5th Cir. 2002) (15%); Temple v. United States, 2006 U.S. Dist. LEXIS 16171 (E.D. Tex. 2006) (12.5%).

105. Est. of Bennett v. Comm'r, T.C. Memo. 1993-34 (1993).

106. Est. of Jelke v. Comm'r, T.C. Memo. 2005-131 (2005), *rev'd*, 503 F.3d 1317 (11th Cir. 2007).

107. Est. of Green v. Comm'r, T.C. Memo. 2003-384 (2003).

108. Est. of Thompson v. Comm'r, T.C. Memo. 2004-174 (2004).

109. Hess v. Comm'r, T.C. Memo. 2003-251 (2003).

110. Adams v. United States, 2001 U.S. Dist. LEXIS 13092 (N.D. Tex. 2001).

111. Temple v. United States, 2006 U.S. Dist. LEXIS 16171 (E.D. Tex. 2006).

a limited universe of funds and computed the discount using the 75th percentile of the limited universe. The court preferred the IRS's expert's approach, finding it was more comprehensive.

Robertson[112] involved the valuation of limited partnership interests in determining a Generation Skipping Transfer Tax (GSTT). The taxpayer's expert arrived at a 22% minority discount based on an 8% median discount in closed-end funds, plus 11% based on "structural differences" between closed-end funds and the subject limited partnership, plus 3% for other factors. The court rejected the 3% discount for other factors, finding it was unwarranted, for this was based on six factors unique to the partnership, none of which was empirically quantifiable—and many of which had already been factored into the closed-end fund analysis. The IRS's expert arrived at a 6% discount for lack of control, based on an average discount for closed-end funds. The court not only found that the taxpayer's expert's analysis was more thorough, but also commented that use of the median was more appropriate than the average, which could be unduly influenced by outliers. Thus, a 19% discount for lack of control was allowed.

Blockage

Blockage is a term used in conjunction with publicly traded stock. It denotes a block of stock so large relative to typical daily or weekly trading volume that it would require a long time to release it into the public market slowly enough to avoid depressing the price of the stock.

Blockage discounts tend to be relatively modest, often in the 3% to 10% range. However, sometimes the Tax Court denies the discount totally, sometimes even inexplicably.[113] At the other extreme, the Tax Court allowed a 25% blockage discount on a block of thinly traded public stock of Frederick's of Hollywood.[114] More typical is *Foote*, where the Tax Court concluded a 3.3% discount for blockage.[115] Nonetheless, unique facts and circumstances can lead to a higher discount.[116] In *Adams*,[117] the court applied both a discount for lack of marketability and a blockage discount on the same block of stock.

Key Person Discount

Dependence on a key person introduces a risk of the consequences of the loss of that person's services in case of death, disability, or resignation. This risk sometimes is recognized through a separate discount for the key person factor.

Typical of the Tax Court's position on this issue is the following:

> Where a corporation is substantially dependent upon the services of one person, and where that person would no longer be able to perform services for the corporation by reason of death or incapacity, an investor would expect some form of discount below

---

112. Robertson v. United States, 2006 U.S. Dist. LEXIS 1167 (N.D. Tex. 2006).

113. *See, e.g.*, Est. of Davis v. Comm'r, 110 T.C. 530 (1998), where the court recognized in its decision that it probably would have taken five to six months to sell the stock without depressing the price yet concluded that petitioner failed to satisfy the burden of proof that a blockage discount should be applied.

114. Est. of Mellinger v. Comm'r, 112 T.C. 26 (1999).

115. Est. of Foote v. Comm'r, T.C. Memo. 1999-37 (1999).

116. *See, e.g.*, Est. of Gimbel v. Comm'r, 2006 Tax Ct. Memo. LEXIS 274 (2006) (14.2% net discount rate for restricted and nonrestricted stock).

117. Est. of Adams v. Comm'r, T.C. Memo. 2002-80 (2002).

> fair market value when purchasing stock in the corporation to compensate for the loss of that key employee.[118] Although FIC could have purchased key-person life insurance on Robert's life, a minority shareholder could not compel FIC to purchase such insurance, and FIC had no such insurance in effect.
>
> We have found as facts that Robert was a key person in the management of FIC, that FIC had no second layer of management, and that Robert's contacts, experience, and managerial expertise were critically important to the success of FIC. We therefore agree with petitioners and find that a key-person discount of 10% was appropriate in determining the value of FIC stock as of February 1980 and August 1981.[119]

In *Mitchell*,[120] the Tax Court applied a 10% key person discount but rejected a key person discount in *Renier*,[121] where factual reasons supporting such a discount were absent from the valuation report.

Nonvoting versus Voting Stock

If a company has nonvoting as well as voting stock outstanding, the nonvoting stock may be discounted compared to the value of the voting stock. For public companies that have both voting and nonvoting stock, the discount for nonvoting in most cases is quite small, often less than 5%, and that level of discount often is used for closely held companies and accepted by the IRS and the Tax Court.

In the unusual situation where the voting stock that controls the company is only a tiny percentage of the total stock outstanding, treatment by courts has been mixed. In the case of *Simplot*,[122] a tiny percentage of all the stock was voting, but it was owned by four parties, each a minority. The Tax Court placed a super-premium on the voting stock. On appeal, however, the Ninth Circuit reversed, finding that the Tax Court had based its ruling on speculation by creating a scenario in which a buyer would purchase a minority share of the voting stock, but with time would be able to play a role in the company.[123]

PREMIUMS

Premiums may be added to value for factors such as control, industry risk, or a swing vote. In *Deputy*,[124] the Tax Court accepted a negative industry risk premium. In determining the capitalization rate to apply, the industry risk premium represents the difference between the general industry risk premium for the market and the risk premium for the industry. The taxpayer's expert concluded a 17.5% capitalization rate, including a 3% industry adjustment. The IRS concluded a negative 5.2% industry risk premium, which resulted in a lower capitalization rate of around 10%. The court determined that

---

118. *See* Est. of Huntsman v. Comm'r, 66 T.C. 861, 1976 WL 3635 (1976); Est. of Mitchell v. Comm'r, 250 F.3d 696 (9th Cir. 2001); Est. of Feldmar v. Comm'r, T.C. Memo. 1988-429; Est. of Yeager v. Comm'r, T.C. Memo. 1986-448.

119. Est. of Furman v. Comm'r, T.C. Memo. 1998-157 (1998).

120. Est. of Mitchell v. Comm'r, T.C. Memo. 1997-461 (1997), *vacated*, 250 F.3d 696 (9th Cir. 2001).

121. Est. of Renier v. Comm'r, T.C. Memo. 2000-298 (2000).

122. Est. of Simplot v. Comm'r, 112 T.C. 130 (1999).

123. Est. of Simplot v. Comm'r, 249 F.3d 1191 (9th Cir. 2001).

124. Est. of Deputy v. Comm'r, T.C. Memo. 2003-176 (2003).

the negative industry risk premium was supported by the fact that the company tended to outperform the industry and the economy.

In *Simplot*,[125] the decedent owned a noncontrolling interest in a small control block of stock. The Tax Court, adopting the IRS's position, attributed a 3% premium to the swing vote block and then took a 35% discount for lack of control from the decedent's pro rata share in that block. This resulted in a multimillion-dollar control premium on the noncontrolling interest in the control block. On appeal, the Ninth Circuit reversed, finding that a buyer of the block never could recover the premium. In accepting the taxpayer's application of a zero premium, the court decided that a controlling block of stock is not to be valued at a premium for estate tax purposes unless it can be shown that a purchaser of the block would be able to use it "in such a way to assure an increased economic advantage worth paying a premium for."

In *Maggos*,[126] the decedent's controlling block of stock in a company was repurchased by the company without the benefit of a formal valuation. After applying a 25% discount for lack of marketability, the court applied a 25% control premium based on average premiums paid in the industry at the time of purchase.

In *Wright*,[127] the court refused to apply a control premium asserted by the IRS's expert that was based on a hypothetical scenario in which other investors might purchase decedent's block of stock.

In *Grieve*,[128] the Tax Court rejected the IRS's expert's application of a premium based on his conclusion that a willing seller of units would first look to acquire control of additional interests to avoid the large discounts that a willing buyer would seek for merely buying the particular units being valued. The court looked at the value of the units on the date of the gift and not the value on the basis of the subsequent events (the purchasing of the additional units) that were not reasonably likely to happen and wasn't supported by any empirical data.

TAXES ON TRAPPED-IN CAPITAL GAINS

One of the most dramatic developments in Tax Court decisions, starting in 1998, was explicit recognition of a liability for capital gains taxes on significantly appreciated property.

In cases arising before 1987, a corporation could liquidate its assets, distribute the proceeds, and dissolve within 12 months, and by so doing eliminate the payment of capital gains taxes at the corporate level. The Tax Reform Act of 1986 eliminated that option.

Before 1986, at least partially relying on the tax-free liquidation option (known as the General Utilities Doctrine, named after a case involving the exercise of that option), the Tax Court had steadfastly denied recognition of any trapped-in capital gains tax liability unless liquidation of the appreciated assets was clearly imminent.

After 1986, there were no Subchapter C corporation gift or estate tax valuation cases clearly isolating this issue until *Eisenberg*[129] in 1997, when the Tax Court again denied

125. Est. of Simplot v. Comm'r, 249 F.3d 1191 (9th Cir. 2001).
126. Est. of Maggos v. Comm'r, T.C. Memo. 2000-129 (2000).
127. Est. of Wright v. Comm'r, T.C. Memo. 1997-53 (1997).
128. Pierson M. Grieve v. Comm'r, T.C. Memo. 2020-28 (2020).
129. Eisenberg v. Comm'r, T.C. Memo. 1997-483 (1997).

recognition of a capital gains tax liability as a factor diminishing value, citing several pre-1987 cases as precedent. Then, in 1998, in *Davis*, the Tax Court decided as follows:

> We reject respondent's position that, as a matter of law, no discount or adjustment attributable to ADDI&C's built-in capital gains tax is allowable in the instant case . . . .
>
> We are convinced on the record in this case, and we find that, even though no liquidation of ADDI&C or sale of its assets was planned or contemplated on the valuation date, a hypothetical willing seller and a hypothetical willing buyer would not have agreed on that date on a price for each of the blocks of stock in question that took no account of ADDI&C's built-in capital gains tax.[130]

The court ultimately recognized a diminution in value equal to approximately half the trapped-in capital gains tax liability. Shortly following the *Davis* decision, the Second Circuit Court of Appeals, citing *Davis* favorably, reversed *Eisenberg*:

> In the past, the denial of a reduction for potential capital gains tax liability was based, in part, on the possibility that the taxes could be avoided by liquidating the corporation. These tax-favorable options ended with the Tax Reform Act of 1986 (TRA).
>
> Now that the TRA has effectively closed the option to avoid capital gains tax at the corporate level, reliance on these cases in the post-TRA environment should, in our view, no longer continue.[131]

The Second Circuit concluded by vacating the Tax Court opinion and remanding the case to the lower court to determine the gift tax based on a valuation taking into consideration the capital gains tax liability. The case was settled with a discount of about the same percentage of the trapped-in gains tax as was decided by the court in *Davis*.

Then, in 1999, the Tax Court reached a decision in *Simplot* that reflected a valuation deduction of 100% of the trapped-in capital gains tax on a block of stock owned by the company being valued.[132]

Another 1999 case, citing *Davis*, recognized the trapped-in capital gains tax liability of a company's timber. The court estimated the rate of growth, the rate of inflation, the capital gains tax rate, and the period over which the timber would be sold, using an estimated equity cost of capital (discount rate). It then deducted the full present value of the capital gains liability thus estimated.[133]

The majority of cases that have followed, either at the Tax Court level or on appeal, have permitted discounts for trapped-in capital gains.

The Tax Court in *Welch*[134] denied such a discount, but was reversed by the Sixth Circuit, which found that even though the company was eligible to defer the tax under I.R.C. § 1033, such eligibility—or even the exercise of such deferral rights—did not automatically preclude application of the discount.

Following *Eisenberg* and *Davis*, the applicable focus generally is no longer on whether the built-in gains discount is permissible, but instead is on how much of a discount should be allowed. In *Borgatello*,[135] the Tax Court allowed a 24% discount for

---

130. Est. of Davis v. Comm'r, 110 T.C. 530 (1998).
131. Eisenberg v. Comm'r, 155 F.3d 50 (2d Cir. 1998).
132. Est. of Simplot v. Comm'r, 112 T.C. 130 (1999).
133. Est. of Jameson v. Comm'r, T.C. Memo. 1999-43 (1999).
134. Est. of Welch v. Comm'r, T.C. Memo. 1998-167 (1998), *rev'd*, 208 F.3d 213 (6th Cir. 2000).
135. Est. of Borgatello v. Comm'r, T.C. Memo. 2000-264 (2000).

trapped-in capital gains tax on a controlling interest in a real estate holding company. However, the Fifth and Eleventh Circuits have held otherwise. The Tax Court in *Dunn*[136] permitted only a 5% discount, but on appeal, the Fifth Circuit ruled that a dollar-for-dollar reduction, amounting to a 34% discount, had to be applied to the company's asset-based value.

In *Jelke*,[137] the Tax Court had rejected a dollar-for-dollar reduction for the tax liability on trapped-in capital gains on a minority interest, reasoning that a hypothetical willing buyer of a minority interest would not adjust the purchase price to reflect the entire amount of the company's built-in capital gains tax liability, and that a hypothetical seller would not accept a price that was reduced for such liability. Finding the Fifth Circuit's approach in *Dunn* persuasive, the Eleventh Circuit reversed, essentially assuming that all company assets were sold in liquidation on the valuation date and that 100% of the trapped-in tax liability would be offset against the fair market value of the stock, dollar-for-dollar. The court thus rejected the Tax Court's distinction between a minority and controlling interest for purposes of the discount, noting that "whether or not a majority or minority interest is present is of no moment in an assumption of liquidation setting."

Cases that have rejected the discount for trapped-in capital gains have involved partnership interests, where the capital gains tax could have been avoided by an I.R.C. § 754 election. The courts in those cases have reasoned that a hypothetical buyer and seller would negotiate with the understanding that such an election would be made.[138]

Notwithstanding the foregoing discussion, several recent decisions by appellate courts in different states reminds us that there remains no uniform approach to built-in gain discount applicability.[139]

Finally, courts may be hesitant to approve of valuations that implement tax affecting.[140] In *Jones*,[141] both experts agreed that a hypothetical buyer and seller would consider

---

136. Est. of Dunn v. Comm'r, T.C. Memo. 2000-12 (2000), *rev'd on other grounds*, 201 F.3d 339 (5th Cir. 2002).

137. Est. of Jelke v. Comm'r, T.C. Memo. 2005-131 (2005), *rev'd*, 503 F.3d 1317 (11th Cir. 2007).

138. Est. of Jones v. Comm'r, 116 T.C. 121 (2001); Temple v. United States, 2006 U.S. Dist. LEXIS 16171 (E.D. Tex. 2006).

139. *See* Shop Rite, Inc. v. Gardiner, 2021 WL 1413949 (La. App. 3d Cir. Apr. 14, 2021) ("if the claimed tax consequence is a future one that will arise upon the occurrence of some unknown future event, the future tax consequence . . . should not be considered in determining" fair value); *and* Guge v. Kassel Enterprises, Inc., 962 N.W.2d 764 (Iowa 2021) (affirmed trial court's rejection of proposed built-in gains tax deduction, citing lack of evidence of any plans to sell the business, which applied essentially the same rationale in reversing the lower court's $7 million deduction for built-in gains tax); *and* Bohac v. Benes Serv. Co., 310 Neb. 722 (2022) (Court upheld estate's expert's ten-year deferred gains tax instead of corporation's expert's 100% deduction.).

140. *See* Est. of Jones v. Comm'r, T.C. Memo. 2019-101, at 41–42. *See also* Jackson v. Comm'r, T.C. Memo. 2021–48, at 77, RIA TC Memo 2021-048 ("Other things being equal, an income-producing asset [is] worth more to a pass-through [entity] than to a C corporation. But the complications of the real world intrude. Even with this tax disadvantage, C corporations dominate the financial markets and are by far the largest share of the largest business organizations in America. *See generally* James D. Cox & Thomas Lee Hazen, Business Organizations Law secs. 1.5–1.6 (4th ed. 2016) (describing the advantages and disadvantages of corporations). And that creates a problem for a DCF analysis. Because pass-throughs do not pay tax at the entity level, their projected cashflows will not account for any tax consequences. But almost always—and, in fact, in this case—the rate used to discount projected cashflows to present value is derived from after-tax, publicly available C-corporation information. Proponents of tax affecting argue that this mismatch between pretax cashflows and after-tax discount rates must be corrected, or tax affected.").

141. *Jones* at 39.

the form of business entity in determining the fair market value of a limited-partnership interest.

In *Jackson*,[142] the court clarified that it did "not hold that tax affecting is never called for. But [the] cases show how difficult a factual issue it is to demonstrate even a reasonable approximation of what that effect would be. In Jackson, there was expert evidence on only one side of the question, and that made a difference."[143]

CHARITABLE CONTRIBUTIONS

Regulation § 1.170A-13(c)(5) requires a summary appraisal by a qualified appraiser in conjunction with any charitable contribution in the form of a closely held business interest valued at more than $5,000. The section defines a qualified appraiser as an individual who:

1. Holds himself or herself out to the public as an appraiser or who regularly performs appraisals
2. Is qualified to appraise property because of his or her qualifications
3. Is aware of the appraiser penalties associated with the overvaluation of charitable contributions under I.R.C. § 6701

Certain individuals, however, may not act as qualified appraisers, including:

1. The property's donor (or the taxpayer who claims the deduction)
2. The property's donee
3. A party to the property transfer transaction (with certain very specific exceptions)
4. Any person employed by, married to, or related to any of the preceding persons
5. An appraiser who regularly appraises for the donor, donee, or party to the transaction and does not perform a majority of his or her appraisals for other persons
6. An individual who would otherwise be a qualified appraiser, but the donor has knowledge of facts that would cause a reasonable person to expect the appraiser falsely to overstate the value of the donated property (e.g., the donor and the appraiser make an agreement concerning the amount at which the property will be valued and the donor knows that such amount exceeds the fair market value of the property)

The IRS and the Tax Court enforce this requirement. For example, in one case, the IRS completely disallowed charitable deductions claimed in two years because the donor failed to comply with the appraisal requirement, even though the commissioner conceded that the values claimed as deductions were the same as the fair market value of the stock contributed. The Tax Court upheld the commissioner's determination. The Court of Appeals found that "Congress intended the qualified appraisal requirement to be mandatory." Accordingly, the taxpayer's failure to obtain an appraisal was fatal to any claim of deduction for his charitable contributions.[144]

In addition, other valuation issues arise in the charitable deduction context, such as the appropriate discounts to apply. For example, where shareholders owned a 45% interest in a corporation and simultaneously donated their interest "in lockstep" with the corporation's other noncontrolling/minority shareholders, as part of a prearranged plan, the Tax Court reduced the IRS's proposed 22% noncontrolling (minority) discount to 10%

---

142. *Jackson* at 82–83, RIA TC Memo ¶ 2021-048.

143. *Id.*

144. Hewitt v. Comm'r, 166 F.3d 332 (4th Cir. 1998).

but failed to explain why any minority discount was justified, because collectively 100% of the company was being transferred.[145]

With regard to contributions of qualified appreciated stock, an issue that can arise is whether on the transfer date market quotations with respect to the shares are readily available on an established securities market. In *Todd*,[146] the stock at issue had not been listed on any exchange and the taxpayer based the claimed deductions on subsequent sales of stock that occurred shortly after the contributions were made. The Tax Court disallowed the deductions, holding that the shares were not qualified appreciated stock on the transfer date. Therefore, the taxpayer was subject to substantiation requirements, which the taxpayer failed to provide. The case thus illustrates the importance of obtaining a formal appraisal when shares are not traded on an exchange.

CONTINGENT LIABILITIES

The most common contingent liabilities are environmental liabilities (discovered or potential) and outcomes of lawsuits. The uncertainty, of course, makes it very difficult to quantify the impact on value of these contingencies at a moment in time. In real-world transactions, the solution normally is to create a reserve account in escrow pending resolution of the uncertainties, but in a tax setting one must arrive at a specific number as of the effective valuation date.

A 1999 case involved a paint company that was considered a hazardous-waste producer with potential environmental liability. The court allowed a 10% discount from the value indicated by the discounted cash flow method but no discount from the value indicated by the guideline public company method, on the theory that the guideline company stock market prices probably already reflected the potential environmental liability.[147] In *Mitchell*,[148] the Tax Court took a $1.5 million discount for a pending compensation lawsuit. In *Klauss*,[149] the court permitted a 10% discount for product liability and environmental claims.[150]

SUBSEQUENT EVENTS AND INFORMATION

The principle is clear that only events or information that were known or foreseeable as of the valuation date may be taken into consideration.[151] Clear as the principle may

145. Koblick v. Comm'r, 2006 Tax Ct. Memo. LEXIS 63 (2006).

146. Todd v. Comm'r, 118 T.C. 354 (2002).

147. Est. of Desmond v. Comm'r, T.C. Memo. 1999-76 (1999).

148. Est. of Mitchell v. Comm'r, T.C. Memo. 1997-461 (1997), *vacated*, 250 F.3d 696 (9th Cir. 2001).

149. Est. of Emily Klauss, T.C. Memo. 2000-191.

150. *See also* REG-130975-08, Notice of Proposed Rulemaking, Fed. Reg. Vol. 87, No. 123 p. 38331 (June 28, 2022), which proposed changes to regulations issued under Code § 2053. Current reg. § 20.2053-1(d)(1) generally requires that deductions from a decedent's gross estate allowed under I.R.C. § 2053 for funeral expenses, administration expenses, and certain claims against the estate be "limited to the total amount actually paid in settlement or satisfaction of that item," though there are exceptions if "the amount to be paid is ascertainable with reasonable certainty and will be paid." Reg. § 20.2053-1(d)(4). Part II.B of the 2053 proposed regs. requires the value of an expense or claim deductible under I.R.C. § 2053(a) or Reg. § 20.2053-1(a) that is not paid before the third anniversary of the decedent's date of death to be discounted to present value.

151. *See, e.g.*, Jackson v. Comm'r, T.C. Memo. 2021–48, at 63–64 (2021), RIA TC Memo 2021-048 ("Because property is valued precisely at the moment of death, it is inappropriate, as a general matter, to

be, the admissibility and relevance of post-valuation date information is often a major controversy.

Proximity of Financial Information to Valuation Date

If valuing stock late in a fiscal period, it usually is acceptable to use financial data as of the end of that period. The philosophy is that late in a fiscal period, the performance for the period would be reasonably foreseeable in most cases.

For example, for a valuation date of December 12, 1988, the court stated:

> [we] agree with respondent that it makes more sense to value a gift of stock made in December 1988 using financial data as of December 31, 1988, rather than December 31, 1987.[152]

In *Central Trust*, the subject company prepared financial statements quarterly. Gifts were made on August 3 and October 25. For the August 3 gifts, the court used earnings for the 12 months ended June 30 for the fifth year of a five-year weighted average for both the subject and guideline public companies. For the October 25 gifts, the court used earnings for the 12 months ended September 30 for the fifth year of a five-year weighted average for both the subject and guideline public companies. This is a commonly used procedure, avoiding any subsequent in-formation dispute.[153]

On appeal in *Polack*,[154] the taxpayer used unaudited financials for years subsequent to the valuation date to argue that actual results were significantly lower than projections provided by the IRS at trial. The Eighth Circuit did not admit these, saying that "post-transaction earnings would not have been known to a prospective purchaser" as of the valuation date.

In *Okerlund*,[155] the Federal Circuit affirmed the Court of Federal Claims' ruling that estate plan provisions requiring the purchase of stock upon decedent's death should not have been included in valuing the stock when decedent's death was untimely and unexpected. The court said that valuation must always be made as of the donative date relying primarily on ex ante information; ex post data should be used sparingly. As with all evidentiary submissions, however, the critical question is relevance. The closer the profile of the later-date company to that of the valuation-date company, the more likely ex post data are to be relevant (though even in some cases, they may not be). The greater the significance of exogenous or unforeseen events occurring between the valuation date and the date of the proffered evidence, the less likely ex post evidence is to be relevant—even as a sanity check on the assumptions underlying a valuation model.

In *Noble*,[156] the court permitted the use of a post death event to value noncontrolling/minority shares in a bank. The estate presented as evidence of value an offer by the controlling shareholder to purchase the decedent's shares for $878,004 a few months

---

ascribe value based upon postdeath evidence. The temptation to use hindsight is usually too great. See Estate of Gilford v. Commissioner, 88 T.C. 38, 52 (1987); Estate of Gallagher v. Commissioner, 101 T.C.M. (CCH) 1702, 1706 (2011)").

152. Rabenhorst v. Comm'r, T.C. Memo. 1996-92 (1996).

153. Central Trust Co. v. United States, 305 F.2d 393 (Ct. Cl. 1962).

154. Polack v. Comm'r, T.C. Memo. 2002-145, *aff'd*, 366 F.3d 608 (8th Cir. 2004).

155. Okerlund v. United States, 53 Fed. Cl. 341 (Fed. Ct. Cl. 2002), *aff'd*, 365 F.3d 1044 (Fed. Cir. 2004).

156. Est. of Noble v. Comm'r, T.C. Memo. 2005-2 (2005).

after the date of death. However, the IRS presented evidence of the estate's sale of the shares to the bank for $1.1 million only ten months later. The court noted that there had not been any material change in circumstances between the sale date and the date of death. The court reasoned that

> An event occurring after a valuation date, even if unforeseeable as of the valuation date, also may be probative of the earlier valuation to the extent that it is relevant to establishing the amount that a hypothetical willing buyer would have paid a hypothetical willing seller for the subject property as of the valuation date. Unforeseeable subsequent events which fall within this latter category include evidence, such as we have here.[157]

In *Grieve*, the Tax Court rejected the IRS's expert's conclusion that a willing seller of units would first look to acquire control of additional interests to avoid the large discounts that a willing buyer would seek for merely buying the units at issue.[158] The court looked at the value of the units on the date of the gift and not the value on the basis of subsequent events (the purchasing of the additional units) that were not reasonably likely to happen and was not supported by any empirical data.

Subsequent Sales

Readers should be aware that the Tax Court frequently relies on subsequent sales as evidence of value. The court distinguishes between subsequent sales that *affected* the value and those that are merely *evidence of value*.

A subsequent sale surfaced as an issue in *Jung* in an opinion released in November of 1993. The matter involved the fair market value of a 20% interest in an operating company as of October 9, 1984. In mid-1986, the company was approached about selling its major operating assets, a transaction was completed on December 29, 1986, and the company was liquidated. The Tax Court explained its position as follows:

> Respondent contends that, in valuing Jung Corp. stock, this Court should consider the sale to Kendall, the other sales, and the ensuing liquidation of Jung Corp. Petitioner contends the 1986 sales and the liquidation are irrelevant because the sales and liquidation were unforeseeable at the valuation date.
>
> We agree in part with respondent and in part with petitioner.
>
> A distinction may usefully be drawn between later-occurring events which affect fair market value as of the valuation date, and later-occurring events which may be taken into account as evidence of fair market value as of the valuation date.
>
> If a prospective October 9, 1984, buyer and seller were likely to have foreseen the 1986 sale to Kendall, and the other activities leading to the liquidation, then those later-occurring events could affect what a willing buyer would pay and what a willing seller would demand as of October 9, 1984. We conclude, and we have found that, on October 9, 1984, Jung Corp. was not for sale, the sale to Kendall was not foreseeable, and the liquidation was not foreseeable. Accordingly, we conclude that those later-occurring events did not affect the October 9, 1984, fair market of decedent's stock.[159]
>
> However, we have stated that "for purposes of determining fair market value, we believe it appropriate to consider sales of properties occurring subsequent to

---

157. For an extensive list of notable subsequent events court cases, *see* Exhibit 35-3 in Pratt & ASA Educ. Found., *supra* note 45, at 781–82.

158. Pierson M. Grieve v. Comm'r, T.C. Memo. 2020-28 (2020).

159. Est. of Gilford v. Comm'r, 88 T.C. 38, 51-55 (1987).

> the valuation date if the properties involved are indeed comparable to the subject properties."[160]
>
> Of course, appropriate adjustments must be made to take account of differences between the valuation date and the dates of the later-occurring events. Although any such changes must be accounted for in determining the evidentiary weight to be given to the later-occurring events, those changes ordinarily are not justification for ignoring the later-occurring events (unless other comparables offer significantly better matches to the property being valued).
>
> When viewed in this light—as evidence of value rather than as something that affects value—later-occurring events are no more to be ignored than earlier-occurring events.
>
> Accordingly, we do not consider the sales and eventual liquidation as affecting the October 9, 1984, value of Jung Corp., but we do consider these events as evidence of the October 9, 1984, value.[161]

Ultimately, the Tax Court determined that some of the petitioner's higher indications of value were reconcilable with the subsequent sale.

An extreme case of the Tax Court relying on a sale long after the effective valuation date is found in *Cidulka.*[162] The valuation date was January 25, 1982. Four years later (January of 1986), the company, an outdoor advertising sign company, sold its assets to a major competitor for approximately 2.9 times its gross revenue. The Tax Court used this sale to conclude that the value of the stock should be 2.5 times the company's gross revenue for 1981 (the year prior to the effective valuation date).

In another case, the Tax Court relied on a January 1994 sale to value noncontrolling (minority) stock in an estate as of July 16, 1991. The estate tax return valued the stock at $35.20 per share, based on an update of an appraisal conducted in 1989. The 1994 sale took place at $75.15 per share. The Tax Court reduced the sale price by 30%, resulting in a value of $50.51 per share. The reason for the reduction was because the IRS offered no expert testimony and the court rejected the taxpayer's expert's opinion for several reasons:

- He was unable to explain certain parts of the analysis contained in the reports.
- He arbitrarily applied a 35% marketability discount.
- He made no mention of a hypothetical seller.
- While the 1989 report states that (taxpayer's expert) toured the facilities, there is nothing in his testimony or the 1991 report to suggest that he did likewise before preparing the 1991 report.
- The 1991 report does not adequately account for the fact that the company's 1991 earnings increased dramatically over the years covered by the 1989 report.
- The 1991 report does not adequately take into account that the company began paying dividends after the time covered by the 1989 report.

160. Est. of Thompson v. Comm'r, 89 T.C. 619, 628-629 n.7 (1987), *rev'd on other grounds* 864 F.2d 1128 (4th Cir. 1989). To the same effect are e.g., Krapf v. United States, 977 F.2d 1454, 1458–60 (Fed. Cir. 1992); Est. of Kaplin v. Comm'r, 748 F.2d 1109, 1111 (6th Cir. 1984), *rev'g* T.C. Memo. 1982-440 (1982); Est. of Brown v. Comm'r, 425 F.2d 1406, 1407 (5th Cir. 1970), *aff'g* T.C. Memo. 1969-91 (1969). *See* Est. of Jung v. Com'r, T.C. Memo. 1990-5 and cases cited therein.

161. Est. of Jung v. Comm'r, 101 T.C. 412 (1993).

162. Est. of Cidulka v. Comm'r, T.C. Memo. 1996-149, 71 T.C. Memo. (CCH) 2555 (1996).

- The 1991 report refers to the financial data of publicly traded companies, yet never explains how those companies were selected or in what respects their lines of business were similar to that of the subject company.[163]

The estate tax value filed might well have held up in court had it been adequately supported. In some other valuation context, such as family law, the case may have been remanded because of lack of adequate valuation evidence, but the Tax Court reaches a conclusion based on whatever it has before it.

In another case, the Tax Court relied on a redemption 16 months following the valuation date. Again, the IRS offered no expert testimony and the court rejected the taxpayer's expert's opinion as unpersuasive, noting, among other shortcomings, reliance on companies that were not comparable. The final determination of value was the redemption amount of $1,947,845, compared to $15,335 filed on the decedent's federal estate tax return. The court also upheld the fraud penalty under § 6663(a).[164]

BUY-SELL AGREEMENTS

The value established by a buy-sell agreement may be controlling, may be ignored, or may be a factor to consider.

For buy-sell agreements entered into after October 8, 1990, a buy-sell price is binding for federal estate tax purposes if it meets all the following criteria:[165]

- The price must be fixed or determinable as of a determinable date.
- The agreement must be binding on the parties both during life and after death.
- The agreement must have been entered into for a bona fide business reason.
- It must not be a substitute for testamentary disposition.
- The agreement must result in a fair market value for the subject business interest at the time the agreement is executed.
- Its terms must be comparable to similar arrangements entered into by persons in arm's-length transactions.
- The Tax Court, in *Lauder II*,[166] adopted this test and ruled that the test's elements are conjunctive, meaning that all of them must be independently satisfied to give the buy-sell price dispositive effect.

Regulations § 20.2031-2(h) provides:

> Such price will be disregarded in determining the value of the securities unless it is determined under the circumstances of the particular case that the agreement represents a bona fide business arrangement and not a device to pass the decedent's shares to the natural objects of his bounty for less than full and adequate consideration in money or money's worth.

In *Blount*,[167] the Tax Court disregarded a buy-sell agreement in determining decedent's interest in a closely held company on the date of his death because decedent had

163. Est. of Scanlan v. Comm'r, T.C. Memo. 1996-331 (1996).

164. Est. of Trompeter v. Comm'r, T.C. Memo. 1998-35 (1998).

165. I.R.C. § 2703. For a discussion of § 2703's treatment of buy-sell agreements, see Howard M. Zaritsky & Ronald D. Aucutt, Structuring Estate Freezes, chs. 4 and 8 (1996).

166. Est. of Lauder v. Comm'r (Lauder II), T.C. Memo. 1992-736 (1992).

167. Est. of Blount v. Comm'r, T.C. Memo. 2004-116 (2004), *aff'd*, 428 F.3d 1338 (11th Cir. 2005).

the unilateral ability to modify it, thus failing to satisfy the requirement that it be binding during life. The court also disregarded the agreement under I.R.C. § 2703, which requires that to be included in a valuation, a buy-sell agreement's terms must be "comparable to similar arrangements entered into by persons in an arm's length transaction." Here, the court concluded that the parties were "related" and had not engaged in arm's-length bargaining. The Eleventh Circuit affirmed.

Interestingly in this case, there was a life insurance policy owned by the company that provided $3.1 million to pay off the mandated buyout of the shares. The Tax Court included the full amount of the insurance proceeds as nonoperating assets and also concluded that because the buy-sell agreement had been disregarded, the issue of whether the company's obligation under that agreement to redeem decedent's stock should offset the proceeds was not before the court. As to the insurance proceeds, the Eleventh Circuit ruled that the Tax Court had erred because those proceeds had already been taken into account in the determination of net worth. The court noted that even when a buy-sell agreement is inoperative for purposes of establishing the value of the company for tax purposes, the agreement remains an enforceable liability against the valued company, if state law fixes such an obligation—which it had in this case. Here, the insurance proceeds were offset dollar-for-dollar by the company's obligation to satisfy its contract with the decedent's estate. The court thus concluded that such nonoperating "assets" should not be included in the fair market valuation of a company where, as here, there was an enforceable contractual obligation that offset such assets.[168]

More recently, however, the Eighth Circuit, in *Connelly*,[169] expressly rejected the Eleventh Circuit's approach and included the value of the insurance payable to the corporation in the stock value. The Eighth Circuit instead applied the reasoning from the lower (Tax Court) *Blount* opinion, indicating that the Eleventh Circuit's reasoning's "flaw lies in its premise. An obligation to redeem shares is not a liability in the ordinary business sense . . . . The redemption of stock is a reduction of surplus, not the satisfaction of a liability . . . . Treating it so distorts the nature of the ownership interest represented by those shares."[170]

The *Blount* and *Connelly* appellate decisions thus represented a direct conflict between the Eighth and Eleventh Circuits with respect to the estate tax inclusion of company-owned life insurance proceeds used to purchase the stock of a deceased shareholder pursuant to a buy-sell obligation. On December 13, 2023, the U.S. Supreme Court accepted *Connelly* for review to resolve the conflict between the circuits.

On June 6, 2024, the Supreme Court[171] affirmed the Eighth Circuit's opinion, ruling that a contractual obligation to redeem shares does not diminish the value of those shares:

> An obligation to redeem shares at fair market value does not offset the value of life-insurance proceeds set aside for the redemption because a share redemption at fair market

---

168. *See also* Est. of Cartwright, 183 F.3d 1034 (9th Cir. 1999), which also excluded insurance proceeds from the fair market value of a company when the proceeds were offset by an obligation to pay those proceeds to a shareholder's estate. However, in *Cartwright*, most of the corporate liabilities there were not obligations of the corporation to redeem its own stock. Instead, the bulk of the corporation's liabilities were for compensating the decedent shareholder for services rendered. As a result, *Cartwright* appears to present a different set of facts than *Blount* or *Connelly*.

169. Connelly v. U.S., 131 AFTR 2d 2023-1902 (8th Cir. 1999).

170. *Id.* at 2023-1907.

171. Connelly v. United States, No. 23–146 (June 6, 2024).

> value does not affect any shareholder's economic interest. A simple example proves the point. Consider a corporation with one asset—$10 million in cash—and two shareholders, A and B, who own 80 and 20 shares respectively. Each individual share is worth $100,000 ($10 million ÷ 100 shares). So, A's shares are worth $8 million (80 shares x $100,000) and B's shares are worth $2 million (20 shares x $100,000). To redeem B's shares at fair market value, the corporation would thus have to pay B $2 million. After the redemption, A would be the sole shareholder in a corporation worth $8 million and with 80 outstanding shares. A's shares would still be worth $100,000 each ($8 million ÷ 80 shares).
>
> Economically the redemption would have no impact on either shareholder. The value of the shareholders' interests after the redemption—A's 80 shares and B's $2 million in cash—would be equal to the value of their respective interests in the corporation before the redemption. Thus, a corporation's contractual obligation to redeem shares at fair market value does not reduce the value of those shares in and of itself.

From a practical perspective, the *Connelly* decision requires businesses to reassess whether their entity-owned life insurance policies and additional liquid reserves are sufficient to fund buy-sell obligations.

In *True*,[172] one issue was whether the book value price specified in the buy-sell agreements controlled estate and gift tax values of the subject interests in several family companies gifted and deeded to children. The analysis focused on the *Lauder II* factors. The court found that the fact that the children did not have independent legal or accounting advice, while not dispositive, reasonably suggested less than arm's-length dealings. The court was critical that the companies' buy-sell agreements did not provide a mechanism for periodic review or adjustment to the tax book value formula. The court also considered an analysis under the adequacy of consideration test. This test requires that the formula price (1) be comparable to what persons with adverse interests dealing at arm's length would accept and (2) bear a reasonable relationship to fair market value. As the court said, "[T]hese standards must be applied with the heightened scrutiny imposed on intrafamily agreements restricting transfers of closely held businesses." The court concluded that "[t]he True family buy-sell agreements do not satisfy the *Lauder II* test, because they are substitutes for testamentary dispositions. As a result, under § 2031 and the related regulations, the tax book value buy-sell agreement price does not control estate tax values of interests in the True companies at issue in the estate tax case."[173] The court also determined that the buy-sell agreements were not controlling for the gift tax case. The Tenth Circuit affirmed.

In *Hutchens*,[174] the court upheld the buy-sell price because it found that the negotiations had been at arm's length and in the ordinary course of business. In arriving at this decision, the court noted that a formal appraisal had been conducted and that each of the parties to the agreement had been individually represented by attorneys during negotiations. This case demonstrates the benefit of having an appraisal conducted not only after the buy-sell agreement has been entered into but also to aid in setting a buy-sell price or formula.

---

172. Est. of True v. Comm'r, T.C. Memo. 2001-167 (2001), *aff'd*, 390 F.3d 1210 (10th Cir. 2004).
173. *Id.* at 1212.
174. Hutchens Non-Marital Tr. v. Comm'r, T.C. Memo. 1993-600 (1993).

WEIGHTING OF VALUATION METHOD RESULTS

As discussed in Chapter 19, "Reconciliation of Value Indications," Revenue Ruling 59–60 is opposed to the idea of reconciling two or more indications of value by applying mathematical weights to each. Judge Laro discussed the issue as follows:

> In spite of this, some valuation practitioners apply weights to various factors in reaching their valuation conclusions because this allows them to clearly demonstrate the importance that they attach to various valuation considerations. This approach was used by the Tax Court in *Estate of Feldmar v. Comm'r*, T.C. Memo. 1988-429; *Estate of Titus v. Comm'r*, T.C. Memo. 1989-466; *Estate of Campbell v. Comm'r*, T.C. Memo. 1991-615. The weighing of various methods, however, was squarely rejected by the Court in *Estate of Mueller v. Comm'r*, T.C. Memo. 1992-284.
>
> With what appears to be conflicting judicial positions on this issue, there is some concern about whether the weighting of factors is a proper method of appraisal.
>
> I believe that one should consider carefully all relevant factors but should not assign weights to each factor. However, practitioners may emphasize a few factors that could influence the ultimate valuation.[175]

Another case in which the court ultimately utilized an explicit percentage weighting of factors was the oft-quoted *Central Trust* decision. In this case, the court relied entirely on the guideline public company method and applied 50% of the weight to the price/earnings multiples, 30% to the dividend yield, and 20% to the price/book value multiple.[176]

In *Hess*,[177] the IRS's expert did not assign any weight to the discounted cash flow method because the company's future income was difficult to predict and because valuation conclusions were highly sensitive to small changes in assumptions. The Tax Court indicated that while less weight should be accorded to this method under such circumstances, it nonetheless should be considered in the valuation process. The court did not, however, specify an exact percentage of weight to be accorded to the method.

In *Dunn*,[178] the court indicated that weighting was a key issue. The IRS's expert accorded the asset approach a 100% weight, while the taxpayer's expert weighted the income and asset approaches equally given that no liquidation was planned. The Tax Court decided the appropriate weight was 65% for the asset-based approach and 35% for the income approach, based on various factors, such as the depressed nature of the industry and the company's low profitability and high debt. On appeal, the Fifth Circuit determined that the likelihood of liquidation was a relevant factor for weighting and ruled that the earnings-based method should be weighted at 85% to reflect the low likelihood of liquidation.[179]

---

175. Hon. David Laro, *Judge Laro's Views on "Fair Market Value," in* JUDGES & LAWYERS BUSINESS VALUATION UPDATE 1–3 (May 1999). Quoted from address before the AICPA National Business Valuation Conference (Nov. 17, 1998).

176. Central Trust Co. v. United States, 305 F.2d 393 (Ct. Cl. 1962).

177. Hess v. Comm'r, T.C. Memo. 2003-251 (2003).

178. Est. of Dunn v. Comm'r, T.C. Memo. 2000-12 (2000), *rev'd on other grounds*, 201 F.3d 339 (5th Cir. 2002).

179. Other examples of express weighting are Est. of Freeman v. Comm'r, T.C. Memo. 1996-372, 1996 WL 453872 (1996) (Court accepts IRS's 70% weighting of market approach and 30% of income approach, but

If the expert says, "I accorded more weight to x factor," the judge may ask, "Well, how much weight?" Shannon Pratt previously opined on this dilemma as follows:

> Despite this wording, the method has been used successfully in many gift and estate tax cases both in dealing with the IRS and in cases decided in court. The wording of Revenue Ruling 59–60 indicates concern that the averaging or weighted average method leaves room for omission of pertinent factors. However, it is possible to use the basic weighted average of factors procedure and still, at one stage or another, incorporate consideration of all the pertinent factors mentioned in Revenue Ruling 59–60. Of course, it is important to be careful to demonstrate in each case that all other pertinent factors were actively considered and reflected in the result to the appropriate extent.[180]

All this discussion would seem to lead to the conclusion that neither explicit nor implicit weighting of varying indications of value is clearly superior. If an explicit weighting is used, we suggest a disclaimer to the effect that there is no empirical basis for the weighting; it is presented only to help the reader understand the analyst's thinking regarding relative importance.[181]

PRESSURE TO SETTLE

The Tax Court has consistently urged taxpayers and the IRS to attempt to settle valuation disputes rather than bring them to trial. For example:

> Once again we must advise counsel that valuation cases such as this are better suited for the give and take of the settlement process than adjudication. See *Buffalo Tool & Die Manufacturing Co. v. Commissioner,* 74 T.C. 441, 451 (1980); *Messing v. Commissioner,* 48 T.C. 502, 512 (1967). It is quite clear from the record that the experts have not been permitted to meet to discuss their reports and attempt to resolve their differences. Furthermore, the Court concludes that counsel have failed to meaningfully confer with each other regarding settlement and stipulation as required by the Court's Standing Pretrial Order. The result of this "Rambo" approach to Tax Court litigation is that the parties and the Court have had to spend considerable time and effort in trial, on briefs, and in opinion writing to resolve a question which clearly should have been settled.[182]

In another example:

> Because valuation may not be reduced to the rote application of formulas, and because of the imprecision inherent in determining fair market value of stock that lacks a public market (and the Solomon-like pronouncements that often follow), we again remind the parties that these matters are better resolved by agreement rather than trial by ordeal in which conflicting opinions of the experts are pitted against each other. See *Estate of Hall v. Commissioner,* supra; *Messing v. Commissioner,* 48 T.C. 502 (1967).[183]

---

accords no weight to taxpayer's value); Est. of Smith v. Comm'r, T.C. Memo. 1999-368 (1999) (Court accepts a 70/30% weighting to asset-based/income approaches, respectively).

180. Shannon Pratt et al., Valuing a Business 374 (3d ed. 1996).

181. For further discussion of this issue, *see* Chapter 23, "Weighting of Approaches," in Laro & Pratt, *supra* note 8.

182. Est. of Bruce v. Comm'r, T.C. Memo. 1993-244 (1993).

183. Est. of Furman v. Comm'r, T.C. Memo. 1998-157 (1998), at 9. *See also* Est. of Fleming v. Comm'r, T.C. Memo. 1997-484 (1997); Buffalo Tool & Die Mfg. Co. v. Comm'r, 74 T.C. 441, 1980 WL 4569 (1980).

DEFINED VALUE FORMULA CLAUSES

While this chapter focuses on the particulars of preparing and supporting (and potential risks to) appraised valuations of property, the *Wandry*[184] decision and its line of cases illustrates different but related principles. Once a valuation has been obtained, can a donor define a gift of that property in terms of a specified dollar amount? And if the appraisal used to support the reported gift is successfully challenged on audit (thereby altering the previously believed number of shares or units, etc. transferred), can the taxpayer avoid additional gift taxes? The Tax Court's opinion in *Wandry* suggests "yes."

Generally speaking, formula clauses have historically been used to limit gift tax audit risk by defining (and thus restricting) the gift value of entity interests to a specified dollar amount (as opposed to a specified number of shares or units). If, on audit, the IRS successfully disagrees with the valuation utilized to support the gift, the IRS's new value serves to only confirm that the number of shares or units, etc., initially believed to have been transferred was incorrect (and corrects that misconception). Such an audit does not, in theory, alter the taxable value of the gift.

To the authors' knowledge, formula clauses were first challenged in *Commissioner v. Procter.*[185] In holding a formula clause invalid, the court found that such clauses created a condition subsequent and were contrary to public policy, primarily because upholding such clauses would undermine IRS gift tax collection enforcement efforts (i.e., if the IRS allocated its resources to revaluing undervalued gifts, a formula savings clause would prevent the collection of additional tax and render such efforts meaningless).

Following *Procter*, taxpayers began successfully using formula clauses linked to charitable transfers. Essentially, to prevent an IRS gift tax valuation challenge, donors provided that a charitable organization would receive that portion of a gift in excess of a specific dollar amount. As a result, if the IRS audited the gift tax return to find that the value of the asset exceeded the reported specific dollar amount of the gift, the excess amount of that value would simply pass in a gift-tax deductible manner to a charity as a result of the formula clause. In that event, the taxable portion of the gift remained equal to the originally specified dollar amount, and no benefit accrued to the IRS. In these "charitable lid" cases, courts frequently agreed with the taxpayers, in part because charitable gifts are favored under federal tax law (providing a competing public policy consideration to those discussed in *Procter*), and in part when it is shown that the charities were represented by separate counsel and negotiated the valuation with the taxpayer at arm's length.[186] Accordingly, until relatively recently, many commentators suggested that involving a charity was the safest way to use a formula clause with a lifetime gift.

However, in *Wandry*,[187] the Tax Court expanded the use of defined value formula clauses further by not requiring a charitable gift component. In *Wandry*, the donors made gifts of limited liability company (LLC) units to their children and grandchildren with a specified dollar amount (rather than as a specific number of units or percentage of

184. Wandry v. Comm'r, T.C. Memo. 2012-88.

185. Comm'r v. Procter, 142 F.2d 824 (4th Cir. 1944).

186. *See, e.g.*, Est. of Petter v. Comm'r, T.C. Memo. 2009-280, *aff'd*, 653 F.3d 1012 (9th Cir. 2011); Hendrix v. Comm'r, T.C. Memo. 2011-133.

187. *See also* McCord v. Comm'r, 120 T.C. 358 (2003), *rev'd*, 461 F.3d 614 (5th Cir. 2006); and Est. of Petter v. Comm'r, T.C. Memo. 2009-280, *aff'd*, 653 F.3d 1012 (9th Cir. 2011).

the donor's interest). The number of initially reported units transferred was determined with reference to an appraisal. The assignment documents stated that if the value of the LLC units, as finally determined for gift tax purposes (i.e., after audit), was different than the appraised value, the number of transferred units would be adjusted so that the dollar amount of the taxable gift remained the same. The IRS audited the gift tax returns and found that the LLC interest value was higher than the originally appraised value. The taxpayer contended that the formula clause prevented any increase in the amount of taxable gifts. The IRS instead argued that the gifts were of fixed percentage LLC interests rather than specific dollar amounts, and that the amount of the taxable gifts should be increased.

The Tax Court agreed with the taxpayer, holding that the formula clause validly prevented the IRS from increasing the taxable gifts, because it legitimately required a reallocation of the LLC interests among the donors and donees based on fixed specific values, as finally determined for gift tax purposes. In other words, so long as the gift was defined as a specific dollar amount rather than a fixed number of units, the gift amount was the specific dollar amount, which could not be increased (and have gift tax imposed thereon) if the final value of each unit turned out to be greater than the appraised value.[188] The court stated that the charitable gift in other reported cases was a contributing factor to the taxpayer victories in those cases but was not determinative.

The IRS initially appealed the Tax Court's decision in *Wandry*, but then withdrew its appeal, instead announcing that it believes the case was wrongly decided and that it will not be followed. A.O.D. 2012-004 (November 13, 2012) (non-acquiescence).[189] Nevertheless, while the authors are aware of post-*Wandry* challenges to formula clauses being raised on audit and being settled, the authors are not aware of any successful challenges to defined formula clauses in any post-*Wandry* court decisions.[190] Accordingly, at the time of drafting, *Wandry* remains valid law.

SUMMARY

Valuations for gift, estate, and charitable contribution matters present numerous conceptual challenges. Practitioners must be familiar with the standard of fair market value, adhering to the exhortation of numerous courts to adequately consider the perspective of both willing buyers and sellers, to the neglect of neither hypothetical party. When appraisals are submitted by qualified appraisers for consideration, courts are often focused on how persuasively general valuation principles are applied to the unique facts and circumstances of the case at hand. For example, courts have recognized the general

188. In so doing, the Tax Court distinguished between an impermissible *Procter* savings clause that creates a donor taking property back from a donee, with a permissible formula clause that instead transfers a fixed set of rights (i.e., property of a fixed and certain value) that remains unchanged throughout. The *Wandry* court also evidenced its skepticism with broad application of the judicially created public policy doctrine (which, decades after *Procter*, the U.S. Supreme Court indicated should be applied sparingly in *Commissioner v. Tellier*, 383 U.S. 687 (1966)).

189. An indication of non-acquiescence by the IRS generally indicates that, although no further review is sought, the IRS disagrees with the holding of the court and will generally not follow the decision in cases involving other taxpayers.

190. *But see* Nelson v. Comm'r, 17 F.4th 556 (5th Cir. 2021), which illustrates how drafting *Wandry*-like formula clauses can go wrong.

relevance of valuation methods under the asset-based, income and market approaches to valuation, but occasionally find that certain valuation methods are not applicable to the subject interest being considered.

While some issues can generally be considered beyond dispute, for example, the existence of discounts for lack of control or lack of marketability, consensus regarding other valuation challenges remains elusive. For example, the long-standing controversies regarding the proper treatment of tax pass-through entities and the relevance of embedded capital gains tax liabilities continue to vex both appraisers and courts.

In this chapter, we have referenced many cases to illustrate courts' posture toward certain valuation circumstances. Some challenges, however, such as the weight accorded to events occurring subsequent to the valuation date defy the application of simple heuristics. In any event, the task of appraisers is to provide relevant economic evidence and rationale to courts in view of the relevant facts of the matter at hand. Throughout the cases referenced herein, courts are clearly partial toward thorough and independent analyses of the valuation challenges particular to the case. Appraisers should be acquainted with prior decisions while remaining most focused on presenting a compelling rationale in support of their conclusions regarding the value of the subject interest.

REFERENCES FOR VALUATIONS FOR GIFT, ESTATE, AND CHARITABLE CONTRIBUTION MATTERS

Articles and Books

Bellatti, Robert M., and Shari L. West. Updated Annually. *Estate Planning for Farms and Other Qualified Family-Owned Businesses* (Carrollton, TX, Thomson Reuters). Covers § 2032A and § 2057 special-use valuations.

Feld, Daniel E. 2012 cumulative supplement No. 1. *Estate and Gift Tax Digest*, 4th Ed. (Carrollton, TX, Thomson Reuters). Cites and digests cases and rulings.

Fishman, Jay, Bruce A. Johnson, and Kent D. Pummel. 2023. "Estate and Gift Tax Valuations." In PPC's *Guide to Business Valuations*, 1000–1005 (Carrollton, TX, Thomson Reuters).

Fishman, Jay E., Shannon P. Pratt, and William J. Morrison. 2013. "Fair Market Value in Estate and Gift Tax." In *Standards of Value: Theory and Applications*, 2nd ed. Chap. 2, 35–88 (Hoboken, NJ: John Wiley & Sons).

Hitchner, James R. 2017. "Estate, Gift and Income Tax Valuations." In *Financial Valuation: Applications and Models*, 4th ed., Chap. 14, 681–723 (Hoboken NJ: John Wiley & Sons, Inc.).

Kasper, Larry J. 1997. "Federal Tax Valuations." In *Business Valuations, Advanced Topics*, 211–58. (Westport, CN: Greenwood Publishing).

Mercer, Z. Christopher. 2022. "What Revenue Ruling 59-60 Says (and Does Not Say) About Fair Market Value." Available at https://chrismercer.net (no charge with subscription to blog).

Pratt, Shannon P. and ASA Educational Foundation. 2022. "Valuation for Gift, Estate and Charitable Contribution Purposes" and "Gift, Estate and Charitable Contribution Tax Court Cases." In *Valuing a Business: The Analysis and Appraisal of Closely Held Businesses*, 6th ed., Chap. 34, 743–63; Chap. 35, 765–818 (New York: McGraw-Hill).

Saltzman, Michael J. Updated three times yearly. *IRS Practice and Procedure* (Carrollton, TX, Thomson Reuters). Covers the complete range of IRS procedures from rulings to collection of taxes.

Trugman, Gary. 2022. "Estate and Gift Valuations." In *Understanding Business Valuations*, 6th ed., Chap. 21, 779–803 (Portland OR: Business Valuation Resources).

Zaritsky, Howard M., and Ronald D. Aucutt. 1996. *Structuring Estate Freezes: Analysis with Forms.* Updated twice yearly. Chaps. 4 and 8 (Carrollton, TX, Thomson Reuters).

Website

www.ustaxcourt.gov contains all appealable Tax Court opinions from January 3, 1999, to the present.

CHAPTER 21

Valuations for Federal Income Tax Matters

Roger J. Grabowski, FASA

INTRODUCTION[1]

In this chapter you will learn about:

- Court interpretations of the meaning of *fair market value*
- Valuation of property received/transferred in a transaction
- Determining basis in a property
- Valuation of worthless and abandoned property
- Issues when using financial reporting valuations for income tax purposes
- Corporate distribution of appreciated property to shareholders
- Valuation principles in intercompany transfer pricing

Before delving into the income taxation transactions where a valuation is relevant, a brief discussion is provided of recent tax legislation. This chapter then lists several types of income tax transactions where a valuation is relevant. The chapter will describe the tax-related reason for the valuation requirement—often in terms of a reference to the appropriate statutory authority, administrative rulings, or judicial precedent. Furthermore, an overview is provided of any noteworthy valuation considerations that relate directly to that specific taxation-related valuation requirement.

Finally, a brief discussion of valuation aspects of intercompany transfer pricing is provided. This includes intangible transfers and valuation approaches and the interaction of transfer pricing and legal entity valuations, among other topics.

Valuation considerations for valuations for gift, estate, and charitable contribution matters are discussed in Chapter 20.

Valuation considerations when valuing stock of Subchapter S corporations and interests in other pass-through entities are discussed in Chapter 26.

Valuation-related federal income tax misstatement penalties are discussed in Chapter 38, "Valuation and Appraiser Penalties." Counsel, valuation practitioners, tax practitioners, and taxpayers should all be mindful of these penalties when accounting for a taxable transaction where valuation is relevant.

---

1. The authors thank Noah Gordon, former legal counsel for Shannon Pratt Valuations, for his contribution to the prior edition.

As with all chapters in this book, this chapter is written from a valuation and economic analysis perspective. It is not intended to offer legal, accounting, or tax advice. Appropriate professional advisors should be consulted for such advice.[2]

FEDERAL INCOME TAX REASONS TO CONDUCT AN APPRAISAL

Exhibit 21-1 lists several federal income tax transactions where valuation is relevant. This list is not intended to be exhaustive. It is intended to illustrate many of the more common income tax-related reasons to conduct a valuation.

Exhibit 21-1 Taxable Transactions Requiring Valuations

Abandonment losses—worthless and abandoned property	Exchange of properties
Acquisitions	Foreclosure of mortgaged property
Bargain purchases	Incorporation of a business
Basis of property (for depreciation and amortization)	Insolvent corporation recapitalization (see Chapter 31)
"Boot" in tax-free transfer	Intercompany transfer of goods or services
Buying or selling a business (see Chapter 14 for issues surrounding noncompetition agreements)	Liquidation, when property is received by a shareholder
Cancellation of indebtedness income (see Chapter 31)	Lump sum acquisition of various assets or properties (purchase price allocation)
Casualty losses	Market rate of return for preferred equity
Charitable contributions of property (see Chapter 20)	Mergers
Check-the-box elections	Partnership contributions
Compensation received in the form of property	"Reasonableness" of compensation (determination of) (see Chapter 13)
Conversion of C corporation to S corporation (see Chapter 26)	Recapitalization
Dividends received in the form of property	Rents received in the form of property
Distributions of appreciated property	Residence converted to a rental property
Divestitures	Strike price for options
Employee stock options and other stock-based compensation (see Chapter 13)	Shareholder agreements (see Chapter 29)
Excess accumulated earnings (quantification of)	Stock rights
	Tax shelters
	Threshold for partnership profits interests
	Transfer pricing
	Transfers of intangible property

Source: Adapted from SHANNON PRATT'S VALUING A BUSINESS: THE ANALYSIS AND APPRAISAL OF CLOSELY HELD COMPANIES 837. Used with permission.

2. This chapter is adapted in part from Chapter 37, "Valuation for Income Tax Purposes," and Chapter 38, "Income Tax Court Cases," in SHANNON P. PRATT & ASA EDUC. FOUND., SHANNON PRATT'S VALUING A BUSINESS: THE ANALYSIS AND APPRAISAL OF CLOSELY HELD BUSINESSES (6th ed. 2022). Used with permission.

The following sections describe select income tax-related valuation requirements in greater detail.

STANDARD OF VALUE[3]

The standard of value for federal tax matters is generally *fair market value* (FMV) defined by the U.S. Treasury Regulations as:

> the net amount which a willing purchaser, whether an individual or a corporation, would pay for the interest to a willing seller, neither being under any compulsion to buy or to sell and both having reasonable knowledge of relevant facts.[4]

It is important to understand how the courts have interpreted the fair market value standard.

The definition of fair market value used for property transaction and property basis purposes is the familiar: the most probable price that, at a particular time, will induce a willing buyer to buy and a willing seller to sell, neither being under undue pressure to buy or to sell, and both being informed as to all relevant facts.[5]

This familiar definition of fair market value has been slightly expanded regarding the income taxation valuation of transactional property to include consideration of (1) the availability of a buyer at the time and place and (2) the assumption that the buyer is not only willing but also able to pay for the property involved.[6] This is consistent with the fair market value definition in the Regulations that has become the cornerstone of valuations performed for tax purposes and quoted in many taxation cases.[7]

Court decisions have further refined the definition. For example, in *Pabst Brewing Company* the Tax Court outlined fundamental valuation principles (as delineated in Chapter 1).[8]

The Tax Court later determined that the valuation should consider synergies with a potential buyer. The court indicated that in determining fair market value, the hypothetical buyer and hypothetical seller must be disposed to maximum economic gain, and because there were multiple potential synergistic buyers for the subject business, synergy should be considered:[9]

> Just as determination of fair market value requires assumption of a willing seller, it does not assume hypothetical transactions that are "unlikely and plainly contrary to the economic interests" of a hypothetical buyer.[10]

At times, courts have also provided guidance as to valuation methodology. For example, in *Nestle*, the Second Circuit concluded that the relief-from-royalty method

---

3. For an extensive discussion available on the nuances of fair market value in the federal tax valuation context, see Jay E. Fishman, Shannon P. Pratt & William J. Morrison, Standards of Value: Theory and Applications 35–87 (2d ed. 2013).

4. 26 C.F.R. § 20.2031–3 Valuation of Property in General. *See also* Rev. Rul. 59–60.

5. *See* H.H. Marshman, 279 F.2d 27 (6th Cir. 1960), *cert. denied*, 364 U.S. 918 (1960).

6. *See* Helvering v. Walbridge, 70 F.2d 683 (2d Cir. 1934), *cert. denied*, 293 U.S. 594 (1934).

7. Regulation § 20.2031-1(b).

8. Pabst Brewing Co. v. Comm'r, T.C. Memo. 1996-506 (Nov. 12, 1996).

9. BTR Dunlop Holdings, Inc. v. Comm'r, T.C. Memo. 1999-377 (Nov. 15, 1999).

10. Citing Est. of Hall v. Comm'r, 92 T.C. 312, 337 (1989) (quoting Est. of Curry v. United States, 706 F.2d 1424, 1429 (7th Cir. 1983)); *see also* Est. of Newhouse v. Comm'r, 94 T.C. 193, 232 (1990).

(a commonly used method in valuing certain intangible assets) necessarily undervalues trademarks.[11] That court concluded that the sole use of a relief-from-royalty method in the case of a sale is not appropriate because it is the fair market value of a trademark, and not the cost of its use, that was at issue. The court concluded that the relief-from-royalty method fails to capture the value of all the rights of intangible asset ownership, such as (1) the power to determine when and where the trademark may be used and (2) the ability to move the trademark into or out of product lines.

In another decision, the Tax Court held in *Pierre* that the tax principle where a single-member limited liability company (LLC) is disregarded does not apply for valuation purposes.[12] The court treated the existence of the LLC as a fact supporting valuation discounts.

In transfer pricing, the standard is an *arm's-length standard* defined by Regulation § 482 and discussed later in the chapter.

U.S. INCOME TAX CONSIDERATIONS

Tax legislation and the accompanying issuance of Regulations need to be considered in valuations. Three most recent pieces of legislation with valuation impacts are the 2017 Tax Cuts and Jobs Act (TCJA), effective on December 22, 2017;[13] the Coronavirus Aid, Relief, and Economic Security Act (CARES Act), passed on March 27, 2020, which included many modifications to the TCJA, some permanent and some temporary;[14] and the Inflation Reduction Act of 2022, which created a new corporate alternative minimum tax (CAMT) of 15% on the adjusted *financial statement income* of large corporations (generally applicable to corporations with average annual income exceeding $1 billion).

VALUATION OF PROPERTY RECEIVED/TRANSFERRED IN A TRANSACTION

The statutory regime for transfers of property between buyers and sellers in taxable transactions requires the valuation of any property,[15] other than cash. This basic rule of income taxation valuation in property transactions is presented in Internal Revenue Code (I.R.C.) § 1001. Specifically, § 1001(b) states "The amount realized from the sale or other disposition[16] of property shall be the sum of any money received plus the fair market value of the property (other than money) received."[17]

---

11. Nestle Holdings, Inc. v. Comm'r, Nos. 152 F.3d 83 (2d Cir. July 31, 1998).

12. Pierre v. Comm'r, 133 T.C. 24 (2009).

13. A side-by-side comparison summarizing the changes between the TCJA and prior U.S. tax legislation is available in the Bloomberg Tax, *Tax Reform Guidance Roadmap*, https://pro.bloombergtax.com/reports/tax-reform-guidance-roadmap/ (last visited May 6, 2024).

14. Bloomberg Tax prepared a summary of the key changes in the *Federal Tax & Accounting—Coronavirus Roadmap*, https//pro.bloombergtax.com/reports/federal-tax-accounting-coronavirus-roadmap/.

15. This may even include the valuation of marketable securities, particularly if certain transfer restrictions are attached, the market for the security is thin, or other facts may require adjustment to what might be its freely marketable price.

16. 26 U.S.C. § 1001 Determination of amount of and recognition of gain or loss.

17. With respect to the buyer, its basis is determined by I.R.C. § 1012(a), which states: "The basis of property shall be the cost of such property. . . ." If the buyer pays for the property purchased in other than cash, then its cost is the fair market value of such property given up. It should be noted that there are many

DETERMINING BASIS IN A PROPERTY

When there is a sale or exchange of property, the taxpayer must determine the amount of the property transaction gain or loss, and whether it is taxable or deductible. The amount of gain or loss is determined by the taxpayer's basis in the property it is selling. For income tax reporting purposes, the following formulas typically determine the basis in the property sold and the amount of the property transaction gain or loss:

$$\text{Basis} + \text{Additions} - \text{Reductions} = \text{Adjusted basis}$$

$$\text{Amount realized} - \text{Adjusted basis} = \text{Gain or loss}$$

One can look at "basis" as the measurement of the taxpayer's investment in the property for income tax reporting purposes. A taxpayer must know the property's basis in order to determine such taxation-related elements as depreciation, casualty losses, and gain or loss on the property's sale or exchange. Basis is ordinarily the property's original cost or purchase price (including transaction costs such as sales taxes and delivery costs, for instance). Upon purchase, basis normally includes cash paid, debt assumed, and the fair market value of any other property given up.[18]

Basis is adjusted for such items as capital investment in the property, sales of a portion of the property, depreciation or depletion, and other transactional and taxation events.[19] These events increase or decrease the original basis. The result is often called the "adjusted basis."

In certain situations, the fair market value of property on a particular date is the key factor in determining its basis. For example, when property is transferred between affiliated entities, or received through an estate. When using value to determine basis, actual sales prices of similar property on the open market are typically reliable evidence of fair market value. For example, for this purpose, various courts have concluded that stock exchange quotations represent good evidence of a stock's fair market value. Often, however, there are no readily observable arm's-length transactions in the security or asset to determine fair market value and an appraisal is needed.

A taxable exchange involves an exchange of property in which the gain is taxable, or the loss is deductible. If a taxpayer acquires one property in return for another property in a taxable exchange, then the basis of the property received is generally its fair market value at the time of the exchange, absent some nonrecognition provision in the I.R.C.

There are two allowable methods for determining the basis of property received in exchange for other property:

1. The fair market value of the property when it is received
2. The fair market value of the property exchanged for it, increased by any payments made or decreased by any payments received, when the two properties are of unequal value

---

instances when gain or loss may be deferred. An example of such situation is a like-kind exchange of real property under I.R.C. § 1031 where the buyer and seller record no gain or loss but transfer the old basis in the property given up to the property received.

18. However, if a taxpayer receives property by some other form, such as by gift or inheritance, the taxpayer must normally use the property's basis rather than its cost.

19. I.R.C. § 1016 Adjustments to Basis.

Occasionally, it may be impractical to estimate the fair market value of the property given up (in order to measure the cost of the property received). In these situations, taxpayers may presume the values of the exchanged properties are equal, if the exchange took place at arm's length. In other words, the fair market value for either the buyer or seller may be measured by the fair market value of the property given up or the fair market value of the property received, whichever is more accurately and reliably measured.

If a taxpayer, other than an employee, receives property for services, then the original basis of the property to that taxpayer is its fair market value. According to Regulation § 1.61-2(d), the taxpayer will include this amount in his or her taxable income.[20] The basis of any restricted property received as payment for services is the sum of any amount paid for the property plus any amount the taxpayer includes in gross income when the property is no longer subject to a substantial risk of forfeiture.[21]

Property Received by Employees

Corporations often issue stock options to employees and other service providers as part of their compensation. I.R.C. § 409A, enacted in 2004 in response to abuses exemplified by the Enron corporation, imposes penalties on certain deferred compensation arrangements. Section 409A considers stock options a deferred compensation arrangement but does not apply penalties if the strike price is equal to or greater than the fair market value of the stock at the time the stock option is granted. Therefore, corporations whose stock is not publicly traded must perform (or obtain) "409A valuations" to support the exclusion of their fair market value stock options from 409A penalties. These valuations take into account appropriate discounts for lack of liquidity (marketability) and lack of control of the subject stock.

Since 2004, the term "409A valuation" has come to refer to any valuation of equity in connection with compensation. A common example is that businesses or private equity funds operated in LLC or partnership form issue "profits interests" to employees and other service providers. I.R.C. Revenue Procedure 93-27 provides that if the profits interest would receive nothing if the partnership were liquidated at fair market value, the grant of the profits interest is tax-free even if the profits interest itself has positive fair market value because it participates in future profits and growth in value of the partnership. The value a profits interest would receive on a hypothetical liquidation on the date of grant is referred to as the "liquidation value." Profits interests incorporate a threshold value below which the particular profits interest does not participate in partnership distributions. A partnership might use a determination of liquidation value to establish the threshold applicable to a particular profits interest.

There can also be a need to determine the fair market value, as opposed to the liquidation value, of the profits interest. The fair market value of the profits interest might be relevant to financial reporting of the compensation expense. Partnerships engaged in certain regulated businesses, including healthcare businesses subject to Medicare rules, might want some of their profits interest holders to pay fair market value for their profits interests to comply with regulatory rules. The valuation of a profits interest would

20. The taxation of stock-based compensation can be complex with income recognition deferred until the employee monetizes the stock in certain situations.

21. The results related to restricted property received as payment for services are presented in Regulation § 1.83-4.

normally employ an option model framework (such as using a Black-Scholes model) (discussed in Chapter 13, "Reasonable Compensation").

USE OF FINANCIAL REPORTING VALUATIONS FOR INCOME TAX PURPOSES

Taxpayers should proceed with caution when attempting to use *fair value* measurements prepared for financial reporting (discussed in Chapter 1) for income tax purposes. While the consensus is that valuations performed under guidance provided by Generally Accepted Accounting Principles (GAAP) may be useful in understanding tax valuations, taxpayers are under the obligation to determine their positions to independently support what value is appropriate for income tax purposes.

For example, impairment analyses under GAAP related to certain tangible or intangible property of a company may have associated tax accounting and collateral tax amortization consequences, but it does not necessarily mean that a valuation prepared for financial reporting purposes can be relied upon for tax reporting.[22]

VALUATION OF WORTHLESS AND ABANDONED PROPERTY

When misfortune strikes, leaving a taxpayer with worthless property, the taxpayer normally has a deductible loss equal to the adjusted basis of the worthless property. It is noteworthy, however, that the loss in these situations may not technically arise from a sale or exchange, which could create a need for a valuation as well as addressing technical tax challenges in being able to take the deduction.[23] The following discussion summarizes how taxpayers may seek to justify and to quantify this deductible loss.

Worthless Securities

If a qualifying security becomes worthless[24] at any time during the taxable year, the resulting loss is treated as having arisen from the sale or exchange of a capital asset on the last day of the taxable year. Losses from worthless securities are then treated as either short-term or long-term capital losses, depending on the taxpayer's holding period of the subject securities.

Whether a security becomes worthless during a given year is a question of fact.[25] A clear case is where the security is an interest in an entity that is bankrupt and liquidates, providing only returns to debt holders. If a security is formally abandoned, a valuation concluding that the security has no value may be needed to counter an IRS argument

---

22. *See, e.g.*, Thor Power Tool Co. v. Comm'r, 439 U.S. 522 (1979).

23. One such tax question that comes up is "what is the correct basis in the security or asset that is considered abandoned or worthless?"

24. For purposes of the worthlessness deduction, a security is defined (in I.R.C. § 165(g)(2)) as (1) bonds, debentures, notes, or certificates, or other evidence of indebtedness issued by a corporation (including those issued by a government or its political subdivision), with interest coupons or in registered form; (2) a share of stock in a corporation; or (3) a right to subscribe for, or to receive, a share of stock in a corporation.

25. The courts generally consider a security to be worthless where the investor has no reasonable possibility of receiving anything of value (*see, e.g.*, Drachman, 23 T.C. 558 (1954)). Typically, no deduction is allowed for partial losses, even if permanent.

that the security had positive value, but the taxpayer abandoned the security because the tax benefit from abandoning was greater than the value of the security itself. The tax benefit from abandoning might be greater because abandonment generates an ordinary loss while a loss on sale generates a capital loss. Shareholders, especially corporations, often receive little or no tax benefit from capital losses.

However, there are other circumstances where the worthlessness of the security is not so evident. The burden of proof is on the taxpayer to show that the security became worthless during the tax year in question. As such, it may be important for the taxpayer to present evidence that the security became worthless; one element of evidence may be a valuation or other economic evidence of worthlessness.

Under I.R.C. § 1255 investors in qualifying small business stock are permitted to claim an ordinary loss (rather than a capital loss) on the disposition (including worthlessness) of such stock. These losses are also allowed in computing an individual's net operating loss without being limited by nonbusiness income. The ordinary loss is limited to $50,000 per year ($100,000 if a joint return is filed), with the excess being treated as a capital loss.

Abandoned Property

While the tax law creates a fictional sale or exchange for worthless securities, it takes a different approach for abandoned property. When worthless property (other than stocks and securities) is abandoned (e.g., a vacant, former manufacturing plant), the abandonment is not considered a sale or exchange. Consequently, any loss arising from an abandonment is treated as an ordinary loss rather than a capital loss—a much more favorable tax result. However, the loss is deductible only if the taxpayer can demonstrate that the property has been truly abandoned and not simply taken out of service temporarily.

Valuation Aspects of I.R.C. § 165

Businesses that own worthless assets or worthless security interests should consider the possibility of taking an abandoned asset or worthless security loss deduction under I.R.C. § 165. Particularly as businesses generate taxable income, this deduction would give rise to either current or future income tax benefits. The federal income tax rules for taking the loss deduction vary depending on the type of nondepreciable business asset (e.g., acquisition of exclusive rights for the remainder of the copyright term to a script for use in producing a motion picture) or security interest involved and the taxpayer's actions.

Calculation of the loss is driven by the taxpayer's adjusted basis in the asset. The taxpayer "shall be allowed as a deduction any loss sustained during the taxable year and not compensated for by insurance or otherwise."[26] The amount of the loss equals the adjusted basis of the property calculated under I.R.C. § 1011, as if the asset had been sold or exchanged at a loss. However, the amount of the loss must be adjusted for any salvage value or for compensation received. If the loss arises from a capital asset, I.R.C. §§ 1211 and 1212 (relating to the capital loss limitation and carryover) restrict the deductibility of the loss.

---

26. I.R.C. § 165(a) Losses.

A loss deduction under I.R.C. § 165 is not permitted if the loss results from an actual sale or exchange of the worthless or abandoned property.[27] In addition, to claim an abandonment or worthless net loss incurred by an individual, it must have been incurred in a trade or business, in a transaction entered into for profit, or from an event classified as a casualty or theft. Whether or not an asset is used in a trade or business is a factual examination and has been the subject of much tax litigation.

The worthlessness or abandonment loss is deductible in the year sustained. However, it cannot be deducted if there is a reasonable prospect of recovery. The possibility of recovery is a question of fact that must be determined by the circumstances involved.

Abandonment Loss for Nondepreciable Business Assets

The loss in nondepreciable business assets is deductible when "evidenced by closed and completed transactions and as fixed by identifiable events occurring in such taxable year."[28]

The deduction of a loss is permitted for "the sudden termination of the usefulness in such business or transaction of any nondepreciable property, in a case where such business or transaction is discontinued or when such property is permanently discarded from use therein . . . ."[29]

Accordingly, an abandonment loss on nondepreciable business assets (other than securities) is deductible, even though the assets may not be worthless. The criteria for establishing an abandonment loss for nondepreciable business assets—in cases other than worthlessness—are:

1. The occurrence of a closed and completed transaction coupled with the termination of the asset's usefulness
2. The discontinuance of the use of the asset
3. The discontinuation of the business

An event that meets either of the last two conditions qualifies as the abandonment of the asset. For a taxpayer to claim an abandonment loss for a business asset, there must be the intent to abandon plus an actual act designed to accomplish that intent. The actual proof of an asset's abandonment will be determined based on the facts and circumstances of the event.

The deductibility of an abandoned nondepreciable asset is effective when the taxpayer discontinues the use of the asset or the business in which the asset is used.[30]

Worthless Stock Deduction

I.R.C. § 165(g) allows a deduction for the loss sustained by a taxpayer resulting from the worthlessness of a security. For there to be a deduction without a sale, the security must be worthless and, therefore, unsalable. A valuation analysis supporting the worthlessness of the security may be required to substantiate the deduction and is often recommended even if the asset is unsalable. The loss deduction must be taken only for the year in which the security becomes completely worthless. However, it cannot be deducted if

27. Though this may trigger a loss under other provisions of the I.R.C., such as § 1001.
28. Regulation § 1.165-1(b) and (d).
29. *Id.* § 1.165-2(a).
30. *Id.*

there is a reasonable prospect of recovery. The possibility of recovery is a question of fact that must be determined by the circumstances involved.[31] A partial worthlessness of a security caused simply by a drop in value in the market price is not deductible until the taxpayer has sold the security. If the security is a capital asset, the loss is a capital loss. To determine if the capital loss is treated as long-term or short-term, the taxpayer is considered to have held the worthless stock or security until the last day of the year in which it became worthless.[32]

The determination of worthlessness is a question of fact. In one case, the IRS urged a finding that stock did not become worthless in the year chosen by the taxpayer for want of an *identifiable event*, such as appointment of a receiver, cessation of normal business operations, bankruptcy, or liquidation. The Tax Court held that exceptional circumstances—that is, the lack of liquidating value and potential operating value—justified the taxpayer's choice.[33]

A taxpayer's deduction for a loss sustained on a worthless security is based on his or her adjusted basis in the security. A cash-method taxpayer may deduct, for worthless stock purchased on the installment basis and not entirely paid for, only the amount paid up to the close of the tax year. A corporate taxpayer will have a loss equal to the adjusted basis in the stock of affiliated corporation.

Worthless Securities in Affiliated Corporations

The basic rule for worthless securities is modified for a corporate taxpayer's investment in the securities of an affiliated corporation. If securities of an affiliated corporation become worthless, then the loss is treated as an ordinary loss and the limitations that normally apply if the loss were a capital loss are avoided.[34]

A corporation is considered affiliated with a parent corporation if the parent owns at least 80% of the voting power of all classes of stock and at least 80% of each class of nonvoting stock of the affiliated corporation. In addition, to be treated as an affiliated corporation for purposes of the worthless security provisions, the worthless affiliated corporation must have been truly an operating company. This test is met if the corporation has less than 10% of the aggregate of its gross receipts from passive sources such as rents, royalties, dividends, annuities, and gains from sales or exchanges of stock and securities. This condition prohibits ordinary loss treatment for what are really investments.

Also, the decision of whether stock in an affiliated corporation is worthless can be made at the time a deemed tax liquidation is caused by a check the box election that creates the identified event. In this case, worthlessness can be determined by the fair market value of the subsidiary's assets (including goodwill and going-concern value[35]) being less than the outstanding liabilities that may be considered for tax purposes. As such, the assets of the worthless subsidiary may not have been abandoned or sold and

31. *See, e.g.*, *Appendix 17A, Cost of Capital and the Valuation of Worthless Stock*, *in* Shannon P. Pratt & Roger J. Grabowski, Cost of Capital: Applications and Examples (5th ed. 2014).

32. I.R.C. § 1.165–5.

33. *See* Steadman v. Comm'r, 424 F.2d 1 (6th Cir. 1970), *cert. denied*, 400 U.S. 869 (1970).

34. I.R.C. § 165(g)(3).

35. *See* Chapter 12 for a discussion of goodwill and Chapter 1 for a discussion of going-concern value.

in continued use, so the fair market value of all the assets must be estimated through an appraisal to support the deduction.[36]

CORPORATE DISTRIBUTION OF APPRECIATED PROPERTY TO SHAREHOLDERS

When a corporation distributes property, how should the fair market value of the property be valued? That was the issue in one decision.[37] In this case, the specific issue involved an I.R.C. § 311 distribution (corporate distribution of appreciated property to shareholders).

A corporation contributed appreciated property to a limited partnership controlled through a group of conduit entities by the corporation's shareholders and then the partnership distributed partnership interests to the corporation's shareholders.

The IRS contended that the fair market value should be calculated as if the entire property had been sold by the corporation on the date of distribution with no reference to the interest received by each shareholder, while the taxpayer argued that the value of the interests should be the aggregate of all the individual partnership units. The Tax Court viewed the issue as being one of what property is to be valued: the entire property interest or the fractional interests received by the shareholders.

The Tax Court held that the appropriate perspective is from that of the corporation, and the property should be valued as if the distributing corporation had sold the entire interest in the property on the date of the distribution.

The Ninth Circuit upheld the Tax Court decision and stated that the determination of value of the distributed property in the hands of the distributing corporation does not imply noncontrolling interest discounts (although such discounts may be appropriate in valuing what was received).

A corporate distribution of appreciated property is taxed twice, once to the corporation and again to the receiving shareholders. While the aggregate fair market value determines the gain to the distributing corporation, the fair market value of individual interests received by each shareholder, determined with appropriate discounts, is commonly believed to be the appropriate fair market value to determine the second tax to the shareholder.

Therefore, when a corporation distributes property, the fair market value of the property must be valued based on the aggregate fair market value of the property being distributed held by that corporation or affiliates. That is, the property under common control must be aggregated when determining its fair market value.[38]

In cases where the property distributed by a corporation to its shareholders is a large stock holding of a public company, a blockage discount may be warranted in estimating

---

36. Typically, where a worthless stock deduction is being taken due to an interest in a subsidiary, the tax dispute revolves around the estimate of fair market value of the subsidiary's assets. As such, it is important for the appraiser to consider not only the value as part of the business but also value as if sold, including assets that have yet to be commercialized or monetized that may have value.

37. Pope & Talbot, Inc. v. Comm'r, 104 T.C. 574 (1995), *aff'd*, 162 F.3d 1236 (9th Cir. 1999).

38. Aggregation of interests was also an issue addressed in two estate tax cases: Ahmanson Found. v. United States, 674 F.2d 761,769 (9th Cir. 1981); and Est. of Curry v. United States, 706 F.2d 1424 (7th Cir. 1983).

the fair market value (discussed in Chapter 18). Regardless of whether the distribution occurs in a liquidation or in a nonliquidating context (e.g., a dividend), the I.R.C. provides that the distributing corporation recognizes gain as if the property were sold at its fair market value.[39] Where the property distributed is a block of shares in another corporation, there could be a disparity between the amount considered by each shareholder, on the one hand, and the distributing corporation, on the other, because while any particular shareholder receives a relatively small number of shares that can be sold at the prevailing market price without impacting the price, the corporation likely could not.

The Regulations acknowledge that "the size of the block of stock to be valued in relation to the number of shares changing hands in sales may be relevant in determining whether selling prices reflect the fair market value of the block of stock to be valued."[40] There is quite a lot of case law determining, in various factual situations, the amount of discount properly applied to a block of stock against the normal trading price of the stock.

VALUATION ASPECTS OF INTERCOMPANY TRANSFER PRICING

As part of an intercompany transfer, an explicit or implicit price is used to value the goods, services, or resources exchanged in the transaction. Because this transfer price is agreed upon by two related parties, market forces may not have as much influence as in transactions between unrelated parties. Therefore, there is a risk that an intercompany price could differ from that which would be established by two independent parties engaged in an arm's-length exchange. Thus, the goal of transfer pricing analyses is to estimate a price that would be utilized by unrelated parties for the same goods, assets, or services.

As a result of the intercompany transaction, the revenue or expenses and, therefore, the taxable income of each related party is affected by the magnitude of the transfer price. Absent a regulatory restriction, a multinational company could set its transfer prices to shift income between taxing jurisdictions to take advantage of differences in income tax rates.

I.R.C. § 482 authorizes the Secretary of the Treasury to allocate income, deductions, and other tax items among related taxpayers to prevent the evasion of taxes or to clearly reflect income. The Tax Reform Act of 1986 amended § 482 by providing that the income from a transfer or license of intangible property must be *commensurate with the income* (CWI) attributable to the intangible. Similarly, at the end of 2017, the U.S. Congress passed the TCJA which added new considerations for intercompany services payments (the BEAT, base erosion and anti-abuse tax) and foreign income levels, particularly those associated with intangible income in low-tax jurisdictions (GILTI, global intangible low-taxed income).

Because transfer pricing involves other taxing jurisdictions, one should be aware of the Organization for Economic Co-operation and Development (OECD) international transfer pricing guidelines, aptly called the OECD Guidelines, including relevant

39. I.R.C. §§ 311(b), 336(a).
40. Treas. Reg. § 20.2031-2(e).

guidance on the Application of the Approach to Hard-to-Value Intangibles (HTVI), which include provisions allowing for ex post adjustments similar to those envisioned by CWI.

U.S. transfer pricing guidance remains among the most voluminous and comprehensive in the world. In July 1994, the IRS issued the final regulations on the intercompany pricing of both tangible and intangible property under § 482. Those Regulations codify the *arm's-length standard* (that is, pricing intercompany transactions as if they were conducted at arm's length) as the basis for intercompany pricing involving U.S. taxpayers. Since 1994, Regulations have expanded to include rules related to cost-sharing arrangements (agreements to attribute proportional shares of costs related to developing of intangible property based on their anticipated benefits to be derived from the property), intercompany services, and global financial dealing.

The following section briefly outlines the arm's-length principle and transfer pricing guidance of the final § 482 Regulations and OECD Guidelines, and discusses the prescribed methods for analyzing transfer prices involving both tangible and intangible assets.

The Arm's-Length Principle

The final 1994 transfer pricing regulations elaborate on the issue that may arise when a company transacts with an affiliate on terms that are not at *arm's length*. The construction of *true taxable income* remains the fundamental remedy of § 482. According to the final regulations, true taxable income is a condition that exists when a controlled taxpayer reports financial results that are consistent with the results that an uncontrolled taxpayer would have attained under comparable circumstances.

The 1994 regulations provide that, "if necessary to reflect an arm's length result, a controlled taxpayer may report . . . the results of its controlled transactions based upon prices different from those actually charged."[41] Likewise, the IRS has the right to assert adjustments to intercompany transactions to more properly reflect the arm's-length standard.[42]

Transfer Pricing Guidance

The arm's-length results are established by using methods determined under the *best method rule* in § 482. Rather than being the most accurate measure, the best method under the final IRS regulations provides the most reliable measure of an arm's-length result. As such, there is not strict preferential hierarchy among the methods presented. Both the OECD Guidelines and § 482 Regulations specify the various methods a taxpayer can utilize when producing measures of arm's-lengths results. These methods can be divided into two categories: transactional methods and profit-based methods. Transactional methods compare the actual price paid in a controlled transaction to prices paid in comparable uncontrolled transactions, and profit-based methods compare the profit

41. Regulation § 1.482-1(a)(3).

42. Two recent transfer pricing decisions that are instructive are Medtronic, Inc. & Consolidated Subsidiaries v. Comm'r, T.C. Memo. 2016-112 (June 9, 2016) (8th Cir., Aug. 18, 2016); and Coca Cola v. Comm'r, T.C. No. 31183-15 was decided on November 18, 2020.

levels of the parties involved in the related party transaction to those of parties in uncontrolled transactions.

Under § 482, the series of factors to be considered in searching for the most reliable method under the arm's-length standard of transfer pricing are (1) the particular facts and circumstances of the transaction, (2) the completeness and accuracy of available data, and (3) the degree of comparability between controlled and uncontrolled transactions.

The Regulations include factors to determine comparability. All factors that could affect a financial result are to be taken into account. The factors to be considered in determining comparability include:

1. **Functional analysis.** An analysis of the economically significant activities of the controlled entity and the uncontrolled entity to which it is being compared must be undertaken (including research and development, manufacturing, marketing, distribution, and managerial functions). For the two transactions (i.e., the controlled and the uncontrolled) to be comparable, the entities should perform similar economic functions with respect to those transactions.
2. **Contractual terms.** To be considered comparable, an uncontrolled transaction must have similar significant contractual terms as that of the controlled transaction.
3. **Risk analysis.** The risks borne by each party in the controlled and uncontrolled transactions must be analyzed, including market risks, research and development, financial risks, product liability risks, and general business risks. The economic substance of transactions will be reviewed by the IRS to determine relevant risks.
4. **Economic conditions.** The economic conditions surrounding the transactions must be similar and must consider factors such as (1) alternatives realistically available to the buyer and seller (e.g., make versus buy); (2) the similarity of the geographic markets; (3) the relative size of each market and the extent of economic development; and (4) the level of the market, market share for items transferred, location specific costs, and competition in the market.
5. **Property or services.** The property or services transferred in the controlled transaction (including embedded intangible property or services being transferred) must be substantially similar to those in the uncontrolled transaction.

Intangible Transfers and Valuation Approaches

The preceding guidance applies to transactions of both tangible and intangible property, yet distinctions between the two types of transfers are evident in the Regulations and OECD Guidelines. Intercompany intangible transfers have become increasingly common, and both the § 482 Regulations and OECD Guidelines have been expanded to provide proper guidance on valuation approach and method.

As defined by the § 482 Regulations, intangibles have substantial value independent of the services of any individual and are comprised of patents, inventions, copyrights, trademarks, franchises, licenses, procedures, and other similar items.[43] Additions to the regulations have expanded the definition of compensable intangibles to include such items as foreign goodwill and going-concern value in some cases. The TCJA further

43. Regulation § 1.482-4(b).

expanded the definition of intangibles to include "any other item the value or potential value of which is not attributable to tangible property or the services of any individual."[44]

The HTVI Guidance specifies that a hard-to-value intangible is one for which no reliable comparable exists and for which projections of future cash flows or income expected to be derived from the transferred intangible, or the assumptions used in valuing the intangible, are highly uncertain.[45]

The three widely accepted approaches for valuing intangible assets (i.e., the income, market, and asset-based (cost) approaches) are generally used in transfer pricing analyses but are given different names. The income and market approaches are utilized most often in transfer pricing analyses. The cost approach is sometimes chosen as the selected method in very early-stage intangibles and/or if the relative intangible development costs are a reasonable proxy for the relative value of contributions by each related entity when applying the Residual Profit Split Method or in cost-sharing analyses.

A well-known transfer pricing valuation method introduced in § 482 is a transaction-based method known as the *Comparable Uncontrolled Transaction* (CUT) method (under OECD Guidelines known as *Comparable Uncontrolled Price* (CUP) method). The CUP/CUT method shares characteristics with the market approach, as value of the controlled transaction is determined by market prices from comparable uncontrolled transactions. For example, the license of intangible property from one related party to another can be benchmarked against a comparable license between two third parties.

Other methods used for transfer pricing valuation purposes fall into the category of profit-based methods. One such method is the *Comparable Profits Method* (CPM) (under OECD Guidelines known as the *Transactional Net Margin Method* (TNMM)). This method utilizes income levels of uncontrolled parties that engage in broadly similar businesses as the controlled entity as a benchmark for the controlled entity's profits. The *Profit Split Method* analyzes the split of profits between uncontrolled parties to a transaction as a baseline for splitting profits between related parties.

The CPM/TNMM establishes arm's-length pricing for intangible transactions (i.e., licenses) when the licensee is determined to be undertaking routine functions that can be benchmarked using comparable companies. The arm's-length price for the intangible license in this circumstance is set so that, after payment for the intangibles, the license expects to earn the benchmarked rate of return.

The revised cost-sharing regulations that became effective in 2009 codified the income method, which compares the status quo to the next best alternative for a controlled taxpayer. Though this method may incorporate the CUP/CUT method or the CPM/TNMM method, it is included as an unspecified method for pricing intangibles in both the § 482 Regulations and OECD Guidelines outside of a cost-sharing context. Other specified methods outlined by the IRS in the cost-sharing rules to value intangible contributions made in association with a cost sharing arrangement include the *Acquisition Price Method* and *Market Capitalization Method*.

The TCJA codified two important principles related to valuations of intercompany transfers of intangibles if they are considered to provide a more reliable means to determine value. The first just mentioned is that the valuation may be based on the realistic

44. I.R.C. § 367(d)(4)(G).
45. HTVI Guidance, § 2.18.

alternative to the transfer, such as the value of licensing versus sale. Second, the valuation may be made on an aggregate basis, particularly if the intangible is used with other tangible property, intangible property, or services. If so, an allocation of the value to the intangible assets transferred may be appropriate. One example is when the intangible is part of a network such as a delivery or service business where the intangibles on their own may have limited value but are very valuable as part of the network.

Differences in Intangible Pricing for Transfer Pricing and Financial Reporting

Compliance with the arm's-length standard as two known related parties execute a transaction may cause intangible prices for transfer pricing valuations to deviate from values established for financial reporting purposes.

Intangible pricing for transfer pricing purposes will ultimately be used in income tax matters to determine pretax prices for controlled transactions. Unlike fair values calculated for financial reporting purposes, intangible values priced under the arm's-length standard will be calculated from the perspective of the controlled parties, given their specific characteristics. Thus, transfer pricing experts can look beyond a hypothetical market transaction between market participants and utilize the facts of the actual controlled transaction when calculating the price of an intangible.

Additionally, while valuations for financial reporting purposes tend to focus on a single asset, transfer pricing analyses typically value a bundle of assets. This bundle frequently encompasses assets with varying economic lifespans, including long-lived intangible assets such as platform intangible property (i.e., any resources, capability, or right that a controlled participant has developed, maintained, or acquired externally that will contribute to the future intangible development activity), business assets, and other broadly defined assets. Because transfer pricing analyses value these inclusive asset bundles, the economic life of the bundle, ceteris paribus, is lengthened, possibly to an indefinite end.

It is important to understand that financial reporting often includes values that are associated with intangible property in goodwill. This could include, for instance, value attributable to the rights to continue to invest in identified intangibles as well as the value of buyer-specific synergies driven in whole or in part by the identified intangibles. For transfer pricing purposes, such value is often appropriately included in the determination of the arm's-length price of an intangible asset.

Therefore, intangible pricing for transfer pricing may result in a higher value than if it was determined for financial reporting due to three key differences between the two purposes.

First, buyer-specific synergies may be included in the value under transfer pricing but would typically not be included in the value under financial reporting. For financial reporting purposes, such synergies are reflected in the residual goodwill value to the extent that they were paid for. Since goodwill is excluded from the value of specified assets in a financial reporting context, the aforementioned synergies would rarely manifest in the reported financial price of any specific class of intangible property asset. However, buyer-specific synergies may be included in the arm's-length price to the extent that they affect the overall arm's-length outcome, as goodwill is included in the transfer pricing value. This could cause the value to rise, as the intercompany-defined synergies raise the price.

Second, for financial reporting purposes, existing technology is valued as a wasting asset as it exists at the date of acquisition. But, because of the indefinite economic life of asset bundles and legal entities, the potential future developments from existing technology and related goodwill are taken into consideration when valuing under transfer pricing. Again, this allows for the potential for a higher value under transfer pricing purposes, as the technology becomes more valuable the longer it can work.

Third, transfer pricing valuations differ in the perspective they are valuing from, therefore altering the tax implications, and leading to a higher value found under transfer pricing. Values found for financial reporting purposes are typically on a post-tax basis since the tax implications for the market buyer are considered. For transfer pricing purposes in the United States, § 482 stipulates valuations be made from the perspective of the known seller, therefore creating a pretax valuation. This contributes to a higher value for transfer pricing purposes since the value equation includes an extra argument: future taxes. In practice, transfer pricing in the United States often uses a pretax set of profits discounted by a post-tax discount rate (cost of capital).

Interaction of Transfer Pricing and Legal Entity Valuation

As established, intangible valuations for transfer pricing are distinct as they may look at a bundle of assets or at an entire legal entity as opposed to individual assets. Transfer pricing plays a key role in most legal entity valuations where the legal entity is controlled by a common parent entity because the subject legal entity often has transactions with related entities that are subject to transfer pricing.

Transfer pricing has different assumptions for valuing components of a valuation performed for other purposes, and these differences can affect the final value. For example, for financial statement reporting purposes, legal entity valuations assume the aggregate value of customer relationship, while transfer pricing disaggregates the value between *entrepreneurial returns* and routine *distributor returns*. This is especially important when assuming technology is a primary driver of value, as the method of disaggregating entrepreneur and distributor returns that transfer pricing specialists utilize should be used when valuing customer relationships.

Pricing of Intercompany Debt

The IRS (through Chief Counsel) in late 2023 issued a legal advice memorandum on a transfer pricing issue with respect to intercompany loans.[46] The IRS concluded that if an unrelated lender would consider group membership in establishing financing terms available to a borrower (i.e., implicit support, that is, the fact that if the borrower were unable to pay, the group might step in to help, even without a contractual promise to do so) even in the absence of a formal guarantee, then the IRS may adjust the interest rate in a controlled lending transaction to reflect the implicit support.

SUMMARY

An understanding of valuations for federal tax purposes is important because of the extensive case law, Revenue Rulings, and other literature. Valuation principles, standard of value, and decisions for tax purposes often are cited in valuation reports and court decisions.

46. Office of Chief Counsel, Internal Revenue Service, AM 2023-008, December 29, 2023.

REFERENCES FOR VALUATIONS FOR FEDERAL INCOME TAX MATTERS

Articles and Books

Bogdanski, John. 2023. *WG&L Federal Tax Valuation* (Carrollton, TX: Thomson Reuters). Annual plus two yearly updates. Includes thousands of case citations with discussions.

Kasper, Larry J. 1997. "Federal Tax Valuations." In *Business Valuations, Advanced Topics*, 211–58 (Westport, CN: Greenwood Publishing).

Pratt, Shannon P. and ASA Educational Foundation. 2022. "Valuation for Income Tax Purposes." In *Shannon Pratt's Valuing a Business: The Analysis and Appraisal of Closely held Businesses*, 6th ed., Chap. 37, 835–64 (New York: McGraw-Hill).

Saltzman, Michael J. 2023. *IRS Practice and Procedure* (Carrollton, TX: Thomson Reuters). Annual plus three yearly updates. Covers the complete range of IRS procedures from rulings to collection of taxes.

Website

www.ustaxcourt.gov contains all appealable Tax Court opinions from January 3, 1999, to the present.

CHAPTER 22

Marital Dissolution Valuations

Jay E. Fishman, FASA, FRICS and Kenneth J. Pia, Jr., ASA, CPA/ABV, MCBA

INTRODUCTION

In this chapter you will learn about:

- Standards of value when appraising businesses and business interests in marital dissolution matters
- Considerations in selecting the premise of value
- Treatment of appreciation during marriage—active versus passive
- Valuation date considerations
- Treatment of goodwill as a marital asset
- Impact of buy-sell agreements
- Treatment of covenants not to compete
- Consideration of noncontrolling (minority) interests and lack of marketability discounts
- Treatment of trapped-in capital gains taxes
- Adequacy of evidence
- Access to records
- "Double-dipping"

While business valuations in the context of litigation are performed for many reasons, court guidance on how valuations should be performed is least settled in the area of marital dissolution. This is especially true in terms of the application of different acceptable methodologies from one state to another; however, there can also be inconsistencies across counties within the same state. Even when there is general agreement on broad approaches and their usage, the courts often take contradictory positions on certain issues. One will observe that, in these matters, trial courts have a very high degree of discretion, into which appellate courts are reluctant to intrude.

This chapter is not intended to provide appraisal guidance for any particular state but rather is intended to provide an overview of the business valuation issues arising in marital dissolution matters and to provide a sampling of how various states have treated these issues. A lawyer requiring a business valuation in a marital dissolution matter should ensure that the business appraiser possesses sufficient knowledge of relevant case law, an understanding of its impacts on an appraisal, and the ability to support his or her opinions on cross-examination. As will be presented in this chapter, states borrow widely from decisions in other states in ruling on valuation issues. Therefore, relevant case law may be found in states other than the state in which the case will be tried.

STANDARD OF VALUE FOR MARITAL DISSOLUTIONS[1]

One of the prevalent differences among jurisdictions in valuing businesses or professional practices for marital dissolution purposes is the appropriate standard of value. "Standard of value" is accorded the definition of value as discussed in Chapter 1.

There can be many definitions of value, and interpretations of those definitions. Unfortunately, in many states, the standard of value for marital dissolution purposes may not be clearly defined, leaving room for interpretation. The lack of clear definitions, and accompanying interpretations, challenges appraisers and lawyers to assist the courts in creating sound precedential case law that may clear up much of the existing ambiguity.

Some family law courts use a *fair value* standard of value that can be inferred from the language and rulings in the case law. When this standard is used, usually it is not intended to be synonymous with "fair value" as used in dissenting stockholder actions or financial reporting, although some marital dissolution decisions have expressly referenced the fair value standard applicable to shareholder oppression and appraisal actions.[2] Rather, it generally means something akin to the "fair market value" standard, with some modification(s). Characteristic traits of fair value cases include the fact that property distributions are typically made on a pro rata share of enterprise value,[3] and there are no "shareholder level" discounts, such as discounts for lack of marketability or lack of control. Under this standard, some element of goodwill may be included, a case may emphasize that the spouses are unwilling sellers (or buyers),[4] or a case may require that the distribution of assets must be "fair."

Certain states, including Connecticut, Florida, Hawaii, Illinois, Missouri, Pennsylvania, South Carolina, Texas, and Wisconsin, adhere strictly to the standard of *fair market value*.[5] Other states, such as Arkansas,[6] Illinois,[7] and Louisiana,[8] mandate this standard by statute. When the mandated standard of value is *fair market value*, it is generally accepted in the business valuation profession that the application is as detailed in Internal Revenue Service (IRS) Revenue Rulings 59-60 and 65-192.

The concept of *value to the holder (owner)* is another standard adhered to by certain states, reflecting special circumstances or characteristics that make the property more valuable to the owner than to another holder. Although courts are not consistent in their naming of this type of value, both business appraisers and real estate appraisers typically

---

1. For a thorough discussion of standards of value for marital dissolution purposes *see* Chapter 5, *in* JAY E. FISHMAN, SHANNON P. PRATT, & WILLIAM J. MORRISON, STANDARDS OF VALUE: THEORY AND APPLICATIONS 237–322 (2d ed. 2013).

2. *See, e.g.*, Brown v. Brown, 792 A.2d 463, 2002 N.J. Super. LEXIS 105 (N.J. App. Div. 2002); Piscopo v. Piscopo, 557 A.2d 1040 (N.J. Super. 1989) (indicating that since both shareholder oppression and marital dissolution cases are brought in equity, it would be unreasonable to treat them differently).

3. *See, e.g.*, Bobrow v. Bobrow, State of Indiana, Hamilton Superior Court Cause No. 29D01- 0003-DR-166; Howell v. Howell, 1998 WL 972312 (Va. Cir. Ct. Sept. 4, 1998), *aff'd*, 523 S.E.2d 514 (Va. Ct. App. 2000).

4. Ellington v. Ellington, 842 So. 2d 1160 (La. Ct. App. 2003).

5. The price at which the property would change hands between well-informed, willing buyers and sellers on an arm's-length basis.

6. A.C.A. § 9-12-315(4) (2008).

7. 750 ILCS 5 (Illinois Marriage and Dissolution Act).

8. LA. REV. STAT. § 9:2801-(1)(a) (2008).

classify it as investment value.[9] States that have accepted an investment value standard of value include Arizona, California, Colorado, Kentucky, Michigan, Montana, Nevada, New Mexico, New York, North Carolina, and Washington (however, such use has not necessarily precluded the application of other standards in these states). Due to this standard's reliance on the special circumstances or characteristics of a particular owner, this value tends to be higher than the value to other investors or the value determined under a different standard of value. The rationale under an investment value posits that, if a sale is not imminent, the value upon a sale is irrelevant.

Some states, like Virginia, in relevant court decisions[10] refer to the standard of value as "intrinsic value" but the meaning in practice is more akin to investment value or fair value.

The court, the lawyer, and the appraiser should all be aware that a case decision citing to the use of any applicable standard of value, including *fair market value*, may actually take a position contrary to that of fair market value as defined in Chapter 1 and in Tax Court case law (see Chapters 20 and 21 as to interpretations of the definition).

If the applicable standard of value is fair market value, then goodwill could be a marital asset, but consideration could also only be given to the extent that the goodwill is transferable. Furthermore, if a state's precedent disallows proceeds from future activities of the spouse (or restrictions on future activities) to be subject to property division, then goodwill should have to be transferable without requiring either an employment agreement or a noncompete agreement in order for it to be includible as a marital asset. In other words, the expert needs to consider the existence of personal goodwill and whether or not it could be, and is permitted to be, considered a marital asset.

Typical of language among states using the fair market value standard is the following:

> When dividing and distributing the value of the property of the parties in a divorce case, the relevant value is, as a general rule, the fair market value (FMV) of the parties' interest therein on the relevant date. FMV is defined as being the amount at which an item would change hands from a willing seller to a willing buyer, neither being under any compulsion to buy or sell and both having reasonable knowledge of the relevant facts.
>
> We disagree with the position advanced by Wife, and In re *Marriage of Fleege*, 91 Wash. 2d 324, 588 P.2d 1136 (1979), that the relevant value of a sole professional business is its value to the professional who operates it. Other assets are, as a general rule, valued at their FMV. We know of no valid reason why sole professional businesses should not be valued at their FMVs.[11]

---

9. *See, e.g.*, Golden v. Golden, 270 Cal. App. 2d 401, 1969 Cal. App. LEXIS 1538 (Cal. Ct. App. 1969) (in a community property state, the spouse's contribution to the intangible value of the other spouse's business is treated as an investment in stock).

10. Howell v. Howell, 31 Va. App. 332, 523 S.E. 2d 514 (2000) and Bosserman v. Bosserman, 9 Va. App. 1, 5, 384 S.E.2d 104, (1989).

11. Antolik v. Harvey, 761 P.2d 305 (Haw. Ct. App. 1988).

PREMISE OF VALUE

The premise of value is predicated on whether the business should be valued on a going-concern basis or on a liquidation basis (as defined in Chapter 2). In *Sommers*,[12] the wife's expert valued the husband's orthodontic practice on a going-concern basis, while the husband's expert used a liquidation value. The trial court accepted the valuation proffered by the husband's expert, but on appeal, the North Dakota Supreme Court reversed, finding as support no evidence that the husband intended to sell the practice. In *Bausano*,[13] the husband's expert claimed liquidation value was the appropriate premise of value because the company had operated at a loss in recent years. The court rejected this approach and found the valuation of the wife's expert more credible because it used replacement value and valued the business as a going concern. The court found that the business had potential, especially since the husband indicated he planned to focus his efforts on the business once the divorce was final. In *Hoverson*,[14] the court rejected liquidation value in valuing a farm that had losses of approximately $1 million, finding that the assets had value to the farm as long as the farm continued in business. The court indicated that the business had to be valued as a going concern despite its current financial condition.

The preceding cases illustrate an important point concerning the premise of value in that courts could be reluctant to adopt a liquidation value premise unless a sale or liquidation is contemplated. A second consideration relating to application of a liquidation value premise is that it should only apply to a controlling owner, as minority interest owners cannot compel a sale or liquidation.

APPRECIATION—ACTIVE VERSUS PASSIVE

States are split on whether the appreciation in value of a premarital asset represents a marital asset or not. Of the states that consider such appreciation to be a marital asset, some hold that its classification as marital is dependent on whether the increase resulted from the passive growth of the business (in which case it would be classified as separate property) or from an individual's active participation[15] or active efforts[16] (in which cases it would be classified as marital property). It is not always clear whether appreciation has resulted from "active" efforts or merely passive market forces. Some courts have held that the party seeking to characterize appreciation as "active" must prove that marital efforts resulted in the appreciation.[17]

---

12. Sommers v. Sommers, 660 N.W.2d 586, 2003 N.D. 77 (2003).
13. Bausano v. Bausano, 632 N.W.2d 123, 246 Wis. 2d 987 (Wis. Ct. App. 2001).
14. Hoverson v. Hoverson, 629 N.W.2d 573, 2001 N.D. 124 (2001).
15. *See, e.g.*, Baum v. Baum, 584 P.2d 604 (Ariz. Ct. App. 1978).
16. *See, e.g.*, Brown v. Brown, 913 S.W.2d 163 (Tenn. Ct. App. 1994).
17. In Conway v. Conway, 1998 WL 865157 (N.C. Ct. App. 1998), the court ruled that to demonstrate active appreciation of separate property, there must be a showing of the value of the asset at the time of the acquisition; value of the asset at the time of separation; and the difference between the two values. Applying these criteria, the court determined that whereas marital efforts had led to the acquisition of a medical license, it did not result in the appreciation of the license's value. In Deffenbaugh v. Deffenbaugh, 877 S.W.2d 186 (Mo. Ct. App. 1994), the Missouri court held that where the husband failed to prove that his acumen and effort contributed to the appreciation in the wife's separate mutual fund shares, the appreciation was nonmarital property.

VALUATION DATE

The date of valuation may differ depending on the jurisdiction in which the marital dissolution action is brought or the asset's classification as active or passive. Some courts use the date of trial as the valuation date.[18] Other courts use a date as near as possible to the final divorce decree or date of dissolution.[19] The valuation date in some states is the date on which the complaint was filed.[20] Certain courts utilize the date of separation.[21] In certain jurisdictions, trial courts may exercise discretion in determining the appropriate valuation date(s),[22] which may also be different depending on the classification of each asset.[23]

The valuation date for certain assets may also be set by the parties, if they agree to a cut-off date. Where the valuation date is not set by statute or case precedent, agreed upon by the parties, or declared by the court, the valuation expert may need to be prepared to opine to a value as of two or more valuation dates.

---

18. *See, e.g.*, Hargrave v. Hargrave, 209 Cal. Rptr. 764, 769 (Cal. Ct. App. 1985); Aufmuth v. Aufmuth, 152 Cal. Rptr. 668, 670 (Cal. Ct. App. 1979); Moffitt v. Moffitt, 813 P.2d 674, 678 (Alaska 1991); Ogard v. Ogard, 808 P.2d 815, 818–19 (Alaska 1991); Taylor v. Taylor, 736 S.W.2d 388, 391 (Mo. 1987); Butler v. Butler, No. 82077, 1998 WL 933354, at *2 (N.Y. App. Div. Dec. 30, 1998).

19. For example, *In re* Marriage of Olinger, 707 P.2d 64, 68 (Or. Ct. App. 1985); Koch v. Koch, 874 S.W.2d 571, 576 (Tenn. Ct. App. 1993); Wilson v. Wilson, 741 S.W.2d 640, 643 (Ark. 1987); *In re* Marriage of Talty, 623 N.E.2d 1041, 1046 (Ill. App. Ct. 1993); *In re* Marriage of Thomas, 608 N.E.2d 585, 587 (Ill. App. Ct. 1993); *In re* Marriage of Lopez, 841 P.2d 1122, 1125 (Mont. 1992); *In re* Marriage of Swanson, 716 P.2d 219, 222 (Mont. 1986); Vivian v. Vivian, 583 P.2d 1072, 1074 (Mont. 1978); *In re* Marriage of Wagner, 679 P.2d 753, 758 (Mont. 1984); Dunn v. Dunn, 802 P.2d 1314, 1320 (Utah Ct. App. 1990); *In re* Marriage of Sommerfield, 454 N.W.2d 55, 60 (1990); Skokos v. Skokos, 40 S.W.3d 768 (Ark. 2001).

20. Mallett v. Mallett, 473 S.E.2d 804, 810 (S.C. Ct. App. 1996); Hickum v. Hickum, 463 S.E.2d 321, 323 (S.C. Ct. App. 1995); Hillebrand v. Hillebrand, 546 A.2d 1047, 1049 (N.H. 1988); Rosenberg v. Rosenberg, 510 N.Y.S.2d 659, 662 (App. Div. 1987); Muller v. Muller, 456 N.Y.S.2d 918, 922 (Sup. Ct. 1982); Siegel v. Siegel, 523 N.Y.S.2d 517, 520 (App. Div. 1987) (because possibility of dissipation of corporate assets existed). *But see* Scharfman v. Scharfman, 2005 N.Y. App. Div. LEXIS 6584 (N.Y. App. Div. 2005) (appellate court rejected trial court's acceptance of the date of filing as the valuation date over the trial date where there was no evidence that the husband's efforts caused the appreciation in value of the marital property).

21. Kilbourne v. Kilbourne, 284 Cal. Rptr. 201, 204 (Cal. Ct. App. 1991); *Moffitt*, 813 P.2d at 678; *Ogard*, 808 P.2d at 818–19; Richmond v. Richmond, 779 P.2d 1211, 1214 (Alaska 1989); Carlson v. Carlson, 487 S.E.2d 784, 786 (N.C. Ct. App. 1997); Bergeland v. Bergeland, 2000 Minn. App. LEXIS 952, 2000 WL 1239754 (Minn. Ct. App. 2000); *In re* Marriage of Rubens, 2003 Wash. App. LEXIS 1544 (Wash. Ct. App. 2003); Morton v. Morton, 2005 Mich. Ch. App. LEXIS 1406 (Mich. Ct. App. 2005). *But see, e.g.*, Washington v. Washington, 2005 Va. App. LEXIS 177 (Va. App. 2005) (Court rejected date of separation, instead of date of evidentiary hearing, which occurred two years after the separation, where the husband's business increased in value over the two years, but husband did not present evidence that this increase was the result of his extraordinary efforts).

22. Scalero v. Scalero, 1998 WL 23845, at *3 (Ohio Ct. App. 1998); Wallace v. Wallace, 733 S.W.2d 102, 106 (Tenn. Ct. App. 1987); Reese v. Reese, 671 N.E.2d 187, 191 (Ind. Ct. App. 1996); Favell v. Favell, 957 P.2d 556, 462 (Okla. Ct. App. 1997).

23. Green v. Green, 1998 WL 363840, at *3 (Ohio Ct. App. 1998); Quillen v. Quillen, 671 N.E.2d 98 (Ind. 1996).

GOODWILL[24]

As discussed in greater detail in Chapter 12, the classic concept of goodwill is the propensity of customers to return to the business enterprise. If this propensity is related to the individual practitioner, it is often called *personal goodwill* or *professional goodwill*. If it is because of other factors (such as location) independent of the personal skills, efforts, and reputation of an individual practitioner, it is often called *practice goodwill* or *enterprise goodwill*. Some definitions of goodwill include all intangible value. The inclusion of goodwill as a marital asset may differ from state to state and is a factor the appraiser needs to be aware of.

A key component in marital dissolution cases where goodwill valuation is at issue is whether it is necessary to distinguish between personal goodwill and enterprise goodwill, and, if such a distinction is necessary, which type of goodwill is a marital or distributable asset. Some courts might not make any distinction between personal and enterprise goodwill. These jurisdictions have taken the position that both personal and enterprise goodwill constitute marital property. A minority of courts have taken the position that neither personal nor enterprise goodwill constitute marital property. The majority of states differentiate between enterprise goodwill and personal goodwill and courts in these states take the position that personal goodwill is not marital property, but that enterprise goodwill is marital property.[25]

This section explores positions taken in various court decisions on this issue. At times, the decisions may be inconsistent with the stated definition of value. This presents a challenge to the appraisers, lawyers, and courts to make the treatment of goodwill consistent with the espoused definition of value.

A widely cited case detailing the factors to consider when determining the value of professional goodwill in a divorce is the California case *Lopez v. Lopez*.[26] These factors include:

1. The age and health of the professional
2. The professional's demonstrated past earning power
3. The professional's reputation in the community for judgment, skill, and knowledge
4. The professional's comparative professional success
5. The nature and duration of the professional's practice, either as a sole proprietor or as a contributing member of a partnership or professional corporation[27]

An excellent summary and analysis of the extremes of various positions on the characterization of goodwill as a marital asset is found in a decision by the Supreme Court of Missouri, sitting en banc and issuing the decision without dissent:

> The husbands in the consolidated cases are the sole partners in an oral surgery partnership. In *Hanson v. Hanson*,[28] the Circuit Court of Boone County valued the partnership at $324,862, including $233,727, an amount characterized as "goodwill" by the parties.

---

24. For an extensive discussion of goodwill valuation issues, *see* BVR's Guide to Personal v. Enterprise Goodwill (5th ed. 2012).

25. *Id.* for a comprehensive state-by-state guide of the treatment of goodwill in marital dissolution cases.

26. Lopez v. Lopez, 38 Cal. App. 3d 93, 113 Cal. Rptr. 58 (Cal. Ct. App. 1974).

27. For cases using similar factors, *see, e.g.*, *In re* Marriage of Fleege, 91 Wash. 2d 324, 588 P.2d 1136 (Wash. 1979); Crosetto v. Crosetto, 1996 WL 389337 (Wash. Ct. App. 1996).

28. Hanson v. Hanson 783 S.W.2d 429 (Mo. Sup. Ct. 1987).

> In *Graham v. Graham*,[29] the Circuit Court of Cole County, hearing virtually identical evidence, valued the same partnership at $90,280. In Hanson, the appeals court reversed and remanded to the trial court to assign a value to Dr. Hanson's interest in the oral surgery practice which does not reflect either goodwill or accrued net profits.

In addressing the question of the existence and value of goodwill in a professional context as marital property, the courts have not been uniform.

In *Dugan*,[30] the New Jersey Supreme Court found that goodwill in the law practice of a sole practitioner is property subject to distribution in a dissolution action. The court recognized that reputation is "at the core" of any consideration of professional goodwill.[31] While acknowledging that future earning capacity is not goodwill per se, the New Jersey justices noted that when "future earning capacity has been enhanced because reputation leads to probable future patronage from existing and potential clients, goodwill may exist and have value."[32]

Similarly, *In the Matter of the Marriage of Fleege*,[33] the Washington Supreme Court defined the critical question as

> not whether the goodwill of the practice could be sold . . . but whether it [the goodwill] has value to [the practitioner].[34]

In determining the value of such goodwill, *Fleege* outlined several factors for consideration:

> The practitioner's age, health, past earning power, reputation in the community for judgment, skill and knowledge, and his comparative professional success.[35]

Each of these factors is, in our view, directly attributable to the professional as a person.

Several courts have attempted to chart a course that recognizes that goodwill is marital property, but only insofar as it exists independently of the individual professional's reputation. Characteristic of these cases is *Taylor v. Taylor*.[36] There, the Nebraska Supreme Court concluded that:

> Goodwill must be a business asset with value independent of the presence or reputation of a particular individual, an asset which may be sold, transferred, conveyed or pledged. If a party produces appropriate evidence establishing salability or marketability of goodwill as a business asset of a professional practice, professional goodwill may be considered in determining the value of property in a marital estate to be divided in a dissolution proceeding.[37]

The court continued:

> As we have said, goodwill is recognized as property in this state; that recognition is not dependent on a traditional mercantile setting. Goodwill may exist in both commercial

---

29. Graham v. Graham No. 69067.
30. Dugan v. Dugan, 92 N.J. 423, 457 A.2d 1 (1983).
31. 457 A.2d at 6.
32. *Id.*
33. In the Matter of the Marriage of Fleege, 91 Wash. 2d 324, 588 P.2d 1136 (en banc 1979).
34. 588 P.2d at 1138–39.
35. *Id.* at 1138.
36. Taylor v. Taylor, 222 Neb. 721, 386 N.W.2d 851 (1986).
37. *Taylor*, 386 N.W.2d at 858–59.

> and professional entities. Irrespective of the setting in which it is found, the meaning of goodwill does not change. It is property which attaches to and is dependent upon an existing business entity; the reputation and skill of an individual entrepreneur—be he a professional or a traditional businessman—is not a component of the intangible asset we identify generally as goodwill.
>
> With the caveats which follow, we hold that goodwill in a professional practice acquired during a marriage is marital property subject to division in a dissolution of marriage proceeding. We define goodwill within a professional setting to mean the value of the practice which exceeds its tangible assets and which is the result of the tendency of clients/patients to return to and recommend the practice irrespective of the reputation of the individual practitioner.
>
> Professional goodwill may not be confused with future earning capacity. We have not declared future earning capacity to be marital property.
>
> Proof of the existence of goodwill is particularly troublesome in a professional context. This difficulty is a product of the fact that the reputation of the individual practitioner and the goodwill of his enterprise are often inextricably interwoven. Because of the difficulties inherent in separating the reputation of the professional from that of his enterprise, evidence that other professionals are willing to pay for goodwill when acquiring a practice is, in our view, the only acceptable evidence of the existence of goodwill. Thus, as a matter of proof, the existence of goodwill is shown only when there is evidence of a recent actual sale of a similarly situated professional practice, an offer to purchase such a practice, or expert testimony and testimony of members of the subject profession as to the existence of goodwill in a similar practice in the relevant geographic and professional market. Absent such evidence, one can only speculate as to the existence of goodwill. Division of marital property may not be based on speculation as to the very existence of the property being divided.

The fair market value method is most likely to avoid the "disturbing inequity in compelling a professional practitioner to pay a judicially determined value that could not be realized by a sale or another method of liquidating value." This seems to be the view from other courts based on decisions such as *Holbrook*[38] and *Hanson*[39] where it was stated: "We therefore reject the notion advanced by some courts that goodwill may exist and be subject to division in a dissolution proceeding even though it may not be sold."

Holbrook was subsequently clarified by the court *In Re McReath*[40] where the court indicated that salable professional goodwill could be a marital asset.

A case representative of the majority position is *May v. May.*[41] In that case, the Virginia Supreme Court, ruling on an issue of first impression in that state, held that trial courts in marital dissolution cases must distinguish between personal and enterprise goodwill in a professional practice, ruling that personal goodwill is not a marital asset but enterprise goodwill is. The court specifically noted that enterprise goodwill can exist in a professional practice that is operated as a sole proprietorship. The court also stated that this holding was consistent with its prior ruling that a professional degree or license is not marital property because it represents the future earning capacity of the

38. Holbrook v. Holbrook, 309 N.W. 2d at 355.

39. Hanson v. Hanson, 738 S.W.2d 429 (Mo. 1987).

40. *In re* McReath, 789 N.W.2d 89 (Wis. Ct. App. 2010).

41. May v. May, 2003 W. Va. LEXIS 118 (W. Va. 2003). *See also* Nowzaradan v. Nowzaradan, 2007 Tex. App. LEXIS 1021 (Tex. Ct. App. 2007); Thompson v. Thompson, 576 So. 2d 267 (Fla. 1991).

professional spouse. Likewise, personal goodwill represents the future earning capacity of the professional spouse.

A case representative of the position that either personal goodwill or enterprise goodwill is a marital asset is *Stewart v. Stewart*,[42] in which the Idaho Supreme Court held that "where a professional business is an independent entity . . . goodwill is calculable and divisible in divorce just as goodwill in any other business." In doing so, the court declined to enter the "morass" of distinguishing between the individual attributes of the professional and the value of the goodwill independent of those personal assets, valuing each separately and then dividing the latter but not the former. A strong dissent argued that because the majority had held that a professional's personal attributes—including knowledge, skill, reputation, and so on—are not divisible community property, the court should have required the parties to distinguish whether the husband's ability to earn above-average income was based on his personal attributes or "some other factor."[43]

Once a court has determined whether to distinguish between personal and enterprise goodwill, the next issue becomes how to do so. Indiana's *Yoon v. Yoon*[44] exemplifies a case where a court attempted to distinguish personal from enterprise goodwill. The court ruled that, in determining if goodwill should be included in a marital estate, there must first be a determination as to the portion attributable to the individual, and then the value of that portion must be excluded from the marital estate. In its decision, the court gave the following explanation in finding that enterprise goodwill is subject to equitable distribution, while personal goodwill can only affect the relative distribution of property:

> Before including the goodwill of a self-employed business or professional practice in a marital estate, a court must determine that the goodwill is attributable to the business as opposed to the owner as an individual. If attributable to the individual, it is not a divisible asset and is properly considered only as future earning capacity that may affect the relative property division. In this respect, the future earning capacity of a self-employed person (or an owner of a business primarily dependent on the owner's services) is to be treated the same as the future earning capability and reputation of an employee.[45]

Based on *Yoon*, the matter of *Bobrow v. Bobrow*[46] discussed the enterprise goodwill of the accounting firm Ernst & Young (E&Y). The husband, E&Y's global chief executive officer, held a partnership interest in a division of the accounting firm. Although there was a partnership agreement limiting an owner's interest to the value of the capital account, thus excluding goodwill, the husband conceded that the agreement only applied to a transaction of his partnership interest (upon resignation, retirement, or death). The court recognized that the assets of E&Y were not personal to the partner but belonged to the institution in which each partner had a share. These institutional assets included

42. Stewart v. Stewart, 2007 Idaho LEXIS 17 (Idaho 2007).

43. *See also* Gaskill v. Robbins, 2006 Ky. App. LEXIS 364 (Ky. Ct. App. 2006) (Court ruled that it would be inequitable to hold that the form of the business enterprise can defeat the community's interest in professional goodwill, since such a result ignores the contribution made by the nonprofessional spouse to the success of the professional); Bunkers v. Bunkers, 2007 Ohio App. LEXIS 523 (Ohio Ct. App. 2007) (Court ruled that all goodwill of a solo practitioner is subject to equitable division in divorce).

44. Yoon v. Yoon, 711 N.E.2d 1265 (Ind. 1999).

45. *Id.* at 3.

46. State of Indiana, Hamilton Superior Court Cause No. 29D01-0003-DR-166.

such intangible assets as E&Y's trade name, the entity's favorable business reputation and name recognition, methods and tools for conducting its business, and its relationships with suppliers. All these items were transferable to an outside purchaser. This court's decision, therefore, contrasted with *Yoon*, where the assets were allocated to the doctor personally rather than to the entity, with the court finding that they could not be transferred to another individual. Ultimately, the court included the value of enterprise goodwill in valuing E&Y and awarded the wife a share of the value of the husband's partnership interest in E&Y based on his pro rata share of the value of the enterprise.

One qualitative method to assess the enterprise and personal components of goodwill in the valuation of a professional practice is the multi-attribute utility model (MUM).[47] This method involves several steps. First, the valuator sets forth an objective. Next, the valuator establishes "alternatives." An alternative is a range of percentages that will define the choices "in which the method will result." Each alternative is then assigned a range. After the objective and the alternatives are set, the valuator then must define the "attributes," which are elements of personal goodwill to which the valuator must assign a value. Examples of attributes are personal reputation and business location.[48] This method is purely qualitative and must be used, if at all, with quantitative methods.

Another issue that may arise in valuing goodwill is determining the best method to do so. *May v. May* discusses five major formulas that are used in valuing goodwill:

1. The straight capitalization accounting method
2. The capitalization of excess earnings method
3. The IRS variation of capitalized excess earnings method (based on Rev. Rul. 68-609—the full text of this rule can be found in Exhibit 10-4, in Chapter 10 of this book)
4. The market value approach
5. The buy-sell agreement method[49]

Of these, the excess earnings method is the most commonly used; some courts find that the market approach and buy-sell agreement methods are easily manipulated by the professional spouse. The excess earnings method is discussed at greater length in Chapter 10. The capitalization of excess earnings method focuses on the earning power of the business to determine what rate of return the predicted earnings will yield in light of the risks involved in attaining them. Broadly put, the excess earnings approach is predicated on a comparison of the earnings of the professional in question with that of a peer. To make this comparison, courts may, among other things, determine the annual salary of a nonowner employee whose experience is commensurate with the spouse who is the sole practitioner or sole owner/employee. Alternatively, courts may apply the similarly situated professional standard, under which reasonable compensation is based on the cost of hiring a nonowner third party to perform, for the same compensation, that which other individuals generally receive for performing similar services. Although not necessarily controlling, professional compensation surveys may be used by experts and trial courts as guidelines for determining reasonable compensation of a practitioner's peers. To be

---

47. David Wood, *An Allocation Model for Distinguishing Enterprise Goodwill from Personal Goodwill*, 18(3) AM. J. FAM. LAW 167–73 (Fall 2004), https://www.valusource.com.

48. *In re* Marriage of Alexander, 2006 Ill. App. LEXIS 836 (Ill. Ct. App. 2006); Neary v. Neary, Case No. 06-DR-3254 (18th Cir., Seminole, Fla.).

49. *See, e.g.*, May v. May, 2003 W. Va. LEXIS 118 (W. Va. 2003).

relevant, however, the surveys must account for similarly situated professional practices and practitioners.

Other cases have clarified that personal goodwill and enterprise goodwill can be a part of a going-concern value, but that going-concern value and goodwill cannot be the same, for the latter may be subsumed within the former. Going-concern value is the intangible value attached to the physical assets of the business, including the business's fixtures, equipment, and its assemblage of personnel, as well as its goodwill.[50]

Several courts, in attempting to determine what constitutes personal goodwill, have ruled that personal (professional) goodwill is indistinguishable from earning capacity, which is not a distributable asset.[51] These courts view goodwill in a professional practice as merely assuring the continuation of earnings in the future. This view has been criticized on the grounds that, at least when it comes to equitable distribution in marital dissolutions, the contributions of each spouse to specific assets must be recognized. Others, however, take the opposite view and argue that goodwill is not a product of a marital partnership. Some courts have ruled that goodwill is separate from earning capacity where the professional's interest in a practice is transferable and separable from reputation.[52] In such instances, it must be proven that goodwill is separate from earning capacity to avoid double counting the same asset. Still, other courts view goodwill as supplementing earning capacity rather than merging with it.[53]

Another goodwill valuation issue is to what degree goodwill inheres in a noncompete agreement. It is sometimes difficult to determine the value that should be assigned to a practice's goodwill and the value that should be assigned to a noncompete agreement.[54]

Yet another issue, discussed at greater length in a section that follows, is that of double counting or "double-dipping." This issue arises when a court in a matrimonial dispute considers the same stream of cash flow from the business in determining the value of a business as well as in setting an alimony (maintenance) award.

The California Business and Professions Code § 14100 defines goodwill as "the expectation of continued public patronage." However:

---

50. Gaydos v. Gaydos, 693 A.2d 1368 (Pa. Super. Ct. 1997).

51. *See* Holbrook v. Holbrook, 103 Wis. 2d 327, 309 N.W.2d 343, 1981 Wis. App. LEXIS 3322 (Wis. Ct. App. 1981) ("The concept of professional goodwill evanesces when one attempts to distinguish it from future earning capacity."); Donahue v. Donahue, 299 S.C. 353, 384 S.E.2d 741 (S.C. 1989); and Hickum v. Hickum, 463 S.E.2d 321 (S.C. Ct. App. 1995).

52. Peerenboom v. Peerenboom, 433 N.W.2d 282 (Wis. Ct. App. 1988).

53. *See, e.g., In re* Bookout, 833 P.2d 800 (Colo. Ct. App. 1991), *cert. denied*, 846 P.2d 189 (Colo. 1993); *In re* Hall, 103 Wash. 2d 236, 692 P.2d 175 (Wash. 1984).

54. *See, e.g., In re* the Marriage of Monaghan, 899 P.2d 841 (Wash. Ct. App. 1995) (covenant not to compete is personal property of the practitioner); Kricsfeld v. Kricsfeld, 588 N.W.2d 210, 8 Neb. App. 1 (Neb. Ct. App. 1999) (noncompete agreement is personal to the practitioner and can never be a marital asset); Held v. Held, 2005 Fla. App. LEXIS 14138 (Fla. Ct. App. 2005) (for the purpose of distinguishing enterprise goodwill from personal goodwill in the valuation of a business, there is no distinction between a "non-solicitation/non-piracy agreement" and a covenant not to compete, which is attributable to the personal reputation of the seller/spouse and not to the enterprise goodwill of the business); Sweere v. Gilbert-Sweere, 534 N.W.2d 294, 1995 Minn. App. LEXIS 912 (Minn. Ct. App. 1995) (to the extent that the purpose of a noncompete agreement is to prevent the spouse from interfering with the transfer of goodwill, the agreement is representative of marital goodwill).

> The philosophy of the community property system is that a community interest can be acquired only during the time of the marriage. It would then be inconsistent with that philosophy to assign to any community interest the value of the post-marital efforts of either spouse (*In re Marriage of Fortier*).[55] Since a community interest can only be acquired during the time of the marriage, the value of the goodwill must exist at the time of the dissolution and that value must be established without dependence on the potential or continuing net income of the professional spouse.[56]

The wording in a frequently quoted California case states:

> We believe . . . the good will of the husband's professional practice as a sole practitioner should be taken into consideration . . . [I]n a matrimonial matter, the practice of the sole practitioner will continue, with the same intangible value as it had during the marriage.[57]

Considering these quotes, one might think that, on the one hand, value cannot be based on the spouse's post-marital efforts while, on the other hand, value is based on the assumption that the practicing spouse will continue to practice. California courts' attempts to reconcile these positions are embodied in a long and confusing series of decisions.

These seeming internal contradictions are prevalent in many family law case decisions. Courts espouse the position that the valuation of a business or practice should not depend on future efforts (or restrictions on future efforts) of the operating spouse. Having said this, the same courts often go on to accept appraisal methodology that, in fact, reflects earnings that could only be achieved if the operating spouse continues in the business or practice.[58]

BUY-SELL AGREEMENTS

A *buy-sell agreement* is a contract between an owner and the company, or between two or more owners, setting forth the terms under which one party may (or must) buy or sell his or her interest to the other. The valuation issues relating to buy-sell agreements are discussed in greater length in Chapter 29. The agreement normally incorporates a price, or a mechanism for determining the price, for such a sale. As such, the buy-sell agreement price is the price that the business-owner spouse could realize such a transaction.

---

55. 34 Cal. App. 3d 384, 109 Cal. Rptr. 915 (1973).

56. *See In re* Marriage of Foster (1974) 42 Cal. App. 3d 577 at 582, 117 Cal. Rptr. 49. *See also In re* Marriage of King, 197 Cal. Rptr. 716 (Cal. Ct. App. 1983).

57. Golden v. Golden, 75 Cal. Rptr. 735 (Cal. Ct. App. 1965).

58. *See* Shannon P. Pratt, *Contradictions in Family Law Cases, in* JUDGES & LAWYERS BUSINESS VALUATION UPDATE 1, 4–5 (Dec. 1999). *See also, e.g.*, Poore v. Poore, 75 N.C. App. 414, 331 S.E.2d 266 (N.C. Ct. App. 1985), which lists as acceptable methods the following:

The price a willing buyer would pay
Capitalization of excess earnings
One year's average gross income
Evidence of sales of comparable practices

All of these imply continued participation to some degree, or a noncompete agreement. Those who argue there is no contradiction point to the fact that reasonable compensation adjustments reflect the efforts of a proxy and not necessarily the owner-spouse.

From the company's viewpoint, the agreement provides control over who will participate in ownership. From the owner's viewpoint, the agreement usually provides liquidity if he or she leaves the company or for the owner's estate in the event of death.

A frequent issue is whether a buy-sell agreement price is controlling for marital property valuation purposes. Some courts hold that the price may be controlling.[59] Others, especially in states where professional (personal) goodwill is a marital asset, find that the buy-sell agreement price generally is not binding and often look at the so-called economic reality. A Washington court decision is typical of this position:

> Professional goodwill has been recognized in Washington as intangible property subject to division in a marital dissolution.[60] The important consideration is not whether the goodwill could be sold without the personal services of the professional, but whether it has value to him.[61]
>
> Both parties cite cases from other jurisdictions as authority. Some cases hold the non-shareholder spouse should be bound by the buy-sell agreement or that the buy-sell agreement should at least be considered.[62]
>
> Other courts have held the non-shareholder spouse is not bound by the terms of the withdrawal agreement and, in some cases, even where the non-shareholder spouse cosigned the withdrawal agreement.[63]

---

59. *See* Pratt, *supra* note 58. *Also see, e.g.*, Rosenberg v. Rosenberg, 510 N.Y.S.2d 659, 662 (App. Div. 1987); Hertz v. Hertz, 657 P.2d 1169, 1174–75 (N.M. 1983); Johnson v. Johnson, 771 P.2d 696, 698 (Utah Ct. App. 1989).

60. *Hall*, 103 Wash. 2d at 238–39, 692 P.2d 175.

61. *In re* Marriage of Fleege, 91 Wash. 2d 324, 327, 588 P.2d 1136 (1979) (goodwill of husband's solo dental practice was a community asset).

62. Hertz v. Hertz, 99 N.M. 320, 657 P.2d 1169, 1174 (1983) (a non-shareholder spouse was bound by the goodwill valuation clause in corporate bylaws for purposes of establishing the valuation of corporate goodwill in a dissolution action. This ensured that the non-shareholder spouse did not receive a greater value than the shareholder.). *See also In re* Marriage of Ondrasek, 126 Wis. 2d 469, 377 N.W.2d 190, 192 (Ct. App. 1985) (in a dissolution, value of a partner's interest in a professional partnership is determined by the monetary consequences of that partner withdrawing from the business); Holbrook v. Holbrook, 103 Wis. 2d 327, 309 N.W.2d 343, 355 (Ct. App. 1981) (capital account was the only value that should be assigned to a lawyer's partnership as an asset where lawyer was entitled to receive only his capital account value on withdrawal and any goodwill is reflected in his salary, which can be considered in setting the family support award); and Hanson v. Hanson, 738 SW2d 429, 436 (Mo. 1987) (value of goodwill of professional practice, subject to division in dissolution proceeding, is determined by the price the practice would bring if sold on open, relevant market to qualified professional; under certain circumstances value may be established by buy-sell agreement).

63. *In re* Marriage of Slater, 100 Cal. App. 3d 241, 160 Cal. Rptr. 686 (1979) (on theory withdrawal agreement was not signed for dissolution purposes); Mitchell v. Mitchell, 152 Ariz. 317, 732 P.2d 208, 210 (1987) (partnership agreement provided that no value was to be placed on goodwill of the firm; however, it did contain provisions for payments to a partner upon retirement or death which were not limited to the firm's tangible assets and accounts receivable, but included a share of net profits for a limited period. A buy-sell agreement had been considered in establishing the valuation of goodwill but was not dispositive. At best it created a presumptive value which either spouse could rebut); Stern v. Stern, 66 N.J. 340, 331 A.2d 257, 260, 74 L.R.3d 613 (1975) (of the four payment plans found in the partnership agreement applicable to a partner who withdraws from a firm, becomes disabled, dies, or retires, the formula applicable on a partner's death is presumptively the value to be used in dissolution; here, the partner was entitled to the value of his capital account plus a fixed sum appended to the partnership agreement which was revised quarterly). *But cf.* Rogers v. Rogers, 296 N.W.2d 849, 852–53 (Minn. 1980) (It was a reversible error not to consider the terms of the buy-sell agreement that create contingencies that affect the value, such as the possibility the shareholder might die or be disabled before he realizes the full value of his interest.).

> Our state has not considered whether a buy-sell agreement not made in close proximity to a divorce is binding on the non-shareholder spouse in a dissolution action. Hall did not reach this issue but held that, at least in some circumstances, buy-sell agreements are not binding in a dissolution action. In light of Hall and Fleege (that it makes no difference whether the goodwill can be sold) we hold the Court did not err in valuing goodwill even though it was assigned no value in the Brooks & Larson, P.S. corporation bylaws.[64]

In the preceding case, the spouse had practiced law for four years before the marriage and 13 years since. The court decided that the interest in the practice the husband bought (and was subject to the buy-sell agreement) was separate property and that his goodwill (valued at $93,115 by the excess earnings method) was community property.

Sometimes a buy-sell price may be a factor to be considered, but not completely controlling.[65] In one case, the husband purchased stock, subject to a buy-sell agreement, for $65,567 from funds borrowed from his mother. In three years, the stock paid $251,000 in dividends, and the buy-sell formula price increased to $82,000. In rejecting the trial court's valuation at the buy-sell price, the Court of Appeals explained:

> It is unreasonable to assume the value of the stock to Darrell was only what he could sell it to the company for, in light of the fact it was producing such generous dividends. It stretches the bounds of reasonableness to value a goose for slaughter price when it lays golden eggs.[66]

The appellate court declined to value the stock at $1.6 million, as claimed by the wife's expert based on capitalization of earnings, but did award the wife an additional $40,000, representing her interest during the marriage.

One case that rejected a buy-sell agreement price as controlling the value of a minority interest noted the following:

- There was evidence that another family member had been bought out at a price that exceeded the value set by the buy-sell agreement.
- The buy-sell agreement was taken into consideration to some extent by the expert's reduction of 35% in value for minority interest and lack of marketability.[67]

Similarly, in another case where stock was subject to a buy-sell agreement at book value, the court "decreased the unrestricted fair market value substantially more

---

64. *In re* Marriage of Brooks, 756 P.2d 161 (Wash. Ct. App. 1988). *See also* In the Matter of Overbey, 2007 Wash App. LEXIS 1651 (Wash. Ct. App. 2007), which continued this state's approach and indicated that a buy-sell agreement was not a binding separation contract, and that while the formula contained therein was relevant, it was not determinative of the company's value.

65. *See, e.g., In re* Marriage of Herlitzke, 2006 Wis. App. LEXIS 972 (Wis. Ct. App. 2006) (buy-sell agreement may establish fair market value of partnership or S corporation, but does not do so as a matter of law); Herron v. Herron, 2004 Ohio App. LEXIS 5209 (Ohio Ct. App. 2004) (Court gave weight to the closely held company's buy-sell agreement because "[a]ny willing buyer would certainly take into account the buy/sell agreement before making any offer on the stock"); R.V.K. v. L.L.K, 2002 WL 31421572 (Tex. Ct. App. 2002); Harmon v. Harmon, 2000 WL 286718 (Tenn. Ct. App. 2000); Howell v. Howell, 46 Va. Cir. 339; 1998 Va. Cir. LEXIS 256 (1998), *aff'd*, 31 Va. App. 332, 523 S.E.2d 514 (Va. Ct. App. 2000).

66. *In re* Marriage of Dieger, 584 N.W.2d 567 (Iowa Ct. App. 1998).

67. Berenberg v. Berenberg, 474 N.W.2d 843 (Minn. Ct. App. 1991).

than it increased the book value to arrive at a valuation for purposes of the marriage dissolution."[68]

Another case summarized the most typical position:

> A majority of courts which have considered a buy-sell agreement in a closely held corporation setting the stock value for equitable distribution purposes has determined that such agreement should not be considered as binding, but rather should be weighed along with other factors in making a determination as to the value of such stock.[69] It is apparent that buy-sell agreements in a closely held corporation can be manipulated by the shareholders to reflect an artificially low value. This is why caution should be exercised in accepting their value for equitable distribution purposes.[70]

A Connecticut court ruled similarly, rejecting the notion that fair market value of a corporation was properly based on the underlying governing shareholder agreement where none of the triggering events outlined in the shareholder agreement had occurred.[71]

A New Mexico court found the buy-sell price in a law firm's stockholder's agreement controlling, even though it was computed completely on a cash basis, and even though the court had, in a previous case, found goodwill using a capitalization of excess earnings method in a medical practice that had no buy-sell agreement.[72]

In a Washington case involving a minority interest in an insurance agency, the court did find the buy-sell agreement price controlling. The court noted that the minority status was not likely to change, there was no evidence that the company was likely to be sold, and it was reasonable to conclude that if the husband were to sell his stock, he would do so subject to the buy-sell agreement formula.[73]

Buy-sell agreements involving key persons often are funded with life insurance benefits payable to the designated purchaser under the agreement, providing liquidity to exercise the buy-sell agreement in the case of the death of the owner of the interest. The amount of the "key person" insurance sometimes is presented as evidence of the partners' idea of the value of the interest. Such evidence could be supportive of an appraised value, at best, but certainly no substitute for an appraisal.

In almost any situation where a buy-sell agreement is taken into consideration, the extent to which the agreement was entered into on an arm's-length basis also should be considered.

---

68. Lyon v. Lyon, 439 N.W.2d 18 (Minn. 1989).

69. *See, e.g., In re* Marriage of Melnick, 127 Ill. App. 3d 102, 82 Ill. Dec. 228, 468 N.E.2d 490 (1984); *In re* Marriage of Moffatt, 279 N.W.2d 15 (Iowa 1979); Rogers v. Rogers, 296 N.W.2d 849 (Minn. 1980); Bowen v. Bowen, 96 N.J. 36, 473 A.2d 73 (1984); Amodio v. Amodio, 70 N.Y.2d 5, 516 N.Y.S. 2d 923, 509 N.E.2d 936 (1987); *In the Matter of the* Marriage of Belt, 65 Ore. App. 606, 672 P.2d 1205 (1983); Bosserman v. Bosserman, 9 Va. App. 1, 384 S.E.2d 104 (1989); Arneson v. Arneson, 120 Wis. 2d 236, 355 N.W.2d 16 (Wis. Ct. App. 1984).

70. Bettinger v. Bettinger, 396 S.E.2d 709 (W. Va. 1990). *See also* Barton v. Barton, 2007 Ga. LEXIS 21 (Ga. 2007), where the Georgia Supreme Court joined the clear majority of states on this issue and held that the value of stock set forth in a buy-sell agreement for a closely held corporation is not binding for purposes of property division in divorce proceedings. The court reasoned that "[t]he buy-sell price in a closely held corporation can be manipulated and does not necessarily reflect true market value."

71. Dahill v. Dahill 1998 Conn. Super. LEXIS 846 (Conn. Super. Ct. 1998).

72. Hertz v. Hertz, 657 P.2d 1169 (N.M. 1983).

73. *In re* Marriage of Gillespie, 948 P.2d 1338 (Wash. Ct. App. 1997).

COVENANTS NOT TO COMPETE

A *covenant not to compete*, or *noncompete agreement*, is a contract preventing an individual (or group of individuals) from competing with a given entity or person. For example, a dentist selling a practice may agree not to practice dentistry for a certain amount of time in the metropolitan area of the location of the subject practice. In other cases, some partnerships or corporations require the sellers to enter into a covenant not to compete as a condition of ownership. The covenant usually enhances the value of the entity by reducing the risk of certain individuals taking away business. The valuation issues relating to covenants not to compete are discussed in greater length in Chapter 14.

Treatment of an actual or prospective covenant not to compete is controversial. Many courts take the position that such a covenant restricts the post-marital activities of the spouse and therefore is separate rather than marital property.[74] Some courts find that such covenants are marital property.[75] Others take the position that sales of most small businesses and professional practices require covenants not to compete, and the court may value the enterprise assuming a covenant, or even order the spouse to execute a covenant, with no separate compensation to the spouse.[76] Still others hold that adjustments for hypothetical noncompete agreements are impermissible, even though comparable transactions include such agreements of similar duration, where the appraiser does not present evidence on the nature of such agreements or their impact on value.[77] A covenant not to compete, by definition, restricts the post-marital efforts of the spouse. In most jurisdictions, this would be considered a nonmarital asset. If the analyst uses the market approach to value the business or practice, and the comparable sales include a covenant not to compete, it could be argued that the value of the covenant should be deducted from the comparable company or practice sales before they are used for comparison.[78]

---

74. *See, e.g., In re* Marriage of Monaghan, 899 P.2d 841 (Wash. Ct. App. 1995) (the portion of sale price attributable to covenant is husband's separate property); Kricsfeld v. Kricsfeld, 588 N.W.2d 210, 1999 Neb. App. LEXIS 1 (Neb. Ct. App. 1999); Ellerbe v. Ellerbe, 323 S.C. 283, 473 S.E.2d 881 (S.C. Ct. App. 1996); Cutsinger v. Cutsinger, 917 S.W.2d 238 (Tenn. Ct. App. 1995) (Court excluded monetary amounts for covenant not to compete from purchase price of chiropractic practice); Hoeft v. Hoeft, 74 Ohio App. 3d 809, 600 N.E.2d 746 (Ohio Ct. App. 1991) (Court determined that while proceeds received for the sale of the husband's dental practice were marital property, monies received from a covenant not to compete were nonmarital); Johnston v. Johnston, 778 S.W.2d 674 (Mo. Ct. App. 1989) (covenant not to compete properly excluded in the valuation of dental practice); Donahue v. Donahue, 299 S.C. 353, 384 S.E.2d 741 (1989) (goodwill of a professional practice is not subject to equitable distribution); Lucas v. Lucas, 621 P.2d 500 (N.M. 1980) (the right to compete is a personal right and the separate property of its owner).

75. Reese v. Reese, 671 N.E.2d 187 (Ind. Ct. App. 1996); Sweere v. Gilbert-Sweere, 534 N.W.2d 294, 1995 Minn. App. LEXIS 912 (Minn. Ct. App. 1995) (to the extent that the purpose of a noncompete agreement is to prevent the spouse from interfering with the transfer of goodwill, the agreement is representative of marital goodwill).

76. *See, e.g.,* Carr v. Carr, 701 P.2d 304 (Idaho Ct. App. 1985) (Court ordered husband to enter into sales agreement including covenant not to compete, with no allowance to husband for the covenant). *But see In re* Marriage of Mally, 2001 WL 539669 (Iowa Ct. App. 2001) (Court accepted that a noncompete agreement was essential to the sale of the practice and reduced the practice's value by $329,000).

77. Duncan v. Duncan, 90 Cal. App. 4th 617 (Cal. Ct. App. 2001).

78. The database *DealStats* (formerly *Pratt's Stats*; *see* References at end of Chapter 8) shows how much was allocated to a covenant not to compete when one was involved in the sale of a business or practice.

NONCONTROLLING INTEREST AND LACK OF MARKETABILITY DISCOUNTS

As discussed in Chapter 18, "Discounts and Premiums," a noncontrolling (oftentimes termed a *minority*) interest usually is worth less than its pro rata share of the value of the entity as a whole. This is because a controlling owner can make many decisions that a noncontrolling owner cannot—decisions that can affect both the value of the company as a whole as well as the relative values of the controlling versus the noncontrolling interests. See the Levels of Value chart, Exhibit 2-1, in Chapter 2.

Therefore, if the valuation methodology produces a controlling interest value and the interest being valued is a noncontrolling interest, a discount for lack of control (DLOC) is usually applied. Because noncontrolling interests often are harder to sell than controlling interests, the discount for lack of control might be compounded by also subtracting a discount for lack of marketability (DLOM) (see Chapter 18). Whether or not discounts are applicable is driven in part by the applicable standard of value.

A frequent issue is whether a discount for lack of control should be applied (and if so, how much) if the interest owned is less than controlling.

In one case, an expert for the husband testified that a 15% discount for lack of control was appropriate for a 50% interest.[79] An expert for the wife testified that no discount for lack of control was appropriate in a divorce settlement context because generally there is no change of ownership. The court rejected the wife's expert's opinion, with several references to decisions in other states:

> We reject [wife's expert's] view as a matter of law. The concept of value is keyed to the price that a prospective buyer would pay.[80] Sherwin's testimony runs counter to this concept. We also note that courts in many jurisdictions have recognized that a minority discount is frequently appropriate in divorce proceedings.[81]

In one case, the discount for lack of control was eliminated because the noncontrolling owner had a purchase right that would enable him to obtain control of the corporation sometime within the next seven to ten years.[82] Nonetheless, there have been many marital dissolution cases that have accepted discounts for lack of control[83] and many that

---

79. According to the *International Valuation Glossary—Business Valuation*, a 50% interest is not a minority interest, but it may lack control. *See International Valuation Glossary—Business Valuation* 3, "Discount for Lack of Control" (jointly published by the ASA, CBV Institute Royal Institute of Chartered Surveyors, and Saudi Authority of Accredited Valuers, Feb. 24, 2022).

80. Moffitt v. Moffitt, 813 P.2d 674 (Alaska 1991).

81. *See* Arneson v. Arneson, 120 Wis. 2d 236, 355 N.W.2d 16, 22 (App. 1984) (not clearly erroneous for trial court to apply minority discount); *In re* Marriage of Jorgensen, 180 Mont. 294, 590 P.2d 606, 610 (1979) (not an abuse of discretion to apply minority discount); *In re* Marriage of Belt, 65 Ore. App. 606, 672 P.2d 1205, 1207–08 (1983) (trial court's valuation modified to include minority discount where the only credible evidence produced at trial favored discount); *In re* Marriage of Reiling, 66 Ore. App. 284, 673 P.2d 1360, 1364, 1365 (1983) (same); *In re* Marriage of Hoak, 364 N.W.2d 185, 192–93 (Iowa 1985) (not error to apply minority discount, but discount allowed by the trial court was too large and must be reduced); Bowen v. Bowen, 96 N.J. 36, 473 A.2d 73, 76–77, 81 (1984) (trial court should appoint independent expert to advise it in deciding whether to apply minority discount).

82. *In re* Marriage of Harrington, 935 P.2d 1357 (Wash. Ct. App. 1997).

83. *See, e.g.*, Priebe v. Priebe, 556 N.W.2d 78 (S.D. 1996) (40%); *In re* Marriage of DeCosse, 936 P.2d 821, 1997 WL 19374 (Mont. 1997) (20%); Arneson v. Arneson, 355 N.W. 2d 16 (Wis. Ct. App. 1984) (25%); Rattee v. Rattee, 767 A.2d 415, 146 N.H. 44 (N.H. 2001); L.R.M. v. R.K.M., 46 S.W.3d 24 (Mo. Ct. App. 2001) (32% combined discount); Anderson v. Anderson, 2006 Tenn. App. LEXIS 592 (Tenn. App. 2006) (38.3%).

have not.[84] As with discounts for lack of control, many courts in marital dissolution cases have accepted discounts for lack of marketability,[85] while many have not.[86] In one case, the court ruled that discounts for lack of marketability are not precluded as a matter of law in marital dissolution cases.[87] Much of the application of shareholder-level discounts is a function of the standard of value used in a particular state. A state that uses the fair value standard (e.g., Massachusetts, New Jersey) may preclude, unless there are special circumstances, the application of such discounts.

TAX ON TRAPPED-IN CAPITAL GAINS

In many cases, the marital estate includes property that is worth more than its cost basis. In this case, if the subject property were disposed of, it would be subject to federal and state capital gains taxes. This is a liability referred to as *trapped-in capital gains taxes*.[88]

Whether to consider tax liabilities that would be triggered by the sale of assets is one of the most common issues in marital property divisions. For the most part, family law courts have been unwilling to make any allowance for trapped-in capital gains on appreciated property unless a sale of the property is imminent.[89] Because family law

84. *See, e.g.*, Howell v. Howell, 46 Va. Cir. 339, 1998 Va. Cir. LEXIS 256 (Va. Cir. Ct. 1998), *aff'd*, 31 Va. App. 332, 523 S.E.2d 514 (Va. Ct. App. 2000); Oatey v. Oatey, No. 67809, 67973 Ohio Ct. App., 1996 WL 200273, at *22 (Apr. 25, 1996); Nardini v. Nardini, 414 N.W.2d 184, 189 (Minn. 1987); Cross v. Cross, 586 P.2d 547, 549 (Wyo. 1978); Ferraro v. Ferraro, 2000 WL 251678 (Va. Ct. App. 2000); Brown v. Brown, 348 N.J. Super. 466, 792 A.2d 463, 2002 N.J. Super. LEXIS 105 (2002) (discounts disallowed absent extraordinary circumstances); Baltrusis v. Baltrusis, 113 Wash. App. 1037 (Wash. Ct. App. 2002); Hanson v. Hanson, 2005 Alaska LEXIS 166 (Alaska 2005) (no discount where majority spouse acquires the minority spouse's interest).

85. *See, e.g.*, *In re* Marriage of Tofte, 895 P.2d 1387, 1392 (Or. Ct. App. 1995) (35%); Ellis v. Ellis, No. 77407 N.Y. App. Div., 1997 WL 35218, at *2 (Jan. 30, 1997) (25%); Michael v. Michael, 469 S.E.2d 14, 17 (W. Va. 1996) (25%); Kapp v. Kapp, 2005 Ohio App. LEXIS 6144 (Ohio App. 2005) (litigation contingency discount accepted where proof of a pending lawsuit was presented); Rattee v. Rattee, 767 A.2d 415, 146 N.H. 44 (N.H. 2001); L.R.M. v. R.K.M., 46 S.W.3d 24 (Mo. Ct. App. 2001) (32% combined discount); Collier v. Collier, 790 So. 2d 759 (La. Ct. App. 2001) (25% combined discount for lack of marketability and contingent liabilities).

86. *See, e.g.*, Howell v. Howell (no amount specified); Neuman v. Neuman, 842 P.2d 575, 579 (Wyo. 1992) (35%); Hanson v. Hanson, 86 P.3d 94, 192 Or. App. 422 (Or. Ct. App. 2004) (25%); Brown v. Brown, 348 N.J. Super. 466, 792 A.2d 463, 2002 N.J. Super. LEXIS 105 (2002); Baltrusis v. Baltrusis, 113 Wash. App. 1037 (Wash. Ct. App. 2002) (25%); Ferraro v. Ferraro, 2000 WL 251678 (Va. Ct. App. 2000); Anderson v. Anderson, 2006 Tenn. App. LEXIS 592 (Tenn. App. 2006) (10% for marketing costs associated with only a hypothetical sale of minority interest); Hanson v. Hanson, 2005 Alaska LEXIS 166 (Alaska 2005); Kapp v. Kapp, 2005 Ohio App. LEXIS 6144 (Ohio App. 2005) (no discount for contingent transaction costs—broker, legal, accounting fees—where no sale is being contemplated); Bertuca v. Bertuca, 2007 Tenn. App. LEXIS 690 (Tenn. Ct. App. 2007) (discount disallowed where a sale of the husband's interest was not "necessary or desirable").

87. Erp v. Erp, 2007 Fla. App. LEXIS 18726 (Fla. Ct. App. 2007).

88. *See* section titled "Tax on Built-in Capital Gains Adjustment" in Chapter 18.

89. *See, e.g.*, Buzanell v. Miller, 590 S.E.2d 332, 162 N.C. App. 180, 2004 WL 26524 (N.C. Ct. App. 2004) (consideration of taxes too speculative); *In re* Marriage of Black, 2001 WL 57999 (Iowa Ct. App. 2001); Guill v. Guill, 2001 WL 770942 (Neb. Ct. App. 2001); Skokos v. Skokos, 40 S.W.3d 768, 344 Ark. 420 (Ark. 2001); Kaiser v. Kaiser, 555 N.W.2d 585 (N.D. 1996) (the deduction of hypothetical tax liabilities rejected); *In re* Marriage of Czapar, 232 Cal. App. 3d 1308, 284 Cal. Rptr. 41 (1991) (it is improper to take into consideration the tax consequences of an order dividing a community asset unless the tax liability is immediate and specific and will arise in connection with the division of the community property).

courts often take Tax Court positions into consideration, perhaps the Tax Court's sharp turnaround on this issue in 1998, directing reflection of trapped-in capital gains taxes in valuation may lead family law courts to give some consideration to this issue.

Typical of how certain courts view this issue occurred in a Washington case ruling. The trial court adjusted the gross value of the parties' interest in a real estate partnership from $119,049 to $101,000 to reflect the capital gains tax that would be paid if it were sold. The Court of Appeals reversed, noting, "There is no Washington case specifically addressing whether capital gains tax consequences should be a factor in determining the value of marital assets."[90] Thus, the court looked to other states for precedent, citing cases in seven other states. The court then concluded:

> Courts have generally found that consideration of tax consequences is either required or at least appropriate where the consequences are immediate and specific and/or arise directly from the court's decree, but find they are not an appropriate consideration where speculation as to a party's future dealings with property awarded to him or her would be required. We agree with the rule adopted by most jurisdictions.
>
> Mr. Hay testified at trial that he had no plans to sell his partnership interest and we remand to enable the trial court to consider the property division without regard to the capital gains tax consequences of a hypothetical sale of H&L Investments.[91]

The practice of reviewing decisions from other states is very common. Typical of a decision reached after such a review is that the court should consider potential tax consequences in valuing marital assets only if:

1. The recognition of a tax liability is required by dissolution or will occur within a short time;
2. The party's future dealings with the assets are definite enough that the court need not speculate; and
3. The future consequences are definite enough that the court need not speculate, and the tax liability can be reasonably predicted.[92]

The courts usually factor in the tax consequences when it is clear that they will be triggered as part of the divorce action. However, an Indiana trial court ordered the husband to pay a mortgage, a car loan, and a cash judgment to the wife from the sale of at least one of two laundromats owned. The court reduced the marital estate by the $53,200 tax liability to be incurred on the sale of the laundromats. The court explained that, although it did not specifically order the sale of the laundromats, sale was the only way that the husband could comply with the orders of the court. Nevertheless, the Appellate Court found that the sale of both laundromats was not an immediate consequence of the property disposition and that the trial court erred in reducing the marital estate by the amount of the tax liability.[93]

There are, however, cases where the tax consequences on sale have been deducted in valuing the marital estate, even when no immediate sale was contemplated. For example, in one case, it was concluded that it was proper to deduct the amount of capital gains tax that the husband would have to pay on the anticipated sale of limited partnership

---

90. *In re* Marriage of Hay, 907 P.2d 334 (Wash. Ct. App. 1995) at 2.
91. *Id.*
92. Kaiser v. Kaiser, 474 N.W.2d 63 (N.D. 1991).
93. Granger v. Granger, 579 N.E.2d 1319 (Ind. Ct. App. 1991).

interests. The wife objected to reducing the value by the impounded taxes, claiming that they were "hypothetical, speculative, imaginary, unfair, and arbitrary."[94] Evidence was introduced to show that the partnership was a tax shelter that would have lost its desirability in five to seven years and probably would be sold. The court concluded that the date of sale was not imaginary or hypothetical.

The court then offered an interesting broader statement that "partnerships ought to be reduced by future capital gains taxes" where the partnerships were investments that "were only valuable as long as other investments were not more desirable," and the husband "was more likely to sell his interest in the partnerships than die owning them," and would, therefore, incur a capital gains tax from the sale of the partnerships.[95] From the viewpoint of a financial analyst, it is reasonable to assume that this reasoning should apply to any investment asset.

Another interesting decision upholding subtraction of capital gains tax involved a commercial building. The appellate court held that the trial court did not abuse its discretion in subtracting the capital gains tax that would be incurred on the sale, even though there was no evidence that the property was going to be sold. The court found that experts for both parties attested to the property's fair market value and that the concept of fair market value assumes the sale of the property to an interested buyer. Thus, the court was reluctant to find any error by the trial court in presuming a sale of the real estate with its attendant tax consequences in order to value that marital asset.[96] In another case, where the husband would effectively have been forced to purchase the wife's shares in a company, the court permitted a credit for capital gains taxes, even though there was no evidence of an imminent sale.[97]

Some courts hold that tax consequences may be considered if the court determines that the property division award will force a party to sell the business to generate the cash needed to pay the court-imposed obligations.[98]

The holdings in these and similar cases suggest that if the sale of the assets is so remote a possibility as to eliminate consideration of the capital gains tax liability, the asset approach should not be the only primary valuation approach used; that perhaps an income approach would be more appropriate or maybe an income approach blended with an asset-based approach.[99]

ADEQUACY OF EVIDENCE

Trial courts have wide discretion in deciding factual matters, such as value, but appellate courts expect trial courts to have an adequate evidentiary basis for reaching their conclusions of fact.[100] There is also a possibility that "expert" evidence at the trial court level

94. Liddle v. Liddle, 410 N.W.2d 196 (Wis. Ct. App. 1987).

95. *Id.*

96. Hogan v. Hogan, 796 S.W.2d 400 (Mo. Ct. App. 1990).

97. Hamilton v. Hamilton, 2002 Ohio 2417 (Ohio Ct. App. 2002).

98. *See, e.g.*, Schuman v. Schuman, 658 N.W.2d 30, 265 Neb. 459 (2003).

99. *See* Shannon P. Pratt, *Trapped-in Capital Gains Affects Real-World Value*, *in* SHANNON PRATT'S BUSINESS VALUATION UPDATE 1, 3 (Feb. 1996).

100. *See, e.g.*, Zerbe v. Zerbe, 2005 Ohio 1180 (Ohio Ct. App. 2005) ("A finding of value must be supported by competent, credible evidence. The Court cannot take the two extremes presented by the evidence and choose a value somewhere between those two extremes"); Augoshe v. Lehman, 2007 Fla. App. LEXIS 6367 (Fla. Ct. App. 2007) ("simply splitting the difference" between two divergent appraisals is an "improper

could be so inadequate that the appellate court remands the case for new hearings and evidence on the value of a business or practice.[101] This usually means that all the money and time spent on "experts" and the related lawyer fees have been wasted. This can be avoided if competent business valuation experts are retained at the beginning of the case, and the lawyer and expert work together to ensure a good record at trial—especially because courts tend to give significantly greater weight to the valuations of qualified, independent business appraisers.[102] This also means that the attorney must obtain the full cooperation of, and disclosure from, the client.[103]

ACCESS TO RECORDS

It is common for an operating spouse to restrict access to the records necessary for the nonoperating spouse's expert to conduct a thorough valuation. Because the nonoperating spouse has a financial interest in the property, their lawyer almost always can obtain a court order compelling production of the information needed by the expert to carry out a thorough valuation (see Chapter 36 on discovery).

In a case that went all the way to the Supreme Court of Connecticut, a radiologist filed a motion to exclude the wife's expert's report and testimony because the report had not been produced prior to trial. The expert testified that the delay in preparing his report was attributable to a lack of cooperation on the part of the husband in failing to make the pertinent financial records available. In denying the motion, the court declared:

> If anybody is playing cat and mouse, it's the [husband]. It is virtually frivolous for the husband to suggest that the Court abused its broad discretion by failing to impose the sanction of excluding testimony because of delay in furnishing the report of an expert witness, after concluding that the delay was largely attributable to the husband's failure to comply with the order for disclosure of his financial records.[104]

---

method of valuation"); *In re* Marriage of Keener, 2007 Iowa Sup. LEXIS 13 (Iowa 2007) ("anecdotal evidence is simply an insufficient basis upon which to determine fair market value"); Pickard v. Pickard, 2006 N.Y. App. Div. LEXIS 9961 (N.Y. App. Div. 2006) (discount rate was rejected where the rate was selected arbitrarily without support for it).

101. *See, e.g.*, Crosetto v. Crosetto, 918 P.2d 954 (Wash. App. Ct. 1996) ("Because the trial Court here did not state how it reached the valuation figure, we remand . . .").

102. *See, e.g.*, *In re* Marriage of Bidwell, 12 P.3d 76, 170 Or. App. 239 (Or. Ct. App. 2000) (the court accepted the wife's expert's opinion over the husband's opinion since husband had not presented expert evidence); *In re* Marriage of Gabriel, 2005 Cal. App. Unpub. LEXIS 8101 (Cal. Ct. App. 2005); Miller v. Miller, 14 S.W.3d 903, 70 Ark. App. 64 (Ark. Ct. App. 2000); Ballas v. Ballas, 2004 Ohio 5128, 2004 WL 2334329 (Ohio App. 7 Dist. 2004) (expert's opinion given greater weight than that of business manager); Dunn v. Dunn, 2005 Miss. App. LEXIS 637 (Miss. Ct. App. 2005) (appeals by both spouses were unavailing where neither had hired a business valuation expert); Mace v. Mace, 818 So. 2d 1130 (Miss. 2002) (where neither spouse hired a business valuation expert, the court recommended that they provide expert valuation evidence on remand).

103. *See, e.g.*, Weinstein v. Weinstein, 2005 Conn. LEXIS 348 (Conn. 2005) (husband's failure to disclose the true value of his company's intellectual property resulted in a finding of blatant and deliberate misrepresentation and reversal); Stribling v. Stribling, 2005 Miss. App. LEXIS 58 (Miss. Ct. App. 2005) (where "a party fails to provide accurate information, or cooperate in the valuation of assets," the trial court is "entitled to proceed on the best information available").

104. Eslami v. Eslami, 591 A.2d 411 (Conn. 1991).

THE PERSISTENT PROBLEM OF "DOUBLE-DIPPING"

One of the most prevalent problems in family law cases involving a business or professional practice valuation is a concept referred to as "double-dipping." Double-dipping means computing a value based, at least in part, on the spouse's future earnings for property division and then also using the future earnings capacity as a basis for determining spousal support or alimony payments.

The potential for this problem arises when an income approach (see Chapter 6), an excess earnings method (see Chapter 10), or a market approach (see Chapter 8) is used for the valuation. If these methods reflect an implication that the operating spouse will continue to operate and receives a normalized (reasonable) level of compensation (see Chapter 13), the value of that spouse's future efforts is impounded, at least to some extent, in the distributive value. If payments for maintenance/alimony are then ordered out of the total earnings from that spouse's efforts (and not based solely on the operating spouse's reasonable compensation), double counting is a potential result.

This problem is exacerbated in those jurisdictions that consider *personal goodwill* a marital asset. Personal goodwill is a function of future earning power resulting from persistence of patronage of the individual. If this value is fully reflected in the distributive asset, then this earning power is being used twice if it is also the basis for future payments to the nonoperating spouse.

This problem can be avoided if the valuation methodology truly follows the philosophy of not depending on future efforts (or restrictions on efforts) of the operating spouse. However, as noted earlier, many court decisions espouse this philosophy but then accept a valuation methodology that actually incorporates an assumption of the operating spouse's continuing efforts or restrictions on those efforts.

In *Steneken*,[105] the trial court determined that the husband's annual compensation was excessive and normalized the compensation in determining the value of his company using the excess earnings method. The court then determined alimony using the husband's actual annual compensation—which was $50,000 more. The husband argued that distributing his excess earnings as the goodwill portion of the value of his business, and also considering it for alimony purposes, was impermissible double counting.

The New Jersey intermediate Appellate Court ruled that the value of the business was as of the date of dissolution and was based on past excess earnings, while the alimony determination was based on future income. The court also noted that even if this was double counting, it was not banned by New Jersey law, which bans only the double counting of pensions.

The New Jersey Supreme Court expressly rejected the premise that, because alimony and equitable distribution are interrelated, a credit on one side of the ledger mandates a debit on the other side. Instead, the court focused on the "bedrock proposition" that all alimony awards and equitable distribution determinations must satisfy basic concepts of fairness, and that, although clearly interrelated, the structural purposes of alimony and equitable distribution are different.

Accordingly, the court rejected the husband's assertion of double counting, stating that the husband "mistakenly equates the statutory and decisional methodology applied in the calculation of alimony with a valuation methodology applied for equitable

105. Steneken v. Steneken, 843 A.2d 344 (N.J. App. Div. 2004), *aff'd*, 873 A.2d 501, 183 N.J. 290 (2005).

distribution purposes that requires that revenues and expenses, including salaries, be normalized so as to present a fair valuation of a going concern."[106] The court concluded that it is not inequitable to use a valuation method that normalizes salary in an ongoing closely held corporation for equitable distribution purposes and to use actual salary received in calculating alimony—the valuation methodology chosen for equitable distribution purposes should not alter the alimony award. According to the court, the "interplay of those two calculations does not constitute 'double counting.'"[107] The final judicial inquiry must be whether the ultimate result, both in toto as well as in its constituent parts, is fair under the circumstances and congruent with the standards set forth in the alimony and equitable distribution statutes. The court also rejected the distinction made by the Appellate Court between the fact that "valuation of the corporate asset was based on [the husband's] past earnings, not his future earnings," while "[the husband's] actual current and future compensation may be treated as income for alimony purposes.[108]

Justice Long, in a dissenting opinion, agreed with the husband that the majority's holding would allow the impermissible double counting of income (albeit not dollar for dollar). Justice Long's position was that the majority converted a certain amount of the husband's projected future income stream into an asset and then calculated the amount of alimony based on that asset. According to Justice Long, this was improper, as "[o]nce a court converts a specific stream of income into an asset, that income may no longer be calculated into the maintenance formula and payout."[109] Instead, Justice Long's solution would have used the appellate court's approach, which neither allows the unfettered dual use of a single income stream, nor requires the use of the same figure for both calculations. "Rather, judges should be able to use the 'real' income for alimony and the 'normalized' income for the corporate valuation so long as the ultimate outcome recognizes that a single income source (the difference between the real and normalized income) played a part in both."[110]

It is arguable that, to the extent the court used excess compensation as the basis for alimony, the court used that money twice: once to value the distributed value of the business and again to determine the amount of alimony—a classic case of double-dipping.

In the Connecticut decision of *Oudheusden*, a ruling that went to both the state's Appellate Court and then, ultimately, its Supreme Court, the latter ultimately found that double counting was not improper provided such awards are consistent with the state's statutory purposes and are fair and equitable.[111]

In *Sampson*,[112] the value of the wife's insurance agency was offset in the husband's property distribution and then was counted as credit toward his alimony support obligations. The wife argued that this was double counting. Because there were inconsistencies in the experts' reports concerning the owner's salary, the court was unable to determine whether double counting had occurred and it remanded the case for further factual determinations on this issue.

---

106. *Id.* at 6.
107. *Id.*
108. *Id.* at 7.
109. *Id.* at 9.
110. *Id.*
111. Oudheusden v. Oudheusden, 259 A.3d 598, 338 Conn. 761 (2021).
112. Sampson v. Sampson, 2004 Mass. App. LEXIS 1223 (Mass. App. Ct. 2004).

The court in *Champion*,[113] noting that there is a split among jurisdictions on the issues of what constitutes double-dipping and whether it ought to be prohibited as a matter of law, rejected a claim of double-dipping and found the business to be both a marital asset and a source of income.

In *Keane*,[114] New York's highest court held that the prohibition against double counting applies only to intangible assets, such as professional licenses or goodwill, or the value of a service business, not income-producing tangible assets such as rental property.

In *Sander*,[115] the court ruled that it is not double counting to assign a value to a business as well as to attribute gross income from that business to the spouse, without adjusting either. Where the trial court, in its discretion, valued the company at a value it would have to a buyer who would pay a manager's salary, the court's decision was upheld as both logical and supported by the record.

SUMMARY

Many aspects of valuations for marital dissolution purposes can differ substantially from valuation assignments for other purposes. For example, the valuation expert may become involved in assisting in the determination as to whether certain property should or should not be included in the marital estate, or whether appreciation in the value of a business during marriage is classified as active or passive.

The applicable standard of value is generally less clear in the context of marital dissolution than for practically any other valuation purpose. The valuation expert needs to be conversant with each state's criteria from a valuation point of view, but it is also imperative to seek direction from counsel. The valuation date is also very important. The valuation expert may have to prepare valuations for more than one date. However, sometimes the court will rule on the valuation date well in advance of trial.

Discovery is often more of an issue in marital dissolution cases than in other types of valuation engagements because the business-owning spouse may resist providing access to records, premises, and/or management, or may even conceal relevant information. The issue of goodwill tends to loom larger in family law valuations than in other areas of valuation. The problem is not just the measurement of the value of goodwill, but its classification as enterprise or personal. Sometimes an allocation must be made between enterprise and personal goodwill.

Owners' compensation adjustments are typically a bigger issue in marital dissolutions than in other types of cases. Reasonable compensation is often one of the most important considerations in providing valuation services for matrimonial dissolution purposes. The issue of reasonable compensation also weighs heavily when considering the concept of double-dipping.

The value of noncompete covenants and employment agreements is another major issue being accorded growing recognition. Such agreements may be an indicium of personal goodwill rather than marital property.

---

113. Champion v. Champion, 54 Mass. App. Ct. 215, 764 N.E.2d 898, 2002 Mass. App. LEXIS 363 (Mass. App. Ct. 2002).

114. Keane v. Keane, 2006 N.Y. LEXIS 3751 (N.Y. 2006).

115. Sander v. Sander, 2006 Conn. App. LEXIS 280 (Conn. Ct. App. 2006).

Deduction of the contingent liability for taxes on trapped-in capital gains on appreciated assets is often an issue. Family law courts have also generally disallowed a deduction for hypothetical taxes on the sale of a business unless a sale has occurred or is contemplated.

Family law courts may treat valuation discounts and premiums differently than they would be treated in a conventional fair market value context. The valuation expert should be conversant in the relevant case law and be well-versed on such issues when it comes to including a discount or premium.

The valuation expert should be objective and must avoid any inclination or pressure toward bias in favor of the client. Although this applies to all types of cases, a reading of the opinions suggests that lack of objectivity may be a more prevalent problem in family law than in other types of cases. The valuation expert should be an advocate for their own opinion only.

The role of the valuation expert is critical, and an increasing number of valuation professionals are specializing in the matrimonial field. It is important to bring in a competent, experienced valuation expert early in the case and to have the valuation expert involved at every step as an integral part of the team.

REFERENCES FOR MARITAL DISSOLUTION VALUATIONS

Business Valuation Resources, www.BVLaw.com. Contains the complete text of all major state appellate decisions involving business valuation decisions, searchable by case name, key word, and state. Also contains full texts of relevant laws and regulations and unpublished conference presentations.

Business Valuation Resources. 2020. *Business Valuation in Divorce Case Law Compendium,* 5th ed. (Portland, OR: Business Valuation Resources, LLC).

Business Valuation Resources. 2011. *BVR's Guide to Fair Value in Shareholder Dissent, Oppression, and Marital Dissolution* (Portland, OR: Business Valuation Resources, LLC).

Business Valuation Resources. 2012. *BVR's Guide to Personal v. Enterprise Goodwill,* 5th ed. (Portland, OR: Business Valuation Resources. LLC).

Fishman, Jay E., et al. 2023. "Valuations for Divorce Engagements." In *PPC's Guide to Business Valuations,* 12-1 to 12-40 (Carrollton, TX: Thomson Reuters).

Fishman, Jay E., Shannon P. Pratt, and William J. Morrison. 2013. "Standards of Value in Divorce." In *Standards of Value,* 2nd ed. Chap. 5, 237–322 (Hoboken, NJ: John Wiley & Sons, Inc.).

Goldberg, Barth. *Valuation of Divorce Assets.* 2022–23 ed. (Carrollton, TX: Thomson Reuters).

Kleeman, Jr., Robert E., James R. Alerding, and Benjamin D. Miller. 1999. The *Handbook for Divorce Valuations* (Hoboken, NJ: John Wiley & Sons, Inc.).

Pratt, Shannon P. and ASA Educational Foundation. 2022. "Valuation for Marital Dissolution Purposes" and "Marital Dissolution Court Cases." In *Shannon Pratt's Valuing a Business: The Analysis and Appraisal of Closely Held Businesses,* 6th ed., Chap. 43, 1015–28 and Chap. 44, 1020–63 (New York: McGraw-Hill).

Rosoff, Charles T., ed. 2019. *Valuation Strategies in Divorce,* 5th ed. (Philadelphia: Wolters Kluwer Legal & Regulatory U.S.).

CHAPTER 23

Shareholder and Partner Disputes

David G. Clarke, ASA, William P. McInerney, ASA, and Elise Scoles

INTRODUCTION

In this chapter you will learn about:

- Shareholder, limited liability company (LLC) member, and partnership litigation involving valuation of interests in the most common situations:
    - Dissenting stockholder actions
    - Minority oppression actions
    - Claims of breach of fiduciary duty, which can accompany either of the preceding
- Disputes among partners in entities such as partnerships and among members of LLCs that may be treated differently based on the partnership agreement, LLC agreement, and/or state laws

All states and the District of Columbia have dissenting stockholder statutes. These statutes essentially provide that if a company effects an extraordinary corporate action—typically identified in the statutes—stockholders may dissent from the action and be paid the *fair value* of their shares.

Dissenters' rights are triggered by major corporate actions, such as mergers, acquisitions, or liquidations, the criteria for which vary from state to state. Dissenters' rights apply in all states if a stockholder is forced to give up their stock, such as in a cash-out merger (sometimes called a squeeze-out). In many states, dissenters' rights are triggered by the sale of major corporate assets, as defined in the respective states' statutes. Stockholders who dissent may not block or reverse the corporate action but are entitled to be paid the *fair value* of the shares immediately before the action has been put into effect, excluding any anticipatory appreciation or depreciation.[1]

Most states require that if a minority (i.e., noncontrolling) stockholder wishes to dissent from a corporate action, the stockholder must register their dissent in writing at or within a few days following the stockholder meeting at which a majority of stockholders approve the action. This process often is referred to as *perfecting* the dissenters' appraisal rights. Courts are virtually unanimous in prohibiting dissenters' appraisal rights unless dissenters perfect their rights within the time and in the manner the relevant statute

1. This chapter is adapted from Chapter 41, "Valuations in Shareholder and Partner Disputes," and Chapter 42, "Shareholder and Partner Dispute Court Cases," in Shannon P. Pratt & The ASA Educ. Found., Shannon Pratt's Valuing a Business: The Analysis and Appraisal of Closely Held Companies (6th ed. 2022). Used with permission.

specifies. In addition, there typically are other procedural hoops through which a stockholder must jump.

Numerous states also have enacted judicial dissolution statutes. Such statutes generally allow noncontrolling shareholders to sue for dissolution of the business entity if they can demonstrate oppression by the controlling shareholder(s) or a decision-making deadlock. Most states also provide for alternative remedies, particularly a compulsory buyout of the minority shareholder(s), either by the majority shareholder(s) or the company, at fair value. Criteria required to trigger a finding of oppression or irreconcilable differences vary.

"FAIR VALUE" STANDARD IN MOST DISSENT AND DISSOLUTION SUITS

State statutes define stockholder appraisal rights and also designate the standard of value to be applied. In virtually all states, the statutory standard of value is *fair value*.[2] The Revised Model Business Corporation Act (RMBCA), which many states have adopted, defined fair value in its 1984 revision as:

> The value of the shares immediately before the effectuation of the corporate action to which the dissenter objects, excluding any appreciation or depreciation in anticipation of the corporate action unless exclusion would be inequitable.[3]

In other words, the dissenting stockholder has a right to receive what was taken away from them. According to the Official Comment of the Model Business Corporation Act, the definition of fair value under state statutes leaves to the parties (and, ultimately, to the courts) the details by which fair value is to be determined within the broad outlines of the definition. However, the 2016 revision of the RMBCA noted that a court "should give great deference to the aggregate consideration accepted or approved by a disinterested board of directors for an appraisal-triggering transaction."[4] Case law precedent provides additional guidance as to how each individual state interprets the standard of fair value.[5] The interpretations vary greatly, but virtually no state specifically equates fair value with fair market value. In some cases, the ultimate value standard that is applied is fair market value, but this is a consequence of following the fair value guidance rather than the other way around. Many states have no precedential case law on fair value, in which case decisions from other states may provide guidance.

In 2016, the RMBCA was revised so that the definition of fair value reads as follows:

> [T]he value of the corporation's shares determined: (i) immediately before the effectiveness of the corporate action to which the shareholder objects; (ii) using customary and current valuation concepts and techniques generally employed for similar businesses in the context of the transaction requiring appraisal; and (iii) without discounting for lack of marketability or minority status except, if appropriate, for amendments to the articles of incorporation pursuant to section 13.02(a)(4).[6]

---

2. Fair market value, not fair value, is the standard for appraisals in California and Ohio.
3. Model Business Corporation Act (1984 Revision) § 13.01(3).
4. Model Business Corporation Act (2016 Revision), Official Comment at 309.
5. For additional details, see Appendix B.
6. Model Business Corporation Act (2016 Revision) § 13.01.

Although still not outlining a specific method of calculating value, the 2016 RMBCA definition adds two important concepts to the framework: (1) the use of customary and current valuation techniques and (2) the rejection of the use of marketability and non-control discounts except, "if appropriate, for amendments to the articles of incorporation pursuant to section 13.02(a)(4)."

In addition, the 2016 RMBCA was amended to include market exceptions to appraisal rights if both conditions are met:

1. The underlying shares were traded in a liquid market.
2. "[T]he value of the shares established by the appraisal-triggering event" is "the result of a process reasonably calculated to arrive at a price reflective of an arm's length transaction."

If those conditions were met, appraisal rights would not be triggered in the corporate event. However, the market exception would not apply if the transaction constituted an *interested transaction*.[7] Also, the 2016 RMBCA added various protections for directors of corporations in terms of fiduciary duty matters.

Approximately one-third of states have incorporated this revision into their statutes either directly or through a hybrid approach through references to rejecting noncontrol and marketability discounts. Exhibit 23-1 groups the states by the definition they have adopted.

Exhibit 23-1 Dissenting Shareholders—Fair Value Definition by State

States with Pre-1999 Definition	Applicable Statute	States with 2016 Definition	Applicable Statute
Alabama	§ 10-2B-13.32	Colorado	§ 7-113-101
Arizona	§ 10-1301	Connecticut	§ 33-855 (3)
Arkansas	§ 4-27-1301	District of Columbia	§ 29-311.01(4)
Georgia^	§ 14-2-1301(5)	Idaho	§ 30-1-1301(5)
Hawaii	§ 414-341	Iowa	§ 490.1301(4)
Indiana	§ 23-1-44-3	Louisiana	RS § 12:1-1301
Kansas*	§ 17-6712	Maine	§ 1301(4)
Kentucky	§ 271B.13-010	Mississippi	§ 79-4-13.01
Maryland^	§ 3-202(b)(2)	Nebraska	§ 21-2,171
Massachusetts	156D § 1301	New Hampshire	§ 293-A:13.01
Michigan	§ 450.1761(d)	South Dakota	§ 47-1A-1301(4)
Minnesota^	§ 302A.473(c)	Virginia	§ 13.1-729
Missouri	§ 351-870(4)	West Virginia	§ 31D-13-1301(4)
Montana	§ 35-1-826(4)	Wyoming	§ 17-16-1301 (2013)
New Jersey^	§ 14A:11-3		
New Mexico^	§ 53-15-4(A)		
North Carolina	§ 55-13-01(5)		

7. *Id.* § 13.02, Official Comment.

States with Pre-1999 Definition	Applicable Statute	States with Hybrid	Applicable Statute
North Dakota^	§ 10-19.1-88	Florida	§ 607.1301(4)
Oklahoma*	§18-1091(h)	Illinois	§ 805 ILCS 5/12.70
Oregon	§ 60.554(4)	Nevada	§ 92A.320
Pennsylvania*	§ 1572	Texas	§ 10.362
Rhode Island^	§ 7-1.2-1202.a	**States with Other**	
South Carolina	§ 33-13-101 (3)	Alaska	§ 10.06.630
Tennessee^	§ 48-23-101 (4)	California	§ 1300(a)
Utah^	§ 16-10a-1301(4)	Delaware	§ 262(h)
Vermont	§ 13.01	New York	§ 623(h)(4)
Washington	§ 23B.13.010	Ohio	§ 1701.85(C)
Wisconsin	§ 180.1301(4)		

* Statute contains relevant factors language.
^ Statute excludes inequitable language.
Source: SHANNON PRATT'S VALUING A BUSINESS: THE ANALYSIS AND APPRAISAL OF CLOSELY HELD BUSINESSES, Exhibit 42-1. Extracted from primarily individual state legislative websites.

Florida, Illinois, Nevada, and Texas use hybrids of the pre-1999 and 2016 definitions. Each of these states uses language from the pre-1999 definition and couples it with language prohibiting the use of discounts for lack of control (commonly referred to as DLOC) and discounts for lack of marketability (commonly referred to as DLOM).

The states with *other* definitions are not based on either the pre-1999 or 2016 versions of the RMBCA. California (in its appraisal statute but not its oppression statute) and Ohio use the term *fair cash value* rather than *fair value.*

Appendix B describes the statutory guidance provided for determining fair value (or other standard of value) in states whose statutes include the use of customary and current valuation concepts and techniques, all relevant factors, or other guidance relating to the method of valuation. Appendix B is displayed at the end of this book.[8]

Market Exception

Appraisal rights are broadly available for shareholders of closely held companies. However, 38 states now restrict or deny appraisal rights of shareholders of publicly traded companies through a provision in their appraisal statutes called a "market exception."[9] With varying specifics, these statutes deny shareholders of publicly traded companies the right to the court-awarded assessment to which similarly situated closely held company shareholders are entitled. The states' positions as to the market exception can be grouped in four general categories.

8. Gilbert E. Matthews, *Most States Reject Discounts in Appraisal and Oppression Cases—But There Are Important Exceptions*, 41(2) ASA BUS. VALUATION REV. 67–80 (Summer 2022). Updated by Matthews.

9. Mary Siegel, *An Appraisal of the Model Business Corporation Act's Appraisal Rights Provisions*, 74 J. LAW & CONTEMPORARY PROBLEMS 231 (2011); Gilbert E. Matthews, *The "Market Exception" in Appraisal Statutes*, HARVARD LAW SCHOOL FORUM ON CORPORATE GOVERNANCE & FINANCIAL REGULATION (Mar. 30, 2020).

Eleven states deny appraisal rights for public shareholders regardless of interested party involvement or the form of consideration received, while 12 states have no market exception. The other 27 states deny appraisal to shareholders of publicly traded corporations who receive publicly traded common stock in stock-for-stock mergers[10] but permit appraisal for public shareholders who receive cash, debt, preferred stock, or warrants as all or part of the consideration. The District of Columbia and 14 of these states additionally permit publicly traded companies' shareholders to retain appraisal rights when interested parties are materially involved, regardless of the form of consideration received.

The definition of publicly traded or marketable shares varies from state to state. Appendix C (displayed at the end of this book) summarizes, for each jurisdiction, whether a market exception applies, the definition of publicly traded shares, the scope of the exception, and the terms of any exemption that allows public shareholders to have appraisal rights.

INTERPRETATION OF THE FAIR VALUE STANDARD IN DISSENT CASES

That Which Has Been Taken

A typical interpretation of the philosophy of fair value in a dissenting stockholder situation is the following:

> Fair value, in an appraisal context measures "that which has been taken from [the shareholder], viz., his proportionate interest in a going concern."[11]

The Delaware Block Method

This statutory valuation "method" involves calculating indications of value using three measures (one related to market value, one related to asset value, and one related to investment or earnings value) and determining a weighted average of the three. The method is akin to a formula-based calculation of value used in a buy-sell agreement among shareholders of a closely held company. The Delaware Block method is now largely considered outdated and has been largely unused by U.S. courts over the past decades.[12] Ironically, the Delaware Block method has not been applied in the Delaware Court of Chancery in more than two decades.

Should Consider All Relevant Factors

In the landmark case *Weinberger v. UOP*, the Delaware Court of Chancery decided that the traditional factors considered under the Delaware Block method alone were not necessarily

---

10. Some of these states permit appraisals in stock-for-stock mergers with parent companies.

11. In Matter of Shell Oil Co., 607 A.2d 12B (Del. 1992), citing Tri-Continental Corp. v. Battye, 74 A.2d 71, 72 (Del. 1950).

12. A small number of exceptions have been observed. *See, e.g., In re* Athlon Sports Comm'ns, Inc., v. Stephen C. Duggan, et al. (Ct. App. Tenn. Oct. 17, 2016) (The Tennessee Supreme Court subsequently ruled that the Delaware Block Method was no longer the exclusive valuation method in dissenters' rights cases.) *See* Athlon Sports Communications, Inc. v. Duggan, 549 S.W.3d 107 (Tenn. 2018). *See also* Utah Resources Int'l, Inc. v. Mark Technologies Corp., 342 P.3d 761, 771 (Utah 2014).

sufficient; instead, "all relevant factors" should be considered.[13] In that case, the court specifically made the point that projections of future earnings should be considered.[14]

In another Delaware appraisal matter, the court noted that "[i]n using 'all relevant factors' to determine fair value, the court has significant discretion to use the valuation methods it deems appropriate, including the parties' proposed valuation frameworks, or one of the court's own making."[15]

The interpretation of fair value is a subject of continued debate and is difficult to generalize. Most states, however, have embraced the notion that "all relevant factors should be considered," following the lead of the Delaware Court of Chancery.

Consideration of Deal Price

When performing a fair value analysis for an appraisal action arising out of a merger, it is important to analyze the process by which the transaction occurred. As noted earlier, the 2016 RMBCA specifically suggested that a court rely on deal price when the price established by the appraisal-triggering event is "the result of a process reasonably calculated to arrive at a price reflective of an arm's length transaction." That condition was coupled with the underlying shares being traded in a liquid market, but one can extrapolate the importance of deal price if the company was sold in a robust process to a third party without conflicts of interests (e.g., sold to a third party without special consideration to management or the controlling shareholder). The 2016 RMBCA further states that "A court determining fair value . . . should give great deference to the aggregate consideration accepted or approved by a disinterested board of directors for an appraisal-triggering transaction."[16] Based on recent Delaware appraisal decisions that have valued several companies based on the transaction price, a valuation submitted in support of an appraisal action should include an explanation of whether the transaction price is indicative of fair value.

REQUIREMENT FOR ENTIRE FAIRNESS

There are many subtleties to the application of fair value for corporate law purposes. For example, some states consider the concept of *entire fairness*. There are two major aspects of entire fairness:

1. Fair consideration
2. Procedural fairness

Fair Consideration

The notion of fair consideration within the context of entire fairness also encompasses two criteria:

1. Absolute fairness
2. Relative fairness

---

13. Weinberger v. UOP, Inc., 457 A.2d 701, 712 (Del. 1983).

14. *Id.* at 714.

15. *In re* Appraisal of DFC Global Corp., 2016 Del. Ch. LEXIS 103 (Del. Ch. July 8, 2016); *rev'd, on other grounds*, DFC Global Corp. v. Muirfield Value Partners, L.P., 172 A.3d 346 (Del. 2017).

16. Model Business Corporation Act (2016 Revision) § 13.01, Official Comment.

Absolute fairness generally addresses whether the consideration received was adequate relative to the value of the interest that was given up.

Relative fairness means whether the consideration received was fair in comparison with what other stockholders received or company management received. For example, are the controlling stockholders receiving some consideration that should be shared with all stockholders (e.g., an employment agreement for which no services are required, and which contributes nothing to the company)?

Procedural Fairness

Within the concept of procedural fairness, there generally are two broad criteria:

1. Independence
2. Competence and thoroughness

Independence refers both to parties affiliated with the company and to outside legal and financial advisors.

If there are potentially conflicted board members, some companies appoint a committee of outside directors with authority to retain independent legal counsel and independent financial advisors, and to negotiate on an arm's-length basis (often referred to as a *Special Committee*). A Special Committee has the fiduciary responsibility to protect the interests of all the stockholders, especially those not part of the controlling group.

Independence with respect to outside advisors means retaining legal counsel and financial advisors who are independent of the controlling parties. This generally means professional advisors who do not have a direct or indirect financial interest in the company or a financial or other relationship with the parties to the dispute that might influence their ability to exercise independent judgment. However, it should be noted that the financial advisors to a transaction may have compensation tied to the consummation of the transaction (i.e., have an incentive to see the transaction completed).[17]

Competence and thoroughness similarly apply to parties affiliated with the company and their outside advisors. It is not expected that board members themselves be experts in legal matters, financial valuation, income tax matters, or deal structuring. It is expected, however, that they use prudent diligence and care in evaluating the qualifications of the experts that they choose to retain. It is also expected that they exert the time and effort necessary to understand and evaluate the recommendations of the outside experts in exercising their fiduciary responsibility to make recommendations in reliance on those experts. The experts merely provide advice. It is the directors who have the fiduciary responsibility to take or recommend action based on that advice.

The following cases illustrate how the Delaware Court of Chancery has applied the entire fairness standard.

- Violations of the preceding criteria caused Delaware Vice Chancellor Jacobs to deny a motion for summary judgment to dismiss a class-action suit that allowed plaintiffs only the appraisal remedy in *Seagraves*. Among the facts cited by Judge Jacobs:
    - The company did not obtain a fairness opinion at the time of the cash-out merger.

17. *See, e.g.*, Inter-Local Pension Fund GCC/IBT v. Calgon Carbon Corp., 2019 WL 479082, at *12 (Del. Ch. Jan. 25, 2019).

- The board did not establish an independent committee to safeguard the interests of the noncontrolling (i.e., minority) stockholders.
- There had been a series of private purchases at prices higher than the cash-out price, a fact that was undisclosed.

  Judge Jacobs concluded that because there was evidence that the entire fairness test was not met, "the Court must reject the defendants' argument that appraisal is the exclusive remedy."[18]

- In *Kahn*, the Delaware Supreme Court found that "the Special Committee [of the board] chose as its financial advisor a bank which had lucrative past dealings with . . . related companies."[19] Furthermore, the special committee's legal advisor was previously retained by two related companies. The court concluded that the special committee did not act in an independent and informed manner. Therefore, the case was remanded for a new fairness determination, with the burden of proof shifted to the defendants.
- A classic example of lack of fairness is found in *Ryan*. First, the controlling stockholders arranged an asset sale of the corporation's major holding, a six-store New York restaurant chain, with employment and noncompete contracts of $1 million each. It then did a squeeze-out merger. One attorney acted as a board member, represented the corporation in the transactions, and represented the controlling stockholders personally in negotiating their employment and noncompete agreements. The board did not retain any unaffiliated law firm, financial advisor, or other independent representative to represent or negotiate the merger on behalf of the noncontrolling shareholders.

  The opinion states,

  > Normally this Court will defer to a decision involving the business judgment of a corporation's directors. However, that presumption vanishes in cases where the minority shareholders are compelled to forfeit their shares in return for a value that is determined as a result of a bargaining process in which the controlling shareholder is in a position to influence both bargaining parties.[20]

  The dissenters ultimately were awarded $23.86 per share versus the $13.36 per share originally offered.

- Another Delaware case finding a lack of entire fairness was *M.G. Bancorporation*,[21] which found that the directors' failure to establish an independent committee of directors to represent the noncontrolling shareholders' interests, while on its own did not constitute evidence of unfair dealing, when combined with other pleaded facts, could support a claim of unfair dealing. The court also found that the difference between the stock's $85 per share fair value and the $41 per share merger price, combined with the other pleaded unfairness claims, created an inference that the merger was the product of unfair dealing.

Lack of entire fairness usually occurs when controlling stockholders approve transactions that benefit them at the expense of other stockholders without independent oversight. The most common scenario is a transaction without an independent appraisal, often coupled with not having an independent committee of the board of directors to

18. Seagraves v. Urstadt Prop. Co., 1996 Del. Ch. LEXIS 36, at *24 (Del. Ch. Apr. 1, 1996).
19. Kahn v. Tremont Corp., 694 A.2d 422, 429 (Del. 1997).
20. Ryan v. Tad's Enters., 709 A.2d 682 (Del. Ch. 1996).
21. M.G. Bancorp. v. Le Beau, 1998 Del. Ch. LEXIS 9 (Del Ch. Jan. 29, 1998); *aff'd*, M.G. Bancorp. v. Le Beau, 737 A.2d 513 (Del. 1999).

evaluate the transaction from the perspective of fairness to noncontrolling stockholders. Directors or controlling shareholders who stand on both sides of a transaction have the burden of establishing the transaction's entire fairness.[22]

In *Gesoff*,[23] the plaintiffs argued that a going-private merger, intended by a foreign parent corporation to remove the noncontrolling shareholders of its U.S. subsidiary, was a product of unfair dealing, producing an unfair price for the subsidiary. Notwithstanding the defendants' argument that the merger was fair because any irregularities in the merger dealings did not affect the fairness of the merger price, the Delaware Court of Chancery found that the merger process was marked with grave examples of unfairness and led to a plainly unfair price for the going-private transaction. Consequently, the court awarded damages to the class and to those stockholders seeking appraisal based on the court's determination of fair value at the time of the merger—a figure significantly greater than the consideration offered in the going-private transaction. In reaching its conclusion, the court determined that the process established by the defendants unilaterally imposed on the noncontrolling (i.e., minority) stockholders a price of the parent's own choosing, established a deceptive negotiation between the parties, and left the noncontrolling stockholder's putative special committee almost entirely powerless against its parent.

There are two recent notable Chancery Court decisions that have narrowed the applicability of the entire fairness standard of review.

- In 2014, the Delaware Supreme Court affirmed the Delaware Court of Chancery's ruling in *M&F Worldwide*[24] in which the Chancery Court allowed the controlling shareholder in a transaction to avoid the entire fairness standard of review. In that case, the controlling stockholder effectively relinquished control over the approval of a self-dealing transaction to an independent committee of disinterested directors. There was also a nonwaivable, fully informed vote of a majority of the noncontrolling shareholders. In this case, the Delaware Supreme Court reasoned that the transaction reflected arm's-length bargaining and afforded noncontrolling shareholders the opportunity to decide for themselves whether to approve the transaction.
- The second case is *Corwin.*[25] The key takeaway from this case is that in the absence of a controlling shareholder, a fully informed vote of disinterested and uncoerced stockholders will extinguish breach of fiduciary claims.

As a result of these decisions, corporate boards of directors may overcome breach of fiduciary duty claims if they can demonstrate a fully informed vote of disinterested and uncoerced stockholders. Even with this roadmap, however, there continue to be cases that do not meet this standard, and thus the Chancery Court determines that an entire fairness review may be appropriate.

22. Weinberger v. UOP, Inc., 457 A.2d 701, 712 (Del. 1983).
23. Gesoff v. IIC Indus., Inc., 902 A.2d 1130 (Del. Ch. 2006).
24. Kahn v. M&F Worldwide Corp., 88 A.3d 635 (Del. 2014).
25. Corwin v. KKR Fin. Holdings LLC, 125 A.3d 304 (Del. 2015).

CONSEQUENCES OF LACK OF ENTIRE FAIRNESS

Lack of entire fairness implies that the directors violated some duty owed to the shareholders. If the plaintiffs establish such liability, then the measure of damages may go beyond simply fair value as contemplated in appraisal actions pursuant to the dissenters' rights statutes.

As explained by former Vice Chancellor Jack Jacobs, then of the Delaware Court of Chancery (and later a justice of the Delaware Supreme Court):

> The statutory appraisal case limits damages, on the upside, in that the value is fixed at one point in time, and is not supposed to include any synergies. There is no issue of burden of proof. If the Court does not accept the valuation presented by one side or the other, it must perform independently its own valuation.[26]

In a breach of fiduciary duty case, the traditional burden of proof rules apply, whereby if the evidence on both sides is even (or in *equipoise*) then the party that has the burden of proof loses.

Another bright line difference is that in a fiduciary duty action, other measures of damages may be available, including damages calculated as of a date after the transaction. Rescissory damages[27] would be an example. Damages measured by that method would be available in a breach of fiduciary duty action, but not in a statutory appraisal case.[28]

NONCONTROLLING INTEREST DISSOLUTION ACTIONS

Numerous states have enacted *judicial dissolution* statutes in one form or another. Such statutes generally allow noncontrolling shareholders to sue for dissolution of the business entity if they can demonstrate oppression by the controlling shareholder(s) or a decision-making deadlock. In some states, the noncontrolling shareholder bringing suit must hold some minimum percentage of the ownership, while other states have no minimum percentage requirement. Most states also provide for alternative remedies, particularly a compulsory buyout of the noncontrolling shareholder(s), by the majority shareholder(s), or by the company, at fair value.

In California, the leading state in noncontrolling shareholder dissolution actions, if stockholders owning one-third or more of a corporation's stock can demonstrate "minority oppression," their remedy is a dissolution of the corporation. However, the majority stockholder(s) can prevent such a dissolution by paying, in cash, the fair value pursuant to California Corporations Code § 2000. The following is the process involved:

1. Noncontrolling stockholder(s) sue for dissolution.
2. Court determines whether conditions warranting the dissolution have occurred.

---

26. Shannon P. Pratt, *Fair Value: A View from the Delaware Court of Chancery Bench* (interview with Vice Chancellor Jack B. Jacobs), *in* 5(9) Business Valuation Update 2 (Sept. 1999).

27. Where rescission has been rendered impossible or impractical, rescissory damages may be awarded; the purpose of rescissory damages is to restore the plaintiff to the position occupied before the defendant's wrongful act.

28. Pratt, *supra* note 26.

3. If so, and parties cannot agree on a price to buy out the controlling stockholders, majority stockholders move to stay the dissolution pending valuation to determine how much the noncontrolling stockholders would receive if liquidation proceeded.
4. Court appoints three appraisers. Parties can agree upon, and seek court confirmation in an appointee process, or can allow the court to select the appraisers. Unless otherwise agreed by the parties, the conclusion of the appraisers is advisory to the court rather than binding.
5. Court adopts a value.
6. Court enters a decree "which shall provide in the alternative for winding up and dissolution of the corporation unless payment is made for the shares within the time specified by the decree."
7. Controlling stockholder(s) may elect to pay the amount in cash prior to the deadline.
8. If the controlling stockholder(s) declines to pay, the company is liquidated, and all shareholders receive a proportionate share of the resulting cash proceeds.[29]

INTERPRETATION OF THE FAIR VALUE STANDARD IN DISSOLUTION CASES

Courts in different states vary from one another (and sometimes from one case to the next in the same state) in their interpretation of fair value for dissolution cases, and may not interpret this standard in the same manner as for dissenting stockholder cases.

California has what might seem at first reading an internally contradictory definition of fair value in the context of its dissolution statutes:

> The fair value shall be determined on the basis of the liquidation value as of the valuation date but taking into account the possibility, if any, of sale of the entire business as a going concern in a liquidation.[30]

While this may seem abstruse at first blush, the evolution of case law makes it clear. The value may be based on a liquidation of assets and/or selling all or parts of the operations as a going concern if that would produce higher net proceeds.

In any case, as with fair value in the context of dissent cases, the definition of fair value in dissolution cases is missing some of the elements of the traditional definition of fair market value. As the previously cited article points out, many of the assumptions underlying fair market value are not present:

- There is no willing seller. In the dissolution the seller is involuntarily disposing of the assets.
- The seller is under compulsion to sell.
- The involuntary seller under compulsion does not have the luxury of waiting for a top offer; the sale must be completed under the adverse conditions of a corporate dissolution conducted in accordance with California law.
- Implicitly, the buyer is aware of the seller's weakened position.

---

29. Arthur J. Shartsis, *Dissolution Actions Yield Less Than Fair Market Enterprise Value*, https://www.sflaw.com/wp-content/uploads/2016/02/AShartsis-Fair-Market-Value.pdf.

30. Cal. Corp. Code § 2000(a).

READERS MUST INTERPRET CASES CAREFULLY

Delaware has by far the most comprehensive body of case law in the realm of dissenting stockholder actions. When other states lack their own precedent, they often look to other states for precedent.[31] Delaware tends to be the leader, but states also look at decisions in other states that have the same or similarly worded statutes.[32] This chapter section provides example cases on valuation issues primarily from the Delaware Court of Chancery.

A primary purpose of appraisal statutes is to protect noncontrolling shareholders and, to this end, courts generally award a proportionate share of the going concern value of the business prior to the triggering action, without consideration of discounts (e.g., discount for lack of control or discount for lack of marketability).[33]

A study of the relevant case law is an essential prerequisite to estimate fair value for either a dissenting stockholder action or a suit for dissolution in any jurisdiction. Rarely will the reader of precedent cases have clear-cut guidance as to the court's likely posture on every possible valuation issue.

The facts and circumstances of cases vary significantly. Thus, while prior cases provide guidance, one must resist interpreting them as providing for bright-line rules or as being the final authority on an issue.

Vice Chancellor Jack B. Jacobs of the Court of Chancery (later, Justice on the Delaware Supreme Court) clearly sounded this warning:

> Both my Court and the Delaware Supreme Court recognize that valuation cases are extremely fact-driven. Very few conclusions on valuation issues have universal applicability, though statements found in some opinions may have the appearance, and might be interpreted by some, as having sweeping generality.[34]

Regardless of case law, appraisers should adhere to best practices as espoused by valuation professional organizations, peer-reviewed valuation articles, and business valuation texts when performing appraisals whenever practical.

HIGH RISK ASSOCIATED WITH APPLYING NOVEL THEORIES

Courts in general appear highly skeptical of unproven financial models and theories. Triers of fact typically do not have formal training in finance (let alone business valuation) and prefer well-established methods generally accepted in the valuation community and/or applied in prior case law. Moreover, the *Weinberger* decision that liberalized valuation methodologies for appraisal actions directed the Court of Chancery to accept valuations based on methodologies "generally considered acceptable in the financial community."[35] Thus, in *Dunmire*, Chancellor Andre G. Bouchard rejected the use of an equity risk premium based on an online survey that had never been

31. *See, e.g.*, Casey v. Amboy Bancorporation, 2006 N.J. Super. Unpub. LEXIS 1355 (N.J. Supr. App. Div. Aug. 8, 2006) and Reynolds Am., Inc. v. Third Motion Equities Master Fund Ltd., 2020 NCBC 35 (N.C. Super. Apr. 27, 2020).

32. Because statutes of several states undergo revision from time to time, it is impractical to publish even summaries of all of them in a book such as this. Most, if not all, states' government web pages provide their statutes. Exhibit 23-1 lists statutes as of May 2023.

33. *See* Chapter 18, "Discounts and Premiums."

34. Pratt, *supra* note 26.

35. Weinberger v. UOP, Inc., 457 A.2d 701, 712 (Del. 1983).

relied upon by a court before and was well outside the range of 5% to 7% used in prior Court of Chancery decisions.[36] Also, in *SourceHOV Holdings*, Vice Chancellor Joseph R. Slights III noted that an expert "undermine[d] his credibility" with a novel method to estimate the subject company's beta.[37]

While innovation in the field of business valuation is encouraged, testing in a court setting new theories and methods that are not generally accepted in the financial community can be a high-risk venture when providing expert witness opinions.

FAIR VALUE UNDER STATE STATUTES IS NOT FAIR MARKET VALUE

While various states interpret fair value differently from one another, and sometimes within the same state differently under differing facts and circumstances, they consistently do not equate fair value with fair market value. This point is illustrated well by a New York court's rejection of an expert's valuation report that relied on fair market value in a dissenting stockholder case. The court stated:

> [B]ecause the petitioner's expert . . . in its valuation report (on title page) and on 15 occasions refers to its valuation to be based on Fair Market Value, the Court considers it a threshold question as to whether Fair Value and Fair Market Value are synonymous. Section BCL 623(H)(4) of the Business Corporation Law only uses the term Fair Value and does so eleven times. . . . The Court may give no weight to market value if the facts of the case so require.[38]

That court ultimately rejected the report based on fair market value (concluding $52 per share) and awarded the dissenters fair value of $99 per share.

In *M.G. Bancorp*, the investment banker had issued a fairness opinion on a squeeze-out merger based on fair market value rather than on fair value. The Court of Chancery stated that this was *legally flawed* as evidence regarding fair value.[39]

In *Pueblo Bancorporation*, the Colorado Supreme Court, after an extensive review of the law in other jurisdictions, stated, "We are convinced that 'fair value' does not mean 'fair market value.'"[40] The New Jersey Supreme Court has expressed a similar sentiment,[41] as have a majority of courts in other jurisdictions.[42]

---

36. Dunmire v. Farmers & Merchants Bancorp of Western Pa., Inc., 2016 Del. Ch. LEXIS 167 (Del. Ch. Nov. 10, 2016).

37. Manichaean Capital LLC v. SourceHOV Holdings, Inc., 2020 WL 496606 (Del. Ch. Jan. 30, 2020), *aff'd*, SourceHOV Holdings, Inc. v. Manichaean Capital, LLC, 246 A.3d 139. In this decision, Vice Chancellor Slights went as far as calling it grounds for a *Daubert* motion (i.e., disqualification) in other jurisdictions.

38. Matter of Slant/Fin. Corp. v. Chicago Corp. (unpublished) (N.Y. Supr. Ct. Oct. 26, 1995), *aff'd*, 236 A.D.2d 547 (N.Y. App. 1997). The text of the decision was printed in the N.Y.L.J. (Nov. 8. 1995).

39. M.G. Bancorp. v. Le Beau, 1998 Del. Ch. LEXIS 9 (Del Ch. Jan. 29, 1998); *aff'd*, M.G. Bancorp. v. Le Beau, 737 A.2d 513 (Del. 1999).

40. Pueblo Bancorporation v. Lindoe, Inc., 63 P.3d 353, 361 (Colo. Jan. 21, 2003).

41. In Lawson Mardon Wheaton, Inc. v. Smith, 716 A.2d 550, 558 (N.J. App. 1998); *aff'd*, 734 A.2d 738 (N.J. 1999), the N.J. Supreme Court concurred with the appellate court, which, quoting J. Anthony & K. Boraas, *Betrayed, Belittled . . . But Triumphant: Claims of Shareholders in Closely Held Corporations*, 22 Wm. Mitchell L. Rev. 1173, 1186 (1996), said, "Fair Value carries with it the statutory purposes that shareholders be fairly compensated, which may or may not equate with the market's judgment about the stock's value. This is particularly appropriate in the close corporation setting where there is no ready market for the shares and consequently no Fair Market Value."

42. *See* Swope v. Seigel-Robert, Inc., 243 F.3d 486, 493 (8th Cir. 2001); Wenzel v. Hopper & Galliher, P.C., 779 N.E.2d 30, 38 (Ind. App. 2002); First Western Bank Wall v. Olsen, 621 N.W.2d 611, 617 (S.D. 2001);

In another Colorado case involving a noncontrolling shareholder's challenge of a transaction as "unfair," in response to the shareholder's contention that no discounts should be allowed, the court admonished that "this case is not a dissenters' rights action. . . . It involves the question of whether a transaction was fair, not the 'fair value' of dissenters' shares." Accordingly, that court held it was proper to apply a DLOM of 15% to 20%.[43] The case demonstrates the importance not only of being clear as to which standard of value is being applied but also as to what kind of case is involved.

PREMISE OF VALUE/EXCLUSION OF SYNERGIES

In a dissenters' rights action, Delaware case law provides that a shareholder is entitled to a proportionate share of the corporation as a going concern based on the operative reality of the company at the time of merger, rather than on a liquidation basis.[44] The exclusion of any benefit that may arise from the triggering event is consistent with a significant majority of statutory definitions of fair value in dissenting shareholder matters.

A related issue decided by the Delaware courts is that the value of change-of-control synergies must be excluded from a merger price in determining the value of a company on a going-concern basis. One of the first cases in which the Court of Chancery subtracted a synergy discount was *Union Illinois*, in which the court applied a 13% deduction for synergies to the merger price.[45] The Court of Chancery now commonly applies a synergy discount from the deal price in those cases where the court finds the deal price a reliable indicator of value and has sufficient evidence regarding synergies transferred to the seller.[46] Other items that are excluded in determining going-concern value are prospective tax benefits,[47] actions planned by a third-party acquirer,[48] and improperly issued shares.[49] However, unless there is a derivative claim attacking it, excessive compensation is deemed to be part of operative reality and is not excluded.[50]

In *Medpointe*,[51] the Court of Chancery ruled that where an asset sale and merger were contingent on each other, capital gains taxes and other expenses related to the asset sale should be deducted in determining the value of the merged company. The court

---

Matthew G. Norton Co. v. Smyth, 51 P.3d 159, 165 (Wash. App. 2002); HMO-W, Inc. v. SSM Health Care Sys., 611 N.W.2d 250, 255 (Wis. 2000).

43. Kim v. The Grover C. Coors Trust, 179 P.3d 86, 97 (Colo. App. 2007). In contrast, Delaware case law generally equates the *fair value* prong of the entire fairness standard with fair value in appraisal. *See* Gesoff v. IIC Indus., Inc., 902 A.2d 1130 (Del. Ch. 2006).

44. *See, e.g.*, Paskill Corp. v. Alcoma Corp., 747 A.2d 549 (Del. Supr. 2000) ("Operative reality" speaks of what was actually occurring at the time of the challenged corporate action. Operative reality depends on the facts of each specific case.).

45. Union Illinois 1995 Investment Ltd. P'ship v. Union Fin. Grp., Ltd., 847 A.2d 340 (Del. Ch. 2003).

46. *See, e.g.*, *In re* Appraisal of Solera Holdings, Inc., 2018 WL 3625644 (Del. Ch. July 30, 2018) and *In re* Appraisal of Panera Bread Co., 2020 WL 506684 (Del. Ch. Jan. 31, 2020).

47. Ng v. Heng Sang Realty Corp., 2004 Del. Ch. LEXIS 69 (Apr. 22, 2004); *aff'd*, Heng Sang Realty Corp. v. Ng, 867 A.2d 901 (Del. 2005).

48. ACP Master, Ltd. v. Sprint Corp., 2017 Del. Ch. LEXIS 125 (Del. Ch. July 21, 2017); *aff'd*, 184 A.3d 1291 (Del. 2018).

49. Gentile v. SinglePoint Fin., Inc., 2003 Del. Ch. LEXIS 21 (Del. Ch. Mar. 5, 2003).

50. Gonsalves v. Straight Arrow Publishers, 701 A.2d 357, 363 (Del. Ch. 1997).

51. Cede & Co., Inc. v. Medpointe Healthcare, Inc., 2004 Del. Ch. LEXIS 124 (Del. Ch. Aug. 16, 2004).

reasoned that the asset sale was a part of the merged company's operative reality on the valuation date.

The operative reality concept results in the exclusion of deferred taxes on built-in capital gains on assets that management does not currently intend to sell. In *Paskill*, the Delaware Supreme Court ruled:

> The record reflects that a sale of its appreciated investment assets was not part of Okeechobee's operative reality on the date of the merger. Therefore, the Court of Chancery should have excluded any deduction for the speculative future tax liabilities that were attributed by Alcoma to those uncontemplated sales.[52]

In contrast, the Delaware Supreme Court approved deferred taxes in *Technicolor*. The difference is that, in *Technicolor*, the built-in gain was operative reality on the valuation date because the company's management had already decided to sell the relevant assets.[53]

Although the Delaware courts usually exclude changes planned by a third-party acquirer, they will take a different view if the buyer gains control before a second-stage merger (a squeeze-out merger that follows a tender or exchange offer) that does not close promptly after the first stage. The Delaware Supreme Court's 1996 *Technicolor* decision ruled that dissenting shareholders were entitled to benefit from changes being made or planned by a new management that had assumed control prior to the valuation date.[54]

In the New York corporate dissolution matter of *Ferolito*,[55] the plaintiff interpreted fair value in New York as follows:

> [I]n fixing fair value, the courts should determine the minority shareholder's proportionate interest in the going concern of the corporation as a whole, that is, "what a willing purchaser, in an arm's length transaction, would offer for the corporation as an operating business."

The plaintiff advocated strategic control value be used (see Chapters 2 and 18 for discussions of the strategic control level of value).

The court did not consider that strategic value was appropriate for its determination of fair value, concluding that:

> These principles make clear that the Court may not consider AriZona's "strategic" or "synergistic" value to a hypothetical third-party purchaser, as [plaintiff] urges. A valuation that incorporates such a "strategic" or "synergistic" element would not rely on the actual facts that relate to AriZona as an operating business, but rather would force the Court to speculate about the future.[56]

---

52. Paskill Corp. v. Alcoma Corp., 747 A.2d 549 (Del. Supr. 2000).

53. Cede & Co. v. Technicolor, 684 A.2d 289, 298–99 (Del. 1996).

54. The Official Comments to MBCA § 13.01 (2008) cite *Cede & Co. v. Technicolor* and state, "[I]n a two-step transaction culminating in a merger, the corporation is valued immediately before the second step merger, taking into account any interim changes in value."

55. Ferolito v. Vultaggio, 2014 N.Y. Misc. LEXIS 4709, at *17 (N.Y. Supr. Oct. 14, 2014), quoting Matter of Blake v. Blake Agency, 107 A.D.2d 139, 146 (N.Y. App. 1985).

56. *Id.* at *18.

BREACH OF FIDUCIARY DUTY EXPANDS PLAINTIFFS' POTENTIAL DAMAGES

As already noted, the concept of *entire fairness* includes both procedural fairness and fair consideration paid. If the test of entire fairness is not met, then plaintiffs' damages may go beyond the simple dissenting stockholder appraisal rights remedy. The remedies for breach of fiduciary duties can vary between appraisal-based damages (i.e., fair value) and other damages (e.g., rescissory). The appropriate measurement will be case specific and developed with the assistance of counsel to the litigation.

SOME STATES USE ACQUISITION VALUE INSTEAD OF GOING-CONCERN VALUE

Most states follow the Delaware interpretation of fair value, valuing a company as it exists on the valuation date. The case law of some states, however, defines going-concern value more expansively. In 1986, the Supreme Judicial Court of Massachusetts ruled:

> As a going concern, the value of an enterprise such as the Old Patriots is the price a knowledgeable buyer would pay for the entire corporation, including the National Football League (NFL) franchise, the stadium lease, various contracts, goodwill, and other assets and liabilities.[57]

The high court of Maine concluded in the *McLoon* case:

> Especially in fixing the appraisal remedy in a closely held corporation, the relevant inquiry is what is the highest price a single buyer would reasonably pay for the whole enterprise, not what a willing buyer and a willing seller would bargain out as the sales price of a dissenting shareholder's share in a hypothetical market transaction.[58]

In *Trapp Family Lodge*, the Vermont Supreme Court ruled:

> [T]o find fair value, the trial court must determine the best price a single buyer could reasonably be expected to pay for the corporation as an entirety and prorate this value equally among all shares of its common stock.[59]

New York similarly defines *fair value* as the amount that would be paid by an arm's-length non-synergistic buyer (i.e., acquisition value):

> [I]n fixing fair value, courts should determine the minority shareholder's proportionate interest in the going concern value of the *corporation* as a whole, that is, "what a willing purchaser, in an arm's length transaction, would offer for corporation as an operating business."[60]

---

57. Sarrouf v. New England Patriots Football Club, Inc., 492 N.E.2d 1122, 1125 (Mass. 1986).
58. *In re* Val. of Common Stock of McLoon Oil Co., 565 A.2d 997, 1004 (Me. 1989).
59. Trapp Family Lodge, 725 A.2d 927, 931 (Vermont 1999).
60. Friedman v. Beway Realty Corp., 87 N.Y.2d 161, 168 (N.Y. 1995), quoting Matter of Blake v. Blake Agency, 107 A.D.2d 139, 146 (N.Y. App. 1985).

Other states that have cited *McLoon* and valued companies at the presumed acquisition value include Connecticut,[61] Florida,[62] Indiana,[63] Iowa,[64] Missouri,[65] and Virginia.[66]

OTHER STATES CONSIDER MARKET VALUE, ASSET VALUE, AND INVESTMENT VALUE

In Utah's dissenters' case of first impression, *Oakridge Energy*,[67] the Supreme Court of Utah reviewed and cited case law from other states that had similar statutes, including Iowa, Maryland, Maine, Delaware, and Massachusetts. The company (which was public before the triggering event) paid dissenting stockholders $2.75 per share, based on a $2.50 market price plus a $0.25 dividend. Plaintiffs claimed $3.57 per share based on a pro forma balance sheet after taking the effect of the proceeds of the asset sale that triggered dissenters' rights.

The court noted that the consensus of the cases cited is that the component elements to be relied on in estimating fair value are market value, net asset value, and investment value, and "the courts have traditionally favored investment value, rather than asset value, as the most important of the three elements."[68] The court "conclude[d] that the trial Court erred in using the stock market price of the Oakridge shares as the sole criterion for determining the fair value of the dissenters' shares."[69] It explained, "We agree with the courts cited above that a dissenting shareholder disclaims both the burden and the benefit of the disfavored corporate action.[70]

> [U]nder the plain language of the statute, any effect of the Cometra sale must be excluded. . . . No informed expert even ventured to suggest the Oakridge assets could be valued at $21.5 million prior to Cometra's offer. . . . The $21.5 million sale price suggests that the South Texas properties had some unique value for Cometra, inflating the value of the assets above their realistic pre-sale value. "However, 'fair value' is not measured by any unique benefits that will accrue to the acquiring corporation, any more than the compensable value of property taken by eminent domain is measured by its special value to the condemner." Moreover, the sale price here was not reinforced by several buyers bidding against each other.[71]

The defendants had introduced testimony that net asset value before the events was $2.13 per share. Neither side had introduced evidence of investment value. Therefore, the Supreme Court concluded:

---

61. Devivo v. Devivo, 2001 Conn. Super. LEXIS 1285 (May 7, 2001).
62. G & G Fashion Design, Inc. v. Garcia, 870 So. 2d 870, 872 (Fla. App. 2004).
63. Lees Inns of Am., Inc. v. Lee, 924 N.E.2d 143, 156 (Ind. App. 2010).
64. Northwest Investment Corp. v. Wallace, 741 N.W.2d 782, 791 (Iowa 2007).
65. Swope v. Siegel-Robert, Inc. 74 F. Supp. 2d 876 (E.D. Mo. 1999).
66. U.S. Inspect, Inc. v. McGreevy, 57 Va. Cir. 511, 526 (2000).
67. Oakridge Energy, Inc. v. Clifton, 937 P.2d 130 (Utah 1997).
68. *Id.* at 133. Investment value, as used here, is defined as a value based on earnings, as opposed to the definition of investment value in contexts other than fair value determinations—that is, the value to a particular buyer or seller.
69. *Id.*
70. *Id.*
71. *Id.*, quoting *In re* Valuation of Common Stock of Libby, McNeill & Libby, 406 A.2d 54, 63 (Me. 1979).

> The stock market price and a reasonable approximation of the asset value were before the trial Court, each supported by substantial evidence of investment value. . . . Absent evidence of investment value, the trial Court should at least have considered the asset value as well as the market price of the stock. However, since the per share value based on asset value ($2.13) is less than the stock market price ($2.50), no choice of weighting would have resulted in a per share value greater than $2.50 for the Oakridge stock. Thus, the trial Court's error is harmless, indeed beneficial to the dissenters since Oakridge has not sought an adjustment of the $2.75 already paid.
>
> We affirm the judgment of the trial Court.[72]

Unfortunately, courts' interpretations of market value, investment value, and asset value vary. For example, asset value usually, but not always, means the net assets adjusted to some premise of current value. In a New York judicial dissolution/oppression case, investment value based on the capitalization of excess earnings via a cash flow analysis was accepted for a determination of fair market value.[73] The court ruled that evidence of corporate wrongdoing was relevant to a valuation using investment value since, if proven, the alleged misappropriation of corporate funds would have had a detrimental effect on the corporation's earning power and its value under that method. Specifically, net income would have to be adjusted by eliminating excess compensation and the unauthorized purchase of personal life insurance and rental of a luxury car.

Consideration of all these major elements, that is, market value, investment value, and asset value, does not necessarily mean that all three will be utilized in the final analysis. In some cases, weight will be accorded to all three, in some cases, only two, and some cases will be decided entirely on the basis of one of the three major elements. Investment value typically is accorded the greatest weight, followed by market value, with asset value usually accorded the least weight.

THE IMPACT OF APPRAISAL ARBITRAGE IN RECENT DELAWARE DECISIONS

In May 2007, Chancellor William B. Chandler III rendered a decision clarifying that investors who bought shares *after* an announced transaction were eligible to seek appraisal. *Transkaryotic* held that new beneficial owners of shares held in street name need not prove that their shares had not been voted in favor of the merger at the direction of a previous beneficial owner.[74] *Transkaryotic* effectively created a market for trading and aggregation in appraisal actions, opening an arbitrage opportunity for hedge funds.

Following *Transkaryotic*, there was a surge in Delaware appraisal cases in which funds bought publicly traded shares of a company following the announcement of its acquisition and then sought appraisal rights. This phenomenon became referred to as *appraisal arbitrage*. The basis of this investment strategy was that the announced deal price in a merger or acquisition of a publicly traded company was inadequate, and that through use of recognized valuation methods such as a discounted cash flow method (DCF), a valuation expert could demonstrate to the court that the fair value was above the deal price. This strategy also became potentially more profitable after the 2007

72. *Id.* at 135.

73. Matter of Dissolution of Exterior Delite, Inc., 831 N.Y.S. 656 (N.Y. Supr. 2006).

74. *In re* Appraisal of Transkaryotic Therapies, Inc., 2007 Del. Ch. LEXIS 57 (Del. Ch. May 2, 2007).

codification of prejudgment interest at 5% plus the federal discount rate, which likely factored into these investors' potential returns.

Appraisal arbitrage investors between 2007 and 2016 won victories with several decisions above deal price based on petitioners' DCF analyses. However, in 2017, the Delaware Supreme Court reversed two Court of Chancery decisions that relied upon petitioners' experts' DCF analyses that were significantly higher than the deal price.[75] It reasoned that if stock markets are efficient and trading prices of public company stocks reflect the collective wisdom of market participants, then it was not plausible that the market's assessment of value is not the best basis for determining fair value (as opposed to the value conclusion of an expert's DCF, for example). As will be discussed later in this chapter, the Court of Chancery has recently and regularly opined that unless a deal process (i.e., the process by which a company was sold) was somehow flawed, the deal price, excluding the value of potential transferred synergies, if any, included in the deal price, is the best indicator of fair value. Likely, it is only when the market for the underlying target's stock is not efficient and/or the deal process is flawed that the court will consider the use of analytical valuation methods such as a DCF to determine fair value.

It is also important to note that the Court of Chancery, which can be skeptical of valuation expert testimony, will often look to other contemporaneous indications of equity value such as valuation performed for Internal Revenue Code (I.R.C.) § 409A, to determine the fair market value of options for income tax reporting. A § 409A valuation is necessary when companies grant stock-based compensation and must perform and report the fair market value of their outstanding options. The Court of Chancery may give weight to the results of a previously prepared § 409A valuation as a non-litigation-driven indicator of a company's value.[76]

Dell Compliance/Approach to Valuation

In a series of decisions between 2017 and 2020, the Delaware courts strongly affirmed that market pricing is the best evidence of fair value.[77] In determining the fair value of public companies, this implies that if the appraisal action results from a sale of the company to a third party, then great deference will be given to the deal price unless there are extenuating circumstances (e.g., conflicts of interest). It is therefore important that

75. Dell Inc. v. Magnetar Global Event Driven Master Fund Ltd, 2017 Del. LEXIS 518 (Del. Dec. 14, 2017), *reversing In re* Appraisal of Dell Inc., 2016 Del. Ch. LEXIS 81 (Del. Ch. May 31, 2016); DFC Global Corp. v. Muirfield Value Partners, L.P., 172 A.3d 346 (Del. 2017), *reversing In re* Appraisal of DFC Global Corp., 2016 Del. Ch. LEXIS 103 (Del. Ch. July 8, 2016); *modified*, C.A. No. 10107-CB (Del. Ch. Sept. 14, 2016) [unpublished].

76. *See, e.g.*, Basho Technologies HoldCo B, LLC v. Georgetown Basho Investors, LLC, 2018 WL 3326693 (July 6, 2018). Note that the Court of Chancery views stock-based compensation as a non-cash expense in DCF analyses but approves it being a charge against income. *See* Merion Capital, L.P. v. 3M Cogent, Inc., 2013 Del. Ch. LEXIS 172, at *44–*45 (Del. Ch. July 8, 2013).

77. In 14 of 15 recent appraisal decisions involving the acquisitions of publicly traded companies, the final opinion of fair value was equal to or less than the merger consideration. The one exception, *Norcraft*, had a fair value conclusion less than 3% in excess of deal price. Blueblade Capital Opportunities LLC v. Norcraft Cos., Inc., 2018 WL 3602940 (Del. Ch. July 27, 2018).

valuation experts analyze the process surrounding the transaction to determine if the process resulted in a *Dell Compliant* transaction.[78]

The term Dell Compliant arose from the Delaware Supreme Court's reversal of the Court of Chancery's *Dell* appraisal. The lower court had rejected the transaction price because, among other things, the shopping process was inadequate.[79] The Supreme Court reversed the decision, rebutting each point made by the lower court and explaining why the shopping process was satisfactory.[80]

If a transaction is Dell Compliant, then the deal price provides the best basis for determining fair value. As laid out in the *AOL* decision:

> Where, however, transaction price represents an unhindered, informed, and competitive market valuation, the trial judge must give particular and serious consideration to transaction price as evidence of fair value. Where information necessary for participants in the market to make a bid is widely disseminated, and where the terms of the transaction are not structurally prohibitive or unduly limiting to such market participation, the trial court in its determination of fair value must take into consideration the transaction price as set by the market. I will refer to transactions compliant with such conditions by the shorthand "Dell Compliant."[81]

If the Court of Chancery determines that a transaction is not Dell Compliant, it will consider all three broad approaches to value (income, market, and asset) in dissenting stockholder cases. When the court declines to defer to the deal price and employs traditional valuation methods, the court has expressed a preference for the DCF method. However, the court recognizes that the reliability of a DCF analysis depends on reasonable projections, which are not always available. Also, note that while the court has rarely given weight (if at all) in recent years to the guideline public company and guideline transaction methods (under the market approach),[82] when appropriate to do so, one should use these valuation methods, so that the court may decide what weight to give the results in its fair value determination.

Exhibit 23-2 lists the Delaware appraisal and fiduciary cases decided from 2010 through late 2023 where the DCF (or capitalized cash flow) method or guideline public company (GPC) method was given weight in the court's determination of fair value.[83]

---

78. *In re* Appraisal of AOL, Inc., 2018 WL 1037450 (Del. Ch. Feb. 23, 2018); *modified*, 2018 WL 3913775 (Del. Ch. Aug. 15, 2018).

79. Dell Inc. v. Magnetar Global Event Driven Master Fund Ltd, 2017 Del. LEXIS 518 (Del. Dec. 14, 2017), *reversing In re* Appraisal of Dell Inc., 2016 Del. Ch. LEXIS 81 (Del. Ch. May 31, 2016).

80. *Id.*

81. *In re* Appraisal of AOL, Inc., 2018 WL 1037450 (Del. Ch. Feb. 23, 2018); *modified*, 2018 WL 3913775 (Del. Ch. Aug. 15, 2018).

82. In the past 12 years, the Court of Chancery has used the guideline public company method in only two appraisal cases, DFC Global Corp. v. Muirfield Value Partners, L.P., 172 A.3d 346 (Del. 2017), and HBK Master Fund L.P. v. Pivotal Software, Inc., 2023 Del. Ch. LEXIS 332 (Del. Ch. Aug. 14, 2023). Over the same period, the court has additionally used the guideline public company method for valuation in two fiduciary duty cases, *In re Southern Peru Copper Corp. S'holder Derivative Litigation*, C.A. No. 961-CS (Del. Ch. 2011) and *Ramcell, Inc. v. Alltel Corp.*, WL 16549259 (Del. Ch. Oct. 31, 2022). It has not used the guideline transaction method.

83. This updated exhibit is adapted from Exhibit 42-2 in SHANNON PRATT'S VALUING A BUSINESS. *See also* Joseph Thompson, ASA, CFA, & Paul Skluzak, *Implied Control Premiums through Delaware Appraisal Decisions*, 42(1) ASA BUS. VALUATION REV. (Spring 2023).

Exhibit 23-2 Selected Chancery Court Decisions Relying on Valuation Methods from 2010 to 2023*

Subject Company	Original Decision Date	Premium (Discount) to Deal Value	Case Citation
Sunbelt Beverage Corporation	1/5/2010	148.8%	*In re Sunbelt Beverage Corp. Sh'holder Litig.*, 2010 Del. Ch. LEXIS 1 (Del. Ch. Jan. 5, 2010)
Golden Telecom, Inc.	4/23/2010	19.5%	*Global GT LP v. Golden Telecom, Inc.* 993 A.2d 497 (Del. Ch. 2010); *aff'd, Golden Telecom v. Global GT LP*, 11 A.3d 214 (Del. 2010)
Pubco Corporation	5/10/2010	11.8%	*Berger v. Pubco Corp., et al.*, C.A. No. 3414-CC, (Del. Ch. 2010)
Hanover Direct, Inc.	9/24/2010	0.0%	*In re Hanover Direct, Inc. Sh'holders Litig.*, 2010 Del. Ch. LEXIS 201 (Del. Ch. Sept. 24, 2010)
Hazelett Strip-Casting Corp.	1/21/2011	135.2%	*Reis v. Hazelett Strip-Casting Corp.*, 28 A. 3d 442, 466 (Del. Ch. 2011)
Minera México, S.A. de C.V.	10/14/2011	(34.4%)	*In re Southern Peru Copper Corporation Shareholder Derivative Litigation*, C.A. No. 961-CS, (Del. Ch. 2011)
Just Care, Inc.	4/30/2012	(14.4%)	*Gearreald v. Just Care, Inc.*, 2012 Del. Ch. LEXIS 91 (Del. Ch. Apr. 30, 2012)
Orchard Enterprises, Inc.	7/18/2012	127.8%	*In re Appraisal of The Orchard Enterprises, Inc.*, 2012 Del. Ch. LEXIS 165 (Del. Ch. July 18, 2012)
Cox Radio, Inc.	6/28/2013	19.8%	*Towerview LLC v. Cox Radio, Inc.*, 2013 Del. Ch. LEXIS 159 (Del. Ch. June 28, 2013)
Cogent, Inc.	7/8/2013	3.5%	*Merion Capital, L.P. v. 3M Cogent, Inc.*, 2013 Del. Ch. LEXIS 172 (Del. Ch. July 8, 2013)
Hesco Bastion USA	5/12/2014	75.5%	*Laidler v. Hesco Bastion Environmental, Inc.*, 2014 Del. Ch. LEXIS 75 (Del.Ch. May 12, 2014)
Rural/Metro Corporation	10/10/2014	22.4%	*In re Rural/Metro Corporation Stockholders Litigation*, 102 A.3d 205 (Del. Ch. 2014)
Ancestry.com, Inc.	1/30/2015	0.0%	*In Re Appraisal of Ancestry.com, Inc.*, 2015 Del. Ch. LEXIS 21 (Del. Ch. Jan. 30, 2015)
Remaining 49% in Southern LNG and El Paso Elba Express and additional 15% in Southern Natural Gas	4/20/2015	(18.4%)	*In re El Paso Pipeline Partners, L.P. Derivative Litigation*, 2015 Del. Ch. LEXIS 116 (Del. Ch. Apr. 20, 2015)

Subject Company	Original Decision Date	Premium (Discount) to Deal Value	Case Citation
Energy Services Group, Inc.	6/17/2015	N/A	*Owen v. Cannon,* 2015 Del. Ch. LEXIS 165 (Del. Ch. June 17, 2015)
Dole Food Company, Inc.	8/27/2015	20.3%	*In re Dole Food Co., Inc. Stockholder Litig.,* 2015 Del. Ch. LEXIS 223 (Del. Ch. Aug. 27, 2015)
BMC Software, Inc.	10/21/2015	0.0%	*Merion Capital LP v. BMC Software, Inc.,* 2015 Del. Ch. LEXIS 265 (Del. Ch. Oct. 21, 2015)
Dell Technologies Inc.	5/31/2016	28.1%* reduced to ~0%	*In re Appraisal of Dell Inc.,* 2016 Del. Ch. LEXIS 81 (Del. Ch. May 31, 2016); *rev'd, Dell Inc. v. Magnetar Global Event Driven Master Fund Ltd,* 2017 Del. LEXIS 518 (Del. Dec. 14, 2017)
DFC Global Corp.	7/8/2016	7.5%* reduced to ~0%	*In re Appraisal of DFC Global Corp.,* 2016 Del. Ch. LEXIS 103 (Del. Ch. July 8, 2016); *modified,* C.A. No. 10107-CB [unpublished] (Del. Ch. Sept. 14, 2016); *rev'd, DFC Global Corp. v. Muirfield Value Partners, L.P.,* 172 A.3d 346 (Del. 2017)
Lender Processing Servicing, Inc.	12/16/2016	0.0%	*Merion Capital LP v. Lender Processing Servicing, Inc.,* 2016 Del. Ch. LEXIS 189 (Del. Ch. Dec. 16, 2016)
ISN Software Corp.	8/11/2016	157.8%	*In re ISN Software Corp. Appraisal Litig.,* 2016 Del. Ch. LEXIS 125 (Del. Ch. Aug. 11, 2016); *aff'd, ISN Software Corp. v. Ad–Venture Capital Partners, L.P.,* 173 A.3d 1047 (Del. 2017)
F&M Bancorp of Western Pa., Inc.	11/10/2016	10.7%	*Dunmire v. Farmers & Merchants Bancorp of Western Pa., Inc.,* 2016 Del. Ch. LEXIS 167 (Del. Ch. Nov. 10, 2016)
SWS Group, Inc.	5/30/2017	(19.0%)	*In re Appraisal of SWS Group, Inc.,* 2018 WL 3625644 (Del. Ch. May 30, 2017)
Clearwire Corporation	7/21/2017	(57.4%)	*ACP Master, Ltd. v. Sprint Corp.,* 2017 Del. Ch. LEXIS 125 (Del. Ch. July 21, 2017); *aff'd,* 184 A.3d 1291 (Del. 2018)
Aruba Networks, Inc.	2/15/2018	(30.6%)* reduced to (22.6%)	*Verition Partners Master Fund Ltd. v. Aruba Networks, Inc.,* 2018 LEXIS 52 (Del. Ch. Feb. 15, 2018); *rev'd,* 210 A.3d 128 (Del 2019)
AOL, Inc.	2/23/2018	(5.8%)	*In re Appraisal of AOL Inc.,* 2018 WL 1037450 (Del. Ch. Feb. 23, 2018); *modified,* 2018 WL 3913775 (Del. Ch. Aug. 15, 2018

Subject Company	Original Decision Date	Premium (Discount) to Deal Value	Case Citation
Jarden Corporation	7/9/2018	(18.4%)	*In re Appraisal of Jarden Corp.*, 2019 WL 3244085 (Del. Ch. July 19, 2019); *aff'd, Fir Tree Value Master Fund, LP v. Jarden Corp.*, 236 A.3d 313 (Del. 2020)
Norcraft Companies, Inc.	7/27/2018	2.6%	*Blueblade Capital Opportunities LLC v. Norcraft Cos., Inc.*, 2018 WL 3602940 (Del. Ch. July 27, 2018)
Domain Associates, Inc.	8/13/2018	NA	*Domain Associates, Inc. v. Shah*, 2018 WL 3853531 (Del. Ch. Aug. 13, 2018)
Trussway Holdings, Inc.	2/28/2019	4.7%	*Hoyd v. Trussway Holdings, LLC*, 2019 WL 994048 (Del. Ch. Feb. 28, 2019)
SourceHOV Holdings, Inc.	1/30/2020	9.9%	*Manichaean Capital, LLC v. SourceHOV Holdings, Inc.*, 2020 WL 496606 (Del. Ch. Jan. 30, 2020); aff'd., SourceHOV Holdings, Inc. v. Manichaean Capital, LLC, 246 A.3d 139
Synapse Wireless, Inc.	7/14/2020	(46.9%)	*Kruse v. Synapse Wireless, Inc.*, 2020 WL 3969386 (Del. Ch. July 14, 2020)
Happy Child World, Inc.	9/29/2020	60.8%	*In re Happy Child World, Inc.*, 2020 WL 5793156 (Del. Ch. Sept. 29, 2020)
Cellular Telephone Co.	3/9/2022	226.0%	*In re Cellular Telephone Partnership Litigation*, 2022 WL 698112 (Del. Ch. Mar. 9, 2022)
Jackson Cellular Telephone Co., Inc.	10/31/2022	286.9%	*Ramcell, Inc. v. Alltel Corp.*, 2022 WL 16549259 (Del. Ch. Oct. 31, 2022)
Pivotal Software, Inc.	8/14/2023	(1.1%)	*HBK Master Fund L.P. v. Pivotal Software, Inc.*, 2023 Del. Ch. LEXIS 332 (Del. Ch. Aug. 14, 2023)

* Reversed on appeal.

OPPRESSION REMEDIES SOMETIMES DIFFER FROM APPRAISAL

Unlike in appraisal cases, many states permit the courts to use *fair market value* in oppression cases.[84] Oppression actions, like appraisal actions, are based on state law. These are cases where noncontrolling shareholders alleged to have been oppressed by the majority. Most states (but not Delaware) have enacted oppression statutes. In states lacking oppression statutes, oppressed shareholders may be able to obtain relief based on a claim of breach of fiduciary duty.

84. *See* Sandra K. Miller, *Discounts and Buyouts in Minority Investor LLC Valuation Disputes Involving Oppression and Divorce*, 13(3) UNIV. PENN. J. BUS. LAW app. E (2011).

The RMBCA's definition of fair value in oppression cases differs from its definition in appraisals because of the differing circumstances of majority conduct in oppression and dissent cases. The RMBCA's comment to § 14.34 (oppression) states:

> The two proceedings [appraisal and oppression] are not wholly analogous . . . and the Court should consider all relevant facts and circumstances of the particular case in determining fair value. For example, liquidating value may be relevant in cases of deadlock but an inappropriate measure in other cases. If the Court finds that the value of the corporation has been diminished by the wrongful conduct of controlling shareholders, it would be appropriate to include as an element of fair value the petitioner's proportional claim for any compensable corporate injury. *In cases where there is dissension but no evidence of wrongful conduct, fair value should be determined with reference to what the petitioner would likely receive in a voluntary sale of shares to a third party, taking into account his minority status.* If the parties have previously entered into a shareholders' agreement that defines or provides a method for determining the fair value of shares to be sold, the Court should look to such definition or method unless the Court decides it would be unjust or inequitable to do so in light of the facts and circumstances of the particular case.[85]

For example, a U.S. District Court, interpreting Louisiana law, recently concluded that "the application of marketability and minority discounts in valuing a withdrawing LLC member's interest is not contrary to [Louisiana] law."[86] New Jersey's dissolution statute permits equitable adjustments to fair value in cases of oppression, but not for appraisal, and it has applied. Unlike in appraisal, an oppression action permits consideration of the degree and circumstances of oppression and misconduct by the majority.

The wording of shareholder agreements can also impact a noncontrolling shareholder's award. In a recent Indiana case, the shareholder agreement provided that the company pay a former officer "appraised market value" of his shares. A state appellate court had interpreted this phrase to mean that no discount for lack of control or marketability could be applied. The Indiana Supreme Court reversed the decision, ruling that the phrase meant that the noncontrolling shareholder shares should be valued at fair market value and that the discounts were applicable.[87]

CORPORATE DISSOLUTION IN SHAREHOLDER DEADLOCK

Entrepreneurs start businesses with the best of intentions. Sometimes, despite good intentions, over time the owners disagree about how to run things. Ideally, an operating agreement would address how the owners should deal with major decisions when they are at an impasse, commonly referred to as a *deadlock*. Deadlock occurs when a business's board of directors is so divided on managing the corporation's affairs that the

---

85. *Changes in the Revised Model Business Corporation Act: Appraisal Rights*, A Report of the Committee of Corporate Laws, American Bar Association, 54 The Business Lawyer 209 (1998) (emphasis added).

86. Complete Logistical Svcs., LLC v. Rulh, 394 F. Supp. 3d 625, 640 (E.D. La. 2019). In contrast, the Louisiana Supreme Court ruled with respect to limited partnerships that "discounts must be used sparingly and only when the facts support their use." [Cannon v. Bertrand, 2 So. 3d 393, 396 (La. 2009)].

87. Hartman v. BigInch Fabricators & Construction Hldg. Co., 161 N.E.3d 1218 (Ind. 2021), *reversing* 148 N.E.3d 1017 (Ind. App. 2020).

votes required for action simply cannot be obtained. At the owner level, deadlock occurs either when the owners are so divided that the votes required for the election of directors cannot be obtained or there is internal dissension and owner factions are so divided that dissolution would be beneficial to the owners. States offer remedies in such situations.[88]

For example, in New York, the law offers a solution for a nonpublic corporation owned by a limited number of shareholders (a close corporation)—a judicial dissolution. In such an action it does not matter which party is at fault. If the existence of the deadlock is undisputed, the court can order dissolution. One remedy is a buyout of one of the parties.

In one such matter, *Ferolito*,[89] the court determined that the appropriate standard of value was fair value without consideration of strategic or synergistic value and the appropriate method to apply was the discounted economic income method, where economic income was measured as net cash flow in valuing the subject company, AriZona.

In arriving at its opinion, the court applied an income tax rate based on the sum of the marginal personal tax rate and marginal state tax rates because of the corporation's Subchapter S corporation (S corp) income tax status. The court also allowed for consideration of a key man discount in development of the discount rate. The court applied a DLOM of 25% based on the facts that AriZona did not have audited financial statements for many years prior to the valuation date; the extensive litigation between the shareholders; the uncertainty about the company's continuing S corp status; and the transfer restrictions in the Owner's Agreement.

PARTNERSHIP AND LIMITED LIABILITY COMPANY DISPUTE CASES

Many partnership agreements and LLC operating agreements have buy-sell agreements that specify the standard of value and procedure for determining the price at which a partnership interest is acquired, sold, or otherwise transferred. Disputes often arise over ambiguities related to the standard of value or lack thereof. Even in those cases where the standard of value and procedures for determining value are well defined, there can be disputes. For example, in a case where there are two 50% partners, the partnership agreement may provide no guidance regarding whether a discount for lack of control or discount for lack of marketability should apply. Even with significant potential for litigation, there are very few court cases that illustrate these disputes. The following provides a few examples.[90]

The *Kinder Morgan* matter involved a transaction where the general partner of a master limited partnership (MLP) orchestrated a reorganization whereby the limited partners were forced to convert their interests in the MLP into cash or interests in the parent of the general partner. While Vice Chancellor Laster noted that the general partner was "conflicted" in the transaction, the limited partnership agreement "eliminates all common law fiduciary duties and substitutes in their place a contractual duty under which the General Partner 'must reasonably believe that its action is in the best interest

88. Jay E. Fishman, Shannon P. Pratt & William J. Morrison, Standards of Value: Theory and Applications 110–15 (2d ed. 2013).

89. Ferolito v. Vultaggio, 2014 N.Y. Misc. LEXIS 4709, at *17 (N.Y. Supr. Oct. 14, 2014), quoting Matter of Blake v. Blake Agency, 107 A.D.2d 139, 146 (N.Y. App. 1985).

90. Buy-sell agreements are discussed in further detail in Chapter 29.

of, or not inconsistent with, the best interests of the Partnership.'"[91] The *Kinder Morgan* decision illustrates a key difference that the legal remedies of investors in limited liability partnerships (LLPs) or LLCs can vary significantly from remedies for shareholders in C corps, since LLPs and LLCs can contractually limit or even eliminate fiduciary obligations.

The *Smith*[92] matter involved an LLC with a single governance document that provided for the repurchase of the plaintiff's interest in the LLC. In that matter, the Court of Chancery was required to opine on the value of the interest with considerations as to which entity was responsible for paying the withdrawing member and the valuation of the operating entity without consideration of the value contributed by the withdrawing member. This matter illustrated the importance of governance documents when operating an LLC.

The *Regency*[93] matter involved the merger of Regency Energy Partners L.P. into Energy Transfer Partners L.P. Both entities were controlled by Energy Transfer Equity, L.P. In a class-action suit, the limited partners of Regency contended that they were damaged by receiving inadequate consideration. The damages expert for the plaintiff could only quantify their damages claim by using a dividend discount model (DDM) to measure the value of a unit Regency limited partners had given up and comparing that to the stock market value of the unit value received in the exchange.

The rebuttal expert presented three analyses (two versions of DDM-to-DDM analyses and market-to-market analysis) that showed no damages were suffered. Chancellor Bouchard agreed and criticized the "apples-to-oranges" analysis (i.e., mismatching methodologies) used by the plaintiff's damages expert.

DISCOUNTS FOR LACK OF CONTROL AND LACK OF MARKETABILITY

Many state appraisal statutes expressly bar discounts for lack of control. Since the courts generally view appraisals as protecting the right of shareholders to a pro rata share of equity value, particularly in transactions initiated by controlling shareholders, courts that have addressed the issue almost always decided that discounts for lack of control (i.e., minority interest discounts) are inconsistent with the basic concept of fair value.[94]

The Delaware Court of Chancery is one venue that has regularly rejected discounts for lack of marketability. For example, in *ISN Software Corporation* and *Doman Associates*, the court did not apply such discounts in determining the fair value of interests in closely held companies.[95]

The RMBCA rejects both discounts for lack of control and discounts for lack of marketability with de minimis exceptions. Under the RMBCA fair value is determined

91. *In re* Kinder Morgan, Inc. Corp. Reorg. Litig., 2015 WL 4975270 (Del. Ch. Aug. 20, 2015), *aff'd*, Haynes Fam. Tr. v. Kinder Morgan G.P. Inc., 135 A.3d 76 (Del. 2016).

92. Smith v. Promontory Fin. Grp., LLC, 2019 WL 1934854 (Del. Ch. Apr. 30, 2019).

93. Dieckman v. Regency GP LP, 2021 WL 537325 (Feb. 15, 2021).

94. For further discussion, on a state-by-state basis, of the rejection and acceptance of discounts for lack of control and lack of marketability in appraisals and oppression cases, *see* Matthews, *supra* note 8.

95. *In re* ISN Software Corp. Appraisal Litigation, C.A. No. 8388-VCG (Del. Ch. 2017); Domain Associates, et al. v. Nimesh Shah, C.A. No. 12921 (Del. Ch. 2018).

"without discounting for lack of marketability or noncontrolling status except, if appropriate, for amendments to the certificate of incorporation."[96] Delaware has not permitted any noncontrolling (i.e., minority) or marketability discounts in appraisal cases since rejecting them in the seminal 1989 *Cavalier* decision.[97] Most states now concur. Appellate courts in several states have reversed earlier decisions that had permitted them. Some states prohibit discounts for lack of marketability in their statutes, and others leave the decision on discounts to the judgment of the courts.

In most states, discounts that are customarily weighed in determining fair market value, such as discounts for restricted stock, or non-voting or low-vote shares, or for limitations imposed by shareholder agreements, are not relevant for fair value. The Utah Supreme Court commented, "Because dissenting shareholders are unwilling sellers with no bargaining power, it would be unfair to penalize them for the lack of marketability of their shares or their lack of control."[98]

Several states do not mandate that discounts for lack of control and discounts for lack of marketability cannot be applied in appraisals. For example, a Michigan court observed:

> Michigan has not adopted the requirement that fair value be ascertained without a discount for lack of marketability or minority status. Conversely, the definition contained in § 761 does not *require* a court to discount the value of minority shares.[99]

The Missouri Supreme Court ruled in 2020:

> [Appellant] is correct that the rationale for applying a minority and marketability discount usually would have limited application in the case of a court-ordered sale to a majority stockholder. But the Circuit Court below did not say otherwise. It did not purport to determine any broad principle of law as to the application of these discounts. It simply agreed with the defendants' expert that, *on these particular facts* . . . a discount was proper.[100]

Some states permit the use of discounts for lack of marketability in certain oppression cases when the court decides that it would be inequitable not to do so. For example, as discussed earlier, New Jersey permits equitable adjustments to fair value in oppression cases.

In a Minnesota case in which a noncontrolling shareholder sought dissolution as a counterclaim to the closely held company's suit against him for breach of fiduciary duty, an equitable adjustment was applied. In *Advanced Communication Design*, the Minnesota Supreme Court ruled that it would be unfair to the company not to apply a discount for lack of marketability. To do otherwise, it determined, would cause:

---

96. Revised Model Business Corporation Act § 1301.4(c).

97. Cavalier Oil Corp. v. Harnett, 564 A.2d 1137, 1145 (Del. 1989), noting that a discount for lack of control or marketability "unfairly enriches the majority shareholders who may reap a windfall from the appraisal process by cashing out a dissenting shareholder, a clearly undesirable result."

98. Utah Resources Int'l, Inc. v. Mark Technologies Corp., 342 P.3d 761, 773 (Utah 2014).

99. Schimke v. Liquid Dustlayer, Inc., 2009 WL 3049723 (Mich. App. Sept. 24, 2009).

100. Robinson v. Langenbach, 599 S.W.3d 167, 185 (Mo. 2020).

> an unfair wealth transfer from the remaining shareholders to respondent because it places unrealistic financial demands on the corporation . . . and in all probability strips ACD of necessary cash flow and earnings for future growth.[101]

In a Connecticut oppression case, *Devivo*, the subject company had large debt, material capital expenditures, and a declining growth rate. The court cited the Minnesota *Advanced Communication Design* decision and applied a 35% discount for lack of marketability to its valuation of a 50% interest.[102]

New York bars discounts for lack of control but applies discounts for lack of marketability in most cases.[103] Other states with published appraisal decisions that permit discounts for lack of marketability at the court's discretion include Florida, New Mexico, Oregon, and Wisconsin. The Office of the Comptroller of the Currency, which regulates appraisals of national banks, explicitly accepts discounts for lack of marketability.[104] Discounts for lack of marketability at the corporate level have been applied in a few appraisal cases and many oppression cases. Corporate- or entity-level discounts apply to the company as a whole and are deducted from the corporate valuation before considering shareholder-level discounts and premiums. They can arise for several reasons, including a portfolio discount, factors that affect the marketability of the company, contingent liabilities, or a key-man discount. Vice Chancellor (later Justice) Carolyn Berger accepted a 20% key-man discount in *Hodas*, based on her conclusion that the founder's "departure would mean the demise of the company."[105]

In *Wright*, Vice Chancellor Glasscock applied a 10% DLOM to the valuation of the businesses. He noted that he was not valuing a proportional interest of a going concern but rather a specific 50% interest in the subject companies.[106] He stated that "a lack of marketability is inherent in the property the Petitioner owns."[107]

The New Jersey Supreme Court applied a corporate-level discount in *Balsamides*, because the oppressed shareholder would be remaining with the corporation and would bear the illiquidity risk.[108] It commented:

> To secure a "fair value" for Perle's stock, a marketability discount should be applied. To do otherwise would be unfair, particularly since Perle was the oppressor and Balsamides was the oppressed shareholder. . . . When Balsamides eventually sells, he will suffer the full effect of any marketing difficulties. Because the "equities" of this case quite clearly lie with Balsamides, it would be unfair to allow Perle to receive Protameen's undiscounted value.[109]

101. Advanced Comm'n Design, Inc. v. Follett, 615 N.W.2d 285, 293 (Minn. 2001).

102. Devivo v. Devivo, 2001 Conn. Super. LEXIS 1285 (May 7, 2001).

103. Friedman v. Beway Realty Corp., 87 N.Y.2d 161, 168 (N.Y. 1995), quoting Matter of Blake v. Blake Agency, 107 A.D.2d 139, 146 (N.Y. App. 1985). Many of the New York decisions are unclear as to whether the DLOM is at the entity level or the shareholder level. Some cases have rejected discounts, e.g., Zelouf International Corp. v. Zelouf, 45 Misc. 3d 1205(A) (N.Y. Supr. Oct, 6, 2014) and 47 Misc. 3d 346 (N.Y. Supr. Dec. 22, 2014).

104. Office of Comptroller of the Currency, Comptroller's Licensing Manual: Business Combinations 45 (July 2018).

105. Hodas v. Spectrum Tech., Inc., C.A. 11, 265 (Del. Ch. 1992).

106. Wright v. Phillips, 2017 Del. Ch. LEXIS 857 (Del. Ch. Dec. 21, 2017).

107. *Id.* at *9.

108. Balsamides v. Protameen Chemicals, Inc., 734 A.2d 721 (N.J. 1999).

109. *Id.* at 736.

The New Jersey Appellate Division affirmed a 25% discount for lack of marketability in an oppression case in the buyout price to be paid to the shareholder due to his bad behavior while managing the business.[110] The matter involved three siblings, Frank, Norbert, and Patricia. Frank built the trucking business started by their father. Frank was sent to prison for several years during which time Norbert took over control of the business. Following Frank's return, Frank and Patricia sued over certain acts committed by Norbert to be evidence that Norbert was oppressing Frank and Patricia. The Chancery Court had held that Norbert was the oppressing shareholder and ruled that he should be bought out. In addition to the discount for lack of marketability, the Chancery Court had previously found that a corporate-level discount of 15% key-person discount should be applied for Frank's importance to the success of the business in determining the price at which Norbert should be bought out; that ruling was not appealed by Norbert.

TIMELY ACTIONS ESSENTIAL

Courts usually hold assiduously to requirements for timeliness of filings and other procedural matters in dissenting stockholder actions. If the dissent is not filed within the statutory period, dissenters' rights are almost always considered waived.

When dissenters' rights actions are filed, most state statutes then require the corporation to commence a proceeding to determine the fair value of the shares within 60 days after receiving the demand. If it doesn't commence the proceeding within 60 days, it must pay the dissenters the amount demanded.

In a Georgia case, for example (where the statute was based on the Model Business Corporation Act), the trial court awarded the dissenters the amount demanded because the corporation failed to initiate the valuation proceeding within the statutory period. The corporation appealed and the trial court's judgment was affirmed.[111]

SUMMARY

Shareholder, limited liability company member, and partnership suits involving valuation of interests arise in a variety of situations: dissenting stockholder actions; minority oppression actions; and claims of breach of fiduciary duty, which can accompany either of the preceding.

In addition to stockholder disputes, disputes among partners in entities such as partnerships and among members of LLCs can also arise but may be treated differently based on the partnership agreement, LLC agreement, and/or state laws.

All states and the District of Columbia have dissenting stockholder statutes. These statutes essentially provide that if a company effects an extraordinary corporate action—typically identified in the statutes—stockholders may dissent from the action and be paid the *fair value* of their shares.

Dissenters' rights are triggered by major corporate actions, such as mergers, acquisitions, or liquidations, the criteria for which vary from state to state. Dissenters' rights apply in all states if a stockholder is forced to give up their stock, such as in a cash-out

---

110. Wisniewski v. Walsh, 2015 N.J. Super. Unpub. LEXIS 3001 (App. Div. Dec. 24, 2015).

111. Riddle-Bradley, Inc. v. Riddle, 459 S.E.2d 576 (Ga. Ct. App. 1995).

merger (sometimes called a squeeze-out). In many states, dissenters' rights are triggered by the sale of major corporate assets, as defined in the respective states' statutes. Stockholders who dissent may not reverse the corporate action but are entitled to be paid the *fair value* of the shares immediately before the action has been put into effect, excluding any anticipatory appreciation or depreciation.

Most of the relevant case law in these matters comes from the Delaware state courts. Whether a company's board of directors will face a breach of fiduciary claim will depend on whether the issues in the case demonstrate that the entire fairness standard applies. The Delaware Supreme Court through the *MFW* and *Corwin* rulings has limited the circumstances under which the entire fairness standard applies.

In recent cases in which the Delaware Court of Chancery made a determination of fair value, significant weight has been given to the company's publicly traded stock price (if available) and/or the deal price resulting from a robust deal process, reasoning that market evidence provides a strong basis for determining value or damages.

The *Kinder Morgan* decision in the Delaware Court of Chancery illustrates a key difference that the legal remedies of investors in LLPs or LLCs can vary significantly from remedies for shareholders in C corps, since LLPs and LLCs can contractually limit or even eliminate fiduciary obligations. Therefore, a careful reading of the partnership or LLC governing documents is important in understanding the rights of limited partners or LLC members.

REFERENCES FOR SHAREHOLDER AND PARTNER DISPUTES

American Bar Association, A *Report of the Committee of Corporate Laws*, "Changes in the Revised Model Business Corporation Act: Appraisal Rights," *The Business Lawyer* 54:1 (1998): 209–83.

______. Corporate Laws Committee, Model Business Corporation Act (2016 Revision).

Fishman, Jay E., Shannon P. Pratt, and William J. Morrison. 2013. "Fair Value in Dissent and Oppression Chart." In *Standards of Value*, 2nd ed. Appendix B, 359–442 (Hoboken, NJ: John Wiley & Sons, Inc.).

Carney, William J., and Keith Sharfman. "The Death of Appraisal Arbitrage: Ending Windfalls for Deal Dissenters." *Delaware Journal of Corporate Law* 43 (2018).

Gordon, Noah J. "Standards of Value for Partnership and Limited Liability Company Buyouts." In Fishman, et al. 2013. *Standards of Value*, 2nd ed. Chap. 4, 197–235 (Hoboken, NJ: John Wiley & Sons, Inc.).

Hamermesh, Lawrence A., Michael L. Wachter, and William B. Johnson. "Finding the Right Balance in Appraisal Litigation: Deal Price, Deal Process, and Synergies." *The Business Lawyer* 73:4 (Fall 2018).

Matthews, Gilbert E., and Matthew L. Miller. "Fair Price for Delaware Fiduciary Actions Can Exceed Appraisal Fair Value." *Harvard Law School Forum on Corporate Governance and Financial Regulation* (April 7, 2021).

Matthews, Gilbert E., and Michelle Patterson. "Fair Value in Shareholders Dissent and Oppression." In Fishman, et al. 2013. *Standards of Value,* 2nd ed. Chap. 3, 89–195 (Hoboken, NJ: John Wiley & Sons, Inc.).

Matthews, Gilbert E. "Fairness Opinions, Experts, and the Courts: A Comparison of Valuation Methods in Delaware Appraisals." *Financial Valuation and Litigation Expert* (October/November 2018).

_____. "Highlights of 2021 to 2023 Delaware Valuation Decisions." *Business Valuation Update* (June 2024).

_____. "Impact of Contractual Rights on Preferred Stock Valuations in Delaware." *Business Valuation Review* (Winter 2019).

_____. "Most States Reject Discounts in Appraisals and Oppression Cases—But There Are Important Exceptions." *Business Valuation Review* 41:2 (Summer 2022).

_____. "Stale Fairness Opinions in Related Party Transactions Should Be Updated." *Business Valuation Update* (September 2018).

_____. "Statutory Fair Value in Dissenting Shareholder Cases (Parts I and II)." *Business Valuation Review* (Spring 2017 and Summer 2017).

_____. "The 'Market Exception' in Appraisal Statutes." *Harvard Law School Forum on Corporate Governance and Financial Regulation* (March 30, 2020).

_____. "Valuation of Dual Class Shares." *Business Valuation Update* (October 2017).

McRoberts, Franklin C. "Pitfalls for Corporate Counsel in Business Divorce Disputes." Farrel Fritz Attorneys (April 24, 2023). Available at https://www.nybusinessdivorce.com/2023/04/articles/attorney-disqualification/pitfalls-for-corporate-counsel-in-business-divorce-disputes/.

Miller, Sandra K. "Discounts and Buyouts in Minority Investor LLC Valuation Disputes Involving Oppression and Divorce." *University of Pennsylvania Journal of Business Law* 13:3 (2011).

Pratt, Shannon P. and the ASA Educational Foundation. 2022. "Valuations in Shareholder and Partner Disputes," and "Shareholder and Partner Dispute Court Cases." In *Valuing a Business: The Analysis and Appraisal of Closely Held Businesses*, 6th ed., Chap. 41, 973–80; Chap. 42, 981–1013 (New York: McGraw-Hill).

Pratt, Shannon P. "Fair Value: A View from the Delaware Court of Chancery Bench" (interview with Vice Chancellor Jack B. Jacobs). *Business Valuation Update* 5:9 (Sept. 1999).

Shartsis, Jr., Arthur. 1999. "Dissolution Actions Yield Less Than Fair Market Enterprise Value." Available at https://www.sflaw.com/wp-content/uploads/2016.02/AShartsis-Fair-Market-Value.pdf.

Shishido, Zenichi. "The Fair Value of Minority Stock in Closely Held Corporations." *Fordham Law Review* 62 (1993).

Thompson, Joseph, and Paul Skluzak. "Implied Control Premiums through Delaware Appraisal Decisions." *Business Valuation Review* 42:1 (Spring 2023).

Website

Delaware Court of Chancery database of decisions. https://courts.delaware.gov/opinions/index.aspx?ag=court%20of%20chancery

CHAPTER 24

Valuations for Employee Stock Ownership Plans

Jeffrey S. Tarbell, ASA, CFA and Arlene L. Ashcraft, ASA, CFA

INTRODUCTION

In this chapter you will learn about:

- The nature and purpose of an employee stock ownership plan (ESOP)
- Legal and regulatory frameworks underpinning ESOPs
- How leveraged and unleveraged ESOPs are typically structured
- Some of the unique advantages of ESOPs as a corporate finance tool
- The role of the ESOP trustee
- Differences and complexities encountered when valuing ESOP stock
- Important case law providing guidance on ESOP stock valuation[1]

The Employment Retirement Income Security Act of 1974 (ERISA) permits an employer to create an ESOP—a type of defined contribution benefit plan designed to invest primarily in the stock of the employer corporation. An ESOP is not a traditional retirement plan—like an IRA or 401(k)—that is designed to maximize participants' retirement savings. Rather, the ESOP's primary purpose is "to serve as an incentive for corporations to structure their financing in such a way that employees can gain an ownership stake in the company for which they work."[2] ESOPs provide a means for employers to incentivize employees by linking the employees' performance to the growth and value of the business. ESOPs also provide a means to provide liquidity to existing company shareholders.

Public policy since 1974 has strongly encouraged employee ownership, especially through ESOPs. At the time of this writing, there are more than 6,500 ESOPs in the United States, holding assets worth more than $2.1 trillion. Approximately 14.7 million U.S. workers are ESOP participants.[3]

---

1. This chapter is adapted from Chapter 39, "Valuations for Employee Stock Ownership Plans," and Chapter 40, "ESOP Court Cases," in SHANNON P. PRATT & THE ASA EDUC. FOUND., SHANNON PRATT'S VALUING A BUSINESS: THE ANALYSIS AND APPRAISAL OF CLOSELY HELD COMPANIES (6th ed. 2022). Used with permission.
2. 129 Cong. Rec. S16629, 16637.
3. Employee Ownership by the Numbers, National Center for Employee Ownership (February 2014).

ESOP LEGAL AND REGULATORY FRAMEWORK

The legal framework of ERISA protects the interests of participants in employee benefit plans by "establishing standards of conduct, responsibility, and obligations for fiduciaries of employee benefit plans, and by providing for appropriate remedies, sanctions and ready access to the federal courts."[4] These standards include the twin fiduciary duties of loyalty and prudence to which ESOP fiduciaries are subject.[5]

Of particular relevance to ESOPs, ERISA § 406 bars any nonexempt transaction involving the "sale or exchange . . . of any property between the plan and a party in interest"—a category that encompasses virtually all ESOP acquisitions of employer stock.[6] ERISA's exemption relevant to ESOP transactions is known as the *adequate consideration* exemption. It provides that ESOP stock purchase transactions are permissible so long as the ESOP does not pay more than adequate consideration for the acquired employer stock.[7]

For closely held securities (i.e., those without a generally recognized market), ERISA defines adequate consideration as

> the fair market value of the asset as determined in good faith by the trustee or named fiduciary pursuant to the terms of the plan and in accordance with regulations promulgated by the Secretary [of Labor].[8]

Aside from its requirement that ESOP valuations use the standard of fair market value—a well-defined concept in the appraisal profession—ERISA provides little guidance on how a determination of adequate consideration should be made, instead directing the Department of Labor (DOL) to provide regulatory guidance for fiduciaries to follow. Yet, as of this writing, nearly 50 years after the passage of ERISA, the DOL has not issued final regulations as to how an adequate consideration determination should be made.[9]

In April 2023,[10] the DOL announced that it would move forward with a public notice and comment rulemaking on a regulation to clearly define adequate consideration under ERISA, § 408(e), 29 U.S.C. § 1108(e). This process will include publication of the proposed draft regulation, with the opportunity for stakeholder/public comments. The agency must respond to those comments before issuing any final regulation. As of publication, the expected timeline for issuance of the proposed regulations on ESOP adequate consideration requirements is the second half of 2024. This will be followed by a multimonth comment period and additional time for approval.

The lack of clear guidance on the issue of adequate consideration over the past 50 years has caused significant confusion among ESOP companies, their advisors and

4. 29 U.S.C. § 1001(b).

5. *Id.* § 1104.

6. ERISA's definition of a party-in-interest includes an employee, officer, director, or a 10% or more shareholder of the company. *See id.* § 1002(14)(H).

7. *Id.* § 1108(e)(1).

8. *Id.* § 1002(18)(B) (emphasis added).

9. The DOL has proposed, but never enacted, regulations defining "adequate consideration." Proposed Regulation Relating to the Definition of Adequate Consideration, 53 Fed. Reg. 17, 632, 17, 633 (proposed May 17, 1988) (to be codified at 29 C.F.R. pt. 2510).

10. As required by the WORK Act (part of the SECURE 2.0 Act of 2022), the DOL (specifically the Employee Benefit Security Administration) will issue formal guidance on valuation of employer stock in employee stock ownership plans.

appraisers, and the DOL. The vacuum of guidance has resulted in frequent litigation by the DOL (and the class action plaintiffs' bar) to enforce the DOL's interpretation of adequate consideration, even though that interpretation is yet to be codified in regulation. Between 2013 and 2022, 68 ESOP litigation cases resulted in monetary settlements or judgments totaling $385 million.[11]

ESOP STRUCTURAL FRAMEWORK

A basic understanding of common ESOP structural frameworks is important in order to properly understand the dynamics of ESOPs and the valuation of their stock. An ESOP's initial acquisition of employer stock is often made by way of a stock purchase transaction whereby the ESOP acquires a block of stock from the company founder(s) or other significant shareholder(s). Such transactions may be leveraged or unleveraged, depending on whether the ESOP uses borrowed funds to acquire the stock.

Leveraged ESOP Transaction

The typical (albeit simplified) steps to an initial leveraged ESOP transaction are set forth here and illustrated in Exhibit 24-1:

1. **External loan.** The sponsor company (employer) borrows funds from a bank or other financing source.[12]
2. **ESOP (or internal) loan.** The sponsor company funds the ESOP.
3. **Stock purchase.** The ESOP then purchases stock from the existing shareholders using the ESOP loan proceeds. The stock is held in a "suspense account" as collateral for the ESOP loan.

Exhibit 24-1 Simplified Steps to an Initial Leveraged ESOP Transaction

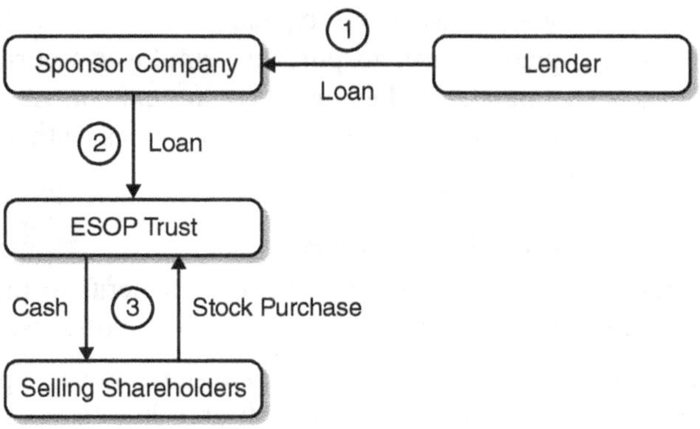

11. Corey Rosen, Bryan Flemming, Mitchell Miller, Kenneth J. Pia, & Patrice Radogna, *Lessons from Recent ESOP Litigation*, National Ctr. for Employee Ownership 1 (2023).

12. For instance, seller financing is often used when it is not possible to finance the desired ESOP transaction solely with senior bank financing.

Subsequent to the initial stock purchase transaction, typical (simplified) steps are set forth here and illustrated in Exhibit 24-2:

1. **Plan contribution.** The sponsor company makes annual tax-deductible cash contributions to the ESOP.
2. **Payment on ESOP loan.** The ESOP uses the plan contribution to make a payment of principal and interest on the ESOP loan.
3. **Payment on external loan.** The sponsor company uses the cash received from ESOP loan service to make a payment of principal and interest on the external loan.
4. **Share release and allocation.** As the ESOP loan is repaid, employer securities are released from the suspense account and allocated to ESOP participant accounts.

Exhibit 24-2 Simplified Steps Subsequent to the Initial Stock Purchase Transaction

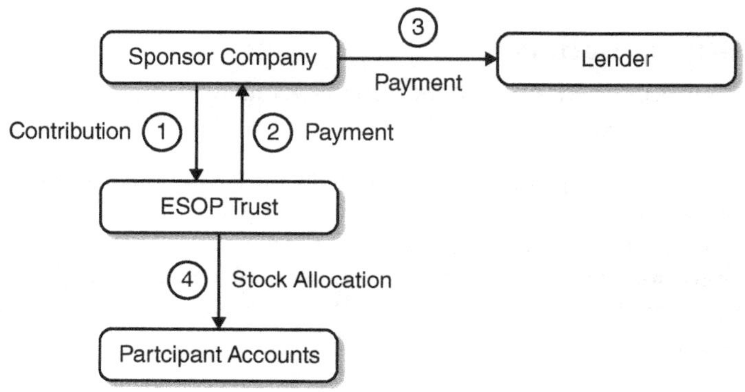

Unleveraged ESOP Transaction

In an unleveraged transaction, the ESOP acquires the employer stock without using borrowed funds. Rather, the nonleveraged ESOP typically uses tax-deductible stock or cash contributions, or a 401(k) plan rollover to purchase employer securities. Such stock is attained gradually each year based on the company's annual contribution amount, and the ESOP's percentage ownership of the company increases with each contribution. Thus, debt financing is not necessary.

Unique Advantages of ESOP Transactions

An ESOP is a unique corporate finance tool, providing benefits to the transaction participants that are not otherwise available, several of which are discussed next:

1. **Benefits to the employee.** The principal benefit to employee participants is the ability to participate economically in the company's equity growth, with no cash investment made by the employee. Academic research has demonstrated that ESOP stock ownership has made retirement more secure and accessible for participants. For instance, data shows that ESOPs have outperformed 401(k) plans and employee owners have greater compensation, job security, and job satisfaction than nonemployee owners.[13]

13. Brief of Amicus Curiae National Center for Employee Ownership in Support of Defendant-Appellees for Affirmance, Lee v. Argent Tr. Co., No. 19–2485 (4th Cir. June 9, 2020), Appendix A.

2. **Benefits to the seller.** The principal benefit for a shareholder selling stock to an ESOP is the ability to defer the recognition of capital gain. I.R.C. § 1042 provides an individual selling Subchapter C corporation (C corp) stock to an ESOP with the ability to defer the associated capital gain tax so long as certain conditions are met. This may allow the shareholder to realize greater net after-tax proceeds when selling to an ESOP as compared to a different taxable transaction.
3. **Benefits to management.** The typical goal of an ESOP transaction is for the plan to acquire on behalf of the employees an equity interest in a successful company with the intent of allowing the existing management team and board of directors to continue to execute its proven operating strategy as long as possible. An ESOP is a financial investor without intent to participate in the day-to-day management of the sponsor company.[14] This concept is consistent with congressional intent for ESOPs but may be inconsistent with the DOL's views.[15]
4. **Benefits to the C corporation.** The principal benefit to a C corp is the tax savings associated with annual employer contributions to the ESOP. These tax benefits also increase the company's leverage capacity and thus enhance the ability to obtain financing. Additionally, the employer may experience productivity gains due to employee ownership, and the ESOP may be helpful in attracting and retaining employees.
5. **Benefits to the S corporation.** Perhaps the biggest economic benefit of the ESOP ownership structure is available only to Subchapter S corporations (S corps), where the company's income is not taxable at the corporate level, but rather flows through to the company's stockholders who are responsible for paying the related taxes. Since 1997, ESOPs have been allowed to hold the stock of S corps and to exempt the company's earnings from unrelated business income tax at the ESOP level.[16] As a tax-qualified benefit plan, the ESOP is tax-exempt and pays no federal income tax on its share of the company's income (though in some states, a state income tax is levied). This can result in a significant economic benefit to the ESOP-owned company over time. In fact, for an S corp that is 100% ESOP-owned, the company's earnings are entirely exempt from federal (and most state) income taxes.

The ESOP Trustee

ESOP stock is held in a trust for the benefit of the employee participants. Like any other trust, the employee stock ownership trust has a trustee with a fiduciary obligation to act on behalf of the trust and its beneficiaries and in a manner consistent with the ESOP plan documents. In a typical ESOP stock purchase transaction, it is the trustee—in consultation with its professional advisors—who conducts diligence and negotiates with the selling shareholder(s) to arrive at a purchase price when an ESOP initially acquires employer stock. As previously discussed, the plan trustee must determine, in good faith, the fair market value of the to-be-acquired securities, to demonstrate that the plan did not pay more than adequate consideration for those securities.

The trustee's actions on behalf of the ESOP and its participants are judged against ERISA's prudent man standard of care, requiring it to act "with the care, skill, prudence, and diligence under the circumstances then prevailing that a prudent man acting in a like capacity and familiar with such matters would use in the conduct of an enterprise of

---

14. Pratt & ASA Educ. Found., *supra* note 1, at 920.

15. Brief of Amicus Curiae National Center for Employee Ownership in Support of Defendant-Appellees for Affirmance, Lee v. Argent Tr. Co., No. 19-2485, at 22 (4th Cir. June 9, 2020).

16. Tax Relief Act of 1997 § 1523.

a like character and with like aims."[17] Under this standard, "the focus is on whether the process the trustee used to determine fair market value is consistent with professional norms and its ERISA fiduciary obligations."[18]

Trustees are not required to become experts in the field of business valuation—they are entitled to rely on the expertise of others, provided that the trustee (1) ensures that any such advisor is qualified (i.e., experienced especially with valuing ESOPs), (2) provides the advisors with all necessary information, and (3) ensures that reliance on the advisor's opinion is reasonable. Trustees typically retain an independent appraiser (sometimes referred to in this context as a financial advisor) to provide an opinion as to the fair market value of the company's stock, as well as legal counsel to advise it on the legal terms of the transaction.

FIDUCIARY PROCESS AGREEMENTS

As of the date of this writing, at least six independent ESOP trustees have entered into settlement agreements with DOL that are commonly referred to as fiduciary process agreements.[19] Each of the six publicly available fiduciary process agreements sets forth procedures that the applicable trustee must follow, and serve as guidelines for other ESOP trustees to consider. Even though these agreements are not regulations, and are formally binding only on the parties thereto, they represent the best available insight as to what the DOL internally believes to be "best practices" for the valuation of company stock in an ESOP purchase transaction that, if followed, could serve as evidence that the trustee fulfilled its fiduciary duty in connection with an ESOP transaction.[20]

A high-level summary of the guidelines follows.

Selection and Oversight of the Financial Advisor

The agreements require the trustee to use a financial advisor (i.e., appraiser) who is independent and specifically has not previously provided services to the plan sponsor and shall make (and document) a prudent investigation of the financial advisor's qualifications. Additionally, the trustee shall take reasonable steps to ensure the advisor receives complete and accurate information regarding the plan sponsor, and prudently determine that reliance on the advisor's valuation analysis is reasonable. The trustee shall monitor the financial advisor and ensure that various items are documented in the appraisal report.

Fiduciary Review Process

The agreements require the trustee to read and understand the valuation report, identify and question the report's underlying assumptions, and ensure that the valuation report is internally consistent as well as consistent with facts known to the trustee. Additionally,

---

17. 29 U.S.C. § 1104(a)(1)(B).

18. Brundle *ex rel.* Constellis Emp. Stock Ownership Plan v. Wilmington Tr. N.A., 241 F. Supp. 3d 610, 633 (E.D. Va. 2017).

19. Certain of these agreements are available in the online appendix to PRATT & ASA EDUC. FOUND., *supra* note 1, Chapter 39, at www.appraisers.org/VAB6.

20. While the basic principles set forth in the various Fiduciary Process Agreements are largely consistent, the agreements themselves differ on certain points, and are in some instances contradictory.

the trustee shall ensure that, together with its advisors, the trustee has sufficient time to "fully, completely, and accurately" review and analyze the contemplated transaction prior to closing.

The most recent agreements included guidance related to issues of control, with two key requirements:

- The trustee will only approve a transaction where the ESOP pays for a controlling interest if, in fact, the ESOP obtains the right to control the company whose stock it acquires.
- If considering a transaction in which the ESOP does not acquire the degree of control of the company commensurate with the ownership interest it is acquiring, or that restrictions are placed on the ESOP's ability to exercise its right to control the company, the trustee will ensure that the purchase price paid by the ESOP will reflect the ESOP's lack of control.

In certain instances, the fiduciary process agreements depart from generally accepted valuation principles and practice. Where these issues are relevant to a particular ESOP transaction, it is important that such issues are discussed among the financial advisor, the trustee, and the trustee's counsel, and that the trustee document the rationale for how such issues were treated in the financial advisor's appraisal.

VALUATION ISSUES WITH ESOP STOCK

The appraisal of ESOP stock is largely consistent with any other fair market value determination, and most of the concepts discussed in other chapters of this book are applicable. There are, however, some added complexities associated with ESOP valuations, and a thorough understanding of ESOPs and ESOP valuation requires knowledge of not only valuation theory but also relevant aspects of ERISA, trust and fiduciary law, tax law, finance, and accounting issues. The following discussion focuses on some of the specific valuation issues and requirements affecting ESOPs.

Independence of the Appraiser

Tax regulations require the appraisal of employer stock held by an ESOP to be made by an "independent appraiser" meeting requirements similar to those prescribed for valuations of property donated to charity, including:

- Has earned an appraisal designation from a recognized professional appraiser organization or has otherwise met minimum education and experience requirements set forth in regulations prescribed by the secretary
- Regularly performs appraisals for which the individual receives compensation
- Meets such other requirements as may be prescribed by the secretary in regulations or other guidance[21]

Additionally, the DOL's proposed regulations require that the ESOP's appraiser be independent of all parties other than the plan trustee.

21. 26 U.S.C. § 170 (F)(11)(E)(ii).

When Appraisals Are Required

Aside from the ESOP's initial purchase of employer stock, tax regulations require the stock held by an ESOP to be valued at least annually—although some ESOP companies have their stock valued semiannually or quarterly—by an independent appraiser.[22]

General Valuation Considerations

The DOL's 1988 proposed regulation addresses the types of considerations fiduciaries and appraisers should contemplate with respect to ESOP transactions. However, since that proposed regulation has never been finalized, it has no force or effect. Further, no court has adopted that proposed regulation as the standard for the adequate consideration exemption's requirements, but some courts have considered it persuasive. With respect to appraisers, the DOL Guidelines provide that the following considerations and factors—largely modeled after IRS Revenue Ruling 59-60—be considered as part of the valuation analysis and any written report containing such valuation analysis:

- The nature of the business and the history of the enterprise from its inception.
- The economic outlook in general, and the condition and outlook of the specific industry in particular.
- The book value of the securities and the financial condition of the business.
- The earning capacity of the company.
- The dividend-paying capacity of the company.
- Whether or not the enterprise has goodwill or other intangible value.
- The market price of securities of corporations engaged in the same or a similar line of business, which are actively traded in a free and open market, either on an exchange or over the counter.
- The marketability, or lack thereof, of the securities. Where the plan is the purchaser of securities that are subject to "put" rights and such rights are considered in reducing the discount for lack of marketability, such assessment shall include consideration of the extent to which such rights are enforceable, as well as the company's ability to meet its obligations with respect to the "put" rights (considering the company's financial strength and liquidity).
- Whether or not the seller would be able to obtain a control premium from an unrelated third party with regard to the block of securities being valued, provided that in cases where a control premium is taken into account:
  - Actual control (both in form and in substance) passes to the purchaser with the sale, or will pass to the purchaser within a reasonable time pursuant to a binding agreement in effect at the time of the sale.
  - It is reasonable to assume that the purchaser's control will not be dissipated within a short period of time subsequent to acquisition.

Level of Value Issues

Control premiums and discounts for lack of control are discussed in detail in Chapter 18. In the ESOP context, the attributes and definition of control remain unsettled. The debate centers on whether an ESOP—even one that owns 100% of a company's voting common stock—can ever really have a true controlling ownership position. Those arguing that the ESOP cannot be a true controlling shareholder point to the fact that many

22. *Id.* § 401(a)(28)(C).

ESOP trustees are "directed" as to how to vote the ESOP shares on certain matters and that selling shareholders and/or management often serve on the ESOP company's board of directors. On the other hand, many practitioners believe that the issue of control is dictated principally by the aggregate voting rights held by the ESOP, noting that an ESOP trustee has the right—under ERISA and most plan documents—to refuse any direction that is not deemed to be consistent with the plan agreements or with ERISA.[23] Further, any party providing direction to an ESOP trustee assumes a fiduciary role in doing so, and thus owes the same duties to the plan and its participants as the trustee.[24]

The DOL proposed regulation provides some guidance on the ESOP's ability to pay a control premium. The regulation generally restricts the ESOP's payment of a control premium unless: (1) a third-party investor would pay a premium and (2) the ESOP receives voting control and control in fact (although the latter phrase is not defined). In addition, if the ESOP plans to purchase control over time, the proposed regulation allows the ESOP to pay the control price if there is an actual binding agreement obligating the employer to pass control within a reasonable period. The proposed regulations also state that a plan does not "fail to receive control merely because individuals who were previously officers, directors or shareholders of the corporation continue as plan fiduciaries or corporate officials after the plan has acquired the securities."[25]

ESOP Financial Statement Adjustments

There are two financial statement adjustments that are unique to the context of ESOP valuations. The first is the recognition that in an ESOP, the annual cash contributions to the plan may be greater than those made to a non-ESOP employee benefit plan. The second includes recognition of the additional tax benefits and leverage that result when ESOP debt is incurred as part of the initial purchase.

Because, in the case of leveraged ESOPs, the magnitude of the ESOP contribution is tied to the amount of ESOP debt, this contribution may not be commensurate with a normal employee benefit expense. The appraiser needs to have an understanding of the level of normal employer contributions both before the ESOP is established and once the ESOP debt is repaid. The typical income statement adjustment would eliminate the ESOP contribution as an expense (that is, add the amount back to earnings) and subtract the expected level of employee benefit expense. If the ESOP contributions were equivalent to the normal level of employee benefit expense, this adjustment would not be necessary. The objective is to arrive at a normalized level of earnings for the company's operations.

The second adjustment considers the income tax benefits associated with the deductibility of the ESOP contributions used to pay ESOP debt. The treatment of this item may vary from one case to another based on the valuation method employed. For example, debt-free valuation methods provide for a subtraction of the ESOP debt from the market value of invested capital. However, as the ESOP debt payments are deductible, this debt is tax-advantaged. Recognition of this can be quantified by calculating the present value of the income tax savings created by this debt instrument and adding it back to the equity value.

---

23. *See, e.g., id.* § 1002(21)(A)(i) (defining functional fiduciaries) and § 1104(a)(1)(A), (B) (defining fiduciary duties).

24. *Id.* § 1103(a)(1).

25. 53 Fed. Reg. 17632–01, at 10 (proposed May 17, 1988).

In addition, the appraiser should consider the effect of the additional financial risk placed on the company after the ESOP transaction in subsequent annual valuations when deciding on discount or capitalization rates in the income approach to value (discussed in Chapter 7) and on valuation multiples in the market approach to value (discussed in Chapter 8).

Discount for Lack of Marketability

IRS regulations require that the sponsor company provide liquidity for the employer securities allocated to a participant's account upon the participant's termination from the plan when the employer securities are not "readily tradable on an established market."[26] This liquidity right is typically referred to as the *ESOP Put Right* even though it is substantively different than a true put option. The company's general obligation to provide liquidity to departing participants is often referred to as the *repurchase obligation*. While that obligation formally accrues to the company, in certain cases the opportunity to repurchase the departing participant's shares may be delegated to the ESOP.

It is widely recognized that the ESOP Put Right greatly enhances the liquidity of stock held by an ESOP vis-à-vis non-ESOP closely held company stock that does not enjoy such rights. With respect to ESOP valuations, the DOL's proposed regulations state that the appraiser should consider the extent to which the ESOP Put Right is enforceable, as well as the company's ability to meet its obligation with respect to these rights (considering the company's financial strength and liquidity). To summarize, the following factors should be considered by the appraiser when selecting the magnitude of the discount for lack of marketability:

- The provisions of the ESOP documents, including ESOP Put Right
- The financial strength and solvency of the company
- The size of the ownership interest held by the ESOP
- The company's liquidity from a balance sheet perspective
- The borrowing capacity of the business
- The repurchase liability and funding thereof
- The company's past repurchase of ESOP shares
- The form and timing of payment by the company to departing participants
- The overall priority of acknowledged and contingent financial claims that may conflict with achieving liquidity for the participants over time

Accordingly, most appraisers assign significantly lower discounts for lack of marketability to stock held by—or to be acquired by—an ESOP than they would apply otherwise. While such discounts depend on various company-specific attributes, they are generally between 0% and 15%. When the ESOP stock represents a controlling ownership interest, the selected discount for lack of marketability is typically at or near the bottom of that range, reflecting the generally accepted notion that a controlling interest does not suffer from any meaningful discount for lack of marketability. The discount for lack of marketability in general is discussed in detail in Chapter 18.

26. I.R.C. § 409(h)(1)(A) and (B).

Repurchase Liability: Redemption or Recirculation

As mentioned earlier, the ESOP Put Right creates a repurchase obligation on the part of the sponsor company. There are two basic methods that can be used by the company to satisfy this obligation, and the company must make a strategic decision as to which method it will implement. The general effect of each of these methods on fair market value is discussed next.

Redemption. A redemption is a direct acquisition by the company from the departing participant, typically followed by the retirement of the repurchased shares. In terms of the effect on per share value, the aggregate company value will decrease by the amount of cash spent on the repurchase, and the number of shares will decrease by the shares redeemed. Thus, if the shares are redeemed at fair market value, then the net effect on the per share fair market value of the ESOP stock will be negligible (i.e., non-dilutive).

Recycling. Also known as recirculation, a share recycling transaction involves the purchase of shares by the ESOP itself—as opposed to the sponsor company—typically using cash received from the company in the form of a tax-deductible contribution and/or dividend. Following such a repurchase, the shares are reallocated to other ESOP participants remaining in the plan. In terms of the effect on per share value, the aggregate company value will decrease by the amount of cash contributed to fund the repurchase, and the number of shares will remain constant since the shares were not retired. Thus, a recycling transaction may be dilutive to the per share value, although the ESOP will benefit by maintaining its collective ownership interest in the company.

RELEVANT CASE LAW

Since the passage of ERISA in 1974, a robust body of litigation decisions has developed, providing guidance as to the roles and responsibilities of ESOP fiduciaries and their financial advisors, principally in connection with ESOP purchase transactions. In the absence of finalized regulations to rely on, practitioners look to these decisions—as well as the fiduciary process agreements—in order to interpret the DOL's stance toward valuation, diligence, and fiduciary process issues.

The remainder of this chapter presents overviews of some of the most important litigation decisions. These overviews are purposefully succinct, presenting very limited background and focusing on the key takeaways.

Sommers v. Corrigan[27]

Sommers v. Corrigan provides useful guidance regarding the factors a valuation advisor should consider in the valuation of closely held stock for ERISA compliance purposes. In this case, the court found the advisor applied the wrong standard of value (i.e., asset or liquidation value versus fair market value), and effectively disregarded the valuation factors delineated in Revenue Ruling 59-60.

In late 1977, the trustee of the Sommers Drug Stores Company (Sommers) employee profit-sharing trust accepted an offer to sell the trust's holdings of Sommers stock back to the company. Before the stock sale, Sommers had sold its drug store operations, becoming a holding company owning cash and real estate. The trust owned approximately 20%

27. Sommers Drug Stores v. Corrigan Enterprises, 793 F.2d 1456 (5th Cir. 1986).

of the outstanding stock. At issue was the fair market value of the stock. The trust sued Sommers and its principal stockholder for breach of fiduciary duty under ERISA in connection with the stock sale. At the trial court level, the trust's expert witness testified that the stock was worth more than the purchase price based on an asset-based analysis, while the defendants' expert testified that the stock was worth less than the offer price. At trial, the jury found that both the principal stockholder and Sommers had breached their fiduciary duty under ERISA, finding that the stock was worth more than the purchase price.

The ruling was appealed. The defendants' principal contention was that the testimony of the plaintiff's expert lacked probative value because his valuation conclusion was inappropriately based on an asset or liquidation value rather than on the fair market value of the business. The appeals court agreed with the defendants' position, citing that the valuation advisor ignored most of the factors mentioned in Revenue Ruling 59-60, and other relevant factors, including the noncontrolling interest position, lack of a discount for marketability, and prior transactions in the stock.

U.S. News & World Report

This case involves two related decisions. *Foltz*,[28] a class action case, dealt with the years 1973 through 1980. *Richardson*,[29] not a class action case, covered 1981. Although the *U.S. News & World Report* cases concerned a profit-sharing plan and a stock bonus plan, the issues were similar to—and are deemed relevant to—those involving ESOPs.

Suits were brought by retirees who claimed that they were underpaid at retirement because the closely held stock of U.S. News & World Report, Inc. (U.S. News) was undervalued by independent appraisers in the years 1973 through 1981. There were numerous valuation issues in the case, including the following matters:

- Controlling versus noncontrolling ownership interest level of value
- Discount for lack of marketability
- Treatment of real estate and other assets
- Subsequent events
- Financial statement adjustments

The court's decision involving the first two issues was as follows:

- A series of noncontrolling interest transactions did not mandate that the appraiser add a control premium for valuation purposes even if the plan eventually gained control. The court emphasized the fact that while the participants' combined interests represented a majority position, this did not entitle them to a pro rata percent of a control value.
- The 10% discount for lack of marketability applied by the appraiser was accepted in light of the fact that the company was under no obligation to repurchase the stock (there was no put option) and the company exercised the stock's call provision from time to time.

---

28. Foltz v. U.S. News & World Report, Inc., 106 F.R.D. 338 (D.C. Cir. 1984), *aff'd in part and vacated in part, remanded*, 760 F.2d 1300 (D.C. Cir. 1985), *on remand*, 613 F. Supp. 634 (D.D.C. 1985) (distributions for 1973 through 1980).

29. Richardson v. U.S. News & World Report, Inc., 623 F. Supp. 350 (D.C. Cir. 1985) (1981 distributions). Note: This 80+ page opinion is highly instructive reading on both ESOP valuation issues and noncontrolling interest (i.e., minority) stock valuation issues in general.

Eyler v. Commissioner[30]

In *Eyler*, Gary L. Eyler, the sole or majority shareholder of Continental Training Services (CTS), Inc., disputed the IRS's determination that the ESOP paid more than fair market value and thus he had engaged in a "prohibited transaction" with the CTS ESOP.

This case provides useful guidance with respect to (1) ESOP share purchase valuation issues (i.e., how much analysis is required to determine fair market value) and (2) ESOP fiduciary issues (i.e., how much due diligence is required to assess adequate consideration). With regard to the fiduciary aspect, the court stated that the fiduciary did not seek independent information, nor up-to-date information regarding the fair market value of the stock. Touching on the issue of lack of marketability, the court rejected the notion that the ESOP's put option reduces the discount for lack of marketability, citing the rationale that the put option did not have a fixed price and it could be paid out over five years under the terms of the ESOP. This aspect of the case has drawn attention to marketability discounts in the ESOP context. Because it has been acceptable among ESOP valuation professionals to reduce or even eliminate the discount for lack of marketability because of the ESOP Put Right, this case is often viewed as controversial on that topic.

Dole v. Farnum[31]

The Wardwell Braiding Machine Company adopted an ESOP in 1985, whereby the ESOP acquired 2,600 shares of Wardwell common stock for $5.46 million. The ESOP purchased the stock with funds borrowed from the company, which in turn borrowed funds from a group of lenders. The ESOP was to repay the acquisition loan using future cash contributions from Wardwell to the plan. In 1990, the DOL filed suit against the Wardwell board, the ESOP administrative committee, and the ESOP trustees, claiming that the transaction was improper because the ESOP agreed to pay more than adequate consideration for the acquired stock. The DOL's principal argument was that the stock valuation failed to consider the drain on Wardwell's cash flows that would result from repayment of the acquisition debt principal and interest.

Unsurprisingly, observers immediately recognized that the DOL's position in the complaint was at odds with basic corporate finance principles—specifically, that valuation is independent of financing. If this notion was applied to the purchase of a residence, the purchase price would need to be reduced by the mortgage payments that the buyer would pay over time—a nonsensical argument. Ultimately, the DOL withdrew the lawsuit and stated that, in the future, it "will not consider the obligations assumed by a company in connection with the establishment of an ESOP in determining whether the plan paid adequate consideration for employer securities."[32]

Henry v. Champlain Enterprises[33]

The court in *Henry v. Champlain Enterprises* rejected the financial advisor's valuation of convertible preferred stock contributed to an ESOP on the grounds that the valuation

30. Eyler v. Comm'r, T.C. Memo. 1995-123 (T.C. 1995), *aff'd*, 88 F.3d 445 (7th Cir. 1996).
31. Dole v. Farnum, No. 90-0371 (D.R.I. filed July 30, 1990).
32. Joel Chernoff, *Withdrawal of Suit Hurts Labor Department*, Pensions & Investments (Oct. 29, 1990).
33. Henry v. Champlain Enters., 334 F. Supp. 2d 252 (N.D.N.Y. 2004).

was biased. In addition, because the trustee failed to document that it had challenged some aspects of the valuation, the district court found the trustee failed to prove it had not breached its fiduciary duties. As to the adequate consideration exception, the court found that the ESOP trustee failed to prove that it had made a good-faith, independent determination of fair market value.

The trustee appealed the district court's decision and was successful. In 2006, the Second Circuit vacated the district court's decision and damages award and remanded for the district court to "(i) identify the specific errors, if any, that occurred in the $60 million valuation of the CommutAir stock; (ii) determine whether a prudent fiduciary would have detected those errors under the circumstances prevailing at the time of the 1994 transaction; (iii) articulate reasons for its specific award of prejudgment interest; and (iv) if the District Court did award damages on remand, explain why those damages would not result in a windfall to the ESOP."[34]

On remand, the district court dismissed all claims against the trustee on the ground that any award of damages would be a prohibited windfall to the ESOP.[35] Nonetheless, the case demonstrates the importance of documenting conduct and decision-making in an ESOP transaction.

Reich v. Valley National Bank of Arizona[36]

Reich v. Valley National Bank of Arizona involved an action brought by the DOL against Valley National Bank of Arizona for its service as trustee of the ESOP sponsored by Kroy, Inc.

The Kroy ESOP transaction involved an ESOP and other equity investors. The non-ESOP investor paid a per-share price that was significantly less than the per-share price paid by the ESOP. This involved a 1986 transaction in which Kroy, Inc. was taken private in a management-led leveraged ESOP transaction. Some takeaways or major points of the case were as follows:

- The ESOP fiduciary must be an active participant in the negotiations regarding the transaction price and terms.
- The independent financial advisor should be retained directly by the fiduciary.
- Diligence pertaining to the company and security being purchased should be thorough, and the fiduciary should not rely solely on its advisor's diligence.

Chao v. Hall Holding Co., Inc.[37]

In *Chao v. Hall Holding Co., Inc.* the DOL brought suit against Hall Holding Co. (Hall Holding) and others on various grounds, including that they breached their fiduciary duty by purchasing Hall Holding stock for the ESOP without conducting a prudent and independent investigation to determine the stock's fair market value. Key aspects include failing to actively negotiate a transaction and oversee the financial advisor's process.

---

34. Henry v. Champlain Enters., Inc., 445 F.3d 610, 621, 623–24 (2d Cir. 2006).
35. Henry v. Champlain Enters., Inc., 468 F. Supp. 2d 368, 373, 372–73 (N.D.N.Y. 2007).
36. Reich v. Valley Nat'l Bank of Arizona, 837 F. Supp. 1259 (S.D.N.Y. 1993).
37. Reich v. Hall Holding Co., Inc., 990 F. Supp. 955, 958 (N.D. Ohio 1998).

The Sixth Circuit[38] affirmed a lower court's finding, concluding that the plan trustees had failed to prove that they had made a good-faith inquiry into fair market value when (1) the trustees relied on a valuation by an individual who had valued the wrong company; (2) the trustees generally were "unaware of what was going on"; (3) the trustees were not consulted on major decisions, such as the price to pay for the stock; (4) the trustees did not engage in any negotiation as to the price of the stock; and (5) the trustees caused the plan to be charged several thousands of dollars simply to enable the trustees to communicate using round numbers.

Keach v. U.S. Trust Co.[39]

Key aspects of the *Keach v. U.S. Trust* decisions include exclusion of fiduciary liability of valuation providers and issues related to the reliance of an ESOP's trustee on an appraiser's diligence.

Foster & Gallagher, Inc. (F&G) was a direct mail marketing company that declared bankruptcy in 2001 after an ESOP was put in place. ESOP participants sued due to a drop in the value of the stock compared to the original purchase price. In the district court case, the plaintiffs asserted that the valuation provider was a fiduciary to the ESOP plan because it (1) exercised control over plan assets and (2) rendered investment advice with respect to the property of the plan. The district court agreed with the valuation provider's position that it was not a fiduciary. The court first observed that a showing of authority or control requires actual decision-making power rather than the type of influence a professional advisor may have with respect to decisions made by trustees. In light of a DOL advisory opinion indicating that appraising the value of closely held stock for an ESOP does not constitute the rendering of investment advice, the court held that the valuation provider should not be a party to the action. With regard to a major change in the industry subsequent to the valuation date, the court stated ERISA's fiduciary duty of care "requires prudence, not prescience."

This case demonstrates that a thorough independent valuation, conducted in light of all known facts as of the valuation date, will withstand ERISA's bad-faith or breach of the duty of care claims. The case also is consistent with the principle that valuation professionals do not need to be "fortune-tellers" to provide defensible valuations.

Eckelkamp v. Beste[40]

In *Eckelkamp v. Beste*, the court rejected a valuation by the plaintiff's valuation advisor, finding it was fundamentally unsupported. The case covers compensation issues and related adjustments made in the valuation, as well as control and the application of a control premium.

Adjustments made to a sponsor company's historical financial statements are an area scrutinized by the DOL and courts, and this case outlines the due diligence performed by the defendant's financial advisor. In this case, the plaintiff's valuation advisor asserted that company management was overcompensated, and a downward adjustment was

---

38. Chao v. Hall Holding Co., Inc., 285 F.3d 415 (6th Cir. 2002).

39. Keach v. U.S. Trust Co., 239 F. Supp. 2d 820 (C.D. Ill. 2002); Keach v. U.S. Trust Co., 419 F.3d 626, 2005.

40. Eckelkamp v. Beste, 201 F. Supp. 2d 1012 (E.D. Mo. 2002).

therefore necessary. However, the court found such an adjustment to be unsupported. The court also cited the plaintiff's financial advisor's application of a control premium as a flaw, criticizing the use of a 15% "control premium." Though positing that a hypothetical buyer might pay to obtain control of the company, the court noted no evidence that the company was likely to be sold, disallowing the premium. The court also found that adjusting management compensation downward was unsupported and were only savings that would accrue if the compensation of the individual defendants were, in reality, reduced. The court questioned this adjustment to actual compensation, citing there was no indication that the company's compensation policies would change.

Armstrong v. LaSalle Bank National Association[41]

In *Armstrong v. LaSalle* a key issue was whether an ESOP trustee breached its fiduciary duty by failing to apply a discount for lack of marketability to a stock redemption.

LaSalle served as ESOP trustee for Amstead Industries, Inc., a manufacturer of transportation equipment. In this case, the employer had liquidity issues due to a recent acquisition, a growing repurchase obligation due to an aging employee base, an ESOP plan that allowed employees to redeem stock immediately (and nine months after the plan year-end to redeem stock at the plan year-end value), and a "run on the bank" situation as a result. The district court found that the trustee's decision not to apply a discount for lack of marketability was reasonable, but the appeals court overturned that decision, stating "one way to pose the question . . . is to ask whether it was unreasonable for LaSalle, in the circumstances that confronted it, to fail to apply a 'marketability discount' to the redemption price."[42] However, the court did not mandate one should always be applied. Rather, it depends on the circumstances.

Kennedy v. Trustmark[43]

Kennedy v. Trustmark addressed the potential of an upcoming sale of the sponsor company, and how this should be incorporated into an ESOP update appraisal with an effective valuation date before the eventual transaction.

At issue was the redemption of shares at the annual ESOP administration price, with a subsequent sale of the company at a higher per share price. The court noted that the appraiser was aware of discussions for a sale, but there had been no letter of intent, no final terms, and no settled transaction as of the valuation date. This case demonstrates that a thorough, independent valuation, conducted in light of all known facts at the time, should withstand claims of bad faith or breach of fiduciary duty. The case also espouses the principle that valuation professionals do not need to be able to see the future in order to provide defensible valuations. In other words, the court held that the appraised fair market value of the stock did not need to consider a sale that was, on the date of valuation, purely "speculative and uncertain."

41. Armstrong v. LaSalle Bank Nat'l Ass'n, 446 F.3d 728 (7th Cir. 2006).
42. Armstrong v. Lasalle Bank National Association, No. 05-3417 446 F.3d 728 (2006).
43. Kennedy v. Trustmark Nat'l Bank, Case No. 3:05cv220-RS (N.D. Fla. Jan. 17, 2006).

Perez v. Bruister[44]

Aside from fiduciary and independence issues, *Perez v. Bruister* touched on several key valuation issues, including the use of financial statements not prepared in accordance with generally accepted accounting principles (GAAP), client concentration, and the development of projections. The DOL brought a civil action claiming a breach of fiduciary duty under ERISA for engaging in prohibited transactions and for failure to monitor.

In this case, the conduct of the trustees with respect to the stock sale, the financial advisor's independence, and whether the trustees' reliance on the valuations was reasonably supported were in question. The Fifth Circuit Court of Appeals[45] reiterated that the trustees conducted an insufficient investigation into the financial advisor's background and qualifications, noting that the valuer had a prior felony conviction for fraud and was operating under an assumed name, but did not determine that the appraiser was "per se unqualified to appraise any company." The Fifth Circuit found that the trustee (1) overlooked the potential lack of independence of the financial advisor, (2) failed to inform its financial advisor of significant information and risk factors for the company, and (3) failed to double-check or significantly review the valuer's ultimate conclusions. The court found that the "flawed valuation process" led to a fair market value determination that was not supported, despite the fact that the transacted value fell within the range of values provided by expert witnesses in the case.

Fish v. GreatBanc[46]

In *Fish v. GreatBanc*, employees of the Antioch Company (Antioch) brought suit against GreatBanc Trust Company, an independent fiduciary, and members of the Antioch board and internal ESOP Advisory Committee (EAC), alleging breach of fiduciary duty causing a prohibited transaction claiming that the ESOP overpaid for the acquired stock.

Within five years of the ESOP transaction, Antioch filed for bankruptcy. Plaintiffs contended that the EAC was a fiduciary, that it failed to provide material information to the trustee and its financial advisor, and that the board failed to monitor the independent trustee. In terms of the valuation, a central matter in the case, the focus was on the forecast utilized and the ESOP repurchase obligation. Overall, the case highlights what can be termed "best practices" by all parties to the transaction, and the court found entirely for the defendants, citing the detailed documentation of the process and practices of the parties involved.

The court found no issue with the warrants that were included as part of the transactions, citing evidence of robust negotiations and advocacy for the ESOP participants, mentioning the fact that the trustee negotiated down the number of warrants issued in conjunction with the transaction.

The court highlighted several aspects of the due diligence process in its opinion that it found favorable, pointing to a thorough process for the development of the forecast, with broad-based management input and analysis and vetting of the forecast by both the trustee and Antioch's financial advisors through their own research and comparison to

---

44. Perez v. Bruister, 54 F. Supp. 3d 629 (S.D. Miss. 2014).
45. Perez v. Bruister, 823 F.3d 250 (5th Cir. 2016) (internal citations omitted).
46. Fish v. GreatBanc Trust Co., No. 09 C 1668 (N.D. Ill. Aug. 17, 2009).

historical performance. The court also recognized the evidence of rigorous negotiations, with modifications made to several aspects of the transaction, perceived as favorable to the ESOP participants.

Brundle v. Wilmington Trust[47]

Brundle v. Wilmington Trust centers on Constellis Holdings, Inc. (Constellis), which formed an ESOP and was soon thereafter sold to another party at an enterprise value that was slightly less than what the ESOP paid.

Fiduciary issues focused on the transaction process and oversight. Valuation issues were central to the case and included the application of a control premium by the trustee's financial advisor, a prior valuation for financial reporting purposes that opined a lower share price than the purchase price, financial projections, Constellis's perceived high client/contract concentration, and the structure of stock appreciation rights. The court in its opinion also focused on the selling shareholders' ability to elect the majority of the board, the prior relationships between the ESOP trustee, its financial advisor, and Constellis's investment banker, citing that the investment banker was the referral source for more than 50% of the trustee's ESOP projects, calling into question the trustee's independence.

The court ruled in favor of Brundle, finding that the trustee inadequately investigated its financial advisor's report, citing failure to consider a prior appraisal, failure to probe management's forecast, number rounding that in total increased the price paid by the ESOP, and a perceived short timeline for the due diligence and decision-making process. However, the court awarded the plaintiff less than one-third of the claimed damages.

The American Society of Appraisers (ASA) filed an amicus curiae (friend of the court) brief in support of the ESOP trustee's appeal to the Fourth Circuit.[48] The brief addressed several issues important to financial advisors, with highlights including:

- The district court's analysis of the control premium was contrary to accepted appraisal theory and practice
- The district court's rejection of management projections
- The district court's misunderstanding of the concept of beta and related errors in its damages calculation

Pizzella v. Vinoskey[49]

Pizzella v. Vinoskey involved a second-stage ESOP transaction with multiple valuation issues. The district court focused mainly on valuation issues affecting the transaction price and the trustee's process and oversight of its financial advisor, including (1) the level of value used (control versus lack of control); (2) adjustments to historical financial statements; (3) the use of a single-period capitalization method as opposed to a discounted cash flow method; (4) the lack of projections, with changes in the appraisal's methodologies and procedures for the transaction valuation as compared to the annual ESOP updates in prior (and subsequent) years; (5) the lack of documented negotiation

47. Brundle v. Wilmington Trust, N.A., 258 F. Supp. 3d 647 (E.D. Va. 2017).

48. https://www.appraisers.org/docs/default-source/6.-publications/vab6/ch-40-asa-amicus-brief-brundle-v.-wilmington-trust.pdf?sfvrsn=bdd4a93_5.

49. Pizzella v. Vinoskey, 409 F. Supp. 3d 473 (W.D. Va. 2019).

of the transaction price; and (6) that the ultimate purchase price was similar to that discussed in trustee correspondence prior to its engagement of the financial advisor.

Much of the court's focus was on the appraisal, with control being a central issue. The court found that the ESOP did not obtain sufficient control, noting that there was no change in leadership post-transaction and no independent board members added as had been discussed during the due diligence process. The judge also found issue with the transaction diligence timeframe, questioning whether it was adequate for the trustee to perform its duties. The case was appealed to the Fourth Circuit Court of Appeals, with a partial reversal of the district court's calculation of damages. The Fourth Circuit found that forgiveness of a portion of the seller's note from the ESOP did offset the damages calculated, citing specific circumstances in this case.

The ASA filed an amicus curiae brief in support of Vinoskey's appeal to the Fourth Circuit.[50] The brief addressed a number of statements in the district court's opinion that were contrary to fundamental principles of valuation, including the following highlights:

- The discounted cash flow method (DCF) is not intrinsically superior to the single-period capitalization of cash flow method, nor is it more widely used.
- The DCF method is not an inherently more reliable method than the single-period capitalized cash flow method.
- The DCF method is not inherently done on a controlling interest basis.
- An ESOP need not acquire total and unfettered control for the valuation to reflect some level of control rights.
- Proper valuation techniques for a damage calculation requires one to consider the mitigating effect of any loan forgiveness obtained by the ESOP.

Remy v. Lubbock National Bank[51]

In *Remy v. Lubbock National Bank*, a novel legal issue arose from what was otherwise a typical breach of fiduciary duty claim against an ESOP trustee. This issue involved whether a trustee's financial advisor might be jointly liable with the trustee for any financial liability associated with an alleged overpayment in an ESOP stock purchase transaction.

The financial advisor was dismissed from the suit, affirming that appraisers are not fiduciaries when providing valuations and fairness opinions to ESOP trustees.

Lee v. Argent Trust[52]

This case pertained to a December 2016 transaction whereby the Choate Construction Company (Choate) ESOP acquired 80% of the Choate common stock in a leveraged transaction. The plaintiff alleged, among other things, that Argent, the ESOP's institutional trustee, breached its fiduciary duty by causing the ESOP to enter into a prohibited transaction by paying more than fair market value to acquire the Choate stock.

The court outlined a clear understanding of the mechanics of a leveraged ESOP transaction and how such leverage would unsurprisingly result in a post-transaction

---

50. https://www.appraisers.org/docs/default-source/6.-publications/vab6/ch-40-asa-amicus-brief-pizzella-v.-vinoskey.pdf?sfvrsn=d7d9c4e0_5.

51. Remy v. Lubbock Nat'l Bank, No. 5:17-CV-460-FL (E.D.N.C. Mar. 20, 2019).

52. Lee v. Argent Tr. Co., 5:19-CV-156-BO (E.D.N.C. Aug. 6, 2019).

drop in the company's equity value. The judge held that the Choate ESOP seemed to have acquired the stock "at a discount," explaining:

> The purchase price was $198 million and the Choate ESOP took on $198 million in debt to obtain the stock. The expected value of the Choate ESOP's shares—at least in the short term—would be $0. Instead, the $64.8 million valuation at the end of December 2016 reflects the fact that the Choate ESOP, like the hypothetical buyer, realized an immediate equitable benefit. That benefit has only grown since, as the Choate ESOP's value was pegged at $107.2 million by the end of 2017.[53]

Notable in conjunction with this case is another ASA Amicus Curiae Brief[54] that relied on extensive research of congressional materials produced during the establishment of ERISA and the formative years of ESOPs. The brief sought to address many misapprehensions regarding ESOPs and ESOP trustees' fiduciary obligations, including the misunderstanding that an ESOP is principally a retirement plan. The brief cites the Congressional Record in support of the view that ESOPs are a mechanism of corporate finance to transfer beneficial ownership in stock to employees and promote stock ownership. The brief also argued that Congress required the use of fair market value as the standard of value for ESOP transactions, and not "investment value," which some plaintiffs have put forth by arguing that the process of determining a company's value be aligned with methods used by private equity buyers. The brief also touched on the use of warrants, due diligence practices, and control.

Walsh v. Bowers & Kubota[55]

In this case, the DOL sued Bowers and Kubota Engineering (B+K) in 2018 based on an alleged overstatement of value in violation of ERISA, essentially alleging manipulation of various facts (e.g., inflation of forecasted earnings) to obtain a value greater than adequate consideration. The DOL's central contention was that the ESOP purchase consideration exceeded adequate consideration and thus violated ERISA.

The court considered several important valuation issues. Based on the testimony of the defendants' valuation expert, the court recognized that the DOL's valuation expert's "failure to follow Uniform Standards of Professional Appraisal Practice (USPAP) introduced substantial errors into [his] analysis." A central issue was the expert's failure to interview company management. Other notable aspects of the case touch on control, trustee's versus director's duties and obligations, and the reliance on a nonbinding indication of interest as an indication of fair market value.

In addition to these valuation issues, the court made clear that the responsibilities of an appraiser are well laid out, and to shirk them is irresponsible. Regardless of the purpose of the engagement or by whom one is engaged, it is necessary to use diligence and follow established standards in developing an opinion of value.

SUMMARY

ESOPs are unique and require a specialized understanding of their unique issues and history, as well as the associated aspects of valuation, tax, accounting, and relevant law.

---

53. *Id.* at 7.

54. https://www.appraisers.org/docs/default-source/6.-publications/vab6/ch-40-asa-amicus-brief-lee-v.-argent-trust.pdf?sfvrsn=5deb8ec9_7.

55. Walsh v. Bowers, U.S. Dist. LEXIS 177184 (Sept. 17, 2021).

The DOL has proposed but never enacted regulations defining "adequate consideration" and there has been substantial litigation in the ESOP space, and the selected cases outlined in the previous sections producing at times contradictory rulings. The Fiduciary Process Agreements provide some insight into the DOL's view on certain valuation issues and procedures, but some aspects run counter to prevailing appraisal practice.

REFERENCES FOR VALUATION FOR EMPLOYEE STOCK OWNERSHIP PLANS

"Analyzing Financial Projections as Part of the ESOP Fiduciary Process," Mercer Capital (2014).

Aschwald, Kathryn F., Barbara M. Clough, Brian D. Hector, Matthew G. Keene, Thomas Roback, Jr., Corey Rosen, Donna J. Walker, and Carolyn F. Zimmerman. 2014. *S Corporation ESOPs: Tax Issues, Plan Design, Administration, Valuation, and Management*, 4th ed. (Oakland, CA: National Center for Employee Ownership).

Carls, Regina, Philip J. Carstens, Vaughn Gordy, Dan Kaczmarek, William Merten, Scott Rodrick, Corey Rosen, and David Solomon. 2020. *Leveraged ESOPs and Employee Buyouts*, 7th ed. (Oakland, CA: National Center for Employee Ownership).

El-Tahch, Aziz, Matthew Hricko, Isaiah Aguilar, Lars Golumbic, and Andrew Salek-Rahem. 2022. "Warranting Further Discussion: Why the Use of Financing Warrants in ESOP Transactions Benefits American Workers," In *Business Valuation Review* 41:1.

Hirschfeld, Christopher. 2002. "ESOPs as an Estate Planning Vehicle for Business Owners." *Journal of Financial Planning* 15:11 (November 30): 92–97.

Pratt, Shannon P. and ASA Educational Foundation. 2022. "Valuations for Employee Stock Ownership Plans" and "ESOP Court Cases." In *Valuing a Business: The Analysis and Appraisal of Closely Held Companies*, 6th ed. Chap 39, 917–38; Chap. 40, 939–72 (New York: McGraw Hill).

Reilly, Robert F. and Robert P. Schweihs. 2007. *Guide to ESOP Valuation and Financial Advisory Services*, 2nd ed. (Portland, OR: Willamette Management Associates).

Rodrick, Scott. 2023. *An Introduction to ESOPs*, 20th ed. (Oakland, CA: National Center for Employee Ownership).

Rosen, Corey, Bryan Flemming, Mitchell Miller, Kenneth J. Pia, and Patrice Radogna. 2023. *Lessons from Recent ESOP Litigation* (Oakland, CA: National Center for Employee Ownership).

Rosen, Corey, Chris Kramer, and Timothy R. Lee. 2020. *The Fiduciary's Guide to ESOP Valuation* (Oakland, CA: National Center for Employee Ownership).

Rosen, Corey, John Case, and Martin Staubus. 2005. *Equity: Why Employee Ownership Is Good for Business* (Cambridge, Mass.: Harvard Business School Press).

Staubus, Martin, David Binns, and Ron Bernstein. 2005. *Transitioning Ownership in the Private Company: The ESOP Solution*, 2nd ed. (San Diego, CA: The Beyster Institute at the Rady School of Management, University of California).

Smiley, Jr., Robert W., Ronald J. Gilbert, David M. Binns, Ronald L. Ludwig, and Corey M. Rosen (editors). December 2006–January 2007, as updated through 2012. *Employee Stock Ownership Plans: ESOP Planning, Financing, Implementation, Law, and Taxation* (San Diego, CA: Beyster Institute at the Rady School of Management, University of California).

CHAPTER 25

Valuing Professional Practices and Small Service Businesses

Alina Niculita, ASA, ARM, CFA

INTRODUCTION

In this chapter you will learn about:

- Differences between small businesses and professional practices and larger types of businesses
- Trade-off between cash and terms in the sale of a small business or professional practice
- Valuation approaches and methods for small businesses and professional practices

The primary attribute that distinguishes professional practices and small service businesses from larger businesses is the personal involvement of the owner(s) in day-to-day operations. This impacts both the way that they are bought and sold and the mechanics of the valuation.

Small businesses and most professional practices usually are sold either in private transactions among acquaintances or through "main street business brokers" (i.e., a professional who helps facilitate the sale of a business), though, in some industries, larger entities have acquired certain professional practices (e.g., hospitals acquiring medical practices) in what is often termed a "roll-up." There are brokers who specialize in certain types of businesses, such as restaurants, or certain types of professional practices, such as dental practices.

TRADE-OFF BETWEEN CASH AND TERMS

Fair market value is a cash or cash equivalent concept. Therefore, when the standard of value is fair market value, when using the market approach (while data is often abundant, it is oftentimes incomplete), it usually is necessary to convert the "price" from whatever the terms are to a cash-equivalent value. Obviously, the more lenient the terms (i.e., terms that are easier for the buyer to make payments), the higher the face amount of the price is relative to the cash-equivalent value.

The smaller the business or practice, the more likely it is to sell on terms rather than for cash. This is because the buyers for such businesses or practices consist largely of individuals, most of whom are not cash rich.

There are two common departures from all-cash transactions:

1. Easy terms
2. Earnouts

Easy Terms

It is common for small businesses and practices to sell for low down payments (the usual range is 20% to 40% of the intended purchase price) with the balance paid over an extended period (usually two to five years, with monthly, quarterly, or annual installments) mostly at a rate of interest that is below what could be attained in a market rate loan, if such a loan could be attained at all. Generally, the only collateral is the business or practice itself.

To convert these extended payments to a cash equivalent value, it is necessary to discount the payments at a market rate. To illustrate with a simple example, assuming annual payments of $10,000 at the end of each year for three years for a total of $30,000 including principal and interest at 6% and a market rate of 15%, the computation would be as follows:

$$PV = \frac{\$10{,}000}{1.15} + \frac{\$10{,}000}{(1.15)^2} + \frac{\$10{,}000}{(1.15)^3}$$

$$PV = \frac{\$10{,}000}{1.15} + \frac{\$10{,}000}{1.32} + \frac{\$10{,}000}{1.52}$$

$$= \$8{,}696 + \$7{,}561 + \$6{,}575$$

$$= \$22{,}832$$

If we assume that the down payment was $20,000, the cash-equivalent value would be $42,832 ($20,000 + $22,832).

Exhibit 25-1 is a table of the present value of each $1,000 at various market interest rates over 60 months.

Exhibit 25-1 Present Value of $1,000 at Various Market Rates of Interest

Market Rate/ Month Received	10%	11%	12%	13%	14%	15%	16%	17%	18%	19%	20%
1	991.74	990.92	990.10	989.28	988.47	987.65	986.84	986.03	985.22	984.41	983.61
2	983.54	981.92	980.30	978.68	977.07	975.46	973.86	972.26	970.66	969.07	967.48
3	975.41	973.00	970.59	968.19	965.80	963.42	961.04	958.68	956.32	953.97	951.62
4	967.35	964.16	960.98	957.82	954.66	951.52	948.40	945.28	942.18	939.10	936.02
5	959.36	955.40	951.47	947.55	943.65	939.78	935.92	932.08	928.26	924.46	920.68
6	951.43	946.72	942.05	937.40	932.77	928.17	923.60	919.06	914.54	910.05	905.58
7	943.56	938.12	932.72	927.35	922.01	916.72	911.45	906.22	901.03	895.87	890.74
8	935.77	929.60	923.48	917.41	911.38	905.40	899.46	893.56	887.71	881.90	876.14
9	928.03	921.16	914.34	907.58	900.87	894.22	887.62	881.08	874.59	868.16	861.77
10	920.36	912.79	905.29	897.85	890.48	883.18	875.94	868.77	861.67	854.62	847.65
11	912.76	904.50	896.32	888.23	880.21	872.28	864.42	856.64	848.93	841.30	833.75
12	905.21	896.28	887.45	878.71	870.06	861.51	853.05	844.67	836.39	828.19	820.08
13	897.73	888.14	878.66	869.29	860.03	850.87	841.82	832.87	824.03	815.28	806.64
14	890.31	880.07	869.96	859.98	850.11	840.37	830.74	821.24	811.85	802.57	793.41
15	882.95	872.08	861.35	850.76	840.31	829.99	819.81	809.77	799.85	790.07	780.41

Market Rate/ Month Received	10%	11%	12%	13%	14%	15%	16%	17%	18%	19%	20%
16	875.66	864.16	852.82	841.64	830.62	819.75	809.03	798.46	788.03	777.75	767.61
17	868.42	856.31	844.38	832.62	821.04	809.63	798.38	787.30	776.39	765.63	755.03
18	861.24	848.53	836.02	823.70	811.57	799.63	787.88	776.30	764.91	753.70	742.65
19	854.13	840.82	827.74	814.87	802.21	789.76	777.51	765.46	753.61	741.95	730.48
20	847.07	833.19	819.54	806.14	792.96	780.01	767.28	754.77	742.47	730.38	718.50
21	840.07	825.62	811.43	797.50	783.82	770.38	757.18	744.22	731.50	719.00	706.72
22	833.12	818.12	803.40	788.95	774.78	760.87	747.22	733.83	720.69	707.79	695.14
23	826.24	810.69	795.44	780.50	765.84	751.47	737.39	723.58	710.04	696.76	683.74
24	819.41	803.32	787.57	772.13	757.01	742.20	727.69	713.47	699.54	685.90	672.53
25	812.64	796.03	779.77	763.86	748.28	733.03	718.11	703.50	689.21	675.21	661.51
26	805.92	788.80	772.05	755.67	739.65	723.98	708.66	693.68	679.02	664.69	650.66
27	799.26	781.63	764.40	747.57	731.12	715.05	699.34	683.99	668.99	654.33	640.00
28	792.66	774.53	756.84	739.56	722.69	706.22	690.14	674.43	659.10	644.13	629.51
29	786.10	767.50	749.34	731.63	714.36	697.50	681.06	665.01	649.36	634.09	619.19
30	779.61	760.52	741.92	723.79	706.12	688.89	672.09	655.72	639.76	624.20	609.04
31	773.16	753.62	734.58	716.03	697.97	680.38	663.25	646.56	630.31	614.47	599.05
32	766.78	746.77	727.30	708.36	689.93	671.98	654.52	637.53	620.99	604.90	589.23
33	760.44	739.99	720.10	700.77	681.97	663.69	645.91	628.63	611.82	595.47	579.57
34	754.15	733.27	712.97	693.26	674.10	655.49	637.41	619.84	602.77	586.19	570.07
35	747.92	726.61	705.91	685.83	666.33	647.40	629.03	611.19	593.87	577.05	560.72
36	741.74	720.01	698.92	678.48	658.65	639.41	620.75	602.65	585.09	568.06	551.53
37	735.61	713.47	692.00	671.21	651.05	631.52	612.58	594.23	576.44	559.20	542.49
38	729.53	706.98	685.15	664.01	643.54	623.72	604.52	585.93	567.92	550.49	533.60
39	723.50	700.56	678.37	656.90	636.12	616.02	596.57	577.74	559.53	541.91	524.85
40	717.52	694.20	671.65	649.86	628.79	608.41	588.72	569.67	551.26	533.46	516.25
41	711.59	687.89	665.00	642.89	621.53	600.90	580.97	561.72	543.12	525.14	507.78
42	705.71	681.65	658.42	636.00	614.37	593.48	573.33	553.87	535.09	516.96	499.46
43	699.88	675.45	651.90	629.19	607.28	586.16	565.78	546.13	527.18	508.90	491.27
44	694.09	669.32	645.45	622.44	600.28	578.92	558.34	538.50	519.39	500.97	483.22
45	688.36	663.24	639.05	615.77	593.36	571.77	550.99	530.98	511.71	493.16	475.30
46	682.67	657.21	632.73	609.17	586.51	564.71	543.74	523.57	504.15	485.47	467.50
47	677.03	651.24	626.46	602.64	579.75	557.74	536.59	516.25	496.70	477.91	459.84
48	671.43	645.33	620.26	596.19	573.06	550.86	529.53	509.04	489.36	470.46	452.30
49	665.88	639.47	614.12	589.80	566.45	544.06	522.56	501.93	482.13	463.13	444.89
50	660.38	633.66	608.04	583.48	559.92	537.34	515.68	494.92	475.00	455.91	437.59
51	654.92	627.90	602.02	577.22	553.47	530.71	508.90	488.00	467.98	448.80	430.42
52	649.51	622.20	596.06	571.04	547.08	524.15	502.20	481.19	461.07	441.81	423.36
53	644.14	616.55	590.16	564.92	540.77	517.68	495.59	474.47	454.26	434.92	416.42
54	638.82	610.95	584.31	558.86	534.54	511.29	489.07	467.84	447.54	428.14	409.60
55	633.54	605.40	578.53	552.87	528.37	504.98	482.64	461.30	440.93	421.47	402.88

Market Rate/ Month Received	10%	11%	12%	13%	14%	15%	16%	17%	18%	19%	20%
56	628.30	599.90	572.80	546.95	522.28	498.74	476.29	454.86	434.41	414.90	396.28
57	623.11	594.45	567.13	541.08	516.26	492.59	470.02	448.51	427.99	408.43	389.78
58	617.96	589.05	561.51	535.29	510.30	486.51	463.84	442.24	421.67	402.07	383.39
59	612.85	583.70	555.95	529.55	504.42	480.50	457.73	436.06	415.44	395.80	377.11
60	607.79	578.40	550.45	523.87	498.60	474.57	451.71	429.97	409.30	389.63	370.92

Earnouts

An *earnout* is a contingency payment based on achieving some level of performance, such as sales or profitability. It would be more prudent for the seller for an earnout to be based on sales rather than profits because sales are more difficult to manipulate compared to profit. The sales figure may be based on total sales or on "retained" sales (that is, revenue attributable to customers that existed prior to the sale). When an earnout is in place, the conversion to a cash-equivalent value requires an estimate of the amount to be received before discounting it to a present value. In the previous simple example, we will assume that the estimated amounts to be received are $8,000 at the end of the first year, $7,000 at the end of the second year, and $6,000 at the end of the third year. Again, assuming the 15% market rate of interest, the computation would be as follows:

$$PV = \frac{\$8,000}{1.15} + \frac{\$7,000}{1.15^2} + \frac{\$6,000}{1.15^3}$$

$$PV = \frac{\$8,000}{1.15} + \frac{\$7,000}{1.32} + \frac{\$6,000}{1.52}$$

$$= \$6,957 + \$5,293 + \$3,945$$

$$= \underline{\underline{\$16,195}}$$

Adding this amount to the $20,000 down payment would give us a cash-equivalent value of $36,195 ($20,000 + $16,195).

VALUATION APPROACHES AND METHODS

When valuing a small business or professional practices, it is important to know exactly what is being sold. It is common practice for sellers to take out all the cash from the business before the transaction takes place. Most transactions do not include receivables; the seller usually collects the receivables. The transaction may or may not include inventory. The databases of private transactions may report prices including or not including inventory. For instance, *DealStats* transaction price includes inventory, whereas *BIZCOMPS* shows but does not include the amount of the inventory. The transaction prices almost never include real estate.

Income Approach

It is not common to use the discounted cash flow method because most small businesses and practices do not have formal forecasts or reliable enough forecasts to provide a basis for valuation.

If the income approach is used, the method usually is a capitalization of the cash flow or earnings. Capitalization of net cash flow generally is preferred, for reasons given in Chapter 6, "The Income Approach." However, frequently, it does not make much difference which variable is used, because many small businesses do not have significant capital expenditures, depreciation, or working capital needs that would cause net cash flow to differ very much from net income when reported on a cash basis.

Market Approach

As noted earlier, there is sufficient data to consider the market approach when valuing most small businesses and professional practices. Among the available databases (such as *DealStats, BIZCOMPS*, and *ValuSource Market Comps* (previously the IBA Market Database), there are literally tens of thousands of sales of small businesses and practices reported.

When the market approach is used, the underlying variables for the valuation multiples usually are sales and/or owner's discretionary earnings (all compensation, benefits, and discretionary expenses to one owner, as discussed in Chapter 8, "The Market Approach").

There are four reasons for this:

1. These are the only two operational variables in either *BIZCOMPS* or *ValuSource Market Comps*.
2. Frequently, these are the only two reliable variables on the financial statements of these small businesses and practices.
3. Owner's discretionary cash flow is "what you get" (i.e., what the owner can take out of the business).
4. Frequently, when the owner's compensation is taken out, there are no remaining earnings available to capitalize. In other words, rather than buying the business for a return on investment, the buyer is just buying a job.

Excess Earnings Method

Many valuations of small businesses and professional practices are based on the excess earnings method, especially for marital dissolution litigation. This method has many variations and pitfalls, as discussed in Chapter 10.

Asset-Based Methods

Sometimes small businesses and practices are based on an adjusted asset value method, as discussed in Chapter 9.

Rules of Thumb

Small businesses and professional practices prices sometimes are arrived at by loose application of rules of thumb. These rules can be in the form of a range of multiples of sales or owner's discretionary income to "assets plus something."[1] Rules of thumb for a variety of industries are shown in Chapter 11.

Rules of thumb tend to become part of the folklore of an industry. Frequently, they represent what owners *hope* to get when they sell. Moreover, they frequently represent prices on typical terms with seller financing and/or earnouts. If rules of thumb are widely used in an industry, they may be considered as part of a comprehensive analysis. A rule

---

1. For an extensive list of rules of thumb, see *Rules of Thumb, in* THE BUSINESS REFERENCE GUIDE (33th ed. 2023).

of thumb can be used as a check for reasonableness but should not be used as the only method in an appraisal.

SUMMARY

This chapter has provided a very brief introduction to the issues in the valuation of small businesses and professional practices. The primary differentiating factor between a large business and a small business or professional practice is the personal involvement of the owner(s) in day-to-day operations. While the main valuation approaches are applicable to small businesses and professional practices, certain methods may be more appropriate than others.

REFERENCES FOR VALUING PROFESSIONAL PRACTICES AND SMALL SERVICE BUSINESSES

Fishman, Jay E., Bruce A. Johnson, Kent Pummel, et al. 2023. "Valuing Professional Practices." In PPC's *Guide to Business Valuations*, 1100.

Hitchner, James R. 2017. "Valuation Issues in Small Businesses," and "Valuation Issues in Professional Practices." In *Financial Valuation: Applications and Models*, 4th ed. Chap. 20: 853–66; Chap. 21: 867–87 (Hoboken, NJ: John Wiley & Sons).

Trugman, Gary. 2022. "Professional Practice Valuations." In *Understanding Business Valuation*, 6th ed. Chap. 23: 915–71 (Portland, OR: Business Valuation Resources).

CHAPTER 26

Valuing Stock of S Corporations and Interests in Other Pass-through Entities

Roger J. Grabowski, FASA

INTRODUCTION[1]

In this chapter you will learn about:

- Relationship of taxes to value
- Debate in the valuation profession and the courts concerning the appropriate methodology to use in valuing shares of Subchapter S corporation (S corp) stock and other pass-through entities (PTE)
- Example of why S corp stock may be worth more than stock of an otherwise identical Subchapter C corporation (C corp) in the hands of an investor
- Considerations when applying other valuation methods

Value and Taxes

Fair market value, the construct under which valuation analysts most frequently determine value, is viewed from the perspective of a hypothetical investor. The investors, albeit hypothetical, have characteristics of real investors; therefore, hypothetical investors are affected by the relevant tax consequences just like real investors.[2] We know this phenomenon is true in our personal investing patterns. *In addition to general investment risk considerations*, whether an investor is considering investing in a public stock, a state municipal (muni) bond, or a U.S. government bond, the investor considers their *after-personal-tax returns*—the amount of money that eventually will end up in their pockets. For instance, hypothetical investors are willing to earn a different (lower) rate of return on the municipal bond than on the public stock, in part, because a municipal bond bears no federal income taxes and likely no state tax.[3] Investors look for a higher rate of return

1. This chapter in the prior edition was adapted from Chapter 2, *Cost of Capital Fundamentals and the Effect of Income Taxes, in* Fannon's Guide to the Valuation of Subchapter S Corporations (2007).

2. Merton H. Miller, *Debt and Taxes*, J. Tax'n (May 1977). In 1977, Merton Miller introduced the effects of personal taxes on investment returns and capital structure in his seminal work, *Debt and Taxes*. Miller argued that investors base their returns on the *after-personal-tax returns* of different investments.

3. I.R.C. § 103(a).

on publicly traded stocks, in part because they bear both federal and state income taxes (again, risk is a key consideration as well).

Anyone who has done any amount of investing understands this simple concept: If an individual investor has to pay taxes on the income received from an investment, the investor ends up with less in the pocket than if the investor didn't have to pay taxes. Therefore, all things being equal, if one investment has taxes levied on it and another does not, an investor will choose the one that does not.

The concept is no different with an investment in a closely held business. Investors invest in closely held businesses because they expect they will end up with a certain amount of money in their pockets *after payment of all taxes.* This issue has formed the heart of the S corp valuation debate: An investment in an S corp *must* be worth more than an investment in a publicly traded C corp simply because investors in an S corp avoid a level of taxes.[4] To understand what tax the S corp shareholder avoids, a simple example is in order.

UNDERSTANDING THE TAX AVOIDED BY THE S CORP

Exhibit 26-1 demonstrates how taxation differs between a C corp and a S corp.

Exhibit 26-1 Traditional Corporate Valuation Model for Identical C and S Corps

	C Corp	S Corp
Income before corporate tax	$100	$100
Corporate income tax	27%	0%
Available earnings	$ 73	$100
Value by capitalizing using 15% discount rate	**$487**	**$667**

The C corp pays income taxes at the corporate level and the shareholders pay income taxes on any dividends received. The S corp pays no income taxes at the corporate level but the shareholders pay the income tax at personal income tax rates on the taxable income passed through to the shareholders (regardless of the amount of any distribution the shareholder receives). In this example, the S corp shareholder realizes 18% more in total after-tax income than the shareholder would have realized had the investment been made in an otherwise identical C corp. Assuming that the same discount rate and expected growth rate were appropriate for each investment (say, 15% capitalization rates), the result would cause the shares in the S corp to be worth more ($100 / 0.15 = $666.67) than the shares in the C corp ($73 / 0.15 = $486.67).

4. The "S corporation debate" refers to the debate in the valuation profession and in the courts brought about by a series of court decisions beginning with in *Gross*, *Heck*, *Wall*, *Adams*, and *Dallas* decisions, cited in footnotes 5 and 9. The debate initially centered on the issue of whether or not to tax-affect S corporation earnings, after the Tax Court rejected the tax-affecting of S corporation earnings in *Gross* and subsequent decisions.

The commonly used valuation procedure in valuing stock of S corps before the *Gross* decision was to tax-affect the S corp taxable income at an assumed C corp income tax rate.[5] The rationale was that discount rates used in the income approach were developed using rates of return from public company stock (i.e., rates of return from investments in C corp stock) and market multiples used in the guideline public company method were drawn from public company stock multiples. Therefore, one wanted to match the characteristics of the discount rate and multiples with the market's pricing of the subject interest.

In *Gross*,[6] the U.S. Tax Court rejected tax affecting of a noncontrolling interest in an S corp. In *Gross*, the estate's expert applied a 40% corporate income tax rate to tax affect the company's (S corp) projected earnings in applying the discounted cash flow method. The expert asserted that a willing buyer "would have tax affected the stock by 40% in determining the purchase price"[7] because (1) there was risk that shareholders would not receive enough distributions to cover their tax obligations, (2) there was danger the S corp might lose its favorable S status, and (3) there were disadvantages to S corps in raising capital because of ownership restrictions. The Tax Court rejected each of these arguments.

While the court ruled in favor of the IRS in *Gross*, it is important to note that the court did not reject the concept of tax affecting. Rather, the court, in its memorandum decision, asserted that the critical factor is to correctly match earnings with an appropriate discount rate.

> If, in determining the present value of any future payment, the discount rate is assumed to be an after-shareholder-tax rate of return, then the cash-flow should be reduced ("tax affected") to an after-shareholder-tax amount. If, on the other hand, a pre-shareholder-tax discount rate is applied, no adjustment for taxes should be made to the cash-flow.[8]

The court ruled in favor of the IRS because the court viewed the discount rate used by the IRS's expert to be a pre-investor tax level, and thus appropriately matched with income before investor-level taxes. The court did not explain how it determined that the expert's discount rate was pre-investor-level taxes. Remember, the subject interest was a noncontrolling interest, not a controlling interest or 100% of the subject business.

In a series of decisions[9] (the *Gross*, *Heck*, *Wall*, *Adams*, and *Dallas* cases), the Tax Court eliminated *any* deduction for corporate income taxes in the valuation of shares of S corps. Other courts have taken differing views as to tax affecting. Exhibit 26-2 lists the decisions in which tax affecting was discussed by the court and how the court dealt with the issue.

---

5. Gross v. Comm'r, T.C. Memo. 1999-254, *aff'd*, 272 F.3d 333 (6th Cir. 2001).
6. *Id.*
7. Gross v. Comm'r (II), 2001, U.S. App. Lexis 24803 (6th Cir., Nov. 19, 2001).
8. *Gross*, T.C. Memo. 1999-254, *aff'd*, 272 F.3d 333.
9. *Id.*; Wall v. Comm'r, T.C. Memo. 2001-75; Adams v. Comm'r, T.C. Memo. 2002-80; Heck v. Comm'r, T.C. Memo. 2002-34; Dallas v. Comm'r, T.C. Memo. 2006-212.

Exhibit 26-2 Significant Cases Related to Pass-through Entity Valuations

Case	Case Type	Year	State/ Jurisdiction	Court	Summary
Gross v. Commissioner	Estate Tax	1999	Federal	U.S. Tax Court	Rejected tax affecting
Wall v. Commissioner	Gift Tax	2001	Federal	U.S. Tax Court	Rejected tax affecting
Heck v. Commissioner	Estate Tax	2002	Federal	U.S. Tax Court	Rejected tax affecting
Adams v. Commissioner	Estate Tax	2002	Federal	U.S. Tax Court	Rejected tax affecting
Dallas v. Commissioner	Gift Tax	2006	Federal	U.S. Tax Court	Rejected tax affecting
Delaware Open MRI Radiology Associates, PA v. Howard B. Kessler	Dissenting Shareholder	2006	Delaware	Court of Chancery	Accepted tax affecting
Vicario v. Vicario	Marital Dissolution	2006	Rhode Island	Supreme Court	Rejected tax affecting
Gallagher v. Commissioner	Estate Tax	2011	Federal	U.S. Tax Court	Rejected tax affecting
Bernier v. Bernier (II)	Marital Dissolution	2012	Massachusetts	Family Court	Accepted tax affecting
Hamelink v. Hamelink	Marital Dissolution	2013	Minnesota	State Court	Did not reject tax affecting
Giustina v. Commissioner (I)	Estate Tax	2011	Federal	U.S. Tax Court	Rejected tax affecting
Giustina v. Commissioner (II)	Estate Tax	2014	Federal	U.S. Court of Appeals 9th Circuit	Acknowledged tax affecting was unsettled matter of law
Bank of America, N.A. v. Veluchamy (In re Veluchamy)	Bankruptcy	2014	Federal/Illinois	Bankruptcy Court	Accepted rationale but rejected execution of tax affecting
Wright v. Philips	Judicial Dissolution	2017	Delaware	Court of Chancery	Accepted tax affecting
Aaron Jones v. Commissioner	Gift Tax	2019	Federal	U.S. Tax Court	Accepted tax affecting
Kress v. United States	Gift Tax	2019	Federal/ Wisconsin	U.S. District Court	Passively accepted tax affecting
R.D. Clark & Sons, Inc. v. Clark	Judicial Dissolution	2019	Connecticut	Appellate Court of CT	Rejected tax affecting
Jackson v. Commissioner	Estate Tax	2021	Federal	U.S. Tax Court	Rejected tax affecting
Cecil v. Commissioner	Estate Tax	2023	Federal	U.S. Tax Court	Accepted tax affecting

Source: Updated exhibit from SHANNON PRATT'S VALUING A BUSINESS: THE ANALYSIS AND APPRAISAL OF CLOSELY HELD BUSINESSES 703 (6th ed.). Used with permission.

In the most recent decision where tax affecting was an issue, the Tax Court accepted tax affecting because experts on both sides applied tax affecting in reaching their valuation conclusions.[10] The court commented:

> We emphasize, however, that while we are tax affecting here, given the unique setting at hand, we are not necessarily holding that tax affecting is always, or even more than not, a proper consideration for valuing an S corporation.[11]

It should be noted that all of the Tax Court decisions to date are T.C. memo opinions. T.C. memo opinions are not officially published but are reproduced by commercial publishers. They generally address cases that do not involve novel legal issues and the law is settled, or the result is factually driven. Although these opinions are technically not precedential, they are often cited by litigants, and the Tax Court does not ignore these opinions lightly.[12]

So how do investors—who are looking for the amount of cash that will end up in their pockets—view shares of an S corp in reality? No corporate income taxes are being avoided by the S corp investment as they are owed by the S corp investors. *However, investors will not have to pay dividend tax on any amount that is distributed to them.* Therein lies the benefit of investing in an S corp.

VALUING S CORPS BY THE INCOME APPROACH REQUIRES USAGE OF MARKET RETURN RATES DERIVED FROM PUBLICLY TRADED C CORPS

In a perfect world, we would not have to go to the public markets to get a rate of return to value the stock of an S corp; instead, we would have rates of return that were appropriate for S corp investors. Why do we need a rate of return to value of shares of an S corp? Because, as shown in Chapter 6, value using the discounted cash flow (DCF) method of the income approach is estimated using the following formula (repeating Formula 6-7):

$$PV = \frac{E_1}{(1+k)} + \frac{E_2}{(1+k)^2} + \cdots + \frac{E_n}{(1+k)^n}$$

Where:

PV = Present value

$E_1 \ldots E_n$ = Expected economic income in each of periods 1 through n

k = Discount rate (cost of capital)

In this formula, the future cash flows usually are available from management's forecasts or budgets for the future. The discount rate (cost of capital) is estimated by the business valuation analyst using empirical data on observed returns in the public market (i.e., risk-free rates, equity risk premium, size premia, industry risk premium). The

10. Est. of William A.V. Cecil, Sr. v. Comm'r, T.C. Memo. 2023-24 (Feb. 28, 2023).

11. *Id.*

12. Kevin Spencer, *Types of Tax Court Opinions and Their Precedential Effect (Updated)*, McDermott Will & Emory, https://www.taxcontroversy360.com (last visited May 22, 2024).

observed returns in the public market are returns of publicly traded C corps, and a mismatch occurs when applying these returns to estimate discount rates for valuing stock in closely held S corps. The mismatch is that although the observed returns from public C corps are returns after corporate taxes, but before personal taxes on dividends, they still reflect the individual investor's expectation that he or she will have to pay the taxes on dividends received from the C corp stock. In other words, it is the return that the investor accepts, fully knowing that they will have to pay another layer of taxes on dividends at the personal level. As we saw in the previous section of this chapter, an investor in the stock of an S corp does not have to pay a second level of tax on dividends.

If we had such a rate of return empirically investing in shares of S corporations, we could use it to value the income realized by an S corp investor directly. At present, valuation analysts do not have such a rate of return available; they only have the rates obtained from the public markets. (Note that even if such rates of return were available, they would need to be adjusted to account for the added risks given the quality of reported small company earnings.) Rates of return in the marketplace are set using investors' expectations of paying a dividend tax, but the S corp investor avoids those taxes. In using the rates of investors in publicly traded stocks to value the S corp, we must adjust for the different tax expectations of the S corp investor.

PUBLIC C CORPORATION VERSUS S CORP PRICING UNDER THE INCOME APPROACH—AN EXAMPLE

Expressed in its simplest form, value is a function of two things:

1. How much cash flow a company produces
2. How much an investor will require for a rate of return to invest in that cash flow

Compare how that analysis applies to two companies: Publico, a company whose stock is publicly traded, and SubSco, a closely held S corp.

- Assume an individual investor invests $1,000 in Publico stock and becomes an owner of Publico, just like the other hundreds (or thousands) of owners. Yet, the investor does not have to pay income taxes on the earnings of Publico because, as a publicly traded C corp, Publico pays taxes at the corporate level. Assume further that in a given year, Publico reports $178 of pretax earnings per share, pays $48 of income taxes (27%) per share, and reports net income of $130 per share, which it pays to the investor as a dividend.[13] Therefore, the $130 comes to the investor after payment of corporate income taxes—a 13% ($130/$1,000) return on your investment. The investor only has to pay taxes on the $130 dividend that the investor received, at the investor's individual tax rate (assume 15%). Accordingly, after paying $20 (15% of $130) in dividend tax, the investor pockets $110 ($130 - $20). Publico reports a 13% rate of return[14] (the $130 dividend it paid out divided by $1,000 the investor invested).

13. This is just for illustration purposes, since it is widely acknowledged that public companies rarely pay out 100% of their earnings as dividends.

14. For simplicity's sake, this analysis focuses only on dividend returns assuming that (1) all earnings are distributed and (2) net income equals cash flow (note public and private returns are actually made up of dividends and capital gains). The S corporation valuation models available in practice distinguish between current returns and retained net income.

- Now assume that instead of investing in Publico, that individual investor wants to consider investing in the stock of SubSco, a closely held Subchapter S corp. It is identical to Publico, except that it is closely held. The CFO predicts that the investor's share of the company's pretax earnings for that year will be $178, which the investor will report as taxable income on their personal tax return and which the investor will receive in cash. As an S corp shareholder, the investor will have to pay income tax on the corporate income allocated to the investor from SubSco. At the investor's personal income tax rate, they will pay $57 (32% equals 40% in federal and state income tax adjusted for the Qualified Business Income Deduction), leaving the investor with a net $121. Because it is an S corp, the investor won't have to pay any dividend tax, so the investor will pocket the entire $121—$11 more than if they had invested in Publico.

How do we value stock in SubSco? If one is using a public market-derived rate of return, value in the public markets is determined by looking into the future and trying to figure out how much cash will be produced *after taxes on corporate income have been satisfied, but before shareholder dividend taxes are assessed*, that is, before the "second level" of tax.[15] In the case of Publico, the cash flow we would measure is $130, and this would be the same cash flow if Publico were a closely held C corp.[16] When it comes to SubSco, *the impact of taxes on its corporate earnings is no different, because those taxes on earnings must be paid; where they are paid from makes no difference to the investor.*[17] Therefore, when one values the stock of an S corp, we would similarly measure the $130 of income available to the investor. However, SubSco's shareholder will not have to pay the dividend tax.

Once we predict how much cash we believe the investment will produce before shareholder-level (dividend) taxes, we then have to determine an appropriate rate of return for the investment. This rate of return is the second part of the value equation.

In our calculations for Publico, we determined the return to the shareholder as follows:

Amount invested	$1,000
Times Publico rate of return	×13%
Equals dividend to investor in Publico	$ 130

The most basic way to calculate value is to reverse this calculation and use a capitalization of dividends method, as follows:

Dividend to investor in Publico	$ 130
Publico rate of return	÷13%
Equals value of investment in Publico	$1,000

15. We ignore, for this discussion, the impact of capital gains on the rate of return. However, both the public rates and the S corporation models have a capital gain component. For S corporations, we recognize this as the buildup in basis component, which will be discussed in a later section.

16. For the moment, this discussion sets aside the differences in how investors typically receive their returns from publicly traded C corporations versus private C corporations.

17. This statement sets noncontrol and control issues aside, which may affect control over payment of distributions.

If you know the dividend you expect to receive and the company's rate of return, you can calculate how much you should be willing to invest. These calculations for Publico confirm that value, rate of return, and the cash dividend to the investor are in sync with each other. Note that in deciding to accept the investment in Publico at a 13% rate of return, the investor expects to pay a dividend tax on the $130 dividend whether he or she receives it.

When we value stock of an S corp, we obtain information about its future cash flow from the company, factoring in the current industry and economic outlook. We reduce that cash flow by the taxes on corporate income that the individual investor will bear. Again, these taxes will be paid, and who pays them makes no difference to the investor. This is because the investor only cares about the amount that will end up in his or her pocket. The net (after-tax) amount is the amount that will be available as a dividend (the same as a "distribution" when we're talking about an S corporation) to the investor.[18] Thus, it is the net, after-tax cash flow that we will value. *We will set aside for the moment (but will not forget) the avoided dividend tax—a benefit that we will come back to later.* For now, we need to find information that helps us predict an investor's rate of return for the S corp's net cash flow.

For this, the only place we can go for meaningful, substantive guidance is the public stock markets. In our example, the rate of return from the public stock markets is 13%.[19] Remember, this is a rate of return after corporate income taxes and before the investor's dividend taxes. From an investor in the public market's point of view, this rate is acceptable and is one that would induce a $1,000 investment in Publico, knowing that after payment of dividend taxes, $110 will end up in the investor's pocket.

Returning to our example, if we use this same rate of return to value SubSco's after-corporate tax income, we would get the same answer—that the investment is worth $1,000. However, we know that the cash that would end up in your pocket is more for your investment in SubSco than for one in Publico—so all things being equal, you should be willing to pay more than $1,000. Why? Because you get to keep $11 more than if you invested in Publico.

This is the benefit of the avoided dividend tax. But how much more should you be willing to pay? And how do you measure that in terms of value? Understanding the two-part answer to these questions is the foundation for the value differential between the publicly traded C corp shareholder and the closely held S corp shareholder.

---

18. The degree to which the company pays out the available cash flow as current dividends influences the valuation in terms of (1) current recognition versus retained net income (basis), which may be deferred, and (2) control versus noncontrol issues.

19. Returns in the public markets are made up of dividends and capital appreciation; in valuing stock in an S corp, we recognize the corresponding benefits as (1) the avoided dividend tax and (2) retained net income, which the models assume equals (dollar-for-dollar) capital appreciation. The example in this chapter focuses solely on the avoided dividend portion of the valuation model. Once understood, the concept (and the discussion) extends to the benefit of the retained net income.

VALUE OF THE AVOIDED DIVIDEND TAX

In simple terms, the additional cash in the investor's pocket leads to additional value. For SubSco, we calculate the additional value the same way we always do: additional cash flow divided by rate of return. In this simple example, we have:

Dividend tax avoided (equals additional cash to investor compared to publicly traded C corporation)	$11
Divided by rate of return from public markets	÷13%
Equals value of dividend tax avoided	$85

Adding this to the value determined for Publico tells us that you should be willing to invest $1,085 in SubSco—the $1,000 that you would be willing to invest in Publico plus $85 for the value of the avoided dividend tax.[20]

This calculation results in a premium for the shares of the S corporation of 8.5%, relative to the publicly traded C corp stock, for the value of the avoided dividend.[21]

In conclusion, when we value stock of an S corp using the income approach, the only rate of return data we have available comes from publicly traded C corps. Immediately, we find the rate of return does not match the cash flows. The public stock market investors set their rate of return requirements based on an expectation of having to pay a dividend tax when they receive their cash returns.

We use this same rate of return to value the S corp cash returns, yet investors pay no dividend tax. Thus, for the income approach, we have to account for this benefit. Obviously, the benefit is a function of the relative income tax rates at the time of the valuation and changes that may be anticipated.

In *Delaware MRI*, the Delaware Court of Chancery, in concluding the fair value of a noncontrolling interest in a S corp, recognized the benefit and adjusted the value of the pass-through entity by comparing the after-tax income available to a C corp investor and an S corp investor.[22] The court acknowledged that tax affecting the pass-through company's income at a full C corp tax rate would result in too low of a value, as there is a benefit that should be recognized in avoiding the dividend tax. However, the court also understood that not taxing the company's earnings would result in too high a value for the company. In order to resolve this discrepancy, the court solved for the income tax rate to be applied to the pass-through company's income (under the assumption that both entity types pay dividends) that matched to the effective income taxes saved.

20. Another issue that is part of the S corp valuation method is the value derived from the ability to build up retained net income. The calculations presented so far assume that the company pays out 100% of its profits to the investor. It gets a little more complicated when the company retains some of the earnings, increasing the investors' basis in the stock. In that case, the benefit of the avoided dividend tax is balanced by the avoidance of a portion of capital gains taxes when the investor sells the S corp stock in the future. While this discussion is beyond the scope of this text, more details can be found in the Sellers and Fannon book included in the references at the end of this chapter.

21. This is a simple example of a capitalization model, as opposed to a discounted cash flow model. As such, it assumes perpetual S corp benefits. This important and material built-in assumption in a capitalization model is one the analyst should make only after understanding the facts and circumstances of the subject company and assessing its implications on the valuation.

22. Delaware Open MRI Radiology v. Kessler, 898 A.2d 290 (Del. Ch. 2006).

Until the 2017 Tax Cuts and Jobs Act (TCJA) lowered the C corp tax rate, the difference was stark. However, the change in tax rates from the TCJA muddied the conversation significantly. The TCJA reduced corporate income tax rates; kept dividend, capital gains, and personal income tax rates largely unchanged; and introduced a temporary cut in taxes for some pass-through businesses through the Qualified Business Income (QBI) deduction. Using the same comparison technique as in *Delaware MRI*, it appears that pass-through entity owners face lower effective earnings than C corp owners, though the QBI deduction may still create a benefit for some business owners through 2025.

SPECIFIC S CORPORATION ISSUES UNDER OTHER VALUATION APPROACHES AND METHODS

When applying a guideline public company method, it is appropriate to consider a benefit of a similar magnitude as we already discussed for the income approach, for the multiples are derived from the public marketplace, where, once again, investors pay a dividend tax.

What about the transaction method when valuing the entire entity? Essentially, when we value an S corp using the transaction method, particularly when compared directly to other S corps, we have already valued the entity by comparison to other, similar closely held corporations, which are most likely subject to the same or similar benefits. This is unlike an income approach valuation, where the purpose of the S corp adjustment is to measure the difference in cash flow expectations inherent in the rate of return from the public marketplace (which does not include data from S corps, but this is what analysts typically use in the income approach) compared to the cash flow expectations of an investor in a S corp. Therefore, when using a transaction method where we compare transaction prices for entire S corp or other pass-through entities to the subject S corp, we need not take any additional premium or detriments into account.

Similarly, in the asset-based approach, net asset value (NAV) method, one is accounting for the fair market value of the subject company's assets and liabilities. Because we are not valuing the net assets by reference to a publicly traded C corp stock, we need add no premium.

SUMMARY

Beginning with the *Gross* decision in 1999, the issue of valuing stock of S corps and other pass-through entities has caused significant confusion and conflict for courts, taxing authorities, business owners, and the business valuation community in general. The key issue has been whether investor-level taxes impact share values and, if so, how to measure that impact.

REFERENCES FOR VALUING STOCK IN S-CORP AND INTERESTS IN PASS-THROUGH ENTITIES

Fannon, Nancy J. "Valuing Controlling Versus Minority Interests in S Corporations." *Business Valuation Review* 26:4 (March 2008).

Grabowski, Roger J. "S Corp Valuations in the *Post Gross* World—Updated," *Business Valuation Review* (September 2004): 139–166.

Hitchner, James R. 2017. "Valuation of Pass-Through Entities." In *Financial Valuation: Applications and Models*, 4th ed., Chap. 13, 607–79 (Hoboken, NJ: John Wiley & Sons, Inc).

Kasper, Larry. "S Corporation Valuations—An Analysis in Search of a Solution." *Business Valuation Review* 26:4 (March 2008).

Laro, David, and Shannon P. Pratt. 2015. "Valuation of S Corporations and Other Pass-Through Tax Entities: Minority and Controlling Interests." In *Business Valuation and Taxes: Procedure, Law and Perspective* 2nd ed. Chap. 8., 88–111 (New York: John Wiley & Sons).

Mercer, Z. Christopher. "Are S Corporations Worth More Than C Corporations?" *Business Valuation Review* (September 2004): 117–38.

Pratt, Shannon P. and ASA Educational Foundation. 2022. "Valuing Interests in S Corporations and Other Pass-through Entities." In *Shannon Pratt's Valuing a Business: The Analysis and Appraisal of Closely Held Businesses* 6th ed., Chap. 31, 697–711 (New York: McGraw-Hill).

Pratt, Shannon P., and Roger J. Grabowski. 2014. Chapter 25, "Cost of Capital of Interests in Pass-Through Entities." In *Cost of Capital: Applications and Examples*, 5th ed., Chap 25. 663–79 (New York: John Wiley & Sons, Inc.).

Sellers, Keith, and Nancy Fannon. 2015. *Taxes and Value: The Ongoing Research and Analysis Relating to the S Corporation Valuation Puzzle* (Portland, OR: Business Valuation Resources).

Treharne, Chris D. "Valuation of Minority Interests in Subchapter S Corporations," *Business Valuation Review* (September 2004): 105–16.

Trugman, Gary. 2022. "Valuation of Pass-Through Entities." In *Understanding Business Valuations*, 6th ed., Chap. 18, 679–722 (Portland, OR: Business Valuation Resources).

VanVleet, Daniel R. "The S Corporation Economic Adjustment Model," *Business Valuation Review* (September 2004): 167–80.

VanVleet, Daniel R. and William R. McInerney, "Valuing C Corps and Pass-Through Entities Under the New Tax Law," *Business Valuation Review* (Spring 2018): 3–14.

CHAPTER 27

Valuing Interests in Real Property Holding Entities

Bruce A. Johnson, ASA and Roger J. Grabowski, FASA

INTRODUCTION[1]

In this chapter you will learn about:

- Basic issues when valuing interests in entities whose principal assets are direct interests in real estate
- What real property appraisers value in a real estate appraisal
- What real estate appraisers consider as going-concern properties and how they value them
- Issues when valuing interests in real estate investment trusts (REITs)
- Issues when valuing noncontrolling interests in limited partnerships and limited liability companies
- Common issues in valuing interests in real property holding entities

There are many holding companies and real estate development and operating companies whose principal assets are direct interests in real estate: real estate investment trusts (REITs), limited partnerships (LPs), limited liability companies (LLCs), and corporations. In some states, it is more advantageous to use one type of entity versus the other due to state income tax laws.

It is important to understand that owning an interest in an entity that owns real property is different than owning the real estate directly. The primary difference is that the entity's underlying assets includes the physical property (real estate) and owner of a noncontrolling interest in an entity cannot manage or control:

- The sale of the underlying real estate or other assets
- The operations of the entity
- The distributions of earnings
- The liquidation of the entity

Of course, an investor would have these rights if they owned the real estate directly (fee simple) or owned a controlling interest in the entity that owns the real estate.

1. This chapter is adapted in part from Chapter 32, "Valuing Interests in REITs and Other Real Property Holding Entities," and Chapter 33, "Valuing Real Property with a Business Component," in SHANNON P. PRATT & ASA EDUC. FOUND., SHANNON PRATT'S VALUING A BUSINESS: THE ANALYSIS AND APPRAISAL OF CLOSELY HELD BUSINESSES (6th ed. 2022). Used with permission.

Often the owner of an interest in a real property entity begins the valuation by engaging a real estate appraiser to value the real property without considering the relationship of the interest in the entity to the underlying real property.

WHAT DO REAL PROPERTY APPRAISERS DO?

The job of a real estate appraiser is to provide his or her opinion of the value of the rights inherent in the ownership of real estate. Through a series of research, methodologies, and procedures (known as the appraisal process) the appraiser arrives at a value opinion.[2]

In business valuation, business appraisers consider three approaches—income, market and asset-based. In real estate appraisal, three similar approaches are considered—income, sales comparison, and cost (asset).

The concluded value is usually based on a *fee simple* concept meaning the asset itself, at *market value*, unencumbered by any existing leases. If the conclusion of market value assumes that an existing lease of the property (i.e., the lease conveys the rights of use and occupancy at a contractual rent) will remain in place, the market value is concluded subject to the existing lease and is termed a *leased fee* interest. If lease terms are at current market as of the valuation date, the fee simple and leased fee interest values are identical. While market value is not technically the same as the business valuation term *fair market value*, they are often used interchangeably.[3]

The sales comparison approach may be the most important method of value for real estate. It is based on the principle of substitution, which states a buyer would likely not pay more for the property than they would for an equal substitute property. The data used for sales comparison are normally derived from published sources showing past sales in various locations.

These comparable sales may be adjusted (plus or minus) for factors such as time, location, and physical differences, including personal property, *along* with a consideration of other economic attributes. This is normally done on a *sales grid* or *adjustment grid* with up or down adjustments (based on market information) to the known subject property/entity from each comparable for market-recognized differences. The conclusion can use price-per-square foot or price-per-unit depending on the type of property, as the units of comparison and are applied to each comparable to arrive at an indicated value for the subject entity.

The cost approach of reconstructing the improved property is often considered. Real estate appraisers refer to a cost manual to estimate the replacement (or sometimes the reproduction) costs new (RCN), deduct the market depreciation, and then add the land value to arrive at an opinion of value via the cost approach.

The income approach often constitutes a capitalization or discounting of net operating income (NOI). NOI is similar to earnings before interest, income taxes, depreciation, and amortization (EBITDA) used in business valuations because it also does not include subtractions for interest expense, income taxes, depreciation, or amortization. NOI also

2. Most people identify with the term *real estate* as opposed to real property, although many use the terms *real property appraisal* and *real estate appraisal* interchangeably. Technically, they are not the same, as real estate refers only to the physical property while real property refers both to the physical property and the bundle of rights that come with it.

3. *See* Pratt & ASA Educ. Found., *supra* note 1, at 29–30, for a discussion of the differences.

does not include rent, suggesting the term *EBITDAR* (earnings before interest, income taxes, depreciation, amortization, and rent charges). Once the NOI is estimated, a capitalization rate is applied to the NOI, which then produces an indication of value. NOI is calculated as follows:

Formula 27-1

		Potential Gross Income (e.g., Rent)
Less:		Vacancy Adjustment
	=	Expected Effective Gross Income
Less:		Fixed and Variable Expenses
	=	Net Operating Income

Capitalization rates are typically extracted from actual sales with reported NOI, which, when divided by the comparable sale price, produces a capitalization rate. Additional sources for capitalization rates can be obtained by various publications, which report observed capitalization rates. Lastly, real estate appraisers can use mathematical calculations to develop a capitalization rate.

HOW DO REAL PROPERTY APPRAISERS ANALYZE GOING-CONCERN PROPERTIES?

Real estate appraisers generally do not value businesses, business interests, or operating entities that own real property. In a real estate centered entity (RECE) property (also called real property with a business component), they value the going concern and extract the value of the real estate of a going concern—and what is *left over* is identified as the business or intangible component.[4] In essence, it is a residual result of valuing the entire going concern then extracting the real estate value and the personal property value. Some refer to it as the going concern value, and others refer to it as the value of the going concern. That value includes the land, improvements, personal property that may be attached, and, if any, the intangible component. While there is no business component (intangible) in a home, there could be such a component in a car wash that is an operating business. This activity, usually translated into earning power, is what differentiates the raw land and structures into a RECE that is often bought and sold as a component of real property.

Typically, RECEs are types of businesses that emphasize services rather than manufacturing and embody more tangible assets rather than intangible assets. What constitutes a RECE or going-concern property? There are some real estate appraisers who truly believe that almost every commercial real property has a business component. Examples of RECEs are lodging properties, fueling stations, and senior housing and nursing homes.

---

4. It is often difficult for a real estate appraiser to imply value of fractional control or minority interests, although there is a body of knowledge to gauge fractional value through the cost to partition into component pieces. This is not reflective of discounts for lack of control or lack of marketability, which are business valuation concepts.

Issues with valuation of the business component arise often in connection with real estate assessment tax purposes. Most state and county jurisdictions do not allow the assessment of tax on an intangible component of a RECE. If the real estate appraiser can prove a lodging property, for example, has a business component as part of the total value, that intangible value is deducted from the taxable base, and could reduce the lodging property owner's real estate tax liability.[5]

While real estate appraisers have valued RECEs for decades, there is new language in the SBA SOP 50[6] that uses the term *going concern* for these types of businesses, and that language is often used by lenders. Real estate appraisers are asked to do *going concern* valuations, implying real estate value as an operating entity, with equipment improvements, and likely continuing customer patronage. They value the entire subject property as a going concern property. The allocated values of the real property and personal property are then deducted from the going concern value, leaving the intangible component as the residual.

The real estate appraiser does not consider liabilities, cash, accounts payable or receivable, covenants-not-to-compete, goodwill, or other typical items valued by the business appraiser. The real estate appraiser is not valuing the equity of the entity operating the going concern. Their goal is to give an opinion of the value of the real property only, and the intangible is a byproduct of that appraisal.

Not understanding what a real estate appraiser does can lead to confusion, as is discussed in the following example.

Example

In 2005, Harvey Evenchick donated to charity 15,534.67 shares of Chateau Apartments, Inc., a company that owned two apartment complexes in Arizona. This donation constituted 72% of the company's stock and was estimated to be worth $1,045,289.

Harvey and Deanna Evenchick reported the donation on their joint income tax return and submitted two real estate appraisals of the underlying assets in the corporation in support of the donation. Neither appraisal addressed the individual shares or the petitioner's 72% interest in those shares. Furthermore, there was no indication that the appraisals were prepared for income tax purposes. As a result, when the Evenchick's return was audited, the entire deduction was disallowed. A notice of deficiency was issued.

Harvey Evenchick died after the case was filed and his estate became the petitioner in the case. The question to be answered at trial was: did the donors obtain a qualified appraisal of the donation, which in this case was shares in a company?[7] Treasury Regulations govern the deductibility of charitable donations.[8] A taxpayer making a charitable contribution of closely held company stock of more than $10,000 must file a Form 8283 with a qualified appraisal attached to his or her tax return.[9]

---

5. This topic has been the subject of much litigation. See Appraisal Institute, The Appraisal Journal, which has a myriad of articles presenting all the various arguments dating back many years.

6. Office of Financial Assistance, U.S. Small Business Administration Lender & Development Company Loan Program (Apr. 1, 2019).

7. Est. of Harvey Evenchick, Gregory V. Gadarian, Personal Representative, and Deanna Evenchick, Petitioners, v. Comm'r, T.C. Memo. 2013-34 (U.S.T.C. Feb. 4, 2013).

8. *See* Chapter 20, "Valuations for Gift, Estate, and Charitable Contribution Matters."

9. Treas. Reg. § 1.170A-13(c)(3).

The problem for the estate was the issue that the appraisals presented were not of the interest donated, but of the underlying real estate held by the company. The court acknowledged that a partial interest may have an impact on the total value to be determined. Furthermore, the Regulations necessitate a valid appraisal to include certain details, such as the property description, transaction date, terms between the donor and donee, appraiser qualifications, and how the appraisal was performed. Unfortunately, the petitioner had not supplied most of this data.

The Tax Court concluded that a proper business appraisal of the stock was not conducted, and the real estate appraisals of the underlying assets were not a qualified appraisal for purposes of valuing a charitable income tax deduction for a contribution of the corporation's stock. The estate was denied all deductions taken from the donation.

The case illustrates the problem when taxpayers confuse valuing the underlying real estate with valuing the interest in the corporate entity that owns the real estate.

HOW DO BUSINESS APPRAISERS VALUE INTERESTS IN REAL ESTATE INVESTMENT TRUSTS?

A real estate investment trust (REIT) is an entity that owns, finances, and/or operates real estate. Some REITs own direct interests in real estate properties, including retail, industrial, office, and residential properties. Other types of REITs, known as mortgage REITs (MREITs), hold loans collateralized by real estate properties. REITs that own both real estate and mortgages are known as hybrid REITs.

REITs were created in 1960 by the U.S. Congress to provide a financial instrument that would enable investors to participate in the development and ownership of commercial, industrial, and residential real estate properties. Today, REITs, both public and private, are appreciated by investors for their regular income streams, diversification, and potential for capital appreciation.

Using REIT Information for the Income Approach

Historical rates of return for publicly held REITs are often used as a basis for estimating a discount rate for an interest in a noncontrolling real estate entity. The business appraiser can then value the interest directly using the income approach by discounting the forecasted cash flows (i.e., distributions) and discounting those expected distributions with an appropriate discount rate.[10]

In the public market, noncontrolling investors buy and sell their equity interests based primarily on the expected rate of return of the interest. A basic theory of valuation is that an investor will require a rate of return on an investment equivalent to the rate of return on alternative investments with equivalent risk. Given two investment choices with equal risk, an investor will choose the investment with the greater expected rate of return, everything else equal.

A build-up method can be used to estimate a discount rate using this data.[11]

---

10. *See* Partnership Profiles, Inc. 2021 Rate of Return Study. Annual data on historical rates of return (back to 1972) for public equity REITs.

11. This is a form of the build-up method discussed in Chapter 7 adapted for REITs.

Formula 27–2

$$\text{Build-up method} = \text{Risk-free rate} + \text{Real estate risk premium} + \text{Specific risk premium}$$

The initial step in this process is to determine the rate of return an investor would require on a risk-free investment (e.g., using the 20-year U.S. government bond yield as of the valuation date). Added to the risk-free rate is a real estate risk premium, which is calculated by subtracting the long-term average income return for government bonds from the observed long-term average return for REITs. When summed with the current risk-free rate, this is equivalent to a required rate of return for investors holding a diversified portfolio of publicly traded REITs.

The final step in determining the discount rate is to adjust this rate depending on whether the subject interest exhibits more risk or less risk than a diversified portfolio of publicly traded REITs. In comparison, publicly traded REITs generally:

- Have a greater diversification of properties
- Own investment grade properties
- Use debt to finance operations
- Have greater depth in management
- Make more consistent distributions than does a closely held REIT

In addition, a REIT has the statutory requirement to pay out 90% of its taxable income in the form of distributions to shareholders. The management of most closely held real estate entities are under no such requirement. An additional risk premium should be considered in addition to the base rate depending on the level of specific risk.[12]

The next step in estimating a noncontrolling value of a closely held entity using the discounted cash flow method is to forecast expected cash flows (i.e., distributions). If an appraiser chooses to use the capitalization of net cash flow method, the expected net cash flow should be based on historical annual returns.[13]

Using REIT and Closed-End Fund Information for the Market Approach

Since publicly traded REITs have no specific date when they will terminate, their pricing multiples are not commonly used for valuing noncontrolling interests in closely held real estate entities in the market approach. Most closely held real estate entities are limited life entities, meaning they will liquidate after a set number of years (or certainly when and if the real property owned by the REIT is sold). In the public market, REITs are valued using a ratio of price-to-funds from operations (FFO, a measure of net income plus depreciation less gains on the sale of any depreciable property). This pricing multiple assumes the business is a going concern. It does not include a possible liquidation of the assets that would enable a noncontrolling interest to realize the value of the appreciated underlying assets. Therefore, the preferred methods are to use REIT information for determining a discount rate to use in the direct equity procedure of the income approach and use price-to-net asset value (NAV) ratios for the market approach.

---

12. Bruce A. Johnson, Spencer J. Jefferies & James R. Park, Comprehensive Guide for the Valuation of Family Limited Partnerships 68 (5th ed. 2017).

13. 2021 Rate of Return Study, *supra* note 10, at 10–16.

Certain closed-end, real estate–focused funds own investments in real estate operating companies (REOCs), REITs, and other securities with ongoing real estate activities. If the subject closely held entity owns interests in REOCs or REITs, using these types of closed-end funds in the market approach is appropriate. But if the subject closely held entity only owns direct interests in real property, it is not appropriate to use the types of closed-end funds that own investments in other real estate companies when valuing a noncontrolling interest in the closely held entity.

HOW DO BUSINESS APPRAISERS VALUE INTERESTS IN LIMITED PARTNERSHIPS AND LIMITED LIABILITY COMPANIES?

A common entity used for owning real property is a limited partnership. If the partnership is closely held by members of a single family, the limited partnership is commonly called a family limited partnership (FLPs); these have become a popular business entity for asset management and planning purposes. LLCs are also used in a similar manner. A FLP is simply a limited partnership used to consolidate and manage multiple types of family-owned assets. Some of the primary advantages of using FLPs include the ability to make gifts to other generations, protect assets from creditors, efficiently manage multiple assets, educate younger family members about family-owned investments, and provide tax benefits.[14]

Indirect Procedure for Valuing the Subject Interests

In valuing closely held limited partnerships, business appraisers typically valued noncontrolling interests by simply using the asset-based procedure: calculating the net asset value of the partnership and then deducting discounts for lack of control (DLOC) and discounts for lack of marketability (DLOM) when appropriate to reflect the characteristics of the subject interest. The problem with this procedure is that the discounts were typically based on general averages reported in published studies or specific discounts cited in court cases (see Chapter 18, "Discounts and Premiums"). This practice often resulted in poor comparisons between the data and the subject interest. When these appraisals reached the U.S. Tax Court, the values were sometimes rejected because the discounts were subjectively determined and based on "leaps of faith." When rejected, the court indicated that appraisers generally had insufficient knowledge of the underlying data contained in the discount studies to explain to the court how the studies compared to the specific interest being valued.

While sometimes subject to criticism, the methodology of starting from net asset value and then applying discounts for lack of control and lack of marketability is still used by business appraisers and often used at the audit level by the Internal Revenue Service (IRS) due to its simplicity. However, it is often difficult for the appraiser (or the IRS) to defend the size of the discounts applied, which can be seen as arbitrary.

As seen in more recent U.S. Tax Court decisions, the court has preferred the income approach and the market approach method when valuing closely held limited partnerships.

14. *Id.*

Direct Procedure for Valuing the Subject Interests

When valuing a noncontrolling interest that has limited marketability, it is typically not a question of whether discounts are appropriate, but rather how the amounts of these discounts have been determined that raises concerns. When making investment decisions in the real world, arm's length buyers and sellers of minority interests do not rely on general averages from published discount studies. Similarly, business appraisers should not use raw averages from such studies to determine a specific discount.

The objective of valuation analysis is to continue to gather supportable empirical data and apply a valuation methodology that demonstrates sound reasoning and logic. It is important to understand that the discounts reported in such studies are the direct result of the specific facts and circumstances that affect the risk and future benefits of each noncontrolling interest. Accordingly, appraisers should identify the specific risk/reward relationship of the interest that is being valued and consider a more empirical method for valuing the subject noncontrolling, nonmarketable interest.

To that end, the procedure of directly valuing the subject interest using the income approach and the market approach generally provides a more direct manner to value a noncontrolling interest in a real estate holding entity. Rate of return information from noncontrolling interests owning real estate can be used for valuing an interest using the income approach. Price-to-net asset value ratios can be used to value an interest using the market approach.

Because a noncontrolling interest typically does not have the ability to partition or sell the underlying assets of an entity, the use of the asset-based procedure is not usually a best practice when valuing a noncontrolling interest that is not expected to liquidate in the near term. But the asset-based procedure can still be used for valuing controlling interests that have significant tangible assets and little or no value added due to services from labor.

In contrast to operating companies, there is an abundant amount of direct empirical data demonstrating that the market of buyers and sellers discounts net asset value for lack of control for noncontrolling ownership interests in holding companies, such as publicly held limited partnerships, closed-end funds, and non-listed REITs. The best source for identifying comparative data, determining rates of return, and pricing multiples (price-to-net asset value) for valuing noncontrolling interests in closely held limited partnerships and LLCs that are comprised primarily of real estate or real estate–related assets is the secondary market for syndicated or publicly held limited partnerships and non-listed REITs.

One of the early studies of discounts for lack of control in real estate holding companies demonstrated that (1) the size of the discounts is related to the risk and rate of return of the publicly held limited partnerships, and (2) the average discount of the study was not applicable when valuing a privately held interest.[15] This study noted that an interest in a publicly held limited partnership is highly comparable to a noncontrolling interest except for the liquidity of the interests.

The conclusion of the research is that the return required by an investor on a limited partnership interest is what ultimately determines the amount the investor is willing to

---

15. Bruce A. Johnson & James R. Park, *Study of Discounts for Limited Partnership Units Traded in a Secondary Market*, 14(3) Bus. Valuation Rev. 99–101 (Sept. 1995).

pay for the interest. The study illustrated that investors price noncontrolling interests based on the degree of perceived risk and projected return. The discount for lack of control was the product of investors reducing the price paid to compensate for the risk of the investment.

Liquidity Considerations

Interests that trade in the secondary market are actively marketed and then sold to the highest bidders. Although the limited partnership interests and non-listed REIT interests that change hands in this market do not trade as often as exchange-listed securities, it is important to understand that there are multiple third-party investors that actively buy and sell almost any publicly held partnership or non-listed REIT interests.

One study measured the extent to which discounts observed in the secondary market reflect a discount for lack of marketability.[16] The study considered the amount of time it takes to sell a publicly held interest and collect the proceeds from the sale, a period—according to one of the leading secondary market firms—that is typically 44 days after the sale of the units or shares. Using a time-value of money approach, the study indicated that the vast majority of the overall discount is due to lack of control. Specifically, the estimated portion of the discount due to lack of marketability was determined to be 9.1% of the overall discount.[17]

Accordingly, most appraisers consider an adjustment for lack of marketability after determining the noncontrolling, marketable value using the income and market approaches. If Partnership Profiles data is used for the calculation of the discount rate in the income approach and/or the selection of a price-to-net asset value ratio of the market approach,[18] an additional adjustment for lack of marketability is still warranted if the entity is closely held.

Using Limited Partnership Information for the Income Approach

Data published by Partnership Profiles includes historical rates of return for publicly held limited partnerships and non-listed REITs (the overall rate of return and rate of return data categorized by leverage and the level of historical distributions):

- **No to low debt versus moderate to high debt.** No to low debt entities are well capitalized and typically have no more than 50% debt-to-net asset value (with many having no debt). Moderate to high debt entities have higher levels of interest-bearing debt.
- **Distributing partnerships.** This group includes entities that make regular distributions on at least an annual basis.
- **Nondistributing partnerships.** This group includes entities that do not historically make distributions on an annual basis.

Similar to the use of publicly traded REITs, the rate of return expectation of real estate limited partnerships and nontraded REITs can also be used to calculate a real estate risk premium. In using these real estate entities, the average return expectation on the real estate partnerships over their complete published historical period (1994 to

---

16. 2021 Rate of Return Study, *supra* note 10, at 10.

17. For example, using an observed discount of 25%, the portion of the discount due to lack of marketability was 2.3% or 9.1% of the total discount.

18. 2021 Rate of Return Study, *supra* note 10.

present) can be compared to the income return of the long-term government bonds for the corresponding time period to determine a real estate risk premium.[19]

Using Limited Partnership Information for the Market Approach

When using the market approach to value a closely held limited partnership or LLC interest, where the holdings of the entity are principally comprised of real estate, the appraiser must first identify guideline public entities in which noncontrolling interests have traded between third parties. As discussed in earlier sections, publicly held limited partnership and non-listed REIT interests published by Partnership Profiles are a source for such comparative data.

Noncontrolling interests in publicly held limited partnerships and non-listed REITs trade in the secondary market at a discount to net asset value because an investor does not control:

- The management of the entity
- The liquidation of the underlying assets
- The distribution of earnings

Because of the increased risk related to lack of control, a noncontrolling investor requires a greater rate of return. To achieve the desired level of return on investment, an investor discounts the net asset value of the noncontrolling interest to a level sufficient to produce a return that is commensurate with the risk of the investment.

Discount for Lack of Marketability

In deriving a noncontrolling, marketable value, the appraiser can apply the income approach using alternative rates of return from publicly held investments (REITs and publicly held limited partnerships and non-listed REIT interests). And the appraiser can apply the market approach using pricing multiples (price-to-net asset value ratios) of publicly held investments (publicly held limited partnerships and non-listed REIT interests). Both the income and market approaches result in a value that is based on comparisons with investments in the public market.

Because a nontraded limited partnership or LLC interest does not have access to a secondary market, it is necessary to adjust the indicated values estimated using the income and market approaches by a factor that reflects the additional investment risk of holding an illiquid investment.

The quantification of a discount for lack of marketability can be measured by using an analytical method, which takes into consideration the unique characteristics of the subject interest in order to determine a value based on the impact of the discount for lack of marketability on the rate of return.[20] The inability to readily sell an interest in a closely held limited partnership or LLC increases the owner's exposure to changing market conditions and increases their risk of ownership. Because of the lack of marketability and the resulting increased risk associated with ownership of a privately held interest, an investor would demand a higher return in comparison to a similar but publicly traded

---

19. 2021 RATE OF RETURN STUDY, *supra* note 10, at 14–16.

20. *See*, for example, the Johnson/Park empirical method. For a discussion of discounts for lack of marketability, *see* Chapter 18, "Discounts and Premiums."

interest. Consequently, the closely held interest trades at a discount or a value less than it would if it were publicly traded.

The question for the courts is not whether discounts for lack of control and lack of marketability exist, but rather how the amounts of these discounts are calculated. In the *Peracchio* decision, the court's opinion regarding the selection of a discount for lack of marketability was made clear when it stated:

> [The taxpayer's expert] makes no attempt whatsoever to analyze the data from those [restricted stock] studies as they relate to the transferred interests. Rather, he simply lists the average discounts . . . asking us to accept on faith the premise that the approximate average of those results provides a reliable benchmark for the transferred interests. Absent any analytical support, we are unable to accept that premise. . . .[21]

An appraiser should objectively determine a discount for lack of marketability that compensates an investor for the additional risks associated with the ownership of the closely held interest based on how much the adjustment increases the rate of return of the noncontrolling interest.

COMMON ISSUES IN VALUING INTERESTS IN BUSINESSES WHOSE PRINCIPAL ASSETS ARE REAL PROPERTY INTERESTS

Disputes arise among owners as to the value of an interest in an entity whose primary assets are either entire or partial interests in real property. Typically, the first issue is "what is the correct standard of value" related to valuing the interest in question. Once the standard of value is determined, then the issue becomes what is the appropriate methodology.

Example of a Shareholder Dispute

The dispute involved shareholders of a closely held Subchapter S corporation that developed a business park and continues to lease the buildings owned by the corporation to tenants. Two noncontrolling shareholders contended shareholder oppression and sued to be bought out. At the valuation date, the capital stock consisted of common stock of which approximately 99.5% was nonvoting shares, distributed among members of the families of the original owner. There is no written shareholder agreement.

Counsel specified that the standard of value is *fair value*.[22] In developing an opinion of fair value, the appraiser should, in addition with consulting with counsel, read the applicable state statute, read applicable opinions of the state courts, and consult any learned treatises on the subject as to the applicable standard of value and its interpretation in this case under the state law the dispute is being adjudicated under.

Valuation Issues

The plaintiff expert incorrectly treated the subject shares of capital stock as a direct interest or partitionable interest in real estate by simply valuing the entity at net asset value, substituting real estate appraised values for book values in the balance sheet. The subject shares are a noncontrolling interest in a closely held corporation, which could

---

21. Peracchio v. Comm'r 2003 T.C. Memo. 280.
22. *See* Chapters 1, 23, and 30.

have a value greater than net asset value if there is intangible value and less if the corporation has liabilities such as imbedded tax liabilities. By assuming that the value of the corporate entity equals the net asset value, one is implicitly assuming a liquidation of the properties rather than valuing interests in the entity as a going concern.[23]

Any valuation of interests in a business entity assumes that all expenses associated with the management and operations of the business are applicable to the valuation of that business. The income to be capitalized or present-valued is the income of the entity, not the sum of the incomes of the individual properties alone as if they were hypothetically sold at the valuation date with, say, new triple-net leases. Further, a willing buyer of a noncontrolling interest would discount the value of underlying net asset values due to the existence of the potential tax on the built-in gain.

Moreover, simply using the net asset value for the value of the entity ignores that, as an S corporation, the entity faces a risk of incurring entity-level income taxes if a nonqualified owner were to obtain shares (discussed in Chapter 26, "Valuing S Corporation Stock and Interests in Pass-through Entities").

Now consider an alternative set of assumptions. Assume that the subject entity is a C corporation formed years earlier and, due to the number of heirs that now own stock, cannot qualify as a Subchapter S corporation. In valuing the underlying real property, the net asset value must be adjusted to account for the fact that it is owned by a C corporation. Real estate appraisers determine the value of the real property as "free and clear," which is typical of ownership outside of a corporation. Simply using a net asset value reflects values as if owned "free and clear" of the corporate structure. To properly apply the asset-based approach to this entity, the appraiser must include an adjustment for the imputed difference between holding the real properties "free and clear" outside of a C corporate structure and holding the properties through a C corporation.

In valuing the real estate "free and clear," the indicated value reflects that the buyer will obtain a new tax basis for the depreciable portion of the value upon acquisition. The assets held in the corporation reflect the historical tax basis. The market would discount the appraised values of real properties as determined in the real estate appraisals ("free and clear" values) for the fact that they were held in a C corporation.[24]

VALUING BUSINESS INTERESTS WHEN REAL PROPERTY USED IN THE BUSINESS IS OWNED BY A RELATED ENTITY

Many closely held businesses are structured with the operating business being owned by one entity and the real estate in which the business operates being owned by another separate entity, with rent being charged to the business. Sometimes the ownership of the entities are identical; in other instances, the ownership may be different. The following are examples where different facts impact the application of valuation methodology.

23. Also simply using the net asset value implicitly assumes a new stepped-up income tax basis equal to the values acquisition price of the total of the real estate properties. A buyer of the capital stock in the entity would not obtain this new, stepped-up income tax basis for the properties owned by the entity.

24. One measure of this discount would be the cost to a seller to deliver the properties "free and clear." This is equivalent to applying a corporate-level tax on the real property holding entity—the embedded tax liability on the built-in capital gains which represents the tax liability that a seller would incur if it sold the real property assets at the appraiser value.

Example 1: Ownership Is Identical

One approach to valuation of the entities is to obtain a valuation of the real estate by a real estate appraiser, with the business appraiser adjusting that value for the other assets and liabilities of the entity owning the real estate. The business appraiser then values the operating business.

In engaging a real estate appraiser, one must specify the valuation that needs to be done—if the real estate appraiser is engaged to perform an appraisal of the fee simple interest (assuming the property can be rented at current market rents), the analysis of the operating business needs to consider the rent that has been charged historically and adjust that rent to the market rent used in the real estate appraisal.

If the real property appraiser is engaged to value a leased fee interest assuming continuation of the existing lease rate, then the operating business can be valued assuming the existing rents continue.

If the entity that owns the real estate is structured as a C corporation, the pretax income of that entity is subject to an entity-level income tax that will not be considered by the real property appraiser regardless of his or her assignment. The business appraiser then needs to take the input from the real property appraiser and arrive at a business valuation of the entity owning the real property. Similarly, if the entity that owns the real estate has elected to be a Subchapter S corporation (subject to built-in gains tax if the real estate were to be sold within a specified period of time), the business appraiser needs to adjust the value of the entity for the built-in capital gains tax liability.

An alternative approach is for the business appraiser to value the entirety of the business as a going concern, with the real property simply being one asset of the consolidated entity.

Example 2: Ownership Is Intermingled

In this example, the older generation owns a controlling interest in the entity that owns the real property that houses the automobile dealership (assuming that the real property is owned through a pass-through entity like an LLC), while the younger generation owns a noncontrolling interest in the real property entity but owns 100% of the dealership.

A real estate appraiser can be engaged to value the leased fee interest in the real estate, which assumes continuation of the existing rent. A business appraiser can use that resulting value in valuing the applicable partial interest in the real property-holding entity.

SUMMARY

This chapter covered various topics on valuing entities whose principal assets are interests in real property:

- Real estate appraisers will provide either a fee simple interest value or a leased fee interest value of the real property and will not typically address other assets or liabilities of the entity owning the real property.
- The asset-based approach results in a control value. Applying a discount for lack of control and a discount for lack of marketability to the net asset value to adjust the value to a noncontrolling interest value may be difficult to defend, especially if the discounts are based on averages from studies. Accordingly, the income approach and the market

approach are recommended for the valuation of noncontrolling interests in real estate FLPs and LLCs.

- Discounts from net asset value are the result of an increase in the overall rate of return sought by an investor. In capital markets, investors determine how much they will pay for an investment based on a desired rate of return that reflects the perceived benefits and risk of the investment, not based on a discount. Investors typically do not apply discounts to determine market value. The discount is the result of an investor seeking a higher rate of return based on their evaluation of the expected risk of the investment.
- When valuing a partial interest in an entity that owns real estate, the income and market approaches often provide the best methods for objectively estimating the value of a noncontrolling interest.

REFERENCES FOR VALUING INTERESTS IN REAL PROPERTY HOLDING ENTITIES

Articles and Books

Johnson, Bruce A. 2021. *Comprehensive Guide for the Valuation of Family Limited Partnerships and LLCs*, 6th ed. (Portland, OR: Business Valuation Resources).

Partnership Profiles Partnership Guideline Reports™ (updated annually): six different reports that provide concise research on various segments in which noncontrolling interests have traded in the secondary market: (1) Equity Distributing—Low to No Debt; (2) Equity Distributing—Moderate to High Debt; (3) Non-Income Producing Real Estate Programs; (4) Equity Nondistributing Real Estate Programs; (5) Oil & Gas Partnerships; (6) Triple Net Lease Real Estate Programs.

Pratt, Shannon P. and ASA Educational Foundation. 2022. "Valuing Real Property with a Business Component." In *Shannon Pratt's Valuing a Business: The Analysis and Appraisal of Closely Held Businesses*, 6th ed., Chap. 33, 727–39 (New York: McGraw-Hill).

Webb, Dennis A. 2021. *Valuing Fractional Interests in Real Estate 2.0* (Los Angeles, CA: Milonguero Press).

Wilson, L. Deane and Robin G. Wilson. 2012. *Going Concern Valuation: for Real Estate Appraisers, Lenders, Assessors and Eminent Domain* (Bloomington: iUniverse Inc.).

Databases

Partnership Profiles Minority Interest Discount Database™: interactive online database that includes detailed data on over 400 publicly held real estate LPs and non-listed REITs. The database provides sale transactions and historical financial information for interests in publicly held real estate LPs and non-listed REITs going back to 1994. In addition to its query capabilities, it also includes instant access to the latest SEC Form 10K filings.

CHAPTER 28

Valuing Intellectual Property and Intangible Assets

Christopher Bakewell, ASA, CLP, Julia Rowe, CPA, and Jill Kosonen

INTRODUCTION

In this chapter you will learn about:

- Valuation of legally protected intellectual property in litigation
- Rights of publicity
- Income tax and transfer pricing considerations for intangible assets
- Differences in valuing intangible assets for financial reporting
- Strategy and licensing valuations

This chapter pertains to intangible assets, which can be defined as an identifiable nonmonetary asset without physical substance. Examples include goodwill, brand recognition, trademarks and trade names, and other types of intellectual property. Intellectual property rights are a subset of intangible assets representing the legal protection (patents, copyrights, trademarks, and trade secrets) granted by statue in most developed countries. There are many reasons to value intellectual property.

This chapter also addresses rights of publicity, a form of intellectual property with unique considerations.

VALUATION OF LEGALLY PROTECTED INTELLECTUAL PROPERTY IN LITIGATION

In the United States, intellectual property (IP) owners may request damages for infringement of patents, copyrights, trademarks, and trade secrets. In general, damages are considered to be the amount of money that would compensate a plaintiff for the actual loss or injury from infringement. The recoverable damages available for each intellectual property type are summarized in Exhibit 28-1.

Exhibit 28-1 Economic Damages Categories by Intellectual Property (IP) Type

IP Type	Reasonable Royalty	Lost Profits	Defendant Profits	Statutory Damages
Utility Patent	✓	✓	–	–
Design Patent	✓	✓	✓	–
Trade Secret	✓	✓	✓	–
Trademark	✓	✓	✓	✓
Copyright	✓	✓	✓	✓
Rights of Publicity	✓	✓	✓	✓

Generally, damages are computed on a pretax basis (i.e., before subtracting income taxes on the damage claim). Judgments or settlements of litigation are typically taxed after receipt.

In practice, damages are often based on past infringement. If an award is granted, prejudgment interest may apply. Prejudgment interest is typically determined on a case-by-case basis, and some jurisdictions have standard rules that apply.

In some cases, additional penalties, sometimes referred to as judicial damages, apply, and attorneys' fees may be awarded, as well as a multiplier on damages for willful infringement. In general, judicial damages are not directly tied to the economic valuation of the intellectual property rights at issue. These penalties are at the discretion of the court and are not addressed in this chapter.

PATENT INFRINGEMENT

According to the U.S. Patent and Trademark Office (USPTO), a patent for an invention is the grant of a property right to the inventor, issued by the USPTO.[1] U.S. patent grants are effective within the United States, U.S. territories, and U.S. possessions. The USPTO states that the term of a new patent is 20 years from the date on which the application for the patent was filed in the United States or, in special cases, from the date an earlier related application was filed, subject to the payment of maintenance fees.[2]

The statutory basis for damages in patent infringement cases is provided in Chapter 29 of the U.S. Patent Act. This provision states in part:

> Upon finding for the claimant the court shall award the claimant damages adequate to compensate for the infringement but in no event less than a reasonable royalty for the use made of the invention by the infringer, together with interest and costs as fixed by the court.[3]

In general, economic patent damages fall into two categories: lost profits and reasonable royalties. These measures are available for both utility patents and design patents.

---

1. U.S. Patents & Trademark Office, General Information Concerning Patents (2014), https://www.uspto.gov/sites/default/files/inventors/edu-inf/BasicPatentGuide.pdf.
2. Under certain circumstances, patent term extensions or adjustments may be available. *See id.*
3. 35 U.S.C. § 284.

Damages for design patent infringement may alternatively be calculated under 35 U.S.C. § 289, which provides for recovery of the infringer's "total profit."

Damages Period Considerations

Generally, patent damages apply starting once a patent has issued and the alleged infringement has begun. Accordingly, the damages period begins at the latter of the following dates: (1) the issuance of the patent or (2) the start of infringement by the defendant. Patent damages are also subject to a six-year statute of limitations, which may cause the damages period to be shorter than the infringement period.

Another consideration that impacts the starting point for damages is patent marking, or patent notice, which may further limit the damages period. According to 35 U.S.C. § 287:

> Patentees, and persons making, offering for sale, or selling within the United States any patented article for or under them, or importing any patented article into the United States, may give notice to the public that the same is patented, either by fixing thereon the word "patent" or the abbreviation "pat.," together with the number of the patent [. . .]. In the event of failure so to mark, no damages shall be recovered by the patentee in any action for infringement, except on proof that the infringer was notified of the infringement and continued to infringe thereafter, in which event damages may be recovered only for infringement occurring after such notice. Filing of an action for infringement shall constitute such notice.

Practically speaking, this means that for a patent owner that practices its invention, damages may begin when the patentee marked its own articles, marked licensed, or otherwise allowed articles, or when the patentee provided notice to the infringer of its patent rights (such as through filing a complaint).[4]

The same notice requirement does not apply to patents directed toward a process or a method. Patents containing only method claims do not require marking. This is because, generally, there is not a tangible item to mark. Patents containing both method and apparatus claims still typically require marking.

For the most part, patent damages only apply for the term of the patent, but one exception is provisional patent damages. Provisional patent damages can accrue between the issuance of the patent and the publication of its application if actual notice of the published application is given.

As for the end date of the damages period, damages are typically awarded for past infringement through the date of trial. Some damages models that would apply for the statutory life of the patent have been accepted. Post-trial damages through the expiration of the patent-at-issue may be addressed through an ongoing royalty determined by the court.

Reasonable Royalty Damages

Reasonable royalty damages envision a hypothetical negotiation wherein the alleged infringer obtained a license to the patent on the eve of infringement. In general, the parties to the negotiation involve the patentee at the time of first infringement and the infringer at the time of first infringement. The 15 factors laid out in the seminal 1970

4. Arctic Cat Inc. v. Bombardier Recreational Prod. Inc., 950 F.3d 860 (Fed. Cir. 2020).

case *Georgia-Pacific*[5] provide an accepted framework that is often used to assess reasonable royalty damages. These *Georgia-Pacific* factors (G-P Factors) are summarized in Exhibit 28-2.

Exhibit 28-2 Summary of the *Georgia-Pacific* Factors

G-P Factor 1	The royalties received by the patentee for the licensing of the patent in suit, proving or tending to prove an established royalty.
G-P Factor 2	The rates paid by the licensee for the use of other patents comparable to the patent in suit.
G-P Factor 3	The nature and scope of the license, as exclusive or non-exclusive; or as restricted or nonrestricted in terms of territory or with respect to whom the manufactured product may be sold.
G-P Factor 4	The licensor's established policy and marketing program to maintain his patent monopoly by not licensing others to use the invention or by granting licenses under special conditions designed to preserve that monopoly.
G-P Factor 5	The commercial relationship between the licensor and licensee, such as, whether they are competitors in the same territory in the same line of business; or whether they are inventor and promotor.
G-P Factor 6	The effect of selling the patented specialty in promoting sales of other products of the licensee; that existing value of the invention to licensor as a generator of sales of his nonpatented items; and the extent of such derivative or convoyed sales.
G-P Factor 7	The duration of the patent and the term of the license.
G-P Factor 8	The established profitability of the product made under the patent, its commercial success, and its current popularity.
G-P Factor 9	The utility and advantages of the patent property over the old modes or devices, if any, that had been used for working out similar results.
G-P Factor 10	The nature of the patented invention, the character of the commercial embodiment of it as owned and produced by the licensor, and the benefits to those who have used the invention.
G-P Factor 11	The extent to which the infringer has made use of the invention, and any evidence probative of the value of that use.
G-P Factor 12	The portion of the profit or of the selling price that may be customary in the particular business or in comparable businesses to allow for the use of the invention or analogous inventions.
G-P Factor 13	The portion of the realizable profit that should be credited to the invention as distinguished from nonpatented elements, the manufacturing process, business risks, or significant features or improvements added by the infringer.
G-P Factor 14	The opinion testimony of qualified experts.

5. Georgia-Pacific Corp. v. U.S. Plywood Corp., 318 F. Supp. 1116, 1120 (S.D.N.Y. 1970), *modified and aff'd*, 446 F.2d 295 (2d Cir.), *cert. denied*, 404 U.S. 870 (1971).

G-P Factor 15	The amount that a licensor (such as the patentee) and a licensee (such as the infringer) would have agreed upon (at the time the infringement began) if both had been reasonably and voluntarily trying to reach an agreement; that is, the amount which a prudent licensee—who desired, as a business proposition, to obtain a license to manufacture and sell a particular article embodying the patented invention—would have been willing to pay as a royalty and yet be able to make a reasonable profit and which amount would have been acceptable by a prudent patentee who was willing to grant a license.

The hypothetical license is generally considered to involve a non-exclusive license to the patents-in-suit, and no other technology, patents, or know-how. The scope of the license is also limited to U.S. infringement.

Despite being well accepted, *Georgia-Pacific* is often criticized as being a legal fiction. However, from a financial and valuation point of view, the concept of the hypothetical negotiation follows the framework laid out in the well-known definition of fair market value. Fair market value has long been defined as "the price at which the property would change hands between a willing buyer and a willing seller, neither being under any compulsion to buy or to sell and both having reasonable knowledge of relevant facts."[6] This can be readily compared to the paradigm of *Georgia-Pacific*, which calls for the evaluation of the amount that a licensor (such as a patentee) and a licensee (such as the infringer) would have agreed upon (at the time the infringement began) if both had been reasonably and voluntarily trying to reach an agreement.[7] Both frameworks focus on four common considerations: (1) assessing particular property rights, (2) at a certain date, (3) between willing parties, and (4) considering relevant facts.

Georgia-Pacific is also analogous to valuations of patent assets, which fall into three common valuation approaches: cost, market, and income. Each approach has different considerations and inputs that should be considered.

The cost approach is based on the *principle of substitution*. Patents are one-time grants of exclusivity that are unique and cannot be exactly replicated. Accordingly, in patent infringement matters, analysis of a reasonable royalty often involves consideration of noninfringing alternatives. In patent damages, the cost approach does not measure the cost to create or protect an intellectual property right, but instead measures, at the time of the hypothetical negotiation, the cost to re-create and develop next-best, noninfringing alternatives to the assets under consideration.[8] Comparing the patented invention to

6. Treas. Reg. § 20.2031-1 (b).

7. *Id.*

8. This valuation approach is based on the premise that no party involved in an arm's-length transaction would be willing to pay more to use the property than the cost to replace or recreate the property (G.K. Leonard & L.J. Stiroh, Economic Approaches to Intellectual Property: Policy, Litigation and Management 55 (2005)). An agreement to license a patent is similar to most business agreements in that, when evaluating whether such an agreement is economically justified, the parties involved conduct an economic analysis of the expected benefits and costs associated with the transaction. If both parties expect to benefit from the agreement (i.e., if the expected benefits to each party exceed the anticipated costs), the transaction is likely to occur. If one or both parties do not expect the benefits to exceed the anticipated costs, a transaction is not likely to occur. In the context of a hypothetical negotiation for a naked patent license before any infringement, the licensee would not enter into the license if it could achieve the same benefit at lower cost

its next-best alternative allows one to effectively isolate the incremental value the patent owner could have expected in the absence of infringement.[9] This approach is similar to the consideration of noninfringing alternatives, which is a standard consideration in a damages determination, as well as *Georgia-Pacific* Factors 9 and 10.

The consideration of noninfringing alternatives includes (1) whether the materials needed to implement the noninfringing alternatives were readily available; (2) whether the noninfringing alternatives were well known in the field at the time of first infringement; and (3) whether all of the necessary equipment, know-how, and experience to use the noninfringing alternatives was available at the time of first infringement.[10]

The market approach is based on the *principle of comparison*. The market approach considers arm's-length transactions between unrelated parties for comparable assets.[11] In a reasonable royalty analysis, the market approach considers the terms of licenses and other transactions involving the patents-in-suit or comparable technology.

There is an extensive body of case law, and special rules have emerged in the patent infringement damages world. In a reasonable royalty analysis, it is generally accepted that a patentee cannot rely on license agreements that were "radically different from the hypothetical agreement under consideration" to determine a reasonable royalty, holding that evidence of royalty rates from licenses without a relationship to the claimed invention could not form the basis of a reasonable royalty calculation.[12] "Prior licenses or settlements need to be 'sufficiently comparable' for evidentiary purposes and any differences must be soundly accounted for."[13]

One challenge with the market approach is that real-world transactions are often not specific to the patent rights at issue. For licenses that include other patents in addition to the patents-in-suit, the "extent to which these other patents contributed to the royalty rate" must be addressed.[14]

Outside of patent infringement matters, courts are generally wary of considering settlement agreements. But in the patent damages, in certain circumstances, licenses involving the settlement of litigation can provide the "best evidence" of a reasonable

---

by using a noninfringing alternative. This approach is one way to measure the incremental contribution of an intellectual property asset.

9. Roman L. Weil, et al., Litigation Services Handbook ¶ 20.6 (d) (6th ed. 2017).

10. LaserDynamics, Inc. v. Quanta Comput., Inc., 2011 WL 197869, at *3 (E.D. Tex. 2011), citing Grain Processing Corp. v. American Maize-Products Co., 185 F.3d 1341, 1353–54 (Fed. Cir. 1999). Licensees or alleged infringers do not simply switch to an existing alternative or develop new available alternatives each and every time they are accused of infringement. To do so any time there is disagreement about validity, enforceability, or infringement would be unreasonable and disruptive. The decision not to switch to an alternative is not, by itself, evidence that such a switch was not possible or would not have occurred.

11. Gordon V. Smith & Russell L. Parr, Valuation of Intellectual Property and Intangible Assets 170–71 (3d ed. 2002).

12. Lucent Technologies, Inc. v. Gateway, Inc., 580 F.3d 1301, 1327 (Fed. Cir. 2009); ResQNet.com, Inc. v. Lansa, Inc., 594 F.3d 860, 870–72 (Fed. Cir. 2010).

13. Elbit Sys. Land & C4I Ltd. v. Hughes Network Sys., LLC, 927 F.3d 1292, 1300 (Fed. Cir. 2019) (quoting VirnetX, 767 F.3d 1308, 1330). *See also* MLC Intellectual Prop., LLC v. Micron Tech., Inc., 10 F.4th 1358 (Fed. Cir. 2021). Also, the "licenses relied on by the patentee in proving damages [must be] sufficiently comparable to the hypothetical license at issue in suit." *Lucent Technologies*, 580 F.3d 1301; Apple Inc. v. Wi-LAN, Appeal No. 2020-2011, 2022 WL 333666, at 16–17 (Fed. Cir. Feb. 4, 2022); and California Inst. of Tech. v. Broadcom Ltd., No. 2020-2222, 2022 WL 333669, at *11 (Fed. Cir. Feb. 4, 2022).

14. *Apple Inc.*, 2022 WL 333666, at *8–9.

royalty. Since litigating is the legal avenue to enforce patent rights, some companies use this path in licensing; for these companies, agreements that involve litigation are part of the business and can be like a hypothetical license.[15] Litigation also has a benefit of having discovery mechanisms that can make the economics more transparent, and a claim construction process that can make the legal boundaries of a patent right clearer. As a case progresses, there can be additional clarity about the scope of patent rights.

The income approach is based upon the *principle of anticipation*. The income approach is a valuation technique that provides an estimation of the fair market value of an asset based on the cash flows the asset can be expected to generate over its remaining useful life.[16] In a reasonable royalty analysis, the income approach must be specific to the patent-in-suit and the result of reliable methodologies. That is because where small elements of multicomponent products or systems are accused of infringement, "calculating a royalty on the entire product carries a considerable risk that the patentee will be improperly compensated for non-infringing components of that product."[17] There are multiple ways to assess the income approach, including conducting surveys or regression analyses.

Ultimately, whether it is the 15 *Georgia-Pacific* factors that are used, the three valuation approaches, or both, a reasonable royalty must "carefully tie proof of damages to the claimed invention's footprint in the marketplace."[18]

Additional Considerations for Standards-Essential Patents

In general, if a patent is necessary to implement either an optional or mandatory provision of a standard, the patent is referred to as "essential."[19] Standards-setting organizations (SSOs) coordinate the inclusion of a participant's technology in a formal standard. In exchange for participating in the standard-setting process, some SSOs require commitments by participants to license patents essential to the implementation of the standard on reasonable and nondiscriminatory (RAND) terms.[20] Licensing on RAND[21] terms is often conditioned upon reciprocity by other firms participating in the standards-setting process.[22]

RAND terms may "vary from case to case," while considering "what commitments have been made."[23] One difference between a "reasonable" royalty and a RAND royalty is the inclusion of the word "nondiscriminatory." A widely accepted definition of a "non-

---

15. Prism Techs. LLC v. Sprint Spectrum LP, 849 F.3d 1360, 1456, 1457 (Fed. Cir. 2017).

16. Robert F. Reilly & Robert P. Schweihs, Valuing Intangible Assets 160–61 (1999).

17. LaserDynamics, Inc. v. Quanta Comp., Inc., 694 F.3d 51, 67 (Fed. Cir. 2012).

18. ResQNet.com, Inc. v. Lansa, Inc., 594 F.3d 860, 870–72 (Fed. Cir. 2010); Uniloc USA, Inc. v. Microsoft Corp., 632 F.3d 1292, 1320 (Fed. Cir. 2011).

19. Microsoft Corp. v. Motorola, Inc., No. C10-1823JLR, 2013 U.S. Dist. LEXIS 60233, at *12–13 (W.D. Wash. Apr. 25, 2013).

20. Carl Shapiro, *Setting Compatibility Standards: Cooperation or Collusion?*, *in* Expanding the Bounds of Intellectual Property 85 (Rochelle Dreyfuss, Diane Zimmerman & Harry First, eds., 2001).

21. RAND is also known as FRAND (fair, reasonable, and nondiscriminatory), more often in a European licensing context.

22. *See, e.g.*, *ETSI Rules of Procedure*, Annex 6: ETSI Intellectual Property Rights Policy (Nov. 18, 2015), http://www.etsi.org/images/files/ipr/etsi-ipr-policy.pdf.

23. Ericsson, Inc. v. D-Link Sys., 773 F.3d 1201, 1231 (Fed. Cir. 2014). Although RAND licenses may include terms apart from a royalty rate, this chapter focuses on the royalty rate.

discriminatory" license is that substantially the same royalty terms will be offered to similarly situated licensees.[24] The notion exists because if a patent holder was allowed to charge substantially different rates to different licensees who were similarly situated, it may influence the outcome of which companies would succeed or fail in the market.[25]

The term "reasonable" is also included in RAND. But relative to general reasonable royalties, some additional considerations apply to apportionment in the context of SEPs:

> When dealing with SEPs, two special apportionment issues can arise. First, the patented feature must be apportioned from all of the unpatented features reflected in the standard. Second, the patentee's royalty must be premised on the value of the patented feature, not any value added by the standard's adoption of the patented technology. These steps can ensure that the royalty award is based on the incremental value that the patented invention adds to the product, not any value added by the standardization of that technology.[26]

It is generally recognized that a RAND royalty should reflect the incremental value of the patent, and not the value attributable to other technologies or the value conferred by standardization. Assessing RAND royalties on an ex post basis, after industry participants choose a standard and take steps to implement it, generally makes it more difficult to change to alternative technologies. This creates a risk of overvaluing the patent right.

There are different schools of thought regarding RAND royalties. One involves a "top down" approach, while the other involves a "bottom up" approach. A "top down" approach looks to calculate available royalties and divide them up among the patents. According to an ITU-T publication,

> [t]here is a school of thought that RAND royalties must be reasonable in the aggregate—that is, the sum of royalties collected for all SEPs covering a given standard should not be so high as to remove the incentives to make and sell products using the standard, or, where such costs are passed on to the customers, to undermine the desirability of and market for standardized end-products.[27]

Standards can "implicate hundreds, if not thousands of patents, and the cumulative royalty payments to all standard-essential patent holders can quickly become excessive and discourage adoption of the standard."[28]

In contrast, a bottom up approach involves looking at a single patent right, or collection of patent rights, separate and apart from everything else. Like traditional patent infringement damages, this could include analysis of noninfringing alternatives at the time the standard was implemented, looking at incremental income, or comparable licenses.[29]

---

24. Daniel G. Swanson & William J. Baumol, *Reasonable and Nondiscriminatory (RAND) Royalties, Standards Selection, and Control of Market Power*, 73(1) Antitrust L.J. 29–31 (2005). *See Microsoft Corp.*, 2013 U.S. Dist. LEXIS 60233, at *12–13; *Ericsson, Inc.* 773 F.3d 1201, 1231.

25. Philip B. Nelson, *Patent Pools: An Economic Assessment of Current Law and Policy*, 38 Rutgers L.J. 542, 549–50 (2007).

26. *Ericsson, Inc.*, 773 F.3d at 1231.

27. Understanding Patents, Competition & Standardization in an Interconnected World, ITU Policy Manual 66–67 (2014), https://www.itu.int/en/ITU-T/Documents/Manual_Patents_Final_E.pdf.

28. *In re* Innovatio IP Ventures, LLC, 2013 U.S. Dist. LEXIS 144061, at *66 (N.D. Ill. Sept. 27, 2013).

29. Litigation Services Handbook, *supra* note 9, ¶ 20.6 (d); Thomas F. Cotter, Erik Hovenkamp, & Norman Siebrasse, *Demystifying Patent Holdup*, 76 Wash. & Lee L. Rev. 1501, 1519 (2019); Commonwealth Sci. & Indus. Rsch. Org. v. Cisco Sys., Inc., No. 2015-1066 (Fed. Cir. Dec. 3, 2015), slip op. at 20–21.

Lost Profits Damages

A patentee may be entitled to an award of lost profits if it can demonstrate that, had the infringement not occurred, it likely would have made the sales that were made by the infringer.[30] Price erosion damages are a type of lost profits that can apply when a patentee had to reduce its own prices in order to compete with an infringer.

At a high level, a lost profits analysis requires reconstructing a market with the same considerations "but for" the alleged infringement, or to model the market under an assumption that the alleged infringement not occurred. Basic elements of this analysis include estimating revenues and deducting appropriate costs associated with these revenues to arrive at lost profits. For a discussion of measuring lost profits damages, see Chapter 32, "Valuation in Lost Profits Damages Matters."

The long-standing *Panduit* decision provides a widely used framework for lost profits damages in patent cases. This includes analysis of four prongs: (1) demand for the patented product, (2) absence of acceptable noninfringing substitutes, (3) adequate manufacturing and marketing capability, and (4) lost profits that can be readily quantified.[31]

Evaluation of noninfringing alternatives, the second *Panduit* factor, often drives the analysis.[32] As the Federal Circuit explained:

> a rational would-be infringer is likely to offer an acceptable, non-infringing alternative, if available, to compete with the patent owner rather than leave the market altogether.[33]

In markets where there are more than two suppliers (and other suppliers provide noninfringing alternatives), one accepted method for quantifying lost profits damages is known as a *Mor-Flo* approach.[34] This method involves using the patentee's market share in relation to the market share of others to estimate the re-allocated percentage of infringing sales that the patentee could have sold "but for" the infringer's sales. This method generally assumes that the infringer would not have been able to participate in the relevant market without the infringing product, and its sales are re-allocated.

Lost profits damages can involve economic considerations, such as market segmentation[35] and price elasticity of demand.[36] One tool, known as critical elasticity, quantifies the highest elasticity of demand that a patentee could face and still find a "but-for" price increase profitable.[37] One should also consider marketing and manufacturing capacity. See Chapter 32 for a discussion of valuing lost profits damages.

---

30. Del Mar Avionics v. Quinton Instrument, 836 F.2d 1320, 1326 (Fed. Cir. 1987).

31. Panduit Corp. v. Stahlin Bros. Fibre Works, Inc., 575 F.2d 1152, 1156 (6th Cir.), *cert. denied*, 439 U.S. 856 (1978) (Markey, C.J., sitting by designation).

32. Although noninfringing alternatives are important considerations in both reasonable royalty analyses and lost profits analyses, the analysis of noninfringing alternatives generally serves a different purpose in lost profits analyses than they do in reasonable royalty analyses. As discussed previously, in reasonable royalty analyses, noninfringing alternatives evaluate the value of the patented invention through envisioning a hypothetical design around of the patented invention.

33. Grain Processing v. Am. Maize-Products, 185 F.3d 1341, 1351 (Fed. Cir. 1999).

34. State Indus., Inc. v. Mor-Flo Indus., Inc., 883 F.2d 1573, 1577–80 (Fed. Cir. 1989).

35. BIC Leisure Prods., Inc. v. Windsurfing Int'l, Inc., 1 F.3d 1214, 1219 (Fed. Cir. 1993).

36. Crystal Semiconductor Corp. v. Tritech Microelectronics Int'l, Inc., 246 F.3d 1336, 1357–59 (Fed. Cir. 2001).

37. Jeffrey Church and Roger Ware, Industrial Organization: A Strategic Approach 608 (2000); James F. Nieberding, *Lost Profits and Price Erosion in Patent Infringement Cases*, 16(1) J. Forensic Econ. 37–49 (2003).

Considerations Unique to Design Patents

Design patents cover a "new, original, and ornamental design of articles of manufacture."[38] In addition to the remedies available for utility patents under § 284, that is, a reasonable royalty or lost profits,[39] a design patent holder may be able to claim an infringer's total profits for an article of manufacture depicted in a design patent.[40] The design patent owner is permitted to recover either total profits, known as "disgorgement," or the other damages measures (i.e., lost profits or reasonable royalties).

Design patents can involve considering the "article of manufacture" for disgorgement purposes. This may be an entire product or, in some cases, an element of the product sold in the marketplace.[41] In general, the infringer's total profits are equal to the dollar amount the infringer generated from sales of the infringing article minus the costs associated with the sales, with costs being determined on a case-by-case basis.[42] Generally, it is the infringer's burden to establish costs that are applicable to the infringer's net profit.[43]

TRADE SECRET MISAPPROPRIATION

Trade secrets were initially enforced via state statutes. But the Uniform Trade Secrets Act (UTSA) is a "model law" drafted by the National Conference of Commissioners on Uniform State Laws. Only a couple of states, New York and North Carolina, have not adopted the UTSA at the time of this writing.[44]

Trade secret damages may include plaintiff's actual losses, defendant's unjust enrichment (or disgorgement of defendant's profits), and a reasonable royalty.[45]

Trade secret damages issues can involve the entire toolkit of a valuation practitioner. Courts have accepted standard valuation methodologies when estimating damages based

---

38. 35 U.S.C. § 171.

39. *Id.* § 284.

40. *Id.* § 289.

41. Samsung Elecs. Co. v. Apple Inc., 137 S. Ct. 429, 436 (2016).

42. Colin B. Harris & Andrew M. Ollis, *Design Patent Damages: An Additional Remedy and Other Considerations*, 2(5) LANDSLIDE (May/June 2010), https://www.oblon.com/A11960/assets/files/News/Design-Patent-Damages-May-June-2010.pdf; Nike, Inc. v. Wal-Mart Stores, Inc., 138 F.3d 1437, 1447–48 (Fed. Cir. 1998).

43. *Nike, Inc.*, 138 F.3d at 1448, *aff'g* 41 U.S.P.Q.2d (BNA) 1146 (E.D. Va. 1996). *See also, e.g.*, In Univ. of Colo. Found., Inc. v. Am. Cyanamid Co., 342 F.3d 1298 (Fed. Cir. 2003) the affirming award based on incremental profits opinion that accounted for "production and marketing/distribution costs"; In Roberts Tech. Grp., Inc. v. Curwood, Inc., 695 Fed. App'x 48, 51 (3d Cir. 2017) "The term 'net profit' refers to the difference between the sale price of a product and each of the expenses incurred as part of the sale process (e.g., the purchase price of the product, marketing costs, etc.)."; Restatement (Third) of Restitution & Unjust Enrichment § 51(4) (2020) defines "the unjust enrichment of a conscious wrongdoer, or of a defaulting fiduciary without regard to notice or fault, is the net profit attributable to the underlying wrong."

44. *Trade Secrets Act*, UNIFORM LAW COMM'N, https://www.uniformlaws.org/committees/community-home?communitykey=3a2538fb-e030-4e2d-a9e2-90373dc05792#LegBillTrackingAnchor (last visited May 22, 2024).

45. Uniform Trade Secrets Act § 3(a). In May 2016, the Defend Trade Secrets Act (DTSA) was signed into law and provided federal protection of trade secrets. The DTSA did not displace protections provided under the UTSA. 18 U.S.C. § 1838. Similar to the UTSA, the DTSA addresses compensatory damages to the trade secret owner in the form of plaintiff's actual losses, defendant's unjust enrichment (or disgorgement of defendant's profits), and a reasonable royalty. U.S.C. § 1836(b)(3).

on the value of the trade secret at the time of the misappropriation, especially where the value has been essentially destroyed as a result of the misappropriation.[46]

Courts have referred to cases involving patent infringement in assessing damages in trade secret misappropriation matters.[47]

Like in design patent cases, profits disgorgement of the defendant is also available. Generally, the plaintiff has the burden of identifying applicable revenues attributable to the misappropriation, and the defendant has the burden of identifying applicable incremental costs.[48]

TRADEMARK AND TRADE DRESS INFRINGEMENT

A trademark or trade dress registrant may seek remedies available under the Lanham Act. The Lanham Act explains that plaintiffs are entitled to "(1) defendant's profits, (2) any damages sustained by the plaintiff, and (3) the costs of the action."[49] The plaintiff generally will not be entitled to recover both plaintiff's losses and infringer's profits for the same sale.[50] Under the Lanham Act, it is the defendant who bears the burden of proof as to the allowance of any deductions from its accused sales.

Like other ways of measuring damages, standard valuation tools can be used in the right circumstances. One available measure is to value the mark at the time of infringement.[51] A reasonable royalty also may be used to measure the trademark owners' damages. The 15 *Georgia-Pacific* factors from patent law have been accepted by the courts as a framework for measuring a reasonable royalty for a trademark.[52] A damages analysis can also involve valuing what the parties would have agreed on as compensation for the trademark had the alleged wrongful acts not occurred. Such a "but for" analysis can involve analyzing a reasonable bargain between the parties as willing parties at arm's length for rights to use a trademark.

Unlike in patent infringement damages, the relief from royalty method has been an accepted method for valuing a trademark.[53] But in *Nestle Holdings*, the Second Circuit

---

46. In Univ. Computing v. Lykes Youngstown Corp., 504 F.2d 518 (5th Cir. 1974), the court held that "the value of the secret to the plaintiff is an appropriate measure of damages only when the defendant has in some way destroyed the value of the secret."

47. It has been held that "the proper measure of damages in the case of a trade secret appropriation is to be determined by reference to the analogous lines of cases involving patent infringement. . . ." International Indus., Inc. v. Warren Petroleum Corp., 248 F.2d 696, 699 (3d Cir. 1997); *see also Univ. Computing*, 504 F.2d 518.

48. Restatement (Third) of Unfair Competition § 45 cmts. b, f (Am. Law Inst., 1995).

49. 15 U.S.C. § 1117.

50. *E.g.*, in Nintendo of America, Inc. v. Dragon Pacific Int'l, 40 F.3d 1007, 1010 (9th Cir. 1994), the court held that "the recovery of both plaintiff's lost profits and disgorgement of defendant's profits is generally considered a double recovery under the *Lanham Act*."

51. Terence P. Ross, Intellectual Property Law: Damages and Remedies (2019).

52. Sands, Taylor & Wood Co. v. Quaker Oats Co., 978 F.2d 947, 963 (7th Cir. 1992); Taco Cabana Int'l, Inc. v. Two Pesos, Inc., 932 F.2d 1113, 1125–26 (5th Cir. 1991); Ramada Inns, Inc. v. Gadsden Motel Co., 804 F.2d 1562, 1565 (5th Cir. 1986).

53. The relief from royalty method is based on the premise that a mark's value can be measured by what the owner of the mark would pay in royalties if he/she did not own the property, but rather had to license it from a third party. The amount of the hypothetical payment is used as a surrogate to measure the portion of economic income attributable to the mark. Gordon V. Smith, Trademark Valuation 148 (1996).

found that because a licensee has less control over the use of a mark than a trademark owner has, an analysis based on the licensing royalty rates can understate the value of a mark in some circumstances.[54]

When using empirical data, consideration of differences between the hypothetical license of the subject intellectual property and the comparable license agreements is appropriate.[55] It is also relevant to consider how established the product is in its market, how profitable the product is compared with similar products, and any evidence of premium pricing.[56]

In trademark infringement cases, lost profits are generally associated with the past. However, there is some authority that the plaintiff may also prove and recover future lost profits based on elimination of markets that were once potentially available.[57] In these or similar circumstances, reasoned determination of cost of capital can affect the final monetary award.[58]

COPYRIGHT INFRINGEMENT

The Copyright Act of 1976 governs damages in copyright infringement matters. Damages in copyright infringement matters may include actual damages to the copyright

---

54. In Nestle Holdings, Inc. v. Comm'r, 152 F.3d 83, 88 (1998), the court found that "A relief-from-royalty model fails to capture the value of all of the rights of ownership, such as the power to determine when and where a mark may be used, or moving a mark into or out of product lines. . . . Ownership of a mark is more valuable than a license because ownership carries with it the power and incentive both to put the mark to its most valued use and increase its value. A licensee cannot put the mark to use beyond the temporal or other limitations of a license and has no reason to take steps to increase the value of a mark where the increase value will be realized by the owner."

55. Relevant comparisons for trademark licenses include (1) restrictions on how and where to use the trademark, including geographic limits or limits restricting the use of the mark to certain products; (2) whether the license is for the exclusive or nonexclusive use of the trademark; (3) how the burden of supporting the trademark is shared between licensor and licensee (for example, some licensors may provide advertising or other promotional support during the license period); (4) who will carry the burden of enforcing the trademark, should it be infringed upon by a third party; (5) any minimum royalties to limit the downside for the licensor; (6) the term of the license and whether the license has any option to extend the term; and (7) any other provisions, including side agreements between licensee and licensor, that are designed to induce either party to enter into the licensing arrangement. Espen Roback, *Lessons from Nestle v. Comm'r: Second Circuit Rejects Popular Trademark Valuation Method*, J. CORP. TAX'N (Summer 1999).

56. *Id.*

57. In Taco Cabana Int'l, Inc. v. Two Pesos, Inc. 932 F.2d 1113, 1126–27 (5th Cir. 1991), a case involving trade dress infringement, the defendant's infringement of the trade dress of the plaintiff's restaurant and its entry into the Houston market effectively "foreclosed" the market from the plaintiff causing the plaintiff to lose anticipated future profits.

58. *See* Chapter 30, "Cost of Capital for Fair Value Reporting of Intangible Assets," in SHANNON P. PRATT & ROGER J. GRABOWSKI, COST OF CAPITAL: APPLICATIONS AND EXAMPLES (5th ed. 2014) for a discussion of the cost of capital for valuing assets for financial reporting purposes. However, determining the discount rate applicable to a trademark will often result in a discount rate that differs from a business or a division of a corporation. This can be shown by way of the following hypothetical example. In a trademark case involving an e-commerce business, a risk-adjusted discount rate of 20% was considered when assessing damages based on the value of the mark at the time of the infringement. Some of the factors that led to the selection of a discount rate of 20% included a "core" cost of capital for the industry of 15%, together with an adjustment of 5% specific to the economic attributes of the mark as used in the context of the dispute.

owner, infringer's profits (i.e., unjust enrichment), and statutory damages.[59] However, a copyright owner is generally not permitted to recover both plaintiff's losses and defendant's profits on the same sale.

Statutory remedies are available for copyright infringement where the copyright has been federally registered. A copyright owner can elect to recover statutory damages instead of actual damages and/or profits of the infringer.[60] The amount of statutory damages that a copyright owner can elect to receive ranges from $750 to $30,000 per infringed work.[61]

Damages in music infringement cases can be measured through evaluating music licensing rights that could have or should have been obtained from a clearinghouse "but for" the infringing act. Clearinghouses offer the ability to obtain licenses from several rights holders under one agreement.

In copyright infringement cases, damages are generally associated with the past. Infringement is usually contested through the date of trial. An injunction may be issued by the court as an equitable remedy for the wrongful act. Therefore, the concept of future damages is rare. It follows that discount rates do not receive substantial explicit attention during the damages phase of copyright cases. However, interest rates are used for determining awards of prejudgment interest.

RIGHTS OF PUBLICITY

Recent estate tax issues involving the *Michael Jackson*[62] and the *Prince*[63] estates, coupled with the National Collegiate Athletic Association (NCAA) decision to allow college athletes to enter into endorsement contracts, have focused new attention on an individual's *right of publicity* (ROP), often also referred to as *name, image, and likeness* (NIL).

The statutory right that privacy is personal gives rise to a person's ability to commercially exploit "that which is theirs." The right of publicity relates to the personal control over commercial display and exploitation of their personality and the exercise of their talents. In a 1953 case involving Topps Chewing Gum, the court found that a person has a right to commercially exploit the value of his photograph; the court went on to call this the ROP.[64]

---

59. 17 U.S.C. § 504 (b).

60. *Id.* § 504 (a).

61. *Id.* § 504 (c). If the copyright owner proves willful infringement, the court can increase the amount of statutory damages to a maximum of $150,000 per infringed work. In a case where an infringer establishes it was not aware of the copyright infringement and had no reason to believe that its acts constituted a copyright infringement, the court in its discretion may reduce the award of statutory damages to a sum of not less than $200.

62. Est. of Michael Jackson, T.C. Memo, 2021-48.

63. Petition in Est. of Prince R. Nelson v. Comm'r, No. 11442-20 (T.C. 2020) settled in Nov. 30, 2021, order.

64. In Haelen Labs v. Topps Chewing Gum, 202 F.2d 866 (2d Cir. 1953), *cert. denied*, 346 U.S. 816 (1953) the Court ruled that "[A] man has a right in the publicity value of his photograph, i.e., the right to grant the exclusive privilege of publishing his picture. . . . This right might be called a 'right of publicity.' For it is common knowledge that many prominent persons (especially actors and ball players), far from having their feelings bruised through public exposure of their likenesses, would feel sorely deprived if they no longer received money for authoring advertisements, popularizing their countenances, displayed in newspapers, magazines, buses, trains and subways."

More recently, basketball player Ed O'Bannon's lawsuit against the NCAA eventually led to profound changes in providing student-athletes with economic rights to their NIL.

Rights of publicity can be protected in most states, with California being the leading example due to the entertainment business based in Hollywood. As illustrated by the cases involving *Jackson* and the *Prince* estate, a celebrity does not even have to be alive to have right of publicity as their property. In the *Jackson* case, the estate's rights were preserved under California Statute § 3344.1. Federal law does not yet protect the right of publicity.

Generally, an individual can control commercial use of their name, likeness, or other aspects of identity. A business cannot use a person's name or likeness without consent, and a business cannot indicate without authorization that a celebrity has endorsed their product or service.[65] Courts can implement injunctions and assess damages.

Generally, measures of damages are relatively flexible, recognizing that circumstances can differ greatly. One concept is that a plaintiff can seek damages for each unlawful use of a likeness or persona. One can consider the profits enjoyed by the defendant from use of the plaintiff's likeness.

California law provides that any person who misappropriates a right of publicity "shall be liable to the injured party or parties in an amount equal to the greater of seven hundred fifty dollars ($750) or the actual damages suffered by him or her as a result of unauthorized use, and any profits from the unauthorized use that are attributable to the use and are not taken into account in computing the actual damages."[66]

Like other forms of intellectual property rights, there is some burden shifting as to deductibility of costs. In California, California Civil Code § 3344 states that "the injured party or parties are required to present proof only of the gross revenue attributable to such use, and the person who violated this section is required to prove his or her deductible expenses."[67] The plaintiff shows applicable revenues; the defendant shows applicable expenses. Defendants may also respond to the applicability of the revenue stream identified by the plaintiff.

In rights of publicity cases, there can be significant evidence regarding licensing. Advertising campaigns often involve more than one likeness, and there can be payments to, for example, other models or celebrities who appeared in analogous print ads. Likewise, the celebrity may have appeared in other print ads before. This is "market approach" type information, as discussed earlier. However, from an economic perspective, challenges can occur if a celebrity does not want his or her likeness used at all, or if the misuse of the likeness somehow diminishes the value of the likeness. As a result of these considerations, rights of publicity damages analyses require some flexibility, and potential consideration of a wide range of theories and models using the full economic toolkit of a valuation practitioner.

---

65. J. Thomas McCarthy, The Rights of Publicity and Privacy § 1:3 (2d ed. 2014). While everyone possesses a right of publicity, right of publicity contracts often involve celebrities, and increasingly, sports figures.

66. Cal. Civil Code § 3344 (a).

67. *Id.*

Valuation Considerations

When analyzing a celebrity's right of publicity, a valuation expert may need to distinguish between compensation for "personal services" and the exploitation of the celebrity's "image rights." A celebrity's right of publicity can be valued within the appropriate circumstances. Common approaches would be a discounted cash flow (DCF) method (income approach) or using sale/transaction multiples (market approach). However, the outright sale of a celebrity's right of publicity is uncommon, and finding comparable transactions can be challenging.

In the context of the right of publicity for celebrities who are still living, there are commonly two means of generating revenue, personal services and/or image rights. Personal services include services actually provided by a celebrity, including personal appearances, product advertising at trade shows, autograph signing events, and concerts. Image rights generate revenue from licensing name, image, and likeness for commercial use.

For a living celebrity, personal services and image rights can be intertwined. For example, celebrity endorsements may require a specified number of personal appearances. An issue in those circumstances is the allocation of revenue between the two (i.e., apportioning economic income between compensation for their personal services versus the licensing of their name, image, and likeness). This requires an allocation between personal services and name and likeness. This has been addressed in a U.S. Tax Court decision involving the golfer, Sergio Garcia.[68]

In the *Garcia* case, there was a dispute over Garcia's taxable income, and the allocation of monies received between personal services and the monies received for his name and likeness. Garcia had an annual endorsement contract with a golf company that required his personal services in order to qualify for additional bonuses. When paying U.S. income taxes, Garcia had allocated 85% of the endorsement revenue to the right of publicity, meaning only the remaining 15% allocated to personal services would be subject to U.S. income taxes. Based on the facts and circumstances of the case and Mr. Garcia's contract, the court ultimately allocated a greater percentage to personal services (35%). There were ten factors considered in coming to this allocation:

- Licensee history
- Budget for prospective use
- Type/nature of use
- Role of the celebrity in the campaign
- Geographical scope (population exposure)
- Type of media used
- Length of the campaign
- Exclusivity
- Other intellectual property rights held by third parties or entities
- Synergy with the company/product

Celebrities and their estates also have the ability to continue to generate income after their death through the exploitation of their right of publicity. The estates of Elvis Presley, Marilyn Monroe, James Dean, and Michael Jackson have benefited from the ability to generate revenue from their right of publicity. However, after passing, the ability to generate income often decreases due to the loss of personal services and lack of public

68. Garcia v. Comm'r, 140 T.C. No. 6 (U.S.T.C. Mar. 14, 2013).

presence. And not every state provides protection for the image rights of deceased celebrities. In valuing the right of publicity in an estate of a deceased celebrity, one has to be cognizant of the applicable law in the state where the celebrity was domiciled.

Over the years, some living celebrities have sold portions of their right of publicity. Perhaps the most famous example was the 1999 sale of the name "George Foreman," purchased by Salton. George Foreman sold the rights to use his name in connection with the marketing and sale of food preparation products worldwide into perpetuity to Salton Inc., which related to the "George Foreman Grill."

Other examples include Shaquille O'Neil, Julius Erving, and Jessica Simpson who sold portions of their right of publicity.[69] Muhammad Ali also sold a portion of his image rights.

INJUNCTIVE RELIEF

Injunctive relief is a remedy sought outside of monetary damages to protect intellectual property assets. Injunctions are not as common in copyright and patent cases. In patent cases, in particular, there are some unique considerations.

In 2006, the Supreme Court's ruling in *eBay*[70] made it more challenging for permanent injunctions to be granted in patent cases. With this decision, the Supreme Court ruled that a four-factor test must be applied in order for a permanent injunction to be granted following a validity and infringement verdict. Prior to this, permanent injunctions were almost always granted when liability was found.

Some patentholders turn to the U.S. International Trade Commission (USITC) for something analogous to injunctive relief. According to the USITC, unfair import, or § 337, investigations "most often involve claims regarding intellectual property rights, including allegations of patent infringement and trademark infringement by imported goods."[71] The "primary remedy available in Section 337 investigations is an exclusion order that directs Customs to stop infringing imports from entering the United States."[72] Section 337 investigations, which are conducted pursuant to 19 U.S.C. § 1337 and the Administrative Procedure Act, include trial proceedings before administrative law judges and review by the Commission.

Automatic injunctions are potentially available in other jurisdictions, including in Europe. Since supply chains are global in nature today, an injunction in one geography can have global implications. For this reason, patentholders will often focus on Europe or assert parallel litigations.

69. Simpson famously bought the majority of her image rights back in 2021.

70. eBay Inc. v. MercExchange, L.L.C, 547 U.S. 388 (2006).

71. Both utility and design patents, as well as registered and common law trademarks, may be asserted in these investigations. Other forms of unfair competition involving imported products, such as infringement of registered copyrights, mask works or boat hull designs, misappropriation of trade secrets or trade dress, passing off, and false advertising, may also be asserted. Additionally, antitrust claims relating to imported goods may be asserted. *See About Section 337*, USITC, https://www.usitc.gov/intellectual_property/about_section_337.htm (last visited May 22, 2024).

72. *About Section 337*, *supra* note 71.

INCOME TAX AND TRANSFER PRICING CONSIDERATIONS FOR INTANGIBLE ASSETS

For income tax purposes, U.S. multinational taxpayers who engage in intercompany transfers of intangible property across international borders must assign a value to the price at which these transfers occur. These "transfer prices" are internal prices for intangibles that influence the taxable income reported by the legal entities involved in the transaction and the overall effective tax rate of the consolidated organization.

Transfer pricing for income tax purposes is governed by local country tax authorities, many of which have issued formal rules regulating transfer pricing practices, to provide a conceptual framework for pricing intercompany transactions and ensuring an appropriate allocation of income between the various tax jurisdictions in which a multinational company operates. The more a multinational's income is allocated or earned in low-tax jurisdictions, the more its overall effective tax rate is favorably influenced, and vice versa.

Valuing intangibles for transfer pricing purposes requires knowledge of the methods available to a taxpayer in a particular jurisdiction for this purpose and therefore differs from valuing intangibles in the context of litigation or financial reporting. The focus in this section is on the methods available from the perspective of a U.S. taxpayer.

Arm's-Length Standard

The fundamental concept behind pricing intercompany transactions is the arm's-length standard. The arm's-length standard is the basis for evaluating transactions between members of a controlled group in the United States and virtually all other tax jurisdictions. The arm's-length standard is the general standard behind the laws and regulations that govern intercompany pricing for multinational companies and is contained in § 1.482-1(b)(1) of the Treasury Regulations that were finalized in 1996 and last revised in 2015, as follows:

> In determining the true taxable income of a controlled taxpayer, the standard to be applied in every case is that of a taxpayer dealing at arm's length with an uncontrolled taxpayer. A controlled transaction meets the arm's-length standard if the results of the transaction are consistent with the results that would have been realized if uncontrolled taxpayers had engaged in the same transaction under the same circumstances (arm's-length results).

Intangible Property Transactions

Intercompany transactions involving intangible property is one of five broad categories of transfer pricing transactions within a multinational.[73] The question, what constitutes an intangible, is common in transfer pricing. As defined under the U.S. transfer pricing rules under § 1.482-4 and codified by the Tax Cut and Jobs Act (TCJA),[74] an intangible includes

---

73. The remaining categories include tangible, services, financing and insurance, and cost sharing arrangements.

74. LB&I Training Tax Cuts & Jobs Act (TCJA), Official IRS Training Material (Oct. 2019), https://www.irs.gov/pub/newsroom/lbi-tcja-participant-guide-367-and-91-14102-and-14221.pdf.

any asset that comprises any of the following items and has substantial value independent of the services of any individual:[75]

- Goodwill
- Patents, inventions, formulae, processes, designs, patterns, or know-how
- Copyrights and literary, musical, or artistic compositions
- Trademarks, trade names, or brand names
- Franchises, licenses, or contracts
- Methods, programs, systems, procedures, campaigns, surveys, studies, forecasts, estimates, customer lists, or technical data
- Other similar items. An item is considered similar to those above if it "derives its value not from its physical attributes but from its intellectual content or other intangible properties."[76]

Identifying a transfer of intangibles can be difficult since it is often possible for a legal entity within a controlled group to "use" certain rights without ever having documented any licenses or transfers in the form of an intercompany agreement, invoice, or other traceable item.[77]

Methods for Determining the Arm's-Length Price

Under Treasury Regulations § 1.482, there are specific methods used to evaluate the arm's-length nature of an intangible transaction. The regulations also contain a best method rule. The rule states, "the arm's-length results of a controlled transaction must be determined under the method that, under the facts and circumstance, provides the most reliable measure of an arm's-length result."[78] As such, there is not strict preferential hierarchy among the methods presented. The § 482 regulations specify the various methods a taxpayer can utilize when producing measures of arm's-length results. These methods can be divided into two categories: transactional methods and profit-based methods. Transactional methods compare the actual price paid in a controlled transaction to prices paid in comparable uncontrolled transaction, and profit-based methods compare the profit levels of the parties involved in the related party transaction to those of parties in uncontrolled transactions.

---

75. Treas. Reg. § 1.482-4(b).

76. With regards to the outbound transfer of intangibles, there are other specific rules prescribed in I.R.C. § 367. The definition of intangible property outlined in § 367(d)(4) and codified in the TCJA includes workforce in place, goodwill (both foreign and domestic), and going concern value as well as the residual category of "any similar item," the value of which is not attributable to tangible property of the services of an individual. The TCJA also introduced into the statute the need to consider realistic alternatives (of buyer and seller) as part of the valuation of intangibles for transfer pricing. In 2018, § 482 was revised to codify the use of an aggregation approach for the valuation of the intangible property being transferred when this approach achieves a more reliable result than an asset-by-asset approach.

77. Potential sources of information available within an organization that can aid in identifying intangible property transfers includes intercompany agreements, tax returns, interviews with personnel such as accounting controllers and business executives in research and development, engineering, design, technology, marketing, and advertising, and information from public sources such as annual reports, SEC filings, and the company's website.

78. Treas. Reg. § 1.482-1(c)(1). There is no strict hierarchy of methods under the U.S. transfer pricing framework, and no single method is considered better than another ex-ante.

To determine which method provides the best or most reliable measure of an arm's-length result, the taxpayer must take into account the degree of comparability between the controlled transaction and any uncontrolled transactions, and the quality of the data and assumptions used in the analysis.

There are four methods available to evaluate the arm's-length nature of pricing for the transfer and use of intangible property. These methods include the (1) Comparable Uncontrolled Transaction (CUT) method,[79] (2) the Comparable Profits Method (CPM),[80] (3) the profit split method,[81] and (4) unspecified methods. These methods are discussed in "Intangible Transfers and Valuation Approaches," in Chapter 21, "Valuations for Federal Income Tax Matters."

Methods not specified may be used to evaluate whether the amount charged in a controlled transaction is arm's length. As with any method, an unspecified method will not be applied unless it "provides the most reliable measure of an arm's-length result."

DIFFERENCE IN VALUING INTANGIBLE ASSETS FOR FINANCIAL REPORTING

This chapter focuses on valuing intellectual property and intangible assets in the context of litigation. There are a few key differences between valuing intangible assets in the context of litigation compared to doing so for the purpose of financial reporting.

In the context of financial reporting, intangible assets are often valued by companies at the time they are acquired as part of a business combination. Accounting regulatory bodies, such as the Financial Accounting Standards Board (FASB) and the American Institute of Certified Public Accountants (AICPA), provide extensive guidance for companies to follow when valuing intangibles. Under U.S. Generally Accepted Accounting Practices (GAAP), companies must value intangible assets at fair value at the time they are acquired. Subsequently, the assets are subject to amortization or impairment. For intangible assets that are internally developed, GAAP requires that development costs be expensed as incurred, resulting in these intangible assets not often appearing on a company's balance sheet. See section, "Fair Value for Financial Reporting," in Chapter 1, "Defining Value in the Relevant Context: Standards of Value," for a discussion of valuation considerations.

The scope for valuing intellectual property and intangible assets for financial reporting often differs from that of valuing them in the context of litigation. When valuing intangible assets for financial reporting, assets are often valued as part of a group rather than as individual assets. For example, when a company acquires a group of intangible

---

79. The intangible involved in the uncontrolled transaction is considered comparable to the controlled intangible when each has a similar profit potential, and each is used in connection with similar products or processes within the same general industry or market. Other factors to be considered are the terms of the transfer, the stage of development, rights to receive updates, revisions, or modifications, uniqueness of the property, duration of the license, economic and product liability risks, existence of collateral transactions, general economic conditions, and functions performed by the transferor (i.e., licensor) and transferee (i.e., licensee). Source: Treas. Reg. § 1.482-4(c)(2)(iii)(B)(2)(vi).

80. Treas. Reg. § 1.482-5(a).

81. There are two types of profit split methods: the comparable profit split method and the residual profit split method.

assets such as the intellectual property portfolio of another business, the assets are valued on the company's books as a group. This differs from valuing intangible assets for litigation because litigation valuations are typically focused on one individual asset, such as a single patent being litigated.

Generally, the methodology for valuing intangible assets for financial reporting and litigation is the same, with some unique considerations. The three main valuation approaches, the income approach, market approach and cost approach may be utilized as a framework for valuing intangibles in each context.[82] Each of these approaches for valuing intangible assets for the purpose of financial reporting also shares similarities with valuation in the context of litigation.

The income approach considers earnings and cash flows, including relative to substitutes, as well as the relief from royalty method. Under the market approach, there are three common methods for valuing intangible assets, including assessing comparable arm's-length transactions and the relief from royalty method.[83] Valuing an intangible asset under the cost approach outside of litigation considers either reproduction costs or replacement costs.

The relief from royalty method relates to both the market approach and the income approach. It is based on the concept that owning an intangible asset relieves the owner from having to pay license fees to a third party for a similar asset if they did not own a comparable asset.[84] The relief from royalty valuation estimates cost savings uses a royalty rate that the company who owns the intangible assets would be obligated to pay a hypothetical third-party licensor for use of that intangible asset.[85] This is comparable to the approach for estimating reasonable royalties, however, the scope is broader.

According to the AICPA, the income approach is considered the primary approach, followed by the market approach, for valuing intellectual property such as patents and copyrights.[86]

STRATEGY AND LICENSING VALUATIONS

Valuations for the purposes of strategy and licensing decisions need not follow a prescribed valuation methodology and may be informed by the valuations in other contexts. In general, strategic valuations (including for licensing) may involve the same cost, market, and income considerations in the form of the consideration of noninfringing alternatives, market transactions, and incremental income attributable to the rights at issue.

Real-world transactions involving intellectual property may provide operating freedom to the licensee and may have more inclusive rights than an agreement in the hypothetical negotiation context just described. Rights may be worldwide, whereas intellectual property protection in other contexts may be specific to a specific country or state. Rights may also be exclusive or non-exclusive, where exclusive rights tend to

82. FASB ASC 820-10-35-24B; AICPA, *Statement on Standards for Valuation Services* VS Section 100 (SSVS No. 1).

83. *Id., Statement on Standards for Valuation Services.*

84. *Id.* at 4–5, https://www.aicpa-cima.com/resources/download/three-approaches-to-valuing-intangible-assets.

85. *Id.*

86. *Id.* at 6.

garner higher royalties (ceteris paribus, or all else equal). Most-favored nations clauses may provide some licensees assurance that they receive comparable terms to their competitors. Springing licenses may provide some protection in the event that the intellectual property changes hands after the initial transaction.

Overall, strategic and licensing valuations are by design flexible and based on the circumstances applicable to the analysis.

SUMMARY

Intellectual property provides a unique legal benefit to exclude others from engaging in certain activities. The fundamental principles of intellectual property valuation were addressed in this chapter, though case-specific and venue-specific considerations apply.

REFERENCE FOR VALUING INTELLECTUAL PROPERTY AND INTANGIBLE ASSETS

Pratt, Shannon P. and ASA Educational Foundation. 2022. "Valuing Intangible Assets." In *Shannon Pratt's Valuing a Business: The Analysis and Appraisal of Closely Held Businesses* 6th ed., Chap. 25, 569–88 (New York: McGraw-Hill).

CHAPTER 29

Valuation Provisions in Buy-Sell Agreements

Z. Christopher Mercer, FASA, CFA, ABAR and Jeffrey S. Tarbell, ASA, CFA

INTRODUCTION

In this chapter you will learn about:

- Drafting an effective agreement, with emphasis on the valuation portions
- Dealing with the agreement when the triggering event occurs
- The effect of the buy-sell agreement on valuation for purposes other than the agreement itself

Buy-sell agreements are contractual agreements between and among the owners of closely held businesses and the business itself. These agreements dictate what happens to ownership—that is, who buys and who sells—when "triggering events" occur. Such triggering events might include the termination, death, disability, or divorce of a shareholder, among other things.

There are hundreds of thousands of buy-sell agreements in existence today. Clients and their attorneys will have to deal with these agreements when triggering events occur. And as new businesses with multiple owners are formed, they will likely establish buy-sell agreements.

Attorneys that have clients with existing buy-sell agreements could do their clients a considerable favor by reviewing the agreement in light of this chapter and modifying the agreement as necessary. They might even retain a qualified business appraiser to review the agreement from business and valuation perspectives.

TYPES OF BUY-SELL AGREEMENTS

Entity Purchase Agreements

Under entity purchase agreements, the company buys the ownership interest from the departing owner upon the occurrence of the triggering event. Unless the entity resells the interest, the proportionate ownership interests of all the remaining owners are increased.

Cross-Purchase Agreements

Under cross-purchase agreements, one or more individuals or entities buys the ownership interest from the departing owner. Cross-purchase agreements can become quite complex as the number of owners increases, and they are not often found in sizeable private companies.

Hybrid Agreements

Hybrid agreements can take on a variety of forms, but usually give the entity the first right of refusal to buy ownership interests of departing owners. If the entity declines, the interests are typically offered to other owners on a pro rata basis. If the other owners decline, the entity may still retain a final right of refusal to ensure control over the shares of departing owners.

Tag-Along Rights

Tag-along rights grant noncontrolling (i.e., minority) owners the right to sell at the same price and the same terms offered to controlling owners. The corollary might be that controlling owners may have *drag-along rights*, which require noncontrolling shareholders to sell along with them, again at the same price and on the same terms.

TYPES OF VALUATION PROVISIONS

Fixed Price

Fixed price agreements state a certain price at which transactions occurring pursuant to buy-sell agreements will occur. Fixed-price agreements are intuitively attractive. The parties to an agreement initially agree on a fixed price for the agreement and then agree to update that price, for example, every year. Unfortunately, owners seldom have the discipline to reset the price over time, even over many years. This creates an inherent problem when transactions occur and the "real" value of the company, or the ownership interest being purchased, vary widely from the fixed price stated in the agreement.

Such agreements need a provision for how the value will be determined in case the parties cannot agree on a price in their meeting or (as frequently happens) the parties fail to meet and agree upon a value. This additional provision must be negotiated by the parties.

Attorneys should be aware of this potential issue with fixed price buy-sell agreements.

Formula Pricing

In formula pricing, the parties agree on a formula for setting the price when triggering events occur. The problem with this form of pricing is that it is seldom possible to create a formula that will be fair to all parties at the time of future triggering events given that company, industry, and economic conditions will surely change over time.

Attorneys should be aware of this potential issue with formula pricing agreements.

"Shotgun" Agreements

Under a common form of *shotgun agreements*, one party can offer to buy (or sell) ownership interests to the other party and the other party then has the right to sell (or buy) the interest at the price offered. Like with fixed-price agreements, shotgun pricing can appear to be intuitively appealing. What could seemingly be fairer than being able to buy or sell at the offered price? The problem lies in that owners subject to the shotgun agreement are seldom of similar age, financial capacity, or physical capacity, and often do not have similar knowledge about the operations of the operating business. These differences can create distinct advantages for one party over the other in terms of achieving a "fair" pricing.

Valuation Process Pricing Agreements

Perhaps the most prevalent type of valuation provision is found in what are commonly referred to as *valuation process agreements,* whereby one or more independent appraisers determines the price when the triggering event occurs. Valuation process agreements can be further divided into those involving a single-appraiser (single appraiser agreements) and those involving more than one appraiser (multiple appraiser agreements).

DRAFTING A GOOD BUY-SELL AGREEMENT

The authors recommend that parties and their attorneys retain a qualified business appraiser at the drafting stage of new buy-sell agreements. Many pitfalls can be avoided by gaining the insight of an appraiser who has dealt with resolving buy-sell agreement pricing under many diverse wordings regarding the establishment of the price for an agreement. It may also be helpful to have an appraiser provide an initial value so that all parties can see the valuation implications of the language in their agreements.

Definition of Value

Perhaps the most critical element of the valuation provisions in a buy-sell agreement is the *standard* (or *definition*) *of value.* (See Chapter 1 for definitions of *value.*) The most prevalent standard of value is fair market value. This generally is desirable, because fair market value is the most widely used and understood standard of value. It is defined in the *International Valuation Glossary—Business Valuation* as:

> **Fair Market Value**—a Standard of Value considered to represent the price, expressed in terms of cash equivalents, at which property would change hands between a hypothetical willing and able buyer and a hypothetical willing and able seller, each acting at arms-length in an open and unrestricted market, when neither is under compulsion to buy or to sell and when both have reasonable knowledge of relevant facts.[1]

The definition of value should be included in each valuation process buy-sell agreement to ensure clarity and to avoid any future confusion regarding the intent of the parties as to the standard of value.

However, once the standard of value has been specified, it still is necessary to define the *level of value* (see Exhibit 29-1, repeat of Exhibit 2-1) to be determined in the appraisal. When parties actually negotiate over the level of value, they most often agree on what can be called the financial control level of value. Potential buyers cannot afford to pay a strategic price that they may never receive for an ownership interest. And

---

1. *International Valuation Glossary—Business Valuation* 5, jointly published by ASA, Chartered Business Valuators Institute, Royal Institution of Chartered Surveyors, and Saudi Authority for Accredited Valuers (Feb. 24, 2022).

potential sellers cannot afford to be offered a discounted price. Given these facts, the financial control value is the most often agreed upon.

Exhibit 29-1 Levels of Value

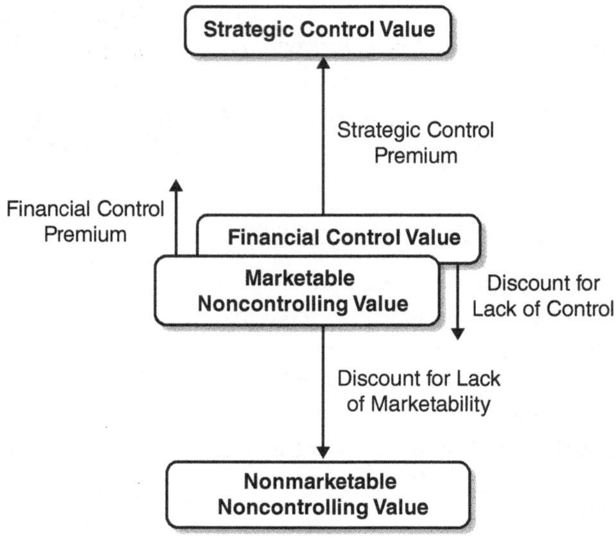

Source: Shannon Pratt's Valuing a Business: The Analysis and Appraisal of Closely Held Businesses 55 (6th ed.); adapted from Z. Christopher Mercer & Travis W. Harms, Business Valuation—An Integrated Theory 37 (3rd ed.). Used with permission.

The desired level of value for any buy-sell agreement should be clearly spelled out in the document language in order to avoid misinterpretation of the parties' intent. To that end, the parties to the agreement may want to ask the following questions:

- Is the desired value that of a pro rata share of the equity value of the entire business? If that is the case, the financial control value will likely be the desired level of value.
- Is the desired value that of the noncontrolling (minority) ownership interest? In that case, the desired level of value will likely be the noncontrolling (minority) nonmarketable level, or the bottom level in Exhibit 29-1.

The language of many buy-sell agreements is unclear and may be subject to more than one interpretation. It is important to understand that there is a significant conceptual difference between these two levels of value, and they often lead to significant differences in valuation conclusions when two or more appraisers interpret the language differently.

Most clients think of fair market value as a proportionate share of the value of the company as a whole. One of the biggest problems with buy-sell agreements is when the agreement simply states, "the fair market value of the interest." This vague language often leads to the selling party being unpleasantly surprised to learn that this language refers to the noncontrolling (minority) nonmarketable level in Exhibit 29-1, with the interest subject to potential discounting.

The valuation provisions may be different for different triggering events. For example, the definition of value for death or normal retirement may be a pro rata share of the fair market value of the equity as a whole, while the value under any other triggering event might be discounted by some agreed-upon percentage from that value.

The Valuation Date

The date as of which the interest is to be valued is a critical piece of information in the buy-sell agreement. The values of businesses and business interests can change significantly, even over short periods of time, because of both internal and external factors (e.g., stock market conditions). Specification of the valuation date is of great importance when—as is often the case—disagreements, disputes, and even litigation between the parties delay the valuation process.

It is common to have the date of the triggering event serve as the valuation date. However, as a matter of convenience, the valuation date is often set on a date when financial statements normally would be prepared, such as the end of the month prior to the triggering event.

Appraiser Qualifications and Business Appraisal Standards

If the buy-sell agreement is a valuation process agreement, the issue of appraiser qualifications should be addressed. There are three principal credentialing organizations for business appraisers in the United States and one in Canada (see Chapter 37, "Business Valuation Standards and Credentials"). The selection of appraiser qualifications determines, in part, the business appraisal standards that the appraisers must follow.

- **American Society of Appraisers (ASA).** Members must follow the ASA *Business Valuation Standards* and the *Principles of Appraisal Practice and Code of Ethics* of the ASA, as well as The Appraisal Foundation's *Uniform Standards of Professional Appraisal Practice* (USPAP).
- **AICPA.** Credentialed appraisers (ABV designation) must follow the *Statement on Standards for Valuation Services* (VS Section 100).
- **NACVA.** Credentialed appraisers (CVA and CBA designations) must follow the *Professional Standards* of NACVA.
- **CBV Institute (Canada).** Credentialed appraisers (CBV designation) must follow the *Practice Standards and Practice Bulletins* of the CBV Institute.

Specifying that the appraisers have appropriate experience and credentials from one or more of these organizations should go a long way toward avoiding undesirable outcomes in valuation appraisal processes.

Note: These organizations issue credentials to individuals, not to firms. Thus, if a firm is named in the buy-sell agreement, it is essential that the lead appraiser be accredited.

APPRAISER SELECTION AND PROCEDURES

Single Appraiser

If there is to be a single appraiser, he or she might be named in the buy-sell agreement itself. If so, it may be preferable to name a firm rather than an individual because an individual may have a higher likelihood of being unavailable when the triggering event occurs.

Of course, there needs to be a process by which the appraiser can be chosen in the event that the named firm or individual is not available. If the parties cannot agree on an appraiser, it may be necessary to retain the services of a neutral party, such as an arbitrator, which process should be set forth in the agreement.

If the parties do not name a firm or individual in the agreement, a common procedure is, when a triggering event occurs, to have each side submit several qualified nominees (either firms or individuals) and then reach agreement on a single appraiser, who then performs the appraisal required for the agreement. It is generally helpful if the appraisers charged with selecting a third appraiser agree upon "ground rules" for the selection process. For example, they might agree in advance as to the number of nominations to be made by each side, and that the third appraiser be selected from that universe of initial appraiser nominations. The selection process can spiral into disarray if each of the appraisers reject the opposing side's initial (and presumably most-qualified) nominations. Any valuation analyst that is nominated by both sides should automatically be selected as the third appraiser.[2] Of course, there still has to be a procedure in the agreement to break a deadlock.

There also should be a reasonable time limit on the appraiser selection process. This can be enforced in the agreement in several ways, including (1) the side not meeting the time requirement defers by default to the side that does, or (2) if the time deadline is not met, the selection process automatically reverts to the named neutral party. Of course, these provisions can be subject to modification by mutual agreement of the parties.

Multiple Appraisers

Two appraisers and a third only if necessary. Some agreements call for two appraisers, with one appointed by each side (i.e., the company and the selling shareholder(s)), each providing appraisals pursuant to the agreement. If the two appraisers' conclusions are within an agreed upon percentage of each other, then the average of the appraised values would serve as the conclusion. The agreed upon percentage set in most buy-sell agreements is 10%. If the conclusions vary by more than this percentage, then the first two appraisers will select a third appraiser.

The authors suggest that the percentage limits be set more broadly, perhaps at 20%, because it is common that even the most competent business appraisers are likely to arrive at value conclusions that are apart by more than 10%. Closely held businesses and business interests do not lend themselves to such precise tolerances.

Anticipating the possibility that a third appraiser becomes necessary, some parties prefer to contingently select the third appraiser at the outset of the appraisal process, before it becomes apparent that the third appraiser will be required. When appraisers have reached disparate conclusions, it is often difficult at that time to agree on a third appraiser. Then, if the difference between the two appraisal conclusions is greater than the stated percentage, the preselected third appraiser would conduct the third appraisal.

The choice of the third appraiser is typically left to the judgment of the first two appraisers. Making the choice subject to the parties' approval tends to unnecessarily delay the process, sometimes substantially, and can cause increased contentiousness.

---

2. Shannon P. Pratt & ASA Educ. Found., Shannon Pratt's Valuing a Business: The Analysis and Appraisal of Closely Held Companies 831 (6th ed. 2022).

The role of the third appraiser varies, but the third appraiser usually is provided access to the work of the first two appraisers, and generally is allowed to contact them.

Sometimes the value arrived at by the third appraiser serves as the final value. At times, it is bounded by the high and low values established by the first two appraisers. Other times the value of the third appraiser is averaged with the closer one of the first two appraisers.

Three-appraiser panel. Sometimes a three-appraiser (or more) panel is appointed at the outset. In this case, it is common for each side to select a qualified appraiser and the two to select a third qualified appraiser. The same admonitions apply as in the previous section.

When a three-appraiser (or more) panel is selected, it is rare that the three appraisers will reach unanimous agreement. If a consensus cannot be reached, it may be possible to reach a majority opinion between two of the three appraisers. If this is not possible, then the average of the closest two may best constitute the final value.

A valuation process pursuant to a buy-sell agreement is tantamount to an arbitration process. In fact, in some cases, the process may consist of an actual arbitration. It is always helpful if the appraisers appointed by each side enter the process with open minds rather than being biased toward their client's interest.

Funding and Payment Mechanisms

Cash and/or promissory notes. Payment terms for purchases of ownership interests should be spelled out in buy-sell agreements. Payment terms can range from cash, likely for smaller interests, to promissory notes of varying structures. Typical terms for promissory notes include:

- A specified down payment
- The rate of interest, whether fixed or variable over time
- The payment structure, which could include equal quarterly or annual payments, or perhaps equal amortization of principal with interest paid each period on the remaining balance
- Any security for the promissory note and any provisions that would prevent its subordination to other borrowings by a company

The company is often provided with the ability to pre-pay buy-sell agreement promissory notes. Correspondingly, note holders may have the right to demand prepayment in the event that a company sells or merges with another entity.

Life insurance as funding. If funded by life insurance, the buy-sell agreement should specify whether any insurance proceeds are to be used as a funding vehicle for the repurchase of ownership interests or as a corporate asset. The treatment of company-owned life insurance can have a significant effect on the resulting position of a company or a selling shareholder following receipt of the insurance proceeds. It can also affect the company's ability to repurchase the stock of a deceased shareholder. The choice of treatment can also impact the resulting position of any remaining shareholders. The differences in treatment can be summarized in an example.[3]

---

3. The example is taken from the broader discussion in Chapter 15, "Treatment of Life Insurance Proceeds," *in* Z. Christopher Mercer, Buy-Sell Agreements for Closely Held and Family Business Owners (2010).

- Harry and Charles each own a 50% interest in High Point Software and have been partners for many years.
- The company owns term life insurance policies on the lives of Harry and Charles in the amount of $6 million each. Assume for simplicity that there would be no corporate income taxes due on the receipt of insurance proceeds.
- The buy-sell agreement states that the company will purchase the shares of stock owned by Harry or Charles in the event of the death of either. The agreement is silent with respect to the treatment of life insurance proceeds and calls for the company to be appraised by an appropriately qualified and experienced appraiser.
- Now assume Harry is killed in an accident. Further assume that the company's aggregate equity value is determined by appraisal to be $10 million prior to consideration of the proceeds of life insurance. Earnings have been normalized in the valuation to adjust for the expense of the insurance policies.
- Before finalizing the appraisal, the appraiser carefully reviews the buy-sell agreement for direction on treatment of the life insurance proceeds. Unfortunately, it is silent on the issue. The appraiser realizes that the choice of treatment of this issue will make a significant difference to Harry's estate, the company, and to Charles personally as the remaining shareholder.[4]

When life insurance proceeds *are not* a corporate asset. The valuation impact of each treatment is developed next in the context of the High Point Software example. In Exhibit 29-2, the proceeds are not treated as a corporate asset but as a funding vehicle.

Exhibit 29-2 Proceeds Are NOT a Corporate Asset

		Company	Harry (Estate)	Charles
1	Stock Ownership (Shares)	100.0	50.0	50.0
2	Stock Ownership (%)	100.0%	50.0%	50.0%
3	Pre and Post Life Insurance Value ($m)	**$10,000.0**	**$5,000.0**	**$5,000.0**
4	Life Insurance Proceeds	$6,000.0		
5	Repurchase Liability	($5,000.0)		
6	Post-Life-Insurance Value	**$11,000.0**		
7	Repurchase Stock	($5,000.0)	$5,000.0	
8	Retire / Give Up Stock	(50.0)	(50.0)	
9	Remaining Stock	50.0	0.0	50.0
10	New Stock Ownership (%)	100.0%	0.0%	100.0%
11	Post-Life Insurance Value of Co.	$11,000.0	$0.0	**$11,000.0**
12	Post-Life Insurance Proceeds		**$5,000.0**	
13	Net Change in Value from Repurchase	**$1,000.0**		

4. *See* Section "Buy-Sell Agreements" in Chapter 20, "Valuations for Gift, Estate, and Contribution Matters," for discussion of court's treatment of corporate-owned life insurance and its impact on the valuation of decedent's stock redeemed pursuant to a buy-sell agreement.

The company is valued at $10 million, which provides $5 million of value for each of the 50% owners (line 3 in Exhibit 29-2). The company receives the $6 million of life insurance proceeds and repurchases the shares held by Harry's estate (lines 4 to 7 in Exhibit 29-2). The interesting aspect of this situation is that the estate gets exactly its share of Harry's predeath value, or $5 million. However, the incremental $1 million of insurance is added to the value of the company, and Charles now owns 100% of High Point Software, which is now worth $11 million.

When life insurance proceeds *are* a corporate asset. In Exhibit 29-3, life insurance proceeds are treated as a corporate asset and added to company value before Harry's estate value is calculated.

Exhibit 29-3 Proceeds Are a Corporate Asset

		Company	Harry (Estate)	Charles
1	Stock Ownership (Shares)	100.0	50.0	50.0
2	Stock Ownership (%)	100.0%	50.0%	50.0%
3	Pre-Life Insurance Value ($m)	**$10,000.0**	**$5,000.0**	**$5,000.0**
4	Life Insurance Proceeds ($m)	$6,000.0	$3,000.0	$3,000.0
5	Post-Life Insurance Value ($m)	$16,000.0	**$8,000.0**	$8,000.0
6	Repurchase Liability	($8,000.0)		
7	Post-Life-Insurance Value	**$8,000.0**		
8	Repurchase Stock	($8,000.0)	$8,000.0	
9	Retire / Give Up Stock	(50.0)	(50.0)	
10	Remaining Stock	50.0	0.0	50.0
11	New Stock Ownership (%)	100.0%	0.0%	100.0%
12	Post-Life Insurance Value of Co.	$8,000.0	$0.0	**$8,000.0**
13	Post-Life Insurance Proceeds		**$8,000.0**	
14	Net Change in Value from Repurchase	**($2,000.0)**		

The $10 million company value is split evenly between Harry's estate and Charles (line 3 in Exhibit 29-3), or $5 million each. However, the additional $6 million of life insurance proceeds is added to the company value (line 4 in Exhibit 29-3) and also split evenly between Harry's estate and Charles. The result is that Harry's estate has a value of $8 million, which is equal to the value of Charles' shares (line 5 in Exhibit 29-3).

We see a difference at the level of remaining company value. Life insurance proceeds were $6 million and the cost of repurchase from Harry's estate was $8 million. That result is substantially greater than the $5 million the estate would receive if life insurance were a funding vehicle.

The result is that the company had to issue a note of $2 million as part of the repurchase, which reduced the remaining value of the company by that amount. The company is now worth $8 million, and Charles is the company's 100% owner. Again, this is a significant reduction from the $11 million of value he would have had if the life insurance was a funding vehicle and not a corporate asset.

The point of this discussion is not to suggest that one treatment is preferable to the other. That is up to the owners to decide when they draft or review their buy-sell agreement. If the agreement is not clear on the treatment, it may be left for the appraiser(s) to decide.

Payment of Appraisers

The buy-sell agreement also should specify what party is responsible for the appraisers' fees. Sometimes the company pays the fees of each party's appraiser. More commonly, in a multi-appraiser scenario, each side pays the appraiser it selects, and the company pays the third appraiser.

Some owners and attorneys think that selling shareholders should pay their own expenses. If they do, however, they arguably are not receiving the full fair market value of their ownership interests. There is a solid logic for companies to pay all or most expenses. The company and the remaining owners receive a proportionate pickup in ownership based on agreement repurchases. There is no corresponding benefit for selling owners.

DEALING WITH THE AGREEMENT WHEN THE TRIGGERING EVENT OCCURS

If the foregoing suggestions have been followed in drafting the buy-sell agreement, subsequent appraisals and appraisal processes will hopefully incur minimal issues. More often, however, there are ambiguities in the existing buy-sell agreements that must be resolved.

The parties and their appraisers should resolve any ambiguities before starting the valuation process (except for preparing the engagement letter specifying that the appraisal is in accordance with the buy-sell agreement as of a given date and document specification). The parties and their attorneys should make every effort to resolve the ambiguities among themselves and give the appraisers clear and unambiguous instructions. Otherwise, the appraisers may be left to interpret the agreement for themselves, which may lead to unintended consequences.

THE EFFECT OF THE AGREEMENT ON VALUATIONS FOR PURPOSES OTHER THAN THE AGREEMENT ITSELF

As noted in Chapter 20, "Valuations for Gift, Estate, and Charitable Contribution Matters," the buy-sell agreement valuation may be binding for other purposes, may be given no weight at all, or may be given some weight along with other valuation approaches and methods. In some situations, the buy-sell agreement may be binding on the estate, yet the IRS may value the ownership interest so much higher that the estate has to pay more in taxes than it received for selling the interest back to the company.

In the preceding example, the most important factor in determining the weight accorded to a buy-sell agreement may be whether it was negotiated on an arm's-length basis. Alternatively, if the buy-sell agreement is among family members, would unrelated parties be agreeable to similar terms?

Chapter 14, § 2703, of the Internal Revenue Code, enacted October 8, 1990, requires that, in order to be binding for estate, gift, or generation-skipping tax purposes, any buy-sell agreement created or significantly modified after that date must meet the following criteria:

- It is a bona fide business arrangement
- It must not be a device to transfer the property to the natural objects of the transferor's bounty (such as family members) for less than adequate and full consideration in money or money's worth
- Its terms must be comparable to similar arrangements entered into by persons in an arm's-length transaction

SUMMARY

Buy-sell agreements are like a prenuptial contract between business owners. Their purpose is to provide a definitive process by which the buyout price and terms of a departing owner's interest can be determined. However, buy-sell agreements can be a source of confusion, dispute, inconsistent valuation determinations, and protracted litigation.

To avoid valuation-related issues, the valuation provisions and process of buy-sell agreements should be drafted unambiguously and using terminology that reflects the core elements of business valuation—such as those described herein. Buy-sell agreements should also encourage the parties to retain appropriately qualified valuation analysts who will develop their value estimates consistent with recognized appraisal standards. The buy-sell agreement should also provide for a process that will provide for a decisive reconciliation of any competing value conclusions and eliminate any inherent advantage that might otherwise accrue to one party or the other.

REFERENCES TO VALUATION PROVISIONS IN BUY-SELL AGREEMENTS

Mercer, Z. Christopher. 2010. *Buy-Sell Agreements for Closely Held and Family Business Owners* (Memphis, TN, Peabody Publishing, LLC).

Pratt, Shannon P. and ASA Educational Foundation. 2022. "Valuation Provisions in Buy-Sell Agreements" In *Shannon Pratt's Valuing a Business: The Analysis and Appraisal of Closely Held Companies,* 6th ed. Chap. 36, 819–34 (New York: McGraw Hill).

CHAPTER 30

Valuation in Fairness Matters

Jeffrey S. Tarbell, ASA, CFA

INTRODUCTION[1]

In this chapter you will learn about:

- Principles of corporate law relevant to fairness opinions
- The role of corporate directors and their fiduciary duties
- Directors' responsibilities and decision-making in a transactional context
- When and why boards of directors often seek fairness opinions
- Standards, regulation, and disclosure requirements
- Common valuation methods and other financial analyses used in fairness opinions
- Important issues affecting the fairness opinion scope of work

In evaluating a corporate control transaction, a corporation's board of directors will often seek a fairness opinion.[2] Such transactions might include a sale, merger, acquisition, leveraged buyout, leveraged recapitalization, employee stock ownership transaction, going private, or de-SPAC transaction.[3] As described further herein, a sell-side fairness opinion addresses the fairness, from a financial point of view, of the consideration to be *received* by the target company or its stockholders in the transaction. On the buy side, a fairness opinion addresses the fairness, from a financial point of view, of the consideration to be *paid* by the target company in the transaction.

Fairness opinions are issued by an investment bank or another firm with appropriate expertise in corporate finance, valuation, and transactional issues, such as a larger business valuation firm.

Fairness opinions provide important information to the corporation's board, enabling the directors to make better informed decisions on the matters at hand. Fairness opinions also serve as indicia of the exercise of care by the corporation's board,

1. This chapter is adapted from Chapter 47, "Fairness Opinions," *in* Shannon P. Pratt & ASA Educ. Found., Shannon Pratt's Valuing a Business: Analysis and Appraisal of Closely Held Businesses (6th ed. 2022). Used with permission.

2. Fairness opinions are sometimes issued to board committees, trustees, or other parties acting in a fiduciary decision-making role on behalf of an entity's stockholders. For simplicity, this chapter is written from the perspective of the corporation board as the fairness opinion recipient.

3. A de-SPAC transaction is one in which closely held companies go public by merging with special purpose acquisition companies (SPACs)—shell companies with no tangible assets other than the cash received from investors.

demonstrating that the directors used "reasonable business judgment" in contemplating the transaction to which the fairness opinion pertains.[4]

Fairness opinions are not required by either regulation, law, or statute. Yet they serve a vital role in a board's deliberation of a corporate transaction. This importance stems from the legal environment in which a board's decision-making process occurs, and that by which the process is often evaluated in hindsight. Thus, while a fairness opinion is a *financial* rather than a *legal* opinion, experienced fairness opinion providers tend to have a thorough understanding of corporation law pertaining to director's duties and decision-making processes. This particularly includes the state law of Delaware, under which many entities are incorporated, as further discussed herein.

CORPORATE LAW RELEVANT TO FAIRNESS OPINIONS

Corporations with registered securities are regulated by various federal laws, most notably the Securities Act of 1933 and the Securities and Exchange Act of 1934, each as amended. The Securities Act regulates public offerings and sales of securities, whereas the Securities and Exchange Act addresses a variety of subjects, including requirements regarding periodic disclosure of information by public or so-called reporting or listed companies (i.e., companies with securities listed on a national securities exchange). Neither the Securities Act nor the Securities and Exchange Act directly regulates the management of a corporation; however, indirectly, both laws exert significant influence over corporate governance by mandating disclosure of many facets of a corporation's internal affairs.

Listed companies are also subject to the rules promulgated by the stock exchange on which its shares trade. For instance, to list its securities on the New York Stock Exchange (NYSE) or NASDAQ, a company must agree to abide by specific corporate governance rules that mandate, among other things, that a majority of the directors of a listed company be comprised of independent directors.[5]

Additionally, each U.S. state has its own laws pertaining to the organization and governance of corporations formed in that state. Such law is comprised of each state's corporation statute and the body of decisions rendered by the courts of that particular state. Such corporation law applies to both closely held and public corporations.

The commonwealth of Delaware has an outsized influence on corporation law affecting fairness opinions. Delaware has become the principal state of incorporation for large U.S. corporations. Indeed, over 65% of the so-called Fortune 500 entities are incorporated in Delaware. Delaware is known for its sophisticated and efficient judicial system. In particular, disputes over the internal affairs of Delaware corporations are adjudicated in a specialized business court known as the Delaware Court of Chancery (the Chancery Court). Cases brought before the Chancery Court are heard and decided by seven "chancellors" highly experienced in corporate, transactional, and governance issues. Decisions by the Chancery Court can be appealed to the Delaware Supreme Court.

As a result, Delaware has an extensive body of corporate law, which provides managers and directors of Delaware corporations, as well as their legal counsel, with a

4. Sec. & Exch. Comm'n (Release No. 34-56645; File No. SR-NASD-2005-080) (Oct. 11, 2007).

5. Generally, an independent director is one who is not part of company management and who has no material financial relationships with the corporation on whose board they sit.

"roadmap" as to how the Delaware courts are likely to rule on key matters of corporate governance.[6] In fact, the influence of the Delaware courts is such that other states often look to Delaware case law when their own state courts have not addressed a particular issue. Given this primacy, the following discussion focuses on Delaware law as set forth in the Delaware General Corporation Law (DGCL) and the decisions of the courts.

The Role of the Board of Directors

Stockholders in a Delaware corporation have important albeit limited rights associated with their ownership interest in the corporation. Typically, stockholders have rights to transfer their shares, participate in annual and special meetings, nominate and elect directors, propose bylaws, receive certain information about the corporation, and approve actions by the board in connection with fundamental changes, such as a sale of the corporation. Stockholders also have the right to assert so-called derivative claims on behalf of the corporation against its directors and officers.

Stockholders also enjoy limited obligations and exposure to potential personal liability. Stockholders who own less than a controlling interest in the corporation owe no legal duty to the corporation or their fellow stockholders. Moreover, stockholders are shielded from personal recourse for the debts and other obligations of the corporation.

The DGCL and cases decided by the Delaware courts make it clear that the board is ultimately responsible for the management of the corporation's business and affairs. In discharging this statutory responsibility, a board will typically act in a supervisory capacity and will delegate the day-to-day management of the business to the officers of the corporation. One of the board's key responsibilities will include approving major corporate actions such as raising financing, issuing securities, entering into a merger, or disposing of substantially all of the assets of, or dissolving the corporation.

A board has the power under the DGCL to designate (and public companies are required to designate) one or more committees of directors (e.g., audit committee, nominating committee, compensation committee). Generally, such committees consist of independent directors within the meaning established by the applicable stock exchange rules.

DIRECTORS' FIDUCIARY DUTIES

Under Delaware law, a corporation's directors have "fiduciary duties" to the corporation and its stockholders. These duties constitute the fundamental principles to which directors must adhere in managing the business of the corporation and they require that the paramount consideration of the corporation and its stockholders be the best interests of the corporation and its stockholders. In Delaware, such fiduciary duties consist of (1) the duty of care and (2) the duty of loyalty. However, the DGCL does not directly address the nature and scope of directors' fiduciary duties. Instead, the contours of such duties have been defined by decisions of the courts.

---

6. The body of Delaware law is enhanced by the fact that all decisions are effectively deemed to be "published," in contrast to other jurisdictions where lower court decisions are infrequently published and unpublished cases are not considered precedential.

The duty of care. The duty of care deals with the responsibility of directors to oversee the corporation. Directors are required to perform their duties in good faith in a manner that they reasonably believe to be in the best interest of the corporation, and with such care that a person in a like position would reasonably believe appropriate under similar circumstances. The "person in a like position" standard does not require that a board be aware of every aspect of the corporation's business, but rather requires that a board be reasonably informed as to material matters affecting the corporation.

Compliance with the duty of care requires active involvement by the members of the board. Directors have an obligation to inform themselves of all material information reasonably available to them before making a business decision and to act with the requisite degree of care in making such decisions.

In discharging their duty of care, directors are generally allowed to rely in good faith on information prepared by those reasonably believed to be knowledgeable in the matter under consideration. This would include the recommendations and advice of experts (such as accountants, valuation analysts, investment bankers, and attorneys) provided that such reliance is reasonable and in good faith. However, a board needs to exercise due care in the selection of its experts, who among other things, should be both qualified and independent. Directors are not entitled to blindly rely on experts' findings. Rather, directors need to probe and test an expert's assumptions, analysis, and conclusions. If a director has reason to know that the information presented by the expert is incorrect, such reliance is not reasonable and the duty of care may not be satisfied.

Courts have generally held that a director's action (or inaction) will constitute a breach of his or her fiduciary duty of care only if such director's conduct rises to the level of "gross negligence." For example, in the landmark *Van Gorkom* case, the Delaware Supreme Court found that the board of Trans Union Corporation (Trans Union) was grossly negligent when it approved the sale of the company after only a few hours of deliberation.[7] The Delaware Supreme Court was highly critical of the fact that the Trans Union board failed to hire an outside opinion provider to render a fairness opinion or to help inform the board as to the inherent value of the company. The fact that the Trans Union stockholders approved the merger, and that the consideration represented a substantial premium to the market price, did not cure the board's gross negligence. The directors of Trans Union were found to be personally liable for an aggregate of $25 million in damages, principally because the stockholders were found to not have been fully informed.

The duty of loyalty. Directors also owe a fiduciary duty of loyalty to the corporation and its stockholders. This duty requires that the directors (1) act in good faith, (2) act in the best interests of the corporation and its stockholders, and (3) refrain from receiving improper personal benefits as a result of their relationship with the corporation. As the Delaware Supreme Court noted, "[E]ssentially the duty of loyalty mandates that the best interest of the corporation and its stockholders takes precedence over any interest possessed by a director, officer, or controlling [stock]holder and not shared by the shareholders generally."[8]

7. Smith v. Van Gorkom, 488 A.2d 858 (Del. 1985).
8. Cede & Co. v. Technicolor Inc., 634 A.2d 345, 361 (Del. 1993).

A breach of the duty of loyalty occurs most often in situations where a director has an economic or other interest in the outcome of a contemplated transaction, even though the director had no direct personal financial interest in the transaction. A director can also be found guilty of a breach of duty of loyalty by approving a transaction that benefits a controlling stockholder to the detriment of noncontrolling stockholders. Additionally, directors have been found to have violated the duty of loyalty when they fail to act in the face of a known duty to act, indicating an abdication of their responsibility to the corporation.

Importantly, a conflict of interest does not per se result in a breach of the duty of loyalty. Rather, it is the manner in which the director handles that conflict and the processes invoked to ensure fairness to the corporation and its stockholders that will determine the propriety of the director's conduct. Moreover, the courts have emphasized that only material personal interests or influences will taint a transaction with duty of loyalty implications.

Duty of loyalty issues can be mitigated if actions involving potential conflicts are approved by a special committee comprised of disinterested and independent directors. However, where no independent decision-maker is present and where the business judgment rule does not apply, duty of loyalty challenges can nevertheless be overcome if the directors and officers can demonstrate that the transaction at issue was "entirely fair" to the corporation and its stockholders (see discussion of entire fairness standard of review later in the chapter).

Good faith. The Delaware Supreme Court has clarified that the duty of good faith is an element of the duty of loyalty and not (as once thought) an independent fiduciary duty. The court stated that "the obligation to act in good faith does not establish an independent fiduciary duty that stands on the same footing as the duties of care and loyalty. Only the latter two duties, where violated, may directly result in liability, whereas a failure to act in good faith may do so, but indirectly."[9]

The Delaware Supreme Court further clarified that bad faith is not simply bad judgment or negligence; rather bad faith implies conscious wrongdoing, and the court observed that bad faith conduct may be found where a director "intentionally acts with a purpose other than that of advancing the best interests of the corporation, . . . acts with the intent to violate applicable positive law, or . . . intentionally fails to act in the face of a known duty to act, demonstrating a conscious disregard for his duties."[10]

Fiduciary duties relative to insolvent companies. A bedrock principle of Delaware corporate law is the notion that directors of *solvent* companies owe fiduciary duties of loyalty and care to the corporation and its stockholders, but not to its creditors. Creditors are presumed to be able to protect themselves contractually or through creditors' rights laws. Similarly, the directors of a solvent company do not owe fiduciary duties to holders of the shares of a Delaware corporation's preferred stock. Again, such holders are deemed able to protect themselves through the negotiated provisions of the certificate of designation and/or the stock purchase agreement by which they became holders.

A corporation is deemed insolvent under Delaware's fraudulent transfer statute when the sum of its debts is greater than all of its assets at a fair valuation (market values). A

9. Stone v. Ritter, 911 A.2d 362 (Del. 2006).
10. *Id.*

company is also presumed to be insolvent if it is generally not paying its debts as they come due. Under Delaware case law, the test is forward-looking: it is not enough for a corporation to meet its current obligations; it must be able to meet its future obligations as well.[11]

The state of insolvency, in and of itself, does not change the focus of directors' duties, which is the corporation itself. Even in times of distress, a director's duty is to preserve and maximize the value of the corporation "for the benefit of all those having an interest in it."[12]

However, the Delaware Supreme Court has made it clear that when a corporation is insolvent, creditors have standing to assert derivative (but not direct) claims against directors for breach of their fiduciary duties. The logic underpinning this conclusion is that, upon insolvency, creditors take the place of stockholders as the "residual beneficiaries" of the corporation's value and are the parties injured by any fiduciary breaches that diminish that value.

Thus, when a corporation becomes insolvent, the board's fiduciary duties are to all of the corporation's residual claimants, which include both creditors and stockholders. Accordingly, directors must continue to make decisions based on what they believe will be in the best interests of the corporation but with the consideration directed to the interests of creditors as well as stockholders.

However, because creditors of an insolvent company can bring derivative actions for breach of fiduciary duty, directors' actions, even though protected by the business judgment rule, can be subject to litigation. Indeed, when a company is financially distressed, many otherwise ordinary course decisions by the board of directors will be subject to increased scrutiny by stakeholder constituencies and, potentially, by the courts. Thus, directors of financially distressed companies need to consider whether the corporation could, in hindsight, be viewed as having been insolvent at the time the board made its decisions and should take special care to ensure that they have built a record of staying informed and taking actions that best serve the entire enterprise rather than any single group of stakeholders. In this regard, professional advice in the form of a capital adequacy opinion may be needed to assess the solvency of the company at the time of the board's decision-making.

BOARD DECISIONS IN A TRANSACTIONAL CONTEXT

The Business Judgment Rule

When a corporation proposes to undertake a material transaction, a stockholder derivative lawsuit may be brought alleging that, among other things, (1) the price to be received by stockholders in the transaction is unfair or inadequate, (2) the price the corporation will pay in the transaction is unfair to the acquiring corporation and its stockholders, (3) the process by which the transaction was negotiated was flawed, and/or (4) the information received by stockholders regarding the board's reasons for recommending the transaction for stockholder approval was misleading or insufficient.

---

11. The U.S. Bankruptcy Code and state fraudulent conveyance statutes require, in addition, consideration of whether a company received reasonably equivalent value and was left with reasonable capital to conduct its business.

12. N. Am. Catholic Educ. Programming Found. v. Gheewalla, 930 A.2d 92 (Del. 2007).

In the face of such a lawsuit against the corporation, directors' decisions are generally protected by the so-called business judgment rule, which has been described by the courts as "a presumption that in making a business decision the directors of a corporation acted on an informed basis, in good faith and in the honest belief that the action taken was in the best interests of the company."[13] Under the business judgment rule, directors' decisions will be respected by the courts unless the directors were interested or lacked independence relative to the decision, did not act in good faith, acted in a manner that cannot be attributed to a rational business purpose, or reached their decision by a grossly negligent process that included the failure to consider all material facts reasonably available.

The business judgment rule reflects the acknowledgment that courts generally lack the information and skill necessary to evaluate complex business decisions. Given that businesses are inherently risky, courts have expressed concern that a low threshold for negligence liability would unduly discourage a board from making those inherently risky decisions that are at times necessary for a successful enterprise. Courts understand that the DGCL entrusts the management of corporate affairs to directors, not to the courts and judges. Courts also appreciate that a corporation's stockholders elected the directors, not a judge, to supervise the management of the corporation.

When the business judgment rule applies, a court will not substitute its own views for those of directors or second-guess the outcome of business decisions by holding a director personally liable for a mistake in judgment. As the Chancery Court observed,

> Business decision-makers must operate in the real world, with imperfect information, limited resources, and an uncertain future. To impose liability on directors for making a "wrong" business decision would cripple their ability to earn returns for investors by taking business risks. Indeed, this kind of judicial second guessing is what the business judgment rule was designed to prevent. . . . It is well established that the mere fact that a company takes on business risk and suffers losses—even catastrophic losses—does not evidence misconduct, and without more, is not a basis for personal director liability.[14]

When the presumption of the business judgment rule applies, a plaintiff will bear the burden of rebutting the presumption and producing evidence that demonstrates that the directors breached one of their fiduciary duties. If the presumption of the business judgment rule is not rebutted, the court will not second-guess the business decisions of the board. However, should a plaintiff succeed in rebutting the presumption of the business judgment rule, the burden then shifts to the directors to prove that the challenged action was *entirely fair* to the corporation and its stockholders. A plaintiff can rebut the business judgment rule presumption by alleging facts from which a reasonable inference can be drawn that a majority of the board was interested or lacked independence with respect to the relevant decision.

In order to claim the protection of the business judgment rule, a board must actively participate in the decision-making process and seek to inform itself of all of the factors relevant for the consideration of the proposed transaction. Courts will consider the level of diligence exercised by the board (including, among other things, reliance on advice

13. Aronson v. Lewis, 473 A.2d 805, 812 (Del. 1984).
14. *In re* Citigroup S'holder Litig., 964 A.2d 106, 130 (Del. Ch. 2009).

from experts) in assessing whether the board's deliberative process is entitled to the presumption of the business judgment rule.

Conflict Transactions and Going Private

The business judgment rule will not protect directors who are not independent, or who are deemed to be interested. A lack of independence can be shown by alleging facts that support a reasonable inference that the director is beholden to a controlling person or "so under [the controlling person's] influence that their discretion would be sterilized."[15] By way of example, a lack of independence can be shown to exist when, for example, a member of the board is the acquirer or is the designee of a significant stockholder.

Questions concerning directors' independence and disinterestedness are frequently raised in context of transactions between a controlling stockholder and the controlled corporation.[16] In such situations, the conduct of directors is subject to careful scrutiny by the courts because of the inherent risk of self-dealing where one person or group is on both sides of a transaction. This risk is of the greatest concern to the courts in the context of so-called going-private transactions.

A going-private transaction is generally one in which a controlling or significant stockholder and/or the corporation's management and an outside investor acquires all of the corporation's stock held by the public. Going-private transactions are subject to the fiduciary issues just described, as well as by Rule 13e-3 under the Exchange Act. Rule 13e-3 defines a going-private transaction as any transaction with an affiliated party that has a reasonable likelihood of, or the purpose of, causing the termination of reporting obligations under the Securities and Exchange Act or causing the securities to be neither listed on any exchange nor authorized to be quoted on an inter-dealer quotation system. Rule 13e-3 requires an issuer and its "affiliates" engaging in a going private transaction to disclose extensive information about the fairness and terms of the transaction. Included in the required information are plans or proposals of the issuer and its affiliates regarding extraordinary or other material corporate transactions and the past contacts, transactions, or negotiations with the target company. Such information must be included in a Schedule 13e-3, which is filed with the SEC and disseminated to the corporation's stockholders.

Entire Fairness[17]

In situations in which directors are denied the presumption of the business judgment rule, they will be required to establish the "entire fairness" of the transaction in question. The Delaware Supreme Court, in 1983, enunciated a two-pronged test against which an interested party transaction would be judged: fairness in a substantive sense (i.e., fair price) and fairness in a procedural sense.[18]

A rebuttal of the business judgment rule most frequently occurs when a director may have an interest in the transaction, or when there is evidence that the directors may have breached their fiduciary duties. In addition, the entire fairness test will be applied

15. Rales v. Blanshard, 634 A.2d 927, 936 (Del. 1993).

16. A controlled corporation is an entity that is effectively owned or controlled by another corporation or party.

17. A more detailed discussion of the "entire fairness" concept is found in Chapter 23.

18. Weinberger v. UOP Inc., 457 A.2d 701, 711 (Del. 1983).

when a corporation consummates a transaction with a controlling stockholder, unless the transaction satisfies certain requirements.[19] If both prongs of this test—fair price and fair dealing—are met, the business judgment rule will apply. If only one of the tests is met, the burden of proof will shift to the plaintiff, who would then be required to demonstrate that the transaction was not entirely fair. A shift in the burden of proof can have a significant impact on whether the court ultimately declares that the transaction was entirely fair.

A board's failure to demonstrate entire fairness under the analysis just described is a basis for a finding of substantive liability.

Fair dealing. In assessing fair dealing under the entire fairness standard of review, a court will examine the process that a board followed, the quality of the result it achieved, and the quality of the disclosures made to the corporation's stockholders in soliciting their approval.

Courts have made it clear that a board's ability to demonstrate fair dealing is enhanced where a majority of the board consists of independent outside directors or where authority to act is delegated to a special committee. The role of the special committee is to replicate a transaction between the corporation and an unrelated party acting at arm's length. As already noted, the utilization of a properly functioning special committee provides evidence of fairness and, in and of itself, shifts to the plaintiff the burden of proving that the transaction is not entirely fair. However, the legal benefits resulting from special committee approval of a transaction will accrue only if the special committee:

- Has real bargaining power and the ability to reject to any transaction proposed by the controlling stockholder
- Has the authority to choose its own financial and legal advisors
- Actively negotiates for the highest or best available transaction for the minority stockholders
- Is fully informed of all relevant information

The legal obligations of directors serving on a special committee are similar to their duties as directors generally. Their duty of care obligates them to act as an ordinary prudent person would under the circumstances. In this regard, directors may rely on the opinions of experts—including fairness and other financial opinion providers—and legal counsel, as to matters that are reasonably within the professional or competence of such experts.

Fair price. In addition to evaluating whether a board engaged in fair dealing, the courts will consider whether a fair price was obtained. "Fair price" examines the economic and financial considerations relied upon when valuing the proposed transaction, including assets, market values, future prospects, earnings, and other factors that affect the value of the securities involved in the transaction. A fair price, however, does not mean the highest price that could be financed or that the party could afford to pay. Rather, it means a price

---

19. In Kahn v. M&F Worldwide Corp., 88 A.3d 65 (Del. 2014), the Delaware Supreme Court affirmed that the business judgment rule standard of review applies to a controlling stockholder merger when it is conditioned, from the outset, on (1) negotiation and approval by an independent, fully functioning and duly empowered special committee that fulfills its duty of care; and (2) the uncoerced, fully informed vote of a majority of the minority stockholders.

that a reasonable seller, under all of the circumstances, would regard as within the range of fair value (i.e., one that such a seller could reasonably accept).

The receipt of a credible fairness opinion can be a critical element convincing a court that a fair price was paid or received in a transaction.

OVERVIEW OF FAIRNESS OPINIONS

Boards often seek fairness opinions when evaluating material corporate control transactions. A fairness opinion addresses the fairness, from a financial point of view, of the consideration to be paid or received in a transaction. The scope of a fairness opinion is limited. For instance, a fairness opinion should not address the fairness of the transaction as a whole, or aspects of the transaction other than the proposed consideration, as such other aspects do not likely lend themselves to credible quantification and may be outside the expertise of the opinion issuer. In fact, the phrase "from a financial point of view" is designed to make clear that the opinion issuer is not opining that the transaction is fair from a legal or process point of view or is the best alternative strategically.

It is important to note that a fairness opinion is not a substitute for the ultimate judgment of the board and is not, among other things:

- A valuation analysis or appraisal
- An evaluation of the business rationale underlying the proposed transaction
- A recommendation to proceed with the proposed transaction
- An opinion that the proposed transaction was the result of a fair process or is otherwise fair from a legal point of view

A fairness opinion is typically delivered to a board at the time that the board makes its decision whether to approve a proposed transaction.

Why Do Boards Seek Fairness Opinions?

Prior to the mid-1980s, fairness opinions were not a prominent feature of the transaction landscape. However, as previously described, the Delaware Chancery Court found in the 1985 *Van Gorkom* case that the Trans Union board had been grossly negligent and personally liable in approving the sale of the company in a cash-out merger. One of the bases for the court's holding was the failure of the board to obtain or consider a fairness opinion or a well-prepared financial analysis as to the intrinsic worth of Trans Union. The court stated:

> Several defendants testified that [they were advised by counsel] that Delaware law did not require a fairness opinion or an outside valuation of the company before the board could act on the [merger] proposal. If given, the advice was correct. However, that did not end the matter. Unless the directors had before them adequate information regarding the intrinsic value of the company, upon which a proper exercise of business judgment could be made, mere advice of this type is meaningless. . . .[20]

The court held that the board's failure to obtain anything more than a rough and unquestioned estimate of possible value from the corporation's chief financial officer did not satisfy the board's duty of good faith. The court indicated that while a fairness opinion,

20. *Van Gorkom*, 488 A.2d at 881.

was not per se required to satisfy the duty, a well-prepared financial analysis was required. The court strongly implied that obtaining a thoroughly prepared valuation study or a fairness opinion would have satisfied not only the board's duty of care to be duly informed as to corporate value but would establish sufficient basis to rely on DGCL § 141(e).

Since *Van Gorkom*, receipt of a fairness opinion has become a necessary and integral aspect of the decision-making process of any corporate board or committee making a corporate control decision. In numerous cases, where a board's decision-making process has been challenged, the courts have noted the receipt of a fairness opinion as a strong, if not dispositive, factor indicating that the board properly acted in making the relevant decision to proceed with the transaction.

Although there is no legal requirement to obtain a fairness opinion, the courts have looked with favor on a board's receipt of such an opinion in connection with the evaluation of merger and acquisition proposals. In the court's view, the receipt of a fairness opinion provides an indication that the board was fully informed as to whether the financial terms of a transaction were within a reasonable range for a corporate control transaction of this nature and, therefore, should be accorded the presumption of the business judgment rule.

When Do Boards Seek Fairness Opinions?

Drawing from the prior discussion on directors' fiduciary duties, boards are typically advised to seek fairness opinions when they face decisions pertaining to corporate control transactions. The desirability of receiving a fairness opinion is particularly high in situations where:

- The terms and conditions depart from customary ones in similar transactions
- The transaction did not result from a competitive sale process
- The transaction is material to the company
- The company has multiple classes of equity with different rights
- A corporate affiliate is a party to the transaction
- The transaction involves a SPAC[21]
- The transaction is driven by expected synergies

Apart from corporate control transactions, fairness opinions are also rendered in connection with transactions that raise the specter of a conflict of interest, such as going-private transactions and other transactions involving controlling stockholders or other corporate affiliates. In addition, fairness opinions are also sought by other fiduciaries that have the responsibility to protect their group's interests (e.g., the trustee of an employee stock ownership plan). Because of the nature of a fiduciary's responsibilities, as well as exposure to potential liabilities, a fiduciary will want an outside expert to confirm his or her own judgment.

What Do Fairness Opinions Say?

Most often, the fairness opinion is delivered verbally to the board and followed with a formal written opinion letter. Generally, written fairness opinions follow a fairly standard format and will include the following items:

---

21. Andrew F. Tuch, *Fairness Opinions and SPAC Reform*, 1 Wash. Univ. L. Rev. 100 (2023).

- Description of the transaction (including the amount and type of consideration to be paid or received in the transaction)
- Description of the opinion that has been requested
- Description of the nature and extent of the review undertaken by the fairness opinion provider, including the documents and information reviewed
- Description of the relevant assumptions and qualifications, including:
  - An assumption that all information reviewed is complete and accurate in all materials respects without any responsibility for independent verification
  - An assumption that the financial forecasts reviewed (including any estimates of cost savings and synergies) have been reasonably prepared on bases reflecting the best currently available estimates and judgments of management as to future financial performance of the relevant companies and, if applicable, the cost savings and synergies expected to result from the transaction
- Description of the relevant limiting conditions, including:
  - A statement that the opinion does not constitute an independent evaluation or appraisal of the target's assets or liabilities and that no such evaluation or appraisal has been provided
  - A statement that the opinion is limited by the information available and upon financial, economic, market, and other conditions as of the date of the opinion
  - Other assumptions and qualifications applicable to the specific companies and the transaction
- Description of any additional services the opinion may offer in the transaction and whether it will receive fees for such services
- Description of any past, current, and expected future materials relationships between the opinion provider and any parties to the transaction (and their respective affiliates), as well as an acknowledgment, if relevant, that the opinion issuer may actively trade the securities of the participants if they are public companies
- Description of the limited purpose of the opinion including and a statement of the parties who are entitled to rely upon the opinion
- A statement that the opinion has been approved by an internal committee of the issuer
- The opinion provider's conclusion regarding fairness

In a corporate control transaction, the operative language of the opinion is that the consideration paid or received in the transaction is fair from a financial point of view to a specified party. The identity of that party is dependent upon the form of the transaction but is typically the party receiving or paying the transaction consideration. For example, in a sale of corporate assets, a standard fairness opinion would address the fairness to the company of the price being received in connection with the sale. In a merger or other sale of the company, the language would address the fairness of the consideration being received by the company's stockholders in the transaction.

No objective metric has been established by the courts or any regulatory agency to determine what *fair* or *from a financial point of view* actually mean in the context of a fairness opinion. However, an offer price is generally deemed to be fair to an acquisition target's stockholders if it falls within or above the range of fair values for the target determined by the opinion provider. Conversely, an offer price is generally deemed to be fair to an acquirer if it falls within or below the valuation range. It is important to note, however, that a determination of fairness does not indicate whether the offer price is the best price a target could achieve or the lowest price at which an acquirer could buy in a competitive auction framework.

In addition to the formal letter expressing the opinion, fairness opinions are typically accompanied by a presentation (often referred to as a "board book") that details the underlying analyses conducted by the opinion provider in arriving at its opinion. It is in these analyses that the meaning and worth of the fairness opinion lies, and a well-advised board will carefully review the board book in connection with their receipt of the fairness opinion.

Standards and Regulation

A fairness opinion is not a valuation or appraisal and, thus, generally falls outside the purview of appraisal standards such as the ASA *Business Valuation Standards*, The Appraisal Foundation's *Uniform Standards of Professional Appraisal Practice* (USPAP), or AICPA's *Statement on Standards for Valuation Services* (VS Section 100). Because a fairness opinion is not an appraisal or appraisal practice under USPAP, Standards 9 and 10 are not applicable. However, USPAP does consider fairness opinions to be valuation services, and thus,

> When providing valuation services, the obligation for an individual recognized in some circumstances as an appraiser is not to misrepresent his or her role.[22]

Fairness opinion issuers that are members of the Financial Industry Regulatory Authority (FINRA), such as broker-dealers, are required to follow FINRA Rule 5150, which addresses fairness opinions and mandates disclosure of potential conflicts and minimum procedures governing the internal review and approval procedures with respect to fairness opinions.[23] The rule applies when a member firm issues a fairness opinion that is to be disclosed to public stockholders. In such instances, the rule requires that the fairness opinion disclose: (1) any compensation payable to the member investment bank that is contingent upon the successful completion of the transaction; (2) any material relationship that existed during the two years prior to issuance of the fairness opinion or is contemplated between the investment bank and the company; (3) whether the opinion has been approved by a fairness review committee; and (4) the categories of information that formed a substantial basis for the fairness opinion and whether any such information in each category was independently verified by the opinion issuer.

While Rule 5150 strictly applies only to FINRA member firms, many consider the rule to represent industry best practices. Accordingly, nonmember firms issuing fairness opinions would be well-advised to be familiar with the disclosure and procedure processes set forth in the rule.

SEC Disclosure Requirements

The SEC requires companies to disclose all material information to shareholders when issuing a proxy solicitation for purposes of obtaining a shareholder vote. Because the SEC considers fairness opinions (and the underlying financial analyses) to be *material information* if they are presented to the board during the process of approving a merger, fairness opinion details must be disclosed to public company stockholders in merger proxy statements.

---

22. The Appraisal Found., 2024 USPAP Guide and Reference Manual 52, *Advisory Opinion 21*.

23. Jeffrey S. Tarbell, *New Fairness Opinion Rule Now in Effect*, Deal Points: The Newsletter of the Committee on Negotiated Acquisitions (Spring 2008).

Historically, the disclosure in proxy statements with respect to fairness opinions was confined to a short summary of the opinion letter itself. However, in 1986, the SEC revised the proxy rules and adopted more stringent disclosure requirements for fairness opinions provided in corporate control transactions. Subsequently, the SEC staff has become more aggressive in its review of proxy statements, and such statements now regularly contain several pages of description as to the analyses undertaken by the opinion provider. SEC staff generally requires disclosure in the proxy statement of the methodologies utilized in preparing a fairness opinion, the results of such methodologies, and the basis for selecting each one. For instance, SEC staff often requires disclosure of the discount rates and terminal values used in discounted cash flow analyses and the companies and transactions referred to in selected companies and selected transaction analyses, respectively.

In addition, fairness opinion issuers are required to disclose in the opinion potential conflicts of interest and any material relationship that existed during the past two years or is mutually understood to be contemplated between the corporation receiving the fairness opinion and the opinion provider (and its affiliates). The compensation received or to be received by the opinion provider as a result of any such relationship must also be disclosed.

If the transaction in question is a going private transaction, Rule 13e-3 imposes even greater disclosure and filing obligations with respect to any fairness opinion received by a board. For instance, the filer is required to furnish any underlying written analyses (e.g., the board book) or other report prepared by the opinion provider in connection with the fairness opinion. The SEC will carefully review disclosures relating to valuation and the fairness of the transaction consideration.

While fairness opinions are regularly published in proxy materials relating to major transactions, the primary intended beneficiaries of fairness opinions are not the corporation's shareholders, but rather the board. Accordingly, a fairness opinion is not intended to constitute a recommendation as to how stockholders should vote on any transaction, nor is it a recommendation as to the investment merit of the company's securities. It does not attest to the anticipated tax consequences of the transaction, nor does it address the relative merits of the transactions versus any other possible transaction the company might consider.

Opinion providers preparing a fairness opinion that is anticipated to be publicly disclosed will regularly retain outside legal counsel to review, among other things, the opinion provider's engagement letter, fairness opinion letter, supporting board book, and—perhaps most importantly—the description of the opinion provider's analysis appearing in the proxy statement or other documents distributed to stockholders and publicly filed with the SEC.

UNDERLYING FINANCIAL ANALYSES

The foundation of a fairness opinion is a series of financial analyses, undertaken by the opinion provider, designed to present a range of values and other indications that can then be compared to the proposed consideration.

The core financial analyses used in fairness opinions include a discounted cash flow analysis, a guideline public company analysis (often referred to as a selected companies analysis), and a guideline transaction analysis (often referred to as a selected transactions analysis). These core valuation methods are covered in Chapter 3, "Overview of Business Valuation Approaches, Methods, and Procedures"; Chapter 6, "The Income Approach"; and Chapter 8, "The Market Approach."

Various other financial analyses are sometimes used in the development of fairness opinions, including those described next. While these additional analyses are not valuation methods, they can provide additional and useful information to the board. Such miscellaneous financial analyses may include:

- **Analysis of the proposed consideration.** If the consideration to be received by the selling stockholders is equity, rather than cash, the opinion issuer's analysis will likely include, at minimum, a quantitative analysis of the proposed equity consideration.
- **Prior share price analysis.** When the target company's stock is publicly traded, the opinion issuer will typically analyze the stock's prior trading price range, trading volume, and other market-observed data.
- **Premiums-paid analysis.** When the target company's stock is publicly traded, the opinion issuer may compare the implied premium to be paid in the contemplated transaction with observed premiums paid in other selected marketplace transactions. However, this analysis may reflect a selection bias since the universe of relevant transactions forming the basis for the premiums paid method includes only companies that were acquired at a premium—presumably reflecting that the buyer deemed the target stock to be undervalued prior to the transaction.
- **Leveraged buyout analysis.** Like a discounted cash flow analysis, a leveraged buyout (LBO) analysis generates an estimate of business value based on the entity's estimated future financial performance. The analysis assumes that (1) a financial buyer acquires the subject company using a combination of debt and equity; (2) each component of such debt and equity earns a particular return over the expected holding period (typically five to seven years); and (3) the buyer exits the investment through an entity sale at the end of the holding period, at a valuation typically based on guideline public company multiples. Ultimately, the implied entity value from the leveraged buy-out analysis is indicated as the acquisition price that satisfies the required rates of return and exit price assumptions.
- **Present value of future share price analysis.** This analysis is designed to provide an indication of the present value of a theoretical future trading price of an entity's shares. Necessary inputs include estimates of (1) the entity's future earnings, (2) a future multiple of earnings, and (3) a range of equity discount rates. Circularity notwithstanding, this method remains widely used by a few of the largest investment banks in their fairness opinion practices.
- **Contribution (has-gets) analysis.** This analysis measures the relative value of two companies that are combining in a merger transaction. It is independent of the companies' respective market prices and is of particular relevance when the two companies have similar business operations. A contribution analysis examines each of the individual company's relative contribution to the post-merger entity.
- **Accretion/dilution analysis.** This analysis examines whether the proposed merger transaction will be accretive or dilutive to the target company shareholders, usually measured on an earnings per share basis. An accretion/dilution analysis may be more meaningful when it includes an examination of projected earnings in future years.

A study of more than 3,000 publicly disclosed fairness opinions issued between 2006 and 2016 found, not surprisingly, that the most prevalently used valuation methods were the selected companies (i.e., guideline public company) method, discounted cash flow method, and selected transactions (i.e., guideline transaction) method. Other financial analyses were utilized with less frequency than the core three valuation methods.[24]

Unlike business valuations where the objective is often to determine a single indicated value, the valuation methods used to develop fairness opinions are frequently structured to develop a range of indicated values. For instance, in a fairness analysis, the selected company method would often employ a range of selected multiples rather than a single selected multiple, and the discounted cash flow analysis would typically utilize a range of estimated discount rates and terminal value inputs. A fairness opinion further differs from a valuation or appraisal in that it does not reconcile the indicated value ranges derived from the underlying valuation analyses into a concluded range of values or a concluded single value (as described in Chapter 19). Rather, the fairness of the proposed consideration to be paid or received in the transaction is assessed by comparison to an indicated value range resulting from each valuation method utilized in the analysis. That comparison is typically presented in a graphical format commonly referred to as a "football field," such as the illustrative example shown in Exhibit 30-1, where the columns represent the indicated value ranges, and the horizontal line represents the proposed transaction consideration.

Exhibit 30-1 Implied Target Company per Share Reference Ranges

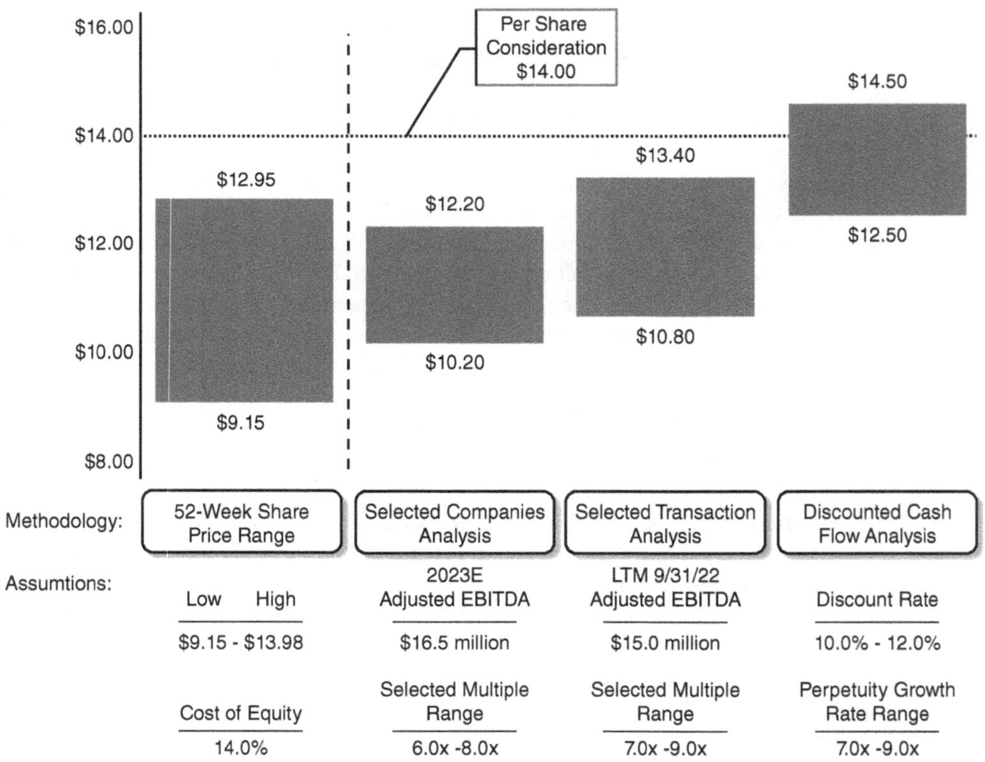

24. Kroll LLC, In Defense of Fairness Opinions: An Empirical Review of Ten Years of Data (2017).

SCOPE OF WORK ISSUES

Defining the concept of fairness. How does one determine whether the proposed consideration is fair, from a financial point of view? This can be a difficult question to answer, in part because the conclusion itself represents an opinion, rather than a factual statement. Courts have not specified which definition of fair price fairness opinion issuers should use.[25] As previously mentioned, fairness opinion providers tend to define a proposed consideration as fair if the proposed consideration falls within a range of reasonably determined fair market values of the securities to be transferred in the transaction.

One noted expert on fairness opinion matters has expanded on this premise, as follows:

> The minimum level of financial fairness in a proposed transaction is a function of the amount that dissenting shareholders to the transaction could reasonably expect to obtain in a statutory appraisal action. . . . [A] financial adviser should not render a positive fairness opinion in a transaction if the consideration is materially below the price that the shareholders would be awarded in an appraisal action. This is true whether or not the structure of the transaction permits shareholders to avail themselves of the appraisal remedy.[26]

Accordingly, the fairness opinion issuer must familiarize themselves with relevant appraisal statutes in the jurisdiction where the subject company is incorporated. Chapter 23 discusses such statutes in additional detail.

Effective date. A fairness opinion, like a business valuation, has an effective date. Unlike a business valuation, however, a fairness opinion always speaks to a determination of fairness that is effective as of the date of the opinion letter itself. In the context of a fairness opinion, the opinion is typically provided to the board or other recipients at the time of its consideration of the transaction.[27] It is important to note that the board's decision to proceed with a transaction may precede by several months the stockholder vote to approve the transaction. Some commentators have expressed concern that this timing discrepancy can lead to stale opinions.[28] Nonetheless, fairness opinions are rarely updated to the date of the shareholder vote or the transaction closing date.

Standard of value. A customary fairness opinion does not state any standard of value that has been followed in the underlying valuation analysis. Obviously, this is a major differentiator from a typical business valuation where standards require the identification of the applicable standard of value. Following the guidance described earlier, the applicable standard of value would appear to be *fair value*, or the analogous standard applicable to dissenting shareholder matters in the subject company's state of incorporation.[29]

---

25. Lucian Arye Bebchuk & Marcel Kahan, *Fairness Opinions: How Fair are They and What can be Done About It?*, 27 Duke L.J. 30 (1989).

26. M. Mark Lee & Gilbert E. Matthews, *Fairness Opinions*, *in* The Handbook of Advanced Business Valuation 16–17 (Robert F. Reilly & Robert P. Schweihs eds., 2000).

27. Steven M. Davidoff Solomon, *Fairness Opinions*, 55 Am. Univ. L. Rev. 1563 (2006).

28. Gilbert E. Matthews, *Stale Fairness Opinions in Related Party Transactions Should Be Updated*, 24(9) Bu. Valuation Update (Sept. 2018).

29. Lee & Matthews, *supra* note 26.

Premise of value. A customary fairness opinion also does not state any premise of value that has been followed in the underlying valuation analysis. Since fairness opinions are typically issued in connection with corporate control transactions—as opposed to bankruptcies or restructurings—it is difficult to imagine a scenario where the applicable premise of value would be anything other than going-concern value.

Relative level of value. While not typically stated outright in the opinion letter, the valuation analyses underlying most fairness opinions reflect a financial control level of value (see Chapter 2 and Chapter 18 for additional discussion on levels of value). This observation derives from two factors. First, most fairness opinions are issued in connection with change-in-control transactions, where valuation discounts for lack of control and lack of marketability are irrelevant. Second, as already described, where the applicable standard of value is fair value (e.g., in the state of Delaware), such standard is generally interpreted to represent a pro rata ownership interest (i.e., a controlling level of value), again eliminating the need for valuation discounts.

SUMMARY

Fairness opinions play a critical role in corporate transactions; they provide important decisional information to boards and other corporate fiduciaries as well as evidence that the board has satisfied its duty of care in the determination of whether or not to proceed with a proposed transaction.[30] While required by neither law nor statute, fairness opinions are pervasive in transactions involving issues of corporate control and/or possible conflicts of interest. Experienced fairness opinion issuers benefit from a deep understanding of relevant corporation law and directors' duties, corporate transaction dynamics, as well as the prerequisite expertise in principles of business valuation and corporate finance.

A fairness opinion is not an appraisal and does not specify an opinion of value. Rather, a fairness opinion presents a reasoned opinion that a proposed transaction consideration is fair, from a financial point of view. While there is no universally accepted definition of what constitutes a fair price, there is a general consensus among practitioners that a price can be considered fair if it is consistent with the range of values that an investor might otherwise expect to receive by way of a sale resulting from an effective auction process.

Because fairness opinions—at least those related to public companies—are often publicly disclosed, opinion issuers are well-advised to seek the advice of legal counsel with appropriate experience and expertise. Fairness opinion issuers manage the inherent risk of publicly disclosed opinions by making sure opinions are subject to a rigorous internal review process, akin to that described in FINRA Rule 5150.

30. Davidoff Solomon, *supra* note 28, at 1558–59.

REFERENCES TO VALUATION IN FAIRNESS MATTERS

Business Valuation Resources. *Fairness Opinion Research Service.* https://www.bvresources.com/products/fairness-opinion-research-service.

Pratt, Shannon P. and ASA Educational Foundation. 2022. "Fairness Opinions" *Shannon Pratt's Valuing a Business: The Analysis and Appraisal of Closely Held Companies*, 6th ed. Chap. 47, 1119–39 (New York: McGraw Hill).

Tarbell, Jeffrey S. "New Fairness Opinion Rule Now in Effect," In *Deal Points: The Newsletter of the Committee on Negotiated Acquisitions* (American Bar Association, Spring 2008).

CHAPTER 31

Valuation in Solvency Matters

Bob Bartell, CFA

INTRODUCTION[1]

In this chapter you will learn about:

- Claims of fraudulent conveyance/transfers—how and when they occur, and the role valuation plays within the context of those claims
- *Reasonably equivalent value* and how it is estimated
- Solvency opinions
- Director duties and how they may shift as a company approaches insolvency
- Cancellation of debt income—what it is and how it is calculated, and the exemption of cancellation of debt income for income tax purposes in cases of technical insolvency

The use of corporate debt in capital structures has been in a steady state of increase over the past two decades. In that time, the amount of outstanding corporate debt has increased by approximately 160%, to approximately $12.6 trillion as of December 31, 2022.[2] While the prevalence of solvency matters increased markedly following the Global Financial Crisis of 2007–2008 and the 2020 recession caused by the Covid-19 pandemic, solvency matters remain a constant consideration for companies, their boards and officers, and their legal and financial advisors as many companies continue to operate with significant financial leverage. The goal of this chapter is to understand when the issue of solvency arises, what issues become subject of disputes, and the actions companies and boards can take to protect themselves in situations of high financial leverage.

CLAIMS OF FRAUDULENT CONVEYANCE/TRANSFERS

In cases of bankruptcy, transactions completed in the years leading up to a bankruptcy filing are subject to scrutiny and potential reversal. Those transactions can include asset sales, debt restructurings or incurrence, stock repurchases, or dividends, and generally involve transactions whereby assets that could be used to support financial liabilities leave the company. Creditors and aggrieved parties may claim that those transactions

1. The author thanks Chris Swiecicki for his assistance in assembling this chapter.

2. Board of Governors of the Federal Reserve System (U.S.), *Nonfinancial Corporate Business; Debt Securities and Loans; Liability, Level*, FRED, Federal Reserve Bank of St. Louis, https://fred.stlouisfed.org/series/BCNSDODNS (last visited June 10, 2023).

rendered the company insolvent, whether they were intentionally fraudulent transactions or transactions that are considered constructive fraudulent transfers.

In the United States, fraudulent transfer claims are governed by two sets of laws, (1) the Federal Bankruptcy Code (specifically, § 548) and (2) the Uniform Fraudulent Transfer Act (UFTA) or the Uniform Fraudulent Conveyance Act (UFCA), as adopted by that state of incorporation.

1. Intentional fraudulent transfers. Transactions in which there is an actual intent to hinder, delay, or defraud any creditor of the debtor. Successful claims must prove that there was intent by the debtor to defraud.
2. Constructive fraudulent transfers. Transactions in which there are two conditions:
    a. In exchange for the transfer, the debtor (company) received less than *reasonably equivalent value*; and
    b. The debtor (company) was "insolvent" on the date that such transfer was made or became insolvent as a result of such transfer; had an unreasonably small amount of capital for the business in which it is engaged; or intended to incur debts that would be beyond its ability to pay such debts as they matured.

The U.S. Bankruptcy Code, UFTA, or UFCA does not define reasonably equivalent value and thus, whether value is reasonably equivalent must be determined on a case-by-case basis in the courts. In making its assessments, the courts have generally considered reasonably equivalent value and *fair consideration* to have effectively the same meaning and have often adopted fair market value as a starting point in its analysis. As a result, determining whether an asset was transferred at reasonably equivalent value is an area of dispute by the parties to the bankruptcy litigation. Often, independent valuation experts are engaged to assist the parties and provide support regarding their assessment of the fair market value of the assets or businesses that were transferred.

Companies that are acquiring assets or businesses from highly leveraged selling entities will often engage independent valuation experts before the closing of proposed transaction, to value the acquired assets contemporaneously with the acquisition process and provide an opinion as to the reasonably equivalent value, potentially providing protection from future claims of constructive fraudulent transfer claims. Valuation experts will utilize commonly accepted valuation methodologies in their analyses, which may include the income approach, the market approach, and the asset-based approach to support their assessments.

Several types of transactions or situations may constitute potential constructive fraudulent transfers, including:

- An asset is sold, leased, or otherwise conveyed
- Debt incurrence or debt restructuring
- Dividends or other distributions
- Stock repurchases or exchanges
- Additional collateral is provided to secure a debt
- A guarantee is given

Successful fraudulent transfer claims have the potential of unwinding the transaction in question, even years after the transaction was completed. Selling shareholders may have to repay sale proceeds or dividend proceeds, directors may face significant personal liability, professional advisors may have to return fees, and secured lenders may have their liens attacked. Companies, their board of directors, and legal advisors have a range of preemptive actions available to address solvency-related concerns in connection with leveraged transactions. Hiring independent valuation experts experienced in such matters to provide objective and rigorous advice on issues relating to reasonably equivalent value and solvency—through solvency opinions—can provide a strong defense against fraudulent transfer claims.

Solvency opinions address key components of the Federal Bankruptcy Code and state law regarding fraudulent transfers. The determinations that encompass a solvency opinion cover both aspects of valuation and aspects of cash flow generation: whether (1) the value of the company's assets exceeds its liabilities; (2) the company can pay its debts as they become due; and (3) the company has a reasonable amount of capital to operate the business.

In addition to addressing claims of fraudulent transfer, solvency opinions are designed to address the legality of dividends and distributions as governed by state law. For instance, Delaware law addresses this by requiring that corporations only pay dividends to their shareholders from a capital surplus. In Delaware law, surplus is defined as (1) the fair value of a corporation's total assets less its stated liabilities, less (2) the corporation's stated capital (which is generally defined as the aggregate par value of the company's stock). Each state has its own statutes that ultimately reflect a variation of the Delaware language. The company's legal counsel, in consultation with the solvency opinion provider, will need to address the specific aspects of each company and transaction on an individual basis.

Solvency opinions provide protections to corporations and boards and assist corporate directors in carrying out their fiduciary duties. In accordance with Delaware law, a member of the board shall be fully protected in relying in good faith upon the records of the corporation and upon opinions by experts (any other person as to matters the director reasonably believes are within such other person's professional or expert competence, and who has been selected with reasonable care by or on behalf of the corporation), as to the value and amount of the assets, liabilities, and/or net profits of the corporation and amount of surplus or other funds from which dividends might properly be declared and paid, or with which the corporation's stock might properly be purchased or redeemed.

The use of solvency opinions by companies, their board of directors, and their legal advisors has increased in the past decade amid heightened awareness surrounding corporate governance, and has become best practice in assessing leveraged transactions.[3]

CLAIMS REGARDING BREACHES OF FIDUCIARY DUTIES IN THE CONTEXT OF INSOLVENCY

A claim for a breach of fiduciary duty against directors and officers generally has several elements: there was a fiduciary duty owed by directors and officers to a party; they breached that duty; the plaintiff suffered damages as a result; and the breach caused those damages. In a solvent company, officers and directors owe a fiduciary duty to the

3. For a more extensive discussion on solvency opinions, *see* Chapter 48 *in* Shannon P. Pratt & ASA Educ. Found., Shannon Pratt's Valuing a Business: The Analysis and Appraisal of Closely Held Companies (6th ed., 2022).

company and its shareholders. Fiduciary duties are not owed to creditors of a solvent corporation. However, when a company experiences financial distress and enters what is known as the zone or vicinity of insolvency, the number of parties to whom the directors owe their fiduciary duties increases to include the corporation's creditors. It is often difficult to determine at which point a company is technically insolvent or in the zone of insolvency. The tests used by courts for determining insolvency are similar to those previously discussed, principally, a balance sheet test (are the value of the company's assets greater than its liabilities) or a cash flow test (can the company pay its debts as they come due and is there adequate capital).

Unless there is a specific determination made that the company is insolvent, its directors and officers may not necessarily know, in real time, when insolvency actually begins. In some states, boards of directors' primary fiduciary duty shifts to the creditors once a company is in the zone of insolvency. In other states, the fiduciary duty does not shift to creditors until a company is officially insolvent. In the remaining states, boards of directors are not required to make creditors' interests a priority over shareholder interests, but they are required to protect the rights of creditors. In these complicated situations, it is important for directors and officers to seek legal advice to understand where their duties stand.

VALUATION ASPECTS OF CANCELLATION OF INDEBTEDNESS INCOME

In times of financial distress, companies will often work with their creditors in an attempt to restructure their liabilities to improve their liquidity and financial standing. Debt restructuring transactions can take many forms, whether it's simply a reduction in the principal outstanding, a more complex exchange of existing unsecured debt for a new priority lien security, or even a significant modification to the terms of the debt other than the principal amount (extension of maturity, changes in interest rate, altering collateral, etc.). If a taxpayer is able to discharge debt that is owed for less than the original amount, that taxpayer must recognize taxable income, subject to certain exclusions or special rules within the tax code. This form of taxable income is often referred to as "discharge of indebtedness" or "cancellation of debt income" (CODI).

Internal Revenue Code (I.R.C.) § 61(a)(12) was enacted in 1954 to codify the discharge of indebtedness or cancellation of debt income as gross income. Simultaneously, Congress added I.R.C. § 108 to provide overriding and supplemental rules to I.R.C. § 61(a)(12), including how to calculate the precise amount of cancellation of debt income. The rational for adding I.R.C. § 108 was to prevent the recognition of a tax liability that a taxpayer would be unable to pay and provide an economically distressed taxpayer the opportunity for a fresh start.

Determining the amount of cancellation of debt income is guided by I.R.C. § 108. If a debt is simply discharged in exchange for a cash payment that is less than the full amount of the outstanding debt, the amount of cancellation of debt income is the amount by which the debt exceeds the cash payment. For example, if $1,000,000 of outstanding debt is discharged with a $800,000 cash payment, $200,000 of CODI is recognized. However, there are many other ways that debt might be reduced, and determining the amount of CODI in those situations can be more complicated. For example, in a situation where there is an exchange of debt instruments, and existing debt is exchanged into new debt with a lower principal amount and issued at a discount to par, the calculation also incorporates the original issue discount of the new debt. Under I.R.C. § 108, the taxpayer's cancellation of debt income is the excess of the adjusted issue price of the original obligation, computed over the issue price of the new obligation, rather than merely the reduction in the face amount of the debt. For example, if a $1,000,000 debt instrument is exchanged into a new $800,000 debt instrument that is issued at a 25% discount to par ($600,000), the cancelation of debt income includes both the $200,000 reduction in principal and the $200,000 original issue discount, resulting in a total gain of $400,000. There are numerous rules within I.R.C. § 108 that provide guidance on the amount of cancellation of debt income to be recognized, and a tax advisor should be consulted to determine the appropriate amount.

There are exclusions or special rules to the recognition of cancellation of debt income that are principally based on whether the company is either in bankruptcy proceedings or technically insolvent. When debt is cancelled under bankruptcy proceedings, there is no taxable income recognized but rather a reduction in tax benefits to which the debtor would otherwise be entitled. The tax benefits that would be reduced include:

1. Net operating losses (NOLs) and NOL carryovers
2. The general business credit
3. The minimum tax credit
4. Capital loss carryovers
5. The basis of the taxpayer's property
6. Passive activity loss and credit carryovers
7. Foreign tax credit carryovers

Another principal exemption on the recognition of cancellation of debt income hinges on whether the taxpayer is technically insolvent—that is, whether its liabilities (that may be considered for tax purposes) exceed the fair market value of the taxpayer's assets immediate before the discharge of indebtedness. If a business remains insolvent after the debt cancellation, the decrease in debt is offset by the seven tax items just listed. If, however, the business is insolvent before, but solvent after the debt cancellation, the taxpayer may not record income associated with the debt cancellation to the extent of the insolvency (i.e., the amount by which the company is technically insolvent or the amount by which liabilities exceed assets). The determination of insolvency and the technical amount of insolvency is entirely a valuation matter. This determination requires the fair market value appraisal of all of the assets owned by the borrower immediately before the debt forgiveness.

The statutory and judicial precedent related to I.R.C. § 108 is clear that all of the taxpayer's assets are subject to appraisal in the determination of insolvency. These assets include tangible personal property (e.g., machinery and equipment), tangible real estate (e.g., land and buildings), intangible real property (e.g., leasehold interests and easements), and intangible personal property (e.g., trademarks and goodwill). Valuation experts can utilize commonly accepted valuation approaches and methodologies in their appraisals. A rigorously prepared and thoroughly documented independent appraisal is required to support a claim of insolvency under I.R.C. § 108.

The I.R.C. does not define liabilities in the determination of insolvency, and thus the determination of what liabilities are included in the insolvency test is a matter of judicial and administrative interpretation, and guidance from tax counsel is required.

There are costs to consider related to income exclusion resulting from I.R.C. § 108. Taxpayers will not recognize income from the cancellation of debt income if they are in bankruptcy, or to the extent that they are insolvent, as discussed. However, in exchange for this income exclusion, taxpayers are required to reduce certain favorable tax attributes. These tax attributes are reduced by the amount of the CODI. For example, general business credits and foreign tax credits are reduced at the rate of 33.3 cents for every dollar of excluded cancellation of debt income.

Unless the taxpayer elects to reduce the basis in their depreciable assets (e.g., real estate) before reducing other tax attributes, the taxpayer must reduce tax attributes in the following sequence:

1. NOLs and NOL carryovers
2. Carryovers of the general business credit
3. Capital losses and carryovers
4. The basis of the taxpayer's depreciable and nondepreciable assets
5. Foreign tax credit carryovers

As an alternative to the reduction of tax benefits, the borrower may elect to reduce the basis of any depreciable assets, but not below his or her basis in the assets.[4]

SUMMARY

Valuation plays an important role in the context of solvency matters, whether it be to defend or refute claims of fraudulent conveyance/transfer or to claim an exemption of the gain related to cancellation of debt. Working with experienced valuation experts in the context of leveraged transactions can help mitigate the risk of economic loss and transactions being unwound.

REFERENCE TO VALUATION IN SOLVENCY MATTERS

Pratt, Shannon P. and ASA Educational Foundation. 2022. "Solvency Opinions," *Shannon Pratt's Valuing a Business: The Analysis and Appraisal of Closely Held Companies*, 6th ed. Chap. 48, 1141–54 (New York: McGraw Hill).

4. For a more extensive discussion on cancellation of debt income, *see* PRATT & ASA EDUC. FOUND., *supra* note 3, at Chapter 37.

CHAPTER 32

Valuation in Lost Profits Damages Matters

William W. Thomsen, ASA, CFA

INTRODUCTION

In this chapter you will learn about:

- Situations requiring an estimate of lost profits or lost business value
- Prerequisites to damage recovery
- Key concepts in damage calculations
- Methods used in measuring damages: lost profits and lost business value
- When to use lost profits, lost business value, or both
- Key differences between lost profits and lost business value analyses
- When lost profits might be greater than lost business value damages
- Using the damages expert

In most commercial litigation settings, the primary source of monetary relief for the plaintiff comes from a damages award for lost profits, lost business value, or both.

SITUATIONS REQUIRING CALCULATION OF LOST PROFITS OR LOST BUSINESS VALUE

In commercial litigation, the award of lost profits or lost business value is a remedy that a plaintiff can seek for the damages caused by the wrongful act of a defendant. Typical claims requiring such a calculation include breach of contract, torts (e.g., fraud, misrepresentation, and unfair competition), and infringement of intellectual property (e.g., patent, copyright, or trademark infringement).

PREREQUISITES TO DAMAGE RECOVERY

An economic damages claim related to lost profits or lost business value will likely be rejected by the court unless the plaintiff establishes three elements: (1) proximate cause, (2) reasonable certainty, and (3) foreseeability.

Proximate Cause

As the name implies, proximate cause relates to causation. The plaintiff's damages must be traced to, and result directly from, the defendant's wrongful act. In other words, there must be sufficient evidence showing that, but for the defendant's alleged wrongful act, there would have been no injury. Thus, plaintiff must establish that the wrongful act was the primary, if not the sole, cause of the damages. If, for example, defendant can show that some other event—say, a severe economic downturn—significantly contributed to plaintiff's losses, then proximate cause might not be established.

In most cases, it is not the damages expert's role to prove causation. Nevertheless, the expert can provide valuable assistance if causation can be proved or supported with financial analysis. For example, the expert might identify other factors potentially contributing to plaintiff's lost profits—such as a weak economy, increased competition, waning demand for plaintiff's products, or plaintiff's own mistakes—and assess their relative impact on plaintiff's financial and operational performance.

Reasonable Certainty

Reasonable certainty refers to the requirement that lost profits damages must be estimated using reliable methods and evidence.[1] This means that the damages calculation must not be remote, speculative, or hypothetical. Somewhat more uncertainty is allowed in quantifying damages versus proving liability—hence the standard of reasonable, not absolute, certainty for the damage calculation.

Foreseeability

Foreseeability refers to the requirement that the losses claimed by the plaintiff are the predictable consequence of defendant's alleged misconduct. This means that the damages were reasonably foreseeable, or within the contemplation of the parties. The foreseeability requirement does not demand absolute certainty that damages would occur as a result of the wrongful act, but rather a reasonable anticipation of their likelihood. The purpose is to prevent speculative or remote claims for damages that could not have been reasonably expected at the time the contract was made or the wrongful act occurred. As an example, losses due to a sudden unexpected downturn in market prices would not be reasonably foreseeable.

KEY CONCEPTS IN DAMAGE CALCULATIONS

Several important considerations underpin any lost profits or lost business value calculation. They are (1) mitigation, (2) the period of damages, (3) time value of money, and (4) ex ante versus ex post calculations.

---

1. Specifically, Federal Rules of Evidence Rule 702–Testimony of Expert Witnesses states:

> A witness who is qualified as an expert by knowledge, skill, experience, training, or education may testify in the form of an opinion or otherwise if <u>the proponent demonstrates to the court that it is more likely than not that:</u>
>
> (a) the expert's scientific, technical, or other specialized knowledge will help the trier of fact to understand the evidence or to determine a fact in issue;
> (b) the testimony is based on sufficient facts or data;
> (c) the testimony is the product of reliable principles and methods; and
> (d) the ~~expert has reliably applied~~ <u>expert's opinion reflects a reliable application of</u> the principles and methods to the facts of the case.

The underline and strike through reflect the amendment effective December 1, 2023.

Mitigation

The damage award is designed to place the plaintiff in a position that is economically equivalent to the plaintiff's position in the absence of the defendant's wrongful acts. This means the plaintiff is to be made whole, though not placed in a better or worse position than prior to the alleged wrongful act.

Plaintiffs therefore have the obligation to *mitigate* damages. Specifically, an injured party cannot recover damages that it could have reasonably avoided with a reasonable, good faith effort. The plaintiff's failure to mitigate does not eliminate the claim for damages. However, damages must be calculated considering reasonable mitigation efforts. This also means that costs of mitigation can be a key component of economic damages.

Of course, parties can and do disagree on what constitutes reasonable mitigation.

Period of Damages

The relevant period of damages typically starts at the date of the alleged wrongful act, and ends depending on case facts and legal issues. This period may include past damages, future damages, or both. *Past damages* cover the time from the onset of the damages period through the date of judgment or trial. *Future damages* encompass losses experienced after that date. Future damages might end at a point in time—for example, when a breached license agreement would have expired, when recoverable damages are constrained by the length of an insurance policy, or when damages are anticipated to be fully mitigated. Alternatively, future damages might go into perpetuity. In a lost business value calculation, the damage period is almost always perpetual by definition.

Time Value of Money

Associated with the period of damages is the concept of time value of money. Damages are almost never calculated by simply summing nominal amounts to get a total. Instead, damages must be converted to a present value, typically as of the date of judgment or trial.

Past damages are brought forward to the present by applying some sort of prejudgment interest calculation (i.e., adding interest to the past damages). The greater the interest rate applied, the greater the present value compared to the total nominal amount of past damages.

Future damages are brought back to the present value by discounting the losses using a risk-adjusted discount rate. The greater the discount rate used, the lesser the present value compared to the total nominal amount of future damages.

Ex Ante versus Ex Post Calculations[2]

Although damages are typically computed starting as of the date of alleged wrongdoing, the date of trial or damage measurement is usually much later. Thus, damages can be computed in two ways:

1. By considering only information that was known and knowable as of the date of the wrongful act. This is known as an *ex ante* calculation.
2. By considering all information available through the present or date of trial. This is known as an *ex post* calculation.

---

2. *Ex ante*, Latin for "from before," refers to before the event. *Ex post*, Latin for "from after," refers to after the event.

A loss of business value damage calculation is, by definition, an ex ante calculation, as a valuation will consider only what was known or knowable as of the valuation date. Lost profits calculations, on the other hand, can be computed on either an ex ante or ex post basis. The decision to use one or the other may depend on the court's guidance.

Proponents of the ex ante approach argue that it is theoretically correct to value damages based on what was known and knowable as of the date of injury. Advocates of the ex post approach, on the other hand, would argue that it is better to use all information available to determine damages.

Even if an expert uses an ex ante approach to determine damages, the expert might be required to look at ex post data to ensure the ex ante calculations are reasonable. Consider, for example, the calculation of the lost value of a business where a wrongful act occurred just prior to the onset of the Covid-19 pandemic. Clearly, in that case, a trier of fact would almost certainly require consideration of ex post data in the computation of damages.

The present value of damages is treated differently depending on whether the damages are computed on an ex ante or ex post basis.

For ex ante calculations, past and future damages are discounted back to the date of injury. They are then brought forward, with prejudgment interest, to the date of trial. In the ex ante damages calculation shown in Exhibit 32-1, total undiscounted damages of $715,000 result in a present value as of the date of trial equaling $612,941.

Exhibit 32-1 Ex Ante Damages Calculation Example

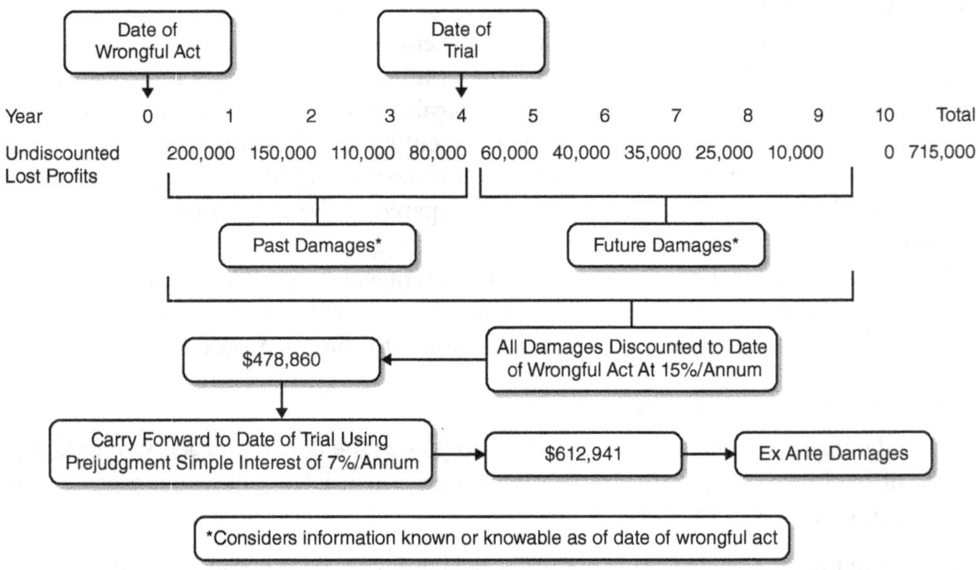

For ex post calculations, past damages are brought forward to the date of trial with prejudgment interest, whereas future damages are discounted back to the date of trial. In the ex post damages calculation shown in Exhibit 32-2, total undiscounted damages of $715,000 result in a present value as of the date of trial equaling $739,179.

Exhibit 32-2 Ex Post Damages Calculation Example

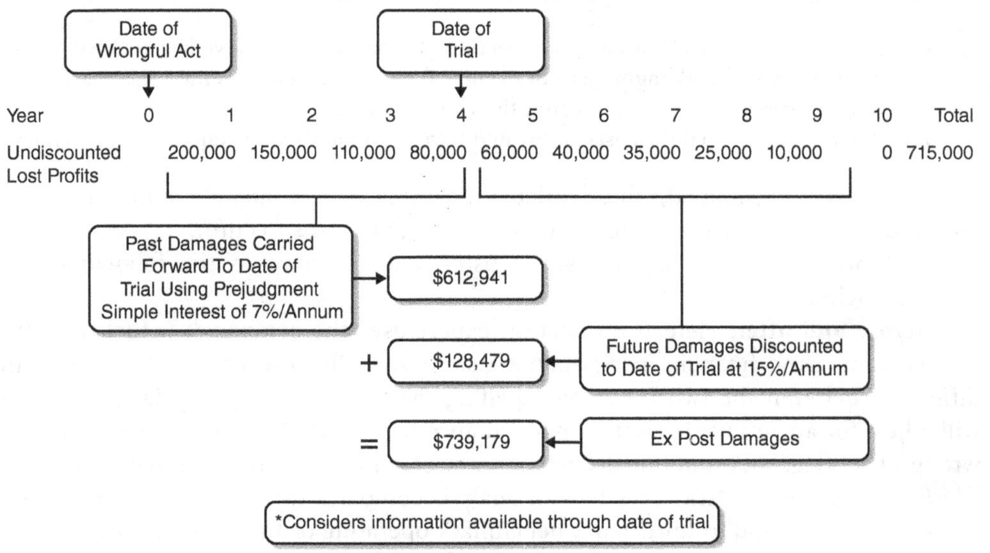

Since the prejudgment interest rate is usually different from the discount rate used to compute damages, ex ante and ex post damage calculations can look very different, even if identical projections of damages are used. This is the case in the preceding example, where the present value of ex post damages is greater than that of ex ante damages despite the amounts being identical on an undiscounted basis. In fact, only when the prejudgment interest rate and damage discount rate are the same would ex ante and ex post damage calculations be similar.[3]

DAMAGE CALCULATION METHODS: LOST PROFITS AND LOST BUSINESS VALUE

In a commercial litigation setting, an expert will consider one of two methods to compute damages: lost profits or lost business value. Each calculation is briefly described next.

Measuring Lost Profit Damages

Lost profits are usually computed using one of the following formulas.

Formula 32-1

Lost profits = "but-for" profits less "actual" profits, where:

- "But-for" profits equal past and/or future profits that would have occurred had the wrongful act not occurred.
- "Actual" profits equal past and/or future profits, taking into account the wrongful act.

3. As damages are typically carried forward using simple interest and discounted on a compounded basis, ex ante and ex post calculations will vary even if identical discount rates are applied.

Formula 32-2

Lost profits = lost revenues less avoided costs, where:

- Lost revenues equal "but for" revenues (i.e., past and/or future revenues that would have occurred had the wrongful act not occurred) minus "actual" revenues (i.e., past and/or future revenues taking into account the wrongful act).
- Avoided costs equal the costs that would have been incurred to generate lost revenues.

As already mentioned, these calculations might also include additional costs incurred by plaintiff as a result of the wrongful act (e.g., costs to cure).

Lost profits are typically measured using one or more of the following three methodologies.

Before and after. Here the valuation expert uses the company's actual operating results, comparing financial performance before and after the wrongful act, with the difference between the two measures equaling the loss. When appropriate, the expert will adjust for any events impacting performance that would have been unrelated to the wrongful act (e.g., an economic decline or entry of competitors into the marketplace).

Benchmark/yardstick. This type of analysis compares the company's actual results during the loss period to third-party benchmark operating or financial metrics that estimate what the revenues and profits of the affected business could have been had the wrongful act not occurred. Benchmarks may be based on industry statistics, performance of the plaintiff's business at separate unimpacted locations, performance of similar unaffected companies, or some other measure. A key consideration is the correlation between the benchmark/yardstick and revenues being analyzed; the less reliable the benchmark, the less credible the lost profits calculation using this technique.

Projections.[4] This analysis is based on projections created prior to, or independent of, the wrongful act. These projections, typically made by company management, portray how the business *would have* performed but for the wrongful act. The reliability of this calculation is of course dependent on the credibility of the projections used. For example, if management projections are used, the extent to which past projections accurately predicted actual results will likely impact the reliability of this technique. Additionally, projections created solely for the purpose of the subject litigation would likely be accorded less weight by a trier of fact than projections prepared prior to the harmful act or for purposes unrelated to the dispute at hand.

Once lost profits are measured, they are adjusted to present value. The lost profits may consist of:

1. *Past* lost profits that are brought forward to the date of trial using a prejudgment interest rate;

4. The terms "forecast" and "projection" are often used interchangeably, yet refer to two different categories of prospective financial information. Forecasts are defined as prospective financial information based on the conditions and course of actions that are expected to exist during the forecast period. Projections reflect expected future conditions given one or more hypothetical conditions, answering the question "what would happen if. . . ." *See* AICPA Guide for Prospective Financial Information, AT-C Section 305.09, for formal definitions of forecasts and projections.

2. *Future* lost profits that are discounted back to the date of trial using a risk-adjusted rate; or
3. A combination of *past and future* lost profits.

As already discussed, lost profits are usually computed on an ex post basis.

Measuring Lost Business Value Damages

Economic damages from a loss of business value are expressed as:

Lost business value = *but-for* business value less *actual* business value, where:

- But-for business value is the appraised value of the business, assuming the wrongful act never occurred.
- Actual business value equals the value of the business, taking into account the wrongful act.

Business value is typically computed using one or more of the business valuation approaches (discussed in Chapter 3): income approach, market approach, asset-based approach.

The asset-based approach measures the value of an asset as the estimated cost to reconstruct or replace it with another of like utility. When applied to businesses, this value is typically calculated as the sum of the fair market values of the entity's underlying assets minus liabilities. Unlike the other two approaches, the asset-based approach is usually best suited for holding companies or entities that are being liquidated, since application of this approach often neglects intangible, going concern, or goodwill values. Nevertheless, the asset-based approach may become relevant when a business has been effectively destroyed by a wrongful act and all that remains is the salvage value of its assets.

As discussed earlier, lost business value is, by definition, computed on an ex ante basis.

WHEN TO USE LOST PROFITS, LOST BUSINESS VALUE, OR BOTH

When Is a Loss of Profits Calculation Preferred?

Generally, when a finite period of loss is at issue, a lost profits analysis is best. A typical situation is when a plaintiff suffers an economic loss due to a wrongful act for a finite period, after which damages are fully mitigated. This situation is graphed in Exhibit 32-3.

Another situation that might call for a loss of profits calculation when only a fractional loss of revenue is at issue. For a very large company that suffers a relatively small partial loss of revenue, a lost business value calculation would likely be too complex compared to a lost profits computation.

When Is a Loss of Business Value Calculation Preferred?

If a business is expected to be permanently impacted by a wrongful act, a lost business value calculation is typically the preferred measurement technique. These cases usually fall into one of two categories:

1. The impacted business suffers a permanent loss of revenue and profits but is still operational (as depicted in Exhibit 32-4); or
2. The impacted business is no longer viable and hence suffers a total loss of value (as depicted in Exhibit 32-5).

Exhibit 32-3 Damage Calculation: Finite Loss Period

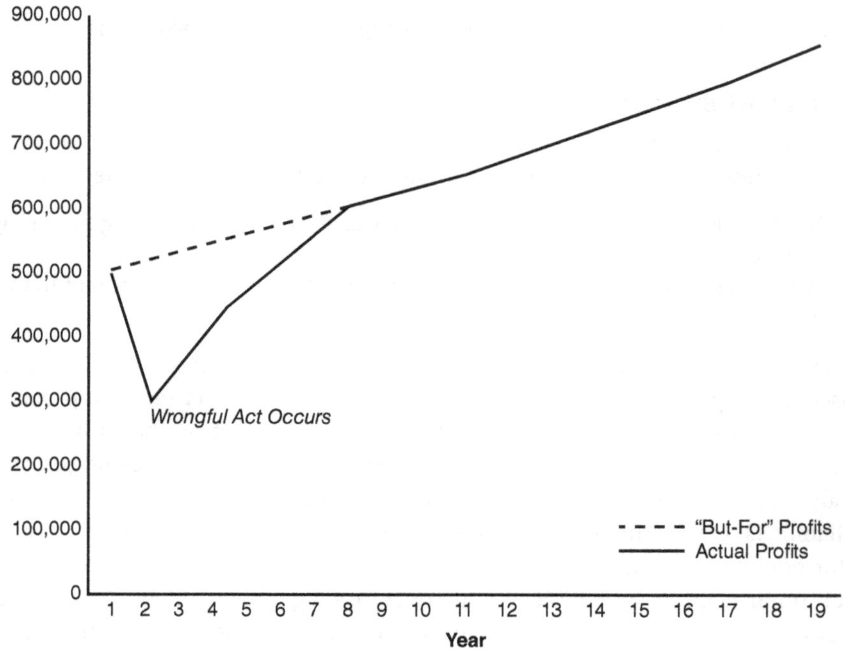

Exhibit 32-4 Damage Calculation: Permanent Loss (Business Still Operational)

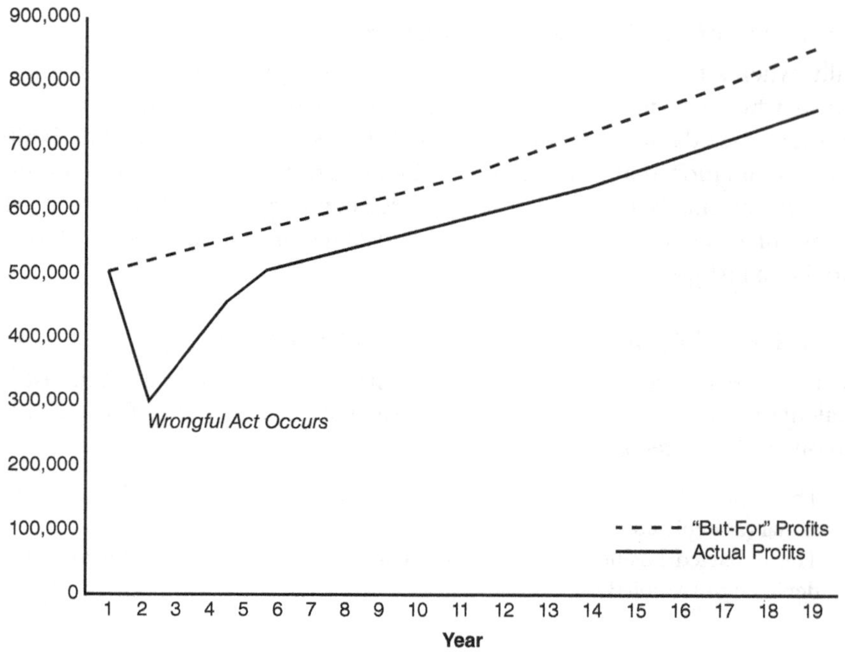

Exhibit 32-5 Damage Calculation: Permanent Loss (Business Destroyed)

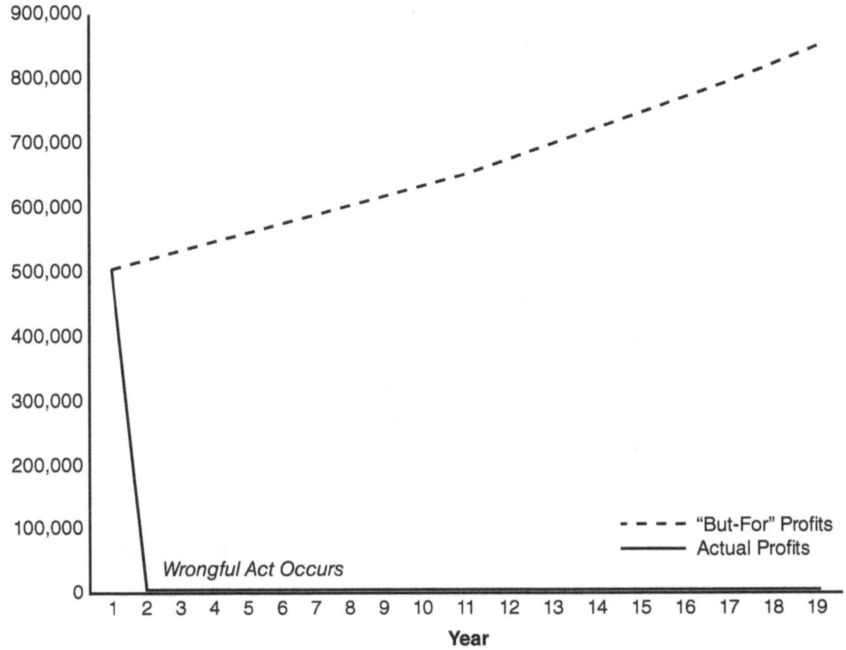

When Should Both Lost Profits and Lost Business Value Calculations Be Used?

Some situations might require both lost profits and lost business value calculations. Consider the "slow death" situation, where the business in question initially suffers a loss of profits due to a wrongful act, yet through mitigation efforts remains operational for a period. Nevertheless, the business eventually succumbs and closes. In such a situation, the damage calculation may involve a calculation of lost profits up to the point where the business permanently closes, at which date the lost business value is computed (see Exhibit 32-6). Care must, of course, be exercised to avoid double counting the loss period so that the lost profits and lost business value calculations do not overlap.

KEY DIFFERENCES BETWEEN LOST PROFITS AND LOST BUSINESS VALUE CALCULATIONS

Business value reflects the present value of future economic benefits, so it would be logical to assume that a loss of profits, if calculated over a long term, would yield the same damages measure as a lost business value calculation. In practice, however, this is not the case. Differences in how these methods are applied can result in significantly different conclusions. These are discussed next.

Exhibit 32-6 Damage Calculation: Permanent Loss (Business Destroyed—"Slow Death")

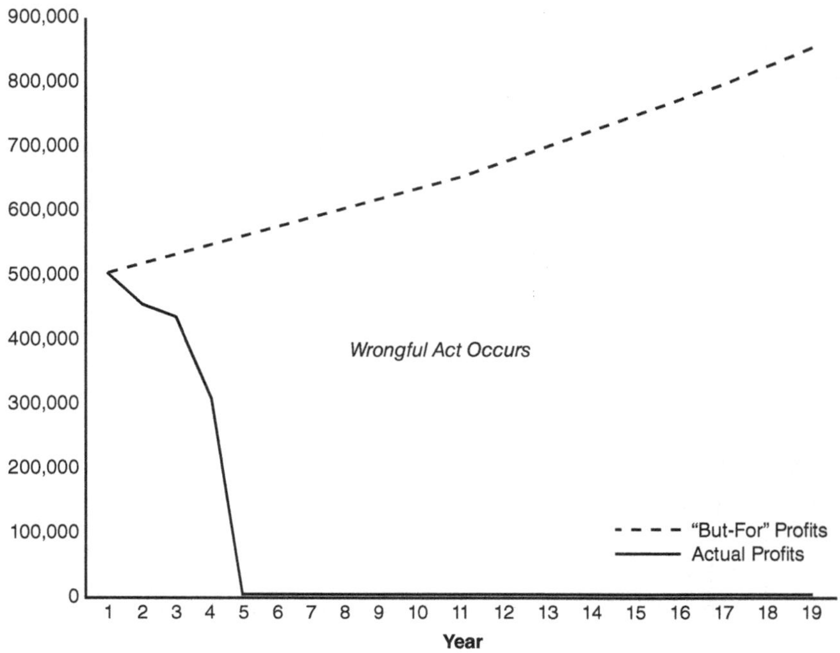

Benefit Stream: Profit versus Cash Flow

The metric for a loss of profits calculation is profit. In contrast, the primary measure of business value under the (analogous) income approach is net cash flow. These two measures can differ substantially. Consider an early-stage business for which substantial investments in working capital and capital equipment are required to support the high anticipated growth. In this situation, net cash flow may differ substantially from profit. The opposite may be true for a mature business with declining sales. Here one can imagine that working capital might actually be returned to the business, making net cash flow higher than profit.

Additionally, a loss of profits calculation is typically concerned with incremental benefit and will omit overhead. In contrast, a lost business value analysis will typically consider all overhead and other non-incremental costs in the loss calculation.

Income Tax Treatment: Pretax versus After Tax

A lost profits calculation typically measures profits on a pretax basis because damage awards are generally taxable. On the other hand, a business typically measures net cash flow on an after-tax basis. Therefore, a lost business value calculation will be based on after-tax profits and net cash flow.

In theory, one might expect that this should not make a big difference, since the discount rate for pre-tax lost profits ought to be adjusted to a pre-tax equivalent, and therefore should be proportionately greater than the after-tax discount rate used to value a business's after-tax net cash flows. In practice, however, these rates do not necessarily line up, and can result in a significant discrepancy between the discounted measures of (pretax) lost profits and (after-tax) lost business value.[5]

Discount Rate Calculation: Incremental versus Entire Business

The discount rate used in valuing a business is typically a cost of capital that reflects the risk of the entire operation. In contrast, a lost profits analysis will utilize a discount rate that only accounts for the risk in a specified lost profits stream, which may have a risk profile quite different from that of the entire operation. For example, suppose a dispute relates to a relatively new line of business that is inherently riskier than the overall business. In this situation, the discount rate used to calculate lost profits may be greater than the discount rate used to value the entire business. Conversely, if the lost profit stream is less risky than that of the rest of the business, the discount rate used to calculate lost profits would logically be less than the one used to value the business as a whole. The use of different discount rates can result in materially different damage measures.

Furthermore, while the discount rate used in a lost business value analysis is typically tied to the discount rate for equity capital or a weighted average cost of capital (WACC, reflecting the overall rate of return for both equity and debt capital), the discount rate used to compute the present value of lost profits may be based on other factors, such as the cost of borrowing, opportunity costs, or even a risk-free rate (if profits are adjusted to be on a certainty-equivalent basis). These differences in discount rate selection can also result in a discrepancy between damages measured via lost profits versus lost business value.

Use of Hindsight: Ex Ante versus Ex Post

As discussed earlier, a business valuation is typically performed as an ex ante analysis that considers only what is known or knowable to a hypothetical investor as of that point in time—that is, hindsight is not allowed. This assumption can result in a significantly different damage conclusion than in an ex post lost profits calculation, where the but-for and actual profits fully consider what has occurred up to the date of trial.

An ex post analysis might also mean use of a lower (less risky) discount rate, since there might be less uncertainty about a projection that takes into consideration all information up to the date of trial. This too could result in a greater lost profits calculation compared to lost business value.

Standard of Value/Investor Perspective: Actual versus Hypothetical Investor

The standard of value and related valuation discounts may also result in a divergence between damages measured by lost business value and lost profits. For example, a typical standard of value for a business valuation is fair market value. This standard implies a hypothetical investor whose expectations and risk tolerance may differ from

5. *See* Chapter 19, "Discount Rates in Theory," *in* Everett P. Harry III & Jeffrey H. Kinrich, Lost Profits Damages: Principles, Methods and Applications 548–49 (2d ed. 2022) (methodology for converting an after-tax discount rate to its pretax equivalent).

the current owner of the business in question, and who might not anticipate synergies currently enjoyed.

Additionally, the fair market value standard typically considers the marketability of the subject business, either through application of a discount for lack of marketability or as implied by a market-based valuation multiple. In contrast, a lost profits calculation typically would not consider such expectations or potential marketability issues. Thus, depending on the working definition of business value used, the standard of value and valuation discounts could result in a different damage measurement obtained through a lost business value analysis compared to that yielded by a lost profits calculation.

Present Value Calculations: Carrying Forward versus Discounting Back

Lost profits and lost business value calculations may yield different damage measures depending on factors related to timing and discounting to present value. For example, a lost business value calculation performed as of the date of the wrongful action will typically discount all cash flows to that date of value, and then bring the loss calculation current (to the trial date) using statutory prejudgment interest. As statutory interest rates are usually much lower than the discount rates used to value businesses, this serves to understate damages compared to a lost profits analysis that merely discounts future losses to the trial date. If the time between the date of the wrongful act and the date of trial is substantial, treatment of discounting can result in a significant difference in damage conclusions.

Exhibit 32-7 summarizes the key differences between lost profits and lost business value calculations.

Exhibit 32-7 Summary of Key Differences between Lost Profits and Lost Business Value Damage Calculations

Assumption	Lost Profits	Lost Business Value
Benefit Stream	Profit	Cash Flow
Use of Hindsight	Ex Post	Ex Ante
Damage Period	Finite	Indefinite (business destroyed or permanently impaired)
Income Tax Treatment	Pre-Tax	After-Tax
Discount Rate	Incremental	Overall Business
Standard of Value/Investor Perspective	Investor-Specific	Hypothetical Investor
Present Value Calculations	Amounts Are Carried Forward or Discounted to Date of Trial	Amounts Are Discounted Back to Date of Injury, Then Carried Forward to Date of Trial

WHEN LOST PROFITS MIGHT BE GREATER THAN LOST BUSINESS VALUE DAMAGES

One might think that the value of the business prior to the wrongful act would be the upper limit on the value of lost profits. However, that is not necessarily true. Examples of ways a calculation of lost profits might be greater than a lost business value calculation are listed here.

- **Use of hindsight.** If a lost business value calculation does not consider a significant increase in "but-for" cash flows that were not known or knowable at the date of the wrongful act, lost profits that incorporate actual results may exceed total business value computed as of the valuation date.
- **Income tax treatment.** A (pretax) lost profits calculation can exceed lost business value (based on an after-tax benefit stream) if the (pretax) discount rate used to compute lost profits is not adequately *grossed up* (i.e., adjusted to pretax equivalent; see Chapter 7) relative to the corresponding (after-tax) discount rate used to compute business value.
- **Discount rate.** The discount rate used to compute lost profits might be much lower than the overall rate used to value the business.
- **Standard of value/investor perspective.** A lost profits calculation might consider plaintiff-specific synergies that a business valuation performed under the fair market value standard would not. In such a case, lost profits may exceed lost business value. Furthermore, a lost business value calculation might include discounts for lack of marketability and other adjustments not considered in a lost profits calculation, further depressing lost business value relative to lost profits.
- **Present value calculations.** If a business is valued as of the date of a wrongful act and then carried forward to the trial date using prejudgment interest, lost business value may be less than lost profits if the discount rate used to value the business is significantly greater than the prejudgment interest rate used to bring the value to the present.
- **Damages relating to incrementally profitable revenue stream.** In certain situations, a company might be unprofitable or minimally profitable overall, yet can still claim damages for the loss to an incrementally profitable revenue stream. Under these circumstances, the value of lost profits will likely exceed overall business value.

Additionally, if the cost of mitigation efforts exceeds the potential loss of business value, lost profits might exceed the total value of the subject business. Most courts would justifiably review such mitigation expenses with a critical eye. For example, it would not appear reasonable to spend $1 million to save a $250,000 business. Nevertheless, delays, uncertainty, and other circumstances might justify prolonged good faith mitigation expenses even if a business ultimately fails. Under such circumstances, lost profits can exceed business value.

Recognizing the preceding, a lost profits calculation that exceeds the value of plaintiff's business may still be considered a "reg flag" and at the minimum require a trier of fact to question the damages conclusion.

USING THE DAMAGES EXPERT

Depending on the nature and timeline of the litigation, the role of a damages expert may include the following:

- **Framing economic issues.** The expert can assist the attorney in reconciling facts and legal theories, and in assessing the economic substance of damage claims.
- **Discovery assistance.** The expert can identify documents required to perform an analysis, ensure relevant documents are obtained, and assist in the development of questions to ask of key individuals.

- **Causation analysis.** The expert may be required to assess the extent to which other factors (e.g., the economy or new competitors) may have had a material impact on the plaintiff during the damage period.
- **Damage calculation.** The expert will provide calculations of lost earnings, lost business value, or both.
- **Expert testimony.** Testimony can take place in deposition, trial, mediation, or arbitration.
- **Rebuttal testimony.** A retained expert will often be required to review and rebut an opposing expert's analysis of damages.

SUMMARY

This chapter discusses valuation issues in the context of lost profits damages matters. Issues addressed included key concepts and considerations in performing a calculation of lost profits or lost business value, how lost profits and lost business value damages are calculated, and key differences in the calculations.

The specific circumstances of a case, including fact patterns and legal considerations, suggest which technique is most appropriate, or if some combination is required. Although theoretically similar, the practical application of these methodologies—including consideration of ex ante versus ex post computations—can result in significantly different damage conclusions, including the counterintuitive result where a lost profits calculation exceeds total business value.

REFERENCES FOR LOST PROFITS DAMAGES

Harry, Everett P. III and Jeffrey H. Kinrich. 2022. *Lost Profits Damages: Principles, Methods and Applications* 2nd ed. (Ventnor City, NJ: Valuation Products and Services, LLC.).

Fannon, Nancy J. ed. 2023.*The Comprehensive Guide to Lost Profits Damages for Experts and Attorneys* 4th ed. (Portland OR: Business Valuation Resources LLC).

CHAPTER 33

Appraisal Reports

Jay E. Fishman, FASA, FRICS and Jeffrey S. Tarbell, ASA, CFA

INTRODUCTION[1]

In this chapter you will learn about:

- Different types of appraisal reports
- Differences between an appraisal report and a restricted appraisal report
- Typical components of a comprehensive appraisal report
- Oral appraisal reports

The conclusions of a business valuation are expressed in an appraisal report, and such reports may vary greatly in the level of detail they present. In some cases, the appraisal report may consist of an oral presentation to the client. And in other cases, the report may be expressed in a written document consisting of as many as hundreds of pages of narrative and exhibits.

Under The Appraisal Foundation's *Uniform Standards of Professional Appraisal Practice* (USPAP) the appraiser has two reporting options for written reports: an appraisal report or a restricted appraisal report.[2] In addition, professional organizations have issued business valuation standards. Specifically, the American Society of Appraisers (ASA), the American Institute of Certified Public Accountants (AICPA), and the National Association of Certified Valuators and Analysts (NACVA) have developed their own reporting standards (and terminology) which provide for different levels of report detail.[3] The following sections provide an overview of the different types of reports a reader may see.

COMPREHENSIVE APPRAISAL REPORTS

Each of the three major appraisal standards provides for a form of "comprehensive" business appraisal report. USPAP provides for an appraisal report, ASA *Business Valuation Standards* refers to a "Comprehensive Written Business Valuation Report," and the AICPA refers to a "Detailed Report."

1. The authors would like to thank Nicholas J. Mastracchio, Jr., PhD, CPA, Associate Professor, University of South Florida, Sarasota-Manatee Campus, for his contribution to the prior editions of this chapter.

2. USPAP Standards Rules 10.

3. NACVA publishes charts comparing standards, including reporting standards. Domestic standards (ASA, USPAP, NACVA, AICPA) are compared in a chart available at https://www.nacva.com/Files/DomesticStandardsChart_2023_Final.pdf. In addition, several international organizations issue standards, including reporting standards. These are discussed in Chapter 37, "Business Valuation Standards and Credentials."

The following paragraphs discuss the typical elements of a comprehensive-style report and the data and information commonly included therein.

Introduction

This section of the appraisal report should provide sufficient information to enable the reader to understand the valuation engagement and includes, at a minimum:

Identity of the client and other intended users. The report should clearly disclose the identity of the client and any other intended users.[4] Under USPAP, the client is always an intended user, but the report may designate other intended users as well.

Note: A party who might receive or obtain a copy of the appraisal report is not an intended user unless identified as such in the report.

Intended use of the valuation. The reader needs to know the intended use of the valuation to understand the standard of value used and other decisions made by the appraiser.

What is being valued. This section identifies whether an entire company or a partial interest is being valued. The subject of the appraisal is commonly referred to as the "subject interest."

Effective (valuation) date. The date of the valuation, also known as the effective date, must be identified. This is the specific point in time at which the conclusion of value applies. Generally, the appraiser should base the appraisal only on information that is available or could have become known at the date of the valuation. However, statistical information released after this date that compiles information prior and up to this date usually is permitted.

Degree of control of the subject interest. If the valuation is of a partial interest, the degree of control is important in normalization decisions, lack of control discounts, and/or control premium considerations. The report discloses the subject interest and the distribution of the remaining interests in order to allow the reader to appreciate the governance environment.

Marketability of the subject interest. The size of the company and its ability to go public, along with any restrictions by government regulation, supplier restrictions, or shareholder agreements, are provided for the reader to understand the appraiser's consideration of any lack of marketability discount.

Standard of value being utilized. The appraisal report must state the standard of value (e.g., fair market value, fair value) used in the analysis. USPAP also requires the appraisal report to define the standard of value and cite the source of that definition.

Premise of value being utilized. The appraisal report must state the premise of value (e.g., going concern value, liquidation value) used in the analysis. USPAP also requires the appraisal report to define the premise of value and cite the source of that definition.

4. The Appraisal Found., 2024 USPAP Guide and Reference Manual *Advisory Opinion 36*, line 30, states "In instances where the client wishes to remain anonymous, the appraiser must still document the client's identity in the workfile but may omit the client's identity in the appraisal or appraisal review report . . . . When the client's identity has been withheld from the report, the report must state that the client's identity has been withheld at the client's request."

Scope of work. Any scope limitations experienced in conducting the appraisal and the appraiser's assessment of the consequences on the opinion are disclosed.

Specialists. If the appraiser relied on the work of any specialists, the appraisal report describes their work and explains how it is incorporated in the analysis. (See discussion in the section "Reliance on Experts" in Chapter 9.)

Hypothetical conditions or extraordinary assumptions used. If the appraiser relied on hypothetical conditions[5] or extraordinary assumptions,[6] they should be disclosed in the report.

Professional standards followed. Frequently used standards include USPAP as well as standards published by organizations such as ASA, AICPA, and NACVA. (Standards are discussed in Chapter 37, "Business Valuation Standards and Credentials.")

Any other information that assists the intended user(s) of the report in understanding the engagement should be included in the introduction.

Sources of Information

This section of the report discloses the extent of the appraiser's research and typically includes the following:

Persons interviewed and extent to which the facilities were visited. It is considered a best practice for the appraiser to have interviewed individuals knowledgeable about the business. In this case, the report should identify the names and positions of those interviewed. If the appraiser also visited the company's facilities (also a best practice when possible), the report should identify which facilities are visited.

Financial information. The company's financial statements and/or income tax returns should be discussed. If the company has financial statements prepared by an independent certified public accountant, there will normally be a cover letter describing whether those financial statements were compiled, reviewed, or audited. If no financial statements were available, the report should discuss the company's tax returns, at a minimum. If the valuation firm is associated with the preparation of those financial statements or tax returns, that also should be disclosed. The financial information referred to in the report may have been acquired from or reconciled with income tax returns. If so, the income tax returns, and whether they are prepared internally or by an outside professional, should be noted.

Economic conditions. The report should discuss the general economic conditions that affect the company including the risks associated with the company being valued. The sources, both government and private, should be identified in the report.

Industry data. The specific attributes of the industry in which the company operates should be researched by the appraiser. The data obtained and its relevance should be discussed here.

---

5. "Hypothetical Condition" is defined as: a condition directly related to specific assignment, which is contrary to what is known by the appraiser to exist on the effective date of the assignment results but is used for the purpose of analysis. The Appraisal Found., *Definitions*, *Uniform Standards of Professional Appraisal Practice* 4 (2024 ed.).

6. *Id.* "Extraordinary assumption" is defined as: an assignment-specific assumption as of the effective date regarding certain uncertain information used in an analysis which, if found false, could alter the appraiser's opinions or conclusions.

Other empirical information. There may be information available in industry publications regarding the segment of the industry that the company specializes in, for instance, information on the specific products and possible substitute products or other empirical information the appraiser finds meaningful. Other empirical information also includes sources of information for guideline public companies, guideline transactions, and cost of capital data.

Qualitative Analysis of the Company

The valuation report should include a description of the company along with a qualitative analysis discussion of the nature and history of the business and the appraiser's assessment of the company's strengths, weaknesses, opportunities, and threats (commonly referred to a SWOT analysis). This analysis is useful in the process of estimating the appropriate discount rate or capitalization rate in the income approach. The qualitative analysis section in a report may include the following sections:

Background and history. The history of the company including the operational changes over the years and the ownership description and changes are discussed here. The organizational structure of the company and management depth also should be discussed.

Product and services. This section discusses the main business activities that generate the company's revenues and cash flows.

Demographics. This section discloses the company's geographical markets and their economic status.

Customers and suppliers. This section discusses the bargaining power of the company relative to its customers and suppliers. This may include the company's risk of reliance on a small number of customers or suppliers.

Threat of new entrants. The ability of new companies to enter the company's business field is a factor of risk and may be discussed in the report.

Technological risk. An analysis of the technological risk the company is facing may be discussed if it is significant to the operations.

Environmental risks. Although most reports will typically contain a disclaimer on environmental compliance, environmental risks should be considered, if significant to the operations.

Regulatory risks. If a relevant factor for the business, the current and potential regulatory environment should be discussed.

Risk of changing preferences. Trends in products (e.g., preference for low-fat foods, natural fabrics in clothing, casual dress at more formal occasions) may have an impact for the company and, if so, should be discussed.

Global risk. Imports of products and outsourcing of services may have an impact on the company and should be assessed and disclosed if necessary.

Strategic plans. Management's future plans for the company, including critical success factors, should be discussed to fully understand the forecast and risks. Even in cases where management does not prepare a formal strategic plan, the business appraiser should describe the plans the owner(s) and management have for dealing with competitive pressures.

Human resources. The intellectual value of the workforce skills established in the company in many cases is a factor that affects risk and may need discussion.

Subject Ownership Interest

If the valuation subject is a partial ownership interest in the company, the company's capital structure, and the impact on the interest being valued should be discussed. Additionally, the report should discuss any restrictions on the sale of the subject interest or other material terms of any shareholder or other agreements.

Quantitative Analysis

The historical financial data of the company is analyzed in a valuation to determine trends in profitability, financial health, and comparison with industry statistics. The report will typically include the following information, recent trends, and an analysis and discussion of each:

Liquidity ratios. These ratios measure the ability of the company to meet current obligations with cash or assets that can quickly be turned into cash.

Profitability ratios. These ratios measure the ability of the company to generate net income.

Activity ratios. These ratios measure how efficiently the company manages its resources.

Leverage ratios. These ratios measure the degree the company relies on debt financing and the ability to survive a downturn in profitability.

Sales and profit trends. The relative size (e.g., sales, profits), trends, and performance (e.g., growth) of the subject company are presented and typically compared to guideline public companies and industry trends and reconciled with any forecasts used in the valuation.

Normalization and Control Adjustments

The purpose of the normalization adjustments is to make the historical results reflect amounts that approximate economic reality for valuation purposes. As discussed in Chapter 15, one can categorize financial statement adjustments as follows:

Normalization adjustments. Adjustments reflecting unusual or nonrecurring items (i.e., items that would not be expected to reoccur in the normal course of business), which would generally be made for all valuation purposes.

Personal expenses and related-party transactions. Transactions between the owners and the company that may be personal expenses and/or may not be at arm's length (i.e., do not reflect market rates); to the extent that they are not at arm's length and could be eliminated by the holder of the subject interest.

Control adjustments. Adjustments that a typical control owner could influence, usually to assess the economic income that would potentially be available to a controlling ownership interest; generally made only if valuing a controlling ownership interest.

Nonoperating adjustments. Nonoperating items should be adjusted from the balance sheet and/or income statement and treated separately for valuation purposes.

Accounting basis adjustments. Converting cash-basis financial statements to an accrual-basis[7] based equivalent.

---

7. The goal is for the appraiser to adjust cash basis or income tax basis financial statements to Generally Accepted Accounting Principles (GAAP) for purposes of comparability to statements of guideline public companies.

The normalization adjustments are based on the financial analysis previously conducted and consideration of the ownership interest being valued.

Valuation Approaches and Methods Considered

The report should provide sufficient information for the reader to determine what valuation methodologies are considered by the appraiser, including both those that are used and those that are rejected. The basic categories of methodology include:

Income approach. The basic principle is that a business is worth the present value of its future benefits. One of the two following methods usually is used:

- **Capitalization of cash flow.** Most business appraisers use net cash flow as the measure of economic income rather than income as reported in financial statements. It is a single (usually normalized) number divided by a capitalization rate.
- **Discounted cash flow.** This method projects annual cash flow for a number of years and then determines a value at the end of the discrete forecast period, referred to as a terminal value, when the business's cash flows have stabilized.

Market approach. Another approach that can be persuasive compares the subject interest at hand to other known transactions. Potential methods include the following:

- **Sales of ownership interest in the same company.** The appraiser's explanation of the circumstances of any recent transactions in the subject company stock is included here.
- **Sale of ownership interest in similar companies.** Sales of entire companies or controlling interests in companies. Some would divide this into two subcategories: companies that were publicly traded before the transaction and companies that were closely held before the transaction. In some cases, the appraiser may be able to obtain data on transactions for interests in similar closely held companies.
- **Guideline public companies.** Often the company operates in an industry where there are publicly traded companies. If so, the appraiser will discuss the possibility of utilizing selected publicly traded company data to derive valuation multiples to value the closely held company.

Note: While use of rules of thumb (pricing multiples) is not recommended for business valuation, in the instance when a rule of thumb is widely used and recognized for an industry, they can be useful to estimate a "ballpark" range of value, or as a "check" on values obtained from traditional business valuation methods.

Asset-based approach. The asset-based approach should be considered, particularly when there is significant capital investment or the entity holds assets (or investments). The premises of value in the asset-based approach are as follows:

- **Assets in use.** This premise of value and resulting method considers the value of the assets in a going concern.
- **Liquidating value.** This premise of value and resulting method considers the liquidation of the assets in either a forced or orderly manner.

Valuation Approaches and Methods Used

This section of the valuation report provides a detailed discussion of the valuation methods used in reaching an opinion of value.

Income approach. The selection of which method is used under the income approach is explained here. The income approach can be on an invested capital basis or on an equity basis.

- **Definition of measure of economic income used.** The report should explain what is used as a measure of future benefits. This may be pretax or after-tax net income or net cash flow or some other measure the appraiser deems appropriate.
- **Appropriate discount and capitalization rates.** The report should explain the derivation of the discount and capitalization rates used. This may be an explanation of the buildup method, the capital asset pricing model or modified capital asset pricing model, the weighted average cost of capital, or other methods of estimating the discount rate. The report should explain how the data is obtained and how the discount and capitalization rates are estimated.

Market approach. The selection of which method(s) used under the market approach is explained here. The market approach can be on an invested capital basis or on an equity basis.

- **Sales of ownership interest in the same company.** The report should discuss the size of ownership percentage, the timing of the transactions, the extent that the transactions are utilizing the same standard of value, and the changes in the company since the transactions occurred; all will influence the relevance of these types of transactions.
- **Sale of ownership interest in similar companies.** If the appraiser decides the information gathered on sales of entire companies or controlling interests in companies is worth consideration, it should be discussed here.
- **Guideline public companies.** If multiples derived from guideline public companies are used, the following information will be presented:
  - **Value being estimated.** Depending on the comparison of the subject company with the guideline public company, and the nature of the valuation, the appraiser will select either the total invested capital value of the firm, including debt, or the equity value, or both.
  - **Profile of the guideline public companies.** The selection criteria used to identify these companies and descriptions of the companies will be provided to assess the comparability of the company in risk, size, and diversity. Financial data and ratios should be provided and compared with the company being valued.
  - **Multiples considered.** The appraiser will typically consider several multiples in determining what the indicators of value are. These include sales, book value, net income, net income before tax, cash flow, earnings before interest and taxes, and earnings before interest, taxes, depreciation, and amortization. The report should discuss which indicators are selected and why.
  - **Adjustment of the multiples.** When the appraiser decides that the multiples should be adjusted to reflect the differences between the subject business and the guideline public companies, an explanation of the adjustments should be provided.

Asset-based approach. The selection of which method to use under the asset-based approach is explained here.

- **Assets in use.** The use of the asset value is typically not very persuasive as it does not consider the value of any goodwill of the company. It may be provided by the business appraiser to indicate a minimum floor value or be a value used if, in fact, there is no goodwill.
- **Liquidating value.** If the company is in or is expected to be in liquidation, the value will be the liquidating value of the assets, and the business appraiser will explain the values determined in this section.

Valuation Adjustments

Often the valuation, to this point, is of the entity without adjustment for the characteristics of the specific ownership interest being valued. At this point, the report should discuss any adjustments applied in order to arrive at the value of the subject interest. Such adjustments may result from factors including the following:

Shareholder agreements. The report should discuss restrictions on control (e.g., ability of noncontrolling owners to select members of the board of directors, percentage ownership approvals for certain actions, restrictions on transferability) contained in either the articles of incorporation, the bylaws, or in a separate shareholder agreement.

Discount for lack of control. If the interest being valued is a noncontrolling interest, the report should discuss any discount applied for this factor.

Discount for lack of marketability. The appraiser will decide the extent the value should be reduced because the interest does not benefit from liquidity in the form of dividends or distributions and is not readily marketable.

Key person discount. In some circumstances, the loss of an owner who is vital to the business may produce a discount. If so, the appraiser should discuss the discount taken and rationale thereof.

Tax on trapped in capital gains. If the appraiser determines that a reduction in value needs to be made because the basis in the assets is lower than their fair market value, the calculation of the reduction should be provided here.

Control premium. If the interest is a controlling ownership interest, the business appraiser may decide that a control premium should be applied. If so, the rationale for the premium and its quantification should be discussed in this section.

Excess or Deficient Operating Assets

If there are excess (i.e., surplus) operating assets, the report should discuss additions to the value. Conversely, if there are deficiencies that need to be adjusted for, the business appraiser should discuss reductions to the value.

Nonoperating Items

If there are assets or liabilities that are not necessary to the operations, the appraiser would have taken them out of consideration in the normalization process. At this point, the appraiser would explain how they affect the value of the company.

Certification of the Appraiser Responsible for the Opinion

The report should include a certification and the signature of the appraiser taking responsibility for the opinion of value and the entire appraisal report. This may be accomplished in this section or in other places in the report. The certification should include the following:

Assumptions and limiting conditions. The report should provide what assumptions and limitations exist. This may appear in an appendix with reference in the main report.

Reliability of the sources. The report should acknowledge that the sources used are deemed reliable and disclose whether any independent validation is performed.

Restricted use. Any restrictions on the use of the report should be noted.

Fee arrangement. The report should disclose whether the appraiser's fee is independent of the conclusions (opinions of value require that the fee is independent of the conclusions; however, there are certain other services which may appropriately have a contingent fee).

Outside specialist. If the appraiser used an outside specialist, this should be disclosed along with the degree of responsibility the appraiser is taking for the specialist's work.

Updates. Unless agreed to otherwise with the client, the business appraiser will typically disclaim any responsibility to update the report.

Prior work. USPAP requires the appraiser to disclose whether the appraiser has performed any valuation services regarding the property that is the subject of the report during the three-year period prior to the agreement to perform the valuation.

Conclusion of Value

The report will typically have a section either near the front or at the back (or both) that will provide the conclusion of value.

Qualifications of the Appraiser

A summary of the background and qualifications of the appraiser should be provided.

SUMMARY LEVEL REPORTS

USPAP provides two reporting options for a appraiser: an appraisal report and a restricted appraisal report. A restricted appraisal report may be provided when the client is the only intended user, or when the additional intended users are identified by name. In a restricted appraisal report, the appraiser only needs to state (as opposed to summarize) facts and findings and can limit the explanations.[8]

CALCULATION REPORT

The appraiser may be engaged to perform specific calculations for a client, which are then expressed in a calculation report. Because the engagement scope is limited to the calculations requested, under the AICPA standards, reporting on the results of agreed upon calculations is not considered an opinion of value. Under USPAP and its terminology (with definitions that sometimes differ from those of AICPA standards), a calculation is still considered an opinion of value, but one completed under a restricted scope of work, which must be disclosed.

ORAL REPORT

USPAP and the AICPA standards also address requirements for an oral report. When the appraiser takes on the role of a testifying expert, their report, in many cases, may be delivered orally. However, care should be taken to minimize the risk of misunderstanding. The oral presentation should include all the information the appraiser believes necessary to adequately provide information regarding the scope, assumptions, limitations, and results of the engagement.

8. 2024 USPAP Guide and Reference Manual, *supra* note 4, *Advisory Opinion 38*.

SUMMARY

There are several types of valuation reports. An example of a detailed report is the Comprehensive Written Business Valuation Report as defined in the ASA's *Business Valuation Standards*. It discloses sufficient information for the reader to understand the data gathered, the analysis and rationale used, and how the estimate of value is determined. However, appraisers often prepare appraisal reports that are of a more summary nature. An oral report also may be rendered.

Readers seeking further guidance on report content should refer to USPAP Standards Rule 10-2, Content of a Business Appraisal Report; ASA BVS-VIII, Comprehensive Written Business Valuation Report; and AICPA VS100, paragraph 48, describing a detailed report, a summary report, and a calculation report.

REFERENCES FOR APPRAISAL REPORTS

Hitchner, James R. 2017. "Report Writing." In *Financial Valuation: Applications and Models*, 4th ed. Chap. 11, 495–582 (Hoboken, NJ: John Wiley & Sons).

Laro, David and Shannon P. Pratt. 2011. "Business Appraisal Reports." In *Business Valuation and Federal Taxes: Procedures, Law and Perspective*, 2nd ed. Chap. 25, 399–419 (Hoboken, NJ: John Wiley & Sons).

Pratt, Shannon P. and ASA Educational Foundation. 2022. "Reviewing a Business Valuation Report." In *Shannon Pratt's Valuing a Business: The Analysis and Appraisal of Closely Held Businesses*, 6th ed. Chap. 24, 553–65 (New York: McGraw-Hill).

The Appraisal Foundation. 2023. "Understanding the Differences: Conclusion of Value vs. Value Calculations." In *Valuation Brief 2023-1.*

Trugman, Gary. 2022. "The Valuation Report." In *Understanding Business Valuation*, 6th ed. Chap. 17, 637–77 (Portland, OR: Business Valuation Resources).

CHAPTER 34

Checklist for Reviewing a Business Valuation Report

Timothy R. Lee, ASA and Lucas M. Parris, ASA, CFA

INTRODUCTION

This chapter is free from copyright restrictions. Readers are free to make copies of it to use as worksheets when reviewing reports of their own appraisers and/or opposing appraisers. Copies also may be distributed to others—attorneys, clients, judges, and so on.

The checklist is organized in sequence with the content typically contained in most valuation reports, although the order of presentation may vary by the type of report and its author.

When comparing one valuation report with another, it might be convenient to place these sheets side by side for an item-by-item comparison. This checklist is applicable to a Comprehensive Written Business Valuation Report, but also may be used for more concise report formats. The chapter references are provided to direct the reader to specific chapters in this book that provide additional detail.

CREDENTIALS OF REPORT PREPARER (CHAPTER 37)

Even though this usually is in an appendix in the back of a report, most attorneys like to review it first so that they can understand the background and qualifications of the business appraiser who prepared the report.

Academic Degrees

- ❏ PhD Doctor of Philosophy
- ❏ DBA Doctor of Business Administration
- ❏ MS Master of Science
- ❏ MBA Master of Business Administration
- ❏ BS Bachelor of Science
- ❏ BA Bachelor of Arts
- ❏ Other ________________________

Professional Designations (See Chapter 37 for explanations of the various business valuation standards, professional organizations, and their respective credentials/designations)

- ❑ ASA — Accredited Senior Appraiser
- ❑ FASA — Fellow of the ASA
- ❑ AM — Accredited Member of the American Society of Appraisers
- ❑ ARM — Appraisal Review and Management
- ❑ CBV — Certified Business Appraiser (credential sunset in 2016)
- ❑ MCBA — Master Certified Business Appraiser (credential sunset in 2016)
- ❑ ABAR — Accredited in Business Appraisal Review
- ❑ CPA/ABV — Certified Public Accountant/Accredited in Business Valuation
- ❑ CPA/CFF — Certified Public Accountant/Certified in Financial Forensics
- ❑ CVA — Certified Valuation Analyst
- ❑ CFA — Chartered Financial Analyst
- ❑ CBV — Certified Business Valuer (Canada) Chartered Business Valuator (Canada)
- ❑ MRICS — Member of the Royal Institution of Chartered Surveyors
- ❑ FRICS — Fellow of the Royal Institution of Chartered Surveyors
- ❑ Other ______________________________

REPORT INTRODUCTION (CHAPTERS 1 AND 2)

Name of entity (and d/b/a if applicable)

____

State of incorporation or registration

____

Type of entity (e.g., C corp, S corp, LLC, limited/general partnership, etc.)

____

Ownership interest to be appraised (if less than 100 percent, specify exact percentage or number of shares; if more than one class of ownership, e.g., common/preferred, voting/nonvoting, should have a diagram showing the capitalization)

____

Relevant dates: effective valuation date(s) and date of report issuance

____

Standard (definition) of value (e.g., fair market value, fair value, intrinsic value; see Chapter 1)

___

Sources of authority for the standard of value (e.g., federal or state statute, revenue ruling, company articles/bylaws, buy-sell agreement, other)

___

Was the stated standard of value appropriate for the situation?

___

What is the level of value (e.g., control, marketable minority, nonmarketable minority; see Chapter 2) in the valuation?

___

What is the purpose of valuation (e.g., gift/estate tax, marital dissolution, shareholder transaction, other)?

___

Who is the client for the appraisal?

___

Who (what entity) performed the appraisal?

___

ECONOMIC ANALYSIS (CHAPTER 17)

Are the factors and analysis relevant to the subject company (versus boilerplate)?

___

Is the analysis/outlook as of the effective date (e.g., contemporaneous or dated)?

___

INDUSTRY ANALYSIS (CHAPTER 17)

Are the factors and analysis relevant to the subject company (versus boilerplate)?

___

Is the analysis/outlook as of the effective date (e.g., contemporaneous or dated)?

___

INTERVIEWS AND SITE VISITS (CHAPTER 5)

Nature of the interviews and/or site visits (e.g., in-person, teleconference, video)

___

Names/positions of individuals interviewed

If no interviews or site visits were conducted, is there an explanation of why not (e.g., limitations, impracticality, passage of time, etc.)?

FINANCIAL STATEMENT ADJUSTMENTS (CHAPTER 15)

Are the company's historical financial statements presented in the report or in exhibits with sufficient detail and history to review for possible adjustments (if missing, is there an explanation for their absence)?

Is there an adequate explanation of what adjustments were made to the company's financial statements or an explanation of why none were necessary?

If the market approach was used, is there an adequate explanation of any financial statement adjustments made to the guideline company statements or an explanation of why none were necessary?

FINANCIAL STATEMENT ANALYSIS (CHAPTER 16)

Is financial statement analysis performed on adjusted or pre-adjusted statements (it normally should be performed on statements after adjustments)?

Are the company's financial ratios, income statement, balance sheet, and so on, compared with themselves over time to identify trends?

Are the company's financial ratios compared with those of peers in the same industry or with selected ratios of guideline companies?

Are the subject company's relative strengths and weaknesses reflected in the valuation multiples and/or discount rates employed in the valuation?

REASONABLE COMPENSATION (CHAPTER 13)

If an adjustment for reasonable owner/manager compensation was made, was it addressed adequately?

What are the sources of information used for any compensation adjustments (e.g., name of source, date, comparability by industry or company size, other)?

____

If no adjustment for reasonable owner/manager compensation was made, is there an explanation of why none was necessary?

____

DISCOUNTS AND PREMIUMS (CHAPTER 18)

Does the subject valuation include a control premium, and if so, what is it (%)?

____

What data, models, and/or rationale were used to quantify the control premium, and are they adequately cited, explained, and applied?

____

Does the subject valuation include a discount for lack of control (sometimes called a minority discount), and if so, what is it (%)?

____

What data, models, and/or rationale were used to quantify the discount for lack of control, and are they adequately cited, explained, and applied?

____

Does the subject valuation include a discount for lack of marketability, and if so, what is it (%)?

____

What data, models, and/or rationale were used to quantify the discount for lack of marketability, and are they adequately cited, explained, and applied?

____

Does the subject valuation include any other premiums or discounts? Are they adequately cited, explained, and applied?

____

VALUATION METHODS USED (CHAPTER 3)

Income Approach (Chapters 6 and 7)

❑ Discounted cash flow
❑ Capitalization of cash flow
❑ Other ____________________

Market Approach (Chapter 8)

- ❑ Guideline public company method
- ❑ Guideline transactions method
- ❑ Past transactions method
- ❑ Rules of thumb
- ❑ Other ______________________

Asset-Based Approach (Chapters 9 and 10)

- ❑ Adjusted net asset value
- ❑ Excess earnings method
- ❑ Other __________________

INCOME APPROACH (CHAPTERS 6 AND 7)

Discounted Cash Flow Method

What is the source of the forecasts (e.g., management-prepared, appraiser-prepared, industry forecasts, etc.)?

____

When were the forecasts prepared (e.g., contemporaneous with the valuation, historical, subsequent to the valuation date, etc.)?

____

Potential items for additional review and/or adjustment (see additional discussion of these items in Chapter 15):

- ❑ Management/owner compensation
- ❑ Rent
- ❑ Nonrecurring items
- ❑ Discontinued items
- ❑ Inventory accounting
- ❑ Depreciation/amortization/depletion
- ❑ Net operating loss carryforwards
- ❑ Excess assets (excess cash and/or nonoperating assets)
- ❑ Taxes
- ❑ Other

Additional considerations:

- ❑ Does the forecast contain any partial year cash flows and how does the model account for these?
- ❑ What discounting convention is used in the analysis (end-of-year or mid-period convention)?
- ❑ What is the basis for calculating the terminal value (Gordon growth model, multiple of a financial variable, other)?
- ❑ Is the terminal value discounted by the proper number of periods?
- ❑ What percentage of the overall value does the terminal value represent?

Discount/Capitalization Rates

Build-up method components. For each, does the report contain adequate sourcing and explanation for the selected input?

- ❑ Risk-free rate
- ❑ Equity risk premium
- ❑ Size premium
- ❑ Industry risk adjustment
- ❑ Specific company risk adjustment
- ❑ Overall equity discount rate
- ❑ Long-term growth rate

Modified capital asset pricing model (MCAPM) components. For each, does the report contain adequate sourcing and explanation for the selected input?

- ❑ Risk-free rate
- ❑ Equity risk premium
- ❑ Beta (industry, guideline companies)
- ❑ Size premium
- ❑ Specific company risk adjustment
- ❑ Overall equity discount rate
- ❑ Long-term growth rate

Weighted average cost of capital components. For each, does the report contain adequate sourcing and explanation for the selected input?

- ❑ Cost of equity (also referred to as an equity discount rate. See previous pages.)
- ❑ Cost of debt (typically expressed on a pretax basis)
- ❑ Income tax rate
- ❑ Capital structure: weight ascribed to equity
- ❑ Capital structure: weight ascribed to debt
- ❑ Overall weighted average cost of capital
- ❑ Long-term growth rate

GUIDELINE PUBLIC COMPANY METHOD (CHAPTER 8)

Criteria for Selection

Are the criteria for selection of the guideline public companies clearly defined?

- ❑ Population(s) or database(s) searched
- ❑ Line of business
- ❑ Industry classification code (SIC or NAICS)
- ❑ Size (e.g., in terms of market capitalization, revenue, assets)
- ❑ Position in the industry
- ❑ Profitability
- ❑ Capital structure
- ❑ Geography/territory
- ❑ Maturity of company
- ❑ Type of customers served
- ❑ Date of stock price and financial statement information
- ❑ List of companies ultimately selected
- ❑ List of companies ultimately rejected
- ❑ Rationale for the companies rejected

Financial Metrics

What financial metrics (valuation multiples) are used in the valuation and what time-frame was selected for each (e.g., latest 12 months, latest fiscal year, next 12 months' forecast)?

- ❑ Market Value of Invested Capital (MVIC) / revenue
- ❑ MVIC / EBITDA
- ❑ MVIC / EBIT
- ❑ MVIC / book value of invested capital
- ❑ MVIC / adjusted book value of invested capital
- ❑ MVIC / other
- ❑ Price / revenue
- ❑ Price / earnings before income taxes
- ❑ Price / earnings (net income)
- ❑ Price / book value
- ❑ Price / adjusted book value
- ❑ Price / other

Statistics and Weightings

For each selected financial metric, what statistics are evaluated and used in the valuation?

- ❑ Mean/average (the mean can sometimes be unduly influenced by extreme observations, especially on the upside. Sometimes analysts avoid this bias by eliminating ratios they consider nonmeaningful.)
- ❑ Median (generally considered a preferable measure of central tendency among ratios)
- ❑ Standard deviation (measures how dispersed the data is in relation to the mean)
- ❑ Coefficient of variation (a measure of relative dispersion calculated as the ratio of the standard deviation to the mean. A lower value indicates a tighter clustering of data.)
- ❑ Does the analyst adequately justify where each multiple applied to the subject company falls relative to the range of observed multiples?
- ❑ Does the analyst adequately justify which variable is accorded the most weight?

GUIDELINE TRANSACTION METHOD (CHAPTER 8)

Criteria for Selection

Are the criteria for selection of the guideline transactions clearly defined?

- ❑ Population(s) or database(s) searched
- ❑ Line of business
- ❑ Industry classification code (SIC or NAICS)
- ❑ Size (e.g., in terms of market capitalization, revenue, assets)
- ❑ Position in the industry
- ❑ Profitability
- ❑ Capital structure
- ❑ Geography/territory
- ❑ Maturity of company
- ❑ Type of customers served
- ❑ Date of transaction and relevant financial metrics
- ❑ List of transactions ultimately selected
- ❑ List of transactions ultimately rejected
- ❑ Rationale for the transactions rejected

Financial Metrics

What financial metrics (valuation multiples) are used in the valuation and what time-frame was selected for each (e.g., latest 12 months, latest fiscal year, next 12 months' forecast)?

- ❑ Market Value of Invested Capital (MVIC) / revenue
- ❑ MVIC / EBITDA
- ❑ MVIC / EBIT
- ❑ MVIC / book value of invested capital
- ❑ MVIC / adjusted book value of invested capital
- ❑ MVIC / other
- ❑ Price / revenue
- ❑ Price / earnings before income taxes
- ❑ Price / earnings (net income)
- ❑ Price / book value
- ❑ Price / adjusted book value
- ❑ Price / other

PAST TRANSACTION METHOD (CHAPTER 8)

This may be a good method for acquisitions made *by* the subject company as well as transactions of interests in the subject company.

Criteria for Selection

Are the criteria for selection of the transactions clearly defined?

- ❑ Date of transaction
- ❑ Percentage of company transacted
- ❑ Any special terms (specify)
- ❑ Values indicated by the subject transaction

Financial Metrics

What financial metrics (valuation multiples) are used in the valuation and what time-frame was selected for each (e.g., latest 12 months, latest fiscal year, next 12 months' forecast)?

- ❑ Market Value of Invested Capital (MVIC) / revenue
- ❑ MVIC / EBITDA
- ❑ MVIC / EBIT
- ❑ MVIC / book value of invested capital
- ❑ MVIC / adjusted book value of invested capital
- ❑ MVIC / other
- ❑ Price / revenue
- ❑ Price / earnings before income taxes
- ❑ Price / earnings (net income)
- ❑ Price / book value
- ❑ Price / adjusted book value
- ❑ Price / other

EXCESS EARNINGS METHOD (CHAPTER 10)

Is there a satisfactory explanation of why the excess earnings method was used?

____

What is the basis for adjusting or reclassifying line items to fair market value?

- ❑ Accounts receivable
- ❑ Inventory
- ❑ Plant and equipment
- ❑ Land
- ❑ Other assets
- ❑ Notes payable
- ❑ Other liabilities
- ❑ Off-balance sheet assets and/or liabilities brought onto balance sheet

Is there a satisfactory explanation of the estimate of the market's required rate of return on the company's assets?

- ❑ Rate of return on tangible assets
- ❑ Rate of return on intangible assets

Is the variable being capitalized clearly defined and supported?

- ❑ Net cash flow
- ❑ Net income
- ❑ Other

Is there a test-of-reasonableness (sanity check) employed to assess the indication of value?

____

Is there a reconciliation of the blended rate of return with the capitalization rate derived from the buildup method or capital asset pricing model?

____

RULES OF THUMB (CHAPTER 11)

Does the valuation report rely on a rule of thumb to develop an indication of value? If so, what are they?

____

If the valuation report employs rules of thumb, are they adequately cited, explained, and applied?

____

If the valuation report employs rules of thumb, what data, models, and/or alternative analyses were used to corroborate and/or support the indications developed?

____

GOODWILL (CHAPTER 12)

Does the entity have goodwill? If so, how is the total amount of goodwill derived?

Does the report distinguish personal goodwill from enterprise goodwill? If so, what are the relative amounts?

If there is an allocation between personal and enterprise goodwill, what data, models, and/or rationale were used to quantify the amounts? Are they adequately cited, explained, and applied?

RECONCILIATION OF INDICATED VALUES (CHAPTER 19)

If a single method dominated the conclusion, did the analyst make a convincing case that that was the best method?

If multiple methods were used, did the analyst use mathematical weighting or subjective weighting?

Were the weights convincingly supported and are reasons given for using and not using various approaches to value?

OVERALL ASSESSMENT

Were the steps taken in the report consistent with the stated standard of value? If not, where did they diverge?

Were there any contradictions (e.g., industry section not supporting valuation section)?

Are there any noticeable biases (e.g., tendency toward unsupported high or low valuation multiples and/or discount rates)?

Were any mathematical errors identified?

Was the report well documented (e.g., could another analyst find the source materials and replicate it)? If not, where is documentation lacking?

CHAPTER 35

Admissibility and Impact of Expert Business Valuation Evidence

Anita M. Ventrelli, JD

INTRODUCTION[1]

In this chapter you will learn about:

- Rules governing admissibility
- Choosing an appraiser, including different credentials
- Court challenges to appraisers
- Keeping opinions within the appraiser's area of expertise
- Information the appraiser can rely upon
- Documenting statements
- Taking shortcuts and their perils and pitfalls
- Incorrect application of accepted methodologies affecting reliability
- Dangers of using valuation methods that are not generally accepted and consistent with valuation standards
- The question of admissibility as opposed to weight of testimony

As the chapter title suggests, expert business valuation reports and testimony present two critical hurdles:

1. Will the report and/or testimony be admitted into evidence?
2. If so, what weight will the court accord it?

Two threshold questions determine the outcome of the first of these hurdles and affect the second one:

1. Will the court find the expert qualified on the subject for which counsel presents the expert?
2. Do the opinions state a sufficient basis to support a court finding the expert opinion reliable?

Courts may also excercise discretion in determining the relevance of the proffered expert report and testimony to the question(s) at bar.

1. The author thanks Michele G. Miles, author of *The Business Appraiser and Litigation Support* (Wiley, 2001) and former executive director at the Institute of Business Appraisers, and Noah J. Gordon, former legal counsel for Shannon Pratt Valuations for their contributions to this chapter's content in the prior edition(s).

SUPREME COURT AFFIRMS COURTS' "GATEKEEPER" ROLE

Daubert v. Merrell Dow Pharmaceuticals

In *Daubert*,[2] surely the most quoted case of the 1990s, the U.S. Supreme Court affirmed the trial court's decision to exclude expert evidence regarding causation of a medical problem on grounds of lack of reliability.

The Court in *Daubert* explained:

> Faced with a proffer of expert scientific testimony, then, the trial judge must determine at the outset, pursuant to Rule 104(a), [FN10] whether the expert is proposing to testify to (1) scientific knowledge that (2) will assist the trier of fact to understand or determine a fact in issue. [FN11] This entails a preliminary assessment of whether the reasoning or methodology underlying the testimony is scientifically valid and of whether that reasoning or methodology properly can be applied to the facts in issue. We are confident that federal judges possess the capacity to undertake this review. Many factors will bear on the inquiry, and we do not presume to set out a definitive checklist or test. But some general observations are appropriate [FN10].

Rule 104(a) provides:

> "Preliminary questions concerning the qualification of a person to be a witness, the existence of a privilege, or the admissibility of evidence shall be determined by the court, subject to the provisions of subdivision (b) [pertaining to conditional admissions]. In making its determination it is not bound by rules of evidence except those with respect to privileges." These matters should be established by a preponderance of proof [FN11].

Rule 104(a) also provides:

> Although the *Frye* decision itself focused exclusively on "novel" scientific technique, we do not read the requirements of Rule 702 to apply specifically or exclusively to unconventional evidence. Of course, well established propositions are less likely to be challenged than those that are novel, and they are more handily defended. Indeed, theories that are so firmly established as to have attained the status of scientific law, such as the laws of thermodynamics, properly are subject to judicial notice under Federal Rule of Evidence 201.

The Court then listed four factors to consider:

1. Whether the theory or technique can be (or has been) tested
2. Whether the theory or technique has been subjected to peer review and publication
3. Whether there is a known potential rate of error
4. Whether the theory or technique enjoys general acceptance within the relevant professional community[3]

Since this decision, numerous trial courts have applied the *Daubert* factors, and several appellate court decisions have sustained, expanded, and interpreted them. The cases

---

2. Daubert v. Merrell Dow Pharmaceuticals Inc., 509 U.S. 579 (1993).

3. *Id.* at 580. While the *Daubert* standard focuses on a Federal Rule of Evidence, those states whose rules of evidence are modeled upon or have similar language to Rule 702 are allowing trial courts discretion in applying these criteria. *See, e.g.*, Leaf v. Goodyear Tire & Rubber Co., 590 N.W.2d 525, 532–33 (Iowa 1999), which stated that the observations in *Daubert* will be helpful to a court in assessing reliability of evidence in complex cases, and Iowa trial courts accordingly may use the criteria at their discretion.

make it clear that the *Daubert* factors apply not only to scientific testimony, but also apply to valuation and economic analysis. However, in a 2004 Ninth Circuit decision, the court stated that factors 1 and 3, related to reliability, "are not applicable to [nonscientific testimony], whose reliability depends heavily on the knowledge and experience of the expert, rather than the methodology or theory behind it."[4]

In 2000, the Supreme Court further amended Federal Rule of Evidence 702 in response to *Daubert*. The amendment affirmed the trial court's role as gatekeeper and provided some general standards that trial courts must use to assess the reliability and helpfulness of proffered expert testimony. The amended rule provided that all types of expert testimony present questions of admissibility for the trial court in deciding whether the evidence is reliable and helpful (this is consistent with the result in *Kumho*, discussed later).

The Supreme Court further amended 702 effective December 1, 2023, as follows (new language is underlined and deleted language is struck through):

> A witness who is qualified as an expert by knowledge, skill, experience, training, or education may testify in the form of an opinion or otherwise if the proponent demonstrates to the court that it is more likely than not that:
>
> (a) the expert's scientific, technical, or other specialized knowledge will help the trier of fact to understand the evidence or to determine a fact in issue;
>
> (b) the testimony is based on sufficient facts or data;
>
> (c) the testimony is the product of reliable principles and methods; and
>
> (d) the ~~expert has reliably applied~~ expert's opinion reflects a reliable application of the principles and methods to the facts of the case.

Consequently, the principles of Rule 104(a) govern the admissibility of all expert testimony. Under that rule, the proponent bears the burden of establishing that the pertinent admissibility requirements are by a preponderance of the evidence.

Since *Daubert* the number of challenges to the admissibility of experts dramatically increased, to the point where business valuation experts should expect to be challenged, almost as a matter of course.[5]

A great majority of courts have admitted the testimony and report evidence presented by proffered business valuation witnesses who have demonstrated their expertise in compliance with *Daubert*. There are, nonetheless, maverick courts that have ruled that business valuation is "junk science." The federal bankruptcy court in *Med Diversified*,[6] which had previously qualified one of the more recognized authorities in the healthcare valuation field, not only retracted its prior ruling on the basis that the expert's report was biased but took the opportunity to seemingly discredit the entire business valuation

---

4. Hangarter v. Provident Life & Acc. Ins. Co., 373 F.3d 998, 1017 (9th Cir. 2004).

5. PwC, *Daubert Challenges to Financial Experts: A Yearly Study of Trends and Outcomes (2000–2021)*, https://www.pwc.com/us/en/services/consulting/deals/library/daubert-study.html. *See also* Carol Krafka et al., *Judge and Attorney Experiences, Practices, and Concerns Regarding Expert Testimony in Federal Civil Trials*, 8(3) Psychol. Pub. Pol'y, & L. 309–32 (2002). This article, based on surveys of judges and attorneys, indicates that judges are much more likely to scrutinize expert evidence in the wake of *Daubert*—and that the rate of exclusion has correspondingly increased.

6. *In re* Med Diversified, Inc., 346 B.R. 621 (Bankr. E.D.N.Y. 2006).

profession as based on "junk science." The court expressed "fundamental skepticism" about certain business valuation methodologies such as the comparison of data from public companies with that of a closely held business, the discounted cash flow method, control premiums, marketability discounts, and other generally accepted methods and data. The court also slighted the entire business valuation profession by characterizing it as a small coterie of self-certifying and self-validating individuals:

> The dominant citations are to the writings of two or three consulting firms which hold themselves out as valuation experts either by self-designation or by designation through the very small professional valuation societies they have formed for themselves.[7]

Other courts have not followed this line of reasoning. Another federal bankruptcy court, faced with the admissibility of one of the experts who had been excluded in *Med Diversified,* referred to the case as "isolated" and as not having any impact on the admissibility of the expert; that court also in no way questioned accepted business valuation methodologies.[8]

General Electric Co. v. Joiner

In *General Electric,*[9] the Supreme Court concluded that courts of appeals must apply an abuse-of-discretion standard when they review a trial court's decision to admit or exclude expert testimony. The Supreme Court ruled that standard applies as much to the trial court's decision about how to determine reliability as to its ultimate conclusion. The Court also held that whether the specific *Daubert* factors are appropriate measures of reliability in a particular case is a matter the law grants the trial judge broad latitude to determine, the same broad latitude that the trial judge enjoys with respect to his or her ultimate reliability determination. In other words, "The permissible scope of expert testimony is quite broad, and district courts are vested broad discretion in making admissibility determinations."[10]

Kumho Tire Co. v. Carmichael

In *Kumho,*[11] the U.S. Supreme Court clearly ruled that the *Daubert* factors and the trial court's "gatekeeping" function regarding the admission of expert testimony do not apply only to scientific experts. Rather, they apply to all technical or other specialized experts. However, in a 2004 Ninth Circuit decision, the court stated that factors 1 and 3, related to reliability, "are not applicable to [nonscientific testimony], whose reliability depends heavily on the knowledge and experience of the expert, rather than the methodology or theory behind it."[12]

The Supreme Court amended Rule 702 in 2000, affirming the trial court's role as gatekeeper, as stated in *Garner.*[13]

---

7. *Id.* at 632.
8. *In re* Doctors Hosp. of Hyde Park, 360 B.R. 787, 173 (Bankr. N.D. Ill. 2007).
9. Gen. Elec. Co. v. Joiner, 522 U.S. 136 (1997).
10. Hill v. Reederei F. Laeisz G.M.B.H. Rostock, 435 F.3d 404, 423 (3d Cir. 2006).
11. Kumho Tire Co. v. Carmichael, 526 U.S. 137, 138 (1999).
12. *Hangarter,* 373 F.3d 998, n.4.
13. State *ex rel.* Garner v. Wright, 562 S.W.3d 311 (2018).

Writing for the Supreme Court in the *Kumho* opinion, Justice Breyer made the following unambiguous statement:

> The *Daubert* "gatekeeping" obligation applies not only to "scientific" testimony, but to all expert testimony. Rule 702 does not distinguish between "scientific" knowledge and "technical" and "other specialized" knowledge, but makes it clear that any such knowledge might be the subject of expert testimony. The word "knowledge" used in the Ruling, not the words (like "scientific") that modify the word, establishes a standard of evidentiary reliability.

Explaining the Court's agreement with the trial court's decision, Justice Breyer concluded:

> In *Daubert*, this Court held that Federal Rule of Evidence 702 imposes a special obligation upon a trial judge to "ensure that any and all scientific testimony . . . is not only relevant, but reliable." The initial question before us is whether this basic gatekeeping obligation applies only to "scientific" testimony or to all expert testimony. We, like the parties, believe that it applies to all expert testimony.

Two attorneys, who also are business appraisers, commented on the implications of *Daubert* for appraisal experts:

> The *Kumho* decision holds good news for business appraisal experts. The trial court, at least in cases where Federal Rules of Evidence apply, has wide latitude to apply whatever criteria it needs to fulfill its duty to make the threshold determination that the appraisal expert's opinion will be reliable. The underlying standard seems to be the same level of intellectual rigor that characterizes practice as a competent business appraiser.
>
> This suggests strongly that, instead of focusing efforts on meeting the four very specific criteria applied to the scientific testimony in *Daubert*, the business appraisal expert should concentrate his efforts on maintaining a degree of professional competence. The appraisal expert should be prepared to offer evidence that his appraisal has employed the same level of intellectual rigor that characterizes the practice of an expert in business valuation.
>
> Certainly, no single rubric exists that will meet this evidentiary requirement in every single case, but evidence that the appraisal expert has performed his analysis and formed his opinion in conformance with the *Uniform Standards of Professional Appraisal Practice* (USPAP), the *Business Appraisal Standards* of the Institute of Business Appraisers (IBA), and the *Business Valuation Standards* of the American Society of Appraisers (ASA) must be viewed by anyone as probative.[14]

The authors went on to suggest several suitable areas for inquiry by the court:

- **Lack of bias, or objectivity.** Indicated by adherence to the type of independence mandated by the appraisal and ethical standards of principal professional appraisal societies.
- **Adequacy of inquiry.** Refers to the completeness of the appraisal expert investigation of the business and its financial condition.
- **Consideration of accepted methods.** The appraisal expert should be able to show that he or she has considered every appraisal method that is applicable and appropriate to the subject company.

14. Deirdre Russell & Steven F. Schroeder, *Implications of Kumho for Business Appraisal Experts* (Apr. 11, 2001) (abbreviations added), www.bvlibrary.com/bvresearch. Note: Upon the merger of IBA into NACVA, IBA standards were merged into NACVA standards.

- **Logical support for analysis.** Appraisal procedures and techniques in accord with fundamental financial theory have evolved over the years and are reflected in the authoritative publications of professional appraisers. Unless otherwise supported, the expert's analysis should fall within the framework of this current body of knowledge.[15]

In addition to the standards cited by these authors, the standards of other organizations that accredited business valuation professionals, such as the American Institute of Certified Public Accountant's (AICPA's) *Professional Standards* and *Statement on Standards for Valuation Services* (SSVS) or the National Association of Certified Valuation Analysts' (NACVA's) professional standards, also might support a claim that an expert who adheres to them is professionally competent.[16]

While *Daubert* challenges sometimes surface in limine after expert disclosure, they can also occur as late as at trial.[17] A successful challenge could hurt a case or even derail it entirely if the case rests primarily on the appraiser's theory or opinion.[18] To avoid expert disqualification, whether for a lack of requisite expertise or because of issues with the expert's work, carefully select an appropriate expert well in advance of disclosure deadlines and direct the expert to provide comprehensive and detailed support for their position as well as professional competence. The expert should emphasize that they used peer-reviewed (i.e., generally accepted and consistent with valuation standards) methods widely accepted in the financial and business valuation community. In responding to a *Daubert* challenge, the expert should detail the data gathered and assumptions used, rather than focusing on the results.

SELECTING AND EVALUATING THE APPRAISER

Business appraisers may have a range of backgrounds, including finance, accounting, academic, brokerage, investment banking, and consulting experience. However, when engaging a business appraiser who may offer expert testimony in a litigated (or

15. *See* Chapter 1, "Business Valuation Standards and Credentials," *in* SHANNON P. PRATT & ASA EDUC. FOUND., SHANNON PRATT'S VALUING A BUSINESS: THE ANALYSIS AND APPRAISAL OF CLOSELY HELD BUSINESSES xxxv–viii, 3–16 (6th ed. 2022).

16. *See id.* Chapter 1 for a discussion of the professional organizations that offer accreditation in business valuation.

17. *See, e.g.*, Club Car, Inc. v. Club Car (Quebec) Imp., Inc., 362 F.3d 775, 780–81 (11th Cir 2004) *abrogated on other grounds by* Innovative Clinical & Consulting Servs., LLC v. First Nat'l Bank of Ames, 279 Ga. 672 (2005), where the court of appeals upheld the district court's holding of the *Daubert* hearing at trial, rejecting the argument that the hearing had been untimely and late. *Compare* FMS Inc. v. Volvo Constr. Equip. N. A. Inc., No. 00-8143, 2007 U.S. Dist. LEXIS 19517, at *25 (N.D. Ill. Mar. 20, 2007) (the court rejected an attempt to resurrect a *Daubert* challenge post-trial as "sandbagging" and, quoting from another case (Alfred v. Caterpillar, Inc., 262 F.3d 1083, 1087 (10th Cir. 2001)), said "*Daubert* generally contemplates a 'gatekeeping' function, not a 'gotcha' function."); CADCO Inc. v. Fleetwood Enters., 220 S.W.3d 426, 434–35 (Mo. Ct. App. 2007) (appellate court, finding no plain error, rejected the attempt to review an expert's admissibility on appeal, noting that the party seeking review had ample opportunities below to challenge the expert's admissibility, but failed to do so).

18. *See, e.g.*, Zenith Elecs. Corp. v. WH-TV Broad. Corp., 395 F.3d 416 (7th Cir. 2005), where the plaintiff's appraisal expert was disqualified because the trial court found that the expert was unable to adequately explain the theory supporting his testimony. The expert's testimony was key to the case, and without it, the plaintiff lost. The Seventh Circuit affirmed, concluding that the expert was not truly an expert where he relied on his own theory rather than on widely accepted analytic strategies that he could have deployed.

arbitrated) matter, the attorney should focus on qualifications, training, experience in business appraisal, ability to thoroughly understand how the business operates, and the ability to communicate effectively. Detailed inquiry must be made into the following:

- As a preliminary matter, whether the appraiser has a conflict of interest (i.e., a business interest in the subject company or a relationship with the parties).
- Efforts made by the appraiser to gain formal training in the theory and application of business appraisal methodology, including continuing education.
- Active participation in professional activities and organizations, such as presenting at or attending professional seminars, authoring articles for professional publications, or authoring professional treatises and books. Such activities help the valuation expert keep up with the latest developments in the profession and also subject the appraiser's positions and methods to constant review by peers. Engaging in such activities will bolster the professional's standing as an expert and credibility for litigation purposes.
- Look at reports the appraiser prepared. While not every assignment calls for a written report, formal work product demonstrates competence and evidence of the appraiser's ability to present a credible and organized conclusion. For example, in *Med Diversified*,[19] although the offered expert averred that his expert report was not to be read as a certified business valuation and indicated that his support staff were certified business valuators who provided input into the report, the court precluded his testimony, among other reasons, because those valuators were not available for cross-examination. The court indicated it was not prepared to admit an expert report submitted by a corporate entity, saying that "the person who signs the report has to testify until the admission of his Report for all evidentiary purposes has been stipulated to."[20]
- Knowledge of the appraiser in the subject type of business. Regulatory, statutory, and geographic factors can dramatically affect business values, and the appraiser must have sufficient expertise to identify these factors and apply appropriate adjustments to value. However, be cautious with the business appraiser whose background is extensive within one industry if his or her main qualification is as an owner, chief executive officer, or other officer of a business within the industry.[21] Such "industry" people may perform appraisals by substituting their own judgment for that of the market and lack the needed objectivity. The essential element is knowledge of business appraisal. A good business appraiser can get the necessary industry knowledge, but an industry person without knowledge of the business appraisal discipline probably will not be able to do a comprehensive job.[22]

---

19. *In re* Med Diversified, Inc., 346 B.R. 621, 642–43 (Bankr. E.D.N.Y. 2005).

20. *Id.* at 643.

21. *See, e.g.*, KW Plastics v. United States Can Co., 131 F. Supp. 2d 1289, 1291–94 (M.D. Ala. 2001) (company's CFO excluded from testifying because his testimony was not based with any degree of certainty in sound economic principles used in a reliable way—the court noted that it was not unilaterally prohibiting an in-house employee serving as an expert from relying upon his own experience, but that an employee serving as an expert must exercise the same professionalism and thoroughness as any other expert in the field); Life-Wise Master Funding v. Telebank, 374 F.3d 917, 928–29 (10th Cir. 2004) (CEO was excluded from testifying because the Court determined that he was not an expert in damage calculations and could not explain the model he used; the model was not regularly used for projecting future profits, was not peer reviewed, was not uniformly used in any industry, and was capable of manipulation).

22. *See, e.g.*, Guang Dong v. ACI Int'l, Inc., No. 03-4165-JAR, 2008 U.S. Dist. LEXIS 3881, at *12 (D. Kan. Jan. 17, 2008) (the court admitted the expert, saying that the expert did not need "firsthand knowledge about [the defendant's] business structure" for his opinions to be admissible).

- Whether the appraiser relies on third-party business appraisal software.[23] The appraiser who relies on such software may substitute the programmer's judgment for his own, or rely on a cookie-cutter approach to business appraisal.

  Business appraisers who have developed their own appraisal software present different problems for counsel because they have to be capable of laying an adequate foundation for the computer program as well as their work product. Unless the appraiser is willing to divulge all the details of the software (and even provide a copy to the opposing appraiser), the valuation conclusion may not be sufficiently replicable to pass scrutiny under professional standards governing business appraisal.[24] The appraiser should thoroughly understand and be able to replicate and defend any of the component processes the computer has performed in determining the value of the subject firm.
- The professional standards the business appraiser follows. The expert should employ the same methods and standards, whether or not the opinion is intended for courtroom presentation.[25]
- Whether the expert can communicate effectively is a key consideration for litigated (or arbitrated) matters. "No matter how brilliant the expert is or how impressive the resume, an expert is of little value if an average juror cannot understand the testimony."[26] Ask a potential expert about his or her track record as an expert witness. Inquire about the expert's reputation and litigation experience. Pay attention to whether the individual is articulate, communicates without using excessively technical jargon, and is likable, and not condescending, arrogant, or patronizing.
- Whether the appraiser has ever been barred from testifying incident to a *Daubert* challenge? If so, ask to see any transcript, order, or opinion so you can evaluate whether the situation would affect the appraiser's credibility. If the court disagrees with the method and does not criticize the appraiser for attempting use, the decision to use the expert might be different than if the court criticizes the expert.

Professional Certifications and the Case for Peer Review

Whatever the background of the business appraiser, they should possess or be working toward one or more of the professional certifications available. Counsel should note the substantial differences among these designations. For example, one difference is the requirement of peer review. Some appraisal designations do not require the appraiser to submit a report for peer review prior to receiving the designation. Even though the designation requires demonstrated experience with appraisal assignments, it may be that the business appraisals performed may have involved flawed methodology. For these reasons, designations that involve peer review offer some assurance that the business appraiser's work product has passed juried scrutiny.

---

23. A distinction must be made between software written specifically for the performance of business appraisals and common spreadsheet software, such as Microsoft Excel®. Statistical software and graphics programs are a normal and appropriate tool for organization and evaluation of financial data, although their utility, like that of business appraisal software, depends on the skill of the user.

24. *See* the Appraisal Standards Board's *Advisory Opinion 18 on the Use of an Automated Valuation Module* (AVM), *in* THE APPRAISAL FOUNDATION, UNIFORM STANDARDS OF PROFESSIONAL APPRAISAL PRACTICE (2008–2009).

25. *See Kumho Tire Co.*, 526 U.S. 137.

26. Robert A. Zupkus, *Using Experts Expertly*, GPSOLO 48–50 (AM. BAR ASS'N. July/August 2004).

The CPA as Business Appraiser

While engaging someone with specific training in financial statement preparation as an appraiser offers peculiar advantages, be aware that not all Certified Public Accountants (CPAs) are qualified to perform a credible business valuation. There were approximately 670,000 CPAs in the United States in 2021. Of this number, as of early 2010, around 2,800 had earned the Accredited in Business Valuation (ABV) designation awarded by the AICPA. In addition, as of 2021, only about 5,000 members of NACVA whose members are predominantly CPAs, had the Certified Valuation Analyst (CVA) designation. It defies logic to assume that the remaining CPAs are just as qualified.

Advantages

- The general practitioner's typical client list generally includes a number of businesses whose financial statements are issued on a regular basis. Where the client list contains similar businesses, the accountant may have accumulated industry expertise. For example, in *Rossi*,[27] the appellate court upheld the trial court's admission of expert testimony on profitability figures offered by the bookkeeper. The bookkeeper's client list included 200 service stations, a factor in the determination that he was "skilled" in the area. In *Floorgraphics*,[28] the court denied a motion to exclude the proposed testimony of a CPA with a CVA credential, finding that these accreditations, along with his many years of experience, rendered him an expert who could testify on business damages and lost profits. Similarly, in *Guang Dong*,[29] the court admitted the testimony of an expert who was a CPA with an ABV credential, had provided expert testimony in several previous lawsuits, and had worked in the field of "forensic accounting litigation" for approximately seven years. Based on the expert's experience and education, the court found the expert more than qualified to testify regarding lost profits, even though he did not have prior experience with the industry involved.[30]
- The full-time involvement with numbers, balance sheets, profit and loss statements, and tax laws.
- The availability of resources on the topic from membership organizations such as the AICPA.
- A good CPA likely possesses a general understanding of the operations of closely held businesses, their style of management, and financing needs and sources.
- Some CPAs are active in industry trade associations, which may offer extra insight for a particular industry.

Disadvantages

- The likelihood that the accountant (except for those who specialize in business appraisal) spends only a small percentage of time on business appraisal (a possible qualification issue in court).[31] The nature of most accounting training emphasizes the objective histor-

27. Rossi v. Mobil Oil Corp., 710 F.2d 821, 830 (Temp. Emer. Ct. App. 1983).

28. Floorgraphics, Inc v. News Am. Mktg. In-Store Servs., Inc., 546 F. Supp. 2d 155, 172–74 (D.N.J. 2008).

29. *Guang Dong*, No. 03-4165-JAR, 2008 U.S. Dist. LEXIS 3881, at *12.

30. *See also* Trugreen Cos., LLC, Inc. v. Scotts Lawn Serv., 508 F. Supp. 2d 937, 958–59 (N.D. Utah 2007) (expert who was a CPA, certified fraud examiner, and certified insolvency advisor with 25 years of experience, while not possessing the "ideal" background to opine on lost profits and damages, nonetheless was qualified. The court said that "his lack of certain training or certification does not necessarily mean that he does not have the required expertise.").

31. *See, e.g., In re Med Diversified, Inc.*, 346 B.R. 621 (the court, excluding an offered expert, rejected the argument that substantive experience over 20-plus years as an accountant and as a liquidating agent or

ical perspective of compliance reporting. Business appraisal, on the other hand, typically involves, either directly or indirectly, the analysis of more subjective future projections. CPAs who have earned the ABV designation should be amply sensitive to these different orientations. CPAs without this designation may or may not have a background that supports the type of analysis required in most valuation assignments. There is nothing in the typical college accounting curriculum that addresses business appraisal.

- The possible current involvement of the accountant with the subject business. While economy and familiarity with the business might argue in favor of retaining the business's regular accountant to perform the appraisal, business appraisal standards could be construed to define the accountant's continued relationship with the client as "a contemplated future benefit," which might disqualify the appraisal opinion.

  A second reason that weighs against the use of the regular accountant in the role of business appraiser arises when the appraisal involves the interests of parties who, while joint when the accountant performed the work, may, for purposes of the business appraisal, now be adverse. Consider, for example, the accountant who has compiled the financial statements and prepared the tax returns for a corporation that is now the subject of a shareholder oppression action. Representing the minority shareholder, the accountant as business appraiser would scrutinize the corporate financial statements and might recast expenses charged to the business (such as travel, promotion, and entertainment expenses) as income that should be imputed to the shareholders, and, in such a situation, it is possible that the majority shareholders would have more income imputed to them. The accountant-as-business-appraiser situation may create the impression that the accountant will cast the financial statements in favor of whomever is cutting the check for services. Although this impression may be completely wrong, the risk of raising such a red flag should be weighed carefully against the benefit of having a business appraiser who is familiar with the financials of the business.

  This scenario also may arise when the accountant prepares not only the tax returns for the business but also the personal returns of the husband and the wife. When the parties decide to separate and the accountant is asked to serve as business appraiser for only one spouse, the question of divided loyalties must inevitably arise. It is also likely that the accountant knows where too many skeletons are buried in both the business and personal financial profiles to be truly objective in the appraisal assignment.

---

bankruptcy trustee in bringing avoidance actions in the bankruptcy court added up to a satisfactory substitute for formal education and training in business valuations and in peer recognition in business valuations, especially in the unique and highly regulated business of in-home health care services.). However, *see also In re Doctors Hospital of Hyde Park*, 360 B.R. 787 (the Court admitted the same expert who had been excluded by the *Med Diversified* court as an insolvency expert (but not a business valuation expert per se), noting that he had been qualified as an expert in insolvency in numerous other cases).

See also, e.g., Acker v. Burlington N. & Santa Fe Ry. Co., 347 F. Supp. 2d 1025, 1031 (D. Kan. 2004) (CPA admitted he was not qualified as an expert in lost profit projections); Sun Ins. Mktg. Network, Inc. v. AIG Life Ins. Co., 254 F. Supp. 2d 1239, 1245 (M.D. Fla. 2003) (testimony of expert as to the value of a business stricken because he "is a forensic accountant, not a business appraiser"); Beverly Hills Concepts, Inc. v. Schatz & Schatz, 717 A.2d 724, 732 (Conn. 1998) ("[A]n accounting degree alone should not qualify a witness to testify that a given volume of sales, for example, will continue in the future.") (internal quotations omitted); Santa Monica Picture, L.L.C. v. Comm'r, T.C. Memo. 2005-104, 404-05 (2005) (CPA with national firm and with extensive experience with corporate NOLs excluded as to valuation of NOLs because "[this expert] . . . has no specific background in valuation; nothing in his testimony or report indicates that he is qualified to value the NOLs.").

The Financial Analyst as Business Appraiser

To clarify, financial analyst in this context means a securities analyst, or someone schooled or experienced in corporate finance, not someone who has performed some type of clerical analysis of various records. For example, in 2023 about 190,000 individuals worldwide possessed the professional designation Chartered Financial Analyst (CFA), awarded by the CFA Institute, but of these the minority also have experience in closely held company valuation. Many of these also have one or more business valuation professional designations.

Advantages

- The discipline of business valuation is, in fact, an exercise in financial analysis. While business appraisal uses the tools of accounting (much as an engineer uses the tools of mathematics), it is the financial analysis of the accounting, industry, and economic data that leads to a conclusion of value.
- The CFA designation requirements are extremely rigorous. You can be sure that the CFA is well schooled in the analysis of public company securities, which forms the basis of the guideline public company method.
- If the person also has an academic degree with a major in finance, they should have a good grasp of what drives value. Many economists and corporate finance gurus take the position that the major objective of any firm should be to maximize shareholder value. Financial analysts are well trained in the analysis of shareholder value.
- If the person is an investment banker with specific valuation experience and has testimony experience (e.g., someone active in mergers and acquisitions and/or with extensive experience in rendering and defending fairness opinions), that person might be a well-qualified expert with respect to valuations of public companies or very large closely held companies.

Disadvantages

- Both the business school courses in finance and CFA study materials tend to be oriented to large companies, especially publicly traded companies. Some people with large-company orientations have trouble relating to smaller companies, often subjects of business appraisals. Small companies often do not have accounting/finance departments; they may lack forecasts, sophisticated accounting, and other systems; and may have owners with less financial acumen. This transitioning can be difficult for the CFA, and usually takes some time to occur.
- Financial analysts oriented to larger companies are proficient in the use of public company databases for market transactions, but often are not proficient with private company transaction databases, such as *Deal Stats*, *Done Deals*, and *BIZCOMPS*.
- Financial analysts often lack the specialized training in valuing closely held businesses and partial interests in closely held businesses.[32]

---

32. *See, e.g.*, Kohler v. Comm'r, T.C.M. 2006-152 (July 25, 2006) (the court criticized the government expert who had a doctorate and held a CFA designation because he was not a member of the ASA nor The Appraisal Foundation, his report was not submitted in accordance with USPAP, and he did not provide the customary USPAP certification (which assures readers that the appraiser has no bias regarding the parties, no other persons besides those listed provided professional assistance, and that the conclusions in the report were developed in conformity with USPAP)).

- Financial analysts and investment bankers often lack experience as testifying experts and may not be familiar with valuation literature, especially with regard to the valuation of closely held businesses or partial interests in closely held businesses.

The Broker as Business Appraiser

If the business recently has been offered for sale, a broker may already be involved, and the client may be interested in using the broker as the business appraiser. Brokers in the community may offer appraisal services as an outgrowth of their practice. Many brokers who perform business appraisals have substantial experience and additional training and may have earned one or more professional accreditations in business appraisal; however, many have no formal training and a "shoot from the hip" approach may not match the assignment, especially for tax or litigation assignments. Before agreeing to use a broker, ask if the person has the Certified Business Intermediary (CBI) designation offered by the International Business Brokers Association (IBBA). Requirements for this designation include two days of recasting financial statements for business pricing and two days of business valuation.

Advantages

- The broker may have a "nose" for discerning the economic earnings of the business (as contrasted with the reported earnings). In many closely held businesses that depend on cash payments, including restaurants, retail stores, service businesses such as auto repair shops, and even professional practices where some patients pay in cash, the reported income may have only a tangential relation to actual revenues. By spotting those issues early, counsel can evaluate not only the real value of the business but also the ramifications of going forward with a valuation when the client may not have reported (and paid taxes) on all the income.
- Brokers deal in the world of "comparables" (i.e., sales of similar companies) and may have internal sources of information for the application of the market approach, in addition to the sources already mentioned.

Disadvantages

- Many business brokers have practices that include business brokerage as part of larger real estate brokerage practices, and business sales may not constitute the majority of their activity. Not only may their expertise in business sales be limited, but the broker who does mostly real estate sales or appraisals may not properly apply the market approach in the context of a business appraisal. Furthermore, in the course of discovery, the broker may be required to disclose confidential information about prior transactions that formed the basis of their opinion.
- Unless the broker has made a concerted effort to become educated by taking courses from a valuation professional organization such as ASA, he or she may have little formal training in the review and adjustment of financial statements or other issues beyond the normal experience of business brokerage. This places the opinion at risk for errors and means the expert may not be able to replicate the appraisal process credibly for the trier of fact.
- If the broker is or has been involved in listing the business, or hopes to list the business in the future, they have a conflict of interest that may discredit or disqualify the valuation conclusion.

The Academic as Business Appraiser

Universities with schools of business, economics, or finance may have faculty members who perform business appraisals in addition to their academic loads. These academics may have backgrounds that include statistics or a focus on a particular industry that will suit the appraisal assignment. Even a small local college may have adjunct faculty members for whom teaching is only part of a day-to-day practice that includes financial, appraisal, and consulting services.

Advantages

- The academic may be published on business appraisal issues or may have performed academic studies in the particular industry that includes the subject business. This enhances their credibility.
- The academic typically will have resources readily available for research and analysis. They will be exposed to the latest writings on the topic and may have more time to follow trends in the development of appraisal methodology.
- Some academics (and not only those who are adjunct faculty members) perform "real-world" business consulting assignments as part of their academic role. For example, if the university has a Small-Business Development Center, the academic may have daily interaction with business start-ups and acquisitions as a counselor. Many graduate schools reach out to the local business community and offer continuing education to established professionals or targeted education to the lending industry or other professional groups. These real-life interactions can produce an expert who is simultaneously versed in the latest theory and grounded in the pragmatic world of business.
- Some academics' education, combined with the courses they teach and their work history, may qualify them as business valuation experts.[33]

Disadvantages

- The academic can be well versed in theory but have little practical experience in its application. This may be particularly true of the "career academic" who may have impressive credentials and a long list of writing credits, but who may not ever have performed an actual appraisal assignment.
- The academic appraiser may have natural teaching abilities that *should* enable him or her, as an expert witness, to communicate effectively and credibly to the trier of fact. However, academics may not possess the necessary translation ability to make important points in simple terms. Even an undergraduate business student will have a grasp of the terms that is far above the technical vocabulary of many jurors. Unless the academic can abandon jargon to state facts and opinions in simple language (and without giving the

33. *See, e.g.*, Tidwell Indus., Inc. v. Diversified Home Products, Inc., No. SA-06-CA-0264 FB, 2007 U.S. Dist. LEXIS 78227 (W.D. Tex. Oct. 19, 2007) (the court admitted as an expert to value lost profits of a cabinet distribution company a finance professor whose master's program included courses relevant to corporate valuation—specifically, managerial accounting, accounting for financial decision-making, and financial management; whose doctorate program included courses in advanced financial management, the theory of finance, and a seminar in corporate finance; who taught finance and corporate valuation at the university level; and who, prior to teaching, had been a bank's senior vice president, served on the bank's loan committee, and assessed the capacities of businesses and individuals to repay loans. The court said, "Even though [the expert] has not previously done a valuation of a cabinet distribution business, he has the knowledge, skill, experience, training, or education to enable him to conduct such a valuation.").

impression that the testimony is "dumbed down" for the audience), little will be gained from his or her impressive credentials.

- If the academic appraiser goes through life steeped in academia, there may be a tendency to apply radical or cutting-edge methodology rather than the tried-and-true business appraisal approaches with which the court has some comfort. Developing theories may merit close monitoring and eventually may be adopted into the conventional body of knowledge, but those who pioneer such methods in court without considering established approaches put the client at risk.
- An academic appraiser may be subject to challenge if he or she has no real-world transaction or business valuation experience.

Engaging the Business Appraisal Expert

It is critically important that the counsel and the business appraisal expert accurately and properly define their assignment, and that the expert and counsel agree on that definition of assignment (sometimes referred to as the *scope of work*). The value of an orange last year is of no relevance if the assignment is to value an apple as of today.[34]

Defining the appraisal assignment is the logical beginning of the valuation process, providing focus for all the considerations and efforts to be undertaken. Identifying and clearly defining the intended purpose and objective of the appraisal assignment helps eliminate many of the problems that can occur with the conclusions of valuation engagements. While it seems simple—and should be simple to understand—failure to clearly define the elements of the appraisal assignment at the beginning of the process is one of the greatest sources of errors, delays, excess costs, and misunderstandings between counsel and expert in a business valuation.

The reason for this failure may be that the attorney lacks sufficient knowledge to realize all the details that should be included in the appraisal assignment or has not thought through the implications of some aspects of the valuation. People who do not engage in business appraisals on a regular basis are unlikely to consider all the key elements of an appraisal assignment. The business appraisal expert should help the attorney (and/or the attorney's client) with these details. However, business appraisers are not lawyers and do not practice law. When legal issues are involved, it is the ultimate responsibility of the attorney, not the appraiser, to frame those issues.

Regardless of why the shortcomings occur, time spent at the outset in being thorough and explicit in defining the appraisal assignment is time well spent.

COURT CASES INVOLVING APPRAISER CHALLENGES

Sometimes courts err on the side of allowing proffered appraisers to testify; then the court accords little or no weight to the testimony. This is often the case with industry experts or academics without business valuation credentials. A person with business valuation expertise is trained to gain familiarity with a new industry, but the industry

34. The section was excerpted from Pratt & ASA Educ. Found., *supra* note 15, at 54–55. Used with permission. *See also id.* Chapter 2, "Defining the Assignment." A sample Engagement Letter is available at https://www.appraisers.org/docs/default-source/6.-publications/vab6/ch-02-sample-engagement-letter.pdf?sfvrsn=af66c6d0_5.

expert or academic without business valuation credentials is not trained to gain business appraisal expertise.

The opinion of the Third Circuit in *Unisys*[35] illustrates the pitfalls of unwise appraiser selection. In an action brought by Unisys employees who participated in individual account pension plans maintained by their employer, the trial court excluded the testimony of the plaintiff's expert witness. The appellate court held that the witness was properly excluded. In its rationale, the court cited the criteria in *Paoli*:[36] the court must find that the witness must be qualified to opine, that testimony of the expert will be reliable, and that the testimony will assist the trier of fact. The *Unisys* court applied this test to the credibility of the expert and decided that the witness's testimony did not "fit" for the following reasons:

1. The "education credentials were not of the highest caliber." (The expert witness in *Unisys* received his PhD from a correspondence school.)
2. The witness's credential statements during voir dire were not consistent with prior deposition testimony.
3. The witness's expertise was in a related but not identical field. Life insurance was the subject of the proffered testimony, but the witness's expertise was in property and casualty insurance. Furthermore, substantial differences between the two were admitted by the witness. Industry specialists are particularly vulnerable on this issue. Often, the desire to continue to build an appraisal practice will tempt the industry specialist or general consultant to accept assignments beyond his or her expertise. Consider, for example, the dental industry specialist (whose credentials may be mainly a life career as a dentist) who appraises the practice of an orthopedic surgeon.

A similar pitfall awaits the accountant with no formal business appraisal training, as any reasonable accountant would admit that not all accounting work involves appraisal. The broker who does few business appraisals is also at risk, as any reasonable broker should admit that there are substantial differences between brokerage and appraisals. The academic economist, statistician, or analyst may fare no better.

These "substantial differences" can even exist within a particular industry. Much has been written, for example, on the differences between publicly traded companies of moderate size and smaller closely held businesses within the same industry. For example, in *University of Pennsylvania*,[37] the appellate court upheld the trial court's disqualification of a claims examiner who offered expert testimony on the reasonableness of a $7 million settlement in a medical malpractice action. The court found that the witness had several years' experience as a claims adjuster, but insufficient experience in claims of this magnitude.

Notwithstanding the need in some cases for appraisers to have knowledge of, or experience with, a particular industry or even with certain aspects of a specific industry, often the appraiser does not need such industry-specific knowledge or experience if the appraiser has significant experience in business valuation and has peer-reviewed professional certifications. For example, in *Physicians Dialysis*,[38] the business being valued

35. *In re* Unisys Savings Plan Litig., 173 F.3d 145 (3d Cir. 1999).
36. *In re* Paoli R.R. Yard Litig., 35 F.3d 717 (3d Cir. 1994).
37. Trustees of the Univ. of Pennsylvania v. Lexington Ins. Co., 815 F.2d 890, 903 (3d Cir. 1987).
38. Physicians Dialysis Ventures, Inc. v. Griffith, No. 06-2468 (MLC), 2007 U.S. Dist. LEXIS 78879 (D.N.J. Oct. 24, 2007).

was a dialysis center. Although the challenged expert had no experience with the dialysis business, the court did not hesitate to admit the expert, who, in addition to being an author on lost profits calculations, was actively involved in the preparation of business valuations for more than seven years, was certified by both the ASA and NACVA, and held the CPA/ABV credential from the AICPA. Her prior employers included "Big 4" accounting firms, and, at the time of trial, she was senior manager of her firm's business litigation group. In addition, she had appraised a distributor, manufacturer, professional practice, physician's practice, outpatient surgical center, car dealership, restaurant, photofinisher, specialized metallurgical manufacturer, foreign sales corporation, and minority interest in a family limited partnership. Throughout her career, she formulated opinions in 60 valuation engagements, signed 17 reports, and made "significant contributions" to others. Thus, the court easily concluded that the expert "has developed specific expertise in the appraisal of business damages both in the form of lost profits and lost business value."[39] This reasoning also applies to the valuation of technology (i.e., the expert does not need to have technical know-how, provided he or she has business valuation know-how).[40]

In contrast, business experience alone may not qualify an individual as a business appraisal expert. In *Rosvold*,[41] the court did not admit as an expert a business executive who was a graduate of the Wharton School of Business, a leading business school, to value a minority corporate interest. The court indicated that the proposed expert lacked any professional experience or credentialing in business valuation.

Even extensive experience in a particular industry may not suffice to qualify an individual to value an entity in that industry. For example, in *24/7 Records*,[42] the proposed expert had more than 40 years of experience as a consultant in the music industry, with a particular specialty in creating and developing start-up music companies. Nonetheless, the court found that the music consultant was "not licensed by any organization as a qualified appraiser, has no formal training in valuation, accounting, or finance, and has never read any scholarly treatises or materials on valuation." The court excluded this expert as well as an attorney who practiced in the music industry and had experience in the valuation, negotiation, and sale of assets similar to those of the subject record company, finding that he, too, was neither licensed by an accredited appraisal organization, nor specifically educated in business valuation.

---

39. *See also, e.g.*, Popovich v. Sony Music Ent., Inc., 508 F.3d 348, 359 (6th Cir. 2007) (the court admitted an expert who had minimal experience valuing certain intangible assets, but had extensive experience as a business valuation professional "sufficient to qualify him as an expert on the value of the contract right in this case"); Henry v. Champlain Enters., Inc., 288 F. Supp. 2d 202, 220 (N.D.N.Y. 2003) (in an ESOP valuation case, the court stated, "While some measure of wariness is indeed expressed as to . . . [this expert]'s qualifications, it is here found, certainly at this stage of the proceedings, that his experience in the financial/securities field is sufficient. As noted, the fact that his experience is not exclusively or largely devoted to valuing stock on behalf of a purchasing ESOP is not enough to exclude his testimony.").

40. *See, e.g.*, Tharo Sys., Inc. v. cab Produckttechnick GMBH & Co. KG, 196 Fed. Appx. 366, 375–76 (6th Cir. 2006) (valuation expert who lacked technical expertise on thermal transfer printers was qualified to testify on the value of the technology).

41. Rosvold v. LSM Sys. Eng'g, Inc., No. 04-75009. 2007 U.S. Dist. LEXIS 82061, at *6–7 (E.D. Mich. Nov. 6, 2007).

42. 24/7 Records, Inc. v. Sony Music Ent., Inc., 514 F. Supp. 2d 571, 574 (S.D.N.Y. 2007).

Ultimately, the court usually will base its decision largely on the proposed expert's education and experience.[43]

The diverse backgrounds of business appraisers all have merits and demerits; often these qualities are not apparent until too late in the appraisal process. For these reasons, there is no real substitute for professional certification, particularly those certifications that include peer review. Proper planning and supervision are essential because an appraiser generally does not perform every aspect of a valuation. Also, staff who have different skill sets and different education, training, and experience also can provide a breadth of quality control not available to small "solo" appraisers. Having a staff that works cooperatively as a "team" yet considers each person's perspective (even challenging other team members views) can provide new and important insights that can produce a more objective value conclusion.

THE APPRAISAL OPINION MUST STAY WITHIN EXPERTISE

Business appraisers are not a source of "one-stop shopping" for expert opinions. Areas on which the appraiser should *not* be asked to render an opinion include the following:

- The standard of value appropriate to the claim. For example, the issue of whether fair value or fair market value is the standard in dissenting shareholder cases is a legal issue that the attorney should provide to the business appraiser.[44] It is neither the appraiser's job nor within the appraiser's expertise to determine the standard of value. Failure to provide the business appraiser with the applicable standard of value (which should be cited in the report with attribution to the attorney) may render the appraisal conclusion useless. Of course, a professional appraiser probably has a good idea of the appropriate standard of value. This is an issue that the attorney and the appraiser should agree on at the outset of the assignment and should be included in the engagement letter.
- Similarly, the appraiser will need the attorney to provide information on the legal questions of whether an agreement pertinent to the business, such as an operating agreement or a buy/sell agreement, can impact the valuation in the particular case, something that arises in dissolution of marriage actions.

---

43. *See, e.g.*, Rogers v. Alexander, 244 S.W.3d 370 (Tex. Ct. App. 2007) (The court qualifies a CPA and certified managing accountant (CMA) as an expert in valuing home-health agencies where he has had experience with strategic planning, budgeting, cash management, book value, market value, and economics, and has specialized in Medicare matters and advised clients on buying/selling home-health agencies.).

44. City of Tuscaloosa v. Harcross Chemicals, 158 F.3d 548, 567 (11th Cir. 1998) includes a scathing commentary on an economic expert overstepping (Testimony of this particular expert was not even challenged on these grounds, the court noted that the "testimony does indeed appear to warrant exclusion: specifically, [the expert's] opinions regarding the legal standards applicable to the case are outside of his competence as an economist and should be excluded. The same is true of [his] characterizations of pieces of documentary evidence as tending to show collusion; such judgments are for the Court to make at summary judgment and for the trier of fact to make at trial. Furthermore, we point out that [his] professed market definition is clearly wrong." The court also noted that the expert's opinion may have been "one with an apparent eye toward litigation," perhaps explaining their pains to critique the expert unasked.) Another court disagreed stating that the *dicta* in *Tuscaloosa* holding that the court not requiring a statistician to opine on the presence of collusion did not govern all circumstances involving collusion. *See, In re* Processed Egg Prods. Antitrust Litig., 815 F. Supp. 3d 412, 420 where the court stated "The more convincing and widely followed approach allows economic experts to testify about whether certain conduct is indicative of collusion. *See, e.g., In re* Titanium Dioxide Antitrust Litig., No. 10-0318, 2013 WL D.MD. (May 1, 2013)."

- Interpretation of contractual rights of parties that may give them a right to buyout, first refusal, or appraisal, or that determine liabilities or ultimate facts. For example, in *Morse/Diesel*,[45] a CPA attempted to testify regarding which party was responsible for construction delays and impact of various change orders. The trial court excluded the testimony under Federal Rule of Evidence 703, holding there was no foundation for the CPA to have such an opinion. The appellate court agreed with the trial court's statement that:

> [I]n each and every one of the four examples given . . . the proffered testimony is qualitative testimony relating to the reasonableness of including certain work with [Morse/Diesel's construction expert's] calculation. We find that this witness is not qualified by knowledge, skill, experience, training, or education to render these sorts of qualitative opinions under *Daubert*.[46]

The attempt to use the CPA to bootstrap the construction expert's calculations on damages, or to add testimony lacking from another expert, was unavailing.

In *Dering*,[47] the court struck the expert's opinion on punitive damages, indicating that it is the jury's role to set the amount of punitive damages and that to have an expert opine on these would invade the jury's "sacrosanct" role.

The structuring of an appraisal report to follow the organization of a statute, and that incorporates language from the statute, does not necessarily go beyond the scope of an appraiser's expertise. In *Joy Recovery*,[48] the business appraisal expert had referred to the Illinois Uniform Fraudulent Transfer Act (IUFTA) in his written report and lifted language directly from the statute. The court concluded that although the expert organized the disputed section of his report to correspond to subsections of the IUFTA, the actual analysis was consistent with principles of accountancy and therefore did not render it an impermissible legal conclusion.

SOURCE DOCUMENTS MUST BE THOSE "TYPICALLY RELIED UPON" BY APPRAISAL EXPERTS

The initial phases of a business appraisal assignment include the review of financial records on the subject business. Throughout the assignment, the appraiser continues to analyze and apply information gleaned from these records. When the appraiser relies on inappropriate or incomplete information, the entire opinion can fail for lack of a credible basis. If the appraiser knows that they lack complete information, they should note it in the limiting conditions. This will enable the appraiser to testify about what they requested and lacked if the failure to consider the missing material becomes a subject of cross-examination.

The risk of relying on the wrong type of documents is illustrated in *Target Market*.[49] In that case, the parties entered into a joint venture to produce and market direct-mail advertising for auto dealers. The venture failed within six months, never made it beyond

45. Morse/Diesel v. Trinity Industries, 67 F.3d 435 (2d Cir. 1995).

46. *Id.* at 444.

47. Dering v. Service Experts Alliance, LLC, No. 1:06-CV-00357-RWS, 2007 U.S. Dist. LEXIS 89972, at *25 (N.D. Ga. Dec. 6, 2007).

48. *In re* Joy Recovery Tech. Corp., 286 B.R. 54, 67–69 (Bankr. N.D. Ill. 2002).

49. Target Market Publ'g, Inc. v. ADVO, Inc.,136 F.3d 1139, 1142–45 (7th Cir. 1998).

the first initial market, and never attracted more than 15 advertisers. In establishing lost profits, the plaintiffs' expert used a marketing plan that was not a market projection but rather was used only to establish target revenues as a forecasting tool. The expert projected that had the contract term continued, the venture would have made $1.4 million in first-year profits.

In attempting to bootstrap their expert's opinion, the plaintiffs pointed to "the long experience and voluminous credentials of the report's author."[50] In rejecting the expert's opinions as "completely untenable,"[51] the court noted the expert's extraordinary assumptions that, contrary to its actual six-month history, the venture (as it was hoped in the market projections) "would penetrate into a total of forty-nine marketing zones, that each zone would generate fourteen advertisers per monthly issue, and that virtually all of those advertisers would pay the full price for their ads."[52] Reviewing the facts against the assumptions, the appellate court agreed with the trial court assessment that the opinion "relies upon mere assumptions—from which no reasonable inference of lost profits could be drawn,"[53] leading the court to reject the testimony under *Daubert*. The marketing department's motivation document was not a reliable basis for the forecasting of the appraiser.

Use of some categories of documents, despite not being completely representative of the conditions of the business, can be a reliable enough basis for appraisal projections to get admitted into evidence. For example, in *Rossi*,[54] the expert used monthly financial statements he prepared for the business that contained expense estimates based on industry averages and also included data on a combination of businesses, some of which were not involved in the suit.

The testimony that relied upon these documents was admitted, even though they were not compilations of "regularly kept business records." That said, the court stated that the court did not approve of what it termed "concealment throughout discovery of their use of industry averages, rather than actual expenses."[55]

Experts are entitled to rely on inadmissible hearsay evidence, provided the information is of a type reasonably relied upon by experts in the particular field in forming opinions or inferences upon the subject. The court found that the documents met the requirements of Federal Rules 703 and 704. This case makes an interesting contrast with the trial court's Memorandum Opinion in *Whelan*.[56] In this district court decision, the judge excluded the financial expert valuation done using only a discounted cash flow analysis that the court found relied upon speculative financial projections. It certainly creates a credibility problem for a witness to testify that an expert could properly rely upon a speculative document.

50. *Id.* at 1443.
51. *Id.* at 1144.
52. *Id.*
53. *Id.* at 1142.
54. *Rossi*, 710 F.2d 821.
55. *Id.* at 830.
56. Andrew J. Whelan et al. v. Tyler Abell et al., U.S. District Court, District of Columbia, civil action nos. 87-442 and 87-1763 cited in *The Implications of Recent Daubert-Related Decisions on Valuation Expert Testimony*, J. AM. BANKR. INST. (June 1999) Value and Cents Column.

Courts also have permitted otherwise qualified business appraisers to rely on the reports of other business valuation professionals. In *Greater Southeast*,[57] the court admitted the net asset valuation and insolvency opinion of a business appraiser who had an extensive background in business valuation and who had relied on third-party appraisals, indicating that all he needed to show was the "requisite knowledge, skill, experience, training, or education to competently render a net asset valuation opinion based on the opinions of others." It is permissible for business valuation analysts to rely on third-party reports, the court said, "so long as those appraisals are of the type experts in the field of business valuation would reasonably rely on."[58]

SUBJECTIVE STATEMENTS MUST BE DOCUMENTED

Discussing the trial court's rejection of the expert opinion, the court in *Kumho* focused on the expert's fallback position, that his subjective analysis (i.e., personal opinion) provided the basis for his conclusions. Note that neither the Supreme Court nor the trial court doubted the expert's qualifications. However, they had no comfort level with the expert's repeated subjective judgments.

> [T]hese concerns might have been augmented by [the expert]'s repeated reliance on the "subjectiveness" of his mode of analysis in response to questions seeking specific information regarding how he could differentiate between a tire that had actually been overdeflected and a tire that merely looked as though it had been.[59]
>
> [N]othing in either Daubert or the Federal Rules of Evidence requires a district court to admit opinion evidence that is connected to existing data only by the ipse dixit of the expert.[60]

In *City of Tuscaloosa*,[61] the appellate court upheld the exclusion of a CPA's testimony on a bid-rigging conspiracy based on his subjective analysis of bids that were signals to co-conspirators. Not only was the judgment of the witness solely his personal conclusion, it also fell beyond the realm of expertise an accountant normally possesses.[62] However, testimony within the accountant's competency, particularly his statistical testimony, was allowed to stand where it used "well-established and reliable methodologies."[63]

Prediction of future events also calls the subjective judgment of the business appraiser into question. Any number of future contingencies can be created to affect the value of the business interest; however, the appraiser must be able to show that those

57. *In re* Greater Southeast Cmty. Hosp. Corp., No. 02-02250, 2007 Bankr. LEXIS 1, at *11–13 (Bankr. D.D.C. Jan. 2, 2007).

58. *See* section "Reliance on Experts" in Chapter 9. *See also* Southwire Co. v. JP Morgan Chase & Co., 528 F. Supp. 2d 908, 934 (W.D. Wis. 2007) (challenged expert's work was a continuation of data collection and compilation initiated by a third-party accounting firm. The Court declined to exclude her testimony, saying, "Analyzing data assembled by another is neither illicit nor unusual, even if the data were prepared for litigation by an interested party.").

59. *Kumho Tire Co.*, 526 U.S. 137.

60. *Id.* at 157 (quoting Gen. Elec., 522 U.S. 136).

61. *City of Tuscaloosa*, 158 F.3d 548.

62. *See also* Santa Monica Picture, L.L.C. v. Comm'r, 89 T.C.M. (CCH) 1157 (T.C. 2005) (expert excluded because his analysis was infected with speculation, advocated his client's position, addressed issues beyond the scope of his valuation engagement, and testified to the ultimate legal issue).

63. *Kumho Tire Co.*, 158 F.3d at 565.

contingencies are somewhat likely to occur. In *Eisenberg*,[64] the court rejected a valuation that considered the ability of a Subchapter C corporation to convert to a Subchapter S corporation, finding no evidence of such intent and, where such an election could produce other consequences, causing the court to characterize such a choice as "practically remote."

Weighting methods to arrive at a conclusion (the averaging of values gained through the various methods) is another sore spot for subjective challenge.[65] In assigning the weights, the appraiser must be prepared with clear reasoning and as much related factual material as possible to substantiate the choice or risk of having the weight assignment appear as expert advocacy or client direction. Either one will taint the conclusion beyond acceptable limits.

An expert's failure to adequately explain the business valuation theory used also can lead a court to conclude that the opinion is subjective. In *Zenith*,[66] the appraisal expert was disqualified because the trial court found that he was unable to adequately explain the theory supporting his testimony and concluded that his opinion was subjective. The court of appeals affirmed, concluding that the expert was not truly an expert where he relied on his own theory.

SUPERFICIAL TREATMENT OF ISSUES: THE "DOWN AND DIRTY" APPRAISAL

Economic and time factors also can play a part in choices of methodology, which can result in the appraisal expert's testimony being excluded for failure to meet *Daubert* and *Kumho* criteria. A "down and dirty" appraisal used for initial case analysis should not become the opinion that the expert renders at trial. Such initial work (often substituted for final work product when money runs short) rarely will employ the methodology that experts in valuation find essential or the "intellectual rigor" discussed in *Kumho*.

Incomplete work cloaked in technical jargon will not pass a savvy opposing expert. In *Frymire-Brinati*,[67] the appellees (plaintiffs), claiming to be bilked investors in a limited partnership, alleged that the appellant's certification of partnership financial statements failed to disclose that the investments were worth less than represented on the books. The defendant's "star witness," using a discounted cash flow analysis, valued the projects at ten times annual cash flow. However, because the historical cash flow of many projects was minimal or even negative, the expert assigned them a value of zero.

The appellate court determined that the expert testimony was inadmissible because it failed to meet *Daubert*'s requirement that the testimony be "not only relevant, but reliable." The trial judge did not conduct any preliminary assessment of the reasoning or methodology used by the expert. The appellate court noted that had such a preliminary

64. Eisenberg v. Comm'r, 155 F.3d 50, 55 n.14 (2d Cir. 1998).

65. It is also true that appraisers can be criticized for failing to use all the approaches to valuation. *See, e.g.*, Est. of Bennett v. Comm'r, 65 T.C.M. (CCH) 1816 (T.C. 1993); Est. of Campbell v. Comm'r, 62 T.C.M. (CCH) 1514 (T.C. 1991); and Est. of Andrews v. Comm'r, 79 T.C. 938 (1982). However, these criticisms are generally not for failure to use a weighted approach, but rather for failure to consider the applicability of all available approaches—a different abuse of subjectivity.

66. Zenith Elecs. Corp. v. WH-TV Broad. Corp, 395 F.3d 416 (7th Cir. 2005).

67. Frymire-Brinati v. KPMG Peat Marwick, 2 F.3d 183 (7th Cir. 1993).

assessment been undertaken, the trial court could not properly have admitted the valuation testimony, for it failed to satisfy the requirements of Federal Rule of Evidence 702. The specific shortcomings of the expert's method lay in the admittedly surface treatment given to the assignment. Normally, to determine market value using a discounted cash flow analysis, the expert considers the *potential* cash flows of the asset, not merely the historical cash flow.

Commenting on the view of the defendant's expert's scenario as explained by the plaintiff's expert, the court noted that "raw land would be worthless and that a large office building in the final stages of construction also has no value even though it is fully leased out and could be sold for a hundred million dollars."[68] Even the defendant's expert conceded that his valuation was not an attempt to determine the market value of the asset (a fundamental necessity of the plaintiff's claims) but merely "a fairly simple pass at what the magnitude of the problem was."[69] Often, testimony that may be flawed in method or that may lack credibility can be admitted with proper instruction to the trier of fact. However, the *Frymire* appellate court was reluctant to admit the testimony and allow the trier of fact to assign it an appropriate weight, finding it problematic to admit this "fairly simple pass" into evidence simply because it was offered by an expert witness qualified in accounting matters. Ultimately, it was the lack of conventional methodology that persuaded the appellate court that the testimony was not reliable, for the expert "conceded that he did not employ the methodology that experts in valuation find essential."[70] Such a concession prevented the testimony from meeting the criteria for reliability and relevancy set forth in *Daubert.*

Another aspect of the "down and dirty" business appraisal is the assignment that heavily relies on off-the-shelf or personally developed business appraisal software. Can the business appraiser discuss the software in a manner that will satisfy the requirements of *Daubert*? Who tested the software? Who has peer reviewed it? What has been published on it? Are there standards governing its use? What are the default presets and how were they determined? Is the software generally accepted? How many people use it and what are their credentials? Who developed the software and what are their credentials? If the appraiser cannot answer these questions, the conclusion of value may have no real basis.

It also may fail to comply with the USPAP and its competency requirement. The Appraisal Standards Board's *Advisory Opinion on the Use of an Automated Valuation Model* (AVM) provides specific guidelines on AVM use:

> In an appraisal assignment, an appraiser must have a basic understanding of how the AVM works in order to reasonably determine that:
>
> 1. use of the AVM is appropriate for the assignment;
> 2. the output of the AVM is credible for use in the assignment; and
> 3. the AVM does not exclude relevant market measures or factual information necessary for a credible calculation.[71]

68. *Id.* at 186, *citing Daubert*, 113 S. Ct. at 2786.
69. *Id.*
70. *Id.*
71. The Appraisal Found., *Uniform Standards of Professional Appraisal Practice*, Adv. Op. 18 (2010–2011).

Finally, with the advent of artificial intelligence used to determine whether an author gave proper attribution to material from other sources, attorneys should make sure that experts give required attribution. Attorneys should also ask their appraisers if the appraiser consulted their firm's counsel about attribution. When in doubt, give the attribution and check all sites for their policies on reproducing the material they offer.

INACCURATE OR INADEQUATE USE OF ACCEPTED METHODOLOGIES—THE EXPERT MUST BE RELIABLE

The expert not only must use accepted or supportable methodologies, but also must do so in a way that evinces a comprehensive understanding of them or that correctly applies them. One study has shown that the primary reason for expert challenges are directed at the expert's reliability.[72] For example, in *Med Diversified*,[73] the court said that even if the proposed expert were otherwise qualified, it nonetheless would exclude his testimony because the expert "showed a discernible measure of negligence in purportedly applying the alleged professional standards and techniques found in the published practical treatises, including the standards and techniques published in the writings of Dr. Shannon Pratt and his co-authors, which were repeatedly propounded by both the Defendants and the Plaintiffs."[74]

The court concluded that it could not accept the testimony of an alleged expert in business valuations when he failed to employ the necessary peer-reviewed methods of business valuation, when he based his analysis on inadequate data, and when he thoroughly mixed up the discreetly different concepts of gross cash flow and net cash flow from operations. The court also concluded that his failure to use the discounted cash flow method and to offer a satisfactory explanation as to why he omitted this method amounted to a material flaw in his methodology sufficient to bar his testimony as an expert witness, because his conclusions lacked "good grounds."

Moreover, the court found that the data on which his conclusions were based were inadequate because he did not conduct any independent analysis as part of a comparable companies approach and did not independently analyze the data from the databases from which he derived his figures in choosing the comparable companies and transactions upon which his analysis was based; the expert admittedly never had considered the nature or products of the businesses or the market in which these businesses operated.

In *Club Car*,[75] the Eleventh Circuit upheld the exclusion of an expert because he based his opinion on gross figures without reducing them to net figures, which, the court found, did not comport with state law requirements that lost profits be calculated net of expenses. The court stated, "The trial court reasonably concluded his lost profit calculation was based on flawed methodology that was not accepted in the accounting community."[76]

---

72. *See* PwC, *Daubert Challenges to Financial Experts, supra* note 5. *See also* https://www.dauberttracker.com/.

73. *In re Med Diversified, Inc.*, 346 B.R. 621.

74. *Id.* at 98.

75. *Club Car, Inc.*, 362 F.3d 775.

76. *Id.* at 780.

In a case involving the Disney corporation, *Children's Broadcasting*,[77] the court initially admitted the expert, but after the expert made highly unrealistic assumptions, the court changed its mind on a motion for judgment as a matter of law, saying that the expert's "damages projections went so far beyond realistic optimism as to be 'fairy-tale-like.'"[78] The court concluded that it erred by admitting the testimony of the expert and should have excluded it under *Daubert*, for his "testimony 'tainted' the trial by exposing the jury to an 'exaggerated sum' of damages."[79] On appeal, the Eighth Circuit agreed that the expert should not have been permitted to testify because his opinion was speculative and based on conjecture.

In another Eighth Circuit decision, *Eckelkamp*,[80] the court again upheld the trial court's decision to exclude expert evidence where the trial court found several methodological flaws, including the expert's use of comparable companies that were not, in fact, comparable; the expert's failure to conduct a site visit and employee interviews; the expert's failure to consider certain market factors; double counting in arriving at a control premium; and other flaws.

Another case where faulty assumptions and data resulted in exclusion of the expert evidence is *Fisherman Surgical*.[81] In this case, the court concluded that there was no factual support for the expert's key assumptions and that this "hole" in his models rendered all his damages calculations unreliable. Similarly, in *Heary Bros.*,[82] the court excluded the expert's lost damages conclusions because the expert made faulty assumptions about market conditions as of the valuation period. In this antitrust case, the expert assumed there were only two market participants at the time, but, in fact, there were many more. The court ruled that this failure of the initial market share assumption rendered the rest of the calculations unreliable and, therefore, inadmissible.

The valuation experts' "numerous outright . . . errors" lost the plaintiffs' case in *Lippe*.[83] The court found significant deficiencies in the analyses of two experts, including the failure to explain why a discounted cash flow valuation was not performed as a check against a comparable company valuation; failure to explain the assumptions used in the valuation including the selection of price-to-earnings multiples, the selection of guideline public companies, and income projections; failure to account for differences between the guideline public companies and the subject companies; failure to independently select guideline public companies (instead utilizing companies suggested by counsel); and failure to explain the selection of control premiums, among others.[84]

---

77. Children's Broad. Corp. v. The Walt Disney Co., 245 F.3d 1008 (8th Cir. 2001).

78. *Id.* at 1015.

79. *Id.* at 1017.

80. Eckelkamp v. Beste, 315 F.3d 863 (8th Cir. 2002).

81. Fisherman Surgical Instruments, LLC v. Tri-Anim Health Servs., Inc., 502 F. Supp. 2d 1170 (D. Kan. 2007).

82. Heary Bros. Lightning Prot. Co., Inc. v. Lightning Prot. Inst., 287 F. Supp. 2d 1038, 1066–68 (D. Ariz. 2003).

83. Richard A. Lippe v. Bairnco Corp., 99 Fed. Appx. 274, 278–80 (2d Cir. 2004).

84. *See also Trugreen Cos.*, 362 F.3d 775 (expert's report was not sufficiently reliable where there was "an impermissible analytical gap . . . between the premises and conclusions" and "this methodology does nothing more than assume the conclusion").

ORIGINAL AND PERSONALLY DEVELOPED APPRAISAL METHODS CREATE RISK

Viewing the expert's opinion as presented to the *Kumho* trial court, the Supreme Court noted there was:

> [n]o indication in the record that other experts in the industry use [the expert]'s particular approach or that [other experts] normally make the very fine distinctions necessary to support his conclusions, nor are there references to articles or papers that validate his approach.[85]

Appraisers, weary of searching among the proven approaches for one best suited to an assignment, may be tempted to combine approaches or create an untried approach or method to cure what they perceive as deficiencies in the currently sanctioned methodology. Authors, wanting to sell books, may invent new theories. Over time, some of these methods may be evaluated and accepted by the technical community. Until that time, however, the business appraiser uses them at his or her own risk.

In *Moore*,[86] the court discussed that:

> [u]nder Rule 702 the "knowledge" of each discipline is both its principles and methodology, and the theories, techniques or inferences produced through its methodology. Thus, the proffered opinion of any expert in a field of knowledge, in order to be evidentially reliable, must either be based soundly on the current knowledge, principles and methodology of the expert's discipline or be soundly inferred or derived therefrom. . . . [Moreover,] the focus must be on the principles and methodology upon which the expert's opinion is based, not on the merits of the expert's conclusion.[87]

Experts who depart from known principles and methodology, therefore, may develop an incredible conclusion, regardless of its apparent merit.

One of the cardinal rules enunciated in the standards of appraisal organizations is that a valuation conclusion should be replicable. If the method has not been validated and studied, it may not be a replicable method. It certainly will not pass the "indicia of reliability" criteria set forth in *Daubert*. "Simple pass" methods, individual or brand-name methods, and software appraisals are no substitutes for the developed body of appraisal knowledge.[88]

In *Nellson*,[89] one of the experts essentially invented the methodology of using EBITDA minus capital expenditures to determine a company's terminal value under a discounted cash flow analysis. The expert admitted that he had never used such a method before and could point to no professional source that validated it. Because the expert's conclusion of terminal value constituted the bulk of his ultimate conclusions regarding value and was, in fact, "inseparable" from his ultimate conclusion, the court struck the entirety of his testimony and report from the record. In *Haupt*,[90] a state case

---

85. *Kumho Tire Co.*, 526 U.S. at 157.

86. Moore v. Ashland Chem., 126 F.3d 679 (5th Cir. 1997); *appeal after remand*, Moore v. Ashland Chem., Inc., 151 F.3d 269 (5th Cir. 1998).

87. *Id.* at 687–88.

88. The body of knowledge for business appraisal, reflecting USPAP and the core courses of all four of the U.S. professional business appraisal organizations, is contained in Pratt & ASA Educ. Found., *supra* note 15.

89. *In re* Nellson Nutraceutical, No. 06-10072 (CSS), 2006 Bankr. LEXIS 3186 (Bankr. D. Del. 2006).

90. Haupt v. Heaps, 131 P.3d 252 (Utah Ct. App. 2005).

interpreting a state analogue of *Daubert* standards, the court found the method relied on by the expert lacked reliability for valuation purposes. The method, known as the Straight-Line Ramp-up (SLR) method, had been used by the company's auditors, but the expert admitted that despite his many years as an economics expert, his extensive training, and his experience in business valuation, he had never seen the SLR method used in valuation prior to reviewing the audit documents and that he had not been able to verify it independently or investigate the auditors' intent in utilizing it. Thus, the court held that SLR was not "an accepted method of business valuations" and excluded it. This conclusion was affirmed on appeal.

ADMISSIBLE EXPERT EVIDENCE VERSUS THE WEIGHT ACCORDED TO IT

Despite the court's role as gatekeeper, "the rejection of expert testimony is the exception rather than the rule."[91] Often, challenged expert testimony will be admitted on the basis that the proffered expert qualifies as an expert and the methods used by the expert are recognized by other experts in the field, even if the challenge to admissibility is made on the grounds that the expert has omitted relevant factors or has made wrong assumptions that are essential to the methodology. In such a case, the court may decide that what is called for is an adjustment to the expert's result and will leave the decision of how much weight to accord to the expert's opinion to the jury. Because the court's gatekeeper role "is not intended to serve as a replacement for the adversary system,"[92] the challenging party has the burden of providing expert evidence that counters or adjusts the faulty results, and the challenging party's attorney must take the expert to task on cross-examination. Merely because the evidence can be critiqued as a matter of fact does not mean it should be stricken entirely as a matter of law if it otherwise satisfies the requirements of *Daubert* and Federal Rule 702.

For example, in *Floorgraphics*,[93] the plaintiff had alleged that the defendants had engaged in various business torts that resulted in plaintiff's damages and lost profits. The plaintiff offered six witnesses as experts, and the defendants moved to exclude the trial testimony of all six. Of these, two were to quantify damages using business valuation methodologies. The first offered expert used a "before and after" methodology. The defendants claimed that the expert's use of this methodology was fatally flawed because it omitted a fundamental step and failed to account for key factors. The defendants contended that the expert's testimony should, accordingly, be excluded because it rested on flawed assumptions and did not reflect real-world conditions. The court rejected this contention.

The court found that the "before and after" method is recognized by experts in the field as an acceptable method to calculate lost profits (citing Dr. Shannon Pratt, the original author of this book) and it agreed with the plaintiffs that to the extent the expert failed to account for certain factors, it was up to the defendants to demonstrate that

91. Fed. R. Evid. 702, 2000 Amendments.

92. United States v. 14.38 Acres of Land, More or Less Situated in Leflore County, State of Miss., 80 F.3d 1074, 1078 (5th Cir. 1995).

93. *Floorgraphics, Inc.*, 546 F. Supp. 2d 155.

those factors mattered. The court said, "When challenging the admissibility of Plaintiff's expert testimony, a party must move beyond empty criticisms and demonstrate that a proposed alternative approach would yield different results."[94] The court concluded that even assuming the defendants' objections were material and relevant, at most, the expert's testimony could be critiqued by the defendants' expert and should not be stricken. The expert's results would have to be adjusted if his key assumptions were wrong, but not excluded entirely, because in the end the expert's testimony would assist the trier of fact. The court said:

> Under Rule 702, it is not the Court's province to determine who is the best expert or the most qualified. Defendants will have an opportunity to vigorously cross-exam [the expert] in addition to presenting their own expert witness at trial.[95]

The defendants also sought to exclude the second business appraisal expert on the ground that his methodologies suffered from flaws. Again, citing Dr. Pratt, the court disagreed that the expert's use of business valuation methodologies was flawed and concluded that, in fact, it comported with accepted business valuation methodologies. Finding that not only did the expert have a reliable methodology, but that his testimony would assist the trier of fact, the court declined to preclude his testimony. In *Guang Dong*,[96] the court ruled that the expert's discount of 50%, based on a pricing email, and the expert's reliance on "ballpark" sales estimates from deposition testimony, did not render his report unreliable. Instead, the court indicated that these issues went to weight and not admissibility, and that a jury would be able to evaluate whether the expert properly used the email and sales data in reaching his opinion of damages.

In *Southwire*,[97] the defendants challenged defects to the plaintiffs' expert's multiple regression model but did not challenge the model itself. The court declined to exclude the expert, finding it more significant that the defendants had questioned neither the model nor the expert's credentials. The court said, "Although [the expert's] judgment may not be correct, his errors are fodder for cross-examination, not summary judgment."[98]

In another case, the business appraisal expert was challenged because he was a de facto contingent witness, that is, the party that retained him ran out of money to pay his fees and owed him an undisclosed sum. The expert admitted that he would not be paid unless the trustee prevailed. The court, however, admitted the expert, finding that this issue went to credibility and the weight of the evidence. The court distinguished between state ethics rules, which prohibit attorneys from using contingent fee experts, and evidentiary rules, which say nothing about contingent witnesses. The court concluded that there was no authority for the proposition that contingent fee experts are incompetent to testify in federal court or that evidence obtained from such witnesses is inadmissible. Merely showing that the expert may have an incentive to exaggerate his testimony is

94. *Id.* at 172.
95. *Id.* at 174.
96. *Guang Dong*, No. 03-4165-JAR, 2008 U.S. Dist. LEXIS 3881.
97. Southwire Co. v. J.P. Morgan Chase & Co., 528 F. Supp. 2d 908 (W.D. Wis. 2007).
98. *Id.* at 930.

insufficient to bar that testimony. Instead, this is a nondispositive consideration in the assessment of his credibility.[99]

Echoing the sentiments of many courts that decline to exclude expert testimony, the court in *Humetrix*[100] said:

> To the extent Gemplus sought to challenge the correctness of Humetrix's experts' testimony, its recourse is not exclusion of the testimony, but, rather, refutation of it by cross-examination and by the testimony of its own expert witnesses. Gemplus availed itself of both of these opportunities.

Similarly, in *KSP*,[101] where the challenged expert had used the same generally accepted methodologies as the challenging party's expert but had merely pointed out problematic assumptions and substituted different data in the same formulas, the court indicated that issues with the expert's testimony could be resolved through cross-examination. Likewise, in *ProtoComm*,[102] the court rejected challenges to each party's experts, saying,

> It appears to this Court that [the parties] are really arguing that . . . [the] opinions are inaccurate in light of the facts. In other words, they focus not on whether the reasoning is valid and the methodology reliable, but rather on whether the conclusions themselves are *correct*. That is not the proper inquiry in a test for admissibility.

The court added that any perceived weakness in the experts' opinions should be challenged through traditional trial tactics.

The defendants in *Tharo*[103] first challenged the plaintiffs' expert qualifications, claiming that the international auditor (with nearly 100 trial appearances) was not familiar with German accounting principles. However, they failed to rebut his assertion that there were no material differences between German and typical U.S. financial statements. And even though the expert had made a translation error, which caused him to exclude 80% of certain salaries from his calculations, he had admitted the error on cross-examination, and the jury had resolved the fact question in its damages award. In the end, his error or lack of familiarity with German accounting statements went to the "weight" of his testimony, according to the court of appeals, not to its admissibility.

COMMON ERRORS

More and more business owners and their counsel try to participate in the valuation process. While doing so aids the appraiser in knowing whether a court will understand their reports, attorneys who direct appraisers not to consider factual material that the appraiser would normally consider or that the other appraiser will consider can create credibility problems and compromise their appraiser's objectivity. Attorneys who instruct

---

99. *In re* Joy Recovery Tech. Corp., 286 B.R. 54. *See also* Physicians Dialysis Ventures, Inc. v. Griffith, No. 06-2468 (MLC), 2007 U.S. Dist. LEXIS 78879 (D.N.J. Oct. 24, 2007) (expert's references to businesses not in existence as of the valuation date did not render her methodologies or opinions unreliable, but went to the weight, not the admissibility, of her opinion).

100. Humetrix, Inc. v. Gemplus, S.C.A., 268 F.3d 910, 919 (9th Cir. 2001).

101. KSP Invs., Inc. v. United States, No. 1:07-CV-857, 2008 U.S. Dist. LEXIS 7383 (N.D. Ohio Jan. 17, 2008).

102. ProtoComm Corp. v. Novell Advanced Servs., Inc., 171 F. Supp. 2d 473, 481 (E.D. Penn. 2001).

103. Tharo Sys., Inc. v. cab Produckttechnick GmbH & Co. KG, 196 Fed. Appx. 366, 375 (6th Cir. 2006).

the appraiser to use a particular position on a contested legal issue risk findings that the expert's product lacks reliability.

SUMMARY

This chapter has discussed a sample of the hundreds of cases where a court either barred an expert from testifying or allowed the testimony but disregarded or gave little weight to the expert's testimony. Hopefully, these examples and the related discussion will provide attorneys guidance so that they will select appropriate experts and not fall into the same trap.

REFERENCES FOR EXPERT WITNESS TESTIMONY

Brinig, Brian Peter. 2022. *Mastering the Art of Expert Witness Testimony* (Burlington Business Press).

Mangraviti, James J. Jr., Steven Babitsky, and Nadine Nasser Donovan. 2015. *A-Z Guide to Expert Witnessing* 3rd ed. (Falmouth, MA: SEAK, Inc.).

Posner, Richard A. 1999. "The Law and Economics of the Economics Expert Witness." In *Journal of Economic Perspectives* 13(2) 91–9 (Spring 1999).

CHAPTER 36

Discovery and the Business Valuation Expert

Anita M. Ventrelli, JD

INTRODUCTION[1]

In this chapter you will learn about:

- Discovery rules pertaining to experts
- Disclosure requirements and reports
- Discovery methods and application to expert witnesses
- Strategy considerations for using the expert in discovery

This chapter discusses discovery rules in cases where attorneys introduce business valuation expert testimony. It also discusses the business valuation expert's role in the discovery process. The discovery devices discussed include the following:

- Witness disclosure and written report requirements
- Requests to the opposing party for production of documents and for entry upon land or premises
- Interrogatories to the opposing party
- Subpoenas served on third parties
- Depositions, including depositions on written questions
- Requests to admit facts and genuineness of documents

With respect to each discovery device, this chapter covers the relevant Federal Rule of Civil Procedure (FRCP), jurisdictions that follow the Federal Rules, and jurisdictions that have a discovery rule that differs from the Federal Rules. A table summarizing all federal, state, and territorial rules relating to the discovery devices discussed here is included as Exhibit 36-1.

1. The author thanks Linda L. Kruschke and Noah J. Gordon for their contributions to this chapter's content in the prior edition(s).

Exhibit 36-1 Summary of Discovery Rules

Jurisdiction	Written Report Required	Interrogatories Allowed Re: Expert	Limit on Number of Interrogatories	Deposition of Expert Allowed	Limit on Number of Depositions
Federal Rules Fed. R. Civ. P. 26, 30, 33 Dec. 1, 2022	Yes	Yes	25	Yes	10
Alabama Ala. R. Civ. P. 26, 33 Dec. 21, 2018	No	Yes	40	With court order only	No
Alaska Alaska R. Civ. P. 26 Jul. 20, 2019	Yes	Yes	30	Yes	No
Arizona Ariz. R. Civ. P. 26 Jan. 1, 2020	No	Yes	40	Yes	No
Arkansas Ark. R. Civ. P. 26 Nov. 1, 2022	No	Yes	No	Yes	No
California Cal. Civ. Pro. Code §§ 2034.270, 2034.030, 2034.410 Jan. 1, 2023	On demand	Yes	35	Yes	No

Jurisdiction	Written Report Required	Interrogatories Allowed Re: Expert	Limit on Number of Interrogatories	Deposition of Expert Allowed	Limit on Number of Depositions
Colorado Colo. R. Civ. P. 26, 33 Jul. 1, 2022	Yes	Yes	30	Yes	No
Connecticut Conn. Practice Book § 13 Jan. 1, 2017	Summary	Yes	No	Yes	No
Delaware Del. R. Civ. P. Super. Ct. 26 Aug. 1, 2019	No	Yes	No order only	With court order only	No
District of Columbia D.C. Super. Ct. R. Civ. P. 26 June 1, 2017	Yes	Yes	40	Yes	10
Florida Fla. R. Civ. P. 1.340, 1.390 Apr. 27, 2023	No	Yes	30	Yes	No
Georgia Ga. Code Ann. §§ 9-11-26, 9-11-33 May 1, 2023	No	Yes	50	Yes	No
Guam Guam R. Civ. P. 26, 33 Aug. 1, 2022	Yes	Yes	50	With court order only	No

Jurisdiction	Written Report Required	Interrogatories Allowed Re: Expert	Limit on Number of Interrogatories	Deposition of Expert Allowed	Limit on Number of Depositions
Hawaii Haw. R. Civ. P. 26, 30, 33 Jan. 1, 2022	Yes	Yes	60	Yes	10
Idaho Idaho R. Civ. P. 26, 33 Jul. 1, 2016	No	Yes	40	Yes	No
Illinois Ill. Sup. Ct. R. 213 May 14, 2021	If interrogatory served	Yes	30	Yes	No
Indiana Ind. R. Trial 26; Ind. R. Evid. 702 Jan. 1, 2023; Jan. 1, 2020	No	Yes	No	With court order only	No
Iowa Iowa R. Civ. P. 1.500(2), 1.509 Apr. 1, 2021	Yes	Yes	30	Yes	No
Kansas Kan. Stat. Ann. § 60-226 Jul. 1, 2012	Summary	Yes	No (30 in damage actions)	Yes	No
Kentucky Ky. R. Civ. P. §§ 26.02, 33.01 Feb. 1, 2023	No	Yes	30	Must serve interrogatories first	No

Jurisdiction	Written Report Required	Interrogatories Allowed Re: Expert	Limit on Number of Interrogatories	Deposition of Expert Allowed	Limit on Number of Depositions
Louisiana La. Code Civ. Proc. arts. 1450, 1457 Jan. 1, 2000	No, allowed with a court order	Yes	35	Yes	No
Maine Me. R. Civ. P. 26, 33 Feb. 15, 2023	No	Yes	30	Yes	No
Maryland Md. R. Civ. P. Cir. Ct. 2-402, 2-421 Jan. 1, 2023	If interrogatory served	Yes	30	Yes	No
Massachusetts Mass. R. Civ. P. 26, 33 Sept. 1, 2022	No	Yes	30	With court order only	No
Michigan Mich. Ct. R. 2.303 May 10, 2023	No	Yes	Yes	Yes	No
Minnesota Minn. R. Civ. P. 26, 33 Jul. 1, 2018	Yes	Yes	50	With court order only	No
Mississippi Miss. R. Civ. P. 26, 33 Jan. 1, 2020	No	Yes	30	With court order only	No
Missouri Mo. R. Civ. P. 26 Sept. 2, 2021	No	Yes	25	Yes	No
Montana Mont. R. Civ. P. 26, 33 Dec. 16, 2014	No	Yes	50	Yes	No

Jurisdiction	Written Report Required	Interrogatories Allowed Re: Expert	Limit on Number of Interrogatories	Deposition of Expert Allowed	Limit on Number of Depositions
Nebraska Neb. Sup. Ct. R. §§ 6-326, 6-333 Jan. 1, 2022	No	Yes	50	With court order only	No
Nevada Nev. R. Civ. P. 16.1, 26, 33 Sept. 29, 2021	Yes	Yes	40	Yes	No
New Hampshire N.H. Rev. Stat. § 516:29-b; N.H. R. Super. Ct. 23 Jan. 1, 2014; June 1, 2023	Yes	Yes	25	Yes	No
New Jersey N.J. Ct. R. 4:10 Sept. 1, 2016	if interrogatory is served	Yes	No	Yes	No
New Mexico N.M. R. Civ. Dist. Ct. 1-026, 1-033 May, 15, 2023	No	Yes	50	Yes	No
New York N.Y. C.P.L.R. 3101 Feb. 24, 2022	No	Yes	25	With court order only	No
North Carolina N.C. Gen. Stat. §§ 26, 33 Oct. 15, 2022	No	Yes	50	Yes	No

Jurisdiction	Written Report Required	Interrogatories Allowed Re: Expert	Limit on Number of Interrogatories	Deposition of Expert Allowed	Limit on Number of Depositions
North Dakota N.D. R. Civ. P. 26 Mar. 16, 2022	No	Yes	50	Yes	No
Ohio Ohio R. Civ. P. 26, 33 Jul. 1, 2022	Yes	Yes	40	Only after the mutual exchange of reports	No
Oklahoma Okla. Stat. tit. 12, §§ 12-3226, 12-3233 Jan. 1, 2019	No	Yes	30	Must serve interrogatories first	No
Oregon Or. R. Civ. P. 36 Dec. 3, 2017	No	No	-	No	No
Pennsylvania 231 Pa. Code § 4003.5 Aug. 9, 2014	if interrogatory is served, discretionary with answering party	Yes	No	With court order only	No
Puerto Rico P.R. R. Evid. 23.1 Mar. 1, 2023	No	Yes	No	With court order only	No
Rhode Island R.I. Super. Ct. R. Civ. P. 26, 33 Dec. 1, 2020	No	Yes	30	Must serve interrogatories first	No
South Carolina S.C. R. Civ. P. 26, 33 May 1, 2019	No	Yes	50	Yes	No

Jurisdiction	Written Report Required	Interrogatories Allowed Re: Expert	Limit on Number of Interrogatories	Deposition of Expert Allowed	Limit on Number of Depositions
South Dakota S.D. Codified Laws § 15-6-26 Feb. 23, 2021	No	Yes	No	Yes	No
Tennessee Tenn. R. Civ. P. 26.02 Jul. 1, 2011	No	Yes	No	Yes	No
Texas Tex. R. Civ. P. 195 June 1, 2023	If requested	No	-	Yes	50 hours
Utah Utah R. Civ. P. 26 May 4, 2022	Yes	Yes	No	Yes	No
Vermont Vt. R. Civ. P. 26 Sept. 22, 2022	No	Yes	No	Yes	No
Virginia Va. R. Sup. Ct. 4:1, 4:8 Aug. 12, 2022	No	Yes	30	Yes	No
Virgin Islands V.I. R. Civ. P. 26, 33 Oct. 27, 2022	Yes	Yes	25	Yes	No
Washington Wash. Sup. Ct. Civ. R. 26 Apr. 28, 2015	No	Yes	No	Yes	No

Jurisdiction	Written Report Required	Interrogatories Allowed Re: Expert	Limit on Number of Interrogatories	Deposition of Expert Allowed	Limit on Number of Depositions
West Virginia W.Va. R. Civ. P. 26, 33 Oct. 4, 2001	No	Yes	40	Yes	No
Wisconsin Wis. Stat. Ann. § 804.01 Apr. 5, 2018	No	Yes	25	Yes	1
Wyoming Wyo. R. Civ. P. 26, 33 Dec. 1, 2019	Yes	Yes	25	Yes	10

Expert Witnesses: Disclosure Requirements and Written Appraisal Report

Generally, business valuation experts should provide a written report explaining their opinion of the value of the business interest or intangible asset that is the subject of litigation, and the basis of that opinion. The attorney should discuss the general content and points to be covered in the report with the business valuation expert before they prepare the report. The attorney (and the expert) should review the procedural rules of the jurisdiction that govern the disclosure of expert witnesses and the requirements relating to written appraisal reports to ensure that the expert covers all the information required. The attorney should also review the rules to ensure that they timely disclose the expert and make the expert aware of the timing of sitting for deposition so he or she may testify at trial, if desired. Finally, the attorney should thoroughly prepare the expert before testimony of any sort.

Federal Rule of Civil Procedure 26(a)(2)

Federal Rule of Civil Procedure 26(a)(2) requires each party to disclose the identity of any expert witness the party intends to call to testify at trial under Federal Rule of Evidence (FRE) 702. As discussed in Chapter 35, the opinion of value of a business valuation expert falls into this witness category.

This disclosure requirement includes disclosure of a written report "prepared and signed by the witness" unless otherwise stipulated or ordered by the court.[2] The required content of the written report as specified in the rule includes the following:

- A complete statement of all the expert's opinions
- The basis and reasons for the opinions
- The facts or data considered in forming the opinions
- Any exhibits that will be used to summarize or support the opinions
- The qualifications of the witness
- A list of all publications authored within the past ten years
- The compensation to be paid
- A list of all cases the expert has testified in at trial or by deposition within the past four years
- A statement of the compensation to be paid for the study and testimony in the case

Absent a stipulation or a court order, the identity of the expert and his or her written report must be provided to opposing counsel and filed with the court within 90 days before trial or for the case to be ready for trial. This timeframe is shortened, however, in the case of expert testimony intended only to rebut expert evidence on the same subject matter disclosed by another party. In this instance, the identity and written report of the rebuttal expert must be provided within 30 days of another party's disclosure of the expert to be rebutted.

Under FRCP 37(c)(1), a party who fails to disclose the identity and written report of an expert witness "is not allowed to use that information or witness to supply evidence on a motion, at a hearing, or at a trial, unless the failure was substantially justified or is harmless." Other appropriate sanctions may be imposed at the discretion of the court. For example, in *Batchelor-Robjohns*,[3] the United States had sued transferees of assets

2. Fed. R. Civ. P. 26(a)(2)(B).
3. United States v. Batchelor-Robjohns, 2005 U.S. Dist. LEXIS 13552, at *7–13 (S.D. Fla. June 3, 2005).

from a corporate taxpayer, alleging that the transfers rendered the taxpayer insolvent and that, therefore, the transferees were liable for the corporation's unpaid taxes. The government's valuation expert had valued the taxpayer's assets and rendered an opinion concerning the corporation's income-generating capacity, but the government refused to disclose information concerning allegedly proprietary computer models used to value the assets. The transferees accordingly moved to strike the expert's report and to exclude witnesses under FRCP 37 for the expert's failure to disclose underlying data as required by FRCP 26(a)(2)(B). The court agreed with the transferees and excluded the expert's opinion, for neither the court nor the transferees were able to test the reliability of the opinion in the absence of the data and methodology upon which the opinion was based. In addition, because the transferees had made good-faith efforts to resolve the dispute before seeking court intervention and because admission of the expert's opinion would clearly have prejudiced the transferees' ability to cross-examine the expert and rebut his opinion, the court excluded the testimony of other experts whose opinions concerning the solvency and foreseeable tax liability of the taxpayer relied on the conclusions of the valuation expert, as well as any testimony to the extent that it relied on the expert's opinion.

However, the court also has significant discretion to permit the expert's testimony notwithstanding a failure to substantially comply with the requirements of FRCP 26(a)(2)(B). For example, in *Audubon*,[4] the defendant submitted a report that was not signed by the expert. The report contained columns of figures without any conclusions or defined sources, it was missing exhibits and a list of the expert's qualifications, and it was not even certain that the expert had written the report. Accordingly, the plaintiff moved to strike the report for failing to comply with FRCP 26. Although the district court found that the plaintiff had made a strong argument for striking the report, given that the suit was "purely about the value of the plaintiff's business interruption insurance claim" and the expert's report was "crucial," the court declined to preclude the expert from providing evidence in the case. It gave the defendant ten days to comply fully with FRCP 26 and ordered it to pay the plaintiffs' costs of deposing the expert.

Jurisdictions That Follow or Deviate from FRCP 26(a)(2)

Only 13 jurisdictions—Alaska, Colorado, District of Columbia, Guam, Hawaii, Iowa, Minnesota, Nevada, New Hampshire, Ohio, Utah, the Virgin Islands, and Wyoming—require a written report of an expert witness under rules similar or identical to FRCP 26(a)(2). Other jurisdictions require a written report of an expert witness:

- If demand is made (California)
- Summary (Connecticut and Kansas)
- If requested in discovery (Texas)
- If an interrogatory is directed to the party who will call the witness (Illinois (only for controlled opinion witnesses, i.e., retained experts), Maryland, New Jersey, Pennsylvania)
- Upon contradictory motion of any party or on the court's own motion (Louisiana)

4. Audubon Veterinary Hosp., Inc. v. U.S. Fidelity & Guarantee Co., 2007 U.S. Dist. LEXIS 46301 (E.D. La. June 25, 2007).

All these jurisdictions provide for the sanction of barring the expert's testimony at trial, at a hearing, or on a motion if the party does not comply with the written report or summary requirements.

Pennsylvania provides that the party answering an interrogatory may provide the expert's report in response or have the expert answer the interrogatory.

The remaining jurisdictions do not require a party to serve or provide a written expert report or summary by an expert witness to other parties. However, each jurisdiction, with the exception of Oregon, provides parties with some discovery device to learn about an expert's opinion.

REQUESTS FOR PRODUCTION OF DOCUMENTS AND ENTRY FOR INSPECTION AND INTERVIEWS

To perform a thorough business valuation, the appraiser needs to review corporate and financial documents of the business to be valued, usually including (but not limited to) articles of incorporation, bylaws, buy-sell agreements, financial statements, and income tax returns. Depending on the nature of the business, it often is important for the business valuation expert to view the business premises and to interview management, even in situations where it might not seem needed.

Documents

Exhibit 5-1 in Chapter 5 is a typical documents and information request list.[5] It should be modified to fit the specific situation.

Site Visit and Interviews[6]

Whenever practical, and in all cases where standards require, the business valuation expert should visit the subject company's major operating location(s) and conduct interviews with key personnel. In some instances, it may be useful for the business valuation expert to visit and conduct interviews with those affiliated with, who provide services to, or who are customers (with prior approval) of the company. The principal objective of such a visit is to gain a broader perspective of the business and its operations than is possible from only a study of documents and telephone interviews. A site visit usually provides an opportunity for the business valuation expert to fill in details missing from an analysis of the written material, and the expert's physical presence may trigger relevant questions and lines of inquiry that would not have been brought up by a mere review of the documents or a diligence meeting that took place only via telephone or video conference. This in-person site visit ideally should be conducted early in the valuation process—after obtaining and reviewing enough preliminary information provided by the client and through discovery and research to create an overview of the company. If the valuation expert is to provide testimony, the expert's credibility will be enhanced by having conducted a site visit, for courts tend to give more credibility to experts who

---

5. For a discussion as to why the appraiser requests certain documents, *see* Chapter 5, "Company Information, Site Visits, and Interviews."

6. *Id.*

have visited the premises of the company to be valued and have interviewed individuals who are key to the valuation.

Attorney's Role

Most business valuation experts prefer to do interviews without attorneys present, as this may result in more candid information gathering. However, experts are accustomed to having attorneys present when strategy requires. It often is desirable for experts on both sides of a case to do site visits and management interviews together, for a combined visit will be less disruptive to operations and personnel and ensure that both experts will have access to the same information on which to base an independent valuation. One can also gain insights into factors the other expert may consider that one's own expert has not yet raised.

Preparation

Generally, the business valuation expert will want to prepare a thorough list of questions in advance of the site visit. By studying the written materials, including financial statements and other basic information, the expert can gain an overview of the company and prepare a list of specific questions that will make the fieldwork more meaningful, productive, and efficient, and also minimize the inconvenience to the company that might be associated with the management interviews.[7]

Mission

As discussed in Chapter 5, "Company Information, Site Visits, and Interviews," the site visit and interviews should focus on establishing the relationship between the information gathered and the existing and prospective company situation and economic environment. The business valuation expert will also want to lay the groundwork for future communication with company personnel and related individuals if permitted by the company. Developing a level of comfort with these personnel and individuals is an important objective of the site visit, so that if the expert requires additional information after completing the fieldwork, it can be more readily obtained.

Information to Be Gathered

Chapter 5 discusses the kind of information the business valuation expert will want to gather through the field visit, which usually includes information related to the company's strengths, weaknesses, opportunities, threats, operations, history, customers, products, and so on. The questions can also be useful to discover nonoperating assets like art. The actual topics and sequence of coverage will vary considerably from one situation to the next, but regardless of which topics are most pertinent to a particular valuation, the expert's goal will be to gather as much information as possible to maximize his or her understanding of all major factors that affect the value of the subject company. Additionally, the field trip can be a convenient time to review some of the documents that would be cumbersome or inconvenient to supply to the expert away from the premises for businesses that do not maintain electronic records in an easy to turnover format.

---

7. Management interviews are discussed in Chapter 5 and examples of questions are included in Exhibits 5-2 and 5-3.

Individuals to Be Interviewed

The categories of topic knowledge matter more than the official title of any interview subject. As discussed in Chapter 5, the expert may need to interview a company's owner(s), president, chief operating officer, sales/marketing officer, or chief financial officer (CFO). In some companies, these job titles are all the responsibility of one person. In other companies, these responsibilities are carried out by individuals who are not employees of the subject company (e.g., an outside accountant serves in the capacity of the CFO). Ultimately, the expert will want to work with the client to determine exactly who should be interviewed to gain an understanding of the important information that affects the company's value and to adjust the list of individuals interviewed once the expert knows who possesses the requisite knowledge.

Confidentiality

Appraisers frequently must handle confidentiality problems carefully during on-site meetings. A company can have many good reasons for their confidentiality concerns. Experienced business valuation experts have learned to work around this problem. They can dress and act unobtrusively, at a minimum. If they must be introduced or identified to an employee not privy to the lawsuit situation, one can introduce them as "consultants," an accurate and adequately benign label. As a last resort, the expert can visit the premises without employees present after working hours. However, this will not give the expert as good a visual of operations as seeing the facility in operation.

All professional business appraisal organizations have provisions in their respective codes of ethics prohibiting dissemination of confidential information obtained during an appraisal assignment. Counsel should be sure to identify information as confidential to avoid issues, to enter protective/confidentiality orders to protect proprietary information if available in the jurisdiction and, failing an order, to have the expert sign a confidentiality agreement. Most courts will accommodate requests to put portions of the court record that include confidential material under seal.

Adversarial Proceedings

Business valuation experts may also face opposition to an adequate facility visit (or sometimes any facility visit at all) in the case of an adversarial proceeding. Undoubtedly, this problem most commonly occurs in appraisals done for the purpose of dividing property in divorces. Some attorneys and clients will try to stonewall the experts retained by the "outside" party (e.g., nonoperating spouse, minority stockholder, damage plaintiff) from interviewing the "inside" party and management. However, this is the opportunity for "inside" parties to present their side of the story. To the extent that their story is credible, a good expert will take it into account. To the extent they are denied information or refused a site visit or interview done at the same time as the opposing expert, the expert should note such events in their report so that they can testify about the circumstances.

In these circumstances, the client's attorney bears responsibility to make the necessary arrangements for the expert to visit the facilities and interview the appropriate people. Case law generally supports site visits as essential to do the job properly.[8] The

8. This issue is discussed in BARTH GOLDBERG & JOSEPH N. DUCANTO, VALUATION OF DIVORCE ASSETS (supplement 2004).

parties must understand that the site visit is a standard part of the business valuation expert's work, and that the expert, even when hired by the opposing side, is neither an adverse party nor an advocate for either party. Rather, the expert has been retained to render an independent opinion about value. When using a reputable professional business valuation expert, the parties should not have to be concerned with confidentiality. Furthermore, the party who is in the adversarial position to the expert's client should welcome the opportunity to tell his or her side of the story to the expert.

If all discovery must proceed through interrogatories and court orders, the process will be much more time-consuming, costly, and disruptive to the business operation. It is usually a good decision for parties on both sides of a dispute to cooperate with any experts since, if even one of the parties does not cooperate, costs generally escalate. Lack of cooperation may give a judge the impression that the non-cooperating party has something to hide or is practicing gamesmanship in the process. This may negatively affect the weight and credibility of the expert testimony engaged by the non-cooperating party.

Federal Rule of Civil Procedure 34

Proper methods for obtaining information to the business valuation can include a request for production of documents and electronically stored information (ESI) and for entry upon the premises for inspection under FRCP 34 or the corresponding rule of the appropriate jurisdiction. The documents or ESI requested and the premises to be inspected must be in the possession or control of a party to the litigation. (If the material needed is not in the possession of a party to the litigation, see the section on subpoenas that follows.)

Limitations on the Scope of Discovery

FRCP 26 limits the scope of available discovery under FRCP 34 to:

> any nonprivileged matter relevant to any party's claim or defense—including the existence, description, nature, custody, condition, and location of any documents or other tangible things and the identity and location of persons who know of any discoverable matter. For good cause, the court may order discovery of any matter relevant to the subject matter involved in the action while protecting against the disclosure of mental impressions, conclusions, and opinions or legal theories of the party's attorney or other representative concerning the litigation. Relevant information need not be admissible at the trial if the discovery appears reasonably calculated to lead to the discovery of admissible evidence.

Attorneys should always be careful to designate communications needed to assist in developing their attorney work product as "confidential attorney work product" and distinguish them from information the expert needs to consider in performing the valuation.

All jurisdictions have a similar limitation on the scope of documents that can be obtained or purposes for which premises may be entered and inspected.

Before drafting a request for production of documents or ESI, discuss with the business valuation expert the specific documents or ESI he or she will need to perform the valuation analysis. Request only those documents or ESI that are relevant to a determination of value or to proof of an element of one of your claims or defenses. FRCP 34(b)(E) provides, regarding ESI, that if a request does not specify a form of production, a party must produce it in a form or forms in which it is ordinarily maintained or in a reasonably usable form or forms, but a party is not required to produce the same ESI in more than one form. Keep in mind that under FRCP 26(b)(1), parties are allowed to obtain discovery on any matter, not privileged, that is relevant to the claim or defense of any party. Relevance within the meaning of FRCP 26(b)(1) is considerably broader than relevance for trial purposes. For discovery purposes, relevance means only that the materials sought are reasonably calculated to lead to the discovery of admissible evidence.

Nonetheless, the other party will likely be able to resist a request that is overbroad[9] and obtain a protective order quashing discovery seeking documents not relevant to the issues actually before the court[10] or a protective order that requires the expert to keep documents confidential.[11] These cases did not present facts regarding protective orders but rather situations where a party moved to compel, and the ultimate outcome supported denying the party the right to the information.

In *Lane*,[12] a dissenting shareholder appraisal suit, the issue was the value of the plaintiffs' interest in Cancer Treatment Centers. The plaintiffs served a request for production of documents that read:

> All financial statements, stock valuations, asset appraisals, and all documents relating to financial data, concerning any of [Cancer Treatment Centers, RJS, Cancer Care Centers] and/or any of their Affiliated Corporations, including without limitation all financial models, budgets (proposed or otherwise) and pro formas.

The Delaware Chancery Court agreed with the defendant's objection that the request was overbroad and was not limited to the narrow issue of valuation of Cancer Treatment Centers. The court required the plaintiffs to rewrite the requests so that they did not include financial documents and information on companies other than Cancer Treatment Centers unless they related specifically to business dealings with Cancer Treatment Centers.

In *Perry*,[13] the issues included whether the defendants had received unfair distributions from the corporation. The plaintiff's request for production of documents sought the defendant's individual income tax returns and personal financial statements. The trial court's denial of the plaintiff's motion to compel was upheld by the Minnesota Court of Appeals on the grounds that the information sought could be obtained from the corporate books and records, to which the plaintiff had full access.

Sanctions for Failure to Comply with a Discovery Order

If a party fails to respond to a request for production of documents or ESI or for entry upon premises for inspection, the other party may move for an order compelling discovery. Before filing such a motion, however, the party must make a good faith effort to confer with opposing counsel to resolve the problem.

---

9. Lane v. Cancer Treatment Centers of Am., 1994 Del. Ch. LEXIS 67 (Del. Ch. May 25, 1994).

10. Picerne Dev. v. Tasca & Rotelli, 635 So. 2d 149 (Fla. Dist. Ct. App. 1994); Perry v. Perry, 1995 Minn. App. LEXIS 1207, 1995 WL 550902 (Minn. Ct. App. Sept. 19, 1995).

11. Oliver v. Stone, 940 So. 2d 526; 2006 Fla. App. LEXIS 17631 (Fla. Ct. App. 2006) (appraiser could not reveal discovered materials underlying the valuation report even to the party that retained and paid him).

12. *Lane*, 1994 Del. Ch. LEXIS 67, at *7.

13. Perry v. Perry, 1995 Minn. App. LEXIS 1207, at *7–8.

Trial courts have broad discretion to impose sanctions for failure to comply with discovery orders, especially where the other party is prejudiced by the failure to comply. Motions and orders to compel discovery and sanctions for failure to comply are governed by FRCP 37. All U.S. jurisdictions have a similar provision. Under these rules, sanctions can include the following:

- An award of attorneys' fees and costs to the party that made the request and obtained the discovery order[14]
- An order "directing that the matters embraced in the order or other designated facts be taken as established for purposes of the action, as the prevailing party claims"[15]
- An order "prohibiting the disobedient party from supporting or opposing designated claims or defenses, or from introducing designated matters in evidence"[16]
- Striking a pleading or portion of a pleading
- Dismissing the suit or one or more claims or counterclaims
- Rendering a default judgment against the noncomplying party
- Treatment of the failure as contempt of court[17]

However, absent exceptional circumstances, a court may not impose such sanctions on a party for failing to provide ESI lost as a result of the routine, good-faith operation of an electronic information system.[18]

Before one of the harsher sanctions, such as dismissal, may be imposed, the trial court must weigh the following factors:

1. The public's interest in the expeditious resolution of litigation
2. The court's need to manage its docket
3. The risk of prejudice to the party seeking sanctions
4. The public policy favoring disposition of cases on their merits
5. The availability of less-drastic sanctions[19]

In *Anheuser-Busch*,[19] the defendant failed to produce business records, claiming that they were destroyed in a fire. After many months of stonewalling, the defendant produced the legible documents that survived the fire. Nonetheless, the trial court dismissed the defendant's counterclaim as a sanction for its conduct, and the Ninth Circuit upheld the dismissal, stating:

> This court has squarely rejected the notion that a failure to comply with the rules of discovery is purged by belated compliance.[20]

SUBPOENA FOR PRODUCTION OF DOCUMENTS, ELECTRONICALLY STORED INFORMATION, OR TANGIBLE THINGS, OR TO PERMIT THE INSPECTION OF PREMISES

Often a business valuation expert will need to review documents, ESI, or tangible things, or inspect business premises that are in the possession or control of someone not a party

14. Fed. R. Civ. P. § 37(b)(2)(C).
15. *Id.* § 37(b)(2)(A)(i).
16. *Id.* § 37(b)(2)(A)(ii)
17. *Id.* § 37(b)(2)(A)(vii).
18. *Id.* § 37(e).
19. Anheuser-Busch, Inc. v. Natural Beverage Distribs., 69 F.3d 337, 348 (9th Cir. 1995).

to the action. Under the Federal Rules, this can be accomplished with a subpoena.[20] As with a request for production or entry upon premises directed at a party, the request must pertain to relevant non-privileged information. All U.S. jurisdictions similarly provide for the issuance of a subpoena to nonparties.

With respect to ESI, the subpoena can designate a form or forms for production of electronic data,[21] but the person served with the subpoena may object to the requested form or forms. In addition, if the subpoena does not specify the form or forms for ESI, the person served with the subpoena must produce ESI in a form or forms in which it is usually maintained or in a form or forms that are reasonably usable.[22] However, the person producing ESI does not have to produce the same information in more than one form unless so ordered by the court for good cause.[23] New Jersey, for example, provides that a party need not provide discovery of ESI from sources that the party identifies as not reasonably accessible because of undue burden or cost.[24]

A nonparty served with a subpoena may object to the subpoena and have it quashed or modified if:

- It does not allow a reasonable time for the nonparty to comply
- It requires the nonparty to travel more than 100 miles
- It requires the nonparty to disclose privileged or protected matter, including trade secrets, confidential research, development or commercial matter, if no exception or waiver applies
- It subjects the nonparty to undue burden, including financial burden
- It is overbroad or not related to a claim or defense of the party serving the subpoena
- It requires disclosure of "an unretained expert's opinion or information that does not describe specific occurrences in dispute and results from the expert's study that was not requested by a party"[25]

Subpoena of Expert's Work Papers

Although a business valuation expert may be directly involved in litigation, the expert is, of course, not a party to the litigation. Nonetheless, it is important to obtain the work papers that the expert created and used in preparing a final valuation report and all of the other documents and information the expert received. Frequently, a party's valuation expert will find errors in the opposing expert's calculations or assumptions that are not apparent on the face of the valuation report and could only be discovered through a review of the work papers. Detection of these errors can bring the opposing valuations much closer and lead to settlement of the case.

Because the expert is not a party, the appropriate means of obtaining the work papers is a subpoena,[26] sometimes called a subpoena duces tecum. The same reasons for objecting to any other subpoena of a nonparty apply when serving a subpoena on an expert witness. Strategy demands issuing this type of subpoena after the expert tenders

20. Fed. R. Civ. P. § 45.
21. *Id.* § 45(a)(1).
22. *Id.* § 45(c)(2).
23. *Id.* § 45(d)(1)(B).
24. *Id.* § 45(d)(1)(C).
25. *Id.* § 45(c)(3)(A) to (B).
26. *Id.* § 45.

their report or answers interrogatories or makes another disclosure of their conclusions and in a manner that allows enough time to receive the document production and to review it before taking the expert's discovery deposition.

INTERROGATORIES: TIMING OF SERVICE AND LIMITATIONS

Expert witness interrogatories can compel a party to identify experts and disclosure of their opinions, conclusions, and the bases for both. They cannot take the place of expert depositions as a means of finding out what an expert has done because they are not interactive, that is, one question cannot be followed up by a series of other questions depending on the answer. However, interrogatories can be a useful discovery tool to obtain information about a business appraisal expert. This is especially true in those jurisdictions that do not require a written report of the expert to be served on other parties or that do not allow a party to depose an expert witness without a court order.[27] Only two jurisdictions, Oregon and Texas, do not allow interrogatories to be used as a discovery device with respect to expert witnesses.

Interrogatories Depend upon Written Report Requirement

In jurisdictions where the parties are required to provide the written report of an expert witness to all other parties, interrogatories can be used to obtain supplemental information about the expert or the report, such as the following:

- Educational background
- Professional designations
- Prior experience testifying as an expert witness
- Prior business valuation experience that is not litigation related
- Books or articles written by the expert
- Clarification of facts recited in the report and the source of those facts

By using interrogatories, a party who is not entitled to a written report can inquire regarding all of the information just listed, as well as require the other party to the following:

- Identify each expert expected to testify at trial
- State the subject matter of the testimony
- State the facts relied on by the expert
- State the substance of the expert's opinions
- Provide a summary of the grounds for each opinion

Timing of Service

Under FRCP 33(a) and 26(d), and the rules of four other jurisdictions—Colorado, Nevada, Utah, and the Virgin Islands—a party may serve interrogatories at any time after the parties have met and conferred on a plan of discovery and have filed a case conference report (i.e., plan of discovery). Most jurisdictions[28] allow a party to serve

27. Eight jurisdictions have both of these limitations: Alabama, Delaware, Indiana, Massachusetts, Mississippi, Nebraska, New York, and Puerto Rico.

28. Alabama, Alaska, Arizona, Arkansas, Delaware, District of Columbia, Florida, Georgia, Hawaii, Idaho, Indiana, Iowa, Kansas, Kentucky, Louisiana, Maine, Massachusetts, Michigan, Minnesota, Mississippi,

interrogatories on the plaintiff at any time after commencement of the action or on any other party with or after service of the summons and complaint on that party. In other jurisdictions, timing for service of interrogatories by plaintiff varies and may be:

- Ten days after service on or appearance by defendant (California)
- At any time after the return day (Connecticut)
- After all defendants have appeared (Illinois)
- After defendant's time for serving a responsive pleading (New York)
- Sixty days after service of summons and complaint upon the party (Rhode Island)
- After the summons and copy of the complaint have been served upon the defendant or the complaint filed (Washington)
- At any time (Maryland and New Hampshire)

Limits on Number of Interrogatories That Can Be Served

Many jurisdictions limit the number of interrogatories that can be served on another party and others authorize only court form interrogatories. These limitations should be kept in mind when deciding what information is most important to obtain about a business valuation expert or their work product. Limitations can be modified by leave of court or written stipulation of the parties.

Under FRCP 33(a), a party can serve "no more than 25 written interrogatories, including all discrete subparts. Leave to serve additional interrogatories may be granted to the extent consistent with Rule 26(b)(2)." Seven other jurisdictions—Missouri, New Hampshire, New York, Utah, Wisconsin, Wyoming, and the Virgin Islands—follow the Federal Rules limitation. The number of interrogatories allowed in other jurisdictions includes the following:

- Sixty (Hawaii)
- Fifty (Georgia, Guam, Minnesota, Montana, Nebraska, New Mexico, and North Carolina)
- Up to 50 in addition to the standard interrogatories provided case criteria met or for good cause shown (South Carolina)
- Forty (Alabama, Arizona, District of Columbia, Idaho, Nevada, Ohio, and West Virginia)
- Thirty-five (Louisiana and California)
- Thirty-five specially prepared and any additional form interrogatories (California)
- Thirty (Alaska, Colorado, Florida, Illinois, Iowa, Kentucky, Maine, Maryland, Massachusetts, Mississippi, Oklahoma, Rhode Island, and Virginia)

Form of Response

Some states have started to require that responses to discovery requests are made in electronic format. Indiana requires that the party making a discovery request serve the request or response in an electronic format (either on a disk or as an electronic document attachment) in any commercially available word-processing software system or certify by verified statement that the party does not have the equipment necessary to comply with this rule. Similarly, with respect to interrogatories, Ohio requires a party to

Missouri, Montana, Nebraska, New Jersey, New Mexico, North Carolina, North Dakota, Ohio, Oklahoma, Pennsylvania (permits service prior to service of complaint for purpose of preparing the complaint), South Carolina, South Dakota, Tennessee, Vermont, Virginia, West Virginia, Wisconsin, Wyoming, Guam, and Puerto Rico.

provide the party served with an electronic copy of the interrogatories unless otherwise agreed or seek leave of court to be relieved of this requirement if it is unable to comply.

REQUESTS FOR ADMISSION

Federal Rule 36 allows a party to serve the other party with a written request to admit the truth of any matters relating to facts, including either the application of law to fact or opinions about either and the genuineness of any document described in the request. Such requests must be accompanied by a copy of the document whose genuineness a party seeks to admit.

- A party will have 30 days after being served to respond, otherwise the matters stated in the request become admitted. While the parties may stipulate to a shorter or longer time for responding, best practices dictate planning to respond within 30 days unless one secures an immediate agreement for more time.
- When answering, if a party does not admit a fact, the answer must specifically deny the fact or state in detail why they cannot truthfully admit or deny the fact. Parties should qualify answers or deny only part of a matter when good faith so requires. A party may also assert a lack of knowledge or information as a basis for not admitting or denying a request, but only if the party states that they made reasonable inquiry and that the information the party knows or can readily obtain will not enable the party to admit or deny.
- Requests to admit only serve a purpose with respect to expert discovery if the questions one wants answered lend themselves to admissions or denials or are targeted toward seeking the admission to the genuineness of documents. They, too, cannot substitute for taking the experts discovery deposition.

DEPOSITIONS: TIMING OF REQUEST AND SPECIAL RULES

Frequently, an attorney will want to depose the other party's appraiser. The deposition is often the most important event during the course of business litigation because most cases settle before trial based on the opposing attorney's evaluation of the testimony and the demeanor of witnesses.[29] Several issues must be considered: whether the expert will be designated as a testifying expert, the timing of requirements for disclosure of expert reports and opinions, the timing of the request for deposition, limitations upon the taking of depositions, and whether the jurisdiction allows depositions of expert witnesses. Attorneys should review these rules with experts at the outset of the engagement to set expectations. They should also review what communications become discoverable.

Federal Rules of Civil Procedure 26(b)(4), 30, and 31

Under FRCP 26(b)(4)(A), a party may depose a business valuation expert whose testimony may be offered at trial. However, the deposition of an expert may be taken only after the parties have met and conferred regarding a plan of discovery as required by FRCP 26(f) and any required written report has been provided, unless leave of court is granted to depose sooner or the parties so stipulate. Other limitations on depositions of testifying experts under FRCP 30 (oral depositions) and FRCP 31 (depositions by

29. Brian Brinig, *Business Valuation Litigation: Developing, Documenting, Presenting and Defending Your Opinion*, Business Valuation Resources (June 22, 2000), www.bvlibrary.com.

written questions) require leave of court or stipulation of the parties to conduct a deposition if the proposed deposition would result in more than ten depositions by the party; the person to be deposed already has been deposed in the case; or the party seeks to take the deposition before the time specified in FRCP 26(d)—generally only after the parties have conferred under FRCP 26(f)—unless the party certifies in the notice, with supporting facts, that the deponent is expected to leave the United States and will be unavailable for examination in this country after that time.

Unless otherwise stipulated or ordered by the court, a deposition is limited to one day of seven hours.

Under FRCP 26(b)(4)(B), if a party hires a business valuation expert in anticipation of litigation or preparation for trial but does not intend to offer the testimony or opinion of that expert at trial, then the other parties may depose that expert only "on showing exceptional circumstances under which it is impracticable for the party to obtain facts or opinions on the same subject by other means."

A minority of U.S. jurisdictions follow the Federal Rules of Civil Procedure requirement that the parties meet and confer to develop a plan of discovery (also referred to as a case management order or case conference report) before depositions may be taken. In others, the rules provide for the court to conduct a case management conference within a certain period after filing. In many jurisdictions, if the plaintiff seeks to take a deposition prior to the expiration of a certain number of days after service of the summons and complaint upon any defendant or related service, the party needs to seek leave of court, except that leave is not required (1) if a defendant has served a notice of taking deposition or otherwise sought discovery or (2) if the plaintiff provides a notice that states the person to be examined is about to go out of the state or out of the country and will be unavailable for examination unless the person's deposition is taken before expiration of the period and sets forth facts to support the statement. Time limitations on the plaintiff for serving a request for deposition in various jurisdictions, irrespective of whether the jurisdiction also requires a court order for the taking of an expert's deposition, vary and some examples follow. This list does not attempt to identify other preconditions to seeking discovery, for example, service of a completed financial disclosure:

- A designated period after service of summons and complaint
- Cannot be initiated before the defendant has had a reasonable time to obtain an attorney, and
- A designated period after the return day for a party to appear

Any time limits can generally be shortened by leave of court or if the defendant seeks discovery earlier.

Some jurisdictions limit the total number of depositions that a party may take without leave of court or stipulation. Other jurisdictions require leave of court to depose an expert witness who already has been deposed in the same case or limit the amount of time any deponent must sit for deposition without an agreement or order of court. Even in a state without such a rule, a basis exists to seek a protective order quashing a subpoena to depose the same individual twice absent some changed circumstance. Some states put a limit on the number of independent expert witnesses that may testify about the same issue.[30]

30. *E.g.*, Alaska (3); Arizona (1).

DEPOSITIONS ON WRITTEN QUESTIONS

Federal Rule 31 allows an attorney to conduct depositions by written questions without leave of court except as provided in Rule 31(a)(2). A party must obtain leave of court if the parties have not stipulated to the deposition and the deposition would result in more than ten depositions being taken by either plaintiff, defendant, or by the third-party defendants; if the deponent has already been deposed in the case; or if the party seeks to take a deposition before the time specified in Rule 26(a)(i)(D), which prohibits a party from seeking discovery before the parties have conferred except in a proceeding exempted from initial disclosure. From a strategy perspective, this method of convening a deposition suffers from the same infirmity as issuing interrogatories, namely the absence of any ability to interact with the witness and to probe further.

States That Do Not Allow Depositions of Expert Witnesses as a Matter of Course

The right to depose an expert witness may be viewed as a matter of course. However, some U.S. jurisdictions[31] do not allow taking the deposition of an expert witness expected to testify at trial without a court order for further discovery beyond interrogatories. Some require service of interrogatories before taking an expert's deposition or leave of court, and one state (Oregon) still does not allow a deposition of an expert witness under any circumstances.

Ensuring an Expert Is Deposition Ready

It goes without saying that any expert who will provide deposition testimony must be thoroughly prepared to do so. However, as *Phase 2*,[32] illustrates, an unprepared expert can torpedo an entire valuation case. In that case, the expert had prepared his report four years prior to being deposed. At deposition, the expert testified that "he had not done any preparation for the deposition and had not looked at the material in the opinion binder since [preparing the report]." As a result of his being ill-prepared, the expert was not able to provide meaningful responses to questions about his assumptions and other valuation matters. Thereafter, the opposing party filed a motion in limine to exclude this expert's testimony and further sought nonsuit if the testimony was stricken. The trial court, determining that the expert's inability to testify at deposition regarding his opinion was sufficient to exclude his testimony, granted both motions.

On appeal, the party retaining the expert argued that the expert's inability to give adequate deposition testimony resulted from the four-year delay between the completion of the report and the deposition and that, in any event, the answers to all the questions asked by the opposing party at deposition could be found in the expert's report, which had been supplied to it. The appellate court rejected these arguments, stating that "the delay in taking the deposition does not eliminate the expert's obligation to be prepared adequately for the deposition."[33] Moreover, it stated, "it is not sufficient for an expert to

31. Alabama, Delaware, Indiana, Massachusetts, Minnesota, Mississippi, Nebraska, New York, Pennsylvania, South Dakota, Guam, and Puerto Rico.

32. Phase 2 Developers Corp. v. Citicorp Real Estate, 2004 Cal. App. Unpub. LEXIS 117, at *7–13 (Cal. Ct. App. 2004).

33. *Id.* at *9.

produce work papers and tell the opposing party to search through them for the answers to questions."[34] Thus, it determined that absent meaningful deposition testimony, the trial court properly excluded this expert.

Timely Disclosure and Duty to Supplement

If requested disclosure is not timely made, although it could be, the court may not permit a subsequent disclosure to remedy the original deficiency. In *AMP*,[35] the plaintiffs sought economic damages. The defendants sought information pertaining to the amount and calculation of the independent sales representatives' damages. The plaintiffs, however, did not provide any information relating to damages, except to indicate that they were engaging an economic expert. Supplemental responses to the defendants' interrogatories were not forthcoming and, eventually, the defendants brought a motion for summary judgment on the basis that the plaintiffs could not establish the amount of damages, a required element to their claim. In response to this motion, the plaintiffs provided the court with a declaration from their economic expert. This declaration listed the documents utilized and people interviewed in connection with the report. It further reported the amount of damages in terms of lost profit and lost value of business. The defendants moved to exclude the expert's declaration as without sufficient basis because it did not include any information on how the damages were calculated. The plaintiffs countered this argument by claiming that the insufficiency of the declaration went to the weight of the evidence rather than to admissibility. The trial court agreed with the plaintiffs that the expert's declaration was insufficient to overcome its motion for summary judgment because it did not provide sufficient detail. It particularly noted that the declaration did not explain the formulas or methods used to calculate the loss, disclose the period used to assess lost profits, or indicate whether the amounts were gross or net profits. Only then did the plaintiffs provide the court with an amended declaration from their expert, including the missing data. The court declined to reopen the matter because it found no reason why the missing data could not have been provided in the original declaration from the expert. On appeal, the appellate court affirmed.

In *Perry*,[36] the appraisal expert was timely disclosed, but the expert's report was not and was provided to counsel three weeks after the due date for its disclosure. Counsel moved to extend the disclosure deadline for the report, arguing that it was late as a result of the unexpected illness of one of the parties and a language barrier. Counsel also argued there was no failure of due diligence, and the opposing parties would suffer neither prejudice nor unfair surprise given that the trial was 73 days away and there was ample time to respond to the report. Nonetheless, counsel for the opposing party objected to the motion, claiming this did not constitute good cause for the late disclosure. The trial court agreed with the opposing party, denied the motion, and precluded the expert from testifying at trial. The court concluded that good cause for delaying docket deadlines does not exist simply because there is a lack of surprise to the other side or counsel inadvertently misjudges the need for an expert. Here, the court reasoned that the expert had commenced work on the report, could have supplied a draft by the disclosure

34. *Id.*
35. AMP Enters. v. Price Pfister, Inc., 2003 Cal. App. Unpub. LEXIS 10830 (Cal. Ct. App. 2003).
36. Estate of Perry, 2007 Tex. App. LEXIS 6465, at *49–52 (Tex. Ct. App. 2007).

deadline, and could have subsequently amended the draft. On appeal, the appellate court affirmed, holding that given the failure to comply in any fashion with the disclosure time limits—and given the "wide latitude" afforded a trial court to maintain its trial docket and discovery orders—there was no abuse of discretion in precluding the expert.

In *Hammers*,[37] a marital dissolution action, the trial court excluded the husband's valuation expert on the grounds that the expert had been disclosed too late—one week, rather than 60 days before trial. Early on, the wife disclosed that she had engaged a valuation expert to value the marital business. The expert's report was submitted by the discovery deadline. After reviewing the business appraisal submitted by the wife, the husband realized that he needed a valuation expert and notified the wife's attorneys that he would secure an independent appraisal. However, it was not until the week before trial that the husband designated his valuation expert. The trial court excluded the husband's valuation expert for failure to timely disclose the expert, and, on appeal, the appellate court affirmed. The appellate court reasoned that the husband could have petitioned the lower court to amend the discovery deadline but instead chose to wait until the week before trial. Accordingly, the court concluded that the wife would be prejudiced if the husband were permitted to bring the expert in on such short notice.

Similarly, in *Letendre*,[38] the trial court excluded the husband's valuation expert's report. Prior to trial, the wife requested disclosure of the husband's valuation expert, but the husband did not comply. Subsequently, the wife moved in limine to preclude the husband from presenting an appraisal or valuation expert's report or testimony not disclosed by the discovery deadline. The trial court granted the motion, and the husband did not provide any expert information to the wife prior to the close of discovery. On appeal, the husband contended that he had disclosed his expert's identity to the wife's attorney nearly a year before trial and, therefore, the wife had ample opportunity to depose him. He also contended that he believed that the discovery deadline was meant "as the date to exchange expert reports provided the exchange was mutual."[39] The state's highest court ruled that the trial court's decision to exclude the husband's expert from testifying was sustainable on the record because he did not comply with the discovery deadline mandated by the trial court and because, even if he misunderstood the meaning of the discovery date, he failed to comply with the wife's repeated requests for information in violation of discovery rules. The court concluded that the husband's failure to provide the wife with complete information bearing directly on the valuation of the business prevented the wife from adequately preparing for trial.

Many jurisdictions require a party who has made a disclosure or who has responded to an interrogatory, request for production, or request for admission—to supplement or correct its disclosure or response in a timely manner if the party learns that in some material respect the disclosure or response is incomplete or incorrect, and if the additional or corrective information has not otherwise been made known to the other parties during the discovery process or in writing or as ordered by the court. FRCP 26(e) provides that for an expert whose report must be disclosed under FRCP 26(a)(2)(B), the party's duty to supplement extends both to information included in the report and

37. Hammers v. Hammers, 890 So. 2d 944, 956 (Miss. Ct. App. 2004).
38. *In re* Letendre, 815 A.2d 938 (N.H. 2002).
39. *Id.* at 37.

to information given during the expert's deposition. Any additions or changes to this information must be disclosed by the time the party's pretrial disclosures under FRCP 26(a)(3) are due. Iowa, for example, expressly requires supplementation as to experts, as soon as practicable, but in no event less than 30 days prior to the beginning of trial except on leave of court.

If required supplemental disclosure is not timely made, a court has broad discretion to craft appropriate sanctions for such failure, up to and including the exclusion of the expert's testimony, or it may make such orders in regard to the nondisclosure as are just. In *Linsell*,[40] the Michigan Court of Appeals affirmed a trial court's decision to not strike a party's expert even though the party had failed to timely supplement interrogatory answers regarding the expert witness. The trial court had ruled that the moving party was not prejudiced because the documents that formed the basis of the expert's testimony were supplied by the moving party, and the appellate court agreed. It concluded that the trial court had not abused its discretion where not only had the documents relied on by the expert been provided by the moving party, but the expert's charts also were provided to the moving party shortly after they had been completed, and the trial court had given the moving party an opportunity to depose the expert.

In *Sharp*,[41] the court determined that a business valuation expert's effort to revise her reports and calculations through supplementation did not necessarily render her methods or opinions unreliable. The court found that no adverse inferences were to be drawn about the quality of her work product under FRCP 26(e) because, in an effort to provide complete and accurate disclosures, she satisfactorily explained the cause of mathematical errors in her business valuation and the basis for revising her calculations through proper and timely supplementation, which did not alter her ultimate opinion that the debtor businesses were insolvent. To the contrary, the court was impressed with the expert's diligence in seeking to ensure that her opinion was based on demonstrable facts (some of which were overlooked in prior reports or only came to light after the reports were issued), that her reports were internally consistent and consistent with each other, and that her analysis could withstand a rigorous review. As a result of her explanations, the court concluded that the corrections were not of the type to cause suspicion that the expert was influenced by the need to reach a particular result for the purpose of the litigation.

Another court addressed the issue of a request for sanctions where the late disclosures resulted from the opposing party failing to provide necessary financial information. In *Liszka*,[42] the appellate court held that the trial court abused its discretion in barring the husband's valuation expert as a sanction for the husband's failure to disclose the expert's opinions and report until just four days before the marriage dissolution trial. The appellate court found (1) the husband had sought to have an expert testify as to the value of the company that husband and wife had started together, (2) the husband disclosed the expert more than 60 days before trial, and (3) the late disclosure of opinions and report was not caused by the husband's bad faith or abusive discovery practices but

40. Linsell v. Applied Handling, Inc., 697 N.W.2d 913, 924–25 (Mich. Ct. App. 2005).
41. Sharp v. Chase Manhattan Bank, 2005 Bankr. LEXIS 3045, at *91–95 (Bankr. N.D. Okla. 2005).
42. *In re* Marriage of Liszka, 2016 Ill. App. (3d) 150238.

rather by the wife's failure to provide the husband and the expert with necessary financial information.

Scope of Discovery—Some Specific Examples

- **Post valuation date events.** In *Maxon*,[43] the New York Supreme Court ruled that discovery of post valuation date events was appropriate in a breach of fiduciary case involving the valuation of a corporation.
- **Confidentiality of underlying data and methodologies.** In *Manship*,[44] a federal district court ruled that pre-IPO studies relied on by a valuation expert to value a corporation for estate tax purposes were discoverable, finding that there was nothing confidential about them. In another federal case, *Batchelor-Robjohns*,[45] the court ruled that the government's refusal to disclose certain valuation models underlying its expert's valuation opinion would require exclusion of that opinion. In that case, the government's valuation expert provided a valuation of the taxpayer's assets and an opinion concerning the taxpayer's income-generating capacity, but the government refused to disclose information concerning the allegedly proprietary computer models used to value the assets. Finding that the government had failed to substantively justify its failure to disclose, the court excluded the expert's opinion, reasoning that neither the court nor transferees to whom the assets had been transferred were able to test the reliability of the valuation opinion in the absence of the data and methodology upon which the opinion was based. In addition, the court concluded that admission of the expert's opinion would clearly have prejudiced the transferees' ability to cross-examine the expert and rebut his opinion. Finally, the court excluded the reports and testimony of other government valuation experts to the extent they had relied on the opinion based on the nondisclosed models.
- **Waiver of attorney-client privilege.** In a case related to *Manship*, but brought in a different jurisdiction, the federal district court held that documents disclosed by an expert, who obtained them from the estate's attorney, although initially covered by the work product or attorney-client privilege, lost the privilege and were discoverable because (1) the estate waived the privilege by voluntarily disclosing the documents and because (2) by listing the appraiser as a testifying expert, FRCP 26(a)(2)(B) permitted discovery of "all documents 'considered' by those experts in rendering their valuation opinions" "regardless of when those materials were received, generated, reviewed and/or used."[46] The court also noted that because the estate placed the valuation *in issue* and intended to rely on it at trial, any privilege connected with the reports and related documents submitted by the estate in connection with the estate tax return was waived. Lastly, the court noted that the IRS would be unable to adequately cross-examine or present rebuttal expert testimony without full access to the documents that the estate's expert considered in forming his opinion of value.

In a subsequent proceeding,[47] the court ruled that, where yet a different court had ruled that the estate's rebuttal witness (the valuation expert) could not claim the attorney-client privilege as to consulting work the expert had conducted for the estate, because even though the expert would only testify at trial to criticize the methodology employed by the United States' valuation expert, the subject matter of that trial testimony involved

---

43. Maxon v. Mirror Show Mgmt., Inc., 7 Misc. 3d 1015A (N.Y. Sup. 2005).
44. Est. of Manship v. United States, 2006 U.S. Dist. LEXIS 96334 (N.D. Ga. 2006).
45. U.S. v. Batchelor-Robjohns, 2005 U.S. Dist. LEXIS 13552.
46. Est. of Manship v. United States, 236 F.R.D. 291 (M.D. La. 2006).
47. Est. of Manship v. United States, 2007 U.S. Dist. LEXIS 81922 (M.D. La. 2007).

the "same topics on which he was engaged in a consulting capacity dealing with the same properties,"[48] a protective order should issue *to limit* the government's questions to those (1) concerning the expert's consulting agreement with the estate (which were questions the expert had refused to answer on grounds of privilege during his previous deposition) and (2) questions arising out of documents produced by the estate related to the prior consulting engagement.

- **Distinguishing opinion from work product.** In *Greenlight*,[49] the Delaware Court of Chancery ruled in a fair value case that a deposition of a valuation witness may be taken even though the valuation report was protected from discovery under work product immunity. The court concluded that "as a logical matter it would seem that the 'bottom line' valuation range, and any intermediate data and calculations leading thereto, would not contain such protected information. Accordingly, I perceive no reason why Emerging's counsel would be unable to frame deposition questions that will elicit the discoverable information . . . without eliciting, directly or indirectly, 'disclosure of an attorney's mental impressions or theories of the case.'"[50]
- **Postproduction assertions of privilege.** Minnesota has a rule dealing with assertions of privilege that are made following production of information in discovery. The rule creates a mandatory obligation to return, sequester, or destroy information that is produced in discovery if the producing party asserts that it is subject to a privilege or work product protection. The information cannot be used for any purpose until the privilege claim is resolved. The rule provides a mechanism for the receiving party to have the validity of the privilege claim resolved by the court. The rule does not create any presumption or have any impact on the validity of the claim of privilege, nor does it excuse the inadvertent or regretted production. If the court determines that that production waived an otherwise valid privilege, then the information should be ordered for production or release from sequestration of the information.
- **Discovery of draft reports and email.** The defendants in *University of Pittsburgh*[51] sought to exclude the testimony of plaintiff's experts on the grounds that they had destroyed prior drafts of their expert reports as well as email with counsel, on a theory of spoliation and destruction of evidence. The defendants had requested the plaintiff to produce

  > [a]ll [d]ocuments provided to or by [y]ou to, revised by, relied upon, or otherwise used in consultation with or as a basis for consultation with, any expert witness identified by [y]ou pursuant to Fed. R. Civ. Proc. 26(a)(2).

  In its response, the plaintiff objected to this request as premature and stated that

  > [r]esponsive documents will be produced in accordance with Federal Rule of Civil Procedure 26(a)(2) and the Case Management Order applicable to this matter.

Around a year and a half later, the defendants deposed the experts, subpoenaing "any and all" documents related to the preparation of their reports, including all drafts

48. *Id.* at *4.
49. Greenlight Capital Qualified, L.P. v. Emerging Comm'ns, Inc., 2001 Del. Ch. LEXIS 170 (Del. Ct. Ch. Feb. 23, 2001).
50. *Id.* at *3–4.
51. Univ. of Pittsburgh v. Townsend, 2007 U.S. Dist. LEXIS 24620 (E.D. Tenn. 2007).

and correspondence with the attorneys. However, the experts had, on counsel's advice, destroyed all prior drafts up to that point as well as e-mails they had exchanged with counsel. Accordingly, the defendants contended that FRCP 26(a)(2) imposes an affirmative duty upon an expert "to preserve all documents, including e-mails and drafts of a report."[52] The defendants also contended that because the plaintiff's experts and counsel destroyed discoverable evidence, the plaintiff should be sanctioned by precluding the experts from testifying at trial.

The plaintiff countered that until the subpoenas were served on the plaintiff's experts shortly before their depositions, there was no outstanding discovery request asking for the drafts of any expert reports and that no documents were destroyed once the subpoenas were served. Furthermore, the plaintiff contended that the requested email communications and draft reports were not "evidence" and raised inherent issues of privilege and work product. Finally, the plaintiff argued that the defendants had not suffered any prejudice because they had the opportunity to fully depose the plaintiff's experts and the experts specifically identified the portions of their reports where they received assistance or input from counsel.

As to the discovery of the draft reports, the court ruled that FRCP 26(a)(2) does not impose an "affirmative duty" upon experts to preserve "all documents," particularly draft reports, and that experts are not obligated to provide copies of draft reports as part of their required 26(a)(2)(B) disclosures. The court added, however, that although draft reports are not "technically" required to be disclosed, they are "certainly discoverable." The question was one of timing. The defendant's discovery request was too "awkwardly worded" to clearly require the production of draft reports, but even a more specific request would have been "unreasonable." Served more than a year before the FRCP 26(a)(2)(B) deadlines, the request would have imposed a "continuing obligation on a party to disclose any document from an expert—whether it be a letter or a draft—as it is received through the consultation process."[53] Moreover, "such a requirement would virtually nullify the expert disclosure deadline established by the Court."[54] Because the defendants clearly requested the draft reports in their deposition subpoenas, "[o]nly at that point were the experts under a duty to retain any drafts and produce them,"[55] and because the experts had destroyed the drafts prior to the subpoenas, they would not be subject to sanctions.

As for the e-mail, the court reasoned that because FRCP 26(a)(2)(B) requires the disclosure of "the data or information considered by the [expert] in forming the opinions," to the extent that correspondence between counsel and the experts contained any factual assumptions or background used in the reports, such correspondence had to be disclosed. Because such data or information expressly is not immune from disclosure by any privilege or work product protection, it was improper "for plaintiff's counsel to have instructed and/or otherwise suggested to the experts that such communications should be destroyed."[56] Nonetheless, the court found no fraudulent intent (plaintiff's counsel, had, in fact apologized for erroneously instructing the experts to destroy the

52. *Id.* at *8.
53. *Id.* at *11.
54. *Id.*
55. *Id.*
56. *Id.* at *14.

communications). The court also concluded that the defendants were not prejudiced by the destruction of these communications, for the defendants were able to fully cross-examine the witnesses, both during depositions and at a *Daubert* hearing, on the substance of these communications and, particularly, counsel's input into their respective reports. Furthermore, the court noted that any prejudice that might have incurred (essentially depriving the defendants of a document with which to cross-examine and possibly impeach these experts) was minimal, given the collateral nature of the issue involved. For these reasons, the court declined to impose the harsh sanction of excluding the experts.

Some states have expressly addressed the discoverability of expert draft reports. Louisiana provides that the expert's drafts of a report, if required by motion, and communications, including notes and electronically stored information or portions thereof that would reveal the mental impressions, opinions, or trial strategy of the attorney for the party who has retained the expert to testify, shall not be discoverable except, in either case, on a showing of exceptional circumstances under which it is impractical for the party seeking discovery to obtain facts or opinions on the same subject by other means.

INVOLVING THE BUSINESS VALUATION EXPERT IN DISCOVERY[57]

Many attorneys do not involve their business appraisal experts in the discovery process in cases involving the value of a business or professional practice. However, an expert can provide support in the discovery process in several ways that will assist in refuting the opposing expert's position.

Preparing Discovery Requests

Business appraisers provide an important service in the preparation of discovery requests to get the information necessary for the appraisal. The appraiser usually will know what to request for companies in the industry or line of practice involved.

The attorney does not want to be in the position of not having requested some information that would be pertinent to a good appraisal and then not being able to obtain it. On the other hand, an overly broad discovery demand gives the other side excuses for delay and objections about the request being unreasonably onerous.

Preparing Deposition and Interrogatory Questions

As mentioned previously, depending on the nature of the business or practice and the rules of the jurisdiction, in addition to the site visit and management interviews, there may be depositions involving employees, outside advisors (e.g., bankers or CPAs), and, especially, the opposing expert. The business appraisal expert can help formulate the initial questions to ask these individuals, as well as general lines of inquiry that will help elicit important information about the opposing expert's valuation conclusion. Depositions generally are preferable to interrogatories because of their interactive nature. The answer to one question may well lead to another question or series of questions. In

---

57. This section was adapted with permission from Shannon P. Pratt, *Involve Your Business Appraiser in Discovery*, DEFENSIBLE BUSINESS VALUATIONS™ (Fall 2007).

circumstances where interrogatories are the only option, however, it is even more critical that the business appraiser be involved in formulating the questions to be sure important information is obtained and that terms of art do not result in answers that do not provide the information sought.

Presence at Opposing Expert's Deposition

If you are deposing an opposing expert, having your expert present usually is a huge benefit. This will help to evaluate the other expert's valuation work product and glean the information needed for effective cross-examination and rebuttal testimony.

Your expert can study the opposing expert's work papers (which you will have demanded be produced via subpoena) and develop questions that delve into the technical nature of what was covered in the appraisal. Your expert can provide follow-up questions, depending on the answers given to the basic questions that already were anticipated.

Many attorneys do not have the financial expertise to totally probe exactly what was determined by the other expert, in a technical sense, to evaluate the strengths and weaknesses of the work and prepare effective cross-examination and rebuttal. Having your expert present should overcome this problem.

Rules in many states only allow counsel and parties to attend depositions, so it helps for counsel to seek agreements to allow experts to attend early on so that time remains for making motions if counsel do not reach agreement.

Involving Your Expert in Depositions of Opposing Experts

The primary purpose of depositions of opposing experts is to find out the opinions to which they intend to offer at trial, and the details of the information and procedures they relied on to reach those opinions. There are a number of topics that attorneys should address in the deposition, including the opposing expert's qualifications, who the opposing expert interviewed, and what other information the expert needs to finish or double-check his or her report.[58] Because opposing experts rely on specialized knowledge, it usually requires the input of someone with comparable specialized knowledge to formulate initial and follow-up questions, and to determine when the line of questioning has been answered sufficiently for a complete understanding of the expert's opinion and the basis therefore.

At the conclusion of the deposition, an expert should be able to replicate the work of the opposing expert and identify any flaws that may be present.

Normally, this necessitates the expert not only reading the opposing expert's report and advising counsel on what needs to be covered but also being present at the deposition of the opposing expert. The reason for this is that it is nearly impossible to create a complete list of deposition questions; follow-up questions are almost always necessary, depending on the answers to the initial questions—often a series of technical questions on details about which the attorney is unlikely to possess the necessary specialized knowledge.

---

58. *See* Gerald Nissenbaum, *Seven 'Knockout Punch' Questions for Cross-Examining Appraisal Experts*, Judges & Lawyers Bus. Valuation Update 1–3 (Feb. 2000).

To take it to the extreme, consider the following:

Q: Why did the subject company's sales decline 25% in 2008 from 2007?
A: The company had a bad year. Customers just didn't seem to be willing to part with their money.

Counsel has not learned anything. This needs to be probed in detail. In a more technical sense:

Q: Where did you get your guideline public company information?
A: SEC filings.

This question is inadequate. Someone knowledgeable about Securities and Exchange Commission filings needs to ask which forms, which dates (which are likely to vary from company to company), and what medium was used to obtain the filings. It is even better if such information (and, indeed, the expert's entire work file) is available at the deposition so that your expert can examine it and raise questions that may never otherwise have been considered. Such questions may include, for example, why did you use the sources and dates that you did? Also, *why didn't* you use. . .? Generally, only an expert would know what to ask about what the other expert *did not* use, procedures not performed, or information provided but *not considered or relied upon.*

Counsel may retain a testifying expert to present valuation opinions at trial and may also retain a consulting expert to prepare counsel and the testifying expert for trial. Alternatively, counsel may elect to retain separate experts to provide affirmative and rebuttal opinions at trial. In some jurisdictions, as soon as a consulting expert is designated as a testifying expert, they remain for all time subject to the discovery rules of a testifying expert including having to disclose communications with counsel and opinions and conclusions. In at least one jurisdiction, a court allowed counsel to re-designate a disclosed testifying expert as a consultant and to shield that expert's reports and opinions from discovery.[59]

Another big advantage of thorough technical probing at deposition is that it often facilitates settlement. Once the expert's differences are totally clarified, there is at least a framework to try to resolve them.

Rebutting the Opposition

The two primary ways that the expert can help refute the opposition are by:

1. Helping the attorney prepare effective cross-examination
2. Providing a rebuttal report and testimony

Any weaknesses of the opposition's expert should be brought to the court's attention. The expert can help to identify these weaknesses by listening to the other expert and helping the attorney to formulate questions that will educate the court convincingly about such weaknesses.

It is often true that effective rebuttal of an opposing expert's testimony is of great importance at trial. Having the expert attend and observe the initial testimony of the opposing expert and then provide rebuttal testimony can be crucial in getting a fair

59. Dameron v. Mercy Hosp. & Med. Ctr., 2019 Ill. App. (1st) 172338.

outcome for your client. There are far too many valuation cases where one side's weak, or even clearly erroneous, testimony carried the day because it was allowed to stand without challenge.

Sometimes, if the case is large enough, counsel may wish to have a rebuttal expert separate from the direct testimony expert. This provides several advantages. For one, it lessens the possibility that the court may feel a taint of bias on the part of the direct expert because of his or her criticism of the opponent's expert's work. Second, the rebuttal expert may have extra credibility with the court by "out-credentialing" the opposing expert. Also, the rebuttal expert may lend extra support to the methodology employed by the direct testimony expert.

COMMON ERRORS

Discovery presents competing considerations for both valuators and attorneys. While temptation might prompt the desire to keep site visits and management interviews separate, closing valuation gaps will always be easier with fewer variables. Making sure the experts all see and hear the same information and receive the same documents narrows the differences to how they use the information.

Confidentiality ought not to be a reason to prohibit having a court reporter or recording of interviews since that limits any chance of misquotation or arguments at trial over what an interviewee said. Better to have the court rule on the issue than to compromise the ability to accurately document interviews.

While rules of procedure generally only require a party to produce what the other side requests, if the expert has access to other documents and information that they rely upon and may also rely upon for testimony, produce it even though not requested. To do otherwise might jeopardize the testimony of the valuation expert.

Keep track of what the expert tenders in lists that can be accessed quickly when objections arise at trial. The same goes for abstracts of deposition testimony from the expert in order to quickly find where they talked about anything that the other side objects to them testifying about. The inability to quickly meet objections of nondisclosure quickly and efficiently, may result in losing on those objections and going back later makes for a disjointed record.

Remember that an attorney for any party can ask questions at a deposition. If the expert needs to supplement their disclosures or to disclose any critique of the opposing expert's work, the attorney can ask questions to draw out those disclosures during their own expert's deposition. That way the other side can hear the information and follow up on it in real time.

SUMMARY

Discovery presents an important and powerful tool both for learning what the other parties intend to present as evidence of the value of a business interest and for obtaining information to assist the business appraiser in their analysis of value and testimony. It should not be conducted lightly or haphazardly; both attorney and expert must give careful thought to every discovery request to ensure that it is both comprehensive and relevant. While it is tempting to use form requests to save time, doing so with valuation issues risks missing the mark on much relevant and useful information or losing battles over quashing requests for information if overbroad.

Giving good depositions (that is presenting powerful testimony when one's own expert testifies at their deposition) can establish the strength of one's case, with a view to encouraging an earlier and more favorable settlement. A conventional instruction to witnesses, including experts, might be: "Just answer the question; don't volunteer information." However, with a strong case and a strong expert, giving the expert leeway to use judgment in volunteering information sometimes helps lead to a settlement.

Also, it is beneficial to use the business appraiser to formulate discovery requests and cross-examination questions, as well as to rebut the other side's expert opinions and reports.

REFERENCE FOR DISCOVERY AND THE BUSINESS VALUATION EXPERT

Kuhne, Cecil C., III. 2019. *A Litigators Guide to Expert Witnesses*, 2nd ed. (Chicago: ABA Book Publishing).

CHAPTER 37

Business Valuation Standards and Credentials

Jay E. Fishman, FASA, FRICS and Kenneth J. Pia, Jr., ASA, CPA/ABV, MCBA

INTRODUCTION

In this chapter you will learn about:

- Organizations offering professional accreditation
- Other organizations offering business valuation guidance
- Business valuation professional standards
- Other professional organization standards
- Internal Revenue Service authority

ORGANIZATIONS OFFERING PROFESSIONAL ACCREDITATION

There are three major professional organizations based in the United States that offer education and examinations leading to accreditation for a professional designation in business valuation. There are organizations based in the United Kingdom and Canada that offer accreditation as well. The organizations based in the United States are the American Society of Appraisers (ASA), the American Institute of Certified Public Accountants (AICPA), and the National Association of Certified Valuators and Analysts (NACVA). In Canada, there is the Chartered Business Valuators (CBV Institute and formerly the Canadian Institute of Chartered Business Valuators), based in the United Kingdom, and the Royal Institution of Chartered Surveyors (RICS). Each of these organizations requires varying accreditation requirements and offers varying forms of education.

Information on each of the organizations, including their education offerings and accreditation requirements, can be found in the Appendix to Chapter 1 of *Shannon Pratt's Valuing a Business: The Analysis and Appraisal of Closely Held Businesses* 6th ed., available on ASA's website, www.appraisers.org/VAB6. All of the organizations publish membership directories, which are available to members or may be obtained for a nominal charge. (Note: Not all members are necessarily accredited by the organization.)

The course curricula of these five[1] organizations largely concern the valuation of closely held businesses (businesses with no public trading market for their securities),

1. Previously, there was another business appraisal organization, the Institute of Business Appraisers (IBA). The IBA offered the Certified Business Appraiser (CBA) and Master Certified Business Appraiser

partial interests in closely held businesses, and intangible assets. In certain instances, they also address matters such as discounts for fractional interests in tangible assets such as real estate.

All the organizations also sponsor valuation training courses, continuing education webinars, seminars, and conferences. The offerings tend to focus on narrower issues in greater depth than do the basic courses; examination of issues about which professional controversy exists; and updated reports on matters such as changes in law and regulation, new precedential case law, and new and expanded sources of empirical data used in valuation.

Each of the credentialing organizations discussed has varying requirements for the certifications offered, including requirements for the number of professional hours devoted specifically to the field of business valuation. However, the ASA is the only professional organization that requires a peer review of appraisal reports prior to the grant of the certification.

Other Organizations Offering Business Valuation Guidance

In addition to the five organizations just discussed, several other organizations offer various forms of education and guidance in aspects of business valuation.

Of particular importance is the CFA Institute (formerly the Association for Investment Management and Research (AIMR)), which awards the Chartered Financial Analyst (CFA) professional designation. This designation requires passing three rigorous full-day examinations primarily covering the analysis of publicly traded securities and portfolio management concepts. The curriculum also includes content on valuing closely held businesses. A small number of the CFA Institute's 190,000-plus charter holders specialize in closely held business valuation. Some individuals also hold the designation of ASA (Accredited Senior Appraiser of the ASA). This cross-designation may be especially relevant for engagements such as when a private company is acquired by a public company, a public company is going private, or dissenting stockholder actions involve public companies. CFA members are concentrated in the United States and Canada, but there are members throughout the world.

The other often-mentioned group is the International Business Brokers Association (IBBA), which is the largest international nonprofit association operating exclusively for the benefit of people and firms engaged in the various aspects of business brokerage and mergers and acquisitions. Today, the IBBA has more than 1,800 cooperative business brokers and intermediaries across Canada, Mexico, Asia, Europe, Australia, and the United States. The IBBA has more than 2,700 members who act as intermediaries in the sales of businesses. Some members also offer business appraisal services. The IBBA awards the professional designation of Certified Business Intermediary (CBI). Required education includes attending one IBBA conference and earning 68 credit hours of IBBA University-offered or other recognized courses on valuation and establishing company sale prices.

(MCBA) designation. In 2008, NACVA acquired IBA and in 2016, NACVA suspended IBA's activities. Although new CBA and MCBA designations are no longer offered, there are active professionals who still maintain the CBA and MCBA designations.

The ESOP Association consists of member companies that sponsor Employee Stock Ownership Plans and the professionals that provide various advisory services to them, including independent business appraisers, who are required to value the share prices of closely held ESOP-owned companies at least annually. The ESOP Association does not issue standards, nor does it offer accreditation. It does publish materials containing valuation guidance for ESOP shares developed by its Advisory Committee on Valuation, which consists of experienced ESOP share appraisers. The ESOP Association also offers continuing education seminars, including sessions relating to ESOP valuation issues. Business appraisers who perform such valuations should also be familiar with all regulatory guidance regarding the valuation of shares in ESOP-owned companies.

Exhibit 37-1 lists the various professional designations offered by the organizations discussed in this chapter.

Exhibit 37-1 Professional Accreditation Quick Reference List

ABAR	Accredited in Business Appraisal Review (Institute of Business Appraisers)
AM	Accredited Member (ASA)
ARM	Appraisal Review and Management (ASA)
ASA	Accredited Senior Appraiser (ASA)
AVA	Accredited Valuation Analyst (National Association of Certified Valuation Analysts)
BVAL	Business Valuator Accredited for Litigation (Institute of Business Appraisers)
CBA	Certified Business Appraiser (Institute of Business Appraisers)
CBI	Certified Business Intermediary (International Business Brokers Association)
CBV	Chartered Business Valuator (The Canadian Institute of Chartered Business Valuators)
CFA	Chartered Financial Analyst (CFA Institute)
CPA/ABV[2]	Certified Public Accountant Accredited in Business Valuations (American Institute of Certified Public Accountants)
CVA	Certified Valuation Analyst (National Association of Certified Valuation Analysts)
FASA	Fellow of the ASA (American Society of Appraisers)
FCBI	Fellow Certified Business Intermediary (International Business Brokers Association)
FCBV	Fellow of the Canadian Institute of Chartered Business Valuators
FRICS	Fellow Royal Institute of Chartered Surveyors
IA	Intangible Asset (American Society of Appraisers)
MCBA	Master Certified Business Appraiser (Institute of Business Appraisers)
MRICS	Member of the Royal Institute of Chartered Surveyors
RICS	Royal Institute of Chartered Surveyors

BUSINESS VALUATION PROFESSIONAL STANDARDS

Uniform Standards of Professional Appraisal Practice

The most widely recognized and cited set of professional appraisal standards is the *Uniform Standards of Professional Appraisal Practice* (USPAP), published by The Appraisal Foundation (TAF). TAF was founded in 1987 by a group of leading professional appraisal organizations serving a variety of appraisal disciplines, including real estate, personal

2. The ABV designation is now also available to non-CPAs who qualify.

property, and business and intangible asset appraisal. It is funded by Congress, member organizations, donations, and proceeds from sales of publications.

TAF is governed by a 21-member board of trustees consisting of appointees of sponsoring organizations and trustees at large. The trustees appoint two boards, the Appraisal Standards Board (ASB) and the Appraiser Qualifications Board (AQB), each of which then acts autonomously in developing and promulgating appraisal standards and appraiser qualifications. The Appraisal Standards Board develops USPAP.

USPAP contains four basic components:

1. Prefatory material (definitions, preamble, ethics, competency rule, and jurisdictional exceptions).
2. Standards Rules 1 through 10 (3 and 4 apply specifically to appraisal review, development, and reporting, and 9 and 10 apply specifically to business and intangible asset appraisals).
   Standard 3 is directed toward developing a credible opinion of the quality of another analyst's work.
   Standard 4 is directed toward developing a credible opinion of the quality and content of another analyst's report.
   Standard 9 includes requirements for procedures and comprehensiveness in conducting an appraisal of a business, business interest, or intangible asset.
   Standard 10 states what needs to be included in a report of an appraisal of a business, business interest, or intangible asset.
3. Statements on Appraisal Standards, which contain further elaboration on points made in the standards themselves. Compliance with the Statements on Appraisal Standards is mandatory for appraisals that purport to conform to USPAP. However, there are few Statements on Appraisal Standards that actually apply to business and intangible asset valuations. All of these have been retired but are instructive.
4. Advisory Opinions, which contain commentary that is advisory in nature. Again, there is little in the Advisory Opinions that is applicable to business or intangible asset appraisals.

USPAP has historically been updated biannually by the ASB, with each edition usually released in November and applicable to appraisals performed in the following calendar years. Note that the edition of USPAP that applies is the edition for the year in which the appraisal is performed, which may be a later year than the year of the effective valuation date if an appraisal is performed retrospectively. The most recent edition is the 2024 edition, which will remain in force until another edition is published.

Compliance with USPAP is legally mandatory for real estate transactions of more than $250,000 involving federally related agencies, and for conversions of mutual savings and loans to stock companies; otherwise, as of this writing, compliance with USPAP is followed only if so stipulated in the engagement agreement between the appraiser and the client or if the appraiser is a member of an organization requiring compliance therewith. Nevertheless, whether required or not, USPAP is widely accepted in the professional appraisal community. Most leading appraisal authorities consider it a valid set of standards against which to measure the minimum requirements for an appraisal.[3]

TAF's other board, the Appraisal Qualifications Board (AQB), has promulgated qualifications for real estate appraisers and personal property appraisers. As of this

3. Currently, printed and electronic versions of USPAP cost $35. Contact The Appraisal Foundation, www.appraisalfoundation.org.

writing, the AQB has no plans to develop qualifications for appraisers of businesses and intangible assets.

Other Professional Organization Standards

All five of the professional associations listed in the first section of this chapter have promulgated professional business valuation standards of their own. As many business valuation professionals are members of the AICPA (CPAs), one such set of commonly applied professional standards is known as the *Valuation of a Business, Business Ownership Interest, Security, or Intangible Asset* (VS Section 100). The various sets of professional standards may be accessed free of charge from each association's respective website.

None of the individual associations' standards are in direct conflict with USPAP. In general, each set of standards goes into more detail than does USPAP.

Internal Revenue Service Authority

Revenue Rulings issued by the Internal Revenue Service are often cited as authority for business valuation standards. The most commonly cited ruling related to business valuation is Revenue Ruling 59–60, which addresses criteria that should be considered in the valuation of closely held company stock.

Revenue Rulings certainly contain some business valuation wisdom. However, three caveats are important:

- Revenue Rulings are not legally binding, they are merely an expression of the IRS's position on an issue. They are usually, but not always, upheld when tested in court.
- Revenue Rulings reflect conditions as of the time they were written and are not typically updated to reflect current conditions (for example, Revenue Ruling 59–60 was written in 1959).
- Revenue Rulings are written for valuations for tax purposes (for example, estate tax, gift tax, charitable contributions, income taxes) and therefore reflect valuation theory in the context of the legal standard of fair market value as defined by the U.S. Treasury Department. In valuations for other purposes under other legal definitions of value (for example, fair value for a shareholder dispute), some aspects of Revenue Rulings may not be applicable.

In 2004, the IRS issued the *IRS Business Valuation Guidelines*. This guidance is very similar to USPAP. The latest version of the IRS Business Valuation Guidelines, released in 2020, can be found online at www.bvresources.com.

SUMMARY

Because of its application to various appraisal disciplines (real property, personal property, business valuation, and mass appraisal), USPAP is an oft referred to set of standards. There are also standards that specifically address business valuation.

Specifically, three U.S. valuation professional associations offer education and accreditation business valuation and publish business valuation standards. These are ASA, AICPA, and NACVA.[4] For example, the AICPA standard VS Section 100 is often used in practice by CPAs.

---

4. NACVA publishes charts comparing standards, including reporting standards. Domestic standards (ASA, USPAP, NACVA, AICPA) are compared in a chart available at https://www.nacva.com/Files/DomesticStandardsChart_2023_Final.pdf.

In Canada, the CBV Institute issues standards. Organizations responsible for standards and educational materials on a global basis include the International Valuation Standards Council (IVSC), RICS, and the International Institute of Business Valuers (iiBV).

In all cases, the standards published by these organizations are considerably more detailed than USPAP. While there are differences, they do not conflict with USPAP. For example, the AICPA's VS Section 100 is similar to USPAP in focusing on two basic standards: Development of the Appraisal (or Analysis) and Reporting.

When assessing the qualifications of a potential expert witness proffering opinions on the value of a closely held business, an interest in a closely held business, or intangible assets, counsel needs to be aware of the many different credentials business appraisers may possess and the qualifications indicated by a given credential. However, counsel should assess credentials with caution, as professional experience, education, and training are equally as important as the credential that an appraiser may possess. Counsel should also have their expert verify that the opposing expert has followed all applicable business valuation professional standards, that is, USPAP, AICPA's Statement of Standards for Valuation Services (VS Section 100), and so on, adequately.

REFERENCES FOR BUSINESS VALUATION STANDARDS AND CREDENTIALS

Hitchner, James R., Shannon P. Pratt and Jay E. Fishman. 2016. "Business Valuation Standards and Ethics." In *A Consensus View—Q&A Guide to Business Valuation*, 257–318 (Ventnor City, NJ: Valuation Products and Services).

Pratt, Shannon P. and the ASA Educational Foundation. 2022. "Business Valuation Standards and Credentials." In *Shannon Pratt's Valuing a Business: The Analysis and Appraisal of Closely Held Companies*, 6th ed. Chap. 1, 3–16 (New York: McGraw-Hill).

CHAPTER 38

Valuation and Appraiser Penalties

Michael A. Gregory, ASA, CVA

INTRODUCTION

In this chapter you will learn about:

- Relationship of standards and valuation penalties at the federal level
- Overall history of the penalty on appraisers and definitions
- Qualified appraiser and appraisal
- IRS Penalty Handbook
- Examples of penalty calculations

This chapter addresses some additional commentary on standards beyond Chapter 37, "Business Valuation Standards and Credentials," with a focus on penalties, the regulatory framework that valuers and appraisers need to navigate, and the implications of not meeting certain standards with the application of penalties and other ramifications. In this chapter, the focus is on penalties on appraisers at the federal level. Some insight is offered on penalties associated with real estate appraisals at the state level and penalties on the taxpayer associated with undervaluation associated with estate and gift tax valuations.

STANDARDS

Chapter 37 addresses business valuation standards. To be clear, appraisers need to meet certain standards associated with professional societies and/or governmental regulations. Governmental regulations are generally at the federal and/or state level and either specify standards or reference standards similar to or associated with the *Uniform Standards of Professional Appraisal Practice* (USPAP). Regarding business valuers (hereafter all business valuers will be referred to as appraisers), the National Association of Certified Valuers and Analysts (NACVA) has developed a comparison chart that compares standards from the American Society of Appraisers (ASA), USPAP, NACVA, and the American Institute of Certified Public Accountants (AICPA).[1]

Real property appraisers may be certified at the state level and have one of several designations based on experience, education, and testing levels with various professional societies. Federal level jurisdiction is directed by The Appraisal Foundation (TAF). The

1. Business Valuation/Appraisal Standards Comparison Chart, https://www.nacva.com/Files/DomesticStandardsChart_Jun2022.pdf.

Appraisal Standards Board is the independent board of TAF responsible for promulgation of minimum appraisal standards for federally related transactions. The Appraiser Qualification Board is the independent board of TAF responsible for promulgation of qualification criteria for licensure of real estate appraisers authorized to conduct appraisals on federally related transactions, and for issuing or endorsing a uniform state real estate appraiser qualification examination.[2]

HISTORY OF THE § 6695A PENALTY ON APPRAISERS AND DEFINITIONS

The Internal Revenue Service (IRS) mission is to:

> Provide America's taxpayers top-quality service by helping them understand and meet their tax responsibilities and enforce the law with integrity and fairness to all.[3]

With the IRS tasked with addressing valuation issues and enforcing the tax laws, Congress determined that the Office of Professional Responsibility (OPR) with Internal Revenue Code (I.R.C.) § 6700 was not able to address abuses by appraisers alone. Under § 6700, IRS applications were rare, and the penalties were small.

With the application of § 1219 of the Pension Protection Act (PPA) of 2006, and an amendment to specifically include estate and gift tax returns,[4] the law was intended to apply to real estate easements for charitable deductions and expanded to include estate and gift tax returns. Today the IRS applies this penalty to all types of appraisals. This I.R.C. § 6695A penalty on appraisers pertains to "Substantial and Gross Valuation Misstatements Attributable to Incorrect Appraisals." Highlights of this act, its history, and implications, are described later.

QUALIFIED APPRAISER AND QUALIFIED APPRAISAL DEFINED

Qualified Appraiser

I.R.C. § 1.170A-17 defines a Qualified Appraiser as follows:

> **(b)** ***Qualified appraiser***—(1) *Definition.* For purposes of section 170(f)(11) and § 1.170A–16(d)(1)(ii) and (e)(1)(ii), the term *qualified appraiser* means an individual with verifiable education and experience in valuing the type of property for which the appraisal is performed, as described in paragraphs (b)(2) through (4) of this section.
>
> **(2)** ***Education and experience in valuing the type of property***—(i) *In general.* An individual is treated as having education and experience in valuing the type of property within the meaning of paragraph (b)(1) of this section if, as of the date the individual signs the appraisal, the individual has—
>
> **(A)** Successfully completed (for example, received a passing grade on a final examination) professional or college-level coursework, as described in paragraph (b)(2)(ii)

2. The Appraisal Foundation, https://www.appraisalfoundation.org/imis/TAF/TAF_Boards.aspx.

3. The IRS Mission Statement, https://www.irs.gov/irm/part1/irm_01-001-001#:~:text=The%20IRS%20mission%3A,IRS%20should%20perform%20that%20role.

4. The Pension Protection Act (PPA) of 2006, Pub. L. No. 109-280 and Tax Technical Corrections Act of 2007, Pub. L. No. 110-172, § 3(e), the application of appraisal penalties under § 6695A(a) of the PPA was amended to include instances of "substantial estate or gift tax valuation understatement[s]."

of this section, in valuing the type of property, as described in paragraph (b)(3) of this section, and has two or more years of experience in valuing the type of property, as described in paragraph (b)(3) of this section; or

(B) Earned a recognized appraiser designation, as described in paragraph (b)(2)(iii) of this section, for the type of property, as described in paragraph (b)(3) of this section.

(ii) *Coursework must be obtained from an educational organization, generally recognized professional trade or appraiser organization, or employer educational program.* For purposes of paragraph (b)(2)(i)(A) of this section, the coursework must be obtained from—

(A) A professional or college-level educational organization described in section 170(b)(1)(A)(ii);

(B) A generally recognized professional trade or appraiser organization that regularly offers educational programs in valuing the type of property; or

(C) An employer as part of an employee apprenticeship or educational program substantially similar to the educational programs described in paragraphs (b)(2)(ii)(A) and (B) of this section.

(iii) *Recognized appraiser designation defined.* A *recognized appraiser designation* means a designation awarded by a generally recognized professional appraiser organization on the basis of demonstrated competency.[5]

Qualified Appraisal

A Qualified Appraisal is defined as follows:

(a) *Qualified appraisal*—(1) *Definition.* For purposes of section 170(f)(11) and § 1.170A–16(d)(1)(ii) and (e)(1)(ii), the term *qualified appraisal* means an appraisal document that is prepared by a qualified appraiser (as defined in paragraph (b)(1) of this section) in accordance with generally accepted appraisal standards (as defined in paragraph (a) (2) of this section) and otherwise complies with the requirements of this paragraph (a).

(2) *Generally accepted appraisal standards defined.* For purposes of paragraph (a)(1) of this section, *generally accepted appraisal standards* means the substance and principles of the Uniform Standards of Professional Appraisal Practice, as developed by the Appraisal Standards Board of the Appraisal Foundation.[6]

ADDITIONAL REQUIREMENTS RELATING TO NON-CASH CHARITABLE CONTRIBUTIONS

Regarding non-cash contribution for federal tax purposes, I.R.C. Regulations § 1.170A-15, § 16, and § 17 further define a Qualified Appraiser and Qualified Appraisal, require an appraisal declaration, and provide examples of when an appraiser is not qualified.[7]

---

5. 26 C.F.R. § 1.170A-17, Qualified appraisal and qualified appraiser.

6. *Id.*

7. Noncash Charitable Contributions Additional Requirements, https://www.federalregister.gov/documents/2018/07/30/2018-15734/substantiation-and-reporting-requirements-for-cash-and-noncash-charitable-contribution-deductions; https://www.govinfo.gov/content/pkg/CFR-2020-title26-vol4/pdf/CFR-2020-title26-vol4-sec1-170A-15.pdf.

2010 DEVELOPMENTS

The major appraisal organizations requested an open session hearing with the IRS to discuss the IRS's process for identifying an appraiser for a penalty violation as specified in a Letter 4477[8] as being detrimental to that appraiser being able to hold himself or herself as an expert witness in court. Just the allegation on a penalty could be detrimental to that appraiser.[9] As a result, the IRS issued a revised Letter 4477 indicating that the appraiser was not accused of a violation, but rather that the IRS was initiating an investigation of a potential penalty on that appraiser.

The IRS established a procedure whereby if any agent or specialist (valuer or appraiser) makes an accusation that a penalty should be applied to an appraiser, and obtains their manager's concurrence, then the facts associated with that case should be submitted to the Engineering Valuation Penalty Coordinator Manager (EVPCM). The EVPCM would then reach out to two experienced valuers or appraisers with expertise in the specified area of valuation to each independently assess the facts and determine if they unanimously (all three) agreed that a penalty investigation should be initiated. If there was a unanimous agreement, then a Letter 4477 would be issued, and a penalty investigation would be initiated. This would involve obtaining all agent or specialist (valuer or appraiser) work papers including administrative files, interviewing the appraiser, and preparing a documented analysis.

January 2020 Developments

On January 22, 2020, the Small Business Self Employed (SBSE) Office of Policy Director and the Director of the Engineering Program (where business valuers are located at the IRS) jointly agreed to eliminate the procedure requiring review by members of the IRS Engineering Program requiring the EVPCM to decide whether there should be an investigation as indicated earlier.[10] The memo referenced in footnote 10 was obtained through a Freedom of Information Request.[11] The IRS provided no reason why the procedure was changed and provided no public workshop or hearing relative to the change.

Reaction by Professional Organizations

A letter was sent by various appraisal-related organizations to the Commissioner of the IRS and to the Assistant Secretary, Tax Policy at the Department of the Treasury on May 18, 2010, raising concerns associated with (1) the absence of due process, (2) absence of checks and balances, (3) emotional and financial impact on appraisers, (4) the statement "more likely than not" in the regulations would result in bias (this will be explained later), (5) the reduction of the number of individuals involved from five to two with the two having no valuation experience, and (6) and no stakeholder notice or engagement.[12]

8. *BVWire Issue #90-1* "ASA Asks IRS to eliminate Letter 4477 and establish due process for appraiser penalties" (Mar. 3, 2010), https://www.bvresources.com/blogs/bvwire-news/2010/03/02/asa-asks-irs-to-eliminate-letter-4477-and-establish-due-process-for-appraiser-penalties.

9. *Id.*

10. Control Number LB&I 20-0120-001 (Jan. 22, 2020).

11. The memo has since been removed from the IRS website.

12. *ASA, Others Send Letter to IRS and Treasury Questioning Recent Changes in 6695A Pre-penalty Review Process*, ASA (May 28, 2020), https://www.appraisersnewsroom.org/?p=6945ASA, ASFMARA, AI, AAA, AMEA, EAANA, ISA, MBREA | The Association of Valuation Professionals, NACVA, NAJA, RICS.

Follow Up to Letter 4477

On April 24, 2020, an internal IRS document that has the "From" and "To" blacked out and is identified as Number 202129009 with subject line "RE: 6695A" states in part:

> Thank you for your question: Can Penalty Examiners assess the section 6695A penalty without having sent the L4477/IDR (Information Document Requests) and not conducted an interview? (e.g., short statute but we may be able to assess penalty through the CCP)
>
> There is no case law or guidance on the issue, but our position is that in order to assess the 6695A penalty, the IRS is not legally required to send the L4477, to send an IDR, or to conduct an interview with the appraiser, but it may be a good policy decision to do so. As I'm sure you're aware, the IRM is not legally binding on the IRS.[13]

With that commentary the IRS can now issue a § 6695A penalty by an agent signed off by his or her manager, not issue a Letter 4477, not request any information including work papers or interview the appraiser, and simply issue the penalty. This allows for streamlining the process for the IRS but may well have detrimental impacts on the appraiser.

Summary of the History

The § 6695A penalty was initially introduced to address real estate easements and amended to address estate and gift tax cases. A process was put in place by the IRS to ensure that the application by IRS personnel had a fair vetting to avoid application that may have involved bias or a perception of bias by an agent, valuer, appraiser, or their managers. That process involved five IRS employees. The notification Letter 4477 was changed to ensure no negative impact on an appraiser by only stating the application of the potential penalty with an investigation and not that a penalty was being applied to the appraiser. The IRS in January 2020 eliminated the review process allowing any agent with their manager's approval to apply the penalty. In July 2023, an internal document indicated that the application of Letter 4477 was a "good idea" in terms of policy, but there was no requirement to send the letter, to issue an IDR, or to conduct an interview of the appraiser to apply the penalty. In other words, any agent with their manager's approval could apply a § 6695A penalty with no valuer assigned to the case.

KEY ELEMENTS OF THE IRS PENALTY HANDBOOK

The *IRS Penalty Handbook* 20.1.12 "Penalties Applicable to Incorrect Appraisals"[14] (Handbook) provides the program scope and objectives, background, authority, responsibilities, fair and consistent approach to penalty administration, program management review, terms/definitions/acronyms, related resources, who asserts the penalty, asserting the § 6695A penalty, statute of limitations, power of attorney (POA), field exam procedures, referrals and penalty case review procedures, penalty case file, I.R.C. § 6695 case file assembly, appeal rights, case processing and assessment instructions, and pro forma

---

13. Text published by *Tax Analysts*, August 19, 2021, "IRS Addresses Requirements for Assessing Appraiser Penalties" citation ECC 2021129009.

14. Internal Revenue Manual of the IRS Part 20. Penalty and Interest Chapter 1. Penalty Handbook Section 12. Penalties Applicable to Incorrect Appraisals, https://www.irs.gov/irm/part20/irm_20-001-012.

explanation of items among other subsections. As of this writing (December 2023) this chapter in the Handbook was last updated October 6, 2021.

The Handbook applies to cases in the Small Business/Self Employed (SBSE), Large Business and International (LB&I), and Tax Exempt and Governmental Entities (TEGE) divisions. Section 1219 of the PPA of 2006, "Substantial and Gross Valuation Misstatements Attributable to Incorrect Appraisals" was enacted to assert penalties against any person who prepared an appraisal of the value of property and who knew, or reasonably should have known, the appraisal would be used for federal tax purposes. The penalty applies to appraisals prepared with respect to returns filed after August 17, 2006. For façade easements, the penalty applies to returns filed after July 25, 2006.

In terms of authority, the IRS can now seek injunctions and penalize appraisers. Prior to passage of the PPA of 2006, appraisers were only subject to § 6700 and § 6701 penalties for promoting abusive tax shelters, and penalties for aiding and abetting understatement of tax liabilities.

Each IRS organization is responsible for establishing its own internal policies for managing procedures and developing their own guidance. For example, SBSE and LB&I engineering agreed to formally suspend the three valuers from determining the facts and making a recommendation. After this went public, as indicated earlier with a response from appraisal organizations and the AICPA, it is not clear what the IRS may have initiated as policy in LB&I or TEGE with no written policy memo having been released to the public.

An IRS publication states:[15]

> **(4)** All employees should keep the following objectives in mind when handling each penalty case:
>
> a. Similar cases and similarly situated taxpayers should be treated alike.
>
> b. Each taxpayer should have the opportunity to have his or her interests heard and considered.
>
> c. Strive to make a right decision in the first instance. A wrong decision, even though eventually corrected, has a negative impact on voluntary compliance.
>
> d. Provide adequate opportunity for incorrect decisions to be corrected.
>
> e. Treat each case in an impartial way (i.e., approach the job, not from the government's or the taxpayer's perspective, but in the interest of fair and impartial enforcement of the tax laws).
>
> f. Use each penalty case as an opportunity to educate the taxpayer, help the taxpayer understand his or her legal obligations and rights, and assist the taxpayer in understanding his or her appeal rights.
>
> g. Endeavor to promptly process and resolve each taxpayer's case.
>
> h. Resolve each penalty case in a manner which promotes voluntary compliance.
>
> (5) All actions will be done in accordance with the Taxpayer Bill of Rights as listed in IRC 7803(a)(3).[16]

15. *Id.* at 20.1.12.1.3.(4) (Oct. 6, 2021), https://www.irs.gov/irm/part20/irm_20-001-012.
16. "Taxpayer Bill of Rights from IRS," http://www.irs.gov/taxpayer-bill-of-rights.

The application of penalties should be consistent, accurate, and impartial. Instead of an interaction with dialogue, in more recent audits, the IRS has opted to use what they call "listening sessions." That is, the penalty group listens to the commentary from the appraiser and makes a determination. With that, the IRS believes it has met its obligation to allow the taxpayer to be heard.

In theory, penalties are applied to promote voluntary compliance. Penalties should be applied consistent with Policy Statement 20-1[17] and philosophy. The analysis is to be consistent, unbiased, and a proper application to the facts and law.

The penalty is asserted by examiners, engineers, business valuers, and attorneys. The penalty guide indicates that "examiners and attorneys should submit a referral for Engineering Program Assistance and/or consultation related to potential penalties, prior to asserting a potential penalty, when assistance of an IRS appraiser or valuation specialist is needed, and a potential I.R.C. § 6695A penalty recommendation from an examining appraiser was not received."[18] However, as indicated earlier it appears that SBSE Policy and the LB&I Engineering Program have agreed that no review process is required and any agent with the approval of their manager can apply a § 6695A penalty. There is no written policy shared with the public on this process at this time.

It should be noted that the penalty is a distinct case separate from the related tax examination. The penalty is not proposed in the presence of the taxpayer. The Handbook states:

> Generally, an IRC 6695A penalty against an appraiser will not be proposed until the related tax examination is completed at the group level. The appraiser penalty case can proceed when the related tax examination case is closed agreed, closed no response after default, is in Appeals or is in Tax Court.
>
> Caution:
>
> If the statute of limitation on the IRC 6695A penalty will expire within 180 days, then the penalty case file should be worked, or a statute extension should be obtained so a protective assessment can be made if needed. See *IRM 20.1.12.4*, Statute of Limitations.[19]

However, feedback from practitioners would seem to indicate that the penalty is being applied well before a final determination is made on the case. For example, an unagreed case may be sent to Appeals while the penalty is being applied well before settlement at Appeals or before a decision by the courts.

There is an exception for application to the penalty, as will be discussed next.

I.R.C. § 6695A AND TWO EXAMPLES

26 U.S.C. § 6695A, Substantial and gross valuation misstatements attributable to incorrect appraisals, states:[20]

> **(a)** Imposition of penalty If—

17. IRM Part 1. Chapter 2. Section 1 (Aug. 8, 2023), https://www.irs.gov/irm/part1/irm_01-002-001#idm140160043413664.
18. IRM 20.1.12.2 (Oct. 6, 2021), https://www.irs.gov/irm/part20/irm_20-001-012.
19. *Id.* at 20.1.12.3 (4).
20. 26 U.S.C. § 6695A Substantial and gross valuation misstatements attributable to incorrect appraisals, https://www.law.cornell.edu/uscode/text/26/6695A.

(1) a person prepares an appraisal of the value of property and such person knows, or reasonably should have known, that the appraisal would be used in connection with a return or a claim for refund, and

(2) the claimed value of the property on a return or claim for refund which is based on such appraisal results in a substantial valuation misstatement under chapter 1 (within the meaning of section 6662(e)), a substantial estate or gift tax valuation understatement (within the meaning of section 6662(g)), or a gross valuation misstatement (within the meaning of section 6662(h)), with respect to such property, then such person shall pay a penalty in the amount determined under subsection (b).

(b) Amount of penalty

The amount of the penalty imposed under subsection (a) on any person with respect to an appraisal shall be equal to the lesser of—

(1) the greater of—

(A) 10 percent of the amount of the underpayment (as defined in section 6664(a)) attributable to the misstatement described in subsection (a)(2), or

(B) $1,000, or

(2) 125 percent of the gross income received by the person described in subsection (a)(1) from the preparation of the appraisal.

(c) Exception No penalty shall be imposed under subsection (a) if the person establishes to the satisfaction of the Secretary that the value established in the appraisal was more likely than not the proper value.

A substantial valuation misstatement is a value by the taxpayer of greater than 150% of the proper value for an income tax return or less than 65% of the proper value for an estate or gift tax return.[21] A gross valuation misstatement is a value by the taxpayer of greater than the 200% of the proper value for an income tax return or less than 40% of the proper value for an estate or gift tax return.[22,23] Whether there is a substantial valuation misstatement or a gross valuation misstatement, the same penalty computation applies.

Example One

For an estate tax return:

- The taxpayer fair market value is $2 million.
- The appraisal fee was $20,000.
- The IRS fair market value is $6 million.
- The taxpayer fair market value of $2 million is less than 65% of the IRS fair market value ($6,000,000 × 0.65 = $3,900,000) so the penalty is applicable.
- The income tax rate is 40%.

Applying the penalty:

(1)(A) The greater of 10% of the underpayment of tax or 0.10 × 0.40 × $4,000,000 = $160,000 or

(1)(B) $1,000

21. Michael A. Gregory & Renee Marino, *IRS Oversight of CPAs Who Provide Valuation Services*, The Tax Adviser (Nov. 1, 2013), https://www.thetaxadviser.com/issues/2013/nov/gregory-nov2013.html.

22. Michael A. Gregory & Renee Marino, *IRS Oversight of CPAs Who Provide Valuation Services*, J. Accountancy (Nov. 30, 2013), https://www.journalofaccountancy.com/issues/2013/dec/20138779.html.

23. IRM 20.1.12.3 (7).

Result of step (1) is $160,000

(2) 125% of the fee paid to the appraiser is $20,000 × 1.25 = $25,000

The lesser of step (1) $160,000 or step (2) $25,000 = $25,000 penalty

The penalty in this instance would be $25,000 to the appraiser.

Example Two

In the case of normal taxes or surtaxes:

- The taxpayer fair market value is $5 million.
- The appraisal fee was $40,000.
- The IRS fair market value is $1 million.
- The taxpayer fair market value of $5 million is more than 150% of the IRS fair market value ($1,000,000 × 1.50 = $1,500,000) so the penalty is applicable.
- The income tax rate is 40%.

Applying the penalty:

(1)(A) The greater of 10% of the underpayment of tax or 0.10 × 0.40 × $4,000,000 = $160,000 or

(1)(B) $1,000

Results of step (1) is $160,000

(2) 125% of the fee paid to the appraiser is $40,000 × 1.25 = $50,000

The lesser of step (1) $160,000 or step (2) $50,000 = $50,000 penalty

The penalty in this instance would be $50,000 to the appraiser.

An Exception to the Application of the Penalty

> The penalty does not apply if the appraiser can establish the appraisal value "more likely than not" was correct. Pending further guidance, consult Counsel regarding "more likely than not" determinations.[24]

This can be a difficult hurdle since the IRS examiner who came up with their number is also being asked to decide whether their number or the taxpayer's number is "more likely than not" correct. Being the examiner, enforcer, judge, and jury, it may be inferred that the IRS could have a difficult time remaining unbiased. That was the reason for the IRS to have had an IRS EVPCM and two other independent IRS valuers to review the potential application of the investigation of a penalty. That process has been eliminated officially in SBSE and it is unclear what is or is not being applied in the LB&I and TEGE divisions.

The term "correct amount" is very important.[25] Note that a valuer or appraiser conducts their appraisal applying appropriate standards and with an analysis of the facts in the case. There are occasions when the appraiser does not have all of the facts for various reasons (e.g., client did not share, records were not available at the time, the other party

24. IRM 20.1.12.3 (5) (Oct. 6, 2021), https://www.irs.gov/irm/part20/irm_20-001-012.
25. IRM 20.1.12.3 (7).

refused to provide the information). During audit, the IRS may become aware of this information directly, with the application of a summons, or by other means.

Appraisers typically include assumptions and limiting conditions within their reports. Generally, a statement is included within the assumptions and limiting conditions so that if additional information were to surface it could change the valuation determination. For this reason, simply looking at the IRS determination of fair market value and comparing it to the valuer or appraiser's valuation number should proceed with caution by the IRS. What was known or knowable to the taxpayer's appraiser may not have included information the IRS obtained on audit from various sources. Appraisers should consider including a list of all information provided and all information considered as an attachment to the appraisal to limit later disagreement with the IRS. This is why the term "proper value" was included in the code section.

Statute of Limitations

> The statute of limitations on assessment for an IRC 6695A penalty expires three years from the date on which:
>
> A. The return, with respect to which the penalty is assessed, was filed (a return filed prior to the due date is deemed to be filed on the due date), or
>
> B. The claim for refund, with respect to which the penalty was assessed, was filed.
>
> The statute on the appraiser penalty case under IRC 6695A can be extended using Form 872-AP, Consent to Extend the Time on Assessment of IRC Section 6695A Penalty.
>
> Note:
>
> Extension of the statute on the related tax case does **not** extend the IRS 6695A penalty statute.[26]

Penalty Case File

There should be a separate case file associated with the § 6695A penalty. This penalty case file[27] should contain all of the relevant documentation and work papers used by the IRS in the development of the penalty. There are also other specific elements that should be included in the case assembly file.[28] If the case should proceed unagreed to IRS Appeals or the appraiser files a claim for refund, an appraiser may want to request a copy of the penalty and assembly file to ensure proper development of the facts. The IRM provides an Exhibit 20.1.12-1 entitled "IRC 6695A—Pro forma Explanation of Items," but that link was inoperable at the time of publication. This is a link from another source of that material from the IRS.[29]

---

26. IRM 20.1.12.4 (Dec. 18, 2017), https://www.irs.gov/irm/part20/irm_20-001-012.
27. IRM 20.1.12.8 (Oct. 6, 2021), https://www.irs.gov/irm/part20/irm_20-001-012.
28. IRM 20.1.12.9 (Aug. 27, 2010), https://www.irs.gov/irm/part20/irm_20-001-012.
29. Manual Transmittal 20.1.12 (Aug. 27, 2010), https://mfford.com/assets/applets/Appraiser_PENALTIES_IRM20.1.12.pdf.

CONCLUSION § 6695A

The IRS has indicated that they intend "aggressive IRS enforcement" related to applying penalties on appraisers.[30] As a result, IRS has stepped up its efforts with penalties on appraisers with a more aggressive application of § 6695A. The process has been simplified for expediency. At the same time, the review process by experienced valuers has been eliminated.

Appraisers and any other valuers should be aware, follow their standards, know where the IRS concentrates its efforts, and ensure reasonableness with their determinations. The most common penalty application for an overvaluation of 150% or more (normal tax return) or an understatement of under 65% or less (estate or gift tax return) results in a penalty of 125% of the fee for service as demonstrated in the two examples in this chapter.

VALUATION PENALTIES ON THE TAXPAYER AND/OR APPRAISER

An estate or gift tax return may be susceptible to an undervaluation of assets penalty. This falls under § 6662.[31] The penalty is applicable if the asset valuation is undervalued as a percentage of the tax payment. However, if the IRS determines that the taxpayer operated in good faith and has a reasonable basis, the IRS may decide not to apply this penalty. On the other hand, if valuation is found to be associated with an Abusive Tax Avoidance Transaction (ATAT) (formerly called a tax shelter), there may be no exception considered.[32]

As an overview, the undervaluation penalty for estate and gift taxes over $1,000 for the value claimed on the tax return as a percentage of the value finally determined is 0% penalty with a value over 65%, 20% penalty with a value between 40% and 65%, and 40% penalty with a value under 40%.

Under § 6701 an appraiser may be subject to a penalty of $10,000 for corporate matters and $1,000 for other than corporate tax matters for aiding and abetting an understatement of tax liability. In addition, under Circular 230, the IRS may bar the appraiser from practicing before the IRS.

SUMMARY

Penalties are a serious concern for appraisers and taxpayers related to valuation. The taxpayer should engage a qualified appraiser to prepare a qualified appraisal for federal tax purposes. The appraiser needs to meet professional standards. I.R.C. § 6695A applies to the appraiser and, as demonstrated in the examples presented, this may likely result in a

30. Hale Sheppard, Esq., *No Notice, No Examination, No Problem: IRS Further Deprives Appraisers of Procedural Protection* (IRS drastically and unilaterally changed its procedures for reviewing appraisals) J. Taxation (Jan. 2022).

31. 26 U.S.C. subtit. F Procedures and Administration, Chapter 68—Additions to the Tax, Additional Amounts, and Assessable Penalties, Subchapter A—Additions to the Tax and Additional Amounts, Part II—Accuracy-Related and Fraud Penalties, https://www.govinfo.gov/content/pkg/USCODE-2011-title26/html/USCODE-2011-title26-subtitleF-chap68-subchapA-partII.htm.

32. Regulations Governing Practice before the Internal Revenue Service Treasury Department Circular No. 230 (Rev. 6-2014) Catalog Number 16586R, https://www.irs.gov/pub/irs-pdf/pcir230.pdf.

penalty applied to the appraiser amounting to 125% of the fee paid to the appraiser. The Handbook further elaborates on the elements to consider and the application of penalties on appraisers. Finally, both taxpayers and appraisers have to be concerned with undervaluation penalties on estate and gift tax returns with potential aiding and abetting penalty ramifications. Note the commentary here addresses the most common penalty considerations regarding valuations but does not include all possible penalties associated with a tax return and valuations.

REFERENCES FOR VALUATION AND APPRAISER PENALTIES

Fishman, Jay E., et al. 2023. "Estate and Gift Tax Valuations—Penalties for Undervaluation on Estate and Gift Tax Returns." In PPC's *Guide to Business Valuations*, 1001.48 to .66. (Carrollton, TX; Thomson Reuters).

Laro, David, and Shannon P. Pratt. 2011. "Penalties and Sanctions." In *Business Valuation and Taxes: Procedure, Law and Perspective* 2nd ed. Chap. 6, 76–85 (New York: John Wiley & Sons, Inc.).

CHAPTER 39

Alternative Dispute Resolution

Eric Rowen, JD, and Neil Beaton, ASA, CFA, CPA/ABV/CFF

INTRODUCTION

In this chapter you will learn about:

- Background of using alternative dispute resolution (ADR) procedures
- Advantages of arbitration instead of litigation through the courts
- Suggestions for selecting arbitrators or mediators
- Suggested instructions to arbitrators
- How arbitration conclusions are reported
- Using alternative dispute resolution in marital disputes
- Using alternative dispute resolution in federal tax disputes

The development of law can be traced back to the 6th century BC when the Ten Commandments were said to have been handed down by God to Moses. In the book of Deuteronomy in the Bible, Moses instructed the people of Israel to appoint judges and officials in their various towns upon entering the promised land in the pursuit of justice.[1] These Biblical roots were added to in the secular realm by the Greek philosophers, Socrates and Plato, in the 4th century BC. Plato was especially keen on the law as demonstrated in his three books, the *Statesman*, the *Republic*, and the *Laws*.[2]

Since then, law has developed from social authority to monarchy, dictatorship, plutocracy, and democracy. Closer to home, after the United States declared its independence from England in July 1776, the Articles of Confederation were drafted in 1777 and adopted in November 1777. However, even though the Articles of Confederation were ratified by the 13 original colonies in 1780, they proved ineffective. Because of this, the founding fathers set out to draft a new constitution, which was completed at the Constitutional Convention between May and September 1787. Two years later, the Constitution of the United States was adopted.[3] ADR followed closely thereafter.[4]

Although ADR existed informally in the colonies before the Constitution was adopted, the first formal application of ADR was found in the Patent Act of 1790 wherein Congress provided for an arbitration system of competing claims. Similar to what we

1. In die Skriflig 55:3 (2021).
2. Nicholas R. Baima, *Plato: the Laws*, The Internet Encyclopedia of Philosophy, https://iep.utm.edu/pla-laws/ (last visited May 22, 2024).
3. *See* Owings v. Speed, 18 U.S. 420, 5 L. Ed. 124 (1820).
4. See generally Deborah R. Hensler, *Our Courts, Ourselves: How the Alternative Dispute Resolution Movement Is Re-Shaping Our Legal System*, 122 Dickinson L. Rev. 349–82 (2017).

have today, the act authorized the creation of an adjudicative board, consisting of one member appointed by each patent applicant and another by the secretary of state. "Decisions by the board were binding and, should an applicant opt out of this arbitration, the other applicant's patent would be summarily approved."[5] However, while these early developments were helpful, ADR did not receive formal institutionalization until 1918 when the U.S. Conciliation Service was formed at the Department of Labor followed by the formation of the Federal Mediation and Conciliation Service in 1947.[6] ADR truly was institutionalized in the 1920s after Congress passed the Federal Arbitration Act in 1925.[7] In 1926, the American Arbitration Association was founded.[8]

While traditional litigation is still very much alive,[9] ADR continues to rise in popularity[10] as a way to lower costs[11] and avoid going to court, and it is becoming used more frequently to settle valuation[12] and other litigated issues.[13] The two primary types of alternative dispute resolution are arbitration and mediation, each with many variations. Private judging, a hybrid of traditional courtroom litigation and ADR,[14] also has had success in resolving certain types of matters.[15]

---

5. Michael McManus & Brianna Silverstein, *Brief History of Alternative Dispute Resolution in the United States*, Cadmus (Nov. 1, 2011), http://cadmusjournal.org/node/98.

6. Fed. Mediation & Conciliation Serv., *A Timeline of Events in Modern American Labor Relations*, https://www.fmcs.gov/aboutus/our-history/.

7. https://en.wikipedia.org/wiki/Federal_Arbitration_Act.

8. Am. Arbitration Ass'n, *About Us*, https://www.adr.org/about-us.

9. Hensler, *supra* note 4, at 350.

10. *Id.* at 349–50 ("Today, interest in dispute resolution is high. This interest cuts across many domains, ranging from the family, to the schoolyard, to workplaces and sales transactions, to community decision making, and to the courts. It is reflected in academic degree programs, law school and business school curricula, executive training, and continuing legal education. The dispute resolution procedures of interest include negotiation, mediation, arbitration, and hybrids such as 'med-arb' and 'reg-neg.' While in some domains, such as schools and neighborhoods, dispute resolution procedures are championed as alternatives to individual or social violence, in the business and legal sectors the primary stated objective of alternative dispute resolution is to avoid litigation and trial."); Russ Bleemer, *The Law Is Enforced by ADR Processes. They Work*, 41(2) Alternatives to High Cost Litigation 19–24 (2023) (describing how mediation has been key in the resolution of ADA cases).

11. *See* Theodore M. Baum et al., *Effective Use of Arbitration*, 54 Tort Trial & Ins. Prac. L.J. 211, 243–48 (2019) (offering a detailed analysis on how to control expenses while in arbitration).

12. *See* Gauthier Vannieuwenhuyse, *The Rise of M&A Arbitration*, Kluwer Arbitration Blog (Apr. 6, 2021), https://arbitrationblog.kluwerarbitration.com/2021/04/06/the-rise-of-ma-arbitration/; Hon. Alan D. Scheinkman (Ret.), *Valuation Disputes and Disagreements—ADR Could Be the Solution for Dissolution*, Nat'l Arbitration & Mediation (Aug. 2022), https://www.namadr.com/publications/valuation-disputes-and-disagreements-adr-could-be-the-solution-for-dissolution/.

13. *See, e.g.*, C. Steven Bradford, *Online Arbitration as a Remedy for Crowdfunding Fraud*, 45(4) Fla. St. U. L. Rev. 1165–210 (2018) (suggesting a "simplified, cost-effective arbitration remedy to deal with crowdfunding fraud); Miki Someya, *Resolving Data Breach Dispute: Automated Negotiation, E-Mediation, and Arbitration Assisted by Technology*, 34(2) Ohio St. J. on Disp. Resol. 393–418 (2019) (advocating for arbitration as an improved alternative to privacy class action suits, both for companies and the consumer); Victoria Dalcourt Angle, *Innovation in Government Contracting: Increasing Government Reliance on Other Transaction Agreements Mandates a Clear Path for Dispute Resolution*, 49(1) Pub. Cont. L.J. 87–122 (2019) (arguing that certain disputes arising from "other transaction agreements" or "OTAs" ought to be resolved through alternative dispute resolution).

14. *See* Sy First Fam. Ltd. P'ship v. Cheung, 70 Cal. App. 4th 1334, 1341 (1999) (outlining the differences between contractual arbitration and private judging in California); Amy L. Litkovitz, *The Advantages of Using a "Rent-a-Judge" System in Ohio*, 10(2) Ohio St. J. on Disp. Resol. 491–506 (1995).

15. Shiela Nagaraj, *The Marriage of Family Law and Private Judging in California*, 116(7) Yale L.J. 1615–23 (May 2007); *see also* Christina Fox, *Contracting for Arbitration in Custody Disputes: Parental Autonomy vs.*

Another ADR vehicle is a minitrial, which generally does not follow formal rules of procedure or evidence but rather depends on commonsense arguments and a few key witnesses.[16] This process is most successful for business disputes in which the person hearing the matter is experienced in the economics of the business affected.[17]

Disputes over the value of an interest in a business lend themselves particularly well to arbitration because there is often a single, clear-cut issue: What is the amount of money needed to settle the case? Some areas where arbitration has worked well are marital dissolutions,[18] corporate and partnership dissolutions, dissenting stockholder actions, and damage cases.[19]

The authors have been involved extensively as advocates, arbitrators, or expert witnesses in arbitration, especially in shareholder disputes, and in arbitration and mediation of business valuation disputes. The results generally have been quite good, providing there are qualified business valuation experts on the arbitration or mediation panels, or the arbitrator has extensive business experience. However, there have been some lopsided valuation decisions when the panels were comprised of inexperienced attorneys and/or industry people rather than qualified business appraisers.

ALTERNATIVE DISPUTE RESOLUTION ACT OF 1998

The practice of ADR was further bolstered by the enactment of House Resolution 3528, the Alternative Dispute Resolution Act of 1998.[20] The act directs every federal district

---

State Responsibility, 12(2) CARDOZO J. CONFLICT RESOL. 547–72 (2011) (advocating for the expansion of New York's private judging scheme to include child custody cases).

16. Thomas J. Klitgaard & William E. Mussman, III, *High Technology Disputes: The Minitrial as the Emerging Solution*, 8(1) SANTA CLARA HIGH TECH. L.J. 1–18 (1992) (defining minitrials); Douglas A. Henderson, *Avoiding Litigation with the Mini-Trial: The Corporate Bottom Line as Dispute Resolution Technique*, 46(2) S.C. L. REV. 237–62 (1995); *A Taxonomy of Judicial ADR*, 9 ALTERNATIVES TO HIGH COST LITIGATION 97 (1991).

17. Henderson, *supra* note 16, at 237, 242 ("The presence of senior executives with the power and desire to settle the dispute is, by definition, essential to the success of the mini-trial process. It is because of this top management participation that the mini-trial becomes 'an extra-judicial procedure which converts a legal dispute from a 'court-centered' problem to a 'businessman-centered' problem. The mini-trial puts resolution of a business legal dispute back into the hands of the businessman litigants.' By blending these two approaches—the legal and the corporate—the mini-trial provides business managers the opportunity 'to use their developed skills—assessing risk and negotiating—to resolve the dispute. . . . [It] places a premium on brevity and relevancy.'").

18. See, e.g., Andrew Schepard et al., *If We Build It, They Might Come: Bridging the Implementation Gap between ADR Services and Separating and Divorcing Families*, 24 HARV. NEGOT. L. REV. 25–81 (2018) (describing the Institute for the Advancement of the American Legal System's successful model for an alternative resolution of family disputes).

19. Scheinkman, *supra* note 12 ("Some of the most contentious legal disputes that confront attorneys center on valuation of property that is the subject of competing claims. Avoiding coming to grips with detailed valuation issues, and the concomitant need for expert testimony, by putting the property up for sale, and letting the market determine the value, is often not possible, or not feasible, or simply undesirable to one or more of the parties. There may be no market, or only a limited one, or it may not be possible to establish a protocol to assure that a sale is fair, and the best price obtained. The parties may disagree as to an appropriate listing or asking price. Even if a sale is in hand, there may be resistance to concluding the deal on the ground that the price does not represent true value or that the sales process was tainted in some fashion. What this all means is that in many instances an agreement needs to be arrived at, or a determination made, as to what the value of the property actually is.").

20. 28 U.S.C.A. § 652.

court to establish its own ADR program by local rule and requires litigants in each case to consider the use of ADR.[21] Around this same time, database providers began publishing directories of ADR practitioners and firms.[22]

ADR services can be divided into three general categories: adjudicative, evaluative, and facilitative.[23] Under adjudicative ADR, a "neutral" serves as the adjudicator, who can render binding, nonbinding, or advisory opinions depending on the agreement of the parties.[24] Under evaluative ADR (also known as a mock trial), both parties present their versions of the case to a neutral who can serve as a "judge," a "panel," or even a "jury" to explore how their side of the story might be perceived in a real trial or arbitration.[25] Finally, in facilitative ADR, the neutral does not render any opinion, but rather attempts to build consensus.[26]

ADVANTAGES OF ARBITRATION VERSUS LITIGATION

The following are the primary advantages of arbitration over litigation in the courts (that is, a courtroom trial):

- Usually less formal and less stressful on all participants, especially the principals to the controversy
- Scheduling generally can be made more convenient for all parties
- Less likelihood of a lopsided result—in favor of one side over the other—assuming the arbitrators are qualified valuation professionals or have a solid command of valuation principles
- Usually takes less elapsed time from start to finish
- Usually costs less—attorneys' time generally is reduced, and experts' fees usually are less than for a courtroom, trial, though the appraisal process itself, however, may not be less expensive
- The award of the arbitrators in most situations is final and binding, and it can be confirmed in court

Under the Uniform Arbitration Act, an arbitrator's award is subject to attack only on the following grounds:

- The award was procured by corruption, fraud, or other undue influence
- An arbitrator was partial or used corruption or misconduct, which prejudiced the rights of either party
- The arbitrator exceeded his or her authority
- The arbitrator refused to postpone the hearing although sufficient cause for postponement was shown, or the arbitrator refused to hear material evidence or failed to conduct the hearing, which resulted in substantial prejudice to a party
- There was no agreement to arbitrate, and the objection was raised during the arbitration[27]

21. *Id.*
22. McManus & Silverstein, *supra* note 5.
23. *Id.*
24. *Id.*
25. *Id.*
26. *Id.*
27. Uniform Arbitration Act § 12(a) (1997).

One of the authors was involved in an arbitration wherein, after the ruling was rendered, it was discovered that the arbitrator failed to disclose prior case work for one of the parties that clearly prejudiced the final order. The order was appealed, and the appeal was granted and remanded for a new arbitration with a different arbitrator. As a result of the remand, the injured party was able to recalculate damages more accurately, because four years had passed from the prior ruling and updated financial information was available.

CHOOSING ARBITRATORS OR MEDIATORS

A practicing litigator offers the following observations on selecting arbitrators and mediators:

> In arbitration, as opposed to litigation, you have the luxury of choosing someone who has knowledge in the particular area of law or fact involved in your dispute. Conversely, a mediator's technical legal competence and familiarity with the business area of the dispute is less important than in arbitration where the arbitrator must render a decision. The focus on mediation should be on a mediator with good experience and skills in mediation, regardless of his or her knowledge of the specific area of law. It is helpful for the mediator to be knowledgeable enough to ask questions and point out weaknesses in each party's position, but since mediation is nothing more than a formalized settlement procedure, the real value of a mediator is being able to bring the parties together and in suggesting alternative solutions to the dispute.[28]

Arbitrators

Given the rather complex and technical nature of business valuation, the arbitrators in business valuation disputes should have a well-qualified, seasoned business appraiser on the panel or at least available for consultation. It is rare to see an unfair decision in a business valuation arbitration when the arbitrator (or a majority of a panel of arbitrators) was a qualified business appraiser.[29] However, there have been inequitable results when industry experts, economists, accountants, and attorneys lacking the technical training to deal professionally with esoteric business valuation issues dominate the arbitration decision.

Mediators

It is also desirable to have senior business appraisal expertise involved in mediating business valuation disputes. The problem here is that there are few business appraisers who are trained and experienced in mediation skills, which has traditionally been the realm of attorneys and retired judges.

---

28. Steven A. Weiss, *ADR: A Litigator's Perspective: Viewing the Plusses and Minuses*, Bus. Law Today 34 (Mar./Apr. 1999); see also E. Norman Veasey & Grover C. Brown, *An Overview of the General Counsel's Decision Making on Dispute-Resolution Strategies in Complex Business Transactions*, 70(2) Bus. Law 407–36 (Spring 2015). ("If a dispute may be headed to arbitration, one wants to be able to select arbitrators with expertise either in the subject matter or in managing disputes, including those likely to arise in discovery. In the end, one would want arbitrators who have great management skills, keep things on track . . . get you in and out, and . . . manage what's going on in front of them in a way that won't let the arbitration get out of control.").

29. Baum et al., *supra* note 11, at 211, 237 (listing qualities to look for in an arbitrator, including "impartiality [,e]xperience as a judge or arbitrator in management of cases of the type at issue [,s]ubject matter expertise . . .").

One solution to this problem is to employ an excellent mediator and a top-level business appraisal expert as a co-mediator, even if the appraiser does not have a great deal of mediation experience.

Process for Selecting Arbitrators

In the case of a sole arbitrator, the person usually is agreed on by the parties. There should be a mechanism in place for appointment by a neutral party if the parties to the action cannot come to agreement; and that mechanism must be followed.[30] The neutral party may be a court or some government official (for example, the state banking commissioner in the case of appraising a financial institution).

When the parties are deadlocked and one party submits a list of qualified business appraisers and the other party submits industry people or others without business appraisal expertise, the neutral party would be better served selecting from the list of individuals with business appraisal expertise.

It is common for each party to appoint one arbitrator and have the two arbitrators select a third.[31] That selection of the third should not be subject to the parties' approval, which could delay the process unduly. If possible, the arbitration agreement should specify that the third arbitrator be a qualified business appraiser. To avoid arguments about the definition of "qualified," the agreement should specify one or more credentials, such as Accredited Senior Appraiser (ASA), Chartered Financial Analysis (CFA), or Accredited in Business Valuation, as discussed in Chapter 37, "Business Valuation Standards and Credentials."

Again, in the event the two arbitrators cannot agree on a third, there should be a procedure in place to break the deadlock. If one party insists on selection from a group of qualified business appraisers with no conflicts and the other side wants someone else, it is highly unlikely that the neutral party would not pick from the list of qualified appraisers.

INSTRUCTIONS TO ARBITRATORS

Business appraisers generally advocate giving business valuation arbitrators as much flexibility to set their own rules as possible. However, certain factors should be specified to the arbitrators. They are:

- Definition of the asset, security, or property to be appraised
- The effective valuation date and whether subsequent events can be considered
- The standard (definition) of value (see Chapter 1)
- Any legal aspects of the case that the appraisers need to be aware of (often, a provision that the non-legally trained arbitrator be allowed to hire or consult legal counsel is provided)
- What constitutes a conclusion by the arbitrators, such as:
    - Agreement by a majority (most common)
    - Average of two closest to each other
    - The conclusion of the third (neutral) arbitrator (somewhat akin to a "special master" situation)

---

30. *See* PoolRe Ins. Corp. v. Organizational Strategies, Inc., 783 F.3d 256, 263–64 (5th Cir. 2015) (holding that the district court properly vacated an award rendered by an arbitrator chosen in a manner different than provided in the arbitration agreement).

31. Baum et al., *supra* note 11, at 236.

- The written report format and procedure for rendering the conclusion
- Some guidance on timing (may require some flexibility)

It may be helpful to have an appraiser experienced in arbitration assist in drafting the arbitration agreement and/or instructions. Obviously, the documents controlling the arbitration should be as clear and complete as possible. However, there should be a provision to request clarification if there are questions after the arbitrators have finished their initial review of the controlling documents.

The following factors typically are left to the arbitrators' discretion:

- Procedures to communicate with each other and scheduling of work and meetings (within the specified timing guidance)
- The valuation approaches, methods, and procedures to apply (within the confines of the designated definition of value and anything mandated in controlling documents)
- The extent to which each arbitrator considers it necessary to develop information independently or is willing to rely on information provided by the company or parties or by another member of the arbitration panel
- Rules regarding contacting the parties or their attorneys (although some attorneys are uncomfortable about giving up control of contacts with the parties)

Communications with Parties and Attorneys

It is often desirable to be very liberal in allowing arbitrators to communicate with parties and attorneys. However, if one learns a fact that might be considered material to the valuation, that information should be shared with the other arbitrators as soon as practically possible.

Site Visit

In many cases, arbitrators may want to visit the operating premises and interview relevant principals and/or management, especially if the subject of the dispute is an operating company with significant assets. This works out best if the arbitrators can conduct this on-site visit together rather than separately; so that they will see the same things at the same time and benefit from hearing each other's questions and answers firsthand. A joint site visit also gives the arbitrators an opportunity to address any items not fully covered in their previous communications and gives any previously unacquainted arbitrators an opportunity to get to know each other and to form a basis for working together.

Hearings

The arbitrators should offer each party the opportunity to present oral and written information and opinions if they so desire. It frequently is convenient to hold a meeting to accommodate such input in conjunction with the site visit. This meeting may be conducted with the parties jointly or separately.

REPORTING AN ARBITRATION CONCLUSION

If there is a sole arbitrator, the parties can specify how they wish the conclusion presented.[32] This can range from a single sentence to a full report in accordance with The

---

32. *Id.* at 248–50.

Appraisal Foundation's *Uniform Standards of Professional Appraisal Practice* (USPAP) or other professional business valuation standards.

However, if there is a panel of arbitrators, the report is usually a brief letter that says that the arbitrators have completed their work in accordance with the arbitration agreement and states the conclusion that was reached. The letter, called an *award* in the parlance of arbitration, is signed by the arbitrators concurring in the conclusion. In many cases, the principals on both sides want a brief report explaining how the valuation conclusion was reached. In arbitration parlance, this is called an *opinion* and it is usually the sole responsibility of the third appraiser. To make such a report a joint effort of two or more arbitrators, each of whom probably judged various factors a little differently, would most likely be an unnecessarily complicated and costly exercise.

It is most desirable to come to a conclusion that can be endorsed as fair by all members of the arbitration panel. This usually can be achieved if all the arbitrators are qualified professional business appraisers. If unanimous agreement cannot be reached, the arbitrator in the minority position may render a dissenting opinion for the record, if he or she so desires.

ALTERNATIVE DISPUTE RESOLUTION IN MARITAL DISSOLUTIONS

Arbitration has been used successfully to resolve financial issues in marital dissolutions.[33] Generally speaking, the cases have held that property division may be arbitrated with the result being final and binding on the parties.[34] The general rationale upon which this conclusion is based is that parties may release property rights by contract.[35] Because parties agree by contract to arbitration, the agreement concerning the process can be enforced. The decision (or award) resulting from arbitration has limited review and limited appeal rights, not unlike arbitration awards in other areas.

Awards by arbitrators of spousal support, maintenance, and/or alimony are almost always final and binding because they, too, are contracts to determine a property right.

33. Elizabeth A. Jenkins, *Annotation, Validity and Construction of Provisions for Arbitration of Disputes as to Alimony or Support Payments or Child Visitation or Custody Matters*, 5(38) Am. Law Reports 69, 78–79 (1996).

34. *See, e.g.*, Spencer v. Spencer, 494 A.2d 1279 (D.C. 1985); *In re* T.B.H.-H., 188 S.W.3d 312 (Tex. Ct. App. 2006) (trial court has limited authority when reviewing an arbitration award in a property settlement case; the courts are limited to analyzing the integrity of the arbitration, not the award itself) [Footnote not in original quote.]; Taylor v. Taylor, 517 P.3d 380, 391 (Utah 2022) ("Arbitrations concerning alimony and division of marital property do not differ substantially from the types of cases that are routinely arbitrated. . . . In both camps of cases, adult parties-often aided by counsel-agree to have a neutral third party decide what is equitable.") (citation omitted).

35. Hill v. Hill, 380 S.E.2d 540, 545 (1989) ("A valid property settlement agreement which waives rights to equitable distribution 'will be honored by the courts and will be binding upon the parties.'"); *but see* Franke v. Franke, 674 N.W.2d 832, 844, 846 (Wis. 2004) ("[W]hen a circuit court enters a judgment confirming an arbitration award in a property division, the same public policy considerations are implicated as would arise if the parties had stipulated to a particular division of property . . . . We do not determine whether Wis. Stat. § 806.07 vests power in circuit courts to open all final judgments incorporating arbitral awards. Divorce judgments are different. A circuit court is statutorily required to perform an independent, substantive review of the parties' agreement before incorporating it in the divorce judgment.").

Such arbitration decisions, consistent with other arbitration awards, are subject to limited review and appeal rights.[36]

In fact, some states regulate such arbitration by statute,[37] and the American Academy of Matrimonial Lawyers has promulgated a model family law arbitration act.[38] As one author indicated:

> ADR is great for promoting property division agreements by (a) facilitating the exchange of relevant information regarding property and debts, (b) helping spouses together apply the [state's] property division model to their own marital estate, and (c) providing a means for couples to tailor their divorce economics to meet the family's specific needs and use their resources most effectively.[39]

For these reasons, arbitration in most divorce matters has gained increased acceptance and use.[40]

While many see the final and binding nature of arbitration as a benefit of that procedure, all family law courts may not necessarily view it as final and binding. While approving the concept of arbitration of alimony and property division, a Massachusetts intermediate appellate court held that any "award must, of course, be subject to review by the judge, who has the authority and the obligation . . . , to make a fair and equitable distribution of property."[41]

ALTERNATIVE DISPUTE RESOLUTION IN FEDERAL TAX DISPUTES

The Internal Revenue Service (IRS) Office of Chief Counsel issued Notice N(35)000-135 dated October 13, 1995, "to outline general considerations for the use of mediation to resolve Tax Court cases." Since the issuance of Notice N(35)000-135, the Office of Chief Counsel published a directives manual setting forth detailed procedures for arbitration and mediation prior to a tax court trial.[42]

---

36. Joan F. Kessler, Kessler et al., *Why Arbitrate Family Law Matters?* 14 J. Am. Acad. Matrim. Law. 333–51 (1997).

37. *See, e.g.*, Michigan's Domestic Relations Arbitration Act, Mich. Comp. Laws §§ 600.5070 *et seq.* (2009); Indiana's Family Law Arbitration provisions, Ind. Code Ann. §§ 34-57-5 *et seq.* (2009); North Carolina's Family Law Arbitration Act, N.C. Gen. Stat. §§ 50-41 *et seq.* (2009); Arizona's Uniform Family Law Arbitration Rule, Ariz. Fam. Law Proc. R. 67.2 (2018); Montana's Uniform Family Law Arbitration Act, Mont. Code Ann. § 40-16-101 (2021); Hawaii's Uniform Family Law Arbitration Act, Haw. Rev. Stat. Ann. §§ 658J-1 27 (2017); N.D. Cent. Code, tit. 32, ch. 32-29.4 (2019); H.R. 917 (Pa. 2023).

38. The Model Family Law Arbitration Act, promulgated in 2005, is meant to be a companion to the Revised Uniform Arbitration Act, drafted by the National Conference of Commissioners on Uniform State Laws, focusing on civil law matters, which has been adopted in at least eight states and is under consideration in several more.

39. William C. Darrah, *ADR Spotlight: A Divorce ADR Primer for the Non-Family Law Attorney*, Hawaii Bar J. (Nov. 2006).

40. *See, e.g.*, George K. Walker, *Arbitrating Family Law Cases by Agreement*, 18 J. Am. Acad. Matrim. Law. 429–533 (2003); Hon. R. Mark Browning & James K. Hoenig, *Hawaii's Family Court Promotes Innovative Divorce Resolutions*, Hawaii Bar J. (July 2006); Schepard et al., *supra* note 18.

41. Reynolds v. Whitman, 40 Mass. App. Ct. 315 (Mass. App. Ct. 1996); *see also* Franke v. Franke, 674 N.W.2d 832, 844, 846 (Wis. 2004).

42. IRM 35.5.5.

Even after a case has been calendared for trial in the U.S. Tax Court, the court may grant an extension based on an agreement between the taxpayer and IRS District Counsel to submit the matter to nonbinding mediation.[43]

The IRS, in Rev. Proc. 2002–44, formally established an appeals mediation procedure, which is a nonbinding process that uses the services of a mediator to help the IRS's Office of Appeals (Appeals) and the taxpayer reach a negotiated settlement.[44] The mediator acts as a facilitator to assist in defining the issues and promote settlement negotiations.[45] He or she will not have settlement authority and will not render a decision regarding any issue in dispute.[46] The goal of this mediation process is to resolve issues while they are in the jurisdiction of the Appeals office and may only be used after Appeals settlement discussions are unsuccessful and, generally, when all other issues are resolved but for the issue to be mediated.[47]

In addition to the mediation program discussed in Rev. Proc. 2002–44, which occurs at the Appeals level, there are two other mediation programs available to certain qualifying taxpayers at the compliance level. They are the "fast-track settlement" (FTS) mediation programs for certain small businesses and self-employed (see IRB 2006-36, Announcement 2006-61) and the FTS program for large and midsize businesses (see Rev. Proc. 2003–40). The program for small businesses and self-employed enables taxpayers who currently have unagreed issues in at least one open year under examination to work together with the compliance section and Appeals to resolve outstanding disputed issues while the case is still in compliance jurisdiction. The FTS process is used to resolve factual and legal issues and may be initiated at any time after an issue has been fully developed, preferably before the issuance of a 30-day letter or equivalent notice. The FTS program for large and midsize businesses offers qualifying taxpayers a way to resolve audit issues during the examination process in less than 120 days. Working with the compliance section and Appeals, taxpayers can use the settlement authority and mediation skills of Appeals to shorten their overall experience with the IRS by as much as two years.[48]

The authors gained new appreciation and respect for a well-done mediation by participating as an expert witness in one such process. The arbitration succeeded because of a mediation team consisting of an attorney highly skilled in mediation and a senior business valuation expert. There were also well-prepared expert witnesses on both sides.

SUMMARY

ADR has had a rich history in the United States over the past 100 years and is still going strong. The benefits of lower cost, faster and more convenient hearings, and the ability to select knowledgeable arbitrators and mediators make ADR a viable alternative to the regular court system. ADR has been codified through the Uniform Arbitration Act as

43. *Id.* 35.5.5.3.
44. *Id.* 35.5.5.4.
45. *Id.*
46. *Id.* 35.5.5.6.
47. *Id.* 35.5.5.5.
48. For additional IRS guidance, *see* IRS Publication 4167, *Appeals: Introduction To Alternative Dispute Resolution*, https://www.irs.gov/pub/irs-pdf/p4167.pdf.

well as solid precedent. There are a large number of organizations and resources available to identify and select competent and just participants. The authors of this chapter have participated in numerous mediations and arbitrations and find them excellent for specific situations, if not all.

Pre-litigation and/or pre-arbitration (early) mediation using a strong mediator, fully informed experts, and attorneys well versed in mediation protocols almost always is an appropriate strategy and protocol for early resolution of disputes. Such a protocol will give the parties an excellent opportunity to resolve their dispute on their own terms, i.e., without a resolution being forced upon them by a judge, jury, or arbitrator, and without incurring the often extremely significant expense of full-blown litigation or alternative dispute resolution.

Whether to choose a court or arbitrator to resolve any dispute that cannot be resolved by early mediation will depend upon the facts and circumstances. If the parties are bound to arbitrate by contract, arbitration likely will be required unless waived by all parties. If arbitration is not required by contract, a decision to resolve any dispute by arbitration will require the agreement of all parties.

Even if arbitration is available, caution should be exercised before choosing arbitration; in that, an arbitrator is not bound by the rules of law or evidence and, generally speaking, so long as the arbitrator allows the parties to introduce their evidence and there is no fraud or collusion involved in any decision, an arbitrator's award is binding even if it is contrary to the parties' underlying contract and even if it is contrary to the law, and there is no allowable review of the merits by a court of appeal. So, if a party is concerned about making sure that the parties' underlying contract is followed and the law is correctly applied, that party should opt for a court proceeding over arbitration, because a court judgment will be subject to appellate review for compliance with the parties' contractual expectations and for compliance with the law.

REFERENCES FOR ALTERNATIVE DISPUTE RESOLUTION

Books and Publications

Diana, James C. 1995. "The New Mediation Procedure in Appeals: The Latest Development in the IRS' ADR Initiative." In *Tax Management Memorandum* (November 13): 331–9.

Fiore, Nicholas. 1996. "Pros and Cons of the New IRS Mediation Program." In *Journal of Accountancy* (May): 36.

Ford, David J. 2000. "CPAs and ADR: A Civilized Alternative to Litigation." In *CPA Litigation Service Counselor* (February): 1–5.

Iwanyshyn, Deborah. 1998. "Mediation as a Form of Dispute Resolution." In *Shannon Pratt's Business Valuation Update* (October): 5–6.

Kessler, Joan F., Allen R. Koritzinsky, and Steven W. Schlissel. 1997. "Why Arbitrate Family Law Matters." In *Journal of the American Academy of Matrimonial Lawyers—Alternative Dispute Resolution Processes for Family Law Matters.* 35 14:2 (Chicago: American Academy of Matrimonial Lawyers).

Kaufman, Steve. 1992. "See You Out of Court: Mediation Used in Resolving Business Disputes." In *Nation's Business* (June): 58–60.

Klinefelter, Stanard T., and Sandra P. Gohn. 1995. "Alternative Dispute Resolution: Its Value to Estate Planners." In *Estate Planning* (May/June): 147–54.

Kratchman, D. Michael, and William P. Walsh. 1995. "Mediation Instead of Litigation for Resolution of Valuation Disputes." In *Michigan Business Law Journal* (Winter): 15–17.

Pratt, Shannon P. and ASA Educational Foundation. 2022. "Alternative Dispute Resolution." In Shannon Pratt's *Valuing a Business: The Analysis and Appraisal of Closely Held Businesses*, 6th ed. Chap. 51, 1203–15 (New York: McGraw-Hill).

Saltzman, Michael I. 1996. "Tax Court Mediation: A Case Study." In *Tax Executive.* (November/December): 449–53.

Professional Arbitration and Mediation Organizations

American Arbitration Associates
120 Broadway, New York, NY 10019
800-778-7879, www.adr.org

American Bar Association Section of Dispute Resolution
1050 Connecticut Ave. N.W., Suite 400 Washington, D.C. 20036
(800) 285-2221, https://www.americanbar.org/groups/dispute_resolution/

Association for Conflict Resolution
P.O. Box 5 | Eagle, NE 68347-0005
614-262-2724, www.acrnet.org

Association of Family and Conciliation Courts
6525 Grand Teton Pl., Madison, WI 53719
(608) 664-3750, www.afccnet.org

CPR, The International Institute for Conflict Prevention and Resolution
30 East 33rd St., 6th Floor, New York, NY 10016
(212) 949-6490, www.cpradr.org
Publishes training modules, videotapes, and books.

Jams/Endispute, Inc.
18881 Von Karman Ave., Suite #350, Irvine, CA 92612
(800) 352-5267, www.jamsadr.com

The Keystone Policy Center
1628 St. John Rd., Keystone, CO 80435
(970) 513-5800, www.keystone.org

CHAPTER 40

Examining a Business Valuation Expert in Depositions and at Trials

Anita M. Ventrelli, JD

INTRODUCTION[1]

In this chapter you will learn about:

- The difference between deposition testimony and trial testimony
- The difference between structuring questions for direct examination and cross-examination at trial
- Redirect examination
- Goals for each type of testimony
- Sample questions for discovery depositions that can also be used for constructing direct examination questions
- Discovery rules that apply to business valuation expert testimony, including requests as well as disclosures
- Information gathering in interviews and site visits
- Discovery goals
- Confidentiality issues in discovery
- Third party discovery requests

Attorneys principally use discovery depositions to find out what opinions the expert intends to offer at trial, the bases for those opinions, and what work the expert did to arrive at those opinions. They can also establish what instructions or assumptions were provided to the expert, the expert's scope of work, definitions for the terms they use in their opinion or report, identify who provided assistance in developing the opinions, what standards they followed, the expert's fees, and anything else pertinent to the assignment. Depositions seek information that accounts for differences between the work of the opposing expert and an attorney's own expert.

Trial testimony tells the story of the valuation issues through direct examination of the party's expert and through cross-examination of the opposing expert. The subject matter and types of questions differ for each type of examination.

---

1. When originally written, Dr. Pratt did not design this chapter with a distinction between taking discovery deposition testimony and eliciting trial testimony from expert witnesses. This updated chapter will differentiate between the two to illustrate how treating each differently aids discovery and structuring trial testimony.

When the parties exchange reports, document production, and witness interrogatory answers or subpoena the opposing expert's complete file ahead of the deposition, the expert can give the attorney a great deal of help in suggesting what areas to explore in deposition and specific questions—and follow up questions—to ask. Responses provided at deposition should enable an expert to replicate the work of the opposing expert and to identify the differences in process and judgment responsible for differences in value. In other words, the attorney directs the questions with a goal of understanding everything the expert did and what every word of the report means. An optimal deposition exhausts the expert's recollection about everything that factored into every professional judgment the expert made to reach the conclusion of value or any other conclusion so that the expert cannot testify to any other opinions, conclusions, or any other bases for opinions or conclusions at trial. This is the best way to enable the attorney's expert to identify weakness in the opposing expert's work that can be brought out at trial.

The expert or a member of the expert's professional staff should be present during the deposition of the opposing expert. This accomplishes two goals. First, the answer to one question may lead to another question that may not occur to the attorney to be sure the expert cannot later add to why they did what they did. Second, it is useful in preparing for court, both in helping the attorney prepare his or her own expert's examination (direct and rebuttal) and helping the attorney prepare the cross-examination of the opposing expert because the expert can observe the opposing expert's tendencies and personality traits when answering questions. For court preparation, an expert should always read the deposition of the opposing expert(s) as well as his or her own deposition.

TRIAL TESTIMONY CONSIDERATIONS

Experts, like other witnesses, require thoughtful guidance in testifying, to give the attorney the needed information to tell the valuation story. What follows includes explanations and considerations for testifying at trial.

- **Credentials.** Mapping out credentials testimony so that the testimony highlights the credentials without boring the judge or reading the expert's entire CV into evidence.
- **Elements of direct exam.** Direct testimony needs to come out using direct examination questions that do not lead the witness (i.e., suggest the answer). Judges can differ in ruling on whether questions that call for a "yes" or "no" answer constitute leading questions. Direct exam questions typically ask:
    - Who?
    - What?
    - When?
    - Where?
    - Why?
    - How?
- **Elements of cross-examination.** Many experts do not understand—and many attorneys take for granted—the principle that good cross-examinations only allow the witness to answer with a "yes" or a "no." Questions that include adjectives and adverbs and that include more than one new fact per question give an expert the chance to avoid a yes or no answer or to give an unexpected "yes" or "no" where the attorney will not be able to easily see which part of the question created the surprise. Cross-examination questions need to use these principles:

- One fact per question
- No adjectives or adverbs
- Precise language from either the report or the deposition
- No compound questions

At the start, counsel should attempt to box the witness into admitting that his or her report includes all the relevant information about what the expert reviewed, what the expert considered, and what the expert relied upon to reach their conclusions, opinions, and the basis for those conclusions and opinions. This limits an expert's ability to later claim that he or she considered other things that the expert did not include to remediate deficiencies.

- **Redirect examination.** Effective cross-examination frustrates witnesses who want to give explanations. Witnesses need to know that their client-attorney can let them explain things on redirect if they recognize that the cross-examination testimony needs further explanation. For effective redirect, the attorney must understand the reports to be able to understand the testimony that the other side brings out on cross-examination, because the attorney cannot ask the witness leading questions on redirect and cannot be assured time to speak to the expert about what the expert thinks requires explanation before undertaking the redirect examination.
- **Experts are the same as other witnesses.** Experts need to know the rules for testifying that an attorney would give to any other witness, for example, how to stop talking when they hear an attorney say "objection," that they are not allowed to ask the examiner questions but they can say they do not understand or cannot answer a questions as worded, that they cannot look at documents while testifying unless allowed by rule or invited by the attorney examining them.
- **Outlines.** If attorneys have outlines of how judges in the jurisdiction are accustomed to receiving testimony, they need to go over them with the expert because expert logic might be different than "attorney logic" about how to tell the valuation story.
- **Practice.** Attorneys should practice asking the questions they want to ask at trial and to listen to the way the expert answers. If there are things in the answers that do not make sense to the attorney or that the attorney knows will need further explanation, the attorney should tell the expert during practice and experiment with the simplest ways to construct the conversation.
- **Offers of proof.** They work during expert testimony too! Offers of proof enable the appellate court to decide whether the trial court correctly ruled on evidentiary objections. Object if the opposing attorney tries to use them to include material barred as a discovery sanction in the record.

The following areas of inquiry use open-ended questions to learn everything needed to replicate the expert's work to prepare for cross-examination. They can also serve as proper, non-leading, open-ended questions for the direct exam of the attorney's own expert. The high-level goals of direct exam include:

- Admitting your expert's conclusion of value.
- Explaining the information sources gathered; the process, methods, and approaches the expert considered; and which the expert relied upon for conclusions.
- Explaining the differences between your expert's report and the opposing expert's report and the resulting differences in valuation. These can include different information, different periods of time and timing conventions, different methods, different approaches, different rates (i.e., the discount rate or tax rate) used in approaches,

and different discounts to value conclusions for things like lack of marketability and minority interests.

- Explaining differences in credentials and experience that can impact comparative expert credibility.

If the expert and counsel agree that the report and other disclosures from the opposing party and expert lack the sufficiency required to support the court admitting the expert's conclusion into evidence, counsel may consider not taking any deposition or action that would allow the opposing expert to supplement an insufficient report or disclosures of basis for conclusions and opinions.

While working with technical terms of art can be tempting, try to help experts structure their reports and all types of testimony to include lay definitions or analogies to explain valuation terms of art. One can never know what prior valuation experience any judge possesses. The art of presenting valuation testimony includes the attorney making sure the judge is on the same page, literally. The attorney should provide the judge with a written copy of all reports and request to note things on their report copy. In this way, the attorney will be sure points hit home and that the judge will not lose the context of the examination points or have to rely on toggling between transcripts and reports when drafting opinions.

The following sections outline the areas that need to be covered in the examination of business valuation experts.

BACKGROUND AND QUALIFICATIONS (CHAPTER 37)

Education

- School attended with dates degrees were earned
    - Majors or special emphasis

Note: Many practitioners who provide business valuation services have an educational background that has nothing to do with business valuation. Also, an accounting degree or certification has no business valuation content whatsoever (that is why the AICPA created the additional designation ABV—Accredited in Business Valuation) and a major in economics may have little or no content in business valuation. That said, experience counts and can be the basis of qualifying an expert.

Professional Credentials and What the Expert Did to Attain the Credential

- ASA (American Society of Appraisers)
    - FASA
    - ASA
    - AM
    - ARM
- American Institute of Certified Public Accountants (AICPA)
    - CPA/ABV

- Institute of Business Appraisers (IBA) (now part of NACVA)
  - MCBA
  - CBA
  - AIBA
  - BVAL
  - ABAR
  - FIBA
- National Association of Certified Valuation Analysts (NACVA)
  - CVA
  - AVA
  - CFFA
- CFA Institute
  - CFA
- CBV Institute
  - CBV
  - FCBV
- Others

Note: The preceding are the primary recognized credentials in business valuation. Attorneys now know more about the various designations and what they mean and use that information to educate courts so that when credibility and judgment differ, the court may be able to better distinguish between the experts. Experts without valuation credentials have greater exposure to criticism by courts. It usually is very helpful to be able to demonstrate that your expert is more qualified than the opposing expert.

Experience

- Company, job description, dates (The attorney should consider exploring how much of each position is related to business valuation.)
- Valuations in similar industries/types of properties

Note: This is nice but not necessary. See *Guang Dong*,[2] *Physicians Dialysis*,[3] and *Popovich*,[4] where the court said industry experience was not a necessary qualification.

- Prior testimony

Note: It can be especially helpful if you can locate prior testimony that can be considered contradictory to the testimony in the case at hand or if you can locate prior court criticism of the expert.

---

2. Guang Dong v. ACI Int'l, Inc., No. 03-4165-JAR, 2008 U.S. Dist. LEXIS 3881 (D. Kan. Jan. 17, 2008).
3. Physicians Dialysis Ventures, Inc. v. Griffith, No. 06-2468 (MLC), 2007 U.S. Dist. LEXIS 78879 (D.N.J. Oct. 23, 2007).
4. Popovich v. Sony Music Ent., Inc., 508 F.3d 348, 359 (6th Cir. 2007).

ASSIGNMENT (CHAPTERS 1 AND 2)

- When were you retained? Who retained you?
- What was the assignment?
- Valuation date or dates property to be appraised
- Name of entity
- Property within entity to be appraised (e.g., shares of voting common stock out of shares outstanding—describe any other equity class in the capital structure)
- State of incorporation or registration
- What definition of value did you use for this appraisal assignment (e.g., fair market value, defined as . . .)?
- What is the source of that definition?
- Why is that definition of value appropriate for this valuation assignment (e.g., statutory definition, definition from precedential case(s) [which should be cited if relied on as authority], definition from binding contractual agreement)?
- What premise about the company's operations did you use when doing your appraisal (e.g., going-concern premise, liquidation premise, some other premise)? Why?
- What assumptions were you instructed to make?
- Written documentation of assignment (e.g., engagement letter)
- Any changes to assignment?

WORK DONE

- Total number of hours spent working on this engagement
- Hourly rates
- Hours by testifying expert and others (specify); Who did what?
- Total billing
- Total payment received to date
- Overdue amounts
- Unbilled amounts
- Amounts written off
- What other work anticipated?

SOURCES OF INFORMATION

Economic and Industry Information (Chapter 17)

- To assess the *status of the national (or regional) economy at the valuation date,* what data did you consider? Which sources did you rely upon? Why did you rely on/not rely on this information for this purpose?
- Which sources did you use to form an opinion about the *national (or regional) economic outlook*?
- At the valuation date, which leading indicators and other factors did you rely upon in the economic forecasts? Why?
- To assess the *status of the relevant industry at the valuation date,* what data did you consider? Which sources did you rely upon? Why did you rely upon this information for this purpose?
- Did these sources include the periodicals from one or more relevant trade associations? If not, why not?
- Which aspects of the economy did you rely upon when assessing the performance of the industry? Why?

- What other factors (e.g., developing technology, emerging substitute products, changes in the composition of the industry, foreign competition) did you cite as having a current and potential influence on the industry? Why?
- Did you have any reason to believe the industry benchmarks derived from composite company data may have been biased in some fashion (such as including too few firms, firms with extreme characteristics, or firms that are largely unrepresentative of the subject company's product line)? If so, what steps did you take to eliminate the effect of the bias?
- What ratios and/or other measures did your analysis identify as being particularly relevant in the analysis of the industry or the individual companies making up the industry? Why?
- How did you incorporate the factors identified in the preceding questions into the analysis supporting the future projections for the subject company?
- To what extent did you use your economic and industry analysis to assess the future projections for the subject company? Why or why not?
- How did you take the economic and industry information into account in the valuation?

Company Information (Chapter 5)

- Site visits: who, where, and when. How long did any site visits take? How many times did you or a member of your team visit the company?
- Interviews: who, where, when, and who else present? Did anyone record or transcribe the interview? Did you take notes?
- Financial statements: what statements, who prepared, compiled, reviewed, or audited?
- Income tax returns (what periods)
- Articles of incorporation, organization
- What contracts (noncompete/employment agreements, buy-sell agreements, supplier/customer contracts, union contracts) and did any make specific mention of valuation for the type of litigation the parties now have?
- Company literature

FINANCIAL STATEMENT ADJUSTMENTS (CHAPTER 15)

- Did you make any adjustments to the subject company's balance sheets? To the income statements? Please describe each adjustment, the reasons for it, and how you quantified the amount of each.
- Why were those financial statement adjustments appropriate?

  [If the market approach was used,] did you make any adjustments to the statements of any of the guideline companies' financial statements? Please describe. If not, why not? (When guideline public companies are used, it is a common error to adjust the subject company's statements and overlook whether any comparable adjustments to the guideline companies' statements should be considered.)
- Were there any adjustments for which there would be tax implications? (If so, how did you take the tax implications into account?)

  [If valuing a noncontrolling interest,] were all your adjustments of a "normalizing nature" (for example, eliminate nonrecurring items to put accounting on a basis comparable with guideline companies or industry standards) or were some of the adjustments things that only a control owner could change? (It is a common error, when valuing noncontrolling interests, to make adjustments that only a control owner could cause to happen and that do not reflect the actual expected ongoing operations of the company.)

COMPARATIVE FINANCIAL STATEMENT ANALYSIS (CHAPTER 16)

- What ratio or trend analysis, if any, did you undertake? For the subject company? For guideline public companies? For industry averages?
- What unusual occurrences came to light from comparing financial statements from one year to the next (horizontal analysis) over recent history? What, if any, explanations did you learn about for these occurrences?
- Have common-sized financial statements been prepared for the subject company over a period of five years or more (if possible)?
- What significant changes have been noted in the proportionate composition of the subject company's assets, liabilities, and equity, and income statement over the period for which common-sized financial statements were prepared? What explanations have been given for these changes?
- How do the current common-sized financial statements of the subject company compare to the industry benchmarks? What explanations have been given for any significant differences noted?
- Which ratios did you use to assess the subject company's profitability? How, if at all, have these changed over the recent past? How do they compare to the industry benchmarks?
- Which ratios did you use to assess the subject company's liquidity? How, if at all, have these changed over the recent past? How do they compare to the industry benchmarks?
- Which ratios did you use to assess the subject company's long-term solvency? How, if at all, have these changed over the recent past? How do they compare to the industry benchmarks?
- Did you treat the amounts by which sales or profits have increased over the recent past differently for different years, such as giving greater weight to exceptionally good or bad years? (a question designed to investigate bias in the calculations or percentages)
- What part of the analysis of the subject company's recent financial history did you deem relevant to the assessment of its future performance? Why?
- What part of the analysis of the subject company's recent financial history did you deem not relevant to the assessment of its future performance? Why?
- Where in your report do you show how the financial statement analysis impacted your valuation conclusion?

Note: Some analysts go through an elaborate financial statement analysis and never again refer to it.

- Did you do the ratio/trend analysis on the statements before or after the adjustments?

Note: The analysis usually should be done on the statements after adjustments. Pre-adjustment ratio analysis has different uses and can be very helpful in identifying performance measurements that appear unusual and require additional inquiry.

OVERALL VALUATION METHODOLOGY (CHAPTER 3)

- What approaches did you consider using (income, market, asset-based)?
- What approaches did you rely upon?
- Why did you choose the approaches you relied upon? Why did you not rely upon . . . ?
- Did you do the valuation on an enterprise basis? On an equity basis? Or both? Why? (If the answer is different for different approaches, specify which and why.)

- Within the valuation approach, what method or methods did you consider? Rely upon? Why did you rely on the method(s) you selected as better than any alternative method(s) for the purpose of the valuation?

INCOME APPROACH (CHAPTER 6)

- Did you conduct your income approach on an equity basis or on an invested capital basis? Why is that basis more appropriate for this assignment?
  [If on an invested capital basis,] what components did you include in your capital structure? Why?
- What economic income variable did you use in the income approach (e.g., net cash flow, net income, pretax income, etc.)? Why?
- What method(s) did you use (e.g., discounted cash flow, capitalized cash flow)? Why?

Note: Experts typically use either a discounting or a capitalizing method, but not both. Capitalizing is just a short version (one period of earnings and one growth rate assumed) of discounting (multiple periods of earnings and multiple possible growth rates assumed) which attorneys should understand does not yield optimum results when company growth fluctuates. If the analyst uses both methods it might signal a lack of sophistication on the part of the expert.

- How did you forecast your net cash flow (or other economic income variable) that you discounted or capitalized?
- What assumptions did you make? What did you rely upon to make each assumption?
- What did you do (if anything) to check for the reasonableness of the assumptions and resulting forecasts?

DEVELOPING A DISCOUNT RATE (CHAPTER 7)

- If a discounted economic income method was used, how did you develop the discount rate? If capitalizing, how did you develop the capitalization rate? Why did you do it in that way?

Note: The capitalization rate equals the discount rate minus the growth rate in perpetuity. If a capitalization rate was developed some other way, the witness should have a good explanation.

- If either discounting or capitalizing, how did you estimate the growth rate, if any?
- Why did you choose that particular growth rate?

Note: Growth rates are in perpetuity, which is a long time. Research has shown that long-term organic growth rates in excess of about one-third forecasted real GNP growth plus inflation (1% plus 2% to 3% long-term inflation most of the time) are very likely unsustainable in the long run.

- What level of value did your income approach produce (e.g., control, noncontrolling marketable; see Chapter 2)?

Note: The control or noncontrolling level of value usually is determined by the level of projected cash flow (i.e., if the cash flows are what a control owner would expect to get, the result would be a control value; if the cash flows would be what a noncontrolling owner would expect, the result would be a noncontrolling (i.e., minority interest) value). Where the company is operated efficiently and all owners are treated in proportion to their ownership interests, the control and noncontrolling values might be equal or close to equal.

- What procedure did you use to estimate your terminal value? (This usually will be a capitalization of income procedure (also referred to as the Gordon Growth Model) or a market multiple of some income variable.) [If a market multiple,] why is that procedure better than a capitalized income model? [If a capitalized income procedure,] why is that procedure better than a market multiple model? What percentage of your total present value is attributable to your terminal value? Did you test your conclusion for reasonableness?
- Will you please define in simple terms exactly what a *discount rate* is? (This question tests the analyst's knowledge and understanding of what the discounting method is all about, and whether the analyst thinks that he or she has captured what he or she should in the rate, that is, *the total rate of return that the market would demand* to place money in this investment, apart from liquidity considerations.)
- [If an invested capital procedure was used,] please explain exactly how you computed your weighted average cost of capital (WACC).
- What percentage weight was assigned to each component of your capital structure? How did you arrive at these weights? Are the weights based on book value of equity or market value of equity? (If book value, the WACC is virtually meaningless; but this is a common error.) What source list did you use to derive the weights you used for each component of the capital structure? (If some comparative financial statement source, such as RMA *Financial Statement Studies* or the *Almanac of Business and Industrial Financial Ratios*, was used and the equity percentage was at market value, there will be a problem, because those sources are at book value.) Why are these weights appropriate to use in this particular valuation assignment? If the analyst is valuing a noncontrolling interest and uses some weights other than the company's own actual weights—for example, some industry average weights—he or she has injected an element of control into the valuation, because the noncontrolling stockholder cannot cause a change in the company's capital structure. (This generally would not be appropriate under the standard of fair market value and may or may not be appropriate under other standards of value.)
- Did you apply any premiums or discounts to your indicated value from the income approach? Why or why not?

MARKET APPROACH (CHAPTER 8)

- What method(s) did you use within the market approach (e.g., guideline public company method, guideline transaction method, prior transactions method)? For each method, why or why not?
- For the guideline public company and transaction methods, what criteria did you use for the selection of guideline companies? What was the population of companies that you searched to make your selections? Why? What steps did you take to make sure that there were no guideline companies in the selected population that met your criteria but were omitted?

- Why did you not use (*EDGAR*, *BIZCOMPS*, *Deal Stats* (formerly *Pratt's Stats*), or other references listed in this book or suggested by opposing expert)?
- What steps did you take to determine whether there were any prior transactions, offers to buy, or buy-sell agreements regarding ownership of the company or interests in it? What information did you receive regarding whether buy-sell or operating agreements bind courts in the jurisdiction on valuation questions?
- Did the subject company make any recent acquisitions?
- What steps did you take to investigate the arm's-length nature of these transactions and what did you find out?
- What use did you make of these transactions?
- What sources did you use for developing fundamental financial information for your guideline companies? If your expert used others, ask whether they considered them and why they did not rely on them.
- What adjustments, if any, did you make to the financial statements of your subject company for comparison with the guideline companies? (Explain and justify adjustments; if none, what procedures did you employ to determine that none were necessary?) If your expert made other adjustments, ask whether they considered them and why they did not make those adjustments.
- What adjustments, if any, did you make to the financial statements of the guideline public companies for comparison with your subject company? (Explain and justify adjustments; if none, what procedures did you employ to determine that none were necessary?) If guideline companies were closely held, there rarely is enough information to make meaningful adjustments. However, if guideline companies were public, whether based on stock market transactions or acquisitions of public companies, there often is information that would suggest adjustments, such as removing a nonrecurring gain or loss even though it was not technically "extraordinary" under the rules of generally accepted accounting principles. Failing to make this analysis is a common error. This is one of the reasons it is better to use SEC filings than more condensed secondary sources for public guideline companies.
- What market multiples did you choose to use? Why? How did you decide where within the range of observed multiples the subject company should fall? How did you weigh the indications of value from the various multiples? Why?
- If you used multiple methods within the market approach, how did you weigh the respective methods? Why?
- Did you apply any premiums or discounts to the results indicated by any of the market methods? Why or why not?

THE ASSET-BASED APPROACH (CHAPTER 9)

- What methods did you use within the asset-based approach (e.g., adjusted net asset value, excess earnings method)? Why?
- What assets did you adjust on the balance sheet? For each adjustment, why did you make the adjustment and how did you arrive at the amount of the adjustment? Did you bring any off-balance-sheet assets or liabilities onto the balance sheet? For each, why, and how did you arrive at the amount?
- For the excess earning method (Chapter 10), how did you estimate the required return on tangible assets? How did you estimate the capitalization rate for intangibles? What checks for reasonableness, if any, did you perform?
- Did you apply any discounts or premiums? Why or why not?

DISCOUNTS AND/OR PREMIUMS (CHAPTER 18)

- Did you apply a discount for lack of control (or a control premium)? Why or why not?
- What database(s) did you use to help you estimate the amount of the discount/premium? Why did you use that particular database? Describe the data from which the database is compiled and the mechanism of computation.

Note: Many analysts use databases blindly, that is, without knowing what does or does not go into them or how they are constructed. Analysts should be able to explain any data they are using. It often is helpful to the attorney's case to test this knowledge (or lack of it).

- How did you estimate the amount of the control premium (or lack of control discount)?
- Did you apply a discount for lack of marketability? If so, the same questions that are listed for the discount for lack of control are appropriate. There are many studies and a number of databases that provide data for the expert to estimate an appropriate discount for lack of marketability and this is the most common area for widely divergent opinions in business valuation cases. Frequently, a good line of questioning is "Why didn't you use the [__________] database?" especially if your expert used it and the opposing expert did not. This may bring out some points to be defended in response to rebuttal.
- Did you apply any other discounts or premiums (e.g., key person, "portfolio," trapped-in capital gains, contingent liabilities, blockage, voting versus nonvoting)? If so, use the same line of questioning.

RECONCILIATION OF VALUE INDICATIONS (CHAPTER 19)

- If only one approach/method was used, why was that approach/method the best and why did you not use other approaches/methods?
- If multiple approaches/methods were used, what weight was given to each and why?
- If you were advising a client about selling or buying the subject interest, would you advise him or her to sell/buy at the price that you concluded for this appraisal?
- What, if anything else, that we have not talked about in your answers formed a basis for your opinion of value?

CONCLUDING INQUIRIES AND PRINCIPLES

- Did anyone give you any directives, instructions, or assumptions about carrying out your work on this engagement? Who gave them to you? How were they communicated to you? Were you provided with any authority for legal principles? What impact did they have on your work?
- Did you and those you worked with on this assignment retain all notes taken and information provided to you? If not, what no longer exists, who decided not to retain anything that no longer exists and why?

COMMON ERRORS

While the procedures attendant to deposing and examining valuation experts in direct and cross-examination at trial mirror those applicable to other witnesses, these experts require a heightened level of care with terminology and phrasing questions. The expert speaks in an entirely different language with its own terms of art. Attorneys err in deposing experts when they either treat the discovery deposition like a cross-examination, limiting the answers they get from the expert to what the attorney can think about asking, or when they attempt to get the expert to use terms the attorney defines as opposed to being sure the attorney understands the definitions the experts use.

Deciding to depose an expert with a deficient report and giving that expert the ability to supplement inadequate disclosures will give them the chance to cure their disclosure defects, so consider not deposing them and involve the expert so you can be sure of having enough points to cross-examine without having deposition testimony. On direct examination, common errors include attempting to lead the expert and not using questions that start with who, what, when, where, why, and how. Conversely, the most common errors in cross-examination consist of using these same open-ended questions and letting the expert control the examination, failing to ask questions that include only one fact per question, using questions that include adjectives or adverbs susceptible to many different meanings, and failing to use terms of art correctly (for example, asking about a method when the correct question would be using the term "approach").

Other common errors in questioning experts consist of not differentiating between what an expert considers and what an expert relies upon in reaching their conclusion of value. Finding out why an expert did not rely upon something will determine whether the point makes for appropriate direct or cross-examination.

SUMMARY

Expert witness testimony requires tailoring for the particular purpose: discovery depositions and trial testimony. The attorney should use his or her own expert to review documents produced regarding the business and to review any report done by the opposing expert to determine where gaps exist that would prevent the attorney's own expert from replicating the work of the opposing expert. Discovery deposition questions targeted toward filling those gaps and clarifying any terms used that could be susceptible to multiple interpretations or that the attorney's own expert does not recognize as valuation terms of art will limit what the other expert can say to cure any problems created by the gaps. Deposition testimony targeted at boxing in the expert to exactly what their report means will work best when using open-ended questions much like the questions used in direct examinations at trial. If an attorney asks questions with lots of specifics, the attorney may miss out on information the opposing expert would provide in answer to an open-ended question.

- Attorneys defending the deposition of their own expert must understand the testimony to determine whether or not to ask questions when the other parties finish their examinations to be sure their expert discloses all opinions conclusions and bases for their opinions and conclusions.
- Attorneys should structure direct examine testimony of their own experts using open-ended questions targeted at explaining what an expert did and simplifying the processes while making sure the judge follows along. This testimony should offer the expert an opportunity to bolster things the expert did that differ from what the opposing expert did to give the judge a basis to differentiate the attorney's own expert as the better authority, the expert who knew the business best, chose the best approaches and

methods, and applied them to the facts most accurately and using the most impartial studies and statistics.

- Conversely, attorneys should structure cross-examination to short, one-fact, no adjectives questions organized to both bolster their own expert judgment calls and to undermine the opposing expert's judgment calls. Attorneys should restrict their use of open-ended who, what, when, where, why, and how questions to only those questions where the attorney need not worry how the expert answers.

REFERENCE FOR CROSS-EXAMINING BUSINESS VALUATION EXPERT

Berman, Kenneth R. 2018. *Reinventing Witness Preparation: Unlocking the Secrets to Testimonial Success* (Chicago: ABA Book Publishing).

APPENDIX A

Glossary of Business Valuation Terms

Terms with an asterisk are from *International Valuation Glossary* (updated February 24, 2022) as jointly published by the ASA (American Society of Appraisers), CBV Institute (Chartered Business Valuators Institute), RICS (Royal Institution of Chartered Surveyors), and TAQEEM (Saudi Authority for Accredited Valuers).

Reference abbreviations are as follows:

VAB6—Shannon P. Pratt and ASA Educational Foundation, *Valuing a Business*, 6th ed., McGraw-Hill, 2022.

Guide—Jay E. Fishman, Bruce Johnson, and Kent Pummel, *PPC's Guide to Business Valuations*, 33d ed., Thomson Reuters, 2023.

VT—Internal Revenue Service, *Valuation Training for Appeals Officers Coursebook*, 1997 ed., available online at http://onlinestore.cch.com.

BB—William J. Morrison and Jay E. Fishman, *The Business Valuation Bench Book*, Business Valuation Resources, 2017.

Acquisition Premium

The difference between transaction price and the unaffected price before the transaction.

Source: Valuing a Business, 6th ed.

Reference: VAB6 410–15

Adjusted Book Value

The book value that results after one or more asset or liability amounts are added, deleted, or changed from their respective book amounts.

Source: ASA Business Valuation Standards

Adjusted Book Value Method

A method within the asset-based approach whereby all assets and liabilities (including off-balance sheet, intangible, and contingent) are adjusted to their fair market values. (Note: In Canada, on a going-concern basis.) Also termed *asset-accumulation method.*

Source: Valuing a Business, 6th ed.

References: VAB6 363; BB 108

Adjusted Net Asset Value Method*

See Adjusted Book Value Method

Adjusted Present Value (APV)*

A method typically used to estimate the value of a levered business as the sum of the value of an unlevered business (i.e., 100% equity financed) and the value of the tax benefits associated with debt financing.

Reference: VAB6 168

Appraisal*

The act or process of estimating value.

Source: Uniform Standards of Professional Appraisal Practice
See Valuation*

Appraisal Date

See Valuation Date*

Appraisal Method

See Valuation Method*

Appraisal Procedure

See Valuation Method*

Asset (Asset-Based) Approach*

A general way of determining a value indication of a business, business ownership interest, or security using one or more methods based on the value of the assets net of liabilities.

References: VAB6 53–54, 361–81, 770–71, 925, 1005, 1022, 1050; BB 108

Basis of Value*

See Standard of Value*

Beta*

A measure of systematic risk of a stock; the tendency of a stock's price to correlate with changes in a specific index.

References: VAB6 222–32, 187–89, 293; Guide 505.4; BB 109

Blockage Discount*

An amount or percentage deducted from the current market price of a publicly traded security to reflect the decrease in the per share value of a block of stock that is of a size that could not be sold in a reasonable period of time given normal trading volume.

References: VAB6 476–77, 788–89, 911; BB 109

Book Value

See Net Book Value*

Business Enterprise

An entity pursuing an economic activity.

Source: Uniform Standards of Professional Appraisal Practice

Reference: BB 110

Business Equity

The interests, benefits, and rights inherent in the ownership of a business enterprise or a part thereof in any form (including but not necessarily limited to capital stock, partnership interests, cooperatives, sole proprietorships, options, warrants).

Source: Uniform Standards of Professional Appraisal Practice

Reference: VAB6 24

Business Risk

The degree of uncertainty of realizing expected future returns of the business resulting from factors other than financial leverage.

See Financial Risk

References: VAB6 140–41; BB 110

Business Valuation

The act or process of determining the value of a business enterprise or ownership interest therein.

References: VAB6 43–61; BB 110

Build-up Model (Method)*

The definition of a discount rate applicable for discounting economic income to equity capital, generally as the sum of a risk-free rate and risk premia (equity risk premium, industry risk premium, size premium, and company-specific risk premium).

Reference: VAB6 212–13

Capital Asset Pricing Model (CAPM)*

A model in which the cost of capital for any stock or portfolio of stocks equals a risk-free rate plus a risk premium that is proportionate to the systematic risk of the stock or portfolio.

References: VAB6 210–12; BB 110

Capital Market Theory

A body of economic theory that divides risk into two components: systematic and unsystematic. This theory assumes that investors hold, or have the ability to hold, common stocks in large, well-diversified portfolios, which eliminates the unsystematic risk attached to an individual company's stock. Therefore, the only risk pertinent to a study of capital asset pricing theory is systematic risk.

Reference: VAB6 222

Capital Structure*

The composition of the invested capital of a business enterprise, the mix of debt and equity financing.

References: VAB6 92, 166–69, 227–30; BB 110

Capitalization*

A conversion of a single-period stream of economic benefits into value.

References: VAB6 182–83; BB 110

Capitalization Factor

Any multiple or divisor used to convert anticipated economic benefits of a single period into value.

Reference: BB 110

Capitalization Rate*

Any divisor (usually expressed as a percentage) used to convert anticipated economic benefits of a single period into value.

References: VAB6 182–83; BB 110

Cash Flow*

Cash inflows or outflows that are generated over a period of time by an asset, group of assets, or business enterprise. It may be used in a general sense to encompass various levels of specifically defined cash flows. When the term is used, it should be supplemented by a qualifier (for example, "discretionary" or "operating") and a specific definition in the given valuation context.

See Equity Net Cash Flows, Invested Capital Net Cash Flows

References: VAB6 161–63; BB 110

Cash Flow Analysis

A study of the anticipated movement of cash into or out of an investment.

Source: Uniform Standards of Professional Appraisal Practice

Client

The party or parties who engage an appraiser (by employment or contract) in a specific assignment.

Source: Uniform Standards of Professional Appraisal Practice

Reference: VAB6 20–21

Coefficient of Variation

The standard deviation divided by the mean.

References: VAB6 312; BB 111

Common-Size Statements

Financial statements in which each line is expressed as a percentage of the total. On the balance sheet, each line item is shown as a percentage of total assets, and on the income statement, each item is expressed as a percentage of sales.

References: VAB6 135; BB 111

Company-Specific Risk Premium*

An adjustment to the cost of equity to account for company-specific risk, the risk that is unique to a specific investment in a business, in excess of the equity risk premium, size risk, and/or country risk.

References: VAB6 246–48

Control*

The power to direct the management and policies of a business enterprise and disposition of a business enterprise.

References: VAB6 391–99; BB 112

Control Premium*

An amount or a percentage by which the pro rata value of a controlling interest exceeds the pro rata value of a noncontrolling interest in a business enterprise, to reflect the power of control. [Confusingly, however, Delaware decisions have also used the phrase "control premium" with two other meanings (in addition to the inverse of the minority discount). The phrase has been used by the Delaware Court of Chancery not only to describe the inverse of the minority discount but also to portray the premium above the Financial Control Value that would be paid by a synergistic buyer for control of a company.]

References: VAB6 410–15; BB 112

Cost Approach*

A general way of determining a value indication of an individual asset by quantifying the amount of money required to replace the future service capability of that asset.

References: VAB6 369, 586–87; BB 112

Cost of Capital*

The expected rate of return that the market requires in order to attract funds to a particular investment.

References: VAB6 208–10; Guide 509; BB 112

Discount for Lack of Control*

An amount or percentage deducted from the pro rata share of the value of 100% of an equity interest in a business to reflect the absence of some or all of the powers of control.

References: VAB6 401–02, 415; BB 113

Discount for Lack of Liquidity*

An amount or percentage applied to the value of an ownership interest to reflect a relative lack of liquidity.

References: VAB6 421–22, 448–50, 455–59; BB 113

Discount for Lack of Marketability*

An amount or percentage deducted from the value of an ownership interest to reflect the relative absence of marketability.

References: VAB6 423–24, 424–50; BB 113

Discount for Lack of Voting Rights*

An amount or percentage deducted from the per share value of a minority interest voting share to reflect the absence of voting rights.

References: VAB6 395, 474–76; BB 113

Discount Rate*

A rate of return used to convert a future monetary sum into present value.

References: VAB6 163–66, 208–10; Guide 503.1; BB 113

Discounted Cash Flow Method*

A method within the Income Approach whereby the present value of future expected net cash flows is calculated using a discount rate.

References: VAB6 161–63, 173–76; BB 113

Discounted Economic Income Method*

A method within the Income Approach whereby the present value of future expected economic benefits is calculated using a discount rate.

References: VAB6 155–80

Economic Income*

Monetary inflows such as revenues, net income, net cash flows, and so on, resulting from business activity. Also known as *economic benefits.*

References: VAB6 156–63l; BB 114

Economic Life

The period of time over which property may generate economic benefits.

References: VAB6 579; BB 114

Economic Obsolescence*

A type of external obsolescence that occurs when there is a deterioration in the level of operating income or the rates of return on investment that is attributable to factors external to the property itself.

Reference: VAB6 1101–06

Effective Date*

See Valuation Date*

Employee Stock Ownership Plan (ESOP)

A statutorily defined qualified employee pension benefit plan designed to invest primarily in the employer's securities, thus providing a means for employees to have an ownership interest in the company for which they work.

References: VAB6 41, 917–38, 940–72; BB 114

Enterprise Value*

The Market Value of Invested Capital, typically adjusted to remove all or a portion of cash and cash equivalents, and other nonoperating assets.

Reference: VAB6 24

Equity

The owner's interest in property after deduction of all liabilities.

References: VAB6 24, 161–63; BB 114

Equity Net Cash Flows*

Those cash flows available to pay out to equity holders (in the form of dividends) after funding operations of the business enterprise, making necessary capital investments, and increasing or decreasing debt financing.

References: VAB6 161–63; BB 114

Equity Risk Premium*

A rate of return added to a risk-free rate to reflect the additional risk of equity instruments over risk-free instruments (a component of the cost of equity capital or equity discount rate).

References: VAB6 216–21; Guide 505.11; BB 114

Excess Earnings*

That amount of anticipated economic benefits that exceeds an appropriate rate of return on the value of a selected asset base (often net tangible assets) used to generate those anticipated economic benefits.

References: VAB6 346, 349–50, 357; Guide Section 704; VT Lesson 7; BB 114

Excess Earnings Method*

A specific way of determining a value indication of a business, business ownership interest, or security determined as the sum of (1) the value of the assets derived by capitalizing excess earnings and (2) the value of the selected asset base. Also frequently used to value intangible assets.

See Excess Earnings*

References: VAB6 345–53: BB 115

External Obsolescence

A reduction in the value of the subject property due to the effects, events, or conditions that are external to, and not controlled by, the current use or condition of the property. The impact of external obsolescence is typically beyond the control of the property owner. For that reason, external obsolescence is usually considered incurable. There are two types of external obsolescence: location obsolescence and economic obsolescence.

Reference: VAB6 1101

Fair Market Value*

The price, expressed in terms of cash equivalents, at which property would change hands between a hypothetical willing and able buyer and a hypothetical willing and able seller, acting at arm's length in an open and unrestricted market, when neither is under compulsion to buy or sell and when both have reasonable knowledge of the relevant facts. (Note: In Canada, the term *price* should be replaced with the term *highest price.*)

References: VAB6 28–30, 33, 200, 404–05, 457–59, 847–47; BB 115

Fair Value (Statutory Fair Value)

A judicial concept, defined differently in different states and countries. It refers to an equitable, just, and reasonable value for property determined without reference to a simulated or real market transaction, since the property holder has no interest in entering the market at all. In a Delaware appraisal, fair value is the value of a company with no premium for control and no discount for minority interest or liquidity.

References: VAB6 32–33, 983–88; Guide 201.5; BB 115

Fairness Opinion*

An opinion as to whether or not the consideration in a transaction is fair from a financial point of view.

References: VAB6 1120–39; BB 115

Financial Risk

The degree of uncertainty of realizing expected future returns of the business resulting from financial leverage.

See Business Risk

References: VAB6 141–42; BB 116

Forced Liquidation Value*

Liquidation value at which the asset or assets are sold as quickly as possible, such as at an auction.

References: VAB6 34; BB 116

Functional Obsolescence*

A form of depreciation in which the loss in value or usefulness of an asset is caused by inefficiencies or inadequacies of the asset itself, when compared to a more efficient or less costly newly developed asset.

References: VAB6 369, 1097

Going Concern*

An ongoing, operating business enterprise.

References: VAB6 34, 289; BB 116

Going Concern Value*

The value of a business enterprise that is expected to continue to operate in the future. The intangible elements of going concern value result from factors such as having a trained work force; an operational plant; and the necessary licenses, systems, and procedures in place.

References: VAB6 34, 374, 574–75; BB 116

Goodwill*

That intangible asset arising as a result of name, reputation, customer loyalty, location, products, and similar factors not separately identified.

References: VAB6 91, 120, 572–74, 575–76, 1020–21, 1036–46; BB 116

Goodwill Value

The value attributable to goodwill.

References: VAB6 344–45, 1045–46; BB 116

Guideline Public Company Method*

A method within the Market Approach whereby market multiples are derived from market prices of stocks of companies that are engaged in the same or similar lines of business, and that are actively traded on a free and open market.

References: VAB6 50–52, 284–323; BB 117

Guideline Transaction Method*

A method within the Market Approach whereby the value of a business is estimated by application of multiples derived from one or more transactions of controlling interests in companies engaged in the same or similar lines of business as the subject business. Sometimes known as guideline merger and acquisition method.

References: VAB6 50–52, 325–41; BB 117

Income (Income-Based) Approach*

A general way of determining a value indication of a business, business ownership interest, security, or intangible asset using one or more methods that convert anticipated economic benefits into a present single amount.

References: VAB6 50–52, 155–206; Guide 203.3; VT Lesson 1; BB 117

Intangible Asset*

An asset that lacks physical substance such as franchises, trademarks, patents, copyrights, goodwill, equities, mineral rights, securities, and contracts (as distinguished from physical assets) that grant rights and privileges and have value for the owner.

References: VAB6 91, 374, 570–88; Guide 1701.4; VT Lesson 13; BB 118

Intellectual Property*

A legal concept that refers to creations of the mind that are derived from intellectual or creative effort for which exclusive or fractional rights are recognized (e.g., trademarks, trade names, trade secrets, patents, copyright, design rights, and proprietary information). Intellectual property rights generally give the owner the right to prohibit others from using the property without permission.

Reference: VAB6 570, 863

Internal Rate of Return*

A discount rate at which the present value of the future cash flows of the investment equals the cost of the investment.

Reference: BB 118

Intrinsic Value*

The value that an investor considers, on the basis of an evaluation or available facts, to be the "true" or "real" value that will become the market value when other investors reach the same conclusion. When the term applies to options, it is the difference between the exercise price or strike price of an option and the market value of the underlying security.

References: VAB6 31–32, 1018; BB 118

Invested Capital*

The sum of equity and debt in a business enterprise. Debt is typically (1) all interest bearing debt or (2) long-term interest bearing debt. When the term is used, it should be supplemented by a specific definition in the given valuation context.

References: VAB6 24, 193; BB 118

Invested Capital Net Cash Flows*

Those cash flows available to pay out to equity holders (in the form of dividends) and debt investors (in the form of principal and interest) after funding operations of the business enterprise and making necessary capital investments.

References: VAB6 24, 161–63; BB 118

Investment Risk*

The degree of uncertainty as to the realization of expected returns.

References: VAB6 49, 140–42, 209–10, 221–22; BB 118

Investment Value*

The value to a particular investor based on individual investment requirements and expectations. (Note: In Canada, the term used is *Value to the Owner.*)

References: VAB6 30–31, 33, 200, 327, 406, 969, 1006–07, 1017, 1031–33; Guide 201.16; BB 118

Key Person Discount*

An amount or percentage deducted from the value of an ownership interest to reflect the reduction in value resulting from the actual or potential loss of a key person in a business enterprise.

References: VAB6 466–69, 789–90; BB 119

Letter (Restricted) Stock

Stock identical to a freely traded stock of a public company except that a letter stock is restricted from trading on the open market for a certain period of time.

References: VAB6 426–27; BB 124

Levered Beta*

The beta reflecting a capital structure that includes debt.

References: VAB6 227–30; BB 119

Liquidation Value*

The net amount that would be realized if the business is terminated and the assets are sold piecemeal. Liquidation can either be "orderly" or "forced."

References: VAB6 34, 289, 298, 328; BB 119

Liquidity*

The ability to quickly convert property to cash or pay a liability.

References: VAB6 57, 421–22, 448–50; BB 119

Locational Obsolescence

A type of external obsolescence related to the physical environment or neighborhood in which the property is located.

Reference: VAB6 1101

Majority Control

The degree of control provided by a majority position.

References: VAB6 394; BB 119

Majority Interest

An ownership interest greater than 50% of the voting interest in a business enterprise.

References: VAB6 394; BB 119

Market (Market-Based) Approach*

A general way of determining a value indication of a business, business ownership interest, security, or intangible asset by using one or more methods that compare the subject to similar businesses, business ownership interests, securities, or intangible assets that have been sold.

References: VAB6 50–2; BB 119

Market Capitalization of Equity*

The share price of a publicly traded stock multiplied by the number of shares outstanding.

References: VAB6 50–52, 285–85; BB 119

Market Capitalization (Market Value) of Invested Capital*

The market capitalization of equity plus the market value of the debt component of invested capital.

References: VAB6 50–52, 285–87; BB 119

Market Multiple

The market value of a company's stock or invested capital divided by a company measure (such as economic benefits, number of customers).

References: VAB6 50–52, 285–87; BB 119

Marketability*

The ability to quickly convert property to cash at minimal cost.

References: VAB6 26, 56–57, 298, 420–24, 669; Guide 803.59; BB 120

Merger and Acquisition Method

See Guideline Transaction Method*

Midyear (Mid-Period Discounting) Discounting*

A convention used in the Discounted Economic Income Method that reflects economic benefits being generated at midyear, approximating the effect of economic benefits being generated evenly throughout the year.

References: VAB6 170–71; Guide 502.72; BB 120

Minority Discount

See Discount for Lack of Control*

Minority Interest

An ownership position less than 50% of the voting interest in a business enterprise.

References: VAB6 394–99; BB 120

Multiple*

The inverse of the capitalization rate.

References: VAB6 285–87; BB 120

Net Assets

Total assets less total liabilities.

Source: ASA Business Valuation Standards

Net Asset Value*

The difference between a business's total assets and liabilities restated at a particular standard of value rather than accounting book values.

References: VAB6 131, 308, 345, 365–67, 714, 723, 1005

Net Book Value*

With respect to a business enterprise, the difference between total assets (net of accumulated depreciation, depletion, and amortization) and total liabilities as they appear on the balance sheet (synonymous with Shareholder's Equity). With respect to a specific asset, the capitalized cost less accumulated amortization or depreciation as it appears on the books of account of the business enterprise.

References: VAB6 362; BB 120

Net Cash Flow*

When the term is used, it should be supplemented by a qualifier.

See Equity Net Cash Flows*, Invested Capital Net Cash Flows*

Net Income

Revenue less expenses and taxes.

Source: ASA Business Valuation Standards

References: VAB6 146, 162; BB 121

Net Present Value*

The value, as of a specified date, of future cash inflows less all cash outflows (including the cost of investment) calculated using an appropriate discount rate.

References: VAB6 160–61; BB 121

Net Tangible Asset Value

The value of the business enterprise's tangible assets (excluding excess assets and non-operating assets) minus the value of its liabilities.

References: VAB6 347–49; BB 121

Net Working Capital

See: Working Capital*

Current assets less current liabilities.

References: VAB6 138–39, 162

Nonoperating Assets*

Assets not necessary to ongoing operations of the business enterprise. (Note: In Canada, the term used is *Redundant Assets*.)

References: VAB6 125, 315–16, 337, 349; BB 122

Nonreporting Company

A company whose stock is publicly traded over-the-counter but that is not subject to the same reporting requirements as a reporting company.

Reference: VAB6 Appendix to Chapter 19

Normalizing Adjustments*

Adjustments to a business's financial statements for nonoperating assets and liabilities, and/or for extraordinary, nonrecurring, non-economic, or other unusual items in order to eliminate anomalies and facilitate comparisons.

Reference: VAB6 109–11

Normalized Earnings*

Economic benefits adjusted for nonrecurring, non-economic, or other unusual items to eliminate anomalies and/or facilitate comparisons.

References: VAB6 349–50; BB 122

Normalized Financial Statements

Financial statements adjusted for nonoperating assets and liabilities and/or for nonrecurring, non-economic, or other unusual items to eliminate anomalies and/or facilitate comparisons.

References: VAB6 108–11; Guide Section 404

Orderly Liquidation (Disposition) Value*

Liquidation value at which assets are sold over a reasonable period of time to maximize proceeds received.

References: VAB6 34; BB 122

Pass-through Entities

Businesses that pass earnings through to their owners, subject only to federal taxation at the owner's personal income tax rate.

Reference: VAB6 698

Physical Obsolescence*

The reduction in the value of an asset due to wear and tear resulting from continued use. Also called *physical depreciation*.

Reference: VAB6 369

Portfolio Discount*

An amount or percentage deducted from the value of a business enterprise to reflect the fact that it owns dissimilar operations, or assets do not fit well together.

References: VAB6 472–3; Guide 803.51; BB 123

Preemptive Right

Stockholders' privilege to subscribe to new issues of voting stock, usually the common stock or securities convertible into voting stock, before such offerings are made to non-stockholders. Also known as a *privileged subscription right.*

Reference: VAB6 397

Premise of Value*

An assumption regarding the most likely set of transactional circumstances that may be applicable to the subject valuation; for example going concern, liquidation.

References: VAB6 34, 58–59; BB 123

Present Value*

The value, as of a specified date, of future economic benefits and/or proceeds from sale, calculated using an appropriate discount rate.

References: VAB6 158–61; BB 123

Price-to-Earnings Multiple

The price of a share of stock divided by its earnings per share.

References: VAB6 1050–51; BB 123

Prior Transaction Method*

A method within the Market Approach that uses previous transactions involving the subject business as an indicator of value.

Reference: VAB6 335–36

Put Option

An option that gives the holder the right to sell the underlying stock by a certain date at a certain price.

Reference: VAB6 443–45

Range

A measure of dispersion that is defined as the spread between the highest and lowest observations.

Reference: VAB6 488–91, 95

Rate of Return*
An amount of income (loss) and/or change in value realized or anticipated on an investment, expressed as a percentage of that investment.

References: VAB6 164; BB 123

Redundant Assets
See Nonoperating Assets

Replacement Cost Method*
A method under the Cost Approach that estimates the value of an asset by calculating the cost, as of the Valuation Date, to recreate the functionality or utility of a similar asset.

Reference: VAB6 369

Replacement Cost New*
The current cost of a similar new property having the nearest equivalent utility to the property being valued.

References: VAB6 369; BB 124

Report
Any communication, written or oral, of an appraisal, appraisal review, or appraisal consulting service that is transmitted to the client upon completion of an assignment.

Source: Uniform Standards of Professional Appraisal Practice

References: VAB6 18–19, 36–37, 500–13; Guide Ch. 9, VT Lesson 16

Report Date*
The date on which conclusions are transmitted to the client.

Reference: BB 124

Reproduction Cost New
The current cost of construction of an exact replica of the subject asset.

References: VAB6 369; VT Lesson 13; BB 124

Required Rate of Return*
The minimum rate of return acceptable by investors before they will commit money to an investment at a given level of risk.

References: VAB6 209; BB 124

Residual Value
See Terminal Value*

Return/Rate of Return

The total yield to the investor, reflecting all dividends, interest, or other cash and cash equivalents received, plus or minus any realized or unrealized appreciation or depreciation in the investment's value.

Reference: VAB6 164

Return on Equity

The amount, expressed as a percentage, earned on a company's common equity for a given period.

References: VAB6 165; BB 124

Return on Investment

See Return on Invested Capital, Return on Equity

Return on Invested Capital

The amount, expressed as a percentage, earned on a company's total capital for a given period.

References: VAB6 165–69; BB 124

Risk

The degree of uncertainty as to the realization of expected future returns.

References: VAB6 209–10; Guide Section 502

Risk-Free Rate*

The rate of return available in the market on an investment free of default risk.

References: VAB6 213–16; BB 125

Risk Premium*

A rate of return added to a risk-free rate to reflect risk.

References: VAB6 209–10; BB 125

Rule of Thumb

A mathematical formula developed from the relationship between price and certain variables based on experience, observation, hearsay, or a combination of these factors, usually industry specific.

References: VAB6 336–37; BB 125

Special-Interest Purchasers

Acquirers who believe they can enjoy post-acquisition economies of scale, synergies, or strategic advantages (buyer-specific synergy) by combining the acquired business interest with their own.

See Investment Value*

References: VAB6 388, 410; BB 126

Stand-alone Value*

The value of an asset, business, or investment estimated without consideration of potential synergies.

Reference: VAB6 390

Standard of Value*

The identification of the type of value being used in a specific engagement; for example, fair market value, fair value, investment value.

References: VAB6 28–33; Guide Section 1202; BB 126

Strategic Acquisition

A purchase by a buyer who expects to benefit from synergies with the purchased company, such as horizontal and vertical integration, elimination of redundant overhead, or better prices through reduced competition.

Reference: VAB6 410

Strategic Control Premium

That premium, over and above the standard control premium, associated with a unique buyer and a unique seller that would relate to a unique set of beneficial synergies or circumstances between that buyer and seller.

Reference: VAB6 388

Synergies*

The concept that the performance and value of two assets or businesses combined will be greater than the sum of the separate individual parts, resulting from the expectation of economies of scale or post-acquisition benefits.

Reference: VAB6 874–75, 986–87

Synergistic Value*

The expected value resulting from a combination of two or more assets or businesses, which is greater than the sum of the separate individual parts.

Reference: VAB 54–56, 404–06

Systematic Risk*

The risk that is common to all risky securities and cannot be eliminated through diversification. The measure of systematic risk in stocks in the CAPM is the beta coefficient.

References: VAB6 221–30; BB 126

Tangible Assets*

Physical assets (such as cash, accounts receivable, inventory, property, plant and equipment, etc.).

Terminal Value*

An estimate of the value of economic income of a business beyond the discrete forecast period in the Discounted Economic Income Method. Also known as *residual value* or *continuing value.*

Reference: VAB6 169–70

Unlevered Beta*

The beta reflecting a capital structure without debt.

References: VAB6 227–30; BB 127

Unsystematic Risk*

The risk specific to an individual security that can be avoided through diversification.

References: VAB6 221–22; BB 127

Valuation*

The act or process of determining the value of a business, business ownership interest, security, or intangible asset.

References: VAB6 44; BB 128

Valuation Approach*

A general way of determining a value indication of a business, business ownership interest, security, or intangible asset using one or more valuation methods.

References: VAB6 50–54; BB 128

Valuation Date*

The specific point in time as of which the valuator's opinion of value applies (also referred to as *effective date* or *appraisal date*).

References: VAB6 27; BB 128

Valuation Method*

Within approaches, a specific way to determine value.

References: VAB6 50–54; BB 128

Valuation Procedure (Model)*

The act, manner, and technique of performing the steps of an appraisal method.

References: VAB6 51; BB 128

Value to the Owner

See Investment Value*

Voting Control

De jure control of a business enterprise.

Reference: VAB6 392–94

Weighted Average Cost of Capital (WACC)*

The cost of capital (discount rate) determined by the weighted average, at market value, of the cost of all financing sources in the business enterprise's capital structure.

References: VAB6 165–69; Guide Section 509; BB 129

Working Capital*

The amount of current assets minus current liabilities held in a business for its day-to-day operational needs. Also known as *debt-free net working capital* when all or a portion of cash and the current portion of interest-bearing debt is excluded.

See Net Working Capital

APPENDIX B

Fair Value in Dissent and Oppression

State	**Alabama**	**Alaska**	**Arizona**	**Arkansas**
Valuation Term	Fair Value	Dissent: Fair Value Dissolution: Fair Value (under Liquidation)	Fair Value	Fair Value
Precedent in Allowing Discounts	(Case law) Rejects discounts	No case law	(Case law) Rejects discounts	(Case law) Rejects discounts
Cases Addressing Discounts	*Ex parte Baron Services, Inc.* 874 So. 2d 545 (Ala. 2003) No discounts applied		*Pro Finish USA v. Johnson* 63 P.3d 288 (Ariz. App. 2003) No discounts applied	*General Securities Corp. v. Watson* 477 S.W.2d 461 (Ark. 1972) Dissenters entitled to "aliquot proportion" *Winn v. Winn Enterprises, L.P.* 265 S.W.3d 125 (Ark. App. 2007) Rejects DLOM for party withdrawing from partnership
Definition of Valuation Term in Appraisal	§ 10A-2-13.01(4): Fair value excludes any appreciation or depreciation in anticipation of the corporate action unless exclusion would be inequitable.	§ 10.06.580(c): In fixing the fair value of the shares, the court shall consider the nature of the transaction giving rise to the right to dissent, its effects on the corporation and its shareholders and other relevant factors.	§ 10-1301(4): Fair value excludes any appreciation or depreciation in anticipation of the corporate action unless exclusion would be inequitable.	§ 4-27-1301(3): Fair value is the value of the shares immediately before the effectuation of the corporate action to which the dissenter objects, excluding any appreciation or depreciation in anticipation of the corporate action unless exclusion would be inequitable.

State	Alabama	Alaska	Arizona	Arkansas
Appraisal Valuation Date	§ 10A-2-13.01(4): Immediately before the effectuation of the corporate action to which the dissenter objects	§ 10.06.580(c): The close of business on the day before the date on which the vote was taken approving the proposed corporate action	§ 10-1301: Immediately before the effectuation of the corporate action to which the dissenter objects	§ 4-27-1301(3): Immediately before the effectuation of the corporate action to which the dissenter objects
Dissolution by shareholder as a remedy for oppression or oppressive behavior?	Yes - § 10A-2-14.30(2)(ii)	Yes - § 10.06.628(b)(4) ["Oppression" not used as term in statute.]	Yes - § 10-1430 (B)(2)	Yes - § 4-27-1430(2)(ii)
Buy-out election in lieu of dissolution?	Yes - § 10A-2-14.34(d)	Yes - § 10.06.630	Yes - § 10-1434	No
Definition of Valuation Term in Oppression		§ 10.06.630(a): Fair value shall be determined on the basis of the liquidation value, taking into account the possibility of sale of the entire business as a going concern in a liquidation.		
Dissolution Valuation Date	§ 10A-2-14.34(d): The day before the date the petition was filed or as of the other date the court deems appropriate under the circumstances		§ 10-1434(D): The day before the date the petition was filed or as of another date as the court deems appropriate under the circumstances	

State	**California**	**Colorado**	**Connecticut**
Valuation Term	Dissent: Fair Market Value Dissolution: Fair Value (under Liquidation)	Fair Value	Fair Value
Precedent in Allowing Discounts	(Case law) Rejects minority discounts in dissolution	(Case law) Rejects discounts	(Statute) Rejects discounts
Cases Addressing Discounts	*Brown v. Allied Corrugated Box Co.* 154 Cal. Rptr. 170 (Cal. App. 1979) Rejected minority discount in dissolution	*Pueblo Bancorp. v. Lindoe, Inc.* 37 P.3d 492 (Colo. App. 2001), *aff'd*, 37 P.3d 492 (Colo. 2003) No minority discount and, except under extraordinary circumstances, no marketability discount	*R.D. Clark & Sons, Inc, v. Clark* 222 A.3d 515 (Conn. App. 2019) Denied minority and marketability discounts in oppression case, ruling that "fair value" when company elects to repurchase minority shares in lieu of dissolution has the same meaning as "fair value" in appraisal statute
Definition of Valuation Term in Appraisal	Appraisal: § 1300(a): Fair market value excludes any appreciation or depreciation in consequence of the proposed action, but adjusted for any stock split, reverse stock split, or share dividend which becomes effective thereafter. LLCs: § 17711.07(b) Fair market value LPs: § 15908.02(c) Fair market value	§ 7-113-101(4): Fair value is the value of the shares immediately before the effectuation of the corporate action to which the dissenter objects, excluding any appreciation or depreciation in anticipation of the corporate action unless exclusion would be inequitable.	§ 33-855(4): Fair value is the value of the shares immediately before the effectuation of the corporate action to which the shareholder objects and without discounting for lack of marketability or minority status except, if appropriate, for amendments to the certificate of incorporation.
Appraisal Valuation Date	§ 1300(a): The day before the first announcement of the terms of the proposed reorganization or short-form merger	§ 7-113-101(4): Immediately before the effective date of corporate action	§ 33-855(4): Immediately before the effectuation of corporate action
Dissolution by shareholder as a remedy for oppression or oppressive behavior?	Yes* - § 1800(b)(4) ["Oppression" not used as term in statute.]	Yes - § 7-114-301(2)(b)	Yes - § 33-896(a)(1)(B)

State	California	Colorado	Connecticut
Buy-out election in lieu of dissolution?	Yes - § 2000	No	Yes - § 33-900
Definition of Valuation Term in Oppression	§ 2000(a): The fair value shall be determined on the basis of the liquidation value as of the valuation date but taking into account the possibility, if any, of the sale of the entire business as a going concern in liquidation.		
Dissolution Valuation Date	§ 2000(f): In the case of a suit for involuntary dissolution under Section 1800, the date upon which that action was commenced		§ 33-900(d): The day before the date on which the petition was filed or as of such other date as the court deems appropriate under the circumstances

State	Delaware	District of Columbia	Federally Chartered Banks
Valuation Term	Fair Value	Fair Value	None
Precedent in Allowing Discounts	(Case law) Rejects discounts	(Statute) Rejects Discounts	Office of the Controller of the Currency (OCC) rules say it will normally not apply a minority discount, but that a marketability discount is applicable to shares that are closely held or have a limited market
Cases Addressing Discounts	*Cavalier Oil Corp. v. Harnett* 564 A.2d 1137 (Del. 1989) Minority and marketability discounts are improper under Delaware law		
Definition of Valuation Term in Appraisal	§ 262(h): Fair value is the value exclusive of any element of value arising from the accomplishment or expectation of the merger or consolidation. In determining such fair value, the Court shall take taking into account all relevant factors.	§ 29-311.01(4): Immediately before the effectuation of the corporate action to which the shareholder objects without discounting for lack of marketability or minority status except, if appropriate, for amendments to the articles pursuant to § 29-311.02(a)(5)	OCC, *Comptroller's Licensing Manual – Business Combinations*: The OCC may apply a marketability discount due to the lack of marketability for stock that is closely held or has a limited trading history. The use of a marketability discount for stock that is not readily marketable is a standard practice in the business valuation industry. The OCC has determined that where the facts warrant the inclusion of this type of discount, such a discount is helpful in reaching the best possible determination of the value. The OCC normally does not apply certain minority discounts to the fair valuation of the dissenting shares of stock.

State	Delaware	District of Columbia	Federally Chartered Banks
Appraisal Valuation Date	§ 262(h): Date at the point before the effective date of the corporate action	§ 29-311.01(4): Immediately before the effectuation of the corporate action to which the shareholder objects	OCC, *Comptroller's Licensing Manual – Business Combinations*: The date of consummation of the consolidation or merger, with the exception of transactions subject to the requirements of 12 USC 214a, in which case the value is determined as of the date the shareholders' meeting was held authorizing the transaction.
Dissolution by shareholder as a remedy for oppression or oppressive behavior?	No - § 275: Majority of directors plus majority of shareholders, or all shareholders by written consent	Yes - § 29-312.20(a)(2)(B) [corporations]; § 29-807.01(a)(5)(B) [LLCs]	
Buy-out election in lieu of dissolution?	No	Yes - § 29-312.24	
Definition of Valuation Term in Oppression			
Dissolution Valuation Date		§ 29-312.24(d): The day before the date on which the petition was filed or as of such other date as the court deems appropriate under the circumstances	

State	**Florida**	**Georgia**	**Hawaii**
Valuation Term	Fair Value	Fair Value	Fair Value
Precedent in Allowing Discounts	(Statute) Rejects discounts	(Case law) Rejects discounts	No case law
Cases Addressing Discounts	*Agnelli v. Miami Lennox Corp.* 2022 WL 2788875 (S. Dist. Fla. July 15, 2022) The term "fair value" is not defined in Florida's judicial dissolution statute but is defined in the analogous appraisal rights statute to expressly disallow discounts for lack of control and lack of marketability.	*Blitch v. People's Bank* 540 S.E. 2d 667 (Ga. App. 2000) No discounts permitted	
Definition of Valuation Term in Appraisal	Corporations: § 607.1301 "Fair value" is the value of the corporation's shares determined without discounting for lack of marketability or minority status LLCs: § 605.106 "Fair value" is the value of the member's membership interest determined without discounting for lack of marketability or minority status. Partnerships: § 620.2113 "Fair value" is the value of the limited partner's partnership interests; for a limited partnership with ten or fewer limited partners, determined without discounting for lack of marketability or minority status.	§ 14-2-1301(5) [corporations] & § 14-11-1001(3) [LLCs]: Fair value is the value of the shares immediately before the effectuation of the corporate [LLC] action to which the dissenter objects, excluding any appreciation or depreciation in anticipation of the corporate [LLC] action	§ 414-341: Fair value is the value of the shares immediately before the effectuation of the corporate action to which the dissenter objects, excluding any appreciation or depreciation in anticipation of the corporate action unless exclusion would be inequitable.

State	Florida	Georgia	Hawaii
Appraisal Valuation Date	§ 607.1301(4)(a) [corporations]: Immediately before the effectiveness of the corporate action to which the shareholder objects § 608.4351(4)(a) [LLCs]: Immediately before the effectuation of the corporate action to which the member objects § 620.2113(4)(a) [partnerships]: Immediately before the effectuation of the appraisal event to which the partner objects	§ 14-2-1301(5) [corporations]; § 14-11-1001(3) [LLCs]: Immediately before the effectuation of corporate [LLC] action	§ 414-341: Immediately before the effectuation of corporate action
Dissolution by shareholder as a remedy for oppression or oppressive behavior?	Yes - § 607.1430(1)(b) ["Oppression" not used as term in statute.]	Yes - § 14-2-1430(2)(B): must be brought by holders of at least 20% of shares ["Oppression" not used as term in statute.]	Yes - § 414-411(2)(B)
Buy-out election in lieu of dissolution?	Yes -§ 607.1436(1)	Yes - under articles of a close corporation - § 14-2-942(b)(1)	Yes - § 414-415
Definition of Valuation Term in Oppression		§ 14-2-942(b)(1): For close corporations, in determining fair value, the court must consider going concern value	
Dissolution Valuation Date	§ 607.1436(4): The day before the date the petition was filed or as of such other date as the court deems appropriate under the circumstances		§ 414-415(d): The day before the date the petition was filed or as of the other date the court deems appropriate under the circumstances

State	Idaho	Illinois	Indiana
Valuation Term	Fair Value	Fair Value	Fair Value
Precedent in Allowing Discounts	(Statute 2015) Rejects discounts	(Statute 2007) Rejects discounts	(Case law) Rejects discounts
Cases Addressing Discounts	*Hall v. Glenn's Ferry Grazing Assn.* 2006 U.S. Dist. LEXIS 68051 (D. Idaho) Minority discount applied by federal court applying Idaho law in oppression case	*Murchie v. Sorenson* 2015 IL App (1st) 133719-U (Ill. App 2015) *Bone v. Coyle Mechanical Supply, Inc.* 2017 IL App (5th) 150117-U (Ill. App. 2017) Although fair value not defined in oppression statute, discounts denied based on the definition in the appraisal statute	*G&N Aircraft, Inc. v Boehm* 743 N.E.2d 227 (Ind. 2001). No discounts in oppression case because it would improperly benefit control shareholder *Hartman v. BigInch Fabricators & Construction Hldg. Co., Inc.* 161 N.E.3d 1218 (Ind. 2021) For a withdrawing shareholder, a shareholder agreement calling for fair market value takes precedence and permits discounts
Definition of Valuation Term in Appraisal	§ 30-29-1301(5): "Fair value" is the value of the corporation's shares determined without discounting for lack of marketability or minority status.	§ 805 ILCS 5/11.70(j)(1): Fair value is the proportionate interest of the shareholder in the corporation, without discount for minority status or, absent extraordinary circumstance, lack of marketability, immediately before the consummation of the corporate action to which the dissenter objects excluding any appreciation or depreciation in anticipation of the corporate action, unless exclusion would be inequitable.	§ 23-1-44-3: Fair value mean the value of the shares excluding any appreciation or depreciation in anticipation of the corporate action unless exclusion would be inequitable
Appraisal Valuation Date	§ 30-28-1301(5)(a): Immediately before the effectuation of the corporate action	§ 805 ILCS 5/11.70(j)(1): Immediately before the consummation of the corporate action	§ 23-1-44-3: Immediately before the effectuation of the corporate action

State	Idaho	Illinois	Indiana
Dissolution by shareholder as a remedy for oppression or oppressive behavior?	Yes - § 30-1-1430(2)(b)	Yes - 805 ILCS 5/12.55(2)	No - IN Code § 23-1-47-1 : Only in deadlock
Buy-out election in lieu of dissolution?	Yes - § 30-1-1434	Yes § 805 ILCS 5/12.55(3)	No
Definition of Valuation Term in Oppression			
Dissolution Valuation Date	§ 30-1-1434(4): The day before the date the petition was filed or as of the other date the court deems appropriate under the circumstances	§ 805 ILCS 5/12.55(3)(d): Such date as the court finds equitable	

State	**Iowa**	**Kansas**	**Kentucky**	**Louisiana**
Valuation Term	Fair Value	Fair Value	Fair Value	Fair Value for appraisal and oppression Fair Market Value for withdrawal from LLC
Precedent in Allowing Discounts	(Statute) Rejects discounts except for banks and bank holding companies (Case law) Control premium may be accepted for banks	(Case law) Rejects discounts	(Case law) Rejects shareholder-level discounts	(Statutes) Rejects discounts for appraisal and oppression; accepts minority and marketability discounts for withdrawal from LLC
Cases Addressing Discounts	*Rolfe State Bank v. Gunderson* 794 N.W.2d 561 (Iowa 2011). Discounts rejected for bank's reverse stock split *Northwest Investment Corp. v. Wallace* 741 N.W.2d 782 (Iowa 2007) Control premium accepted in valuing a bank	*Arnaud v. Stockgrowers State Bank of Ashland, Kansas* 992 P.2d 216 (Kan. 1999) Discounts are not appropriate when purchaser is the corporation or the majority.	*Shawnee Telecom Resources v. Brown* 354 S.W.3d 542 (Ky. 2011) Discounts rejected	*Wall v. Bryan* 251 So.3d 650 (La. App. 2018) In withdrawal from LLP, court may apply minority and marketability discounts

State	Iowa	Kansas	Kentucky	Louisiana
Definition of Valuation Term in Appraisal	For companies other than banks: § 490.1301(4): Fair value is the value of the shares without discounting for lack of marketability or minority status except for amendments to 490.1302(1)(e). For banks: § 524.1406(3(a): In determining the fair value of shares of a bank or a bank holding company, due consideration shall be given to valuation factors recognized for federal tax purposes, including discounts for minority interests and discounts for lack of marketability. However, any payment shall be in an amount not less than the stockholders' equity in the bank as disclosed in its last statement of condition.	§ 17-6712(h): Fair value is the value exclusive of any element of value arising from the accomplishment or expectation of the merger or consolidation. In determining such fair value, the Court shall take taking into account all relevant factors.	§ 271B.13-010(3): Fair value is the value of the shares excluding any appreciation or depreciation in anticipation of the corporate action unless exclusion would be inequitable.	§ 12.1-1-1301(4) (corporations): Fair value is the value of the corporation's shares without discounting for lack of marketability or minority status. § 12:1-1435(C) (oppression): Same as for corporations § 12:1-1325(C) (withdrawal from LLC): Fair market value
Appraisal Valuation Date	§ 490.1301(4)(a): Immediately before the effectuation of the corporate action to which the shareholder objects	§ 17-6712(h): Date at the point before the effective date of the corporate action	§ 271B.13-010(3): Immediately before the effectuation of corporate action	§ 12.1-1-1301(4) (corporations): Immediately before the effectuation of the corporate action to which the shareholder objects

Page Intentionally Left Blank

State	Iowa	Kansas	Kentucky	Louisiana
Dissolution by shareholder as a remedy for oppression or oppressive behavior?	Yes - § 490.1430 (2)(b)	No - § 17-6804: Voluntary	Yes - § 271B.14-300 (2)(b) ["Oppression" not used as term in statute.]	Yes - § 12:1-1435(A)
Buy-out election in lieu of dissolution?	Yes - § 490.1434	No	No	Yes
Definition of Valuation Term in Oppression				§ 12:1-1435(C) (oppression): Fair value is the value of the shares without discounting for lack of marketability or minority status § 12:1-1325(C) (withdrawal from LLC): Fair market value.
Dissolution Valuation Date	§ 490.1434: The day before the date the petition was filed or as of the other date the court deems appropriate under the circumstances			§ 12:1-1435(C) (oppression): Effective date of the notice of withdrawal § 12:1-1325(C) (withdrawal from LLC): Date of the member's withdrawal or resignation

State	**Maine**	**Maryland**	**Massachusetts**	**Michigan**
Valuation Term	Fair Value	Fair Value	Fair Value	Fair Value
Precedent in Allowing Discounts	(Statute) Rejects discounts	(Case law) Rejects discounts	(Case law) Rejects discounts	(Case law) Court's discretion
Cases Addressing Discounts	*In re Val. of McLoon Oil Co.* 565 A.2d 997 (Me. 1989) Rejected discounts *In re Val. of Penobscot Shoe Co.* 2003 Me. Super. LEXIS 140 Rejected discounts *Kaplan v. First Hartford Corp.* 603 F. Supp. 2d 195 (D. Me. 2009) Federal court rejected discounts and adjusted market prices to reverse built-in discounts	*American General Corp. v. Camp* 190 A. 225 (Md. App. 1937) Shareholders entitled to aliquot portion of net asset value *East Park L.P. v Larkin* 893 A.2d 1219 (Md. App. 2006) Rejected application of minority and marketability discounts with respect to withdrawing partners	*BNE Massachusetts Corp. v. Sims* 588 N.E.2d 14 (Mass. App. 1992) No discounts applied *Spenlinhauer v. Spencer Press, Inc.* 959 N.E.2d 436; Mass. App. 2011 No discounts applied	*Schimke v. Liquid Dustlayer, Inc.* 2009 WL 3049723 (Mich. App. Sept. 24, 2009) No requirement that fair value be ascertained without a discount for lack of marketability or minority status, but definition contained in statute does not require any discount
Definition of Valuation Term in Appraisal	§ 12.1-1301(4): Fair value is the value of the shares without discounting for lack of marketability or minority status.	Corp. & Ass'ns § 3-202(b): Fair value is the value of the shares excluding any appreciation or depreciation in anticipation of the corporate action.	Ch. 156D, § 13.01: Fair value is the value of the shares excluding any appreciation or depreciation in anticipation of the corporate action unless exclusion would be inequitable.	§ 450.1761(d): Fair value is the value of the shares excluding any appreciation or depreciation in anticipation of the corporate action unless exclusion would be inequitable.

State	Maine	Maryland	Massachusetts	Michigan
Appraisal Valuation Date	§ 1301(4): Immediately before the effectuation of the corporate action	Corp. & Ass'ns § 3-202(b)(1)(i) (short-form merger): On the day notice of a merger is given Corp. & Ass'ns § 3-202(b)(1)(ii) (other transactions): On the date of stockholder vote	Ch. 156D, § 13.01: Day immediately before the effective date of the corporate action to which the shareholder demanding appraisal objects	§ 450.1779: The latter of the day prior to the date of the vote and 20 days before the business combination, or the date of the business combination if there is no vote
Dissolution by shareholder as a remedy for oppression or oppressive behavior?	Yes - § 13-C-1430 (2)B	No - Corp. & Ass'ns § 3-413(b)(2); Yes - Corp. & Ass'ns § 4-602(a) (close corporations)	No - Ch. 156D, § 14.30 - .34: Deadlock	Yes - § 450.1489(1)
Buy-out election in lieu of dissolution?	Yes - § 13-C-1434	Yes (close corporation) - Corp. & Ass'ns § 4-603	No	Yes - § 450.1489(1)
Definition of Valuation Term in Oppression		Corp. & Ass'ns § 4-603(b)(2) (close corporations): Same as for appraisal		§ 450.1489(1)(e): Fair value
Dissolution Valuation Date		Corp. & Ass'ns § 4-602(b)(2) (close corporations) - As of the close of business on the day on which the petition for dissolution was filed		

State	Minnesota	Mississippi	Missouri
Valuation Term	Fair Value	Fair Value	Fair Value
Precedent in Allowing Discounts	(Case law) Rejects minority discounts; marketability discounts at court's discretion	(Statute) Rejects discounts	(Case law) Court's discretion
Cases Addressing Discounts	*MT Properties, Inc. v. CMC Real Estate Corp.* 481 N.W. 2d 38 (Minn. App. 1992) Prohibited minority discounts *Foy v. Klapmeier* 992 F.2d 774 (8th Cir. 1993) Federal court rejected minority discount *Advanced Communication Design, Inc. v. Follett* 615 N.W.2d 285 (Minn. 2000) Marketability discount accepted *Lund v. Lund* 924 N.W.2d 274 (Minn. App. 2019) In oppression case, declined to apply marketability discount, because circumstances not extraordinary	*Dawkins v. Hickman Family Corp.* 2011 U.S. Dist. LEXIS 63101 (N.D. Miss.) Federal court rejected discounts based Mississippi statute	*King v. F.T.J., Inc.* 765 S.W.2d 301 (Mo. Ct. App. 1988) Accepted discounts *Swope v. Siegel-Robert, Inc.* 243 F.3d 486, 492 (8th Cir. 2001) Federal court rejected discounts *Hunter v. Mitek Indus.* 721 F. Supp. 1102 (E.D. Mo. 1989) Federal court rejected discounts, but noted that discounts are at court's discretion.
Definition of Valuation Term in Appraisal	302A.473(c) [corporations]; 322B.386 subd. 1(c) [LLCs]: Fair value is the value of the shares of a corporation [LLC] immediately before the effective date of the corporate [LLC] action.	§ 79-4-13.01(4): Fair value is the value of the shares without discounting for lack of marketability or minority status.	§ 351.870: Fair value is the value of the shares excluding any appreciation or depreciation in anticipation of the corporate action unless exclusion would be inequitable.

State	Minnesota	Mississippi	Missouri
Appraisal Valuation Date	§ 302A.473 [corporations]; 322B.386 subd. 1(c) [LLCs]: Value of the shares of a corporation [LLC] immediately before the effective date of the corporate [LLC] action	§ 79-4-13.01(4)(i): Immediately before the effectuation of the corporate action to which the shareholder objects	§ 351.455(1): As of the day prior to the date on which the vote was taken
Dissolution by shareholder as a remedy for oppression or oppressive behavior?	Yes - § 302A.751 subd. 1(b)(3) [corporations]; § 322B.833 subd. 1(1)(iii) [LLCs]	Yes - § 79-4-14.30(2)(ii)	Yes - § 351.494(2)(b)
Buy-out election in lieu of dissolution?	Yes - § 302A.751 subd. 2 [corporations]; § 322B.833 subd. 2 [LLCs]	Yes - § 79-4-14.34	No, except close corporation § 351.790
Definition of Valuation Term in Oppression	§ 302A.751 subd. 2 [corporations]: Fair value, unless the court determines that the price or terms are unreasonable under all the circumstances of the case	§ 79-4-14.34: Fair value.	§ 351.860(2)(1): for close corporations, in determining fair value, the court must consider going concern value
Dissolution Valuation Date	§ 302A.751 subd. 2 [corporations]; 322B.833 subd. 2 [LLCs]: The date of the commencement of the action or as of another date found equitable by the court	§ 79-4-14.34(d): The day before the date the petition was filed or such other date the court deems appropriate under the circumstances	

State	**Montana**	**Nebraska**	**Nevada**
Valuation Term	Fair Value	Fair Value	Fair Value
Precedent in Allowing Discounts	(Case law) Rejects discounts	(Case law) Rejects discounts	(Statute) Rejects discounts
Cases Addressing Discounts	*Hansen v. 75 Ranch Co.* 957 P.2d 32 (Mont. 1998) Minority discounts inapplicable when the shares are purchased by the company or an insider.	*Rigel Corp. v. Cutchall* 511 N.W.2d 519 (Neb. 1994) Discounts rejected *Camino Inc. v. Wilson* 59 F. Supp. 2d 962 (D. Neb. 1999) Federal court rejected discounts based on Nebraska case law *Bohac v. Benes Service Co.* 969 N.W.2d 103 (Neb. 2022) Although statute re repurchase in lieu of dissolution does not define fair value, it has same meaning as in appraisal statute.	*McMinn v. MBF Operating Acq. Corp.* 164 P.3d 41 (N.M. 2007) Discounts rejected *American Ethanol Inc. v. Cordillera Fund, L.P.* 252 P.3d 663 (Nev. 2011) No discounts applied
Definition of Valuation Term in Appraisal	§ 35-1-826(4): Fair value is the value of the shares excluding any appreciation or depreciation in anticipation of the corporate action unless exclusion would be inequitable.	§ 21-20,137(4): Fair value is the value of the shares excluding any appreciation or depreciation in anticipation of the corporate action unless exclusion would be inequitable.	§ 92A.320: Fair value is the value of the shares excluding any appreciation or depreciation in anticipation of the corporate action unless exclusion would be inequitable, and without discounting for lack of marketability or minority status.
Appraisal Valuation Date	§ 35-1-826(4): Immediately before the effectuation of the corporate action to which the shareholder objects	§ 21-20,137(4): Immediately before the effectuation of the corporate action to which the shareholder objects	§ 92A.320: Immediately before the effectuation of the corporate action to which the shareholder objects

State	Montana	Nebraska	Nevada
Dissolution by shareholder as a remedy for oppression or oppressive behavior?	Yes - § 35-1-938(2)(b) [corporations]; § 35-8-902(1)(e) [LLCs]; § 35-9-501(1)(a) and § 35-9-504 (close corporations)	Yes - § 21-20,162(2)(a)(ii) [corporations]; § 21-147(5)(a) [LLCs]	No
Buy-out election in lieu of dissolution?	Yes - § 35-1-939(1)(d) [corporations]; § 35-9-503 [close corporations] No - LLCs	Yes - § 21-20,166 [corporations]; § 21-147(5)(b) (LLCs—the court may order a remedy other than dissolution)	No
Definition of Valuation Term in Oppression			
Dissolution Valuation Date		§ 21-20,166: The day before the date on which the petition was filed or as of such other date as the court deems appropriate under the circumstances	

State	**New Hampshire**	**New Jersey**	**New Mexico**
Valuation Term	Fair Value	Dissent: Fair Value Oppression: Fair Value + Equitable adjustments, if any	Fair Value
Precedent in Allowing Discounts	No case law	(Case law) Rejects discounts except in oppression; allows control premiums on a case by case consideration.	(Case law) Rejects discounts; permits control premiums at court's discretion
Cases Addressing Discounts		*Lawson Mardon Wheaton Inc. v. Smith* 734 A.2d 738 (N.J. 1999) No discounts applied *Balsamides v. Protameen Chemicals, Inc.* 734 A.2d 721 (N.J. 1999) Marketability discount applied because if oppressor instigates problem, oppressor should not benefit at expense of oppressed *Casey v. Brennan* 780 A.2d 553 (N.J. Super. 2001) Control premium permitted but cannot include future benefits of merger	*McMinn v. MBF Operating Acq. Corp.* 164 P.3d 41 (N.M. 2007) Discounts rejected *Peters Corp. v. New Mexico Banquest Investors Corp.* 188 P.3d 1185 (N.M. 2008) Control premium rejected based on facts of case

State	New Hampshire	New Jersey	New Mexico
Definition of Valuation Term in Appraisal	Corporations: § 293-A:13.01(3): Fair value is the value of the shares excluding any appreciation or depreciation in anticipation of the corporate action unless exclusion would be inequitable. LLC and LPs: § 304-C:22-a(II) [LLCs]; § 304-B:16-c(II) [LPs]: Fair value' is the value of the dissenter's interest excluding any appreciation or depreciation in anticipation of the limited liability [partnership] action.	§ 14A:11-3: Fair value shall exclude any appreciation or depreciation resulting from the proposed action.	§ 53-15-4(A): Fair value is the value excluding any appreciation or depreciation in anticipation of the corporate action.
Appraisal Valuation Date	§ 293-A:13.01(3 [corporations]: Immediately before the effectuation of the corporate action to which the shareholder objects; § 304-C:22-a(II) [LLCs]: immediately before the effective date of the limited liability action	§ 14A:11-3(3): The day prior to the day of the corporate action	§ 53-15-4(A): The date prior to the day on which the vote was taken for the corporate action
Dissolution by shareholder as a remedy for oppression or oppressive behavior?	Yes - § 293-A:14.30(b)(iii) [corporations]; § 304-C:134.C.III ["Oppression" not used as term in statute.]	Yes - § 14A:12-7(1)(c) (for corporations with 25 or less shareholders)	Yes - § 53-16-16(A)(1)(b)
Buy-out election in lieu of dissolution?	Yes - § 293-A:14.34 [corporations] No - LLCs	Yes -§ 14A:12-7(8)	No
Definition of Valuation Term in Oppression		§ 14A:12-7(8)(a): Plus or minus any adjustments deemed equitable by the court	
Dissolution Valuation Date	§ 293-A:14.34: The day before the date on which the petition was filed or as of such other date as the court deems appropriate under the circumstances	§ 14A:12-7(8)(a): The date of the commencement of the action or such earlier or later date deemed equitable by the court	

State	New York	North Carolina	North Dakota
Valuation Term	Fair Value	Fair Value	Fair Value
Precedent in Allowing Discounts	(Case law) Allows marketability discounts; rejects minority discounts in corporations but not in partnerships	(Statute) Rejects discounts in appraisal (Case law) Court's discretion in oppression	(Case law) Discounts in oppression cases at court's discretion
Cases Addressing Discounts	*Matter of Blake v. Blake Agency* 107 A.D.2d 139 (N.Y. App. 1985) Rejected minority discount, marketability discount is appropriate *Friedman v. Beway Realty Corp.* 87 N.Y.2d 161 (N.Y. 1995) Marketability discount must be considered in all fair value cases *Zelouf Intl. Corp. v. Zelouf* 2014 N.Y. Misc. LEXIS 4341 (N.Y. Sup., Oct.6, 2014) DLOM rejected because it was unlikely that the company would ever actually be sold. *Congel v Malfitano* 101 N.E.3d 341 (N.Y. 2018) Minority discount permitted in partnership	*Garlock v. South Eastern Gas & Power, Inc.* 2001 NCBC LEXIS 9 (N.C. Super. 2001) In oppression case, rejected minority and marketability discounts as inequitable but permitted key man discount *Finkel v. Palm Park, Inc.* 2020 NCBC 84, 2020 WL 6802470 (N.C. Super. 2020) Concluded in its discretion that value should not be adjusted for lack of marketability or control	*KBM, Inc. v. MacKichan* 438 N.W.2d 181, 184 (N.D.1989) Failure to apply minority discount was not error *Puklich v. Puklich* 930 N.W.2d 593, 600 (N.D. 2019) Trial court ascertaining fair value of minority shares should not automatically discount their value.
Definition of Valuation Term in Appraisal	§ 623(h)(4): In fixing the fair value of the shares, the court shall consider the nature of the transaction giving rise to the shareholder's right to receive payment for shares and its effects on the corporation and its shareholders, and all other relevant factors.	§ 55-13-01(3) [corporations]: Fair value is the value excluding any appreciation or depreciation in anticipation of the corporate action unless exclusion would be inequitable, without discounting for lack of marketability or minority status. § 57D-6-03(d) [LLCs]: Fair value is not defined	§ 10-19.1-88(1)(b) [corporations]: Fair value of the shares is the value of the shares the day immediately before the effective date of a corporate action.

State	New York	North Carolina	North Dakota
Appraisal Valuation Date	§ 623(h)(4): The close of business on the day prior to the shareholders' authorization date	§ 55-13-01(3): Immediately before the effectuation of the corporate action to which the shareholder objects	§ 10-19.1-88(1)(b) [corporations]; § 10-32-55(1)(a) [LLCs]: Day immediately before the effective date of action objected to
Dissolution by shareholder as a remedy for oppression or oppressive behavior?	Yes - § 1104-a (a)(1)	Yes - § 55-14-30(2)(ii) [corporations]; § 57D-6-02(2) [LLCs] ["Oppression" not used as term in statute.]	Yes - § 10-19.1-115(2)(b)(3) [corporations]; § 10-32-50(e)[LLCs] ["Oppression" not used as term in corporation statute.]
Buy-out election in lieu of dissolution?	Yes - § 1118	Yes - § 55-14-31(d)[corporations]; § 57D-6-03(d)[LLCs]	Yes - § 10-19.1-115(4) [corporations]; § 10-32-50(2) [LLCs]
Definition of Valuation Term in Oppression	§ 1118(b): Exclusive of any element of value arising from such filing but giving effect to any adjustment or surcharge found to be appropriate		
Dissolution Valuation Date	§ 1118(b): The court may award interest from the day prior to the date on which the petition was filed.		§ 10-19.1-115(4)(a) [corporations]: The date of the commencement of the action or as of another date found equitable by the court

State	Ohio	Oklahoma	Oregon
Valuation Term	Fair Cash Value	Fair Value	Fair Value
Precedent in Allowing Discounts	(Statute) Fair market value standard (Case law) Permits discounts	(Case law) Rejects discounts	(Case law) Rejects discounts
Cases Addressing Discounts	*Armstrong v. Marathon Oil Co.* 513 N.E.2d 776 (Ohio App. 1987) Valued dissenters' shares at pre-announcement market price *English v. Artromick Intl., Inc.* 2000 Ohio App. LEXIS 3580 (Ohio App. 2000) Discounts applied, distinguishing "fair cash value" standard from "fair value"	*Woolf v Universal Fidelity Life Ins. Co.* 849 P.2d 1093 (Okla. App. 1992) Discounts rejected	*Columbia Mgt. Co. v. Wyss* 765 P.2d 207, 209 (Ore. App. 1988) [pre-*Cavalier*] Rejected minority discount in appraisal but accepted marketability discount *Chrome Data Systems, Inc. v. Stringer* 820 P.2d 831 (Ore. App. 1991) [post-*Cavalier*] No discounts discussed in appraisal decision *Hayes v. Olmsted & Associates, Inc.* 21 P.3d 178 (Ore. App. 2001) Discounts rejected in oppression case. *Marker v. Marker* 242 P.3d 638 (Ore. App. 2010) No discounts applied in oppression case.

State	Ohio	Oklahoma	Oregon
Definition of Valuation Term in Appraisal	§ 1701.85(C) [corporations]; § 1705.42(B) [LLCs]; § 1782.437(B) [LPs] Fair cash value is the amount that a willing seller who is under no compulsion to sell would be willing to accept and that a willing buyer who is under no compulsion to purchase would be willing to pay, but in no event shall the fair cash value exceed the amount specified in the demand of the particular shareholder [member] [partner]. Any appreciation or depreciation in market value resulting from the proposal [merger, consolidation, or conversion] shall be excluded. (corporations only) Any control premium or any discount for lack of marketability or minority status shall be excluded. The fair cash value of a share listed on a national securities exchange shall be the closing sale price immediately before the effective time of a merger or consolidation.	§ 1091(H): Fair value is the value exclusive of any element of value arising from the accomplishment or expectation of the merger or consolidation. In determining such fair value, the Court shall take taking into account all relevant factors.	§ 60.551(4): Fair value is the value of the shares excluding any appreciation or depreciation in anticipation of the corporate action unless exclusion would be inequitable.

State	Ohio	Oklahoma	Oregon
Appraisal Valuation Date	§ 1701.85(C) [corporations]; § 1705.42(B) [LLCs]; § 1782.437(B) [LPs]: The day prior to that on which the shareholders' [members'] [partners'] vote on the transaction was taken or the day before the day on which the request for approval or other action was sent	§ 1091: Effective date of the merger or consolidation	§ 60.551(4): Immediately before the effectuation of the corporate action to which the shareholder objects
Dissolution by shareholder as a remedy for oppression or oppressive behavior?	No - § 1701.91: Attorney general if corporation has acted unlawfully, voluntary dissolution; when it is established that it is beneficial to the shareholders that the corporation be judicially dissolved	No - § 1096: Majority of shareholders	Yes - § 60.661(2)(b); § 60.952(1)(b)
Buy-out election in lieu of dissolution?	No	No	Yes - § 60.952(1)(k) (close corporations only)
Definition of Valuation Term in Oppression			
Dissolution Valuation Date			

Page Intentionally Left Blank

State	**Pennsylvania**	**Rhode Island**	**South Carolina**	**South Dakota**
Valuation Term	Fair Value	Fair Value	Fair Value	Fair Value
Precedent in Allowing Discounts	No case law	(Case law) Rejects discounts in oppression	(Case law) Rejects discounts in oppression	
Cases Addressing Discounts		*Charland v. Country View Golf Club* 588 A.2d 609, 613 (R.I. 1991) Marketability discount is inapposite when corporation elects to buy out shareholder who filed for dissolution; however, the Court said that this differs from determining fair value in appraisal. [Discounts have not been discussed in any published R.I. appraisal case.]	*Morrow v. Martschink* 922 F. Supp. 1093 (D. S.C.1995) Federal court found that discounts inapplicable in intra-family transfers in closely held company or in forced sale under S.C. law [Discounts have not been discussed in any published S.C. appraisal case.]	*First Western Bank Wall v. Olsen* 621 N.W.2d 611, 619 (S.D. 2001) Rejected discounts in appraisal [Predates statute]
Definition of Valuation Term in Appraisal	C.S.A. § 1572: The fair value of shares taking into account all relevant factors, but excluding any appreciation or depreciation in anticipation of the corporate action	§ 7-1.2-1202(a): Fair value is the value of the shares excluding any appreciation or depreciation in anticipation of the corporate action.	§ 33-13-101(3): Fair value is the value of shares excluding any appreciation or depreciation in anticipation of the corporate action to which the dissenter objects, excluding any appreciation or depreciation in anticipation of the corporate action unless exclusion would be inequitable.	§ 47-1A-1301(4): Fair value is the value of the shares and without discounting for lack of marketability or minority status.

State	Pennsylvania	Rhode Island	South Carolina	South Dakota
Appraisal Valuation Date	C.S.A. § 1572: Immediately before the effectuation of the corporate action to which the shareholder objects	§ 7-1.2-1202(a): As of the day prior to the date on which the vote was taken approving the proposed corporate action	§ 33-13-101(3): Immediately before the effectuation of the corporate action to which the dissenter objects	§ 47-1A-1301(4): Immediately before the effectuation of the corporate action to which the dissenter objects
Dissolution by shareholder as a remedy for oppression or oppressive behavior?	Yes - C.S.A. § 1676 (a)(2) (close corporations only)	Yes - § 7-1.2-1314(a)(1)(ii)	Yes - § 33-14-300(2)(ii) [corporations]; § 33-18-400(a)(1) & § 33-18-430 (close corporations); § 33-44-801(4)(e) [LLCs]	Yes - § 47-1A-1430(2)(b)
Buy-out election in lieu of dissolution?	No	Yes - § 7-1.2-1315	Yes - § 33-14-310(d)(4) [corporations] (in court's discretion); § 33-18-420 [close corporation] No - LLCs	Yes - § 47-1A-1434
Definition of Valuation Term in Oppression			§ 33-18-420(b)(1): for close corporations, in determining fair value, the court must consider going concern value	
Dissolution Valuation Date		§ 7-1.2-1315: The day on which the petition for dissolution was filed		§ 47-1A-1434.3: The day before the date on which the petition was filed or as of such other date as the court deems appropriate under the circumstances

State	**Tennessee**	**Texas**	**Utah**
Valuation Term	Fair Value	Fair Value	Fair Value
Precedent in Allowing Discounts	(Case law) Rejects discounts	(Statute) Rejects discounts (Case law) Permitted discounts when shareholder had intent to sell to third party	(Case law) Rejects discounts
Cases Addressing Discounts	*Raley v. Brinkman* 2020 WL 4360052 (Tenn. App. July 30, 2020)	*Ritchie v. Rupe* 339 S.W.3d 275 (Tex. App. 2011) Discounts are applicable when minority shareholder has expressed intent to sell.	*Hogle v. Zinetics Medical, Inc.* 63 P.3d 80 (Utah 2002) Discounts rejected *Utah Resources Int'l, Inc. v. Mark Technologies Corp.* 342 P.3d 761 (Utah 2014) Marketability discount impermissible
Definition of Valuation Term in Appraisal	§ 48-23-101(4) [corporations] & § 48-231-101(2) [LLCs]: Fair value is the value of the shares excluding any appreciation or depreciation in anticipation of the corporate [LLC] action.	§ 10.362 (a): Any appreciation or depreciation in the value of the ownership interest occurring in anticipation of the proposed action or as a result of the action must be specifically excluded from the computation of the fair value of the ownership interest. (b) Consideration must be given to the value of the domestic entity as a going concern without including in the computation of value any control premium, any minority ownership discount, or any discount for lack of marketability.	§ 16-10a-1301(4): Fair value is the value of the shares excluding any appreciation or depreciation in anticipation of the corporate action.

State	Tennessee	Texas	Utah
Appraisal Valuation Date	§ 48-23-101(4) [corporations]; § 48-231-101(2) [LLCs]: Immediately before the effectuation of the corporate [LLC] action to which the dissenter objects	§ 10.362(a): The date preceding the date of the action that is the subject of the appraisal	§ 16-10a-1301(4): Immediately before the effectuation of the corporate action to which the dissenter objects
Dissolution by shareholder as a remedy for oppression or oppressive behavior?	Yes - § 48-24-301(2)(B)	No	Yes - § 16-10a-1430(2)(b) [corporations]; § 48-3-701(5) [LLCs]
Buy-out election in lieu of dissolution?	No	No	Yes - § 16-10a-1434 [corporations]; § 48-3-702 [LLCs]
Definition of Valuation Term in Oppression			
Dissolution Valuation Date			§ 16-10a-1434 [corporations]; § 48-3-702(4) [LLCs]: The day before the date the petition was filed or as of any other date the court determines to be appropriate under the circumstances and based on the factors the court determines to be appropriate.

State	**Vermont**	**Virginia**	**Washington**
Valuation Term	Fair Value	Fair Value	Fair Value
Precedent in Allowing Discounts	(Case law) Rejects discounts, accepts control premiums	(Statute) Rejects discounts	(Case law) Rejects discounts
Cases Addressing Discounts	*In re Shares of Trapp Family Lodge, Inc.* 725 A.2d 927 (Vt. 1999) Control premium applied *Waller v. American Intl. Distrib. Corp.* 706 A.2d 460 (Vt. 1997) No minority discount when oppression is found. *In re Shares of Madden, Fulford and Trumbull* 2005 Vt. Super. LEXIS 112 (Vt. Super. 2005) Control premium applied.	*U. S. Inspect, Inc. v. McGreevy* 2000 Va. Cir. LEXIS 524 (Va. Cir. 2000) Discounts rejected [Predated statute]	*Matthew G. Norton Co. v. Smyth* 51 P.3d 159 (Wash. App. 2002) No marketability discount can be applied at the shareholder level except in extraordinary circumstances.
Definition of Valuation Term in Appraisal	11A V.S.A. § 13.01(3): Fair value is the value of the shares excluding any appreciation or depreciation in anticipation of the corporate action unless exclusion would be inequitable.	§ 13.1-729: Fair value is the value of the shares immediately before the effectuation of the corporate action to which the shareholder objects, without discounting for lack of marketability or minority status.	§ 23B.13.010(3) [corporations]; § 25.15.425(3) [LLCs]; § 25.10.831(2) [LPs]: Fair value is the value of the shares excluding any appreciation or depreciation in anticipation of the corporate action [merger] unless exclusion would be inequitable.

State	Vermont	Virginia	Washington
Appraisal Valuation Date	11A V.S.A. § 13.01(3): Immediately before the effectuation of the corporate action to which the dissenter objects	§ 13.1-729: Immediately before the effectuation of the corporate action to which the dissenter objects	§ 23B.13.010(3) [corporations]; 25.15.425(3) [LLCs]; § 25.10.831(2) (LPs): Immediately before the effectuation of the corporate action [merger] to which the dissenter objects
Dissolution by shareholder as a remedy for oppression or oppressive behavior?	Yes - 11A V.S.A. § 14.30(2)(B) [corporations]	Yes - § 13.1-747(A)(1)(b)	Yes - § 23B.14.300(2)(b)
Buy-out election in lieu of dissolution?	No, except close corporations 11A V.S.A.§ 20.15 (b)	Yes - § 13.1-749.1	No
Definition of Valuation Term in Oppression		§ 13.1-749.1.D - fair value shall consider all relevant facts and circumstances, including, unless it would be unjust or inequitable to do so, (i) petitioner's minority status, (ii) marketability of the petitioner's shares, (iii) relevant terms of any shareholders' agreement, and (iv) if value of corporation has been diminished by wrongful conduct of controlling shareholders, petitioner's proportionate claim for any compensable corporate injury	
Dissolution Valuation Date	11A V.S.A.§ 20.15(b) [close corporations]: As of the close of the business on the day on which the petition for dissolution was filed.	§ 13.1-749.1(D): The day before the date the petition was filed or as of such other date as the court deems appropriate under the circumstances.	

State	West Virginia	Wisconsin	Wyoming
Valuation Term	Fair Value	Fair Value	Fair Value
Precedent in Allowing Discounts	(Statute) Rejects discounts	(Case law) Rejects discounts	(Statute) Rejects discounts
Cases Addressing Discounts		*HMO-W Inc. v. SSM Health Care System* 611 N.W.2d 250 (Wisc. 2000) Minority discounts are impermissible in appraisal *Edler v. Edler* 745 N.W.2d 87 (Wisc. App. 2007) Discounts rejected in oppression case *Albert Trostel & Sons Co. v. Notz* 2010 U.S. Dist. LEXIS 108778 (E.D. Wis., Sept. 28, 2010); *aff'd,* 679 F.3d 627 (7th Cir. 2012) Marketability discounts are impermissible in appraisal	*Brown v. Arp and Hammond Hardware Co.* 141 P.3d 673 (Wyo. 2006) Minority discount rejected, marketability discount not applied by lower court [Predates statute]
Definition of Valuation Term in Appraisal	§ 31D-13-1301(4): Fair value is the value of the shares using customary and current valuation concepts and techniques generally employed for similar businesses in the context of the transaction requiring appraisal and without discounting for lack of marketability or minority status except for amendments to § 31D-13-1302(5)(a)	For business combinations (as defined in § 180.1130 (3)): § 180.1130(9)(a): Fair value is market value. If shares are publicly traded, it is the highest closing sales price per share during the valuation period. If not publicly traded, the market value as determined in good faith by the board of directors. For all other transactions: § 180.130(4): Fair value is the value of the shares immediately before the effectuation of the corporate action to which the dissenter objects, excluding appreciation or depreciation in anticipation of the corporate action unless exclusion would be inequitable.	§ 17-16-1301(a)(iv): Fair value is the value of the shares without discounting for lack of marketability or minority status.

State	West Virginia	Wisconsin	Wyoming
Appraisal Valuation Date	§ 31D-13-1301(4): Immediately before the effectuation of the corporate action to which the shareholder objects	§ 180.1301(4): Immediately before the effectuation of the corporate action	§ 17-16-1301(a)(iv)(A): Immediately before the effectuation of the corporate action to which the dissenter objects
Dissolution by shareholder as a remedy for oppression or oppressive behavior?	Yes - § 31D-14-1430(2)(B) [corporations]; § 31B-8-801(b)(5)(v) [LLCs]	Yes - § 180.1430(2)(b) [corporations]; § 183.0701(1)(d)(3) [LLCs]; § 180.1833(1)(a) [close corporations]	Yes - § 17-16-1430 (a)(ii)(B) [corporations]; § 17-17-140(a)(i) (close corporations); § 17-29-701(a)(v)(B) [LLCs]
Buy-out election in lieu of dissolution?	Yes - § 31D-14-1434	Yes - close corporations - § 180.1833(3) No - corporations & LLCs	Yes - § 17-16-1434 [corporations]; § 17-17-142 (close corporations)
Definition of Valuation Term in Oppression		§ 180.1833(3): for close corporations, in determining fair value, the court must consider going concern value.	§ 17-17-142: for close corporations, in determining fair value, the court must consider going concern value.
Dissolution Valuation Date	§ 31D-14-1434(d): The day before the date the petition was filed or as of another date as the court deems appropriate under the circumstances		§ 17-16-1434: The day before the date the petition was filed or as of such other date as the court deems appropriate under the circumstances.

APPENDIX C

Terms of the Market Exception

In this exhibit, a "listed" company is a company traded on the New York Stock Exchange or the NYSE MKT LLC. The term "national securities exchange" also includes Nasdaq and other national securities exchange registered with the SEC. "Marketable shares, as defined" refers to the definition in the center column.

	Definition of publicly traded shares	Market exception applies if consideration is:	Exemption from the market exception:
Alabama	[No market exception]	–	–
Alaska	Shares of company listed on a national securities exchange.	Any form of consideration.	–
Arizona	Shares of company listed on a national securities exchange or with 2,000 shareholders of record.	Any form of consideration.	–
Arkansas	[No market exception]	–	–
California	Shares of company listed on a national securities exchange.	Shares of company listed on a national securities exchange.	If shares have transfer restrictions or if shareholder receives anything but marketable shares, as defined. Cash for fractional shares does not trigger appraisal rights.
Colorado	Shares of company listed on a national securities exchange or with 2,000 shareholders of record.	Shares of company listed on a national securities exchange or with 2,000 shareholders of record.	If shareholder receives anything but marketable shares, as defined. Cash for fractional shares does not trigger appraisal rights.
Connecticut	Shares of company traded in an organized market with 2,000 shareholders and market value of $20 million, excluding shares held by senior executives, directors, and 10% beneficial shareholders.	Shares of company traded in an organized market with 2,000 shareholders and market value of $20 million, excluding shares held by senior executives, directors, and 10% beneficial shareholders.	If transaction is with interested party, as defined, or if shareholder receives anything but cash or marketable shares, as defined.

	Definition of publicly traded shares	Market exception applies if consideration is:	Exemption from the market exception:
Delaware	Shares of company listed on a national securities exchange or with 2,000 shareholders of record.	Shares of company listed on a national securities exchange or with 2,000 shareholders of record.	If shareholder receives anything but marketable shares, as defined, or short-form merger other than second step of a two-step transaction. Cash for fractional shares does not trigger appraisal rights.
District of Columbia	Shares of company traded in an organized market with 2,000 shareholders and market value of $20 million, excluding shares held by senior executives, directors, and 10% beneficial shareholders.	Shares of company traded in an organized market with 2,000 shareholders and market value of $20 million, excluding shares held by senior executives, directors, and 10% beneficial shareholders.	If transaction is with interested party, as defined, or if shareholder receives anything but cash or marketable shares, as defined.
Florida	Shares of company listed on a national securities exchange or with 2,000 shareholders and market value of $10 million excluding shares held by senior executives, directors, and 10% beneficial shareholders.	Shares of company listed on a national securities exchange or with 2,000 shareholders and market value of $10 million excluding shares held by senior executives, directors, and 10% beneficial shareholders.	If transaction is with interested party, as defined, or if shareholder receives anything but cash or marketable shares, as defined.
Georgia	Shares of company listed on a national securities exchange or with 2,000 shareholders of record.	Shares of company listed on a national securities exchange or with 2,000 shareholders of record.	If shareholder receives anything but marketable shares, as defined, or if shareholder receives shares different in type or exchange ratio from shares offered to others of same class. Cash for fractional shares does not trigger appraisal rights.
Hawaii	[No market exception]	–	–

	Definition of publicly traded shares	Market exception applies if consideration is:	Exemption from the market exception:
Idaho	Shares of company listed on a national securities exchange or with 2,000 shareholders and market value of $20 million excluding shares held by senior executives, directors and 10% beneficial shareholders.	Shares of company listed on a national securities exchange or with 2,000 shareholders and market value of $20 million excluding shares held by senior executives, directors, and 10% beneficial shareholders.	If transaction is with interested party, as defined, or if shareholder receives anything but cash or marketable shares, as defined.
Illinois	[No market exception]	–	–
Indiana	Shares of company listed on a national securities exchange.	Any form of consideration.	–
Iowa	Shares of listed or Nasdaq company or company with 2,000 shareholders and market value of $20 million excluding shares held by senior executives, directors, and 10% beneficial shareholders.	Shares of listed or Nasdaq company or company with 2,000 shareholders and market value of $20 million excluding shares held by senior executives, directors, and 10% beneficial shareholders.	If acquisition is by beneficial owner of 20% or by party with right to elect 25% of directors, or if shareholder receives anything but cash or marketable shares, as defined.
Kansas	Shares of listed or Nasdaq company or company with 2,000 shareholders of record.	Shares of listed or Nasdaq company or company with 2,000 shareholders of record.	Short-form merger, or if shareholder receives anything marketable shares, as defined. Cash for fractional shares does not trigger appraisal rights.
Kentucky	[No market exception]	–	–
Louisiana	Shares of company traded in an organized market with 2,000 shareholders and market value of $20 million, excluding shares held by senior executives, directors, and 10% beneficial shareholders.	Shares of company traded in an organized market with 2,000 shareholders and market value of $20 million, excluding shares held by senior executives, directors, and 10% beneficial shareholders.	If transaction is with interested party, as defined, or if shareholder receives anything but cash or marketable shares, as defined.

	Definition of publicly traded shares	Market exception applies if consideration is:	Exemption from the market exception:
Maine	Shares of company traded in an organized market with 2,000 shareholders and market value of $20 million, excluding shares held by senior executives, directors, and 10% beneficial shareholders.	Shares of company traded in an organized market with 2,000 shareholders and market value of $20 million, excluding shares held by senior executives, directors, and 10% beneficial shareholders.	If transaction is with interested party, as defined, or if shareholder receives anything but cash or marketable shares, as defined.
Maryland	Shares of company listed on a national securities exchange.	Shares of a corporation (but with no marketability requirement).	Merger with interested party, as defined, or if directors and executive officers were the beneficial owners, in the aggregate, of 5%, or if directors and executive officers receive stock on terms not available to all holders. Cash for fractional shares does not trigger appraisal rights.
Massachusetts	Shares of listed or Nasdaq company, or company traded on a regional securities exchange or interdealer quotation system that has least 250,000 outstanding shares and market value of $5,000,000, excluding shares held by officers, directors, and affiliates.	Shares of listed or Nasdaq company, or company traded on a regional securities exchange or interdealer quotation system that has least 250,000 outstanding shares and market value of $5,000,000, excluding shares held by officers, directors, and affiliates.	If transaction is with interested party, as defined, or if shareholder receives anything but cash or marketable shares.
Michigan	Shares of company listed on a national securities exchange.	Any form of consideration; also, if shares of company listed on a national securities exchange are sole consideration to private company shareholders.	If shareholder receives anything but cash or marketable shares, as defined.

	Definition of publicly traded shares	Market exception applies if consideration is:	Exemption from the market exception:
Minnesota	Shares of listed or Nasdaq company.	Shares of listed or Nasdaq company.	If shareholder receives anything but marketable shares, as defined. Cash for fractional shares does not trigger appraisal rights.
Mississippi	Shares of listed or Nasdaq company or company with 2,000 shareholders of record and market value of $20 million excluding shares held by senior executives, directors, and 10% beneficial shareholders.	Shares of listed or Nasdaq company or company with 2,000 shareholders of record and market value of $20 million excluding shares held by senior executives, directors, and 10% beneficial shareholders.	If transaction is with interested party, as defined, or if shareholder receives anything but cash or marketable shares, as defined.
Missouri	[No market exception]	–	–
Montana	[No market exception]	–	–
Nebraska	[No market exception]		–
Nevada	Shares of listed or Nasdaq company or company with 2,000 shareholders.	Shares of listed or Nasdaq company or company with 2,000 shareholders.	If shareholder receives anything but marketable shares, as defined. Cash for fractional shares does not trigger appraisal rights.
New Hampshire	Shares of company traded in an organized market with 1,000 shareholders and market value of $20 million, excluding shares held by senior executives, directors, and 10% beneficial shareholders	Shares of company traded in an organized market with 1,000 shareholders and market value of $20 million, excluding shares held by senior executives, directors, and 10% beneficial shareholders	If transaction is with interested party, as defined, or if shareholder receives anything but cash or marketable shares, as defined.

	Definition of publicly traded shares	**Market exception applies if consideration is:**	**Exemption from the market exception:**
New Jersey	Shares of company listed on a national securities exchange or with 1,000 shareholders of record.	Shares, obligations or other securities which will be listed on a national securities exchange or by held 1,000 holders of record.	If shareholder receives any consideration other than shares, obligations or other securities which will be listed on a national securities exchange or by held 1,000 holders of record
New Mexico	[No market exception]	–	–
New York	Shares of company listed on a national securities exchange.	Shares of company listed on a national securities exchange.	Merger with parent company, or if shares are not entitled to vote on transaction, or if shareholder receives anything but marketable shares, as defined.
North Carolina	Shares of company traded in an organized market with 2,000 shareholders and market value of $20 million, excluding shares held by senior executives, directors, and 10% beneficial shareholders.	Shares of company traded in an organized market with 2,000 shareholders and market value of $20 million, excluding shares held by senior executives, directors, and 10% beneficial shareholders.	If transaction is with interested party, as defined, or if shareholder receives anything but cash or marketable shares, as defined.
North Dakota	Shares of company listed on a national securities exchange.	Shares of company listed on a national securities exchange.	If shareholder receives anything but marketable shares, as defined. Cash for fractional shares does not trigger appraisal rights.
Ohio	[No market exception]	–	–
Oklahoma	Shares of company listed on a national securities exchange or with 2,000 shareholders of record.	Shares of company listed on a national securities exchange or with 2,000 shareholders of record.	Short-form merger, or if shareholder receives anything but marketable shares, as defined. Cash for fractional shares does not trigger appraisal rights.

	Definition of publicly traded shares	Market exception applies if consideration is:	Exemption from the market exception:
Oregon	Shares of company listed on a national securities exchange.	Any form of consideration.	–
Pennsylvania	Shares of listed or Nasdaq company or company with 2,000 shareholders.	Any form of consideration, unless other members of the class receive special treatment.	–
Rhode Island	Shares of listed or Nasdaq company or company with 2,000 shareholders of record.	Any form of consideration.	–
South Carolina	Shares of company listed on a national securities exchange.	Any form of consideration.	–
South Dakota	Shares of company listed on a national securities exchange or with 2,000 shareholders and market value of $20 million excluding shares held by senior executives, directors, and 10% beneficial shareholders.	Shares of company listed on a national securities exchange or with 2,000 shareholders and market value of $20 million excluding shares held by senior executives, directors, and 10% beneficial shareholders.	If transaction is with interested party, as defined, or if shareholder receives anything but cash or marketable shares, as defined.
Tennessee	Shares of company listed on a national securities exchange.	Any form of consideration.	–
Texas	Shares of company listed on a national securities exchange or with 2,000 shareholders of record.	Shares of company listed on a national securities exchange or with 2,000 shareholders of record.	Merger with parent, or if shareholder receives anything but marketable shares, as defined. Cash for fractional shares does not trigger appraisal rights.
Utah	Shares of company listed on a national securities exchange or with 2,000 shareholders of record.	Shares of company listed on a national securities exchange or with 2,000 shareholders of record.	If shareholder receives anything but marketable shares, as defined. Cash for fractional shares does not trigger appraisal rights.

	Definition of publicly traded shares	Market exception applies if consideration is:	Exemption from the market exception:
Vermont	[No market exception]	–	–
Virginia	Shares of company traded in an organized market with 2,000 shareholders and market value of $20 million.	Shares of company listed on a national securities exchange or with 2,000 shareholders and market value of $20 million excluding shares held by senior executives, directors and 10% beneficial shareholders.	If transaction is with interested party, as defined, or if shareholder receives anything but cash or marketable shares, as defined.
Washington	[No market exception]	–	–
West Virginia	Shares of company listed on a national securities exchange, or with 2,000 shareholders and market value of $20 million excluding shares held by senior executives, directors, and 10% beneficial shareholders.	Shares of company listed on a national securities exchange, or with 2,000 shareholders and market value of $20 million excluding shares held by senior executives, directors, and 10% beneficial shareholders.	If transaction is with interested party, as defined, or if shareholder receives anything but cash or marketable shares, as defined.
Wisconsin	Shares of listed or Nasdaq company	Any form of consideration.	–
Wyoming	Shares of company traded in an organized market with 2,000 shareholders and market value of $20 million, excluding shares held by senior executives, directors, and 10% beneficial shareholders.	Shares of company traded in an organized market with 2,000 shareholders and market value of $20 million, excluding shares held by senior executives, directors, and 10% beneficial shareholders.	If shareholder receives anything but cash or marketable shares, as defined.

Index of Court Decisions

24/7 Records, Inc. v. Sony Music Entm't, Inc., 514 F. Supp. 2d 571 (S.D.N.Y. 2007), 570 n.42

A

Acker v. Burlington N. & Santa Fe Ry. Co., 347 F. Supp. 2d 1025 (D. Kan. 2004), 564 n.31

ACP Master, Ltd. v. Sprint Corp., 2017 Del. Ch. LEXIS 125 (Del. Ch. July 21, 2017), *aff'd*, 184 A.3d 1291 (Del. 2018), 386 n.48, 394

Active Wear, Inc. v. Parkdale Mills, Inc., 331 B.R. 669 (W.D. Va. 2005), 13 n.24

Adams v. Commissioner, T.C. Memo. 2002-80, 435, 436

Adams v. United States, 2001 U.S. Dist. LEXIS 13092 (N.D. Tex. 2001), 308 n.110

Advanced Communication Design, Inc. v. Follett, 615 N.W.2d 285 (Minn. 2001), 400 n.101, 700

Agnelli v. Miami Lennox Corp., 2022 WL 2788875 (S. Dist. Fla. July 15, 2022), 690

Ahern v. Ahern, 2008 Me. LEXIS 1 (Jan. 3, 2008), 159

Ahmanson Found. v. United States, 674 F.2d 761 (9th Cir. 1981), 292 n.3, 338 n.38

Ala. By-Products Corp. v. Neal, 588 A.2d 255 (Del. 1991), 150 n.4

Albert Trostel & Sons Co. v. Notz, 2010 U.S. Dist. LEXIS 108778 (E.D. Wis., Sept. 28, 2010), 718

American Ethanol Inc. v. Cordillera Fund, L.P., 252 P.3d 663 (Nev. 2011), 702

American General Corp. v. Camp, 190 A. 225 (Md. App. 1937), 698

Amodio v. Amodio, 70 N.Y.2d 5, 516 N.Y.S.2d 923, 509 N.E.2d 936 (1987), 361 n.69

AMP Enters. v. Price Pfister, Inc., 2003 Cal. App. Unpub. LEXIS 10830 (Cal. Ct. App. 2003), 608 n.35

Anderson v. Anderson, 2006 Tenn. App. LEXIS 592 (Tenn. App. 2006), 363 n.83, 364 n.86

Andrew J. Whelan et al. v. Tyler Abell et al., U.S. District Court, District of Columbia, civil action nos. 87-442 and 87-1763, 573

Anheuser-Busch, Inc. v. Natural Beverage Distribs., 69 F.3d 337 (9th Cir. 1995), 601 n.19

Antolik v. Harvey, 761 P.2d 305 (Haw. Ct. App. 1988), 158, 349 n.11

Apple Inc. v. Wi-LAN, Appeal No. 2020-2011, 2022 WL 333666 (Fed. Cir. Feb. 4, 2022), 464 n.13

Arctic Cat Inc. v. Bombardier Recreational Prod. Inc., 950 F.3d 860 (Fed. Cir. 2020), 461 n.4

Armstrong v. LaSalle Bank National Association, 446 F.3d 728 (7th Cir. 2006), 420

Armstrong v. Marathon Oil Co., 513 N.E.2d 776 (Ohio App. 1987), 708

Arnaud v. Stockgrowers State Bank of Ashland, Kansas, 992 P.2d 216 (Kan. 1999), 694

Arneson v. Arneson, 355 N.W.2d 16 (Wis. Ct. App. 1984), 361 n.69, 363 n.81, 363 n.83

Aronson v. Lewis, 473 A.2d 805 (Del. 1984), 499 n.13

Audubon Veterinary Hosp., Inc. v. U.S. Fidelity & Guarantee Co., 2007 U.S. Dist. LEXIS 46301 (E.D. La. June 25, 2007), 595 n.4

Aufmuth v. Aufmuth, 152 Cal. Rptr. 668 (Cal. Ct. App. 1979), 351 n.18

Augoshe v. Lehman, 2007 Fla. App. LEXIS 6367 (Fla. Ct. App. 2007), 366 n.100

B

Balicki v. Balicki, 837 N.E.2d 532 (Ind. App. 2005), 159
Ballas v. Ballas, 2004 Ohio 5128, 2004 WL 2334329 (Ohio App. 7 Dist. 2004), 367 n.101
Balsamides v. Protameen Chemicals, Inc., 734 A.2d 721 (N.J. 1999), 704
Baltrusis v. Baltrusis, 113 Wash. App. 1037 (Wash. Ct. App. 2002), 364 n.84, 364 n.86
Bank One Corp. v. Comm'r, 120 T.C. 174, 2003 U.S. Tax Ct. LEXIS 13, 120 T.C. No. 11 (2003), *rev'd and remanded*, 2006 U.S. App. LEXIS 20430 (7th Cir. 2006), 293 n.12
Barton v. Barton, 2007 Ga. LEXIS 21 (Ga. 2007), 361 n.70
Basho Technologies HoldCo B, LLC v. Georgetown Basho Investors, LLC, 2018 WL 3326693 (July 6, 2018), 391 n.76
Baum v. Baum, 584 P.2d 604 (Ariz. Ct. App. 1978), 350 n.15
Bausano v. Bausano, 632 N.W.2d 123, 246 Wis. 2d 987 (Wis. Ct. App. 2001), 350 n.13
Berenberg v. Berenberg, 474 N.W.2d 843 (Minn. Ct. App. 1991), 360 n.67
Bergeland v. Bergeland, 2000 Minn. App. LEXIS 952, 2000 WL 1239754 (Minn. Ct. App. 2000), 351 n.21
Berger v. Pubco Corp., et al., C.A. No. 3414-CC (Del. Ch. 2010), 393
Bertuca v. Bertuca, 2007 Tenn. App. LEXIS 690 (Tenn. Ct. App. 2007), 364 n.86
Bettinger v. Bettinger, 396 S.E.2d 709 (W. Va. 1990), 361 n.70
Beverly Hills Concepts, Inc. v. Schatz & Schatz, 717 A.2d 724 (Conn. 1998), 564 n.31
BIC Leisure Prods., Inc. v. Windsurfing Int'l, Inc., 1 F.3d 1214 (Fed. Cir. 1993), 467 n.34
Black Industries, Inc. v. Commissioner, 1979 T.C. Memo. 61, 11 n.22
Blitch v. People's Bank, 540 S.E.2d 667 (Ga. App. 2000), 690
Blueblade Capital Opportunities LLC v. Norcraft Cos., Inc., 2018 WL 3602940 (Del. Ch. July 27, 2018), 391 n.77, 395
BNE Massachusetts Corp. v. Sims, 588 N.E.2d 14 (Mass. App. 1992), 698
Bobrow v. Bobrow, State of Indiana, Hamilton Superior Court Cause No. 29D01-0003-DR-166, 348 n.3, 355
Bohac v. Benes Service Co., 310 Neb. 722 (2022), 313 n.139, 702
Bolan v. Bolan, 32 Ark. App. 65, 796 S.W.2d 358 (1990), 153 n.8
Bone v. Coyle Mechanical Supply, Inc., 2017 IL App (5th) 150117-U (Ill. App. 2017), 692
Bosserman v. Bosserman, 9 Va. App. 1, 384 S.E.2d 104 (1989), 361 n.69
Bostwick v. Bostwick, 1991 WL 42628 (Del. Fam. Ct. 1991), 153 n.8
Bowen v. Bowen, 96 N.J. 36, 473 A.2d 73 (1984), 361 n.69, 363 n.81
Brown v. Allied Corrugated Box Co., 154 Cal. Rptr. 170 (Cal. App. 1979), 686
Brown v. Arp and Hammond Hardware Co., 141 P.3d 673 (Wyo. 2006), 718
Brown v. Brown, 348 N.J. Super. 466, 792 A.2d 463, 2002 N.J. Super. LEXIS 105 (N.J. Super. 2002), 274 n.59, 348 n.2, 350 n.16, 364 n.84, 364 n.86
Brundle *ex rel.* Constellis Emp. Stock Ownership Plan v. Wilmington Tr. N.A., 241 F. Supp. 3d 610 (E.D. Va. 2017), 410 n.18
Brundle v. Wilmington Trust, N.A., 258 F. Supp. 3d 647 (E.D. Va. 2017), 422
Brusach v. Brusach, Mich. App. LEXIS 1619 (2017), 159
BTR Dunlop Holdings, Inc. v. Commissioner, T.C. Memo 1999-377 (Nov. 15, 1999), 283 n.4, 294 n.18, 331 n.9
Buffalo Tool & Die Manufacturing Co. v. Commissioner, 74 T.C. 441 (1980), 323
Bump v. Stewart, Wimer & Bump, P.C., 336 N.W.2d 731 (Iowa), 141
Bunkers v. Bunkers, 2007 Ohio App. LEXIS 523 (Ohio Ct. App. 2007), 355 n.43
Butler v. Butler, 63 A.2d 148 (Pa. 1995), 160, 351 n.18
Buzanell v. Miller, 590 S.E.2d 332, 162 N.C. App. 180, 2004 WL 26524 (N.C. Ct. App. 2004), 364 n.89

C

CADCO Inc. v. Fleetwood Enters., 220 S.W.3d 426 (Mo. Ct. App. 2007), 560 n.17
California Inst. of Tech. v. Broadcom Ltd., No. 2020-2222, 2022 WL 333669 (Fed. Cir. Feb. 4, 2022), 464 n.13
Camino Inc. v. Wilson, 59 F. Supp. 2d 962 (D. Neb. 1999), 702
Cannon v. Bertrand, 2 So. 3d 393 (La. 2009), 396 n.86
Caracci v. Comm'r, 118 T.C. 379, 118 T.C. No. 25, 2002 U.S. Tax Ct. LEXIS 25 (2002), 296 n.27
Carr v. Carr, 701 P.2d 304 (Idaho Ct. App. 1985), 362 n.76
Casey v. Amboy Bancorporation, 2006 N.J. Super. Unpub. LEXIS 1355 (N.J. Supr. App. Div. Aug. 8, 2006), 384 n.31
Casey v. Brennan, 780 A.2d 553 (N.J. Super. 2001), 704
Cavalier Oil Corp. v. Harnett, 564 A.2d 1137 (Del. 1989), 399 n.97, 688
Cecil v. Comm'r, T.C. Memo. 2023-24, 269 n.44, 276–277
Cede & Co., Inc. v. Medpointe Healthcare, Inc., 2004 Del. Ch. LEXIS 124 (Del. Ch. Aug. 16, 2004), 386 n.51, 387 n.53, 496 n.8
Central Trust Co. v. United States, 305 F.2d 393 (Ct. Cl. 1962), 293 n.9, 316 n.153, 322
Champion v. Champion, 54 Mass. App. Ct. 215, 764 N.E.2d 898, 2002 Mass. App. LEXIS 363 (Mass. App. Ct. 2002), 370
Chao v. Hall Holding Co. Inc., 285 F.3d 415, 2002 U.S. App. LEXIS 5929 (6th Cir. 2002), 283 n.8, 418
Charland v. Country View Golf Club, 588 A.2d 609 (R.I. 1991), 712
Children's Broad. Corp. v. The Walt Disney Co., 245 F.3d 1008 (8th Cir. 2001), 578
Chrome Data Systems, Inc. v. Stringer, 820 P.2d 831 (Ore. App. 1991), 708
City of Tuscaloosa v. Harcross Chemicals, 158 F.3d 548 (11th Cir. 1998), 571 n.44, 574 n.61
Clary Hood, Inc. v. Commissioner, 177–178
Club Car, Inc. v. Club Car (Quebec) Imp., Inc., 362 F.3d 775 (11th Cir. 2004), 560 n.17, 577 n.75
Coca Cola v. Commissioner, T.C. No. 31183-15, 341 n.42
Collier v. Collier, 790 So. 2d 759 (La. Ct. App. 2001), 364 n.85
Columbia Mgt. Co. v. Wyss, 765 P.2d 207 (Ore. App. 1988), 708
Commissioner v. Procter, 142 F.2d 824 (4th Cir. 1944), 324
Commissioner v. Tellier, 383 U.S. 687 (1966), 325 n.188
Commonwealth Scientific & Indus. Research Org. v. Cisco Sys., Inc., No. 2015-1066 (Fed. Cir. Dec. 3, 2015), 465 n.29
Complete Logistical Svcs., LLC v. Rulh, 394 F. Supp. 3d 625 (E.D. La. 2019), 396 n.86
Congel v. Malfitano, 101 N.E.3d 341 (N.Y. 2018), 706
Connelly v. United States, No. 23–146 (June 6, 2024), 320 n.171
Connelly v. U.S., 131 AFTR 2d 2023-1902 (8th Cir. 1999), 320 n.169
Conway v. Conway, 1998 WL 865157 (N.C. Ct. App. 1998), 350 n.17
Corwin v. KKR Financial Holdings LLC, 125 A.3d 304 (Del. 2015), 381 n.25
Crooker v. Crooker, 432 A.2d 1293 (Me. 1981), 130 n.3
Crosetto v. Crosetto, 918 P.2d 954 (Wash. App. Ct. 1996), 352 n.27, 367 n.101
Crystal Semiconductor Corp. v. Tritech Microelectronics Int'l, Inc., 246 F.3d 1336 (Fed. Cir. 2001), 467 n.36
Cutsinger v. Cutsinger, 917 S.W.2d 238 (Tenn. Ct. App. 1995), 362 n.74

D

Dahill v. Dahill, 1998 Conn. Super. LEXIS 846 (Conn. Super. Ct. 1998), 361 n.71
Dallas v. Commissioner, T.C. Memo. 2006-212, 435 n.9, 436
Dameron v. Mercy Hosp. & Med. Ctr., 2019 IL App (1st) 172338, 616 n.59
Daubert v. Merrell Dow Pharmaceuticals Inc., 509 U.S. 579 (1993), 556–557, 556 n.3, 559, 575, 576 n.68

Dawkins v. Hickman Family Corp., 2011 U.S. Dist. LEXIS 63101 (N.D. Miss.), 700
Deffenbaugh v. Deffenbaugh, 877 S.W.2d 186 (Mo. Ct. App. 1994), 350 n.17
Delaware Open MRI Radiology v. Kessler, 898 A.2d 290 (Del. Ch. 2006), 436, 441 n.22
Dell Inc. v. Magnetar Global Event Driven Master Fund Ltd., 2017 Del. LEXIS 518 (Del. Dec. 14, 2017), *reversing In re* Appraisal of Dell Inc., 2016 Del. Ch. LEXIS 81 (Del. Ch. May 31, 2016), 391 n.75, 392 n.79
Del Mar Avionics v. Quinton Instrument, 836 F.2d 1320 (Fed. Cir. 1987), 467 n.30
Dering v. Service Experts Alliance, LLC, No. 1:06-CV-00357-RWS, 2007 U.S. Dist. LEXIS 89972 (N.D. Ga. Dec. 6, 2007), 572 n.47
Devivo v. Devivo, 2001 Conn. Super. LEXIS 1285 (Conn. Super. May 7, 2001), 389 n.61, 400 n.101
DFC Global Corp. v. Muirfield Value Partners, L.P., 172 A.3d 346 (Del. 2017), *reversing In re* Appraisal of DFC Global Corp., 2016 Del. Ch. LEXIS 103 (Del. Ch. July 8, 2016), 378 n.15, 391 n.75, 392 n.82
Dieckman v. Regency GP LP, 2021 WL 537325 (Feb. 15, 2021), 398, 398 n.93
Dole v. Farnum, No. 90-0371 (D.R.I. filed July 30, 1990), 417
Domain Associates, et al. v. Nimesh Shah, C.A. No. 12921 (Del. Ch. 2018), 395, 398 n.95
Donahue v. Donahue, 299 S.C. 353, 384 S.E.2d 741 (S.C. 1989), 357 n.51, 362 n.74
Dugan v. Dugan, 92 NJ 423, 457 A.2d 1 (1983), 160, 353 n.30
Duncan v. Duncan, 90 Cal. App. 4th 617 (Cal. Ct. App. 2001), 362 n.77
Dunmire v. Farmers & Merchants Bancorp of Western Pa., Inc., 2016 Del. Ch. LEXIS 167 (Del. Ch. Nov. 10, 2016), 385 n.36, 394
Dunn v. Dunn, 802 P.2d 1314 (Utah Ct. App. 1990), 276, 351 n.19

E

East Park L.P. v. Larkin, 893 A.2d 1219 (Md. App. 2006), 698
eBay Inc. v. MercExchange, L.L.C., 547 U.S. 388 (2006), 474 n.70
Eckelkamp v. Beste, 201 F. Supp. 2d 1012 (E.D. Mo. 2002), 419–420, 578
Edler v. Edler, 745 N.W.2d 87 (Wisc. App. 2007), 718
E.E.C. v. E.J.C., 457 A.2d 688 (Del. 1983), 158
Eisenberg v. Commissioner, 155 F.3d 50 (2d Cir. 1998), 130 n.3, 311, 312, 575
Elbit Sys. Land & C4I Ltd. v. Hughes Network Sys., LLC, 927 F.3d 1292 (Fed. Cir. 2019), 464 n.13
Ellington v. Ellington, 842 So. 2d 1160 (La. Ct. App. 2003), 348 n.4
Elliotts Inc. v. Commissioner, 716 F.2d 1241 (1983), 170 n.8
Ellis v. Ellis, No. 77407 N.Y. App. Div., 1997 WL 35218 (Jan. 30, 1997), 364 n.85
Endres v. Endres, 532 N.W.2d 65 (S.D. 1995), 161
English v. Artromick Intl., Inc., 2000 Ohio App. LEXIS 3580 (Ohio App. 2000), 708
Ericsson, Inc. v. D-Link Sys., 773 F.3d 1201 (Fed. Cir. 2014), 465 n.23
Erp v. Erp, 2007 Fla. App. LEXIS 18726 (Fla. Ct. App. 2007), 364 n.87
Eslami v. Eslami, 591 A.2d 411 (Conn. 1991), 158, 367 n.104
Estate of Adams v. Comm'r, T.C. Memo. 2002-80 (2002), 309 n.117
Estate of Andrews v. Commissioner, 79 T.C. 938 (1982), 15 n.26, 255 n.5, 306 n.92, 307 n.97, 575 n.65
Estate of Bennett v. Commissioner, 65 T.C.M. (CCH) 1816 (T.C. 1993), 299 n.42, 302 n.65, 308, 575 n.65
Estate of Berg v. Comm'r, T.C. Memo. 1991-279 (1991), 295 n.22
Estate of Blount v. Comm'r, T.C. Memo. 2004-116 (2004), *aff'd*, 428 F.3d 1338 (11th Cir. 2005), 319 n.167
Estate of Borgatello v. Comm'r, T.C. Memo. 2000-264 (2000), 312
Estate of Brookshire v. Comm'r, T.C. Memo. 1998-365 (1998), 300 n.49, 303 n.72

Estate of Brown v. Commissioner, 425 F.2d 1406 (5th Cir. 1970), *aff'g* T.C. Memo. 1969-91 (1969), 318 n.160
Estate of Bruce v. Comm'r, T.C. Memo. 1993-244 (1993), 298 n.38, 323 n.182
Estate of Campbell v. Commissioner, 62 T.C.M. (CCH) 1514 (T.C. 1991), 322, 575 n.65
Estate of Cartwright, 183 F.3d 1034 (9th Cir. 1999), 320 n.168
Estate of Cidulka v. Comm'r, T.C. Memo. 1996-149, 71 T.C. Memo. (CCH) 2555 (1996), 318 n.162
Estate of Cloutier v. Comm'r, T.C. Memo. 1996-049 (1996), 307
Estate of Curry v. United States, 706 F.2d 1424 (7th Cir. 1983), 331 n.10, 338 n.38
Estate of Davis v. Commissioner, 86 T.C. 1156 (U.S.T.C. 1986), 130 n.3, 275 n.63, 305 n.86, 309 n.113, 312
Estate of Deputy v. Comm'r, T.C. Memo. 2003-176 (2003), 304 n.79, 306 n.94, 310 n.124
Estate of Desmond v. Comm'r, T.C. Memo. 1999-76 (1999), 307 n.103, 315 n.147
Estate of Dougherty v. Comm'r, 59 T.C. 772 (1990), 307
Estate of Dunn v. Comm'r, T.C. Memo. 2000-12 (2000), *rev'd and remanded*, 301 F.3d 339 (5th Cir. 2002), 308 n.104, 313, 322
Estate of Elsie Church v. United States (Cause No. SA-97-CA-0774-OG), 272 n.52, 306 n.93
Estate of Emily Klauss, T.C. Memo. 2000-191, 272 n.53, 306 n.93, 315 n.149
Estate of Etta H. Weinberg et al. v. Comm'r, T.C. Memo. 2000-51 (2001), 268 n.38
Estate of Feldmar v. Commissioner, T.C. Memo. 1988-429 (1988), 275 n.60, 310 n.118, 322
Estate of Fleming v. Comm'r, T.C. Memo. 1997-484 (1997), 307 n.95, 323 n.183
Estate of Foote v. Comm'r, T.C. Memo. 1999-37 (1999), 277 n.74, 309 n.115
Estate of Ford v. Comm'r, 53 F.3d 924 (8th Cir. 1995), 296 n.24
Estate of Frazier Jelke III v. Commissioner, 507 F.3d 1317 (11th Cir. 2007), 276 n.67
Estate of Freeman v. Comm'r, T.C. Memo. 1996-372, 1996 WL 453872 (1996), 302 n.63, 322 n.179
Estate of Furman v. Commissioner, T.C. Memo. 1998-157 (1998), 275 n.60, 293 n.11, 306 n.94, 310 n.119, 323 n.183
Estate of Gallagher v. Commissioner, 101 T.C.M. (CCH) 1702 (2011), 316 n.151
Estate of Gallo v. Comm'r, T.C. Memo. 1985-363 (1985), 111 n.3, 300 n.50, 303 n.70
Estate of Gilford v. Commissioner, 88 T.C. 38 (1987), 316 n.151, 317 n.159
Estate of Gimbel v. Comm'r, 2006 Tax Ct. Memo. LEXIS 274 (2006), 277 n.74, 305 n.88, 306 n.90, 309 n.116
Estate of Giustina v. Commissioner, T.C. Memo. 2011-141, *aff'd*, 1586 Fed. Appx. 417 (9th Cir. 2014), 258 n.14, 269 n.43, 305 n.86
Estate of Green v. Comm'r, T.C. Memo. 2003-384 (2003), 254 n.4, 305 n.85, 308 n.107
Estate of Hall v. Commissioner, 92 T.C. 312 (1989), 111 n.4, 300 n.50, 303 n.70, 323, 331 n.10
Estate of Harvey Evenchick, Gregory V. Gadarian, Personal Representative, and Deanna Evenchick, Petitioners, v. Commissioner, T.C. Memo. 2013-34 (U.S.T.C. Feb. 4, 2013), 283 n.3, 448 n.7
Estate of Heck v. Comm'r, T.C. Memo. 2002-34 (2002), 300 n.52
Estate of Hendrickson v. Comm'r, T.C. Memo. 1999-278, 1999 Tax Ct. Memo. LEXIS 318 (1999), 302 n.62, 307 n.98
Estate of Huntsman v. Commissioner, 66 T.C. 861, 1976 WL 3635 (1976), 310 n.118
Estate of Jameson v. Comm'r, T.C. Memo. 1999-43 (1999), 302 n.68, 312 n.133
Estate of Jelke v. Comm'r, T.C. Memo. 2005-131 (2005), *rev'd*, 503 F.3d 1317 (11th Cir. 2007), 130 n.3, 303 n.73, 308 n.106, 313
Estate of Jones v. Commissioner, T.C. Memo. 2019-101 (2019), 258 n.14, 269 n.45, 313
Estate of Josephine Thompson v. Comm'r, T.C. Memo. 2004-174 (2004), *aff'd*, 499

F.3d 129 (2d Cir. 2007), 296 n.29, 297 n.33
Estate of Jung v. Comm'r, 101 T.C. 412 (1993), 302 n.64, 317, 318 n.160, 318 n.161
Estate of Kaufman v. Commissioner, T.C. Memo. 1999-119 (1999), 294 n.14, 299 n.46
Estate of Kelly v. Comm'r, T.C. Memo. 2005-235 (2005), 304 n.75
Estate of Lauder v. Comm'r (Lauder II), T.C. Memo. 1992-736 (1992), 319 n.166
Estate of Lehmann v. Comm'r, T.C. Memo. 1997-392 (1997), 294 n.16, 302 n.66
Estate of Leichter v. Comm'r, T.C. Memo. 2003-66 (2003), 299 n.48
Estate of Maggos v. Comm'r, T.C. Memo. 2000-129 (2000), 307 n.102, 311
Estate of Magnin v. Comm'r, T.C. Memo. 2001-31 (2001), 306 n.94
Estate of Manship v. United States, 236 F.R.D. 291 (M.D. La. 2006), 611 n.44, 611 n.46
Estate of Mellinger v. Commissioner, 112 T.C. 26 (1999), 309 n.114
Estate of Michael Jackson, T.C. Memo. 2021-48, 471 n.62
Estate of Mitchell v. Commissioner, T.C. Memo. 2002-98, 275 n.60, 306 n.94, 310, 315 n.148
Estate of Mueller v. Comm'r, T.C. Memo. 1992-284, 322
Estate of Newhouse v. Commissioner, 94 T.C. 193 (1990), 331 n.10
Estate of Noble v. Comm'r, T.C. Memo. 2005-2 (2005), 316 n.156
Estate of Perry, 2007 Tex. App. LEXIS 6465 (Tex. Ct. App. 2007), 608 n.36
Estate of Peter S. Perrachio v. IRS, T.C. Memo 2008-280, 268 n.39
Estate of Petter v. Comm'r, T.C. Memo. 2009-280, *aff'd*, 653 F.3d 1012 (9th Cir. 2011), 324 n.186, 324 n.187
Estate of Renier v. Comm'r, T.C. Memo. 2000-298 (2000), 310
Estate of Richmond v. Commissioner, T.C. Memo. 2014-26, 276
Estate of Scanlan v. Comm'r, T.C. Memo. 1996-331 (1996), 319 n.163
Estate of Simplot v. Commissioner, 112 T.C. No. 13, 1999 WL 152610 (1999), 130 n.3, 292 n.4, 295 n.21, 310–312
Estate of Thompson v. Commissioner, 89 T.C. 619 (1987), *rev'd on other grounds*, 864 F.2d 1128 (4th Cir. 1989), 254 n.4, 296 n.26, 308 n.108, 318 n.160
Estate of Titus v. Comm'r, T.C. Memo. 1989-466, 322
Estate of Trompeter v. Comm'r, T.C. Memo. 1998-35 (1998), 319 n.164
Estate of True v. Comm'r, T.C. Memo. 2001 167 (2001), *aff'd*, 390 F.3d 1210 (10th Cir. 2004), 321
Estate of Watts v. Comm'r, T.C. Memo. 1985-595 (1985), *aff'd*, 823 F.3d 483 (11th Cir. 1987), 300 n.55
Estate of Welch v. Comm'r, T.C. Memo. 1998-167 (1998), *rev'd*, 208 F.3d 213 (6th Cir. 2000), 312
Estate of William A.V. Cecil, Sr. v. Commissioner, T.C. Memo 2023-24 (Feb. 28, 2023), 300 n.53, 437 n.10
Estate of Williams v. Comm'r, T.C. Memo. 1998-59 (1998), 303 n.72
Estate of Wright v. Comm'r, T.C. Memo. 1997-53 (1997), 311
Estate of Yeager v. Commissioner, T.C. Memo. 1986-448, 310 n.118
Exacto Spring Corp. v. Commissioner, 196 F.3d 833 (7th Cir. 1999), 169 n.6
Eyler v. Comm'r, T.C. Memo. 1995-123 (T.C. 1995), *aff'd*, 88 F.3d 445 (7th Cir. 1996), 417 n.30

F

Favell v. Favell, 957 P.2d 556 (Okla. Ct. App. 1997), 351 n.22
Ferolito v. Vultaggio, 2014 N.Y. Misc. LEXIS 4709 (N.Y. Supr. Oct. 14, 2014), 387 n.55, 397 n.89
Ferraro v. Ferraro, 2000 WL 251678 (Va. Ct. App. 2000), 364 n.84, 364 n.86
Finkel v. Palm Park, Inc., 2020 NCBC 84, 2020 WL 6802470 (N.C. Super. 2020), 706
First Western Bank Wall v. Olsen, 621 N.W.2d 611 (S.D. 2001), 385 n.42, 712

Fisherman Surgical Instruments, LLC v. Tri-Anim Health Servs., Inc., 502 F. Supp. 2d 1170 (D. Kan. 2007), 578 n.81
Fish v. GreatBanc Trust Company, No. 09 C 1668 (N.D. Ill. Aug. 17, 2009), 421
Floorgraphics, Inc. v. News Am. Mktg. In-Store Servs., Inc., 546 F. Supp. 2d 155 (D.N.J. 2008), 563 n.28, 580 n.93
FMS Inc. v. Volvo Constr. Equip. N. A. Inc., No. 00-8143, 2007 U.S. Dist. LEXIS 19517 (N.D. Ill. Mar. 20, 2007), 560 n.17
Foltz v. U.S. News & World Report, Inc., 106 F.R.D. 338 (D.C. Cir. 1984), 416
Foltz v. U.S. News & World Report, Inc., 106 F.R.D. 338 (D.C. Cir. 1984), *aff'd in part and vacated in part, remanded*, 760 F.2d 1300 (D.C. Cir. 1985), *on remand*, 613 F. Supp. 634 (D.D.C. 1985), 22 n.5, 283 n.4, 283 n.5, 293 n.9
Ford v. Ford, 782 P.2d 1304 (Nev. 1989), 160
Forward Communications Corp. v. United States, 608 F.2d 485 (Ct. Cl. 1979), 185 n.8
Foy v. Klapmeier, 992 F.2d 774 (8th Cir. 1993), 700
Franke v. Franke, 674 N.W.2d 832 (Wis. 2004), 644 n.35, 645 n.41
Friedman v. Beway Realty Corp., 87 N.Y.2d 161 (N.Y. 1995), 388 n.60, 400 n.103, 706
Frymire-Brinati v. KPMG Peat Marwick, 2 F.3d 183 (7th Cir. 1993), 575, 575 n.67

G

Gallun v. Comm'r, T.C. Memo. 1974-284, 33 T.C. Memo. (CCH) 1316 (1974), 277 n.74
Garcia v. Commissioner, 140 T.C. No. 6 (U.S.T.C. March 14, 2013), 473 n.68
Garlock v. South Eastern Gas & Power, Inc., 2001 NCBC LEXIS 9 (N.C. Super. 2001), 706
Gaskill v. Robbins, 2006 Ky. App. LEXIS 364 (Ky. Ct. App. 2006), 159, 355 n.43
Gaydos v. Gaydos, 693 A.2d 1368 (Pa. Super. Ct. 1997), 357 n.50
Gearreald v. Just Care, Inc., 2012 Del. Ch. LEXIS 91 (Del. Ch. Apr. 30, 2012), 393
General Electric Co. v. Joiner, 522 U.S. 136 (1997), 558, 558 n.9
General Securities Corp. v. Watson, 477 S.W.2d 461 (Ark. 1972), 684
Gentile v. SinglePoint Financial, Inc., 2003 Del. Ch. LEXIS 21 (Del. Ch. Mar. 5, 2003), 386 n.49
Georgia-Pacific Corp. v. U.S. Plywood Corp., 318 F. Supp. 1116 (S.D.N.Y. 1970), *modified and aff'd*, 446 F.2d 295 (2d Cir.), *cert. denied*, 404 U.S. 870 (1971), 462 n.5
Gesoff v. IIC Indus., Inc., 902 A.2d 1130 (Del. Ch. 2006), 381 n.23
G & G Fashion Design, Inc. v. Garcia, 870 So. 2d 870 (Fla. App. 2004), 389 n.62
Global GT LP v. Golden Telecom, Inc., 993 A.2d 497 (Del. Ch. 2010), *aff'd*, Golden Telecom v. Global GT LP, 11 A.3d 214 (Del. 2010), 393
G&N Aircraft, Inc. v. Boehm, 743 N.E.2d 227 (Ind. 2001), 692
Golden v. Golden, 75 Cal. Rptr. 735 (Cal. Ct. App. 1965), 349 n.9, 358 n.57
Goldman v. Goldman, 554 N.E.2d 860 (Mass. App. 1990), 159
Gonsalves v. Straight Arrow Publishers, 701 A.2d 357 (Del. Ch. 1997), 386 n.50
Graham v. Graham, No. 69067, 353
Grain Processing Corp. v. American Maize-Products Co., 185 F.3d 1341 (Fed. Cir. 1999), 467 n.33
Granger v. Granger, 579 N.E.2d 1319 (Ind. Ct. App. 1991), 365 n.93
Greenlight Capital Qualified, L.P. v. Emerging Communications, Inc., 2001 Del. Ch. LEXIS 170 (Del. Ct. Ch. Feb. 23, 2001), 612 n.49
Green v. Green, 1998 WL 363840 (Ohio Ct. App. 1998), 351 n.23
Grieve v. Commissioner, T.C. Memo. 2020-28, 257 n.10, 273, 273 n.55, 306 n.93, 311, 317
Gross v. Comm'r, T.C. Memo. 1999-254, 435 n.5, 436
Grunfeld v. Grunfeld, 94 N.Y.2d 696 (2000), 176

Guang Dong v. ACI International, Inc., No. 03-4165-JAR, 2008 U.S. Dist. LEXIS 3881 (D. Kan. Jan. 17, 2008), 561 n.22, 563 n.29, 581 n.96, 653 n.2
Guge v. Kassel Enterprises, Inc., 962 N.W.2d 764 (Iowa 2021), 313 n.139
Guiffre v. Baker, 1996 WL 535254, 1996 Ohio App. LEXIS 3673 (Ohio Ct. App. 1996), 60 n.3

H

Haelen Labs v. Topps Chewing Gum, 202 F.2d 866 (2d Cir. 1953), *cert. denied*, 346 U.S. 816 (1953), 471 n.64
Hall v. Glenn's Ferry Grazing Assn., 2006 U.S. Dist. LEXIS 68051 (D. Idaho), 692
Hamilton v. Hamilton, 2002 Ohio 2417 (Ohio Ct. App. 2002), 276 n.69, 366 n.97
Hammers v. Hammers, 890 So. 2d 944 (Miss. Ct. App. 2004), 609 n.37
Hangarter v. Provident Life & Acc. Ins. Co., 373 F.3d 998 (9th Cir. 2004), 558 n.12
Hansen v. 75 Ranch Co., 957 P.2d 32 (Mont. 1998), 702
Hanson v. Hanson, 86 P.3d 94, 192 Or. App. 422 (Or. Ct. App. 2004), 160, 352, 354, 359 n.62, 364 n.84, 364 n.86
Hargrave v. Hargrave, 209 Cal. Rptr. 764 (Cal. Ct. App. 1985), 351 n.18
Hartman v. BigInch Fabricators & Construction Hldg. Co., 161 N.E.3d 1218 (Ind. 2021), *reversing* 148 N.E.3d 1017 (Ind. App. 2020), 396 n.87
Haupt v. Heaps, 131 P.3d 252 (Utah Ct. App. 2005), 579–580, 579 n.90
Hayes v. Olmsted & Associates, Inc., 21 P.3d 178 (Ore. App. 2001), 708
HBK Master Fund L.P. v. Pivotal Software, Inc., 2023 Del. Ch. LEXIS 332 (Del. Ch. Aug. 14, 2023), 392 n.82, 395
Heary Bros. Lightning Prot. Co., Inc. v. Lightning Prot. Inst., 287 F. Supp. 2d 1038 (D. Ariz. 2003), 578 n.82
Heck v. Commissioner, T.C. Memo. 2002-34, 435 n.9
Held v. Held, 2005 Fla. App. LEXIS 14138 (Fla. Ct. App. 2005), 357 n.54
Helvering v. Walbridge, 70 F.2d 683 (2d Cir. 1934), *cert. denied*, 293 U.S. 594 (1934), 331 n.6
Hendrix v. Comm'r, T.C. Memo 2011-133, 324 n.186
Henry v. Champlain Enterprises, Inc., 445 F.3d 610 (2d Cir. 2006), 417–418, 417 n.33, 570 n.39
Herron v. Herron, 2004 Ohio App. LEXIS 5209 (Ohio Ct. App. 2004), 360 n.65
Hertz v. Hertz, 657 P.2d 1169 (N.M. 1983), 359 n.62, 361 n.72
Hess v. Comm'r, T.C. Memo. 2003-251 (2003), 254 n.4, 299 n.47, 300 n.54, 308 n.109, 322
Hewitt v. Comm'r, 166 F.3d 332 (4th Cir. 1998), 314 n.144
Hickum v. Hickum, 463 S.E.2d 321 (S.C. Ct. App. 1995), 351 n.20, 357 n.51
Hillebrand v. Hillebrand, 546 A.2d 1047 (N.H. 1988), 351 n.20
Hill v. Hill, 380 S.E.2d 540 (1989), 644 n.35
Hill v. Reederei F. Laeisz G.M.B.H. Rostock, 435 F.3d 404 (3d Cir. 2006), 558 n.10
HMO-W Inc. v. SSM Health Care System, 611 N.W.2d 250 (Wisc. 2000), 718
Hodas v. Spectrum Technology, Inc., C.A. 11 (Del. Ch. 1992), 400 n.105
Hoeft v. Hoeft, 74 Ohio App. 3d 809, 600 N.E.2d 746 (Ohio Ct. App. 1991), 362 n.74
Hogan v. Hogan, 796 S.W.2d 400 (Mo. Ct. App. 1990), 366 n.96
Hogle v. Zinetics Medical, Inc., 63 P.3d 80 (Utah 2002), 714
Holbrook v. Holbrook, 103 Wis. 2d 327, 309 N.W.2d 343, 1981 Wis. App. LEXIS 3322 (Wis. Ct. App. 1981), 354, 357 n.50, 359 n.62
Hoverson v. Hoverson, 629 N.W.2d 573, 2001 N.D. 124 (N.D. 2001), 350 n.14
Howard v. Shay, 100 F.3d 1484 (9th Cir. 1996), 256 n.9
Howell v. Howell, 1998 WL 972312 (Va. Cir. Ct. Sept. 4, 1998), *aff'd*, 523 S.E.2d 514 (Va. Ct. App. 2000), 348 n.3
Howell v. Howell, 31 Va. App. 332 (2000), 161, 349 n.10

Howell v. Howell, 46 Va. Cir. 339, 1998 Va. Cir. LEXIS 256 (Va. Cir. Ct. 1998), *aff'd*, 31 Va. App. 332, 523 S.E.2d 514 (Va. Ct. App. 2000), 360 n.65, 364 n.84, 364 n.86
Howell v. Howell, 523 S.E.2d 514 (Va. Ct. App. 2000), 60 n.3, 349 n.10
Hoyd v. Trussway Holdings, LLC, 2019 WL 994048 (Del. Ch. Feb. 28, 2019), 395
Humetrix, Inc. v. Gemplus, S.C.A., 268 F.3d 910 (9th Cir. 2001), 582
Hunter v. Mitek Indus., 721 F. Supp. 1102 (E.D. Mo. 1989), 700
Hutchens Non-Marital Trust v. Comm'r, T.C. Memo. 1993-600 (1993), 321
H.W. Johnson, Inc. v. Commissioner, T.C. Memo 2016-95 (U.S.T.C. May 11, 2016), 176 n.11

I

In Matter of Shell Oil Co., 607 A.2d 12B (Del. Supr. 1992), 377 n.11
Innovative Clinical & Consulting Servs., LLC, v. First Nat'l Bank of Ames, 279 Ga. 672 (2005), 560 n.17
In re Appraisal of Ancestry.com, Inc., 2015 Del. Ch. LEXIS 21 (Del. Ch. Jan. 30, 2015), 393
In re Appraisal of AOL, Inc., 2018 WL 1037450 (Del. Ch. Feb. 23, 2018), *modified*, 2018 WL 3913775 (Del. Ch. Aug. 15, 2018), 392 n.78, 394
In re Appraisal of Dell Inc., 2016 Del. Ch. LEXIS 81 (Del. Ch. May 31, 2016), 391 n.75, 392 n.81, 394
In re Appraisal of DFC Global Corp., 2016 Del. Ch. LEXIS 103 (Del. Ch. July 8, 2016), *rev'd on other grounds*, 378 n.15, 391 n.75, 394
In re Appraisal of Jarden Corp., 2019 WL 3244085 (Del. Ch. July 19, 2019), 395
In re Appraisal of Panera Bread Co., 2020 WL 506684 (Del. Ch. Jan. 31, 2020), 386 n.46
In re Appraisal of SWS Group, Inc., 2018 WL 3625644 (Del. Ch. May 30, 2017), 394
In re Appraisal of The Orchard Enterprises, Inc., 2012 Del. Ch. LEXIS 165 (Del. Ch. July 18, 2012), 393
In re Appraisal of Transkaryotic Therapies, Inc., 2007 Del. Ch. LEXIS 57 (Del. Ch. May 2, 2007), 390 n.74
In re Athlon Sports Communications, Inc., v. Stephen C. Duggan, et al., Court of Appeals of Tennessee (Oct. 17, 2016), 377 n.12
In re Bookout, 833 P.2d 800 (Colo. Ct. App. 1991), *cert. denied*, 846 P.2d 189 (Colo. 1993), 357 n.53
In re Cellular Telephone Partnership Litigation, 2022 WL 698112 (Del. Ch. Mar. 9, 2022), 395
In re Citigroup S'holder Litig., 964 A.2d 106 (Del. Ch. 2009), 499 n.14
In re Doctors Hospital of Hyde Park, 360 B.R. 787 (Bankr. N.D. Ill. 2007), 558 n.8
In re Dole Food Co., Inc. Stockholder Litig., 2015 Del. Ch. LEXIS 223 (Del. Ch. Aug. 27, 2015), 394
In re El Paso Pipeline Partners, L.P. Derivative Litigation, 2015 Del. Ch. LEXIS 116 (Del. Ch. Apr. 20, 2015), 393
In re Greater Southeast Cmty. Hosp. Corp., No. 02-02250, 2007 Bankr. LEXIS 1 (Bankr. D.D.C. Jan. 2, 2007), 574 n.57
In re Hall, 103 Wash. 2d 236, 692 P.2d 175 (Wash. 1984), 357 n.53
In re Hanover Direct, Inc. Sh'holders Litig., 2010 Del. Ch. LEXIS 201 (Del. Ch. Sept. 24, 2010), 393
In re Happy Child World, Inc., 2020 WL 5793156 (Del. Ch. Sept. 29, 2020), 395
In re Innovatio IP Ventures, LLC, 2013 U.S. Dist. LEXIS 144061 (N.D. Ill. Sep. 27, 2013), 465 n.28
In re ISN Software Corp. Appraisal Litigation, C.A. No. 8388-VCG (Del. Ch. 2017), 394, 398 n.95
In re Joy Recovery Tech. Corp., 286 B.R. 54 (Bankr. N.D. Ill. 2002), 572, 582 n.99
In re Kinder Morgan, Inc. Corp. Reorg. Litig., 2015 WL 4975270 (Del. Ch. Aug. 20, 2015), *aff'd*, Haynes Fam. Tr. v. Kinder Morgan G.P. Inc., 135 A.3d 76 (Del. 2016), 397, 398 n.91

In re Letendre, 815 A.2d 938 (N.H. 2002), 609 n.38
In re Marriage of Alexander, 2006 Ill. App. LEXIS 836 (Ill. Ct. App. 2006), 355 n.48
In re Marriage of Bauer, 2011 WL 4337093 (Cal. App. 4 Dist.), 153 n.9
In re Marriage of Bidwell, 12 P.3d 76, 170 Or. App. 239 (Or. Ct. App. 2000), 367 n.101
In re Marriage of Black, 2001 WL 57999 (Iowa Ct. App. 2001), 364 n.89
In re Marriage of Brooks, 756 P.2d 161 (Wash. Ct. App. 1988), 360 n.64
In re Marriage of Czapar, 232 Cal. App. 3d 1308, 284 Cal. Rptr. 41 (1991), 364 n.89
In re Marriage of DeCosse, 936 P.2d 821, 1997 WL 19374 (Mont. 1997), 363 n.83
In re Marriage of Dieger, 584 N.W.2d 567 (Iowa Ct. App. 1998), 360 n.66
In re Marriage of Fleege, 91 Wash. 2d 324, 588 P.2d 1136 (Wash. 1979), 352 n.27, 353, 359 n.61
In re Marriage of Fortier, 34 Cal. App. 3d 384, 109 Cal. Rptr. 915 (1973), 358
In re Marriage of Foster, 42 Cal. App. 3d 577, 117 Cal. Rptr. 49 (1974), 358 n.56
In re Marriage of Gabriel, 2005 Cal. App. Unpub. LEXIS 8101 (Cal. Ct. App. 2005), 367 n.101
In re Marriage of Gillespie, 948 P.2d 1338 (Wash. Ct. App. 1997), 361 n.73
In re Marriage of Hall, 692 P.2d 175 (Wash. 1984), 161
In re Marriage of Harrington, 935 P.2d 1357 (Wash. Ct. App. 1997), 363 n.82
In re Marriage of Hay, 907 P.2d 334 (Wash. Ct. App. 1995), 130 n.3, 365 n.90
In re Marriage of Head, 652 N.E.2d 1246 (Ill. App. 1995), 158
In re Marriage of Herlitzke, 2006 Wis. App. LEXIS 972 (Wis. Ct. App. 2006), 360 n.65
In re Marriage of Hoak, 364 N.W.2d 185 (Iowa 1985), 363 n.81
In re Marriage of Hogeland, 448 N.W.2d 678 (Iowa App. 1989), 159
In re Marriage of Huff, 834 P.2d 244 (Colo. 1992), 158
In re Marriage of Hull, 219 Mont. 480 (1986), 950 P.2d 1373 (Mont. 1997), 160
In re Marriage of Jorgensen, 180 Mont. 294, 590 P.2d 606 (1979), 363 n.81
In re Marriage of Keener, 2007 Iowa Sup. LEXIS 13 (Iowa 2007), 367 n.100
In re Marriage of King, 197 Cal. Rptr. 716 (Cal. Ct. App. 1983), 358 n.56
In re Marriage of Liszka, 2016 IL App (3d) 150238, 610 n.42
In re Marriage of Lopez, 38 Cal. App. 3d 93 (1974), 158, 351 n.19
In re Marriage of Mally, 2001 WL 539669 (Iowa Ct. App. 2001), 362 n.76
In re Marriage of Melnick, 127 Ill. App. 3d 102, 82 Ill. Dec. 228, 468 N.E.2d 490 (1984), 361 n.69
In re Marriage of Moffatt, 279 N.W.2d 15 (Iowa 1979), 361 n.69
In re Marriage of Monaghan, 899 P.2d 841 (Wash. Ct. App. 1995), 357 n.54, 362 n.74
In re Marriage of Olinger, 707 P.2d 64 (Or. Ct. App. 1985), 351 n.19
In re Marriage of Ondrasek, 126 Wis. 2d 469, 377 N.W.2d 190 (Ct. App. 1985), 359 n.62
In re Marriage of Reiling, 66 Ore. App. 284, 673 P.2d 1360 (1983), 363 n.81
In re Marriage of Rubens, 2003 Wash. App. LEXIS 1544 (Wash. Ct. App. 2003), 351 n.21
In re Marriage of Slater, 100 Cal. App. 3d 241, 160 Cal. Rptr. 686 (1979), 359 n.63
In re Marriage of Sommerfield, 454 N.W.2d 55 (1990), 351 n.19
In re Marriage of Swanson, 716 P.2d 219 (Mont. 1986), 351 n.19
In re Marriage of Talty, 623 N.E.2d 1041 (Ill. App. Ct. 1993), 351 n.19
In re Marriage of Thomas, 608 N.E.2d 585 (Ill. App. Ct. 1993), 351 n.19

In re Marriage of Tofte, 895 P.2d 1387 (Or. Ct. App. 1995), 364 n.85
In re Marriage of Wagner, 679 P.2d 753 (Mont. 1984), 351 n.19
In re McReath, 789 N.W.2d 89 (Wis. Ct. App. 2010), 354 n.40
In re Med Diversified, Inc., 346 B.R. 621 (Bankr. E.D.N.Y. 2005), 557–558, 563 n.31, 564 n.31, 577 n.73
In re Nellson Nutraceutical, No. 06-10072 (CSS), 2006 Bankr. LEXIS 3186 (Bankr. D. Del. 2006), 579 n.89
In re Paoli R.R. Yard Litig., 35 F.3d 717 (3d Cir. 1994), 569 n.36
In re Processed Egg Prods. Antitrust Litig., 815 F. Supp. 3d 412, 571 n.44
In re Rural/Metro Corporation Stockholders Litigation, 102 A.3d 205 (Del. Ch. 2014), 393
In re Shares of Madden, Fulford and Trumbull, 2005 Vt. Super. LEXIS 112 (Vt. Super. 2005), 716
In re Shares of Trapp Family Lodge, Inc., 725 A.2d 927 (Vt. 1999), 388 n.59, 716
In re Southern Peru Copper Corp. S'holder Derivative Litigation, C.A. No. 961-CS (Del. Ch. 2011), 392 n.82, 393
In re Sunbelt Beverage Corp. Sh'holder Litig., 2010 Del. Ch. LEXIS 1 (Del. Ch. Jan. 5, 2010), 393
In re T.B.H.-H., 188 S.W.3d 312 (Tex. Ct. App. 2006), 644 n.34
In re Titanium Dioxide Antitrust Litig., No. 10-0318, 2013 WL D.MD. (May 1, 2013), 571 n.44
In re Unisys Savings Plan Litig., 173 F.3d 145 (3d Cir. 1999), 569 n.35
In re Val. of Common Stock of McLoon Oil Co., 565 A.2d 997 (Me. 1989), 388 n.58, 698
In re Val. of Penobscot Shoe Co., 2003 Me. Super. LEXIS 140, 698
In re Valuation of Common Stock of Libby, McNeill & Libby, 406 A.2d 54 (Me. 1979), 389 n.71
In re Watterworth, 821 A.2d 1107 (N.H. 2003), 160
Inter-Local Pension Fund GCC/IBT v. Calgon Carbon Corp., 2019 WL 479082 (Del. Ch. Jan. 25, 2019), 379 n.17
International Indus., Inc. v. Warren Petroleum Corp., 248 F.2d 696 (3d Cir. 1997), 469 n.47
In the Matter of Overbey, 2007 Wash. App. LEXIS 1651 (Wash. Ct. App. 2007), 360 n.64
In the Matter of the Marriage of Belt, 65 Ore. App. 606, 672 P.2d 1205 (1983), 361 n.69, 363 n.81

J

Jackson v. Comm'r, T.C. Memo. 2021–48, RIA TC Memo 2021-048, 314, 315 n.151
Janda v. Comm'r, T.C. Memo. 2001-24 (2001), 273 n.56, 304 n.80, 306 n.94
Johnson v. Johnson, 771 P.2d 696 (Utah Ct. App. 1989), 359 n.59
Johnston v. Johnston, 778 S.W.2d 674 (Mo. Ct. App. 1989), 362 n.74

K

Kahn v. Kahn, 536 N.E.2d 678 (Ohio 1987), 160, 380 n.19
Kahn v. M&F Worldwide Corp., 88 A.3d 635 (Del. 2014), 381 n.24, 501 n.19
Kaiser v. Kaiser, 474 N.W.2d 63 (N.D. 1991), 365 n.92
Kaplan v. First Hartford Corp., 603 F. Supp. 2d 195 (D. Me. 2009), 698
Kaplin v. Comm'r, 748 F.2d 1109 (6th Cir. 1984), *rev'g* T.C. Memo. 1982-440 (1982), 318 n.160
Kapp v. Kapp, 2005 Ohio App. LEXIS 6144 (Ohio App. 2005), 364 n.85
KBM, Inc. v. MacKichan, 438 N.W.2d 181 (N.D. 1989), 706
Keach v. U.S. Trust Co., 419 F.3d 626 (2005), 419
Keane v. Keane, 2006 N.Y. LEXIS 3751 (N.Y. 2006), 370
Kennedy v. Trustmark National Bank, Case No. 3:05cv220-RS (N.D. Fla. Jan. 17, 2006), 420

Kilbourne v. Kilbourne, 284 Cal. Rptr. 201 (Cal. Ct. App. 1991), 351 n.21
Kim v. The Grover C. Coors Trust, 179 P.3d 86 (Colo. App. 2007), 386 n.43
King v. F.T.J., Inc., 765 S.W.2d 301 (Mo. Ct. App. 1988), 700
Koblick v. Comm'r, 2006 Tax Ct. Memo. LEXIS 63 (2006), 315 n.145
Koch v. Koch, 874 S.W.2d 571 (Tenn. Ct. App. 1993), 351 n.19
Koffler v. Commissioner, 1978 T.C. Memo. 159, 275 n.61
Kohler v. Comm'r, T.C. Memo. 2006-152, 2006 Tax Ct. Memo. LEXIS 156 (2006), 56 n.7, 296 n.25, 297 n.32, 298 n.39, 565 n.32
Krapf v. United States, 977 F.2d 1454 (Fed. Cir. 1992), 318 n.160
Kress, James F. v. U.S. (2019, DC WI), 123 AFTR 2d 2019-1224, 2019-1 USTC ¶ 60711, 372 F. Supp. 3d 731, 304 n.84
Kricsfeld v. Kricsfeld, 588 N.W.2d 210, 1999 Neb. App. LEXIS 1 (Neb. Ct. App. 1999), 162 n.4, 357 n.54, 362 n.74
Kruse v. Synapse Wireless, Inc., 2020 WL 3969386 (Del. Ch. July 14, 2020), 395
KSP Invs., Inc. v. United States, No. 1:07-CV-857, 2008 U.S. Dist. LEXIS 7383 (N.D. Ohio Jan. 17, 2008), 582 n.101
Kumho Tire Co. v. Carmichael, 526 U.S. 137 (1999), 558, 559, 562 n.25, 574 n.59, 579
KW Plastics v. United States Can Co., 131 F. Supp. 2d 1289 (M.D. Ala. 2001), 561 n.21

L

LabelGraphics, Inc. v. Commissioner, T.C. Memo 1998-343 (Sept. 28, 1998), *aff'd*, 221 F.3d 1091 (9th Cir. 2000), 169 n.5
Laidler v. Hesco Bastion Environmental, Inc., 2014 Del. Ch. LEXIS 75 (Del. Ch. May 12, 2014), 393
Lane v. Cancer Treatment Centers of Am., 1994 Del. Ch. LEXIS 67 (Del. Ch. May 25, 1994), 600
Lappo v. Comm'r, T.C. Memo. 2003-258 (2003), 304 n.77
LaserDynamics, Inc. v. Quanta Comp., Inc., 694 F.3d 51 (Fed. Cir. 2012), 464 n.10, 465 n.17
Las Vegas Dodge v. United States, No. CV LV 79-7, RDF, 1985 WL 6366 (D. Nev. Mar. 20, 1985), 301 n.58
Lawson Mardon Wheaton, Inc. v. Smith, 716 A.2d 558 (N.J. App. 1998), 385 n.41, 704
Leaf v. Goodyear Tire & Rubber Co., 590 N.W.2d 525 (Iowa 1999), 556 n.3
Le Beau v. M.G. Bancorporation, Inc., 1998 Del. Ch. Lexis 9, 1998 WL 44993 (Del. Ch. Jan. 29, 1998), 2 n.5, 262 n.23
Lees Inns of America, Inc. v. Lee, 924 N.E.2d 143 (Ind. App. 2010), 389 n.63
Lee v. Argent Tr. Co., 5:19-CV-156-BO (E.D.N.C. Aug. 6, 2019), 423–424
Leibowitz v. Comm'r, T.C. Memo. 1997-243 (1997), 295 n.20
Liddle v. Liddle, 410 N.W.2d 196 (Wis. Ct. App. 1987), 366 n.94
LifeWise Master Funding v. Telebank, 374 F.3d 917 (10th Cir. 2004), 561 n.21
Linsell v. Applied Handling, Inc., 697 N.W.2d 913 (Mich. Ct. App. 2005), 610 n.40
Litman v. United States, 78 Fed. Cl. 90 (Cl. Ct. 2007), 304 n.81, 305 n.89
Lloyd B. Sanderson Estate v. Commissioner, 42 F.2d 160 (1930), 143
Lopez v. Lopez, 38 Cal. App. 3d 93, 113 Cal. Rptr. 58 (Cal. Ct. App. 1974), 352
L.R.M. v. R.K.M., 46 S.W.3d 24 (Mo. Ct. App. 2001), 363 n.83, 364 n.85
Lucent Technologies, Inc. v. Gateway, Inc., 580 F.3d 1301 (Fed. Cir. 2009), 464 n.12
Lund v. Lund, 924 N.W.2d 274 (Minn. App. 2019), 700
Lyon v. Lyon, 439 N.W.2d 18 (Minn. 1989), 361 n.68

M

Mace v. Mace, 818 So. 2d 1130 (Miss. 2002), 367 n.101
Mallett v. Mallett, 473 S.E.2d 804 (S.C. Ct. App. 1996), 351 n.20
Mandelbaum v. Comm'r, T.C. Memo. 1995-255 (1995), 268, 303 n.72

Manichaean Capital LLC v. SourceHOV Holdings, Inc., 2020 WL 496606 (Del. Ch. Jan. 30, 2020), *aff'd*, SourceHOV Holdings, Inc. v. Manichaean Capital, LLC, 246 A.3d 139, 385 n.37, 395

Marker v. Marker, 242 P.3d 638 (Ore. App. 2010), 708

Martin Ice Cream Co., 110 T.C. 189 (1998), 164 n.6

Matter of Blake v. Blake Agency, 107 A.D.2d 139 (N.Y. App. 1985), 387 n.55, 388 n.60, 397 n.89, 400 n.103, 706

Matter of Dissolution of Exterior Delite, Inc., 831 N.Y.S. 656 (N.Y. Supr. 2006), 390 n.73

Matter of Slant/Fin. Corp. v. Chicago Corp. (unpublished) (N.Y. Supr. Ct. Oct. 26, 1995), *aff'd*, 236 A.D.2d 547 (N.Y. App. 1997), 2 n.5, 262 n.23, 385 n.38

Matthew G. Norton Co. v. Smyth, 51 P.3d 159 (Wash. App. 2002), 716

Maxon v. Mirror Show Mgmt., Inc., 7 Misc. 3d 1015A (N.Y. Sup. 2005), 611 n.43

May v. May, 214 W. Va. 394 (2003), 161, 354, 355 n.49

McCord v. Comm'r, 120 T.C. 358 (2003), *rev'd*, 461 F.3d 614 (5th Cir. 2006), 304 n.74, 324 n.187

McDiarmid v. McDiarmid, 649 A.2d 810 (D.C. App. 1994), 158

McMinn v. MBF Operating Acq. Corp., 164 P.3d 41 (N.M. 2007), 704

McReath v. McReath, 2011 Wisc. LEXIS 354 (July 12, 2011), 161

Medtronic, Inc. and Consolidated Subsidiaries v. Commissioner, T.C. Memo. 2016-112 (June 9, 2016) (8th Cir. Aug. 18, 2016), 341 n.42

Menard Inc. v. Commissioner, No. 08-2125 (7th Cir. 2009), 170 n.7

Merion Capital, L.P. v. 3M Cogent, Inc., 2013 Del. Ch. LEXIS 172 (Del. Ch. July 8, 2013), 391 n.76, 393, 394

Messing v. Commissioner, 48 T.C. 502 (1967), 323

M.G. Bancorp. v. Le Beau, 1998 Del. Ch. LEXIS 9 (Del. Ch. Jan. 29, 1998), *aff'd*, M.G. Bancorp. v. Le Beau, 737 A.2d 513 (Del. 1999), 380 n.21, 385 n.39

Miami Valley Broadcasting Corporation and Carolina Broadcasting Company v. United States, 204 Ct. Cl. 592 (1974), 499 F.2d 677, 11 n.22

Michael v. Michael, 469 S.E.2d 14 (W. Va. 1996), 364 n.85

Microsoft Corp. v. Motorola, Inc., No. C10-1823JLR, 2013 U.S. Dist. LEXIS 60233 (W.D. Wash. Apr. 25, 2013), 465 n.19

Miller v. Miller, 14 S.W.3d 903, 70 Ark. App. 64 (Ark. Ct. App. 2000), 158, 367 n.101

Mills v. Mills, 167 Vt. 567 (1997), 161

Mitchell v. Mitchell, 719 P.2d 432 (N.M. App. 1986), 160

Mitchell v. Mitchell, 732 P.2d 208 (Ariz. 1987), 158

MLC Intellectual Property, LLC v. Micron Technology, Inc., 10 F.4th 1358 (Fed. Cir. 2021), 464 n.13

Moffitt v. Moffitt, 813 P.2d 674 (Alaska 1991), 351 n.18, 363 n.80

Moll v. Moll, 722 N.Y.S.2d 732 (2001), 160

Moore v. Ashland Chemical, 126 F.3d 679 (5th Cir. 1997), *appeal after remand*, Moore v. Ashland Chem., Inc., 151 F.3d 269 (5th Cir. 1998), 579 n.86

Moore v. Comm'r, T.C. Memo. 1991-546 (1991), 294 n.15

Moore v. Moore, 2015 S.C. LEXIS 343, 161

Moretti v. Moretti, 766 A.2d 925 (R.I. 2001), 160

Morrissey v. Comm'r, 243 F.3d 1145 (9th Cir. 2001), 299 n.43

Morrow v. Martschink, 922 F. Supp. 1093 (D. S.C. 1995), 712

Morse/Diesel v. Trinity Industries, 67 F.3d 435 (2d Cir. 1995), 572 n.45

Morton v. Comm'r, T.C. Memo. 1997-166 (1997), 301 n.61

Morton v. Morton, 2005 Mich. Ch. App. LEXIS 1406 (Mich. Ct. App. 2005), 351 n.21

MT Properties, Inc. v. CMC Real Estate Corp., 481 N.W.2d 38 (Minn. App. 1992), 700

Muller v. Muller, 456 N.Y.S.2d 918 (Sup. Ct. 1982), 351 n.20

Murchie v. Sorenson, 2015 IL App (1st) 133719-U (Ill. App. 2015), 692

N

Nail v. Nail, 486 S.W.2d 761 (Tex. 1972), 161
Nardini v. Nardini, 414 N.W.2d 184 (Minn. 1987), 364 n.84
Neal v. Ala. By-Products Corp., 1990 Del. Ch. LEXIS 127 (Aug. 1, 1990), 150 n.4
Nelson v. Commissioner, T.C. Memo. 2020-8, 269 n.46, 325 n.190
Nestle Holdings, Inc. v. Commissioner, 152 F.3d 83 (2d Cir. July 31, 1998), 331–332, 332 n.11, 470 n.54
Ng v. Heng Sang Realty Corp., 2004 Del. Ch. LEXIS 69 (Apr. 22, 2004), *aff'd*, Heng Sang Realty Corp. v. Ng, 867 A.2d 901 (Del. 2005), 386 n.47
Nike, Inc. v. Wal-Mart Stores, Inc., 138 F.3d 1437 (Fed. Cir. 1998), 468 n.42
Nintendo of America, Inc. v. Dragon Pacific Int'l, 40 F.3d 1007 (9th Cir. 1994), 469 n.50
North American Catholic Educational Programming Foundation v. Gheewalla, 930 A.2d 92 (Del. 2007), 498 n.12
Northwest Investment Corp. v. Wallace, 741 N.W.2d 782 (Iowa 2007), 389 n.64, 694
Norwalk v. Comm'r, T.C. Memo. 1998-279 (1998), 164 n.7
Nowzaradan v. Nowzaradan, 2007 Tex. App. LEXIS 1021 (Tex. Ct. App. 2007), 354 n.41

O

Oakridge Energy, Inc. v. Clifton, 937 P.2d 130 (Utah 1997), 389 n.67
Oatey v. Oatey, No. 67809, 67973 Ohio Ct. App., 1996 WL 200273 (Apr. 25, 1996), 364 n.84
Ogard v. Ogard, 808 P.2d 815 (Alaska 1991), 351 n.18, 351 n.21
Okerlund v. United States, 53 Fed. Cl. 341 (Fed. Ct. Cl. 2002), *aff'd*, 365 F.3d 1044 (Fed. Cir. 2004), 303 n.72, 316
Oliver v. Stone, 940 So. 2d 526, 2006 Fla. App. LEXIS 17631 (Fla. Ct. App. 2006), 600 n.11
Oudheusden v. Oudheusden, 259 A.3d 598, 338 Conn. 761 (2021), 369 n.111
Owen v. Cannon, 2015 Del. Ch. LEXIS 165 (Del. Ch. June 17, 2015), 394
Owings v. Speed, 18 U.S. 420, 5 L. Ed. 124 (1820), 637 n.3

P

Pabst Brewing Company v. Commissioner, T.C. Memo 1996-506 (Nov. 12, 1996), 5 n.12, 331 n.8
Panduit Corp. v. Stahlin Bros. Fibre Works, Inc., 575 F.2d 1152 (6th Cir.), *cert. denied*, 439 U.S. 856 (1978), 467 n.31
Paskill Corp. v. Alcoma Corp., 747 A.2d 549 (Del. Supr. 2000), 283 n.6, 386 n.44, 387 n.52
Peerenboom v. Peerenboom, 433 N.W.2d 282 (Wis. Ct. App. 1988), 357 n.52
Peracchio v. Comm'r, T.C. Memo. 2003-280 (2003), 304 n.78, 455 n.20
Perez v. Bruister, 54 F. Supp. 3d 629 (S.D. Miss. 2014), 421
Perry v. Perry, 1995 Minn. App. LEXIS 1207, 600 n.10
Peters Corp. v. New Mexico Banquest Investors Corp., 188 P.3d 1185 (N.M. 2008), 704
Phase 2 Developers Corp. v. Citicorp Real Estate, 2004 Cal. App. Unpub. LEXIS 117 (Cal. Ct. App. 2004), 607 n.32
Physicians Dialysis Ventures, Inc. v. Griffith, No. 06-2468 (MLC), 2007 U.S. Dist. LEXIS 78879 (D.N.J. Oct. 24, 2007), 569 n.38, 653 n.3
Picerne Dev. v. Tasca and Rotelli, 635 So. 2d 149 (Fla. Dist. Ct. App. 1994), 600 n.10
Pickard v. Pickard, 2006 N.Y. App. Div. LEXIS 9961 (N.Y. App. Div. 2006), 367 n.100
Pierre v. Commissioner, 133 TC 24 (2009), 332 n.12
Piscopo v. Piscopo, 557 A.2d 1040 (N.J. Super. 1989), 348 n.2
Pizzella v. Vinoskey, 409 F. Supp. 3d 473 (W.D. Va. 2019), 422–423
Polack v. Comm'r, T.C. Memo. 2002-145, *aff'd*, 366 F.3d 608 (8th Cir. 2004), 298 n.40, 316

PoolRe Ins. Corp. v. Organizational Strategies, Inc., 783 F.3d 256 (5th Cir. 2015), 642 n.30
Poore v. Poore, 75 N.C. App. 414, 331 S.E.2d 266 (N.C. Ct. App. 1985), 160, 358 n.58
Pope & Talbot, Inc. v. Commissioner, 104 T.C. 574 (1995), *aff'd*, 162 F.3d 1236 (9th Cir. 1999), 338 n.37
Popovich v. Sony Music Entertainment, Inc., 508 F.3d 348 (6th Cir. 2007), 570 n.39, 653 n.4
Prahinski v. Prahinski (II), 75 Md. 227 (1990), 159
Priebe v. Priebe, 556 N.W.2d 78 (S.D. 1996), 363 n.83
Prism Techs. LLC v. Sprint Spectrum LP, 849 F.3d 1360 (Fed. Cir. 2017), 465 n.15
Pro Finish USA v. Johnson, 63 P.3d 288 (Ariz. App. 2003), 684
ProtoComm Corp. v. Novell Advanced Servs., Inc., 171 F. Supp. 2d 473 (E.D. Penn. 2001), 582 n.102
Pueblo Bancorporation v. Lindoe, Inc., 63 P.3d 353 (Colo. Jan. 21, 2003), 385 n.40, 686
Puklich v. Puklich, 930 N.W.2d 593 (N.D. 2019), 706

Q

Quillen v. Quillen, 671 N.E.2d 98 (Ind. 1996), 351 n.23

R

Rabenhorst v. Comm'r, T.C. Memo. 1996-92 (1996), 316 n.152
Rakow v. Comm'r, T.C. Memo. 1999-17, 302 n.67
Rales v. Blanshard, 634 A.2d 927 (Del. 1993), 500 n.15
Raley v. Brinkman, 2020 WL 4360052 (Tenn. App. July 30, 2020), 714
Ramada Inns, Inc. v. Gadsden Motel Co., 804 F.2d 1562 (5th Cir. 1986), 469 n.52
Ramcell, Inc. v. Alltel Corp., WL 16549259 (Del. Ch. Oct. 31, 2022), 395
Rattee v. Rattee, 767 A.2d 415, 146 N.H. 44 (N.H. 2001), 363 n.83, 364 n.85
R.D. Clark & Sons, Inc. v. Clark, 222 A.3d 515 (Conn. App. 2019), 686
Reese v. Reese, 671 N.E.2d 187 (Ind. Ct. App. 1996), 351 n.22, 362 n.75
Reich v. Hall Holding Co., Inc., 990 F. Supp. 955 (N.D. Ohio 1998), 418 n.37
Reich v. Valley Nat. Bank of Arizona, 837 F. Supp. 1259 (S.D.N.Y. 1993), 418
Reis v. Hazelett Strip-Casting Corp., 28 A.3d 442 (Del. Ch. 2011), 393
Remy v. Lubbock Nat'l Bank, No. 5:17-CV-460-FL (E.D.N.C. Mar. 20, 2019), 423
ResQNet.com, Inc. v. Lansa, Inc., 594 F.3d 860 (Fed. Cir. 2010), 464 n.12, 465 n.18
Reynolds American, Inc. v. Third Motion Equities Master Fund Ltd., 2020 NCBC 35 (N.C. Super., Apr. 27, 2020), 384 n.31
Reynolds v. Whitman, 40 Mass. App. Ct. 315 (Mass. App. Ct. 1996), 645 n.41
Richard A. Lippe v. Bairnco Corporation, 99 Fed. Appx. 274 (2d Cir. 2004), 578 n.83
Richardson v. U.S. News & World Report, Inc., 623 F. Supp. 350 (D.C. Cir. 1985), 416 n.29
Richmond v. Richmond, 779 P.2d 1211 (Alaska 1989), 158, 351 n.21
Riddle-Bradley, Inc. v. Riddle, 459 S.E.2d 576 (Ga. Ct. App. 1995), 401 n.111
Rigel Corp. v. Cutchall, 511 N.W.2d 519 (Neb. 1994), 702
Ritchie v. Rupe, 339 S.W.3d 275 (Tex. App. 2011), 714
Robertson v. United States, 2006 U.S. Dist. LEXIS 1167 (N.D. Tex. 2006), 304 n.83, 309 n.112
Robinson v. Langenbach, 599 S.W.3d 167 (Mo. 2020), 399 n.100
Rogers v. Alexander, 244 S.W.3d 370 (Tex. Ct. App. 2007), 571 n.43
Rogers v. Rogers, 296 N.W.2d 849 (Minn. 1980), 359 n.63, 361 n.69
Rolfe State Bank v. Gunderson, 794 N.W.2d 561 (Iowa 2011), 694
Root v. Root, 65 P.3d 41 (Wyo. 2003), 161
Rosenberg v. Rosenberg, 510 N.Y.S.2d 659 (App. Div. 1987), 351 n.20, 359 n.59
Rossi v. Mobil Oil Corp., 710 F.2d 821 (Temp. Emer. Ct. App. 1983), 563 n.27

Rosvold v. LSM Sys. Eng'g, Inc., No. 04-75009, 2007 U.S. Dist. LEXIS 82061 (E.D. Mich. Nov. 6, 2007), 570 n.41
Roth v. Roth, 406 N.W.2d 77 (Minn. App. 1987), 159
R.V.K. v. L.L.K., 2002 WL 31421572 (Tex. Ct. App. 2002), 360 n.65
Ryan v. Tad's Enters., 709 A.2d 682 (Del. Ch. 1996), 380 n.20

S

Sampson v. Sampson, 2004 Mass. App. LEXIS 1223 (Mass. App. Ct. 2004), 369 n.112
Samsung Elecs. Co. v. Apple Inc., 137 S. Ct. 436 (2016), 468 n.51
Sander v. Sander, 2006 Conn. App. LEXIS 280 (Conn. Ct. App. 2006), 370
Sands, Taylor & Wood Co. v. Quaker Oats Co., 978 F.2d 947 (7th Cir. 1992), 469 n.52
Santa Monica Picture, L.L.C. v. Comm'r, 89 T.C.M. (CCH) 1157 (T.C. 2005), 574 n.62
Sarrouf v. New England Patriots Football Club, Inc., 492 N.E.2d 1122 (Mass. 1986), 388 n.57
Scalero v. Scalero, 1998 WL 23845 (Ohio Ct. App. 1998), 351 n.22
Scharfman v. Scharfman, 2005 N.Y. App. Div. LEXIS 6584 (N.Y. App. Div. 2005), 351 n.20
Schimke v. Liquid Dustlayer, Inc., 2009 WL 3049723 (Mich. App. Sept. 24, 2009), 399 n.99, 698
Schulz v. Commissioner, 294 F.2d 52 (9th Cir. 1961), 187 n.12
Schuman v. Schuman, 658 N.W.2d 30, 265 Neb. 459 (Neb. 2003), 366 n.98
Seagraves v. Urstadt Prop. Co., 1996 Del. Ch. LEXIS 36 (Del. Ch. Apr. 1, 1996), 380 n.18
Sergi v. Sergi, 1996 WL 425914, 1996 Ohio App. LEXIS 3241 (Ohio Ct. App. 1996), 60 n.3
Sharp v. Chase Manhattan Bank, 2005 Bankr. LEXIS 3045 (Bankr. N.D. Okla. 2005), 610 n.41
Shawnee Telecom Resources v. Brown, 354 S.W.3d 542 (Ky. 2011), 694
Shooltz v. Shooltz, 498 S.E.2d 437 (Va. Ct. App. 1998), 60 n.4, 135 n.11
Shop Rite, Inc. v. Gardiner, 2021 WL 1413949 (La. App. 3 Cir. Apr. 14, 2021), 313 n.139
Siegel v. Siegel, 523 N.Y.S.2d 517 (App. Div. 1987), 351 n.20
Skokos v. Skokos, 40 S.W.3d 768, 344 Ark. 420 (Ark. 2001), 351 n.19, 364 n.89
Slater v. Slater, 245 P.3d 676 (Ore. Ct. App. 2010), 160
Smith v. Promontory Financial Group, LLC, 2019 WL 1934854 (Del. Ch. Apr. 30, 2019), 398 n.92
Smith v. Smith, 709 S.W.2d 558 (Tenn. App. 1985), 161
Smith v. Van Gorkom, 488 A.2d 858 (Del. 1985), 496 n.7, 502 n.20, 503
Sommers Drug Stores v. Corrigan Enterprises, 793 F.2d 1456 (5th Cir. 1986), 282 n.1, 415–416, 415 n.27
Sommers v. Sommers, 660 N.W.2d 586, 2003 N.D. 77 (N.D. 2003), 160, 350 n.12
Sorensen v. Sorensen, 839 P.2d 774 (Utah 1992), 161
Southwire Co. v. J.P. Morgan Chase & Co., 528 F. Supp. 2d 908 (W.D. Wis. 2007), 574 n.58, 581 n.97
Spencer v. Spencer, 494 A.2d 1279 (D.C. 1985), 644 n.34
Spenlinhauer v. Spencer Press, Inc., 959 N.E.2d 436 (Mass. App. 2011), 698
State *ex rel.* Garner v. Wright, 562 S.W.3d 311 (2018), 558 n.13
State Indus., Inc. v. Mor-Flo Indus., Inc., 883 F.2d 1573 (Fed. Cir. 1989), 467 n.34
Steadman v. Commissioner, 424 F.2d 1 (6th Cir. 1970), *cert. denied*, 400 U.S. 869 (1970), 338 n.33
Steneken v. Steneken, 843 A.2d 344 (N.J. App. Div. 2004), *aff'd*, 873 A.2d 501, 183 N.J. 290 (N.J. 2005), 368 n.105
Stern v. Stern, 66 N.J. 340, 331 A.2d 257, 74 L.R.3d 613 (1975), 359 n.63
Stewart v. Stewart, 2007 Idaho LEXIS 17 (Idaho 2007), 158, 355 n.42

Stone v. Ritter, 911 A.2d 362 (Del. 2006), 497 n.9
Stribling v. Stribling, 2005 Miss. App. LEXIS 58 (Miss. Ct. App. 2005), 367 n.103
Sun Ins. Mktg. Network, Inc. v. AIG Life Ins. Co., 254 F. Supp. 2d 1239 (M.D. Fla. 2003), 564 n.31
Sweere v. Gilbert-Sweere, 534 N.W.2d 294, 1995 Minn. App. LEXIS 912 (Minn. Ct. App. 1995), 357 n.54, 362 n.75
Swope v. Seigel-Robert, Inc., 243 F.3d 486 (8th Cir. 2001), 385 n.42, 389 n.65, 700
Sy First Fam. Ltd. P'ship v. Cheung, 70 Cal. App. 4th 1334 (1999), 638 n.14

T

Taco Cabana International, Inc. v. Two Pesos, Inc., 932 F.2d 1113 (5th Cir. 1991), 469 n.52, 470 n.57
Target Market Publishing, Inc. v. ADVO, Inc., 136 F.3d 1139 (7th Cir. 1998), 572–573, 572 n.49
Taylor v. Taylor, 222 Neb. 721, 386 N.W.2d 851 (1986), 351 n.18, 353, 644 n.34
Taylor v. Taylor, 736 S.W.2d 388 (Mo. 1987), 160
Temple v. United States, 2006 U.S. Dist. LEXIS 16171 (E.D. Tex. 2006), 304 n.82, 306 n.94, 308 n.104, 308 n.111, 313 n.138
Tharo Sys., Inc. v. cab Produckttechnick GmbH & Co. KG, 196 Fed. Appx. 366 (6th Cir. 2006), 570 n.40, 582, 582 n.103
Thompson v. Thompson, 576 So. 2d 267 (Fla. 1991), 158, 354 n.41
Thor Power Tool Company v. Commissioner, 439 U.S. 522 (1979), 335 n.22
Tidwell Indus., Inc. v. Diversified Home Products, Inc., No. SA-06-CA-0264 FB, 2007 U.S. Dist. LEXIS 78227 (W.D. Tex. Oct. 19, 2007), 567 n.33
Todd v. Comm'r, 118 T.C. 354 (2002), 315 n.146
Tortorich v. Tortorich, 902 S.W.2d 247 (Ark. App. 1995), 158
Towerview LLC v. Cox Radio, Inc., 2013 Del. Ch. LEXIS 159 (Del. Ch. June 28, 2013), 393
Traczyk v. Traczyk, 891 P.2d 1277 (Okla. 1995), 160
Tri-Continental Corp. v. Battye, 74 A.2d 71 (Del. 1950), 377 n.11
Trugreen Cos., LLC, Inc. v. Scotts Lawn Serv., 508 F. Supp. 2d 937 (N.D. Utah 2007), 563 n.30, 578 n.84
Trustees of the University of Pennsylvania v. Lexington Ins. Co., 815 F.2d 890 (3d Cir. 1987), 569 n.37

U

Uniloc USA, Inc. v. Microsoft Corp., 632 F.3d 1292 (Fed. Cir. 2011), 464 n.12
United States v. 14.38 Acres of Land, More or Less Situated in Leflore County, State of Miss., 80 F.3d 1074 (5th Cir. 1995), 580 n.92
United States v. Batchelor-Robjohns, 2005 U.S. Dist. LEXIS 13552 (S.D. Fla. June 3, 2005), 594–595, 594 n.3, 611 n.45
University Computing v. Lykes Youngstown Corp., 504 F.2d 518 (5th Cir. 1974), 469 n.46
University of Pittsburgh v. Townsend, 2007 U.S. Dist. LEXIS 24620 (E.D. Tenn. 2007), 612 n.51
Univ. of Colo. Found., Inc. v. Am. Cyanamid Co., 342 F.3d 1298 (Fed. Cir. 2003), 468 n.43
U.S. Inspect, Inc. v. McGreevy, 57 Va. Cir. 511 (Va. Cir. 2000), 389 n.66
U.S. Inspect, Inc. v. McGreevy, 2000 Va. Cir. LEXIS 524 (Va. Cir. 2000), 716
Utah Resources Intl., Inc. v. Mark Technologies Corp., 342 P.3d 761 (Utah 2014), 377 n.12, 399 n.98

V

Verition Partners Master Fund Ltd. v. Aruba Networks, Inc., 2018 LEXIS 52 (Del. Ch. Feb. 15, 2018), 394
VGS Corp. v. Commissioner, 68 T.C. 563 (1977), 11 n.22
Vivian v. Vivian, 583 P.2d 1072 (Mont. 1978), 351 n.19

W

Wallace v. Wallace, 733 S.W.2d 102 (Tenn. Ct. App. 1987), 351 n.22
Waller v. American Intl. Distrib. Corp., 706 A.2d 460 (Vt. 1997), 716
Wall v. Bryan, 251 So. 3d 650 (La. App. 2018), 694
Wall v. Commissioner, T.C. Memo. 2001-75, 435 n.9, 436
Walsh v. Bowers, U.S. Dist. LEXIS 177184 (Sept. 17, 2021), 424
Walter v. Duffy, 287 F. 41 (3d Cir. 1923), 294 n.17
Wandry v. Comm'r, T.C. Memo 2012-88, 324–325
Washington v. Washington, 2005 Va. App. LEXIS 177 (Va. App. 2005), 351 n.21
Watson v. Watson, 882 So. 2d 95 (Miss. 2004), 159
Weinberger v. UOP, Inc., 457 A.2d 701 (Del. 1983), 378 n.13, 381 n.22, 384 n.35, 500 n.18
Weinstein v. Weinstein, 2005 Conn. LEXIS 348 (Conn. 2005), 367 n.103
Wenzel v. Hopper & Galliher, P.C., 779 N.E.2d 30 (Ind. App. 2002), 385 n.42
White Tower System v. White Castle System of Eating Houses Corporation, C.C.A. Mich., 90 F.2d 67, 141
Wilson v. Wilson, 741 S.W.2d 640 (Ark. 1987), 351 n.19
Winn v. Winn Enterprises, L.P., 265 S.W.3d 125 (Ark. App. 2007), 684
Wisniewski v. Walsh, 2015 N.J. Super. Unpub. LEXIS 3001 (App. Div. Dec. 24, 2015), 401 n.110
Woolf v. Universal Fidelity Life Ins. Co., 849 P.2d 1093 (Okla. App. 1992), 708

Y

Yoon v. Yoon, 711 N.E.2d 1265 (Ind. 1999), 355 n.44
Young v. Young, 600 So. 2d 1140 (Fla. Dist. Ct. App. 1992), 153 n.8

Z

Zelouf International Corp. v. Zelouf, 45 Misc. 3d 1205(A) (N.Y. Supr. Oct. 6, 2014) and 47 Misc. 3d 346 (N.Y. Supr. Dec. 22, 2014), 400 n.103, 706
Zenith Elecs. Corp. v. WH-TV Broad. Corp., 395 F.3d 416 (7th Cir. 2005), 560 n.18, 575 n.66
Zerbe v. Zerbe, 2005 Ohio 1180 (Ohio Ct. App. 2005), 366 n.100
Zerbey v. Commissioner (*In re* Estate of Richmond), T.C. Memo 2014-26, 305 n.86

Subject Index

A

abandonment loss, 330, 337
Abbott, Ashok, 271
abuse-of-discretion standard, 558
ABV. *See* Accredited in Business Valuation (ABV)
accounting basis adjustments, 204
Accounting Standards Codification (ASC)
  ASC 805 Business Combinations, 133
Accounting Standards Codification Topic 820, *Fair Value Measurement* (ASC 820), 6
Accredited in Business Valuation (ABV), 563, 642
Accredited Senior Appraiser (ASA), 642
accrual basis accounting, 43–44
acquisition premiums, 253, 257–259, 663
adequate consideration, 5, 14
adequate disclosure, 298
adequate knowledge, 294, 298
adjusted book value, 663
adjusted book value method, 129, 663
adjusted book value of invested capital, 109–110
adjusted net asset value method, 27, 129, 131, 664
adjusted present value (APV), 664
admissibility
  of original and personally developed appraisal methods, 579–580
  reliability and, 577–578
  source documents and, 572–574
  of subjective statements, 574–575
  of superficial work, 575–577
  weight accorded and, 580–582
adversarial proceedings, 598–599
Aguilar, Isaiah, 425
AICPA. *See* American Institute of Certified Public Accountants (AICPA)
AICPA Statement on Standards for Valuation Services VS Section 100 (SSVS No. 1), 478 n.82, 560
Alabama
  discovery rules in, 586
  fair value in, 684–685
  market exception in, 722
Alaska
  discovery rules in, 586
  fair value in, 684–685
  market exception in, 722
Alerding, James, 278, 371
ALFRED. *See* Archival Federal Reserve Economic Data (ALFRED)
alternative dispute resolution (ADR), 638–649
  adjudicative, 640
  arbitration *vs.* litigation in, 640–641
  evaluative, 640
  facilitative, 640
Alternative Dispute Resolution Act of 1988, 639–640
American Arbitration Association, 638
American Bankruptcy Institute, 201
American Institute of Certified Public Accountants (AICPA), 619
American Society of Appraisers (ASA), 559, 619
analytical-based methods, 265, 270
Angell, Joshua B., 278
Angle, Victoria Dalcourt, 638 n.13
Annual Statement Studies & Industry Reports, 236, 247
Appeals and Review Memorandum Number 34 (ARM 34), 137, 142
appraisal, 1–2, 4–5, 8, 13–14
  approaches, 25–30
  defined, 664
  methods, 25–30
  procedures, 25–30
  qualified, 626–627

Appraisal Foundation, The, 2
appraisal organizations, 579, 598, 630
appraisal reports
  calculation report, 541
  comprehensive, 533–541
  detailed report, 533
  as within expertise, 572
  information sources for, 535–536
  normalization and control adjustments in, 537–538
  oral, 541
  qualitative analysis in, 536
  quantitative analysis in, 537
  summary level, 541
  valuation adjustments, 540
  valuation approaches in, 538–539
Appraisal Standards Board (ASB), 622
appraiser. *See also* experts
  challenges, 568–571
  credentials, 543–544
  qualifications, 295–296, 485, 615, 622–624
  qualified, 626–627
  selection, 485–490, 560–569
  standards, 625–626
appraiser certification, 540–541
Appraiser Qualifications Board (AQB), 622–623
appreciated property, 311, 330, 339–340, 364, 371
approach, 25, 29–30
APV. *See* adjusted present value (APV)
AQB. *See* Appraiser Qualifications Board (AQB)
arbitration
  conclusion reporting, 643–644
  litigation *vs.*, 640–641
arbitrator instructions, 642–643
arbitrators, 641
arbitrator selection, 642
Archival Federal Reserve Economic Data (ALFRED), 240
Arizona
  discovery rules in, 586
  fair value in, 684–685
  market exception in, 722
Arkansas
  fair value in, 684–685
  market exception in, 722
Armentrout, Brant H., 71 n.10
arm's length, 26
arm's length negotiations, 122
arm's length standard, 341, 475
arm's length transactions, 298–299
ASA. *See* Accredited Senior Appraiser (ASA); American Society of Appraisers (ASA)
ASB. *See* Appraisal Standards Board (ASB)
Aschwald, Kathryn F., 425
Ashcraft, Arlene L., 405
asset accumulation method, 27, 129–131
asset approach, 302–303
asset-based approach, 26, 28–29, 129, 659, 664
asset build-up method, 129
assets
  capital, 185–186, 194
  identifiable intangible, 184
  income-producing, 21, 108
  intangible, 56, 183–186, 195, 201, 672
  net, 675
  nonoperating, 676
  off-balance-sheet, 50
  tangible, 137–140, 142–146, 680
Assistant Secretary, Tax Policy at the Department of the Treasury, 628
Aucutt, Ronald D., 319 n.165

B

Babitsky, Steven, 583
Baima, Nicholas R., 637 n.2
Bakewell, Christopher, 459
balance sheet, 33, 36–37
balance sheet adjustments, 213
barriers to entry, 187–188
Bartell, Bob, 513
basis in property, 330–331, 332 n.17, 333–335
Baum, Theodore M., 638 n.11
Baumol, William J., 466 n.24
Beaton, Neil, 637
Bebchuk, Lucian Arye, 509 n.25
Bedi, Akanksha, 290
Beige Book, 245
Bellatti, Robert M., 326
Berman, Kenneth R., 662
Bernstein, Ron, 425

beta, 85, 85 n.7, 87–92, 95, 99, 664, 673, 681
bias, lack of, 559
Binns, David M., 425
Bishop, David, 278, 289
BIZCOMPS, 120, 126, 151–152, 155
Blalock, Clarlene M., 181
Bleemer, Russ, 638 n.10
blockage, 309
blockage discount, 5, 7, 664
Bogdanski, John, 346
Bolotsky, Michael J., 264
Bonbright, James C., 2 n.4
Bonner, Paul, 181
book value of invested capital, 96, 109–110, 113, 117, 119, 122, 128
Bordi, Lorena, 71 n.10
Bradford, C. Steven, 638 n.13
breach of contract, 199–200
breakup value, 132
Brinig, Brian Peter, 583
Brown, Grover C., 641 n.28
Browning, Hon. R. Mark, 645 n.40
build-up method, 83, 85–88, 93, 101, 665
built-in capital gains, 252, 312–313, 387
burden of proof, 297–298, 469, 501
Bureau of Economic Analysis *Regional FACT Sheets* (BEARFACTS), 244
Business Brokerage Press, 150
business enterprise, 665
business equity, 665
business interruption insurance claim, 595
Business Reference Guide, 149, 151–153
business risk, 665
business torts, 580
business valuation, defined, 665
business valuation report
  discounts in, 547
  economic analysis in, 545
  excess earnings method in, 552
  financial statement adjustments in, 546
  financial statement analysis in, 546
  goodwill in, 553
  guideline public company method in, 549
  guideline transaction method in, 550–551
  income approach in, 548
  industry analysis in, 545
  interviews in, 545, 546
  introduction, 544–545
  overall assessment in, 553
  past transaction method in, 551
  premiums in, 547
  preparer credentials for, 543–544
  reasonable compensation in, 546–547
  rules of thumb in, 552
  site visits in, 545
  valuation methods in, 547–548
Business Valuation Resources, 243, 371
buy-sell agreements, 27, 124, 319–321, 596
  cross-purchase agreements, 481–482
  drafting, 483–485
  entity purchase agreements, 481
  fixed price, 482
  formula pricing with, 482
  funding and payment mechanisms with, 487–490
  hybrid agreements, 482
  multiple appraisers with, 486–487
  shotgun agreements, 482–483
  single-appraiser process with, 485–486
  tag-along rights, 482
  triggering events with, 481–483, 490
  types of, 481–482
  types of valuation provisions with, 482–483
BVLaw™, 279
BVUpdate™, 279

C

California
  discovery rules in, 586
  fair value in, 686–687
  market exception in, 722
California Corporations Code § 2000, 6, 16
capacity utilization, 240
capital asset pricing model (CAPM), 83, 85, 87, 89–93, 95, 101, 665
capital expenditures, 43
capitalization, 666
capitalization factor, 666
capitalization rate, 26–28, 30, 40, 61–65, 72, 74, 76, 81, 92–93, 100–101, 115, 138–146, 666
capitalizing, 26
capital market theory, 665–666
capital structure, 36, 666
CAPM. *See* capital asset pricing model (CAPM)

CARES Act. *See* Coronavirus Aid, Relief, and Economic Security Act (CARES Act)
Carls, Regina, 425
Carney, William J., 402
Carstens, Philip J., 425
Case, John, 425
case assembly file, 634
cash basis accounting, 43–44
cash-equivalent values, 151–152
cash flow, 39, 59–60, 666
cash flow analysis, 666
cash to accrual basis adjustments, 204
CBI. *See* Certified Business Intermediary (CBI)
CBV Institute, 619
Certified Business Intermediary (CBI), 566, 620–621
Certified Public Accountants (CPAs), 560
Certified Valuation Analyst (CVA), 563
CFA. *See* Chartered Financial Analyst (CFA)
CFA Institute, 620
changes in debt, 43
changes in net working capital, 43
charitable contributions, 283, 314–315, 627–629
Chartered Financial Analyst (CFA), 563, 642
Chernoff, Joel, 425
Chicago Fed Letter, 245
Chincarini, Ludwig B., 102
Church, Jeffrey, 467 n.37
Clarke, David G., 373
closed-end funds, 260–261, 308–309
Clough, Barbara M., 425
coefficient of variation, 667
Colorado
  discovery rules in, 587
  fair value in, 686–687
  market exception in, 722
Commissioner of the IRS, 628
common equity, 34, 36
common-size balance sheets, 217
common-size income statements, 217, 667
common-size statements, 667
company information
  company documents in, 47
  company-specific, 45–46
  external, 46
  financial statements in, 46–49
  gathering of, 45–56
  income tax returns in, 49
  operating information in, 51
  owners' rights and, 51–52
company-specific risk, 83, 85–87, 91–92
company-specific risk premium, 667
comparable company method, 26
comparative analysis, 41, 115–116
  horizontal analysis in, 217–219
  industry data resources in, 236–237
  liquidity analysis in, 233–235
  profitability analysis in, 227–233
  tools, 216–217
comparative financial statement analysis, 656
compounding, 62, 175
condition subsequent, 324
confidentiality, 598
conflicts of interest, 561, 566
Connecticut
  discovery rules in, 587
  fair value in, 686–687
  market exception in, 722
consistent, 30
consulting expert, 560, 616
Consumer Price Index (CPI), 240–241
contingent fee experts, 581
contingent liabilities, 315
contingent payments, 152
control
  defined, 667
  degrees of, 255–256
  lack of, 255–256
  majority, 673
  premium for, 252–253
  voting, 681
control adjustments, 106, 204, 209
controlling interests, 98, 104–106, 255–257, 291, 307
control premium, 251–254, 258–259, 558, 660, 667
conversion from cash to accrual basis, 44
copyright, 470–471
Cornell, Bradford, 71 n.9
Coronavirus Aid, Relief, and Economic Security Act (CARES Act), 332
correct amount, 633–634
cost approach, 175, 667

cost of capital, 60, 81, 667
Cost of Capital Navigator, 73
Cost of Capital Professional, 85 n.10
Cotter, Thomas F., 466 n.29
CountryData Online, 245
covariance, 88
covenant not to compete, 150–152, 162, 183, 188–189, 362
Covrig, Vicentiu, 290
Cox, James D., 313 n.140
CPAs. *See* Certified Public Accountants (CPAs)
CPI. *See* Consumer Price Index (CPI)
credentials, 620, 623, 650
credibility, expert, 561–562, 567
cross-examination, 572, 580–582, 595, 611, 650
cross-examination questions, 650–651
Crow, Matthew R., 125
CRSP Deciles Size Study, 85–86, 90
cumulative voting, 256, 276
current ratio, 234–235, 247–248
CVA. *See* Certified Valuation Analyst (CVA)

D

Darrah, William C., 645 n.39
Daubert challenges, 560, 562
Daubert factors, 556–558
Daubert standards, 556 n.3, 580
DCF. *See* discounted cash flow (DCF)
DealStats, 126, 151
debt free, 96, 100
debt-free cash flow (DFCF), 40, 109
debt-free net income (DFNI), 40, 109
debt-to-equity ratio, 233, 235, 247
defined value formula clauses, 324–325
definitions of value, 1–2, 10, 13–16
De Franco, Gus, 264
degrees of control, 255–256
Delaware
  discovery rules in, 587
  fair value in, 688–689
  market exception in, 723
Department of Labor (DOL), 14
depositions, 603, 605, 614–616, 649, 661
deposition testimony, 569, 581, 607–608, 617, 661
depreciation adjustments, 212–214
desirability, 188–189, 197
Desmond, Glenn, 150, 154
DFCF. *See* debt-free cash flow (DFCF)
DFNI. *See* debt-free net income (DFNI)
Diana, James C., 647
DiMattia, Ronald D., 274
direct equity procedure, 29, 119
direct examination, 650
direct examination questions, 650
direct procedure, 257, 261
disclosure, timely, 608–611
disclosure requirements, 594
discontinued operations, 204
discounted cash flow (DCF), 60, 189
discounted cash flow analysis, 573, 575–576
discounted cash flow method, 430, 435, 577, 668
discounted economic income method, 668
discount for lack of control (DLOC), 251–252, 254, 257–270, 272–274, 277, 302, 308–311, 326, 363, 364, 376, 384, 396–401, 412, 668
discount for lack of liquidity, 668
discount for lack of marketability (DLOM), 251, 254, 263–266, 268–277, 303, 363, 376, 386, 397, 400, 668
discount for lack of voting rights, 668
discounting, 26, 78–79
discount rate, 60, 81–82, 191, 194–196, 199, 668
discovery
  attorney's role in, 597
  confidentiality and, 598
  depositions, 603, 605, 649, 661
  devices, 585
  draft reports in, 612
  email in, 612–613
  experts and, 585–618
  gathering information for, 597
  limitations on, 599–600
  limitations on number of interrogatories in, 604
  privilege and, 611
  rules, 586
  scope of, 599–600
discrete period, 67, 69–72, 75
discretion, 558
discretionary earnings, 39, 108, 120, 126, 150

discretionary expenses, 205–206
dissenting shareholder cases, 571, 600
dissolution statutes, 6, 14
distribution schedule, 50
District of Columbia
  discovery rules in, 587
  fair value in, 688–689
  market exception in, 723
dividend schedule, 50
divorce, personal *vs.* enterprise goodwill in, 158–162
DLOC. *See* discount for lack of control (DLOC)
DLOM. *See* discount for lack of marketability (DLOM)
document request, 596–601
Donovan, Nadine Nasser, 583
double dipping, 176, 179
double taxation, 177
DuCanto, Joseph N., 598 n.8

E

earnings before interest, income taxes, depreciation, amortization, and rent (EBITDAR), 447
earnings before interest, income taxes, depreciation, and amortization (EBITDA), 28, 38–39, 72–73, 109, 113, 119, 121, 150–151, 172, 579
earnings before interest and taxes (EBIT), 39, 109, 113, 119, 121, 172
EBIT. *See* earnings before interest and taxes (EBIT)
EBITDA. *See* earnings before interest, income taxes, depreciation, and amortization (EBITDA)
EBITDAR. *See* earnings before interest, income taxes, depreciation, amortization, and rent (EBITDAR)
economically real, 186
economic considerations, 168
Economic Global Updates, 245
economic income
  capitalizing, 60–61
  defined, 59, 668
  discounting, 61
  in financial statements, 38–42
Economic Indicators, 243
economic information, 654–655
economic life, 668
economic obsolescence, 669
Economic Outlook Update, 243
Economic Report of the President, 243
economic returns, 184, 189, 195
economic unit, 60
economy, national, 240–244
EDGAR. *See* Electronic Data Gathering and Retrieval (EDGAR)
electronically stored information (ESI), 599, 601–603, 614
Electronic Data Gathering and Retrieval (EDGAR), 107, 127
Ellis, J., 102
El-Tahch, Aziz, 425
email, in discovery, 612–613
Employee Stock Ownership Plan (ESOP), 14, 52, 176, 669
Employee Stock Ownership Plan (ESOP) valuation
  adequate consideration and, 406–407, 409, 412, 417–418, 424–425
  benefit plan and, 405–406, 409, 413
  breach of duty and, 419
  capital gains and, 409
  client concentration and, 421
  compensation and, 419–420
  controlling interest and, 416, 423
  damages calculation with, 422
  Department of Labor and, 406–407, 409–411, 424–425
  discounts for lack of control and, 412
  documentation and, 421
  due diligence and, 417
  employee ownership and, 405, 409
  Employment Retirement Income Security Act of 1974 (ERISA), 405–406, 409–411, 413, 415, 421, 424
  Employment Retirement Income Security Act of 1974 (ERISA) compliance and, 415–416
  ESOP financial statement adjustments and, 413–414
  ESOP Put Right and, 415
  ESOP transactions and, 406–411, 414–424
  ESOP trustee and, 406, 409–410
  failure to monitor and, 421

fiduciary and, 406, 409–411, 413, 415–425
fiduciary duty and, 420
fiduciary liability and, 419
fiduciary obligations and, 409–410, 424
fiduciary process agreements and, 410–411
fiduciary review and, 410–411
independence of appraiser and, 411
lack of control and, 411–412, 422
lack of marketability discount and, 414
leveraged ESOP transactions and, 407–408
National Center for Employee Ownership and, 408
negotiation and, 418–419
non-ESOP investors and, 418
plan sponsor and, 410
post-transaction drop and, 424
prior valuation and, 422
prohibited transactions and, 417
projections and, 421
prudence and, 419
redemption and, 415
repurchase liability and, 415
repurchase obligation and, 415
risk factors and, 421
share recycling and, 415
stock appreciation rights and, 422
stock purchase transactions and, 406–409, 423
subsequent events and, 416
tax benefits and, 409, 413
Tax Relief Act of 1997 and, 409
transaction process and, 422
unleveraged ESOP transactions and, 407–408
valuation issues with ESOP stock, 411–415
valuation process and, 421
warrants and, 424
Employee Stock Ownership Plan (ESOP) valuation control premiums and, 412–413
employment agreement, 151–152, 163, 177, 183, 198–201
employment contracts, 163
Employment Retirement Income Security Act (ERISA), 13–14
Encyclopedia of Associations, 246
enforceability, 183–184, 187, 201
Engineering Program, 628, 631
Engineering Valuation Penalty Coordinator Manager (EVPCM), 628
enterprise value, 11–12, 22–23, 108, 167, 175–176, 669
entity-specific, 7
equity
common, 34, 36
defined, 669
incentives in LLCs, 178–179
invested capital *vs.*, 28–29
equity basis, 656–657
equity multiples, 109–110, 117, 119, 122–123
equity net cash flows, 669
equity risk premium (ERP), 84, 84 n.4, 85, 87, 92, 669
ERI Executive Compensation Assessor, 171
ERISA. *See* Employment Retirement Income Security Act (ERISA)
ERP. *See* equity risk premium (ERP)
ESI. *See* electronically stored information (ESI)
Everett, Craig R., 95 n.16, 102
evidentiary reliability, 559
EVPCM. *See* Engineering Valuation Penalty Coordinator Manager (EVPCM)
excess earnings, 669
excess earnings method, 27, 29, 552, 670
applying, 138–141
background of, 137–138
common errors with, 144–146
validity with, 141–144
exit price, 6
expected return, 60, 65, 69, 81
expert disclosure, 560
expert disqualification, 560
expert qualifications, 560
experts
adjusted net asset value and, 659
asset-based approach and, 659
in asset valuation, 132–135
capitalized cash flow and, 657
capital structure and, 654
common errors in examination of, 660–661
company information in examination of, 655
comparative financial statement analysis and, 656

experts, *continued*
consulting, 560, 616
control premium and, 660
court gatekeeper role with, 556–560
credentials of, 650
disclosure requirements with, 594
discounted cash flow and, 657
discount rate and, 657–658
discounts and, 660
discovery and, 585–618
educational background of, 652
equity basis and, 656–657
excess earnings and, 659
exclusion of, 574, 577–578
financial statement adjustments and, 655
growth rate and, 657
guideline companies and, 658
income approach and, 657
independence of, 500, 559
lack of control discount and, 660
level of value and, 657
marketability discounts and, 660
market approach and, 658–659
market multiples and, 658
net cash flow forecast and, 657
opinion within expertise of, 571–572
overall valuation methodology and, 656–657
premiums and, 660
qualifications of, 652–653
reconciliation of value indications and, 660
reliability of, 577–578
selection of, 560–568
source documents used by, 572–574
subjective statements by, 574–575
terminal value and, 658
testifying, 605, 611, 616
weight accorded to, 580–582
work papers of, 602–603
external obsolescence, 670

F

FactSet Mergerstat/BVR Control Premium Study, 126, 279
fair market value, 2–8, 10, 12–13, 16, 122, 483, 571, 623, 670
fairness
business judgment and, 494, 497–503
conflicts and, 506
contribution analysis and, 507
corporate law relevant to, 494–495
Delaware Chancery Court and, 494
disclosure and, 505
duty of care and, 495–496
duty of loyalty and, 495–496
entire, 500–502
fair dealing and, 501
fair price and, 501–502
fiduciary and, 503, 515
fiduciary duty and, 497–498
Financial Industry Regulatory Authority (FINRA) and, 505
FINRA Rule 5150 and, 505
going private and, 500
good faith and, 496–497
has-gets analysis and, 507
insolvency and, 497–498
leveraged buyout analysis and, 507
opinions, 502–506
Rule 13e-3 and, 500
Securities Act and, 494
Securities and Exchange Act and, 494
solvency and, 497–498
SPAC, 493
fairness opinion, 494–495, 565, 670
fair value, 571
absolute fairness and, 378–379
appraisal arbitrage and, 390–395
breach of fiduciary duty and, 373, 381, 388
competence and thoroughness with, 379
deadlock and, 374, 382, 396–397
defined, 373
Delaware Block Method, 377
Dell compliance and, 391–392
dissenters' appraisal rights, 288, 373–377, 390
dissenters' rights, 373, 382, 386, 389, 401–402
dissenting stockholder actions and, 373–375, 377, 384, 389, 392, 399
dissenting stockholder statutes and, 373, 401

fair consideration and, 378–379
for financial reporting, 6–8
going concern basis and, 386
independence and, 379
judicial dissolution statutes and, 382, 390
minority oppression actions and, 382, 401
oppression actions and, 373, 395–396
procedural fairness and, 379–381
relative fairness and, 379
Revised Model Business Corporation Act (RMBCA), 374–376, 378, 396, 398
Special Committee and, 379
under state statutes, 5–6, 684–719
Weinberger v. UOP and, 377–378
family limited partnership (FLP), 451
Fannon, Nancy J., 442, 532
FASB. *See* Financial Accounting Standards Board (FASB)
feasibility, 188–189
Feder, Robert T., 147, 154, 278
Federal Arbitration Act of 1925, 638
Federal Mediation and Conciliation Service, 638
Federal Reserve Archival System for Economic Research (FRASER), 240
Federal Reserve Bank, 240, 243, 245
Federal Reserve Board Index of Industrial Production, 240
Federal Reserve Economic Data (FRED), 240
Federal Rule of Civil Procedure 26(a)(2), 594–596
Federal Rule of Civil Procedure 34, 599
Federal Rule of Evidence 702, 556
Federal Trade Commission (FTC), 185
Fee, E.C., 102
Feld, Daniel E., 326
FFO. *See* funds from operations (FFO)
FIFO. *See* first-in, first-out (FIFO)
50 percent interests, 306–307
Financial Accounting Standards Board (FASB), 6–8
financial reporting valuation, 335
financial risk, 670
financial statement income, 332
financial statements
audited, 48
basic, 33–35
in business valuation report, 546
comparative analysis of, 215–237
compiled, 48
economic income in, 38–42
expense concepts in, 37–38
information from, 46
interim, 34
levels of preparation of, 35
normalized, 676
reasons for adjustments with, 203–204
reviewed, 48
Fiore, Nicholas, 647
first-in, first-out (FIFO), 206–207, 211–213
First Research, 246
First Research—Dunn & Bradstreet, 171
Fishman, Jay E., 17, 23, 31, 58, 79, 101, 125, 135, 147, 157, 214, 237, 250, 278, 289, 347, 371, 402, 432, 533, 619, 624, 636, 663
five-factor test, 169
Flemming, Bryan, 425
Florida
discovery rules in, 587
fair value in, 690–691
market exception in, 723
Florida Statutes § 607.1340, 6
FLP. *See* family limited partnership (FLP)
forced liquidation value, 671
Ford, David J., 647
forecast, 71, 73–74, 78
formula approach, 142–143, 145–146
Fowler, Bradley A., 125
Fox, Christina, 638 n.15
FRASER. *See* Federal Reserve Archival System for Economic Research (FRASER)
Frazier, William H., 251, 272, 277
FRED. *See* Federal Reserve Economic Data (FRED)
free and clear, 456
FTC. *See* Federal Trade Commission (FTC)
functional obsolescence, 671
fundamental analysis, 9
fundamental discount, 117
fundamental value, 1, 3, 9–10
funds from operations (FFO), 450
future capital expenditures, 50–51
future projections, 564, 655

G

GAAP. *See* Generally Accepted Accounting Principles (GAAP)
Garner, Brian A., 1 n.1
gatekeeper role, of courts, 556–560
GDP. *See* gross domestic product (GDP)
Generally Accepted Accounting Principles (GAAP), 43–44, 48, 130
Georgia
  discovery rules in, 587
  fair value in, 690–691
  market exception in, 723
Georgia-Pacific factors, 462–463
Gerger, Richard, 71 n.9
Gilbert, Ronald J., 425
Global Economic Prospects, 245
Goeldner, Richard W., II, 116 n.5, 125
Gohn, Sandra P., 648
going concern, 447–448, 671
going-concern premise, 27
going-concern value, 11, 19, 130, 671
Goldberg, Barth, 371
Golumbic, Lars, 425
goodwill, 56, 671
  in business valuation report, 553
  enterprise, 158–163, 175, 186, 197–198
  income tax and, 164
  personal, 152, 158–163, 175, 198
goodwill value, 671
Gordon, Myron, 65 n.5
Gordon, Noah J., 402
Gordon Growth Model, 65, 68, 77–78
Gordy, Vaughn, 425
Grabowski, Roger J., 1, 19, 25, 59, 79, 81, 101, 129, 137, 147, 281, 329, 433, 443, 445
Greer, Willis R., Jr., 79
Gregory, Michael A., 625, 632 n.21
gross cash flow, 39
gross domestic product (GDP), 71, 75, 240–244, 246–247
gross profit, 190, 192–195
growth rate, 63–65, 69, 71–72, 75–76, 92–93, 99–101
Guam, discovery rules in, 587
guideline companies
  criteria for selecting, 110–111
  developing multiples, 112–113
  number of, 111
Guideline Public Company Comps Tool, 127
guideline public company method, 26, 31, 105, 110, 124–125, 549–550, 671
guideline transaction method, 26, 550–551, 671

H

Hamermesh, Lawrence A., 402
Hann, Rebecca N., 102
Harms, Travis W., 279, 291
Harry, Everett P., 532
Hawaii
  discovery rules in, 588
  fair value in, 690–691
  market exception in, 723
Hazen, Thomas Lee, 313 n.140
Hector, Brian D., 425
Heidt, Paul, 203, 215
Henderson, Douglas A., 639 n.16
Hensler, Deborah R., 637 n.4
Herman, Gregg, 154
highest and best use, 4–5, 210, 293
Hirschfeld, Christopher, 425
history, company, 51
Hitchner, James R., 79, 101, 125, 136, 147, 164, 237, 278, 326, 432, 443, 542, 624
Ho, James K., 645 n.40
Hollis, Erin, 167
horizon risk, 84
horizontal analysis, 217–219
Hovenkamp, Erik, 466 n.29
Hricko, Matthew, 425
hurdle rate, 60, 81
hybrid premise, 27
hypothetical seller and buyer, 293, 293 n.7, 294–295, 299, 313, 317–318, 331

I

IBA. *See* Institute of Business Appraisers (IBA)
Ibbotson, Roger, 102
IBISWorld, 171–172, 246–247
Idaho
  discovery rules in, 588
  fair value in, 692–693
  market exception in, 724

identifiable event, 337–338
identifiable intangibles, 134, 162, 184
Illinois
discovery rules in, 588
fair value in, 692–693
market exception in, 724
illiquidity, 251, 263, 272–273, 303, 400
income approach, 26, 28–29, 59–79, 170, 548, 657, 672
income statement, 33
income statement adjustments, 212, 214, 413
Independent Investor Test, 169–170
Indiana
discovery rules in, 588
fair value in, 692–693
market exception in, 724
indirect procedure, 257
Industry Comparison Approach, 170
industry data, 245–249
industry expertise, 563
Industry Growth Outlook Report, 246
industry information, 654–655
Industry Key Statistics, 247
Industry Profiles, 246
Industry Reports, 246
industry risk premium, 83, 85–86
industry specialists, 569
industry trade associations, 563
inflation, 240–242, 246–247
Inflation Reduction Act of 2022, 332
information sources, 654–655
injunctive relief, 474
insider transaction adjustments, 209
inspection of premises, 601–603
Institute of Business Appraisers (IBA), 555 n.1, 559, 621, 653
intangible property, 475–476
Integra Information Industry Reports, 236, 240, 246–248
intellectual property
arm's length standard and, 475
copyright infringement and, 470–471
defined, 672
financial reporting and, 477–478
income tax considerations, 475–477
injunctive relief with, 474
as intangible property, 475–476
licensing valuation and, 478–479
patent infringement and, 460–468
rights of publicity and, 471–474
trade dress infringement and, 469–470
trademark infringement and, 469–470
trade secret misappropriation and, 468–469
transfer pricing and, 475–477
valuation of legally protected, in litigation, 459–460
intercompany transfer pricing, 340–345
interest coverage ratio, 235
interest rate risk, 84
internal rate of return, 672
Internal Revenue Code (I.R.C.), 13. *See also entries at* I.R.C.
Internal Revenue Service (IRS), 13, 15–16, 239, 626
International Business Brokers Association (IBBA), 620
International Valuation Glossary—Business Valuation (Glossary), 1, 3, 8–12
interrogatories, 614–616
interviews, in discovery, 596–597
intrinsic value, 3, 9–10
inventory adjustments, 206–207, 212–213
invested capital, 25, 28–29, 36, 672
invested capital basis, 539, 657
invested capital multiples, 108–109, 112, 117, 119, 121
invested capital net cash flows, 672
invested capital procedure, 25, 29, 31, 105, 117, 119
investment banker, 496, 565–566
investment value, 1, 3, 8–9, 12, 673
Iowa
discovery rules in, 588
fair value in, 694–695, 697
market exception in, 724
IRB 2006-36, Announcement 2006-61, 646
I.R.C. § 1.170A, 626–627
I.R.C. § 61, 516
I.R.C. § 103, 433 n.3
I.R.C. § 108, 516–517
I.R.C. § 165, 335 n.24, 336–337
I.R.C. § 170, 626
I.R.C. § 197, 134
I.R.C. § 311, 339
I.R.C. § 367, 343 n.44, 476 n.76

I.R.C. § 409, 414 n.26
I.R.C. § 409A, 334, 391
I.R.C. § 482, 134, 340
I.R.C. § 754, 313
I.R.C. § 1001, 332
I.R.C. § 1012, 332 n.17
I.R.C. § 1016, 333 n.19
I.R.C. § 1031, 333 n.17
I.R.C. § 1033, 312
I.R.C. § 1042, 409
I.R.C. § 1255, 336
I.R.C. § 2031, 13, 264 n.29
I.R.C. § 2053, 315 n.150
I.R.C. § 2512, 13
I.R.C. § 2703, 305 n.84, 319 n.164, 320, 491
I.R.C. § 6501, 298 n.35
I.R.C. § 6695, 629–631
I.R.C. § 6695A, 626, 631–636
I.R.C. § 6700, 626
I.R.C. § 6701, 314, 630
I.R.C. § 7491, 297 n.31, 298
I.R.C. § 7803, 630
IRS Business Valuation Guidelines, 623
IRS Office of Appeals, 646
IRS Penalty Handbook 20.1.12, 629–630
IRS Valuation Guide for Income, Estate and Gift Taxes, 262
Iwanyshyn, Deborah, 647

J

Jefferies, Spencer J., 450
Jenkins, Elizabeth A., 644 n.33
Johnson, Bruce A., 17, 23, 31, 58, 79, 101, 125, 135, 147, 237, 250, 251, 445, 458, 663
Johnson, William B., 402
Johnson/Park Empirical Method, 270–272, 303, 306 n.93
Judd, Joshua, 102
junk science, 557–558

K

Kaczmarek, Dan, 425
Kahan, Marcel, 509 n.25
Kansas
  discovery rules in, 588
  fair value in, 694–695, 697
  market exception in, 724
Kasper, Larry J., 326, 346, 443
Kaufman, Steve, 647
Keene, Matthew G., 425
Kentucky
  discovery rules in, 588
  fair value in, 694–695, 697
  market exception in, 724
Kessler, Joan F., 645 n.36, 647
key person, 163, 175, 181, 183–189, 191–194, 197, 201, 252, 275, 277, 309–310, 361, 401
key person discount, 309–310, 673
Kim, Daehwan, 102
Kinrich, Jeffrey H., 532
Klinefelter, Stanard T., 648
Klitgaard, Thomas J., 639 n.16
know-how, 163, 184, 200–201
Koritzinsky, Allen R., 647
Kosonen, Jill, 459
Krafka, Carol, 557
Kramer, Chris, 425
Kratchman, D. Michael, 648
Kroll LLC, 508 n.24
Kuhne, Cecil C., 618
Kumho criteria, 575

L

lack of bias, 559
lack of control, 255–256
lack of control discount, 20, 104, 660
lack of marketability adjustment, 104
Lanham Act, 469
Large Business and International (LB&I), 630, 633
Laro, Hon. David, 58, 79, 125, 136, 165, 209, 214, 237, 250, 278, 289–291, 293, 322, 356, 443, 542, 636
last-in, first-out (LIFO), 211–213
latest 12 months (LTM), 48–49
LB&I. *See* Large Business and International (LB&I)
LEAPS. *See* Long-term Equity Anticipation Securities (LEAPS)
leased fee interest, 457
Lee, Brian, 71 n.10
Lee, M. Mark, 71 n.10
Lee, Timothy R., 425, 543
Leonard, G.K., 463 n.8
Letter 4477, 628–629

letter stock, 673
levels of operating performance, 215
levered beta, 673
liabilities, off-balance sheet, 50
life insurance, key person, 51
LIFO. *See* last-in, first-out (LIFO)
limited liability companies (LLCs), 178–179, 332
limited partnership (LP), 445, 452–454
Linebarger, Kimberly, 239
liquidation premise, 27
liquidation value, 673
liquidity, 19, 23, 673
liquidity analysis, 233–235
liquidity measures, 217
LiquiStat™ Database, 279
litigation experience, 562
Litkovitz, Amy L., 638 n.14
Livingston Survey, 243
locational obsolescence, 673
Long-term Equity Anticipation Securities (LEAPS), 271
Lorie, James H., 10 n.20
lost business value, 519, 525–531, 570
lost profits, 563, 570
  cash flow and, 528
  damage calculation with, 520–525
  damage recovery and, 519–520
  damages expert and, 531–532
  discount rate and, 529, 531
  ex ante calculations with, 521–522, 529
  ex post calculations and, 521–523, 529
  foreseeability and, 520
  income tax and, 528–529, 531
  lost business value and, 519, 525-531
  mitigation and, 521
  period of damages and, 521
  present value and, 529, 531
  proximate cause and, 519–520
  reasonable certainty and, 520
  time value of money and, 521
Louisiana
  discovery rules in, 589
  fair value in, 694–695, 697
  market exception in, 724
LP. *See* limited partnership (LP)
LTM. *See* latest 12 months (LTM)
Ludwig, Ronald L., 425

M

Maine
  discovery rules in, 589
  fair value in, 698–699
  market exception in, 725
majority control, 673
majority interest, 674
management interviews, 53–54
Mangraviti, James J., Jr., 583
Many Hats Approach, 175
Marino, Renee, 632 n.21
marital asset, 135, 137, 162 n.4, 164, 198
marital dissolution, 6, 9, 13–14, 120, 124, 135, 137, 157, 161, 197–198, 644–645
  active appreciation and, 350, 350 n.17
  appreciation and, 350
  buy-sell agreements and, 358–361
  capital gains and, 364–366
  community property and, 355, 358, 360
  covenants not to compete and, 362
  date of separation and, 351
  double-dipping and, 368–370
  enterprise goodwill and, 355–357
  equitable distribution and, 355, 357, 361, 368–369
  excess earnings and, 356, 360, 368
  goodwill and, 348–349, 352–358
  key person and, 361
  multi-attribute utility model and, 356
  passive depreciation and, 350
  personal goodwill and, 349, 352, 354–357, 359, 368
  post-marital efforts and, 350, 358, 362
  professional goodwill and, 352–354, 355 n.43, 357–358
  separate property and, 350, 360, 362 n.74
  standard of value for, 348–349
  tax consequences and, 365–366
  transferable goodwill and, 349
  trapped-in capital gains and, 364–366
  value to holder and, 348–349
marketability, 674
marketability discounts, 534, 558, 660
market approach, 26, 28–29, 170–171, 658–659, 674
  concept and overview, 103–106
  data sources, 106–107
market capitalization of equity, 674

market capitalization of invested capital, 674
marketing materials, 51
market multiples, 103, 105, 107–110, 115, 124, 674
market participant, 6–8
market risk, 85, 87, 91
market value, 1–5, 8–10, 12–13, 15–16
Maryland
  discovery rules in, 589
  fair value in, 698–699
  market exception in, 725
Massachusetts
  discovery rules in, 589
  fair value in, 698–699
  market exception in, 725
Matthews, Gilbert E., 125, 402, 403
MCAPM. *See* modified capital asset pricing model (MCAPM)
McCarthy, J. Thomas, 472 n.65
McConaughy, Dan, 71 n.10
McDermott Will & Emory, 437 n.12
McInerney, William R., 373, 443
McManus, Michael, 638 n.5
McRoberts, Franklin C., 403
mediators, 641
Mercer, Christopher Z., 17, 481, 491
merger and acquisition method, 674
Mergerstat Review, 279
Merten, William, 425
method, 25, 29–30
Michigan
  discovery rules in, 589
  fair value in, 698–699
  market exception in, 725
midyear discounting, 674
midyear discounting convention, 74, 76, 78–79
Miller, Benjamin D., 371
Miller, Matthew L., 402
Miller, Merton H., 433 n.2
Miller, Mitchell, 425
Miller, Sandra K., 403
Miller, Scott R., 181
Minnesota
  discovery rules in, 589
  fair value in, 700–701
  market exception in, 726
minority discount, 674
minority interest, 674
Minority Interest Discount Database, 279
Mississippi
  discovery rules in, 589
  fair value in, 700–701
  market exception in, 726
Missouri
  discovery rules in, 589
  fair value in, 700–701
  market exception in, 726
mock trial, 640
Model Business Corporation Act, 5–6, 13
Model Family Law Arbitration Act, 645
modified capital asset pricing model (MCAPM), 83, 85, 87, 89–93, 95, 101
Moneta, Fabio, 102
Montana
  discovery rules in, 589
  fair value in, 702–703
  market exception in, 726
Montgomery, Ryan, 291
Mor-Flo approach, 467
Morones, Serena, 203, 214, 215
Morris, Katherine E., 278
Morrison, Robert B., 183
Morrison, William J., 17, 31, 79, 125, 147, 326, 402, 663
mortgage REIT (MREIT), 449
MREIT. *See* mortgage REIT (MREIT)
Multifactor Test, 169
multiple, 675
multiple regression model, 581
multiples of gross profit, 153
multiples of revenue, 151
Murphy, Jennifer, 214
Mussman, William E. III, 639 n.16

N

NACVA. *See* National Association of Certified Valuators and Analysts (NACVA)
Nagaraj, Shiela, 638 n.15
NAICS. *See* North American Industry Classification System (NAICS)
Nath, Eric W., 125
National Association of Certified Valuators and Analysts (NACVA), 619
National Economic Trends, 243

national economy, 240–244
NAV. *See* net asset value (NAV)
Nebraska
discovery rules in, 590
fair value in, 702–703
market exception in, 726
Nelson, Philip B., 466 n.25
net asset value (NAV), 450, 675
net asset value method, 129
net book value, 675
net cash flow, 59–60, 63–64, 68, 72–73, 190–192, 194, 196, 675
net cash flow forecast, 657
net cash flow to equity, 42
net cash flow to invested capital, 41–42
net income, 41, 675
net operating income (NOI), 446
net operating losses carried forward, 207
net operating profit, 40, 60, 192–193
net present value, 675
net tangible asset value, 675
net working capital, 37, 675
Nevada
discovery rules in, 590
fair value in, 702–703
market exception in, 726
New Hampshire
discovery rules in, 590
fair value in, 704–705
market exception in, 726
New Jersey
discovery rules in, 590
fair value in, 704–705
market exception in, 727
New Mexico
discovery rules in, 590
fair value in, 704–705
market exception in, 727
New York
discovery rules in, 590
fair value in, 706–707
market exception in, 727
Niculita, Alina, 33, 45, 103, 149, 281, 427
Nieberding, James F., 467 n.37
Nissenbaum, Gerald, 615 n.58
NOI. *See* net operating income (NOI)
noncash charges, 37–38
noncompete agreements, 52, 183
noncontrolling interest, 19, 22, 98–99, 103–106, 109, 124, 129, 134, 175, 209–210, 212–213, 252, 255–260, 262, 264, 269, 272–274, 276–277, 283, 286, 292, 306, 311, 339, 363, 416
noncontrolling owner, 204, 209, 251–255, 257–258, 263, 274, 283, 286–287, 292, 308, 363, 416
noncontrolling parties, 2, 6, 8, 15
nondepreciable business assets, 336–337
Nonmarketable Investment Company Evaluation Method (NICE), 270, 272–273, 303
nonoperating items, 204, 213
nonrecurring items, 204–205
nonreporting company, 676
nonsolicitation agreements, 183
nonvoting shares, 252, 276–277
nonvoting stock, 310
NOPAT (net operating profit after income taxes), 40
normalization adjustments, 204, 208, 213, 676
normalized earnings, 676
normalized net income, 139, 142
North American Industry Classification System (NAICS), 246, 248–249
North Carolina
discovery rules in, 590
fair value in, 706–707
market exception in, 727
North Dakota
discovery rules in, 591
fair value in, 706–707
market exception in, 727

O

objection to subpoena, 600
OCF. *See* owner's cash flow (OCF)
ODCF. *See* owners' discretionary cash flow (ODCF)
offers to buy, 124
Office of Chief Counsel, 645
Office of Financial Assistance, U.S. Small Business Administration, 448
Office of Professional Responsibility (OPR), 626
Ogneva, Maria, 102

Ohio
discovery rules in, 590
fair value in, 708–710
market exception in, 727
Oklahoma
discovery rules in, 590
fair value in, 708–710
market exception in, 727
operating expenses, 186, 190, 193, 195
operating information, 51
opinion of value, 446, 538, 540–541, 594, 611, 660
opportunity cost of capital, 60, 81
oppression, 256, 274, 348, 374, 376, 382, 395–396, 398–401
OPR. *See* Office of Professional Responsibility (OPR)
option pricing models, 270–271, 273
orderly liquidation value, 676
Oregon
discovery rules in, 590
fair value in, 708–710
market exception in, 728
original appraisal methods, 579–580
overvaluation of 150% or more, 635
owner-employee, 167–170
owner's cash flow (OCF), 150
owners' compensation, 38
owners' discretionary cash flow (ODCF), 39
owners' rights, 51–52
Ozbas, Oguzhan, 102

P

Panduit, 467
Panitz, Philip Garrett, 181
Park, James R., 260 n.18
Partnership Profiles, Inc., 260–261, 272, 279
Parr, Russell L., 464 n.11
Parris, Lucas M., 543
Partnership Profiles Partnership Guideline Reports, 458
pass-through entities, 676
past transaction method, 26, 551
Patent Act of 1790, 637–638
patent damages, 460–461
patent infringement, 460–468
Patterson, Michelle, 402
PCAOB. *See* Public Company Accounting Oversight Board (PCAOB)
PCMR. *See* Private Capital Markets Report (PCMR)
Peercomps, 126
peer review, 556, 560, 569, 571, 576, 577
Penalties Applicable to Incorrect Appraisals, 629–630
penalty case file, 635
Penman, Stephen H., 214
Pennsylvania
discovery rules in, 590
fair value in, 712–713
market exception in, 728
Pension Protection Act (PPA) of 2006, 626, 630
Personal Consumption Deflator, 246
personal expenses, 204–206
personal guarantees, 169
personally developed appraisal methods, 579–580
personnel, key, 51
persons, hypothetical, 3–4
Peters, Jerry O., 125
physical obsolescence, 676
Pia, Kenneth, Jr., 157, 347, 425, 619
Pitchbook, 126–127
portfolio discount, 677
Posner, Richard A., 583
post valuation date events, 611
Pratt, Shannon P., 17, 23, 31, 58, 79, 125, 136, 147, 155, 214, 217, 237, 250, 252, 266, 268–269, 278–279, 290–294, 299, 302, 323, 326, 330–331, 338, 346, 348, 358–359, 366, 371, 373, 376, 382, 397, 402–403, 405, 409, 425, 443, 458, 479, 491, 511, 518, 542, 624, 636, 663
preemptive right, 677
Pre-IPO Studies, 269, 300, 303–305, 307
premium for control, 252–253
premium for risk, 82
premiums, 310–311
pretax income, 40–41
price-to-discretionary earnings, 120, 126
price-to-earnings multiple, 63, 115, 677
price-to-funds from operations (FFO), 450
price-to-net asset value (NAV), 450
price-to-sales multiples, 29, 109, 117, 120
principle of anticipation, 465

principle of comparison, 464
principle of substitution, 463–464
prior transaction method, 122–125, 677
prior transactions, 122–124
Private Capital Markets Report (PCMR), 95, 102
privilege, discovery and, 611
professional competence, 559–560
professional organizations, 619–623
professional practices, 427–432
professional standards, 560, 562, 577, 621–623
profitability ratios, 217
profit margin, 228–230, 233, 247
profits interest, 168, 178
projection, 50, 57, 71, 135
proper value, 634
protective orders, 600, 606, 612
PRS Group, 245
Public Company Accounting Oversight Board (PCAOB), 133
public policy, 185
Puerto Rico, discovery rules in, 590
Pummel, Kent, 17, 23, 58, 79, 101, 125, 135, 147, 214, 237, 289, 663
put option, 677
put-option method, 305

Q

qualitative-based methods, 265
Quantitative Marketability Discount Model (QMDM), 270, 273, 303–304
Quarterly Review, 245
quick ratio, 233–235, 248

R

Radogna, Patrice, 425
RAND terms. *See* reasonable and nondiscriminatory (RAND) terms
range, 677
rate of return, 678
RCN. *See* replacement cost new (RCN)
real estate centered entity (RECE), 447–448
real estate investment trust (REIT), 261, 286
real estate operating companies (REOCs), 451
real property appraisers, 446–449
reasonable and nondiscriminatory (RAND) terms, 465–466
reasonable compensation
- adjustment with, 175, 358
- in business valuation report, 546–547
- common errors with, 179
- in corporations, 176–178
- defining, 167–169
- five-factor test with, 169–170
- Job Aid for, 170–175
- resources on, 179–181
- tax court and, 169–170

Reasonable Compensation Job Aid for IRS Valuation Professionals, 170
rebuttal expert, 594, 611, 617
RECE. *See* real estate centered entity (RECE)
reconciliation of value indications, 660
reconciliation process
- correct appraisal and, 282–284
- divergent results and, 284–285
- major considerations in, 284–285
- overview of, 281–282
- weighting in, 285–289

redirect examination, 651
Regional Review, 245
regression analysis, 306–307
Reilly, Robert F., 181
REIT. *See* real estate investment trust (REIT)
relevance, 555, 568, 600
reliability, 577–578
REOCs. *See* real estate operating companies (REOCs)
replacement compensation, 167, 179
replacement cost method, 678
replacement cost new (RCN), 446, 678
report, defined, 678
report date, 678
reporting, asset-based methods in, 133–134
reproduction cost new, 678
requests for admission, 605
requests for production, 596–601
required rate of return, 678
required return, 60, 81
reserve and allowance account adjustments, 208
restricted stock studies, 265–267, 270, 272, 300, 303
return on assets, 228, 233, 235, 248
return on equity, 232–233, 235, 248, 679
return on invested capital, 679

Revenue Procedure 93-27, 334
Revenue Procedure 2002-44, 646
Revenue Ruling 59-60, 59 n.1, 110, 143-144, 239, 288, 300-302, 322-323, 326, 412, 415-416, 623
Revenue Ruling 69-09, 137, 139 n.1, 142, 144-146
Revenue Ruling 77-403, 188-189
Revenue Ruling 81-253, 15
Revenue Ruling 83-120, 29 n.2
Revenue Ruling 93-12, 15
revenues (sales), 38
Rhode Island
  discovery rules in, 590
  fair value in, 712-713
  market exception in, 728
RICS. *See* Royal Institution of Chartered Surveyors (RICS)
rights of publicity, 471-474
risk
  defined, 60, 679
  as expectation, 215
  financial, 670
  horizon, 84
  interest rate, 84
  investment, 673
  market, 85, 87, 91
  with model and, 189
  premium for, 82
  systematic, 680
  without model and, 194-195
risk-free rate, 82-84, 86-87, 89, 91, 679
Risk Management Association (RMA), 217, 247
risk measures, 217
risk premium, 679
Risk Premium Report—Size Study, 85, 87, 90-92, 94
RMA Annual Statement Studies, 236
Roback, Espen, 470 n.55
Roback, Thomas, Jr., 425
Rodrick, Scott, 425
Rosen, Cory, 425
Rosoff, Charles T., 278, 371
Ross, Franz, 125
Ross, Terence P., 469 n.51
Rowe, Julia, 459
Rowen, Eric, 637
Royal Institution of Chartered Surveyors (RICS), 619
rules of thumb, 27, 29, 552, 679
  checking, against actual transactions, 151-152
  court reaction to, 153-154
  disclaimers, 149
  examples, 151
  general nature of, 150
  as not cash-equivalent prices, 151
Russell, Deirdre, 559 n.14

S

Salek-Rahem, Andrew, 425
sales (net revenues), 38
Salter, Roy, 290
Saltzman, Michael J., 327, 346
sanctions for noncompliance, 600-601
Sanders, Michael V., 4 n.11
SARs. *See* stock appreciation rights (SARs)
SBSE. *See* Small Business Self Employed (SBSE)
Scheinkman, Hon. Alan D. (Ret.), 638 n.12
Schepard, Andrew, 639 n.18
Schlissel, Steven W., 647
Schroeder, Steven F., 559 n.14
Schweihs, Robert P., 201
Scoles, Elise, 373
scope of discovery, 599-600
scope of work, 509, 535, 541
S corporation
  C corporations and, 437-440
  dividend tax and, 441-442
  income approach and, 437-440
  as pass-through entity, 436, 441-442
  Qualified Business Income Deduction and, 439, 442
  specific issues, 442
  tax avoided by, 434-437
  value and taxes, 433-434
SDCF. *See* sellers' discretionary cash flow (SDCF)
SDE. *See* sellers' discretionary earnings (SDE)
Seaman, Ronald M., 271
SEC filings, 106-107, 126
Seigneur, Ronald, 181
seller financing, 151-152

Sellers, Keith, 443
sellers' discretionary cash flow (SDCF), 39, 150
sellers' discretionary earnings (SDE), 39
seller's gain, 185–186, 198
Serfling, Matthew, 102
service businesses, 427–432
    adjusted asset value and, 431
    asset-based methods with, 431
    capitalization of cash flow and, 431
    capitalization of earnings and, 431
    earnouts and, 430
    excess earnings method and, 431
    fair market value and, 427
    income approach and, 430–431
    market approach and, 431
    owner's discretionary earnings and, 431
    rules of thumb and, 431–432
    seller financing and, 431
settlement, 460, 464, 569, 602, 616, 618, 631, 641, 644, 646
settlement pressure, 323
seven-factor test, 169
Shah, Ronak P., 277
Shakih, Sarah, 102
Shapiro, Carl, 465 n.20
shareholder level discount, 251, 273, 348, 364, 400
shareholder oppression action, 564
Sharfman, Keith, 402
Shartsis, Arthur J., 16 n.27, 403
Sheeler, Carl L., 125
Shepherd, Leah, 184
Sheppard, Hale, Esq., 635 n.30
Shishido, Zenichi, 403
SIC. *See* Standard Industrial Classification (SIC)
Siebrasse, Norman, 466 n.29
Silverstein, Brianna, 638 n.5
site visits, 45–46, 52–53, 596–597, 643
size premium, 83, 85–87, 90–92
Skluzak, Paul, 403
Slee, Robert T., 93 n.14
Small Business Self Employed (SBSE), 628
Smiley, Robert W., Jr., 425
Smith, Gordon V., 464 n.11
Solo, David, 102
Solomon, David, 425
Solomon, Steven M. Davidoff, 509 n.27
solvency
    cancellation of debt income and, 516–518
    fiduciary duty and, 515–516
    fraudulent conveyance and, 513–515
    insolvency, 515–516
    opinion, 514–515
    reasonably equivalent value and, 514
Someya, Miki, 638 n.13
Sornette, Didier, 102
South Carolina
    discovery rules in, 590
    fair value in, 712–713
    market exception in, 728
South Dakota
    discovery rules in, 592
    fair value in, 712–713
    market exception in, 728
special-interest purchasers, 679
Spencer, Kevin, 437 n.12
S&P Global, 245
spoliation, 612
Spunt, Eric S., 264
Standard Industrial Classification (SIC), 224, 249
standard of value, 1, 3–5, 8, 10, 12, 16, 534, 571
standards
    appraiser, 625–626
    business valuation, 621–623
Staubus, Martin, 425
Stiroh, L.J., 463 n.8
stock appreciation rights (SARs), 178
stock-based compensation, 334 n.20, 391
Stockdale, John J., 306
Stout Restricted Stock Study Database and DLOM Calculator, 279
strategic control premium, 680
strategic value, 10, 12
subpoena duces tecum, 602
Subramanyam, K.R., 214
subsequent sales, 317–319
substantial valuation misstatement, 626, 630, 631–632
sustainable, 30
Swanson, Daniel G., 466 n.24
swing block, 256
swing vote, 256, 310

synergies, 1, 3, 7–8, 12, 680
synergistic value, 1, 8, 12

T

Tadri, Aleza, 278
TAF. *See* The Appraisal Foundation (TAF)
TagniFi, 127
tangible assets, 137–140, 142–146
tangible book value, 37
Tarbell, Jeffrey S., 405, 481, 493, 505 n.23, 511, 533
tax, income
- double taxation and, 177
- goodwill and, 164
- intellectual property and, 475–477
- lost profits and, 528–529, 531
- reporting, 134
- returns, 49
- valuations for, 329–345

Tax Cuts and Jobs Act (TCJA), 332, 340, 342–343
tax disputes, 645–646
Tax Exempt and Governmental Entities (TEGE), 630, 633
Taxpayer Bill of Rights, 630
Tax Reform Act of 1986 (TRA), 275, 311–312, 340
tax reporting, 134
TCJA. *See* Tax Cuts and Jobs Act (TCJA)
TEGE. *See* Tax Exempt and Governmental Entities (TEGE)
Tennessee
- discovery rules in, 592
- fair value in, 714–715
- market exception in, 728

terminal value, 506, 508, 538, 579, 658
Texas
- discovery rules in, 592
- fair value in, 714–715
- market exception in, 728

The Appraisal Foundation (TAF), 621
Thomas, S., 102
Thompson, Joseph, 403
Thompson, Mark S., 264
Thomsen, William W., 519
timely disclosure, 608–611
timing, of deposition request, 603–604
total beta, 95
total book value, 37
total rate of return, 81
TRA. *See* Tax Reform Act of 1986 (TRA)
trade dress infringement, 469–470
trademark infringement, 469–470
trade secrets, 459–460, 468–469
trailing 12 months (TTM), 48–49
transaction method, 104, 125
transfer pricing, 340–345
- acquisition price method, 343
- application of the approach to hard-to-value intangibles, 341
- base erosion and anti-abuse tax, 340
- best method rule, 341
- commensurate with income, 340
- comparable profits method, 343
- comparable uncontrolled price, 343
- comparable uncontrolled transaction, 343
- contractual terms, 342
- cost-sharing regulations, 343
- economic conditions, 342
- functional analysis, 342
- intellectual property and, 475–477
- Internal Revenue Service, AM 2023-008, 345 n.46
- market capitalization method, 343
- Organization for Economic Co-operation and Development, 340–341
- property or services, 342
- relief-from-royalty method, 331–332
- residual profit split method, 343
- risk analysis, 342
- true taxable income, 341

trapped-in capital gains, 276, 302–303, 311–314, 364–366, 371
Travers, Mary Ann, 71 n.10
Treharne, Chris D., 443
trial testimony, 650–652
Trugman, Gary R., 58, 79, 102, 126, 136, 147, 165, 237, 327, 432, 542
TTM. *See* trailing 12 months (TTM)
Tuch, Andrew J., 503 n.21
Turner, Jim, 126 n.6

U

UFTA. *See* Uniform Fraudulent Transfer Act (UFTA)
Ulmann, Florian, 102

uncertainty, 62, 82
understatement of under 65% or less, 635
Uniform Arbitration Act, 640
Uniform Business Corporation Act, 14
Uniform Fraudulent Conveyance Act (UFCA), 514
Uniform Fraudulent Transfer Act (UFTA), 514
Uniform Standards of Professional Appraisal Practice (USPAP), 2, 2 n.3, 4–5, 559, 621, 644
Uniform Trade Secrets Act (UTSA), 468
unleveraged, 96
unleveraged beta, 681
U.S. Bankruptcy Code, 13
U.S. Conciliation Service, 638
U.S. Cost of Capital Module, 84–85, 85 n.10
U.S. Council of Economic Advisors, 243
U.S. Industry Benchmarking dataset, 90, 90 n.13, 98
U.S. International Trade Commission (USITC), 474
U.S. Master Estate and Gift Tax Guide, 279
U.S. Patent Act, 460
U.S. Patent and Trademark Office (USPTO), 460
U.S. Treasury Regulations, 3–4, 14, 167, 292, 295 n.19, 314, 319, 331, 331 n.7, 340 n.40, 334, 334 n.21, 337 n.28, 448, 448 n.9, 463 n.6, 475, 476, 476 n.78, 477 n.80, 623
Utah
  discovery rules in, 592
  fair value in, 714–715
  market exception in, 728
UTSA. *See* Uniform Trade Secrets Act (UTSA)

V

valuation, 1–10, 13–16, 131, 665, 681
Valuation Advisors' Lack of Marketability Discount Study™, 279
valuation approach, 681
valuation date, 485, 681
valuation method, 681
valuation methodology, 22
valuation procedure, 681
value
  acquisition, 10
  basis of, 664
  book, 10–11, 33, 36
  book, per share, 3
  book, tangible *vs.* total, 37
  in continued use, 21, 27, 131, 144
  continuing, 67
  definitions of, 1–2, 10, 13–16
  enterprise, 11–12, 22–23, 108, 167, 175–176, 669
  in exchange, 21, 131
  fair, 684
  fair market, 2–8, 10, 12–13, 16, 670
  financial control, 20
  fundamental, 1, 3, 9–10
  going-concern, 11, 19, 130, 671
  as a going concern, 19, 21–22
  goodwill, 671
  intrinsic, 3, 9–10, 672
  investment, 1, 3, 8–9, 12, 673
  levels of, 19–21, 483–484, 657
  liquidation, 12, 21, 135
  market, 1–5, 8–10, 12–13, 15–16, 34, 36
  marketable noncontrolling, 20
  net book, 10, 36–37
  nonmarketable, 20–21
  orderly liquidation, 676
  to the owner, 8
  in place, 21
  premises of, 21–22, 677
  present, 677
  proper, 634
  residual, 67
  stand-alone, 680
  standard of, 1, 3–5, 8, 10, 12, 16, 22, 680
  strategic, 10, 12
  strategic control, 20
  synergistic, 1, 8, 12, 680
  terminal, 67–71, 506, 508, 538, 579, 658, 681
  transaction, 10, 12–13
value in exchange, 286
ValuSource Market Comps, 126, 151
ValuSource M&A Comps, 126
Van Gorkom, 496, 502
Vannieuwenhuyse, Gauthier, 638 n.12
VanVleet, Daniel R., 443
Veasey, E. Norman, 641 n.28
Ventrelli, Anita M., 555, 585, 649

Vermont
  discovery rules in, 592
  fair value in, 716–717
  market exception in, 729
vertical analysis, 215, 217, 237
Virginia
  discovery rules in, 592
  fair value in, 716–717
  market exception in, 729
Virgin Islands, discovery rules in, 592
voting control, 681
voting stock, 310

W

Wachter, Michael L., 402
Walker, Donna J., 425
Walker, George K., 645 n.40
Walsh, William P., 648
Ware, Roger, 467 n.37
Washington
  discovery rules in, 592
  fair value in, 716–717
  market exception in, 729
Webb, Dennis A., 458
weight, of testimony, 580–582
weighted average cost of capital (WACC), 61, 96–98, 199, 682
Weil, Roman L., 464 n.9
Weiss, Steven A., 641 n.28
West, Shari L., 326
West, Tom, 149
West Virginia
  discovery rules in, 593
  fair value in, 718–719
  market exception in, 729
WFE Statistics Database, 245
Whitehead, Steven, 71 n.10, 203, 215
willing buyer, 3–4, 6, 21, 292–294, 313, 317, 325
willing seller, 3–4, 6, 21, 292–294, 311–312, 317, 325
Wilson, L. Deane, 458
Wilson, Robin G., 458
Wisconsin
  discovery rules in, 593
  fair value in, 718–719
  market exception in, 729
Wise, Richard M., 3 n.8, 126
with and without method, 188, 194, 198–199, 201
witness preparation, 662
Woefel, Charles J., 262
Wood, David, 165, 356 n.47
workforce, 185, 195, 197, 199
working capital, 682
World Bank, 245
World Federation of Exchanges, 245
worthless and abandoned property, 330, 335–339
worthlessness, 337–338
worthless stock deduction, 337–338
write-down and write-off policies, 205–207
written reports, 561, 572, 594
Wyoming
  discovery rules in, 593
  fair value in, 718–719
  market exception in, 729

X

XBRL, 107

Y

Yahoo Finance, 127
Yeanoplos, Kevin, 181

Z

Zaritsky, Howard M., 319 n.165, 327
Zimmerman, Carolyn F., 425
Zupkus, Robert A., 576 n.26